This book is dedicated to
Betty (Margaret Elizabeth) Ewins (1918-1995)
and
Richard Daggett (1938-1993)

WHARRAM

A Study of Settlement on the Yorkshire Wolds, XI

THE CHURCHYARD

by

S. Mays, C. Harding and C. Heighway

With contributions by Craig Barclay, Alex Bayliss, Justine Bayley, E. Ann Clark, G. Cook, Peter Didsbury, Blanche Ellis, Sheila Elsdon, Geoff D. Gaunt, Alison R. Goodall, Ian H. Goodall, Emmeline Marlow-Mann, Gerry McDonnell, Richard T. Porter, Jennifer Price, C. Bronk Ramsey, Jane Richardson, Ian Riddler, Peter Ryder, Bryan Sitch, A.M. Slowikowski, David Stocker, John G. Watt, Susan R. Watts, Hugh Willmott and Stuart Wrathmell

Illustrations by

Emmeline Marlow-Mann, Mark Chisnall, Alison Deegan, D. Honour, Cecily Marshall, Chris Philo and James C. Thorn

York University
Archaeological Publications 13

© Wharram Research Project and Department of Archaeology, University of York, 2007
ISBN 978 0 946722 20 4

Edited by: E. Ann Clark and S. Wrathmell
Published by: University of York
Typeset by: Archaeological Services WYAS
Printed by: Short Run Press Limited, Exeter

This publication has been made possible by a grant from English Heritage

Wharram: A Study of Settlement on the Yorkshire Wolds
General Editor: S. Wrathmell

Vol. I+   *Domestic Settlement 1: Areas 10 and 6* (1979)
             Society for Medieval Archaeology Monograph 8

Vol. II   *Wharram Percy: The Memorial Stones of the Churchyard* (1983)
             York University Archaeological Publications 1

Vol. III*+   *Wharram Percy: The Church of St Martin* (1987)
             Society for Medieval Archaeology Monograph 11

Vol. IV   *Two Roman Villas at Wharram le Street* (1986)
             York University Archaeological Publications 2

Vol. V   *An Archaeological Survey of the Parish of Wharram Percy, East Yorkshire.*
             1. The Evolution of the Roman Landscape (1987)
             British Archaeological Reports, British Series 172

Vol. VI*   *Domestic Settlement 2: Medieval Peasant Farmsteads*
             York University Archaeological Publications 8

Vol. VII   *Two Anglo-Saxon Buildings and Associated Finds* (1992)
             York University Archaeological Publications 9

Vol. VIII*   *The South Manor Area* (2000)
             York University Archaeological Publications 10

Vol. IX*   *The North Manor Area and North-west Enclosure* (2004)
             York University Archaeological Publications 11

Vol. X*   *Water Resources and their Management* (2005)
             York University Archaeological Publications 12

Vol. XI*   *The Churchyard* (2007)
             York University Archaeological Publications 13

Vol. XII   (late and post-medieval vicarage and post-medieval farmstead, in prep.)

Vol. XIII   (synthesis, in prep.)

* These volumes are available from Oxbow Books, Park End Place, Oxford, OX1 1HN

+ These volumes are available from Customer Sales and Services, Maney Publishing, Suite 1C,
  Joseph's Well, Hanover Walk, Leeds LS3 1AB

Cover: detail of an 11th-century grave-cover (No. 3: see pp 271-2 and 279), photograph by
Susan Harrison, English Heritage

Maurice Beresford at Wharram Percy

Maurice Beresford died in Leeds on 15 December 2005. It seems appropriate to include in this, the latest volume on the Wharram Percy excavations, an appreciation of his role in a project which but for him, would never have taken place. It was he who 'discovered' the site in 1948, brought students, spades and shovels to the earthworks in 1950 and 1951, and who handed on the archaeological baton to John Hurst (1927-2003) in 1952. Over the following fifty years both men combined to bring their very different skills and personalities to one of the longest running research projects in Europe.

Maurice Beresford's initial connection with the site is best described in his own words:

On 26 June [1948] *a Saturday ramble in the Yorkshire Wolds from Malton youth hostel took Philip and Eric Lawton and myself up the scarp from Birdsall to the isolated church at Wharram Percy and its surrounding earthworks, more substantial than anything I had seen in the Midlands and with shapes that were more obviously houses. The historical sources had suggested that depopulations were confined to the Midlands but here they now were on my doorstop.* [He had recently been appointed to a lectureship at Leeds].

The possibility of exploring so distant a site as Wharram Percy arose only because on 10 October 1949 the headmaster of the village school at Settrington happened to hear a talk which I broadcast for the BBC Northern Home Service, designed to celebrate the 600th anniversary of the Black Death. I mentioned a record of plague deaths at Settrington and in a letter Mr Winstanley asked whether I know of a nearby village called Wharram Percy which was locally believed to have been a victim of the plague? If I was interested to work there he was sure he could get permission from Lord Middleton, who was the owner of the site and a governor of his school; additionally we could use the schoolroom as a dormitory. The latter was a key facility, making the long journey worthwhile.

On 9 June 1950 Mr Winstanley joined myself and two Leeds students [Peter Tillott and Keith Allison] *at the site*[1]

The first finds were excavated that weekend. The timing was opportune in that this important example of what was later to be termed a deserted medieval village could be included in the text which Maurice was then preparing for *The Lost Villages of England*, his important book of 1954 which drew academic and popular attention

to the number and distribution of such sites and to their potential as evidence for the late medieval population decline. In keeping with his long-standing fascination for maps, Plate 1 shows the Ordnance Survey of 1850-51 of Wharram together with an R.A.F. vertical aerial photograph of the site taken in 1946 which Maurice had located at Medmenham: combined as one plate they dramatically illustrated the surviving earthworks of the site.

It was to Beresford's credit that he did not consider Wharram Percy his exclusive 'patch' but was open and willing to share its potential with a young professional archaeologist, John Hurst, seven years his junior and only just out of Cambridge. In 1952, having handed over the archaeological direction of the dig to Hurst, Beresford concentrated his remarkable energy into organising the annual dig, including recruitment, personnel, accommodation, catering and finance - all this on a shoestring budget. In retrospect, it is fair to say that without Maurice Beresford it is doubtful that the long-standing excavations would ever have taken place. While John Hurst was a gifted and dedicated archaeologist he did not have the skills needed to organise recruitment, run the living side of the excavation and integrate volunteers from a wide range of backgrounds. Maurice, however, relished the challenge of naming everybody at morning briefings (no mean feat when numbers exceeded fifty), allocating daily chores, organising local supplies and excursions, etc. The force of his personality and his experiences in adult education and social work were put to good use. He could and would talk to anyone and could usually find some mutual interest or talking point. Aside from his dogs (a succession over several years) 'Wharramites' almost became his family. He kept in touch with a large number of diggers and followed with interest their subsequent careers, be they lorry drivers, schoolteachers, social workers or professors. Few things gave him greater pleasure than chance meetings with diggers, be it at concerts, on station platforms or on the London underground. He took great pleasure in being the hub of the network, something which became increasingly important to him in his later years when he was less mobile and increasingly dependent upon friends, especially those in Leeds.

Aside from running the annual dig (and occasional weekends on site) Maurice was, most importantly, the historian of the medieval village and of its post-medieval history. In the 1950s and 1960s when the emphasis of the excavation was on peasant houses, the church and the search for origins, he documented the village from medieval sources. Later, in keeping with the widening of the project to the 'total history' of the community, Maurice turned his attention to the documentation of all the townships in Wharram Percy parish and, specifically to the farmhouse and 18th-century vicarage which were found on the site. His evidence, garnered from hearth taxes, glebe terriers, rentals and other estate materials gave more precision to the dating of the excavated remains and to the small finds. The combined historical and archaeological evidence from forty years of work was brilliantly synthesised in 1990 in *Wharram Percy.*

Deserted Medieval Village which he and John Hurst wrote in the Batsford/English Heritage series. By then a remote place which few had heard of in 1948 had become one of the best-known place-names in English medieval studies.

1 Extracts taken from M.W. Beresford, 'A draft chronology of deserted village studies' in *Medieval Settlement Research Group Annual Report* no. 1 (1986), 22-3

Rob Glasscock

Maurice Beresford (left) with John Hurst and Christopher Taylor at Wharram Percy on 18 July 1989.

Contents

List of Plates

List of Figures

xi

List of Tables

Summary

This publication covers excavations in the churchyard of Wharram Percy, North Yorkshire. It complements a previous volume in this series (*Wharram III*), which was concerned with the excavation of the associated church and its interior. An extensive programme of radiocarbon dating indicates that the burial ground was established soon after the mid-10th century, before the first stone church was erected. This volume includes the definitive reports on human remains and associated mortuary practices extending from the 10th century to post-medieval times. Over 900 skeletons were uncovered, and 687 of these were subject to detailed analysis, revealing a wealth of information about the diet, health and mortality of the parishioners.

Zusammenfassung

Diese Veröffentlichung behandelt Ausgrabungen auf dem Friedhof von Wharram Percy in Nord-Yorkshire. Sie vervollständigt einen früheren Band in dieser Reihe (*Wharram III*), der von der Ausgrabung der dazugehörigen Kirche und deren Innenraum handelt. Ein umfangreiches Programm von C14-Datierungen deutet darauf hin, daß der Begräbnisplatz bald nach der Mitte des 10. Jahrhunderts und vor der Errichtung der Steinkirche angelegt wurde. Dieser Band enthält maßgebliche Nachweise menschlicher Überreste vom 10. Jahrhundert bis hin zu nachmittelalterlicher Zeit und damit im Zusammenhang stehender Bestattungspraktiken. Über 900 Skelette wurden freigelegt, von denen 687 detailliert analysiert wurden und reiches Zeugnis über Diät, Gesundheit und Sterblichkeitsziffer der Gemeindemitglieder lieferten.

Résumé

Cette publication couvre les fouilles exécutées dans le cimetière de Wharram Percy, North Yorkshire. Elle s'ajoute à un volume précédent dans cette série (*Wharram III*), qui traitait des fouilles de l'église associée et de son intérieur. Un programme étendu de datation au radiocarbone indique que le cimetière avait été établi peu après le milieu du 10ème siècle, avant la construction de la première église en pierre. Ce volume englobe les rapports définitifs sur les restes humains et les pratiques mortuaires associées, du 10ème siècle à l'époque post-médiévale. Plus de 900 squelettes ont été découverts et 687 d'entre eux ont fait l'objet d'une analyse détaillée, révélant toute une foule de renseignements concernant le régime alimentaire, la santé et la mortalité des paroissiens.

Preface and Acknowledgements

The process of publishing the results of work on Wharram Percy church and churchyard has been lengthy, and in some respects unsatisfactory. The structural history of the church, along with excavations both inside the standing building and in its immediate vicinity, were published exactly twenty years ago in a Society for Medieval Archaeology monograph (*Wharram III*). Omitted from that volume were most of the skeletal remains of over 900 individuals recovered from the various trenches: only those from the nave achieved a measure of publication, as most of the rest had not then been analysed (*Wharram III*, 181-8). Also omitted was any consideration of Site 26, to the north of the present graveyard, where some of the human remains had been uncovered, and of the results from a number of small trenches on the graveyard's southern margin. Again, the analyses had not then been carried out.

Wharram III was deficient not only in content but also in presentation. It was prepared in line with the 1975 'Frere report' on the publication of archaeological excavations. As a result, much of the detail on both the standing structure and the excavations was consigned to a pocket of fiche at the back of the volume. In retrospect, some of the decisions as to what should and should not appear on the printed pages seem ill-judged. For example the 11th-century grave-covers, along with their headstones and footstones, are dismissed in five lines of printed text accompanied by one photograph; whereas the 18th and 19th-century wall monuments to members of the Greame and Wrangham families were furnished with a dozen lines of text, two drawings and two photographs.

The present volume rectifies these omissions, but it does much more than this. At its core is Simon Mays' new, comprehensive analysis of all the skeletal remains from Wharram, an analysis that achieves a level of sophistication which would simply not have been possible twenty years ago. Furthermore, it is supported by over 90 radiocarbon determinations and associated statistical analyses which have mitigated the poor stratigraphy – and indeed, for the early years, the poor stratigraphic records – and have provided the kind of chronological framework that would have been inconceivable in 1987. A number of general conclusions drawn from this analysis have already appeared in relevant journals, many listed in the bibliography at the end of this volume.

This is not, however, simply a 'human bone report'. Among the other highlights is David Stocker's re-examination and reconsideration of the 11th-century grave-covers and associated items. His startling conclusions open up completely new ideological considerations. Among the minor curiosities is the re-identification of a pre-graveyard 'lime kiln' as a probable Middle Saxon *Grubenhaus*. If the new identification is

correct, this, not the one revealed in the 1975 excavation of Site 39 (*Wharram VII*), is actually the first *Grubenhaus* that was excavated at Wharram.

There is, inevitably, some overlap between the contents of this publication and those of other volumes. Site 71, beyond the south-eastern corner of the graveyard, was fully described in the publication of the pond and dam just beyond it (*Wharram X*), but has been summarised here because of the evidence it provides for the development of the churchyard boundary. Site 26, beyond the northern boundary of the present graveyard, was clearly once part of it, but was later incorporated into the vicarage grounds. It is fully described here, but will be considered further in the next volume (*Wharram XII*), dealing with the vicarage and post-medieval farmstead excavations.

Beyond that, only one volume remains to be published: one that will draw together the excavation results on a village-wide basis, including the currently unpublished sites on the Plateau, and a series of local and regional studies which will attempt to provide a wider context for what we know of the development of Wharram and the lives of its inhabitants. Current indications are that it will necessitate a further, radical overhaul of Wharram's settlement history from Iron Age and Roman times to the medieval village's final demise in 1527.

The excavations discussed here were sponsored by the Department of the Environment, later English Heritage, and carried out under the auspices of the Medieval Village (now Medieval Settlement) Research Group. The direction and administration of the project were in the hands of the late John Hurst and the late Maurice Beresford, the latter assisted by Francesca Croft. As always the late Mrs Joan Summerson and the Milner and Veysey families provided valuable organisational assistance throughout.

Charlotte Harding, who, assisted by the late Betty Ewins and Sheila Ely (nee King), supervised Site 26, wishes to thank the following for their assistance, support, patience and good humour during the protracted period of preparation of this report: Alex Bayliss, Rob Bell (ed. *Wharram III*), the late Maurice Beresford, E. Ann Clark, Julie Dunk (especially for her work in phasing the burials), Carolyn Heighway, the late John Hurst, Emmeline Marlow-Mann, Simon Mays, R.T. Porter, Peggy Pullan, Anna Slowiskowski and Stuart Wrathmell. In addition she would like to thank all the excavators of the church sites (acknowledged in *Wharram III*) and those whose site reports are incorporated into this volume: David Andrews (Site 52); Malcolm Atkin (Site 71); Glen and Ann Foard (Site 41); Terry Pearce (Sites 20 and 21); John Wood, David Gilding and Barbara Johnston (Sites 77, 99 and 100).

The excavation was greatly assisted by the work of the late Richard Daggett (who also took many of the photographs), Janet Escritt, Tom Greeves, the late Gill Hurst, Jean Le Patourel, Chris Mahany, Colin Treen, Bob Yarwood and all those volunteers who spent long hours on the sites. Later site photography was by Dan Smith and Sebastian Rahtz, and site survey was by Richard Porter. The on-site processing of finds was supervised first by Dan Smith and then by Ann Clark. Both wish to thank Nicky Gilding and all the others who worked so hard on the processing and preparation of finds, especially washing and recording the numerous skeletons. More recently the project has benefited greatly from the help of English Heritage's Centre for Archaeology staff, notably with the movement, storage and conservation of finds.

Simon Mays thanks G. Müldner (University of Bradford), C. Nielsen-Marsh (University of Newcastle) and T. Molleson (Natural History Museum) for granting access to unpublished data. D. Brothwell (University of York), the late P. Guyer (Radiography Dept, Southampton General Hospital), G. Mann (retired ENT surgeon), J. McEwan (University of Alberta), D. Ortner (Smithsonian Institution) and the late Juliet Rogers (Bristol Royal Infirmary) kindly offered their expertise on the interpretation of some of the pathological changes. Thanks are due to G.M. Taylor (Imperial College London) for the use of Plate 59.

Many specialists have contributed to this volume: we acknowledge their assistance and thank them for their continued commitment to the project. Three of them warrant particular mention: Simon Mays and Alex Bayliss, also of English Heritage's Centre for Archaeology, whose reports are fundamental to this volume, and David Stocker, who contributed a chapter on the 11th-century grave-covers and associated stonework at short notice. The stones had been reburied on site after excavation, and we wish to thank English Heritage's curatorial staff, particularly Kevin Booth and Susan Harrison, for their help last summer in uncovering and moving the grave-covers into English Heritage's Helmsley store. These stones can now be more widely appreciated on the store's open days.

Wharram XI has been sub-edited and desktop published by Chris Philo. The drawings are credited individually within the captions. Paul Gwilliam took the photographs which appear as Plates 119 and 120, Simon Mays, the photographs which appear in Part Three (with the exception of Plate 59) and Susan Harrison Plates 102-118. Susanne Atkin created the index, and the foreign language summaries have been prepared by Klaus and Frederike Hammer, and Charlotte Sheil-Small. Peggy Pullan provided administrative back up, and has prepared the site archive for deposition at Hull City Museums. The editors are grateful to English Heritage's anonymous referees for suggesting a number of improvements to the draft volume, and to Kath Buxton and Dave MacLeod, English Heritage's project monitors, for their guidance and support.

It is, finally, our sad duty to record the death of Ian Goodall during 2006. Ian had been part of the Wharram project for a very long time, and his visits to the site, usually accompanied by his wife Alison and son Edward, were times of instruction and discussion that were anticipated with pleasure by John Hurst and the finds team. Ian was a pioneer in the study of ironwork from medieval sites, and his reports have appeared in our excavation volumes from *Wharram I* onwards, including this volume. The Wharram project will greatly miss an important member of the team, and a good friend.

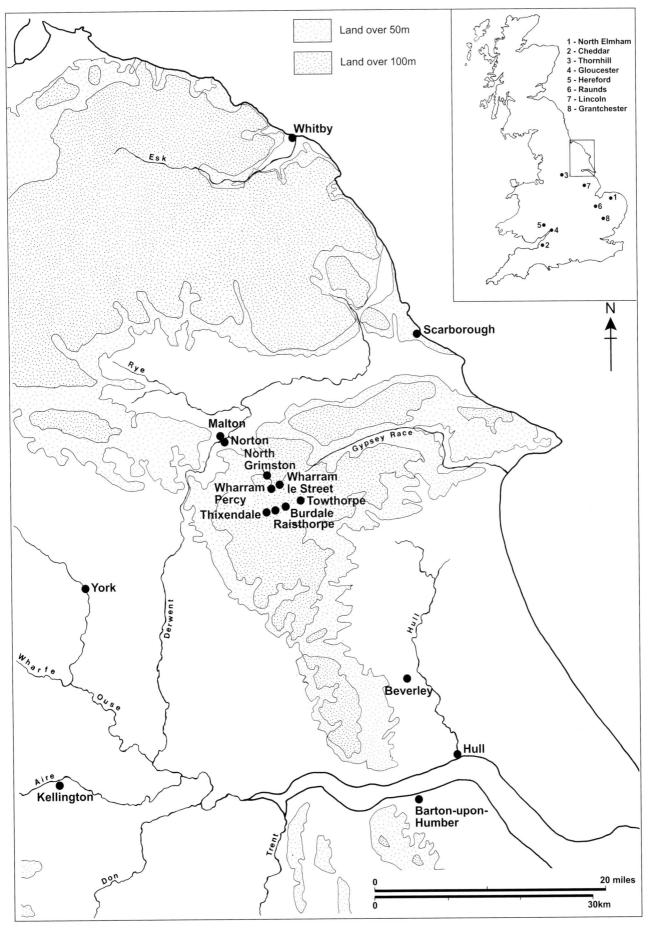

Fig. 1. Map of north-east England showing the position of Wharram Percy and other locations mentioned in the text. (C. Philo)

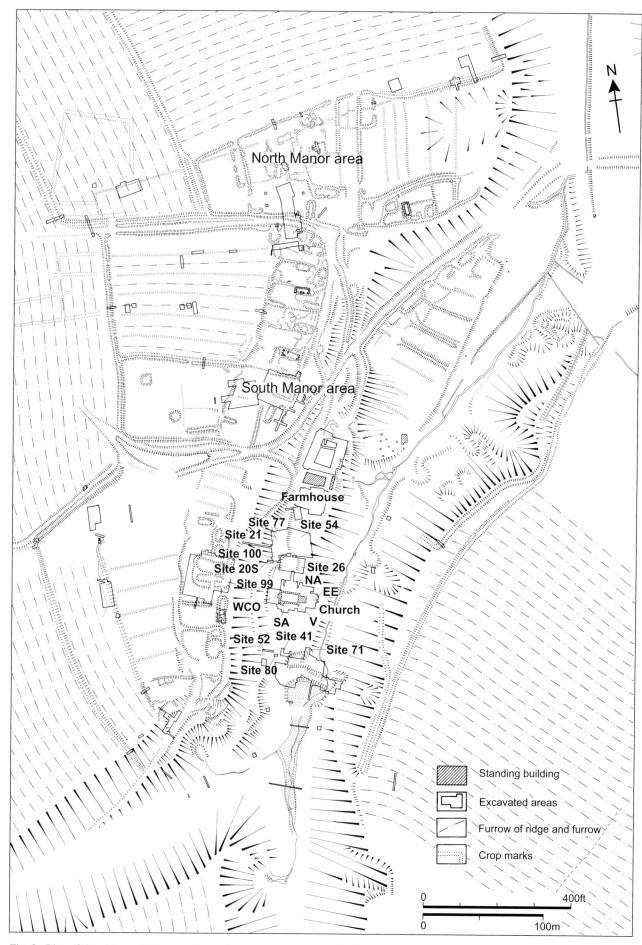

North Manor area

South Manor area

Farmhouse

Site 77   Site 54
Site 21
Site 100
Site 20S   Site 26
Site 99   NA
               EE
WCO   Church
       SA   V
Site 52 Site 41
            Site 71
Site 80

	Standing building
	Excavated areas
	Furrow of ridge and furrow
	Crop marks

0   400ft

0   100m

Fig. 2. Plan of the village of Wharram Percy showing relevant sites. (C. Philo)

Part One

The Churchyard and Glebe Land

1 Introduction

by C. Harding and S. Wrathmell

Wharram Percy lies near the north-west scarp of the Yorkshire Wolds, 7 miles (11 km) south-east of Malton (Fig. 1). The scarp is dissected by a number of deep valleys, mainly dry in their upper courses, the Wharram Percy valley being the longest of these in the northern Wolds. The medieval village, and much of the earlier settlement, was on the chalk plateau on the western side of the valley at about 150m OD. The church and churchyard lie on a narrow, sheltered, fairly level and partly artificial terrace *c*. 4-7m above the valley floor and the beck, and 13-16m below the lip of the plateau. The church of St Martin is at National Grid reference SE 8583 6421 (Fig. 2).

The structure of the earliest church dates to between 950 and 1050, replaced by a new, larger building in the early 12th century. It reached its maximum extent in the early 14th century and was reduced largely to its present form in the early 17th century. The outer face of the tower fell down in 1959, and the vestry, which had been constructed in the mid-19th century, was demolished in 1973.

From at least the 12th century the church served not only the community at Wharram Percy but also the four other townships in the ecclesiastical parish: Towthorpe, Burdale, Raisthorpe and Thixendale, all 2km to 4km distant on the south side of the Wolds watershed, covering an area of some 600ha (Fig. 3). Of the five townships, Burdale and Wharram Percy were deserted by the middle of the 16th century, and Towthorpe and Raisthorpe by the end of the 17th century - their settlements reduced to single farmsteads. Thixendale has survived as a village, and its inhabitants continued to attend Wharram Percy church until at least 1870.

In 1835 Wharram Percy parish was united with the adjacent parish and village of Wharram le Street, to the north-west. The last burial at Wharram took place in 1906, although the church continued in intermittent use, particularly for baptisms, until 1949. The last documented refurbishment of the church was in 1923, accompanied by graveyard clearance and fence repairs. In 1954 the parish and diocesan authorities reluctantly decided that the church fabric was beyond economic repair and the interior fittings and bells were removed to other nearby churches. For further information and a more detailed introduction to the village and parish see *Wharram III*, 1-46 and Beresford and Hurst 1990, 13-26.

One of the conclusions of the analysis of the church fabric is that the building's expansion and contraction were probably due more to liturgical developments and changes in patronage than to the pressures of fluctuations in the population; the decline of the population in the 15th and 16th centuries did not follow from or result in a decline in the wealth of the landlord, whose concerns by then were based on the expanding population of sheep (1180 sheep are recorded in a dispute of 1543: *Wharram III*, 205-9). The depopulation of the parish was a gradual process, evident at Wharram Percy from at least the later 15th century and completed by 1527. This process of gradual depopulation, accelerated in the early 16th century, also took place at Burdale, while Towthorpe and Raisthorpe were not deserted until *c*. 1680.

At Wharram Percy a series of farmsteads on the terrace north of the church (Fig. 2) existed from at least the 17th century until the late 1840s, when all but the south range of the courtyard farm which had been rebuilt in the 1770s was demolished. The south range was converted into three cottages, one of which was permanently occupied until 1976. A new farm on the Wold top south of the village site, also called Wharram Percy Farm, took over. Another farm, Bella Farm on the Wold top, east of the beck, had already been built in the 1770s.

On the terrace between the churchyard and the farmsteads stood the late medieval and post-medieval vicarages. Extending northwards under the farmsteads and along the valley floor beyond, parallel with the beck, lay a sequence of tofts occupied in the 12th to 13th centuries while to the south of the church lay the village pond. This whole assemblage formed the east row of the medieval village, overlooked by the west row on the plateau (Beresford and Hurst 1990, 80)

The natural bedrock on the terrace is hard fractured chalk. As the ground falls to the east, underlying deposits of more clayey 'Red Chalk' and dark blue-grey Upper Jurassic clay are successively exposed. The boundary between the latter formations, which passes immediately beneath the east wall of the present chancel, gives rise to the numerous springs in this section of the valley (see *Wharram X*, fig. 3). The nearest sources of building stone are the beds of Lower Calcareous Grit (yellow sandstone) in the Birdsall Leavening and Acklam region and the outcrop of oolitic limestone (white limestone) at North Grimston and Langton.

That part of the terrace on which the churchyard lies is at a height of 138-141m OD, sloping eastwards at about 1 in 12. On the west side, hillwash from the steep valley

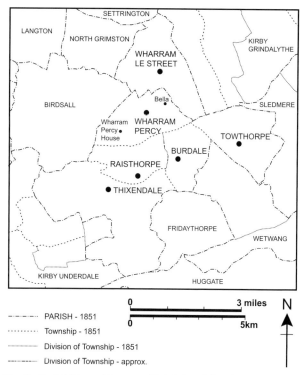

Fig. 3. Parish/Township map. (E. Marlow-Mann)

Legend:
- — · — · — PARISH - 1851
- · · · · · · · · · Township - 1851
- — — — — — Division of Township - 1851
- — — — — Division of Township - approx.

0 _____ 3 miles N
0 _____ 5km

side has accumulated, narrowing the terrace and graduating the slope down from the plateau. To the east the churchyard has built up to form a slight lynchet along its eastern fence-line above the steep slope down to the beck, with a more substantial elevation east of the church over the former chancels. The ground also slopes southwards, reaching its lowest point in the south-east corner at *c*. 137m OD. The persistent use of the churchyard for burial over a period of perhaps 1000 years has raised the ground level into a 'platform' around the church structure and this was particularly noticeable at the points of entry - the north door and south porch.

Work on the terrace in and around the churchyard took place between 1962 and 1978 during the annual three-week excavation season (Fig. 4). Trial trenches were dug to assess the stratigraphy, and then areas were opened each season starting to the north and east sides of the church. This strategy was followed partly because of the unstable fabric of the church, which precluded the excavation of deep open areas, and partly because of the short excavation season. Following the consolidation of the fabric in the 1970s it was possible, for example, to open all the area of the nave at once (1974), and to excavate right up to the west wall and tower (1972). Further areas of the churchyard were examined in the 1970s when increased funding permitted a larger work force and thus the simultaneous excavation of more extensive areas. Even so, it was often not possible to leave sites open over-winter, except within the enclosed churchyard, because of the prospective danger to cattle and the public of deep holes. Areas that were left open could not be totally covered in protective plastic because of the possibility of ingestion by cattle that strayed in to the churchyard.

The circumstances of the excavation and the large number of people involved over such a long period, during which the nature of field archaeology was changing rapidly, hint at the very varied nature of the site records (see *Wharram III*, 48-9). As was general practice in the 1960s, annotated plans and sections were made, and photographs were taken with general working notes written in a notebook. During the course of the 1970s detailed context records in a notebook progressed to context sheets and single context recording. Unfortunately, several of those who carried out much of the work in the 1960s are no longer alive, but for the 1970s it has been helpful to the authors not only in some cases to have seen most of the sites in progress, but also to have consulted some of those involved at the time. It also became clear that over the last two decades some of the site records, which had to be relocated on several occasions, are now missing.

The development of the church fabric, the excavations both within and around the building, and the burials and other finds recovered from these investigations, were all covered to some extent in *Wharram III*. That volume was, however, deficient in various respects. In the first place, the human bone analysis had not been completed by 1984, and so a decision was taken to defer this to a later volume which could also encompass the burials recovered during work in the northern part of the burial ground (Site 26). Secondly, the quantity of data to be accommodated in *Wharram III* led to a decision to consign many of the detailed reports to a wallet of fiche attached (at least initially) to the monograph's cover. Thirdly, not only the quantity but also the variability of the data meant that some of the intricacies of depositional history were omitted in the printed volume. Such variation was inevitable in excavations that ran from 1962 to 1978, given the progress in systematic stratigraphic recording during that period. The present volume addresses these deficiencies.

Work started on the preparation of this volume in the early 1990s with the cataloguing of the site records. A further initial step was the renumbering of burials, moving from sequences with both Roman and Arabic numerals to an alpha-numeric sequence with letter codes for each area of the church and churchyard followed by an Arabic number (e.g. Burial SA034: South Aisle Burial 34). The burials from Site 26 stand alone, having been recorded with an individual context number for each skeleton prefixed by the site code, for example 26/250; these now have a G(lebe) number (e.g. Burial G250). Concordances of old and new burial numbers for all the sites discussed in this volume can be found in Appendix 9.

In 1976 (part way through the excavation of Site 26) a context recording system based on that used by the Central Excavation Unit (now the English Heritage Centre for Archaeology) was adopted at Wharram (see *Wharram VII*, 2 for more details). It must be noted that the original recording techniques used for burials prior to this change, frequently did not differentiate between

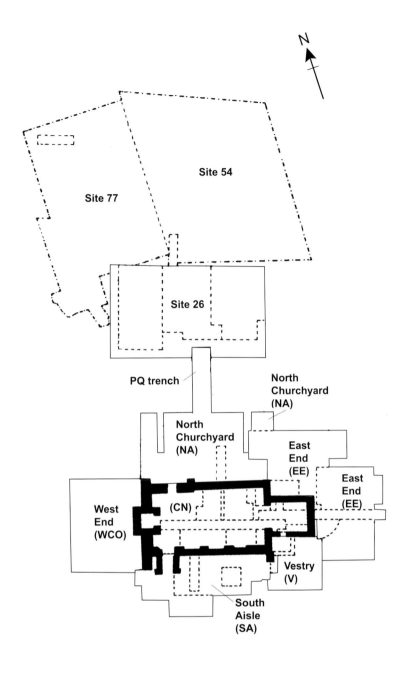

N

Site 54

Site 77

Site 26

PQ trench

North
Churchyard
(NA)

North
Churchyard
(NA)

East
End
(EE)

East
End
(EE)

West
End
(WCO)

(CN)

Vestry
(V)

South
Aisle
(SA)

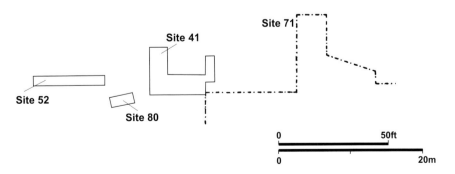

Site 71

Site 41

Site 52

Site 80

0   50ft

0   20m

Fig. 4. Detailed plan of the areas of excavation around the church, showing full site codes. (E. Marlow-Mann)

skeletons and the cuts and fills of their graves – so for example, Burial SA050, where referred to in the text, incorporates skeleton number, grave cut and grave fills which may or may not have originally had separate context numbers. In the finds sections, objects are catalogued with their original context number, often the grave fill, but the Burial number is given as well for clarity.

The letter codes for each area of the church were first used in *Wharram III* where they are used as a prefix to layer and feature numbers. It is therefore possible for the same number to refer to a feature in the church excavations and a burial in the final burial list. To prevent confusion, all references to burials in this volume are always prefixed by the word Burial.

These preliminary stages were followed by the analysis of the skeletal material, and the selection of bones for radiocarbon dating. While this was in progress, a study of the burial practices involved and a detailed examination of the non-burial archaeology were separately prepared. All work ceased for a period in the late 1990s, when English Heritage commissioned the Wharram post-excavation team to prepare a MAP2 Assessment, which could guide the whole analysis and publication programme to a successful conclusion. Work was resumed on the present volume in 2001.

In spite of the nature of some of the records, and the occasional frustrations stemming from those which are known to be missing, much new information could be extracted from the records, on aspects which were not part of the brief for the 1987 church monograph. The substantial radiocarbon dating programme of skeletal material has transformed our understanding of burial chronology and its relationship to the broader depositional history of the sites. Because of this, and with the benefit of hindsight, it has been possible to recognise features that were not identified or understood at the time and put them in context. The greatest difficulty has been the correlation of some layers and features across site boundaries; no attempt has been made to assign more than general site-wide phasing, and where possible to relate it to the church development phases as in *Wharram III*, 52 (see Ch. 3 and Fig. 6). It should be stressed at the outset that nothing has emerged from the new dating evidence and analysis to alter significantly our understanding of the structural chronology of the church itself. The burials which were radiocarbon dated (Ch. 7) are cited in the text as *posterior density estimates* throughout the volume. These are quoted in italics to differentiate them from simple calibrated dates which are quoted in plain type.

The stratigraphic sequence in each separate excavation area and 'site' is described, where possible, by period and phase. The areas and sites have been grouped into three chapters marking the different parts of the graveyard that have been excavated. Each chapter ends with a discussion of chronological development. The finds reports supplement and extend those in *Wharram III*, 147-76, and provide an opportunity for further discussion of key

assemblages, such as the pre-Conquest and later grave-covers and burial markers. It is important to emphasise that within the finds reports, as elsewhere, periods and phases remain specific to each site.

There are two other Wharram volumes, besides the church monograph, that overlap with the present publication. One is the previous volume on Wharram's water resources (*Wharram X*), where the full account of Site 71 has been published. This site lay just within the southern graveyard, and the later phases were crucial for an understanding of the use of the southern pond and its dam during the later medieval period. Here, only a summary account of the site is given. The second overlap is at the northern end of the graveyard, where the late medieval and post-medieval vicarage buildings stood. The boundary between vicarage and graveyard was not static, but changed position over the centuries, resulting in some structural remains and occupation debris from the vicarage lying within Site 26. A full interpretation of these remains will be provided in *Wharram XII*, a volume covering the main vicarage excavations in Sites 54 and 77, along with a review of the history of Wharram Percy's rectory, vicarage and chantries.

2 Cartographic Evidence
by R.T. Porter

Introduction

This chapter provides an analysis of the cartographic and written sources relating to the size, shape, boundaries and internal features of the churchyard and the adjacent glebe land in the 18th and early 19th centuries. It is based on a much longer, detailed archive report prepared by the author, and has been edited for this volume by C. Harding and S. Wrathmell. A broader account of the cartographic evidence for buildings, boundaries, trackways and other features on the terrace will be incorporated in the volume devoted to the excavation of the post-medieval vicarage and farmstead (*Wharram XII*).

In addition to the churchyard and the portion of the glebe where the vicarage buildings were located, early vicars had possessed glebe lands in the open fields. By the early 18th century, some two centuries after the abolition of open-field farming at Wharram, their locations were, however, unknown. A terrier of 1716, the earliest to provide a detailed record of contemporary glebe holdings, states: 'Tis not known where the Glebe land lies. But in lieu thereof the vicar receives from the Farmer Nine Pounds yearly... also five Cow Gates and two Horse Gates, Winter & Summer, in any Part of the Lordship where the Farmers Cows and Horses Goe... [but to stop the Vicar's animals being a nuisance when the farmer is giving his animals feed in the winter] The Vicar by Agreement injoys a piece of Ground opposite to his House called the Wood, by Estimation two Acre of

Land...' (Borthwick, Wharram Percy Glebe Terriers, 1716). This piece of winter pasture occupied the steep valley side east of the Beck and immediately south of Nut Wood. It is parcel 23 on the 1836 plans (see Fig. 5), where it is described as 'glebe'. The plans give the same appellation to the vicarage area (parcel 25) and the churchyard (parcel 26).

The churchyard, too, was used for grazing, and a survey of 1806 gives it a value of £1.10s (Birdsall Estate Office, Bella Estate 1806, 14). By 1853 this area and the rest of the Glebe were let to the neighbouring farmer. A Terrier of that year (Borthwick PR WP1,134) brackets together the churchyard and glebe: 'The site of the old Vicarage House & Stable & the said Orchard & back yard & the Herbage of the Church Yard are now let by the Vicar to Mr W.F. Gofton [farmer of Wharram Percy] at the annual rent of two pounds'.

The churchyard fences and trackways in 1836 (Figs 5 and 159)

Detailed examination of the cartographic and written sources, and comparison with information drawn from the archaeological record, has enabled a number of features relating to the churchyard and glebe to be identified and dated. The accompanying plan (Fig. 5) shows the churchyard area in the first half of the 19th century. It is based primarily on two estate maps of 1836, but also uses data from the Ordnance Survey 1:10560 map of 1854 (surveyed 1851) and 1:2500 map of 1890 (surveyed 1888) in order to decide the exact alignments of boundaries and trackways. The dates cited below are the survey dates. Figure 5 was compiled at 1:120, involving considerable enlargement of some source plans with inevitable uncertainty of up to a metre in some areas. The published figure is at c. 1:600.

The 1836 plans, the earliest known of Wharram Percy township, were made by William Dykes. One of them (Dykes 1836a) is at a scale of 1 inch to 3 chains (1:2376) drawn on several sheets with overall measurements 5ft 5ins (1.65m) (north-south) by 6ft 3¾ins (1.92m). It is coloured, with buildings, fences, roads, tracks, ponds, streams and gates, field names, numbers and acreages all shown. Although unsigned, Dykes 1836a carries the same title as a second, smaller scale plan, in ink on parchment, at a scale of 1 inch to 9 chains (1:7128; Dykes 1836b). This shows similar detail to Dykes 1836a, but omits gates.

The first known reference to churchyard fencing at Wharram occurs in a Visitation of 1586, when Leonard Weddell caused a disturbance at the church with a great dog. The blame for the incident was ascribed to those who ought to have fenced the churchyard, presumably indicating the disrepair rather than the absence of a fence (Borthwick V.1586/CB, f.126r). Further presentments for disrepair of fencing are recorded in other Visitations in the 17th century, for example in 1633 (Borthwick V.1633/CB1 f.329v). The term 'fence' here and in the

Terriers signifies a barrier in general – whether hedge, railing or wall etc. Cartographic evidence may not be sufficient to distinguish between these specifically.

In the 18th century the fences incorporated a number of ash trees, and these trees have been crucial in relating to each other the boundaries shown on the various maps. The 1770 Terrier (reproduced in Beresford and Hurst 1990, 108) recorded 'twenty Small Ashes upon the Glebe, and Church Yard Fence - in Value by Estimation about Twenty Shillings'. The 1786 Terrier used similar wording. All these trees apparently still stood in 1888.

The Terriers enable us to say that most of the churchyard boundaries shown on the 1836 plan in fact date back to at least the 18th century, since the ash trees planted pre-1770 are shown, in the position of the 1836 boundaries, on later maps. A few of them also survived to be recorded by the Wharram Project, their surveyed positions affording assistance and justification for the plotting of the 19th-century boundaries. It is also reasonable to suppose that the 18th-century fence lines on which these trees were planted were in fact hedgerows, since the 1853 Terrier states that the Churchyard 'is fenced round by Hedges which are kept in repair by the Parish' (Borthwick PR WP1,133-4).

Although the 1836 plans are the first at a scale large enough to show the churchyard in any detail, earlier county maps provide some ancillary information. The road running southwards from Wharram Percy village towards Raisthorpe and Thixendale, which is ascribed to the pre-desertion period, is not shown on Jefferys' 1775 map – the first to show roads in the Wharram area. Jefferys does, however, show a short stretch of fenced road running northwards from the church; this passed to the west of two buildings, presumably the vicarage and the farmstead, and then joined the Birdsall-Sledmere road, which is shown crossing the Beck on a bridge very close to the modern accommodation bridge over the railway line.

The continuation of the Jefferys road southwards, across the dam, first appears on the more accurate and detailed Greenwood map of 1818 and Teesdale's 'corrected' version of 1828. The road is also a clear track or bridle way in 1851 and on subsequent Ordnance Survey maps down to 1909 (Fig. 159). Greenwood's scale is, however, too small to show the short stretch of road beside and northwards from the church. The first, and only contemporary, map to show and name the Vicarage house is Bryant's (1829), surveyed 1827-8, but road and buildings were badly mis-orientated.

On Dykes's plans the church is shown with a symmetrical east end (i.e. pre-Vestry), and the churchyard (parcel 26) is given an area of 0a. 3r. 15p. (0.341 ha), just under 1 acre. Fences to the west, south and east are shown belonging to the churchyard, the north fence as belonging to the Glebe.

The north boundary of the churchyard is shown straight on Dykes 1836a but is distinctly convex northwards on Dykes 1836b. In view of this, and to accord with Ordnance Survey 1851, a slight bend has

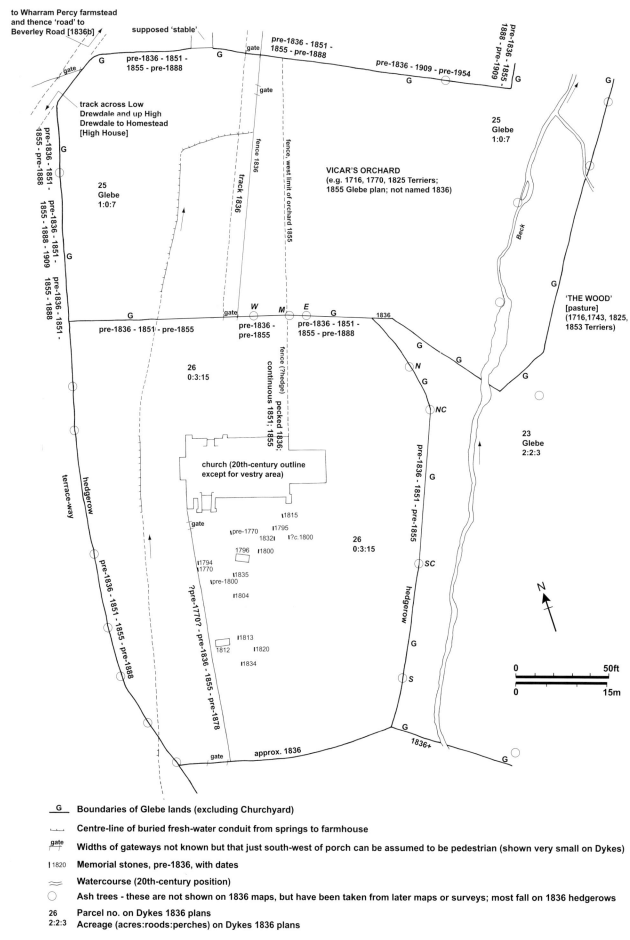

to Wharram Percy farmstead
and thence 'road' to
Beverley Road [1836b]

supposed 'stable'

pre-1836 - 1851 -
1855 - pre-1888

pre-1836 - 1851 -
1855 - pre-1888

pre-1836 - 1909 - pre-1954

pre-1836 - 1855 -
1888 - pre-1909

gate

gate

G

G

G

G

G

G

track across Low
Drewdale and up High
Drewdale to Homestead
[High House]

pre-1836 - 1851 -
1855 - pre-1888

pre-1836 - 1851 -
1855 - 1888 - 1909

pre-1836 - 1851 -
1855 - 1888

25
Glebe
1:0:7

25
Glebe
1:0:7

fence 1836

track 1836

fence, west limit of orchard 1855

VICAR'S ORCHARD
(e.g. 1716, 1770, 1825 Terriers;
1855 Glebe plan; not named 1836)

Beck

G

G

'THE WOOD'
[pasture]
(1716,1743, 1825,
1853 Terriers)

G

G

G

G

G

G

gate

W   M   E   G

pre-1836 -
pre-1855

pre-1836 - 1851 -
1855 - pre-1888

1836

N

NC

G

G

G

pre-1836 - 1851 - pre-1855

26
0:3:15

fence (?hedge)
pecked 1836;
continuous 1851; 1855

church (20th-century outline
except for vestry area)

23
Glebe
2:2:3

26
0:3:15

G

pre-1836 - 1851 - pre-1855

SC

G

terrace-way

hedgerow

pre-1836 - 1851 - 1855 - pre-1888

?pre-1770? - pre-1836 - 1855 - pre-1878

gate

|1815
|pre-1770 |1795
1832| |?c.1800
1796 |1800
|1794
|1770
|1835
pre-1800
|1804

|1813
1812 |1820
|1834

hedgerow

G

S

N

gate

approx. 1836

1836+

G

0   50ft

0   15m

G   Boundaries of Glebe lands (excluding Churchyard)

Centre-line of buried fresh-water conduit from springs to farmhouse

gate   Widths of gateways not known but that just south-west of porch can be assumed to be pedestrian (shown very small on Dykes)

| 1820   Memorial stones, pre-1836, with dates

Watercourse (20th-century position)

○   Ash trees - these are not shown on 1836 maps, but have been taken from later maps or surveys; most fall on 1836 hedgerows

26   Parcel no. on Dykes 1836 plans
2:2:3   Acreage (acres:roods:perches) on Dykes 1836 plans

Fig. 5. Plan of the Churchyard and Glebe boundaries, based on Dykes 1836a and 1836b. (E. Marlow-Mann after R.T. Porter)

6

been introduced on Figure 5 at the point where an internal churchyard fence meets the boundary. Immediately to the east of this the boundary passes through the site of an ash tree (*M*) whose stump was surveyed in 1970. Six metres to the west is a second ash tree (*W*). From a point just west of the latter tree, a fence is shown running northwards through the Glebe, across the site of the then recently demolished vicarage, separating the Orchard (although it is not shown as such until a later, 1855 plan) from the farm road which on Dykes 1836b runs on past the west front of the farmhouse; on Dykes 1836a only the stretch of this road through the Glebe is actually shown. Unlike Ordnance Survey 1851, Dykes does not show any track through the churchyard or across the Dam. From the 1770s the new farmstead at Bella controlled all the plateau east of the Beck so there would have been no need for access for agricultural purposes, and its absence from Dykes implies that this stretch of the route through the churchyard was not by this time defined on the ground – except by the gate in the south face. Although its use as a through route may have been minimal, parishioners from Bella and Wharram Percy farms would have entered the churchyard from the north.

The Dykes plans show the eastern boundary of the churchyard as a gentle curve, concave westwards, and the straight northern section makes an angle of about 80° with the axis of the church. Ordnance Survey 1851, on the other hand, not only has a rounded north-east corner but the northernmost straight section makes an angle of about 95° with the axis of the church. A line joining the two extant ash trees (NC and SC) on this section of the boundary also makes an angle of 95° with the church axis. Since it seems improbable that the boundary in 1836 had deviated from the hedgerow line, only to revert by 1851, Figure 5 gives more weight to the 1851 plan. The trees at *NC* and *SC* mark the top of the steep slope down to the Beck. Towards the south end of the east boundary ash tree *S* is shown in 1888, but it has not been observed on any photographs and had certainly disappeared by the mid-1950s.

The south-east corner of the churchyard is shown somewhat rounded on Dykes 1836a, but not on Ordnance Survey 1851, where the straight lines of the east and south boundaries meet at an angle of 111°. In 1888 ash *S*, unlike those to the north, was plotted virtually on the fence line, where the fence turns south-west; the 1836 line has therefore been taken through this ash, and then the 20th-century line has been followed to the south-east corner.

The ash tree shown just west of the south-west corner in 1888 appears to correspond with the south-west corner on Dykes's plan, and has been used together with the 1888 position of the south-east corner to fix the 1836 southern boundary. Apart from this tree, there are (and were in 1888) no ash trees along the south boundary to provide evidence of its 18th-century alignment. While the 1836 line is convex southwards and the 1851 line is almost straight, there is no obvious reason for rejecting Dykes's line. Near the west end of the south boundary Dykes shows the gate which leads to the dam and beyond.

Most of the western boundary of the churchyard and glebe is shown as an almost straight line on Dykes 1836a, with a slight convex bend to the west. On Ordnance Survey 1851 this bend is much greater (*c*.18°). The positions of the trees on Ordnance Survey 1888 are in agreement with the boundary depiction of 1851. As the two ash trees that survived until 1979 on the western boundary of the churchyard and glebe are insufficient to permit discrimination between the 1836 and 1851 versions, Figure 5 is, on similar reasoning to that used for the east boundary, based largely on the Ordnance Survey alignment.

Ordnance Survey 1888 shows seven trees (and one bush) along what was, by then, the former west boundary of the churchyard. These trees are all taken to be ashes surviving from the 18th century; their positions on Figure 2.1 are all (except for the tree west of the porch) enlarged from the Ordnance Survey map. The west boundary, as plotted, lies below, and a metre or two east of, the present terraced way along the valley side; there is at present no archaeological data to suggest when the terraced way was established. The continuing slippage of the hillside in this area precludes the determination of the relation of this boundary to the west limit of the medieval cemetery.

The south-western part of the churchyard was divided off from the portion used for 18th and early 19th-century burials by an internal fence, running northwards from the east side of the southern gate to the south-west corner of the church. It passes close to five memorial stones; 1770, 1794, pre-*c*.1800, 1812 are more or less parallel or at right angles to it, while the Gofton 1871-78 slab (not shown) straddles the fence line and helps to date its disappearance (*Wharram II*, 3). This suggests that the fence dates back to at least 1770 (the earliest of the dated stones). This fence line produces, incidentally, a truer west-east orientation for the 1770-1812 stones than for the other memorial stones, although some influence of the fence line can be traced in the alignment of the 1835 and 1853 stones. A small gate in the fence immediately south of the porch provided access to the Church from the main north-south route.

Another internal churchyard fence ran north from the north-east corner of the nave to the northern churchyard fence at *M*. It is shown by Dykes as a pecked line, but continuous on the later maps (e.g. the plan of 1885 in the parish register: Borthwick PR WP1, 139). Like the southern internal fence, this may date from the late 18th century or earlier; both were doubtless used to control the grazing of the churchyard (see pp 4-5).

In conclusion, the principal lineaments of the 1836 reconstruction plan would have appeared on a late 18th-century plan, and they continued to subsist until the third quarter of the 19th century, say the early 1860s. Thereafter, a major re-fencing and reduction in area are reflected in the survey of 1888.

Part Two
The Excavations

3 Excavations in the Central Graveyard Area
by C. Harding and E. Marlow-Mann

Introduction

Excavation of the church, and of the graveyard in the immediate vicinity of the church, took place between 1962 and 1973, and the findings were published in *Wharram III*. The focus of that volume was, however, the structural development of the building, and the preparation of the current publication provided an opportunity to review the often complex site records in order to glean further information about the relationship of burials to other activity in the graveyard. This chapter supplements *Wharram III*, but it does not repeat detailed information that can be found there. The two reports should therefore be read together to gain a comprehensive view of the results of excavation in the graveyard immediately around the church. The work was previously reported in *Interim Report* 1962, 2-3; 1963, 2-4; 1964, 3; 1965, 3; 1967, 2; 1968, 2; 1969, 3-4; 1970, 3; 1971, 1-3; 1972, 1-2; 1973, 1-2; 1979, 11.

This chapter groups together the individual units of excavation into areas that are referenced to the church building (see Fig. 4). It starts with investigations outside the east end of the present building, and proceeds clockwise to the areas south of the chancel and nave, the west end and finally to the area north of the nave which was linked by a long trench to Site 26 (Chapter 4). The southernmost area of the graveyard, identified in trenches outside the present churchyard, is described in Chapter 5.

Summary of the church phases in *Wharram III* (Fig. 6)

A summary description of the principal phases of activity identified in *Wharram III* as associated with the church, is a necessary prelude to the details of excavations that follow. All phasing in this summary relates solely to phasing for the church; it does not relate to the subsequent phasing within Sites 26, 41, 52, 71 and 80. Unlike the two chapters which follow, the excavation reports which appear in Chapter 3 are grouped by area in relation to the standing church building, rather than by stratigraphic phase or chronological period. This is because they can, broadly, be related to the phasing of the church as set out in *Wharram III*. The church phases with dating as defined in *Wharram III* are summarised below.

Pre-church Phase (1st century to early 4th century AD) (Fig. 20)

Iron Age and Romano-British activity was recorded during the church excavations. Late Iron Age pottery was present in an area south of the present chancel, in a clay deposit into which Phase II burials had been cut. Pottery found in association with a 'hearth' beneath the present chancel arch, more or less on the central axis of the church, indicates activity in the 1st and 2nd centuries AD; the significance of this find is reviewed later in this chapter. A Late Roman presence was indicated by the recovery of two coins of the late 3rd to early 4th century (*Wharram III*, 174).

Two ditches were revealed in the North Churchyard on an east-west, roughly parallel, alignment, 7.6m apart. They were approximately 1.5m wide and 1.2m deep but were not necessarily contemporary. The northern ditch (ditch 255 in Site 26) contained Romano-British pottery with some residual Iron Age sherds, and medieval material in the upper fill. The southern ditch (NA35) produced no finds.

Phase I (mid/late 10th century)

A series of post-holes was recorded, enclosed by the Phase II nave and extending into the chancel, but their relationship with the Phase II church was uncertain (*Wharram III*, fig. 11). Many of the post-holes were cut into natural chalk and were cut or sealed by Phase II features; they were all therefore assigned to Phase I. Although some almost certainly related to the construction of the Phase II nave, the layout of the post-holes suggested that they may have belonged to a timber structure, 6.7m x 3m, possibly an early timber church.

Phase II (early/mid-11th century)

Several courses of large chalk blocks (EE106; Fig. 9, Section B; *Wharram III*, fig. 11) were recorded 1.4m below the Phase II ground level. These were interpreted as a chalk platform acting as a revetment to consolidate the ground for building; no inner edge of this platform was noted.

The first stone church was constructed as a two-cell building with chancel and nave much smaller than those which followed. The nave measured 8.7m by 6.5m externally and 6.6m by 4.3m internally; the chancel comprised a square with sides of 4.4m externally and 3.2 by 2.5m internally. The complete excavation of the chancel walls was not possible, due to the location of the present chancel, but they were identified by auguring and slot-trenches. The walls were built in foundation trenches. Several post-holes were recorded in positions indicative

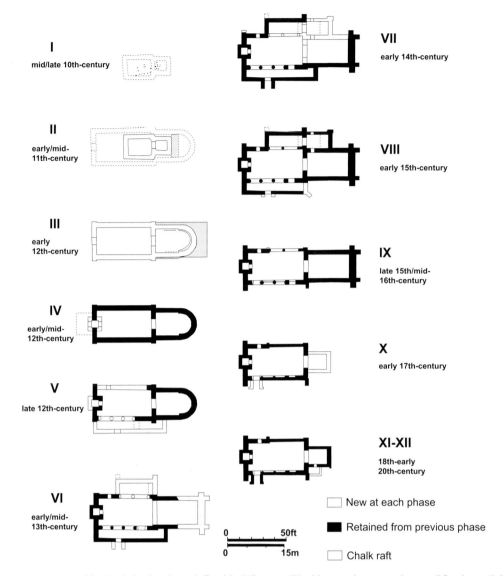

Fig. 6. The phased development of St Martin's church, as defined in *Wharram III* with some interpretative modifications. (J.C. Thorn)

of construction phase scaffolding. The construction of this church was assigned to the 11th century.

Most of the masonry of this first church had been completely robbed, along with almost all the floor surface. No doorways were evident but the entrance was presumably through one of the nave walls.

Phase III (early 12th century)

Phase III marks the construction of the church which is, basically, the nave that still stands. The Phase II nave was almost completely demolished and the Phase III nave was constructed, almost 3¹/₂ times larger, measuring 14.6m by 7.2m internally. It enclosed the earlier building and extended approximately 7m westwards. Attempts were made to create a horizontal floor surface by raising its level towards the east, but the ground continued to slope 0.6m from the west end of the nave to the chancel arch. Unlike that of the Phase II church, this arch was built directly onto the natural chalk. No evidence was found of the chancel arch itself because of later intrusions, and its width is therefore unknown.

The new apsidal-ended chancel was 6.4m wide and had a maximum length of 9.3m, extending over what had previously been external graveyard areas. Internally, it was about seven times larger than the area of the Phase II chancel and was supported by a large raft (EE42; *Wharram III*, fig. 17), constructed of large roughly-coursed chalk blocks; this may have been constructed while the previous chancel was still in use. The inner edge of the raft curved around the inside line of the apse, while the squared outer edge extended 13.7m east of the nave wall, 9.15m wide at its broadest point with a maximum depth of 2.3m. Immediately east of the chancel arch was a stone block (C26; *Wharram III*, fig. 17); evidence of similar blocks forming a line across the entrance to the chancel were noted and, in conjunction with two post-holes, these may have indicated a screen and associated gate.

The building has been dated to the early 12th century. It should be noted, however, that the chancel arch remained in the same position as it had occupied in the previous building, leaving open the possibility of

10

'alternate rebuilding', with the nave and chancel being replaced at slightly different times.

Phase IV (early/mid-12th century)
The tower was added to the Phase III church later in the 12th century. It was constructed in two sections astride and abutting the western nave wall and built straight onto the natural chalk; no early flooring survived. There was some evidence to suggest that a fully external tower had originally been intended but the design may have been modified during construction.

Phase V (late 12th century)
The west wall of the tower was further modified in this phase, and the north nave wall was rebuilt with a reduced thickness. An arcade was inserted in the south nave wall to give access to a new south aisle that extended the full length of the nave and overlapped the west end of the chancel. The aisle, which possibly had a chapel at its east end, was 2.3m wide and an entrance was recorded opposite the central bay of the south arcade.

The nave floor was again raised, particularly at the east end, reducing the west-east slope to 0.4m. Areas of concentrated chalk rubble and occasional burnt sandstone on both sides of the nave suggested the footings of wall benches. These were probably only in use for a relatively short time as they would have been removed for the Phase VI works.

Evidence of intense burning at the foot of the west nave wall, inside the tower and at the base of the west bay of the south arcade suggests the occurrence of a fire. No burning was seen on the north nave wall or beneath the east doorway of the tower, indicating that these were replaced after the event, and that the south arcade was erected before the north wall was rebuilt.

Phase VI (early/mid-13th century)
A porch was added to the south aisle. The Phase III-V chancel arch was removed and replaced by a much wider and taller arch. The jambs and voussoirs of the former chancel arch were then used to form a fourth archway at the east end of the south nave wall, giving additional access to the south aisle.

The apsidal east end of the chancel was replaced by a straight wall, with the north and south walls extended to meet it; the west half of the north wall was rebuilt. This new chancel had an internal length of 10.8m. The Phase III raft was no longer visible indicating that the external ground surface had risen considerably, possibly as a result of grave-digging.

The north aisle was constructed, with an internal length of 8.6m and a width of 2.4m. The stonework was of poorer quality than the south aisle and comprised ashlar interspersed with chalk blocks. Chalk rubble footings indicated the presence of a buttress in the north-east corner, but this did not appear paralleled at the north-west.

Phase VII (early 14th century)
An industrial complex was located within the west half of the nave, consisting of a furnace, bell-casting pit, ash pit and two possible lead-melting hearths. A single line of sandstone blocks along the base of the furnace suggested one side of a flue. The lead-melting hearths may have been associated with plumbing or glazing work. These metalworking features were then sealed by a new floor level.

Part of the north arcade and the nave wall to the east were rebuilt above floor level on a more northerly alignment than previously. The Phase VI arcade column was retained but was moved northwards. A chapel, measuring 5.6m by 3.5m internally, was added at the east end of the north aisle. The north wall contained reused ashlar blocks and abutted the north aisle footings; a gap probably indicated the position of a doorway. A clasping buttress supported the north-east corner.

The Phase VI chancel arch collapsed and the present, much smaller, arch was built in the gap. The old masonry was reused on either side of the new archway, but the smaller size of the arch resulted in too little stone remaining to complete the wall. The upper half was therefore built of chalk, quarried on site.

Phase VIII (early 15th century)
The east end of the south aisle chapel was demolished and a new east end wall built, decreasing the length of the aisle to approximately 15.2m. A diagonal buttress supported its new south-east corner. A single row of sandstone 'lumps' ran the width of the aisle; a slot in the inner face of the south wall indicated that this row was probably the base of an altar screen. The porch may have been demolished in this phase, with the stumps of the walls being converted into short buttresses on either side of the doorway.

Phase IX (late 15th century/mid-16th century)
The two arcades were blocked with courses of sandstone, including a reused chamfered plinth and a number of decorated grave slabs (Ch. 21). An earlier doorway was re-erected within the former west bay of the south arcade, and the aisles and chapel were demolished. Several post-holes were recorded, especially within the nave, but as later layers had been destroyed it was difficult to identify to which phase these post-holes belonged; at least one post-hole may have been associated with the Phase IX alterations due to the presence in its fill of a worn York penny of the third quarter of the 15th century. The demolition of the aisles probably took place between the late 15th to mid-16th centuries.

Phase X (early 17th century)
In the 17th century, the large chancel was demolished, the north-east corner of the nave rebuilt and the present, smaller, chancel erected. This chancel was not precisely rectangular in shape, being 0.1m wider at the east end than at the west, and had a maximum internal length of

5m. Its outer wall faces were supported by large fragments of worked sandstone, probably reused from the demolished large chancel. The chancel was paved with flagstones. The level of the floor within the nave was not clear, but the pew-slots terminated 0.2m above the Phase VII floor.

The present south porch was constructed, extending 2.3m south of the nave; it was 1.5m wide and was supported by large flat chalk slabs. The entrance to the porch was a reused feature, probably salvaged from the large chancel.

Phases XI-XII (18th century to early 20th century)

A series of soakaways was recorded outside the north and south walls of the nave, on the north side cutting through the southern half of the former chapel. At the east end they were 1m deep and 0.6m wide and had caused significant damage to earlier features.

A new floor of large thick flagstones was laid in the nave; new pews stood on a wooden floor supported by rows of bricks and chalk blocks. The damp coursing beneath the floor destroyed many of the earlier floors, except for those protected by the slope towards the chancel arch. The floor of the tower was paved with black and red tiles and the font stood on a plinth of limestone ashlar blocks. Three graves were recorded beneath the floor here, but they may have been moved from the north-west corner of the nave.

In 1847 a vestry was added to the south side of the chancel, abutting the chancel and the east wall of the nave. The floor comprised red and black tiles, set diagonally with a rectangular border of black tiles. Access to the vestry was through a doorway with brick jambs cut through the south wall of the chancel.

The Phase XI drainage system was replaced by a series of ceramic drains associated with the building of the vestry.

Phase XIII (mid-20th century)

After the abandonment of the church, the pews and other fittings were removed from the nave in the 1950s.

The East End, 1962-64, 1971 and 1979 (Fig. 7)

Although many of the original plans of this area were not comprehensive, some of the sections were more detailed and corroborated by the 1979 quadrant excavation at the south-east corner of the existing chancel. Some difficulties of interpretation have arisen because of the conflation of separate contexts for illustrative purposes (and brevity) in *Wharram III*. Comparison with the original site records and archive data sheets provided clarification.

This complex group of trenches and areas occupies the space between two major zones of excavated burials: the Vestry, to the south, and the North Churchyard. Information relating to this area, not covered by *Wharram III*, falls into two categories: the natural topography of the terrace edge, and external ground surfaces. With the

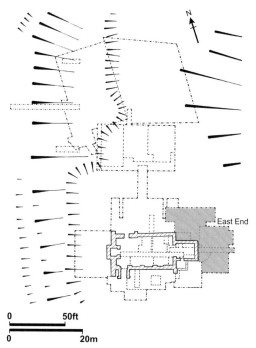

Fig. 7. Location of the East End (EE) excavations. (E. Marlow-Mann)

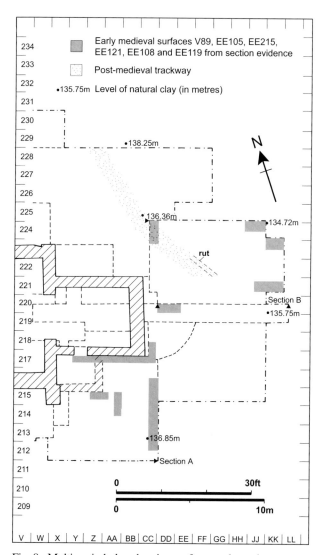

Fig. 8. Multi-period plan showing surfaces and trenches excavated north-east of the standing church. (E. Marlow-Mann)

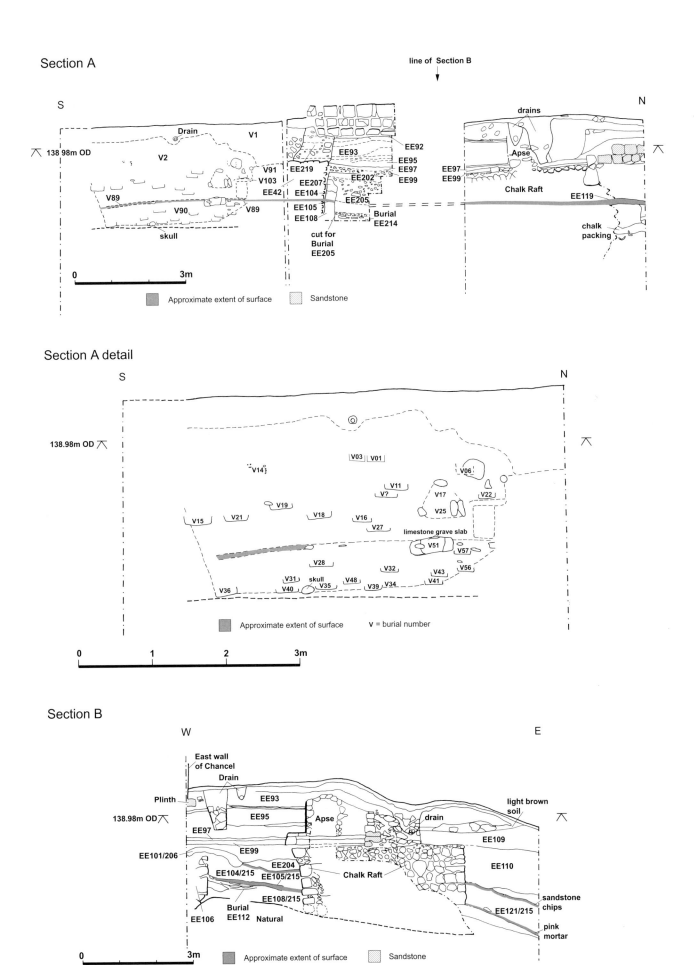

Section A

S   line of Section B   N

138.98m OD

Drain
V1
V2
V91
V103
EE219
EE42
EE207
EE104
V89
V90
EE105
EE108
V89
skull
cut for
Burial
EE205
EE92
EE93
EE95
EE97
EE99
EE202
EE205
Burial
EE214

drains
Apse
EE97
EE99
Chalk Raft
EE119
chalk
packing

0   3m

Approximate extent of surface   Sandstone

Section A detail

S   N

138.98m OD

V14
V03 V01
V06
V11
V?
V17
V22
V19
V25
V15
V21
V18
V16
V27
V28
V31
skull
V48
V32
V43
V36
V40
V35
V39
V34
V41
V56
limestone grave slab
V51
V57

Approximate extent of surface   v = burial number

0   1   2   3m

Section B

W   E

East wall
of Chancel
Drain
Plinth
138.98m OD
EE93
EE95
Apse
EE97
EE99
EE101/206
EE104/215
EE105/215
EE204
Chalk Raft
EE108/215
EE106
Burial
EE112   Natural
light brown
soil
drain
EE109
EE110
sandstone
chips
EE121/215
pink
mortar

0   3m

Approximate extent of surface   Sandstone

Fig. 9. East End sections: A, composite north-south section along Grid CC/DD (approximate position), 212-25 (southern section is along Grid mid-CC) and detail of burials; B., composite east-west section along Grid mid-220, CC-LL. (E. Marlow-Mann)

exception of already published 19th-century drainage schemes around the church and the 'Romano-British hearth' beneath the chancel arch (Fig. 20) there appeared to be no evidence of any activities other than church construction and burial.

Across the excavated area as far east as Grid BB/229 (see Fig. 8), the natural ground surface was identified as chalk, its surface at 138.25m OD. Further south-east, as far as the limit of excavation, natural was a blue-grey clay, its surface recorded in Grid CC/224-25 at 136.36m OD. It sloped down to 134.72m OD in Grid KK, with a steep break of slope east of Grid FF. This pattern of slope was replicated further south, but rising slightly: the surface of the clay was at *c*.135.75m OD in Grid KK 219/20, and in Grid CC/213 it was at *c*.136.85m OD. It appears therefore that the central axis of the church was not quite aligned on the highest ground. The possible significance of these observations will be considered further in the discussion which concludes this chapter.

Deposits located beneath, or cut by, the Phase III chalk raft (EE42; *Wharram III*, fig. 17) supporting the early 12th-century apsidal chancel, and beneath the dumped clay (EE110) displaced by its construction (Fig. 6 and Fig. 9, Sections A and B), include at least one surface which must have been contemporary with the first stone church and may have pre-dated it. Comparison of adjoining sections from the Vestry (below) indicates that context V89, a distinctive surface characterised by frequent 'green' sandstone chips in a mortary matrix, appears to have covered a wide area of the slope descending eastwards and southwards (Fig. 6 and Fig. 9, Section B). This horizon sealed the previously exposed stone grave-covers (Ch. 21, Nos 3 and 2) of Burials V51 and V52 (V82 and V83 in *Wharram III*), as well as Burial V56, the fill of which contained a styca dated to *c*. AD 841-49/50 (Ch. 25, No. 8, and see Fig. 11, and Table 117).

At the East End this horizon was also clear on sections in front of the chancel, where it formed part of the 'layer' numbered EE215 in *Wharram III,* fig. 8, section 1. EE215 as published is in fact an amalgamation of contexts EE104, EE105 and EE108 (Fig. 9, Section B). In *Wharram III*, EE215 is described as a pre-stone church ground surface, but there are in fact two surfaces: EE105 and the top of EE104. In absolute levels the top of EE104 and V89 correspond exactly, but not in content; context EE105, a band of chalk rubble and mortar below EE104, forming the surface of EE108, was more similar to V89.

Figure 9, Section B also indicates a sloping deposit of 'clayey brown with sandstone chips' beyond the raft, on the surface of EE121/215. It also shows 'pink mortar' at the base of this layer, above a layer described as 'blue mixed clay'. It seems likely that the sandstone chips on the surface of EE215 equate to the surface of EE104 further west, whilst the pink mortar below might conceivably be equivalent to EE105. Another area of sandstone surfacing (EE119) was recorded further north, on Figure 9, Section A, located above the early burial layer.

The unifying factor relating these surfaces is the presence of the distinctive sandstone chips. The spread of

this stony deposit suggests the remnants of building debris deliberately distributed as a surface. In Grids CC-DD/218-20 it was overlain by a 0.15-0.3m thick dump of mortar (EE101/206/207: see Fig. 9, Section B), which was assumed to have derived from the construction of the east wall of the first stone chancel (on the further assumption that the coursed chalk blocks EE106 visible on the same section represent a raft that consolidated the ground immediately east of the Phase II chancel, rather than the footing of another wall). If this is the case, then the sandstone surface will have been either earlier than the construction of the first stone church, or contemporary with the work on its foundations. This does not, of course, preclude the continued use of most of this fairly extensive surface after the first stone church had been completed. EE105 might relate to the construction of EE106, the Phase I 'chalk raft'.

Although the use of this area for continual and repeated burial until the 16th century is known from the spread of dated burials (see Figs 117 and 122) some of the sections, particularly towards the north-eastern boundary, show a series of buried turf lines. This suggests intermittent demand for burial space, reflecting the relative density shown on the overall burial plan (Fig. 117) in comparison to the area further west.

Plans of the north-eastern area excavated in 1964 show, directly below the modern turf level, various spreads of chalk and sandstone rubble with occasional flint, brick and tile, some dispersed but others more compact with a distinct eastern edge matched in section by a deposit with a convex surface. This was described as chalk packing with larger chalk beneath. Further south, at a comparable level, were spreads of slate, compacted chalk, larger chalk and sandstone and the line of a possible rut (Fig. 8). While the rubble spreads could just be dispersed demolition material it is possible that they represent deliberate surfacing. This could represent one of the post-medieval trackways known to have crossed the churchyard in the 19th century, for example that running south from Site 26 (Period 6, Phases 1-2) or that on the 1851 map (see Fig. 159).

The Vestry 1973 (Fig. 10)

In 1973 the vestry, which had been constructed in *c*.1847, was demolished, exposing the south doorway into the Phase X chancel. An area 7.3m (east to west) by 7m was opened south of the chancel and east of the east wall of the south aisle, including the area of the former vestry and the south-east chapel. The work produced useful data on the terrace profile and ground surfaces as well as a complete burial sequence. The most significant discoveries were, however, three pre-Conquest burials (Burials V50-52) with stone grave-covers, accompanied by some headstones and footstones. Though described briefly and illustrated in *Wharram III* (fiche only), these grave-covers were not, in retrospect, given adequate consideration. This is now rectified in a discussion provided by David Stocker (Ch. 21).

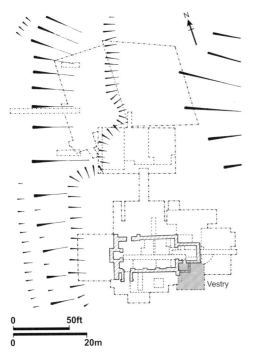

Fig. 10. Location of the Vestry (V) excavations. (E. Marlow-Mann)

The pre-graveyard period was represented by some residual Late Iron Age and early Roman pottery (Grid CC13, context 2004, not illustrated; see *Wharram III*, 53, fig. 10). The published sherds are from a Late Iron Age cooking pot (hand-finished calcite gritted) in 'association' with a sherd of abraded samian (*Wharram III*, 154, fiche 6.D1). This pottery was ascribed to context V90, but was actually located within Burial V36 (Fig. 9, Section A detail).

The earliest phase of burials, including the pre-Conquest stone grave-covers to Burials V50-52 which would previously have been exposed at ground level, was sealed by an external surface of 'green [sand]stone lumps mixed with sandy mortar/sandstone layer' V89 (Fig. 11). V89 was a fairly even deposit 50-78mm thick sloping down slightly to the south but steeply to the east. From its composition it has been identified as probable construction debris, laid as a surface. For discussion of the possible wider extent of this deposit see the previous section on the East End excavations, where it is equated with EE105/108.

The profile of the terrace east of the Phase II chancel, and probably also to the south, was considerably altered by the dumping of clay (EE110) dug out for the construction of the Phase III chalk raft V91. This process cut through and sealed part of the Phase II ground surface represented by deposit V89. To the west, the surface was sealed by a chalky clay which appeared to have been mostly dumped directly east of the raft to compensate for the very steeply sloping ground in this area.

Repeated burial in this zone until the mid-19th century left little evidence of any other activity in this part of the churchyard, including surfaces of 19th-century paths or tracks skirting the east end of the church towards Thixendale. An extensive deposit of sandstone and chalk rubble from the Phase X demolition of the large chancel was evident, however, pre-dating glazed ceramic drains, e.g. V20. For 19th-century drainage (as South Aisle and West End) see *Wharram III*, 77-9.

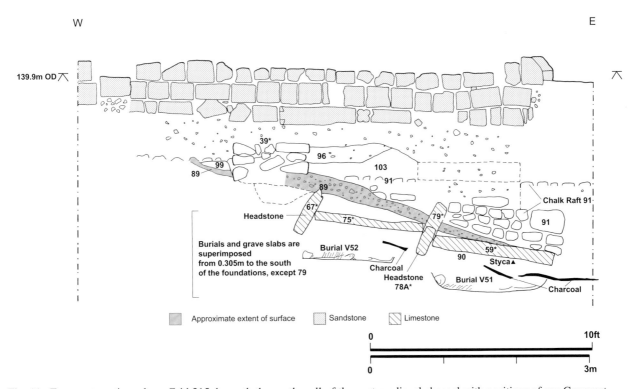

Fig. 11. East-west section, along Grid 215, beneath the south wall of the post-medieval chancel with positions of pre-Conquest gravestones projected from further south. Contexts marked with * are original 1973 contexts; other context numbers are those used in *Wharram III* publication sequence. Burial numbers as present sequence. (E. Marlow-Mann)

15

South Aisle, 1967-69 (Fig. 12)

The slope of natural chalk was observed and the height of natural noted at 0. 46m below the then ground surface in Grid N/O, and 1.52m below at the east end of the Nave. No pre-church features were located due to the extensive disturbance of the natural chalk by graves. The site notebook for a 1967 test-pit (Trench 9) refers to rubble initially identified as a 'medieval soakaway' in Grids O-P/212, but this may well have been a foundation trench for part of the Phase VI porch. Nineteenth-century soakaways (as around the North Aisle and West End) dating to c.1829 and 1847 are described in *Wharram III*, 92.

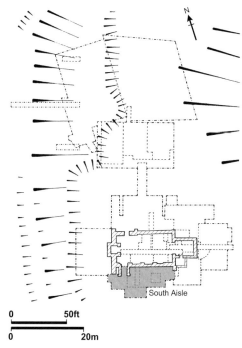

Fig. 12. Location of the South Aisle (SA) excavations. (E. Marlow-Mann)

West End, 1972 (Fig. 13)

An area 12.2 (north to south) by 9.15m was excavated between the west end of the church and the hillside, including the footings of the west wall and tower. The primary objective was to locate any evidence of an earlier tower.

The earliest feature, predating Phase III, was a quarry (WCO239; Fig. 14), extending 2.1 by 3.4m in an irregular oval shape and up to 1.2m deep. Another probable quarry (WCO244) was located in the south-west corner but was not fully excavated. Neither feature contained any datable material. A surface (WCO19) of hard grey packed chalk was identified extending up to 0.91m west from the face of the west wall of the tower and beneath it. A similar deposit, WCO18, was under the west nave wall. Two post-holes (WCO56, which cut through WCO19 and WCO57) were close to the respective corners of the tower, and were probably connected with its construction.

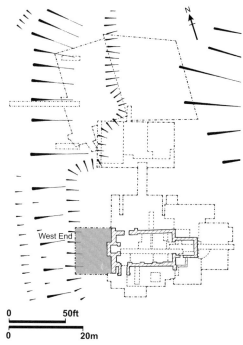

Fig. 13. Location of the West End (WCO) excavations. (E. Marlow-Mann)

In Phases IV-VIII the burials which extended all over the area (see Figs 18 and 115), were cut into and sealed by a 'cemetery soil' (WCO44, not illustrated) up to 0.9m deep, created by the excavation of graves. A few features contemporary with the burials were located, while others which cut through some burials may well have been contemporary overall. These included a shallow pit (WCO28, Fig. 15) with Ceramic Group 5 pottery in the fill (*Wharram III*, 161 no. 12), a second pit (WCO29) and a small post-hole (WCO58) which was not obviously a grave-marker. A very large flint block in Grid F/221 (Fig. 15) appears to have been a head marker for Burial WCO181 and squared sandstone blocks in Grid F/220 (Fig. 15) possibly represent other displaced markers (see Ch. 15). The date range for these burials is wider than expected; and whilst it is not impossible that the latest burials are post-medieval, a late medieval date seems more likely.

In Phases IX-XI, extending c.3m west from the tower and sealing the burials (but possibly contemporary with some of the latest burials), was a deposit of 'hard chalk packing' (WCO24a, Fig. 16), around the perimeter of which were several post-holes (WCO51, WCO52 and WCO53) with another in the middle (WCO50). To the south of WCO52 was a substantial post-hole with a post-pipe, WCO54/55 which had a soft dark fill of charcoal, mortar and fused metal. The disposition of these features suggests a possible stabilising dump/make-up and scaffold pole holes, presumably for repair or rebuilding of the tower. Although nothing is documented until the 19th century there is circumstantial evidence of the poor state of the parapet in the 16th and 17th centuries (*Wharram III*, 115). Sealing WCO24a and extending further north beside the nave wall was a sandy level containing sandstone rubble (WCO251) cut by two further post-

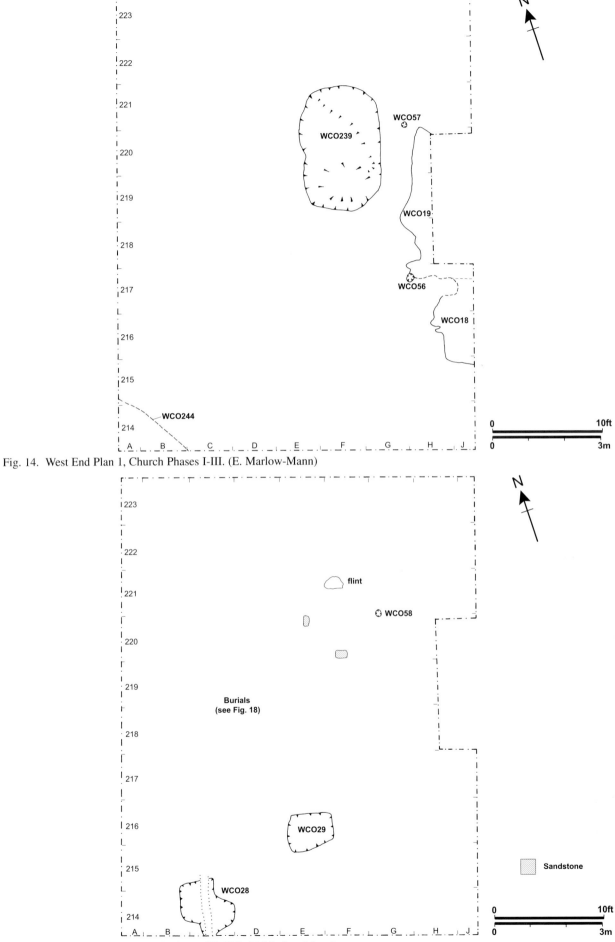

Fig. 14. West End Plan 1, Church Phases I-III. (E. Marlow-Mann)

Fig. 15. West End Plan 2, Church Phases IV-VIII. (E. Marlow-Mann)

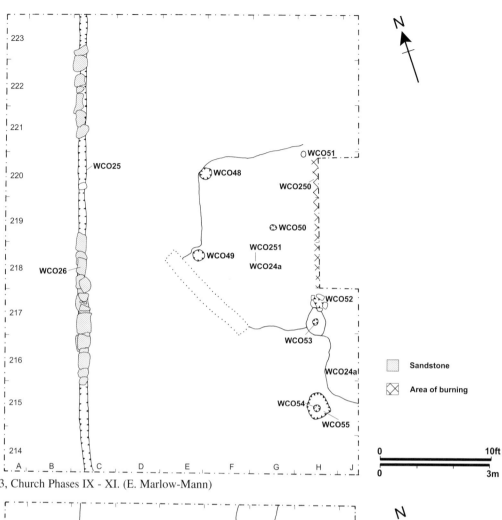

Fig. 16. West End Plan 3, Church Phases IX - XI. (E. Marlow-Mann)

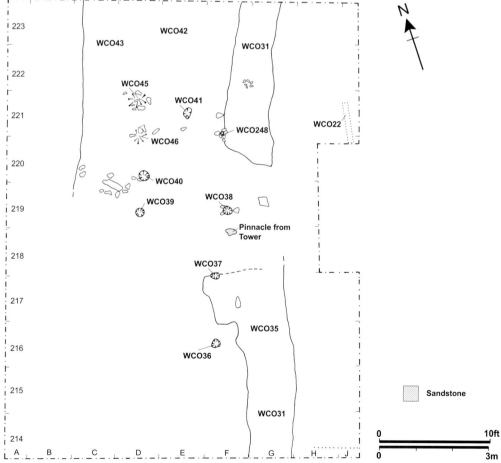

Fig. 17. West End Plan 4, Church Phase XII. (E. Marlow-Mann)

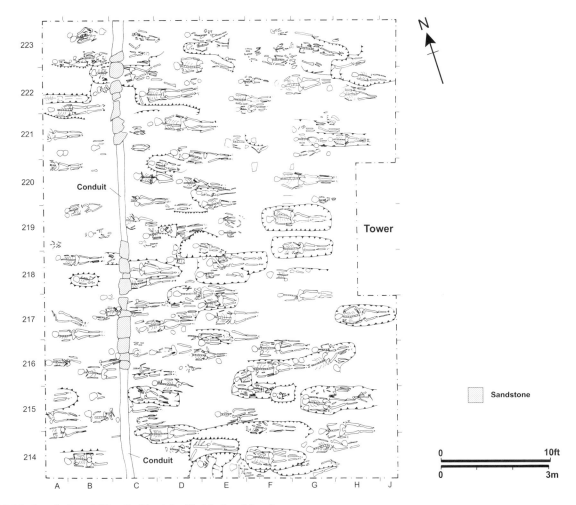

Fig. 18. Multi-phased plan of West End burials. (E. Marlow-Mann)

holes (WCO48 and WCO49). Alongside the tower this deposit and the face of the tower itself were scorched and burnt (WCO250).

Crossing the site from north to south, cutting through an earlier pit (WCO28), was a fresh water conduit (WCO26). It was set in a trench (WCO25) 0.5m wide and 0.6m deep and the sides constructed of 18th-century bricks with a clay lining. It was capped with bricks and sandstone slabs, and 50mm of clean silt lay in the bottom.

In Phase XII a linear surface of chalk pebbles (WCO31, Fig. 17), with patches of larger chalk, brick and tile and worn chalk pebbles (WCO35), crossed the site from north-east to south-east just west of the tower. The profile of this surface was slightly convex and rutted and its width varied from 1m to 1.2m (Plate 1). This clearly served as a pathway or narrow track and is probably that thought to have passed by the west side of the church from the farmhouse (and until 1834 the vicarage) to the north, joining the path to the south from the porch, but not documented until 1851 (Fig. 159). From 1888 a wider trackway skirting the bottom of the west hillside outside the churchyard fence is documented and was probably represented on site by deposits of sandstone blocks and rubble (WCO42) and patches of chalk packing (WCO43) at the north end of the site. Unfortunately, the upper levels of the site were not recorded at the south end, but from

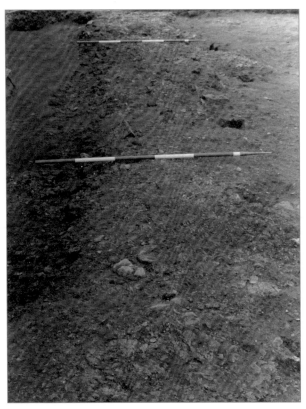

Plate 1. Path in H-F/222-13 and post-holes 36-38, from the north.

19

photographs a similar surface appears to have extended across the site. To the west lay grey chalky material, probably hill wash from the adjacent slope.

Some of the post-holes in the upper levels also appear to correspond with those documented. A row of four (WCO248, WCO38, WCO37 and WCO36) along the west side of the path, or the east side of the trackway, were spaced *c*.1.8m (6ft) apart and are on the line of the fence removed in 1972. Another row of four (WCO39, WCO40, WCO45 and WCO46) cutting through trackway surface WCO42 were spaced *c*. 0.9m (3ft) apart which would have been rather close together for a post and rail fence but may have served some temporary purpose, perhaps during works to the church in the 1880s or 1920s.

Sealing the surfaces (but presumably not all the post-holes) was a black loamy deposit (WCO23) with chalk tile and brick, thickest towards the hillside suggesting that it may have originated as topsoil washed down the hillside. Modern features included a ceramic drain (WCO22) adjacent to the nave wall on the north side of the tower, (see other areas for similar drainage in Phase XII, probably inserted in 1847), a narrow shallow trench possibly dug in 1961 by the RCHM to investigate possibilities of an earlier tower, and debris in the form of sandstone mouldings from the collapse of the west face of the tower in 1961.

North Churchyard, 1962-73 (Figs 19 and 20)

The area north of the church was investigated in a complicated series of interventions over five separate seasons.

This sequence of excavated areas may have been even more complex than indicated on *Wharram III*, fig. 5. For example, slides show the Grid L-M baulk to be wider

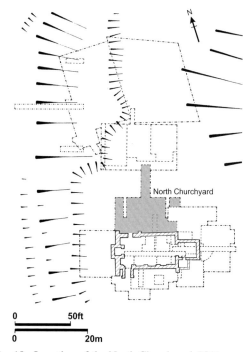

North Churchyard

0   50ft

0   20m

Fig. 19. Location of the North Churchyard (NA) excavations. (E. Marlow-Mann)

north of Grid mid-27 line. It is not known whether this represents a narrower baulk to the south than the 0.9m marked on the plans or a wider baulk to the north. The relative absence of planned burials in Grid M (see Fig. 115) may indicate that the baulk was wider to the north.

The earliest feature appears to be an east-west V-shaped ditch (Figs 20 and 21; Plate 2) identified at the northern end of the 1970 trench in Grids P-Q/ 236-37 (NA96; Fig. 20). The ditch was further recorded in Site 26, as context 255 (see Fig. 31), with Burials NA001, NA001a, NA002 and NA003 (Fig. 21) cut into the top of it. The southern edge was very steep; the northern edge possibly less so, but intrusive burials obscured the top of the ditch. At the highest point at which it was clearly defined, however, the width of the ditch was *c*. 1.5m and the depth 1m, mainly cut through natural chalk. It is possible that the original upper width of the ditch was about 2.3m, at 139.82m OD, giving an original depth of 1.2m.

Plate 2. Section through ditch NA96 along Grid O/P 235-237, looking west.

The finds included Romano-British and Iron Age material, discussed further in the Site 26 report below (p. 34). This ditch is an extremely interesting and important feature, and this is the only recorded section through it, as the southern limit of Site 26 was unfortunately sited along the middle of the ditch cut. Its likely period of use and its possible interpretation are discussed below (p. 60).

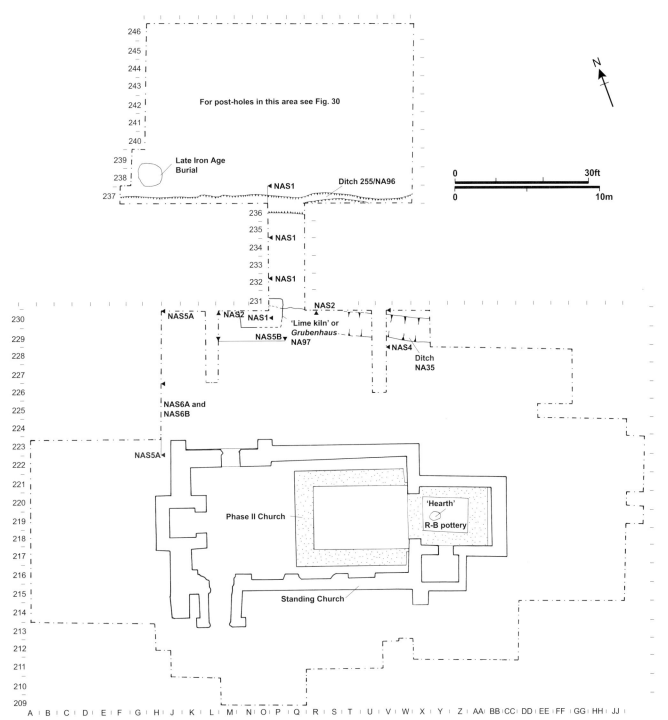

Fig. 20. Plan of pre-church features including location of North Churchyard sections. (E. Marlow-Mann)

Approximately 6.1m to the south was a similar, more or less parallel, and possibly contemporary ditch (NA35), U to V-shaped in profile and with three distinct fills (Figs 20 and 22; Plate 3). The north edge was beyond the limit of excavation; the maximum recorded width was 2m but the projected upper width was *c*. 2.7m. The base of the cut sloped down to the east. The lowest fill (NA38) included much 'red' chalk which had accumulated up the sides as well as over the base.

The ditch appears to have been recut with the deeper part to the north and a second fill (NA37) of mixed 'red' chalk, weathered chalk and darkish 'soil' accumulated to

a depth of more than 0.3m. Above was another fill (NA36) of weathered gravelly chalk. Whether this was the fill of another recut is not clear because of the intrusion of Burial NA113, but the general angle of the deposit suggests that here the ditch was not recut again. The ditch as recorded in Grid U/230, although cut by several burials, shows 'dark ditch fill with chalk blocks' in a U-shaped cut. From the level and description this appears to be the middle fill (NA37) in the recut.

All the profiles suggest that the north face was the steepest, with a more gentle break of slope and a berm on the southern edge. The base of the ditch suggested a slight

21

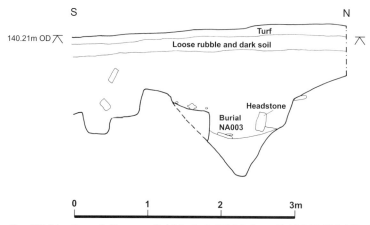

0   1   2   3m

Fig. 21. East-facing section NAS1a, through Romano-British ditch NA96 along Grid O/P 235-237. (E. Marlow-Mann)

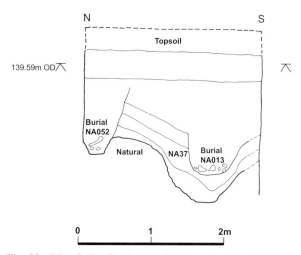

0   1   2m

Fig. 22. West-facing Section NAS4, through ditch NA35 in Grid mid-V, 229-230. (E. Marlow-Mann)

Plate 3. Section through ditch NA35 in Grid mid-V, 229-230, looking east.

north-west to south-east alignment. It must be concluded that the ditch does not seem to have turned in any other direction and thus represents a linear boundary feature across the terrace. A 9th-century zoomorphic strap end from a burial above the ditch is illustrated in *Wharram III*, fig. 191 no. 9. Other finds from the ditch include a trumpet brooch (p. 307, Church catalogue No. 73) of the late 1st to mid-2nd century AD, as well as copper, glass and ceramics of medieval date.

In the area of Grid O/229-30 (Fig. 23) was a clearly defined deposit of chalk and sandstone (NA97) at least 1.1m deep (top at 140.05m OD) and cut by burials. The western extent of this deposit was marked by a charred upright post (Grid mid-N230, *c.* 100mm diameter, at least 0.3m high) cutting through weathered and natural chalk in the north section (Fig. 23). This post is also clearly visible on slides of this section (Plates 4 and 5), which describe this as the area of the 'lime-kiln', a feature noted, but not discussed, in *Wharram III*, 49 and 84. To the south and east, slides show an area of pink, possibly burnt chalk cut by Burials NA091-094 in O-P/230, and deposits of bright green possibly 'rotted' clay/chalk also cut by burials located approximately in Grid O-P/229. The original finds records state that Burial NA092 in Grid P/230 was at the 'level of burnt chalk' (NA51), while

'fragments of plaster' in Grid N/230 were recorded as from a 'sand filled feature' (not identified on the section). The relatively numerous slides of this area in conjunction with plans and sections (Fig. 24, NAS5B and NAS2, and Fig. 25, NAP2 and NAS1) enable a general description and reconstruction (Fig. 23) to be attempted.

This feature (NA97; Fig. 23) was sub-rectangular, covering an area approximately 3m by 2m, with material including small sandstone as well as chalk 'contained'

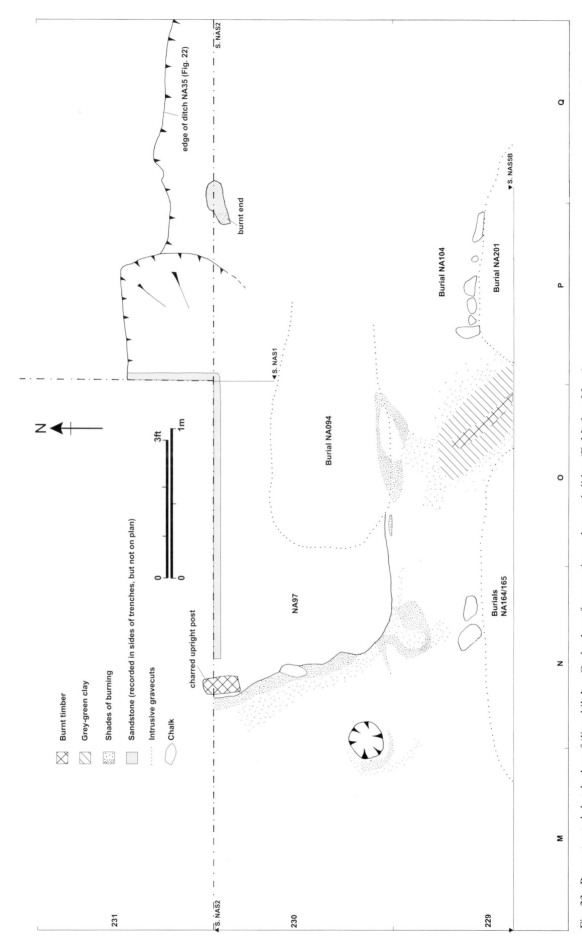

Fig. 23. Reconstructed sketch plan of 'lime kiln' or *Grubenhaus* from sections, plans and slides. (E. Marlow-Mann)

N

Burnt timber

Grey-green clay

Shades of burning

Sandstone (recorded in sides of trenches, but not on plan)

Intrusive gravecuts

Chalk

0   3ft

0   1m

charred upright post

NA97

Burial NA094

Burials
NA164/165

Burial NA104

Burial NA201

edge of ditch NA35 (Fig. 22)

S. NAS2

burnt end

S. NAS1

S. NAS5B

S. NAS2

231

230

229

M   N   O   P   Q

Plate 4. NAS5B through feature NA97, Grid O/P 229, looking south.

within or dumped over the top. The material was 0.9m in depth, above the base which appears to have been small compact chalk (probably natural). The sides or edge of the feature appear to have been distinctively hard, with an almost smooth and vertical inner face and scorching of the chalk around the 'outside'. At Grid P-Q/230, some 0.6m lower than the top of the post, a large sandstone block, burnt on its western face also appears to sit against the edge of the feature.

Against the southern edge the scorching was much more intense (Plates 4 and 5), and in the section immediately to the south (NAS5B, Fig. 24) was a line of intense burning with bands of grey-yellow-green and grey-green possibly 'rotted' or burnt clay to either side. This area of burning was at least 0.6m long but only 0.5m high as it was angled down from the east to the west. It was identifiable in plan up to the southern face of the sub-rectangular feature. All this area was much cut into by later burials, and two of these, Burial NA094 and Burial NA104 from Grid O/230 and Grid P/229, were dated by radiocarbon to *cal AD 950-1050 (86% probability)* or *cal AD (1090-1160 (9% probability)* and *cal AD 950-1040 (95% probability)* respectively (see Ch. 14). These therefore provide a *terminus ante quem* for this feature in the first half of the 11th century. A post-hole to the south-west of the feature also showed signs of burning around the edges.

From the recorded section north-south along Grid O-P/230-37 (NAS1, Fig. 25), photographs and the plan of the base of the Grid P-Q trench (NAP2, Fig. 23) it may be possible to relate this feature NA97 to the ditch NA35. At the south end of the trench in Grid 31 a cut edge, its base 139.36m OD at the south-east corner, was identified in plan as 'line of earlier [i.e. 1965] excavation', but this does not extend to the south-west corner where a deposit of loosely packed chalk rubble including pink possibly burnt sandstone (level top 139.09m OD) appears to fill a feature cutting through this 'line of earlier excavation' and the natural chalk down to the north. It is probable that this 'line of earlier excavation' is in fact a continuation of the northern edge of ditch NA35, and suggests that the so-called 'lime-kiln' was later than the ditch.

The northern edge of the 1965 excavation is unlikely to have eroded quite so far in only one season (see Fig. 25 where the erosion line of the 'old trench' is indicated). Burial NA021 in Grid P/231 (upper edge at 139.82m OD) is shown cutting through a deposit of chalk and sandstone blocks in a feature with sloping sides which is indicated extending down below the limit of excavation at this point (138.98m OD). The loose chalk rubble which fills the cut through the probable ditch line might relate to the lower ditch fills (NA37 and NA38 which included 'red' chalk, but *not* sandstone) or, more probably, to the 'lime-kiln' where sandstone was mixed with the chalk. The

Section NAS5B

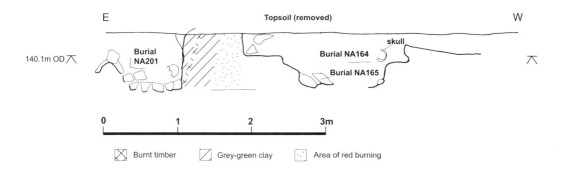

E   Topsoil (removed)   W

skull

140.1m OD

Burial NA201

Burial NA164

Burial NA165

0   1   2   3m

⊠ Burnt timber   ⧄ Grey-green clay   ⬚ Area of red burning

Section NAS2

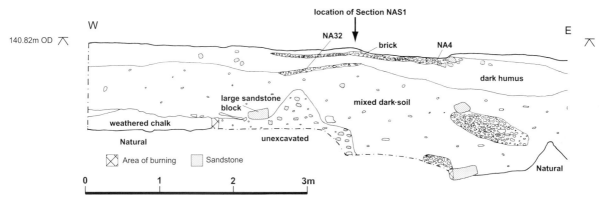

location of Section NAS1

W

140.82m OD

NA32

brick

NA4

E

dark humus

large sandstone block

mixed dark-soil

weathered chalk

Natural

unexcavated

Natural

⊠ Area of burning   ⧄ Sandstone

0   1   2   3m

Fig. 24. North Churchyard sections through lime kiln or *Grubenhaus:* north-facing NAS5B along Grid mid-229, M-P; south-facing NAS2 along Grid 230/31, M-R. (E. Marlow-Mann)

Plate 5. Section NAS5B through feature NA97, Grid O/P 229, looking south-east.

corresponding east-west section along the northern edge of the 1965 excavation (Fig. 24, Section NAS2) shows a large sandstone block at 139.9m OD, possibly a grave-marker but equally likely to have been part of feature NA97. This point in Grid P/231 appears to mark the northern extent of the structure and suggests that the ditch, as previously noted, was on an alignment tending slightly to the north-west.

Feature NA97, if it was associated with lime burning, would have been some type of 'clamp' kiln. Given the dating of the burials which intruded into its fill, it would demonstrate that the first stone church, the earliest building in this part of the site to require lime mortar, was erected before the mid-11th century. The archaeological literature contains a number of examples of excavated pre-Conquest and early post-Conquest lime kilns. Some seem to have been lined with stone walling; others were represented by unlined cuts into the subsoil or bedrock, much like the Wharram feature. These are, however, circular in plan, with two or more flues radiating outwards from the circle: for example the early 12th-century kiln from North Elmham, and the 13th-century kiln from Cheddar – both associated with the construction of ecclesiastical buildings (Wade-Martins 1980, 216-18; Rahtz 1979, 116-19). The lime kilns at Great Paxton

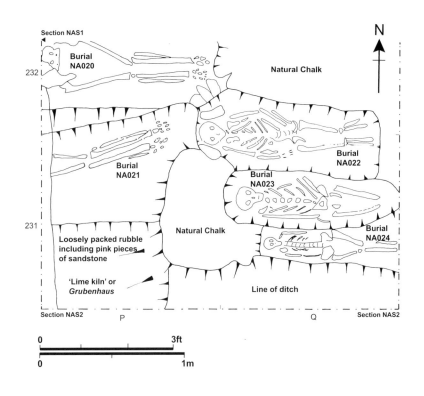

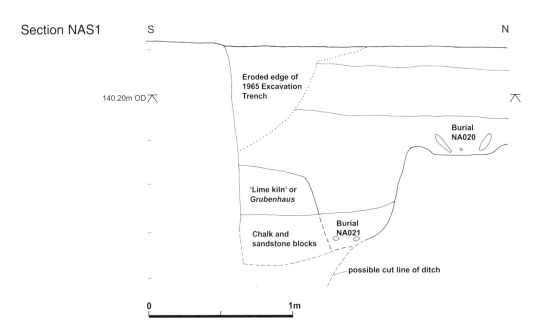

Fig. 25. Plan of south end of 'PQ Trench' 1970 and east-facing section along Grid O/P, 230-32. (E. Marlow-Mann)

Hunts, associated with St Neot's Ware, were circular mounds about 3.05m across (Lethbridge and Tebbutt 1933-4, 97-105). The Wharram structure, whilst it might have had a flue extending southwards, accounting for the more extensive burning in that area and the vertical features in the section (Fig. 24), was definitely sub-rectangular rather than circular in plan.

There is an alternative interpretation of feature NA97, one that would not have occurred to excavators at Wharram before the discoveries made in 1979 on Site 39.

Its size, its base, probably cut into natural chalk, and the occurrence of a post against one of its sides, on what may conceivably have been the axis of the structure, are all characteristics reminiscent of a *Grubenhaus*, similar to those excavated later on the Plateau (*Wharram VII*, 5-12, 18-25, 86-8; *Wharram IX*, 66-71). If it was a comparable structure, it was presumably destroyed by fire, accounting for the burnt chalk along the sides of the structure, and the burnt post at one end. Like the similar structures on the Plateau, this example seems to have been created in the

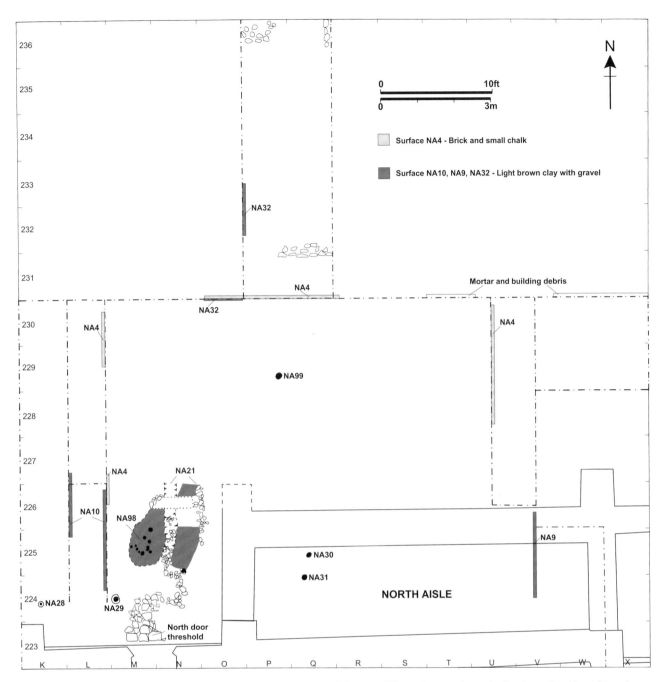

Fig. 26. Composite plan of post-aisle and post-burial surfaces and features. Those shown schematically along the sides of trenches were recorded only in section: their full extents are unknown. (E. Marlow-Mann)

fill of an earlier ditch. With hindsight it is regrettable that the post was not recovered during the excavations, as its date would have been crucial either to the date of the first stone church, or to the continuing debate on the chronology of Wharram's *Grubenhäuser*.

A number of other features, numbered as a group NA21 (see Fig. 26) were located immediately west of the west wall of the north aisle, and although probably post-dating its construction appear to relate to the aisle rather than post-demolition phases. Parallel to the wall-line as surviving and *c.* 0.9m from it, was evidence of a shallow north-south gully (or possibly a robbed sill or foundation trench) 0.2-0.3m wide and deep, with a fill of soft brown soil and chalk and small and medium sandstone. A

photograph of Burial NA214 in Grid N/226 (Plate 6) which may have been in a coffin clearly shows this feature in section cut through by the burial. The general scatter of small and medium rubble in the gully may be merely dispersed demolition material although a small post-hole (unnumbered) with chalk and sandstone packing at the top was located at the south-eastern end of this linear feature, in Grid N/225.

East of the gully, and parallel to it, was a line of small and medium rubble. It is not known how far north this extended, beyond the then (1973) limit of excavation. Other features in this area may be later (see below). Post-holes NA28, NA29 and NA99 (Fig. 26) were not apparently related to burials, nor was a collection of

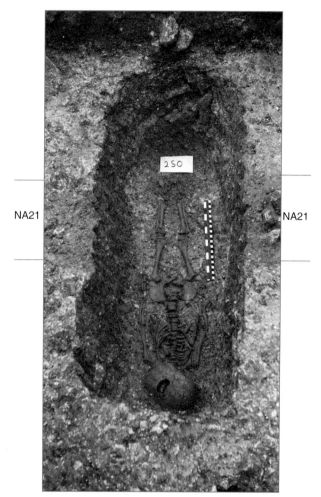

Plate 6. Burial NA214 in N/226, showing the grave cut through linear feature NA21, looking east.

eleven stake-holes (NA98) which may relate to the linear features noted above.

With the exception of the uppermost deposits recorded in the area of the north aisle and doorway the only evidence of later activity in this part of the churchyard comes from the 1970 P-Q trench and some of the sections (see Figs 21 and 25). Some features identified on Site 26 to the north (see Ch. 4) could be traced into the area of the trench. At the north end, photographs (Plate 2) show large blocks of chalk (and probably sandstone) aligned north-south in Grid Q/237 which are also evident in section and likely to be a continuation of wall line 248 in Site 26 (Period 6, Phase 4). This may also relate to a spread of large and medium chalk shown on plan in Grid P236. An east-west line of large chalk and burnt sandstone blocks, 0.3m wide in Grid P-Q/231 (Fig. 26), may mark Burial NA022 (see Fig. 25, NAP2), rather than part of a structure.

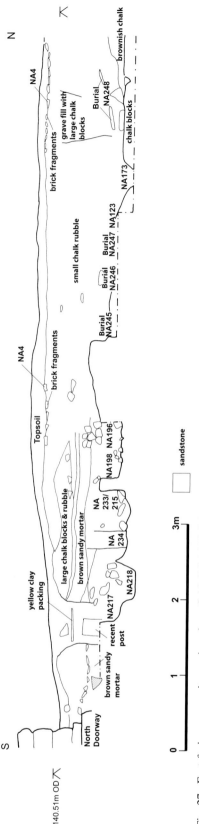

Fig. 27. East-facing composite section along Grids L/M 223-26 and K/L 226-30, incorporating Section NAS6A and B and Section NAS5A. (E. Marlow-Mann)

28

A spread of small packed chalk gravel recorded only in section along the western side of the Grid P/Q trench, in Grid P/232-3, may be part of the surface of a path (NA32 and Site 26 32/54/283; Figs 26 and 39) thought to have been used between the north door of the church and the vicarages. Further deposits of similar material were also noted in the section in Grid O-Q/230 (Fig. 24, NAS2) where it was 75-100mm thick with occasional inclusions of brick and sandstone. Finds records (C873-5, 878) located finds 'under small chalk path' in Grid M-N/224 equated with a 'fine yellow chalk spread', recorded in section only. The material itself is probably a type of 'natural' which is known to have been used as bonding material for walls and a make-up for internal and external surfaces. Its dispersal over this area probably represents post-aisle demolition. The small chalk path may relate to path 32 from Period 5, Phase 1 on Site 26 (see Ch. 4).

An extensive deposit of mortar and 'building debris' (NA4) 50-150mm thick was recorded only in section (Fig. 24, NAS2 and Fig. 26), sloped down to the east and possibly southwards on a section in Grid mid-U 228-30 sloping down slightly to the north. A similar deposit was identified in section to the west (Grid M/226-7, NA10: Fig. 27) at a comparable level, and possibly at Grid O-Q/230. This may be general post-demolition ground levelling but also possibly surfaces of the track ways known to have crossed this part of the churchyard in the 19th century (Fig. 159; *Wharram III*, 85; Site 26 Period 7, and to similar deposits noted in the East End section).

Discussion

The evidence for prehistoric and Roman activity on this part of the terrace is slight, no doubt partly the result of the extensive disturbance caused by later inhumations. Romano-British pottery is scattered all along the terrace, see, for example, the vestry discussed above and Chapters 4 and 5. The parallel east-west ditches north of the church (see also Ch. 4) possibly originated in the later Romano-British period, and may be indicative of settlement or field enclosures. The only feature definitely assigned to the Romano-British period was the hearth discovered beneath the chancel arch, 'associated' with Romano-British pottery (Fig. 20). It is, however, remarkable that this was located precisely on the axis of the church, directly beneath the chancel arch. Could it instead have been related to the first stone church of Phase II, or even part of an earlier structure that then informed the siting of the first stone church?

This part of the graveyard, in common with the rest, seems to have been used first for burial in the second half of the 10th century (see Ch. 14), and the earliest burials can be shown to pre-date the first stone church. There is some evidence of activity in the Middle Saxon period, pre-dating the commencement of burial. Three coins of the mid-8th to the mid-9th centuries were recovered from the central graveyard and church area, with two others of

the same date range from Site 26 (Ch. 4). To these may be added part of a 9th-century strap end, from a grave cut into the top of the southern east-west ditch, NA 35 (*Wharram III*, 54). This scatter of artefacts, all in residual contexts, may be given greater significance if the so-called 'lime-kiln' is reinterpreted as a *Grubenhaus*, comparable with some of the examples from other parts of Wharram which have been dated to the Middle Saxon period (*Wharram VII*, 54-6, 83-4).

With regard to the construction of the first stone church, observations of the surface of natural chalk below and around the building provide two interesting pieces of information. The first is that the eastern part of the church was constructed over the junction of the natural chalk and the underlying clay. The second is that the axis of the church (along Grid 219/220) does not seem to have been located along the highest part of the site. The natural surface of the clay was highest in Grid CC/213, beyond the south-east corner of the church, indicating that prior to the late 20th-century landscaping, the slope down to the north was not merely the result of accumulated debris over demolished apses etc.

Richard Morris has previously suggested that the location of the Wharram church may have been determined by the position of a holy well (Morris 1991, 15-24). The observations, above, could be interpreted as providing a small measure of support for this notion, in that the junction of the chalk and clay is precisely where any spring would have emerged, and the possible slight hollowing of the pre-church ground surface along the axis of the building might indicate the line of a former stream issuing from such a spring. All this is pure speculation, and any spring at this point would have been erased by earth moving associated with later church building. Nevertheless, such springs are a regular feature along both sides of the Wharram watercourse, and one of them, in Wharram le Street, was called *Halykeld,* or Holy Well, when it was granted to Meaux Abbey along with a site for a grange in the mid-12th century (Wrathmell 2005, 2, fig. 3).

The positioning of early ecclesiastical buildings over holy wells must account for the frequent location of medieval churches on sloping sites, with their attendant structural problems. At Wharram, the choice of such a site necessitated the creation of a chalk rubble raft to support the extended chancel of the early 12th-century church. That raft may have been constructed whilst the Phase 2 chancel was still in use (*Wharram III*, 70-71), allowing the formation of layers EE97/99 under the apse wall (*Wharram III*, fig. 12). This is perhaps further evidence in support of the 'alternate rebuilding' of nave and chancel, with the original chancel remaining in use until sometime after the nave had been rebuilt.

Speculation on the overall period of use and density of the graveyard has not been attempted when so much of the area south of the church remains unexcavated. The radiocarbon dating programme has, however, shown that the proposed model of the churchyard contraction and expansion in *Wharram III* was too simplistic. For example, the burials at the West End are not a relatively closely dated group but span a very long period of intermittent use from the pre-Conquest to the post-medieval periods (see also Ch. 32).

The finds from the upper levels of the churchyard have also been re-examined but little can be added to the interpretation and conclusions already published in *Wharram III*. Analysis of the occupation of the whole terrace in the post-medieval period and the influences of the succession of vicarages and farmsteads to the north of the church will follow in *Wharram XII*. Some of the features in the north churchyard (e.g. path NA32) and the rutted road surface (Figs 26 and 8) were also identified on Site 26 to the north (see Ch. 4 Periods 5 and 7). A detailed analysis of the cartographic evidence (Ch. 2) does, however, provide a context for the fences, paths and trackways identified crossing the churchyard in the post-medieval period.

4   Excavations in the Northern Graveyard Area
by C. Harding

Site 26, 1972-8

Introduction (Fig. 28)
A rectangular area adjacent to the track running from the cottages to the church was first opened in 1972. It was extended over the next four seasons to encompass an overall area of 12.2m (north to south) by 19.5m. The coincidence of the Period 7 conduit with the alignment of the western limits of excavation resulted in a section more than 2m deep (Plate 14). The depth of this section beside the track led to the closure, in 1973, of the most westerly grid squares for safety reasons. In the autumn of 1973 a shallow trial trench 1.22m wide was cut northwards from Grid M to locate any possible wall parallel to the Period 5 wall 74, the interpretation of which was then uncertain. During the 1974 season a trench was dug down to natural in Grid 246 to ascertain the overall depth and possible complexity of deposits. The work was covered in *Interim Report 1972*, 2-3; *1973*, 2; *1974*, 1-2, 5-6; *1975*, 1-2; *1976*, 5-6; *1977*, 4-5; *1978*, 9-10.

The stream lies about 6m below the present terrace level, and the western plateau about 13m above the terrace. Variations of 'natural' deposits were found with the chalk rubble; these included pinkish-red stained chalk and fine silty clay, 'rotted' greenish-yellow clay, and yellowish-brown clay with small chalk chips. The level of the top of the natural sloped down from west to east, 139.86 to 138.28m OD (458.85 to 453.72ft). At the east end of the site it was level, without any suggestion of a slope to the south or the east.

The heavy chalk rubble in fine creamy clay which forms most of the 'natural' on the terrace is the result of

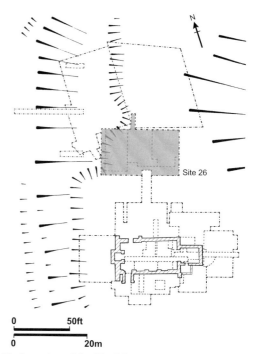

Fig. 28. Location of the Site 26 excavations. (E. Marlow-Mann)

hillwash slumping and mass movement of the valley side. This process is still continuing and deposits at the foot of the western plateau are now known to have moved there in the late medieval or early post-medieval period (*Interim Report 1982*, 29-30; *1983*, 25-6; *1984*, 19; see also Sites 21/22, 41, and 52). It is clear that before this slumping occurred the terrace would have been wider (extending further west), and the slope up to the plateau would have been steeper.

The eastern edge of the natural terrace stopped about 4.27m short of the eastern limit of excavation, at which point the natural chalk dips steeply. Dumping in, and since, medieval times has extended the terrace about 5.5 to 6m further east, thereby compensating for the reduction in the terrace area to the west. No buried soil levels were located and it is probable that terracing activities have removed original as well as later ground surfaces (and truncated some cut features); it is otherwise difficult to suggest why turf and topsoil should have been deliberately removed.

Erosion and truncation of deposits by regular and repeated terracing and levelling (as documented elsewhere along the terrace, see Chapter 5) as well as the mixing and movement of deposits and finds by hill wash, repeated burial, tree roots and small mammal activity resulted in some ill-defined stratigraphy and relationships, and intrusive ceramic finds. The clarity of stratigraphic relationships was further reduced by the prohibition on the use of plastic sheeting to cover the site between excavation seasons - banned to protect grazing cattle. The basis for the division of periods and phases, for example at the truncated lower levels (where stratigraphic links were least clear) is entirely on the recorded relationships unless otherwise stated.

Period 1 (2nd century BC to 4th century AD)

Period 1, Phase 1 (Fig. 29)

Cut into the natural chalk in the south-west corner of the excavation was a sub-circular grave containing a crouched skeleton (Burial G305). The western half of the grave was initially outside the area of excavation, and on location of the burial the excavation area was extended so that the whole of the grave-cut could be excavated. The grave fill was the redeposited natural chalk into which it had been cut. It contained a fragment of animal bone, slag and two snail shells. On the floor of the grave, 0.10m south of the skull was a large piece of flint, measuring 0.15 by 0.10m. The skeleton lay on the south-east side of the grave; the body was aligned north-east to south-west, resting on its left side with its head facing south. It has been identified as the skeleton of an arthritic female aged 25-35 (Bayley 1976), and is dated to cal BC 200 – 120 cal AD (see Table 117 and pp 199-200).

Although isolated burials of this date and type are not unknown, the absence of any grave goods or of any trace of a barrow mound or ditch makes it not only unusual, but difficult to interpret. Subject to the results of any future excavations to the west or south, it must be presumed that this burial is an isolated occurrence and not part of a cemetery. There was no trace of any ditch, or of any contemporary turf (ground) level, but it is possible that a small scraped-up barrow mound has been terraced away or eroded and washed down the hillside. For possible contemporary occupation see Site 41 south of the church (Ch. 5, Period 2).

It has been claimed that this burial was 'respected' by later activity (Rahtz 1981, 6), but the evidence is equivocal. The most westerly row of medieval graves (Period 3) stopped 1.32m to the north-east of Burial G305, but the graves were already less concentrated in this area and cannot really be seen as 'avoiding' the burial. The northern edge of ditch 255 (Period 1, Phase 4; Fig. 31) ran east-west only 0.45m south of Burial G305, and although it may be said to 'respect' the burial, the very proximity of the ditch confirms that no mound of any substance survived at the time the ditch was cut.

Period 1, Phase 2 (Fig. 30)

The variable density of post-holes and other features attributed to this phase is to some extent a reflection of the variable concentration of later graves, which occurred mainly in the southern and eastern parts of the site. The probability of removal or erosion of contemporary ground surfaces also means that at least some features described here may have been truncated and were actually cut from later phases. Nevertheless, the various disparate features cutting the natural chalk and sealed by the Period 1, Phase 3 deposits are thus grouped together here.

With the exception of the eastern line of stake-holes (see below) there was no obvious relationship between many of these post or stake-holes. They shared few common characteristics of shape, few exceeded 0.30m in any dimension and most had vertical sides. More similarity was noted amongst the fills with 662, 616 and 120 showing evidence of considerable burning. Only one post-hole (740) had evidence of possible packing, in the form of large chalk blocks (not retained) in the fill (741).

A row of seven stake-holes (778-84) lay at the top of the valley slope 2.13-2.44m east of the natural edge of the terrace and may have marked a division between land-use on the terrace and on the valley side. Further holes to the south might have been removed by burials.

Some grouping of the features on the basis of their characteristics and spatial arrangements can be suggested. The largest post-holes (615 and 620) both had smaller cuts (661 and 629) at their south-west corners suggesting either a double post arrangement, or replacement posts (629 was cut into the fill of 620). The arrangement of 789 with 127, 122 and 126 and the cluster of 754, 766, 768, 771 and 770 are similar. The position of 615 and 620 relative to the elongated features 618A and 618B may not be coincidental. The fill of 618A spilled out over the edges of both features as a single deposit (619) with frequent pottery, small chalk and burnt sandstone fragments and some large chalk blocks at the top on the east side.

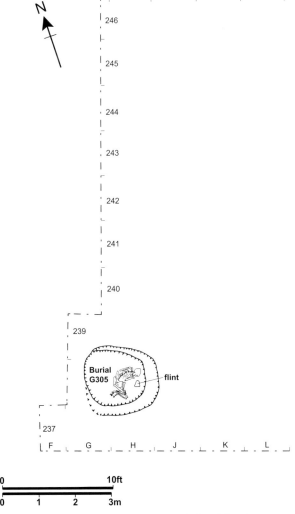

Fig. 29. Site 26 Period 1, Phase 1. (E. Marlow-Mann)

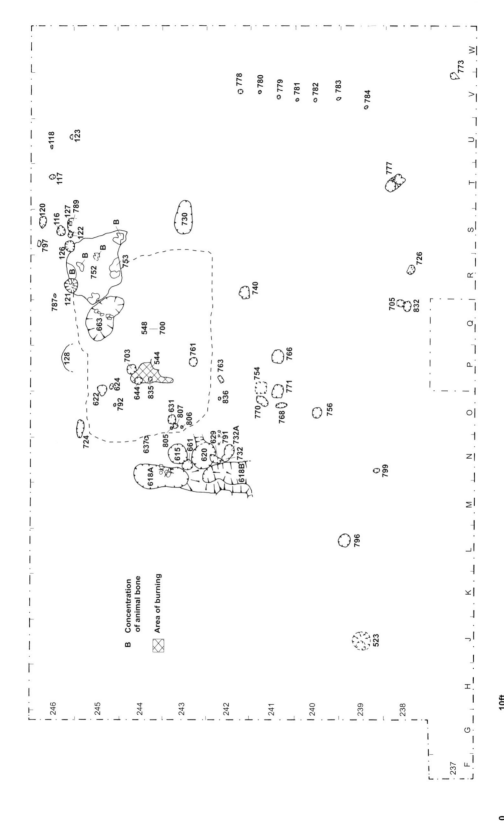

Fig. 30. Site 26 Period 1, Phase 2. (E. Marlow-Mann)

32

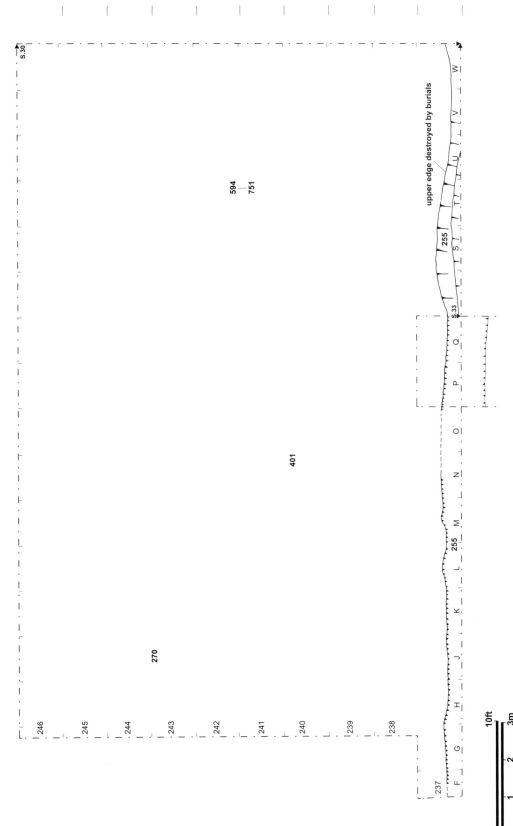

Fig. 31. Site 26 Period 1, Phase 4 (E. Marlow-Mann)

An area of mixed chalk rubble in greyish-brown clay loam with occasional flecks and fragments of charcoal (700) was identified above the natural chalk in the northern half of the site 'within' the area of many of the post-holes. Its edges were not clearly defined and it may have sealed some of the smaller features cut into the natural. A few post-holes (724, 622 and 624) were cut through it but of more interest was an area of burnt clay (544) with associated post and stake-holes (835, 846 (not illustrated) and 703). To the north-east was a dump of dark brown silty humic loam (752), up to 0.55m thick, cut by post-hole 121. Within this deposit were concentrations of animal bone and a patch of pale brown clay (753). Context 700 does not seem to have been a surface, but the presence of what appears to have been a hearth (544) indicates some sort of possible short-term activity. The humic content of 752 suggests that other debris had been dumped along with the bone.

A poorly defined area of compacted brown clay and pea grit resurfacing (548) subsequently sealed much of 700, hearth 544, and some post-holes to the east of 618A and 618B. A wide shallow cut (663) was divided into two parts by a row of medium chalk blocks cut into the edge of dump 752; its fill (664) contained a substantial amount of burnt daub (Appendix 4; A36). To the south-west were a post-hole, 732 and a stake-hole, 732a. The surface showed no signs of prolonged use or exposure.

The concentration of pottery from fill 619 (101 sherds of calcareously tempered Ceramic Group 4 wares) and the deposit sealing it (617 of Period 1, Phase 3, with calcareously tempered and grey wares) contrasts markedly with the almost aceramic character of most of the other feature fills. This quantity of pottery, along with fragments of lava quern from 620, 632 (not illustrated) and 700, parts of two loomweights from 547, and the presence of hearth 544 might represent purely domestic activity. The concentration of animal bone in 752, however, might indicate the deliberate separation of material: pottery into fill 619 and animal bone with possible vegetation in dump 752. With the exception of a piece of slag from 616 (not illustrated) no other diagnostic material survived. The pottery of this phase dated broadly to the late 1st to early 2nd centuries AD and may be contemporary with Site 41 Period 2, Phase 1 (pp 66-7).

Period 1, Phase 3 (not illustrated)
Clay deposits with large and medium chalk rubble (270 and 401) and looser loamy deposits (751, 545, 594, 823 and 617) mark a hiatus between the earlier features and ditch 255 (see below) as well as Period 2 features.

Four of these deposits (270, 545, 594 and 751) contained post-Roman as well as Roman pottery, which might indicate (apart from intrusive or animal disturbance) that the deposits had become mixed during terracing or erosion. The descriptions of the two western deposits suggest hillwash or redeposited natural, the accumulation of which can be rapid. The greatest quantity of post-Roman ceramics was, not surprisingly, in 594 at the bottom of the slope.

Period 1, Phase 4 (Fig. 31)
The northern edge of a substantial ditch, 255 (NA96), ran the length of the excavation west-east, 0.46-0.53m inside the southern limit of excavation. The full extent of this feature is not known. A section across it was recorded in 1970 in the north churchyard trench PQ/237-9 (see Ch. 3) which extended into the area of Site 26 (Fig. 21). Its form is that of a V-shaped ditch up to 2.75m wide and 1.52m deep. West of Grid M/N the depth within Site 26 ranged from 0.46m to at least 0.81m. The north edge sloped fairly steeply but irregularly. East of the M/N grid line the upper edge and fill had been destroyed by successive burials.

At its west end ditch 255 appeared cut into layers (270/401) sealing Period 1, Phase 1 and some Period 1, Phase 2 features, but because of problems of truncation etc noted above, the precise level of its cutting cannot be established. The siting of Site 26 was unfortunate in respect of this feature, and the detail on the section recorded in 1970 (Fig. 21) is not sufficient for precise correlation with Site 26. The absolute level at which it appears cut on the 1970 section is 0.17m higher than that at which it was recognised on Site 26, but much of the upper northern edge in Grids P-Q was cut away by Burials G377 and G381 which were not removed until 1976. No particular differences in the fill were distinguished during excavation but on examination of the sections in 1978 it was noted that the upper half of the fill was more compact than the lower half. The fill was generally 'clean' without large quantities of rubbish or any evidence of recutting. There was, however, a wide range of Romano-British pottery, from early calcite-gritted to 3rd and 4th-century grey wares. This mixture of Romano-British fabrics is comparable to that of the finds from deposits in Period 1, Phase 3. A Romano-British trumpet brooch (Ch. 26, Church 73), dating from the later 1st to mid-2nd century, was found in the 1970 excavation of the PQ trench and within the ditch. The presence of post-Roman pottery (17% of the assemblage) could be entirely explained by the density of later intrusions (burials) in the ditch area and the burrowing of small mammals: although there were over twenty sherds, they ranged from Saxo-Norman through to later 13th and 14th-century types (see Ch. 18). The ditch may have been a field or enclosure boundary, its use confined to the Romano-British period.

Period 2 (5th century to mid-10th century)
Period 2, Phase 1 (Fig. 32)
A series of substantial post-holes (610, 562, 648, 728 and 736) formed an east to west row and with 711, to the north of 736, cut through the natural chalk and deposits of Period 1, Phase 4. The post-holes' dimensions ranged from 0.59-0.81m in length by 0.53-0.69m in width, with vertical sides and depths ranging from 0.43-0.71m. The fills of post-holes 610 and 562 (611 and 563 respectively) contained deposits of looser and less rubbly material in the south and south-west areas of the cuts, indicative of the positions of a post.

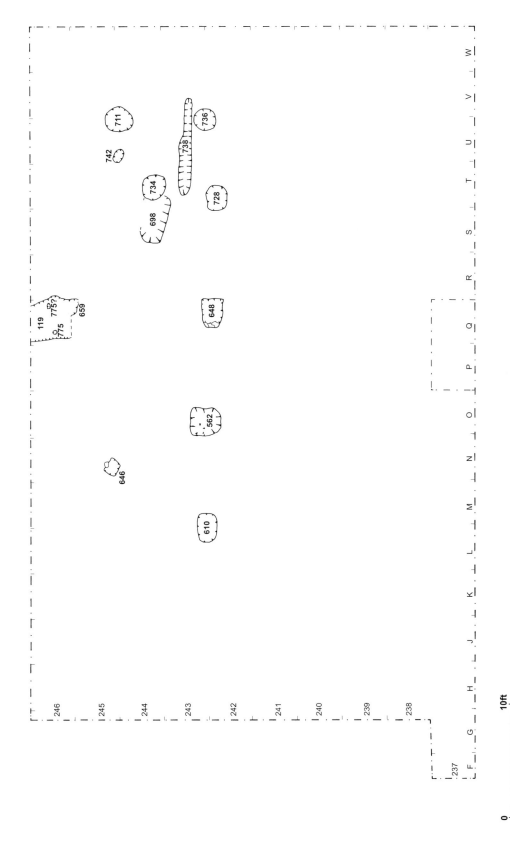

Fig. 32. Site 26 Period 2, Phase 1. (E. Marlow-Mann)

35

A further group of features cut into 594 (Fig. 31), to the north of those above. A linear cut (738) was 2.6m long with rounded ends and gently sloping sides. The width and depth (as recorded) varied from 0.34m wide and 0.18m deep at the west end, narrowing approximately halfway along its length to 0.23m wide and 63mm deep. The base of the cut sloped down to the east with the general level of the ground surface, dropping 0.3m over the length of the feature. A sub-circular post-hole (734) was 0.6m in diameter and 0.53m deep with vertical sides and an irregular base. Within the fill (735) the central area, 0.41m across, was soft and loose with moderate charcoal flecks, suggesting the location of a post-pipe. A rectangular depression (698), 1.22m by 0.71m with gently sloping sides, had been cut away on the north side by a later intrusion and by 734 at the east end. Oval cut 742, 0.36m x 0.28m and 0.15m deep, had fairly vertical but irregular sides. Context 646 was an irregular trapezoid cut (maximum dimension 0.43m) and 0.36m deep, vertical-sided, with a rounded base; some large chalk blocks around the upper edge may have been packing. Features 698, 742 and 646 each had fills of greyish brown with frequent charcoal inclusions (699, 743 and 647 respectively).

Adjacent to the northern edge of excavation was part of a substantial cut feature (119) first located in the 1974 trial trench, *c.* 1.14m wide, at least 1.22m long and 0.46m deep, with sloping sides and a flat base. The dark brown silty loam fill of 119 was relatively rubble-free, with some occasional large blocks of chalk at the top and occasional charcoal flecks. At the south-east corner was the southern edge of an irregular cut (659) which may represent a separate post-hole: its brown loam fill (660/566) had a much higher frequency of rubble inclusions than the fill of 119. In the base of cut 119, towards the sides, were two sub-circular stake-holes (775).

Although the space between them varied from 1.6m-2.36m post-holes 610, 562, 648, 728, 736 and 711 share some characteristics of size and shape and appear to represent part of a structure. Some of the other features discussed above (646, 734 and 742) may also be associated. If it was a roofed building, it was a large one (at least 10.06m by 4.88m); but no recognisable floor surfaces survived and it is possible that the post-holes represent a rather substantial property division and not a building.

Finds from the post-holes were very few and included some residual Romano-British sherds; also an 11th-century gaming counter was recovered from the fill (566) of 659 (Ch. 28, No. 11). Other pottery was from Ceramic Groups 3 and 4, and a date in the late 12th century might have been suggested for the dismantling of the structure if the carbon dated burials of Period 3 cutting through these features had not been earlier. Some contamination by later activity is, however, evident in the fill (699) of feature 698 which produced nine sherds of early and high medieval pottery (Ch. 18, Table 136).

Period 2, Phase 2 (not illustrated)
A deposit of dark greyish-brown silty loam (598) sealed elements of the east side of the structure and surrounding deposits; it was characteristic of an accumulation of rain-washed silt. In the trial trench (Grid 246) deposit 228 was identified at corresponding levels and equated with 598. Although this appears to mark the end of the use of the structure and its (at least partial) dismantling, it has no characteristics or inclusions to suggest building demolition or decay. It included a large quantity of pottery from Ceramic Group 4 (Ch. 18, Table 136). Cutting 598 in the extreme north-east corner of the site (Fig. 40, S.30) was a cut feature (824), possibly a pit, containing substantial chalk blocks. The increasing depth towards the eastern limit of excavation reflects, in part, the steeper slope of the terrace edge south of Grid R and suggests accumulation up against a barrier (possibly a fence, hedge or wall) beyond the eastern limit of excavation.

The dating and relative chronology of Periods 1 and 2 are unlikely to be conclusively established because of problems of residuality of the finds and the factors of erosion and terracing already discussed above. Intensive intrusive activity of later periods increased the likelihood of finds contamination from burrowing animals and plant action, as well as destroying stratigraphic relationships. Whatever the date of the cutting of the east-west ditch, it may have been open, at least at the top, in the post-Roman period, and might thus have had a phase of use contemporary with this Period 2 structure. For further comment on the implications of the radiocarbon sequence on the dating of Ceramic Groups see Chapters 14 and 18.

Period 3 (mid-10th century to late 12th century)
This period marks the first occurrence of medieval burials in the area covered by Site 26. The difficulty in distinguishing contemporary surfaces referred to earlier, and thus the level from which graves were cut, is compounded by the probability that erosion, clearance or terracing activities were already occurring here, possibly in response to build-ups of hill wash. The excavation of the burials was not always straightforward: grave cuts were difficult to distinguish in both very dry and wet conditions, particularly when grave intercutting and non-burial activity obscured relationships. This has possibly resulted in some misphasing, particularly at the west end of the site where erosion and terracing were most evident.

Some of the deposits did have characteristics of 'cemetery soil' or 'grave earth' (Dawes and Magilton 1980, 10; Rodwell 1981, 134). It is clear that there were also definite periods of hiatus. The overall frequency of burial was not high – this area may have been in use for 400 years with, on average, less than one burial every three years. Most of the surfaces identified between the suggested phases of burial had traces of other activity – patches of burning, dumps of domestic material and cut features, but it is obviously not possibe to determine the temporal length of such a phase. Very few of the Period 3, burials intercut which suggests, along with the possibility

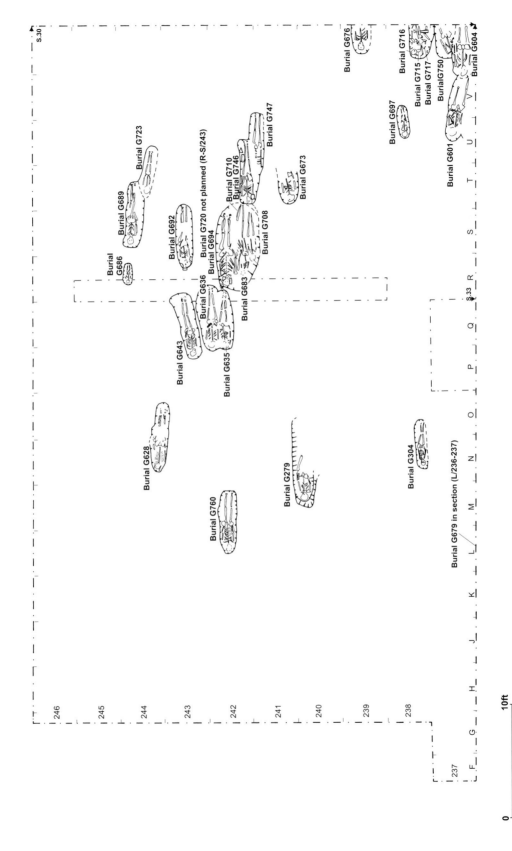

Fig. 33. Site 26 Period 3, Phase 1. (E. Marlow-Mann)

37

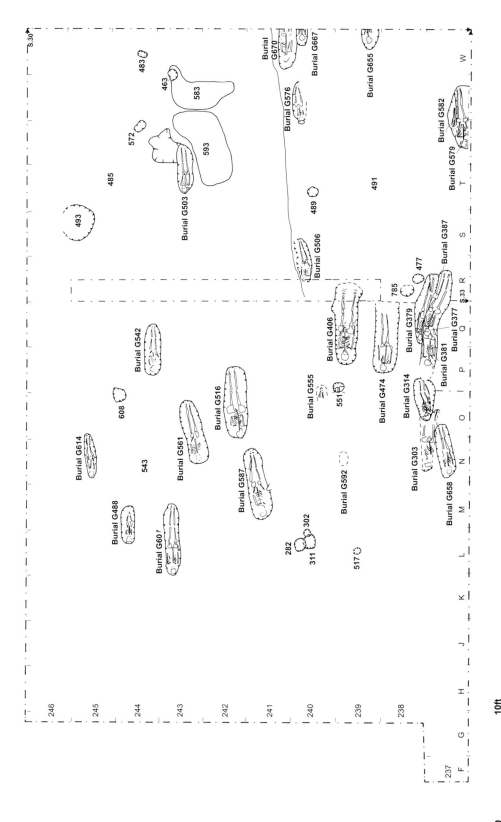

Fig. 34. Site 26 Period 3, Phases 2-3. (E. Marlow-Mann)

38

that they were well-marked, that intervening non-burial activity may have been intermittent or short-lived.

All burials were supine and aligned east to west. There were examples of burials with the head to the side or a body twisted to one side, with stone weights or 'ear-muffs' and of grave cuts part-lined with chalk blocks. See Chapter 15 for the complete catalogue of burial attributes.

Period 3, Phase 1 (Fig. 33)
The earliest burials were spread across the site in no evident arrangement, with some intercutting and clustering. About a quarter were children or juveniles. The double burial (Burials G635 and G636) contained two females, aged 50+ and 21 (p. 341). Burial G746 had an 'ear muff' (to the right Fig. 130), a foot pillow and a weight on its left leg; Burial G760 also had a weight on its left leg. None of the post-holes identified as more or less contemporary (Period 3, Phase 3, below) appeared to be grave-markers.

Period 3, Phase 2 (Fig. 34)
Sealing the Phase 1 burials in the central area of the excavation was a deposit of firm silty clay (543) which became progressively more rubbly down the slope, to the east, with concentrations of compact chalk. The colour also darkened to the east, where it corresponded with 485 (see below). Inclusions and fragments of charcoal (with a concentration in Grids M243-244) and a range of domestic debris suggest the proximity of habitation. In the eastern area of the excavation the burials were sealed by compacted chalk surfaces (485 and 491) resembling cobbles, which were only differentiated on grounds of colour. Their average depth was 0.10-0.13m, increasing to 0.25m deep along the eastern limit of excavation and they were comparatively free from debris. In areas of the site not apparently covered by the extent of these deposits earlier surfaces (see above, Periods 1-2) may well have been contaminated by finds from these later ones.

Period 3, Phase 3 (Fig. 34)
Cutting through Phase 2 surfaces was another phase of burial extending across most of the site interspersed with post-holes, shallow cuts and scoops. Burial G576 had a clear head marker and leg weights. Post-holes 608, 551 and 572 had large blocks of chalk and sandstone in their fills possibly to stabilise the ground after the removal of a post as no post pipes were evident. Post-holes 572 and 483 were not only of similar size and shape but were set at complementary angles, *c.* 1.83m apart, suggesting that they might have shared a related function. None of these post-holes appeared to mark the head or foot of any contemporary or earlier grave and the few finds were from Ceramic Group 4.

Period 3, Phase 4 (Fig. 35)
Sealing the burials and other features were compact surfaces 389 and 412, with frequent small chalk and charcoal flecks and domestic debris - pottery, animal bone and metalwork. Two small roughly circular patches of burnt clay (507 and 454) *c.* 0.3m in diameter overlay 412. The relationship of 389 with 390, a similar deposit to the south, was partly obscured by the settlement of a later wall (325; Period 4, Phase 1; Fig. 36), and in contrast 390 contained only one fragment of oyster shell. Sealing the southern edge of 390, up to the southern limit of excavation were patches of a silty deposit (382) described as resembling ditch fill 255 (Fig. 31 and Fig. 35, S.33). It contained, among domestic debris of later date, a 9th-century styca (Ch. 25, No. 6), together with a clay mould fragment (Ch. 23, No. 6) and a bone comb fragment (Ch. 28, No. 2) both also of Anglo-Saxon date. To the south of 412 were 347, a less rubbly area of medium brown clay, and a mixed area of grey-gingery/brown clay and loam with chalk rubble (342).

The characteristics of these exterior surfaces (with the exception of 347 and 382), and the density of debris, suggests domestic occupation immediately adjacent, to the north or north-west. In composition the deposits were very similar and perceived differences between 390 and 342 were probably mainly the result of the arbitrary baulk. The differences north to south probably reflect other factors. At their junction 389 and 390 were sealed by a later wall (Period 4, Phase 1) and, although there was no evidence of a formal boundary, this continuing division (see Period 3, Phase 2, 485/491, Fig. 34) was already apparent in the differing usage and character of the areas to the north and south. The resemblance of 382 to ditch fill 255 (Period 2, Phase 6) is probably not coincidental; the area above the ditch had been churned up by repeated grave digging into the ditch fill. Again, the bulk of the finds were from Ceramic Group 4, with some intrusive finds from Ceramic Groups 5 and 6 in 389.

Period 3, Phase 5 (Fig. 35)
A further phase of scattered and intercutting graves had been cut through Phase 4 surfaces across the site. The dating of this phase was very close to Period 4, Phase 1, and they could well be contemporary, those of Period 4, Phase 1 merely denoting a discrete group south of the Period 4, Phase 1 footings which were constructed on this level. Burial G565 had weights on the pelvis and right femur.

Period 4 (late 12th century to mid-14th century)
Period 4, Phase 1 (Figs 36 and 49)
Sealing the burials and surfaces of Period 3 were spreads of medium and large chalk rubble with small chalk and clay bonding material. Although much dispersed, these appeared to be the remains of wall footings, the plan and extent of which suggest something more extensive than a simple boundary wall.

Along the eastern edge of the site were large chalk blocks forming the northern edge of a linear spread of mainly chalk rubble and occasional sandstone (388), with larger blocks mostly at the edges. A 51 to 76mm deep deposit of clay and chalk chip 'bonding'-type material

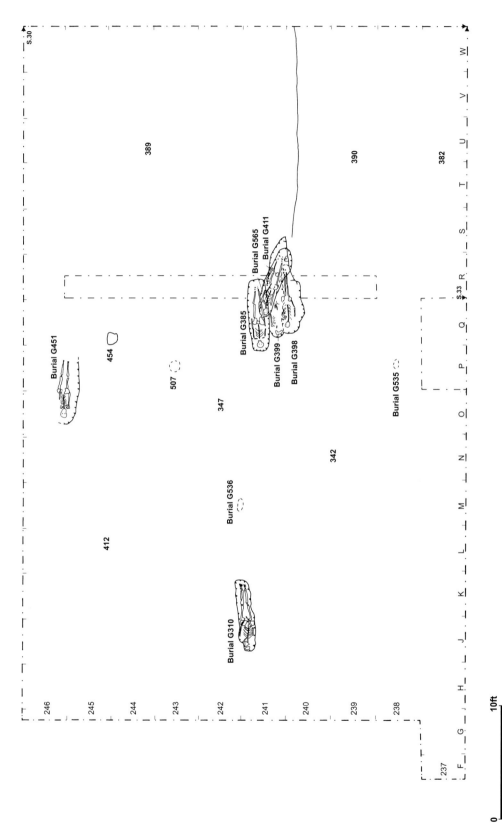

Fig. 35. Site 26 Period 3, Phases 4-5. (E. Marlow-Mann)

40

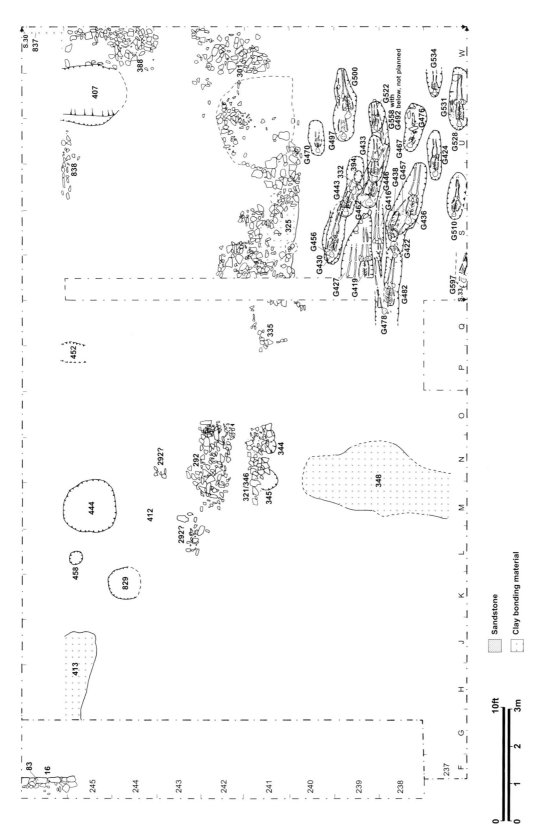

Fig. 36. Site 26 Period 4, Phase 1. All 'G' numbers shown here refer to burial numbers. (E. Marlow-Mann)

41

(837) tipped against its north face and extending northwards beyond the limit of excavation may indicate the former continuation northwards of 388. Chalk chips and 'bonding' material were also noted in the greyish-brown soil matrix of 388. This rubble may have continued westwards but a later intrusion had destroyed the relationship between 388 and chalk rubble 838. To the south of 388 was another linear spread of rubble, 301, in light brown clay with larger blocks on its north edge forming a face.

To the west of 301, beyond a further intrusion, was another area of rubble (325). The clay 'bonding' material beneath and between this rubble formed a well-defined southern edge. The disposition of the large blocks on the north side of 325 suggested a possible corner of wall footings (not separately numbered) distinct from the main spread of rubble and 'bonding' material. The line of the rubble continued through the baulk (Grid R237/245, numbered 335 on the west side). In the baulk the rubble was of two courses, 0.51m wide, with an overall depth of 0.20m.

Further west, two post-holes, 344 (a 'double' cut) and 345, cut into a bedding layer of clay 'bonding' material (346) were sealed by another area of rubble (321) which consisted of mainly large chalk blocks with well-defined edges to the north and south forming a single-course wall-footing 0.51 to 0.56m wide and up to 2.13m long. To the north was a further deposit of mixed rubble, 292, 1.17m wide which extended east-west for up to 3.66m. It comprised large, small and medium chalk with occasional sandstone and roof tile. There was some suggestion of a face to this deposit along its eastern edge. Contemporary with these structural remains were a post-hole (458), several shallow scoops (829, 444, 452 and 407), and areas of compacted clay 'bonding' material (413 and 348).

In the extreme north-west corner of the site and cut by the Period 7 conduit was a short length of wall (83; Plate 7) standing three courses high with sandstone blocks facing a chalk rubble core and an associated compacted chalk surface (16). They have no stratigraphic link to other structural remains on Site 26 because of the conduit, and they cannot therefore be accurately phased, despite being at a comparable level to other Period 4 features.

Plate 7. Site 26 Period 4, Phase 1 Wall 83.

They may, however, be linked with structures on Site 77, immediately to the north, and will be discussed fully in *Wharram XII*.

To the south was another group of burials cutting through surfaces 390/382 (Period 3, Phase 4, Fig. 35). These were much more intercut and closely spaced than earlier burial phases. They were of similar date range to those of Period 3, Phase 5, and some or all are possibly of that phase, pre-dating the structures described above. They were, however, sealed by later surfaces (Period 4, Phase 2) and form a discrete group in what was clearly still a part of the churchyard, now defined by the extent of the structure to the north. The edge of the grave cut for Burial G419 was lined with stone fragments set on edge.

The deposits of rubble described above had some relatively well-defined edges which in conjunction with their 'loose' and uncompacted character suggests that, in spite of their fragmentary survival, they were not surfaces but the collapsed and displaced elements of chalk walls or footings (Fig. 49). It should be noted that this east-west line almost repeats the distinctions observed between 485 and 491 (Fig. 34), and 389 and 390 (Fig. 35) in Period 3, suggesting that the construction of an east-west wall formalised a pre-existing but apparently unmarked boundary between an area primarily used for burial and an area used for 'domestic' or other purposes. At the west end of 325 the area of clay 'bonding' material may actually reflect the line of a wall, and the edges within the rubble to the north might have been those of footings or pads for timber supports of structures built up against the north side of the wall. The pottery 'associated' with these structural remains dates to the late 13th and 14th centuries, but may reflect post-demolition activity rather than the use of the buildings. Access from the vicarage complex to the north door of the church is possibly reflected in the clear edges at the east ends of 321 and 292, following a route close to that recorded in Period 5.

Period 4, Phase 2 (Fig. 37)
A surface of compacted large, medium and small chalk rubble (352) in ginger/brown silty clay loam extended southwards from the limit of excavation over the northern parts of the chalk rubble spreads of Period 3, Phase 1. The degree of compaction resembled that of a cobbled surface. To the south and east this surface corresponded with compacted surface 355 which butted up against wall footings 325 and 388. Both these deposits included much domestic debris, the pottery including small quantities of later 13th to 14th and 15th-century wares. Within 355, 30 joinery nails were recorded but not retained, some in groups of two or three possibly representing part of a decayed or destroyed timber structure. To the north of the nails was an oval post-hole (353). Cutting the southern edge of wall line 325 were some irregularly spaced post-holes (358, 329, 333, 330 and 392), perhaps reinforcement or repair to the wall or a rough fence line.

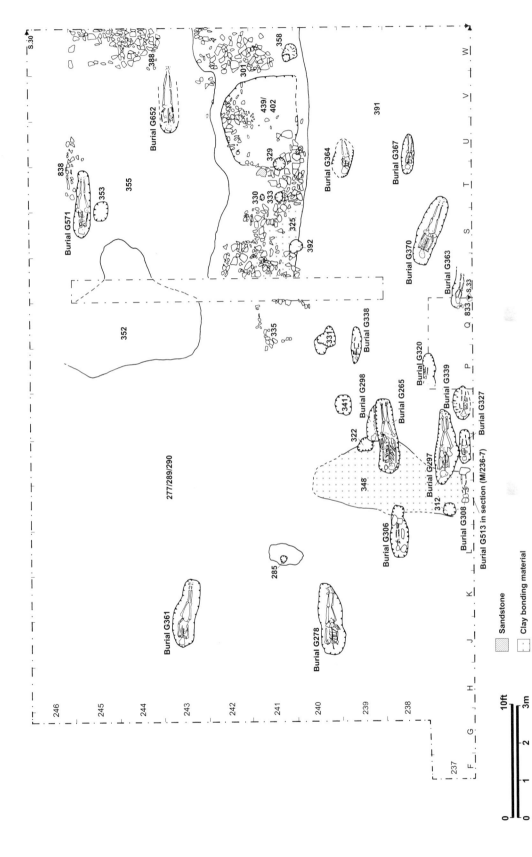

Fig. 37. Site 26 Period 4, Phases 2–3 (structural elements retained from Period 4, Phase 1. (E. Marlow-Mann)

43

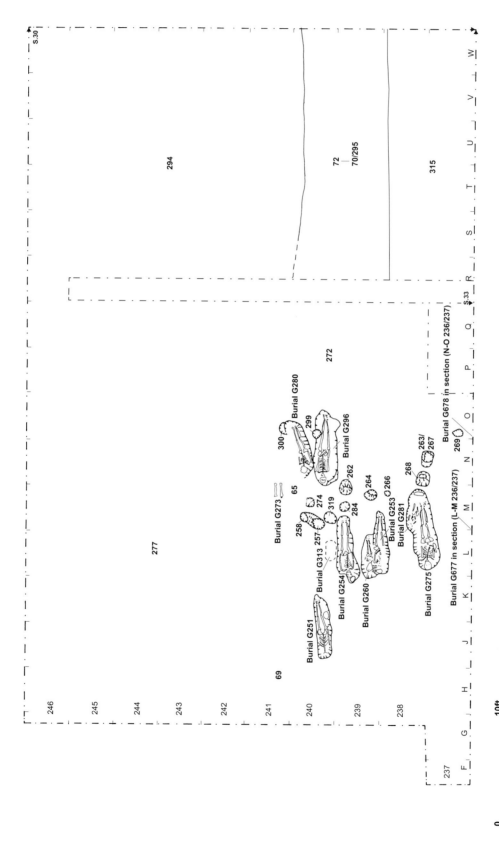

Fig. 38. Site 26 Period 4, Phases 4-5. (E. Marlow-Mann)

44

To the south were more loamy, less compacted deposits, 336, 337, and 391 which sealed the Period 4, Phase 1 burials. Against the southern limit of excavation, sealing 391, was a small area of large and medium chalk rubble with occasional large blocks of flint in brown loamy soil (833). Compacted rubble 277/289/290, in the north-west part of the site sealed wall lines 292/321 (Fig. 36) and had accumulated against the northern edge of 335. The frequent inclusions of domestic debris in these surfaces continued the pattern noted in Period 3.

Period 4, Phase 3 (Fig. 37)
Cutting into the surfaces and features described above were more burials and various cut features. The burials were mostly concentrated towards the southern edge of the site, but three were located north of the Period 4, Phase1 wall line, suggesting that any functional 'division' of this area had more to do with 'domestic' activity and structures spreading southwards from a focus to the north of the site, than a conscious attempt to define or limit the northern edge of the graveyard. Burial G306 of a juvenile was partly stone-lined while another juvenile (Burial G308) had a chalk head marker and a small piece of slag at the foot. None of the post-holes (285, 312, 322, 331 and 341) appeared to mark any of the graves, with the possible exception of 322 marking Burial G298.

Period 4, Phase 4 (Fig. 38)
A series of less compacted loam deposits (295/70/72/315/272/65/69) further sealed the rubble wall lines of Period 4 Phase 1. In the north-east quadrant, deposit 294 was comparable to 277 (Period 4, Phase 2) which continued in use. Both contained much domestic debris, with 294 including roof tile, late medieval pottery, window glass and cames which may have derived from the church. Both appeared to have been well-used external yard surfaces. The southern edge of 294 continued the Period 4, Phase 1 wall line.

Period 4, Phase 5 (Fig. 38)
Cutting through deposits 272 and 65/69 was a final group of burials and contemporary post-holes. Post-holes 257, 319, 284, 264, 266 and 268 were aligned north-west to south-east. Post-holes 258, 274, 262, 263/7 and 269 may also have been related; 299 and 300 were cut through by burials. On the basis of their location, 284 and 268 could have been markers for graves (Burials G254 and G275A respectively).

The burials were fairly evenly spaced and regularly aligned. Given that all but the two post-holes identified above seem not to have been head or foot-markers, they might have marked some kind of division between kinship burial groups. The probable date range of these was relatively short, *cal AD 1230-1330 (95% probability; GU-5543)*. The detached skull in Burial G251 was not related to the body, indicating either a missed later intrusion or subsequent terracing/levelling (p. 358).

Period 4, Phase 6 (not illustrated)
Sealing the last group of burials were some deep accumulations of chalk rubble (62 and 271), up to 0.28m deep. Cutting 62 were two post-holes (204 and 205), both with evidence of burning in their fills. At some point two further burials (Burials G250 and G525 - not dated) were interred; one was the very shallow grave of a baby, the other was only visible in the southern section. The compacted nature of 62 may in part have resulted from the weight of later wall 20 (Period 5, Phase 1): its description and depth do not suggest use as a surface, and there were few finds compared with deposits 'outside' the churchyard. Sherds from an unidentified jug in context 62 might be dated as late as the 16th century.

Period 5 (mid-14th century to early 16th century)
Period 5, Phase 1 (Figs 39 and 40)
Set directly on to Period 4 deposits, an east-west wall (74) (Plate 8) extended almost the whole way across the western half of the site. Though cut away by a Period 7 intrusion against the west baulk, it had originally extended beyond the western limit of excavation (see Site 99, Fig. 48) for a length of 9.14m-9.45m before turning northwards: it will be further discussed in *Wharram XII*. It survived to a height of up to six courses (Plate 9), *c.* 0.84m, near the western baulk but was reduced to one

Plate 8. Site 26 Period 5, Phase 1 Wall 74/20.

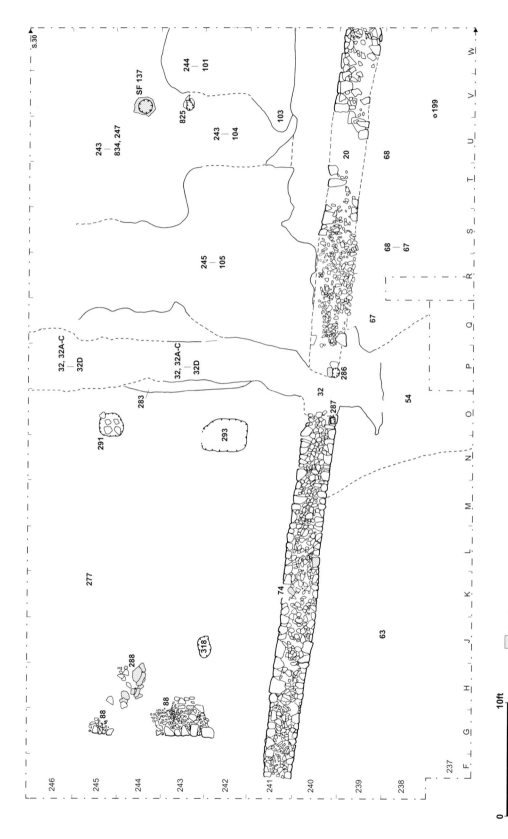

Fig. 39. Site 26 Period 5, Phase 1. (E. Marlow-Mann)

46

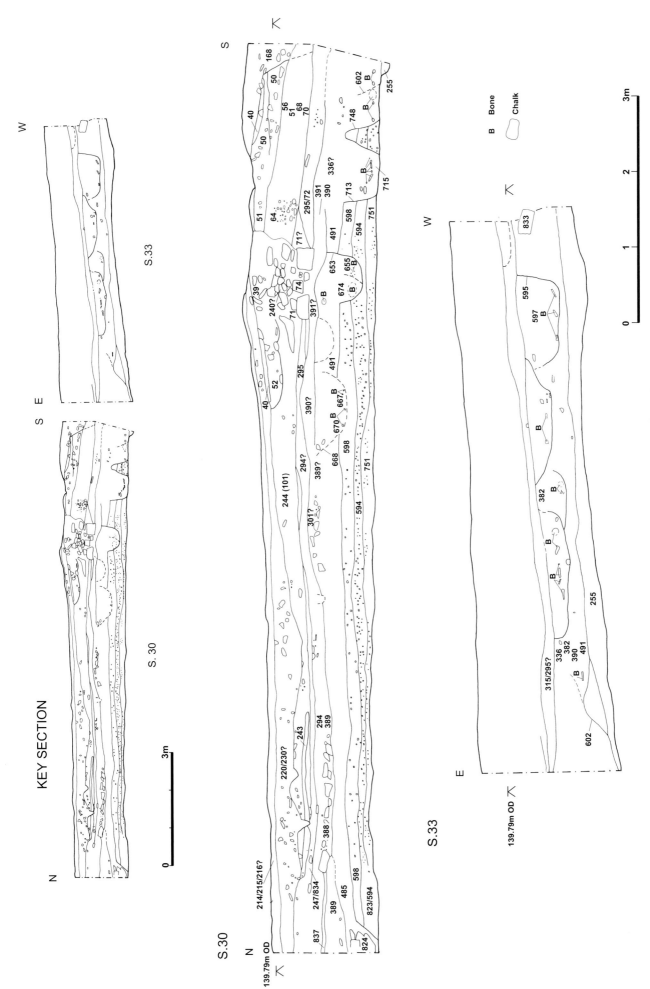

Fig. 40. Site 26 sections: west-facing S.30 along W/X, 237-247; north-facing S.33 along 236/237, R-X. (E. Marlow-Mann)

47

Plate 9. Site 26 Period 5, Phase 1, elevation of wall 74/20.

or two courses at the centre of the site. There was no evidence of a foundation trench, but in places the bottom course was slightly offset to the north and consisted of very large chalk blocks set on yellow-orange bonding material. The upper courses consisted of roughly squared large-medium chalk and very occasional sandstone blocks, facing a core of small and medium chalk rubble, with clay bonding material and very occasional sandstone. The width of the wall varied from 0.84m to 0.99m.

Plate 10. Site 26 Period 5, Phase 1 wall 74/20 showing gap at junction with path 32.

To the east, after a gap of *c*. 2.13m (Plate 10), another stretch of walling, 20, extended on the same alignment for a distance of 9.53m, continuing beyond the eastern limit of excavation. This wall had been extensively robbed, particularly at its west end where only the core of small chalk and clay bonding, remained. Further east down the slope were roughly squared facing blocks of medium and large chalk (and very occasional large sandstone). In the east section three to four courses survived to a height of *c*. 0.61m. At this point the bottom course included some very large chalk blocks offset to the north and south, perhaps to compensate for the natural slope of the ground, which dips very steeply at this point (Period 1, Phase 1).

The construction and width of 20 and 74 were very similar and they are presumed to be contemporary in construction. The gap between walls 20 and 74 was flanked by rectangular post-holes (286 and 287) with large blocks of sandstone and chalk against their sides, presumably marking the position of gateposts. Hillwash deposits (63, 67 and 68) accumulated to the south of the walls; to the east the deposits were more mixed with occasional sandstone and burnt sandstone and patches of very compact chalk in loose grey/brown soil.

North of the gateway between walls 74 and 20 was a deposit of very hard-packed small sandstone and rounded chalk (283) extending at least 5.18m north-south, up to 1.22m wide and 50mm deep. It served as a make-up or foundation layer for 32D, a surface of small compacted chalk varying from 15 to 88mm in depth. Sealing 283/32D was a series of four chalk cobble make-ups and surfaces, 32C, 32B, 32A, and 32 (Plate 11) with an overall depth of 0.15m (north end) to 0.25m. Corresponding to these, to the south, was a deposit of pea grit, gravel and small chalk rubble in light brown clay (54). The surface of 54 sloped down to the north, against the natural incline, towards the gateway. These surfaces served as a pathway, repaired and relaid, running through the wall, apparently linking the vicarages to the north with the north door of the church to the south.

East of path 32 and north of wall 20 were chalk rubble deposits (244, 245 and 247) and clayey gravel surfaces

Plate 11. Site 26 Period 5, Phase 1 path 32.

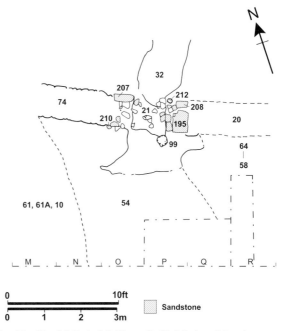

Fig. 41. Site 26 Period 5, Phase 2. (E. Marlow-Mann)

Period 5, Phase 2 (Fig. 41)
Further deposits of brown clay with small chalk and pea grit (61A, 10 and 61), and a compacted surface (57, not illustrated) accumulated against the south face of walls 74 and 20 up to the edge of path 54. East of the path was a very hard compacted surface of chalk in sandy brown soil (64). Its depth averaged 76mm to 100mm increasing towards the south-east, to compensate for the slope, where there was a small area of charcoal burnt wood and burnt sandstone (58).

In the gap between walls 74 and 20 was a patch of hard-packed chalk and sandstone rubble set in a lime mortar, (209, not illustrated), another repair to the surface of path 32. In the four corners of the gateway, partly overlying mortar 209, were fragments of reused sandstone blocks (207, 208, 210 and 195). Block 210 was part of a sandstone shaft (Ch. 22, No. 67), which sealed post-hole 287 (Period 5, Phase 1; Fig. 39), while 195 was a reused window-sill jamb (Ch. 22, No. 70; *Wharram III*, 193, fiche fig. 119). Both these blocks were thought to have come from the north aisle of the church, demolished in the late 15th or early 16th century. To the west of 195 was part of a chamfered sandstone block (252, not illustrated); the top of this was more than 0.1m higher than the top of 209. North of 252, cutting through the path were two post-holes (211, not illustrated and 212) only 76mm apart.

Subsequently sealing 209 and 252 between walls 74 and 20 was a further repair to the path surface of compact chalk cobbles (21), with occasional large and medium chalk and sandstone. Cutting the south-east corner of 21 was an irregular post-hole (99).

The pottery from Period 5 features dates broadly to the late medieval and the early 16th century (Ch. 18, Table 139). On this basis it can be assigned to the late medieval vicarage complex and will be considered further in *Wharram XII*.

(243 and 834). Set on to 243 was a large octagonal piece of sandstone, (SF137) probably a padstone. It was 0.61m x 0.46m with a circular depression 0.38m in diameter in the centre, 90mm deep. Immediately south of this stone feature was a post-hole (825) with large chalk packing. The paths contained pottery of late medieval and 16th-century date, though context 247 incorporated also a number of sherds from a much earlier York Glazed vessel (B18) (Ch. 18, No. 6).

West of the path, features and surfaces were eroded and truncated. Two sections of a north-south wall (88) remained towards the western edge. The full width of the wall, 1.07m, survived in part, for a single course. It was constructed with a facing of large and medium chalk and a rubble core of mostly small chalk. To the east was a deposit (288) of large rubble (mostly sandstone roof tile). These structures relate to vicarage buildings to the north and will be discussed more fully in *Wharram XII*. A sub-circular feature (291) with large flint and limestone blocks, as well as burnt bone and charcoal, may have been a post setting or a hearth (although burning was not noted on the stones). The fill of shallow oval cut 318 included carbonised grain. Scoop 293 may have been a truncated feature.

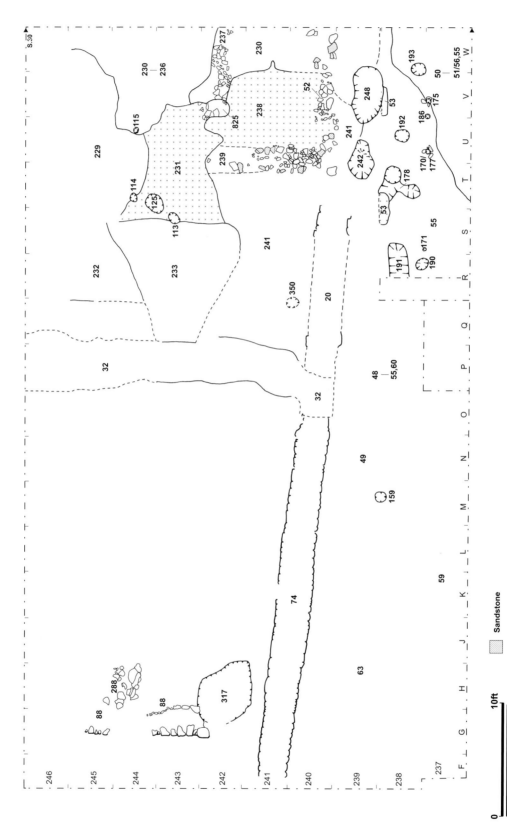

Fig. 42. Site 26 Period 6, Phase 2. (E. Marlow-Mann)

Sandstone

Clay bonding material

50

Period 6 (16th century to 18th century)

Period 6, Phase 1 (not illustrated)

To the north and south of wall 20 were compacted deposits of clay bonding with flint and sandstone chips and some small chalk rubble, spilling out from the core of the wall with rubble from the face. Roof tile and animal bone were also noted. A patch of burnt clay up to 0.18m thick (213) together with loamy brown soils disturbed by animal activity (240 and 180), mark the disuse of the wall.

As wall 74 to the west survived substantially intact it seems likely that the poor survival of 20, mostly as collapsed rubble from the core, was caused by the deliberate robbing of the facing stones rather than by gradual decay, although no discernible cut for this robbing was noted.

Period 6, Phase 2 (Fig. 42)

To the south of the robbed line of wall 20 and east of path 54 (Fig. 41), were surfaces 51 and 56, compacted small chalk which sloped down considerably towards the south and particularly the south-east. Cut through 51 and 56 was a series of post-holes and stake-holes (159, 190, 171, 178, 170/177, 192, 186, 175 and 193) forming an irregular line with three post-holes (179, 182 and 183, not illustrated) cut through the path. Accumulated against the section edge were deposits of silt (55) and loose mixed rubble (50). The increasing depth of 55 suggests accumulation against some sort of barrier further down the slope beyond the limit of excavation. To the north were two patches of clay bonding-type material (53) probably displaced from the wall and two shallow depressions, or possibly, pits (242 and 248) from the robbing of rubble for wall material (see below, 239 etc).

Further west were very soft loose deposits of brown clayey soil with some small chalk rubble (59 and 49), with stone roof tile in 49; these spilled over the line of path 54. Sealing the rest of 54 (and post-holes 179, 182 and 183) was 48, brown earth with small chalk rubble and some compact chalk cobbles. The post-holes, although varying in size and shape, formed a line, regularly enough spaced to have served as some sort of fence, (perhaps temporary) to the churchyard, extending eastwards from path 54 and replacing wall 20. With the abandonment of the path this area of the churchyard was little used and thus deposits did not become compacted. Some of the material may have been hill-wash accumulated over a period of time.

To the north of the line of robbed wall 20 and east of path 32 was a group of distinct surfaces (229, 231 and 238). Edging 238 to the east and south were disturbed wall footings (239/52), comprising large and medium chalk limestone and flint with rammed chalk cobbles, 0.53m to 0.61m wide. To the north and parallel to 52 was another irregular east-west line of chalk rubble (237); this may have formed the bottom course of a wall footing with post-hole 825 retained from Period 5, Phase 1. There was a suggestion of a possible extension northwards of a wall footing beyond post-hole 825.

To the east of these features were areas of rubble (230/236), (230 containing a currycomb handle) (Ch. 27, No. 62), possibly from the collapse of the structure represented by 239/52/237. The edge between internal surface 231 and cobbles 229 was marked by post-holes 114 and 115, and the western edge of 231 by post-holes 113 and 125. West of the structure were further chalk rubble deposits (241, 232 and 233).

The stone, rubble and clay footings (239, 52 and 237) together formed the west end of a building at least 2.44m wide, extending eastwards beyond the limit of excavation. It is also possible that there was an entrance at the north-west corner of the structure onto external cobbled surface 229. There was no indication of the character of any superstructure apart from the clay bonding-type material (238), but the general spread of rubble suggested that the footings were probably more than one course high. These footings, in an area of external yard surfaces, suggest agricultural use. Internal surfaces, or make-up layers for a stone floor, are represented by 238/231. Context 229 produced a shears blade (Ch. 27, No. 7), horseshoes (No. 59), a horseshoe nail and bridle bit (No. 63), indicating the presence of a stable in the vicinity. This stable will be discussed further in *Wharram XII*. With the exception of 241 all these surfaces included moderate quantities of domestic debris - animal bone, pottery, ironwork etc., and in 230 the first recorded occurrence of brick inclusions.

Period 6, Phase 3 (Fig. 43)

West of path 32 and north of the line of wall 74 were rubble deposits (17/35 and 246), possibly from the decay or demolition of wall 88 (Period 5, Phase 1, Fig. 42). A surface of very compact chalk rubble (15) sealed 88, and to the north was a loamy deposit (14).

Set on to 14 at its north-east corner was a rough wall footing or setting of large and medium chalk blocks (814) extending 0.81m from the northern edge of excavation. This narrowed from 0.61m to 0.25m, the width of a single block; it was *c.* 0.28m high. On photographs the rubble appears two courses deep and some of the blocks were fairly regularly laid with a deliberate curve on the eastern (inner) face. There was no indication as to whether it had originally extended further south and been robbed.

To the east of 814 was a deposit of charcoal and burning (813) up to 0.15m deep. The western edge of 813 curved on a line with the projected 'inner' face of 814 and its southern extent on a line projected from the western arm of 34 (see below). Its eastern extent was beyond the limit of the 1972 area of excavation and was not recorded in the extended area of 1973, although from the northern section it clearly extended for at least 0.61m into this area, towards 34.

Beyond 813 was a line of large chalk and sandstone blocks set in clay bonding material, 34, extending 0.91m and turning to the west for 1.22m. Within this area was a deposit of small chalk and brown clay (822). Two small post-holes (97 and 98) were cut against the western face of 34 and into 822.

The combination of 34 and 822, in conjunction with the extents of 814 and 813, suggests that they formed

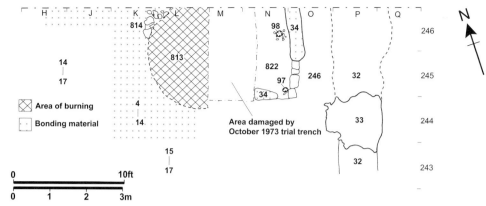

Fig. 43. Site 26 Period 6, Phase 3. (E. Marlow-Mann)

parts of a single structure. The curve on the stub of footing 814 and the edge of 813 would have made an elongated D-shape 3.66m-3.96m long. The burnt material 813 may be the result of some particular agricultural or domestic function, but unfortunately it was not sampled and no finds were present. It is also possible that 813 was itself the remains of a burnt superstructure. Its plan and position suggest that it may have been an external oven relating to a domestic building immediately to the north. The context of these remains will be discussed further in *Wharram XII*.

To the east of 34, set into the top of path 32, was a deposit of sandstone and mixed chalk rubble (33) presumably a repair to the surface. To the south and west of 813 was a deposit of bonding-type material (4). It could have been the remains of another wall footing south of 814 or, more likely, spread as a floor make-up or surface.

Period 6, Phase 4 (Fig. 44)
South of wall 74, sealing Period 6, Phase 2 deposits, were level surfaces of compact chalk with some sandstone in light grey/brown soils (3A, 45, 46 and 47) up to 0.3m deep.

Considerable quantities of domestic debris - pottery, animal bone, iron and copper objects, nails and oyster shell - were noted from 45, 46 and 47. An area of burning (44B), suggestive of burning *in situ* within the churchyard, butted against 148, a feature of large and medium chalk including some very large blocks up to 0.46 x 0.3m, as well as brick, flint, sandstone and burnt sandstone. Although disturbed, the large chalk blocks were faced and regularly arranged in bonding-type material forming a wall footing 0.38m wide, one to two courses high. This structure appeared to have been faced to the west but may have continued southwards.

Photographs (e.g. Plate 2) show that regular large chalk blocks and areas of large and medium chalk rubble in the adjoining grid squares to the east and south were evident at a comparable level, but were not recorded in detail. To the north was clay bonding material (155) up to 0.15m deep associated with rubble facing, bounding a small area of possible internal flooring. Sealing 155 was demolition debris (145 and 146) from this structure.

Plate 12. Site 26 Period 6, Phase 4 wall 76, Grid H/J 239-238.

52

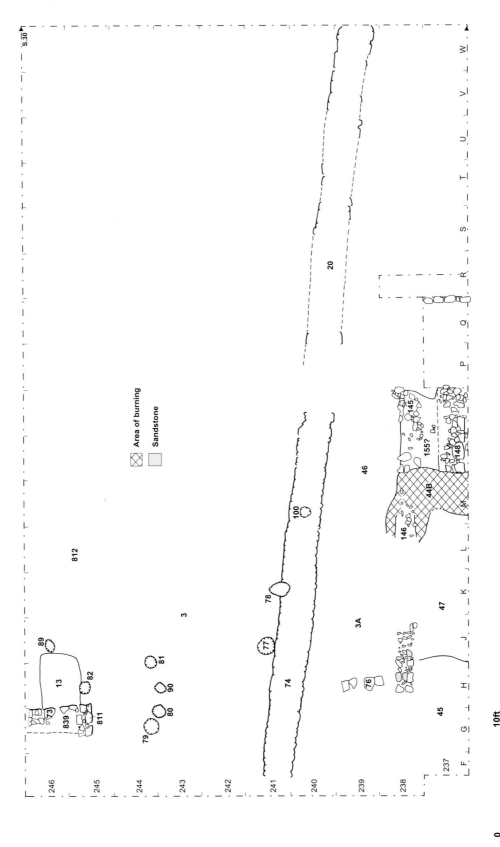

Fig. 44. Site 26 Period 6, Phases 4-6. (E. Marlow-Mann)

53

To the west, set onto 3A, was part of a wall (76; Plate 12) surviving for a length of 1.98m constructed of large chalk and sandstone in two courses over 0.3m high. The roughly squared blocks facing a rubble core had a total width of 0.53m. Although extensively disturbed, and robbed to the north, it appeared that at the south end the wall turned east directly in line with 146.

In spite of the compacted nature of surfaces 45, 46, and 47 and their considerable depth, they appear not to have accumulated over a long period; possibly deliberately dumped as levelling material, which in the case of 45 included a considerable amount of hillwash. Given the unstable nature of the western hillside it is probable that hill-washed deposits were regularly spread out and used for levelling-up.

From the surviving elements of wall footing 148 it is difficult to suggest what form or function the structure or superstructure might have taken. Apart from the spread of clay bonding material in the area between 148 and 155 there were no particular indications that they were necessarily part of the same structure. Their distance apart (0.9m) makes it unlikely that one was a 'lean-to' against the other. A possible function might have been the storage of tools or even a bier by a sexton; this would not have required a structure of size or substance.

Period 6, Phase 5 (not illustrated)
Cutting into the line of wall 148/155 was a robbing cut (144) with a fill of dark brown soil, burnt sandstone, yellow clay, charcoal and brick. To the west, partly sealing wall 76 and spilling out to the north and east was a spread of large and medium chalk, sandstone and burnt sandstone (8) similar to the fill of 144. This deposit was confined more or less to the area within walls 76, suggesting that the wall footings had been pushed in, rather than allowed to decay. To the south of 155 was a rubble spread (44A), up to 0.18m deep, possibly the result of the demolition of 148/155 but not necessarily contemporary with the destruction of 76.

Period 6, Phase 6 (Fig. 44)
Sealing the Period 6, Phase 3 oven and associated surfaces to the west, was a deposit of mixed brown soil with 'heavy' chalk rubble (3) extending south to the line of wall 74 and level with its uppermost surviving courses. A reasonable quantity of domestic debris was included in the deposit, suggesting that it had been either dumped from a zone of occupation or exposed (or in use) for a considerable time. The actual area of the demolished 'oven' was distinguished by large chalk rubble (812).

In the north-west corner, extending south from the north section was part of a wall (73) (Plate 13) surviving up to seven courses (0.72m) high. The bottom course comprised large blocks of chalk, sandstone and burnt sandstone. Above this the east face comprised roughly dressed large and medium chalk and possible reused sandstone blocks; the west face was of medium chalk

Plate 13. Site 26 Period 6, Phase 6 walls 73/811, Grid G245-247.

blocks with a rubble core. Flint, brick, and 'cement stone' were also noted but it is not clear whether from the core or facing. The width of the wall was 0.43m and it survived for a length of 0.38m, although the foundation course continued south for a further 0.84m.

The remaining upstanding southern part of 73 had been robbed, so that it was not clear whether the wall had originally continued further south and been robbed to foundation level or faced, with the foundation forming a threshold. At the point where the foundation course of 73 terminated, another wall (811, Plate 13), aligned east-west, extended to the west for 0.86m. It was of the same width and construction as 73, and survived up to four courses, at least 0.39m high, although the foundation course of 73 was apparently not well-bonded to 811.

The surviving upper courses of wall 811 were fairly regular but slumped at the junction with 73, reinforcing the suggestion that a threshold may have existed at that point. From the section it appears that the foundation course of 73 was probably trench-built into 839, a wall bonding-type material. Again this substantial building relates to structures to the north and its context will be discussed further in *Wharram XII*.

The rest of 839 and wall 811 were both truncated by the later conduit, (Period 7, Phase 1). To the south of 811 and a surface of small chalk cobbles (13) was context 5 (Fig. 45), part dark soil with charcoal to the north, part compressed chalk to the south. Cutting the eastern edge of 13 was a shallow oval post-hole (89) and on the southern edge another post-hole (82) perhaps indicating some sort of porch over the threshold. To the south was a group of four post-holes aligned in a curve (79, 80, 90 and 81), and cut into, or close to, wall 74 were post-holes 77, 78 and 100. At the time of excavation layer 3 was not distinguished from 3A (Period 6, Phase 4); thus Period 6, Phases 4 and 6 may be broadly contemporary.

Period 7 (late 18th century and later)

Period 7, Phase 1 (Fig. 45; Plate 14)

In the north-west corner of the area of excavation a major structural cut (11) was identified, extending deep into the natural chalk and right through the Period 5 wall (74); its total depth was 2.13m. Its fill, including material from earlier levels, marked the destruction of the Period 6, Phase 4 building, with a dump of large chalk, sandstone, flint and brick (810), sealing walls 73 and 811, surface 13, and associated post-holes (Fig. 44). The cut was almost vertical with the west face of wall 73 forming the edge at the top, and the lower half of the cut sloping steeply, except for the bottom 0.36m which was vertical, descending to a level base. The upper west side of the cut was beyond the limit of excavation but this side clearly sloped less steeply down to a point 0.36m above the base, where it formed an offset 0.3m wide and then sloped steeply to the base.

On the natural chalk at the base of this trench a layer of natural grey-green (puddled) clay, 76mm to 180mm thick, had been spread. This layer was not particularly level but between the two ends of the surface exposed here was a maximum differential of 37mm with the slope from the south down to the north. On the clay surface against the sides of the trench were large and medium slabs of chalk and sandstone set edge to edge, forming a stone-lined channel (84). This was 76mm to 180mm

Plate 14. Site 26 Period 7, Phase 1 conduit.

wide; on top rested a continuous capping of large slabs of chalk and sandstone. The length of channel exposed here was 8.03m; it appears to have been empty and no silting was recorded. Sealing the channel and the base of the cut were fills of soft dark soil, mixed chalk and light brown clay tipping down to the east. The uppermost fill (6) was compacted chalk, perhaps a consolidating surface.

This water conduit has been identified on other sites along the terrace (Site 52, see Ch. 5; Sites 54 and 77 see *Wharram XII* (forthcoming); and at the west end of the church, see Ch. 3), and is known to have carried fresh water from the spring on the valley side to the west of the pond along the terrace to the farmhouse (Site 74) north of the vicarage. It is thought to have been constructed in the late 18th century, and will be further discussed in *Wharram XII*.

Period 7, Phase 2 (Fig. 45)

Extending right across the eastern end of the site to a line approximately 1.2m east of path 32 (Fig. 43) was 218/40, an extensive area of small compact chalk cobbles forming a fairly even surface. The thickness of the cobbles varied from 25-76mm at the south end where the surface was also more undulating; the alignment of this surface was roughly north-west/south-east. On the upper surface were discontinuous north-south linear depressions (219 and 43) 76mm-0.11m wide and, although only 25mm deep, quite distinctive (Plate 15). These ruts were aligned over the eastern half of 218 and 40 and were about 1.37m apart (centre to centre). To either side of this surface were mixed deposits including some larger rubble (22/224 and 220) and compact smaller chalk and rubble (225, 223, 42, 31 and 29).

The extensive and well-made surfaces 218/40 were clearly part of a road, and from excavations on adjoining sites to the north (Sites 54 and 49; *Wharram XII*) it is known that this road passed in front (i.e. to the east) of the 18th to 19th-century vicarage. From Site 54 it was also established that the conduit was constructed before the road surfaces were laid. Estate maps dating from 1836 (see Ch. 2) show a sequence of tracks and fences in this area.

Period 7, Phase 3 (Fig. 45)

A series of features (scoops 30 and 222) and post-holes aligned roughly north-south, was cut into the western edge of the road surface 218 of Phase 2. A roughly-edged area of mixed rubble (234) was sealed by 818, a more extensive area of mixed rubble, including brick, with post-holes (91, 102, 94, 95 and 96) around the edge. These features, and some of the other post-holes to the south, are likely to relate to the 18th-century vicarage on Site 54 to the north, and would have abutted its south wall, which lay in the north section of Site 26. They may represent a repair to the main wall or chimney and/or possibly some partial replacement of the Period 6 'oven'. The eastern post-holes (830, 831, 111, 110, 109, 108, 107,

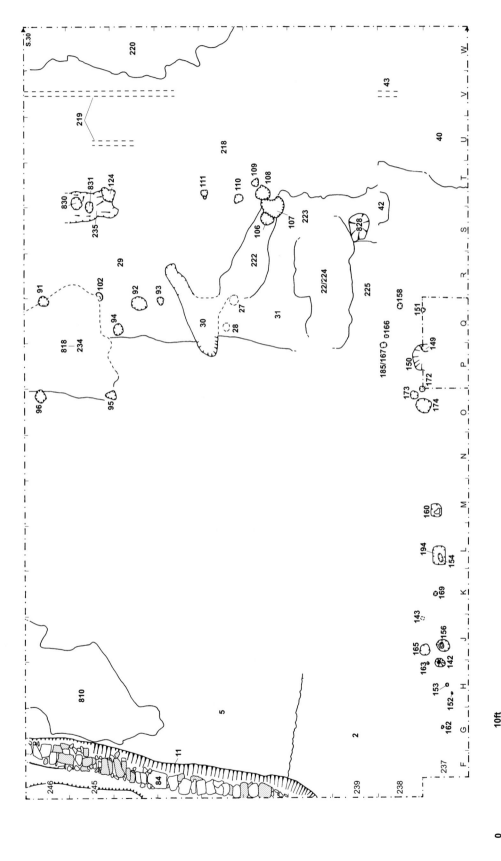

Fig. 45. Site 26 Period 7, Phases 1-3. (E. Marlow-Mann)

56

Plate 15. Site 26 Period 7, Phase 2, road surface and embedded ruts.

828, 106, 27, 28, 93 and 92), although disparate in size and spacing, may have formed 'fence' lines separating the road from the former churchyard to the west.

To the south was a more convincing line of post and stake-holes, (162, 152, 153, 142, 163, 165, 156, 143, 169, 154, 160, 174, 173, 172, 150, 149, 151, 185/167, 166 and 158) although again disparate in size and spacing. Some were clearly repairs and a number retained fragments of wood *in situ*. This established a new northern boundary to the churchyard on much the same alignment as that of the Period 6, Phase 2 posts.

Period 7, Phase 4 (not illustrated)
A series of deposits was laid over road surface 218. These extensive uneven spreads of mostly sandstone and chalk rubble were much disturbed by tree roots against the eastern section at the south-east corner of the site. Against the eastern limit of excavation were two rows of fairly regularly laid, roughly-squared blocks, with two large squared sandstone blocks to the north and one large block of chalk to the south forming a single row at the west end in an overall T-shape. This may have been the vestigial remains of a wall footing or padstone or perhaps the edge of a regularly laid surface or repair.

The uneven nature of most of these deposits and the uncertain interpretation of others suggest the disuse of the road rather than resurfacing, although occasional use as a trackway would not necessarily have resulted in much compaction. The likely source of much of the rubble is the former vicarage to the north, demolished in 1834.

With its removal, much traffic along this route would have ceased.

Period 7, Phase 5 (not illustrated)
Sealing structures and surfaces over the entire area of excavation were deposits of mixed rubble and small frost-shattered chalk in dark, humic soil (215, 216, 9, 36 and 37), marking the disuse of this area north of the church for domestic/agricultural activities.

Sites 20S and 21, 1970-71 (Fig. 46)

An east-west trench (Site 20S), 1.22m wide by 6.1m, was cut in Grid 241 from Grid 5W-5A, as part of a series of exploratory trenches down the hillside, which also included Site 21. The work on these two trenches was initially reported in *Interim Report 1970*, 4 and *1971*, 4-5. Apart from general questions about the nature of the slope and valley side, an earthwork was apparent at the east end of Site 20S. Two structures of considerable interest were found in this trench, and both were left *in situ*.

At the west end of Site 20S a 'revetment' wall was located, extending 0.3m to 0.61m out from the hillside; from the short length exposed it was apparently aligned on the hillside. It was composed of two courses of 'dry laid' chalk blocks and rubble with one piece of burnt sandstone. The top of this feature was at 144.44m OD (473.91ft), just over 0.61m below the turf level (Plate 16). It was not observed further north, in Site 21, and it is

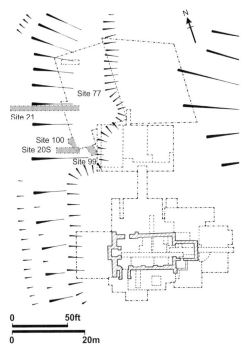

Fig. 46. Location of Sites 20S, 21, 99 and 100 in relation to Site 77. (E. Marlow-Mann)

Plate 16. Site 20S revetment wall.

possible it only continued north as far as the steps (see below, Site 77, context 100).

At the east end of the trench a substantial chalk and sandstone feature was located running north-west to south-east. This feature is now known to be part of a stepped track, the full width of which was exposed on Site 100 in 1990 (see below). The worked sandstone blocks evident on plan and in section, proved to be risers on this flight of steps. A more detailed description of the steps is given below.

In 1970 the Site 21 trench was cut down the hillside from the western plateau to the terrace further to the north. On the more level area of the hillside (in Grids 5P-

5Q), described as terrace 2 there was a build-up of compact chalk and humus at the lowest level above the natural chalk, but no evidence of any surface. This was the suggested route of the terraced track up the hillside from the pond area to the village site (Beresford and Hurst 1990, fig.55), but there was nothing to confirm the line of this proposed track way, and it was assumed that it had been eroded since the medieval period.

The revetment wall is unlikely to have served as a churchyard boundary and is probably post-medieval in date. It was possibly constructed to reduce or prevent the accumulation of hillwash on the trackway below. If projected northwards the western edge of the 'steps' would have met the line of trench Site 21 in Grid 5P-5Q, precisely the suggested location for the trackway.

Sites 100/77, 1989-90 (16th century or later)
(Fig. 46)

The full Site 77 report will appear in *Wharram XII*; features noted here relate to structures identified as relevant to the churchyard and its access. The substantial feature revealed at the south-west corner of Site 77 in 1989, which had previously been recorded on site 20S in 1971 (see above), prompted a small extension to Site 77 known as Site 100. This was opened in 1990 in Grid squares 813-4/241, extending northwards to Grid 245 in order to examine the full extent of contexts and their relationship to Site 20S (see above). Earlier reports are to be found in *Interim Report 1971*, 4-5; *1984*, 19-20; *1989*, 6, 9, fig.5; *1990*, 9-10.

Squared, medium-large sandstone and occasional chalk, small-medium chalk and sandstone with occasional flint (Site 100, context 79) were set in level 'steps' (Plate 17; Fig. 47), the larger material forming the 'treads' of the steps, the other material being infill (Fig. 47). Overall, these were 1.7m wide, increasing to *c.* 2.5m further uphill. Between Grids 242-245 ten shallow 'risers' provided a gentle lift up the slope from 142.6-143m OD, with the level further north in Grid 248 (Site 77, context 176) at 143.25m OD. Although described as 'steps' this feature clearly represents a terraced path or trackway and it was left *in situ*.

Information on the nature of its construction is provided by observations on Site 20S in 1971 where a small area was revealed in plan and in section in Terrace Grid 241/A at the east end of the trench. The squared chalk and sandstone blocks were set on foundations of chalk, flint and sandstone rubble to a depth of 0.61m. At its east end the paving appeared to merge with a surface of small-medium chalk.

There is no further evidence on the full extent of this feature. Presumably it continued down to the bottom of the slope which forms the western edge of the churchyard (along the line of Terrace Grid C/D), where it perhaps joined a path across the churchyard to the north door of the church; and up the hillside to the west as far as the line of the north-south track (see Site 20S, above; Beresford and Hurst 1990, fig. 55).

Plate 17. Site 100/77 'steps'.

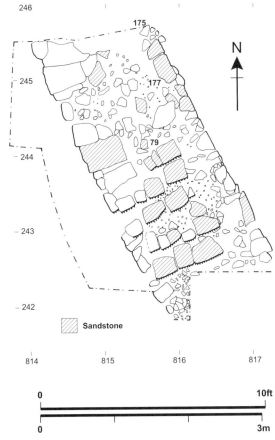

Sandstone

Fig. 47. Site 100: plan of trackway with steps. (E. Marlow-Mann)

No dating evidence was recovered as this feature remains *in situ*, but in terms of the sequence on Site 77 it has been suggested that the vicarage boundary wall 182 (see Site 99, below; Fig. 48), a continuation of Site 26 wall 74 (Period 5, Phase 1; Fig. 39) probably remained in use after the 'steps'. Two points should, however, be noted here: first, that the use of sandstone may well indicate a late or post-medieval date of construction (note that the boundary wall is built of chalk); and secondly, that on Site 26 parts of that wall survived as a substantial feature for a considerable time after its boundary function had ceased.

The construction of such a well-surfaced track diagonally across the slope may reflect an attempt to stabilise an access route down the constantly eroding hillside (see also the revetment wall on Site 20S). If this track had continued upwards in a straight line it would have met a continuation of the revetment wall from Site 20S at the point where the north-south trackway (see Site 21) is thought to have passed along the edge of the hillside. Such well-laid external surfaces have not been encountered elsewhere in the village and this sort of terracing in stone is usually associated with more rocky terrain.

Sites 99/77, 1987-89, 1990 (16th century)

(Fig. 46)

A wall (182), extending in a north-westerly direction from the south edge of Site 77 towards the western end of the excavation, was first revealed in 1987. An extension of Site 77 was opened in 1990, in the area of NG 819-820/242, to trace the wall southwards (Fig. 48). This was numbered Site 99. The results were reported in *Interim Report 1987*, 16, fig. 5; *1988*, 8; *1989*, 6-7, fig. 5.

The wall was not set in a construction trench but laid directly onto the ground surface; stone roof tiles had been used as levelling material where necessary. Large and medium chalk with occasional sandstone blocks faced a core of small and medium chalk rubble forming a structure 0.7m to 0.8m wide standing to a height of four courses. There was no evidence of any lime mortar or apparently, any other bonding material.

One metre to the south of the Site 77 boundary the alignment changed and turned to the south-east for another metre, where it was cut away by the late 18th-century conduit trench (see Site 26 Period 7, Phase 1; 84, Fig. 45). Although some of the facing stones were either missing or irregular at the turn of this wall, the change in alignment was carefully examined and there was no evidence of any change in the core or construction. It is thus clear that this was the original course. An angle in the wall would inevitably have been a weak point and subtle differences in construction here possibly represent repair or stabilisation.

This wall is of considerable interest, as from its position and construction it is clearly a continuation of wall 74 on Site 26. Wall 74 had originally been envisaged as a boundary of the churchyard. It is clear from its

59

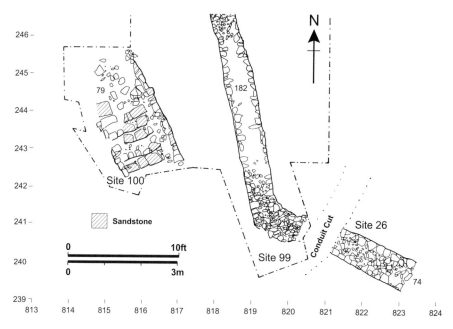

Fig. 48. Sites 99 and 100: plan showing Site 77, wall 182, Site 26, wall 74 and Site 100, 'steps' 79. (E. Marlow-Mann)

continuation in Sites 99 and 77, however, that it must have served as an enclosure wall to the later medieval vicarage, incidentally forming a northern boundary to the churchyard. Detailed discussion of its relationship to the vicarage buildings must await the report on those structures (*Wharram XII*).

Discussion

The earliest firmly dated structural feature in Site 26, defining Period 1, was the Iron Age burial (Burial G305; Fig. 29). Similar crouched and flexed Late Iron Age burials are known widely across the Yorkshire region. Recent discoveries include flexed burials in pits at Gargrave, North Yorkshire (Martin and McCluskey 2004) and a number of flexed and crouched inhumations deposited in the pits of pit-alignments at Ferrybridge, West Yorkshire (Richardson 2005a, 70, table 1). These date broadly to the 2nd and 1st centuries BC and the 1st century AD. They are, however, in small groups, rather than single, isolated interments.

If the Wharram burial really is an isolated occurrence (and only the area to its east and north has been excavated), then it belongs to a much more rarely recorded phenomenon in the region (*pers. comm.* M. Holst). The Wolds area has produced a crouched burial at Driffield (Philips 1960, 183), and another crouched inhumation (female) in an oval grave has recently been discovered at Reighton, near Filey (Signorelli and Wheelhouse 2004).

Such interments have been found near contemporary settlements, often in boundary ditches or pits dug originally for other purposes. It has been suggested that their association with boundaries, tracks and watercourses may be an expression of 'liminality', reflecting the transition from life to death, or of

regeneration (Bevan 1999, 141-2). In this case, proximity to water – perhaps springs as much as the stream – may have been a factor.

Settlement is, however, attested in the 1st and early 2nd centuries AD, with boundary ditches and structural features probably representing buildings both here and on Site 41 south of the church (see below). The absence of a clear chronological sequence, the problems of erosion and truncation, and the paucity of dating evidence make any interpretation necessarily tentative. Though the archaeological record has traditionally emphasised the location of Iron Age and Romano-British settlements on the Wolds plateaux (e.g. *Wharram V*; Beresford and Hurst 1990, 69-72, 89-93), this may simply be a matter of visibility, as the narrow valley floors in this part of the Wolds are sometimes maintained as permanent pasture and therefore immune to the formation of cropmarks (to be discussed further in *Wharram XIII*, forthcoming). Furthermore, even where cultivated, they are liable to have accumulated significant deposits of hillwash in later centuries, obscuring remains of the prehistoric, Roman and early medieval periods.

Ditch 255 (Fig. 31) seems to have been cut after the disuse of features assigned to Period 1, Phase 2. It may still, however, belong to the later Roman period, and it is perhaps significant that its course is broadly parallel with the ditch located about 6m to the south (NA 35, see Ch. 3; Fig. 20). We know very little about NA35, but it is more likely to be post-Roman. Ditch 255 may have been maintained or redefined in the post-Roman Period 2, to create a boundary associated with the Period 2 structure marked by the line of substantial post-holes. Whether, even at that stage, it might have separated the secular from the religious is a matter for speculation, as is the function of the post-holes. In this context, it should be noted that Site 26 produced no pottery and only a few artefacts that could be identified, or even suggested, as being specifically Anglo-Saxon in date or broadly contemporary with the possible *Grubenhaus* in the north churchyard (Ch. 3). There were two Saxon coins from medieval contexts (Ch. 25, Nos 4 and 6) but their presence could be explained in many ways: there was nothing to indicate the type of occupation that would have resulted in considerable quantities of domestic debris, as for example on parts of the plateau (e.g. *Wharram VIII*). It is clear that any surfaces contemporary with Period 2 were eroded or truncated. There is no indication of the extent of any period of use, or the function of the structure, but it might well have been short-lived, early 10th-century for example.

In Period 3, starting (on the evidence of radiocarbon determinations) in the later 10th to early 11th centuries, the graveyard extended from the area immediately north of the church as far as the area of the Period 2 building on Site 26. A sequence of burials interspersed with make-ups, surfaces and features apparently unrelated to burial activity suggests that, although more than 126 individuals were buried here, this does not amount to particularly intense use as it covered a period of some 400 years. Clearly, different parts of the churchyard were in use simultaneously and patterns, family groupings etc are discussed elsewhere (Ch. 15). Unfortunately there was no evidence of any early medieval churchyard boundary on this site, or beyond the limits of excavation to the north on Site 54 (*Wharram XII*). Excavation on Site 77 did not reach early medieval levels and it is possible that further isolated burials may remain there. Site 26 covers approximately 8% of the total churchyard area.

There was no evidence for the accumulation of topsoil and thus turf over these graveyard deposits, but it is possible that repeated use for burial has destroyed the evidence. This might account for the apparently shallow cuts of some graves and post-holes, in that they would have been cut through a destroyed level and thus originally at least 0.15m deeper (see below-next page). During Period 3, Phases 1-5, the northern half of the area of excavation was used for a decreasing number of burials. This may reflect encroachment on the burial ground because of increasing demand for space from domestic or other activities to the north, rather than a simple decreasing demand on burial space. This use for other activities resulted in the very different characteristics of the surfaces in the northern half of the area, as well as the concentration of finds.

Pottery was mostly from Ceramic Group 4 (early medieval) with a few residual sherds from Group 3 and intrusive sherds from Groups 5 and 6. The pottery shows no noticeable progression in date between Period 3, Phases 1 to 5. The radiocarbon dates indicated that the earliest burials from this period dated to *cal AD 960-1030 (95% probability; GU-5545)*; the latest burials were dated to *cal AD 1040-1130 (95% probability; GU-5537, GU-5539, GU-5540, GU-5541)*. In conjunction, with the sequence south of the church (Ch. 5), this appears to suggest a possible earlier starting date for Group 4

ceramics. In general, the range of non-ceramic finds from the burial levels is similar to that from other areas of the graveyard.

In general terms the Period 4 burials were arranged approximately in seven rows, with a greater density towards the southern limit of excavation. The overall arrangement is of some tightly clustered intercutting burial groups interpersed in rows of fairly widely spaced graves (see Ch. 15). The reason for the clustering is not clear. Two contributory factors (not mutually exclusive) could account for these characteristics. First, times of plague or sickness, resulting in sudden concentrations of contemporary deaths (assuming a preference for burying together, possibly in family groups). Secondly, inertia on behalf of the gravedigger who knows that it is easier to dig into an area already disturbed rather than into the natural chalk (note also the concentration of burials in the soft fill of the Period 1 ditch).

As many of the burials in the rows are not of the same phase, some sort of marking of graves (possibly as humps in the ground) must have occurred: few of the numerous post-holes within the graveyard area could be associated with adjacent graves, assuming that they were supposed to be at the head (or foot) and not just anywhere close to the grave. On the other hand, the disturbance of graves where jointed limbs (sometimes articulated, e.g. Burial G689, Period 3, Phase 1; Fig. 33) and skulls were subsequently displaced indicates that by no means all graves were clearly marked. At St Helen-on-the-Walls in York some clustering of burials was evident, but to a lesser degree (Dawes and Magilton 1980, 10-11, figs 6, 7).

The depth of grave cuts varied considerably, from about 0.6m to 0.27m. The problem of truncation in graveyards is discussed by Rodwell (1981, 134) and some sort of truncation levelling/clearance seems likely as no turf levels or humic deposits seem to have accumulated over the surfaces sealing the burials, unless they were entirely removed by the insertion of subsequent burials or eroded by other 'activities'. Some of the horizons sealing burials were so compacted as to suggest considerable traffic across the area, particularly north-south across the western part - towards the possible residential focus identified north of this area.

This raises the question as to whether grass could or would have grown sufficiently for animal grazing. The only use suggested for the not infrequent post-holes occurring between the graves (and sometimes cut through them) is to support posts for tethering animals. The use of graveyards for grazing is well documented (and still occurs: see also Ch. 2). The need to tether would have been greater if there were no formal boundary fence, wall or ditch around the churchyard to contain animals - which may have been the case here before the 16th century.

The alignment of the grave cuts varied considerably from 53° south of east (i.e. south-east to north-west) to true east-west (see also Ch. 15). More than half (56) of those that could be determined (101) were within 4° north or south of the alignment of the church, which itself lies on an alignment of 18° south of east. Some grave cuts were twisted, and in others the bodies were twisted. The church lies more or less at right angles to the terrace, so burials may have been aligned to the terrace, rather than having a more precise relationship to the 'correct' alignment of the church itself. At St Helen-on-the-Walls, York, it was assumed that the 'correct' alignment was that of the church itself. The building's alignment shifted over time, the latest being 40° north of east. Unfortunately it was not possible to phase the burials tightly enough to test this hypothesis (Dawes and Magilton 1980, 13, fig. 8). Distance from the object of alignment is also a factor: the further away the less influence is exerted. Burial alignments relative to sunrise have been thoroughly discussed by Kendall (1983).

It has been noted (e.g. Rodwell 1981, 135) that the northern sides of churchyards were the 'least favoured' for burial, and that a high proportion of those buried would be women or children. Unfortunately, as the entire churchyard was not fully excavated, it has not been possible to test such hypotheses here.

The period of burial on Site 26 has a suggested date range from the second half of the 10th century until the mid-14th century. For only 126 individuals to be buried over such a long period does not amount to concentrated use for burial.

The greater density of burial in Period 4, Phase 1 at the south-east corner of Site 26 is perhaps a consequence of the construction of buildings over the northern half of the site and appears comparable with that in some areas of the north churchyard (see below). The surviving fragments of wall footing are not sufficiently coherent to suggest a plan of the structure, but its likely overall shape and size are indicated on Figure 49. The relative absence of larger chalk bocks redistributed in surrounding deposits suggests that it was robbed and dismantled, rather than allowed to decay. The large amounts of rubbish accumulating in the deposits in this northern part of the site and 'within' the area enclosed or bounded by the structure may reflect the use of this area for casual refuse disposal after the demolition of the building. It is remarkable that the area again came to be used for occasional burials in succeeding phases of Period 4, suggesting that it was still regarded as consecrated ground, although without any sign of formal limits.

Period 5, walls 74 and 20 (Fig. 39), established immediately south of the Period 4 structure(s), formed part of an enclosing wall of the vicarage to the north, a wall also traced beyond the conduit cutting, northwards through Sites 99 and 77. It also defined, apparently for the first time, the northern boundary of the churchyard. In relation to the OS grid, the alignment of wall 74/20 was not east-west, but 24° south of east. Nor was it parallel to the church, which lies at 18° south of east. The apparent truncation of Burial G251 (Period 4, Phase 5; Fig. 38) suggests that there may have been some terracing or levelling down for the construction of the wall, as well as levelling up further east (271, Period 4, Phase 6, not illustrated) The method of construction, using natural

clay with chalk and flint chips as bonding and bedding material and without a foundation trench is a method of wall building in general use at Wharram. A structure built of chalk and clay would not, however, have survived persistent rain and winter frosts unless capped with tiles or perhaps thatch; rendering of the walls was also a possibility.

The arrangement of post-holes 287 and 286 (Fig. 39) suggests support for a timber gate or barrier across the gap between the two lengths of wall. A single or double gate hinged on 286 or 287 and opening into the churchyard, or posts and a rail slotted into the wall, are possible. This point would have given access directly from the vicarage to the north door of the church, traditionally the entrance for the clergy. With the exception of a wall and ditches on the south side of the churchyard (Sites 41 and 71, Ch. 5), further comparison of boundaries is not possible. The steep hillslopes to the west and east of the church served as natural boundaries, where necessary, revetted by walls (Site 20S). The contraction of the graveyard coincides with the contraction of the church during the late 15th and early 16th centuries (*Wharram III*, phase IX) and of the village as a whole (Beresford 1979, 6-9).

The patching and resurfacing of path 32 (Period 5-6; Fig. 42) from the vicarage to the north, through the wall towards the north door of the church suggests regular use. The wider spread of 54 (Fig. 39) inside the churchyard suggests that access was not only directed to the church but also to the rest of the churchyard, particularly to the west end and tower (possibly a route to the pond to the south of the church: see Ch. 2). Given the alignment of the path, the gap between walls 321 and 325 (Period 4, Phase 1; Fig. 36) may indicate an earlier point of access into the churchyard from the vicarage.

The concentration of reused sandstone architectural elements in the remodelling of the gateway contrasts with the chalk fabric of the walls, which may not have weathered very well. The date of the window-sill or jamb 195 is not earlier than *c*.1350 and a suggested provenance of this, and the other stonework, is the north aisle of the church, constructed at that time and demolished in the late 15th or early 16th century (*Wharram III*, 91, phase IX).

The silty deposits that accumulated south of the walls mark the disuse of this area for burial, although it still lay within the churchyard. Heavily compacted surface 64 (Fig. 41), to the east of the path was possibly the result of the passage of animals using the valley slopes below the terrace for grazing, or access to the pond and stream to the south. To the north were surfaces or levelling up material which included a reasonable proportion of domestic debris, indicating continued use for 'domestic' purposes as an exterior yard. West of the path, wall footing 88 (Fig. 39) belonged to a building extending northwards, and will be discussed further in *Wharram XII*.

A relative absence of finds from the path surfaces, or the gateway remodelling, precludes much discussion of the time-span of Period 5. Wall 74 is likely to have been

Fig. 49. Site 26 Period 4, Phase 1: possible reconstruction of wall footings and demolition debris. (E. Marlow-Mann)

63

constructed after the mid-14th century and could be as late as the 16th century: its dating will be considered further in *Wharram XII* in relation to the buildings it enclosed. The path north of the wall line may have continued in use up to the 18th century, when its course would have been blocked by the final vicarage house that was built to the north (Site 54, *Wharram XII*).

The Period 6 features continued the 'domestic' and ancillary use of Periods 4 and 5, with the addition of structures south of the line of the boundary wall, over the area of the reduced burial ground. The latter structures may have had functions relating to the church rather than the vicarage. The collapse of wall 20 (Fig. 42) after the removal of the facing stones must have been gradual, as its alignment seems to have still been apparent for some time. The recorded eastern extent of Period 6, Phase 2 deposits was on much the same alignment as the surfaces beneath, with the southern 'wall' line 52 (Fig. 42) butting against the remains of wall 20, suggesting further elements of continuity in this exterior yard area. The Period 6, Phase 3 oven relates to structures to the north on Site 54, and will be discussed further in *Wharram XII*.

By Period 6, Phase 4, wall 74 had also ceased to have a boundary function; the nature of the surfaces and finds to the south was very similar to those on the north side and this area had now effectively become an extension of the yard area of the vicarage rather than part of the churchyard. The function of the structure(s) here is not clear. The absolute levels of these features close to the line of wall 74 were at the same height as its surviving top, and it is possible that all higher stone courses were removed in this period (perhaps for reuse in walls 76/148 or 73/811; Fig. 44), and that the structures to north and south of it (i.e. Phases 4 and 6) were broadly contemporary. The ceramic material is similar, but with more Ceramic Group 7 material to the north. Walls 73/811 (Phase 3) contrast with all the other structures so far described, in the manner of their construction. Properly laid and bonded and set in a trench they appeared to indicate a fully stone-walled building rather than footings for a superstructure. Their structural, and other associations, will be discussed in *Wharram XII*.

Most of the walls on Site 26 shared one important characteristic: they were bonded with clay rather than lime mortar. 'Puddled' clay mixed with small chalk and flint chips forms a very strong binding element, even if not entirely weatherproof. A mixture of similar composition was also used for floor surfaces (e.g. in Period 6, Phase 2) and bedding for stone floors. The clay and flint are presumed to have been obtained from the area around the construction, although no definite mixing pits have been identified. Chalk chips can be a by-product of frost-shattering and the flint chips were presumably obtained by knapping. This type of wall-footing construction was common at Wharram, but what is not clear is the nature of any timber-framed superstructure, or any cob, wattle or daub infill. Other factors for consideration include the optimum height or width of walls as footings (Milne 1979, 71).

The conduit, Period 7, Phase 1, carried fresh water to the farmhouse and is thought to date to the late 18th century. The construction of the Phase 2 cobbled road which crossed the eastern half of the site marks a major change in land-use. From other excavations (Sites 49 and 54) and from maps (Fig. 159), it is known that an early 19th-century road passed by the western range of the farmyard, in front of the farmhouse and the vicarage and crossed the former churchyard. It then bifurcated and passed as paths to the east of the chancel and to the west of the tower. The road surfaces are also known to have been laid after the conduit.

In 1834 the last vicarage (on Site 54) was 'taken away', and the estate plan of 1836 shows a track on the line of the path, but a little wider, with a fence on the east side crossing the site of the former vicarage and Site 26. No archaeological evidence of such a route, other than the path itself (from Period 5, Phase 1) was recovered. The fence lines could, however, be represented by the north-south post-holes of Period 7, Phase 3. For further comment on the relationship between maps and archaeological evidence see Chapter 2.

5 Excavations in the Southern Graveyard Area
by C. Harding

Site 52, 1978-9 (12th century to 15th century)
(Fig. 50)

A small excavation, 6.1m by 1.2m, was opened at the south-west corner of the churchyard in Grid G-L/182, adjacent to the terraced way from the plateau down to the dam and pond. The ground surface sloped down from 141.99m OD at the north-west corner to 140.3m OD at the south-east corner. The results were reported in *Interim Report 1978*, 10-11; *1979*, 3, 13. The following is a summary and as such does not include detailed phasing.

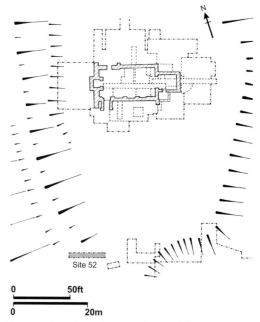

Fig. 50. Location of Site 52. (E. Marlow-Mann)

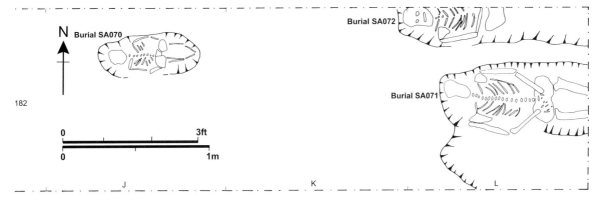

Fig. 51. Site 52 plan of burials. (E. Marlow-Mann)

The purpose of the excavation was to examine the line of the medieval and post-medieval terraced way which skirted the west boundary of the churchyard from the plateau above to the west, down to the dam and pond to the south and east. Damage to this area by heavy earth-moving equipment during backfilling and reconstruction work on part of the dam and pond, had removed the turf and topsoil in the centre of the trench, exposing a 'cliff' of chalk and hillwash. Following excavation this area of the churchyard was to be landscaped.

The natural chalk sloped down from 140.57 to 139.04m dipping sharply down at the east end of the trench. This possibly marks the edge of a shelf or fault which must exist between this site and adjacent Site 41 (see below) where a very different pattern of geology and deposition was recorded. Sealing the natural chalk were deposits of yellow-brown clay and small chalk, and of orange-brown clay (21; not illustrated). There was no evidence on this site, however, of Roman or prehistoric occupation, and only one residual Roman sherd.

No evidence of any medieval or later surface or trackway was evident, but three burials (Burials SA070-072; Phase 3.1; Fig. 51) were located, cut into the hillwash and sealed by similar deposits of yellow-brown to light brown clay loam with small chalk. The burials were not suitable for radiocarbon dating, but are likely to be broadly contemporary with those on adjacent Sites 41 and 80.

Apart from the topsoil where the latest datable material was fragments of imported stoneware, the datable finds from Site 52 were medieval, with most pottery sherds from Ceramic Group 4. This agrees with the general interpretation of this area of the churchyard as mostly undisturbed since the medieval period. The shallow depth of the graves, however, also accords with evidence from Site 41, where it is suggested that some terracing or levelling had taken place in the post-medieval period.

In 1979, Site 52 was extended to the west and the top of the conduit, which runs along the terrace from the spring at the west end of the pond to the farmhouse, was located. The same conduit was recorded in the excavations at the west end of the church (see Ch. 3) and on Site 26 (Ch. 4).

Site 80, 1984 (12th century to 13th century)
(Fig. 52)

In 1984, during drainage work outside the southern boundary of the churchyard and north-west of the reconstructed dam, a trench for a sump was cut approximately 1.5m south of the churchyard gate, in the area of Grid N-P/179-180. At approximately 0.1m below the ground surface an articulated skeleton was discovered (Burial SA080; not illustrated). The trench was extended to about 1.5m x 3.5m to reveal the entire inhumation. The burial was clearly *in situ* with head to west, but truncated below the pelvis by a later post-hole. Although submitted for radiocarbon dating, the sample proved unsuitable. This was reported in *Interim Report 1984*, 4.

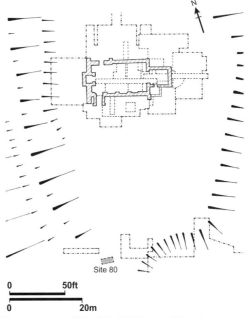

Fig. 52. Location of Site 80. (E. Marlow-Mann)

Site 41, 1975-1978 (Fig. 53)

Initially a north-south trench 1.2m wide was opened in Grid 182-4/X. This was extended in 1976 with an L-shaped area adjoining to the west, but only a part of this area was excavated to natural because of the depths involved. The work was covered in *Interim Report 1975*, 1; *1976*, 6-7; *1977*, 7-8; *1978*, 5-6.

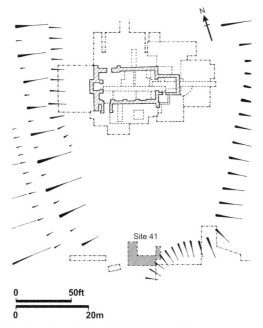

Fig. 53. Location of Site 41. (E. Marlow-Mann)

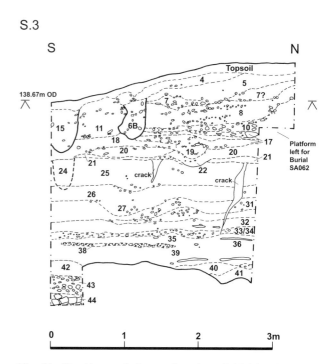

S.3

Period 1 (Middle to Late Bronze Age) (not illustrated in plan; see Fig. 54, S.3)

Evidence of the earliest occupation comprised a series of 'surfaces' with scatters of flint flakes and charcoal, separated by deposits of sterile, silty soils sloping down to the north-west (including contexts 35 and 36 on Fig. 54, S.3). The latest contexts sealing the charcoal levels, contained fragments of Middle and Late Bronze Age pottery. Work at this level was only carried out in a small area in Grids X/182-4, down to 2.7m below the turf level. The unexpected depth of deposits in this area, and the direction of slope of the natural chalk, in the opposite direction to the present-day ground slope, is indicative of considerable topographical change. The survival of these features is due to the subsequent accumulation of hill-washed silts in a 'wedge' against the hillside; this has

protected them from destruction by intrusions and later activity.

Period 2 (1st century to 4th century)

Period 2, Phase 1 (Fig. 55)

The earliest coherent structural remains on this site consisted of a shallow ditch (539/27: see also Fig. 54, S.3), aligned north-east to south-west, up to 1.2m wide and 0.4m deep, with post-holes along the edges: 29/30 (not illustrated), 545 and 547 to the north; 28 (not illustrated), 543, 533 and 532 to the south. Ceramics were of Late Iron Age/Romano-British date, probably 1st to mid-2nd-century. A bronze brooch (Ch. 26, No.1) was found in the

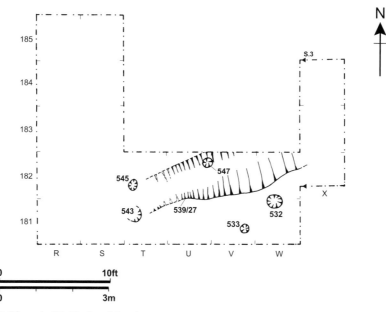

Fig. 55. Site 41 Period 2, Phase 1. (E. Marlow-Mann)

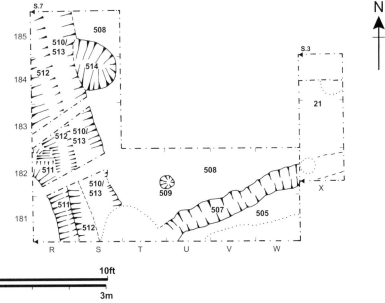

Fig. 56. Site 41 Period 2, Phase 3. (E. Marlow-Mann)

Plate 18. Site 41 Period 2, Phase 3 Ditch 513 and recuts.

fill (544) of the ditch. This complex of features was considered by the excavator as typical of the site of an Iron Age/Romano-British farmstead and may be contemporary with Site 26 Period 1, Phase 2 features (p. 34).

Period 2, Phase 2 (Not illustrated in plan; see Fig. 60, S.7) The Period 2, Phase 1 remains were covered by layers, 0.3-0.6m deep, and chalk surfaces (including 515).

Period 2, Phase 3 (Fig. 56)
The latest phase featured a narrow ditch (507), up to 0.6m wide. It may have been linked to a wider ditch to the west (513) running at right-angles, though their junction had been destroyed by a later intrusion. These ditches had been cut through deposits of compact orange-brown smooth clay and clay loam with thin lenses of chalk fragments (505, 508 and 21) which overlay 515/521 of

Period 2, Phase 2 (see Fig. 60, S.7). Ditch 513 was up to 2.1m wide and 1.2m deep; it was subsequently recut (510, 511 and 512; Plate 18) with a large scoop or cut (514) on its eastern side. In the angle of the two ditches was a post-hole (509). Ceramics from this phase included sherds of late 3rd or 4th-century date, suggesting some activity in the area over an extended period.

Period 2, Phase 4
A deposit of largely sterile silty clays, loam and bands of small chalk, up to 0.4m deep, probably an accumulation of hillwash material, overlay the Period 2, Phase 3 features.

Period 3 (12th century to 13th century)
Period 3, Phase 1 (Fig. 57)
Following this period of abandonment, activity or occupation resumed and the overall direction of downward ground slope shifted slightly, to the north-east, from a high point at the south-west corner of the site. The earliest features were some shallow gullies in the north-west corner (e.g. 168, sealed by 163) and, to the east, a small circular hearth (164A-B) of orange burnt clay c. 0.8m in diameter and sealed by chalky surfaces (uppermost 160).

The hearth was not directly associated with any structural features within the excavated area or artefactual debris; nor did it appear to have been used for long. Some 680 grams of slag was, however, recorded in layer 150 next to post-hole 155. In Grid S a diverse line of post-holes (152, 155, 154, 153, 146B, 148, 149, 145 and 144) crossed the site north-south, cutting through surfaces 150 and 163. They were possibly contemporary with the hearth although some contained medieval pottery in their fills. Context 150 also produced slag and part of a quern (Ch. 22).

A shallow north-south gully (158), 1.2m wide, was cut through surfaces 150 and 160 immediately to the east of

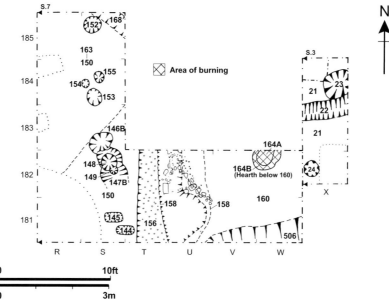

Fig. 57. Site 41 Period 3, Phase 1. (E. Marlow-Mann)

the post-holes. The fill of the gully was mostly small chalk but with some large and medium rubble and a straight-edged deposit of small chalk (156) forming the western side. Crossing the south-eastern quadrant was the northern edge of a substantial ditch (506), which may have been cut from a higher level; it was aligned approximately north-east to south-west and at least 0.6m deep, with charcoal in the fill, particularly at the base. To the north, cutting through chalk surface 21 were a substantial post-hole (23) and an east-west shallow gully or slot (22) up to 0.2m deep. From the short section of ditch 506 it is not possible to get a precise alignment, but it could well have served as a southern graveyard boundary; and some relationship to ditch 263 (Fig. 63), further east on Site 71 but on a similar alignment, is also possible (see Site 71 below).

Period 3, Phase 2 (Fig. 58)
To the west of gully 158 (fill 156), and cutting through it, was a similar feature with regular edges (131/151), 0.6m wide, with a more evenly distributed fill including some sandstone. The depth of the surviving fill increased to the north. It was also noted that the fills of several Period 4 graves, which cut down into these levels, contained large and medium chalk and sandstone blocks. This more clearly-defined feature was perhaps the footing for a boundary wall rather than a structure, and 'gully' 158 may reflect a construction trench or sinkage from its weight. To the north-east, gully 22 was also recut (19) to a depth of 0.3m.

The deposits to the east (132, 133, 134, 20 and 130) and west (130A-D, 136 and 137) of this structure contained varying degrees of small chalk or rubble in fairly loose clay or loam not characterised as surfaces,

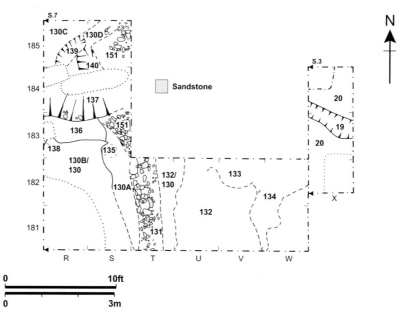

Fig. 58. Site 41 Period 3, Phase 2. (E. Marlow-Mann)

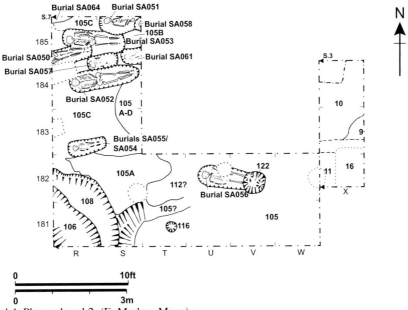

Fig. 59. Site 41: Period 4, Phases 1 and 2. (E. Marlow-Mann)

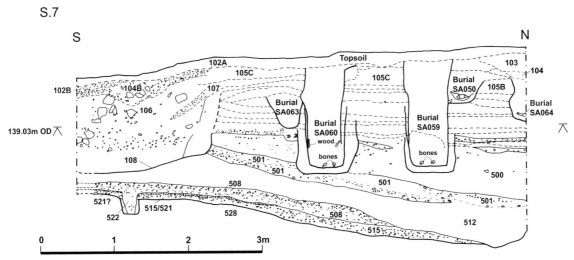

Fig. 60. Site 41: east-facing section along Grid Q/R 181-185. (E. Marlow-Mann)

with depressions and scoops (139, 137 and 140) cutting them. These were all sealed by a series of chalk surfaces (115, 117, 128, 129 and 17B), some with fairly regular north-south edges reflecting the trend of earlier alignments. The ground surface at the end of this period was fairly level in the western part of the excavation but still sloped down to the north-east.

The pottery derived from contexts of this period was mainly from Ceramic Group 4 (probably 12th to 13th-century). There was no residual pre-Conquest ceramic material, suggesting that whatever was happening to the north, around the church, and at the pond to the south and east in the Anglo-Saxon period was limited to those areas.

Period 4 (mid-12th century to 13th century)

Period 4, Phases 1 and 2 (Fig. 59)

Chalk surfaces on the west side of the site (113, 114 (not illustrated) and 112, Period 4, Phase 1) retained elements of the north-south linear divisions seen in Period 3 above, but cutting through them in the middle of the site, east of

the line of the Period 3 'footings', was an adult inhumation (Burial SA056, Period 4 Phase 2), having a radiocarbon date of *cal AD 980-1190 (95% probability; GU-4563)*. It was probably contemporary with another burial (Burial SA063; Fig. 60, S.7) (left *in situ*) in the west section. Surface 17B (not illustrated) to the east was sealed by an extensive dump of large chalk rubble (17A; not illustrated), tipping down from the east. This rubble and the burials were in turn sealed by further chalk surfaces (10, 11, 105, and 105A-D).

A further ten bodies (Period 4, Phase 2) were then interred, close together and intercutting, most of them west of the Period 4 'footing'. Two burials from this phase, Burial SA052 and Burial SA053, were dated to *cal AD 980-1220 (95% probability; GU-5461)* and *cal AD 1020-1220 (95% probability; GU-5462)* respectively (see Ch. 7). Possibly contemporary with the burials was a large pit (108) cut (and later recut, 106) into the south-west corner of the site, with a couple of post-holes (116 and 122) to the east.

69

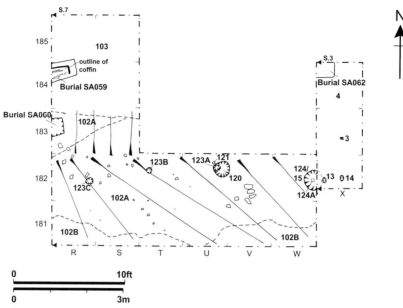

Fig. 61. Site 41 Period 5, Phases 1 and 2. (E. Marlow-Mann)

With the burials mostly confined to the north-west corner of this site, some sort of boundary to the churchyard or constraint on burial must have existed to the south and to the east - even if not apparent on Site 41. One possible constraint to the east would have been the location of a building which may have occupied this area, as evidenced by the dumps of domestic debris on Site 71 (see below). The extensive rubble from context 17A may relate to some aspect of this building although this rubble appears to be too early in date for demolition material. The burial in Site 80 (Burial SA080), located *c.* 6.1m to the south-west in 1984 during drainage works, may well have been outside any formal southern churchyard boundary, or just inside if the boundary was represented by ditch 506 (Fig. 57).

The ceramic material from this period was, as for Period 3, mainly from Ceramic Group 4. Given the date range of the burials, this suggests that Period 4 activity followed on closely after Period 3. The accepted ceramic date range (mid-12th to mid-13th-century) is clearly slightly at variance with the likely date of the burials.

Period 5 (13th century to 14th century) (Fig. 61)

With a series of dumps and make-up deposits (4, 103 and 102B) the ground level started to slope down to the east. An isolated burial (Burial SA062) was located in the northern section of the eastern arm of the site and left *in situ*. Although lacking evidence of a coffin, it was cut from a high level, and was considered late medieval or post-medieval at the time of excavation. The dumps and make-up deposits contained mainly early medieval pottery of the mid-12th to mid-13th centuries, much of it Staxton ware, but with a scatter of later sherds.

A series of post-holes (14, 13, 15/124/124A, 120/123A/121, 123B and 123C), including repair, replacement and the posts actually removed in 1976 prior to the excavation, was located on an east-west alignment

with soil and rubble (102A) accumulating against them on the north side, forming a slight ridge or bank. In the 19th century, from at least 1851 (Ch. 2), a southern boundary fence to the churchyard crossed the southern part of this site. To the north of this fence line two 'modern' (probably early 20th-century) coffined burials (Burials SA059 and SA060) were recorded, set 1.4m deep, in straight-sided cuts with wood remaining. Modern sensibilities at the disturbance of relatively recent remains marked by tombstones, may have resulted in reuse of the outer zones of the churchyard, where there were only unmarked medieval graves (*Wharram II*, 2, fig.1).

The shallow depth of the burials in Period 4 - only about 0.6m below the modern turf level - in comparison to the modern burials in Period 5, suggests that erosion and truncation of deposits occurred in this area sometime in the later medieval or post-medieval period. This explains the almost total absence of post-medieval or modern finds, and was also a feature of neighbouring Site 52 (see above). The ground surface by now sloped down to the south and, more sharply, to the east, marking a complete reversal of the pre-Roman ground form.

Site 71, 1982-3 (Fig. 62)

An area of 98 sq. m crossing the existing graveyard boundary was excavated by M. Atkin to investigate graveyard boundary sequences, and to relate stratification to the activities on Site 30. Work was initially reported in *Interim Report 1982*, 23-4; *1983*, 20-23. This summary deals only with the boundary features and the area within the churchyard; the full excavation report relating to Site 71 has been published in *Wharram X* and the phasing divisions here do not relate to the overall phasing sequence of the current volume.

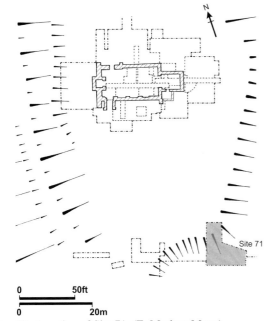

0   50ft

0   20m

Fig. 62. Location of Site 71. (E. Marlow-Mann)

Phase 1 (mid-12th century to mid-13th century)
(Figs 63 and 65)

A channel (263) with a low clay bank raised on its south side (260) ran approximately west to east and fed into a large depression (273). To the north-west side of the angle made by 263 and 273, were the remnants of a chalk platform (245) located on an artificially raised clay surface (258), associated with two post-settings for 0.2m square timbers (270 and 271) and a post-hole (272). Depression 273 and ditch 263 gradually silted up; however, the channel was later reopened with successive recuts (268, 269 and 262).

Phase 2 (mid-13th century to 15th century) (Figs 63 and 65)

Ditch 265 replaced ditch recut 262 on a similar alignment, while the raising of clay bank 260 with another dump of clay (259) suggested that the bank now served as a distinct boundary feature on the north side of the ditch.

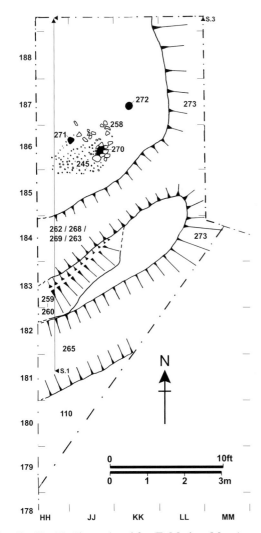

Fig. 63. Site 71, Phases 1 and 2. (E. Marlow-Mann)

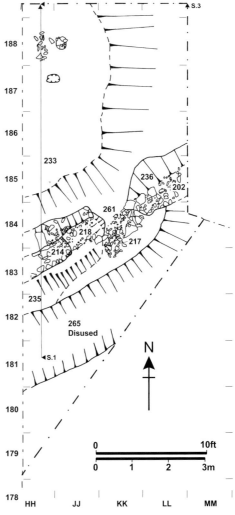

Fig. 64. Site 71, Phase 3. (E. Marlow-Mann)

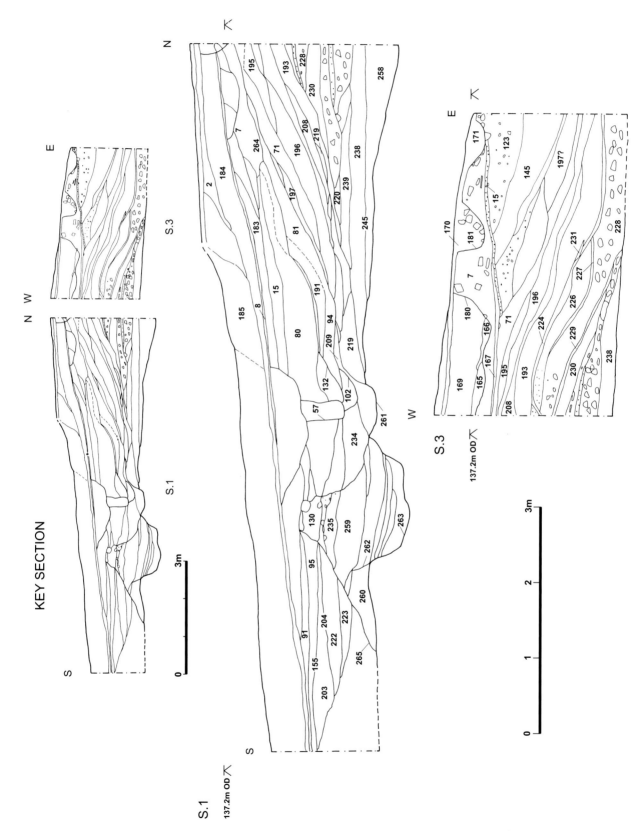

Fig. 65. Site 71 sections: east-facing S.1 along Grid mid-GG, 181-189; south-facing S.3 along Grid mid-189, mid-GG-LL. (E. Marlow-Mann)

Plate 19. Site 71, Wall 202 with centre gap plugged with chalk rubble 217. Ditch 261 is located behind the wall and the disused Ditch 265 is in the foreground, viewed from the south-west.

Phase 3 (mid-13th century to 15th century) (Figs 64 and 65)

The backfill of ditch 262 spread southwards with a series of chalk spreads (219 and 239; Fig. 65, S.1) that formed an extensive rough surface. Although well-rotted and compressed, roughly-squared blocks of chalk were discernible within the layers of chalk. Clay bank 259 was raised and extended eastwards by the addition of clay deposits (235 and 236). A chalk rubble wall (214/218/202), surviving as a single course of flat slabs with rough facing stones, ran along the bank. Initially, a gap was left in this wall to allow drainage from ditch 265 to continue to the north (Plate 19).

A new northward-draining ditch (261) was then dug to the north of the wall line, replacing ditch 265, and the gap was plugged with chalk rubble (217). This ditch appeared to have been regularly cleaned out, with the material piled on the north bank as a mixture of clayey silts (233) and lenses of water-washed gravel (220; Fig. 65, S.1), possibly to provide extra protection for the Phase 2 chalk platform (219/239).

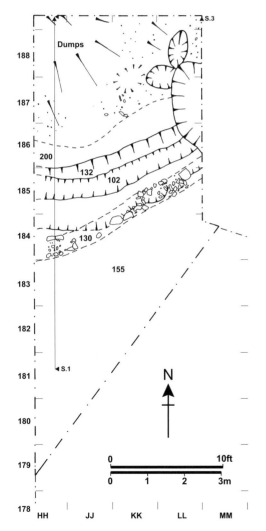

Fig. 66. Site 71, Phase 4. The dump of material includes the following contexts: 70, 81, 191-7, 208, 224 and 227-30. (E. Marlow-Mann)

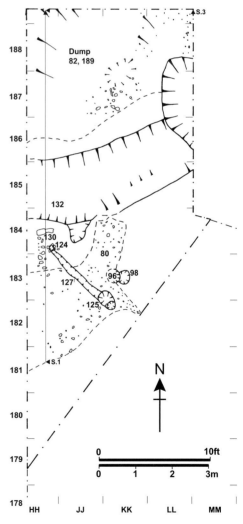

Fig. 67. Site 71, Phase 5. (E. Marlow-Mann)

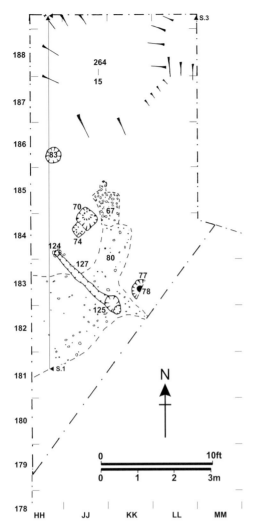

Fig. 68. Site 71 Phase 6. (E. Marlow-Mann)

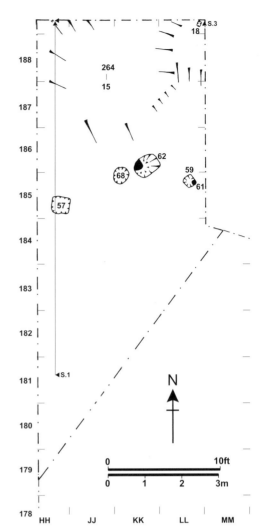

Fig. 69. Site 71 Phases 7-8. (E. Marlow-Mann)

Phase 4 (mid-13th century to 15th century) (Figs 66 and 65)

The topography of the site was now dramatically altered with at least 1.8m of make-up including layers of rubble, ash and carbonised grain being dumped against wall 214/218/202. Drainage ditch 261, north of the wall, had to be repeatedly recut as a series of temporary channels (102 and 132) as this dump of material built up. Several hollows were cut through these channels as they fell into disuse. Pottery from the dumps was mainly of early medieval date (mid-12th to mid-13th century), the bulk being Staxton ware. There were also sherds of the late 13th and 14th centuries, including a handled jar of possibly late 13th to 14th-century date.

A new boundary wall (130) and temporary revetment to the rubble (200) which accumulated against its north face was constructed on top of bank 235. It was built of chalk blocks and curved round to the west. A series of chalk yard surfaces (155) was located to the south; these surfaces probably related to a possible rectory or vicarage house in the vicinity which will be considered in more detail in *Wharram XII* (forthcoming).

Phase 5 (16th century to 18th century) (Figs 67 and 65)

Wall 130 was partly removed while further dumps levelled the existing ground surface to the north (layers 82 and 189), forming the basis of a later trackway (264 in Phase 6). To the south was a further series of compacted yard surfaces (80 and 95). These were cut by a 1.8m long slot (127), 0.15m wide, with a chalk block post-setting (124) at the north end and a post-hole (125) at the south end. This possible fence line and/or gateway would have maintained a boundary between the churchyard and the pond area, almost at right angles to the line of the former demolished boundary features. The relationship of two intercutting post-holes (96 and 98) with this feature was unclear. Pottery was of the later 13th and 14th centuries though again with significant quantities of residual Staxton sherds.

Phase 6 (18th century) (Figs 68 and 65)

Surface 264 consisted of the compacted surface of the upper chalk dumps of Phase 5, on a base of layer 15. The line of the boundary fence of Phase 5 was probably maintained just to the north by post-holes 83, 70/74 and 77. Note that the ground surface was now sloping down from east to west.

Phase 7 and 8 (19th century to 20th century) (Figs 69 and 65)

The line of the graveyard boundary is documented from 1851 (Ch. 2, Fig. 5) and, until its replacement in 1978, would have been represented by the line of post-holes

(57, 62, 68 and 59) at the foot of the slope of the medieval dump, reflecting a shift in the graveyard boundary back to the former medieval alignment. Post-hole 18 was situated at the corner of the 1978-82 fence.

Discussion

The unexpected depth and nature of the deposits in Site 41 represent a considerable challenge to our understanding of the stratigraphic sequence in this part of the valley as well as the ever-extending settlement pattern. Nothing similar was found either immediately to the west on Site 52 or to the south (Site 30). At present, the early prehistoric features located in Site 41 are the only evidence of settlement at this period in the valley. The Late Iron Age and Romano-British features, on the other hand, appear similar in nature and date to those north of the church (see Ch. 4).

Among the Period 3 features on Site 41, the repeated north-south alignment of surfaces and wall footings could be related either to the graveyard and Phase II church, or to activity by the stream to the south. Alternatively, it may represent part of a domestic building or agricultural shelter, associated with the hearth. The Period 5 dumps, though created probably in the 14th century, contained a large quantity of early medieval pottery (mid-12th to mid-13th-century) that may arguably have been associated with this building.

The earlier than expected date of the Period 4 burials on Site 41 forces a re-examination of the model of the development of the church and churchyard. Until the radiocarbon dating programme and the accompanying statistical work, it had not been anticipated that, as early as the 11th century, demand for burial space in the churchyard would have necessitated the use of land this far south of the church or as far north as the early burials on Site 26 (Ch. 4). One explanation of this might be the zoning of the cemetery into family or settlement groups. If the latter, this area might have been used by the inhabitants of those settlements in the parish that lay to the south of the church. The shallow depth of the burials on Sites 52, 80 and 41 is explicable in terms of considerable landscaping and clearance work in this area, as well as probable terracing, in the post-medieval period.

The succession of ditches and walls on Site 71 defined a sequence of east to west boundary features that were in existence from the 11th or 12th century into the 20th century, with the presence of chalk surfaces and associated post-holes to the north of that line in Phases 1 and 2 indicating some sort of structure on the platform at the edge of the pond and adjacent to the graveyard (*Wharram X*, 33). The presence of domestic refuse (which, from its unabraided state, had evidently not travelled far) and the absence of any evidence of burials, suggests that the boundary line defined activities associated with the pond from a domestic structure lying to the south of the church. The burials on Site 41 were confined to the western half of the excavation, perhaps another sign of a structure somewhere between and north of Sites 41 and 71. While domestic refuse is common in churchyards, the quantity here is clearly in excess of casual churchyard use for other activities.

On Site 71, the dump of structural and artefactual debris that was the principal evidence for a domestic focus of activity seems to have been tipped there from the north-west. The pottery was mainly Staxton ware (12th to 13th-century), but the dump included some later material including a large part of a handled jar of late 13th to 14th-century date. The presence of large quantities of nails and domestic refuse in a dump of carbonised grain, more than 3cwt (100kg), suggests that it did not derive from a milling accident but perhaps from a domestic store that had burnt down. The way it was laid down suggests a deliberate extension of the terrace and thus the available building area, perhaps reflecting pressure on space. The bulk of the pottery dated to the mid-12th to mid-13th centuries, and may be associated with the comparable activity evidenced in Site 41. The dumping may have taken place in the late 13th or 14th centuries.

It seems unlikely that the domestic debris had been brought far, and its presence may indicate the existence nearby of a house site occupied broadly in the period 1150-1250. An earlier report (*Interim Report 1983*, 23) noted aerial photograph evidence (unspecified) for the site of a house north-west of Site 71. Whilst there is, indeed, the possible outline of a building in the southern graveyard visible in an aerial photograph of 1956 (CUCAP RX42), nothing convincing is evident on the ground. If it existed, the building could have been an early priest's house; the possibilities will be considered further in *Wharram XII*.

The demolition and erosion of the medieval boundary features in Phase 5, with the re-establishment of a fence line on a different alignment (at right angles to the previous features) may reflect a temporary change in use of the site following the demolition of the postulated building, and possibly an extension of the area intended to be made available for burial. The former line of the boundary features was, however, then re-established in Period 6 and continued into the 20th century.

On the other hand, post-medieval burial may have been confined to the mounded area which contains the surviving memorial stones, and it is conceivable that the remains of a building might survive in the lower area of the churchyard, against the boundary to the east and south-east.

Part Three

The Human Remains

by S. Mays

6 The Nature of the Skeletal Collection

Introduction

The aim of this report is to investigate the demography, growth, physique and health of the population which used Wharram Percy church and churchyard for burial. Comparisons will be made with osteological data from other sites, both to help put the Wharram Percy results in context and to address more specific questions. The collection spans a period of about 900 years from the commencement of burial in the churchyard in about the mid-10th century, to the mid-19th century. Because of this, analysis of change over time is a major focus of the work.

Appendix 1 provides a complete catalogue of the burials, Appendix 2 notes on individual burials and Appendix 3 key words for individual burials.

In this report, when reference is made to individual burials, sex, age at death and phase are generally given, using the following abbreviations:
Sex
M, F, U and J denote male adult, female adult, unsexed adult and unsexed juvenile (juveniles are those aged under 18 years, adults are aged 18 and over) respectively;
? used as a suffix indicates probable sex in adults;
? used as a prefix indicates probable sex in older juveniles.
?? used as a prefix indicates possible sex in juveniles, as indicated by craniofacial morphology (see Chapter 7).
Age
Given in years unless stated.

The skeletal material

An explanation of references to burials
Burials in this volume have been renumbered to an alpha-numeric sequence with letter codes for each area of the church and churchyard, followed by an Arabic number (e.g. Burial SA034: South Aisle Burial 34); the burials from Site 26 are prefixed with G (e.g. Burial G250) (see p. 2 for more details). In 1976 (part way through the excavation of Site 26) a new context recording system was adopted at Wharram (see *Wharram VII*, 2 for more details). It must be noted that the original recording techniques used for burials prior to this change, frequently did not differentiate between skeletons and the cuts and fills of their graves – so for example, Burial SA050, where referred to in the text, incorporates skeleton number, grave cut and grave fills which may or may not have originally had separate context numbers.

Phasing
Skeletal remains of 687 articulated burials from the church and churchyard have been examined. These remains represent those who died at the village of Wharram Percy or elsewhere in this rural parish. They come from seven different parts of the excavated area, denoted with letter prefixes (Fig. 70). With the exception of the church nave (site code CN), these do not relate to divisions present in antiquity but rather represent arbitrary areas selected for excavation in different seasons.

Burials were divided into the phases shown in Table 1.

Table 1. Chronological phases used in the current work.

Phase	Approx. date (AD)	Description
1	950-1066	Late Anglo-Saxon
2	1066-1348	Earlier medieval
3	1348-1540	Later medieval
4	1540-1850	Post-medieval

Division into Saxon, medieval and post-medieval periods follows conventional archaeological divisions and facilitates comparison with published results. The aim of having a dividing point for the medieval material in the mid-14th century was to enable comparison of pre and post-Black Death groups. Documentary data indicate that the depletion of population due to the mid-14th-century Black Death generally resulted in better living conditions for those who survived as labour became scarcer and wages rose (Hatcher 1994). It was hoped to investigate whether there was any evidence for this from Wharram Percy.

Assignment to phase was made for:

a Burials with radiocarbon dates.

b Burials with datable coffin fittings (in practice only post-medieval coffin fittings were datable).

c Burials with direct stratigraphic relationships to a or b. This includes most burials from site area G (Site 26), where field conditions permitted stratigraphic relationships among burials to be recorded.

d Burials from areas of the churchyard which radiocarbon dating indicated had a restricted period of use, at least for adult burials. In practice this means that adult burials from area prefixes EE and NA were assigned to Phase 1-2 unless they could be more closely dated from radiocarbon determinations.

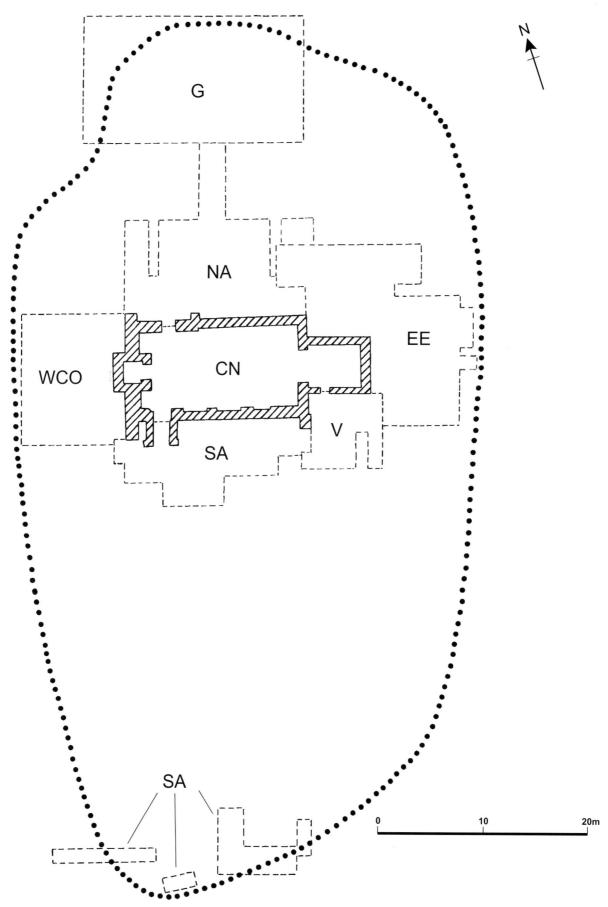

Fig. 70. Plan of the churchyard showing the outline of the standing church and the seven excavated areas with their letter prefixes. The dashed line shows the limits of the excavated areas, the dotted line the likely limits of burial. The number of burials from each area for which bones were received for study is as follows: CN, 39 burials; EE, 98 burials; G, 117 burials; NA, 217 burials; SA, 32 burials; V, 52 burials; WCO, 132 burials. (E. Marlow-Mann)

Table 2. Burials split by phase.

Phase	1	1-2	2	2-3	3	2-4	3-4	4	Total
N	10	167	78	11	0	1	8	51	326

Table 3. Macroscopic bone preservation and skeletal completeness.

Preservation	Approximate skeletal completeness					
	<20%	20-40%	40-60%	60-80%	80%+	Total
Good	59	76	82	131	176	524
Moderate	14	31	37	35	34	151
Poor	3	3	3	2	1	12
Total	76	110	122	168	211	687

In addition to the above, a small number of burials from area prefixes SA and V could be assigned to 'probable' phases on the basis of location of grave cuts in section drawings. For the current purposes, these are regarded as unphased because the aim is to pursue a conservative strategy whereby the study of secular change in osteological features was restricted to those burials for which assignment to phase could be regarded, for practical purposes, as certain (categories a-c, above) and those for which the probability of them coming from particular phases has been quantified as a result of statistical analysis of radiocarbon determinations (category d, above).

The numbers of burials assigned on the above basis to the different phases are shown in Table 2.

The relatively low numbers of burials which are firmly of pre-Conquest date is notable, as is the total lack of any which are of definite later medieval date. This latter effectively precludes direct comparisons between pre and post-Black Death medieval populations. The 326 phased burials comprise 258 adults and 68 juveniles. Of the 68 phased juveniles, the great majority come from Site 26 and date to Phase 2. The lack of a reasonable spread of juveniles over the different phases meant that investigations into change over time were essentially restricted to the adult burials. These form a reasonably large group to look at secular change, albeit at a rather broad-brush level. It is worth noting that all save one of the post-medieval burials were identified as such from the presence of distinctive coffin fittings or via stratigraphic relationships with those thus dated. Because most of the earlier burials lacked datable coffin fittings, it is likely that the greater 'visibility' of post-medieval burials has meant that they are over-represented in the phased sample.

Skeletal completeness, bone survival and macroscopic bone preservation
Of the 687 interments, there was only one showing any survival of soft tissue. Burial SA023 (F, 60+, Phase 4) showed a small amount of hair adhering to the right parietal bone. The hair and the surrounding area of skull were stained green by nearby copper-alloy coffin fittings. The biocidal effects of the copper ions may have helped to preserve the hair. The hair is green to grey in colour. That grey was its original colour is supported by the likely elderly age at death of this individual.

Methods
For each skeleton, an inventory of bones present was compiled. From this, the approximate degree of skeletal completeness was estimated. For each skeleton, overall preservation was scored subjectively as poor, moderate or good based on the level of post-depositional erosion of bone surfaces.

Table 4. Macroscopic bone preservation in adults and infants.

Preservation	Infants	Adults
Good	61 (60%)	273 (76%)
Moderate	38 (38%)	80 (22%)
Poor	2 (2%)	7 (2%)
Total	101	360

(Kolmogorov-Smirnov D statistic = 0.16, $p<0.05$)

Results
The skeletal preservation and completeness data are shown in Table 3.

In general, the level of macroscopic skeletal preservation is very good, with minimal post-depositional erosion of bone surfaces. There is no suggestion of any association between sex and gross bone preservation. The only evidence for an association between preservation and age at death was when infants (defined as those aged under one year) were compared with adults (those eighteen and over). Adult skeletons were in general somewhat better preserved than those of infants (Table 4) and were also more complete (Table 5). This suggests that even at this site, where soil conditions are clearly

Table 5. Skeletal completeness in adults and infants.

| | Approximate skeletal completeness | | | | | |
	<20%	20-40%	40-60%	60-80%	80%+	Total
Adults	41 (11%)	44 (12%)	71 (20%)	76 (21%)	128 (36%)	360
Infants	10 (10%)	29 (29%)	19 (19%)	35 (35%)	8 (8%)	101

(Kolmogorov-Smirnov D statistic = 0.28, p<0.05)

Notes: That some skeletal elements (e.g. patellae) are not ossified in infants was taken into account when estimating skeletal completeness in these individuals.

conducive to good bone survival, the more delicate infant bones suffered somewhat more from post-depositional erosion than have the more robust bones of adults. The lesser skeletal completeness of the infant skeletons may reflect preservation factors but because there was no on-site sieving programme to recover small bones it is also likely to be due to deficiencies of recovery.

Burials from within the church are more poorly preserved than those in the churchyard (Table 6) despite the fact that the former are post-medieval in date and post-date the latter by up to 900 years.

Table 6. Macroscopic bone preservation in church nave and churchyard burials.

| Preservation | Location | |
	Church nave	Other
Good	18 (46%)	506 (78%)
Moderate	14 (36%)	137 (21%)
Poor	7 (18%)	5 (1%)
Total	39	648

Kolmogorov-Smirnov D statistic = 0.32, p<0.05

In addition to showing more superficial erosion, many of the church nave bones were stained red-brown, a feature which was rarely seen in the churchyard burials. The rather different state of the bones from the church presumably reflects some local difference in burial environment connected with being interred beneath a standing building.

The burials at Wharram Percy were densely intercut, as is usual in medieval churchyards. Damage to burials by later features, principally further graves, was undoubtedly a factor behind the incompleteness of many interments. If burials graded 'poor' are ignored because of their small numbers, the Kolmogorov-Smirnov statistic indicates a significant association between skeletal completeness and macroscopic bone preservation (D=0.13, p=0.041), with those judged as showing 'moderate' bone preservation having lower degrees of skeletal completeness than those allocated to the 'good' category. This supports the idea that even in this relatively well preserved collection,

destruction of material in the soil was probably a factor affecting skeletal completeness.

The skeletal inventory data were used to obtain the numbers of each skeletal element in the assemblage. For the present purposes an element was regarded as present if it was represented by a complete or incomplete bone. The results for adults (Table 7) and for the assemblage as a whole (Table 8) are shown below. Figure 71 shows for the adults the numbers of each bone type present expressed as a percentage of that expected if all skeletons were complete.

The general pattern of skeletal representation (Fig. 71) resembles that observed for another medieval site, Ipswich Blackfriars, for which the presence of skeletal elements was recorded in the same way (cf. Mays 1998, fig. 2.6). The bones which are least well represented tend to be the smaller elements. This is as expected with hand-recovered material: unless soil is sieved to recover them they are often overlooked (Keiley 1989). At Wharram Percy, there is also a puzzling tendency for bones from the lower parts of the body to be more poorly represented than those from upper parts. For example, there are fewer femora than humeri, tibiae are less well represented than any of the bones of the arm, and there are fewer tarsals and metatarsals than carpals and metacarpals (Fig. 71). It seems unlikely that this reflects preservation factors as bones from the lower limb are generally more robust than their upper limb counterparts, reflecting the weight-bearing function of the former. It is also difficult to explain it in terms of selective removal of lower elements by intercutting graves as the pattern was not present at Ipswich Blackfriars where burials were also densely intercut.

Chemical and microstructural diagenesis
The aspects considered here are bone nitrogen content, porosity, histological preservation, and infra-red and X-ray diffraction spectra.

Burials analysed for nitrogen content were selected in order to sample different areas of the churchyard as well as the full range of ages at death and both sexes, as part of another study (Mays 2003a). The samples for porosity, histology and the spectroscopic work were selected to cover burials from different parts of the excavated area.

Table 7. Representation of skeletal elements in adult burials (N=360).

Skeletal element	Number
Crania	291
Mandibles	263
Hyoids	104
Cervical vertebrae	1668
Thoracic vertebrae	2986
Lumbar vertebrae	1225
Sacra	254
Sterna	237
Left ribs	2501
Right ribs	2485
Left claviculae	249
Right claviculae	245
Left scapulae	260
Right scapulae	257
Left humeri	251
Right humeri	261
Left radii	244
Right radii	237
Left ulnae	246
Right ulnae	244
Left carpals	922
Right carpals	884
Left metacarpals	1017
Right metacarpals	978
Left hand phalanges	1257
Right hand phalanges	1223
Unsided hand phalanges	851
Left innominates	271
Right innominates	266
Left femora	255
Right femora	247
Left patellae	163
Right patellae	159
Left tibiae	221
Right tibiae	224
Left fibulae	205
Right fibulae	209
Left calcanei	176
Right calcanei	177
Left tali	170
Right tali	170
Left tarsals*	664
Right tarsals*	641
Left metatarsals	721
Right metatarsals	718
Left foot phalanges	507
Right foot phalanges	503
Unsided foot phalanges	403
Foot sesamoids	89

*excluding tali and calcanei

Table 8. Representation of skeletal elements (all burials (N=687)).

Skeletal element	Number
Crania	591
Mandibles	531
Hyoids	144
Cervical vertebrae	3302
Thoracic vertebrae	5506
Lumbar vertebrae	2194
Sacra	443
Sterna	379
Left ribs	4567
Right ribs	4538
Left claviculae	487
Right claviculae	484
Left scapulae	497
Right scapulae	492
Left humeri	490
Right humeri	507
Left radii	467
Right radii	471
Left ulnae	465
Right ulnae	467
Left carpals	1015
Right carpals	985
Left metacarpals	1451
Right metacarpals	1454
Left hand phalanges	1355
Right hand phalanges	1319
Unsided hand phalanges	1945
Left innominates	522
Right innominates	516
Left femora	485
Right femora	479
Left patellae	186
Right patellae	179
Left tibiae	426
Right tibiae	425
Left fibulae	381
Right fibulae	382
Left calcanei	276
Right calcanei	277
Left tali	256
Right tali	244
Left tarsals*	872
Right tarsals*	852
Left metatarsals	1140
Right metatarsals	1143
Left foot phalanges	592
Right foot phalanges	593
Unsided foot phalanges	632
Foot sesamoids	93

*excluding tali and calcanei

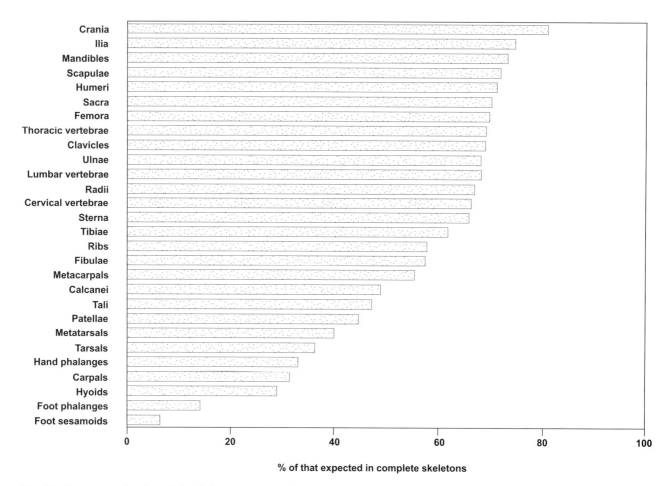

Fig. 71. Frequency of various skeletal elements expressed as a percentage of that expected if all skeletons were complete (adult burials only).

As bone degrades, the amount of collagen falls (Hedges and Law 1989). Whole bone nitrogen content has been shown to reflect the quantity of collagen in the bone provided that the percentage nitrogen exceeds 0.4% (Nielsen-Marsh and Hedges 2000), as was invariably the case in the current material. Whole bone nitrogen is thus a proxy measure of the amount of collagen remaining in a specimen.

Living bone is a rather porous material at the microscopic level. During diagenesis, this porosity increases and there is a shift in the size-distribution of pores with an increase in the number of larger pores, a change which has been referred to as an increase in macroporosity (Hedges *et al.* 1995; Nielsen-Marsh and Hedges 2000).

During diagenesis there is progressive loss of histological structure as a result of microbiological attack (Hackett 1981). Histological preservation was scored according to the six-point scheme of Hedges *et al.* (1995), which ranges from 0 (most severe diagenesis, no original features visible other than Haversian canals) to 5 (very well preserved, virtually indistinguishable from fresh bone).

X-ray diffraction and infra-red spectra each provide a measure of crystallinity of bone mineral. High crystallinity denotes large crystal size and absence of structural defects in a mineral, qualities which tend to be found together (Sillen 1989). Fresh bone shows low crystallinity, but it is well established that in buried bone crystallinity increases during diagenesis (Sillen 1989). An estimate of crystallinity was obtained from the infra-red spectrum using splitting of the phosphate anti-symmetric bending peak (Termine and Posner 1966). Increasing crystallinity is manifested in the X-ray diffraction pattern as a narrowing and sharpening of the peaks (Sillen 1989).

Methods
Nitrogen was measured using a CHN analyser (Mays 2003a). The histological work, porosity and infra-red spectroscopy were conducted at the University of Oxford by Christina Nielsen-Marsh, following published methods (Nielsen-Marsh and Hedges 2000). The X-ray diffraction study was carried out by Gordon Cressey at the Department of Mineralogy at the Natural History Museum, London, using hand-powdered bone samples. Adult burials were used in all analyses. The distribution of nitrogen values does not conform to a normal distribution, and there is no reason to suspect that the other continuous data do so. Thus non-parametric statistical techniques are used to analyse the results.

82

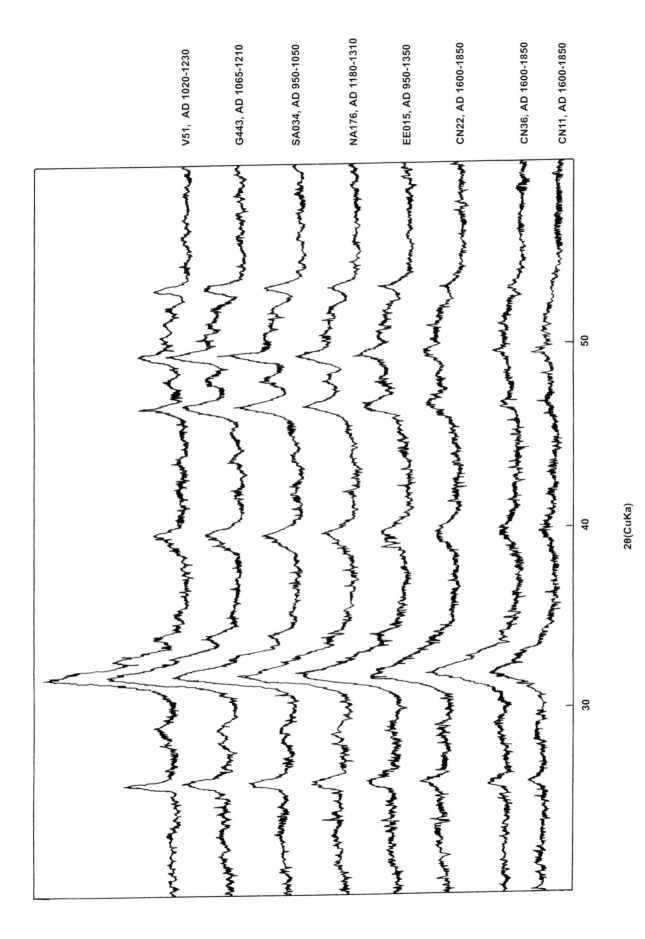

V51, AD 1020-1230

G443, AD 1065-1210

SA034, AD 950-1050

NA176, AD 1180-1310

EE015, AD 950-1350

CN22, AD 1600-1850

CN36, AD 1600-1850

CN11, AD 1600-1850

30   40   50

2θ(CuKa)

Fig. 72. X-ray diffraction pattern.

Results

The X-ray diffraction results are shown in Figure 72.

Table 9 indicates that there is a fall in nitrogen content with increasing age of the specimen, successively earlier phases showing lower median nitrogen levels. A Kruskal-Wallis non-parametric analysis of variance indicates that the variation in nitrogen content across the five sub-groups attains statistical significance (chi-square = 12.35, p=0.015). There is thus a measurable loss of nitrogen over the 900 years covered by the burials. Given the nitrogen content expected in fresh bone (4.8%), there is a drop of about 3.4% over about 1000 years, giving a mean rate of loss of about 0.34% per century. Although the dating of the phases is rather broad, the present results do not give any indications of marked deviation from linearity in the pattern of loss of nitrogen. Other writers (Lynch and Jeffries 1982; Sillen and Parkington 1996) indicate that loss of nitrogen in buried bone generally follows an exponential pattern with initial rapid loss being followed by a slowing in the rate. These workers were dealing with rather older specimens than the current material – the Wharram Percy material may be rather too young yet to show evidence of any appreciable levelling off in the rate of nitrogen loss.

Table 9. Nitrogen content.

Phase	N	% Nitrogen Median	IQR
1	2	1.37	0.07
1-2	15	1.67	1.52
2	8	2.17	1.81
3-4	3	2.28	0.38
4	9	3.63	2.26

Notes: Fresh bone value = 4.8% (Nielsen-Marsh and Hedges 2000)

Table 10. Histology.

Phase	Histology score					
	0	1	2	3	4	5
1		1				
1-2		3	1	1		
2	2					
4		1				4

For the histology (Table 10), the post-medieval burials generally show very good preservation, whereas diagenesis is generally severe in sections taken from earlier material. A Kolmogorov-Smirnov test indicates that this difference attains statistical significance (D=0.80, p=0.039).

Samples from all phases tend to show increased infra-red splitting and increased macroporosity compared with fresh bone (Table 11). Although the data give hints of

lesser change in the more recent material, trends by phase in these parameters failed to attain statistical significance.

Sample size for the X-ray diffraction data was too small to make statistical analysis worthwhile. Inspection of Figure 72 indicates that the peaks from the medieval specimens are in general rather narrower and sharper than those from the post-medieval bone, indicating greater crystallinity in earlier specimens

Table 11. Infra-red spectroscopy and macroporosity.

Phase	N	Infra-red splitting factor Median	IQR	%Macroporosity Median	IQR
1	1	3.4	-	83.0	-
1-2	5	3.2	0.30	86.7	12.9
2	2	3.2	0	84.9	1.0
4	5	3.1	0.85	74.8	35.9

Notes: Fresh bone values: infra-red splitting factor = 2.7, macroporosity = 52.8% (Nielsen-Marsh and Hedges 2000)

Discussion

Macroscopic preservation at Wharram Percy was generally good. This likely reflects the alkaline burial environment: the site lies on chalk geology, resulting in pH levels of 7.3 to 8.3 (Abrahams 1977; Keeley n.d.). These would be expected to be conducive to good bone survival (Mays 1998, 17-20).

Chemically and microstructurally, the post-medieval burials show lesser diagenetic change than older specimens, although even the post-medieval bone differs appreciably from fresh bone in many of the parameters measured here. The Phase 4 burials used in these analyses all derive from within the church. It seems likely that the lesser degree of diagenesis in this material reflects its more recent origin, but because, unlike the other burials, it comes from beneath a standing building, the soil environment may also have been somewhat different. The greater chemical and microstructural integrity of the church post-medieval remains contrasts with their rather poorer macroscopic preservation. This emphasises the point, long noted (e.g. Hanson and Buikstra 1987), that gross bone preservation is not a guide to the degree of diagenesis at the microscopic level.

7 Demography

Methods

For immature individuals, the main technique used to estimate age was dental development. The standards of Schour and Massler (1941) were used, together with supplemental data for the third molars from Garn et al. (1962) and Anderson et al. (1976). More precise age estimates for perinatal infants were obtained from long-bone lengths, using the linear regression equations of Scheuer et al. (1980). For adolescents and young adults,

Table 12. Instances of two inhumations in the same grave.

Burials	Age and sex	Phase	Disposition
G275/ G281	F, 25-25/ J, 4	2	Juvenile alongside legs of adult
G438/ G457	F, 25-35/ J, 30wiu	2	Foetus between femora of adult
G528/ G531	M, 19-21/ J, 1	2	Side by side
NA060/ NA60A	J, 45wiu/ J, 35-36 wiu	-	Unknown
NA103/ NA107	??F, 7/ J, 9mo	-	Infant on chest of child
NA170/ NA170A	F?, 21-25/ J, 42-45wiu	1	'Foetus in situ'
V47/ V53	??M, 12/ J, 0-1	-	Infant between or above legs of child
V51/ V55	M 40-50/ J, 6	1-2	Side by side

Notes: Age, wiu = weeks in utero (i.e. weeks gestation), mo = months, otherwise age in years

epiphysial fusion (Workshop of European Anthropologists 1980) was used as an age indicator. In juveniles where dental elements were missing, long-bone lengths were used to estimate age at death by comparison with juveniles from the assemblage which could be aged using dental development. In adults, dental wear was the primary ageing technique. The rate of wear on the molar teeth was calibrated from wear on juvenile permanent molars using the methodology of Miles (1963). Account was also taken of the degree of ante-mortem tooth loss to help identify older individuals (Mays et al. 1995). Pubic symphysial morphology (Suchey et al. 1987; 1988) and cranial suture closure (Perizonius 1984) were also recorded and used as supplemental age indicators. For analytical purposes, adults were sorted into three age groups: 18-29, 30-49 and 50+ years. Although it is probably possible to age younger adults into narrower age spans than this using dental wear (Mays 1998, 71), placement into these three broad age categories is a conservative strategy and is adequate for the current purposes.

In adults, sex was determined from pelvic and cranial morphology, or if these indicators were missing, from general skeletal robusticity (Brothwell 1981). Although it is acknowledged that sex determination in immature individuals is problematic (Mays and Cox 2000), attempts were made to sex perinatal infants from the morphology of the greater sciatic notch (Mays 1998, 39), and for older children (aged from about 5 to 18 years) from craniofacial morphology (Molleson et al. 1998).

Duration of breastfeeding in infants was estimated using analysis of nitrogen stable isotopes in infant bone collagen (Richards et al. 2002; Mays et al. 2002a). Nitrogen and carbon stable isotope determinations were also used to shed light on childhood and adult diets. Ribs from 99 individuals (70 immature, 29 adult) were analysed using established methodology (Richards and Hedges 1999).

In the sections which follow, relationships between the age and sex of the deceased and certain aspects of burial practices are considered first. Secondly, inferences are made concerning some demographic aspects of the population that used the churchyard. For adults, efforts were made to look for secular trends by comparing results for burials from different phases. Too few juveniles could be assigned to different phases to make this strategy viable for immature individuals, so they are treated as a single group.

Relationship between demographic variables and burial practice

Double burials

As is customary in Christian burial grounds, the great majority of burials at Wharram Percy were single interments. There were a few instances, however, in which two bodies were placed in the same grave. The precise frequency of this practice at Wharram Percy is difficult to evaluate accurately: field notes were often insufficiently detailed, and the difficulty of recognising grave cuts in the reworked soil of the churchyard presented problems in distinguishing true double burials from instances where two separate graves lay close together. Study of the field records reveals eight fairly unequivocal examples of two individuals buried in the same grave (Table 12).

It is notable that all the double interments in Table 12 involve juveniles, either buried with an adult or another juvenile. Although interment of two individuals in the same grave is uncommon in medieval churchyards, when double burials do occur a tendency to feature juvenile individuals has previously been noted (e.g. at St Helen's-on-the-Walls, York (Dawes and Magilton 1980), Hereford Cathedral Green (Stone and Appleton-Fox 1996) and London Guildhall (Bateman 1997)).

In most cases it is impossible to advance a reason why two individuals should have been interred together in the same grave. Sellevold (1997) indicates that it has been the tradition in Norway that infants might be buried with another person who happened to die at the same time. This explanation is perhaps relevant here, and at the least reminds us that we should not assume some family relationship between the individuals in question. In two instances, however, some tentative inferences as to the circumstances can be made.

The placement of the foetus, Burial G457, between the thighs of adult female Burial G438 is strongly suggestive of a mother/infant burial. Birth generally occurs at about 40 weeks gestation (Tanner 1989, 43), so Burial G457 was ten weeks short of full term. Burial G438 showed osteological signs of tuberculosis and was also positive for tuberculosis DNA (see pp 163-6). Given the early stage of development of the foetus it would seem likely that Burial G438 died, presumably of tuberculosis or some secondary opportunistic infection, during pregnancy. One possible explanation for the location of the infant is that it represents a 'coffin-birth', expulsion of the foetus from the abdomen after death by pressure from the gases of putrefaction (archaeological examples of this phenomenon have been tentatively identified (Moller-Christensen 1982; Kósa 1989, 23)). There is no evidence that Burial G438 was interred in a coffin. The phenomenon of post-mortem expulsion of the foetus is more likely in coffined burials as the coffin provides a void space for the foetus to pass into. In addition, given that the foetus lay with its head to the west, it would have to have been expelled in the breech position. Perhaps a more likely explanation is that on the death of the obviously pregnant Burial G438, the baby was cut free from the corpse in the hope that it might live, as was the practice urged of medieval midwives (Hanawalt 1986; Shahar 1990). When the foetus proved dead, or died immediately afterwards, it was interred with its mother.

The other case where there is a clue as to the reason for a double burial is for Burials NA170/NA170A, where the field notes describe the latter as a 'foetus in *situ*'. It is not altogether certain that this means that it was *in situ* in the abdomen of Burial NA170 rather than simply *in situ* in the grave. If it was the former, it is worth noting that, although probably female, Burial NA170 had a rather narrow pelvis showing some male-like character (e.g. a fairly narrow greater sciatic notch). This, coupled with the rather large foetus, Burial NA170A, may well have led to fatal obstetric problems (cf. a similar example of a female burial with foetus *in situ* in the pelvic cavity from medieval London (Wells 1988)).

Coffins and corpse position

Evidence for coffins was fairly uncommon at Wharram Percy, particularly in the medieval period, but when traces were present they could occur with individuals of both sexes and for the full range of ages from pre-term infants to elderly adults. No association with age or sex was found (Table 13). The data should be interpreted with caution as absence of evidence for a coffin cannot be taken reliably to mean that a coffin was absent: in many instances adequate field records are lacking and soil conditions were unfavourable for survival of traces of wood.

There is no evidence that arm position varies with the sex or age of the individual (Table 14).

Table 13. Presence/absence of coffin traces by age and sex.

	Traces of coffin	
	Absent	Present
Male adults	202	9
Female adults	128	12
Unsexed adults	8	1
Juveniles	315	12
Total	653	34

Location of burial

There was no evidence of any relationship between sex of the deceased and location of the burial (Table 15), either in terms of the seven site-area subdivisions, or when interments within the church (all those prefixed CN, plus Burials EE079 and EE080 which were medieval interments in a side chapel since demolished) were compared with those in the churchyard.

Analysis of a cross-tabulation of burial location and age (Table 16) indicates a significant association (chi-square = 81.7, p<0.0001). Adults are more likely than juveniles to be buried within the church. In the churchyard, juveniles were more likely than adults to be interred in area NA, immediately to the north of the church, and there was a preponderance of adults in areas SA and WCO, which lie immediately to the south and west of the church.

Table 14. Cross-tabulation of arm placement of the corpse by age and sex.

				Arm position				
	C	C/S	P	P/S	S/P	S	W	Total
Male adults	3	0	56	5	0	38	1	103
Female adults	0	0	39	3	2	30	1	75
Juveniles	4	1	45	2	1	36	2	91
Total	7	1	140	10	3	104	4	269

Notes: for arm location C = on chest, S = by side, P = on pelvis, W = across waist. Arm placement is symmetrical unless indicated by codes separated by /, in which case these denote position of left arm/position of right arm

Table 15. Cross-tabulation of burial location and sex for adults.

| | Location by area prefix | | | | | | |
---	CN	EE	G	NA	SA	V	WCO
Males	22	36	30	42	13	16	52
Females	13	16	29	28	15	8	31

Table 16. Cross-tabulation of burial location and age.

| | Location by area prefix | | | | | | |
---	CN	EE	G	NA	SA	V	WCO
Adults	35	52	63	70	28	26	86
Juveniles	4	46	54	147	4	26	46

The greater proportion of adults among the burials within the church may be an indication that people were prepared to expend greater resources on the burial of an adult than of a child. Intramural burial traditionally carried greater prestige and cost more than churchyard burial (Daniell 1997). During the post-medieval period (from whence all but two of the internal burials come), documentary sources confirm the greater cost of intramural interment at Wharram Percy. For example, during the period 1770-1825 the fee for church burial was 21/-, for churchyard burial 5/- (Beresford 1987, 26).

Table 17. Age breakdown of juveniles in area prefix NA compared with burials in other areas.

	Location	
Age range	NA	Elsewhere
<40wiu	22 (69%)	10 (31%)
40wiu – 0.49yrs	27 (61%)	17 (39%)
0.5 – 0.99	16 (64%)	9 (36%)
1 – 1.49	6 (46%)	7 (54%)
1.5 – 1.99	9 (52%)	8 (48%)
2 – 2.99	8 (38%)	13 (62%)
3 – 3.99	4 (36%)	7 (64%)
4 – 4.99	8 (38%)	13 (62%)
5 - 17	47 (33%)	96 (66%)
Adult (18+ yrs)	70 (19%)	290 (81%)

Note: wiu = weeks in utero, otherwise age is in years

Turning to burials in the NA area, breakdown of the age distribution (Table 17) shows that about two thirds of children aged under one year were interred here compared with one third of those aged over two years and one fifth of adults. Plotting infants under one year on a plan of the NA area showed that, although they were not buried hard up against the church wall, none was present in the trench connecting the NA area with the area to the north prefixed G, Site 26 (Fig. 70). There was no evidence in area G for a preponderance of infant burials. Thus there was a tendency to bury infants within about 30ft of the north wall of the church nave.

Among juveniles a transition in preferred burial location seems to occur between one and two years of age. One possible explanation is that baptism of infants generally occurred at about this age: the north side of the church is a traditional location for burials of the unbaptised (Grauer 1991, 70; Harding 1996).

In medieval times, baptism was an important sacrement. The infant, born from the carnal lust of his parents, and inheriting the sin of Adam and Eve, needed to be cleansed of the sin of his conception and heritage. Proper baptism was undertaken one week after birth (Shahar 1990, 46). If the life of the newborn appeared in danger it would be baptised immediately. If no priest were present then a lay-person could do this, and it was in fact considered their Christian duty so to do. Indeed, such was the horror of death in an unbaptised state that if, during delivery, it appeared the child might be stillborn, midwives were permitted to baptise any limb that emerged (Shahar 1990, 49). If the mother died in childbirth, the midwife would cut open the abdomen, not only in an attempt to save the baby but to baptise it (Hanawalt 1986, 172).

Given the importance of baptism in the medieval mind, it seems inconceivable that it could have been routinely delayed for one to two years and hence, because of the infant mortality rate (see below), denied to so many infants. Perhaps some other life transition often occurred between one and two years old and was given recognition in burial practice.

There is no evidence for any difference in burial treatment between pre-term infants/foetuses, and infants well into their first year of life. Given that some proportion of premature infants (under about 40 weeks gestation (Tanner 1981, 43)) must have been born dead, it would seem that no distinction was made in burial practices between stillbirths and live births. This is as might be expected if, as suggested above, all were baptised, as in the eyes of the church there would have been no difference between them.

Spatial clustering of infant burials has been reported from a few other medieval churchyards. I have been unable to locate a case where the pattern precisely resembles Wharram Percy, although at Raunds churchyard (Boddington 1996) infants tended to be buried close to the church walls, and a similar pattern has been claimed for Rivenhall (Rodwell and Rodwell 1986) and for St Olav's churchyard, Trondheim (Sellevold 1997).

Table 17 shows that more children aged 2-17 than adults were interred in area NA, a pattern which is statistically significant (chi-square = 14.8, p<0.001). It seems, therefore, that the transition to adulthood was, to some extent, given recognition in burial location. The small numbers of adolescent burials precluded evaluation of the precise age at which this transition occurred.

The demography of the population

The ages of the individuals in the Wharram Percy assemblage range from a foetus of 28 weeks gestation to adult individuals aged well over 60 years. The overall age composition of the assemblage is depicted in Figure 73. A detailed breakdown of the age distribution of juveniles is shown in Table 18.

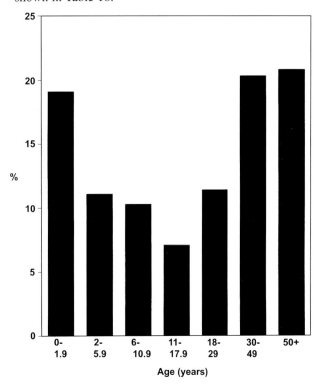

Fig. 73. Overall age composition of the assemblage.

Table 18. The age composition of the juvenile part of the assemblage.

Age group	N
Foetal (<40 weeks in utero)	32
40 weeks in utero – 0.49 years	44
0.5 – 0.99	25
1 – 1.49	13
1.5 – 1.99	17
2 -	21
3 -	11
4 -	21
5 -	23
6 -	25
7 -	12
8 -	13
9 -	6
10 -	15
11 -	14
12 -	6
13 -	6
14 -	5
15 -	3
16 -	8
17 -	7
Total	327

Notes: Age in years unless stated; 3 – denotes 3 – 3.99 and so on

Before discussing the results, a number of caveats on interpretation and some potentially biasing factors need to be considered. Firstly, only about one third of the area used for burial has been subject to archaeological investigation (Fig. 70). The proportion of total interments made in the churchyard represented by the excavated assemblage is likely to be markedly less than one third. Many burials have been destroyed by later activity, as witnessed by the large amount of disarticulated bone encountered during excavation. In most burial areas, not all burials were located and lifted. Using a mixture of documentary evidence and educated guesswork, Bell (1987) suggests that there may have been between 5000 and 10,000 burials in the churchyard. If Bell's figures are to be believed, then we may have less than one tenth of the total interments which were made in the burial area over the nine centuries of its use. In addition, spatial patterning of burials according to age may potentially lead to sample bias. For example, the observation that the excavated parts of the cemetery included an area clearly favoured for infant burial (site area NA) may have increased the numbers of the very young in the assemblage.

The case was made in Chapter 6 that the small bones of infants are more poorly preserved than those of older individuals. Although bone survival at Wharram Percy is generally very good, it may be that there is some minor under-representation in infants due to preservation factors. Of somewhat more concern is deficient recovery. In Chapter 1 the case was made that the under-representation of smaller bones in adults represents deficient recovery of these elements (as is generally true of hand-recovered material (Mays 1998)), and it follows from this that there would likely also have been deficient recovery of the small bones of infants. This was probably a factor in the rather lower levels of skeletal completeness in infants. Further support for the notion that infant burials may have sometimes have been overlooked was provided by the occasional finding of remains of a fairly complete infant boxed mixed with the skeleton of an adult, even when there was no indication of the infant burial having been noticed in the field (e.g. Burials NA121 and NA121A).

Immigration and emigration may affect the age structure of a community. The case will be made below for adult emigration from Wharram Percy to nearby urban settlements such as York. If, as seems likely, most migrants would have left in late adolescence (see below) then this will not affect greatly the adult age distribution, as those who remained could either die young or live to grow old. It may potentially diminish the adult: juvenile ratio.

The balance between birth and death rates in the parish will affect the age structure of the skeletal assemblage. In conditions of population growth, with birth rate exceeding death rate, the age structure will tend to be biased toward younger age groups. The converse is true for a population in decline where the death rate exceeds the birth rate. At Wharram Percy, the burials span both a period of growth of population and, from the 14th century onwards, a period of population decline, as well as doubtless many short term fluctuations. Whether these changes reflect changing birth and death rates, migration patterns, or both is not known. The observation that periods of both increase and decline are covered permits the suggestion that the overall effect on the age structure may be fairly modest.

The above discussion has tentatively identified several factors which may potentially affect the age composition of the skeletal assemblage and may complicate the interpretation of the age structure. Some factors have opposing effects. For example if the inference of out-migration of adults is correct then this will tend to diminish the adult : juvenile ratio, whereas the likely under-recovery of infants may tend to have the opposite effect. Overall, it is suggested that, as a working hypothesis, the age distribution of the skeletons may give a reasonable, if time-averaged impression of age at death in the parish. In addition, attempts are made below to evaluate the possibility of bias in the age structure of the assemblage by making certain comparisons with expectations based on theoretical premises and on documentary data. With regard to the latter, adequate medieval sources are few, so that post-medieval data are sometimes used. Furthermore, many publications of historical demographic data do not present the data in ways which permit comparison with information derived from skeletal series, further constraining the choice of sources.

Age at death in juveniles

In recent societies lacking modern medical care and sanitation, about 20-56% of deaths may occur under 16 years of age (Hewlett 1991). Historical records are generally consistent with this. For example, in a rural parish in 19th-century Dorset, approximately 40% of burials were, according to the parish registers, of those dying under 16 years (Walker 1981). The Wharram Percy data are broadly congruent with this: there are 312 burials aged under sixteen at death, or 45% of the total.

Age-specific mortality in developing countries is high in infancy, declines to a low level during later childhood and adolescence, and gradually rises again with increasing adult age (Waldron 1994). Although such populations are not likely to be exactly comparable to ancient groups, one might expect age at death distributions approximately to conform to this U-shaped profile, and the current data appear to do so (Fig. 73).

Turning to perinatal infants, there is, as I have previously demonstrated (Mays 1993), a fairly even spread of ages at death (Fig. 74). This contrasts with some

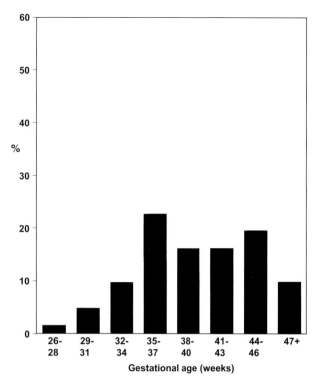

Fig. 74. Age at death distribution of the perinatal infants.

Romano-British assemblages where there is a peak in the perinatal age at death profile at about the age corresponding to full term, a pattern which I have interpreted as suggestive of infanticide (Mays 1993). The rather flat age distribution in Figure 74 is as expected of natural deaths in the perinatal period and does not suggest infanticide (Mays 1993). It is impossible to determine in individual cases whether a perinatal infant was born dead or died in the immediate post-natal period; all that can be said is that the Wharram Percy age distribution is compatible with some combination of stillbirths and natural deaths soon after birth.

Demographers customarily divide infant deaths into neonatal and post-neonatal mortality. The former corresponds to the first four weeks after birth, the latter to the period from one month to the end of the first year (Saunders and Barrans 1999). Neonatal mortality is due both to endogenous factors, such as congenital or developmental defects or birth problems, and to exogenous factors such as infectious disease. Endogenous factors play a negligible role in post-neonatal mortality; it is due almost entirely to exogenous factors and has been observed to increase dramatically under insanitary conditions. In developing countries and, until recently worldwide, post-neonatal mortality exceeded neonatal mortality, and where living conditions are harsh, post-neonatal mortality may even exceed stillbirth and neonatal deaths combined (Saunders and Barrans 1999). Saunders and Barrans (1999) postulate that these patterns may be expected to apply to archaeological societies.

A problem in deriving the above patterns in mortality from skeletal data is that, as stated above, we cannot, in individual cases, ascertain whether, for very young infants, they were stillborn or died in the immediate post-natal period. In a study of material from a 19th-century churchyard in colonial Ontario, Saunders *et al.* (1995) dealt with this problem by excluding infants aged as pre-term from the neonatal category. When they calculated the neonatal:post-neonatal ratio for infant deaths in this way from skeletal material, they found that this strategy was successful in that the proportion matched almost exactly that documented in the church records. In this light, a similar strategy was followed with the current material, with a full term foetus assumed to be aged about 40 weeks gestation. The results are shown in Table 19.

Table 19. Infants split into 'stillbirth', 'neonatal' and 'post-neonatal' categories.

Age category	Description	N
< 40 weeks gestation	'Stillbirths'	32
40 weeks gestation – 1 month post - natal	'Neonates'	16
1 month – 0.99 years	'Post-neonates'	53
Total		101

The way that the infants were sorted into the categories in Table 19 simply using ages at death means that a few of the youngest individuals classed as 'neonates' may well have been born dead. Rather more of those classed as 'stillbirths' were probably born alive but died shortly after birth. Thus, overall, the number of 'stillbirths' in Table 19 is probably something of an over-estimate and the 'neonates' probably somewhat underestimated. Nevertheless, although precise comparisons between expectations based on data from living communities and data from skeletal series are problematic

(Saunders and Barrans 1999), the data do seem broadly consistent with the theoretical postulates of Saunders and associates for early populations. The post-neonatal category exceeds both the neonatal category on its own, and the combined stillbirth and neonatal categories.

The pattern of infant deaths at Wharram Percy is broadly consistent with that which might be expected for a historic population. Direct comparisons with demographic data from the medieval period is problematic. Studies of skeletal series do not customarily break down their infant age data in this way and medieval documentary sources are inadequate to derive meaningful infant mortality patterns (Russell 1948). Looking at 16th-century documentary records, Wrigley (1968) estimates that between about 50 and 60% of all deaths under one year occurred in the first month of life. The Wharram Percy figure is rather lower than this (Table 19) but whether this is a genuine population difference is difficult to determine. Documentary sources have their own problems and biases (discussed by Wrigley 1968), not least the problem of accounting for stillbirths, and Wrigley's figures seem somewhat out of kilter with expectations for historical societies, discussed above.

Comparison of the proportion of infant deaths with those reported from other archaeological sites is shown in Table 20.

Sixteenth-century documentary data collated by Wrigley (1968) suggest that about 12-24% of infants may have died in their first year. The figure for Wharram Percy lies somewhere between 11% and 15% depending upon the proportion of stillbirths. Thus Wharram Percy falls into the lower end of the range derived by Wrigley from 16th-century written sources. In most other medieval skeletal assemblages, infant burials are rather fewer than at Wharram Percy. The reasons for this are at present unclear.

Table 20. Proportion of infants (aged under one year unless stated) at various medieval churchyards.

Site	Proportion of infants	Source
Westerhus, Sweden	32% (120/371)	Gejvall (1960)
Raunds	20% (73/363)	Powell (1996)
Stonar	18% (26/147)*	Eley and Bayley (1975)
Wharram Percy	15% (101/687)	-
Espenfeld, Germany	12% (54/438)	Grupe and Bach (1993)
Trondheim, Norway	7% (26/389)	Anderson (1986)
St Nicholas Shambles, London	5% (12/234)†	White (1988)
Lund, Sweden	5% (160/3305)	Arcini (1999)
Rivenhall	4% (9/229)	O'Connor (1993)
Jewbury, York	3% (13/471)	Stroud *et al.* (1994)
Hereford Cathedral Green	3% (22/851) †	Pinter-Bellows (1996)
St Helen-on-the-Walls, York	3% (33/1041)‡	Dawes (1980)

All sites UK unless stated
* = under 1.5 yrs; † = under 2 yrs; ‡ = under 2.5 yrs

Table 21. Age at death and sex data for the adult part of the assemblage.

	18-29	30-49	50+	Indeterminate adult	Total
Males	35	62	75	39	211
Females	29	52	44	15	140
Unsexed	1	2	0	6	9
Total	65	116	119	60	360

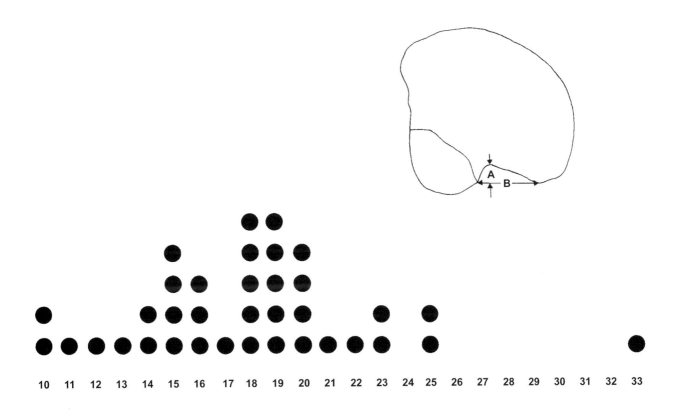

Sciatic notch index (100x A/B)

Fig. 75. Distribution of the greater sciatic notch index for the perinatal infants.

The sex balance in the assemblage and the age at death of adults

The overall age and sex composition of the adult part of the assemblage is shown in Table 21. There is no evidence of variation in the adult age structure or sex ratio by phase, nor is there any significant difference in the age structure between males and females. The overall sex ratio of 211:140 differs significantly from 1:1 (chi-square = 14.36, p<0.0001).

A number of possible explanations for the imbalanced sex ratio among the adult burials needs to be considered. Given that there is no evidence for spatial segregation of burials with regard to sex, it seems unlikely that the 'missing' females are lurking in a cluster in some unexcavated part of the burial area. A more plausible possibility is that there was greater female mortality during infancy and childhood, and it was in order to investigate this that the attempts referred to in the methods section of this chapter were made to determine sex in immature individuals. The results from the measurement of the greater sciatic notch in the ilia of perinatal infants are depicted in Figure 75. When detectable dimorphism is present in the perinatal sciatic notch it generally takes the form of a narrower, deeper notch in males (Boucher 1957; Fazekas and Kósa 1978) paralleling the situation in adults although the degree of dimorphism is very much more slight (Mays and Cox 2000). The Wharram Percy results appear to show a bimodality in sciatic notch index. No evidence was found for an association between sciatic notch index and perinatal age, so the most likely conclusion is that the two peaks correspond to males and females, the males being represented by the group at the higher index value. Although there is likely to be considerable overlap between male and female index values, the relative size of the two clusters probably tells us something about the sex ratio in perinatal deaths: with an even sex ratio, numbers in each cluster should be similar whereas a significant difference in numbers between the two clusters would be suggestive of a biassed sex ratio. Inspection of Figure 75 suggests a dividing line between the two clusters at about an index value of seventeen. There are 21 individuals with indices greater than this (possible males) and fourteen with values lower (possible females). A ratio of 21:14 does not differ significantly from 1:1 by chi-square, so there is no evidence for a sex imbalance in perinatal deaths.

Using craniofacial morphology, it was possible to assess sex in 56 children aged 5-17 years. Thirty-one were assessed as male, 25 as female. On the juveniles of documented sex from Christ Church, Spitalfields, which were used to develop the technique, craniofacial morphology resulted in 78% being correctly sexed (Molleson et al. 1998). The technique has yet to be tested on other documented collections, but at Wharram Percy it was found that those sexed as male using craniofacial morphology showed larger permanent canine crown dimensions than those sexed as female (Molleson et al. 1998). This is as expected if, in general, the sex inferred from the craniofacial skeleton was correct. A sex ratio of 31:25 does not differ significantly from 1:1 by chi-square.

Although the techniques used above require further testing on juvenile remains of documented sex before results on undocumented archaeological material can be accepted at face value, it is noteworthy that neither protocol produced any evidence for a sex imbalance in immature deaths. This argues against the hypothesis that excess female mortality during infancy or childhood lay behind the adult sex imbalance in favour of males. A better explanation may be female-led emigration from the parish.

In the medieval period, urban centres were augmented by immigration from surrounding rural areas (Russell 1948). Documentary evidence (Goldberg 1986) shows that in the late medieval period many urban centres in northern England had imblanced adult sex ratios – for example in Hull the male:female ratio was 0.86 and in York 0.91. Goldberg argued that the skewed sex ratios resulted from female-led migration into urban centres from the surrounding countryside. Migrant female labour was absorbed into domestic service and, to a lesser extent, into craft industries such as weaving (Goldberg 1986). Many migrants probably settled in poorer areas of cities, and it is interesting to note that among the medieval skeletons the churchyard of St Helen-on-the-Walls, York (AD 950-1550), which served the poor district of Aldwark, the sex ratio was 338 males:394 females (Dawes 1980), a significant imbalance in favour of females (chi-square=4.3, p<0.05). Wharram Percy lies about 20 miles from York and there is documentary evidence (Russell 1948) that many probably migrated this sort of distance in medieval times to become resident in cities. Perhaps at Wharram Percy we are seeing the other side of the coin, as female-led emigration left a rural population dominated by males. Although the evidence is slender, textual sources suggest that many girls left during

adolescence (Goldberg 1986). This would be consistent with the lack of evidence for a sex imbalance among the Wharram Percy juveniles (the great majority of those juvenile skeletons which were sexed were younger than this) and with the observation that the sex ratios in the three adult age categories do not differ from one another. If these inferences concerning migration patterns, particularly age at migration, are correct, then this factor should have little effect on the adult age distribution.

Comparison of adult age at death between archaeological assemblages from different sites is problematic due to the myriad different ageing techniques used to generate the data and their varying reliability. Instead, the current figures are compared with documentary sources. Medieval data on adult age at death which are presented in such a way as to be comparable with skeletal data are few, and do not relate directly to the peasant classes. Data collected by Russell (1937), relating to 582 male individuals dating to the period 1250-1348, using the Inquisitions Post Mortem, are used here (Table 22).

Table 22. Adult age distribution among the Wharram Percy burials and in Russell's (1937) historical demographic study.

Age range	Wharram Percy		Russell's data	
	Number	Percent	Number	Percent
18-29†	65	21	58	10
30-49	116	39	232	40
50+	119	40	292	50

† 21-29 for Russell's (1937) data.

Russell's (1937) data appear broadly similar to the Wharram Percy results, although they are in general somewhat older. There are a number of factors which may play a part in this. The Inquisitions Post Mortem give the ages of the heirs of deceased individuals; the age of the deceased must be calculated from his age at the death of his predecessor. Therefore, individuals who predeceased their fathers would not be included, even if they had died in adulthood. This would tend to bias the data towards the older ages, and in particular we might expect deaths in the 21-30 age group to be under-represented. Secondly, Russell's figures refer solely to the wealthy, whose living conditions were doubtless better than those at Wharram Percy. Thirdly, Russell deliberately excluded the great plague years 1348-1350 whilst, of course, the Wharram Percy burials are not purposely selected in this way. It must also be emphasised that care is needed when comparing ages known fairly accurately from documentary sources with those estimated from skeletal remains. Although dental wear, the principal ageing technique for the Wharram Percy adults, is likely to be the most reliable available, no age estimation method for adults can be considered wholly satisfactory (Mays 1998).

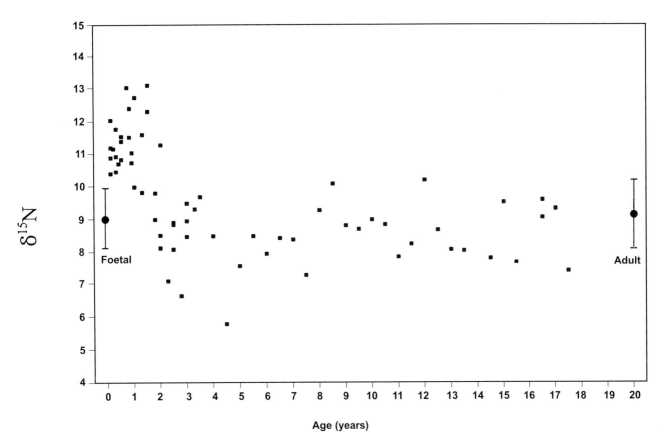

Fig. 76. $\partial^{15}N$ data for immature individuals (aged from birth to 17 years; N=65). Mean values for foetal material (aged 28-39 weeks in-utero; N=5) and adults (N=29) are superimposed.

Despite the above, the Wharram Percy results are not too dissimilar from those obtained from medieval documents, and the discrepancies which do exist are explicable in terms of differences between the datasets. The archaeological data suggest that once adulthood was attained, the inhabitants of Wharram Percy had a fairly good chance of surviving beyond 50 years of age.

Stable isotope analyses

There are two stable isotopes of nitrogen, ^{14}N and ^{15}N, and the ratio of the two, the nitrogen stable isotope ratio, is measured by $\partial^{15}N$, expressed in parts per thousand (‰). $\partial^{15}N$ increases as one ascends a food chain, the magnitude of the trophic level effect being approximately 3-4‰ (Schwarcz and Schoeninger 1991). A foetal or newborn infant would be expected to have a $\partial^{15}N$ similar to that of its mother. Breast-feeding infants are in effect consuming their mother's tissues, so that they are at a higher trophic level. $\partial^{15}N$ rises during breast-feeding to give a collagen $\partial^{15}N$ about 3-4‰ greater than maternal collagen. During the weaning process, as mother's milk is replaced by other foods, $\partial^{15}N$ normally declines (Mays 2000a, 429).

Carbon, like nitrogen, also has two stable isotopes, ^{12}C and ^{13}C. Biological tissues from marine ecosystems are enriched in carbon-13 relative to those from terrestrial ones. As with nitrogen, carbon stable isotope ratios in bone collagen vary with the diet consumed. This means that human bone collagen carbon stable isotope ratios shed light on the ratio of marine:terrestrial foods in diets.

Marine foods also contain elevated levels of ^{15}N. Bone collagen carbon stable isotope values principally reflect the protein part of diets; nitrogen stable isotope values reflect only dietary protein (Mays 2000a).

Duration of breast-feeding

The nitrogen stable isotope results for immature individuals are plotted against individual age in Figure 76. As expected on theoretical grounds, values for skeletons of pre-term foetuses (for the present purposes considered to be those under 40 weeks gestation) resemble those in adults. Immediately after birth there is a rapid rise in $\partial^{15}N$, presumably reflecting the incorporation of the breast-milk signal into the collagen. Highest levels occur at about one year, but there is a rapid fall thereafter so that by two years they once more resemble adult values.

The results suggest cessation of breast-feeding between about one and two years of age. The strong age-related pattern between one and two years, with little spread of data points, indicates relatively little inter-individual variation in timing of weaning. This suggests that breast-feeding duration was generally constrained by community-wide cultural factors rather than decisions being made freely according to individual circumstances. The consistent nature of the pattern despite the long period covered by the Wharram Percy burials suggests that culturally accepted patterns of weaning may long have remained unchanged here (this cannot be analysed further due to the paucity of infants who could be phased).

Breast-feeding has important health benefits for the infant, both because of the milk's immunological content and because it enables early avoidance of potential infection from contaminated food or water (Katzenberg *et al.* 1996). Historically, breast-feeding practices had a major impact on infant mortality. Knodel and Kintner (1977) found that in late 19th to early 20th-century populations, infant mortality was markedly higher in those where infants were not breast-fed or where breast-feeding was discontinued soon after birth. For example, figures from 19th-century Bavaria indicate that in communities where extended breast-feeding was practised less than 20% of liveborn infants perished in their first year; where there was little breast-feeding the figures were 30-40% (Knodel and Kintner 1977). Of course, duration of breast-feeding is only one of many variables which affect the rate of infant mortality in a population. Nevertheless, if it is accepted, as argued above, that the proportion of individuals dying before their first birthday at Wharram Percy (11-15%) is a reasonable indication of pattern of death in this population, then it resembles the rates seen in Knodel and Kintner's (1977) study in adequately breast-feeding populations. That the rate was not higher may reflect the beneficial effects of continuing breast-feeding beyond the first few months of life.

Because lactation suppresses ovulation, duration of breast-feeding is a major determinant of fecundity in societies lacking reliable artificial means of contraception (Vitzthum 1994). Whilst age at menopause appears to have changed little over time (Pavelka and Fedigan 1991), there is good evidence for a secular decline in age at onset of menses – for example menarche occurred on average in the mid-teens in the mid-19th century compared with about twelve years in the 1970s (Tanner 1989). An average age of menarche sometime in the mid-teens seems likely for medieval females (Bullough and Campbell 1980). Menarche is generally followed by a period of up to three years adolescent sterility (Bogin 1988). This would leave a period of about twenty years when a medieval woman was at her most fertile. Although various aspects of breast-feeding behaviour, in addition to its simple duration, are likely to affect post-partum fecundity (Vitzthum 1994), if it is assumed that the mean duration of breast-feeding of eighteen months inhibits conception for that period, then the closest birth interval would have been about two and a half years, meaning that a woman at Wharram Percy could have produced a maximum of about eight children. Given the infant and juvenile mortality rates reconstructed from the age at death data, this would have meant that perhaps six of these children would have survived beyond about two years of age and four to adulthood. Of course, poor nutrition and heavy disease loads are likely to have reduced fertility significantly in practice, quite apart from any deliberate strategies taken to avoid conception such as celibacy, or *coitus interruptus* (this latter is known to

have been practised by medieval people despite being frowned upon by the church (Biller 1982)).

It was noted above that there was a tendency for individuals under about one to two years of age to be buried immediately to the north of the church. Given that breast-feeding also seems to cease at around this age, the question arises as to whether the spatial pattern occurs because what was being accorded recognition in burial placement was whether or not an infant had been weaned. Although the age-related decline in $\partial^{15}N$ in infants is quite consistent there is nevertheless noticeable variation in $\partial^{15}N$ even before the likely cessation of breast-feeding at about eighteen months (Fig. 76). If burial immediately to the north of the church reflected that the infant was still breast-feeding then individuals under about one to two years found in this area ought to have higher $\partial^{15}N$ than those in this age group interred elsewhere. Despite exploring several different ways of partitioning the data by age for those under two years, no evidence was found for such a pattern. It is unclear what the life transition was which was being given recognition in burial location of the Wharram Percy infants, however, it seems clear that it was not whether the child had reached an age when breast-feeding was discontinued.

Diets in adults and children
Among the adults there was no significant variation in $\partial^{15}N$ or $\partial^{13}C$ by sex (Table 23) or by phase, indicating no evidence for any difference in dietary protein sources between the sexes or over time. Interpretation of the human bone collagen stable isotope values is aided by consideration of those derived from analyses of animal bones from the site (Table 24).

Table 23. $\partial^{15}N$ and $\partial^{13}C$ results for adults (data from Richards *et al.* 2002).

	N	$\partial^{15}N$		$\partial^{13}C$	
		Mean	sd	Mean	sd
Males	12	9.48	1.43	-19.48	0.41
Females	17	8.95	0.60	-19.73	0.24
Total adults	29	9.17	1.04	-19.62	0.34

Table 24. $\partial^{15}N$ and $\partial^{13}C$ results for Wharram Percy animal bones (data provided by G. Müldner).

	N	$\partial^{15}N$		$\partial^{13}C$	
		Mean	sd	Mean	sd
Carnivores (cat)	3	7.1	1.1	-20.9	0.2
Herbivores (horse, sheep/goat, cattle)	14	5.6	1.1	-22.1	0.6

Among the faunal remains, the carnivore $\partial^{13}C$ mean value is about 1‰ less negative than the herbivore mean (Table 24). This pattern resembles that found in previous archaeofaunal isotopic studies (references in Richards *et al.* 2002), where a minor (about 1‰) trophic level effect has been reported. Using the Wharram Percy animal bone figures, a $\partial^{13}C$ end-point for humans on a purely terrestrial, mixed diet can be estimated at about –21.5‰. This is in agreement with the value which has been used earlier with archaeological skeletal material from northern England (Mays 1997). The $\partial^{13}C$ data seem, therefore, to suggest a minor but significant role for marine foods in human diets at Wharram Percy. The presence of seafoods in diets here is consistent with the observation that remains of marine fauna were found in excavations of the settlement part of the site (Ryder 1974). The $\partial^{13}C$ end-point for a purely marine diet has been estimated at about -12‰ (Mays 1997). If it can be assumed that $\partial^{13}C$ values vary in an approximately linear fashion with respect to the marine:terrestrial contributions to diet, the Wharram Percy data suggest that about 20% of dietary protein came from marine sources. Given the protein-rich nature of most marine foods, and the likelihood that, overall, medieval peasant diets were low in protein (Gies and Gies 1990, 96-7), the contribution of seafoods to whole diets would clearly have been much lower than this: as might be anticipated for an inland agrarian site, the diet was largely based on terrestrial resources. Freshwater fish from carbonate rich waters may show somewhat less negative $\partial^{13}C$ values than other non-marine foods (Day 1996). Given the calcareous geology, it is possible that consumption of locally caught freshwater fish may be making some minor contribution to human $\partial^{13}C$ values. The $\partial^{15}N$ values for the human remains exceed somewhat those from both carnivorous and herbivorous animals. The slightly elevated $\partial^{15}N$ is presumably associated with the small marine component in human diets.

Table 25. $\partial^{15}N$ and $\partial^{13}C$ results for children, split into four to eight and eight to eighteen years age classes (data from Richards *et al.* 2002).

Age group (years)	N	$\partial^{15}N$ Mean	sd	$\partial^{13}C$ Mean	sd
4 - 7.9	8	7.79	0.94	-20.08	0.50
8 - 17.9	20	8.76	0.79	-19.77	0.34

The scatterplot of $\partial^{15}N$ against age (Fig. 76) appears to indicate that values for middle childhood, particularly between the ages of about four and eight years, may be lower than those of later childhood and adulthood. A t-test shows that the difference in $\partial^{15}N$ between individuals aged four to eight years and individuals eight to eighteen years (Table 25) is statistically significant (t=2.6, p=0.024), as is the difference between those aged four and eight years and adults (t=3.62, p=0.003). In addition, $\partial^{13}C$ in children in the four to eight years class is lower (more negative) than that in either the eight to eighteen

year age group or in adults (Tables 23 and 25), although only the difference with adults reaches statistical significance (t=2.46, p=0.036). Taken together, these results suggest that diets in the four to eight year age group may have been more plant-based, containing a lesser proportion of marine foods and/or meat or other animal products than did those of older individuals.

8 Skeletal Growth

Introduction

Long-bones attain their final adult forms by a process of endochondral and appositional growth. Increase in length occurs via endochondral growth. This involves bone deposition on the end of the diaphysis beneath the epiphysial growth plate. Physiological stress (*sensu* Cox *et al.* 1983), caused by nutritional, disease or psychological factors, may cause interruption of bone growth (references in Mays 1995). The manifestation of interruption of endochondral bone growth is the Harris line, a transverse line visible radiographically in long-bones as a line of increased density, generally in the spongy bone of the diaphysis or metaphysis.

Growth in width of a long-bone is via appositional growth. Long-bone diaphyses take the form of hollow tubes. During growth, bone is added to the sub-periosteal (outer) surface, and, in infancy and childhood, it is simultaneously resorbed from the endosteal (inner) surface of the cortex. During the growth period, the rate of sub-periosteal deposition generally exceeds the rate of endosteal resorption so that as well as increasing in overall width, the cortex of the diaphysis also increases in thickness (Garn 1970).

At Wharram Percy, endochondral and appositional bone growth were studied by plotting various aspects of bone size in juveniles against dental age. Endochondral growth was investigated using long-bone lengths. Bone length data were also used to generate stature estimates in order to permit growth in height to be studied. Interruptions to endochondral bone growth were investigated using Harris lines. Appositional bone growth was analysed using measures of cortical thickness. Comparison with growth in archaeological and recent populations documented in the literature were made by plotting mean values of the different parameters at different ages. Some results of these investigations have previously been published (Mays 1995; 1999a).

Methods

Maximum diaphysial length of immature long-bones was recorded. Stature was calculated from femur length using the methodology of Feldesman (1992). The presence/absence of Harris lines in the distal femur was scored from radiographs as previously described (Mays 1995). Total bone width (T) and medullary width (M) were measured at the femur midshaft from radiographs

Table 26. Diaphysial lengths of juvenile long-bones.

Age	Femur N	Femur Mean	Femur sd	Tibia N	Tibia Mean	Tibia sd	Fibula N	Fibula Mean	Fibula sd	Humerus N	Humerus Mean	Humerus sd	Radius N	Radius Mean	Radius sd	Ulna N	Ulna Mean	Ulna sd	Clavicle N	Clavicle Mean	Clavicle sd
0.25	21	81.8	11.5	16	70.1	11.0	8	65.4	6.8	30	72.0	9.1	22	56.9	6.9	21	64.0	8.4	16	47.3	4.6
1	10	125.5	10.9	11	103.1	6.8	1	103.0	-	9	98.0	8.7	10	76.9	5.5	9	83.0	7.3	15	61.4	4.0
2	10	151.9	10.3	7	121.6	11.9	2	116.0	14.1	12	117.1	9.7	9	88.9	6.6	9	95.7	6.2	13	68.7	2.9
3	11	173.1	12.8	12	136.3	9.6	6	139.8	4.7	15	133.4	8.9	9	98.4	6.2	12	106.1	5.4	14	72.6	3.7
4	11	186.0	12.1	10	149.9	11.1	3	146.0	10.1	10	140.4	10.2	7	101.7	7.3	5	118.0	9.7	7	77.3	4.0
5	6	195.5	9.9	4	154.0	10.9	5	154.4	5.3	8	145.9	7.1	6	107.5	6.1	6	121.0	6.3	4	81.5	5.8
6	21	214.6	12.8	14	174.1	10.2	11	169.9	11.0	25	159.0	9.2	19	118.7	7.1	23	130.9	6.8	20	83.1	4.2
7	8	241.9	23.9	8	195.1	12.7	4	199.3	15.8	11	175.7	13.4	8	130.6	11.1	7	143.6	12.5	8	90.4	4.7
8	4	262.3	16.8	3	207.3	24.0	1	187.0	-	11	184.8	11.5	8	132.9	10.5	7	147.0	13.1	10	93.6	6.9
9	6	272.7	14.1	4	218.8	17.3	3	220.3	21.2	6	201.0	12.7	5	143.2	12.2	4	158.5	12.9	6	96.0	9.6
10	9	285.0	26.4	10	229.2	17.8	5	228.6	8.7	9	203.4	16.2	10	151.3	13.6	8	162.9	13.6	7	100.3	4.9
11	6	300.3	24.0	5	244.6	24.4	4	234.8	22.6	7	220.1	18.5	5	163.6	14.5	7	178.3	12.9	7	103.1	7.3
12	2	306.0	12.7	2	235.0	14.1	2	233.5	12.0	4	229.3	4.7	3	157.3	7.2	4	173.5	5.5	4	107.3	5.2
14	5	346.0	12.0	6	270.5	14.7	3	265.0	16.5	5	243.4	19.3	3	184.3	7.8	2	198.0	0	6	111.8	5.6
17	8	376.9	22.6	8	290.1	18.7	5	288.8	20.6	2	263.5	0.7	4	193.0	9.9	4	215.0	7.3	7	123.0	7.7

Key: Age is mid-point of age category in years (e.g. 0.25 year age class is those which fall into the band neonatal – 0.49 years, 1 years is 0.5 – 1.49 etc). Measurements in mm.

Table 27. Comparative archaeological data for femoral diaphysial length.

Site	Date	N	Source
Poundbury, England	3rd-4th-century AD	55	Mays (unpublished data)
Mikulčice, Czech Republic	9th-century AD	249	Stloukal and Hanáková (1978)
Ensay, Scotland	AD 1500-1850	118	Miles and Bulman (1994)
Belleville, Canada	AD 1821-1874	156	Saunders et al. (1993)

(Mays 1995). Cortical thickness (CT) is given by T-M. Cortical index (CI), a measure of cortical thickness standardised for bone size, is calculated as: CI = 100x(T-M)/T.

Since few juveniles could be assigned to different phases, the growth studies treat the juvenile cohort as a single group.

Results

Long-bone lengths and estimated stature

Long-bone diaphysial lengths are presented in Table 26, and plotted in Figures 77 and 78.

Choice of comparative data used to set the current results in context was constrained by the fact that there are few cemeteries with large numbers of juvenile skeletons for which growth studies have been published, and for which the data are presented in such a way as to be directly comparable with the present results. Femur length data from four archaeological assemblages, representing populations of northern European origin, were selected (Table 78). In addition, the classic study of Maresh (1955) on recent American White children was chosen as a modern comparison. He gives femur lengths measured from radiographs of living subjects. For the present purposes, Maresh's data are adjusted for radiographic enlargement using the factors estimated for that study by Feldesman (1992). For older age groups, Maresh's measurements include epiphyses. So that comparisons could be made with the current data, diaphysial lengths are estimated for Maresh's older subjects from total bone lengths, using previously published methodology (Mays 1999a).

The Wharram Percy femoral length data are shown in Fig. 79, together with the archaeological and modern comparative data. The Wharram Percy femora are generally shorter than those from the recent children studied by Maresh (1955). The differences are quite marked. For example, the diaphysial lengths for fourteen year olds from Wharram Percy resemble those for ten year olds among Maresh's subjects. Archaeological material comprises solely children who failed to survive the growth period, whereas presumably most of the living subjects in Maresh's study survived to adulthood. That we are comparing results from living children with those from dead ones may potentially prejudice comparisons. It might be argued that mortality bias might be in part responsible for the growth deficit seen in the Wharram Percy children – in other words the growth profile might not be fully representative of healthier children at Wharram Percy who did survive into adult life. A recent examination of the problem posed by this in skeletal

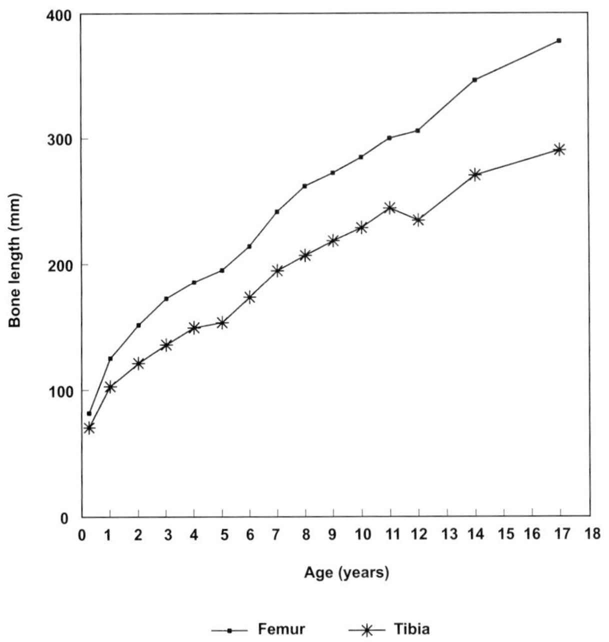

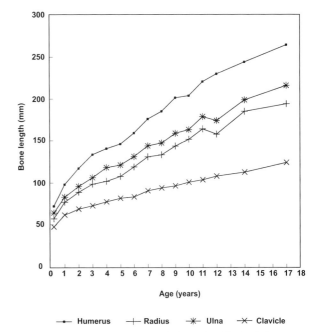

Fig. 77. Femoral and tibial diaphysial lengths versus dental age.

Fig. 78. Humeral, radial, ulna and clavicular diaphysial lengths versus dental age.

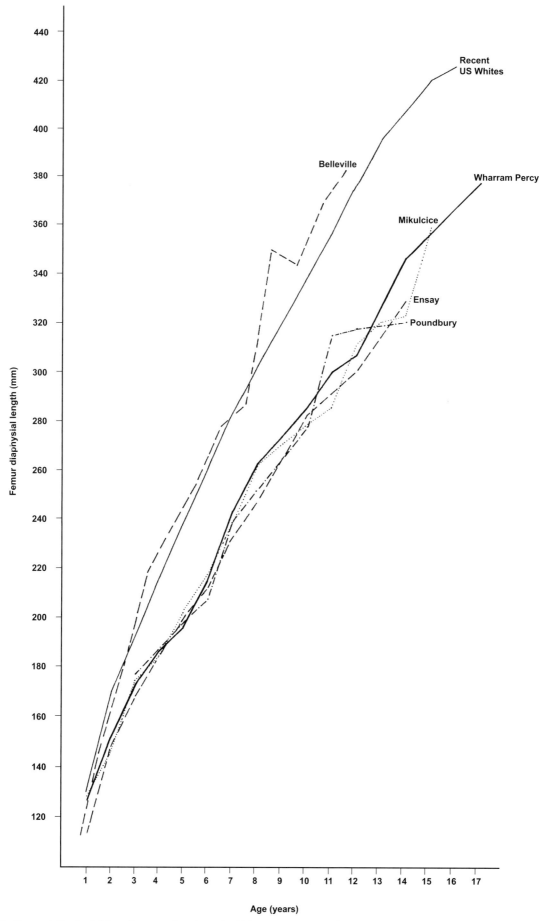

Fig. 79. Femoral diaphysial length versus dental age for Wharram Percy and four other archaeological populations (for sources see Table 27). Data for recent US children (Maresh 1955) have also been included.

98

growth studies (Saunders and Hoppa 1993) indicates that the biasing effect is probably minor. An additional consideration is that, in the Wharram Percy children, age was estimated using dental development, whereas age in Maresh's subjects was known exactly. It has been demonstrated, however, that dental development is little affected by extrinsic factors (Lewis and Garn 1960) and is a highly reliable ageing technique, both for recent (Smith 1991) and archaeological (Liversage 1994) populations.

Turning to the archaeological comparisons (Fig. 79), it is clear that, despite spanning some 1500 years, most of the results closely resemble one another, suggesting that, in the past, patterns of diaphysial growth changed little over many centuries. The exception is the 19th-century Canadian material, where the growth profile resembles the recent data. The marked disparity between the 19th/20th-century data and the earlier material is consistent with a secular increase in stature for age in recent times. That such an increase has occurred is well known from written sources (Tanner 1989). The causes of this are probably multiple, but improvements in nutritional status and lessening of disease are likely to have been of prime importance (Tanner 1989, 156ff).

In order to make comparisons with height data from 19th and 20th-century studies of living British children, stature estimates derived from the Wharram Percy femur lengths were used. Figure 80 shows the stature data in comparison with 19th-century and recent British figures. The 19th-century data come from an 1833 survey of children employed in factories in Manchester and Stockport (data reproduced in Tanner 1981). That work was the first large-scale growth study carried out in Britain. The recent figures are from the mid-20th century (Tanner *et al.* 1966).

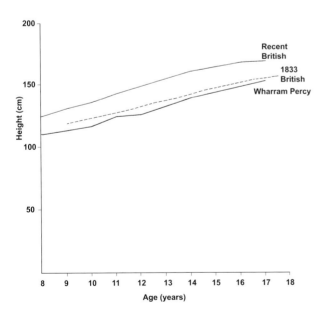

Fig. 80. Estimated stature versus dental age. Stature figures for 19th-century and modern children are included for comparison (for data sources see text).

In addition to the caveats discussed above, which apply generally to comparisons between archaeological data and measurements on living subjects, there is also the consideration that, in the stature comparisons, we are comparing children whose height was measured exactly with those for whom stature has been estimated from femur length. An assumption is that the femur:stature ratio at Wharram Percy was similar to that in the reference groups upon which Feldesman (1992) based his work. Although the potential problems should be kept in mind, some tentative inferences can be made. As was suggested by the femur length data, the height deficit of the medieval children is very striking. At ten years old, the estimated mean stature of Wharram Percy children is fully 20cm less than the recent figure of 137cm. To express it another way, the data suggest that the height of a typical fourteen year old at Wharram Percy would only have been about the same as a modern ten year old. This is in agreement with the comparison of femur lengths with the Maresh (1955) data, and indirectly lends support to the idea that the estimation of stature from femur lengths at Wharram Percy is reliable. The difference between Wharram Percy and the 1833 data is less pronounced. Although the growth profiles lie quite close together, it is perhaps worth noting that for every age class the Wharram Percy mean lies below that of the 19th-century children.

Growth in children is strongly dependent upon disease and nutrition (Eveleth and Tanner 1990), so height is often used as a proxy for health when making comparisons at a population level (Tanner 1989, 163). The results, therefore, suggest that, not surprisingly, the Wharram Percy children had poorer nutrition and suffered a greater disease load than their recent counterparts. That the height of the Wharram Percy children was not greater than the 19th-century subjects suggests that health and nutrition in this medieval community may have been no better than among the urban poor of the Industrial Revolution; given that for every age class the mean stature for the medieval children was less, conditions may even have been worse.

Although children growing up in adverse conditions tend to be short for their ages, the growth period is extended so that final adult stature may be little affected (or at least affected less than height for age in children), but it will be attained at a later age (Eveleth and Tanner 1990). As might be anticipated from this, concomitant with the secular increase in height for age in children, there has also been a trend toward earlier completion of growth. In modern populations in the developed world, growth in height is virtually complete by about eighteen years (Tanner 1989, fig. 4). Records show that in the past final adult stature was not achieved until somewhat later. For example, there are indications that in 19th-century England, growth in height was completed by about 21 years of age in the higher social classes and not until about 29 years in those of low socio-economic status (Morant 1950).

There is some evidence for prolonged growth in the Wharram Percy population. Estimated mean height for ten year olds is 117cm. Mean adult stature is approximately 158cm for females, 169cm for males (see p. 118), giving a mid-sex mean of 163.5cm. Height at ten years is thus about 71% of final adult stature. This compares with a figure of about 81% in recent subjects (Tanner *et al.* 1966). Consistent with this, the deficit in adult height compared with recent subjects is less than that in children. Estimated height for ten year olds at Wharram Percy is 85% of that reported by Tanner *et al.* (1966) for recent ten year olds, but adult height is about 97% of that found by Tanner *et al.* (1966).

Cortical thickness and cortical index

Data on cortical thickness and cortical index in the femur are shown in Table 28, and plotted against age in Figures 81 and 82 in comparison with modern data. The modern data are from a study of living subjects from Finland (Virtama and Helelä 1969); no suitable comparative data are available from a modern British population. Owing to possible differences in the degree of radiographic enlargement, cortical thickness data derived from archaeological skeletons are not, strictly-speaking, directly comparable with data obtained from living subjects, although comparisons of general patterns should be broadly valid. Effects of differential radiographic enlargement on cortical index are likely to be negligible.

Table 28. Cortical thickness and cortical index in juvenile femurs.

Age	N	Cortical thickness		Cortical index	
		Mean	sd	Mean	sd
0.25	19	3.7	0.7	54.3	14.3
1	9	3.9	0.8	37.5	7.0
2	9	4.5	0.9	38.1	7.1
3	11	5.2	1.2	40.4	8.3
4	11	5.1	0.8	38.6	3.4
5	5	5.1	0.5	35.3	1.7
6	21	5.8	1.0	41.1	7.4
7	8	7.3	1.0	46.0	6.9
8	4	8.4	1.3	50.6	7.7
9	6	7.9	1.5	47.1	4.8
10	7	8.9	1.6	48.4	7.0
11	6	9.4	0.8	50.8	3.5
12	2	9.3	1.4	47.7	6.0
14	5	10.5	1.5	48.5	4.8
17	7	12.0	2.0	50.6	6.0

Age is the mid-point of the age category in years, cortical thickness in mm

As with bone length, the Wharram Percy children are markedly deficient in cortical bone compared with their modern counterparts (Figures 81 and 82). For cortical

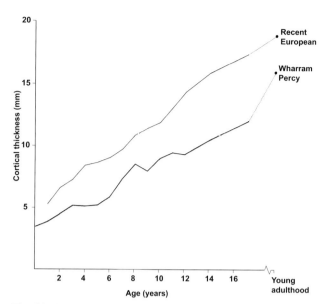

Fig. 81. Femoral cortical thickness versus dental age. Recent data (Virtama and Helelä 1969) are included for comparison.

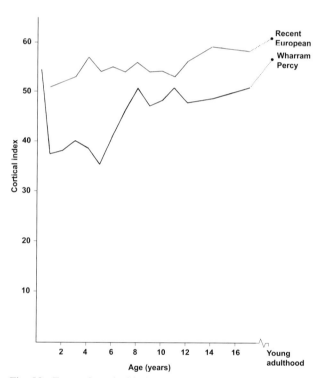

Fig. 82. Femoral cortical index versus dental age. Recent data (Virtama and Helelä 1969) are included for comparison.

thickness, the Wharram Percy individuals seem to lag behind their modern counterparts to a greater extent than was the case for bone length. The difference is about two years at age three, and rises to about seven years at age seventeen. Between the ages of one and seventeen years there is no overlap in the age-group means for cortical index: the highest mean value for any of the Wharram Percy age-groups is lower than the lowest mean for any of the age groups in the modern data.

There is abundant evidence (references in Mays 1999a) for a link between deficient appositional bone growth and poor nutrition during the growth period. The results are therefore consistent with the idea that the

Wharram Percy people suffered poorer nutrition and health during the growth period than recent children. That the deficiency in cortical thickness is greater than in bone length may suggest that cortical bone apposition was more affected by problems experienced during the growth period than was longitudinal bone growth, and hence that the former may be a more sensitive indicator of stress, at least in this group. For cortical thickness, the difference between adult values in modern and medieval samples is less than during childhood (Fig. 81). Just as the stature data suggested prolongation of longitudinal bone growth, it is likely that peak values of cortical thickness were attained somewhat later at Wharram Percy than is the case in modern subjects.

Growth interruption and recovery: Harris lines

Harris lines record episodes of stress sufficient to interrupt longitudinal bone growth. Following a period of arrest, growth will, if sufficient resources are available, restart at an accelerated rate, quickly returning the individual to his or her original growth trajectory (Prader *et al.* 1963). Alternatively, if insufficient resources are available to sustain a period of catch-up growth, growth may restart at a normal or slowed rate, with the result that the individual will be short for their age. Investigation of the relationship between the presence of Harris lines and diaphysial length allows elucidation of whether, following the incidents which gave rise to Harris lines, sufficient resources were generally available to sustain a period of catch-up growth. The relationship between Harris lines and cortical thickness may potentially reveal whether appositional growth resumed its normal trajectory following stress events which gave rise to Harris lines.

Figures 77, 81 and 82 suggest, for those aged about two years and over, approximately linear relationships between age and femur length, cortical thickness and cortical index. This is supported by the results of linear regression analysis (Table 29).

In order to evaluate any relationship betweeen the presence or absence of Harris lines and femur length, cortical thickness or cortical index, controlling for the effects of age, three multiple regression analyses were performed. Femur length, cortical thickness and cortical index were the dependent variables in each case, with the presence/absence of Harris lines (coded 1 and 0 respectively) and age as the independent variables.

Table 30 indicates that the association between the presence of Harris lines and femur length and cortical thickness, controlling for age, is statistically significant. The observation that the partial regression coefficients are less than zero indicates that femur length and cortical thickness tend to be lower in those with Harris lines. For cortical index the partial regression coefficient is also less than zero, but it fails to attain conventional statistical significance.

That the Wharram Percy juveniles with Harris lines were deficient both in bone length and in cortical bone indicates that, following the stress episodes which led to Harris line formation, there were generally insufficient resources to sustain a spell of catch-up growth. This is in contrast to the results of a study (Mays 1985) on juveniles from Romano-British Poundbury, Dorset. In that study, it was found that those with Harris lines were deficient neither in cortical bone nor in bone length, suggesting that there was generally full catch-up growth in both parameters following incidents causing Harris lines. Either the insults causing Harris lines were more severe or chronic at Wharram Percy, or the Wharram Percy children had feebler powers of recovery. In either case, it would appear that chronic poor health was more frequent at Wharram Percy than at Poundbury. In part this may reflect differences in the natural environment in the regions where the two sites are situated. The soils at Wharram Percy are thin and prone to nutrient exhaustion (Hayfield 1988a, 25-6). Wharram Percy's more northerly location and greater elevation mean that it has a harsher climate, hence crop failures and food shortages may have

Table 29. Linear regression analyses of femur length, cortical thickness and cortical index, on age.

Variable	N	Intercept	Slope	Correlation coefficient	F value	Sig. of F
Femur length	102	128.6	15.5	0.966	1400	<0.0001
Cortical thickness	97	3.14	0.55	0.876	313	<0.0001
Cortical index	97	35.6	1.1	0.558	42.9	<0.0001

Notes: Femur length and cortical thickness in mm, age in years. Analysis is over the age range 2-17 years

Table 30. Partial regression coefficients from multiple regression analyses.

Dependent variable	N	Partial regression coefficient	F value	Significance of F
Femur length	89	-10.01	7.29	0.0084
Cortical thickness	89	-0.78	10.65	0.0016
Cortical index	89	-2.39	2.93	0.091

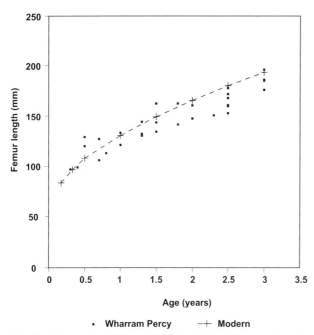

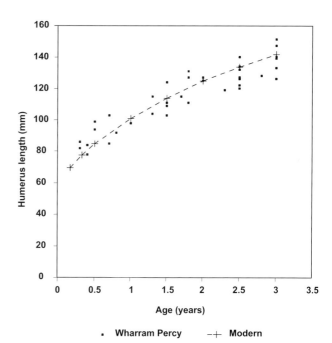

Fig. 83. Scatterplot of femoral diaphysial length versus dental age for infants and young children. Recent data (Maresh 1955), represented by the dashed line, are superimposed.

Fig. 84. Scatterplot of humeral diaphysial length versus dental age for infants and young children. Recent data (Maresh 1955), represented by the dashed lines, are superimposed.

been more common than in lowland southern England where the Poundbury site is located. The results may also reflect the differences in social status. The Poundbury people were a prosperous, heavily Romanised group (Molleson 1992). The Wharram Percy population, on the other hand, represent a lower stratum of a very hierarchical society, and hence might be expected to have been more vulnerable to disease and nutritional stress. Indeed, documentary sources indicate that dietary shortages were common in peasant communities in the medieval period (Gies and Gies 1990, 96-8).

The effects of weaning on growth patterns

Weaning is often thought to be associated with elevated levels of physiological stress. The immunological and nutritional benefits of maternal milk are progressively lost. The inclusion of other foods in diets poses new risks of infection and, in societies where diets are generally poor, post-weaning diets may be nutritionally inadequate.

The stable isotope study (p. 93), suggested breast-feeding continued for between one and two years *post-partum*. This appears consistent with medieval documentary sources, which recommended cessation of breast-feeding at about this age (Fildes 1986). Medieval writers recommended commencing supplementation of breast-milk with other foods some time before this, generally when the infant was some months old or cut its first teeth (i.e. at about six to nine months) (Fildes 1986). Indeed, supplementation often begins at around this time in recent non-Western societies as most women are unable to produce enough milk beyond about six months *post-partum* to sustain the infant's needs, so that supplementation with other foods is necessary to prevent under-nutrition and growth faltering (King and Ulijaszek

1999). Medieval documentary sources suggest the use of cereal-based foods and animal milk as supplements to breast-milk (Fildes 1986). It is difficult to infer from the stable isotope data whether these were introduced into infant diets at Wharram Percy prior to cessation of breast-feeding: animal milk would be expected to be fairly similar to human milk in its ^{15}N content, and low-protein supplements such as cereal foods would be difficult to detect because the ^{15}N signal reflects protein sources only.

In order to investigate whether there is evidence that weaning was a time of particular physiological stress for the Wharram Percy infants, longitudinal bone growth during this period was examined in further detail. Maresh (1955) gives long-bone lengths from two months of age onwards. Wharram Percy long-bone lengths from this age up to three years were studied in comparison with his data. The femur and humerus were selected as they are the limb-bones where sample numbers are greatest for this age range (Figures 83 and 84).

Both the femur and the humerus data indicate that up to about one year of age, bone lengths resemble those reported by Maresh (1955) for recent children. Beyond this age, the ancient and the modern data sets start to diverge. The pattern seems to differ slightly according to whether the femur or the humerus data are examined, but taken together they seem to indicate that the Wharram Percy children begin to show the first signs of falling behind between about one and two years of age.

If it is accepted that failure to supplement infant diets by the time the child is much beyond six months of age is likely to cause growth faltering, then the lack of evidence for this in the first year may support the idea that supplementation must have occurred by about six months, and further that the introduction of such potential

102

sources of infection did not lead to problems sufficient to retard longitudinal bone growth. The stable isotope data suggested cessation of breast- feeding at between one and two years old. That the Wharram Percy bone length data appear to begin to diverge from the modern reference sample at about this age might be interpreted as supporting the notion that there were particular problems associated with weaning. This may, however, be rather simplistic. Firstly, there is no evidence for elevated mortality at about this time (Chapter 7), which might be expected if weaning was a particularly problematic period. Secondly, the growth deficit is greater later on in childhood than it is immediately post-weaning. For example, at two years femur length is 92% of that reported by Maresh (1955), this falls to about 86% by four years and this percentage deficit remains more or less unchanged throughout the rest of the juvenile period. It would thus appear that as far as longitudinal bone growth is concerned, cessation of breast-feeding at between one and two years merely marks the start of a general pattern of deficient growth, which most probably reflects the generally rather poor nature of health and nutrition at Wharram Percy, rather than being any indication of particular stresses concentrated at time of weaning.

Conducting a similar exercise to the above using the cortical thickness and cortical index data is rather more problematic, as Virtama and Helelä (1969) do not give figures for individuals less than one year old. Figures 81 and 82 indicate that by one year old there is already a substantial difference between the ancient and modern children. Figure 82 indicates a marked drop in cortical index during the first year. A fall in cortical index at this time, due to rapid endosteal resorption, is a normal feature of human long-bone growth and appears to have its origin in the prenatal period, so this cannot of itself be taken to indicate any special problems among the Wharram Percy infants (Mays 1999a). If, as seems probable given the protection from environmental insults offered by the intra-uterine environment (Bagchi and Bose 1962), the deficit in cortical bone at one year in the Wharram Percy infants compared with the modern subjects is primarily a result of deficient growth in thickness in post-natal life, it may be that the decline in cortical index in the immediate post-natal period is greater than in modern subjects. The lack of comparative data over this age range for the recent reference group means that this question cannot fully be resolved.

It would seem that, although the medieval infants under one year were able to match modern infant rates of longitudinal growth, they were unable to sustain modern rates of appositional growth. It is unclear, however, when appositional growth began to fall behind. That a deficiency in appositional but not in longitudinal bone growth is observed in these young individuals supports the earlier contention that in this sample appositional bone growth is a more sensitive stress indicator. If it is accepted that the deficit of cortical bone in those under one year reflects post- rather than pre-natal conditions, it would seem that breast-feeding did not shield infants

from their environment sufficiently to ensure appositional as well as longitudinal bone growth proceeded at a similar rate to that observed in recent northern Europeans.

9 Metric and Non-metric Skeletal Variation

Introduction

This chapter comprises a study of metric and non-metric morphological variation in the Wharram Percy skeletal material. In the sections on metric variation, cranial and post-cranial measurements are analysed and the latter used to estimate handedness, stature and body weight. There is also a biomechanical study of humerus diaphysial cross-sectional morphology carried out with the aim of shedding light on activity patterns. Cranial and post-cranial non-metric traits are analysed, and some of the more important developmental variants found in this group are described.

Cranial measurements

The aim of this section is to characterise cranial form at Wharram Percy using a suite of measurements, to investigate any secular trends in the material, and to make comparisons with other skeletal assemblages. Thirty-two linear dimensions and one angle were recorded, and eight indices were derived from them. The results for the whole assemblage are summarised in Tables 31 and 32. With regard to the different phases, only Phases 1-2, 2 and 4 produced sufficient material to make separate presentation of results worthwhile; the results are summarised in Tables 33-36.

For the males, analysis of variance indicates that eight measurements show significant change across the three phase groups (Table 33). Primarily, this appears to represent a narrowing of the cranial vault over time so that crania from Phase 4 are narrower than from preceding phases. Consistent with this, there is significant variation in cranial index across the three phase groups, with Phase 4 having the lowest value (Table 35). Multiple comparison tests using the least significant difference statistic (Howell 1992, 356) indicate that each of the three phase groups differs from the others in cranial index. Cranial index increases between Phase 1-2 and Phase 2, only to decrease again in Phase 4. These patterns are not evident in the female crania, where there are few statistically valid differences in measurements between the three phase groups and no significant differences in the indices (Tables 34 and 36).

In order to investigate in more detail the secular trend in male cranial index, the patterning in the sub-set of the material which had been subject to radiometric dating was examined (Fig. 31). This appears to suggest that cranial index increases from approximately AD 1000, the earliest radiocarbon dated material for which cranial index data are available, until at least the 13th century.

Table 31. Cranial measurements.

Measurement	Symbol	Males N	Males Mean	Males sd	Females N	Females Mean	Females sd
Cranial length	L	125	184.0	7.1	84	177.9	6.9
Cranial breadth	B	116	147.1	6.6	88	143.4	5.9
Basi-bregmatic height	H'	93	132.0	5.5	60	127.7	5.3
Basi-nasion length	LB	89	99.6	5.1	56	95.6	4.4
Maximum frontal breadth	B"	118	123.9	6.9	96	120.3	6.3
Bimaxillary breadth	GB	68	94.2	4.8	41	90.3	3.7
Bizygomatic breadth	J	33	134.8	5.5	21	127.3	5.3
Bifrontal breadth*	FMB	120	99.4	4.1	91	96.1	3.9
Bregma-lambda chord	S'$_2$	134	113.3	6.7	104	108.9	5.7
Lambda-opisthion chord	S'$_3$	133	96.5	5.5	93	94.9	5.4
Mastoid height*	MDH	143	28.6	2.7	102	26.2	2.4
Nasion-bregma chord	S'$_1$	122	112.2	5.0	87	109.6	4.5
Biasterionic Breadth	BiastB	125	112.8	4.9	88	109.9	4.4
Foraminal length	FL	99	36.6	2.5	69	35.5	1.8
Foraminal breadth	FB	96	30.4	2.2	70	29.3	1.9
Simotic chord	SC	57	9.5	1.5	39	9.4	1.8
Orbital breadth	O'$_1$	60	40.3	1.9	33	39.6	1.5
Orbital height	O$_2$	59	33.8	1.8	35	33.4	1.8
Basion-alveolare length	GL	47	91.7	6.2	27	89.8	4.5
Nasion-alveolare chord	G'H	61	69.4	4.6	38	68.3	3.6
Nasal height	NH'	64	51.4	3.1	39	49.7	2.7
Nasal breadth	NB	80	24.7	1.7	50	23.8	1.8
Palatal length	G'$_1$	73	45.2	3.7	46	43.4	2.7
Palatal breadth	G$_2$	101	36.2	2.7	67	34.7	2.6
Bidacrionic chord	DC	46	22.9	2.4	25	22.4	2.2
Bicondylar width	W$_1$	83	123.7	5.9	69	117.8	5.8
Bigonial breadth	GoGo	119	102.8	7.0	87	95.0	5.2
Foramen mentalia breadth	ZZ	130	45.1	2.6	99	43.3	2.3
Minimum ramus breadth	RB'	133	31.5	2.9	101	30.0	2.6
Symphysial height	H$_1$	114	31.8	3.8	85	29.6	3.6
Mandibular length	ML	85	104.8	4.9	70	100.4	4.3
Coronoid height	CrH	124	63.2	5.9	92	57.5	5.2
Mandibular angle†	M<	80	121.9	7.1	63	125.1	5.9

Notes: Measurement definitions and symbols taken from Brothwell (1972), except: *, Howells (1973); † Vallois (1965). All measurements in mm, mandibular angle in degrees

Table 32. Cranial indices.

	Males N	Males Mean	Males sd	Females N	Females Mean	Females sd
Cranial index	112	80.2	4.8	83	80.7	4.4
Cranial module	88	153.9	4.5	57	149.5	3.9
Length-height index	89	72.1	3.8	58	72.0	3.8
Breadth-height index	91	90.1	4.9	59	89.2	4.4
Upper facial index	31	51.5	3.5	17	54.5	3.0
Nasal index	57	48.4	3.8	35	47.9	3.5
Orbital index	59	84.1	5.1	33	84.2	4.8
Palatal index	69	80.2	8.4	44	80.5	7.4

Notes: Indices defined according to Bass (1987)

Table 33. Cranial measurements for males, split by phase.

Measurement	Symbol	Phase 1-2			Phase 2			Phase 4			F
		N	Mean	sd	N	Mean	sd	N	Mean	sd	
Cranial length	L	60	185.1	6.9	15	181.3	7.2	15	185.3	7.7	
Cranial breadth	B	58	148.0	5.9	13	149.9	5.4	15	142.3	5.4	**
Basi-bregmatic height	H'	48	132.4	5.6	9	131.8	5.7	13	128.9	5.9	
Basi-nasion length	LB	46	99.3	5.4	8	97.9	3.6	13	98.9	6.1	
Maximum frontal breadth	B"	56	124.9	6.5	14	125.3	5.8	16	118.3	7.7	**
Bimaxillary breadth	GB	31	95.2	4.7	11	92.6	4.6	7	92.2	4.9	
Bizygomatic breadth	J	16	135.1	5.3	3	136.3	3.4	5	130.6	7.4	
Bifrontal breadth*	FMB	55	100.0	4.2	14	99.1	2.4	16	96.3	4.3	**
Bregma-lambda chord	S'_2	64	114.4	6.3	15	112.0	8.1	15	112.2	6.3	
Lambda-opisthion chord	S'_3	62	97.5	5.5	15	95.6	5.3	16	96.3	6.4	
Mastoid height*	MDH	67	28.6	2.7	15	29.9	2.8	15	28.2	2.8	
Nasion-bregma chord	S'_1	56	112.0	4.7	14	112.4	5.6	15	113.6	5.3	
Biasterionic Breadth	BiastB	60	113.3	4.8	15	114.5	2.7	15	108.7	3.9	***
Foraminal length	FL	52	36.1	2.3	11	37.9	3.1	11	37.1	2.1	
Foraminal breadth	FB	48	29.9	2.3	9	31.6	1.1	11	31.7	1.6	**
Simotic chord	SC	26	9.5	1.3	6	8.9	0.8	10	9.2	2.2	
Orbital breadth	O'_1	31	40.5	1.9	7	40.1	2.3	8	39.8	2.0	
Orbital height	O_2	31	33.8	1.4	7	32.9	1.8	8	34.9	2.5	
Basion-alveolare length	GL	24	93.1	5.4	5	91.1	6.0	7	84.9	3.6	**
Nasion-alveolare chord	G'H	30	69.3	4.0	8	67.2	6.1	9	69.0	4.3	
Nasal height	NH'	33	51.0	2.7	8	50.4	4.4	9	52.7	2.9	
Nasal breadth	NB	40	24.6	1.7	11	24.4	1.7	8	24.2	2.0	
Palatal length	G'_1	38	45.8	3.8	9	45.2	2.1	7	41.4	3.6	*
Palatal breadth	G_2	53	35.9	2.9	13	36.5	2.0	8	35.2	1.7	
Bidacrionic chord	DC	19	22.8	2.3	6	22.2	3.1	6	22.1	2.6	
Bicondylar width	W_1	46	124.0	5.8	8	125.0	4.5	6	119.1	8.2	
Bigonial breadth	GoGo	57	103.8	7.0	16	103.6	6.9	13	97.8	4.9	*
Foramen mentalia breadth	ZZ	60	45.2	2.4	16	44.3	2.4	16	43.8	1.9	
Minimum ramus breadth	RB'	63	31.5	2.8	16	30.5	2.5	16	31.0	2.8	
Symphysial height	H_1	53	31.9	4.0	13	31.1	3.1	14	30.2	2.5	
Mandibular length	ML	47	105.6	4.7	8	105.5	5.5	7	104.9	2.4	
Coronoid height	CrH	58	62.3	6.1	16	62.9	4.3	16	64.5	6.5	
Mandibular angle†	M<	44	123.5	6.8	9	121.7	7.1	6	121.7	10.5	

Notes: as for Table 31, except F = significance of F value from analysis of variance, * 0.05>p>0.01, ** 0.01>=p>0.001, *** p<=0.0001

Beyond this only three male crania for which cranial index could be recorded were radiometrically dated. These date to about the 16th century, and their indices lie in the range 71-5. This suggests that the reduction in male cranial index identified between Phases 2 and 4 (Table 35) may have occurred between about the 14th and the 16th centuries at Wharram Percy.

Multivariate analysis was conducted on the male skulls which could be assigned to phase. Conventional multivariate statistical techniques require there be no missing data. There were only eleven male skulls assigned to phase for which all 32 measurements could be taken. There were a further 48 male skulls for which ten or fewer measurements were missing. Cranial measurements are, to a greater or lesser extent, correlated with one another and this allows missing data to be estimated. For each measurement for which there were missing data among these 48 skulls, the variables which were most strongly correlated with it were identified by analysis of correlation coefficients, and linear regression equations generated. The chosen correlated measurement was treated as the independent variable and the measurement for which we aim to estimate a missing value was treated as the dependent variable. By

Table 34. Cranial measurements for females, split by phase.

Measurement	Symbol	Phase 1-2			Phase 2			Phase 4			F
		N	Mean	sd	N	Mean	sd	N	Mean	sd	
Cranial length	L	35	177.7	5.6	14	179.6	8.7	9	180.9	7.7	
Cranial breadth	B	35	143.7	6.2	15	144.9	4.7	10	142.6	4.9	
Basi-bregmatic height	H'	26	126.9	5.2	9	129.4	5.1	6	124.3	2.2	
Basi-nasion length	LB	27	95.2	4.5	9	94.8	1.3	5	94.4	1.3	
Maximum frontal breadth	B"	36	120.5	5.3	18	120.4	7.1	12	118.8	6.1	
Bimaxillary breadth	GB	18	90.4	3.2	6	88.8	2.8	5	90.1	4.9	
Bizygomatic breadth	J	10	126.7	6.0	3	127.6	3.9	3	126.8	5.7	
Bifrontal breadth*	FMB	34	94.5	3.8	16	96.8	2.4	13	96.7	4.1	
Bregma-lambda chord	S'$_2$	40	109.0	5.6	17	109.1	5.6	13	108.6	7.7	
Lambda-opisthion chord	S'$_3$	37	95.0	4.9	15	96.2	6.8	10	94.1	5.1	
Mastoid height*	MDH	42	25.5	2.5	16	27.4	2.5	10	25.8	2.8	*
Nasion-bregma chord	S'$_1$	34	108.4	4.8	16	110.5	4.5	10	110.6	3.8	
Biasterionic Breadth	BiastB	39	109.8	4.5	13	111.1	4.5	9	108.2	4.8	
Foraminal length	FL	29	35.6	2.0	12	36.0	1.5	7	35.4	2.4	
Foraminal breadth	FB	29	29.5	1.9	11	29.5	1.9	6	28.4	2.3	
Simotic chord	SC	15	9.5	2.2	8	10.2	1.6	6	8.8	1.5	
Orbital breadth	O'$_1$	13	39.2	1.8	6	39.9	1.5	4	39.0	0.7	
Orbital height	O$_2$	14	33.7	2.1	6	33.1	2.1	5	33.5	1.7	
Basion-alveolare length	GL	13	90.5	4.8	5	85.6	3.1	3	87.3	2.1	
Nasion-alveolare chord	G'H	17	68.8	4.2	7	68.3	3.5	4	65.7	2.6	
Nasal height	NH'	17	49.6	2.9	7	49.0	3.2	5	49.7	1.4	
Nasal breadth	NB	22	23.4	1.8	9	24.5	1.6	6	24.4	0.8	
Palatal length	G'$_1$	18	44.9	2.7	7	42.3	2.5	4	40.7	1.0	**
Palatal breadth	G$_2$	24	34.3	2.2	11	34.3	2.3	6	33.9	2.2	
Bidacrionic chord	DC	10	21.0	1.8	6	22.1	3.0	2	22.6	1.7	
Bicondylar width	W$_1$	29	116.5	5.0	11	119.7	4.6	5	120.4	3.1	
Bigonial breadth	GoGo	37	94.9	5.6	14	95.7	5.0	6	94.4	7.0	
Foramen mentalia breadth	ZZ	42	43.3	2.8	16	44.1	1.7	8	42.1	2.0	
Minimum ramus breadth	RB'	44	29.9	2.8	15	29.6	2.7	9	29.2	3.0	
Symphysial height	H$_1$	36	29.4	4.0	13	30.6	2.1	5	28.3	4.6	
Mandibular length	ML	29	100.8	4.5	11	99.7	4.8	5	99.8	2.2	
Coronoid height	CrH	39	56.3	4.9	15	58.7	6.9	9	56.2	5.7	
Mandibular angle†	M<	26	125.6	6.7	10	125.1	5.5	5	121.8	3.6	

Notes: See Table 33

substituting into the regression equation the value for the independent variable, the missing value of the dependent variable could be estimated. In three of the 48 cases this was not a viable strategy as in these instances missing values arose as a result of an entire area of the skull (e.g. the mandible) being absent. This left 45 skulls for which the above procedure resulted in production of a complete suite of measurements, and with the eleven intact skulls this produced a total of 56 skulls for analysis.

The multivariate method used was Principal Components Analysis (hereafter PCA). The purpose of PCA is to produce from the original set of (correlated) measurements a new set of variables, or axes, which are uncorrelated with one another. The axes are composites of the original variables, and are to some extent interpretable in terms of combinations of them. The first new axis, or component, accounts for the most of the sample variance, the next the next most etc. There are as many axes are there were original variables, but the first few axes will often account for much of the original variance and hence provide a simplified, but still useful summary of the data. In the current analysis, the first three principal components account for nearly half the variance and are the only ones discussed. The loadings of

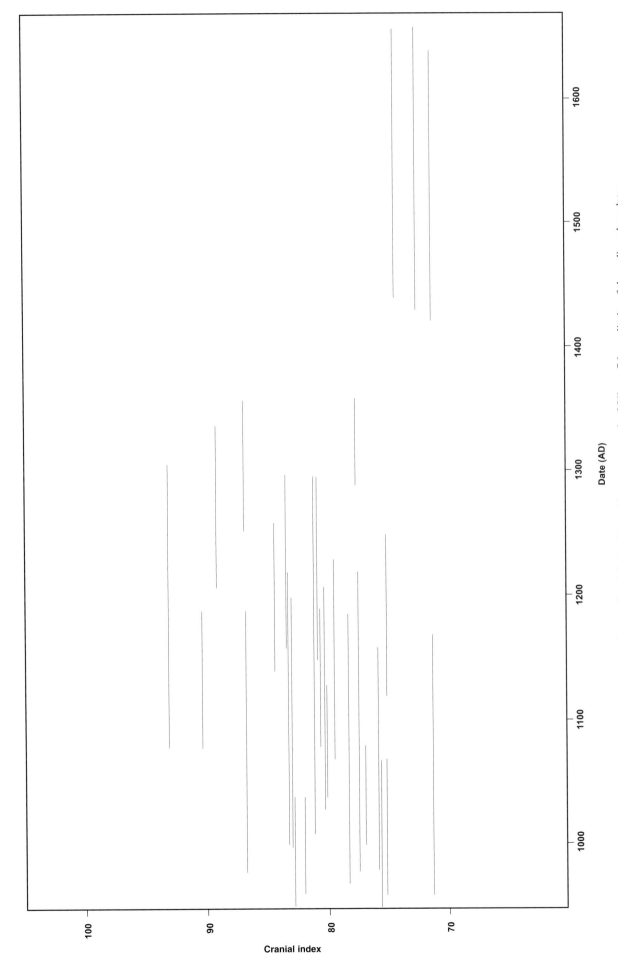

Fig. 85. Plot of cranial index in males versus radiocarbon date. The lengths of the horiziontal bars represent the 95% confidence limits of the radiocarbon dates.

Table 35. Cranial indices for males split by phase.

| | Phase 1-2 | | | Phase 2 | | | Phase 4 | | | |
	N	Mean	sd	N	Mean	sd	N	Mean	sd	F
Cranial index	56	80.2	4.0	13	83.4	5.0	15	77.0	4.6	***
Cranial module	45	155.0	4.5	8	153.1	3.7	13	151.8	4.0	
Length-height index	45	72.0	3.7	9	73.7	4.7	13	70.0	3.2	
Breadth-height index	47	89.6	4.7	8	87.0	4.0	13	90.7	5.5	
Upper facial index	14	50.7	3.9	3	51.5	0.9	5	52.4	4.6	
Nasal index	27	48.9	3.3	8	47.9	5.1	8	46.5	4.3	
Orbital index	31	83.6	3.9	7	82.5	7.0	8	87.9	6.9	
Palatal index	36	77.8	8.6	9	79.7	4.2	7	86.4	8.1	*

Notes: see Table 33

Table 36. Cranial indices for females split by phase.

| | Phase 1-2 | | | Phase 2 | | | Phase 4 | | | |
	N	Mean	sd	N	Mean	sd	N	Mean	sd	F
Cranial index	34	81.0	4.0	14	81.2	4.4	9	78.9	3.7	
Cranial module	25	149.6	4.0	9	150.3	2.4	6	147.7	3.2	
Length-height index	26	71.6	3.4	9	73.7	5.1	6	70.2	2.6	
Breadth-height index	25	88.3	4.6	9	89.1	5.6	6	88.0	4.0	
Upper facial index	8	54.2	3.3	3	55.1	1.2	1	56.7	-	
Nasal index	15	47.9	3.1	6	48.1	2.3	5	49.1	2.1	
Orbital index	13	85.0	4.9	6	82.8	3.0	4	86.4	3.4	
Palatal index	17	76.7	5.4	7	82.1	5.3	4	80.8	4.0	

Notes: see Table 33

the original variables on the first three components are shown in Table 37.

As is often the case in PCA of osteometric data, component one appears to relate primarily to size: all measurements have substantial positive loadings on this component. Turning to component two, several variables which are measures of facial height have substantial positive loadings, whereas a number of breadth measurements, particularly of the cranial vault, have negative loadings. Individuals with higher scores on this component will tend to have higher faces and narrower cranial vaults. Many cranial vault measurements, particularly breadth measurements, have substantial positive loadings on component three, and many facial measurements have negative loadings. Skulls with higher scores on this component will tend to have large, broad vaults in relation to the size of the facial skeleton. The summary statistics for the three phase group scores on components 1-3 are shown in Table 38.

The results for component 1, the putative size component, indicate a trend toward a reduction in cranial size in Phase 4. The increase in component 2 from the Phase 1-2/Phase 2 material to that from Phase 4 indicates a trend toward higher faces and narrower cranial vaults in Phase 4. There is a subtle indication for a reversal of this trend between Phase 1-2 and Phase 2, suggesting wider vaults in

Phase 2 crania than in Phase 1-2 material, although this seems consistent with the observations on cranial index (Table 35), it is not statistically significant. The trend for component 3 does not reach statistical significance, but the

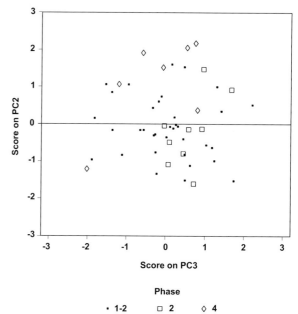

Fig. 86. Principal Components Analysis of craniometric data for male crania: scores for individual crania on components 2 and 3.

Table 37. Principal components analysis of male phased skulls (N=56): eigenvalues, percent variance accounted for, and component loadings for the first three components.

		PC1	PC2	PC3
Eigenvalue		8.6	3.1	2.5
%variance accounted for		26.9	9.6	7.8
		Component loading		
Measurement	Symbol	PC1	PC2	PC3
Cranial length	L	0.637	0.154	-0.158
Cranial breadth	B	0.573	-0.193	0.575
Basi-bregmatic height	H'	0.615	-0.031	0.119
Basi-nasion length	LB	0.636	-0.028	-0.448
Maximum frontal breadth	B"	0.497	-0.470	0.407
Bimaxillary breadth	GB	0.472	-0.072	0.280
Bizygomatic breadth	J	0.782	-0.319	-0.012
Bifrontal breadth	FMB	0.763	-0.485	-0.100
Bregma-lambda chord	S'_2	0.513	0.076	0.033
Lambda-opisthion chord	S'_3	0.204	0.041	0.355
Mastoid height	MDH	0.433	0.086	0.399
Nasion-bregma chord	S'_1	0.439	0.255	0.135
Biasterionic Breadth	BiastB	0.521	-0.239	0.366
Foraminal length	FL	0.340	-0.047	0.132
Foraminal breadth	FB	0.291	0.241	0.274
Simotic chord	SC	0.398	-0.364	-0.394
Orbital breadth	O'_1	0.818	-0.015	0.024
Orbital height	O_2	0.151	0.546	0.194
Basion-alveolare length	GL	0.656	-0.161	-0.440
Nasion-alveolare chord	G'H	0.534	0.639	-0.059
Nasal height	NH'	0.331	0.562	-0.053
Nasal breadth	NB	0.368	-0.326	-0.322
Palatal length	G'_1	0.664	-0.012	-0.195
Palatal breadth	G_2	0.371	-0.040	-0.152
Bidacrionic chord	DC	0.267	-0.494	0.093
Bicondylar width	W_1	0.431	-0.246	0.482
Bigonial breadth	GoGo	0.532	-0.001	0.204
Foramen mentalia breadth	ZZ	0.448	0.282	-0.148
Minimum ramus breadth	RB'	0.387	-0.023	-0.515
Symphysial height	H_1	0.571	0.573	-0.057
Mandibular length	ML	0.663	0.341	0.003
Coronoid height	CrH	0.493	0.357	0.134

somewhat lower mean for the Phase 4 material is suggestive of somewhat smaller vaults and larger facial skeletons in this period. Scores for individual male crania on components 2 and 3 are plotted in Figure 86.

To summarise, the results of the PCA for the male crania support those from the univariate analyses of measurements and indices in indicating narrower crania in Phase 4, and in addition there appears to be a secular trend towards higher faces. Generally, clearer differences exist between Phase 4 and the earlier material than between

Phase 1-2 and 2; this is as might be expected given the temporal overlap between Phase 1-2 and Phase 2 material.

Discussion

Secular trends

It has been noted (Goose 1962; Moore et al. 1968) that there is a reduction in mandibular and maxillary robusticity between medieval and post-medieval times in Britain, with a reduction in the dimensions of the mandibular ramus, an increase in mandibular angle, and a

Table 38. Summary statistics for component scores for phase groups, male crania.

	N	PC1		PC2		PC3	
		Mean	sd	Mean	sd	Mean	sd
Phase 1-2	35	0.22	1.01	-0.09	0.82	0.03	0.99
Phase 2	9	-0.14	0.58	-0.22	0.95	0.60	0.54
Phase 4	7	-0.92	0.76	1.12	1.20	-0.25	1.08
ANOVA		F=4.6, p=0.02		F=5.8, p=0.01		F=1.9, p=0.17	
LSD		1-2vs4		1-2vs4, 2vs4		-	

Notes: ANOVA = analysis of variance; LSD = least significant difference statistic, inter-group differences significant at the 5% level or better are identified

reduction in palate width. This was ascribed to a transition to a softer diet after the medieval period, a change for which there is also documentary evidence. By the 17th century, urban groups were generally consuming bread made from finely milled flour, in contrast to the coarse bran and rye breads which formed the staples of earlier times. Consistent with this, a decrease in the rate of dental wear has also been observed in post-medieval populations (Moore and Corbett 1978). The post-medieval material examined by Goose (1962), Moore *et al.* (1968) and, Moore and Corbett (1978) was from urban contexts. In the current material, there is no evidence for a decrease in mandibular or maxillary robusticity in the post-medieval period (Tables 33 and 34). Consistent with this, even the latest post-medieval burials (early 19th century) continue to show heavy dental wear. In contrast to the findings from urban samples examined by earlier workers, maxillary and mandibular morphology and dental wear provide no evidence for any great change in dietary consistency between medieval and post-medieval periods at Wharram Percy.

It has previously been observed (Buxton 1937; Tattersall 1968a) that in Britain there was an increase in cranial index between the Anglo-Saxon and medieval periods. Dawes (1980) confirmed this pattern for sites in the York area. A trend toward brachycranialisation during the medieval period has also been noted in Continental Western Europe (Rösing and Schwidetzky 1984). There was a subsequent decline in cranial index in British populations, so that values for post-medieval series are less than for medieval assemblages (Buxton 1937; Tattersall 1968a; Brodie 1994). The results for the Wharram Percy males appear consistent with these previously identified trends. The current results are important as they demonstrate them within a single assemblage dated using radiocarbon determinations, whereas previous studies have generally relied on comparing different, often geographically disparate cranial series dated to within rather broad limits on archaeological grounds.

In a British context, the change in cranial form between material from Anglo-Saxon and later medieval sites has led to speculation concerning the possible role of Norman invaders (Buxton 1937). The data from Wharram Percy seem to suggest a continuous trend toward brachycranialisation which appears to have been underway from at least AD 1000 and continued until at least the 13th century (Fig. 85). There is no evidence for any abrupt change at around the time of the Norman conquest. In any event, given that Wharram Percy was a rather remote and poor rural settlement, large scale ingress of population at any time during the medieval period, let alone Norman invaders, seems somewhat unlikely. The change in cranial form which appears to have occurred between about the 14th and the 16th centuries is even more difficult to ascribe to the arrival of migrants on any significant scale – at this time the population of the parish was shrinking not growing.

Rather than reflecting some change in genetic make-up due to influx of migrants from outside the community, it seems more probable that at Wharram Percy secular change in male cranial form occurred within the indigenous population, presumably in response to change in some environmental factor(s). Identifying credible candidates for causal factors from among those known potentially to affect cranial form is problematic. Other than dietary consistency, for which there seems to be no evidence of any change through time at Wharram Percy, climate is a factor which may influence cranial form, including cranial index. Much heat is lost through the head and a brachycranic skull has a lower surface area : volume ratio than a longer, narrower cranium, and hence is better for heat conservation. At a population level, variation in cephalic index (cranial index taken on living subjects) has been interpreted in terms of climatic factors. For example, populations living in regions of the world experiencing winter frosts have a higher mean cephalic index than those from the frost-free tropics (Beals *et al.* 1983).

Mean annual temperature in England increased by about 0.5°C between AD 1000 and AD 1200 and there was a decrease of more than 1°C between AD 1200 and 1600 (Lamb 1984). The Wharram Percy data show an increase in cranial index between about AD 1000 and AD 1200, but a fall between the 13th and the 16th centuries. These are precisely the opposite trends to those expected if climate were an important factor behind the secular trend in cranial form.

It is interesting that it is only the male crania which show evidence for secular change at Wharram Percy. The generally smaller sample sizes for females may have militated against obtaining statistically valid patterns. Although smaller than for males, sample sizes for females were still reasonable (Tables 34 and 36). The observation of morphological change in the male but not the female skulls may support the idea that some extraneous environmental factor(s) rather than genetic change was responsible. Male skeletons tend to show greater plasticity in response to environmental stress during development than do females whose developmental course seems more firmly canalised (Stinson 1985; Tanner 1989). Hence if we are correct in supposing that the changes in cranial form at Wharram Percy reflect the influence of some, as yet unidentified, environmental factors, we might expect changes in males to be more pronounced, and hence more readily detectable, than those for females. Conversely, if genetic change in the population due to immigration was a factor in the changes in cranial form at Wharram Percy, then one might expect changes in female as well as male skulls (this would be so even if migrants were predominantly male as inter-marriage with the local population would produce offspring of both sexes).

Comparison with other assemblages
In order to provide a rigorous multivariate comparison with other assemblages, analysis of the raw data from those assemblages would be needed, and such an exercise is beyond the scope of the current report. Instead, a rough and ready comparison was undertaken using multivariate analysis based on sample means for individual measurements (following Dawes 1980). Choices of comparative assemblages were constrained by the availability of published summary statistics in osteological reports. Of assemblages which potentially form relevant comparative data for the present material, a literature search revealed adequate data from ten populations on seventeen of the measurements used here (L, B, H', LB, GL, G'H, GB, J, NH', NB, O'1, O2, BiastB, SC, S'1, S'2 and S'3).

The following assemblages were used for comparative purposes:

1) York, St Helen-on-the-Walls. Urban cemetery (N=1041 individuals). Date: AD 950-1550. Source: Dawes (1980). Abbreviation: YKSTH.

2) York, Fishergate, period 4. Urban cemetery (N=131 individuals). Date: 11th-12th century AD. Source: Stroud (1993). Abbreviation: YKFGP4.

3) York, Fishergate, period 6. Urban priory (N=271 individuals). Date: 13th-16th century AD. Source: Stroud (1993). Abbreviation: YKFGP6.

4) York, Jewbury. Urban cemetery for Jewish community (N=475 individuals). Date: 13th century AD. Source: Stroud *et al.* (1994). Abbreviation: YKJEW.

5) York, Clementhorpe. Urban nunnery (N=79 crania). Date: 12th-16th century AD. Source: Dawes (1980). Abbreviation: YKCLM.

6) York Minster. Urban cemetery (N=159 crania). Date: Anglo-Scandinavian (pre-12th century AD). Source: Dawes (1980). Abbreviation: YKMIN.

7) Hythe, Kent. Rural ossuary (N=199 crania). Date: 12th-16th century AD. Source: Stoessiger and Morant (1932). Abbreviation: HYTHE.

8) Oslo. Urban cemeteries (N=110 crania). Date: medieval. Source: Dawes (1980). Abbreviation: OSLO.

9) Arras culture, various east Yorkshire cemetery sites (N=246 individuals). Date: 4th-1st century BC. Source: Stead (1991). Abbreviation: ARRAS.

10) London, Spitalfields. Urban cemetery (N=986 crania). Date: 13th-16th century AD. Source: Morant and Hoadley (1931). Abbreviation: SPITS.

For the purposes of comparison, the Wharram Percy data were split into the three major phase groups

Table 39. Dissimilarity matrix (squared Euclidean distance), male crania.

Site	WPP1-2	WPP2	WPP4	YKJEW	YKFGP4	YKFGP6	ARRAS	YKSTH	HYTHE	OSLO	YKCLM	YKMIN
WPP2	49.7											
WPP4	176.4	202.6										
YKJEW	69.3	145.4	208.5									
YKFGP4	102.9	240.1	327.2	125.3								
YKFGP6	36.4	67.4	260.6	84.3	125.8							
ARRAS	349.6	510.4	431.3	323.7	204.9	360.1						
YKSTH	38.0	67.7	136.0	97.6	166.8	48.6	306.5					
HYTHE	100.4	90.3	284.4	165.7	290.6	78.7	514.1	55.4				
OSLO	77.7	197.3	218.3	93.0	63.5	115.0	238.6	97.4	194.3			
YKCLM	43.5	99.5	219.8	115.9	111.1	42.1	318.8	55.4	149.1	135.5		
YKMIN	94.3	225.6	271.4	114.5	47.6	103.9	157.9	111.3	243.4	36.8	94.6	
SPITS	81.7	105.2	190.9	118.5	219.4	98.4	382.0	42.3	40.7	109.8	151.2	162.1

Table 40. Dissimilarity matrix (squared Euclidean distance), female crania.

Site	WPP1-2	WPP2	WPP4	YKJEW	YKFGP4	YKFGP6	ARRAS	YKSTH	HYTHE	OSLO	YKCLM	YKMIN
WPP2	49.6											
WPP4	48.8	61.6										
YKJEW	36.7	140.5	112.3									
YKFGP4	121.7	209.7	160.9	115.2								
YKFGP6	32.8	75.3	88.3	48.6	103.7							
ARRAS	289.7	370.4	309.2	288.8	220.9	228.4						
YKSTH	21.9	58.6	62.5	66.3	153.1	31.5	307.3					
HYTHE	102.6	190.6	160.5	148.5	307.6	127.4	325.3	84.3				
OSLO	114.6	219.1	116.1	110.5	98.9	99.8	97.0	129.3	144.3			
YKCLM	34.0	40.9	77.4	101.6	229.2	61.3	337.9	25.5	103.1	183.4		
YKMIN	120.6	167.1	142.1	117.8	33.5	87.0	159.5	146.8	311.2	92.7	195.0	
SPITS	166.0	253.7	189.9	221.1	369.7	195.7	276.4	158.7	28.9	139.9	166.3	354.9

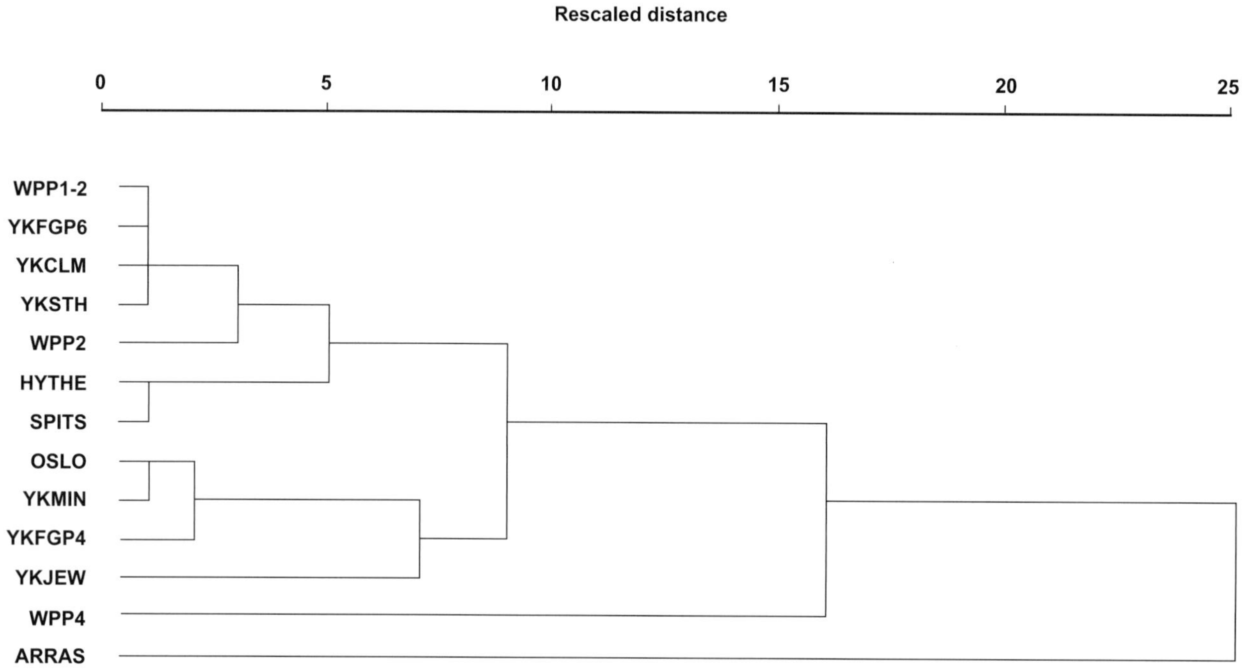

Rescaled distance

Fig. 87. Cluster analysis of craniometric data from Wharram Percy and from some other published sites, male skulls. For site abbreviations and sources for comparative data, see text.

discussed above (1-2, 2 and 4, abbreviated WPP1-2, WPP2 and WPP4).

Dissimilarity coefficients were calculated (squared Euclidean distance) using group means for the seventeen measurements. The dissimilarity data were displayed using a cluster analysis (agglomerative hierarchical, based on average linkage). Analyses were also run after transforming the data to z-scores. Results were similar to those obtained using untransformed data. Only results for the untransformed data are shown (Tables 39 and 40; Figures 87 and 88).

In general, the patterns obtained from the male and female crania resemble one another. Given the nature of the analysis inferences must be made with caution, and it should also be borne in mind that both genetic and

environmental factors influence cranial morphology. Nevertheless, it is notable that the broad pattern in the results is consistent with the geographical and temporal spread of the populations and, in some instances, with relationships which can reasonably be inferred from historical and other data. For the later medieval British material, a regional pattern is evident, with most of the Yorkshire sites resembling one another, but being somewhat separated from their southern counterparts from London and Hythe which cluster together. The York Jewbury material is somewhat separated from other late medieval York sites. Presumably this reflects the distinct ethnic identity of this group within the city of York. The material from the York Minster and Fishergate period 4 burial grounds is somewhat separated from the later

112

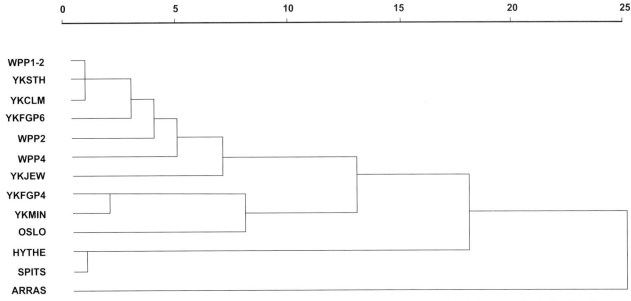

Fig. 88. Cluster analysis of craniometric data from Wharram Percy and from some other published sites, female skulls. For site abbreviations and sources for comparative data, see text.

medieval York material, and resembles the Oslo medieval crania. One might speculate that this reflects a Scandinavian contribution to the population of York during the earlier medieval period, but that this element becomes 'diluted' by migrants into York from the surrounding countryside during the later medieval age so that later medieval samples are less similar to the Oslo group. The Arras culture crania are distinct from the other material. This presumably represents their temporal remoteness from the other groups and, perhaps, the likely foreign origin of the Arras culture.

That the Wharram Percy medieval crania resemble most closely those from later medieval York probably reflects the geographical closeness of these populations. Even among the earliest phased Wharram Percy material there is little resemblance to the Oslo crania, nor indeed to the earlier medieval York crania from Fishergate period 4 and York Minster. This might be interpreted as suggesting any Scandinavian contribution to the Wharram population was minor compared with that to earlier medieval York. In the male results, the Wharram Percy post-medieval crania are distinct from medieval crania, both from Wharram Percy and from other sites. This serves to emphasise the cranial morphological changes, noted above, which occurred over time at Wharram Percy. The post-medieval female crania from Wharram Percy are less different from medieval material; again this is consistent with results discussed above.

Post-cranial measurements

Measurements were made on all major long-bones. The results are shown in Tables 41-46.

Looking at the data split by phase (Tables 43-46), there is no evidence for any great secular change in post-cranial skeletal morphology. The only patterning detectable appears to be a slight increase over time in femoral width measurements, particularly anterio-posterior dimensions. Consistent with this there is also an increase in meric index. These patterns are similar in males and females.

Leg-bone shaft indices may vary with the degree of mechanical stress habitually placed on the bones in life, lower index values (flattened shaft cross-sections) generally tending to indicate greater mechanical forces (Larsen 1997, 222). It has long been noted (e.g. Buxton 1938; Brothwell 1972) that there has been a secular trend toward more rounded femoral and tibial cross-sections in human populations up to the present day, perhaps connected with a very general trend toward increasingly sedentary lifestyles. The secular change in the meric index at Wharram Percy, referred to above, appears consistent with this general trend, although whether this implies lesser activity patterns among the period 4 people is debatable as the meric index is elevated in this phase group by an increase in anterio-posterior width rather than a decrease in medio-lateral width. Cnemic index shows no change. Comparisons of the Wharram Percy cnemic and meric indices with results from some other material are shown in Table 47.

Table 47 indicates that the values for meric and cnemic indices from Wharram Percy resemble those from St Helen-on-the-Walls. There is also a suggestion of a secular trend toward higher indices from the Iron Age to the medieval material, more particularly in meric index.

The brachial and crural indices measure the relative lengths of distal segments of the arm and leg respectively, lower index values corresponding to relatively shorter distal limb segments. At a population level, relative length of distal limb segments varies with mean annual temperature, populations living in colder climes having more abbreviated distal limb segments (Trinkaus 1981).

Table 41. Post-cranial measurements.

Bone	Measurement	Symbol	Males			Females		
			N	Mean	sd	N	Mean	sd
Left humerus	Max. length	HuL$_1$	95	323.9	16.5	77	298.4	14.8
	Max. head diameter*		96	46.7	2.8	75	41.7	2.3
	Max. width at midshaft	HuD$_1$	92	23.2	1.5	76	20.8	1.6
	Min. width at midshaft	HuD$_2$	93	18.5	1.4	76	16.4	1.3
	Epicondylar width*		109	64.1	3.5	89	56.7	3.4
Right humerus	Max. length	HuL$_1$	92	327.7	16.0	70	302.0	14.3
	Max. head diameter*		91	47.8	2.9	72	42.0	2.4
	Max. width at midshaft	HuD$_1$	92	23.7	1.4	70	21.3	1.6
	Min. width at midshaft	HuD$_2$	93	18.9	1.4	70	16.7	1.4
	Epicondylar width*		108	64.6	3.6	89	57.4	3.1
Left radius	Max. length	RaL$_1$	87	242.4	13.9	65	220.7	11.0
Right radius	Max. length	RaL$_1$	92	242.4	13.0	60	221.7	11.6
Left ulna	Max. length	UlL$_1$	81	260.8	14.5	60	238.7	12.4
Right ulna	Max. length	UlL$_1$	80	263.4	14.5	54	241.3	12.6
Left femur	Max. length	FeL$_1$	111	446.7	24.4	74	412.8	20.8
	Vertical diameter of head†		122	48.7	3.2	84	42.7	2.4
	A-p width below lesser trochanter	FeD$_1$	139	26.5	2.4	96	23.7	2.1
	M-l width below lesser trochanter	FeD$_2$	139	32.9	2.3	96	30.8	2.1
	A-p width at midshaft*		109	29.2	2.4	76	26.0	2.0
	M-l width at midshaft*		109	28.6	1.8	76	26.0	1.8
	Bicondylar width	FeE$_1$	110	80.5	4.4	68	72.4	3.5
Right femur	Max. length	FeL$_1$	102	446.7	23.6	78	412.4	20.0
	Vertical diameter of head†		108	49.0	3.3	86	42.9	2.7
	A-p width below lesser trochanter	FeD$_1$	128	26.3	2.4	92	23.3	1.9
	M-l width below lesser trochanter	FeD$_2$	128	32.7	2.2	92	30.4	2.2
	A-p width at midshaft*		101	29.5	2.6	79	26.1	2.0
	M-l width at midshaft*		101	28.5	2.0	79	25.7	1.6
	Bicondylar width	FeE$_1$	90	80.8	4.3	65	72.2	3.2
Left tibia	Max. length	TiL$_1$	100	356.9	23.0	69	334.2	16.7
	A-p width at nutrient foramen	TiD$_1$	111	34.3	3.1	86	29.8	2.1
	M-l width at nutrient foramen	TiD$_2$	111	24.5	2.0	86	21.7	1.8
Right tibia	Max. length	TiL$_1$	104	355.9	22.4	66	331.2	15.4
	A-p width at nutrient foramen	TiD$_1$	114	34.7	3.1	86	30.0	2.0
	M-l width at nutrient foramen	TiD$_2$	114	24.5	2.0	86	21.7	1.6
Left fibula	Max. length	FiL$_1$	58	350.8	23.6	41	328.1	17.2
Right fibula	Max. length	FiL$_1$	55	350.0	20.7	36	332.0	14.9
Left clavicle	Max. length*		86	147.3	8.4	72	138.0	7.7
Right clavicle	Max. length*		81	145.5	8.9	64	137.1	8.1

Notes: Measurements follow the definitions of Brothwell (1981), except *Bass (1987) †Stewart (1968), and are in mm. A-p = anterio-posterior, M-l = medio-lateral. Symbols follow Brothwell (1981)

Table 42. Post-cranial indices.

	Males			Females		
	N	Mean	sd	N	Mean	sd
Cnemic index	124	71.4	6.5	93	72.9	4.9
Meric index	151	81.1	7.6	104	77.6	7.9
Pilasteric index	123	102.5	8.0	91	101.3	8.3
Brachial index	91	74.6	2.4	64	73.6	2.3
Crural index	95	79.9	2.4	71	80.7	2.3
Intermembral index	62	69.9	1.9	44	69.6	1.9

Notes: Cnemic index=100xTiD$_2$/TiD$_1$, Meric index=100xFeD$_1$/FeD$_2$, Pilasteric index=100xmidshaft a-p width/midshaft m-l width,
Brachial index=100xRaL$_1$/HuL$_1$, Crural index=100xTiL$_1$/FeL$_1$, Intermembral index=100x(HuL$_1$+RaL$_1$)/(FeL$_1$+TiL$_1$). Indices calculated using left limbs. If left side missing, right side substituted.

Table 43. Post-cranial measurements split by phase, males.

Bone	Measurement	Symbol	N	Mean	sd	N	Mean	sd	N	Mean	sd	F
			Phase 1-2			Phase 2			Phase 4			
Left humerus	Max. length	HuL_1	39	321.5	15.5	14	330.8	15.1	14	330.7	14.7	
	Max. head diameter*		44	46.4	2.9	11	46.9	2.0	12	47.7	2.1	
	Max. width at midshaft	HuD_1	38	22.8	1.6	13	23.2	1.5	14	24.3	1.4	
	Min. width at midshaft	HuD_2	38	18.3	1.4	13	19.0	1.2	14	19.1	1.2	
	Epicondylar width*		47	63.9	3.9	16	64.6	3.1	12	64.6	2.7	
Right humerus	Max. length	HuL_1	37	326.5	15.3	12	333.3	13.2	20	331.4	13.6	
	Max. head diameter*		40	47.9	2.7	12	47.8	2.1	15	47.7	2.4	
	Max. width at midshaft	HuD_1	37	23.6	1.5	13	23.6	1.2	19	24.3	1.3	
	Min. width at midshaft	HuD_2	37	18.7	1.5	13	18.9	1.3	20	19.2	1.0	
	Epicondylar width*		45	64.5	4.1	16	64.6	3.7	19	64.7	2.5	
Left radius	Max. length	RaL_1	34	243.1	13.4	12	249.3	13.7	14	245.4	11.5	
Right radius	Max. length	RaL_1	33	242.0	12.7	14	249.0	13.4	17	244.7	11.6	
Left ulna	Max. length	UlL_1	33	261.2	13.2	11	266.2	13.6	13	268.3	14.8	
Right ulna	Max. length	UlL_1	30	264.4	13.6	10	266.2	14.6	17	266.4	13.6	
Left femur	Max. length	FeL_1	38	449.2	20.1	13	453.1	27.1	20	452.9	16.6	
	Vertical diameter of head†		41	48.4	3.2	17	48.8	1.8	20	49.8	3.2	
	A-p width below lesser trochanter	FeD_1	48	26.1	1.9	19	26.6	2.9	21	27.9	2.4	*
	M-l width below lesser trochanter	FeD_2	48	33.1	2.3	19	32.7	2.1	21	33.1	2.6	
	A-p width at midshaft*		37	29.5	2.0	12	28.6	2.2	20	29.6	2.2	
	M-l width at midshaft*		37	28.3	1.6	12	28.8	1.1	20	29.2	1.8	
	Bicondylar width	FeE_1	37	79.8	4.1	12	80.9	3.0	20	83.1	4.3	*
Right femur	Max. length	FeL_1	39	448.4	20.6	11	449.5	26.2	18	455.2	12.1	
	Vertical diameter of head†		41	48.8	3.3	12	49.1	2.2	18	50.8	3.5	
	A-p width below lesser trochanter	FeD_1	48	25.9	2.0	17	26.0	3.0	20	27.7	2.5	*
	M-l width below lesser trochanter	FeD_2	48	33.0	1.9	17	32.4	2.3	20	32.9	2.2	
	A-p width at midshaft*		38	29.3	2.7	11	29.7	2.5	17	29.6	2.0	
	M-l width at midshaft*		38	28.0	2.1	11	28.8	1.6	17	29.2	1.6	
	Bicondylar width	FeE_1	33	80.6	4.0	10	80.9	2.8	15	82.9	3.5	
Left tibia	Max. length	TiL_1	33	362.3	22.7	14	358.8	17.9	17	361.5	18.9	
	A-p width at nutrient foramen	TiD_1	38	34.4	3.0	15	33.8	3.7	17	35.0	2.2	
	M-l width at nutrient foramen	TiD_2	38	24.5	1.8	15	24.6	1.7	17	25.1	2.2	
Right tibia	Max. length	TiL_1	32	359.8	21.7	16	360.3	21.3	19	360.3	16.7	
	A-p width at nutrient foramen	TiD_1	38	34.8	3.0	16	34.7	3.4	19	34.7	2.0	
	M-l width at nutrient foramen	TiD_2	38	24.5	1.8	16	24.6	1.9	19	24.7	2.1	
Left fibula	Max. length	FiL_1	20	359.0	23.0	10	360.0	18.6	10	360.2	17.6	
Right fibula	Max. length	FiL_1	17	354.1	20.8	8	361.2	22.2	12	354.5	19.1	
Left clavicle	Max. length*		36	148.0	6.9	11	148.7	8.6	12	144.8	8.5	
Right clavicle	Max. length*		38	147.6	8.4	12	144.6	8.3	7	141.0	9.1	

Notes: as for Table 41, except F = significance of F value from analysis of variance, * 0.05>p>0.01, ** 0.01>=p>0.001, *** p<=0.0001

Table 44. Post-cranial measurements split by phase, females.

Bone	Measurement	Symbol	Phase 1-2			Phase 2			Phase 4			F
			N	Mean	sd	N	Mean	sd	N	Mean	sd	
Left humerus	Max. length	HuL_1	27	299.2	17.5	14	295.4	12.1	6	299.3	12.8	
	Max. head diameter*		27	41.2	2.1	14	42.2	3.2	6	43.0	1.8	
	Max. width at midshaft	HuD_1	28	20.2	1.5	14	21.0	2.0	6	21.3	1.3	
	Min. width at midshaft	HuD_2	28	16.0	1.3	14	16.8	1.5	6	16.3	1.0	
	Epicondylar width*		33	56.6	3.5	16	56.6	4.1	9	56.2	3.1	
Right humerus	Max. length	HuL_1	26	300.0	16.1	11	304.4	16.0	9	308.6	11.6	
	Max. head diameter*		30	41.5	2.6	12	42.4	2.5	6	43.0	1.9	
	Max. width at midshaft	HuD_1	26	20.9	1.5	11	21.7	1.9	9	21.9	1.7	
	Min. width at midshaft	HuD_2	26	16.4	1.7	11	17.0	1.2	9	16.8	0.9	
	Epicondylar width*		34	57.2	3.4	17	57.1	3.3	7	57.2	2.5	
Left radius	Max. length	RaL_1	27	222.0	10.3	11	219.5	9.5	8	217.0	14.6	
Right radius	Max. length	RaL_1	27	222.8	12.3	12	222.5	11.0	5	215.4	12.5	
Left ulna	Max. length	UlL_1	19	241.6	13.0	10	239.9	10.8	7	232.4	13.1	
Right ulna	Max. length	UlL_1	21	242.3	12.6	11	242.6	13.9	5	244.2	13.8	
Left femur	Max. length	FeL_1	21	408.5	22.2	14	405.9	14.2	11	421.7	19.4	
	Vertical diameter of head†		29	41.9	2.4	16	42.3	2.3	9	42.8	1.4	
	A-p width below lesser trochanter	FeD_1	32	23.0	2.0	18	23.9	2.0	13	25.2	2.5	**
	M-l width below lesser trochanter	FeD_2	32	30.5	2.1	18	31.3	2.2	13	29.4	2.3	
	A-p width at midshaft*		21	25.0	1.9	14	26.5	2.4	12	27.1	1.5	*
	M-l width at midshaft*		21	25.3	2.0	14	26.0	1.6	12	26.0	1.9	
	Bicondylar width	FeE_1	19	71.3	3.6	15	72.9	3.2	10	73.4	4.1	
Right femur	Max. length	FeL_1	27	407.6	20.4	16	409.7	15.3	12	422.8	19.2	
	Vertical diameter of head†		29	41.8	2.5	17	42.5	2.6	11	44.3	2.3	*
	A-p width below lesser trochanter	FeD_1	33	22.9	1.9	17	22.9	1.7	11	25.0	2.5	*
	M-l width below lesser trochanter	FeD_2	33	30.1	2.1	17	30.5	2.4	11	29.0	2.4	
	A-p width at midshaft*		27	25.4	1.9	16	26.1	2.1	12	27.1	1.7	
	M-l width at midshaft*		27	25.2	1.7	16	25.5	1.3	12	26.0	2.0	
	Bicondylar width	FeE_1	21	71.7	3.3	15	72.3	3.4	8	73.7	3.9	
Left tibia	Max. length	TiL_1	23	333.0	20.1	15	334.5	14.0	8	341.1	14.3	
	A-p width at nutrient foramen	TiD_1	29	29.5	2.0	16	30.9	1.9	12	29.3	2.2	
	M-l width at nutrient foramen	TiD_2	29	21.2	1.6	16	22.2	1.7	12	21.9	2.1	
Right tibia	Max. length	TiL_1	18	324.1	15.5	16	332.9	14.0	10	338.6	17.4	
	A-p width at nutrient foramen	TiD_1	27	29.3	2.0	16	31.1	2.0	14	29.7	1.5	*
	M-l width at nutrient foramen	TiD_2	27	21.4	1.5	16	21.8	1.3	14	21.7	2.1	
Left fibula	Max. length	FiL_1	14	330.1	18.0	11	324.5	16.7	6	327.0	21.0	
Right fibula	Max. length	FiL_1	10	331.4	11.5	9	330.4	19.0	5	330.0	21.2	
Left clavicle	Max. length*		32	138.0	7.1	10	139.1	8.1	5	139.8	6.5	
Right clavicle	Max. length*		29	136.9	7.7	8	138.3	7.7	4	135.5	7.3	

Notes as for Table 43

116

Table 45. Male post-cranial indices split by phase.

Index	N	Phase 1-2 Mean	sd	N	Phase 2 Mean	sd	N	Phase 4 Mean	sd	F
Cnemic index	41	71.3	6.7	17	72.7	6.4	20	71.7	5.9	
Meric index	54	79.3	6.2	21	81.0	9.7	22	84.4	8.0	*
Pilasteric index	45	103.8	8.5	14	99.8	7.6	20	101.5	7.9	
Brachial index	35	75.4	2.3	13	75.0	2.5	18	74.1	2.7	
Crural index	31	80.4	2.3	13	79.6	2.2	18	80.2	2.0	
Intermembral index	21	69.2	2.1	9	70.3	2.2	14	70.4	1.6	

Notes as for Table 43

Table 46. Female post-cranial indices split by phase.

Index	N	Phase 1-2 Mean	sd	N	Phase 2 Mean	sd	N	Phase 4 Mean	sd	F
Cnemic index	29	72.0	4.9	17	72.1	6.0	14	75.0	4.3	
Meric index	35	76.3	6.9	19	76.6	6.7	15	85.5	11.6	**
Pilasteric index	29	100.9	8.7	17	103.0	8.0	15	103.3	8.1	
Brachial index	26	73.8	2.5	12	74.2	2.2	5	70.7	0.9	*
Crural index	21	80.9	2.6	16	81.8	2.4	10	80.2	1.8	
Intermembral index	14	69.6	2.0	10	70.4	1.7	5	68.6	0.8	

Notes as for Table 43

Table 47. Mean meric and cnemic indices from some cemeteries from east Yorkshire.

Site	Meric index M	F	Cnemic M	F	Source
Yorkshire Arras Culture	70.2	72.2	67.0	69.7	Stead (1991)
West Heslerton	77.1	73.2	69.7	72.4	Cox (1999)
Wharram Percy	81.1	77.6	71.4	72.9	-
York, St Helen on-the-Walls	79.2	77.6	71.8	72.6	Dawes (1980)

Notes: Dates of comparative material: West Heslerton: 5th-7th-century; for dates of other cemeteries see list of comparative sites for craniometric data (above)

Table 48. Asymmetry in arm bone lengths.

Bone(s)	N	Standardised asymmetry Mean	sd	R>	Raw measurements L=R	L>
Humerus	125	1.18	1.29	97	10	18
Radius	107	0.52	1.37	60	17	30
Ulna	85	0.50	1.28	52	9	24
Humerus + radius	81	0.87	1.03	66	2	13

This is in accord with Allen's rule, which holds that organisms native to cold climates should show shorter extremeties than their warmer climate conspecifics, reducing surface area: volume ratios hence conserving heat. At an empirical level, it has been shown that animals raised under conditions of cold stress tend to have shorter extremeties (Trinkaus 1981). At Wharram Percy, brachial index in females is lower in Phase 4 than in the other two major phase groups. Among males, the mean Phase 4 value is lower than that for the other two phase groups, but the trend does not reach statistical significance (p=0.19). The direction of the change in brachial index is as expected if it was in response to climate since mean annual temperature in England was more than 1°C lower in the 'Little Ice Age' of the Early Modern period than during medieval times (Lamb 1984). There is, however, no evidence for any concomitant change in crural index.

The intermembral index is an expression of the relative lengths of lower and upper limbs. In modern populations mean intermembral index varies from about 66.8 to 73.0 (Trinkaus 1981). The Wharram Percy values (Table 42) resemble the mean of 69.0 cited for a modern White (USA) reference group (Trinkaus 1981).

Arm bone length asymmetries

Minor asymmetries in the upper limb of the human skeleton reflect behavioural handedness bias (Steele 2000). In particular, the side of the dominant hand tends to show greater length of the bones (Inglemark 1946; Schulter-Ellis 1980). This probably reflects the greater use of the dominant limb for tasks involving significant mechanical loading (references in Steele 2000). In the present material, asymmetry was expressed, for each individual, as the difference between left and right elements of a pair, standardised by the mean length of left and right elements:

$$\frac{R-L}{(R+L)/2} \times 100$$

The results (adults only, sexes pooled) are given in Table 48, together with raw counts of individuals with longer left bones, longer right bones and where left and right were equal to within readout precision (1mm).

One-sample t-tests indicate that for all three bone lengths, and for humerus + radius length (here used as a proxy for arm length), the mean standardised asymmetry differs significantly from zero (p<0.001 in each case). In each case the mean standardised asymmetry is greater than zero, indicating a rightward bias. Consistent with this the number of individuals with greater right

measurements is greater for each variable than the number with longer left bones.

Inglemark (1946) noted that in living subjects, greater forelimb length (measured by humerus + radius length) was correlated with the side of the dominant hand. At Wharram Percy the combined humerus plus radius length was greater on the right side in 81%, greater on the left in 16% and equal to within 1mm in 3%. These figures imply a rather greater frequency of left-handedness than has customarily been observed in recent populations, where left-handers are reported as making up, on average, about 8% of the total (McManus 1991). Behavioural handedness, particularly for fine motor tasks such as handwriting, may be fairly readily moulded by cultural practices. This usually takes the form of suppression of left- handedness with a consequence that the 'natural' proportion of left-handers may tend to be underestimated when handedness is inferred from hand-preference in living subjects. Consistent with this, the higher reported rates of left-handedness are generally from societies where pressure to conform has been relaxed (references in Steele and Mays 1995). The Wharram Percy data resemble much more closely figures reported for asymmetries in manual skill and grip strength in modern populations than they do figures for hand preference. For example, Annett and Kilshaw (1983) reported that for a peg-moving task 82% were more skilled with the right hand, 15% with the left, and Plato et al. (1980) observed that 77% of male Caucasian adults have a stronger grip with the right hand, 15% with the left. The Wharram Percy results may reflect a distribution of hand use for tasks with significant loading asymmetry which was unconstrained by, or resistant to, cultural pressures for conformity.

Adult stature

Adult stature was estimated from long-bone lengths using the formulae of Trotter and Gleser (1952; 1958, reproduced in Brothwell 1981, 101). (Juvenile stature was discussed on pp 99-100.) The results are shown in Tables 49 and 50 and in Figure 89.

Table 49. Adult stature (cm).

	Males			Females	
N	Mean	sd	N	Mean	sd
169	168.8	5.7	119	157.8	5.1

Analysis of variance indicates no significant variation in stature across the three phase groups for either sex.

Table 50. Adult stature (cm) split by phase.

		Phase 1-2			Phase 2			Phase 4	
	N	Mean	sd	N	Mean	sd	N	Mean	sd
Males	63	169.7	5.3	21	169.6	5.9	23	169.1	4.2
Females	44	157.2	5.6	20	158.1	5.0	16	158.8	4.6

118

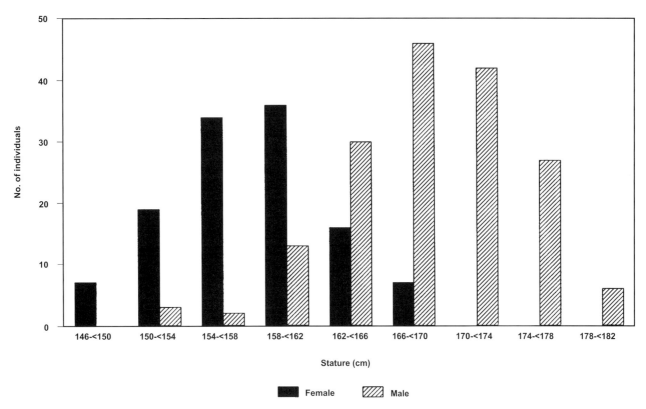

Fig. 89. Distribution of adult stature.

Table 51. Stature comparisons with some large archaeological and historical samples.

	Date	Mean male stature	Mean female stature	Source
East Yorkshire sites				
Yorkshire Arras culture	4th-1st century BC	170.7	158.2	Stead (1991)
York, Trentholme Drive	2nd-4th century AD	170	155	Warwick (1968)
Norton, Cleveland	AD 520-620	173.5	164.1	Marlow (1992)
West Heslerton	5th-7th century AD	173.7	160.0	Cox (1999)
York Minster	Pre-AD 1080	173	161	Stroud et al. (1994)
York Fishergate, period 4	11th-12th century AD	172	158	Stroud (1993)
York Minster	Post-1180 AD	171	158	Stroud et al. (1994)
Wharram Percy	AD 950-1850	168.8	157.8	-
York St Helen-on-the-Walls	AD 950-1550	169.3	157.4	Dawes (1980)
York Clementhorpe	13th-16th century AD	171	156	Stroud et al. (1994)
York Jewbury	13th century AD	167	156	Stroud et al. (1994)
York Fishergate, period 6	13th-16th century AD	171	159	Stroud (1993)
Medieval Scandinavia				
Tirup, Denmark	AD 1100-1320	174.6	161.6	Arcini (1999)
Trondheim, Norway	AD 1100-1600	173.3	157.8	Anderson (1986)
Lund, Sweden*	AD 990-1536	172.8	160.9	Arcini (1999)
Westerhus, Sweden	AD 1025-1375	174.3	161.6	Gejvall (1960)
Historical and recent UK				
'Habitual criminals'	AD 1869-1876	166.2	155.5	Johnson and Nicholas (1995)
'Most favoured classes'	AD 1857-1883	175.0	-	Morant (1950)
Modern	AD 1990	176.4	163.6	Freeman et al. (1995)

Notes: stature in cm. For skeletal material, stature estimated from long-bone lengths using the equations of Trotter and Gleser (1952; 1958) in Brothwell 1981, except: * follows Sjøvold's (1990) method. Historical and recent data are standing heights measured on living subjects.

The stature figures from Wharram Percy most closely resemble those from the coeval site at St Helen-on-the-Walls, which was a churchyard serving a poor parish in York, but they are also fairly similar to those from other late medieval sites in the region (Table 51). Early medieval (i.e. pre-Conquest) period assemblages seem to have rather greater mean figures. Although one should exercise caution when comparing archaeological stature data generated using long-bone lengths with those measured from living subjects, one sample t-tests show that the mean Wharram Percy estimated stature is less than that for modern UK subjects and for the highest social classes in the late 19th century. On the other hand, it exceeds that for 19th-century criminals (likely representative of the lowest social classes).

Adult body weight

Ruff *et al.* (1991) have produced regression equations for estimation of body weight in adults based on dimensions of the proximal femur. They derived their formulae from a radiographic study of living subjects (hospital patients) from Baltimore. Correlations between the femoral dimensions and body weight were generally between 0.5 and 0.6. Their equations for Whites are used here. Ruff (2000a) provides regression equations for estimation of body weight from bi-iliac breadth and stature. These are based upon a study of 56 living world populations and show correlations with body mass of between 0.8 and 0.9 (Table 52).

Table 52. Regression formulae used to estimate body weight from skeletal remains (sources: Ruff *et al.* 1991, table 4; Ruff 2000a, table 1).

Males	
EQM1	3.383 x femur head diameter – 85.8
EQM2	3.105 x femur shaft breadth – 17.3
EQM3	0.0808 x femoral cortical area + 39.4
EQM4	0.373 x stature + 3.033 x bi-iliac breadth – 82.5
Females	
EQF1	0.493 x femur head diameter + 46.2
EQF2	2.70 x femur shaft breadth – 11.8
EQF3	0.0895 x femoral cortical area + 28.3
EQF4	0.522 x stature + 1.809 x bi-iliac breadth – 75.5

Notes: stature and bi-iliac breadths in cm, other measurements in mm

All femoral measurements were taken from anterio-posterior radiographs of the proximal femur following the methods outlined in Ruff *et al.* (1991). Briefly, vertical femoral head diameter was recorded. Femur shaft width and medullary width were taken at a distance equivalent to two-thirds femoral head diameter distal to the centre of the lesser trochanter. To estimate radiographic enlargement, femur head and shaft breadths were re-measured on the specimen. This procedure indicated that

true dimensions were approximately 96% of those recorded radiographically. All three radiographic measurements were corrected for enlargement by multiplying by 0.96. Cortical area in cross-section was estimated from shaft width and medullary width assuming a circular cross-section:

Cortical area = 0.785 x [(femur shaft width)^2 – (medullary width)^2]

Bi-iliac breadth was measured by re-articulating the pelvic girdle. The measurement was taken in the coronal plane between the most lateral points on the iliac crests of left and right innominate bones. Because bi-iliac breadth was taken on living subjects in the reference groups used to derive the body weight estimation formulae the measurement included soft tissue. To adjust for this, 0.5cm was added to the present dry bone values, following Ruff and Walker (1994).

In order that results obtained using the various methods could be compared, only individuals for which all four equations could be applied were included here. Body weight estimates were made for eighteen males and six females. The chief limit on sample size was the paucity of burials with both innominate bones and the sacrum sufficiently intact for accurate measurement of bi-iliac breadth. The results are shown in Tables 53-54.

The three methods based on proximal femur dimensions give fairly similar results to one another, but they are systematically greater than estimates using stature/bi-iliac breadth. The stature/bi-iliac breadth method is a morphometric technique in that it attempts to estimate body weight by reconstructing the general size and shape of the body. The femoral methods may be thought of as partially morphometric, in that femur size will show a positive relationship with overall body size, and partly biomechanical in that dimensions, more particularly of the diaphysis, may be influenced by mechanical forces on the bone (Ruff 2000b).

Ruff *et al.* (1991) indicate that the femoral diaphysial methods will likely over-estimate body weight when used on early skeletal remains. This is because activity levels were likely generally higher in palaeopopulations than in the modern US subjects upon whom the methods were devised. The method based on femoral head diameter will also likely over-estimate body mass when applied to archaeological remains (Ruff *et al.* 1991). This is because femoral head diameter will not change once the epiphysis has fused to the shaft, and although weight gain during adulthood is the norm for modern Westerners which made up the reference sample from which the method was derived, this is not likely to have been the case for pre-industrial cultures (Eaton *et al.* 1988). Like femur head diameter, bi-iliac breadth and stature do not change greatly during adulthood, however the tendency of these parameters to over-estimate body weight may be less marked than for femur head diameter as the reference sample used to derive the stature/bi-iliac breadth technique included non-Western populations for which

Table 53. Estimates of body weight, males.

Burial	Age	Stature		Body weight estimates			
				EQM1	EQM2	EQM3	EQM4
CN14	ADULT	169		75.5	79.9	81.7	68.1
EE013	ADULT	178		83.6	79.1	86.3	65.1
G265	35-45	171		89.1	85.5	95.4	67.8
G297	50+	171		75.9	87.3	92.3	65.3
G436	25-35	168		85.2	76.6	80.8	64.5
G694	25-35	180		100.0	88.4	97.0	76.4
G746	30-50	175		92.8	78.7	89.4	73.5
NA140	ADULT	170		83.7	89.9	97.2	70.0
NA176	circa 25	162		83.7	88.5	98.0	60.6
NA181	50+	165		86.3	99.4	112.9	58.3
NA224	ADULT	168		72.2	90.3	97.5	70.6
SA002	22-24	168		74.3	84.9	90.8	69.4
V38	40-50	167		94.5	88.7	93.5	64.5
V45	40+	166		80.5	87.6	91.1	61.4
WCO059	50+	157		69.1	78.5	84.8	53.4
WCO078	22-30	168		79.8	81.7	84.5	61.8
WCO162	50+	162		62.0	72.7	78.7	54.3
WCO164A	40+	160		79.0	81.5	84.9	59.9
			Mean	81.4	84.4	90.9	64.7
			sd	9.5	6.4	8.2	6.2

Notes: age in years unless stated, stature in cm, estimated body weights in kg

Table 54. Estimates of body weight, females.

Burial	Age	Stature		Body weight estimates			
				EQF1	EQF2	EQF3	EQF4
CN41	40-50	164		67.1	71.0	72.0	57.4
EE018	circa 21	155		66.8	60.5	64.1	53.5
EE043	25-35	155		67.4	81.5	85.1	57.4
G692	50+	160		67.1	74.6	74.8	55.5
WCO036	40+	150		66.1	67.6	71.4	52.3
WCO184	35-45	152		67.4	71.4	79.3	54.0
			Mean	67.0	71.1	74.5	55.0
			sd	0.5	7.0	7.2	2.1

Notes as for Table 53

the tendency for weight gain in adulthood may be somewhat less than is the case with the modern Americans. In addition, the correlation with body weight is rather stronger for the stature/bi-iliac formula than for the femur equations, so the former may be more reliable. To summarise: although the wide divergence in body weight estimates from the four techniques does not lend one very much confidence in the reliability of any of them, the discrepencies between the femur-based methods and the stature/bi-iliac breadth technique are understandable in terms of the nature of the techniques and the reference populations upon which they are based. One would suspect that the figures given by stature/bi-iliac breadth technique are nearest the truth, although it seems likely that even these may over-estimate actual body weight at Wharram Percy.

Biomechanical study of humeri

Within limits, bone adapts its form to the mechanical forces imposed upon it, bone being added where it is needed and removed where it is not. In the shaft of a tubular bone, an increase in mechanical loading may result both in an increase in the amount of cortical bone and in an alteration in its distribution in cross-section so that more is disposed further from the neutral axis of the bone. These changes have the effect of increasing diaphysial strength, particularly in bending and torsion, which are the predominant modes of mechanical stress under physiological conditions. The link with in-vivo mechanical loadings has led to the use of diaphysial cross-sectional morphology to investigate activity patterns in skeletal populations, mostly using estimates of second moments of area (Larsen 1997).

In this study, polar second moments of area in humeral diaphyses are investigated in order to study activity patterns involving the upper limbs. The polar second moment of area, denoted J, is an estimate of torsional rigidity, and may be considered a general measure of overall diaphysial strength (Bridges 1996). Polar second moments of area were estimated for adult individuals with both humeri intact (N=102, 64 males, 38 females). Methods follow Mays (1999b). Briefly, the part of the humerus selected for study is the point 35% of the way from the distal end. Anterio-posterior and medio-lateral radiographs were taken and total bone width (T) and medullary width (M) measured at this point. Second moments of area (I_{ML} and I_{AP}) were calculated from T and M assuming an elliptical cross-section; these were summed to yield the polar second moment of area.

$$I_{ML} = \frac{\Pi}{64} (T_{ML}T^3_{AP} - M_{ML}M^3_{AP})$$

$$I_{AP} = \frac{\Pi}{64} (T_{AP}T^3_{ML} - M_{AP}M^3_{ML})$$

$$J = I_{ML} + I_{AP}$$

For each individual, asymmetry in J values, denoted J_{ass}, was defined as the difference between between the larger and smaller sides divided by the value for the smaller side and expressed as a percentage, i.e. 100 x (max-min)/min. An overall J value, denoted J_{avg}, was calculated for each individual as follows. Firstly, the left and right J values were standardised by bone length raised

to the power of 2.33, and the result multiplied by 10^4, following Trinkaus et al. (1994). This size standardisation, whilst not necessary for asymmetry scores such as J_{ass}, is necessary to permit comparison of absolute J values between assemblages or sub-groups of an assemblage which may differ in terms of bone length. J_{avg} for each individual is simply the mean of left and right standardised J values. J_{ass} is a measure of differential mechanical loading of the two upper limbs. J_{avg} may vary with the overall level of mechanical loading habitually placed on the upper limbs. Unsigned measures of asymmetry, such as J_{ass}, are non-normally distributed (Thomson 1999). Hence results for J_{ass} are summarised using medians and inter-quartile ranges, and are analysed using non-parametric statistical tests. For both J_{avg} and J_{ass}, results are compared with male and female lay burials from York Fishergate, which were the subject of an earlier study (Mays 1999b; Table 55).

Table 55. J_{ass} for Wharram Percy and York Fishergate layfolk.

Site		N	Median	Iqr
Wharram Percy	Males	64	7.4	12.5
	Females	38	7.3	8.1
York Fishergate	Males	66	11.8	15.3
(Mays 1999b)	Females	21	5.4	10.4

For Wharram Percy, a Kruskal-Wallis non-parametric analysis of variance indicates that there is no significant variation in J_{ass} with respect to phase (data not shown). A Mann-Whitney test indicates no significant difference in J_{ass} between the sexes at Wharram Percy; this is in contrast to York Fishergate, where a statistically significant difference was found (Mays 1999b), males having the higher value.

Data from recent Europeans (Virtama and Helelä 1969) indicate that there is loss of cortical bone in both sexes from about middle age onwards. Therefore analysis of J_{avg} is restricted to those under 50 years at death (Tables 56 and 57).

At Fishergate, the greater asymmetry among the men than in the women indicates a greater involvement of males in activities involving differential loading of the

Table 56. J_{avg} for Wharram Percy by phase for adults under 50 years at death.

	Phase 1-2			Phase 2			Phase 4			
	N	Mean	sd	N	Mean	sd	N	Mean	sd	F
Males	14	249.8	48.3	5	240.8	32.7	5	308.7	34.7	*
Females	9	174.5	52.4	3	195.1	49.1	1	186.9	-	

Notes: J_{avg} in $mm^{1.67}$; F=significance of F value from analysis of variance; if this column is blank, p>0.05; *, p<0.05

Table 57. J_{avg} for Wharram Percy and York Fishergate layfolk for adults under 50 years at death.

	Wharram Percy			York Fishergate layfolk			
	N	Mean	sd	N	Mean	sd	t
Males	30	258.4	46.8	47	273.0	52.3	
Females	23	190.3	52.8	15	157.3	29.6	**

Notes: J_{avg} in $mm^{1.67}$, t = t-test for difference between Wharram Percy and York Fishergate; if this column is blank, p>0.05; **, p<0.01

upper limbs. This has been interpreted (Mays 1999b) as suggestive of greater participation of the middle class urban males from this site in craft activities which involved use of tools designed to be used one-handed. At Wharram Percy, the similarity in asymmetry values between the sexes implies little difference in participation in activities which differentially loaded the upper limbs.

In males there is a greater mean J_{avg} among Phase 4 burials. All five Phase 4 burials for which J_{avg} could be calculated came from the church nave. There is abundant evidence linking poor nutrition in the growth period to deficient cortical bone (Himes *et al.* 1975). Therefore, although the greater J_{avg} among Phase 4 individuals may indicate greater strenuous activities involving the upper limbs among men from this period, given the likely higher status of those using the church rather than the churchyard for burial (see Chapter 7), it may also reflect somewhat better nutrition during the growth period.

Although in males no significant difference exists between J_{avg} values from Wharram Percy and York Fishergate, there is a difference among the females, the Wharram Percy women having the higher value. Given the likely higher social status of the those using the Fishergate site for burial, this difference is unlikely to be accounted for by poorer nutritional status among the Fishergate women. It seems more likely that the Wharram Percy women undertook more activities which involved heavy mechanical loading of the upper limbs than did the Fishergate females. Documentary evidence indicates that in medieval peasant communities there was no rigid sexual division of labour, although some activities, particularly involving work centred around the household, tended to be female work. Women also frequently joined men in agricultural labour in the fields (Bennett 1987).

Non-metric variation

Non-metric traits are minor variations of skeletal anatomy. The causation of many remains obscure, but for some at least there is evidence that they are under a significant degree of genetic control. Thirty-three cranial and twenty post-cranial non-metric traits were recorded systematically in the current study material. They were drawn principally from Berry and Berry (1967) and Finnegan (1978). Traits not described by these writers

were taken from Brothwell (1981), Ossenberg (1976) and Hauser and de Stefano (1989). In immature individuals, the occurrence of many traits is age-correlated so many workers omit juveniles from studies of trait frequency. In this light only results for adult skeletons are discussed here. The frequency data are given in Table 58.

For the purposes of analysis, scores for bilateral traits were dichotomised into simple presence/absence scores for individuals by considering scores of 1/1, 1/0, 0/1, 1/- and -/1 as trait presence, and scores of 0/-, -/0 and 0/0 as trait absence.

Of the 53 traits, the frequency of five differed significantly between the sexes. Extra-sutural mastoid foramen, agenesis of mandibular third molar, and plaque formation on the femoral neck were each more frequent in males; accessory sacral facets and humeral septal aperture were more frequent in females. For all these save the last, there is little sign in the literature that they are regularly more common in one sex than the other. For humeral septal aperture, a greater frequency of the trait in females has long been noted, as has a greater frequency in the left than the right humerus (Martin 1928). This latter pattern was also evident at Wharram Percy: in all nine cases where the trait occurred unilaterally it was present on the left (Table 58).

Only one trait (acetabular crease) showed significant patterning by phase. This may be a chance finding, given that with 53 traits one might expect up to two statistically significant results to arise by chance.

A major reason for recording non-metric variants in the current material was to investigate whether there is any evidence that individuals who were closely related genetically tended to be buried near one another. This might occur if, for example, family members were often interred near existing graves of blood relatives or perhaps if there was a tendency for inhabitants of the different settlements in the parish to be buried in specific areas of the churchyard. Nineteen traits were selected as suitable for this part of the work on the basis that a literature review (Mays 1987) provided evidence of a significant genetic component in their causation, and that they occur with reasonable frequency in the current material. These traits are: metopic suture, ossicle at lambda, lambdoid ossicle, sagittal ossicle, parietal notch bone, foramen of Huschke, ossicle at asterion, palatine torus, mastoid foramen extra-sutural, parietal foramen, zygomatic facial foramen, divided hypoglossal canal, supra-orbital foramen complete, maxillary third molar absent, mandibular third molar absent, supra-condyloid process, sacral spina bifida occulta, sixth sacral segment and posterior atlas bridging.

With presence/absence data it is clearly not possible to estimate missing values as could be done for the cranial measurements. For multivariate analysis, only skeletons with data for all nineteen variants could be included. This resulted in a sample of 80 individuals. These 80 were subject to cluster analysis in order to identify sub-groups of individuals bearing similar combinations of traits. The rationale here is that individuals sharing similar

Table 58. Non-metric trait frequencies for adults from the whole assemblage.

Trait	1	0	1/1	1/0	0/1	1/-	-/1	0/-	-/0	0/0
Cranial traits										
Metopic suture	27	232								
Ossicle at lambda	40	199								
Lambdoid ossicle	117	130								
Inca bone	1*	253								
Sagittal ossicle	5	215								
Ossicle at bregma	1	236								
Coronal ossicle	3	237								
Fronto-temporal articulation			2	0	0	1	1	25	15	158
Epipteric bone			6	14	5	2	1	32	10	106
Squamo-parietal ossicle			1	3	1	0	0	24	20	170
Parietal notch bone			6	10	18	2	1	20	11	175
Auditory torus			0	0	0	0	0	15	17	227
Foramen of Huschke			24	12	10	5	4	10	13	181
Ossicle at asterion			4	4	18	2	1	20	16	176
Clinoid bridging			1	2	4	1*	3	18	19	32
Pterygoid bridging			1	2	2	5	1	19	13	37
Palatine torus	12	197								
Maxillary torus	2	216								
Mastoid foramen extra-sutural			48	49	37	7	5	13	9	89
Mastoid foramen absent			5	16	13	1	0	19	12	191
Double condylar facet on occipital			2	2	1	1	0	14	17	202
Parietal foramen			101	36	36	1	3	2	0	73
Accessory infra-orbital foramen			10	5	7	5	9	26	33	78
Zygomatic-facial foramen present			148	6	14	26	26	6	3	17
Divided hypoglossal canal			22+	36#	27~	2	4	9	9	143
Posterior condylar canal patent			95	30	32	20	15	10	6	39
Precondylar tubercle			8	10	1	1	0	6	6	207
Foramen ovale incomplete			1	1	3	6	2	40	34	116
Accessory lesser palatine foramen			57	24	20	21	16	8	7	15
Supra-orbital foramen complete			14*	23†	20‡	3	5*	16	12	156
Maxillary M3 absent			15	5	7	7	2	17	22	149
Mandibular M3 absent			32	12	9	2	2	15	3	178
Mandibular torus	2	242								
Mylohyoid bridging			9^	13^	9#	4	2	17	9	187
Post-cranial traits										
Fossa of Allen			30	9	3	6	5	33	27	131
Plaque formation			46	11	5	16	11	25	18	111
Exostosis in trochanteric fossa			73	13	16	25	15	19	13	81
Supracondyloid process			0	1	2	0	0	33	42	191
Septal aperture			7	9	0	4	5	36	39	167
Acetabular crease			13	6	6	9	7	18	15	176
Accessory sacral facets on ilium			9	5	8	3	3	28	24	144
Sacral spina bifida occulta	7	217								
Sixth sacral segment	49Δ	133								

Table 58 continued.

Trait	1	0	1/1	1/0	0/1	1/-	-/1	0/-	-/0	0/0
Acromial articular facet			2	2	6	3	0	42	35	122
Os acromiale			4	5	6	7	5	37	28	115
Supra-scapular foramen			1*	6^	2*	1	1	47	37	134
Vastus notch			40	5	17	15	18	19	13	57
Vastus fossa			26	13	5	5	13	27	18	76
Emarginate patella			0	3	1	1	0	32	30	118
Anterior calcaneal facet double			56	17	11	5	10	8	10	68
Anterior calcaneal facet absent			1	4	0	1	1	12	19	147
Atlas facet double			9	16	9	0	0	10	10	181
Posterior atlas bridging			9†	7^	7~	1	0	9	7	195
Lateral atlas bridging			1*	4*	1	1*	0	9	13	206

Trait score

Notes. Trait scores: 1 = trait present, 0 = trait absent, - = trait not scored due to element being defective or missing. For bilateral traits, scores given as left side/right side.

* = includes one case of partial manifestation of trait; ^ = includes 2 cases of partial manifestation of trait; ~ = includes 3 cases of partial manifestation of trait; # = includes 4 cases of partial manifestation of trait; † = includes 5 cases of partial manifestation of trait; ‡ = includes 6 cases of partial manifestation of trait; + = includes 7 cases of partial manifestation of trait; Δ = includes 11 cases of partial manifestation of trait. Sacral spina bifida occulta only scored as present if *all* sacral segments show failure of union of the neural arch at the midline.

combinations of traits ought generally to be more closely related genetically than those showing less similar combinations. The results of the cluster analysis (agglomerative hierarchical procedure, based on average linkage and a squared Euclidean distance dissimilarity coefficient) are shown in Figure 90.

The results of the cluster analysis appear to offer no evidence that individuals with similar trait combinations were regularly interred near one another in the burial area. A possible reason for the lack of spatial clustering within the churchyard of individuals with similar trait combinations might be its long period of use. Given the lack of permanent grave-markers it must have been inevitable that newly dead were interred among earlier burials whose identities and locations had long been forgotten. In an attempt to control for this, the analysis was re-run separately on the three major phase groups (Phases 1-2, 2 and 4). This procedure failed, however, to produce evidence for spatial groupings (data not shown).

The above results may indicate that there was no tendency to bury close blood-relatives or inhabitants of particular settlements in spatial groups. It should be emphasised that genetic control over non-metric variants is variable and generally fairly weak (Mays 1998, 106-10). In addition, it seems reasonable to suppose that most individuals interred at Wharram Percy were fairly closely related genetically anyway. These factors would tend to militate against spatial groupings of individuals with similar non-metric trait combinations being evident archaeologically even if spatial organisation of the burials was based to some extent on blood relationship or domicile.

Squatting facets

Habitual extreme movement at a joint promotes extension of the joint surface. Habitual extreme dorsiflexion of the ankle joints (i.e. feet fully bent upwards at the ankles), as occurs in those who adopt habitually the squatting posture, leads to anterior joint extensions at the inferior end of the tibia – squatting facets (Trinkaus 1975). Squatting facets on the distal joint surface of the tibia were scored systematically in the Wharram Percy adults. Facets were scored separately on left and right tibiae but scores were combined, as for the non-metric traits above, in order to dichotomise trait scores into simple presence or absence for individuals.

One hundred and ninety-three adults had one or both distal tibiae intact for recording the trait. Of these, 107 (55%) showed tibial squatting facets. There was no difference in prevalence according to phase. Of the 193 adults, 187 could be sexed. The results split by sex are shown in Table 59.

Table 59. Squatting facets.

	Males	Females
Squatting facets present	50	52
Squatting facets absent	62	23

The prevalence of squatting facets in females (69%) is greater than that in males (45%) (chi-square = 11.1, $p<0.001$).

The frequency of squatting facets at Wharram Percy was compared with that at 18th to 19th-century Christ Church, Spitalfields, London (Table 60).

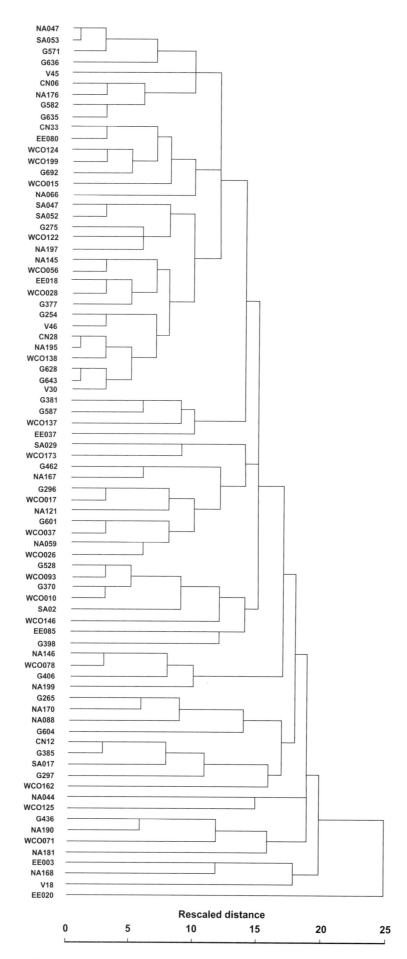

Rescaled distance

Fig. 90. Cluster analysis of non-metric data.

Table 60. Squatting facets at Wharram Percy and London Spitalfields.

	Wharram Percy	Spitalfields
Squatting facets present	107	9
Squatting facets absent	86	455

Notes: Spitalfields data courtesy of T. Molleson

The frequency of squatting facets at Spitalfields (2%) resembles that reported for recent Europeans, whereas that at Wharram Percy (55%) approaches the frequencies of 70-80% seen in recent populations known habitually to squat.

Those buried at Spitalfields were the monied middle classes of Georgian and Victorian London. They would certainly have used chairs rather than reposed in the squatting position. By contrast chairs were a rarity for the medieval peasant (Field 1965), although benches and low stools were known. It would seem that the Wharram Percy people habitually adopted postures which involved hyperdorsiflexion of the feet. The habitual adoption of squatting or similar posture, for example to attend to tasks low to the ground such as tending a fire, is the type of activity which would result in the formation of squatting facets. The sex difference would seem to suggest that women adopted the squatting posture more frequently than men. Documentary evidence suggests that in medieval peasant communities women were more involved in tasks centred around the dwelling such as caring for infants, cleaning, preparing food etc. (Bennett 1987). These tasks might be expected to have often involved working in a squatting or similar position.

Miscellaneous variants
In addition to the traits recorded above, there are a number of other anatomical variants worthy of note.

Dental variants
Hypodontia (one or more congenitally missing teeth) and localised microdontia (reduction in size of one or some few teeth) are thought to be linked phenomena and share a significant genetic component in their causation (Grahnén 1956; Graber 1978; Brook 1984). Instances of hypodontia (other than of the third molars which was included in the analysis above) and localised microdontia are tabulated in Table 61.

Twenty individuals show microdontia alone, thirteen show hypodontia only and four show both. There is no evidence of a sex bias in either condition. In both microdontia and hypodontia, the maxillary dentition is more commonly affected than the mandibular teeth. The maxillary I2 is the most commonly missing tooth, followed by the maxillary PM2. The maxillary I2 is also the most frequently reduced tooth, but reduced premolars are rare. Conversely, first and second molar teeth were on occasion found to be reduced but were never observed to be missing congenitally.

A few other dental variants, besides hypodontia and microdontia, were also observed. Fused teeth arise through the union of two normally separated tooth germs (Shafer et al. 1983, 38). There is one fairly clear example of this. The deciduous left mandibular incisors of Burial NA189 (J, 1-1½, unphased) are fused at their roots and the lower parts of the crowns. A radiograph shows that the two teeth have separate pulp chambers even though they share a single root canal.

Geminated teeth arise when there is an attempt at division during development of a single tooth germ (Shafer et al. 1983, 38). Gemination and fusion are sometimes difficult to distinguish from one another and are together referred to as double teeth (Schuurs and van Loveren 2000). The left deciduous maxillary lateral incisor of Burial NA151 (J, 4-5 , unphased) shows mesio-distal broadening of the crown and root, and the incisive edge shows a double labial convexity. The right maxillary permanent I2 of Burial NA019 (J, 8-9, unphased) shows a vertical groove on the lingual side of its root and a bucco-lingual groove on the incisive edge of the crown. It is also broader in its mesio-distal dimensions than its normal antimere. The erupted tooth counts in the maxillae are normal in each case. These examples appear to represent either gemination or else fusion between a lateral incisor and a supernumerary element.

As well as representing a possible double tooth, the crown on the left maxillary deciduous I2 of Burial NA151 (J, 4-5 years, unphased) shows a supernumerary cusp projecting lingually from the cingulum. Radiography indicates that a horn of the pulp cavity projects into the base of the extra cusp. This is an example of a rare anomaly, talon cusp (Davis and Brook 1986). This individual also shows a supernumerary element in the uneruped permanent anterior dentition in the left maxilla. This case has been discussed in detail elsewhere (Mays 2003b; Mays forthcoming a).

Four individuals (Burial CN27 (M, 40+, Phase 4), Burial G478 (F, 21-23, Phase 2), Burial NA227 (M, 22-25, Phase 1-2) and Burial V07 (?M, 13-14, Phase 4)) show enamel pearls (tiny globules of enamel) on the roots of a total of seven maxillary and one mandibular molar teeth. Enamel pearls are developmental anomalies.

Spinal variants
Spondylolysis
A cleft in the neural arch at the pars interarticularis is termed spondylolysis. In the current material, 31 vertebrae in 27 individuals showed spondylolysis (Table 62). All but one involved the lumbar spine (Table 63).

The prevalence of spondylolysis has been reported at 3-7% in modern Caucasian populations (Resnick and Niwayama 1988). It is most frequently observed in the last lumbar segment, is rare outside the lumbar region, 90% of cases are bilateral (i.e. involve both sides of the neural arch), and the condition seems more frequent in males. It is sometimes a cause of lower back pain, although it may also be symptomless (Merbs 1996). In

Table 61. Hypodontia (other than third molar) and localised microdontia.

Burial	Sex & age	Phase	Microdontia	Hypodontia
CN12	M, 25-35	4	Max I2s	-
CN27	M, 40+	4	R Max M3	-
CN31	M, 40+	4	-	L Max PM1
EE003	M, 25-35	1-2	Max M2s	-
EE027	M, 25-35	1-2	Max I2s	-
EE037	M, 40-50	1-2	-	R Max PM2
EE043	F, 25-35	1-2	Max and mand M1s	-
EE070	F, 40-50	1-2	-	L Max PM1
EE072	??F, 10	-	Max & mand M1s, Max I2s	-
G265	M, 35-45	2	-	R Max I2
G304	??M, 5-6	1	R Max M2	-
G363	J, 2¹/2	2	Dec mand Cs	Dec Max & Mand I2s, Max & Mand I2s
G438	F, 25-35	2	Max I2s	-
G443	F, 21-24	2	Max I2s	-
G500	J, 9-10	2	L Max I2	-
G635	F, 21	1-2	R Max M3	-
G643	F, 25-35	1-2	Max I2s	-
G715	M, 35-45	1-2	R Max M2	-
NA081	M, 35-45	1-2	-	L Max PM2
NA088	F, 40-50	1-2	R Max M3	-
NA100	M?, 40-50	1-2	Max I2s	-
NA105	??M, 13	-	Max I2s	-
NA111	J, 6-7	-	-	L Max PM1
NA145	F?, 25-35	1-2	-	L Max I2
NA154	M?, 18	1-2	Max & mand Cs, max PM1s, mand PM1s & PM2s	Max PM2s
NA167	F, 25-35	2	Mand M3s, R Max M3	-
NA173	F, 21-25	1-2	R Max I2	R Mand PM2
NA176	M, 25	2	Max I2s	-
NA198	?M, 11-12	-	-	R Max I2
NA218	M, 50+	1-2	-	L Mand I2
SA017	F, 21-25	4	-	R Max PM2
SA030	M, 30-40	-	Max I2s	-
V33	F, 35-45	-	R Max I2	-
V42	M, 40-60	4	L Max I2	R Max I2
V62	F, 35-45	-	-	R Max I2
WCO093	F, 21-25	-	-	R Mand PM2
WCO173	F, 40-50	-	-	Max PM1s

Notes: Sex, M=male, F=female, J=unsexed juvenile, ?? denotes sex inferred from craniofacial morphology in juveniles; Age, estimated age in years; Microdontia and hypodontia, all entries refer to permanent dentition unless stated, Max = maxillary, Mand = mandibular, Dec = deciduous

128

Table 62. Spondylolysis.

Burial	Sex & age	Phase	Level	Spondylolysis Bi- or unilateral	Olisthesis
EE003	M, 25-35	1-2	L6	u	No
EE018	F, 21	1-2	L3	b	No
			L4	b	No
EE080	M, 25-35	2	L5	b	No
G275A	F, 25-35	2	L5	b	No
G528	M, 19-21	2	L1	u	No
G565	M?, ADULT	2	L6	b	No
G746	M, 30-50	1-2	L3	u	No
			L4	b	No
G747	F, 21-30	1-2	L4	b	No
NA006	F, 40-50	1-2	L5	u	Yes
NA033	F, 50+	1-2	L5	u	No
NA146	M, 40-50	1-2	L5	b	No
NA157	F, ADULT	1-2	L5	b	No
NA166	M, ADULT	1-2	L4	b	No
NA168	M?, 50+	1-2	L3	b	Yes
NA176	M, 25	2	L4, L5	b	No
NA181	M, 50+	1-2	L5	b	No
NA197	M, 50+	1-2	L5	b	No
NA205	J, 15-18	-	L5	b	No
NA218	M, 50+	1-2	L5	b	No
NA227	M, 22-25	1-2	L5	b	No
SA034	M, 50+	1	L4	b	-
V15	M, 50+	-	L6	b	No
WCO011	J, 11-12	-	L5	b	No
WCO059	M, 50+	-	T12	u	No
WCO093	F, 21-25	-	L5	b	No
WCO130	F, 50+	2-3	L4	b	No
			L5	b	No
WCO174	M, 22-24	-	L5	b	No

Notes: Sex, M=male, F=female, J=unsexed juvenile; Age: estimated age at death, in years unless stated; Level, vertebra(e) showing defect(s); Bi- or unilateral indicates whether one or both sides of the neural arch are affected, u=unilateral lesion, b=bilateral lesion; Olisthesis=forward slippage of body of affected vertebra (see text).

the current material, 25 adults show the condition out of 258 who have at least one lumbar vertebra neural arch present for observation, a prevalence rate of 10% (if the prevalence rate is calculated using only those adult individuals with a complete complement of lumbar vertebra neural arches present for inspection then the frequency is 24/201=12%). The frequency in the Wharram Percy group is higher than that reported in modern Caucasians (frequency in Wharram Percy adults with complete lumbar spines versus a modern frequency taken as 5%: chi-square = 20.6, p<0.001). In terms of favoured location in the spine, the Wharram Percy data

Table 63. Spondylolysis by spinal segment.

Vertebra	No.
T12	1
L1	1
L2	0
L3	3
L4	7
L5	16
L6	3

seem to match expectations based on the literature. There is no evidence of any sex difference in prevalence.

The prevailing view seems to be that the primary lesion in spondylolysis is a fatigue failure of the neural arch but that there is in some instances a genetic predisposition in the form of anatomical features which increase the risk of arch failure (Merbs 1996). When the defect is observed unilaterally, it appears that, in some instances, such cases are in fact partially healed bilateral lesions (Wiltse *et al.* 1975). Conversely, unilateral defects have also been observed to develop into bilateral ones (Fredrickson *et al.* 1984). In the six unilateral cases from Wharram Percy there is no evidence for callus formation on the intact side of the arch, so it seems unlikely that in the present material unilateral cases represent partially healed bilateral lesions. Perhaps they represent lesions which might potentially have progressed to bilateral defects.

In life, the defect at the pars interarticularis is bridged by strong connective tissue, however, should this soft tissue rupture, forward slippage (olisthesis) of the vertebral body may take place, a condition known as spondylolisthesis. In skeletal remains, olisthesis may be manifested by periosteal reactive bone formation on the anterior wall of the slipped vertebral body or its neighbours as a result of activation of the periosteum (Ortner and Putschar 1985, 358). Two cases from Wharram Percy show evidence for spondylolisthesis (Table 62). In one instance the defect at the pars interarticularis was unilateral but was accompanied by a cleft pedicle on the contra-lateral side. In the other, the defect at the pars interarticularis was bilateral. In the latter case, the individual in question showed severe unilateral osteoarthritis of the right hip. Perhaps this is causally associated with the spondylolysis, but whether the hip osteoarthritis developed in response to an altered gait consequent to the spinal problem or whether an abnormal gait induced by the hip osteoarthritis precipitated fatigue failure of the arch is unclear.

At Wharram Percy, spondylolysis is nearly three times as frequent in those showing a sixth lumbar vertebra than in those with the normal complement of five (29% vs 11%), but the small numbers involved mean that the difference fails to attain statistical significance. An association has been reported between spondylolysis and spina bifida occulta (e.g. Roche and Rowe 1951; Eisenstein 1978; Fredrickson *et al.* 1984). No such association was present in the Wharram Percy material.

Spina bifida occulta in the pre-sacral vertebrae
Spina bifida is a cleft in the neural arch at the midline. In spina bifida cystica there is herniation of spinal cord and meninges through the defect. Cleft neural arch with no neural tube defect is often known as spina bifida occulta. This is a symptomless defect which in life would have been bridged by fibrous tissue. Spina bifida cystica was not observed at Wharram Percy. Spina bifida occulta was scored systematically for the sacrum where the frequency of the defect, regarded as present only if all five sacral

segments were affected, was 3% in adults (Table 58). Instances of spina bifida occulta in the pre-sacral vertebrae are detailed in Table 64.

Table 64. Spina bifida occulta in the pre-sacral vertebrae.

Burial	Sex and age	Phase	Vertebra
CN05	M, 50+	4	C1
EE006	??F, 7-8	-	C1
EE062	M, 30-40	1-2	C1
G303	M, 30-40	1-2	L6
G314	J, 5-6	1-2	L5
NA002	??F, 11	1-2	L6
NA025	??F, 5-6	-	L4
NA033	F, 50+	1-2	L5
NA088	F, 40-50	1-2	C1
NA095	??F, 9	-	C1
NA105	??M, 13	-	L5
NA120	J, 6	-	C4, L4, L5
NA235	M?, 17-24	1-2	C2
V15	M, 50+	-	L6
WCO011	J, 11-12	-	L5

Notes: Sex, M=male, F=female, J=unsexed juvenile ?? denotes sex inferred from craniofacial morphology in juveniles; Age: estimated age at death, in years unless stated

Spina bifida occulta appears to reflect both genetic and non-genetic factors, although the relative importance of each has yet to be determined (Papp and Porter 1994). In modern populations, defects in the pre-sacral vertebrae are most common in the last lumbar vetebra, where the frequency is about 1-2% (Schmorl and Junghanns 1971, 84), and the first cervical vertebra, in which Barnes (1994, 120) states that clefts are found in about 5% of adults. At Wharram Percy there does indeed seem to be a predilection for involvement of the last lumbar and first cervical vertebra, however, the frequency in the latter does not reach the heights cited by Barnes for modern adults – the prevalence among Wharram Percy adults is three out of 241 individuals for whom C1 is preserved, a frequency of just over 1%.

Tortuous vertebral artery
The vertebral arteries run through the transverse foramina of the cervical vertebrae, generally C1-C6. The artery may, on occasion, be abnormally coiled or looped where it passes through a vertebral transverse foramen. These tortuosities are considered anatomical variants of arterial form. They may cause pressure defects on the vertebral bone (Brahee and Guebert 2000; Waldron and Antoine 2002). There are two possible examples of this in the current material. Burial G385 (F, 35-45, Phase 2) shows a small (7mm deep), smooth-walled cavity in the right side of the body of the fourth cervical vertebra at the foramen

for the vertebral artery. A similar lesion is present in Burial WCO179 (F, 40+, Phase 1-2) on the left side of the body of the sixth cervical vertebra, also at the foramen for the vertebral artery (Plate 20). The lesion in Burial WCO179 is the deeper of the two, undermining the vertebral body for about half its width, eroding the anterior part of the pedicle, and enlarging the transverse foramen.

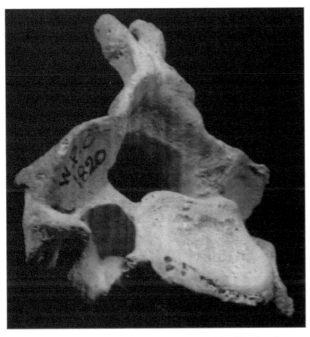

Plate 20. Sixth cervical vertebra, Burial WCO179, showing an erosion in the left side of its body at the transverse foramen, probably due to tortuosity of the vertebral artery.

Cranio-caudal border shifts in the presacral vertebral column
In cranio-caudal border shifts, a vertebra at the border between two different spinal regions takes on the character of an adjacent vertebra in the neighbouring region (Barnes 1994, 79). The lumbo-sacral region is the most frequent site of border shifts. For example, a cranial shift in this region causes partial or complete sacralisation of the last lumbar vertebra so that the sacrum has six instead of the usual five segments. The presence of a sixth sacral segment was scored systematically in the current material, and among adults had a frequency of 27% (Table 58).

In addition to shifts at the lumbo-sacral border, the current material showed evidence for caudal shifting at the occipito-cervical border, resulting in occipitalisation of the atlas vertebra, cranial shifting at the cervico-thoracic border, resulting in cervical ribs on C7, and caudal shifting at the thoraco-lumbar border resulting in lumbar ribs on L1.

There were three examples of occipitalisation of the atlas vertebra (Burials EE073, G438 and NA150). Three

individuals showed cervical ribs, Burials G528 and WCO134, where the ribs were present bilaterally, and Burial NA227 where a left cervical rib was accompanied by an elongated transverse process on the right side of C7. In addition, the C7s of Burials NA115 and NA170 showed elongated left and right transverse processes respectively. An elongated transverse process might be considered a rudimentary cervical rib (Barnes 1994). Lumbar ribs were more common than cervical ribs, occurring in ten individuals. In five cases they are present bilaterally, in three unilaterally; in two instances the material was too damaged to ascertain this.

Block vertebrae
Failure of segmentation during spinal development results in block vertebrae – two or some few vertebrae showing bony union. The occurrence of such defects appears to have a genetic component in its causation (Barnes 1994). Twelve individuals showed block vertebrae (Table 65).

The frequency of block vertebrae is 12/591 in the whole assemblage or 9/304 among adults (denominators are individuals with two or more vertebrae present for study).

Table 65. Block vertebrae.

Burial	Sex & age	Phase	Vertebrae	Site of union
EE015	F, 60+	1-2	T2 & 3	f
EE046	M, 40-50	1-2	C2 & 3	fc
			T3-5	fc
EE079	M, ADULT	2	C2 & 3	f
EE080	M, 35-45	2	C6 & 7	cn
G438	F, 25-35	2	T3 & 4	cn
NA116	J, 2½	-	C2 & 3	fn
NA120	J, 6	-	C3 & 4	fn
NA150	J, 4-5 months	-	2 mid-thoracic vertebrae	fn
NA217	M, 50+	2	C2 & 3	fnc
SA015	M, 50+	-	C5 & 6	nc
SA023	F, 60+	4	T4 & 5	fnc
WCO203	M, ADULT	-	3 mid-thoracic vertebrae	fc

Notes: site of union: parts of vertebrae which show bony union, f=facet joints, n=neural arches, c=centra

Miscellaneous variants
Irregular segmentation of ribs
Two individuals show fused ribs (Burials EE071 and G576). In each, two adjacent middle ribs are united by a bony bridge near their sternal ends. Two individuals (Burials EE039 and WCO144) each show a rib bifurcated at its sternal end.

Tarsal coalitions

Nine individuals show coalitions involving the tarsal bones. None showed bony ankylosis, in all instances the presence of adjacent rough, porotic surfaces indicated soft tissue union. Tarsal coalitions arise when two adjacent bones fail to separate during intra-uterine development (Regan *et al.* 1999). There is a genetic component in their causation (Leonard 1974). At Wharram Percy, six cases involve coalition between the third metatarsal and the lateral cuneiform, one involved the cuboid and the navicular, and two the calcaneus and the navicular. Of these, the calcaneo-navicular coalitions (Burials SA029 and WCO156) are most likely to have been symptomatic. In clinical practice, calcaneo-navicular coalitions are recognised as a cause of a form of painful flat foot called peroneal spastic flatfoot (Chambers 1950).

Bathrocrany

Protrusion of the occipital bone, with a pronounced step in the region of the lambdoid suture, is known as bathrocrany. Its cause appears to be premature synostosis of the posterior part of the sagittal suture (Lin *et al.* 1998). At Wharram Percy there are six fairly clear examples of this (Burials G406, G587, SA023, SA052, WCO010 and WCO146). In five cases the deformity was accompanied by multiple ossicles in the lambdoid suture. In addition to these fairly unequivocal examples, a number of other crania with slight degrees of bathrocrany were also noted, however when its expression is slight, objective scoring of the trait becomes somewhat problematic. Although the trait was not scored systematically, there were 291 adults with complete or partial crania, and if this total is used as the denominator this gives an estimated frequency of 2%. Most recent osteological reports do not report bathrocrany, perhaps because it is considered unimportant. Some studies, particularly those by early workers, do present frequency data for the trait. In large series of medieval crania its frequency has been reported at 1% (St Saviour, Bermondsey – Connell and White forthcoming), 6% (Rothwell, Northamptonshire – Parsons 1910) and 9% (Hythe, Kent – Parsons 1908). Bathrocrany has also been noted in between 1% and 11% of crania from various 17th-century sites in London (MacDonell 1904; 1906; Hooke 1926; White 2002), and in 18% of crania from 16th to 19th-century Ensay, Scotland (Miles 1989).

Dermoid cysts

Burial NA178 (?M, 17, unphased) shows an approximately circular depression, about 28mm diameter in the cranium on the coronal suture (Plate 21). Ectocranially, the edges slope down to a flat area of thin bone which forms the floor of the lesion. The lesion floor is perforated along the line of the coronal suture. There is no pitting or any other sign of infection. The morphology of the lesion is suggestive of the presence of a dermoid cyst (Barnes 1994, 56-7). During embryonic development,

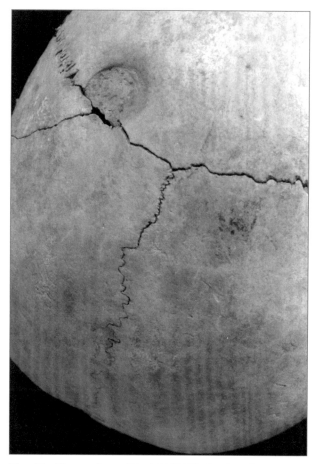

Plate 21. The cranium of Burial NA178. On the left side of the coronal suture lies a depression, approximately 3cm in diameter, with bevelled margins and a flat central floor. The lesion is suggestive of a dermoid cyst.

some surface ectodermal cells (which will form skin and associated structures) may occasionally become trapped in underlying mesenchymal tissue (which ultimately goes on to form, among other things, bone). The result is a cyst containing the various components of dermoid tissue (epithelium, hair follicles, sweat glands, etc) (Barnes 1994, 56). The lesion may develop in the cranial diploe, particularly where two cranial bones meet. The skeletal manifestation is a rounded depression with a thin floor. Another possible example is seen in Burial WCO131 (male, aged 50+, unphased). There is perforation of the occipital bone just to the right of the midline. The lesion is rounded with a maximum diameter of 13mm. The diameter of the lesion is greatest within the diploe. The internal surfaces are of fairly smooth cortical bone. There is no bony reaction or signs of infection. Dermoid cysts are rarely reported in palaeopathology: Barnes (1994) indicates only one published case.

Finally, mention should be made of an unusual anomaly in Burial WCO139 (M, 45-55, Phase 2). There appears to be a failure of formation of most of the maxillary part of the floor of the left orbit. Only the lateral-most part seems to be present, although post-depositional damage means that it is impossible to assess fully the extent of the dysplasia.

10 Dental and Oral Disease

This chapter, and the two which follow, detail the main pathological conditions identified in the study material. The pathological changes evident on a skeleton are to a great extent a cumulative record of the insults suffered during life; the greater the age at death the more years over which the individual was at risk of acquiring skeletal disease or injury. In addition, with regard to disease, it is generally only the more chronic conditions which manifest on the skeleton. Therefore, other factors being equal, assemblages with overall older ages at death will tend to show greater frequencies of most skeletal lesions. It is difficult to control for this directly in comparisons of disease prevalences between Wharram Percy and those reported for other assemblages because of the variety of different adult ageing techniques used by earlier workers and the unreliability of many of these methods. Efforts are made to control for differences in age structure when making internal comparisons within the Wharram Percy assemblage.

Dental caries, ante-mortem tooth loss and dental abscesses

Methods

Caries was scored as present or absent in each tooth, and as present or absent in individuals with one or more erupted teeth present for study. The location of caries cavities on the molar teeth was recorded into one of five categories: on the root surface, at the cemento-enamel junction, on the occlusal surface, on the side of the enamel crown (whether on inter-proximal, buccal or lingual sides) or as gross, where carious destruction of the tooth was too far advanced to determine where the lesion had originated.

Ante-mortem tooth loss was scored on a presence-absence basis for each erupted tooth position, and as present or absent in individuals with one or more erupted tooth positions available for study. Periapical abscess cavities in alveolar bone were scored in a similar fashion. Periapical cavities in alveolar bone, generally referred to by osteologists as 'abscess cavities', form not in response to acute dental abscess but rather to chronic, long-term inflammation (Dias and Tayles 1997).

Results

Dental caries
Among the juveniles, 31 of 194 individuals with one or more erupted teeth present for study showed cavities in one or more teeth. The results for adults are shown in Tables 66-9.

Chi-square tests indicate no evidence for any difference in prevalence of dental caries in terms of its presence/absence in individuals with respect to sex or phase. Turning to frequencies with respect to total teeth, the prevalence rates for males and females are almost identical, but there is a suggestion of a higher frequency in Phase 4 compared with earlier material (Table 68).

Statistical evaluation of this pattern is problematic as data quantified with respect to total teeth are not amenable to standard inferential statistical tests because teeth in a given individual do not constitute independent observations for statistical purposes.

Comparisons of caries prevalences at Wharram Percy with selected other sites are shown in Table 70.

Ante-mortem tooth loss
Of 190 juveniles with one or more erupted tooth positions present for study, four showed ante-mortem tooth loss due to disease. Results for adults are shown in Tables 71-3.

Frequency of ante-mortem tooth loss expressed with respect to observable tooth positions is not amenable to standard statistical analyses since tooth positions within a given mouth do not constitute independent observations for analytical purposes. Chi-square tests indicate no evidence for any difference in frequency of ante-mortem tooth loss, scored as present or absent in individuals, between males and females. There is a difference, however, between phases (chi-square=8.89, 2df, p<0.025), with the condition being more frequent in Phase 4. In Chapter 7 it was indicated that there is no difference in the distribution of adult ages at death between the different phases of the site. However, considering only those adults scored for ante-mortem tooth loss, Phase 4 contained a greater proportion of adults aged over 50 years than the other phases. Ante-mortem tooth loss is strongly age-progressive (Mays 2002), so its greater prevalence in Phase 4 burials may simply reflect the greater age at death among those in this phase scored for the condition.

Dental abscesses
Of 190 juveniles with one or more erupted tooth position present for study, six showed periapical abscess cavities. Results for adults are shown in Tables 74-6.

There is no significant variation in frequency of dental abscesses according to sex or phase.

Discussion

Bacterial breakdown of carbohydrate residues in the mouth produces the acids responsible for caries cavities. Non-carbohydrate food residues do not form acidic breakdown products so are non-cariogenic. Sugars are the most cariogenic foods. Although small amounts of sugar began to be imported into England from the 12th century onwards, sugar in the medieval period was a scarce luxury and its consumption was too low to make an impact on population-level caries rates (Moore and Corbett 1978). The only widely available sweetening agent in the medieval period was honey. Starches were the principal dietary carbohydrate. Although not directly cariogenic, if residues of starchy foods are retained in the mouth (as must have been the case prior to modern standards of oral hygiene), they are broken down into highly cariogenic low molecular weight carbohydrates by enzymatic action. Therefore, even before the introduction of refined sugars, carbohydrate foods would have been

Table 66. Prevalence of dental caries in the adult permanent dentition.

	Individuals			Total teeth		
	Present	Absent	Total	Present	Absent	Total
Males	110	52	162	283	2381	2664
Females	79	38	117	205	1890	2095
Total adults	190	90	280	492	4276	4768

Note: figures for total adults include data from one unsexed adult

Table 67. Distribution of dental caries in the adult permanent dentition.

	Maxilla															
	Left								Right							
	M3	M2	M1	PM2	PM1	C	I2	I1	I1	I2	C	PM1	PM2	M1	M2	M3
Total teeth	89	137	130	158	158	171	123	106	109	125	164	159	153	142	130	92
Carious teeth	23	40	25	17	14	5	4	1	0	2	4	12	11	28	29	26
Total teeth	130	174	160	187	196	192	160	119	126	158	192	187	178	159	180	124
Carious teeth	29	34	35	15	8	4	0	0	0	3	6	3	8	35	39	32
	Mandible															

Table 68. Prevalence of dental caries in the adult permanent dentition, data split by phase.

	Individuals				Total teeth			
	Present	Absent	Total	Prevalence (%)	Present	Absent	Total	Prevalence (%)
Phase 1-2	86	39	125	68.8	214	2169	2383	9.0
Phase 2	28	9	37	75.7	78	703	781	10.0
Phase 4	19	7	26	73.1	57	248	305	18.7

Table 69. Location of caries cavities on molar teeth.

Location	Phase 1-2		Phase 2		Phase 4		All adults	
	N	%	N	%	N	%	N	%
Root	7	4.1	1	1.5	2	5.4	14	3.7
Cemento-enamel junction	81	47.4	36	54.5	13	35.1	161	42.9
Occlusal	31	18.1	15	22.7	11	29.8	92	24.5
Side of crown	12	7.0	3	4.5	2	5.4	22	5.9
Gross	40	23.4	11	16.7	9	24.3	86	22.9
Total	171		66		37		375	

Notes: figures for all adults include unphased material

Table 70. Dental caries prevalence comparisons with other large archaeological assemblages.

Site	Date	Individuals +	-	Prev.	Total teeth +	-	Prev.	Source
East Yorkshire sites								
Yorkshire Arras Culture	4th-1st-century BC	-	-	-	98	5114	2%	Stead (1991)
York, Trentholme Drive	2nd-4th-century AD	102	119	46%	192	3714	5%	Cooke and Rowbotham (1968)
Norton, Cleveland	AD 520-620	18	45	29%	54	1271	4%	Marlow (1992)
West Heslerton†	5th-7th-century AD	19	104	15%	41	1682	2%	Cox (1999)
York Fishergate, period 4	11th-12th-century AD	23	37	38%	59	1347	4%	Stroud (1993)
Wharram Percy	AD 950-1850	190	90	68%	492	4276	10%	-
York St Helen-on-the-Walls	AD 950-1550	-	-	-	345	5311	6%	Dawes and Magilton (1980)
York, Jewbury†	13th-century AD	195	133	59%	-	-	-	Stroud et al. (1994)
York Fishergate, period 6	13th-16th-century AD	103	53	66%	356	2589	12%	Stroud (1993)
Other medieval sites								
Rural								
North Elmham Park	11th-century AD	-	-	-	102	1475	6%	Wells (1980)
Raunds, Northants.	10th-11th-century AD	-	-	-	142	3108	4%	Powell (1996)
Clopton, Cambs.	12th-14th-century AD	-	-	-	95	695	12%	Tattersall (1968b)
Rivenhall, Essex	9th-19th-century AD	-	-	-	203	1013	17%	O'Connor (1993)
Urban								
Ipswich, School Street	10th-11th-century AD	26	21	55%	68	612	10%	Mays (1989)
St Nicholas Shambles, London	11th-12th-century AD	-	-	40%	-	-	6%	White (1988b)
Trondheim, Norway	AD 1100-1600	18	127	12%	33	2257	1%	Mays (1998b)
Post-medieval sites								
London	17th-century AD	-	-	-	132	659	17%	Hardwick (1960)
Gothenburg, Sweden	17th-century AD	38	25	60%	106	810	12%	Lingström and Borrman (1999)
Sevenoaks, Kent	AD 1550-1875	26	32	45%	113	690	14%	Boyle and Keevill (1998)
Spitalfields, London	AD 1729-1852	64	6	91%	311	1316	19%	Whittaker (1993)
Zwolle, Netherlands	AD 1819-1828	72	8	90%	290	1172	20%	Mays (1996b)
Red Cross Way, London	19th-century AD	31	8	79%	161	460	26%	Brickley and Miles (1999)

Notes: adults only except † = includes some juveniles; + = caries present, - = caries absent, prev. = prevalence

Table 71. Prevalence of ante-mortem tooth loss in the adult dentition.

	Individuals			Total tooth positions		
	Present	Absent	Total	Present	Absent	Total
Males	103	58	161	692	3434	4126
Females	65	50	115	427	2631	3058
Total adults	169	108	277	1120	6075	7195

Note: figures for total adults include data from one unsexed adult

Table 72. Distribution of ante-mortem tooth loss in the adult dentition.

				Maxilla												
				Left								Right				
	M3	M2	M1	PM2	PM1	C	I2	I1	I1	I2	C	PM1	PM2	M1	M2	M3
Tooth posns	174	216	223	219	220	224	222	220	216	215	218	210	216	220	213	176
A-m loss	49	61	75	32	23	13	21	17	16	12	8	20	30	64	66	56
Tooth posns	201	252	250	245	243	244	243	243	244	243	245	234	237	239	238	192
A-m loss	51	63	78	26	12	10	17	27	29	16	10	18	26	73	54	47
				Mandible												

Table 73. Prevalence of ante-mortem tooth loss in the adult dentition, data split by phase.

	Individuals				Total tooth positions			
	Present	Absent	Total	Prevalence (%)	Present	Absent	Total	Prevalence (%)
Phase 1-2	71	50	121	58.7	430	2798	3228	13.3
Phase 2	19	18	37	51.4	77	935	1012	7.6
Phase 4	24	4	28	85.7	181	514	695	26.0

Table 74. Prevalence of alveolar abscesses in the adult dentition.

	Individuals			Total tooth positions		
	Present	Absent	Total	Present	Absent	Total
Males	94	67	161	309	3817	4126
Females	61	54	115	168	2890	3058
Total adults	156	121	277	478	6717	7195

Note: figures for total adults include data from one unsexed adult

Table 75. Distribution of alveolar abscesses in the adult dentition.

				Maxilla												
				Left								Right				
	M3	M2	M1	PM2	PM1	C	I2	I1	I1	I2	C	PM1	PM2	M1	M2	M3
Tooth posns	174	216	223	219	220	224	222	220	216	215	218	210	216	220	213	176
Alv. abscess	12	22	38	25	21	7	7	2	5	6	6	22	29	36	33	15
Tooth posns	201	252	250	245	243	244	243	243	244	243	245	234	237	239	238	192
Alv. abscess	7	16	34	9	12	5	5	5	5	8	4	7	10	30	17	18
				Mandible												

Table 76. Prevalence of alveolar abscesses in the adult permanent dentition, data split by phase.

	Individuals				Total tooth positions			
	Present	Absent	Total	Prevalence (%)	Present	Absent	Total	Prevalence (%)
Phase 1-2	65	56	121	53.7	173	3055	3228	5.4
Phase 2	23	14	37	62.2	70	942	1012	6.9
Phase 4	21	7	28	75.0	53	642	695	7.6

136

potentially cariogenic, and diets that relied to a large extent on carbohydrate-rich plant foods will have tended to be more cariogenic than those which placed more emphasis on animal products (Mays 1998, 149-55).

The caries prevalence at Wharram Percy seems to be somewhat greater than those reported for earlier east Yorkshire material, but is fairly similar to frequencies in other medieval assemblages (Table 70). The cariogenicity of Wharram Percy diets differed little from that of contemporary English rural communities.

In a survey of British skeletal material dating from the Iron Age to the late 19th century, Moore and Corbett (1978; 1983) found evidence for a marked increase in the prevalence of caries from about the 17th century, a trend which accelerated during the later post-medieval period. They interpreted this as reflecting the increasing importance of sugar in British diets. The post-medieval material examined by Moore and Corbett was from urban sites, and more recent work has tended to support their findings, urban assemblages from the late post-medieval period tending to show high caries frequencies (Table 70). At present it is unclear whether this trend also applies to rural populations. The evidence from Wharram Percy is equivocal in this respect. On the one hand, the prevalence of dental caries with respect to total teeth is somewhat greater among Phase 4 burials than in earlier material (Table 68), it resembles those reported for other post-medieval assemblages and is greater than those generally found for medieval groups (Table 70). The statistical validity of the secular trend within the Wharram Percy data cannot readily be determined, and the observation that there is no concomitant rise in the prevalence with respect to individuals affected suggests that it may simply be a chance finding.

In modern Western populations, the most favoured sites for carious attack are the occlusal surfaces of the posterior dentition. Modern diets are insufficiently abrasive to scour these surfaces clear of food residues and to remove the pits and fissures which act as foci for decay. Studies of skeletal remains (e.g. Moore and Corbett 1978; 1983) indicate that, prior to the 17th century, the pattern was rather different, with the cemento-enamel junction the favoured site for lesions. This change in caries pattern is probably connected with alterations in dietary consistency. The coarse diets which were universal up to the 17th century meant that dental wear was heavy. As well as scouring the occlusal surfaces clear of food residues and obliterating pits and fissures, this meant that teeth continued to erupt from their sockets throughout life in order to maintain occlusion in the face of continuing loss of crown height. This would have exposed the tooth necks to the oral environment and increased the inter-tooth spaces facilitating the retention there of food residues. Softening of diets in the 17th century due to changes in food-preparation techniques, especially in bread-making, meant that for urban groups at least, the distribution of caries cavities began to move toward the modern pattern (Moore and Corbett 1983).

For all periods at Wharram Percy, the most frequent site of carious attack on the molar teeth is the cemento-enamel junction (Table 69). The post-medieval results here contrast with those of Moore and Corbett (1978; 1983) and other, more recent studies of post-medieval urban groups (Whittaker and Molleson 1996; Lingström and Borrman 1999; Mays 1996b), which report the occlusal surface to be the favoured site of attack.

Although the cemento-enamel junction continues to be the most frequent site of carious attack even in Phase 4, there is nevertheless a rise in the proportion of occlusal cavities and a decline in the proportion of those at the cemento-enamel junction in burials from this period (Table 69). This may indicate that a shift of a similar type to that seen in urban material is taking place here, albeit to a reduced extent. This cannot be confirmed statistically. It should also be mentioned that numbers of individuals, especially for Phase 4, are small, and the proportion of gross cavities, where caries is too far advanced to determine the point of origin of the lesion, is high. These factors further cloud the picture. That dietary consistency may change relatively less over time at Wharram Percy than is the case in many urban populations is supported by the observations that dental wear continues to be heavy in post-medieval burials (although precise observations of its rate are difficult to make due to the lack of a valid independent adult ageing technique) and that there is no reduction in the robusticity of the jaws.

Dental caries, diseases of the periodontal tissues, and heavy dental wear with consequent continued eruption of teeth and weakening of support for them in the jaws, are important causes of ante-mortem tooth loss in earlier populations. Chronic periapical abscesses are generally caused by exposure of the dental pulp to the oral environment, either due to dental caries, trauma to the tooth, or excessive attrition. Figures from other medieval rural sites for ante-mortem tooth loss (expressed with respect to total observable tooth positions) are 11.1% (North Elmham Park), 11.7% (Raunds) and 17.9% (Clopton), compared with 16.8% at Wharram Percy. For alveolar abscesses the figures are 2.0% for North Elmham Park and 9.2% for Clopton, compared with 6.6% at Wharram Percy. As with the caries data, the frequencies of ante-mortem tooth loss and alveolar abscess cavities at Wharram Percy are within the ranges reported for other medieval samples, albeit toward the higher ends (for further comparative data see Roberts and Manchester 1995, tables 4.2 and 4.3).

Dental calculus

Dental calculus is a concretion on the teeth which may be considered as mineralised dental plaque. It is associated with poor oral hygiene. It was scored in the current material using the scale of Dobney and Brothwell (1987) (Tables 77-8).

Table 77. Dental calculus.

	Degree of development				
	0	1	2	3	4
Male adults	18	88	32	20	0
Female adults	11	61	31	5	2
All adults	29	149	63	26	2
Juveniles	145	37	6	0	0

Note: figures for total adults include data from one unsexed adult

Table 78. Dental calculus data for adults, split by phase.

	Degree of development				
	0	1	2	3	4
Phase 1-2	8	73	28	13	1
Phase 2	2	19	12	4	0
Phase 4	6	13	3	1	0

There is no evidence for any association between the degree of calculus development and sex or phase. Deposits are, however, greater and more frequent in adult than in juvenile dentitions, presumably reflecting the greater time for deposits to accumulate in adults. Calculus deposits tend to fall off rather easily during cleaning and handling of skeletal remains, and most of the current material was excavated three decades before it reached the present author for examination. The frequency and extent of development of calculus deposits in the Wharram Percy dentitions is, almost certainly, an underestimate of its true prevalence due to post-excavation losses of deposits.

Dental enamel hypoplasias

Methods
Dental enamel hypoplasias (DEH) appear as transverse bands of depressed (or less commonly, pitted) enamel. DEH represent disturbances to the formation of the enamel crown, generally as a result of disease or poor nutrition. They thus represent a record of poor conditions during childhood. In general, anterior teeth tend to show hypoplasias more frequently than does the posterior dentition (Goodman and Armelagos 1985). In the current material, although defects were on occasion noted in the posterior teeth, they were only recorded systematically in the anterior dentition. No linear dental enamel hypoplasias were seen in the deciduous dentition. In the permanent dentition, individuals with at least one complete incisor or canine enamel crown were scored for dental enamel hypoplasias (thus young individuals where all anterior tooth crowns were incompletely formed, and older individuals where all were heavily worn, were excluded).

The anterior dentition potentially records DEH which formed in the period from approximately one to six years old (Reid and Dean 2000). A more precise estimate of the age at which a DEH formed was obtained from its position on the tooth. Usually when defects were present on one anterior tooth they were also visible on other elements of the anterior dentition in locations suggesting that they were caused by the same event(s). In each individual, one tooth was selected for measuring the location of defects. If not all anterior teeth showed the same number of DEH, the dental element showing the most lines was selected. If, as was generally the case, several teeth showed the same number of defects, then their location was measured on the tooth which showed them most clearly. The age at formation for each DEH was then estimated using the methodology of Reid and Dean (2000). Briefly, crown heights of ten unerupted (and hence unworn) teeth of each anterior tooth type were measured and the mean crown height of each tooth type calculated. The mean crown height was divided into ten equal parts. For each DEH, its location in terms of distance from the cemento-enamel junction was used to determine into which decile of mean crown height it fell. This permitted its approximate age at formation to be estimated using the schedule presented by Reid and Dean (2000).

Results
Frequency

Table 79. Frequency of dental enamel hypoplasias.

	Number of lines				
	0	1	2	3	4
Males	75	30	9	7	1
Females	70	16	5	1	0
All adults	145	46	14	8	1
Juveniles	70	15	7	2	0
Total	215	61	21	10	1

Notes: table cells are numbers of individuals

The frequency with which males and females show one or more lines differs significantly (chi-square = 5.1, p=0.024), with males more often showing defects (39% against 24%). There is no difference in the frequency with which adults and juveniles show DEH (Table 79), nor is there any patterning with respect to phase.

A number of interpretations may be suggested for the finding of a greater frequency of DEH in males. Some (e.g. Arcini 1999) have emphasised that DEH only occur when individuals recover from episodes of arrested crown formation, and suggest that an increased frequency of defects may indicate an increased capacity to overcome disease, perhaps implying better living conditions. This interpretation cannot apply to the patterning seen in the current data. In this study all individuals scored for DEH survived the period of crown formation (and indeed those for which sex was determined survived into adulthood); those without DEH lived through it without suffering events which led to DEH formation, those with defects did suffer such events. The greater prevalence of defects in males either reflects a greater predisposition of males towards expression of DEH or poorer childhood conditions for boys. It appears that males display a greater vulnerability to growth perturbations during development (Stinson 1985; Tanner 1989). A recent review (Guatelli-Steinberg and Lukacs 1999) indicates that any influence on DEH frequency is probably minor. The best interpretation of the sex difference may be that (if the evidence from the cohort who survived to adulthood is anything to go by) males suffered poorer conditions than females during early childhood.

Age at formation
The distribution of age at formation of all DEH (138 defects) and of the first DEH in each individual (N=93) are shown in Tables 80 and 81.

Table 80. Distribution of age at formation for all DEH.

| | Age (years) | | | | |
	1-1.99	2-2.99	3-3.99	4-4.99	5-5.99
Males	1	9	37	23	3
Females	0	7	10	10	2
All adults	1	16	47	33	5
Juveniles	0	17	12	5	1
Total	2	33	59	38	6

Table 81. Distribution of age at formation of the first DEH in each individual.

| | Age (years) | | | | |
	1-1.99	2-2.99	3-3.99	4-4.99	5-5.99
Males	1	9	24	13	0
Females	0	7	10	5	0
All adults	1	16	34	18	0
Juveniles	0	15	6	3	0
Total	1	31	40	21	0

The age at formation for all defects appears to show a unimodal distribution with a peak centred at about three to four years of age. In the anterior dentition, there is evidence that the middle parts of tooth crowns have a general tendency to display greater numbers of hypoplastic defects than apical or cervical parts (Goodman and Armelagos 1985). In the current material, it was the canine teeth in which defects were usually the most frequent and most easily seen, and hence it was

usually on these teeth that the location of DEH was measured in order to estimate timing of events. The middle third of the canine crown forms at about two and a half to four years of age (Reid and Dean 2000). This may account to a great extent for the heaping up of data points in this age range.

There is no evidence for any difference in distribution of age at formation of DEH between the sexes or between phases. There appears to be a tendency for those who died in childhood to show DEH at earlier ages than those who survived into adult life (Tables 80 and 81). DEH within an individual dentition cannot be considered independent events for the purposes of statistical analysis, so the age distribution of all DEH is not a valid basis for standard inferential statistical tests. If just the age at formation of the first defect in each individual is considered, valid statistical analysis can be performed, and this reveals that the age distributions of first DEH in adults and juveniles differ significantly (Kolmogorov-Smirnov test: D_{obs}=0.38, p=0.01). Although for estimating timing of events, more DEH were measured on canines than on first or on second incisors in the material as a whole, this was less true for juveniles than for adults (89% of adult DEH were measured on canines versus 46% for juveniles). The middle third of incisor crowns generally forms earlier than the middle third of canine crowns (Reid and Dean 2000), and so this discrepency may have played a part in the difference in age distribution of defects noted between adults and juveniles. In order to investigate this, the age distribution of defects on the canine teeth alone was tabulated (Table 82).

Table 82. Distribution of age at formation of DEH, canine teeth only.

| | Age (years) | | | | |
	1-1.99	2-2.99	3-3.99	4-4.99	5-5.99
All DEH					
Adults	1	14	46	33	5
Juveniles	0	11	10	7	1
First DEH					
Adults	1	14	33	18	0
Juveniles	0	10	6	4	0

Comparing Table 82 with Tables 80 and 81 indicates a weakening of the difference in the distribution of age at formation of DEH between adults and juveniles when only canine defects are considered, with a shift in the distribution of the juvenile pattern toward older ages. This is as anticipated if the difference in the age distribution of DEH on the anterior dentition as a whole between adults and juveniles was, at least in part, an artefact of the fact that relatively more juvenile defects had, by chance, been measured on the incisor teeth. The juvenile age distribution for canine DEH is still somewhat flatter than that for adults, and the modal age group for juvenile defects is still two to three years as compared to three to four years for adults, however, the difference no longer attains statistical significance.

The episodes which caused DEH are not directly linked to cause of death, as the very fact that a DEH is visible on the tooth indicates that the tooth crown continued to grow after the event. If, however, one accepts that there is a tendency for those who died in childhood to show earlier timing of defects, then it may be that those individuals who experienced episodes of disease or poor nutrition in early life severe enough to cause DEH had an increased chance of dying prior to attaining adulthood compared with those who only experienced events causing DEH later in childhood.

Localised hypoplasia of the primary canines (LHPC)

Although there are no examples of linear dental enamel hypoplasia in the deciduous dentitions, two individuals (Burial NA151, J, 4-5, unphased and Burial V25, J, 3-4, unphased) each showed an approximately 1mm diameter area denuded of enamel on the labial aspects of both mandibular deciduous canine teeth (Plate 22). The lesions appear to represent LHPC (Skinner 1986). In each case, the defects are located at a distance of between about one half and two thirds crown height from the cemento-enamel junction. This suggests that they formed in the immediate post-natal period (Gustafson and Koch 1974). The cause of LHPC is still debated. It has been suggested that it results from abnormal contact between the developing tooth and the wall of an unusually constricted crypt (Lukacs 1999). Alternatively, it may arise from a deficiency of bone in the anterior crypt wall exposing the developing tooth to minor physical trauma (Skinner and Newell 2003). In either case, LHPC is thought to be an indicator of deficient nutrition during the period when the canine tooth was developing within the jaw.

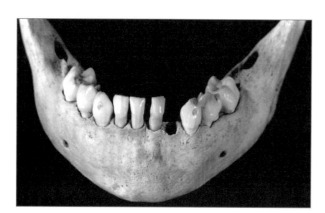

Plate 22. The mandible of Burial V25. Both deciduous canines show localised enamel hypoplasia.

Impacted and embedded teeth

Impacted teeth are those which are prevented from erupting by the presence of some physical impediment. Embedded teeth are those which fail to erupt due to

inherent lack of eruptive force in the tooth (Shafer *et al.* 1983, 66).

In the current study material, eight individuals show impacted third molars. In six individuals this involves the maxillary and in two the mandibular M3s. All cases involved a single tooth. In most cases the third molar was impacted against the neighbouring M2, either because the M3 was angled mesially or because it simply lay too close to the M2 to erupt past it. In one individual (Burial CN15, ?M, 14-15, Phase 4) the maxillary left M3 is impacted against the M2, and the pressure from the M3 seems to have, in turn, impacted the M2 against the M1, so that the M2 was also prevented from erupting fully (Plate 23).

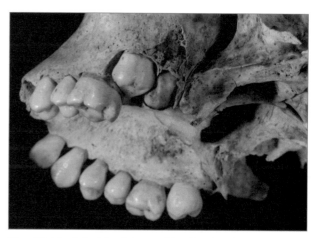

Plate 23. The left side of the maxilla of Burial CN15. There is impaction of both the second and third molars.

Twelve individuals have impacted canines. In nine cases this involves maxillary and in three mandibular teeth. In four individuals, impaction is bilateral. The canines have generally become impacted as a result of being abnormally tilted within the jaw (Plate 24).

There was one individual with an embedded tooth: the right maxillary canine of Burial NA068 had failed to erupt fully although there is no evidence of any physical impediment to the eruption path.

Dental trauma

Ante-mortem dental chipping was identified in four individuals (Table 83). This was differentiated from post-depositional damage by the presence of wear on the broken edges.

Table 83. Dental chipping.

Burial	Sex and age	Phase	Site of dental injury
G406	M, 40-50	1-2	L maxillary M3
G467	J, 4-5	2	R dec maxillary I1
NA031A	J, 2.5	-	L & R dec mandibular M1s, L maxillary dec M1
NA112	M, 50+	1-2	R mandibular I1

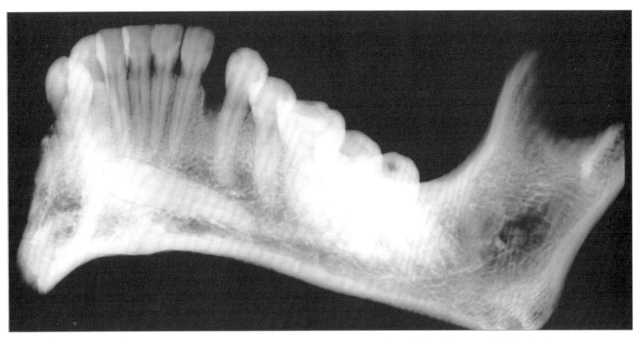

Plate 24. Posterio-lateral radiograph of the mandible of Burial G710. A canine lies tilted and impacted within the jaw.

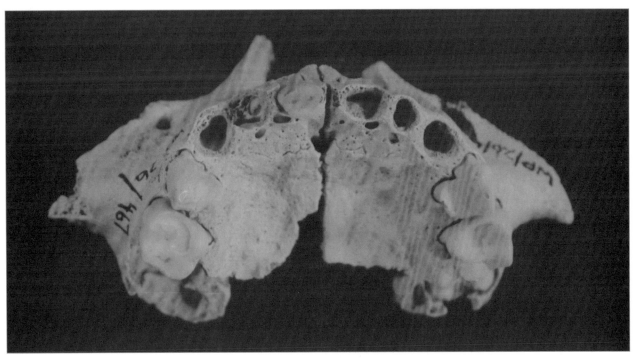

Plate 25. Inferior view of the maxillae of Burial G467. The right deciduous central incisor shows ante-mortem fracture of the crown, with exposure of the horns of the pulp cavity.

Trauma to anterior teeth may have been caused by a blow or fall. Chipping to the posterior dentition was more likely a result of biting upon some hard object inadvertently taken in with the food. In the two cases involving anterior teeth, abscess cavities have formed at the apices of affected teeth. In one instance (Burial G467) this was clearly a result of exposure of the pulp cavity of the broken tooth (Plates 25 and 26).

Activity-related dental alterations

Three individuals show evidence for dental grooves which may be related to habitual use of teeth as tools.

The left maxillary I1 of Burial WCO010 (M, 20, Phase 3-4) shows a shallow groove on its incisive edge (Plate 27). It has the appearance of having been due to habitual gripping of a narrow object (e.g. twine) between the teeth.

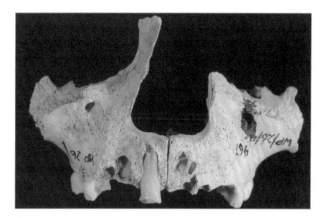

Plate 26. Anterior view of the maxillae of Burial G467. There are periapical abscesses at the socket for the fractured right deciduous central incisor and the sockets for each of the neighbouring teeth. The anterior surfaces of the maxillae are abnormally pitted, suggesting spread of infection from the dental abscesses.

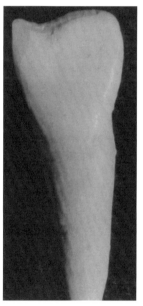 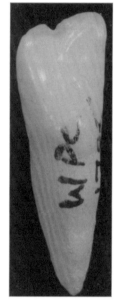

Plate 27. Lingual view of the left permanent maxillary central incisor, Burial WCO010, showing a groove on its incisive edge.

Plate 28. Lingual/distal view of the right permanent maxillary central incisor, Burial WCO016, showing a groove on its incisive edge.

This tooth's occlusal partner is missing post-mortem so it cannot be determined whether it too bore a groove. A somewhat narrower groove (Plate 28) is present on the incisive edge of the right maxillary I1 in Burial WCO016 (F, 18-19, unphased). This tooth's occlusal partner is also missing post-mortem.

A groove of somewhat different character is present on the left maxillary I2 of Burial V26 (F, 50+, unphased). It is about 6mm long, 1mm wide and a maximum of 1-2mm deep, and is located on the lingual/distal surface at the level of the cemento-enamel junction (Plate 29). The groove has a somewhat polished appearance and seems

likely to have been caused by a thread having been habitually passed between this tooth and the neighbouring canine, perhaps in order to help smooth the thread. This is the only element of the maxillary anterior dentition present so it cannot be determined whether other, neighbouring teeth bore grooves. The anterior mandibular dentition bears no similar modifications but is very heavily worn.

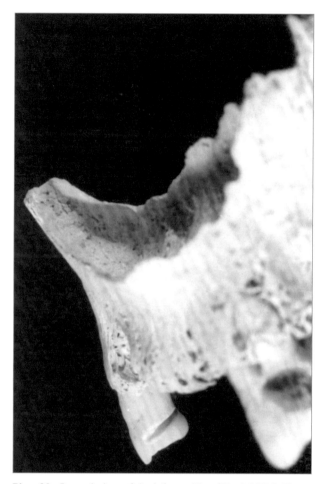

Plate 29. Lateral view of the left maxilla of Burial V26. The lateral incisor shows a horizontal groove at the cemento-enamel junction.

Odontoma

Burial SA029 (F, 21-24, unphased) has a mass consisting of a small dentinous part and a larger enamel portion, measuring about 0.5cm in diameter, situated within the right maxillary bone immediately posterior to the central incisor. A radiograph (Plate 30) shows that it has a curved canal internally, resembling the root canal of an anterior tooth. This probably represents an odontoma, a benign tumour containing both enamel and dentine. Its anatomical resemblance to a normal tooth indicates that it should be classified as a compound composite odontoma (Shafer *et al*. 1983, 308). Odontomas appear during the normal period of dental development, are generally asymptomatic, and are rare in modern dental experience

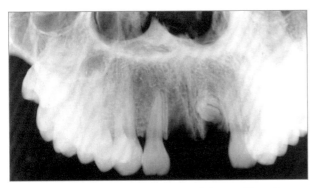

Plate 30. Posterio-anterior radiograph of the maxillae of Burial SA029. An odontoma is visible in the right maxilla.

(Shafer *et al.* 1983, 308-11). Palaeopathological reports of odontomas are few (references in Anderson and Andrews 1993), although some cases have been published from British sites (Anderson and Andrews 1993; Anderson 1994; Brothwell *et al.* 2000).

11 Traces of Injury

Fractures

A total of 72 individuals (69 adults, 3 juveniles) show fractured bones (Table 84). For adults this gives a frequency with respect to individuals of 69/360 = 19.2%, and 162/28799 = 0.6% with respect to total bones present. There is no significant difference in the frequency of fractures with respect to sex or phase.

Cranial fractures

Four individuals show evidence for cranial injuries from edged weapons.

Burial SA034 shows multiple cranial trauma. Some details of the injuries are difficult to reconstruct because of post-depositional damage to the affected area, but the individual appears to have suffered at least three blade injuries and one blunt trauma to the left side of the skull which resulted in death (Plate 31). One cut, about 10cm long, runs approximately horizontally from the left frontal eminence to a point on the left parietal bone. A second, more vertically orientated cut, crosses this one and describes a curve from the left temporal squama to a point near the vertex of the skull (the length cannot be measured due to post-depositional damage to the cranium). A third, approximately 7cm long, runs from the inferior margin of the left temporal bone to a point just above the squamo-parietal suture. A break extends a further 7cm from the superior end of this cut and may represent an associated peri-mortal fracture. Toward the superior end of this putative perimortal fracture is an ovoid hole (approximately 2 x 3cm) which is internally bevelled and has signs of crushing and flaking on the ectocranial margin. This is suggestive of a peri-mortal blunt injury. A further fracture, probably perimortal, extends from this hole to terminate in the region of the bregma. No injury shows any sign of healing.

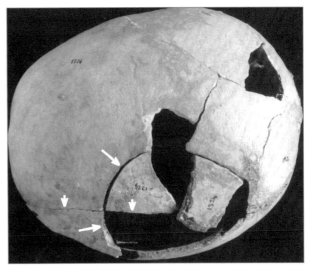

Plate 31: The cranium of Burial SA034, showing blade injuries. The short arrows indicate the first blade injury described in the text, the long arrows the second.

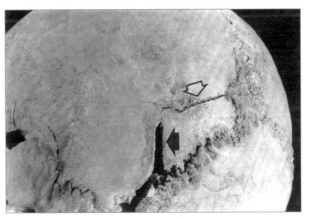

Plate 32. Left/posterior view of the cranium of Burial EE003. The solid arrow indicates the blade injury. The open arrow indicates a probable perimortal fracture running from the superior end of the blade injury.

Burial EE003 has an unhealed blade injury, 2cm long, on the posterior part of the left parietal bone (Plate 32). The internal surface of the cut is bevelled. There is a probable perimortal fracture running medially for a distance of about 3cm from the superior end of the cut. The morphology of the blade injury suggests that it was a result of a blow from a narrow-bladed implement, such as an adze or small hatchet.

Burial V45 shows a linear indentation 11mm long by 2mm wide, and a maximum of 3mm deep, running obliquely across the left frontal bone. This appears to represent a healed superficial blade injury. Burial SA003 shows a fissure in the right zygomatic bone adjacent to, and running parallel with, the zygomaxillary suture (Plate 33). This too is probably a healed blade injury.

In addition to Burial SA034, six other individuals show evidence of blunt injury to the skull. There is a small depression about 5mm deep on the right parietal bone of Burial G304 (Fig. 34). The inner table of the skull

Table 84. Fractures.

Burial	Sex & age	Phase	No. of fractured bones	Location of fractures
CN12	M, 35-45	4	2	R trapezoid, R 2nd metacarpal
CN16	F, 40+	4	1	Body of T6
CN27	M, 40+	4	3	3R ribs
CN33	M, 50+	4	2	Bodies T6, T7
CN39	M, Adult	4	3	3R ribs (2 are ununited)
CN45	M, 50+	4	8	Bodies of L2, L3 and three thoracic vertebrae, 2L ribs, L clavicle (lat 1/3)
EE003	M, 25-25	1-2	1	Skull (unhealed blade injury)
EE004	M, 40+	1-2	3	L acetabulum (fissure fractures), 2R ribs
EE015	F, 60+	1-2	17	L 3rd metatarsal, 9L ribs, 2R ribs, 5U rib fragments
EE018	F, 21	1-2	1	L tibia (d jt surface, fissure fracture)
EE022	F, 50+	1-2	1	1L rib
EE032	M, 50+	1-2	1	Skull (blunt trauma)
EE037	M, 40-50	1-2	1	Neural spine T1 (clay-shoveller's fracture)
EE060	M, 40+	1-2	2	2U rib fragments
G253	F, 18-19	2	2	2U rib fragments (ununited)
G278	M, Adult	2	1	Body T8
G279	M, 50+	1	1	1R rib
G303	M, 30-40	1-2	1	1R rib
G304	??M, 5-6	1	1	Skull (unhealed blunt trauma)
G310	M, 30-40	2	4	L fibula (d jt surface fissure fracture), 2R ribs, 1U rib fragment
G327	J, 1½	2	1	R humerus (p1/3, ?greenstick fracture)
G379	M, 45-60	1-2	1	Skull (depressed fracture)
G451	F?, 50+	2	3	R hand phalanx, L hand phalanx, L tibia (d jt surface fissure fracture)
G482	M, 50+	2	3	L hand phalanx, 1L rib, R acetabular roof
G561	M, 50+	1-2	6	Bodies of T11, T12 & L1, 3L ribs
G565	M?, Adult	2	3	Body of L2, 1R rib, L ulna (p1/3)
G571	F, 40+	2	1	1L rib
G597	F, 21-25	2	1	L 5th metacarpal (d jt surface, fissure fracture)
G607	M, 35-45	1-2	2	2R ribs
G636	F, 50+	1-2	1	R trapezoid (ununited)
G694	M, 25-35	1-2	3	R 1st metacarpal, L ulna (d1/3), skull (blunt injury)
G715	M, 35-45	1-2	1	Skull (blunt injury)
G746	M, 30-50	1-2	1	R acetabular roof
NA33	F, 50+	1-2	1	R 2nd metacarpal (d jt surface, fissure fracture)
NA044	F, 18	1-2	1	1L rib
NA046	M, 50+	1-2	1	L clavicle (m 1/3)
NA091	M?, 40+	1-2	1	1U rib fragment
NA167	F, 25-35	2	1	R fibula (d jt surface, fissure fracture)
NA181	M, 50+	1-2	5	R hand phalanx, bodies C6 & T12, R tibia (m 1/3), R fibula (m 1/3)
NA183	M, Adult	1-2	1	1U rib fragment

Table 84 continued.

Burial	Sex & age	Phase	No. of fractured bones	Location of fractures
NA190	M, 35-45	1-2	2	Bodies T11 & T12
NA197	M, 50+	1-2	7	R hand phalanx, L navicular, L 5th metatarsal, 2L ribs, 2R ribs
NA199	M, 50+	2-3	2	R calcaneus (jt surface for cuboid, fissure fracture), L clavicle (lat 1/3)
NA203	F, 40+	1-2	1	L fibula (d jt surface, fissure fracture)
NA217	M, 50+	2	2	1L rib, 1R rib
NA218	M, 50+	1-2	1	R foot phalanx
SA003	M, 50+	3-4	2	1R rib, skull (blade injury)
SA015	M, 50+	-	1	1R rib
SA034	M, 50+	1	1	Skull (unhealed blade & blunt injuries)
SA052	M, 50+	1-2	1	1L rib
V15	M, 50+	-	1	1L rib
V19	M?, Adult	-	1	Body T12
V24	?M, 14-15	-	1	R clavicle (lat 1/3)
V26	F, 50+	-	1	R foot phalanx
V33	F, 35-45	-	1	L clavicle (lat 1/3)
V37	M, 40-50	-	1	L fibula (d jt surface, fissure fracture)
V38	M, 40-50	2-3	2	R foot phalanx, 1R rib
V44	F?, 35-45	-	5	5R ribs
V45	M, 40+	2	1	Skull (superficial blade injury)
V61	F, 35-45	-	1	R 5th metatarsal (p jt surface)
WCO012	M, Adult	-	1	R 2nd metatarsal
WCO013	M, 50+	-	2	2L ribs
WCO017	F, 50+	-	1	Body of a lumbar vertebra
WCO037	M, 50+	-	1	1L rib (ununited)
WCO045	F, 60+	3-4	8	Bodies of T11, T12 & L1, 2L ribs, 2R ribs, R hand phalanx
WCO117	M, 50+	-	11	L clavicle (med 1/3), R clavicle (m 1/3), 6L ribs, 2R ribs, T7 (transverse process)
WCO137	M, 50+	-	3	1L rib, 2U rib fragments
WCO139	M, 45-55	2	1	1R rib
WCO164A	M, 40+	-	2	L calcaneus (cuboid facet, fissure fracture), L 1st metatarsal
WCO165	F?, 35-45	-	1	Skull (superficial blunt injury)
WCO170	F?, 50+	2-4	1	Axis vertebra
WCO200	M, 50+	-	4	3R ribs, R hand phalanx

Notes: Sex, M=male, F=female, J=unsexed juvenile, ?? denotes sex inferred from craniofacial morphology in juveniles; Age: estimated age at death, in years; Fracture location, L=left, R=right, U=unsided, for vertebrae C=cervical, T=thoracic, L=lumbar, for long-bones location of fracture given as in the midshaft (m), distal, (d), proximal (p) thirds except for the clavicle where location is given as in the medial (med), lateral (lat) or midshaft thirds. All fractures are healed unless stated. For cranial trauma, 'unhealed' denotes perimortal injury with no signs of bony remodelling. For other trauma 'ununited' denotes fractures where there is bony remodelling of broken ends which failed to achieve union.

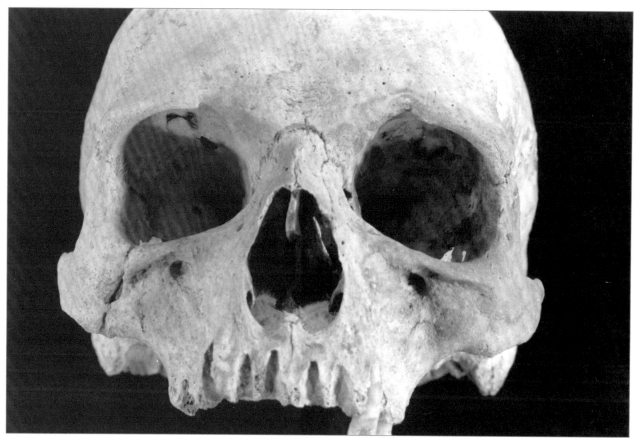

Plate 33. The cranium of Burial SA003. The fissure running approximately vertically in the right zygomatic is probably a healed blade injury.

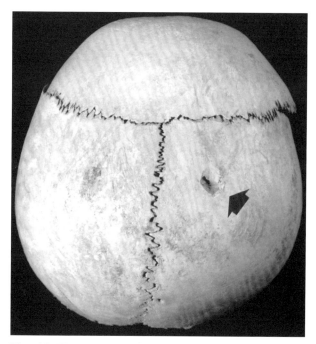

Plate 34. The cranium of Burial G304. The blunt injury is indicated by the arrow.

Plate 35. The internal surface of the cranium of Burial G304 at the site of the injury.

The remaining cases of blunt trauma all show advanced signs of healing and so the injuries were probably unconnected with cause of death. Three of these individuals, Burials EE032, G694 and G715, show extensive cranial fracturing.

There are several intersecting fractures on the cranium of Burial EE032. They do not radiate from particular foci but are distributed over the frontal and parietal bones. This suggests that their cause was a blow from an object with a large contact area. All fractures are healed with well remodelled callus. In the area of the bregma there is

here has splintered away exposing the underlying diploe (Fig. 35). Some fragments of the inner table remain attached and are hinged inwards. There is no sign of bony remodelling. This appears to represent a peri-mortal injury.

pitting suggestive of infection. The pitted area is well remodelled and is confined to the ectocranial surface, suggesting an infection of the scalp which had healed at time of death. There is a transverse depression in the fractured area just behind the coronal suture, so perhaps the cranial injuries were a result of a heavy beam or similar object falling across the head.

Burial G694 shows several intersecting fracture lines on the right parietal and frontal bones focused in the region of the coronal suture about 4cm from the midline. All fractures are firmly healed and there is well-remodelled pitting in the part of the skull where the fractures are situated.

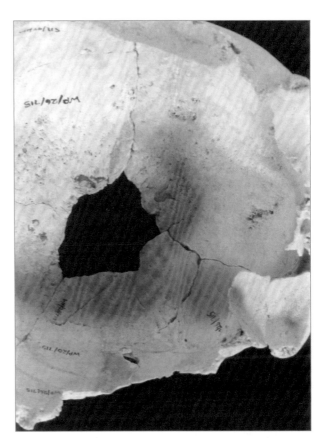

Plate 37. The internal surface of the cranium of Burial G715. Several united fractures are visible, radiating away from the hole in the skull.

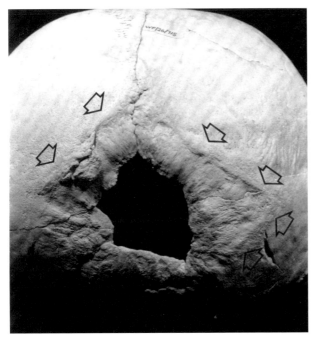

Plate 36. The cranium of Burial G715 showing a large hole surrounded by pitted, roughened bone. The margins of the reactive area are marked by slight ridges of new bone (arrowed), which on three sides are fairly straight, resembling three sides of a rectangle.

There is a large hole approximately 5 by 4cm diameter in the left parietal/frontal bone of Burial G715 (Plate 36). Several fracture lines radiate from the edges of the hole (Plate 37). Most are only a few centimetres long, but one is about 15cm in length, extending over the right parietal bone and terminating on the right temporal squama. There is an area of pitted, roughened bone around the hole on the ectocranial surface suggestive of infection. On three sides, the margins of the pitted, roughened area, marked by slight ridges of new bone, are fairly straight, resembling three sides of a rectangle (Plate 36). The edges of the hole are for the most part bevelled externally, and are thoroughly remodelled and rounded. The radiating fractures are united by smooth callus, and the pitted, roughened bone on the ectocranium is well remodelled. These lesions suggest a blunt injury to the part of the skull now occupied by the hole. The pitted, roughened bone on the ectocranial surface suggests that there was originally

some superficial infection at the injury site. The state of the lesions suggests an old injury occurring long before death. The reason for the hole may be that the blow caused such comminution at point of impact that bone fragments were resorbed rather than united when the wound healed, but a more likely explanation is that the hole represents a trepanation aimed at treating the injury. The externally bevelled edges support this latter explanation: trepanning tends to produce a hole with external bevelling; a hole produced by blunt trauma tends to show internal bevelling (Berryman and Haun 1996). Furthermore, the regular shape of the pitted, roughened area is suggestive of flaps of skin being deliberately folded back from the wound. Few instances of trepanation in Britain can be dated to the late medieval period (Roberts and McKinley 2003). Instances where trepanation to treat cranial injury are fewer still: two medieval examples exist where cranial bone appears to have been cut away to widen a blade injury (Brothwell and Browne 1994; Powers 2004), and there is one case of probable medieval date with a possible trepanation with two linear fractures leading from it (McKenzie 1936).

Two individuals show single depressions in the skull which probably represent healed injuries. Burial G379 has an oval depresion about 1 by 1.5cm on the left side of the frontal bone, with a corresponding bulge endocranially. This is probably a healed depressed fracture. Burial WCO165 has a broad, shallow, linear depression on the right side of the frontal bone 25mm long by 7mm wide. There is no corresponding bulge in the endocranial surface. This lesion may also represent a healed injury. Burial WCO165 is difficult to sex as diagnostic areas of the pelvic bones are missing, but if the tentatively assigned sex is correct, then this is the only female showing cranial trauma.

Post-cranial fractures

The most commonly fractured bones were ribs and vertebrae. There were 85 fractured ribs (33 lefts, 36 rights and 16 of indeterminate side), together accounting for more than half of all fractured bones. Rib fractures are generally caused by a direct impact, such as a fall against a hard object or, when multiple, by crushing injury to the chest. There were 24 vertebral fractures of which all but three were compression fractures of the bodies. Vertebral compression fractures usually result from forced spinal flexion or from vertical compression of the spinal column. In simple compression fractures there is no narrowing of the spinal canal so the spinal cord is undamaged. The three cases of spinal injury which were not simple compression fractures are described below.

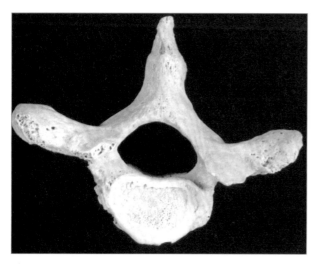

Plate 38. The first thoracic vertebra of Burial EE037, showing a united fracture of the spinous process.

Burial EE037 shows a united fracture of the neural spine of the first thoracic vertebra (Plate 38). The cause of this type of fracture is overload on the spinous process due to forceful muscular action. In recent populations, the overwhelming majority of this type of injury occurs in those whose work entails shovelling, especially when heavy soils are involved. For this reason these fractures are called clay-shoveller's fractures (Knüsel et al. 1996). Although the soils at Wharram Percy are thin and light, injury of this nature may have been incurred when attempting to dig the hard chalk bedrock. Clay-shoveller's fractures are only rarely reported in palaeopopulations. Knüsel et al. (1996) collate six cases from British sites. As with the current example, all were male. They also noted a tendency for injured individuals to be of taller than average stature, and suggest that this may have predisposed them to back strain. The stature of

Burial EE037, estimated from long-bone lengths, is 172.1cm, compared with a male average at Wharram Percy of 168.8cm. In addition, this individual had 25 instead of the usual 24 pre-sacral vertebrae. If one accepts the proposition that a relatively long trunk predisposes to back strain, then the physique of Burial EE037 may have acted as a predisposing factor to his injury.

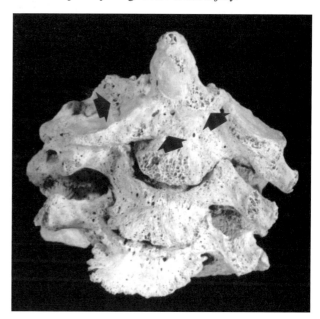

Plate 39. The axis and the third and fourth cervical vertebrae of Burial WCO170. Two united fractures are visible on the axis, one running obliquely across the vertebral body beneath the odontoid process (twin arrows) and one on the right lateral mass, running across the superior articular facet (single arrow).

There are two fractures of the axis vertebra of Burial WCO170 (Plate 39). There is crushing of the right superior articular facet with a fracture line across it. A further fracture runs obliquely across the vertebral body beneath the odontoid process. The fractures are firmly healed but the odontoid process is displaced anteriorly/rightward by a few millimetres and angled about 20 degrees to the right. The axis vertebra is ankylosed to C3 at the right facet joint and there is also bony fusion between C3 and C4 at both facet joints. When placed in its anatomical position (Plate 40), it is clear that the atlas vertebra would have slipped anteriorly/rightward with luxation of the odontoid atlanto-axial articulation. The spinal canal at this level has been narrowed somewhat by the displacement of the atlas and there appears to have been some bony resorption on the anterior surface of its posterior arch, perhaps in response to slight pressure on the structures surrounding the cord. There must have been no injury to the cord itself because at this level in the cervical spine it would have been fatal. When the degree of vertebral dislocation is small, the cord may escape injury as it does not completely fill the spinal canal. It seems likely that the injury was incurred by the neck being forcibly bent forwards and to the right, perhaps as a result of a headlong fall or by a heavy object falling on the head.

148

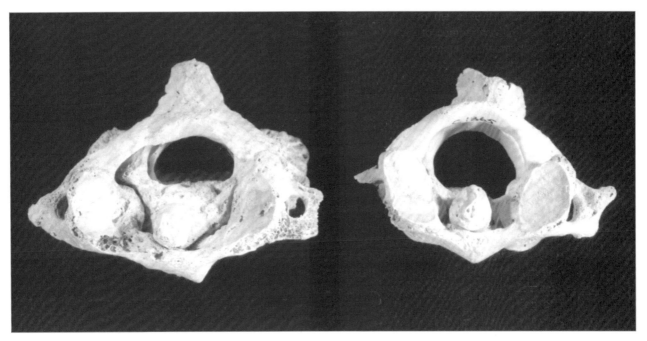

Plate 40. The atlas and axis vertebrae of Burial WCO170 re-articulated (on the left of the photograph), together with a comparative specimen indicative of normal atlanto-axial configuration.

The body of the sixth cervical vertebra of Burial NA181 shows a compression fracture (Plate 41) and it is ankylosed to C5 by osteophytes at the body and at the facet joints. The fifth cervical vertebra has been dislocated forwards on C6 by about 7mm (Plate 42). This has caused angular kyphosis and there is some narrowing of the spinal canal. The post-cranial skeleton in this individual is heavily mineralised, indicating no lasting neurological deficit, so the degree of anterior luxation must have been insufficient to damage the spinal cord. As with Burial WCO170, this injury was probably caused by a headlong fall or by a heavy object landing on the head. Burial NA181 also shows other fractures (Table 84) which may have occurred in the same incident.

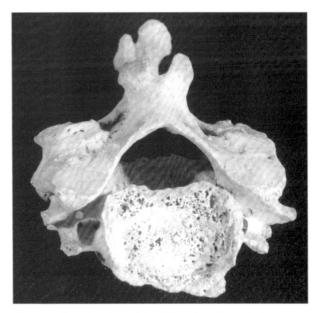

Plate 42. Superior view of the fifth and sixth cervical vertebrae of Burial NA181 to illustrate the anterior slippage of C5.

There are sixteen long-bone fractures at Wharram Percy (Table 85). Of these, six are fissure fractures of the distal joint surface of the tibia or fibula, reflecting trauma to the ankle joint (Plate 43). Of the ten shaft fractures (occurring in eight adults, giving a prevalence of 2.4%), six involve the clavicle, making it the most frequently fractured long-bone.

The long-bone diaphysial fractures are firmly healed with well-remodelled callus. They are generally healed in good alignment so that there is little abnormal angulation of the bone, but most do show some shortening due to over-riding of the broken ends. The lack of marked

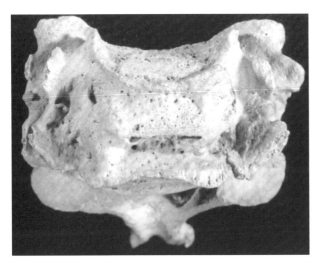

Plate 41. Anterior view of the fifth and sixth cervical vertebrae of Burial NA181. There is a healed compression fracture of the body of C6 and the two vertebrae are ankylosed.

malalignment does not necessarily imply splinting or other treatment: Schultz (1967) observed that many fractures in wild apes heal with little deformity.

Table 85. Long-bone fractures (adults only).

Bones			Individuals		
No. with fractures	Total	%	No. with fractures	Total	%
16	3338	0.5	14	334	4.2

Notes: long-bones comprise, clavicles, humeri, radii, ulnae, femora, tibiae and fibulae. The total for individuals is the number of adults with at least one long-bone present for observation.

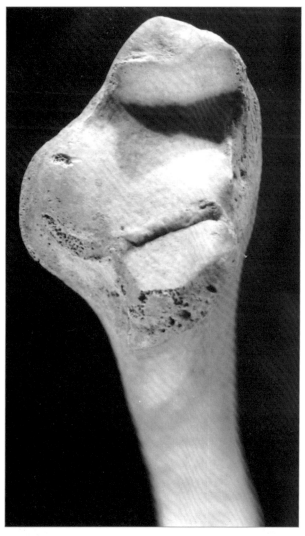

Plate 43. The distal joint surface of the left tibia of Burial EE018, showing a healed fissure fracture.

Comparisons with other sites

The fracture rates for Wharram Percy resemble those for Ipswich Blackfriars which were recorded in a similar way. Burials at that site were not of friars but rather represented middle class lay benefactors who elected to be buried within the religious house. At the Ipswich Blackfriars site, 18.1% of adults showed one or more

fractures, and the fracture frequency with respect to total bones was 0.4% (Mays 1991). As at Wharram Percy, rib fractures were by far the most frequent, a pattern which is commonly found in archaeological material (e.g. Wells 1980; Stroud 1993; Waldron 1993).

Comparisons of fracture rates with those from other sites is problematic as different writers use different methodologies. Judd and Roberts (1999) present fracture data for long-bones from the rural medieval site at Raunds, Northamptonshire. Of 170 adults they found that 33, or 19.4%, showed one or more long-bone fractures. They do not mention any instances of fissure fractures to joint surfaces, and it is unclear whether these were sought but not observed or whether they only studied shaft fractures. Either way, the frequency of long-bone fracture there is markedly greater than that seen at Wharram Percy. Judd and Roberts (1999) give a frequency with respect to total long-bones of 3.5%. In calculating this prevalence they include in their denominator all complete bones plus any incomplete ones that show fractures. The policy of including incomplete bones in the denominator if they show fractures but excluding them if they don't, will tend to produce a higher prevalence than the methodology used here. If, however, the Wharram Percy prevalence with respect to total long-bones is recalculated using Judd and Roberts' (1999) methodology it is, at 0.7%, still far below the Raunds figure.

Grauer and Roberts (1996) report fractures in long-bone shafts (excluding the clavicle) at St Helen-on-the Walls, York. Of 685 adult skeletons, 30 showed one or more diaphysial fractures, giving a prevalence of 4.4%. At Wharram Percy, 332 adults had at least one limb long-bone present for observation; three showed diaphysial fractures, a prevalence of 0.9%.

The above comparisons suggest that long-bone shaft fractures at Wharram Percy are fewer than in a coeval group of low status urban dwellers (York St Helen's) or in a contemporary rural population (Raunds). Looking at a variety of sites, Judd and Roberts (1999) found that long-bone fracture was more frequent among rural than urban medieval groups: the frequency of individuals sustaining long-bone shaft fracture ranged from 10.7% to 19.4% for rural sites and from 4.7% to 5.5% for urban groups. Wharram Percy does not appear to fit this pattern, the long-bone diaphysial fracture frequency by individuals (2.4%) is less than observed by Judd and Roberts (1999) at either type of site.

Dislocation

There is disruption of the right shoulder joint of Burial EE031 (M, 50+, Phase 1-2). There is superior displacement of the humeral head. It remains in articulation with the upper part of the glenoid cavity but there is impingement on the coracoid and the acromion. There is severe osteoarthritis with eburnation on the glenoid, humeral head, coracoid and acromion (Plate 44). There is a depression in the medial side of the humeral diaphysis in the region of the surgical neck. This is

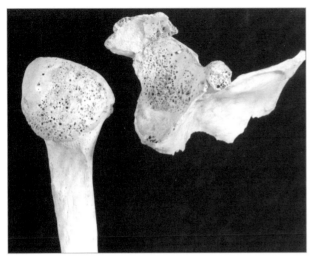

Plate 44. Shoulder joint of Burial EE031 showing subluxation and severe degenerative changes.

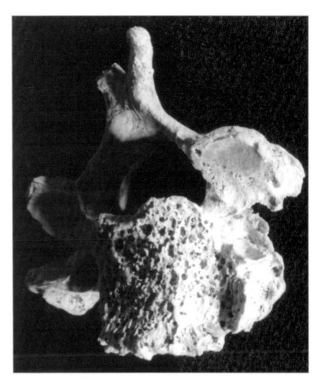

Plate 45. The fourth cervical vertebra of Burial EE031. It shows a smooth-walled erosion in the right side of the body at the transverse foramen.

probably a result of pressure from the inferior border of the glenoid cavity due to the abnormal conformation of the gleno-humeral joint. There is also dislocation of the acromio-clavicular joint. Re-articulation suggests that the displaced, eburnated clavicular face of the joint articulated with the sub-luxated humeral head. There is also severe disc degeneration and osteoarthritis of the facet joints in the cervical spine, especially on the right side. These changes are suggestive of severe trauma to the right shoulder and neck area.

The fourth cervical vertebra of Burial EE031 bears a smooth-walled erosion in the right side of its body at the transverse foramen (Plate 45). There is also erosion of the foramen in the left transverse process of the axis which

has undermined the joint surface so that the subchondral bone is perforated in its central part and is elsewhere paper-thin. Differential diagnosis for these lesions lies between tortuosity of the vertebral arteries and aneurisms. The distinction is very difficult to make in dry bones (Waldron and Antoine 2002) but the severe neck/shoulder

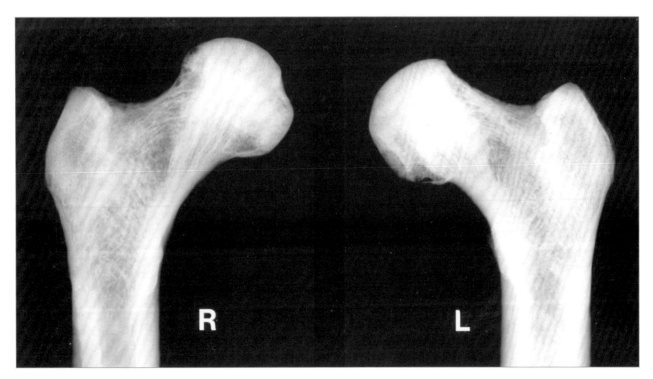

Plate 46. Anterio-posterior radiograph of the femora of Burial G275. The left shows inferior displacement of the head. The pit for the ligamentum teres is preserved but lies closer than normal to the inferior articular margin. Unilateral slipped capital ephiphysis.

151

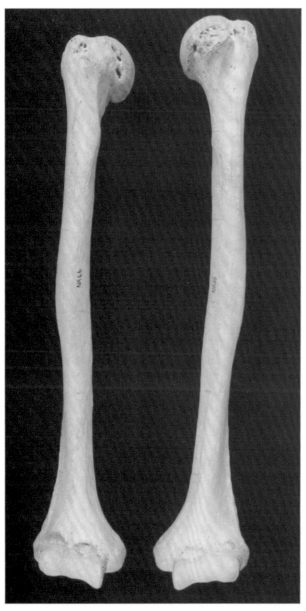

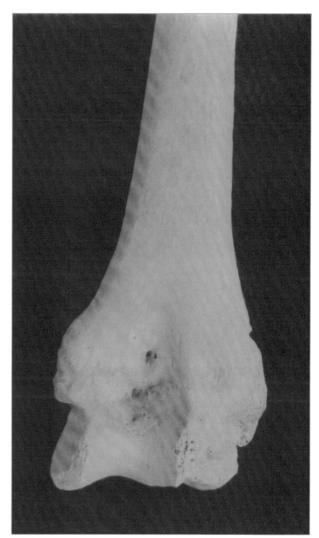

Plate 48. Posterior side of the distal end of the right humerus of Burial WCO201. The deformity probably represents a healed childhood avulsion injury to the epiphysial plates of the condyle and medial epicondyle.

Plate 47. The humeri of Burial NA066.

trauma suffered by this individual leads one toward a diagnosis of aneurism, as does the observation that bilateral and multilevel tortuosities of vertebral arteries are rarely observed (Kricun *et al.* 1992; Braheee and Guebert 2000).

The right elbow of Burial G601 (M, 35-45, Phase 1-2) is grossly disrupted with lateral migration of the ulna so that it articulates with the lateral part of the very asymmetrical humeral condylar surface. There is severe osteoarthritis. This appears to be dislocation, possibly accompanied by fracture of the humeral condyle.

Epiphysial plate injuries
Mechanical strain may cause failure of the epiphysial cartilage in the growing bone. Examples were found in the current material in femora, humeri, vertebrae and, possibly, tibiae. Most cases were identified in adult skeletons, although these are clearly injuries which would have occurred during the childhood/adolescence of these individuals.

Four individuals (Burial G275A, F, 25-35, Phase 2; Burial SA050, F, 40+, unphased; Burial V29, F, 40+, unphased; Burial WCO015, F, 40-50, unphased) show slipped femoral capital epiphyses, with downward displacement of the femoral head (Plate 46). Burial WCO069 (J, 13-15, unphased) may be a further example but the diagnosis is not clear-cut. Slipped femoral capital epiphysis may occur as a result of trauma to the hip joint but it may also arise spontaneously. Burial NA066 (F, 22-30, Phase 1-2) shows an analogous condition in the right humerus, with slippage of the proximal epiphysis so that the joint surface lies below the level of the greater tuberosity (Plate 47). Compared with the normal left bone, the right humerus, measured to the greater tuberosity, is 12mm shorter, indicating that the damage to the epiphysial plate has resulted in deficient growth. This condition is known as humerus varus. The observation that in Burial NA066 this is an isolated deformity, with no evidence of underlying disease such as rickets or osteomalacia, indicates that this is likely due to trauma. This is an injury of early life. It may occur during delivery of the infant,

Table 86. Schmorl's nodes: distribution in the adult spine.

	Total adults			Males			Females		
	Total vert.	No. of vert with nodes	No. of nodes	Total. vert	No. of vert. with nodes	No. of nodes	Total vert.	No. of vert with nodes	No. of nodes
Cervical vertebrae	1337	2	2	726	1	1	603	1	1
Thoracic vertebrae	2566	345	372	1390	216	232	1147	125	135
Lumbar vertebrae	1069	77	94	590	47	60	471	30	34

Note: Figures for total adults includes data from three unsexed adults

especially if she is in the breech position, or as a result of trauma during infancy or early childhood (discussion in Anderson 1997). Burial NA149A (J, 8-9 months, unphased) shows medial bowing of the distal extremeties of both tibiae. There is no evidence of a systemic cause such as rickets. The aetiology of this bilateral varus deformity in the tibiae is unclear but injury to the distal growth plates is a possibility.

The medial epicondyle on the right humerus of Burial WCO091 (M, 25-35, unphased) is absent. There is a large exostosis in the area of the lateral epicondyle. The olecranon fossa is rounded rather than showing the usual ovoid shape. The distal joint surface is enlarged compared with the normal contralateral element. This is probably an example of a healed childhood avulsion injury to the epiphysial plates of the condyle and medial epicondyle (Glencross and Stuart-Macadam 2001). The reason for the enlargement of the distal joint surface is unclear, but it may be a response to altered mechanical forces during the growth period due to the injury. The right distal humerus of Burial WCO201 (U, 20-40, unphased) bears a similar injury (Plate 48).

Three individuals (Burials CN28, NA104 and WCO092) show avulsion injuries of the vertebral endplates of the type described by Maat and Mastwijk (2000). Such injuries are due to abrupt spinal hyperflexion-hyperextension movements (i.e. acceleration/deceleration) such as may occur in falls or other bodily impacts.

Schmorl's nodes

An intervertebral disc consists of a tough outer layer, the annulus fibrosus, surrounding an inner core (the nucleus puplosus) which, until young adulthood, is composed of semi-gelatinous material. In young individuals, excessive spinal compression, such as might result from heavy lifting, may cause extrusion of gelatinous material from the nucleus puposus into the vertebral body, resulting in the formation of a bony pit – the Schmorl's node. In some individuals, congenital weakness in the cartilaginous endplate may pre-dispose to Schmorl's node formation, but there is no doubt that a single trauma may produce a Schmorl's node in a normal vertebra (Schmorl and Junghanns 1971, 158-68). Schmorl's nodes were recorded systematically in the adults. The results are shown in Tables 86-8.

Table 87. Schmorl's nodes: presence/absence in individuals (adults only).

	Present	Absent
Males	70	97
Females	47	82
Total adults	118	181

Note: Figures for total adults includes data from three unsexed adults. For inclusion individuals needed to show at least one vertebral body present for observation.

Table 88. Schmorl's nodes: presence/absence in individuals (adults only) split by phase.

	Present	Absent
Phase 1-2	50	73
Phase 2	11	31
Phase 4	16	18

Chi-square tests indicate no significant difference in the frequency with which individuals show Schmorl's nodes either by sex or by phase.

Other signs of injury

The tibia of Burial V21 bears a smooth, ovoid swelling on the medial/anterior surface of its shaft. This is probably an ossified sub-periosteal haematoma. The right humerus of Burial NA171 shows a smooth swelling on its medial surface, and radiography shows diffuse radiolucency within the lesion. This may be a further example of ossifying haematoma. An alternative diagnosis is osteoid osteoma, but the radiolucency within the lesion is rather less well-circumscribed than is customarily observed in that condition (Ortner and Putschar 1985, 369).

Four burials (Burials CN20, EE098, G482, and NA181) show *myositis ossificans circumscripta*, an ossification which arises through deep muscle injury. In three cases it affected the femur, in one the humerus.

The right humerus and ulna of Burial CN16 are ankylosed and there is severe eburnation of the head of the radius. There are no signs of infection at the joint. The changes here are probably the result of trauma.

12 Bone Disease

Degenerative changes to the joints: osteoarthritis and degenerative disc disease

Most of the movable joints in the body are synovial joints. In a synovial joint, the bone ends are covered with a layer of hyaline articular cartilage and are bathed in synovial fluid which acts as a lubricant. The joints between the vertebral bodies are somewhat different. Although the opposing bone surfaces are each covered by hyaline cartilage, there is no synovial fluid and the bones are connected by a fibro-cartilaginous intervertebral disc, the flexion of which permits some movement of the joint. Degenerative changes at these two types of joint are classified as distinct diseases and so are herein considered separately.

Osteoarthritis is degeneration of the cartilage at a synovial joint. The process of cartilage degeneration may lead to characteristic bony changes to the underlying joint surface. The bony joint surface becomes porous and pitted and, as the cartilage breaks down completely, bone-on-bone friction may cause polishing, a phenomenon known as eburnation. Osteophytes may also form at joint margins.

Degeneration of the intervertebral disc leads to it.s spreading so that its margins may cause traction at the sites at which it attaches to the vertebral body. This may stimulate the periosteum to produce bone, resulting in the formation of marginal osteophytes on the vertebral bodies. In addition, degeneration of the cartilaginous plates which attach the discs to the vertebral bodies may occur in a similar fashion to cartilage degeneration in a synovial joint, leading to analogous changes to the underlying bone.

The causation of osteoarthritis and degenerative disc disease is complex, but mechanical strain on the joints seems to play an important role (Simon *et al.* 1972; Hadler *et al.* 1978; Radin *et al.* 1980; Croft *et al.* 1992).

Methods

Lesions due to osteoarthritis and degenerative disc disease were distinguished from other arthropathies using the criteria of Rogers *et al.* (1987).

Degenerative changes at synovial joints were scored into four categories, based on the scheme of Sager (1969), reproduced in Brothwell (1981, fig. 6.9):

Grade 0: Normal joint morphology
Grade 1: Marginal osteophyte formation only.
Grade 2: Porotic changes to joint surface (with or without marginal osteophyte formation).
Grade 3: Eburnation (with or without marginal osteophyte formation or joint surface porosis).

The implication of Sager's scheme is that it represents a gradient of increasing severity of changes. The exent to which this is valid is unclear. Joint surface porosity may arise in osteoarthritis due to a variety of causes, and it may precede or occur subsequent to eburnation (Jurmain 1999, 33). Porosis and eburnation may be observed in the absence of marginal osteophyte formation, indicating that osteophytes do not necessarily represent an earlier phase of disease. Indeed, although it is clear that ostcophytcs may occur in osteoarthritis, their diagnostic value when they are present in a palaeopathological specimen in the absence of joint surface changes is controversial. Although palaeopathologists have long used marginal osteophytes as an identifier of osteoarthritis (e.g. Edynak 1976; Jurmain 1977; Bridges 1991; Lovell 1994), Rogers and Waldron (1995) strongly oppose this practice, indicating that, in the absence of other pathology, marginal osteophytes are probably not indicative of disease but are a non-pathological accompaniment of ageing (Rogers and Waldron 1995, 25). They thus contend that osteoarthritis should never be diagnosed when marginal osteophytes are the only abnormality observed at a joint (Rogers and Waldron 1995, 44).

A value of the recording scheme used here is that it allows cases where marginal osteophytes are the only abnormality to be distinguished (and analysed separately) from cases where there are joint surface lesions clearly indicative of osteoarthritis. Mindful of the cautions of Rogers and Waldron (1995), osteoarthritis is only inferred as present in the current work when joint surface changes are observed (i.e. grades 2 or 3 in the scoring scheme for synovial joints).

Degenerative disc disease was scored according to the scheme of Sager (1969), reproduced in Brothwell 1981, fig. 6.9:

Grade 0: Normal vertebral body morphology.
Grade 1: Marginal osteophytes only.
Grade 2: Marginal osteophytes and some porotic changes to bone underlying vertebral end-plate.
Grade 3: As above, but changes more advanced.

Results

Degenerative joint disease is not normally observed in the immature skeleton, and in the current material no instances were seen among the juveniles. Results for adults are shown in Tables 89-94.

Table 89. Osteoarthritis: maximum grade in individuals.

	Maximum grade			
	0	1	2	3
Males	86	21	45	59
Females	57	20	27	36
Total adults	149	41	73	97

Note: figures for total adults include data from nine unsexed adults

Table 90. Distribution of osteoarthritis.

Skeletal element	Grade 0	1	2	3
L mandibular condyle	202	2	1	4
R mandibular condyle	185	1	3	2
Cervical vertebrae	1382	74	72	95
Thoracic vertebrae	2505	90	80	140
Lumbar vertebrae	1060	26	44	43
L ribs	2233	142	107	19
R ribs	2197	137	124	27
L medial clavicle	220	1	4	1
R medial clavicle	215	3	5	0
L lateral clavicle	177	9	18	6
R lateral clavicle	151	13	25	7
L glenoid fossa	225	3	0	0
R glenoid fossa	220	5	1	1
L proximal humerus	211	0	1	1
R proximal humerus	211	2	1	2
L distal humerus	223	0	1	2
R distal humerus	223	1	3	5
L proximal radius	201	0	1	3
R proximal radius	196	1	0	5
L distal radius	211	2	1	2
R distal radius	202	1	1	5
L proximal ulna	213	7	1	0
R proximal ulna	212	7	0	3
L distal ulna	177	6	2	2
R distal ulna	177	3	2	4
L carpals	902	1	8	11
R carpals	871	0	3	10
L metacarpals	1006	4	5	2
R metacarpals	956	9	8	5
L hand phalanges	1237	11	2	7
R hand phalanges	1189	18	7	9
Unsided hand phalanges	837	13	1	0
L acetabulum	207	19	10	6
R acetabulum	202	21	11	8
L proximal femur	217	9	1	6
R proximal femur	205	9	5	10
L distal femur	220	1	1	2

Table 90 continued.

Skeletal element	Grade 0	1	2	3
R distal femur	209	2	2	2
L patella	159	3	0	1
R patella	151	6	2	0
L proximal tibia	209	1	2	2
R proximal tibia	200	1	2	2
L distal tibia	198	0	0	0
R distal tibia	200	0	0	0
L proximal fibula	134	0	0	0
R proximal fibula	118	1	0	0
L distal fibula	183	0	0	0
R distal fibula	185	0	0	0
L calcaneus	174	0	1	1
R calcaneus	176	0	1	0
L talus	167	0	2	1
R talus	170	0	0	0
L tarsals*	659	3	2	0
R tarsals*	640	0	1	0
L metatarsals	715	1	4	1
R metatarsals	711	1	4	2
L foot phalanges	507	0	0	0
R foot phalanges	499	0	1	3
Unsided foot phalanges	400	3	0	0

*excluding tali and cancanei

Table 91. Degenerative disc disease: maximum grade in individuals.

	Maximum grade 0	1	2	3
Males	37	58	60	12
Females	34	43	36	16
Total adults	72	102	97	28

Note: figures for total adults include data from three unsexed adults. For inclusion, individuals needed to show at least one vertebral body present for observation

Table 92. Degenerative disc disease: prevalence by vertebrae.

	Cervical 0	1	2	3	Thoracic 0	1	2	3	Lumbar 0	1	2	3
Males	526	87	93	20	887	433	68	2	328	220	38	4
Females	407	78	90	28	758	340	47	2	272	159	33	7
Total adults	939	167	183	48	1667	780	115	4	600	386	72	11

Note: frequencies for total adults include data from vertebrae from three unsexed adults

155

Table 93. Osteoarthritis: maximum grade in individuals, data split by phase.

	Maximum grade			
	0	1	2	3
Phase 1-2	55	15	32	43
Phase 2	22	2	14	7
Phase 4	14	7	4	16

Table 94. Degenerative disc disease: maximum grade in individuals, data split by phase

	Maximum grade			
	0	1	2	3
Phase 1-2	23	32	52	16
Phase 2	15	14	10	3
Phase 4	4	23	6	1

Discussion

The frequency with which individuals show osteoarthritis at one or more joint surfaces does not differ between the sexes, nor does the frequency with which individuals show disc disease. There may, however, be subtle sex differences in the distribution of degenerative joint disease in the skeleton. The sites most frequently affected by osteoarthritis in males and females are summarised in Table 95.

Table 95. The skeletal sites most frequently affected by osteoarthritis in males and females.

Males		Females	
Site	% affected	Site	% affected
Lateral clavicle	18.1%	Lumbar vertebrae	10.4%
Cervical vertebrae	12.1%	Cervical vertebrae	8.5%
Thoracic vertebrae	8.5%	Lateral clavicle	8.4%
Acetabulum	7.8%	Thoracic vertebrae	6.9%
Lumbar vertebrae	5.1%	Acetabulum	6.6%
Ribs	5.0%	Ribs	6.3%
Proximal femur	5.0%	Proximal femur	4.6%
Distal ulna	4.6%	Proximal tibia	3.5%
Distal radius	3.9%	Mandibular condyle	2.9%
Distal humerus	3.2%	Distal femur	2.8%

Note: Osteoarthritis is only regarded as present if there are joint surface changes, i.e. if the joint is assigned grades 2 or 3 in the scoring scheme used in the current work.

The lateral joint surface of the clavicle is a frequent site for changes in both sexes (as indeed it is in modern populations (Resnick and Niwayama 1988)), but this pattern is more marked in males. In addition, several forearm sites appear in the male 'top ten' but are absent from the female list, which is composed entirely of axial and lower limb sites. If one accepts that mechanical factors are an important influence on patterns of skeletal involvement in osteoarthritis at a population level, then it may be that these differences in the distribution of changes between the sexes reflect differences in activity patterns, with more male involvement in tasks placing greater mechanical forces on some of the joints of the upper limb.

Looking specifically at changes to the spine, it is interesting to note that degenerative disc disease and osteoarthritic changes to the (synovial) facet joints show rather different distributions (Tables 92 and 95). The relative frequency of degenerative disc disease in the different segments of the spine in both males and females is lumbar > thoracic > cervical. For osteoarthritis the order is cervical > thoracic > lumbar for males, lumbar> cervical > thoracic for females.

The observation that, at Wharram Percy, degenerative disc disease is most frequent in the lumbar segment matches the findings of most other studies (Bridges 1994). There appears to be little consistency between studies of different human populations concerning which spinal segment is most commonly affected by osteoarthritis (Bridges 1994). Given that both degenerative disc disease and osteoarthritis appear to reflect to a great extent mechanical factors, it may appear surprising that their distributions within the spinal column should differ. This has been noted for other assemblages (e.g. Bridges 1994; Knüsel et al. 1997) and it may reflect functional differences between the vertebral bodies and the neural arch facet joints. The function of the vertebral bodies is primarily support. The apophysial joints provide less in the way of support (especially those in the thoracic spine, which lie behind the centre of gravity in the upright posture) but allow varying degrees of movement so that weight bearing and spinal curvature have less effect on the distribution of facet joint degeneration (Bridges 1994; Knüsel et al. 1997).

In most locations, whether in the appendicular or axial skeleton, there is a tendency for osteoarthritic changes to be more frequent in right elements (Table 90). For each joint surface, frequency of osteoarthritis is too low for bilateral differences in frequency to reach statistical significance. Looking at locations where either left or right element shows osteoarthritis in at least five cases, twelve of the thirteen locations (medial and lateral clavicle, distal humerus, proximal and distal radius, distal ulna, acetabulum, proximal femur, ribs, carpals, metacarpals, hand phalanges and metatarsals) show a greater frequency of osteoarthritic changes in right elements (the exception is carpals for which the frequency is greater in left elements). This 12:1 split is significantly different from an even left/right pattern (chi-square=9.3, p<0.005). The most plausible explanation of the rightward bias is that it is related to handedness with greater mechanical forces being habitually placed on the right upper limb, and hence on this side of the body, during physically demanding tasks.

The evidence for bilateral asymmetry in the occurrence of marginal osteophytes in the absence of other joint changes is less clear. Of the above thirteen sites, seven show a greater right frequency, four a greater frequency on the left side, with two equal. The distribution is not significantly different from an even left-right pattern (chi-square=0.81, non-significant). It would seem therefore that if there is a rightward bias in the occurrence of marginal osteophytes at otherwise normal joint surfaces then it is more weakly expressed than is the bilateral asymmetry in joint surface changes.

There is no evidence for any variation in frequency of osteoarthritis with respect to phase at Wharram Percy. Analysis of the data in Table 94 indicates that there is some variation in the expression of degenerative disc disease by phase (chi-square = 28.8, 6df, p<0.001). Closer analysis of the data reveals that more individuals show degenerative disc disease in later phases but those that do display it show it less severely. The interpretation of this pattern is unclear.

Inter-site comparisons

Detailed comparisons between degenerative joint disease at Wharram Percy and at other sites are problematic due to the different ways in which earlier writers have recorded and presented data. Comparison can be drawn, however, with medieval skeletons from the Ipswich Blackfriars site, for which degenerative joint disease was recorded by the present writer (Mays 1991) in a similar fashion to the current material. The burials from Ipswich Blackfriars date to the period AD 1263-1538 and are not of friars but of lay benefactors of the friary. Because degenerative changes at both the synovial joints and at intervertebral discs tend to be strongly age progressive, differences in age at death between assemblages may potentially prejudice comparisons. The age at death at Wharram Percy is in general somewhat greater than at Ipswich. For example, at Wharram Percy 60% of adults were over 40 years of age compared with about 50% at Ipswich. This would tend to have the effect of raising the prevalence of both conditions at Wharram Percy compared with Ipswich, and this needs to be kept in mind when making interpretations.

Table 96. Osteoarthritis at Wharram Percy and Ipswich Blackfriars, maximum grade in individuals.

| | Maximum grade | | | |
	0	1	2	3
Wharram Percy	149	41	73	97
Ipswich	61	70	35	45

Note: data from Ipswich taken from Mays (1991)

Table 97. Degenerative disc disease at Wharram Percy and Ipswich Blackfriars, maximum grade in individuals.

| | Maximum grade | | | |
	0	1	2	3
Wharram Percy	72	102	97	28
Ipswich	40	82	37	14

Note: data from Ipswich taken from Mays (1991)

Looking first at osteoarthritis, the distribution of grades at the two sites is different (chi-square = 40.8, 2df, p<0.001). This appears principally to reflect two differences between these groups. There is a greater frequency of degenerative changes classed as grade 1 (marginal osteophytes only) in the Ipswich material, where the frequency of individuals showing a maximum change at any joint of grade 1 is 33% compared with 11% at Wharram Percy. There is a greater frequency of individuals showing changes to grade 2 or grade 3 (true osteoarthritis in Rogers and Waldron's (1995) view) at Wharram Percy: 47% of Wharram Percy adults show osteoarthritis versus 38% at Ipswich. Both these patterns are statistically significant (chi-square = 40.4, p<0.001 and chi-square = 4.7, p<0.05, respectively).

It might at this point be suggested that the greater prevalence of osteoarthritis at Wharram Percy may to some extent be an artefact of the somewhat older age at death in that group. To investigate this, analyses were re-run solely on those aged over 40. Although, as expected, the prevalence of osteoarthritis in individuals was greater among this cohort than among all adults from each group, the difference in frequency between the sites remained similar: 72% of the over 40s at Wharram Percy show osteoarthritis on one or more joint surfaces compared with 61% at Ipswich. This suggests that the difference in prevalence of the condition between the two groups is a robust result and not an artefact of the older age at death at Wharram Percy.

For degenerative disc disease, there is a significant difference in the distribution of the different grades between the two sites (chi-square = 9.9, 3df, p<0.025). Closer analysis indicates that this reflects a difference in the number of individuals showing a maximum of grade 1 changes (i.e. marginal osteophytes only), the frequency is 34% at Wharram Percy and 47% at Ipswich. This difference in frequency of grade 1 changes is statistically valid (chi-square = 8.2, p<0.005).

With regard to the synovial joints, the difference in inter-site patterning between the frequencies of individuals showing marginal osteophytes alone and those showing joint surface changes (with or without marginal osteophytes) may support Rogers and Waldron's (1995) contention that marginal osteophyte formation in the absence of joint surface changes is not diagnostic of osteoarthritis and should be treated as a distinct phenomenon.

The higher frequency of joint surface changes indicative of osteoarthritis at Wharram Percy may relate to differences in habitual mechanical strain placed upon the joints by these two groups. For the medieval peasant, work was a ruling fact of life, and given the state of technology of the day, this meant human physical effort. The Ipswich group were probably made up of middle class traders and craftsmen. It seems likely that their lifestyles would have generally involved less in the way of hard physical labour than would that of low status rural people. If the primacy of mechanical factors in determining the prevalence of osteoarthritis at a population level is accepted, then the difference in frequency of the condition between these two assemblages would be consistent with the likely differences in lifestyle.

Rogers and Waldron (1995) have noted that, in some individuals, there may be a tendency toward the formation of osteophytes at various locations in the skeleton, including the margins of the synovial joints. They term such individuals 'bone formers'. It is possible that the greater frequency of individuals showing marginal osteophytes in the absence of any other joint abnormality in the Ipswich material is simply because in this population there was a greater tendency toward bone formation than was the case at Wharram Percy.

Turning to degenerative disc disease, it seems unlikely that the greater proportion of individuals showing grade 1 changes (vertebral body marginal osteophytes only) at Ipswich reflects greater mechanical strain on the spine, as, if this were so, one would expect an overall greater frequency of degenerative disc disease, including grade 2 and 3 changes, but this is not the case. It is also at odds with the inference, above, of greater mechanical strains on the joints of the Wharram Percy people. Perhaps the greater prevalence of vertebral body osteophytes is best taken, along with the greater frequency of marginal osteophytes at synovial joints, as further evidence of a greater inherent tendency toward bone formation in the Ipswich group.

Diffuse idiopathic skeletal hyperostosis (DISH)

DISH is a progressive ossification of the spinal ligaments, particularly in the thoracic segment, leading to ankylosis. There is also ossification at extra-spinal ligamentous and tendinous insertions. At present, the causes of DISH are unknown. Epidemiological studies of living individuals have suggested a number of possible associations and risk factors. Perhaps the most robust of these is an association with obesity and late onset diabetes, but associations with human leucocyte antigen HLAB27, gout and with disturbances to lipid and urate metabolism, have also been suggested (refs in Mays 2000b).

Vertebral osteophytes due to DISH were distinguished from those due to degenerative disc disease and other arthropathies using the criteria of Rogers et al. (1987). In a major population-based study of DISH using radiographs of living subjects (Julkunen et al. 1971) DISH was diagnosed if two compete bony bridges were present between vertebral bodies in the thoracic spine. This same criterion was applied in the current work.

Altogether, 29 individuals showed indications of spinal ligamentous ossification consistent with bone formation due to DISH with a further two showing significant enthesial ossification at extra-spinal locations but not in the spine. Of the 29 with spinal changes, 23 show ossifications in the thoracic spine. In eighteen of these the ossification was insufficiently advanced at time of death to permit diagnosis of DISH according to clinical criteria (Julkunen et al. 1971). Of these eighteen, there were two skeletons in which only two vertebral bodies were united, and sixteen in which osteophyte formation was insufficient to cause any instances of vertebral ankylosis (although in several cases osteophytes interlocked). This leaves five skeletons satisfying the clinical criteria for diagnosis of DISH (Table 98).

In their study, Julkunen et al. (1971) found no cases of DISH in individuals under 40 years old. The current results seem consistent with this. Given the definition of DISH used in the current work, no individual with fewer than three thoracic vertebral bodies present for observation could be scored for the disease. In the light of the above, the prevalence of DISH at Wharram Percy is expressed with respect to the number of adults over 40 with three or more thoracic vertebral bodies available for study (Table 99).

Comparison with archaeological and modern data

The prevalence of DISH at Wharram Percy was compared with that recorded in the Ipswich Blackfriars skeletons (Mays 2000b) and with that reported for modern Europeans (Julkunen et al. 1971) (Table 100).

The prevalence of DISH at Wharram Percy differs significantly from that at Ipswich Blackfriars (chi-square=10.8, p<0.005) with Ipswich having the higher frequency. The prevalence of DISH at Wharram Percy does not differ from that reported for recent Europeans by Julkunen et al. (1971). Julkunen et al. (1971) report a greater male frequency of the disease (the prevalence for males was 3.5% compared with 2.2% for females), as do other writers (references in Mays 2000b). At Wharram Percy, all cases were male. At Ipswich Blackfriars, ten of the eleven cases were male (Mays 2000b). Although numbers are too small for the sex imbalance to attain statistical significance in either archaeological group, when the data from the two sites are combined the sex difference is statistically valid (chi-square=7.44, p<0.01).

Table 98. Summary of cases of DISH.

Burial	Sex	Age	Phase	Ankylosed vertebrae	Vertebrae showing ligamentous ossification without ankylosis
CN05	M	50+	4	C5-C6, T5-T11	C6-T1, T11, T12, L2, L3, L5, S1
CN33	M	50+	4	T6-T7, T8-T10, L1-L2	T11-L1, L3-L5
NA046	M	50+	1-2	T7-T9	T10-T12, L2-S1
NA217	M	50+	2	C5-C6, T4-T5, T7-T11, 2 lumbar	C3, C7, T1, T2, T5-T7, 3 lumbar
WCO013	M	50+	-	T10-T12	T2, T4, T9, T10

Table 99. Prevalence of DISH.

	Males	Females
DISH present	5	0
DISH absent	80	63
Prevalence (%)	5.9	0

Notes: Figures for total adults include one unsexed individual. Tables 98 and 99 are corrected versions of data which were originally published in *Journal of Paleopathology* (Mays 2000b). The data were incorrectly printed in that journal due to printer's errors, which were so profuse that they marred the article. The journal refused to publish an *erratum*.

Table 100. Prevalence of DISH in three populations.

	Wharram Percy	Ipswich Blackfriars	Living Europeans
DISH present	5	11	164
DISH absent	144	58	5765
Prevalence (%)	3.4	15.9	2.8

Notes: All prevalences reported for adults over 40 years old. For the archaeological groups only those over 40 with at least three thoracic vertebrae are included. The Wharram Percy data include one unsexed individual. Ipswich Blackfriars data from Mays (2000b); recent data from Julkunen *et al.* (1971).

Discussion

The archaeological data are consistent with those for living populations in indicating a greater male prevalence of DISH. This shows that the sex difference is not simply an artefact of gender-related exposure to risk factors for the condition due to some aspect of modern lifestyle, but may represent some inherent difference in bone metabolism between the sexes.

A number of palaeopathological studies (e.g. Waldron 1985; Rogers *et al.* 1985; Janssen and Maat 1999; Rogers and Waldron 2001) have claimed a higher prevalence of DISH among burials from monastic sites and have interpreted this as indicative of obesity due to over-eating among monastic orders or among the high status benefactors accorded burial in religious houses. At first sight, the higher prevalence of DISH among the Ipswich Blackfriars skeletons than in those from Wharram Percy might be viewed as consistent with this. Interpreting the current results in terms of different rates of obesity is problematic. The frequency of DISH among the Ipswich Blackfriars group is markedly greater than reported in modern Europeans (Julkunen *et al.* 1971). It is difficult to believe that obesity was more of a problem among the middle class traders and craftsmen interred at the Blackfriars, who were hardly among the wealthiest by medieval standards, than it is among modern Europeans, given the high calorific intake and low activity levels which characterise current Western lifestyles. The growth studies in Chapter 8 indicated that diet was deficient at Wharram Percy, and it is hard to believe that obesity was a problem here, but nevertheless the rate of DISH was no less than it is today.

Given the above, it would seem unlikely that the patterning seen in the DISH data in Table 100 reflects differences in the prevalence of obesity. The higher prevalence at Ipswich Blackfriars than at Wharram Percy may represent an inherently greater predisposition among the Ipswich folk to form bone, a suggestion which is consistent with the greater prevalence of marginal osteophytes at synovial joints and at vertebral body margins discussed above.

Aseptic necroses

Aseptic necroses involve the death of a section of bone, generally at an epiphysis, through deficient blood supply. There is often a history of trauma to the joint, but some cases are idiopathic (i.e. have no identifiable cause). Several types of aseptic necrosis were evident in the current material.

Osteochondritis dissecans

Osteochondritis dissecans is a focal necrosis of bone on the articular surface of a synovial joint. The necrotic fragment cleaves away, leaving in the joint surface a pit with sclerotic margins. In the current material, six cases were identified (Table 101, Plate 49).

Table 101. Osteochondritis dissecans.

Burial	Sex & age	Phase	Location of lesion(s)
CN13	F, 30-40	4	Left talus: posterior sub-talar articular surface
CN17	M, 30-40	4	Left and right tibiae: medial surface of tibial plateaux
G279	M, 50+	1	Left and right tibiae: medial surface of tibial plateaux
NA176	M, c25	2	Left femur: lateral condyle
NA198	??M, 11-12	-	Axis vertebra, left superior articular surface
WCO176	J, 10	-	Left tibia: distal joint surface

Notes: Sex, M=male, F=female, J=unsexed juvenile ?? denotes sex inferred from craniofacial morphology in juveniles; Age: estimated age at death, in years. In addition to the cases listed in the table, there were three further individuals (Burials CN11, EE030 and G406) showing articular surface pits which may be osteochondritis dissecans (see Appendix 2).

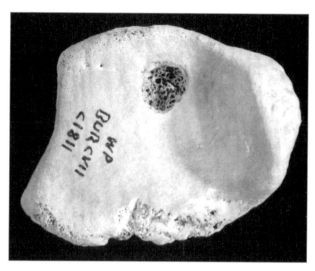

Plate 49. The distal joint surface of the left tibia from Burial WCO176, showing a pit, probably due to osteochondritis dissecans.

In modern subjects, the great majority of osteochondritis dissecans lesions occur on convex joint surfaces. The most common location is on the medial condyle of the femur (Resnick and Niwayama 1988). These patterns are not evident in the current material, but given that there is an association between osteochondritis dissecans and joint trauma, there is no reason to expect distribution of lesions in ancient populations, where activity patterns are very different from those of today, to match those seen in modern cases.

Necrosis of the femoral heads
Burial G601 (M, 35-45, Phase 1-2) shows partial destruction of both femoral heads, focused on the upper parts of the articular surfaces (Plate 50). The lytic lesions penetrate deep within the sub-chondral bone, undermining the joint surface. In the left femur this has led to the beginning of the collapse of the articular surface, with fissure fracturing. The margins of lytic areas are sclerotic. It seems probable that this is an example of bilateral avascular necrosis of the femoral heads (Ortner and Putschar 1985, 236-8).

Interruption of blood supply due to fracture of the femur neck or dislocation of the femur may lead to avascular necrosis of the femoral head. It may also occur in some systemic diseases such as Gaucher's disease (Aufderheide and Rodriguez-Martin 1998). There is, however, no sign of disease or femur neck fracture in Burial G601. Aseptic necrosis may occur following hip trauma even in the absence of fracture or dislocation. Perhaps this is what happened here – this individual had clearly suffered trauma as he had a very disorganised left elbow joint secondary to injury (see Chapter 11). Femoral head aseptic necrosis may also occur idiopathically.

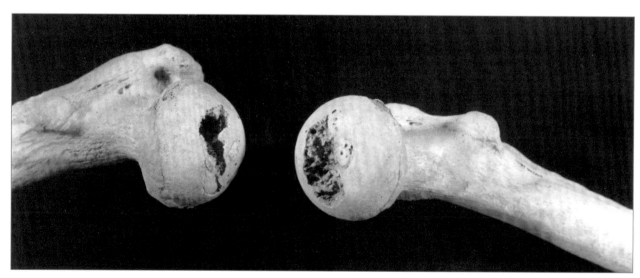

Plate 50. Femoral heads of Burial G601. The cavitation is probably due to avascular necrosis.

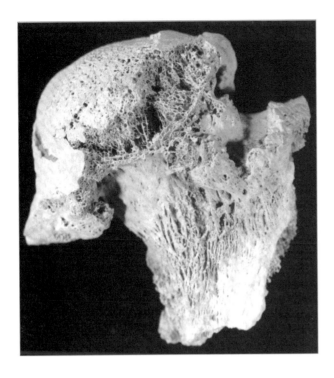

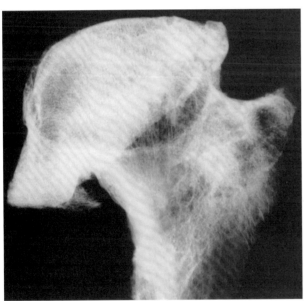

Plate 51. The left femoral head of Burial WCO115. There is flattening of the femoral head and formation of massive osteophytes. The radiograph shows that there is no displacement of the head relative to the neck. Probably Perthes' disease.

Perthes' disease

Perthes' disease is avascular necrosis of the femoral head in children. Its peak age of occurrence is between three and ten years of age and 80% of cases occur in males (Aufderheide and Rodriguez-Martin 1998, 84). Ninety percent of cases are unilateral (Wynne-Davis and Gormley 1978). Burial WCO115 (M, adult, unphased) shows bony changes compatible with Perthes' disease.

There is marked flattening of the left femur head, and both it and the left acetabulum show severe osteoarthritic changes with porosis, eburnation and massive marginal osteophytes (Plate 51). The osteophytes have irritated the periosteum on the femur neck and around the acetabulum, resulting in some new bone deposition. The pit for the ligamentum teres on the femoral head has been obliterated. The length of the femoral neck has been preserved and there is no evidence for displacement of the head with respect to the axis of the neck (Plate 51). Both components of the right hip joint are missing so it is unknown whether changes were bilateral.

Aseptic necrosis of the metacarpal head (Dieterich's disease)

The head of the right third metacarpal of Burial NA202 (F, 60+, Phase 1-2) is flattened and broadened (Plate 52). The distal part of the shaft is thickened and the bone is 2mm shorter than its left side counterpart. It seems likely that this represents a vascular disturbance to the epiphysis of the bone, analogous to Freiberg's disease in the metatarsal. Avascular necrosis of the metacarpal head (Dieterich's disease) is rare and there is usually a history of trauma: effusion of the metacarpo-phalangeal joint or occult fracture of the metacarpal head may compress the blood vessels supplying the metacarpal head, causing necrosis (Wright and Dell 1991; de Smet 1998). As far as I am aware, this is the first time that the condition has been recognised in ancient skeletal remains.

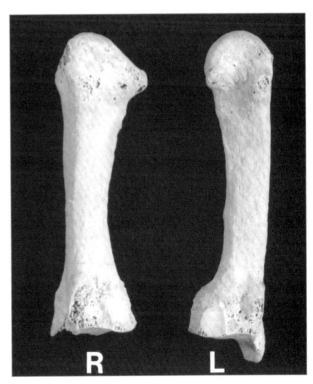

Plate 52. The third metacarpals of Burial NA202. The deformity in the right bone is probably due to avascular necrosis of the head (Dieterich's disease).

Miscellaneous joint disease

Hallux valgus

Hallux valgus is the lateral deviation of the great toe. It generally arises from habitual wearing of footwear which constricts the toes. Since the orientation of the great toe is somewhat variable even in undiseased feet, hallux valgus was only diagnosed if noticeable lateral deviation of the great toe was accompanied by osteoarthritis of the metatarsal head or bony activity on the medial side of the first metatarsal suggestive of the existence of a bunion at this site. Seven individuals (Burials CN18, G265, G278, G636, V21, WCO014 and WCO018) showed this condition. All were adult, five males, one female, one unsexed.

Scheuermann's disease

Defective endochondral ossification of the vertebral bodies is known as Scheuermann's disease. Early theories as to its aetiology involved avascular necrosis of the ring epiphysis. This has not been verified, and the causation of this condition remains uncertain (Wenger and Frick 1999). In dry bones, Scheuermann's disease manifests principally as wedging of vertebral bodies (Scoles *et al.* 1991). Burial SA52/16 (F, 21-23, unphased) shows erosions on the superior and inferior surfaces of the vertebral bodies from T8 to L1, near their anterior margins, producing slight kyphosis. The bone at eroded areas is sclerotic. Many affected vertebrae also bear Schmorl's nodes, depressions due to protrusion of disc tissue into the vertebral end-plates. These changes are consistent with Scheuermann's disease (Scoles *et al.* 1991). Measurement of vertebral bodies, using the methodology of Scoles *et al.* (1991), reveals that only two of them show wedging of greater than 5°. Clinical diagnostic criteria demand that at least three consecutive vertebral bodies show wedging of at least 5° (Scoles *et al.* 1991).

Supra-acetabular cysts

In advanced osteoarthritis of the hip, sub-chondral cyst formation is almost invariably a feature, most probably due to extrusion of synovial fluid under pressure through fissures in the degenerate cartilage into the subchondral bone. Forty innominates in 30 individuals show formation of cystic cavities within the subchondral bone of the ilium, immediately superior to the acetabular roof (Plate 53), in the absence of diagnostic osteoarthritic changes to the superior part of the acetabulum. In the whole assemblage 227 adults show one or both supra-acetabular areas intact for observations. Using this as the denominator gives a prevalence of the cystic changes of 13%. All affected individuals were adults; 22 were male, eight female. This sex imbalance is statistically significant (chi-square = 5.03, p = 0.025). In no case were there corresponding lesions on the femoral head. All cysts showed communication with the joint space via a single or multiple holes (Plate 54). These holes were situated in the upper part of the acetabulum on or adjacent to the rim. Diameters of the cystic defects in the subchondral bone ranged up to 45mm, but most were between 5 and 15mm.

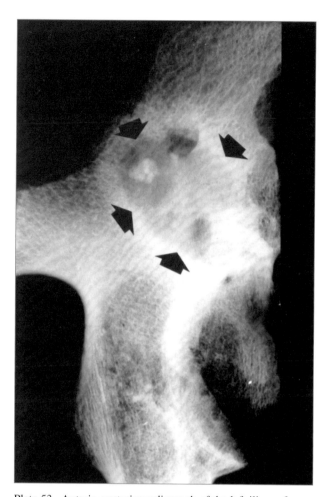

Plate 53. Anterio-posterior radiograph of the left ilium of Burial EE004. There is a large supra-acetabular cyst, the outline of which is indicated by the arrows. The radio-opacity within the defect and the small, sub-circular, radiolucent patch just above it and to the right in the photograph are post-depositional artefacts.

Plate 54. The right acetabulum of Burial G278. There is a pore on the joint surface near to the acetabular rim. The pore communicates with a large, cystic cavity within the ilium. The cleft in the joint surface further away from the acetabular rim is an unconnected anatomical variant.

162

The lesions resemble those described as supra-acetabular cysts by Wells (1976). These lesions are reported in detail elsewhere (Mays forthcoming b). The following is a summary of the interpretations made in that article.

It is suggested that the supra-acetabular cysts in these cases arose due to trauma. In three instances (Burials EE004, G482 and G746) this is supported by the co-existence of healed fractures of the acetabular roof, and in six (Burials CN31, G607, NA031, SA033, WCO059 and WCO200) by the presence of acetabular rim avulsion injuries. In these cases it is suggested that the sub-chondral cysts formed as a result of extrusion of synovial fluid into the subchondral bone as a result of the injury.

In the remaining 31 affected innominates there is no bony evidence for trauma. The supra-acetabular cysts are similar in morphology and location to those in the nine cases which did show acetabular bony injury, suggesting that trauma may also have played a part in their causation. Clinical studies (references in Mays forthcoming b) have shown an association between supra-acetabular cysts and injuries to the acetabular labrum (a fibro-cartilaginous extension of the acetabular rim) and associated structures: synovial fluid may be forced into subchondral bone via a tear at the labral base or in neighbouring cartilage.

In modern populations, injury to the labrum and associated structures of the acetabular rim is most often seen in patients showing acetabular dysplasia, as in the dysplastic acetabulum, mechanical forces are more concentrated near the rim edge than is the case in the normal hip (references in Mays forthcoming b). Of the current examples, only four (Burials EE099, NA031, NA088 and WCO200) show shallow acetabula, in the remaining cases the hips are not dysplastic. Perhaps in the Wharram Percy population the (presumed) higher activity levels meant that a greater proportion of individuals exposed their hip joints to mechanical forces sufficient to cause this type of injury than is customarily the case in (presumed more sedentary) modern European populations. If this argument is accepted, then the greater frequency in male hips suggests greater involvement among males in tasks sufficiently heavy to expose the hip to injury.

Infectious disease

Infection involving the bone surface results in inflammation of the periosteum (periostitis). This stimulates an osteogenic response so that new bone is deposited upon existing cortex. Infection involving the compact bone, and the marrow cavity or trabecular bone within, is termed osteomyelitis. This characteristically results in destructive lesions within the bone, together with reactive bone production, which results in irregular thickening of the affected element, and often in formation of sinuses through which pus exudes from the interior.

In some instances, the morphology and distribution of infectious lesions in a skeleton permit the identification of the particular disease responsible. In others, where a specific diagnosis cannot be made, cases are referred to as instances of non-specific infection. At Wharram Percy both specific and non-specfic infectious lesions were noted. In addition to bone infections, two further conditions, porotic hyperostosis and hypertrophic osteoarthropathy, which likely occurred as a response to soft-tissue infections, were identified in the current material and are discussed in this section.

Specific infections
At Wharram Percy, two specific infectious diseases were identified, tuberculosis and leprosy.

Tuberculosis
Nine individuals showed skeletal changes consistent with tuberculosis. Lesions were principally located in the vertebral bodies or at the hip, were destructive with little new bone formation, and in advanced spinal lesions there was angular kyphosis. The location of lesions is summarised in Table 102. In addition to these nine fairly clear cases, two other burials show lesions which may be tuberculous. Burial SA049 (F, 50+, Phase 4) shows superficial destruction of the left acetabulum and femoral head with minimal bony regeneration, together with a periosteal reaction on the left tibia. Burial CN14 (M,

Table 102. Cases of tuberculosis, summary of lesions.

| Burial | Sex & age | Phase | Lesions | | |
			Spine	Hip	Other
EE056	M?, 50+	1-2	Yes (t,l)	No	Yes (ribs)
G438	F, 25-35	2	Yes (t,l)	No	Yes (ulna, ribs, ilium)
G482	M, 50+	2	Yes (l)	No	No
NA026	F, 35-45	1-2	Yes (t)	-	Yes (ribs, scapula)
NA046	M, 50+	1-2	Yes (l)	No	No
NA112	M, 50+	1-2	No	Yes	No
NA197	M, 50+	1-2	No	Yes	No
SA013	F, 35-45	2-3	Yes (t)	No	Yes (ribs)
WCO142	M, Adult	-	Yes (l,s)	Yes	Yes (ilium, femora, tibiae, fibula, metatarsal, calcanei, foot phalanx)

Notes: Sex: M=male, F=female; Age: estimated age at death, in years unless stated; Lesions: lower case letters give location of lesions in spine t=thoracic, l=lumbar, s=sacral; - = part of skeleton missing

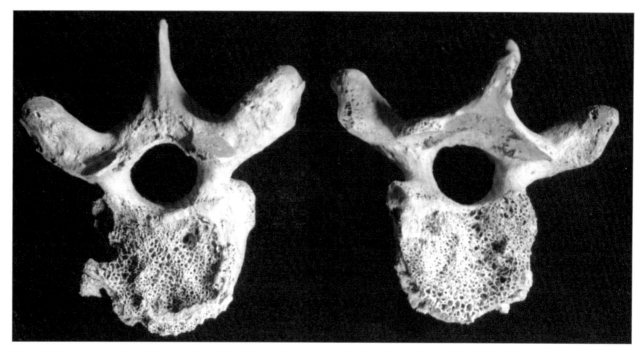

Plate 55. Superior surface of the seventh and inferior surface of the sixth thoracic vertebrae of Burial NA026. The bodies show superficial destruction characteristic of tuberculosis.

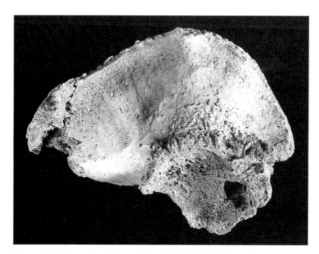

Plate 56. The right ilium of Burial NA197. There is destruction of the acetabulum suggestive of tuberculosis.

adult, Phase 4) shows superficial destruction of the right acetabulum and femoral head, with a little new bone formation around the acetabulum, together with superficial resorptive lesions of both ischial tuberosities.

Examples of spine and hip lesions are illustrated in Plates 55 and 56. The individual with the most widespread skeletal disease was Burial WCO142. Only the lower parts of the skeleton survive, but in addition to destructive spinal and hip lesions, many bones show subperiosteal bone deposition, and there is destruction of the head of the left 5th metatarsal.

Four of the cases listed in Table 102 showed lesions on the ribs. In all instances, changes were confined to the vertebral ends of costal elements and took the form of destructive foci (Plate 57) and/or thickening by subperiosteal new bone deposition. In each case, the rib lesions appear to represent extensions of spinal disease.

No evidence was found in these nine cases for periostitis focused on the visceral surfaces of ribs, of the form described by Kelley and Micozzi (1984) and Roberts *et al.* (1994) as representing direct extension to costal elements of sub-adjacent pulmonary infection (although other skeletons from Wharram Percy do show this type of rib disease – see below).

Tuberculosis is a bacterial disease. In man, the principal causative agents are two members of the *Mycobacterium tuberculosis* complex, *Mycobacterium tuberculosis* and *Mycobacterium bovis*. *Mycobacterium tuberculosis* is almost exclusively a human pathogen. It is transmitted person to person as a droplet infection so that disease caused by this micro-organism generally begins as a respiratory infection. *Mycobacterium bovis* causes disease in diverse animal species (particularly cattle) as well as in man, and it is naturally transmissible between animals and humans. *M. bovis* may be acquired by humans from inhalation of contaminated aerosol from live infected animals or carcasses, producing pulmonary disease. It may also be contracted by consumption of milk or meat from infected animals. In such cases, the primary lesion is in the cervical lymph nodes (due to oropharangeal penetration by ingested bacteria) or in the alimentary tract (Aufderheide and Rodriguez-Martin 1998, 118).

Although disease due to both *M. tuberculosis* and *M. bovis* may affect the skeleton (Davies *et al.* 1984), it is impossible to distinguish the two using osteological criteria as the skeletal lesions produced are similar. This distinction is possible, however, using ancient DNA. In an effort both to confirm the diagnoses of tuberculosis and to identify causative species, DNA analyses aimed at detecting and amplifying *M. tuberculosis* complex DNA were conducted on these nine individuals. This work has

Plate 57. The left sixth rib of Burial SA013. There is a lytic lesion at its head, probably as a result of tuberculosis.

been reported in detail elsewhere (Mays *et al.* 2001a), but in brief the results confirmed the diagnosis of tuberculosis in each case, and in all instances showed the presence of *M. tuberculosis*; there was no evidence for *M. bovis.*

The finding that all cases were *M. tuberculosis* not *M. bovis* infection was somewhat unexpected. *M. tuberculosis* infection is a population density dependent disease (Manchester 1984), whereas close man-animal contact is a risk factor for human acquisition of *M. bovis* infection. It has been suggested (Manchester 1991) that, in earlier human populations, there was a baseline of *M. bovis* infection upon which was superimposed *M. tuberculosis* disease. Although disease caused by both pathogens is likely to have affected both urban and rural populations, the balance between the two may have differed in different communities, *M. tuberculosis* being favoured in crowded urban centres whereas scattered, rural, agrarian communities may have harboured a greater proportion of cases due to *M. bovis.*

The parish of Wharram Percy, and the region in which it is situated, were sparsely populated by medieval standards (Bell 1987; Smith 1988). At Wharram Percy, cattle bones formed about 40-60% of faunal remains (Ryder 1974; Stevens 1992; Pinter-Bellows 1992). Excavations at the settlement at Wharram Percy yielded remains of pottery vessels which would have been used for dairy products, testifying to the importance of these foods in diets (Beresford and Hurst 1990). House-plans uncovered during excavation indicate that humans and cattle shared the same living space, cattle being stalled at one end of a peasant dwelling, the family occupying the other (Beresford and Hurst 1990). Given the above, the expectation was that at least some cases of tuberculosis would have been due to *M. bovis.*

One explanation for the absence of *M. bovis* disease is that the herds at Wharram Percy may have been free of tuberculosis. One way of eliminating this possibility would be to demonstrate, using ancient DNA, that *M. bovis* was present in some diseased animal remains excavated from the site. No faunal remains from Wharram Percy showing destructive lesions resembling those illustrated from recent cases of tuberculous animals

(Lignereux and Peters 1999) could be located. There were, however, a number of cattle rib fragments showing periostitis. In cattle, as in man, chronic lesions in the lungs are a prominent feature of tuberculous disease. In humans, it seems that rib periostitis may be associated with pulmonary tuberculosis (Kelley and Micozzi 1984; Roberts *et al.* 1994), so it seems reasonable to speculate that this may also be the case for cattle, although there is, as yet, no direct evidence confirming this. Although rib periostitis cannot be considered diagnostic for tuberculosis in cattle, just as it is not in humans, these rib fragments seemed to represent the most promising targets available for DNA analysis. We subjected three diseased cattle ribs to PCR assays for tuberculosis DNA but all proved negative (Mays *et al.* 2001a). This may reflect poor DNA survival in those specimens or that the rib periostitis may have been due to some other disease. The results do not permit comment upon whether or not tuberculosis was present in the Wharram Percy cattle.

If domestic stock were not the main source of tuberculosis among the population at Wharram Percy, alternative models for infection from human sources need to be considered. Rural Yorkshire would not appear to have provided an ideal environment for a population density-dependent disease such as pulmonary tuberculosis. Nevertheless, it does appear that tuberculosis can be maintained even in scattered populations (Black 1975), so it might be suggested that the human form of the disease was endemic among rural communities in this area in the medieval period. The degree to which tuberculosis can be maintained in human groups of small size in the absence of an extrinsic reservoir of relatively large size is unclear (Buikstra and Cook 1981). Population aggregates in urban centres may act as reservoirs of tuberculous infection, which may then 'pulse out' to small rural communities in their hinterlands (Buikstra and Cook 1981). York, about 20 miles from Wharram Percy, had a population of about 12,000 in the medieval period making one of the largest cities in England (Goldberg 1986). Excavated human remains from York showing tuberculous lesions (e.g. Stroud 1993) confirm the presence of the disease there in medieval times.

In Chapter 7 it was argued that there may have been emigration from Wharram Percy to urban centres such as York. Furthermore, ceramic and other artefactual evidence from Wharram Percy indicates trade with local towns such as Malton (Hurst 1984). A few remains of marine fauna (Ryder 1974) have also been recovered from Wharram Percy, and consistent with this, stable isotope determinations (Chapter 7) indicate that marine foods were a small but important component of human diets here. Marine foods may have been obtained direct from fishing ports, such as Scarborough or Hull, or from trade with inland market towns.

Perhaps contact with reservoirs of the disease as a result of social and economic links with larger population centres may have helped maintain tuberculosis in the countryside. Models of this nature, which invoke person to person transmission of disease, may be more appropriate for understanding tuberculosis at Wharram Percy than reference to local animal vectors.

Given that *M. tuberculosis* infection is a population density dependent disease, one's *a priori* expectation might be that its frequency would be greater in urban than in rural settlements. There is no indication of this, however, in the present material. Among adults at Wharram Percy, the prevalence of tuberculosis is 9/360 = 2.5%. This compares with 4/312 = 1.3% of adults from York Fishergate (Stroud 1993) and 6/342 = 1.8% of adults at York Jewbury (Brothwell and Browne 1994). No DNA work has yet been done on the York examples, so it cannot at present be confirmed that they represent cases of *M. tuberculosis* rather than *M. bovis*. Even if, as seems likely, all the urban cases do prove to be *M. tuberculosis*, the data still provide no evidence of a greater prevalence of this infection than at rural Wharram Percy.

Leprosy
Burial G708 (??M, 10, Phase 1-2) shows deposits of woven bone upon the superior surface of the hard palate. The margins of the pyriform aperture are thickened and rounded, and there is resorption of the anterior nasal spine

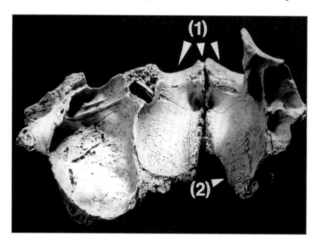

Plate 58. Superior view of the maxillae of Burial G708. There is resorption of the anterior nasal spine and rounding of the pyriform aperture (1), and there is deposition of new bone on the superior surface of the hard palate (2). These changes are strongly suggestive of leprosy.

(Plate 58). These rhino-maxillary changes are typical of those encountered in leprosy (Møller-Christensen 1961; Andersen and Manchester 1992). Only a few hand and foot bones were present; they showed no abnormalities. PCR analysis for *Mycobacterium leprae* DNA proved positive, confirming the diagnosis (Watson *et al.* 2004).

In the medieval period, lepers were usually segregated from the rest of the population by their isolation in leper hospitals, in whose burial grounds they were generally interred at death (Clay 1909). Burial G708 comes from Phase 5.1 of the Glebe area of the churchyard. Radiocarbon determinations indicate that this phase dates to AD 960-1100. The first leper hospitals in England were founded in the late 11th century (Manchester 1984), and during the 12th century segregation of sufferers in leper hospitals began to become routine (Clay 1909). The relatively early date of Burial G708 (perhaps coupled with his young age) may explain why this individual was buried in the churchyard (suggesting he continued to live in the community until his death) despite the fact that the skeletal changes indicate that facial signs of leprosy would have been clearly visible. Although this individual was buried in the northern-most excavated part of the churchyard, he does not lie at the edge of the spatial distribution of interments – burials belonging to the same phase continue to the north. The location of this burial cannot be considered marginal nor is there anything in the treatment of the corpse which would mark this interment out from others.

Non-specific infection
At Wharram Percy, cases of non-specific periostitis and osteomyelitis were observed.

Periostitis
A total of 58 individuals show non-specific periostitis (Table 103). Conditions other than bone infection may elicit periosteal new bone production. These include some forms of bone cancer and hypertrophic osteoarthropathy, and cases of these are tentatively identified further on in this chapter. However, periostitis is generally an indication of bone infection in archaeological material (Ortner and Putschar 1985, 132), so it seems reasonable to consider the 58 cases seen here predominantly as examples of infection.

Among adults, the most frequent site for lesions is in the lower leg. Twenty-one of the 29 adults with periostitis show tibial and/or fibular lesions. In seventeen of these cases, lesions are confined to the lower legs, in four periostitis also occurs in other elements, generally the femur or foot bones. Although periosteal reactions in the lower leg-bones may, on occasion, arise as a result of systemic disease, the patterning here would seem to suggest localised infection of the lower legs may have been an important, if not exclusive, cause of lesions here in adults. Given that the response of bone tissue to infectious disease is fairly slow, this indicates the presence of chronic lower leg infections. The exposed position of the tibia renders it vulnerable to trauma, and in the 18th and 19th centuries, medico-historical records indicate that chronic infection and ulceration of the lower legs, probably initiated by minor injury, was a frequent medical problem (Loudon 1981). It seems reasonable to suppose that local infection following minor injuries to the lower legs might be an important cause of the periostitis at Wharram Percy.

Plate 59. A rib fragment from Burial WCO137, showing a deposit of woven bone upon its visceral surface.

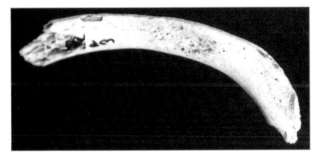

Plate 60. A left upper rib from Burial G723. There is a shallow erosion on the inferior/visceral surface. A minor proliferative lesion is also visible, proximal to this (on the right of the photograph).

Four adults and four juveniles showed periostitis on the visceral surfaces of the ribs (Plate 59). In three individuals (Burials EE016, G658 and G723) the ribs also showed superficial erosive lesions (Plate 60). It seems likely that visceral surface rib lesions of the type seen in the current material are a bony response to underlying pleuro-pulmonary infection (Roberts *et al.* 1998). Studies on modern dissecting hall skeletal collections (Kelley and Micozzi 1984; Roberts *et al.* 1994) have found that visceral surface rib lesions are more frequent in tuberculosis than in other respiratory diseases. In this light, it would be of interest to determine whether the examples in the current material represent cases of tuberculosis. In order to investigate this, analyses for tubercle bacillus DNA were conducted. Full details of this work are given elsewhere (Mays *et al.* 2002b), however in brief, of the six cases which, of the above, have thus far been subject to DNA analyses (Burials EE016, G253, G658, G723, WCO137, and WCO200) only Burial G658 was positive for *M. tuberculosis* complex DNA. It does not appear likely that this simply reflects poor survival of pathogen DNA, because the work discussed above on skeletons showing classical tuberculous lesions demonstrates that *Mycobacterium tuberculosis* complex DNA may survive well in diseased bone under the burial conditions obtaining at the site. A more likely explanation is that, at Wharram Percy, these rib lesions are generally due to respiratory infections other than tuberculosis.

Four individuals with visceral surface rib lesions displayed other bone disease relevant to the interpretation of the rib changes. Burial WCO200 shows bony changes indicative of hypertrophic osteoarthropathy, a condition which normally arises as a result of chronic chest disease, in earlier populations principally infection (see below). This supports the idea that the rib lesions in this individual are a response to pleuro-pulmonary infection but does not allow a more specific diagnosis to be advanced. Burial G253 showed fractures, with woven bone callus, to two rib fragments. Given that the visceral surface rib lesions were also of woven bone, it seems possible that they are a bony response to infection introduced as a result of the chest injury sustained by this individual. Burial G658, in addition to the periosteal reactions on the ribs and leg bones (Table 103), shows several other changes suggestive of bony infection. There is thickening of some proximal rib ends, and superficial erosions beneath the epiphyseal cartilage of the proximal left tibia and distal left femur. There are also minor endocranial resorptive changes (Plate 61). Burial G658 was the only instance where DNA analyses proved positive for M. tuberculosis complex DNA, and the above extra-costal lesions are consistent with those which have been observed, either in documented cases of tuberculosis in the case of the long-bone periosteal reactions (Santos

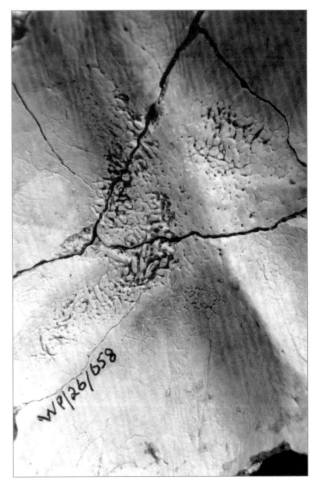

Plate 61. The endocranial surface of the occipital bone of Burial G658 showing sinuous resorptive lesions.

Table 103. Non-specific periostitis.

Burial	Sex & age	Phase	Active or remodelled	Location of lesions
Adults				
CN05	M, 50+	4	r	R fibula
EE016	F, 21-25	1-2	ar	1L, 4R, 1U rib
EE018	F, 21	1-2	r	L & R tibiae
EE070	F, 40-50	1-2	r	R tibia & fibula
EE098	M, Adult	1-2	r	R tibia & fibula
G253	F, 18-19	2	a	3U ribs
G278	M, Adult	2	r	L tibia
G303	M, 30-40	1-2	r	L tibia & fibula
G379	M, 45-60	1-2	r	L & R tibiae
G398	M, 21-24	2	a	R tibia
G411	M, 50+	2	r	R femur, L & R tibiae & fibulae
G462	M, 20-21	2	a	First row phalanx, L hand
G678	M?, Adult	2	r	U tibia
G692	F, 50+	1-2	r	L & R tibiae & fibulae
G747	F, 21-30	1-2	r	L tibia
NA104	M, 25-40	1	a	R radius
NA176	M, 25	2	r	R fibula
NA177	M, Adult	1-2	ra	L & R femora, tibiae & fibulae, R 2nd metatarsal
NA218	M, 50+	1-2	r	L & R tibiae & fibulae, R femur
NA233	M, 40+	1-2	ra	R fibula, R ulna
NA234	M, 40+	2-3	r	L tibia & fibula
SA002	M, 22-24	3-4	a	L & R tibiae
WCO009	M, 25-40	2-3	r	L fibula
WCO039	U, 16-20	-	a	L tibia, R fibula
WCO130	F, 50+	2-3	ar	L tibia
WCO137	M, 50+	-	a	4R & 5U ribs
WCO181	M, 25-35	2-3	a	L & R femora
WCO199	F, 40-50	-	a	L & R scapulae
WCO200	M, 50+	-	a	2L, 1R rib
Juveniles				
EE029	M, 16-18	-	a	Sacrum
EE054	J, 1-3 months		a	L scapula, L & R ilia
EE072	??F, 10	-	a	L femur
G327	J, 1½	2	a	Endocranial surface
G467	J, 4-5	2	a	L fibula
G531	J, 1	2	ra	U fibula, endocranial surface
G658	??M, 11	1-2	ra	10R ribs, L femur, tibia & fibula
G697	J, 2-3	1-2	a	Endocranial surface
G723	??F, 10	1-2	ar	7L, 6R ribs
NA004A	J, 38wiu	-	a	L humerus
NA014A	J, 44-47wiu	-	a	L & R tibiae, ectocranial surface
NA024	J, 5	-	a	Endocranial surface
NA043	J, 46-47wiu	-	a	L & R tibiae & femora
NA043A	J, 6 months	-	a	Ecto- and endocranial surfaces
NA060	J, 45wiu	-	a	Endocranial surface, L & R humeri, R ulna

Table 103 continued.

Burial	Sex & age	Phase	Active or remodelled	Location of lesions
NA103	??F, 7	-	ar	6L, 3R, 3U ribs, L femur, L2, L3
NA117	J, 11-12	-	ar	R femur, L & R tibiae, L fibula, L 4th & 5th metatarsals
NA118	J, 1¹/₂-2	-	ar	Endocranial surface
NA132	J, 2	-	r	L & R tibiae
NA138	J, 11	-	a	Sacrum
NA160	J, 0-3 months	-	r	L tibia
NA174	??F, 11-14	-	a	L femur
NA225	J, 1¹/₂	1	a	Endocranial surface
SA055	J, 2-2¹/₂	-	ar	L humerus, L & R scapulae, R clavicle
V59	J, 7-8	-	ar	L zygomatic
WCO99	??F, 8	-	a	Ectocranial surface
WCO107	J, 12-14	-	a	L & R humeri, L ischium, 2R ribs
WCO115A	J, 1¹/₂	-	ar	L & R tibiae
WCO164	??M, 10-11	-	a	R radius & ulna

Notes: Sex, M=male, F=female, U, unsexed adult, J=unsexed juvenile, ?? denotes sex inferred from craniofacial morphology in juveniles; Age: estimated age at death, in years unless stated, wiu=weeks in utero for foetal or perinatal juveniles; Active or remodelled lesions indicated by a or r, when both types are present the more frequent type is put first.

and Roberts 2001), or which have been interpreted in archaeological material as probable or possible signs of tuberculosis (Baker 1999; Schultz 2001; Hershkovitz *et al.* 2002). Burial NA103, which has yet to be analysed for *M. tuberculosis* complex DNA, shows new bone deposition on L2 and L3, in the region of the pedicles and on the lateral sides of the vertebral bodies, and there is slight erosion of the side of the body of L2. There is also new bone deposition on the left femur shaft. The vertebral lesions may suggest early tuberculosis but the changes are insufficient to support a firm diagnosis.

Among the juveniles, the lower leg bones are, as with the adults, frequent sites for periosteal reactions. The pattern is less marked – 31% of the juveniles with periosteal reactions show lesions in the tibiae or fibulae, compared with 72% of adult cases. A more disparate array of anatomical sites are affected by lesions in the juvenile cohort than in adults (Table 103). If bone disease confined to a particular area of the body (legs, arms, trunk or head) is regarded as localised whereas individuals with lesions in two or more of these areas are regarded as having disseminated disease, then the preference for localised lesions is more marked in the adults (28 of 29 adults versus 22 of 29 juveniles show localised disease under this definition). Another difference between adult and juvenile disease is that in juveniles endocranial lesions are observed (there are a total of eight cases) whereas no periosteal deposits are observed at this anatomical site in adults. In most instances, endocranial new bone deposits are confined to the posterior parts of the skull. In all cases, part or all of the endocranial deposits were unremodelled, suggesting infection active

at time of death. Presumably they represent instances of fatal meningitis.

At this juncture, mention should be made of four individuals (Burial EE017, J, 4, unphased; Burial G658, ??M, 11, Phase 1-2; Burial G720, J, 5, Phase 1-2 and Burial WCO175, J, 1-1¹/₂, unphased) showing sinuous resorptive lesions on endocranial surfaces (Plate 61). In all instances, changes are confined to the occipital bone. It has been suggested that sinuous resorptive endocranial lesions are indicative of meningitis (Schultz 2001) or that they are manifestations of hypertrophic osteoarthropathy, a bony response to intra-thoracic disease (Hershkovitz *et al.* 2002). Neither of these explanations is particularly convincing, but the observation that these lesions were present in Burial G658 gives pause for thought: this burial was identified above as a case of pulmonary tuberculosis, and furthermore, meningitis is often a feature of tuberculosis.

Grauer (1993) recorded the prevalence of periostitis in the material from the cemetery of St Helen-on-the-Walls, York. Comparison between her figures and the results from Wharram Percy are shown below (Tables 104 and 105).

Table 104. Prevalence of periostitis at Wharram Percy and at St Helen-on-the-Walls, York.

	Absent	Present
Wharram Percy	629	58 (8.4%)
St Helen-on-the-Walls	497	144 (22.5%)

Notes: data from St Helen-on-the-Walls from Grauer (1993)

Table 105. Status of periosteal lesions at Wharram Percy and at St Helen-on-the-Walls, York.

	Remodelled	Active
Wharram Percy	21	37 (63.8%)
St Helen-on-the-Walls	98	46 (31.9%)

Notes: data from St Helen-on-the-Walls from Grauer (1993). For Wharram Percy 'active' includes individuals with mixed lesions where, overall, woven bone is the predominant type, 'remodelled' includes individuals with mixed lesions where, overall, remodelled bone is the predominant type. For St Helen-on-the-Walls, lesions were classed by Grauer (1993) simply as remodelled or active.

There is a greater frequency of non-specific infection in the York assemblage (chi-square=50.6, p<<0.001). This suggests a greater pathogen load in the urban environment, doubtless reflecting the unhygienic and crowded conditions of medieval towns. More of the St Helen's group were probably suffering from infectious disease for more of their lives than was the case at Wharram Percy. It takes time for infectious disease to produce skeletal changes, so it is only the longer-lasting conditions which have the potential to leave traces on the bones. The relatively fewer lesions shown by the Wharram Percy group may also mean that fewer individuals had sufficient resistance to infectious disease to survive for long enough when they did contract it for it to affect the skeleton. Perhaps those at Wharram Percy did not have the long-term exposure from birth to a wide array of pathogens that city-dwellers did, so that when infectious disease did strike, often killed quickly, before bone changes had the chance to develop. The higher rate of lesions in the York group, in addition to showing a greater disease load than at Wharram Percy, may also be a testament to these people's resistance to disease, many recovering or at least surviving for extended periods before succumbing. The greater prevalence of remodelled lesions (chi-square=17.4, p<0.001) among the York group than at Wharram Percy would tend to support this interpretation.

Osteomyelitis
Two individuals show evidence for osteomyelitis.

The distal metaphysis and distal part of the diaphysis of the left femur of Burial WCO041 (M, 25-40, unphased) is greatly thickened (Plate 62). A large hole pierces the posterior wall of the shaft and a smaller one penetrates the anterior wall. These represent cloacae through which pus from the bone interior would have drained. Radiography reveals that there is much bony sclerosis and the original cortex at the lesion site has been completely removed by remodelling. The left tibia shows much well-remodelled sub-periosteal new bone on its shaft, presumably as a result of direct infection from the femur lesion.

The distal metaphysis and distal part of the shaft of the right radius of Burial CN31 (M, 40+, Phase 4) is pitted

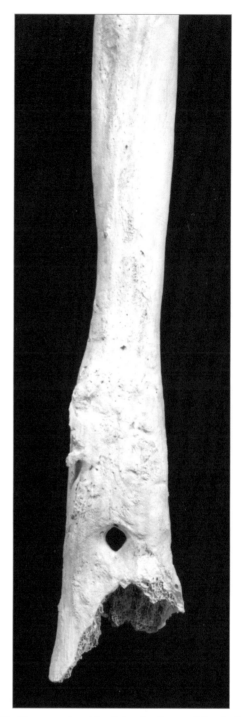

Plate 62. The posterior side of the distal part of the shaft of the left femur of Burial WCO041, showing osteomyelitis. The bone is greatly thickened. The large hole is probably a cloaca through which pus exuded from the interior.

and thickened. Considerable alteration to the contours on the endosteal surfaces of the medullary cavity is visible on X-ray, together with much bony sclerosis.

Osteomyelitis may result from direct penetration of pathogens via a wound, however the most frequent route of infection is haematogenous dissemination from a seat of infection elsewhere in the body. Haematogenous osteomyelitis generally begins during childhood, usually starts at the metaphysis, and generally involves only one bone (Ortner and Putschar 1985, 105-16). The appearance

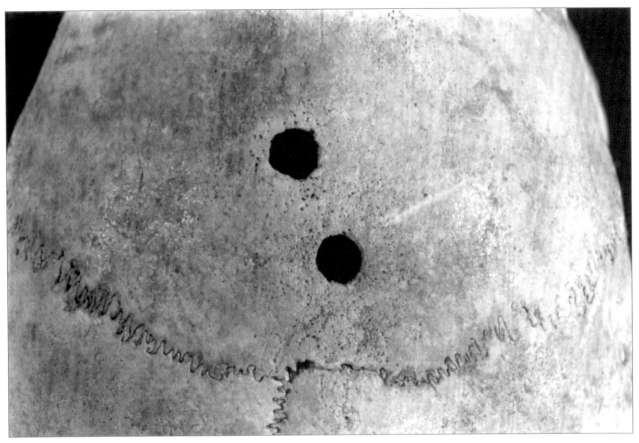

Plate 63. The cranium of Burial CN28. The frontal bone shows two perforations, surrounded by an area of pitting.

of the lesions in the present cases is suggestive of disease of long-standing, so despite the fact they died during adulthood, these individuals may well have acquired their infections as children.

Other probable cases of bony infection

All the cases discussed so far in this section can reasonably be considered examples of infectious disease, even if, in most instances, the specific disease responsible cannot be identified. There is a further subset of five individuals where the lesions, although probably indicative of skeletal infection, were rather ambiguous.

Burial CN28 (M, 22-24, Phase 4) shows two holes, 8mm diameter in the frontal bone (Plate 63). The holes are bevelled internally and there is woven bone on the endocranial surface in the region of the defects. Ectocranially, they are surrounded by an area of pitting. There is periostitis on the right femur (where it takes the form of a fusiform swelling of the diaphysis), on both tibiae, the left fibula, the distal part of the left humerus and proximal part of the left ulna. Some deposits are well remodelled, others are of woven bone. The joint surfaces of the left elbow are smaller than their right side counterparts and the shaft widths of the left ulna are also reduced (the left radius is missing). There is pitting on the right mandibular ramus.

These lesions suggest a systemic infection of fairly long duration which was active at time of death. The reduction in the joint surface dimensions at the elbow

suggests that the lesions here were acquired prior to cessation of growth. Although the holes in the cranium to some extent resemble trephinations, the internal bevel argues against this. The unremodelled endocranial bone suggests that intra-cranial infection was cause of death in this individual. Diagnosis is problematic. Treponemal disease, smallpox and tuberculosis were among the candidates which suggested themselves, but none is convincing. It may even be that more than one disease was responsible for this rather baffling array of lesions.

Burial G296 (M, 35-45, Phase 2) shows a lytic lesion on the left scaral ala which is probably infectious in origin. Burial G398 (M, 21-24, Phase 2) shows superficial destruction of the left zygomatic bone, together with pitting of its medial surface and in the floor of the left orbit. It seems likely that this represents bone infection from a lesion in overlying soft tissue. Burial G677 (U, 35-45, Phase 2) shows ankylosis of the right sacro-iliac joint. The bones have broken apart post-mortem to reveal the presence of superficial cavitation of the iliac face of the joint. There are no other changes in this (rather incomplete) skeleton. These changes probably reflect an infectious process at the joint.

Conditions which are suggestive of soft-tissue infectious disease

In addition to direct signs of skeletal infection, two other conditions, porotic hyperostosis and hypertrophic osteoarthropathy, are also considered in this section.

Although the lesions are not indicative of skeletal infection, their most frequent association is with infectious disease in soft tissues.

Porotic hyperostosis

This is a condition which manifests in skeletal remains as pitting of the ectocranial surface of the skull, particularly the orbital roofs where it is known as cribra orbitalia. Porotic hyperostosis represents an overgrowth of the diploe together with a thinning of the outer table. It appears to be a response to anaemia, in the majority of populations, iron-deficiency anaemia (Stuart-Macadam 1987; 1989). The spongy bone hyperplasia is a result of increased activity of the bone marrow as the body attempts to combat the anaemic condition by raising erythrocyte production. Iron deficiency anaemia is rarely the result of lack of iron in the diet, it generally results from disease, particularly gastro-intestinal parasites or other gut infections: diarrhoea causes food to pass through the gut too quickly for nutrients and minerals such as iron to be absorbed, and parasitic infestations may lead to anaemia through chronic blood loss (Stuart-Macadam 1992; Kent *et al.* 1994; Kent and Dunn 1996).

Cribra orbitalia was scored systematically in the current material. Because lesions, if they occur, are generally present in both orbital roofs, all individuals showing one or both orbital roofs present for study were scored for cribra orbitalia. Other conditions, such as scurvy or rickets, which may cause pitting of the orbital roofs, were distinguished on the basis that they lack the diploic hyperplasia of cribra orbitalia. When cribra orbitalia was observed to be present, lesions were classified as porotic, cribriotic or trabecular, according to the scheme of Brothwell (1981, fig. 6.17). In addition, remodelled and active lesions were distinguished using the criteria of Mensforth *et al.* (1978). This enabled lesion status in individuals to be divided into three classes: active, remodelled or partly remodelled. The results are shown in Tables 106-8.

Table 106. Cribra orbitalia: lesion type.

Lesions	Males	Females	Total adults[1]	Juveniles	Total
Absent	121	83	206	171	377
Porotic	13	17	30	50	80
Cribriotic	9	8	17	18	35
Trabecular	1	1	2	8	10

[1]Includes two adults of unknown sex.

Table 107. Prevalence of cribra orbitalia in adults, split by phase.

Lesions	Phase		
	1-2	2	4
Absent	86	30	25
Present	23	5	5

There is no significant difference in the distribution of lesion types, nor of the frequency of the condition on a presence/absence basis, either between the sexes, or between adults assigned to different phases. Cribra orbitalia is more frequent in juveniles than in adults: it was found in 30.8% of juveniles and 19.2% of adults (chi-square=9.0, p=0.003).

For juveniles, the Kolmogorov-Smirnov test indicates that the occurrence of cribra orbitalia is not random with respect to age (D_{obs}=0.44, p<0.001). Table 108 shows that this largely reflects a paucity of lesions in infants and young children. Among the adults, the patterning with respect to the three age groups fails to attain significance (Kolmogorov-Smirnov test, D_{obs}=0.16, $D_{95\%}$=0.22). If, however, the two older age groups are combined, the frequency differs from that in young adults, aged 18-29 (chi-square=6.6, p=0.01), with the younger group having the higher frequency.

Turning to the status of lesions (i.e. active vs remodelled), there is a difference in the distribution of lesion types between adults and juveniles (Kolmogorov-Smirnov test: D_{obs}=0.39, p<0.001). Table 108 indicates that this reflects a greater tendency for juveniles to show active lesions (73.7% of juveniles showing cribra orbitalia showed lesions classified as active, compared to 34.7% in adults). There is no evidence of any patterning in lesion status with respect to adult age.

The greater frequency of active lesions in juveniles is consistent with findings in most other early skeletal collections (Larsen 1997, 32). The most likely explanation is that, in the growing individual, every cubic centimetre of bone marrow is needed for erythrocyte production, with a result that, in anaemia, the need for blood-forming space will likely exceed normal marrow volume. In adults, there is much more 'spare capacity' in this respect, so that if they do suffer from anaemia, porotic hyperostosis is less likely to result (El-Najjar *et al.* 1976). Some have even ventured so far as to suggest that porotic hyperostosis only forms during childhood (Stuart-Macadam 1985), so that lesions seen in adult skeletons are invariably relics of childhood disease. Assuming that the criteria of Mensforth *et al.* (1978) permit reliable identification of active cases, this cannot be true for Wharram Percy, as lesions classified as active are regularly observed in adults (Table 108).

One interpretation of the greater frequency of lesions in juveniles than in adults is that those suffering from anaemia are more likely to die prematurely. Although this is possible, progressive obliteration of lesions from previous disease by bone remodelling in adult life would also be consistent with the observed pattern.

Iron deficiency anaemia does not normally occur prior to six months of age unless iron stores at birth are inadequate (Mensforth *et al.* 1978). The most important influences on iron stores at birth are prematurity and birth-weight, iron being deficient in premature and other low birth-weight infants. At Wharram Percy, no individual under nine months of age shows cribra orbitalia. The lack of porotic hyperostosis in early infancy may indicate that iron stores at birth were generally

Table 108. Cribra orbitalia by age category.

Age group (years)	Presence/absence of lesions		Status of lesions		
	Absent	Present	Active	Partially remodelled	Remodelled
Juveniles					
Perinatal	45	0 (-)	-	-	-
0-1.9	43	8 (15.7%)	7	0	1
2-	21	7 (25.0%)	5	1	1
4-	20	14 (41.1%)	10	2	2
6-	12	16 (57.1%)	10	4	2
8-	10	7 (41.2%)	6	0	1
10-	7	11 (61.1%)	10	1	0
12-	3	3 (50.0%)	1	1	1
14-	2	4 (66.7%)	3	1	0
16-17.9	8	6 (42.9%)	4	1	1
All juveniles	171	76 (30.8%)	56	11	9
Adults					
18-29	36	16 (30.8%)	8	4	4
30-49	87	14 (13.9%)	4	4	6
50+	79	16 (16.8%)	4	4	8
All adults†	206	49 (19.2%)	17	12	20

†Includes seven adults who could not be more closely aged

adequate and, by implication, that low birth-weight was not a regular problem. It might be suggested that low iron stores at birth were a regular occurrence but that affected infants simply died prior to developing bone lesions. This possibility is less likely as demographic analysis (Chapter 7) suggested that infant mortality was not especially high by pre-modern standards.

As infants are weaned onto adult foods, and hence introduced to a fresh range of gastro-intestinal pathogens, they may develop 'weanling diarrhoea' which is a potential cause of anaemia (Mittler and van Gerven 1994). At Wharram Percy, the frequency of lesions is less during the weaning phase and immediately thereafter (it seems likely that breast milk began to be supplemented with other foods by about six months of age and that breast-feeding ceased at one to two years (Chapter 7)) than in somewhat older children (Table 108), so perhaps weanling diarrhoea was not an especially significant problem. As above, one could argue against this by suggesting that weanling diarrhoea was a significant risk but that infants with it died rapidly before chronic anaemia and associated bone lesions could develop. Again, however, the demographic evidence argues against this being a frequent scenario – elevated mortality in the immediate post-weaning period is not evident (Chapter 7).

In addition to the cases of cribra orbitalia, there were seven examples of porotic hyperostosis elsewhere in the skull (Burials G298, G503, G531, NA135, NA184, SA080 and V10). In all instances lesions were on the cranial vault (where they are known as cribra cranii) and were located toward the back of the skull, principally on the posterior parts of the parietal bones. It seems general that cribra cranii is rather less common that cribra orbitalia (Aufderheide and Rodriguez-Martin 1998, 350), and it may be that cribra orbitalia represents an initial response to anaemia but cranial vault lesions require more prolonged and severe disease in order to develop (Hengen 1971). The present results are broadly consistent with this; in the five cases of cribra cranii with orbital roofs present for study, all but one showed cribra orbitalia.

Grauer (1993) recorded porotic hyperostosis in the St Helen-on-the-Walls collection from York. Her results, in comparison with those from Wharram Percy, are shown in Tables 109 and 110.

Table 109. Prevalence of porotic hyperostosis at Wharram Percy and at St Helen-on-the-Walls, York.

	Absent	Present
Wharram Percy	377	125 (25%)
St Helen-on-the-Walls	193	267 (58%)

Notes: data from St Helen-on-the-Walls from Grauer (1993)

Table 110. Status of lesions of porotic hyperostosis at Wharram Percy and at St Helen-on-the-Walls, York.

	Remodelled	Active
Wharram Percy	52	73 (58%)
St Helen-on-the-Walls	203	64 (24%)

Notes: data from St Helen-on-the-Walls from Grauer (1993). For Wharram Percy the remodelled category combines lesions classed above as remodelled and partially remodelled. For St Helen-on-the-Walls, the data was simply classed by Grauer (1993) as remodelled or active, based on the criteria of Mensforth *et al.* (1978).

The prevalence of porotic hyperostosis differs in the Wharram Percy and St Helen-on-the-Walls material (chi-square = 109.3, p<<0.001), with the site in York having the higher value. In the York material, Grauer used as her denominator individuals with the frontal and/or parietal bones present. Given the previously noted tendency for porotic hyperostosis to be present much more often in the orbital roofs than on the parietal bones, coupled with the observation that parietal bones tend to survive better in archaeological material than the delicate orbital roofs, Grauer's strategy will have the result of depressing the apparent frequency of porotic hyperostosis compared with that calculated here for Wharram Percy. Thus, although there is this discrepency in scoring procedures, the higher rate of porotic hyperostosis at St Helen-on-the-Walls is likely to be a robust result.

Large numbers of people living in close proximity favour the spread of disease. As well as offering increased opportunities for disease transmission between persons, sanitation and hygiene tend to be poorer, mainly due to contamination of water supplies. Crowded, unhygienic conditions characterised many medieval cities, and York was no exception (Grauer 1993). The high rate of porotic hyperostosis in the St Helen-on-the-Walls material may reflect this. The lower frequency at Wharram Percy may testify to the lesser sanitation problems posed in a rural area with a lower population density.

There is also a tendency for porotic hyperostosis more often to be active at time of death at Wharram Percy than in the York material where the majority of lesions were remodelled (chi-square = 44.3, p<<0.001). One might expect the urban environment to be more pathogen-rich, so that individuals raised here might show a greater resistance to infection than those from a rural community. It may be that chronic gut infections more often led to death, either directly or due to weakening of the immune system opening the way to opportunistic infection, at Wharram Percy than in the York group where more tended to recover from such episodes.

Hydatid cyst
One individual showed direct evidence for the presence of gut parasites. Calcified fragments of a hollow spheroid were recovered from Burial G571 (F, 40+, Phase 2). The

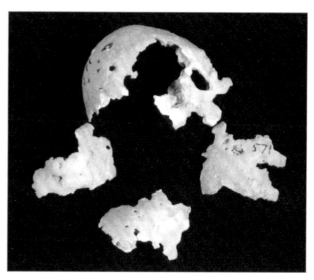

Plate 64. Fragments of a calcified spheroid, from Burial G571. It is probably a hydatid cyst.

curvature of the fragments suggest that it had a diameter of about 4-5cm. The fragments are smooth on their convex (outer) surfaces and rough on their concave (inner) sides, and are penetrated by small holes (Plate 64). They are up to several millimetres thick. This probably represents the remains of a hydatid cyst. This is caused by tape-worm infestation. Ingested tapeworm ovae may be carried to any organ of the body, via the bloodstream (the liver is most often affected). Here the larva forms a cyst, which may calcify (Ortner and Putschar 1985, 230-32). In the present case, it is not known from which area of the body the hydatid cyst remains were recovered, so it is not known within which organ the cyst was located. In hydatid infestation, cysts may also form within the cancellous bone of the skeleton, however radiography revealed no evidence for this in the present case.

Hypertrophic osteoarthropathy
Hypertrophic osteoarthropathy (HPO) is a syndrome consisting of clubbing of the digits of the hands and feet, joint inflammation, and diffuse sub-periosteal bone deposition (Resnick and Niwayama 1981, 2983-96). Digital clubbing and joint changes generally involve soft tissue only (although on occasion there may be some bony proliferation or lysis in phalangeal tufts (Locke 1915; Pineda *et al.* 1985)), so palaeopathological diagnosis of the condition normally rests on the pattern and nature of sub-periosteal bone deposition (Ortner and Putschar 1985, 245-6). Typical features include: sub-periosteal bone deposition without endosteal changes; lesions are widespread in the skeleton and show marked left/right symmetry in paired elements; lesions tend to occur most frequently in the large and small tubular bones of the appendicular skeleton; changes tend to be most pronounced in tubular bones distal to elbow and knee; other frequently involved elements include the skull, claviculae, scapulae and calcanei; sites of musculo-tendinous insertion may act as foci for increased bone deposition (Gall *et al.* 1951; Greenfield *et al.* 1967; Ali *et*

174

al. 1980; Resnick and Niwayama 1981, 2983-96; Ortner and Putschar 1985, 245-6).

In the current material, five individuals (Burial CN33, M, 50+, Phase 4; Burial EE062, M, 30-40, Phase 1-2; Burial G296, M, 35-45, Phase 2; Burial WCO018, M, adult, unphased; Burial WCO200, M 50+, unphased) show bony signs of HPO. Two of these cases (Burials EE062 and WCO200) have been published previously (Mays and Taylor 2002). In four of the five individuals, lesions consist solely of sub-periosteal bone deposits, but in one (Burial WCO018), an additional change consistent with HPO was found: a terminal foot phalanx shows clear signs of bony resorption (Plate 65).

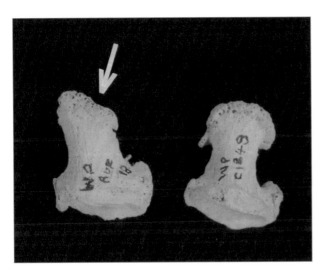

Plate 65. The left terminal hallucial phalanx from burial WCO018, showing osteolysis of the tuft (arrowed). The bone in the right of the photograph is a comparative specimen of normal morphology.

Hypertrophic osteoarthropathy may be primary or secondary. Primary HPO (pachydermoperiostosis) is a rare, genetically transmitted condition in which changes are accompanied by skin lesions. Only about 3 - 5% of cases of HPO fall into this category (Aufderheide and Rodriguez-Martin 1998, 91). The secondary form of the disease is generally a response to intra-thoracic or intra-abdominal disorders, in 90% of cases the former (Locke 1915). Intra-thoracic cancer or chronic chest infections are the most frequent causes. Periostitis in secondary HPO is not due to dissemination of neoplastic metastases or infection to the parts of the skeleton manifesting new bone formation. The mechanism by which the bony response is elicited has yet to be fully understood, although abnormalities in circulating growth factors as a result of the primary infectious or neoplastic disease are implicated (Silveri *et al.* 1996; Silveira *et al.* 2000).

Primary HPO generally appears around puberty and only progresses until the end of adolescence or shortly thereafter (Shneerson 1981). All the cases here show deposits of woven bone, indicating a disease process active at time of death. Given the individual ages, this argues against a diagnosis of primary disease in four of the five examples. In one case (Burial WCO018) no inference could be made in this respect as this individual was an adult for which no more precise age determination was possible.

Today, intra-thoracic cancer, particularly primary lung cancer, accounts for the great majority of cases of secondary HPO (Resnick and Niwayama 1988). Prior to the decline of the chronic infectious lung and pleural diseases in the mid-20th century, about three in four cases of HPO were due to these causes (Locke 1915). Tuberculosis was a particularly important cause of HPO: in a survey of cases up to 1915, 22% of instances of secondary HPO were due to tuberculosis (Locke 1915).

The hypertrophic lesions themselves are of little help in indicating the primary disease process which elicited them, as the cause of HPO has little effect on its character (Rothschild and Rothschild 1998). Burial WCO200 does show some additional bony lesions which are of use in this respect. The rib lesions in this individual are suggestive of chronic pulmonary infection (see above). Given the frequency with which HPO was associated with pulmonary infection in the pre-antibiotic era, it seems reasonable to infer that this was the eliciting factor for HPO in this case.

Given the importance of tuberculosis as a cause of HPO in the pre-antibiotic age, it was of interest to investigate whether tuberculosis was present in these cases. None showed diagnostic signs of tuberculosis, although, as discussed above, Burial G296 shows a lytic lesion on the sacrum, which is probably infectious in origin and could be consistent with tuberculosis. Two individuals (Burials EE062 and WCO200) have, to date, been analysed for *M. tuberculosis* complex DNA (Mays and Taylor 2002). Only Burial EE062 proved positive and, as in the other tuberculosis cases, the infecting micro-organism proved to be *M. tuberculosis* rather than *M. bovis* (Mays and Taylor 2002).

Few cases of HPO have been published in the palaeopathological literature (references in Mays and Taylor 2002), and to my knowledge the current examples are the only cases thus far published from Britain. The paucity of cases in the literature is likely, at least in part, due to under-diagnosis of the disease in ancient human remains. The characteristic symmetrical distribution of lesions is difficult to evaluate in the fragmentary and incomplete material often encountered archaeologically, and there may in addition be a tendency among palaeopathologists to lump together instances of periosteal reactions as non-specific skeletal infection without adequate consideration of other potential causes, such as HPO.

Metabolic disease

Imbalances in bony metabolism may occur as a result of a deficiency in particular components of diet or for other reasons. At Wharram Percy, examples of rickets, osteoporosis, hyperostosis frontalis interna and hyperparathyroidism were found.

Table 111. Rickets.

Burial	NA036	NA108	NA131	NA191	NA194	NA236	V28	V57
Estimated age	18Mo	8Mo	6-12Mo	3Mo	4-6Mo	6-8Mo	12Mo	6-2Mo
Pathological feature								
Cranial vault porosity	A	P	P	P	P	P	P	-
Orbital roof porosity	P	P	-	A	P	P	P	-
Deformed mandibular ramus	-	-	-	A	P	-	P	-
Deformed arm bones	P	A	P	P	A	-	-	P
Deformed leg bones	P	A	A	A	A	-	A	A
Flared costo-chondral ends of ribs	P	P	-	P	P	-	P	-
Cortex of costo-chondral ends of ribs irregular and porous	A	P	-	P	P	-	P	P
Growth plate abnormality of long bones	A	P	P	P	P	-	A	P
Cortex of metaphyses irregular and porous	A	P	P	P	P	P	P	P
Thickening of long-bones	P	A	P	P	A	-	P	A

Ages at death in months; pathological feature, P = condition present, A = condition absent, - = condition not scored due to the relevent skeletal parts being missing or damaged. No burial showing rickets could be phased. Table from Ortner and Mays (1998)

 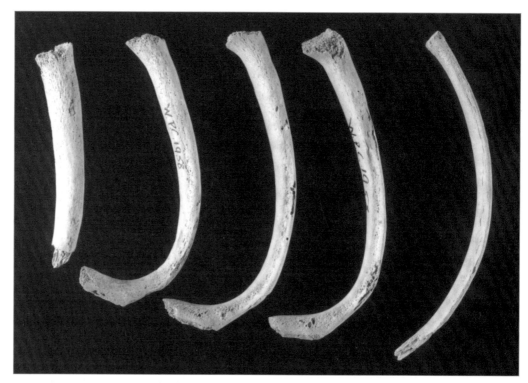

Plate 66. The left radius of Burial V57, showing abnormal angulation of the distal end due to rickets.

Plate 67. Some ribs from Burial V28, together with a normal specimen (extreme right) for comparison. The diseased ribs show thickening towards their sternal ends indicative of rickets.

Rickets

Rickets is a disease of infancy and childhood characterised by inadequate mineralisation of bone. It is caused by a deficiency of effective vitamin D. This is generally not a reflection of dietary deficiencies as most foods contain little vitamin D. Vitamin D is synthesised by the action of sunlight upon a chemical pre-cursor in the skin. Insufficient exposure of the skin to sunlight is the main cause of rickets. The principal palaeopathological manifestations of the disease are bony porosis and deformation of skeletal elements under mechanical force due to muscular contraction and weight-bearing.

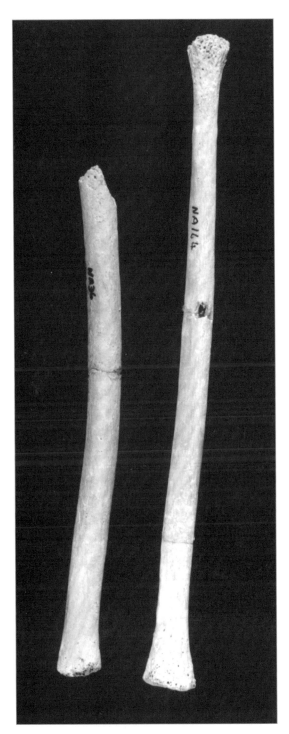

Plate 68. The right fibula from Burial NA036, together with a normal specimen (on the right) for comparison. The diseased fibula shows abnormal curvature due to rickets.

Among the Wharram Percy burials, eight likely cases of rickets were identified (and have previously been published – Ortner and Mays 1998). All were active cases in infants and young children, no cases of healed rickets were found. The major pathological changes seen in these individuals are summarised in Table 111 and some are illustrated in Plates 66-7. In addition to these fairly clear examples, Burial NA092 (J, 4-5 months, unphased) showed porosis of the ectocranial surfaces of the skull vault and of the right ilium, and some sternal rib ends

appear swollen, and Burial NA189 (J, 1-1½, unphased) showed swollen, somewhat porous sternal rib ends, somewhat thickened long-bones and slight bending of the distal tibiae. These may represent further cases of the disease.

Convincing cases of rickets from contexts prior to the post-medieval period in Britain are few (Mays 2003b). Given the outdoor lifestyle which characterised medieval peasant communities, Wharram Percy may not be a population amongst which one might have expected to encounter the disease, yet the site has yielded a larger number of good cases than any other published British site dating from before the Early Modern Age (Mays 2003b). Reasons why it was found here are difficult to determine. One possibility is that the cases encountered were infants and children who were otherwise sickly and for this reason were kept indoors in dark, smoky houses, and so developed the disease. This suggestion is consistent with the fact that all cases were individuals who died in early life with active rickets despite the fact that it is a non-lethal condition, and with the observation that no individuals who survived their early years showed any evidence for healed rickets.

Two cases, aged four to six months and twelve months, showed deformation of the mandibular ramus, presumably as a result of muscle action during chewing. This would appear consistent with the suggestion (Chapter 7) that solid foods were introduced into infant diets by about six months, but it should be recalled that infants often tend to chew on hard non-food objects in an effort to alleviate the discomfort of teething.

In the limbs, most mechanical deformities were seen in arm rather than leg bones. This presumably reflects the greater proportion of body weight born by the upper limbs in the crawling infant. In those infants for which both leg and arm bones were present for study, those showing only arm-bone deformation were aged between three and twelve months at death. In only one case (Burial NA036) were arm-bone deformities accompanied by deformation of the leg bones (Plate 68). This individual was aged eighteen months at death. Infants usually begin to walk by the end of their first year. The pattern of limb-bone deformity in the rickets cases may be consistent with this, the restriction of leg-bone deformity to the eighteen-month old individual may indicate that only this individual had begun to walk before death intervened.

Osteoporosis

Osteoporosis is a condition characterised by a decrease in bone mass and a micro-architectural deterioration in bone tissue, with a consequent weakening of the skeleton and increased susceptibility to fracture (Watts 1996). The bone changes of osteoporosis occur with advancing age in both sexes but are more marked in women. Loss of bone density is symptomless, osteoporosis only manifests clinically when it leads to fracture. Today, osteoporosis tends to be a particularly marked health problem in northern European populations or those of northern European descent. Although both sexes may experience osteoporotic fracture, this is more often a problem in women as their skeletal deterioration is more marked. In both sexes, the most important cause of bone loss in osteoporosis is age-related changes in sex hormones, in women due to the menopause. A number of extrinsic factors, many of which are associated with modern Western lifestyles, are also held to play a part. Among those which are often cited as exacerbating bone loss are sedentary lifestyle, cigarette-smoking, calcium deficiency and perhaps vitamin D deficiency (Eastell 1993; Heaney 1993; Nguyen and Eisman 1999). The investigation of osteoporosis in past populations which are genetically similar to our own but which had rather different lifestyles may help elucidate the importance or otherwise of lifestyle factors in influencing the disease. This was one of the principal factors motivating the work on osteoporosis which has been done on the Wharram Percy collection (Mays 1996; Mays *et al.* 1998; Turner-Walker *et al.* 2000; 2001). What follows is a summary of that work.

Methods
Both thickness of cortical bone and bone mineral density (BMD) were measured. Technical details have already been published (Mays 1996a; Mays *et al.* 1998), but a brief summary is given here.

A measure of cortical thickness was obtained using the cortical index. This gives the percentage of bone width taken up by cortex.

Cortical index = total bone width – medullary width x 100

total bone width

Measurements were taken at the midshaft of the second metacarpal and the femur, from anterio-posterior radiographs.

Bone mineral density was measured at the proximal femur using dual energy X-ray absorptiometry (DXA). A lunar DPX bone densitometer was used to take density measurements at two sites used in clinical studies, the femoral neck (BMDN) and Ward's triangle (BMDW).

Results
The results are shown in Table 112.

Discussion
The results show significant age-related decline in all four parameters for females and in the two BMD measurements for males. In accord with expectations based on modern data, bone losses are greater in females than in males. In females, loss of BMD in the proximal femur sites is seen earlier, and is ultimately greater than loss of cortical bone at the midshaft metacarpal or femur. In males, significant losses could be demonstrated only in bone density at the proximal femur sites and not in the diaphysial cortical bone measures. The proximal femur sites are rich in trabecular bone. Earlier and greater loss of trabecular bone is expected on physiological grounds - its greater metabolic activity means that it is more responsive to changes in mineral homeostasis. Both sexes show greater losses of BMD at Ward's triangle than in the femur neck site, in accordance with modern findings.

The adults are generally markedly deficient in cortical bone compared with their modern counterparts, reflecting the reduced build up of cortical bone during the growth period most probably due to poorer childhood nutrition

Table 112. Bone density and cortical index results.

		BMDN			BMDW			FEMCI			MCCI	
	N	Mean	sd	N	Mean	sd	N	Mean	sd	N	Mean	sd
Females												
18-29	14	1.102	0.115	14	1.089	0.155	14	55.0	6.3	15	49.5	9.7
30-49	21	0.920	0.156	21	0.837	0.181	20	53.7	4.6	29	44.8	8.7
50+	19	0.815	0.181	19	0.723	0.184	18	48.7	9.9	23	41.5	7.9
ANOVA		All			All		50+vs18-29; 50+vs30-49			50+vs 18-29		
Males												
18-29	14	1.149	0.126	14	1.125	0.149	14	57.8	5.0	10	42.9	7.8
30-49	30	1.080	0.145	30	1.018	0.170	28	56.0	5.9	27	45.0	8.8
50+	31	0.944	0.160	31	0.819	0.190	28	53.5	5.9	34	40.4	7.1
ANOVA	50+vs18-29; 50+vs30-49			50+vs18-29; 50+vs30-49			ns			ns		

Key: BMDN = bone mineral density at the femoral neck, BMDW = bone mineral density at Ward's triangle, FEMCI=cortical index at the femoral midshaft, MCCI = cortical index at the second metacarpal midshaft, BMDN and BMDW in g cm^{-2}; ANOVA = analysis of variance, ns=no significant age-related pattern, otherwise the age-related patterning is significant at the 5% level or better and where this is the case entries show between which age-groups significant differences lie according to the least significant difference statistic. Note that MCCI values differ slightly from those previously published (Mays 1996a) due to the addition of a small amount of new data since that work.

Table 113. Bone density and cortical index results compared with recent Caucasian subjects.

	BMDN		BMDW		FEMCI		MCCI	
	Wharram Percy	Recent	Wharram Percy	Recent	Wharram Percy	Recent	Wharram Percy	Recent
Females								
18-29	1.102 (100%)	0.994 (100%)	1.089 (100%)	0.947 (100%)	55.0 (100%)	60.6 (100%)	49.5 (100%)	64.3 (100%)
30-49	0.920 (83.5%)	0.953 (95.9%)	0.837 (76.9%)	0.863 (91.1%)	53.7 (97.6%)	63.1 (104.1%)	44.8 (90.5%)	64.0 (99.5%)
50+	0.815 (74.0%)	0.844 (84.9%)	0.723 (66.4%)	0.705 (74.4%)	48.7 (88.5%)	57.7 (95.2%)	41.5 (83.8%)	52.8 (82.1%)
Males								
18-29	1.149 (100%)	1.107 (100%)	1.125 (100%)	1.022 (100%)	57.8 (100%)	61.6 (100%)	42.9 (100%)	60.6 (100%)
30-49	1.080 (94.0%)	1.022 (92.1%)	1.018 (90.5%)	0.887 (86.8%)	56.0 (96.9%)	61.4 (99.7%)	45.0 (105.0%)	60.3 (99.5%)
50+	0.944 (82.2%)	0.960 (86.7%)	0.819 (72.8%)	0.780 (76.3%)	53.5 (92.6%)	60.0 (97.4%)	40.4 (94.1%)	55.2 (91.1%)

Key: BMDN = bone mineral density at the femoral neck, BMDW = bone mineral density at Ward's triangle, FEMCI=cortical index at the femoral midshaft, MCCI = cortical index at the second metacarpal midshaft, BMDN and BMDW in g cm^{-2}. Figures in brackets are values expressed as a percentage of those for the young adult (18-29 years) groups. Recent BMDN and BMDW data are from Lunar Corporation (1993), recent cortical index data are from Virtama and Helelä (1969).

(see Chapter 8). It is interesting that this deficiency appears less marked in the femur than the metacarpal. This may reflect the weight-bearing role of the femur. Physical activity during the growth period promotes attainment of greater peak bone mass at sites which are loaded (Eastell 1993). Although cortical index was depressed at both the femur and the metacarpal, the effect at the former may have been mitigated by the (presumed) higher activity level among medieval people. BMD levels appear fairly similar in ancient and modern bones but direct comparisons of absolute levels are problematic for a number of reasons, not least the obvious fact that the archaeological specimens lack soft tissue (discussion in Mays *et al.* 1998).

The reduction in metacarpal cortical index in the 50+ age group compared with the 18-29 group is similar to that in recent subjects (Table 113). Bone losses at the three femur sites in the 50+ age group compared with the 18-29 age group are also similar to those observed in modern subjects. Indeed at these femur sites, the losses of bone substance experienced by the Wharram Percy people appear, if anything, somewhat greater than is the case in the recent reference groups, although the nature of the data precludes statistical analysis of the differences.

A possible problem in comparing ancient and modern age-related losses of bone substance is that the imprecision of skeletal ageing methods hinders precise age-matching of samples. In particular, it is regrettable that the 50+ age group could not be further subdivided, as here the amount of bone substance might be expected to show considerable age-related variation. If the composition of the 50+ age group differed between the ancient and modern samples, then it would potentially compromise comparisons. This problem has been tackled using a demographic modelling approach (see Mays 1996a; Mays *et al.* 1998) drawing upon age at death distributions from medieval documentary sources. This procedure indicates that it is likely that the average age of the 50+ group was, if anything, somewhat greater in the

modern samples than in that from Wharram Percy. This means that the direction of any inaccuracies in estimating the degree of bone loss at Wharram Percy relative to that in the modern samples will tend to lead to under rather than over estimation of reduction in bone substance in the medieval group. From this it would seem that the finding that losses of bone substance among the 50+ group at Wharram Percy compared with young adults were no less than in recent Europeans, is a robust result, and the diminution of bone mineral among the Wharram Percy people may even have been greater than seen today.

Most of the differences in lifestyle between medieval and modern people would have been expected to lower rather than raise the risk of osteoporosis in the former. Tobacco was unknown in medieval England and medieval peasants would likely have had a much more physically active lifestyle than their modern descendants. The diet at Wharram Percy was unlikely to have been calcium deficient: the site lies on chalk geology, and many cattle bones and fragments of pottery vessels which would have been used for dairy products were found in excavations on the settlement (Ryder 1974; Beresford and Hurst 1990). Despite the finding of eight active cases of rickets among the infant and young child skeletons, it is not likely that Vitamin D was routinely deficient in this population. The outdoor lifestyle of medieval populations would seem to preclude this, and no clear examples of healed rickets or osteomalacia were found among those who survived their earliest years. The results from the work on osteoporosis in the Wharram Percy remains suggest that lifestyle factors may have no great influence on the degree of bone loss which has occurred by old age.

Although there is no evidence that ultimate losses of bone substance differed very greatly at Wharram Percy from those seen in modern populations of northern European origin, there are hints that among the women, loss of bone mineral may have commenced earlier in life than is the case today. The Wharram Percy women appear to show rather greater losses of BMDN and BMDW

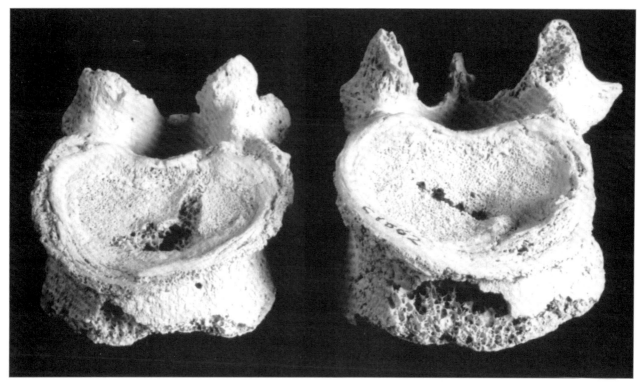

Plate 69. Healed compression fractures in the bodies of the twelfth thoracic and first lumbar vertebrae from Burial WCO045. This individual is an elderly female with a femur neck BMD four standard deviations below the young adult female mean.

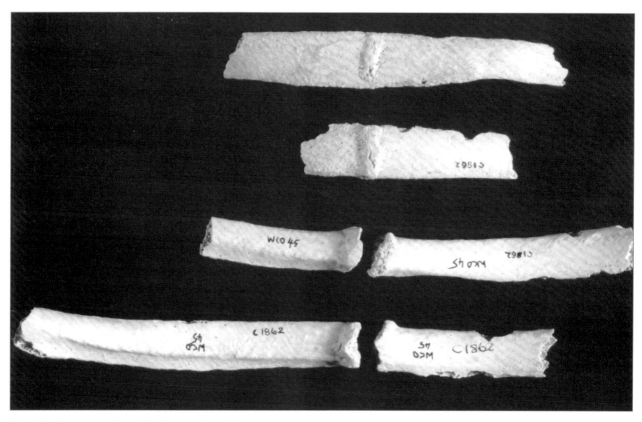

Plate 70. Fractures in four ribs from Burial WCO045. Two right ribs (top) show united fractures. Fractures to two left ribs (bottom) show remodelling but the bony callus has failed to unite the broken ends.

between the 18-29 and 30-49 age groups than is the case for modern female subjects (Table 113), although the nature of the data means that statistical evaluation of this difference between the ancient and modern groups is problematic. No indication of this pattern is seen in the males. We have suggested (Turner-Walker *et al.* 2000; 2001) that this may reflect the effects of high parity and relatively late weaning of their offspring on the Wharram Percy women. In modern populations, minor reductions in BMD may occur during pregnancy and lactation but are quickly recovered (Kohlmeier and Marcus 1995; Kalkwarf and Specker 1995; Laskey and Prentice 1999). We have speculated that in medieval times recovery of bone mass following pregnancy and lactation may have been slowed by poor maternal nutrition (Turner-Walker *et al.* 2001), and that this may explain the apparent greater loss of bone during the reproductive years in the medieval women.

In modern populations, osteoporosis predisposes to fractures at the hip, wrist and the highly trabecular bone of the axial skeleton, principally the vertebral bodies but also the ribs (Aloia *et al.* 1983; Resnick and Niwayama 1988, 2022). At Wharram Percy there are no hip or wrist fractures, but some skeletons do show healed vertebral compression and rib fractures (Plates 69 and 70). Metacarpal cortical index in those with and without vertebral compression/rib fractures is shown in Table 114. Among the females, the difference in metacarpal cortical index between those with and without rib/vertebral fractures attains statistical significance (t=3.35, p=0.028). For the males it does not, and there was no relationship between metacarpal cortical index and fractures of bones other than the ribs or vertebral bodies for either sex. Although we cannot know at what ages individuals sustained their fractures, the most plausible explanation would seem to be that, like modern women, loss of bone substance predisposed medieval women to fractures of the highly trabecular bone of the axial skeleton.

Plate 71. The femoral heads of Burial CN03, showing erosive changes.

Table 114. Metacarpal cortical index in those with and without healed vertebral compression/rib fractures.

	Individuals with RV fractures			Individuals without RV fractures		
	N	Mean	sd	N	Mean	sd
Males	17	40.9	6.5	62	43.6	8.3
Females	4	35.5	5.5	67	45.4	9.0

Notes: Only individuals showing one or more rib or vertebra available for study are included. Note that values differ slightly from those previously published (Mays 1996a) due to the addition of a small amount of new data since that work.

Given the pain and disability which may result from osteoporotic fractures of the axial skeleton (Ettinger *et al.* 1992), it is clear that the health impact of osteoporosis for the medieval women would not have been negligible. It would not have been as great as today due to the lack of hip fractures. Hip fractures are the greatest health threat in osteoporosis and are a significant cause of morbidity and mortality among the elderly today (Parker and Pryor 1993). Reasons for the dearth of hip fractures at Wharram Percy are unclear, but it is worth noting that in modern populations their frequency only begins to rise markedly in those over about 75-80 years of age (Buhr and Cooke 1959). Perhaps too few people survived into advanced old age for hip fractures to be a problem.

Hyperparathyroidism
Burial CN03 (F, adult, Phase 3-4) shows evidence for hyperparathyroidism. The skeleton is very incomplete with only fragments of hip and leg bones surviving. This case has been fully described elsewhere (Mays *et al.* 2001b), but in brief, there are erosive changes at both hip

181

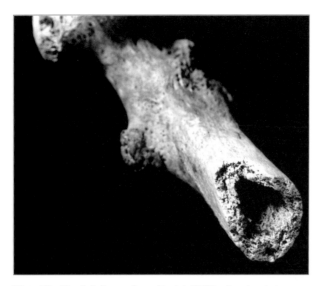

Plate 72. The left femur from Burial CN03, showing intra-cortical resorption, visible as porosity at the post-depositional break.

Plate 73. Hyperostosis frontalis interna, Burial V61

joints (Plate 71), the left sacro-iliac joint, both talo-navicular joints and the distal joint surface of the right fibula. All bones are rather demineralised, and this appears to reflect diminution in cortical bone, the trabecular bone appears fairly normal. Intra-cortical resorption is seen in the femoral shafts (Plate 72) and there is loss of cortico-medullary distinction. The proximal phalanx of the right great toe shows sub-periosteal resorption. These features are typical of hyperparathyroidism, an imbalance in bone metabolism due to hyperactivity of the parathyroid glands in the neck (Resnick and Niwayama 1988, 2219-85). Parathyroid hormone promotes bone remodelling and the release of calcium from bone, hence the demineralisation characteristic of the disease. The preferential site of action of parathyroid hormone is cortical bone, so in hyperparathyroidism there is demineralisation of compacta whilst trabecular bone volume is conserved (Silverberg *et al.* 1989).

Hyperparathyroidism may be primary or secondary. Primary disease is generally a result of a parathyroid adenoma (Horowitz and Nordin 1993). Secondary hyperparathyroidism is most usually a result of kidney disease. Distinguishing primary from secondary disease in skeletal remains is difficult, but the present case lacks the osteosclerosis and periostitis which are not infrequent in secondary disease (Resnick and Niwayama 1988, table 57.4), and this may favour a diagnosis of primary hyperparathyroidism. Today, hyperparathyroidism is one of the most common endocrine diseases, with a frequency of five to ten cases per 10,000. Nevertheless very few cases have been recognised palaeopathologically (references in Mays *et al.* 2001b), and to my knowledge this is the first published palaeopathological case from Britain. The initial skeletal changes of the disease are simply diffuse osteopaenia and the other changes are often subtle, so its apparent low frequency in skeletal remains may simply reflect difficulties in its palaeopathological recognition.

Hyperostosis frontalis interna

Burial V61 (F, 35-45, unphased) shows slight deposits of smooth bone on the internal surface of the frontal bone (Plate 73). Such deposits are termed hyperostosis frontalis interna. This condition is seen 5-10 times more often in females than in males and has a peak incidence in the 40-60 age group (Salmi *et al.* 1962). It has been reported to be more common in modern populations than in skeletal samples, although this is, in part at least, probably an artefact of differences between clinical and palaeopathological diagnostic criteria (Barber and Rogers 1997). Its aetiology is unclear. Hershkovitz *et al.* (1999) favour oestrogen stimulation as the cause of the lesion and, arguing that the lower frequency in ancient populations is a real phenomenon, speculate that this may be because in early populations females were pregnant or lactating for a greater proportion of their reproductive period, implying minimal oestrogen exposure.

Scurvy

Scurvy was scored for in a systematic manner among the juveniles (amongst which skeletal signs are much more likely to occur than in adults), using the diagnostic criteria of Ortner and Eriksen (1997). The disease manifests principally on the cranial bones (especially the greater wing of the sphenoid) and the scapulae, and scorbutic changes were looked for systematically in these elements (Connell 1997). No cases were found (N=183 juveniles with one or both sphenoid bones present for study).

Neoplasms

A neoplasm, or tumour, is an uncontrolled growth of cells. Neoplasms may be benign or malignant. In the former case they tend to be slow-growing and localised, in the latter they may be faster growing and spread to other parts of the body via the bloodstream or lymphatic system. The cause of most is unclear. In the current material, 21 individuals show neoplastic conditions of bone. In all but one case, lesions appear to represent benign tumours.

Eleven individuals show evidence for osteomas. An osteoma is a benign, slow-growing lesion formed of abnormally dense bone, lying on the sub-periosteal surface of a bone (Capasso 1997). Generally, their most frequent location is on the ectocranial surface of the skull vault, where they are referred to by palaeopathologists as button osteomas. At Wharram Percy, six of the ten individuals with osteomas show them in this location (Table 115, Plate 74).

Table 115. Button osteomas.

Burial	Sex & age	Phase	Location	Maximum diameter
G385	F, 35-45	2	L. parietal	10mm
G419	F, 50+	2	R parietal	22mm
G571	F, 40+	2	Frontal bone	7mm
NA218	M, 50+	1-2	R parietal	20mm
WCO080	F, 30-50	-	R parietal	11mm
WCO184	F, 35-45	2	Sagittal suture	20mm
			R parietal	6mm

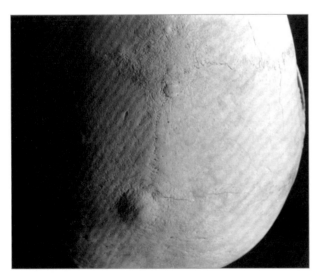

Plate 74. The cranial vault of Burial WCO184, showing at least two button osteomas.

A study of button osteomas in recent skeletal material (Eshed *et al.* 2002) found that they are generally solitary, most often occur on the parietal bones, are more common in older individuals, are generally less than 1cm diameter, and there is no sex bias in their occurrence. The current observations seem consistent with this, although some of the Wharram Percy examples seem to be of rather large size.

Less commonly, osteomas may occur in the paranasal sinuses. There are three examples of this (Burial NA068, F, 50+, Phase 1-2; Burial SA52/18, M, 20-22, unphased; Burial V46, F, 50+, unphased), all in the frontal sinuses. All are small except for Burial NA068, where the osteoma is V-shaped, with a maximum length of 25mm (Plate 75). In this case, there appears to have been localised expansion of the frontal sinus to accommodate the osteoma.

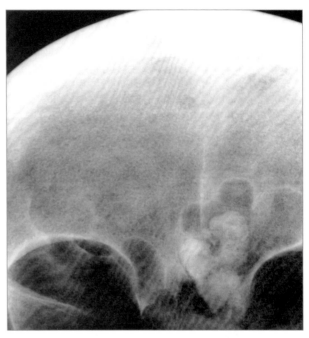

Plate 75. Anterio-posterior radiograph of the cranium of Burial NA068. There is a large osteoma in the frontal sinus.

A right rib of Burial WCO056 (F, 35-45, unphased) bears a hard, dense bony exostosis, rising 4mm proud of the rib surface and measuring about 8 by 5mm in diameter. Radiography indicates that it sits on the normal cortex from which it is demarcated by a radiolucent line (Plate 76). A similar, smaller lesion is present on a rib from Burial G673 (F, 50+, Phase 1-2). These probably represent osteomas.

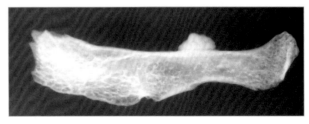

Plate 76. Radiograph of a right rib from Burial WCO056, showing an osteoma.

The next most frequent type of neoplasm at Wharram Percy, after the osteoma, is the osteochondroma. Osteochondromas are bony outgrowths which appear during childhood. They lie close to an epiphysial cartilage and owe their formation to faulty differentiation of the inner layer of periosteum into cartilage. This cartilage undergoes ossification mimicking normal endochondral bone growth and the exostosis normally ceases to enlarge when the nearby epiphysis fuses. In skeletal material osteochondromas manifest as rounded outgrowths of bone. The trabecular bone within is continuous with that of the bone to which they attach. In long-bone metaphyses they generally point away from the adjacent joint (Ortner and Putschar 1985, 371). Six individuals show osteochondroma, in all but one the lesion is solitary. Five individuals show lesions situated at the proximal tibial metaphysis (Burials G462, NA197, SA014, WCO009 and WCO134) and one of these (Burial NA197) also shows an osteochondroma at the distal metaphysis of the humerus. In the sixth individual (Burial WCO041) the lesion is located on the ilium.

Turning to other types of benign tumours, the right radius of Burial CN15 (?M, 14-15, Phase 4) shows an elongated convexity in the endosteal surface of the cortical wall. This endosteal protuberance is about 1cm long and has a sclerotic margin where it borders the medullary cavity. The bone was grossly normal, the abnormality being a chance finding when the bone was radiographed for another purpose. When the remainder of the skeleton was examined radiographically no further lesions were found. This most likely represents a fibrous cortical defect (a lesion which arises due to faulty development of the inner layer of periosteum (Ortner and Putschar 1985, 374)) which has become infilled with bone.

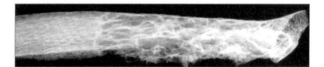

Plate 77. Radiograph of a right rib from Burial G419. The abnormality is probably due to a haemangioma.

A fragment of a right middle rib from Burial G419 (F, 50+, Phase 2) has a rather porous cortex. Radiography reveals coarsening of the bony trabeculae with patchy sclerosis and rarification (Plate 77). The lesion is located about one quarter of the way from the vertebral end. The demarcation between normal and abnormal tissue is sharp. This is probably a haemangioma (a neoplasm formed by abnormal proliferation of blood vessels), with lymphangioma and localised myeloma as possible but less likely, diagnoses (PB Guyer, pers. comm. 1992). A fragment of the body of a lumbar vertebra from this individual shows marked coarsening and thickening of the bony trabeulae. This too is a feature of haemangioma (Ortner and Putschar 1985, 376-7).

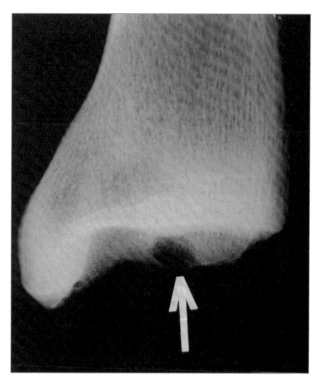

Plate 78. Anterio-posterior radiograph of the distal end of the left tibia of Burial G555. The radiolucency (arrowed) is suggestive of an intra-osseous ganglion.

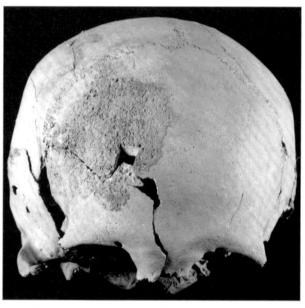

Plate 79. The cranium of Burial NA115, showing a deposit of fine-grained fibre bone.

Burial G555 (U, adult, Phase 1-2) shows a unilocular cavity, 10 by 7mm on the posterior margin of the distal joint surface of the left tibia. Radiographically (Plate 78) its margin shows slight sclerosis. There is no evidence for joint surface disease. Diagnosis of this lesion is difficult, but its solitary nature, epiphysial location, lack of communication with the articular space, well circumscribed nature, and marginal radio-opacity, are

184

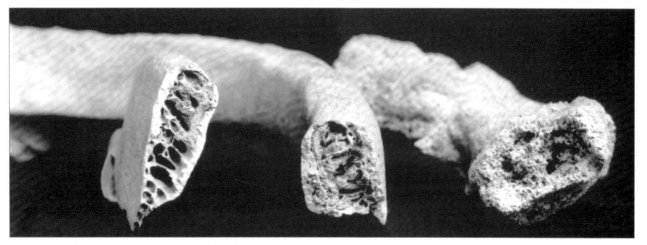

Plate 80. Endosteal fibre bone deposits within three rib fragments from Burial NA115. The rib on the left shows new bone deposition within the spaces of the normal trabecular structure. That in the centre shows greater bone deposits but the normal trabecular structure is still discernible in places. The specimen on the right shows complete obliteration of the normal cancellous bone structure by fine-grained new bone.

suggestive of an intra-osseous ganglion, a benign cystic lesion of bone containing gelatinous material (Feldman and Johnston 1973; Kamboulis *et al.* 1973).

There is a cavity about 6 by 9mm on the medial side of the proximal metaphysis of the right tibia of Burial WCO039 (U, 16-20, unphased). Radiographically, the cavity has sclerotic margins. Diagnosis is difficult, although two possibilities are fibrous cortical defect and intra-osseous ganglion.

There is one case of malignant disease, Burial NA115 (M, 30-45, Phase 1-2). This individual has already been described in detail (Mays *et al.* 1996), but briefly the skeleton shows deposits of fine-grained, sub-periosteal woven bone on the skull vault, mandible, ribs, vertebrae, pelvic bones, humeri and femora. Most of the above elements also show surface pitting and endosteal deposits of fine-grained woven bone (Plates 79 and 80). Although minor lytic lesions are present in a few elements, the skeletal changes are predominantly blastic. The nature and distribution of the lesions are suggestive of metastatic carcinoma, the spread of cancerous lesions to bone from a primary site in soft tissue. The primary sites most likely to develop skeletal metastases are the prostate gland, breast, kidney and, less frequently, the thyroid gland and the lung (Resnick and Niwayama 1988). All these, save the prostate, produce bone lesions which are primarily lytic (Resnick and Niwayama 1988). Bone lesions associated with prostatic carcinoma are mainly blastic in nature (Jacobs 1983). In this light it seems likely that the metastases in Burial NA115 derive from a primary focus in the prostate gland.

Other diseases

Burial NA135 (??M, 8, unphased) shows an extensive lytic lesion in the left side of the mandible destroying the ramus and the posterior part of the left mandibular corpus (Plates 81 and 82). The lesion has a rather irregular shape and there is little bone regeneration, although there is a

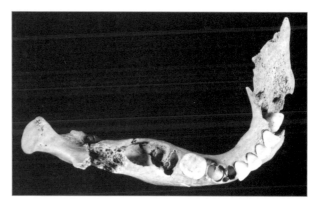

Plate 81. The mandible of Burial NA135. There is a large lytic lesion on the left side

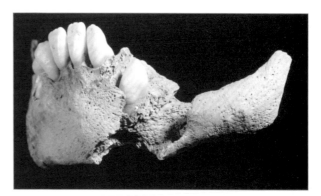

Plate 82. Anterio-lateral view of the left side of the mandible of Burial NA135, showing lytic changes.

little unremodelled sub-periosteal bone at its margin. There is destruction of the mandibular fossa of the left temporal bone and of the pterygoid fossa on the left sphenoid bone. The greater wing of the left sphenoid and the left temporal squama show pitting.

The lesions are suggestive of a single disease focus in the region of the left mandibular ramus. The presence of both remodelled and unremodelled bone deposits suggests a disease process active at time of death but with

Plate 83. The temporal bones of Burial SA023, showing erosions at the external auditory meatuses probably due to external ear canal cholesteatomas.

Plate 84. The left and right ilia of Burial NA119, together with an ilium of normal conformation (right) for comparison. The acetabular surfaces in the ilia of NA119 are more obliquely angled than normal and hence would have formed very shallow fossae for the femoral heads.

which the individual had lived for some time before succumbing. This case has been fully published (Mays and Nerlich 1997), and we argued for a diagnosis of Langerhans' cell histiocytosis.

Langerhans' cell histiocytosis is a disease of unknown cause characterised by abnormal proliferation of histiocytes (cells involved in normal tissue maintenance) in bone and/or various soft tissues. Although it is a tumour-like condition, it is believed to result from dysfunction of the immune system rather than being truly neoplastic. It may have a lethal outcome. Given that the disease process in Burial NA135 was active at time of death, Langerhans' cell histiocytosis, or associated complications, may have led to the death of this child.

Burial SA023 (F, 60+, Phase 4) shows erosions around both auditory meatuses, particularly the inferior and posterior parts. In each case this has resulted in destruction of the inferior wall of the auditory meatus (Plate 83). The lesion on the left side is the larger and it has eroded part of the mastoid process. The surfaces of eroded areas are rather rough. In both temporal bones, the middle ear and tympanic ring are normal. Radiography reveals that the margins of the lesions are sclerotic. The mastoid processes contain a mixture of diploic bone and small air cells and are not abnormally sclerotic. A variety of diagnoses were considered for this case (which has

been presented in detail elsewhere (Mays and Holst, forthcoming)) including benign and malignant tumours, Langerhans' cell histiocytosis, malignant otitis externa and keratosis obturans. The lesions appear most compatible with external ear canal cholesteatomas. A cholesteatoma is an accumulation of dead epithelial cells in the ear which becomes infected with low-grade pathogenic micro-organisms. The gradually expanding mass tends to erode the surrounding bone. External canal cholesteatomas most often arise in the elderly. Their cause is in most instances unclear, but it may be that hard, dry wax produced by ageing cerumen glands becomes firmly adherent to the skin lining the external ear canal, trapping shed, dead epithelial cells (references in Mays and Holst, forthcoming).

Both acetabula of Burial NA119 (J, 6 months, unphased) are very shallow (Plate 84). The condition of the proximal femoral epiphyses could not be established as they were missing post-mortem. The femoral necks are normal. Despite the negligible acetabular concavity, there is no evidence of hip dislocation. The age of the individual indicates the liklihood that he had not begun to walk. Perhaps dislocation would have occurred had he lived long enough to become fully ambulatory.

A further six burials (Burials CN19, EE099, NA031, NA088, NA119 and WCO200) were also noted as having

186

rather shallow acetabulae. Four showed supra-acetabular cysts, and of these, two were accompanied by avulsion injury to the bony rim of the acetabulum. The case was made above that these features reflect increased mechanical forces at the acetabular rim consequent upon the dysplastic acetabulum.

The thoracic spine of Burial NA066 (F, 22-24, Phase 1-2) shows mild scoliosis. The heights of the centra of T2 and 3 are reduced on the right side, as are those of T5-9 on the left side. This combines to produce an S-shaped curvature to the spine, the scoliosis of the upper curve being about 25° to the right, the lower about 30° to the left. Thus the two curves approximately cancel one another out, permitting the head to be maintained approximately in the mid-sagittal plane during life. There is asymmetry of the neural arches, the distance from the pars interarticularis to the midline often being less and the facet joint surfaces smaller on concave sides of the curves. There is osteophytosis of vertebral bodies and osteoarthritis of facet joints on concave parts of curves testifying to the increased mechanical strains imposed here as a result of the spinal deformity. It seems probable that this is an example of congenital scoliosis due to multiple mild hemimetameric hypoplasia (Barnes 1994, 62).

Burial G528 (M, 19-21, Phase 2) shows marked asymmetry of the upper limb bones (Table 116).

Table 116. Upper limb asymmetry in Burial G528.

Bone	Measurement	Left	Right
Humeri	Maximum length	300	314
	Max width at midshaft	18.4	20.7
	Min. width at midshaft	15.4	16.3
Radii	Max width at tuberosity	16.8	19.0
Ulnae	Olecranon breadth	23.8	26.7

Notes: all measurements in mm. Maximum lengths of forearm bones could not be ascertained due to post-depositional damage in these elements

In addition, there is slight asymmetry in femur length, the left being shorter by 9mm.

The cause of these asymmetries is unclear. This individual possesses two cervical ribs and one possibility is that the arm-bone asymmetries are connected with these. Cervical ribs may compress nerves or blood-vessels supplying the upper limb. Both cervical ribs in the present case are rather fragmentary and incomplete, but the right rib is rather slender and the estimated chord is about 45-47mm. Only a fragment about 2cm long, which articulates with the transverse process of the seventh cervical vertebra, remains of the left, but it was clearly much smaller than its counterpart. It is difficult to believe such a diminutive element could cause neurological or vascular problems to the left upper limb (although it

should be recalled that cervical ribs may have a soft tissue component (Black and Scheuer 1997) – even though there is no evidence or articulation with the neighbouring first thoracic rib, the left cervical rib may have born a costal cartilage). In addition this would hardly explain the femur asymmetry, if indeed this is connected with that of the upper limb – a difference in femur length of 9mm is not outside the boundaries of normal skeletal variation. Perhaps a more likely cause is some disease episode (e.g. poliomyelitis) during the growth period. The dental enamel of this individual shows multiple, severe hypoplastic defects corresponding to stress episodes occurring between about one and five years of age. Perhaps they are residues of a childhood disease which led to the asymmetries in skeletal development.

Plate 85. The ilia from Burial WCO058. Sub-periosteal layered new bone deposits are visible.

Burial WCO058 (?M, 13-15, unphased) shows deposits of sub-periosteal bone on the humeri, right radius, ilia (Plate 85), scapulae, the visceral surfaces of the ribs and the necks of the femora. Most deposits show a laminated appearence. This layering of sub-periosteal bone is evident both grossly (Plate 85), and radiographically (Plate 86). There are deposits of new bone within the medullary cavities of the left humerus and right radius (Plate 87). There is also new bone formation within the trabecular structure of most ribs (Plate 88), some scapula fragments, within the body of the third lumbar vertebra and the neural arch of the fourth lumbar vertebra. In flat-bones and metaphyses of long-bones, endosteal bone deposits generally take the form of cancellous new bone formed within spaces in the normal trabecular structure (Plate 88). Internally, the cortices of some long-bones are rather porous. This is evident grossly at post-depositional breaks, and also radiographically as radiolucent striations. In the light of the age at death of this individual, caution should be exercised in interpreting this sign: it may be seen in normal individuals undergoing the adolescent growth spurt (Buckland-Wright et al. 1990).

Infections and hypertrophic osteoarthopathy may cause widespread sub-periosteal bone formation, but they can be excluded here because they do not cause endosteal bone deposition. Fibrous dysplasia is a disease of childhood which involves endosteal deposition of woven

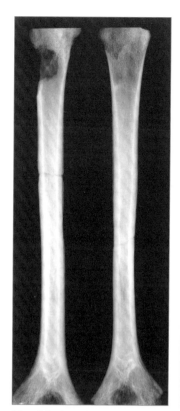

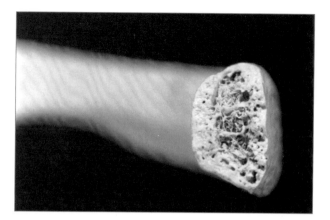

Plate 86. Anterio-posterior radiograph of the humeri of Burial WCO058. Sub-periosteal deposits of new bone are visible on both humeri. Deposits are characteristically separated from the underlying cortex by a radiolucent line. In places, deposits have flaked away post-mortem.

Plate 87. Medio-lateral radiograph of the radii of Burial WCO058. The right bone shows osteosclerosis due to endosteal new bone deposition.

Plate 88. Rib fragments from Burial WCO058. New bone deposits are visible within spaces in the normal cancellous bone structure. The endosteal new bone has a trabecular structure and thus differs morphologically from the endosteal bone observed in Burial NA115, which was fine-grained and amorphous (cf. Plate 80).

bone and which may be polyostotic. The following aspects of the skeletal manifestations of fibrous dysplasia are inconsistent with the changes observed in Burial WCO058. There is generally expansion of the cortex in the region of the endosteal lesions. Sub-periosteal deposits of woven bone are characteristically absent so that the cortical surfaces remain smooth. Affected elements are often bowed. Endosteal bone deposits are generally sharply demarcated. In the polyostotic form of the disease, skeletal involvement often shows marked bilateral asymmetry (Steinbock 1976, 336-40; Ortner and Putschar 1985, 315-22; Aufderheide and Rodriguez-Martin 1998, 420-21).

Some of the cancers of childhood, such as leukaemia, Hodgkin's disease, non-Hodgkin's lymphoma, neuroblastoma and retinoblastoma may metastatise to bone. Although each of the above may, on occasion, produce osteoblastic skeletal metastases, characteristically lesions are mainly or entirely lytic in nature (Parker 1997; Abramson 1997; Silverman and Kuhr 1993). Although rarely seen in children, carcinoid tumours and prostatic carcinoma may produce predominantly blastic skeletal metastases. These are not

likely diagnoses for Burial WCO058. Carcinoid tumour metastases are characteristically composed of spiculated new bone (Peavey et al. 1973), although more diffuse deposits of new bone may also occur, as may localised, focal osteosclerosis (Cookson 1974). Diffuse new bone formation due to metastases from a carcinoid tumour may be difficult to distinguish from those from prostatic carcinoma (Peavey et al. 1973). In prostatic carcinoma, both endosteal and sub-periosteal bone deposits are characteristically fine-grained and amorphous, as exemplified by Burial NA115, above. The new-bone formation in Burial WCO058 resembles skeletal metastases from neither of these primary tumours.

A possible diagnosis is renal osteodystrophy. In this condition, renal insufficiency induces hypocalcaemia, stimulating hyper-activity of the parathyroid glands. Because of the role of parathyroid hormone in skeletal homeostasis (see discussion of Burial CN03, above) bony changes occur as a consequence of this secondary hyperparathyroidism. In untreated cases, the frequency of bone changes in renal disease may reach 25% (Greenfield 1972). As we have seen with Burial CN03, hyperparathyroidism tends to produce internal porosity of cortical bone through tunnelling resorption. If the radiographic and gross appearance of the cortical bone in Burial WCO058 is accepted as abnormal, then it would be consistent with a diagnosis of renal osteodystrophy. Unlike primary hyperparathyroidism, hyperparathyroidism secondary to renal disease frequently leads to sub-periosteal and endosteal deposits of new bone. Although it seems that both the sub-periosteal and endosteal bone deposition in renal osteodystrophy are associated with hyperactivity of the parathyroid glands, the precise mechanism leading to these changes is controversial, and the reasons why they should occur much more often in secondary than in primary hyperparathyroidism are unclear (Resnick and Niwayama 1988, 2036, 2043). In renal osteodystrophy, periosteal deposits are generally polyostotic and their distribution in the skeleton is fairly symmetrical (Resnick and Niwayama 1988, 2036, 2043). A zone of radiolucency characteristically separates new bone deposits from the underlying cortex (Meema *et al.* 1974). Endosteal deposits of bone in renal osteodystrophy take the form of an increase in cancellous bone. Radiographically, this makes the bone look osteosclerotic, and gives it a rather homogeneous, 'ground-glass' appearance (Kaye *et al.* 1960). In renal osteodystrophy, endosteal bone deposition, sub-periosteal bone formation and intra-cortical porosity tend to co-occur (Meema *et al.* 1974).

The above observations support a diagnosis of renal osteodystrophy. The current case, however, seems to lack what is perhaps the most important diagnostic indicator for hyperparathyroidism (whether primary or secondary): sub-periosteal resorption, particularly in the phalanges (Buckland-Wright *et al.* 1990). For this reason, the diagnosis must remain tentative. It should also be noted that renal osteodystrophy in children may lead to skeletal rickets, of which there is no sign in Burial WCO058. Skeletal rickets may often be absent, and it seems that skeletal changes due to hyperparathyroidism are generally the first to develop (Ellis and Peart 1973).

Burial G275A (F, 25-35, Phase 2). The medullary cavities in the clavicles and forearm bones are very narrow and the bones are osteosclerotic on X-ray. Most of the vertebral bodies show two horizontal band-like radiodensities situated toward their upper and lower margins, separated by a band of normal trabeculae in between. The trabecular bone in the innominates is rather sclerotic and the structure is sparser than normal.

This may be another, somewhat less certain, example of renal osteodystrophy. That the lesions in both Burial WCO058 and Burial G275A are compatible with this diagnosis illustrates the great variability which exists in the skeletal manifestation of this condition. The osteosclerosis in Burial G275A, particularly the band-like radiodensities in the vertebral bodies (which are sometimes referred to as 'rugger-jersey spine'), are consistent with the condition (Resnick and Niwayama 1988, 2252; Adams 1997). Interestingly, this individual also shows slipped capital epiphysis (Chapter 11), a recognised complication of renal osteodystrophy (Adams 1997).

13 Summary and Conclusions

Six hundred and eighty-seven burials have been examined. Forty-one represent interments within the church, the remainder are churchyard burials. The burials date from the period AD 950-1850, but the great bulk are medieval. Gross bone preservation was generally very good with minimal post-depositional erosion of bone surfaces. There was a tendency for intra-mural burials to be more poorly preserved than churchyard interments. The church burials are generally of more recent date than those in the churchyard, so the greater soil erosion of bone in the former is presumably due to a different burial environment beneath the standing building. Unlike gross bone preservation, chemical and micro-structural diagenesis tended to increase with the age of the burial, earlier interments showing greater alteration.

Various investigations were carried out into the spatial patterning of burials. There was no evidence for burial together of individuals who were closely related genetically, as might have been expected if families used particular burial plots or if inhabitants of different settlements in the parish tended to use particular areas of the churchyard. The difficulties of detecting such practices using osteological data must be emphasised. By contrast, there were clear age-related spatial groupings. There was a tendency for individuals under about eighteen months old to be buried immediately to the north of the church. The north side of the churchyard is traditionally an area used for burial of, amongst others, the unbaptised, however, it was argued that baptism was unlikely to have been routinely delayed until the infant was eighteen months old. Presumably some other life transition occurred at about this age and was regularly given recognition in burial placement. More children than adults were also interred in this area. Perhaps the transition to adulthood was also being given recognition.

The assemblage was approximately evenly split between immature individuals and adults. About 15% of the whole assemblage were infants. If this is a guide to infant mortality levels then this is a fairly modest rate compared with others documented historically. Analysis of the age distribution of porotic hyperostosis suggested that iron stores in new-born infants were probably adequate, and hence that low birth-weight and prematurity were not regular problems for this population. Nitrogen stable isotope analysis indicated that breast-feeding continued for about eighteen months from birth. If we are correct in inferring a fairly modest rate of infant mortality in this group, it may be, given the well-known beneficial effects of breast-milk, that the extended breast-feeding practised at Wharram Percy played some part in this. Most women are unable to produce adequate milk beyond about six months post-partum to sustain the infant's needs. Unless breast-milk is supplemented with other foods at about this time, growth begins to falter. At Wharram Percy, long-bone growth showed no evidence for faltering at this age, so that it seems likely that women were starting to supplement infant diets with other foods some time before cessation of breast-feeding. Given that there was no change in nitrogen stable isotope ratios prior to about eighteen months of this age it seems likely that supplements were based on cereal foods or animal milk, both of which would have negligible impact on $\partial^{15}N$ and hence would be difficult to detect in diets using the nitrogen stable isotope technique.

Growth in bone length appears to match that seen in modern subjects up to the age of about one year. In this population, appositional growth in cortical bone thickness was more sensitive to retardation by environmental insults than was growth in bone length. Appositional bone growth was deficient even in individuals under one year compared with modern reference data. Despite the evidence for the effectiveness of the infant feeding strategy, this reminds us that breast-feeeding could not completely insulate infants from the problems posed by their environment.

Between one and two years of age the Wharram Percy children start to fall behind modern children in terms of growth in bone length (and hence in stature). This pattern seems to begin with the cessation of breast-feeding. It seems likely that this simply reflects the removal of the beneficial effects of breastmilk, there is no evidence that weaning was an especially problematic time for the Wharram Percy infants. There is no sign of elevated mortality or morbidity at this age, and the growth deficit in bone length is simply the beginning of a pattern which continued in later years.

During childhood, growth was greatly retarded compared with that in children today. For example, a Wharram Percy fourteen-year old was only about the same height as a modern ten-year old. This suggests, not surprisingly, that disease and poor nutrition were greater problems at Wharram Percy than in modern Britain. In addition, comparison with 19th-century figures suggests that Wharram Percy children were no taller than factory children during the Industrial Revolution. This suggests that the health and nutrition of the medieval children may have been no better than that of the 19th-century urban poor. Further evidence of adverse conditions during the growth period is provided by analysis of Harris lines. This showed that children suffering episodes of growth interruption which gave rise to Harris lines subsequently failed to catch up, either in appositional growth or in bone length, so that they remained both short for their ages and deficient in cortical bone. This suggests that chronic poor nutrition and disease were a problem.

Despite the growth problems experienced in childhood in this population, adults were only a little shorter than their modern counterparts. This is probably due to prolongation of the growth period. Rather than growth being complete by the late teens as it is in Western populations today, it probably continued well into the twenties, as was commonly the case until recent times.

Approximately 40% of adult burials were of individuals aged over 50 years. This suggests, even in this low-status population, reasonable longevity once adulthood was attained. Indeed there were sufficient elderly in this group for the diseases of old age to manifest themselves. Loss of bone density in older individuals due to osteoporosis was no less than that seen in the elderly today. This was despite the fact that various aspects of lifestyle held to exacerbate the disease in modern populations, such as sedentary habits and cigarette smoking, were absent at Wharram Percy. Among females, loss of bone density may also have commenced during the reproductive period, which is earlier than its outset in modern Europeans. The explanation for this is unclear but it may reflect the effects of repeated pregnancy and prolonged lactation under conditions of sub-optimal nutrition. Older women suffered rib and vertebral compression fractures as a consequence of osteoporosis, but hip fractures are absent, perhaps because too few survived to the advanced old age at which these fractures tend to occur.

By old age many suffered from osteoarthritis. This may have been a consequence of their physically arduous lifestyle. The frequency of osteoarthritis was greater than that seen in another medieval population composed largely of middle class urban dwellers.

Given the extended time span covered by the burials, the investigation of secular trends in osteological data was a major focus of the work. This was necessarily confined largely to adults given that relatively few juveniles could be assigned to different phases. In general, secular trends in osteological data were rather few. There was little evidence for change over time in health, activity patterns or demographic composition of the population. The only hint of a trend with regard to disease was in dental caries. The frequency appeared to increase in the post-medieval period and a greater proportion of cavities originated on the occlusal surfaces of the teeth. The nature of the data meant that statistical validation of these patterns was problematic, however, they do appear to parallel, albeit in rather more muted fashion, those which have been noted in urban material. When seen by previous workers in urban material, these trends were ascribed to a shift to a somewhat softer and more cariogenic diet in post-medieval times mainly due to increasing imports of cane sugar and changes in food preparation techniques, particularly in flour-grinding and breadmaking. The dental disease data suggest that these dietary changes were much less marked for the Wharram Percy group than for urban populations which have been the subject of study by earlier investigators, and there is other evidence to support this. For example, urban populations have been shown to display a decrease in robusticity in the maxilla and mandible as a consequence of the change in dietary consistency in post-medieval times. This effect is absent at Wharram Percy, post-medieval jaws are indistinguishable from their medieval counterparts in terms of robusticity. Unlike the situation for urban groups, heavy dental wear continued to be a feature in post-medieval burials, although whether the rate of wear truly matched that in medieval teeth is unclear due to the lack of a satisfactory independent skeletal ageing technique for adults.

There is evidence for a change in cranial morphology over time, at least in male skulls. Crudely speaking, cranial vaults were broader during the later medieval period than during either earlier medieval or post-medieval times. This secular change in British skulls has been known about for some time, but this is the first time it has been demonstrated in a single population using radiometrically dated material. Interpretation of this change in British cranial morphology has been controversial, but the current data would appear to strengthen the case for extraneous environmental factors rather than genetic changes due to arrival of migrants.

Comparison of intramural and churchyard burials provided little indication of differences in health according to social status. Likewise, there was scanty evidence for health differences between the sexes, other than in diseases such as osteoporosis and DISH where dissimilarities appear to represent inherent biological differences rather than differences in nutrition or lifestyle. Several aspects of the work, however, helped to shed light on gender-related differences in activity patterns. Biomechanical analyses of humerus morphology in a medieval group from York suggested that males showed greater bilateral asymmetry in bone shaft strength than females, suggesting greater male participation in activities which differentially load the left and right arms. This pattern did not obtain at Wharram Percy, and in addition, sexual dimorphism in overall humerus shaft strength was less at Wharram Percy than in the York group, due to greater diaphysial bone strength in rural than in urban females. Taken together these findings suggest lesser sexual division of tasks at Wharram Percy and a greater female participation in physically demanding work. There were differences in distribution of osteoarthritis between the sexes. In males the joints in the upper limb were favoured sites for lesions. This was not the case for females where lesions were seen more often in the lower limb and trunk. This may suggest that although the distribution of heavy work involving the upper limbs was more equal between the sexes in the rural than the urban environment, males still undertook more of this type of work than females. Although loading on the upper limbs was likely greater in rural than urban females, when compared to male work, female tasks at Wharram Percy more often tended to place stress on the legs and back rather than the arms. Another sex difference is that females more often showed squatting facets than did males. More female work may have involved squatting to attend to tasks close to the ground.

Turning to population comparisons with other skeletal series, cranial morphology shows close similarity with later medieval groups from York. It is, however, distinct from that of earlier medieval York groups. Material from the earlier part of the medieval period in York shows strong resemblance to crania from medieval Oslo, but the Wharram Percy crania do not. This may suggest that any Scandinavian contribution to the population at medieval Wharram Percy was minor compared with that of earlier medieval York.

Demographic analysis may shed further light on relationships between York and Wharram Percy. Among the Wharram Percy adults, males outnumber females, but the reverse is true at the York site of St Helen-on-the-Walls. The favoured interpretation of this pattern was that female-led migration into York was occurring from surrounding rural settlements such as Wharram Percy, a pattern for which there is medieval documentary evidence. Analysis of documentary sources (Goldberg 1986) suggests that this was associated with labour imbalances consequent upon the social disruption caused by the mid-14th-century Black Death, with increased demand for female labour in urban centres. At Wharram Percy, however, the sex imbalance applies for all phases. If a female-led migration pattern is the correct explanation, then this appears to have been something which was already underway well before the Black Death – perhaps the occurrence of the Black Death simply accentuated trends already present before the mid-14th-century outbreak of the disease.

The osteological data also provide evidence for trading links between Wharram Percy and other settlements. Carbon and nitrogen stable isotope analyses indicate that both medieval and post-medieval diets contained small but significant amounts of seafood, which may have been acquired direct from coastal settlements or indirectly via trade with inland towns. Regular links between Wharram Percy and larger settlements may also have impacted upon the disease experience of the community. DNA analyses indicate that tuberculosis at Wharram Percy was acquired not via animal vectors but from other infected humans. The human form of tuberculosis is a population-density dependent disease, and it was suggested that perhaps regular contact with large urban centres helped to maintain the disease even in rather thinly populated countryside.

Despite the evidence for regular contacts with other settlements, comparison with coeval material from York also resulted in the detection of some important differences in health. Both porotic hyperostosis and periostitis were more frequent in the York St Helen-on-the-Walls population than at Wharram Percy. This is consistent with a greater pathogen load in the urban environment due both to crowded living conditions and contamination of water supplies. More of the York group probably suffered from infectious disease for more of the time than the Wharram Percy population. In addition, there was a tendency for more of the York lesions to be healed, whereas a greater proportion of the Wharram Percy cases were active at time of death. This suggests that the conditions which caused these lesions more often led to death at Wharram Percy, whereas at York there may have been greater resistance to disease so that a greater proportion of individuals tended to recover. This too is consistent with the idea of a greater pathogen load in the urban environment; long-term exposure from birth to a pathogen-rich environment might be expected to lead to greater resistance to infectious disease.

The rate of long-bone fractures at Wharram Percy was rather lower than that seen in the York material, or indeed in other medieval rural assemblages. Most fractures at Wharram Percy appeared more likely due to accident rather than violence. There were, however, four individuals showing cranial blade-injuries, and a further six showed blunt injuries to the skull which may also have been due to violence. One individual with blunt injury to the skull vault showed evidence of possible cranial surgery in the form of a trepanation in the injured area. This last indicates that access to complex surgical treatment was not always restricted to the wealthy in medieval society.

Other than the cases already discussed, notable palaeopathological findings include one example of leprosy in a child, an adult showing skeletal metastatic disease due to prostate cancer, and there were several examples of rickets. Some individual cases of diseases rarely encountered in palaeopathology were identified, including hyperparathyroidism, Dietrich's disease, and Langerhans' cell histiocytosis.

Part Four

The Burials

14 Radiocarbon Dating

by A. Bayliss, G. Cook and C. Heighway,
with contributions from C. Bronk Ramsey,
C. Harding and S. Mays

An explanation of burial references

Burials in this volume have been renumbered to an alpha-numeric sequence with letter codes for each area of the church and churchyard, followed by an Arabic number (e.g. Burial SA034: South Aisle Burial 34); the burials from Site 26 are prefixed with G (e.g. Burial G250) (see p. 2 for more details). In 1976 (part way through the excavation of Site 26) a new context recording system was adopted at Wharram (see *Wharram VII*, 2 for more details). It must be noted that the original recording techniques used for burials prior to this change, frequently did not differentiate between skeletons and the cuts and fills of their graves – so for example, Burial SA050, where referred to in the text, incorporates skeleton number, grave cut and grave fills which may or may not have originally had separate context numbers. In the finds sections, objects are catalogued with their original context number, often the grave fill, but the burial number is given as well for clarity. The letter codes were originally used in *Wharram III* as a prefix to layer and feature numbers; it is therefore possible for the same number to refer to a feature in the church excavations and a burial in the final burial list. To prevent confusion, all references to burials in this volume are always prefixed by the word Burial.

Introduction

A total of 99 radiocarbon measurements have been made on material from the cemetery around the church at Wharram Percy. Seven samples were processed at AERE Harwell between 1978 and 1980, with a further 92 measured by the Scottish Universities Research and Reactor Centre at East Kilbride, Glasgow between 1995 and 1997 (see Table 117).

All samples but one were of human bone from articulated skeletons which were excavated between 1963 and 1984. The exception, C238 (HAR-3584), was a combined sample of animal and human bone from layer EE215, the ground surface beneath the mortar foundation of the Phase II chancel of the stone church (see below; *Wharram III*, 54, 179).

Eight samples were submitted as replicate measurements in 1997. All of these were second samples of articulated skeletons which had been dated previously. Archaeologically there is no doubt that these pairs of measurements represent true replicates on material of exactly the same age. The samples were not chosen randomly, but were submitted where the existing measurements were in statistical disagreement with the recorded stratigraphy (Bronk Ramsey 1995) (Burials WCO118 (GU-5503 and GU-5682), WCO162 (GU-5517 and GU-5678) and NA224 (GU-5657 and GU-5677) or where this was suspected (Burial G652 (GU-5557 and GU-5680)). The other replicate samples were submitted because the first measurements were amongst the earliest from the site and so, in addition to their quality assurance function, the extra precision from the replicates would contribute to refining the estimated date for the start of burial on the site (see below).

Radiocarbon analysis

In the laboratory at East Kilbride the bone samples were washed thoroughly to remove adhering material, and then broken up and placed in cold (0.5 molar) hydrochloric acid for about two hours. This dissociates the carbonates, solubilises some of the mineral material, and partly denatures the collagen. The bone fragments were washed again to remove any further adhering material and heated to approximately 90°C in distilled water (with a very small amount of acid added to keep the solution on the acid side of neutrality). This temperature was maintained for many hours until the collagen became solubilised. It was then filtered and dried.

Combustion of the sample in a pure oxygen environment produced carbon dioxide, which was purified and passed over molten lithium. The reaction produces lithium carbide, which was cooled before the addition of distilled water. This yields acetylene which was subsequently purified and converted to benzene by cyclotrimerisation using a chromium based catalyst. The ^{14}C activity in the benzene was measured by liquid scintillation spectrometry. Background and modern reference standards (i.e. ^{14}C free materials, such as ancient carbonates or petroleum derived products, and SRM-4990C (oxalic acid) respectively) are sythesised to benzene and measured for ^{14}C activity in an identical fashion to allow the calculation of ^{14}C ages. Full details of the methods used to process and measure the Wharram Percy samples can be found in Stenhouse and Baxter (1983).

Table 117. The radiocarbon results.

Context	Laboratory Number	Radiocarbon Age (BP)	δ¹³C (‰)	Weighted mean (BP)	Calibrated date range (95% confidence)	Posterior density estimate (95% probability)
C238	HAR-3584	1240±90	-22.7	-	cal AD 640–1000	-
EE038	GU-5452	610±50	-20.1	-	cal AD 1280–1430	cal AD 1280–1360
EE003	GU-5507	940±60	-21.7	-	cal AD 980–1230	cal AD 1000–1220
EE007	GU-5508	730±60	-21.0	-	cal AD 1190–1400	cal AD 1180–1330
EE013	GU-5506	830±50	-19.9	-	cal AD 1040–1290	cal AD 1160–1290
EE019	GU-5510	1070±60	-21.8	-	cal AD 780–1160	cal AD 950–1070 (85%) or cal AD 1080–1160 (10%)
EE020	GU-5511	1080±70	-22.2	1076±53BP; T'=0.0; T'(5%)=3.8; ν=1	cal AD 780–1030	cal AD 950–1040 (91%) or cal AD 1090–1120 (2%) or cal AD 1140–1160 (2%)
EE020	GU-5683	1070±80	-20.3	-	cal AD 780–1160	cal AD 960–1170
EE026	GU-5509	1040±70	-21.5	-	cal AD 890–1220	cal AD 970–1200
EE214	HAR-3575	980±70	-21.6	-	cal AD 1440–1660	-
SA002	GU-5453	340±50	-20.9	-	cal AD 1440–1660	-
SA003	GU-5454	350±50	-20.9	-	cal AD 1430–1660	-
SA012	GU-5455	890±50	-19.2	-	cal AD 1020–1270	cal AD 1030–1220
SA013	GU-5491	630±50	-23.1	-	cal AD 1280–1420	cal AD 1280–1360
SA014	GU-5456	760±50	-20.2	-	cal AD 1180–1380	cal AD 1190–1300
SA033	GU-5457	380±60	-19.0	-	cal AD 1420–1650	-
SA034	GU-5458	1050±50	-19.2	-	cal AD 890–1160	cal AD 950–1050 (85%) or cal AD 1080–1160 (10%)
V38	GU-5460	600±50	-20.7	-	cal AD 1280–1430	cal AD 1280–1360
V41	GU-5669	1010±60	-22.4	-	cal AD 890–1170	cal AD 960–1160
V45	GU-5459	780±50	-20.1	-	cal AD 1160–1300	cal AD 1160–1300
V50	HAR-2672	910±80	unknown	-	cal AD 980–1280	cal AD 1000–1260
V51	HAR-2460	910±70	-20.2	-	cal AD 990–1280	cal AD 1020–1230
V52	HAR-2462	980±70	-21.1	-	cal AD 890–1220	cal AD 980–1220
V56	HAR-2631	890±70	-20.8	-	cal AD 1000–1280	cal AD 1020–1230
SA052	GU-5461	960±70	-21.5	-	cal AD 900–1220	cal AD 980–1220
SA053	GU-5462	930±50	-20.3	-	cal AD 1000–1220	cal AD 1020–1220
SA056	GU-5463	980±70	-20.4	-	cal AD 980–1190	cal AD 980–1190
WCO009	GU-5515	680±50	-21.1	-	cal AD 1260–1400	cal AD 1240–1360
WCO010	GU-5513	400±50	-22.3	-	cal AD 1420–1640	-
WCO028	GU-5512	610±60	-21.0	-	cal AD 1280–1440	cal AD 1270–1360
WCO044	GU-5495	320±60	-21.2	-	cal AD 1440–1800	-
WCO045	GU-5516	230±50	-21.7	-	cal AD 1520–1950	-
WCO070	GU-5494	920±60	-21.1	-	cal AD 990–1260	cal AD 1000–1190
WCO118	GU-5503	1080±70	-21.1	961±46BP; T'=5.2; T'(5%)=3.8; ν=1	cal AD 990–1210	cal AD 1070–1230

Table 117 continued.

Context	Laboratory Number	Radiocarbon Age (BP)	$\partial^{13}C$ (‰)	Weighted mean (BP)	Calibrated date range (95% confidence)	Posterior density estimate (95% probability)
WCO118	GU-5682	870±60	-19.2	-	cal AD 880–1170	cal AD 960–1170
WCO119	GU-5502	1030±70	-22.0	-	cal AD 1290–1440	cal AD 1290–1360
WCO130	GU-5493	570±50	-22.8	-	cal AD 1290–1450	cal AD 1290–1360
WCO138	GU-5499	550±60	-21.6	-	cal AD 1290–1450	
WCO139	GU-5498	790±60	-20.5	-	cal AD 1060–1300	cal AD 1040–1090 (4%) or cal AD 1120–1140 (2%) or cal AD 1150–1300 (89%)
WCO153	GU-5497	350±50	-21.9	-	cal AD 1430–1660	-
WCO156	GU-5496	530±70	-20.9	-	cal AD 1290–1480	cal AD 1280–1360
WCO162	GU-5517	860±70	-20.8	827±41BP; T'=0.3; T'(5%)=3.8; v=1	cal AD 1060–1290	cal AD 1030–1210
WCO162	GU-5678	810±50	-19.6	-	cal AD 1160–1290	-
WCO170	GU-5492	430±70	-22.0	-	cal AD 1330–1640	-
WCO179	GU-5501	820±70	-21.0	-	cal AD 1030–1300	cal AD 1030–1300
WCO181	GU-5500	550±50	-21.1	-	cal AD 1300–1450	cal AD 1290–1350
WCO184	GU-5514	740±50	-21.4	-	cal AD 1210–1390	cal AD 1190–1310
NA002	GU-5641	990±50	-20.8	-	cal AD 970–1170	cal AD 980–1170
NA006	GU-5642	840±90	-23.1	-	cal AD 1010–1380	cal AD 1020–1290
NA013	GU-5643	990±60	-20.3	-	cal AD 900–1210	cal AD 1020–1220
NA014	GU-5644	940±70	-21.9	-	cal AD 980–1260	cal AD 980–1160
NA046	GU-5645	1000±60	-22.4	-	cal AD 890–1190	cal AD 970–1190
NA094	GU-5646	1050±50	-22.1	-	cal AD 890–1160	cal AD 950–1050 (86%) or cal AD 1090–1160 (9%)
NA104	GU-5647	1150±70	-21.1	1094±53BP; T'=1.5; T'(5%)=3.8; v=1	cal AD 780–1030	cal AD 950–1040
NA104	GU-5681	1020±80	-20.7		cal AD 890–1160	
NA112	GU-5648	1020±50	-20.9	-	cal AD 890–1160	cal AD 980–1160
NA127	GU-5649	940±70	-22.0	-	cal AD 980–1260	cal AD 980–1230
NA146	GU-5650	1050±80	-21.5	1022±53BP; T'=0.2; T'(5%)=3.8; v=01	cal AD 890–1160	cal AD 960–1070 (90%) or cal AD 1080–1120 (5%)
NA146	GU-5679	1000±70	-20.4		cal AD 890–1190	
NA167	GU-5651	750±60	-20.1	-	cal AD 1160–1390	cal AD 1160–1330
NA170	GU-5652	1110±60	-20.4	-	cal AD 770–1030	cal AD 940–1040 (94%) or cal AD 1140–1160 (1%)
NA173	GU-5653	1040±60	-21.6	-	cal AD 880–1160	cal AD 960–1070 (74%) or cal AD 1080–1160 (21%)
NA176	GU-5654	750±50	-20.2	-	cal AD 1190–1390	cal AD 1180–1310
NA195	GU-5655	860±100	-21.4	-	cal AD 980–1380	cal AD 1010–1300
NA199	GU-5656	660±50	-20.5	-	cal AD 1270–1410	cal AD 1260–1360

Table 117 continued.

Context	Laboratory Number	Radiocarbon Age (BP)	$\partial^{13}C$ (‰)	Weighted mean (BP)	Calibrated date range (95% confidence)	Posterior density estimate (95% probability)
NA215	GU-5659	1150±70	-21.1	-	cal AD 680-1030	cal AD 950-1030
NA217	GU-5640	700±50	-21.5	-	cal AD 1240-1400	cal AD 1210-1340
NA218	GU-5639	1030±50	-20.6	-	cal AD 890-1160	cal AD 960-1070 (76%) or cal AD 1080-1160 (19%)
NA223	GU-5638	930±50	-21.9	-	cal AD 1000-1220	cal AD 1020-1220
NA224	GU-5657	1050±50	-20.3	1035±35BP; T'=0.2; T'(5%)=3.8; v=1	cal AD 900-1040	cal AD 960-1040
NA224	GU-5677	1020±50	-20.1			
NA227	GU-5658	950±50	-20.4	-	cal AD 990-1220	cal AD 1000-1200
NA233	GU-5637	1030±50	-22.5	-	cal AD 890-1160	cal AD 970-1070 (70%) or cal AD 1080-1160 (25%)
G265	GU-5544	930±50	-21.6	-	cal AD 1000-1220	cal AD 1140-1250
G275	GU-5543	810±70	-24.5	-	cal AD 1030-1300	cal AD 1230-1330
G278	GU-5547	920±60	-20.7	-	cal AD 990-1260	cal AD 1140-1260
G279	GU-5542	1040±50	-22.5	-	cal AD 890-1160	cal AD 960-1040
G297	GU-5546	930±70	-20.9	-	cal AD 980-1270	cal AD 1140-1260
G303	GU-5541	940±50	-21.8	-	cal AD 990-1220	cal AD 1040-1130
G304	GU-5545	1080±50	-21.6	-	cal AD 780-1030	cal AD 960-1030
G305	HAR-2208	2030±60	-21.4	-	cal BC 200-120 cal AD	-
G314	GU-5540	870±50	-21.6	-	cal AD 1020-1280	cal AD 1040-1130
G361	GU-5553	760±60	-22.3	-	cal AD 1160-1390	cal AD 1170-1290
G385	GU-5552	900±50	-21.0	-	cal AD 1020-1260	cal AD 1080-1190
G451	GU-5551	940±70	-20.6	-	cal AD 980-1260	cal AD 1080-1190
G462	GU-5550	930±50	-22.7	-	cal AD 1000-1220	cal AD 1080-1190
G474	GU-5539	930±50	-21.3	-	cal AD 1000-1220	cal AD 1040-1130
G478	GU-5549	960±50	-22.3	-	cal AD 980-1220	cal AD 1080-1180
G528	GU-5548	890±50	-20.8	-	cal AD 1020-1270	cal AD 1080-1190
G571	GU-5538	830±50	-21.3	-	cal AD 1040-1290	cal AD 1160-1270
G582	GU-5537	910±50	-21.4	-	cal AD 1010-1250	cal AD 1040-1130
G601	GU-5554	950±50	-21.5	-	cal AD 990-1220	cal AD 980-1080
G604	GU-5558	910±50	-20.3	-	cal AD 1010-1250	cal AD 1000-1080
G652	GU-5557	770±50	-21.1	803±38BP; T'=1.1; T'(5%)=3.8; v=1	cal AD 1160-1290	cal AD 1180-1280
G652	GU-5680	850±60	-20.1	-	cal AD 900-1160	cal AD 970-1070
G750	GU-5556	1000±50	-20.0	-	cal AD 1010-1270	cal AD 990-1080
G760	GU-5555	900±60	-21.4	-	cal AD 1420-1640	-
CN03	GU-5575	400±50	-18.4	-	cal AD 1640-1955*	-
CN44	GU-5576	170±50	-19.9	-		-

A similar process was used to prepare bone samples for dating at AERE Harwell in the late 1970s (Otlet and Warchal 1978). Once roots and other obviously intrusive material had been physically removed, samples were placed in (3 molar) hydrochloric acid and heated for 30 minutes. This removes carbonates. Contamination by humic acids was removed by heating samples in (4%) sodium hydroxide for 30 minutes. After this the material was washed, dried, and, if enough remained, charred.

The sample was then combusted to carbon dioxide and synthesised to benzene using a method similar to that initially described by Tamers (1965) and a vanadium based catalyst (Otlet 1977). The radiocarbon content was measured using liquid scintillation counting as described by Otlet (1979).

Quality assurance and reliability

The radiocarbon laboratory at East Kilbride maintains a continual programme of quality assurance procedures, in addition to participation in international intercomparisons (Rozanski et al. 1992; Scott et al. 1998). These tests indicate no laboratory offsets and demonstrate the validity of the precision quoted.

Because of the scale of the Wharram Percy dating programme, additional quality assurance measures were taken specifically for this project. These include the programme of blind replicates. One of these samples (Burial NA215) was too small for radiometric dating. The other pairs of results are shown in Table 117. Six of these are not statistically significantly different (Ward and Wilson 1978). The two measurements on Burial WCO118 (GU-5503 and GU-5682) are statistically significantly different at 95% confidence, although the difference is not significant at 99% confidence (T'=5.2; v=1; T'(5%)=3.8; T'(1%)=6.6). This difference on one pair of measurements out of seven pairs is not unexpected, and the replicate programme has provided additional assurance on the consistency of the results quoted.

In 1978 the importance of quality assurance for radiocarbon dating was less widely appreciated, although at this time the first steps towards formal inter-laboratory comparision were being taken within the UK. The results of these measurements were published in 1980 (Otlet et al. 1980) and show that the British laboratories were in good agreement. The seven samples from the cemetery at Wharram Percy which were measured at Harwell were processed at this time.

Although considerable effort has been made to ensure that the radiocarbon content of the samples submitted has been measured accurately, it is also necessary that the sample should relate directly to the event which is of archaeological interest - for it is this date which we wish to estimate. All but one of the samples comes from human bone which was recovered articulated. In these cases there can be little doubt that the date of sample is almost exactly the same as the date of burial, or decay would have set in and the bone become disarticulated. The bones submitted from C238 (HAR-3584) were not articulated and were not from the same individual, or even the same species, as it is recorded that the sample was of 'animal bone and human bone'. For this reason the result cannot be regarded as an accurate estimate of the date of the pre-church Saxon activity on the terrace. There is no guarantee that the bones which constituted the sample were even of the same date, since some could have been residual in the buried soil. Consequently this result can only be regarded as a terminus post quem for the building of the Phase II chancel of the stone church.

All radiocarbon measurements have been corrected for fractionation using the $\partial^{13}C$ values shown in Table 117. Further carbon and nitrogen stable isotope measurements have been measured on human skeletons from Wharram Percy for dietary studies (Mays 1997; Richards et al. 2002). These measurements suggests the protein consumed by the population buried in the cemetery was very largely of terrestrial origin.

Results

The results are given in Table 117, and are quoted in accordance with the international standard known as the Trondheim convention (Stuiver and Kra 1986). They are conventional radiocarbon ages (Stuiver and Polach 1977).

Calibration

The calibrations of these results, which relate the radiocarbon measurements directly to the calendrical time scale, are given in Table 117 and in outline in Figures 99-101, 103-104 and 106-113. All have been calculated using the atmospheric dataset published by Stuiver et al. (1998) and the computer program OxCal (v3.5) (Bronk Ramsey 1995; 1998; 2000). The calibrated date ranges cited in the text are those for 95% confidence. They are quoted in the form recommended by Mook (1986), with the end points rounded outwards to 10 years. Those in italics are ranges derived from mathematical modelling of archaeological problems (see below). The calibrated ranges in Table 117 have been calculated according to the maximum intercept method (Stuiver and Reimer 1986), all other ranges are derived from the probability method (Stuiver and Reimer 1993; van der Plicht 1993; Dehling and van der Plicht 1993).

Aims of the dating programme

The main objective of the dating programme was to discover whether the phasing sequences proposed for the burials in different areas of the site have chronological integrity, and to put absolute dating onto that phasing structure. This approach attempts to date as large a proportion of the burial assemblage as possible, whilst sampling only a proportion of it. This objective is vital, not only for the understanding of the development of the cemetery, but also because many of the research aims for the study of human bones from the site depend on looking for change over time.

Specifically, the principal objectives of the dating programme which relate to the development of the cemetery are:

• When did burial start on the site?

• Did burial occur in different parts of the cemetery at different times? For example, when was the area to the west of the church used for burial? Are burials closer to the church earlier than those further away?

• Does the arrangement of the arms of the corpse change over time?

• Does the use and variety of stone settings change over time?

• Does the use of coffins (and parallel sided burials) vary over time?

The main research objectives relating to the osteology of the population at Wharram Percy which require dating of the cemetery are:

• Looking at changes in craniometric data over time. It has long been noted that there is a change in cranial form between Saxon and medieval sites in Britain (Brothwell 1972). The Wharram Percy collection presents an opportunity to determine whether this change is observable in a group from a single cemetery, and if so to determine what aspects of cranial form change and when these changes occurred. Traditionally changes in skull form have been ascribed to migrations of peoples, but it is now realised that a number of other factors such as diet, nutrition, and climate also exert an influence (Mays 1998).

• The population of Wharram Percy parish was drastically reduced in the mid-14th century, presumably as a result of the Black Death. It is interesting to compare living conditions in the parish pre and post-Black Death to investigate what effect the marked depopulation had on the health of the remaining inhabitants. Historical sources indicate that peasant nutrition was much improved after the Black Death (Platt 1996; Gies and Gies 1990) - was this true at Wharram Percy?

• Studies in urban cemeteries indicate a change in food preparation techniques during the 17th century, so that caries and dental wear patterns move away from those which had seen little change since the Neolithic, and start to resemble those in modern dentitions (Moore and Corbett 1978; Brothwell 1963). It is of interest to look at the Wharram Percy skeletons to determine whether this pattern was followed in this remote rural parish. Carbon stable isotope data will also be used to determine whether more non-local foods reached the parish in post-medieval times.

• A variety of projects have been undertaken to look at bone diagenesis (see discussion on p. 84). The presence of a large, well-dated series like Wharram Percy, spanning about 1000 years, would be very important for increasing our understanding of the rates of various diagenetic processes.

• Comparisons with other collections, particularly those from the nearby city of York, will be vital to place the Wharram Percy results in context. Dating of the Wharram skeletons will enable selection of suitable comparanda.

Sampling

There are 874 recorded burials from the cemetery at Wharram Percy (Fig. 115), and 688 skeletons which were lifted. Of these 361 are adults. The sampling strategy adopted for radiocarbon dating was not random. Firstly we did not choose to date any of the known post-medieval burials, since 89 of these (54 adults and sixteen children with extant bones) had already been identified by associated coffin fittings, or by being stratigraphically later than burials with coffin fittings (see Fig. 124). The burials dated at Harwell in the late 1970s were also not chosen at random, indeed they were chosen specifically because they were associated with late Saxon grave slabs.

A judgmental sampling strategy was applied in choosing the samples for the 1995/6 programme of dating. This varied depending on local circumstances relating to excavation, recording, and lifting in different areas of the site. The basis of the proposed phasing structures also vary in different areas of the site, and so the sampling strategies required to investigate their chronology are different.

Overall, however, there were four criteria which were particularly considered when selecting samples:

• Stratigraphic strands of burials with relative dating were targeted, to maximise the potential for constraining the calibrated date ranges of the results (see below)

• Within each zone of the cemetery we aimed to sample burials spread over all parts of the area, to investigate any difference in chronology within areas

• Since it was thought that depth might be related to date in certain parts of the cemetery, adults were preferred because of the suspicion that children might be buried less deeply

• Skeletons which were well preserved and so could produce the most osteological information were preferred

Almost all the skeletons sampled scored highly by at least three of these criteria, despite the local factors which influenced selection. The rationale behind the specific selection of samples in each area is explained below.

Some burials were also selected partially on the basis of their stratigraphic relationships with parts of the church or boundary ditches within the graveyard. These dates provide corroborative evidence for the dating of these structures independent of architectural or other evidence.

Analysis and interpretation (stage 1)

Although the simple calibrated date ranges of the radiocarbon measurements are accurate estimates of the dates of the samples, this is usually not what we really wish to know as archaeologists. It is the dates of the archaeological events which are represented by those samples which are of interest, or the dates of phases of archaeological activity made up of those events. Fortunately explicit methodology is now available which allows us to combine the results of the radiocarbon analyses with other information which we may have, such as stratigraphy, to produce realistic *posterior density estimates* (dates written in italics to distinguish them from simple calibrated dates) of these dates of archaeological interest. It should be emphasised that these distributions and ranges are not absolute, they are interpretative *estimates*, which can and will change as further data become available and as other researchers choose to model the existing data from different perspectives.

A Bayesian approach has been adopted for the interpretation of the chronology of the site (Buck *et al.* 1996). The technique used is a form of Markov Chain Monte Carlo sampling and has been applied using the program OxCal v3.5 (http://www.rlaha.ox.ac.uk/orau;

Bronk Ramsey 1995; 1998; 2000), which uses a mixture of the Metropolis-Hastings algorithm and the more specific Gibbs sampler (Gilks *et al.* 1996; Gelfand and Smith 1990). Full details of the algorithms employed by this program are available from the on-line manual, and fully worked examples are given in the series of papers by Buck *et al.* (1991; 1992; Buck, Litton *et al.* 1994; Buck, Christen *et al.* 1994). The algorithms used in the models described below can be derived either from the structure shown in Figures 98-101, 104, 108-110, and 112, or from the chronological query language files which are contained in the project archive. An explanation of the index of agreement is provided by Bronk Ramsey (1995).

This report concentrates on the archaeology. The initial hypotheses which drove the sampling strategies adopted are described. The relative chronological sequences recorded through stratigraphic relationships between burials, which have been used to constrain the calibration of relevant radiocarbon results, are discussed. Using these estimates of the dates of the sampled burials, we address wider archaeological questions relating to the use of different areas of the cemetery and to the cemetery as a whole.

The chronology of the burial ground is described by area, starting in the east and progressing around the church clockwise. This not only breaks up the analysis into manageable pieces, but also allows us to tackle the different problems presented by the methods of excavation and recording adopted by excavators over more than fifteen years. The possibility that different parts of the cemetery were in use at different times can also be investigated. One measurement, HAR-2208 (cal

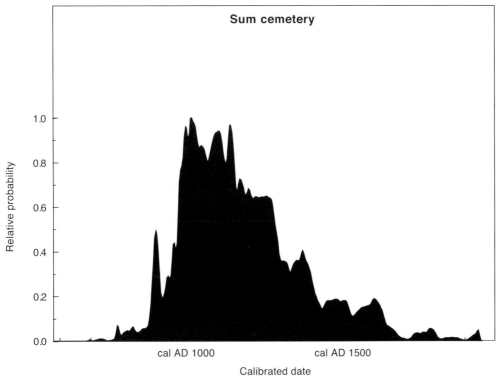

Fig. 91. Sum of the probability distributions of the simple calibrated radiocarbon dates from the medieval cemetery of St Martin, Wharram Percy. A weighted mean has been taken of replicate measurements before calibration (see Table 117). This distribution provides an estimate of the chronological distribution of the events dated by the radiocarbon measurements.

BC 200–120 cal AD; 2030±60 BP), on a Late Iron Age burial from Site 26 (Burial G305) is not included in the mathematical model as it does not form part of the medieval cemetery. The result on bulked bone from beneath the Phase II chancel (HAR-3584; C238) is simply used as a *terminus post quem* for the construction of that part of the church.

Firstly, however, the overall structure of the model for the dating of the cemetery needs to be considered. It has been demonstrated that, when radiocarbon dates are constrained by relative dating information, there is a danger that the posterior density estimates may be spread evenly across plateaux in the calibration curve, irrespective of the actual age of the material dated (Steier and Rom 2000). This is because the statistical weight of a group of measurements naturally favours longer overall spans. This effect can be eliminated by imposing a uniform prior distribution on the spread of the dates while assuming that, within this distribution, the dates are independent and a random sample of a relatively constant level of human activity (Buck *et al.* 1992): see Bronk Ramsey (2000) for details of the implementation in OxCal. This approach also allows us to provide an estimate of the date when burial started on the site, rather than an estimated date of the first dated burial. This is preferable because the probability that we have actually sampled the first burial on the site for radiocarbon analysis is fairly low.

Unfortunately the archaeological assumptions inherent in this approach are demonstrably untrue! For example, post-medieval documents record 399 burials in the period 1570–1699, that is about three burials per year, but only 482 burials in the period 1700–1899, that is about one burial every two years (*Wharram III*, fig. 3). This is not a constant level of human activity. Equally the sample of dated burials is not random, not only because identifiably later burials were deliberately not selected for dating, but because later burials were in the southern churchyard and deliberately not excavated. Figure 117 shows the sum of the probability distributions of all the dated burials. This provides the best estimate of the chronological distribution of the dated events. It can be seen that this distribution is by no means uniform.

It is necessary therefore to assess how far the results of the model depend on the uniform prior distribution, and how far on the relative dating provided by the stratigraphic sequences of burials and radiocarbon results. This can be examined by considering the posterior density estimates for the start of burial on the site from models which incorporate different information.

This problem has been tackled using two alternative modelling approaches. Firstly, a model has been created of the chronology of the burial ground up to the end of the high medieval period, omitting those measurements which calibrate substantially after AD 1400 (i.e. Burials CN03 (GU-5575), CN44 (GU-5576), SA002 (GU-5453), SA003 (GU-5454), SA033 (GU-5457), WCO170 (GU-5492), WCO044 (GU-5495), WCO153 (GU-5497), WCO010 (GU-5513) and WCO045 (GU-5516)), but assuming a uniform distribution for the period from the start of the cemetery to this date (Fig. 92). Secondly, a model has been created which imposes a uniform prior distribution on the entire chronological span of the cemetery, but attempts to alleviate the effect of the

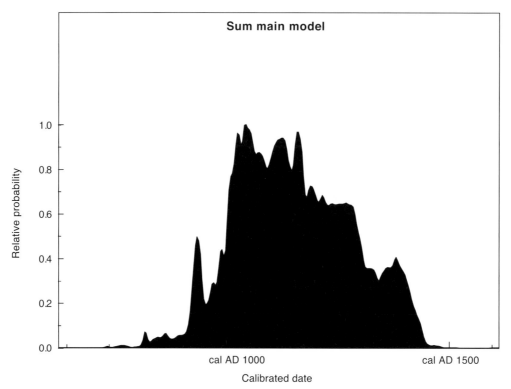

Fig. 92. Sum of the probability distributions of the simple calibrated radiocarbon dates to the end of the high medieval period in the cemetery of St Martin, Wharram Percy excluding those measurements which calibrate substantially after AD 1400 (i.e. GU-5575-6, GU-5453-4,GU-5457, GU-5492, GU-5495, GU-5497, GU-5513, and GU-5516).

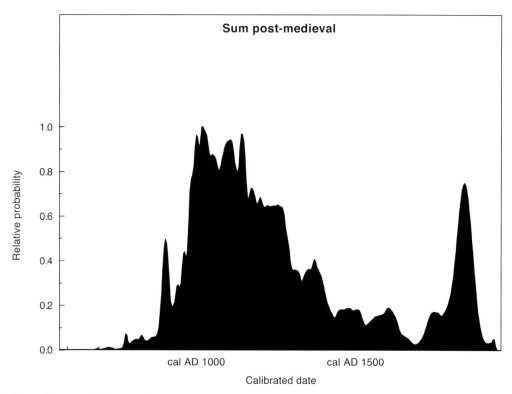

Fig. 93. Sum of the probability distributions of the simple calibrated radiocarbon dates from the medieval cemetery of St Martin, Wharram Percy and the typological dates of burials with coffin fittings from outside the church.

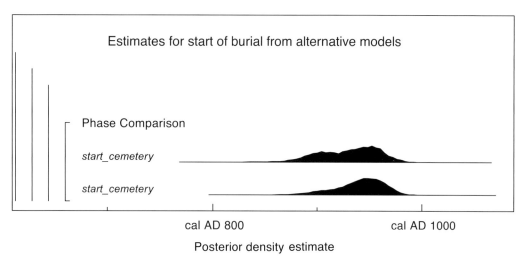

Fig. 94. Posterior density estimates for the date of the start of burial in the churchyard at Wharram Percy. Each distribution represents the relative probability that an event occurred at a particular time. The lower distribution derives from the model described in Figures 98-101, 104, 108-110 and 112. The upper distributions derives from the alternative model described in relation to Fig. 93.

decrease in the number of burials during the 18th and 19th centuries, and the deliberate avoidance of post-medieval burials in the radiocarbon sampling strategy, by incorporating the typological dates of the coffin fittings into the model (Fig. 93; *Wharram III*, 150-51).

The first model provides an estimated date range for the start of burial on the site of *cal AD 940–995 (95% probability)*. It has good overall agreement (A=99.8%). The second model provides a rather less precise, and slightly earlier estimate for this event of *cal AD 870–980 (95% probability)*. It also has good overall agreement (A=93.3%). It can be seen that the models provide very similar estimates for the start date of the cemetery (Fig. 94), with both suggesting that burial is likely to have started during the course of the 10th century. It can be seen from Figure 93, however, that by using graves dated by coffin fittings we have not succeeded in fully compensating for the lack of later burials on the site. The sum of the probability distributions of the dates included in the first model (Fig. 92) more closely approximates to a uniform distribution.

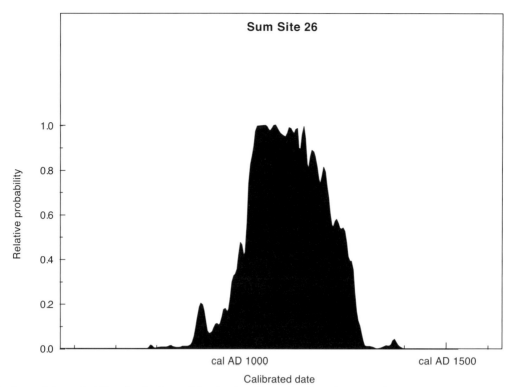

Fig. 95. Sum of the probability distributions of the simple calibrated radiocarbon dates from Site 26.

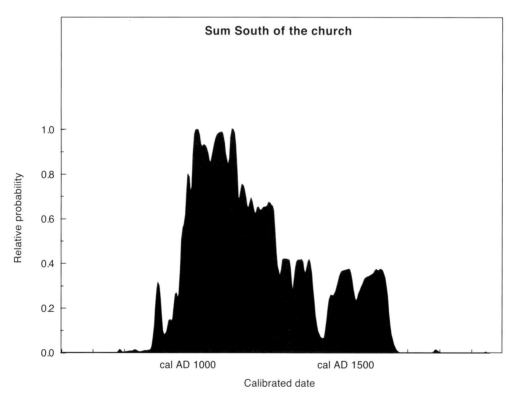

Fig. 96. Sum of the probability distributions of the simple calibrated radiocarbon dates from south of the church.

For this reason, this approach has been adopted for the interpretation of the site chronology presented here.

Other models have also been considered, however. For example, the possibility of assuming a uniform distribution for burial in each area of the site was evaluated. Although this would be a reasonable approach for some areas of the churchyard (e.g. Site 26; Fig. 95), it is clearly inappropriate for other areas (e.g. South of the church; Fig. 96). This makes it difficult to be consistent in applying this approach to modelling of the chronology of the cemetery. Archaeologically, it is also hard to justify the assumption that particular areas of the cemetery are constantly used and then completely abandoned despite ongoing population in the parish.

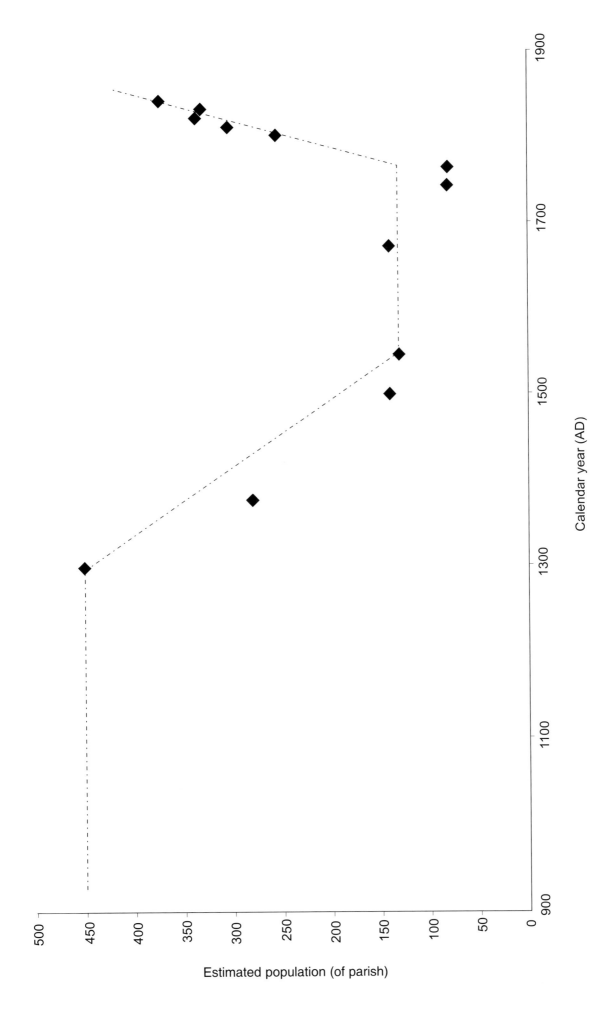

Fig. 97. Estimated population of the parish (after Bell *et al.* 1987, tables 1 and 7).

203

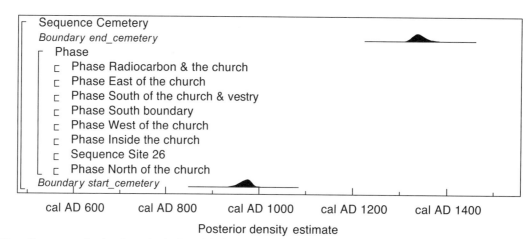

Fig. 98. Overall structure for the chronological model of burial in the churchyard at Wharram Percy. The component sections of this model are shown in detail in Figures 99-101, 104, 108-110 and 112. The large square brackets down the left hand side of these figures, along with the OxCal keywords define the overall model exactly.

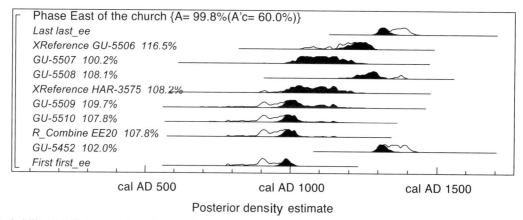

Fig. 99. Probability distributions of dates from burials to the east of the church. Each distribution represents the relative probability that an event occurred at a particular time. For each radiocarbon date, two distributions have been plotted: one in outline which is the result of simple radiocarbon calibration, and a solid one based on the chronological model used; the 'event' associated with, for example, GU-5507, is the growth of the bone of the individual who died and was dated. The other distributions correspond to aspects of the model. For example, the distribution 'first_ee' is the estimated date for the first burial in this area of the churchyard. Measurements followed by a question mark have been excluded from the model for reasons explained in the text, and are simple calibrated dates (Stuiver and Reimer 1993). The large square brackets down the left hand side of the figure, along with the OxCal keywords define the overall model exactly.

Theoretically, perhaps the most attractive approach for modelling the chronology of the cemetery is to use the estimated population of the parish over time as the prior distribution for the analysis. This distribution is shown in Figure 97. Despite the difficulties of estimating population from the documentary sources, this distribution is largely based on historical data. There is no direct documentary evidence for the earlier medieval period, and so little can be done other than assume a population reasonably constant from that first recorded *c.* 1300. Circumstantial support for this approach may be provided by the fact that there were as many arable units in the village at Domesday as there were in the late 13th century (Beresford 1979, 16). There was undoubtedly a large fall in population in the later middle ages, which thereafter remained reasonably constant until the rise in

population in the 19th century. Although we know that the last burial in the Wharram Percy churchyard occurred in 1906, the modelling of this latest period of use of the cemetery is complicated, not only by the avoidance of radiocarbon sampling and excavation for these later burials, but because there was an alternative site for Christian burial in the parish from 1871 when the church at Thixendale was consecrated.

Unfortunately the application of this model is currently beyond the scope of the available analytical software (Bronk Ramsey 1995; Buck *et al.* 1999), and so it has not be applied here. Instead, a pragmatic approach has been adopted, in effect attempting to model simply the earlier medieval period of the use of the cemetery (see above and Figs 98-101, 104, 108-110, and 112).

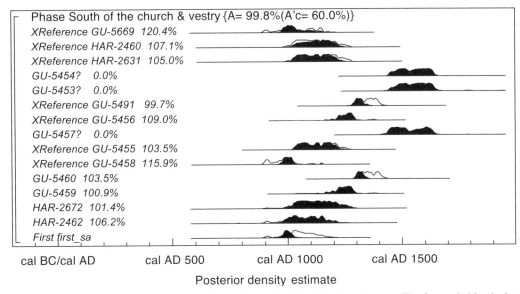

Fig. 100. Probability distributions of dates from burials to the south of the church and vestry. The format is identical to that of Fig. 99.

East of the church and the north-east chapel (Figs 115, 98 and 99)

Selection of samples in this area of the churchyard was particularly restricted because few of the recorded burials were lifted on excavation, and many of the skeletons in the collection have no associated records and so are unlocated. Where possible adult burials which had stratigraphic relationships with each other or with phases of the church structure, were selected. An attempt was also made to select samples from both close to the church and towards the boundary of the eastern area, although the actual distance between these points is very limited since the cemetery does not extend far in this area because of the slope which falls away sharply to the stream.

The only stratigraphic relationship between burials - that Burial EE020 (GU-5511 and GU-5683) lay below Burial EE019 (GU-5510) - has not been used to constrain the calibration of the results (see Fig. 99). This is because it is possible that the burials are in fact contemporary, contained in a double grave. Certainly the radiocarbon results are not statistically significantly different (T'=0.0; T'=(5%)=3.8; v=1; Ward and Wilson 1978).

Burials EE003 (GU-5507) and EE007 (GU-5508) are noted as probably being contemporary with the Phase III chancel apse, which is perfectly possible according to the radiocarbon evidence (see Table 117; *Wharram III*, 52). Burial EE013 (GU-5506), which cut through the apse, was accompanied by a chalice and patten, and so is probably the burial of a priest. The radiocarbon determination demonstrates that this is not the body of Robert Firby (ob.11.11.1464) (*Wharram III*, 30 and 76) as it is considerably earlier. The radiocarbon dating of this burial also suggests that the associated chalice, which has previously been regarded as more likely to be 14th-century in date, may be slightly earlier (*Wharram III*, 150).

Not surprisingly, given the small area involved, there is little evidence of chronological shift spatially across this area of the cemetery (see Fig. 99). Some of the earliest burials (e.g. Burial EE026 (GU-5509)) are on the limits of the excavated area away from the church, but so is the latest (Burial EE038 (GU-5452)). Similarly, there are burials of a range of dates right up close to the chancel itself (e.g. Burials EE003 and EE007 (GU-5507 and GU-5508)). The depth of burial is also no guide to dating, with the latest burials (e.g. Burial EE038 (GU-5452), approx 1.52m below the surface) appearing much lower than some of the earlier ones (e.g. Burial EE019 (GU-5510), approximately 1m below the surface).

The area of the cemetery to the east of the church is very likely to have come into use before the Conquest, the first dated burial occurring *cal AD 955-1020 (95% probability*; Fig. 99; *first_ee*). The last dated burial occurs between *cal AD 1285-1355 (95% probability;* Fig 99; *last_ee*), probably before the Black Death (*95% probability*). All in all this area of the burial ground was probably in use for between *280 and 380 years (95% probability*).

Using this sample of eight burials as a random selection of those in this area of the churchyard, less than 1% of burials are likely to be post-1348 (i.e. one or two of the 53 adults). It is likely that a much larger proportion are pre-Conquest in date (*c.* 52%; 27 or 28 of the 53 adults). Unfortunately it is not possible to identify which burials date to which period from the sample dated by radiocarbon analysis, except for those few skeletons sampled during the present radiocarbon programme or with stratigraphic relationships to those bodies.

South of the church (Figs 98 and 100)

Although there may have been a preference for burial to this side of the church, only a relatively small sample of the existing burials have been excavated in this area (Fig. 115). Trenches were dug close to the church in 1968, 1969, and 1973 to locate the south aisle and examine the area beneath the vestry.

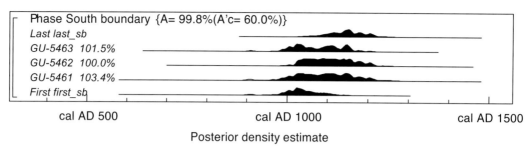

Fig. 101. Probability distributions of dates from burials on the south boundary of the churchyard (Sites 41 and 52). The format is identical to that of Figure 99.

Four samples were submitted for dating in 1977 and 1978 (Jordan *et al.* 1994, 208) because they were under Saxon grave slabs. Burial V41 (GU-5669) was sampled in 1996, because it is stratigraphically earlier than Burial V51 (HAR-2460). Potentially this would not only constrain the calibration of these dates, but also provide a check on the reliability of the previous measurements from the Harwell laboratory. In fact the measurements are in good agreement with each other and with the recorded stratigraphic relationship between the burials (A=120.4% and A=107.1%), which increases our confidence in their accuracy.

Other burials in the area were sampled to counter this specific selection of early graves, although there are 22 adult burials associated with post-medieval coffin fittings which were deliberately not sampled. In addition to the stratigraphic relationships between the burials themselves, some skeletons also have direct physical relationships with the structural sequence of the church. Burials SA002 and SA003 (GU-5453 and GU-5454) are earlier than the Phase X porch. Burial SA034 (GU-5458) is cut by the South Aisle wall (Phase V), which is in turn cut by Burial SA033 (GU-5457). This wall is also earlier than the Phase VI porch. This porch is itself later than Burial SA012 (GU-5455), and earlier than Burial SA014 (GU-5456) which is itself earlier than Burial SA013 (GU-5491). See Figure 118 for a summary of the stratigraphic relationships between dated burials and the church structure.

The estimated dates of these burials, taking both the radiocarbon and stratigraphic evidence into account, are shown in black in Figure 100. From these results we can estimate that the first dated burial occurred between *cal AD 960-1040 (95% probability; first_sa)*. Since the last coffin fittings in this area belong to the mid-19th century, we can therefore estimate that the period of use of this area of the cemetery is 780-920 years (95% probability).

Basically, it is not possible to date any of the undated adult burials in this area by analogy with those which have radiocarbon dates, with the exception of a few burials (e.g. Burial SA046) which have stratigraphic relationships with sampled burials or with dated phases of the church. There are, however, also 22 burials which can be dated from coffin fittings.

The south boundary (Sites 41 and 52; Figs 115, 98 and 101)
Because the recent use of the cemetery prevented excavation, there is a considerable spatial gap between the burials in the South Aisle and Vestry areas, described above, and those on the furthest southern limit of the site (*c.* 33m). Small areas have been excavated to examine this boundary. Three burials have been dated, which again represent a sample of the best preserved examples which were not associated with coffin fittings.

Analysis of these results (see Fig. 101) suggests that the cemetery had reached this furthest extent to the South by *cal AD 975-1125 (95% probability; first_sb)*, probably before the Conquest *(74% probability)*. There was one relatively recent burial in the area (Burial SA062) and two modern burials (Burials SA059 and SA060), but the latest medieval use of the area was probably around *cal AD 1045-1225 (95% probability; last_sb)* certainly well before the Black Death. It appears that this area of the cemetery was first in use for a relatively short time of around 10-200 years (95% probability). Although three dated burials are a relatively small sample, they do represent 25% of the twelve undated burials from this area of the cemetery, and so is probably reasonably representative.

West of the church (Fig. 115, 98 and 101)
This area of the cemetery was excavated in one season in 1972. All 177 burials were excavated, recorded, and lifted. The comparatively neat alignment of the burials and rarity of intercutting, led to the hypothesis during post-excavation analysis that these burials represented one period of deposition of relatively short duration. The absence of coffins, stone settings and post-medieval coffin fittings also seemed to lend weight to this theory. On the basis of the stratigraphy and depth of burial, a preliminary phasing structure had been proposed, consisting of nine phases. The sampling strategy in this area aimed to test the chronological validity of this phasing, and to provide absolute dates for the relatively short part of the medieval period when this area of the site was thought to have been in use.

In accordance with the general sampling strategy (see p. 198) eighteen burials were selected for dating from

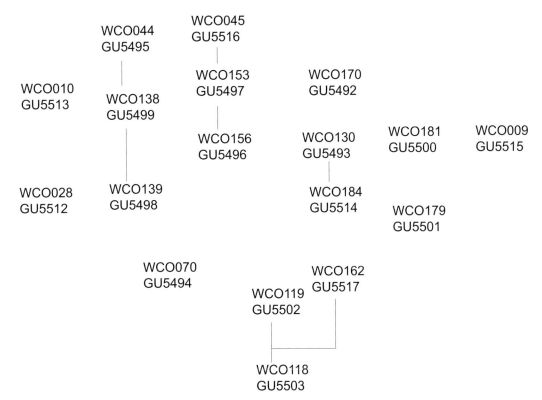

Fig. 102. Matrix showing the stratigraphic relationships between dated burials at the west end of the church.

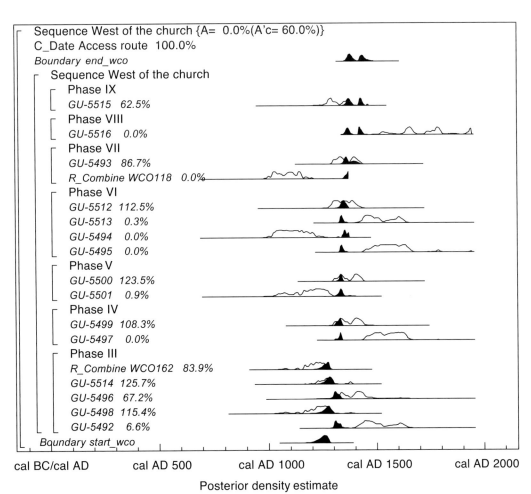

Fig. 103. Probability distributions of dates from burials to the west of the church, incorporating the relative 'chronology' provided by the preliminary phasing structure. The format is identical to that of Figure 99.

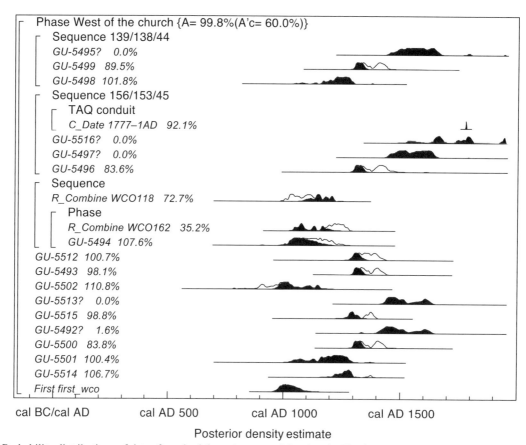

Phase West of the church {A= 99.8%(A'c= 60.0%)}
  Sequence 139/138/44
    GU-5495? 0.0%
    GU-5499 89.5%
    GU-5498 101.8%
  Sequence 156/153/45
    TAQ conduit
     C_Date 1777–1AD 92.1%
    GU-5516? 0.0%
    GU-5497? 0.0%
    GU-5496 83.6%
  Sequence
    R_Combine WCO118 72.7%
    Phase
     R_Combine WCO162 35.2%
     GU-5494 107.6%
  GU-5512 100.7%
  GU-5493 98.1%
  GU-5502 110.8%
  GU-5513? 0.0%
  GU-5515 98.8%
  GU-5492? 1.6%
  GU-5500 83.8%
  GU-5501 100.4%
  GU-5514 106.7%
  First first_wco

cal BC/cal AD   cal AD 500   cal AD 1000   cal AD 1500

Posterior density estimate

Fig. 104. Probability distributions of dates from burials to the west of the church. The format is identical to that of Figure 99.

across the excavated area. Burials within relative dating sequences defined by stratigraphic relationships were preferred (Fig. 102). These sequences are that Burial WCO139 (GU-5498) is earlier than Burial WCO138 (GU-5499) which is earlier than Burial WCO044 (GU-5495) and that Burial WCO156 (GU-5496) is earlier than Burial WCO153 (GU-5497) which is earlier than Burial WCO045 (GU-5516) which is earlier than the conduit. This conduit is dated to the later 18th century on archaeological and other grounds, and may well be part of the rebuilding of the farmhouse to the north of the churchyard which occurred in 1775-9 (Beresford and Hurst 1990, 115). The sequence, Burials WCO070 (GU-5494) and WCO162 (GU-5517 and GU-5678) are earlier than Burial WCO118 (GU-5503 and GU-5682) which is in turn earlier than Burial WCO119 (GU-5502), has been re-examined in light of the radiocarbon results which are in disagreement with this stratigraphic information (A=21.4%; Bronk Ramsey 1995). Osteological examination indicated that the bones from Burial WCO119 (GU-5502) came from a single individual, however, the plan suggests that perhaps the remains were not found articulated, and so they may represent an earlier disturbed burial. The suggested stratigraphic relationship is therefore not necessarily the same as the chronological relationship between the samples. Burial WCO118 (GU-5503 and GU-5682) does appear to consist of the upper body and right side as shown in plan, and so the relationship between this burial and Burial WCO162 (GU-5517 and GU-5678)/WCO70 (GU-5494) would

appear to be valid. In this area we also tried to sample burials from as many of the preliminary burial phases as possible, and three samples were selected simply because they were the only datable burials from their preliminary phases (Burial WCO009 (GU-5515) from Phase IX, and Burials WCO179 (GU-5501) and WCO181 (GU-5500) from Phase V).

Unfortunately this preliminary phasing structure has had to be abandoned in the light of the radiocarbon results which demonstrate that there is no relationship between chronology and the preliminary phasing. Indeed, a model which assumes that the phasing is chronologically significant is so inconsistent with the radiocarbon data that the overall agreement is 0.0% (Fig. 103).

Analysis of the results (Fig. 104) demonstrates that this area of the cemetery was in use for a far longer period than originally assumed, from *cal AD 960-1110 (95% probability; first_wco)* to *cal AD 1515-1600 (20% probability)* or *cal AD 1615-1700 (50% probability)* or *cal AD 1735-1780 (25% probability)*. Burial in the area had almost certainly ceased by the time the area was fenced off as shown on the map of AD 1836 (see Chapter 2). This spans a period 465-785 years (95% probability). Indeed the first dated burial in this area of the site is very likely to predate the Conquest *(83% probability)*, and may well date to before AD 1000 *(77% probability)*.

The estimated dates for these burials, which include the relative dating evidence provided by stratigraphy and the documentary evidence cited above, are listed in Table 117 and shown in black in Figure 103, with the simple

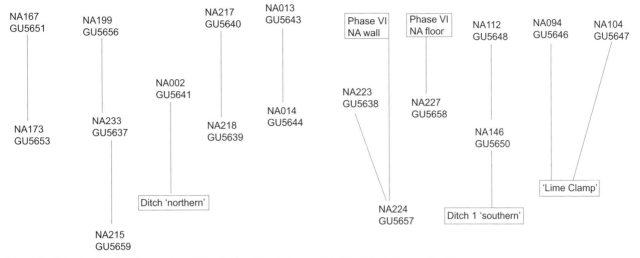

Fig. 105. Matrix showing the stratigraphic relationships between dated burials in the north aisle area.

unconstrained probability distributions of the radiocarbon measurements alone shown in outline.

Analysis of these distributions show that the majority of the burials in this area are medieval (*c.* 79% before AD 1540), although perhaps 36 or 37 of the 177 burials are later than this. The area is used throughout the medieval period however, with a substantial group of pre-Conquest burials (*c.* 11%, perhaps 19 burials), a substantial group of medieval burials (*c.* 49% dating to between AD 1066 and AD 1348, perhaps 87 burials), and a significant group of later medieval skeletons (*c.* 19% dating to between AD 1348 and AD 1540, perhaps 34 skeletons). This last group is particularly important, since burials of this date are conspicuous by their absence in other excavated areas of the cemetery. It should be noted, however, that the proportion of later burials suggested by the model may be rather larger than it was in reality. This is because a uniform prior distribution has only been imposed on burials dating to before AD 1400 (see above). Later burials, without this prior belief, may scatter rather later than they did in reality (Steier and Rom 2000; Bronk Ramsey 2000).

Given the importance of this group, it is particularly unfortunate that, although we can estimate that these chronological groups exist in the skeletal assemblage, it is impossible to identify which of the bodies belong to each group, or to date the undated proportion of the assemblage (90%) by analogy with the dated portion. On this basis the dating programme for the area of the cemetery to the west of the church has been a complete failure, although it is salutary to compare what we thought we knew at the start of the dating programme with the results!

North of the nave (Figs 115, 98 and 108)
This area of the cemetery was excavated in three campaigns, in 1965, 1970 and 1973.

Several stratigraphic sequences of burials were dated (Fig. 105). These sequences are that Burial NA215 (GU-5659) is earlier than Burial NA233 (GU-5637), which is earlier than Burial NA199 (GU-5656). Burial NA218 (GU-5639) is earlier than Burial NA217 (GU-5640), Burial NA173 (GU-5653) is earlier than Burial NA167 (GU-5651), and Burial NA014 (GU-5644) is earlier than Burial NA013 (GU-5643). In addition some results have relationships with the date of the church structure (Burials NA227 (GU-5658) and NA224 (GU-5657 and GU-5677) were cut or sealed by parts of the Phase VI north aisle). Burial NA224 (GU-5657 and GU-5677) is also earlier than Burial NA223 (GU-5638). Other burials are related to the early churchyard boundary ditches (Burial NA002 (GU-5641) cuts the north boundary ditch (14.NA96/26.255) and Burial NA146 (GU-5650 and GU-5679) cuts the south boundary ditch (14.NA35)). Burial NA146 (GU-5650) in turn is cut by Burial NA112 (GU-5648). Two further burials, NA094 (GU-5646) and NA104 (GU-5647 and GU-5681), cut the lime kiln or *Grubenhaus*.

Twelve samples were dated from the 1965 and 1970 excavations. These burials were grouped into five spits by Don Brothwell, and it was hoped that there might be some relationship between these spits and date. A model which supposes a strict chronological sequence through the spits (Fig. 106) shows poor agreement between the relative dating and the radiocarbon measurements (A=0.1%; see Bronk Ramsey 1995). This means that the radiocarbon evidence demonstrates that this theory is incorrect. A more general interpretation of the spits in terms of date does seem to be supported by the measurements. If Burial NA167 (GU-5651) (a child) is omitted, a model which lumps together spits 1 and 2, and spits 3, 4 and 5 together, has acceptable agreement (see Fig. 107; A=153.0%). Moreover the boundary between these two phases of burial is estimated to be *cal AD 990-1040 (68% probability)* or *cal AD 975-1090 (95% probability; Boundary 1-2/3-5)*. Perhaps we can justifiably divide the cemetery population roughly into pre and post-Conquest groups on the basis of the excavated spits.

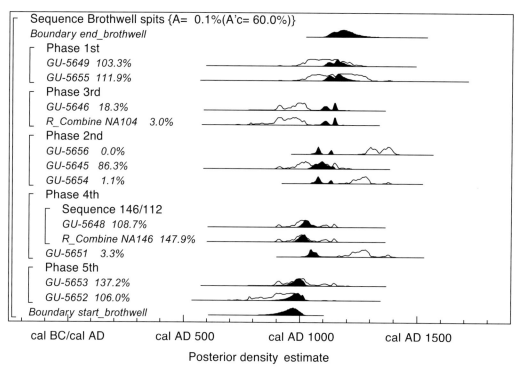

Fig. 106. Probability distributions of dates from burials to the north of the church, incorporating the relative 'chronology' suggested by the division of burials into 'spits' by Don Brothwell. The format is identical to that of Figure 99.

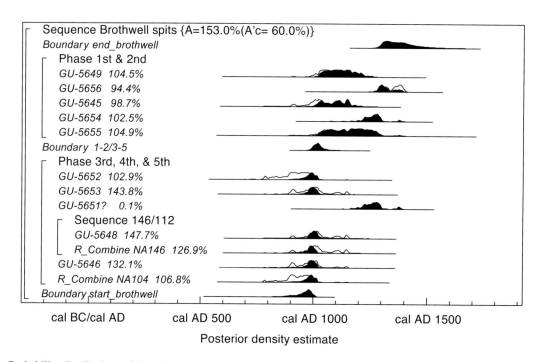

Fig. 107. Probability distributions of dates from burials to the north of the church, incorporating the relative 'chronology' suggested by the division of burials into 'spits' by Don Brothwell (combining 'spits 1 and 2' and 'spits 3-5'). The format is identical to that of Figure 99.

The main model for the chronology of this part of the site is shown in Figure 108. Overall we can estimate that the start of burial in this area was in *cal AD 950-1000 (95% probability; first_na)*. The end of burial in this area was between *cal AD 1280-1360 (95% probability; last_na)* - probably before AD 1348 *(94% probability)*.

Burial was taking place in this area for between *290-385 years (95% probability)*.

On the basis of this evidence the seventeen undated adults in Brothwell's spits 4 and 5 have been allocated to a period between the start of burial in the cemetery and AD 1066, and the nineteen undated adults in Brothwell's spits 1, 2 and 3 to the period AD 1066-1348.

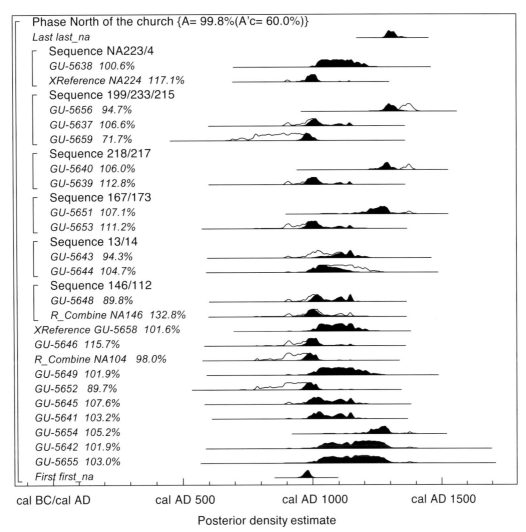

Phase North of the church {A= 99.8%(A'c= 60.0%)}
Last last_na
  Sequence NA223/4
    GU-5638 100.6%
    XReference NA224 117.1%
  Sequence 199/233/215
    GU-5656 94.7%
    GU-5637 106.6%
    GU-5659 71.7%
  Sequence 218/217
    GU-5640 106.0%
    GU-5639 112.8%
  Sequence 167/173
    GU-5651 107.1%
    GU-5653 111.2%
  Sequence 13/14
    GU-5643 94.3%
    GU-5644 104.7%
  Sequence 146/112
    GU-5648 89.8%
    R_Combine NA146 132.8%
  XReference GU-5658 101.6%
  GU-5646 115.7%
  R_Combine NA104 98.0%
  GU-5649 101.9%
  GU-5652 89.7%
  GU-5645 107.6%
  GU-5641 103.2%
  GU-5654 105.2%
  GU-5642 101.9%
  GU-5655 103.0%
  First first_na

cal BC/cal AD   cal AD 500   cal AD 1000   cal AD 1500

Posterior density estimate

Fig. 108. Probability distributions of dates from burials to the north of the church. The format is identical to that of Figure 99.

Site 26 (Figs 115, 98 and 109)

One hundred and twenty five burials were excavated in this area between 1972 and 1978. Bone from 118 of these survives, including one Iron Age flexed burial (Burial G305; HAR-2208; Table 117). The quality of recording in this area, combined with the nature of the deposits, allowed a relatively secure phasing structure to be proposed (see Chapter 4). This provided a good opportunity to utilise this relative chronology and provide precise estimates for the dates of the skeletal assemblage.

The analysis shown in Figure 109 demonstrates that burial in Site 26 began *cal AD 960-1015 (95% probability; first_3.1)*, almost certainly before the Conquest *(more than 95% probability)* and probably before AD 1000 *(83% probability)*. The area went out of use in *cal AD 1235-1330 (95% probability; Fig. 109; end_4.3)*, probably by the Black Death *(more than 95% probability)* and probably by AD 1328 *(more than 95% probability)*. This would be consistent with the hypothesis that the boundary wall, which seals the burials in this area, was built as part of the construction of a new vicarage at that time (see Chapter 4; *Wharram III*, 22). Overall this area of the site was used for burial for between *240 and 350 years (95% probability)*.

The chronological model provides the following estimated dates for the phases of burial within Site 26. The first phase of burials (Period 3, Phase 1) started in *cal AD 960-1015 (95% probability; Fig. 109; first_3.1)* and ended in *cal AD 1030-1100 (95% probability; Fig. 109; end_3.1/start_3.3)*, probably before the Conquest *(probability 67%)*. Burial took place for *30-120 years (95% probability)*. The burials in this phase can be regarded as a late Saxon population. The next phase of burial (Period 3, Phase 3) started at this date and continued until *cal AD 1065-1150 (95% probability; Fig. 109; end_3.1/start_3.3)*, lasting for *10-85 years (95% probability)*. Next come two phases of burial (Period 3, Phase 5 and Period 4, Phase 1) which, in stratigraphic terms are contemporary, and continued from the end of Period 3, Phase 3 until *cal AD 1125-1210 (95% probability; Fig. 109; end_3.3/start_3.5/4.1)*, lasting for *20-105 years (95% probability)*. The phase of burial sealing this (Period 4, Phase 3) continued until *cal AD 1220-1305 (95% probability; Fig. 109; end_3.5/4.1/start_4.3)*, lasting for *40-155 years (95% probability)*. Finally, the single dated burial from Period 4, Phase 5 (Burial G275A; GU-5543), dates to *cal AD 1235-1330 (95% probability)*. These are important not only because

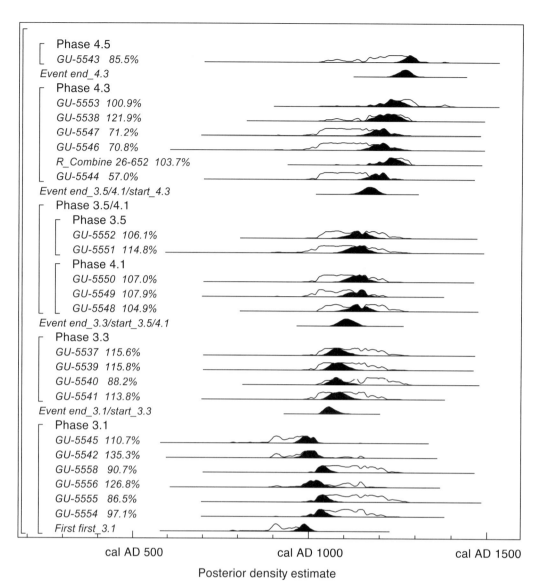

Phase 4.5
GU-5543 85.5%
Event end_4.3
Phase 4.3
GU-5553 100.9%
GU-5538 121.9%
GU-5547 71.2%
GU-5546 70.8%
R_Combine 26-652 103.7%
GU-5544 57.0%
Event end_3.5/4.1/start_4.3
Phase 3.5/4.1
Phase 3.5
GU-5552 106.1%
GU-5551 114.8%
Phase 4.1
GU-5550 107.0%
GU-5549 107.9%
GU-5548 104.9%
Event end_3.3/start_3.5/4.1
Phase 3.3
GU-5537 115.6%
GU-5539 115.8%
GU-5540 88.2%
GU-5541 113.8%
Event end_3.1/start_3.3
Phase 3.1
GU-5545 110.7%
GU-5542 135.3%
GU-5558 90.7%
GU-5556 126.8%
GU-5555 86.5%
GU-5554 97.1%
First first_3.1

cal AD 500   cal AD 1000   cal AD 1500

Posterior density estimate

Fig. 109. Probability distributions of dates from burials in the area of the later Site 26. The format is identical to that of Figure 99.

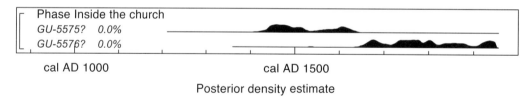

Phase Inside the church
GU-5575? 0.0%
GU-5576? 0.0%

cal AD 1000   cal AD 1500

Posterior density estimate

Fig. 110. Probability distributions of dates from burials within the church. The format is identical to that of Figure 99.

they date the burials, but also because of the make-up layers and surfaces between these phases of burial which contain artefact assemblages whose deposition can be dated using these estimates (see Ch. 18).

Overall the burials in Site 26 are well dated. All those in Period 3, Phase 1 and some of those in Period 3, Phase 3 may be pre-Conquest as the probability that the boundary between them lies before AD 1066 is 67%. The burials from the other phases are high medieval (see Ch. 4), however, but almost certainly pre-date the Black Death (*more than 95% probability*).

In addition to the single Iron Age burial, posterior density estimates for the date of burial can be provided for 116 of the 117 skeletons from this area. Only Burial G525 from Period 4, Phase 6 could not be dated. This has been achieved by dating a sample of 22 burials and integrating the results with the stratigraphic sequence shown in Figure 109.

Inside the church (Figs 115, 98 and 110)
The majority of burials inside the church can be shown to be post-medieval because of their association with coffin fittings, or because of stratigraphic relationships with burials so dated. The latest coffin dates to AD 1839.

Two burials without coffin fittings, which appeared to be stratigraphically the earliest recovered from the church, were dated to determine whether they were the remains of medieval burials which had been almost entirely truncated by later activity. Analysis of these results (see Fig. 110) suggests that at least one of them may be late medieval (the probability that it is before AD 1540 is 64%), which supports the hypothesis that two other burials (Burials CN51 and CN52 from which bones do not survive in the Archive), which appear to be earlier than the Phase II church, are medieval. Burial CN51 has ear-muffs, which are elsewhere argued to date to the 10th to 12th centuries (Ch. 15).

Despite these caveats, the bone assemblage from within the church can be regarded as essentially post-medieval.

Analysis and interpretation (stage 2)

The previous section has described the integration of the stratigraphic and radiocarbon evidence in detail. The model described does, however, also go some way towards achieving the original overall objectives of the dating programme.

The development of the churchyard

The model provides a *posterior density estimate* for the start of burial on the site of *cal AD 940–995 (95% probability*; Fig. 98; *start_cemetery*). The last documented burials in the churchyard were two which occurred in AD 1906 (*Wharram III*, table 12). Burial on the site therefore continued for *910-965 years (95% probability)*.

Figure 111 demonstrates that burial extended to the identified limits of the cemetery very quickly, with the areas to the north of the church (including the area of Site 26), east of the church and south of the church all in use for adult burial before AD 1066 (at more than 95% probability). It is likely that the areas to the west of the church and right down to the southern boundary of the churchyard came into use, if not before the Conquest, shortly thereafter.

Many areas of the graveyard seem to have become disused for adult burial at least by AD 1348, with interment continuing to the west and south of the church and within the building itself. It is possible that infant burial may have continued rather longer in the favoured area north of the church (Ch. 8), although this is not demonstrated by the radiocarbon evidence as no infants were sampled.

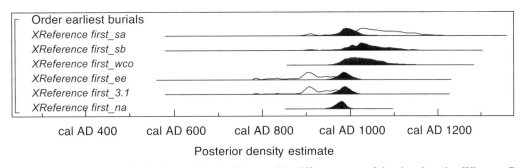

Fig. 111. Posterior density estimates for the dates when burial started in different areas of the churchyard at Wharram Percy. The format is identical to that of Figure 94.

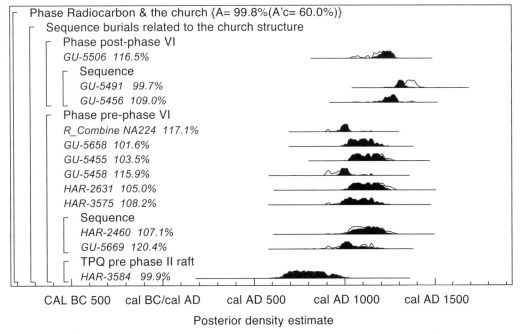

Fig. 112. Probability distributions for dates from burials with stratigraphic relationships with parts of the church structure, included in the model shown in Figure 98. The format is identical to that of Figure 99.

213

Dating the church

The model used to incorporate the stratigraphic information between the church structure and dated burials in the main model for the chronology of the cemetery is shown in Figure 112. A different model has been used to estimate the dates of construction of various phases of the church, one without any assumptions regarding the distribution of the dated events and only including those measurements which are from burials with direct stratigraphic relationships with parts of the church. This model is shown in Figure 113 and has been adopted because a number of these burials date to after AD 1400 (see above). In fact, the estimates for the dates of church building provided by the model are imprecise in comparison with those available from architectural and other evidence, and so the approach to modelling adopted for this objective does not make much difference to the results.

Basically, the radiocarbon evidence is in good agreement with the architectural sequence. The model provides a posterior density estimate for the construction of the Phase II church of *cal AD 1010-1120 (68% probability)* or *cal AD 945-1185 (95% probability*; Fig. 113; *start_church*). This is consistent with the late Saxon or Saxo-Norman date proposed by Bell (*Wharram III*, 59-61). The date of Phase III is estimated as *cal AD 1070-1170 (68% probability)* or *cal AD 1040-1215 (95% probability;* Fig. 113; *phase II*). Again this is entirely consistent with the suggested date of AD 1110-30 proposed on architectural grounds (*Wharram III*, 63). The dates of Phase V, *cal AD 1125-1220 (68% probability)* or *cal AD 1075-1245 (95% probability*; Fig. 113; *phase III*), and Phase VI, *cal AD 1180-1250 (68% probability)* or *cal AD 1135-1270 (95% probability*; Fig. 113; *phase V*), are also consistent with the late 12th century and *c.* 1200 or shortly afterwards proposed for these phases on other grounds (*Wharram III*, 65). Finally, the radiocarbon evidence from two burials provides a *terminus post quem* for the construction of the Phase XI porch of *cal AD 1500-1530* or *cal AD 1545-1630 (68% probability)* or *cal AD 1470-1645 (95% probability*; Fig. 113; *tpq_phase XI*). This also agrees well with evidence from other sources (*Wharram III*, 91).

Although the radiocarbon dating does not substantively add to our knowledge of the dating of the church fabric, it is reassuring to note that the radiocarbon and other forms of evidence are in such good accord.

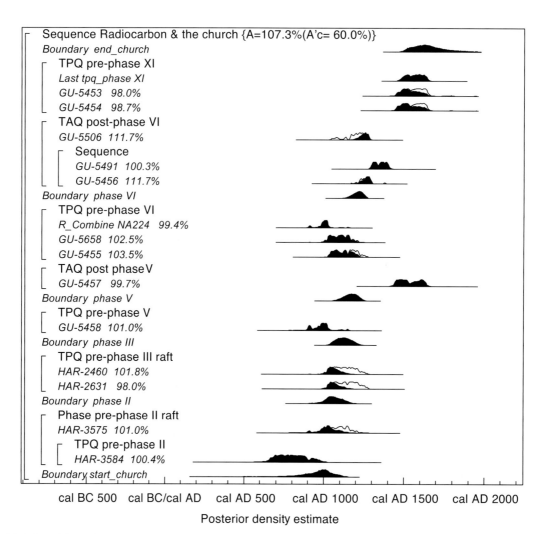

Fig. 113. Model used for estimating the dates of construction for parts of the church structure, showing probability distributions for dates from burials with stratigraphic relationships with the structure. The format is identical to that of Figure 99.

214

Table 118. Chronological summary of burials with extant bone (by area of the churchyard; Fig. 114): √√ (many burials), √(some burial), ? (possibly some burial), - (no known burials).

	pre-AD 1066	AD 1066-1348	AD 1348-1540	post-AD 1540
East of the church and NE chapel	√√	√√	-	-
South Aisle and Vestry	√	√	√	√
Sites 41 and 52	?	√√		√
West of the church	√	√√	√√	√
North of the nave	√√	√√	-	-
Site 26	√	√√	-	-
Inside the church	-	?	√	√√

Dating associated features

Termini ante quos are also provided by burials in the northern churchyard for two boundary ditches. The northern ditch (14.NA96/255.26) is cut by Burial NA002 which occurred in *cal AD 980-1165 (95% probability; GU-5641)* and the southern ditch (14.NA35) is cut by Burial NA146 which occurred in *cal AD 960-1070 (90% probability; weighted mean of GU-5650 and GU-5679)*. It appears that this ditch is securely pre-Conquest in date.

The lime kiln or *Grubenhaus* in the northern churchyard is also demonstrably pre-Conquest in date as it is cut by Burial NA104 which dates to *cal AD 950-1035 (95% probability; weighted mean of GU-5647 and GU-5681)* and by Burial NA094 which dates to *cal AD 955-1050 (85% probability; GU-5646)*.

Burial rites and osteology

The radiocarbon dating programme has affected the phasing and dating of the cemetery. This is discussed by Heighway (Ch. 15). The dating has also enabled the discussion of trends in burial rite through time (Ch. 15) and changes in the population at Wharram Percy over time (Ch. 7).

Dating the cemetery from dating a sample of the burials

The 99 radiocarbon measurements from this site were carried out on 89 articulated burials from the medieval churchyard, one Iron Age articulated burial (Burial G305; HAR-2208), one group of bones which were thought to be articulated on submission but have been reinterpreted as redeposited following the radiocarbon dating (Burial WCO119; GU-5502), and one mixed sample of human and animal bone (C238; HAR-3584).

Of the 89 skeletons dated from the medieval churchyard, three were sampled for radiocarbon dating before full osteological analysis was complete and so are not included in the total figures of selected skeletal remains (Burial V50, V56 and EE214; HAR-2672, HAR-2631, and HAR-3575). Five samples were from children (Burials NA223, NA002, G304, G314 and WCO044; GU-5638, GU-5641, GU-5545, GU-5540, and GU-5495). This means that of the 687 selected skeletons from the churchyard, a sample of 81 was dated from the 360

adults recovered (22.5%), and five were dated from the 327 children recovered (1.5%).

Seventy burials with extant bone (54 adults and sixteen children) can be identified as post-medieval because of the coffin fittings they contained, or their stratigraphic relationships to burials with coffin fittings.

The effectiveness of the sampling strategy in dating burials which were not sampled varies across the site. It was most effective in Site 26, where a sample of 22 burials (twenty adults and two children) provides secure dating for 116 burials (62 adults and 54 children). To the north of the nave a sample of 12 adult skeletons suggests that broad phasing based on the depth of burial is consistent with the radiocarbon evidence, providing broad dating for another 36 adults.

Additionally, it appears that the undated burials on the southern boundary and those in the area to the east of the church can be ascribed to the period between the start of burial in the churchyard and the Black Death. This provides rather imprecise dating for a further 50 adults, in addition to the eleven whose age is known rather more precisely because they were sampled for radiocarbon analysis.

The dating of the area to the west of the church has been most disappointing, as only those burials which were directly radiocarbon dated could be phased from the results of the scientific analyses. This exercise did demonstrate, however, that the preliminary phasing proposed for the area was incorrect; an important, if rather negative, result. It was less surprising that no burials in the south aisle could be dated in addition to those sampled for radiocarbon analysis.

In total the radiocarbon programme provides absolute dating for 190 adults and 57 children with extant bones from the churchyard. In addition, 70 burials are dated by associated coffin fittings (54 adults and sixteen children). Secure dating is now available for 244 of the 360 adults in the collection (68%), and 63 of the 327 children (19%).

The radiocarbon programme also provides precise estimates for the date when burial started on the site and its period of use as a cemetery. It also provides information on the extent of the cemetery at different periods, and gives an indication of the period when it was at its maximum extent. A summary of the dating of the cemetery by area is provided in Table 118.

15 The Attributes of Burials

by C. Heighway

Introduction (Figs 114 and 115)

The first churchyard burials were excavated when the north churchyard was trenched in 1962, and the last major churchyard area to be excavated was Site 26, between 1972 and 1978. In those fifteen years a considerable change had taken place in techniques of burial excavation. In the early 1960s burials were seldom planned and often not photographed. Obvious attributes such as stone-lined graves and stone settings were noted, but no drawn record was made of the precise disposition of the body or its absolute depth. Therefore, data from the different areas are variable and the information to be gained in respect of burial attributes is very limited.

There were some difficulties with identification and location of burials, particularly in the East End. Burials which are mentioned only in the finds record, and therefore not located precisely, are marked with triangles on Figure 115. The archive carries a detailed account of the ways in which some of the difficulties of identification were overcome.

The overall burial distribution plan (Fig. 115) also gives the impression of several 'blank' areas where there

were no burials. It is not possible from the excavation records to state whether these were truly empty or whether they indicated areas where either excavations had not reached the relevant level or where the burials had been destroyed by later activity.

There are 931 burials on the attributes database, though not all these have bones which have been retained for study (see p. 77). Numbering of burials has changed more than once and the burial numbers published in *Wharram III*, chapter X, have been superseded. Areas near the church are distinguished by letter codes (Fig. 114) and the burial numbers are prefixed by these (e.g. Burial EE056). The south boundary sites have burials numbered in the SA series, although the excavations are referred to by their site numbers; 41, 52 and 80. Burials in the several superimposed chancels are numbered as nave burials (i.e. prefixed CN) when internal at the time of excavation; others are prefixed in the EE series. The burials from Site 26 stand alone and are prefixed G. All references to burials in this volume are always prefixed by the word Burial to prevent confusion. Appendix 9 provides concordances of the various numbering systems.

In 1976, part way through the excavation of Site 26, a new context recording system was adopted at Wharram (see *Wharram III*, 2 for more details). It must be noted that the original recording techniques used for burials prior to this change, frequently did not differentiate between skeletons and the cuts and fills of their graves – so for example, Burial SA050, where referred to in the text, incorporates skeleton number, grave cut and grave fills which may or may not have originally had separate context numbers. In the finds sections, objects are catalogued with their original context number, often the grave fill, but the Burial number is given as well for clarity.

Phasing

The allocation of stratigraphic sequences to large numbers of burials is always difficult. With densely-used burial grounds, grave-cuts are hard to see. A solution is to excavate in horizontal spits, recording burials as they are encountered, and deducing their sequence from intercutting of bones (Kjølbye-Biddle 1975, 97). This method requires precise surveying and recording. It also requires area excavation. Neither condition applied to the Wharram excavations (cf. *Wharram III*, 49). Most areas were initially trenched, then excavated again, often piecemeal. Interpretation was made more difficult by the policy (dictated by the Ministry of Works at that time) of leaving in walls, even floor patches, *in situ* whilst excavation continued in the spaces between. This applied to the SA area in particular.

As a result it is nearly impossible, especially in the case of areas NA, SA, and EE, to establish sequences of burial. Except for Site 26, it was not possible to track attributes or pathology through time other than in very general terms. The radiocarbon dates are, however, of immense value. Not only do they provide dates for the limited number of cases where sequences could be distinguished; they also

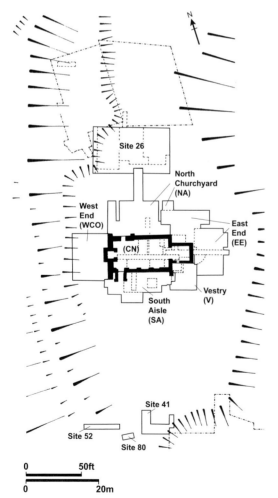

Fig. 114. Areas of excavation with site codes. (E. Marlow-Mann)

provide a range of dates for the various areas of the site. In addition, in the NA area, the series of plans on which the burials were located at the time of excavation can be divided into two groups which appear, from the radiocarbon dates, broadly to represent pre and post-Conquest burials (Ch. 14). This suggests that, here, absolute level is relevant to burial phasing of pre-modern burials, with lower burials being earlier (as long as child burials are not included). This principle was used in the assessment of other areas. In the absence of other evidence, such as plans or levels, burials which were on the same plan as dated burials were phased with the dated burials. Many burials are still of unknown phase.

Using this information it has been possible to produce incomplete plans of pre and post-Conquest burials (Figs 117 and 122). Burials of unknown phase have been omitted from these plans (with the exception of unphased burials in the 1970 PQ trench which are shown on both pre and post-Conquest plans, Figs 117 and 122).

Methodology and problems

The north aisle and north churchyard (NA)
This area included the 13th-century north aisle (demolished in the late medieval period and thus external at the time of excavation), and the cemetery north of the church, including a 2.4m wide trench (the 'PQ' trench) dug in 1970 which linked the north churchyard to Site 26 (Fig. 4; Ch. 3). Most of the NA area and the entire PQ trench were dug to natural, so the burials excavated should be a complete sample.

The burials when excavated in 1965 were plotted diagrammatically as 'stick-men' onto five 1:48 scale plans. The plans were apparently compiled as excavation proceeded down (though there are discrepancies between plans and photos which suggest that the plan was compiled after the burials were lifted). Each one of these five plans was taken to represent an excavation 'spit'. A check on the chronological validity of these five 'spits' achieved poor agreement when checked with radiocarbon dates (p. 209), though grouping some of the 'spits' together achieved better chronological validity. In additional to these five plans, 52 out of the 250 burials also had more detailed drawn plans and 67 were photographed (Plate 89).

The nave and various chancels (CN)
The church nave burials have been illustrated and published (*Wharram III*, 68, figs 16 and 20; Beresford and Hurst 1990, fig. 38; see Appendix 9 for renumbering).

South aisle (SA)
The area includes the late 12th-century south aisle, which became external again upon demolition in the late medieval period, as well as a section of the medieval churchyard beyond. The area was dug over several seasons from 1967 to 1969, with some re-excavation of areas previously opened (*Wharram III*, 49, fig. 5).

Plate 89. Grids J-K/224-30 from north. Burials outside the north of the church near the West End.

The south boundary sites (Sites 41, 52 and 80)
These three trenches were opened on different occasions between 1975 and 1984 (see above, Ch. 3), in order, among other things, to investigate the boundary of the known cemetery. Nineteen skeletons were recorded: some were radiocarbon dated. Unexpectedly, the cemetery here was found to start *cal AD 975-1125 (95% probability; Fig. 101; first_sb)*, and this area of the cemetery was in use for up to 200 years (Ch. 14).

West of the church (WCO)
This was excavated in 1972 and 177 skeletons were excavated (Plate 90). The area had been used for several quarry pits before burial began, though the pits contained no dating evidence. The burials appeared to respect the west end and tower of the church; they were laid in approximate rows. Although all discernible burials were removed and some quarry pits identified there is no certainty that all areas were dug to natural (*Wharram III*, 96): nevertheless, the 177 excavated burials should be a complete record of the sequence of burial in this area. The burials were laid in approximate rows.

Multiple overlaying of burials (implying reuse of the same ground after a period of time sufficient for grave locations to be altogether forgotten) was very rare: there were only six instances where such overlay of skeletons

217

was observed, though there were 'many examples of skeletons cut by later graves' (*Wharram III*, 96). This minor overlapping might represent poor marking of burials; there was no evidence of the dense multiple overlaying of burials which results from the frequent reuse of ground for burial. Grave cuts were not visible, which made it difficult to determine a sequence of burial. Early in the post-excavation analysis an attempt was made to group the burials chronologically, but when this was tested using radiocarbon dates this grouping was shown not to be valid (Fig. 103). The overall site plan (Fig. 18) allows nearly all skeletons to be fitted on plan without major overlap, which might imply that they belong to one phase of burial.

Another characteristic of the western area burials was the absence of headstones, markers, cists, stone settings, coffins or other medieval characteristics which form a small proportion of the burials in all other areas. This suggests that all these WCO burials are late medieval, or exceptionally poor, or perhaps both. The pottery derived from this area was late medieval Humber ware (*Wharram III*, 96). It was concluded that this western part of the cemetery dated to the medieval period and was of relatively short duration.

This interpretation was contradicted by the radiocarbon dates. These indeed suggest that most of the burials were medieval, however there was a group of pre-Conquest burials (perhaps nineteen) and a significant group of later medieval skeletons (p. 209). This area of the cemetery was thus in use from the 10th to 11th centuries for up to seven hundred years (Ch. 14): this implies an average of one burial in this area every three or four years. The other areas of the cemetery also contain medieval burials, and burial in the western area must have been concurrent with burial elsewhere in the churchyard. The reasons for this choice of burial area are unknown. These do not seem to be distinctive burials: the lack of stone settings or coffins makes it seem unlikely that this area was set aside for one high status family. Perhaps it was an area used occasionally for pauper burials. It seems that this burial area was brought back into use from time to time after a few years lapse. A possible similar pattern of use was identified in the North Churchyard (Ch. 4).

A distribution plan of the radiocarbon dated burials (Fig. 116) indicates that no significance can be attached to the date of burial related to its location. The earlier medieval burials (Burials WCO070, 139, 162, 179 and 184) do not occur in the extreme north part of the site: the later medieval burials (Burials WCO009, 028, 130, 138, 156 and 181) occur all over the area.

The chancels, east of the chancels, and the north-east churchyard (EE)

Area east of the chancels (EE)

This was tested by a single 1.2m wide trench in 1962: the north-east quadrant and the apse interior excavated in 1963. In 1964 the north-east chapel and the area north of it was excavated and the whole chancel area re-excavated (see Ch. 3).

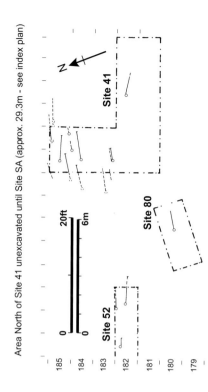

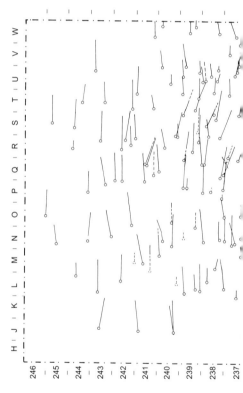

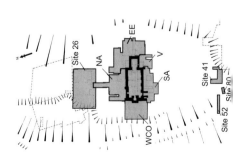

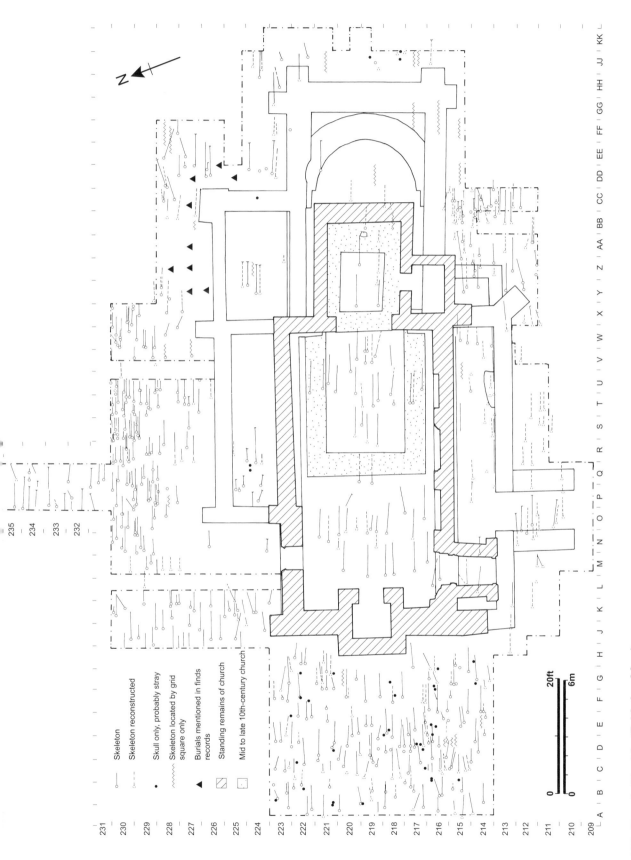

Fig. 115. Plan of all burials. (E. Marlow-Mann)

Skeleton

Skeleton reconstructed

Skull only, probably stray

Skeleton located by grid square only

Burials mentioned in finds records

Standing remains of church

Mid to late 10th-century church

20ft

6m

219

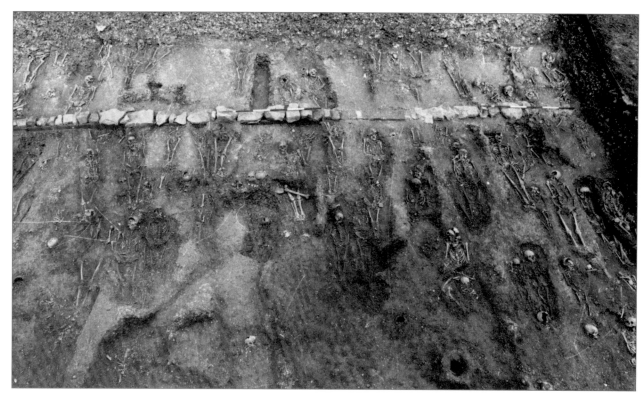

Plate 90. West End area, general view east, showing density of burials.

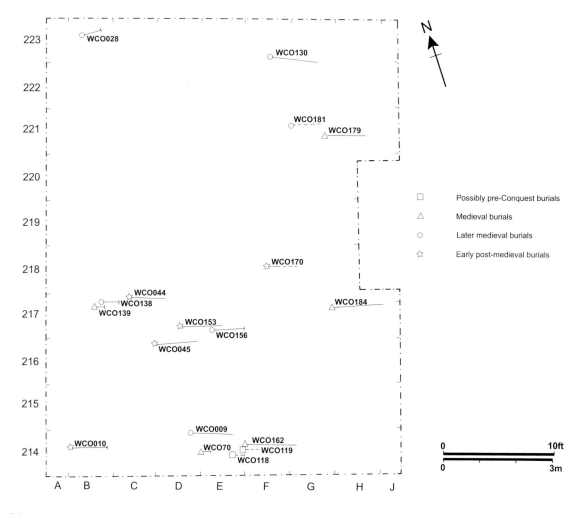

Fig. 116. Diagrammatic representation of those burials west of the church which were dated by radiocarbon. (E. Marlow-Mann)

Plate 91. Stone cist (Burial SA035) under the south aisle wall of Phase V and above the cist Burial SA034 which has been C14 dated to *cal AD 950-1050 (85% probability; GU-5458)*.

The natural ground here slopes steeply down to the east (Fig. 8). At the eastern limit of excavation deposits were up to 3m below ground level. The various upstanding walls in the chancel area meant that the depth as well as the area of excavation was restricted. The earliest burials could not be excavated, and even in the more open area to the north, natural was not reached, except against the north section (EES12). The north-east chapel was only excavated to just below the group of medieval burials in front of the altar. The burials retrieved thus do not include a full sample of burials of all dates.

The area north of the north-east chapel (EE)
Sixty-three skeletons from the churchyard north of the chancels (Grids Y-HH/225-228) were lifted but were not planned. Some of these burials have been numbered twice, once for the skeleton and once for the attributes visible in the photographs (photographs do not carry burial numbers). Some original numbers could be identified by matching photographs with bones, but there remain burial numbers (from Burial EE104 onwards) which may duplicate earlier EE numbers which have bones but no location.

The area of the post-medieval vestry (V)
This was excavated in 1973 (see Ch. 3) and the recording included plans, sections, photographs and detailed site description. The natural slope of the ground descends steeply from west to east. The area was excavated down to, and including, the 11th-century 'grave-cover' burials;

the only area excavated to natural was a 1.2m wide trench on the E side. This provided a very important section (Fig. 9, Section A): it is one of the few places on the site where there is a full section of burials down to natural.

Site 26
This area was excavated between 1972 and 1978 (see Ch. 4). It lay north from the area described as the North Aisle area (see above), linked to it by the 1970 'P/Q' trench. A total of 128 burials were excavated.

The pre-Conquest cemetery (Figs 117 and 118)

The earliest burials at Wharram are identified by radiocarbon dates, and include burials both close to the first church and on the furthest limits of the churchyard. On the southern boundary of the churchyard, there were two pre-Conquest burials (Burial SA052 and Burial SA053), and another ten which span the 11th century.

West of the church, Burials WCO118 and WCO119 (GU-5503/GU5682 and GU-5502) are dated to *cal AD 1070-1230* and *cal AD 960-1170* respectively. It is supposed (see above) that the earliest burials formed a small isolated group of pre-Conquest date (see p. 209). This group is at some distance (about 11m) from the Phase II church, and the intervening space is taken up with the later phases of the western nave and tower, where the earlier archaeological evidence has been destroyed. It is, therefore, not possible to be sure whether there were other burials of this date nearer the Phase II church.

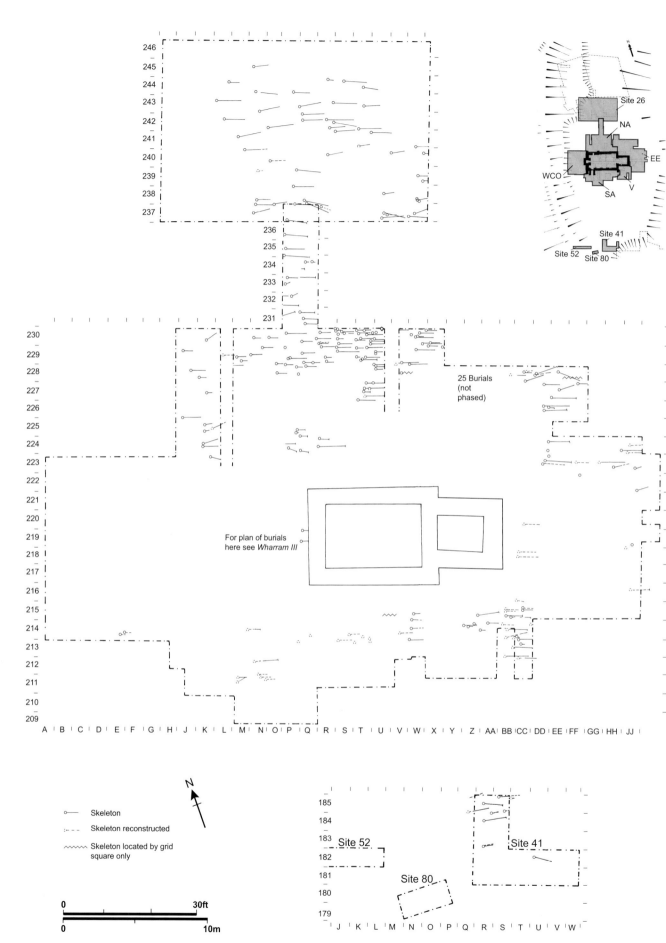

Fig. 117. Plan of the Phase I/II church with pre-Conquest burials. The burials on Site 41, those from Period 3, Phase 3 on Site 26 and some of those in the PQ trench may span the Conquest (see Ch. 14) and are therefore shown on Figs 117 and 122. (E. Marlow-Mann)

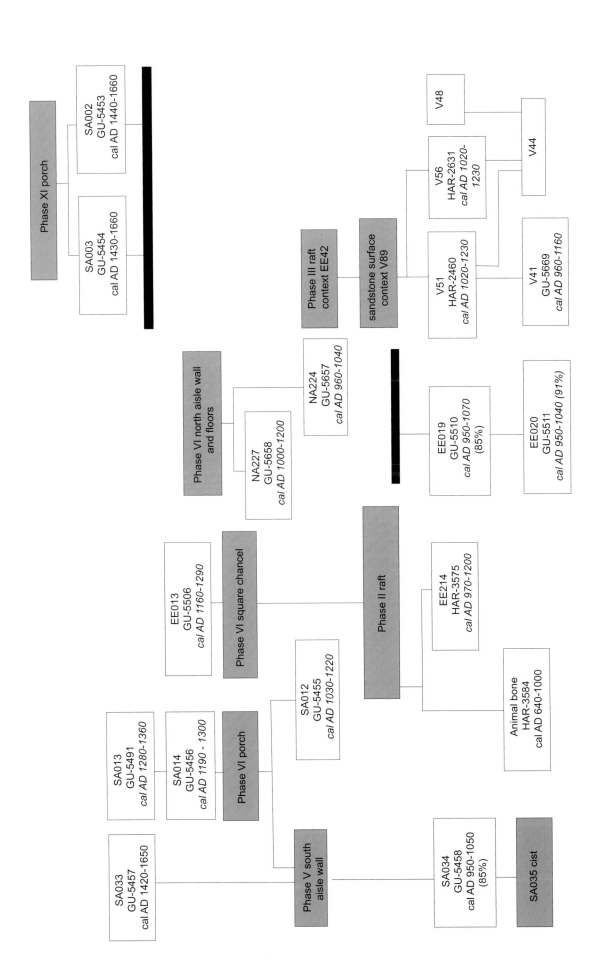

Fig. 118. Diagram to show some C14 dates related to significant structural phases (shaded). Numbers are burial numbers except where stated. Italicised dates are posterior density estimates derived from the chronological model and given 95% probability (except where noted). Non-italicised dates are calibrated ranges given at 95% confidence: (see Ch. 14) Heavy line = no significant stratigraphy known above or below this context.

223

Fig. 119. Early burials cut by the west wall of the Phase II Church. (E. Marlow-Mann)

For burials just south of the church, the radiocarbon dates also provide the pre-Conquest evidence. A stone cist (Burial SA035; Pl. 91), cut by the late 12th-century Phase V south aisle wall, had above it (or possibly in it as a secondary item) a skull (Burial SA034) which was radiocarbon dated to *cal AD 950-1050 (85% probability; GU-5458)* (Ch. 14); the south aisle wall itself incorporated grave-covers of 11th to 13th-century date (*Wharram III*, 58, 86; see Ch. 21). A number of adjacent burials on a similar alignment and at a similar depth have been assigned to the pre-Conquest period.

Inside the church most of the earliest burials had been destroyed by post-medieval ones. Burial CN51 and Burial CN52 (Fig. 119; YY and ZZ in Beresford and Hurst 1990, fig. 38) may be an exception. They appear to be cut by the west wall of the Phase II church. Both were also cut by the RCHM trench of 1962 and by other post-medieval features. The excavators thought that both these burials cut floors of Phase VII-VIII, which would make them post-medieval. One burial, however, clearly has an 'ear-muff' (for these see below) which would suggest it is 10th to 12th century. It seems possible that later disturbances have confused the evidence, and that these two burials belong to the Phase II church, or even to a pre-church phase of burial. The burials are on the church alignment.

There were early burials under the chancel and east of the church, which could not be excavated (see above). There was, however, evidence, albeit fragmentary, of burials here contemporary with or earlier than the Phase II church. Some burials (Burials EE111, EE112 and EE214) were under the Phase II chancel construction (*Wharram III*, 56-7). Other burials were cut by the Phase III raft (EE205 and EE184). Burial EE214 carried a radiocarbon date *cal AD 970-1200 (95% probability; HAR 3575* (Ch. 14) and 10th-12th century dates have been confirmed for a number of burials. The first burials

in the EE area occurred *cal AD 955-1020 (95% probability;* Fig. 99; *first _ee)* (Ch. 14).

In the Vestry area (V) several early burials were excavated. The 31 post-medieval burials had cut away most of the upper 1.2m of soil. Below was a surface of sandstone chippings (V89, Fig. 11, p. 15), apparently an old ground surface, cut by the Phase III chancel raft and sealing a group of 11th-century burials with stone grave-covers, one with a decorated top that was meant to be exposed. The graves under the covers had upright stones

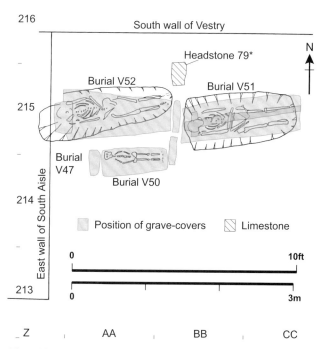

Fig. 120. Plan of 11th-century stone grave-cover burials south of Phase II chancel. Numbers marked with * indicate numbers used within a separate church sequence in *Wharram III*. (E. Marlow-Mann)

224

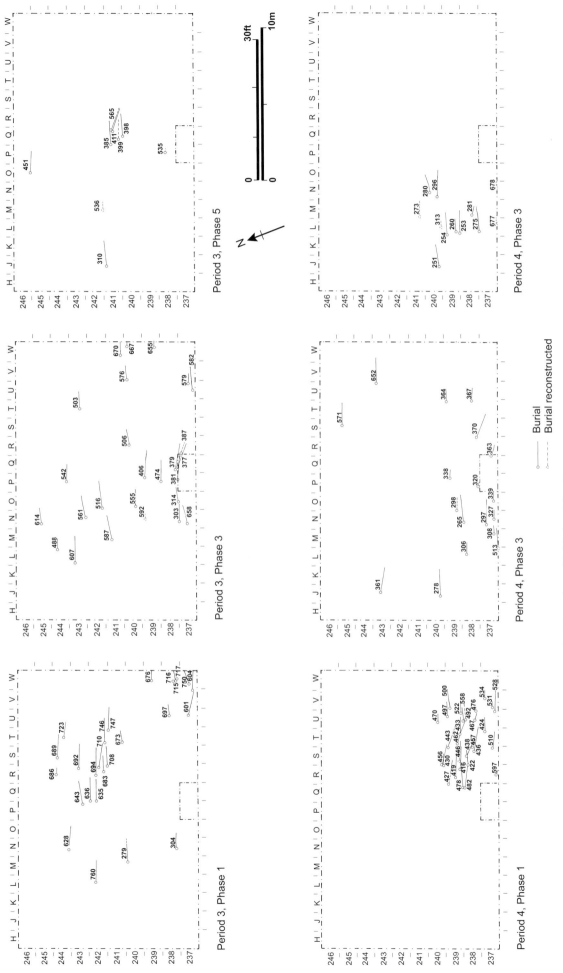

Fig. 121. Site 26 burials by phase. All numbers shown are G burial numbers. (E. Marlow-Mann)

225

Plate 92. North Churchyard – Burials NA112 and NA146 (below), both in 'southern ditch 1' in Grid V-X/229-230, looking north-east.

at head and foot, though the covers did not rest on the stones (Figs 120 and 133). Two of the burials, Burial V41 (GU-5669) and Burial V51 (HAR-2460), gave radiocarbon dates of *cal AD 960-1160* and *cal AD 1020-1230* respectively.

Burial V56 (which predated one of the grave-cover burials) had a line of charcoal-flecked soil over the grave: this might represent a wooden cover, presumably a slightly more economical version of the stone covers. The plan of the whole group of burials below layer V89 (Fig. 120) shows how the covers and headstones all fit neatly together. They are likely, therefore, to be contemporary or closely consecutive. These are surely high-status burials, and their social and ecclesiastical context is explored in Chapter 21. These graves are not however, the earliest: one of them, Burial V51, cut Burial V56 and Burial V41. Burial V51 was accompanied by a juvenile skeleton: for such double burials see pp 85-6.

North of the church (NA) is an area where phasing was difficult. The earliest two generations of burials are, however, likely to be pre-Conquest (Ch. 14). Overall the burials in this area started *cal AD 950-1000 (95% probability;* Fig. 108*; first_na),* and finished *cal AD 1280-1360 (95% probability;* Fig. 108*; last_na),* probably before AD 1348.

The puzzling factor about the burials in area NA is their uneven distribution, with the lower density close to the church. The eastern end of the north aisle, and the area north of the aisle, were excavated to natural. The 1973 re-

excavation of the west end of the north aisle, west of Grid S, presumably went down to natural, and located several burials. Yet none of these areas produced anything like the density at the northern limit of this churchyard area.

Potentially the centre of this clustering of burials was Burial NA146 (male, 40-50; Plates 92 and 93): the burial is radiocarbon dated to *cal AD 960-1070 (90% probability; GU-5650/GU-5679).* It had, as well as stones round the head, a bed of chalk blocks. Such grave lining might be an indication of high status (Daniell 1997, 157-8). A nail in the mouth and an iron nail found with the bones could have come from a cover made from a reused piece of wood which happened to have nails in it. It is possible that this burial was the focus of the clustering; or there may have been a churchyard cross which formed a focus.

The evidence of the radiocarbon dates suggests that this burial (Burial NA146) and the group of burials with stone grave-covers were roughly contemporary. Are there two clusters of burials?

Further north still, on Site 26 (Fig. 121), graves began to be dug *cal AD 960-1015 (95% probability;* Fig. 109*; first_3.1),* and the first two phases of these (Period 3, Phases 1 and 3) are likely to be pre-Conquest. These burials are not densely packed, but they nevertheless extend further north than do medieval burials of the Period 3, Phase 5 and Period 4, Phases 1 and 5.

Overall, the picture is of burial starting in the late 10th to early 11th century, and taking place even then over a

Plate 93. Burial NA146 in detail. This burial had iron nails and rested on a bed of chalk.

wide area. The implications for the development of the churchyard are discussed in Chapter 32 – the cemetery may have begun with scattered multiple foci.

The earliest burials may predate the church. It is becoming increasingly recognised that the earliest graveyards pre-date the establishment of their churches (Hadley 2002, 212-13). The radiocarbon dates indicate a start of burial for the whole cemetery of *cal AD 940-995 (95% probability;* Fig. 98*; start_cemetery)* and some burials are stratigraphically earlier than the Phase II church (see Fig. 119; also *Wharram III*, 56-7). There were no burials inside the church which were contemporary with Phases I and II: but this is to be expected, since it was not the practice to bury in Anglo-Saxon churches (Rodwell 1989, 157; Daniell 1997, 186-7).

The post-Conquest cemetery (Figs 122 and 118)

Burial continued north of the church (area NA) through the medieval period, probably until the Black Death (Ch. 14). At the extreme southern limit of the churchyard, Burial SA080 appears to be medieval, from green-glaze pottery in the grave fill, and Burials SA070-072 are probably also medieval. The latest medieval use of this area would have been around *cal AD 1280-1360 (95% probability;* Fig. 108*; last_na)* (Ch. 14). Towards the north, however, on Site 26, burial, though still continuing, did not extend so far north as it had in the pre-Conquest period.

Plate 94. Child Burial EE072 north of the north-east chapel. Stone at head, stones either side of feet.

227

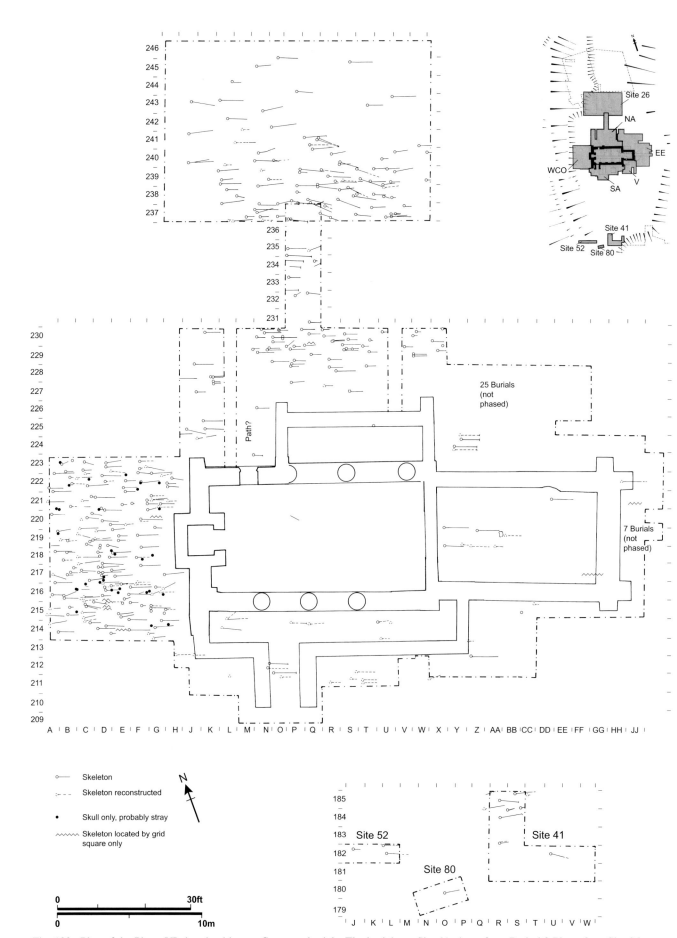

Fig. 122. Plan of the Phase VI church with post-Conquest burials. The burials on Site 41, those from Period 3 Phase 3 on Site 26 and some of those in PQ trench may span the Conquest (see Ch. 14) and are therefore shown on Figs 117 and 122. For post-medieval burials see Fig. 124. (E. Marlow-Mann)

Plate 95. 'Childrens' graveyard'. These burials (Burials EE074-6, EE137 and EE139) were north-east of the north aisle.

In the area west of the Phase III and subsequent churches (area WCO) burial started before the Conquest and continued for several hundred years. There was only one coffin, no stone settings, and no post-medieval burials with coffin fittings. The area must have been used intermittently for many centuries. In the post-medieval period access to this area may have been undesirable due to the unstable hillside (Ch. 3).

The south aisle (SA) area once included medieval burials, though not many were excavated: the blocking of the south aisle arcade included reused 13th to 14th-century grave slabs (pp 289-292; *Wharram III*, 91 and 147).

The children's graveyard (EE)

The area covering approximately grid squares V, W, X 227, was described by the excavators as a 'childrens' graveyard', so it is unfortunate that many burials cannot be located (see above). Of the nine which can be assigned to this area, three are juveniles (Burials EE075 and EE076, both aged 8, and Burial EE072 aged 10: Plates 94 and 95). Half (32 out of 63) of the 'unlocated' skeletons which potentially came from the area in question are of children under 10 or juveniles. In the site as a whole, two-thirds of infants aged under one year were interred within 9.14m of the church north wall (p. 87) and it is clear that an area north of the chancel was set aside for burial of juveniles.

Post-Conquest burial in the church (Fig. 123)

It is not clear exactly when burial in the church began. The many post-medieval nave burials have destroyed much of the evidence and there are very few medieval burials left. One candidate was proposed in Wharram III (71-2): a burial on the central axis of the apsidal end of the Phase III chancel (Burial EE120). In this location it would have been positioned in front of the altar. Its east end was subsequently truncated by the east wall of the present, smaller chancel. At its west end, however, was an apparently associated socket stone (Fig. 123A) reconsidered here by David Stocker (p. 293). The stone may, in fact, mark an early post-medieval burial.

In Phase VI of the church there were also prestigious burials. In the square-ended chancel, Burial EE013 (Plate 96) was placed on the north side of the new chancel. The skeleton, a male adult, was laid in a wooden nailed coffin with chalice and paten resting on the right shoulder (Fig. 123.B; *Wharram III*, 150; cf. Gilchrist and Sloane 2005, 126). The use of a chalice and/or paten in the grave is common in churches and it is taken to denote a priest burial. They may, when buried, have contained consecrated wine and bread (Daniell 1997, 170).

This burial, on the basis of the chalice within it, was thought 'unlikely to be earlier than 1300' and provided a *terminus ante quem* for Phase VI (*Wharram III*, 76, ch. VIF). This burial has now been radiocarbon dated to *cal AD*

229

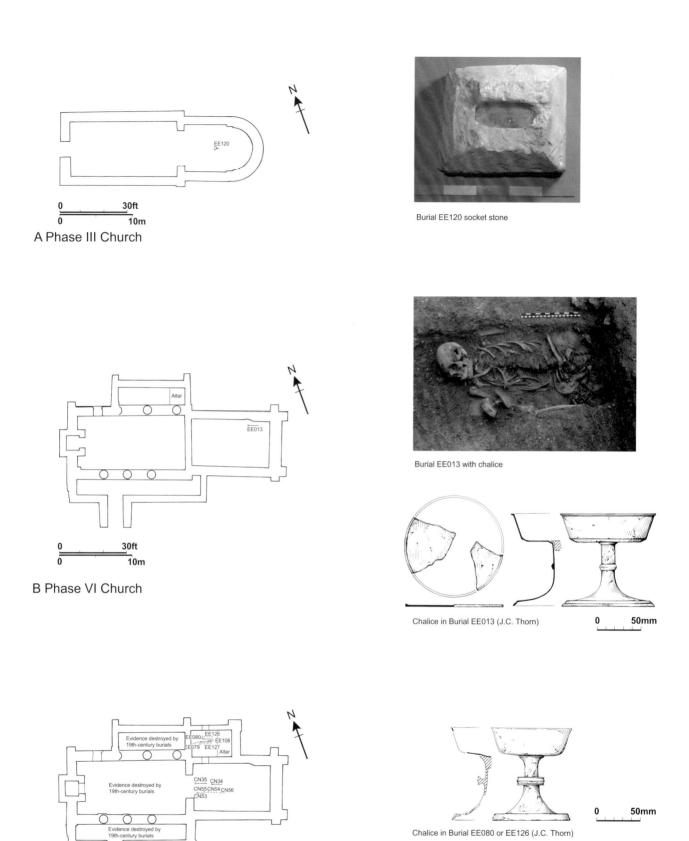

0
30ft
0
10m

A Phase III Church

Burial EE120 socket stone

Altar
EE013

0
30ft
0
10m

B Phase VI Church

Burial EE013 with chalice

Chalice in Burial EE013 (J.C. Thorn)
0
50mm

Evidence destroyed by 19th-century burials
EE126
EE080
EE108
EE079
EE127
Altar
CN35 CN34
CN55 CN54 CN56
CN53
Evidence destroyed by 19th-century burials
Evidence destroyed by 19th-century burials

0
30ft
0
10m

C Phase VIII Church

Chalice in Burial EE080 or EE126 (J.C. Thorn)
0
50mm

Fig. 123. Burials in the medieval church. All numbers shown are burial numbers. (E. Marlow-Mann)

230

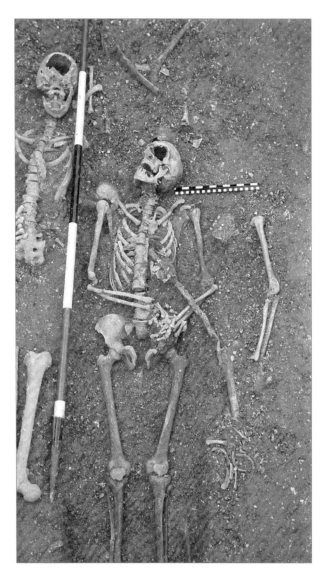

Plate 96. Burial EE013. This burial was set in the north side of the straight-ended chancel of Period VI. The burial was in a cofffin and there was a pewter chalice and paten at the right shoulder. The burial has been C14 dated to *cal AD 1160-1290 (95% probability; GU5506).*

Plate 97. Burials in front of the altar in the north-east chapel. From left to right: Burials EE079, EE080 and EE126 (arm only). The chalice and paten near the left shoulder of Burial EE080 is likely to have belonged to Burial EE126.

1160-1290 (GU 5506). The burial is thus not 14th or 15th century as was thought, but was added close to the time the chancel was constructed in the 13th century. Mortuary chalices are difficult to date precisely; this example could be 13th-century in date (cf. Rodwell 2001, 528). There is a 13th to 14th-century grave slab with an incised chalice (Fig. 138, No. 24) which may have adorned this or one of the other priestly burials in or close to the church (see below).

It is often the case that a church chancel is a popular location for later medieval burials. At Wharram there were a good many intercutting burials in the square chancel of Phases VI-IX (Fig. 123.C). There was a double-width grave containing one skeleton, Burial CN34 (originally context C75, described in *Wharram III*, 76, fig. 18), and there were five other internal burials probably of the same general phase (Burial CN35 and Burials CN53-56). Burials CN53-5 form an intercutting sequence and presumably represent prolonged use of the square chancel for burials.

The 14th-century north-east chapel of the Phase VII church also contained what appears to be a priest burial or burials. The chapel was removed in the late medieval period, and so was external to the church when excavated in 1964. The remains of the altar had, in front of it, Burial EE080 (a male adult) placed centrally; a chalice lay near the left shoulder (Fig. 123.C; *Wharram III*, 150). This burial cut several earlier ones – Burials EE126, EE108, EE079, and EE127. Most of these earlier burials were fragmentary and no bones survive except for Burial EE079, a male adult. Burial EE126, of which only the left arm survived, lay under Burial EE080; it is just possible that this may have been the chalice burial and not Burial EE080. Photographs show the chalice apparently outside the grave limit of Burial EE080, resting approximately on the chest of Burial EE126 (Plate 97). Since the 14th to 15th-century period was the era of chantries, it may be that a succession of chantry priests was buried in front of the altar in this chapel.

231

Burial EE080 in the north-east chapel had a wooden (?) object across it (Plate 97): this might have been a pilgrim staff (cf. Daniell 1997, 167; Gilchrist and Sloane 2005, 171-6) but crosses two graves, Burials EE080 and EE126, so is perhaps just a tree root.

It was common in the late medieval period for burials to be placed in front of a side altar (cf. 16th-century burials in front of the north aisle altar at St Oswald's, Gloucester (Heighway and Bryant 1999, 200, 204 and 219)). There were undoubtedly other burials in the north east chapel at Wharram, and indeed one would expect the whole width of the side chapel to be taken up with burials, rather than a group in the middle. The chalk raft under the south half of the chapel might have inhibited burial there.

Post-medieval burials (Fig. 124)

Post-medieval burials occurred inside the church (*Wharram III*), and were distinguishable by their fittings and coffins. The 45 external post-medieval burials were deeper than medieval ones and had often removed the

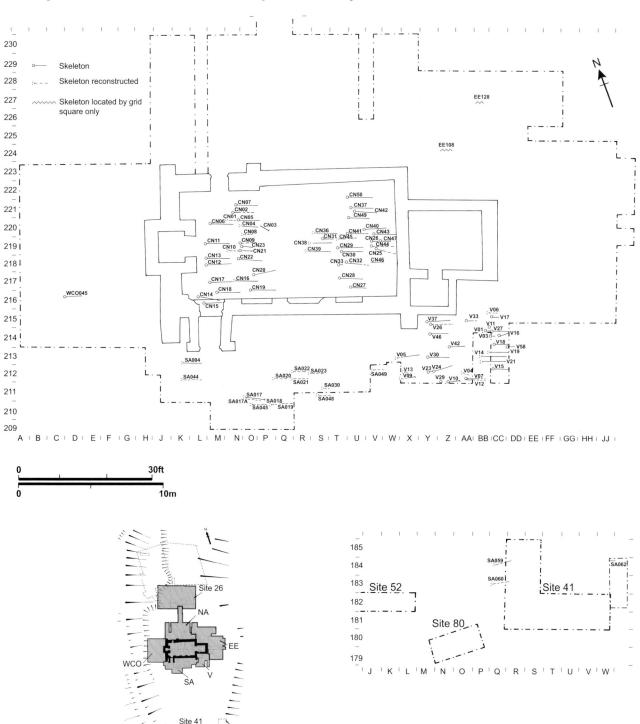

Fig. 124. Post-medieval burials. All numbers shown are burial numbers. (E. Marlow-Mann)

burials immediately beneath (e.g. the Vestry area). The post-medieval burials with fittings are published in *Wharram III*, 79, fig. 20 (see Appendix 9 for renumbering). Originally, the nave burials were all thought to be late medieval or post-medieval. Two burials (Burials CN03 and CN04) had unusual orientations and were cut by other post-medieval burials; nevertheless these too were early post-medieval in date when radiocarbon dated (Ch. 14). Two other burials (Burials CN51 and CN52) are pre-Conquest and probably among the earliest recorded (see above).

The other post-medieval burials were all south of the church. They clustered close to the church just south of the chancel, in the area of the post-medieval vestry, but did not occupy the area of the medieval south aisle, even though the aisle was then demolished. Possibly the 18th and 19th-century sextons were aware that this area was occupied by walls and floors and was therefore hard to dig (C. Harding, pers comm).

There were some post-medieval burials on the south boundary (Site 41). Two of the nineteen burials discovered there (Burials SA059 and SA060; Fig. 61) are late in the sequence and were in coffins; they are probably late 19th-century, though they do not have gravestones (see *Wharram II*, 7 for frequency of burials with tombstones, and *Wharram III*, 38 for loss of tombstones due to tidying). Burial SA062 also appears to be post-medieval from stratigraphic evidence.

In the north-east chapel was a burial (Burial EE108) of a child in a coffin, 0.46m from the ground surface. This might be an isolated post-medieval grave, inserted long after the chapel had been demolished.

The attributes

Despite the small sample and insecure phasing, some observations on the attributes of the burials can be made.

Arm position (Tables 19-22; Figs 125-7)
The burial position of the body may be culturally significant. For medieval burials, legs were usually laid straight, but arms could be:

1   by the sides
2   on the body, with hands on pelvis
3   on the body, with hands crossed on the chest
4   on the body, with arms across the waist
5   one on the body, one by the side

Table 119 gives the overall site information for Wharram. The percentages have been reckoned on available information: data can be obtained only from about a third of all burials.

At Wharram, Positions 1 and 2 form roughly the same proportion in all areas except Site 26 (10th-12th century) and the nave, where burials were mostly post-medieval. Table 120 gives information for Site 26, the only area where burials could be closely phased and so the attributes tracked through time. There, though Position 2 'pelvis' and Position 1 'sides' were equally popular in the

Area	Sides	Pelvis	Chest	Waist
CN	9	19	0	0
Site 26	22	63	6	0
EE	13	13	0	2
NA	18	25	0	0
SA	4	5	0	1
S boundary	2	5	0	1
V	8	9	0	0
WCO	49	40	2	4
Total	125	179	8	8

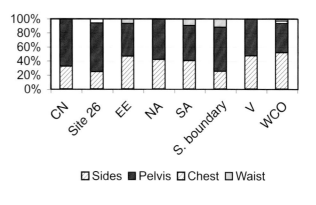

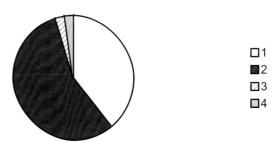

Fig. 125. Data and diagrams for arm positions of burials. The East End includes EE013 in chancel.

late Saxon period, by the late 11th early 12th century the 'pelvis' position constituted the majority of burials. The relationship between Positions 1 and 2 seems to have evened out thereafter.

The small group of burials on the south boundary (Table 121) spans a range of dates; they show that the 'pelvis' position was used from the earliest date. Medieval Burial SA072 had the right arm on the waist, so probably represents a Position 4, but other limbs were missing.

A separate analysis was done of post-medieval burials only (Table 122), but in fact the ratio between Positions 1 and 2 was similar to that for the medieval burials.

Different burial positions seem to be a matter of local or even family custom. At St Oswald's, Gloucester the 'sides' position was most common in the Anglo-Saxon period with the 'pelvis' position a close second. The same was true for 10th to 12th-century burials at St Andrew Fishergate (Stroud and Kemp 1993, 149). At Hereford it

Table 119. Arm positions, omitting burials for which there is no information.

Area	1 Sides	%	2 Pelvis	%	3 Chest	%	4 Waist	%	Total
CN	9	32	19	68	-	-	-	-	28
Site 26	22	24	63	69	6	7	-	-	91
EE	13	46	13	46	-	-	2	7	28
NA	18	42	25	58	-	-	-	-	43
SA	4	40	5	50	-	-	1	10	10
South boundary: sites 41, 52 and 80	2	25	5	63	-	-	1?	12	8
Vestry	8	47	9	53	-	-	-	-	17
West end	49	52	40	42	2	2	4	4	95
Totals	125	39%	179	56%	8	3%	7	2%	320

Table 120. Site 26: analysis of arm position through time.

Phase	date	1 Sides	%	2 Pelvis	%	3 Chest	%	5 Pelvis/ side	5 Chest/ Side	%	Total
3.1	late Saxon	7	32	8	36	4	18	3	-	14	22
3.3	until 1065-1150	6	30	11	55	1	5	2	-	10	20
3.5		2	33	3	50	-	-	1	-	17	6
4.1	until 1125-1210	3	13	19	79	-	-	1	1	8	24
4.3	until 1220-1305	2	17	8	67	-	-	2	-	17	12
4.5	1235-1330	2	33	3	50	-	-	1	-	17	6
4.6		-	-	1	100	-	-	-	-	-	1
Total		22	24%	53	58%	5	5%	10	1	12%	91

Table 121. Arm positions: Sites 41, 52 and 80.

Phase	1 Sides	2 Pelvis	3 Chest	4 Waist	Unknown	Totals
EM	-	1	-	-	1	2
EM/M	-	4	-	-	6	10
M	2	1	-	1?	-	4
PM	-	-	-	-	3	3
Total	2	6	-	1	10	19

EM=pre-conquest, EM/M=11th-12th century; M=medieval, PM=post-medieval

Table 122. Post-medieval burials: arm positions.

	1 Sides	2 Pelvis	3 Chest	4 Waist	5	Unknown	Totals
CN	9	18	-	-	1	22	50
EE	-	-	-	-	-	2	2
SA	1	1	-	1	-	11	14
S Boundary	-	-	-	-	-	3	3
V	7	4	-	-	-	29	40
WCO	-	1	-	-	-	-	1
Total	17	24	0	1	1	67	110

Table 123. Comparison of different burial arm positions from various sites (% of available data).

Site	Date range	1 Sides	2 Pelvis	3 Chest	4 Waist	5 Other
St Oswalds Gloucester	10th-11th-century	42	36	1	10	-
	17th-century				100	-
	Post-medieval	47	20	4	26	-
Jewbury	13th-century	72	5	-	-	22
Fishergate	11th-12th-century	33	49			18
	13th-16th-century	29	53			17
Hereford	Saxon		most popular			
	13th-century				most popular	
	later			most popular		
Raunds	10th-13th-century	79	21	-	-	-
Wharram	10th-15th-century	38	57	3	2	

	Sides	Pelvis	Chest	Pelvis/ Sides	Chest/ Side
3.1	7	8	4	3	0
3.3	6	11	1	2	0
3.5	2	3	0	1	0
4.1	3	19	0	1	1
4.3	2	8	0	2	0
4.5	2	3	0	1	0
4.6	0	1	0	0	0

Sides	Pelvis	Chest	Waist	Other
17	24	0	1	1

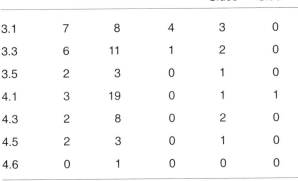

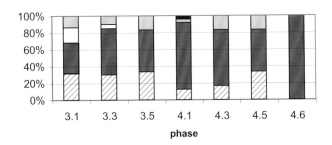

Fig. 127. Data and diagrams for arm positions of post-medieval burials.

Fig. 126. Data and diagrams for arm positions of burials: Site 26.

was the pelvis position that was most common in the Saxon period (Stone and Appleton-Fox 1996, 48). It is possible that the 'pelvis' position indicates that the body was wrapped in a shroud.

Position 5 could have been caused by one arm falling out of position during the moving of the body; this indeed has been the assumption in totalling the Wharram burials where the number of 'Position 5s' is in any case very small. It is, however, possible that such a position was deliberate: at the Jewish burial ground at Jewbury, York, these 'mixed' burial positions form about 30% of the total (Lilley et al., 389-91). Site 26 had better-recorded data and Position 5 could there be separately reckoned. Table 120 shows that this position accounted for 12% of all burials in that area.

Position 3 (with hands crossed on the chest) constituted at St Oswald's, Gloucester, 1% of Saxon burial positions, increasing to 9% of late medieval burials (Heighway and Bryant 1999, 203). This position occurs in the late Middle Ages, perhaps derived from placing the hands in a praying position (Daniell 1997, 118). At Wharram it formed a very small proportion of Saxon and medieval burials; it was not used for post-medieval burials.

Position 4, with arms across the waist, is very rare at Wharram; there was one in the chancel (Burial EE013, the 13th-century 'priest' burial), one from the south aisle, and four from the west end, totalling 6% of the available data and much less as a percentage of the total burials on the site. At St Oswald's, Gloucester this position is predominantly late medieval, though there are some (10% of burials) in the Saxon period (Heighway and Bryant 1999, 204).

Perhaps it is surprising that Positions 3 and 4, if they are a later custom as they seem to be elsewhere, do not appear in post-medieval burials at Wharram; however, few of those excavated belong to the 17th and early 18th century, which is the date they seem to be at Gloucester (Table 123). There is no evidence that arm position varies with the age or sex of the individual (p. 86).

Orientation (Fig. 128)
This aspect cannot be measured for those burials excavated in the earlier years, so there is a high number of unknowns in the data; furthermore, the orientation of

the NA burials in particular shows incompatibility between plans and photographs and so is probably not precise. The table shows only that burials nearer the church were more likely to be closely orientated on it. The burials on the south boundary show a tendency to be orientated towards the north, which no doubt reflects the proximity of a similarly aligned boundary at the time they were made. The burials of Site 26 show most variation of orientation which bears out the assumption that burials furthest from the church were less affected by its orientation.

The table data takes the orientation of the church as 0° and groups the angle of deviation from this, pivoting from the head, west, end, in units of 10 degrees. The table is expressed graphically in Figure 128.

Parallel-sided and displaced skeletons (Fig. 129)
Post-deposition displacement of bodies observed in an Anglo-Saxon cemetery (Reynolds 1976, 142; Boddington 1987, 420-22) indicates that the graves must have been

	EE	NA	South boundary sites	SA	WCO	Site 26	V	CN
26-35N	0	1	0	0	0	0	0	0
16-25N	3	9	0	2	4	1	2	4
6-15N	3	1	5	3	15	18	4	0
5N-5S church alignment 0°	24	219	5	20	108	62	32	47
6-15S	0	4	1	2	9	14	1	0
16-25S	3	2	0	0	3	8	0	1
26-35S	0	0	0	0	0	0	0	0
Total with data	33	236	11	27	139	103	39	52
No data	103	31	5	32	71	20	25	4
Total	136	267	16	59	210	123	64	56

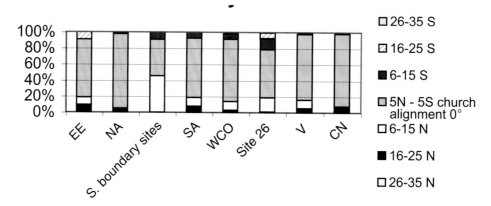

Fig. 128. Orientation of burials: summary of data and comparison between sites.

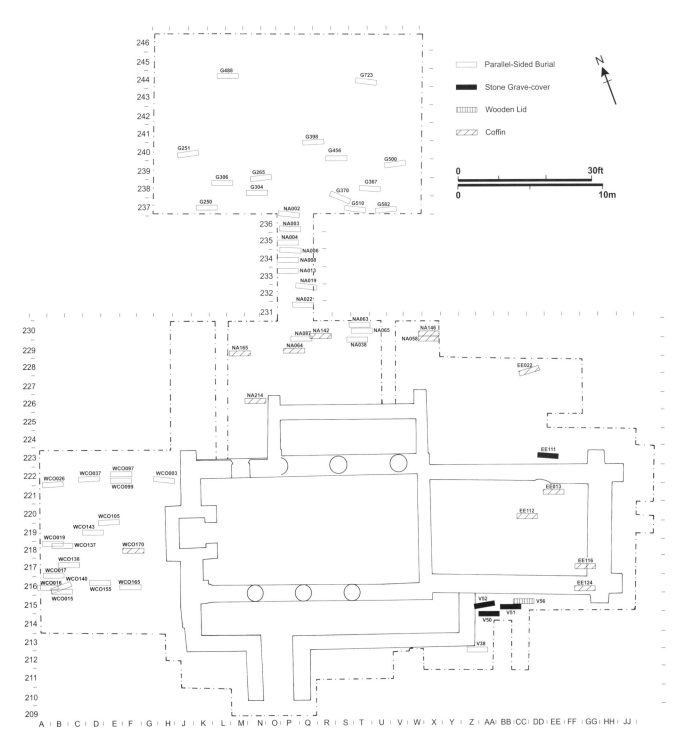

Fig. 129. Coffins and parallel-sided burials (post-medieval excluded). All numbers shown are burial numbers. (E. Marlow-Mann)

boarded over, as the displacement would have been unlikely if there had been earth packed around the bodies, and was more extensive than could possibly have resulted from earth-worm activity. It is now known that much disturbance (e.g. of ribs and vertebrae in the chest and abdomen) is possible as the result of natural decaying processes where there is space around the body. The movement of long bones is possibly the result of small-mammal activity.

The so-called parallel-sided effect as observed on skeletons is characterised by having the arms close to the chest with the hands tight against or over the pelvis and feet close together. Such a disposition is not always conclusively identifiable and many burials are unclassifiable. This effect can indicate coffined burials (Boddington 1996, 35) or may indicate only that the body was enclosed in a shroud.

Evidence for displacement at Wharram has not been plotted as there has been too much other disturbance of burials for this attribute to be observed in a statistically valid number of cases. Some examples were observed from Site 26.

Stone settings (Fig. 130)

Stone settings of some sort are well-known in medieval cemeteries and there is a great variety (Gilchrist and Sloane 2005, 134-9). Many of them were probably originally associated with stone or wooden covers or wooden coffins (Boddington 1996, 38). The following types of stone setting have been distinguished at Wharram:

1   Earmuffs. Here the head is propped by a large cobble either side of the head; there are no other stones (except sometimes at the feet; Plates 98 and 99)

2   Stones around the head. The arrangement varies from one or two stones under or beside the head, to a whole band of stones surrounding the head, halo fashion; this includes

the category sometimes described as 'pillow stones'. At Wharram, where the record often consists of verbal description rather than photographs or detailed drawing, the rite is not always distinguishable from 'earmuffs'.

3   Head and footstones. Two single upright flat slabs are placed at head and foot of the grave, in effect creating an imitation of the ends of a box. Again, this arrangement is distinctive in photographs, but from the written description in the record often cannot be distinguished from 1 and 2.

4   Stone cist. This is where a 'coffin' is created out of a number of stones carefully built around the whole body (Plates 90, 98 and 100)

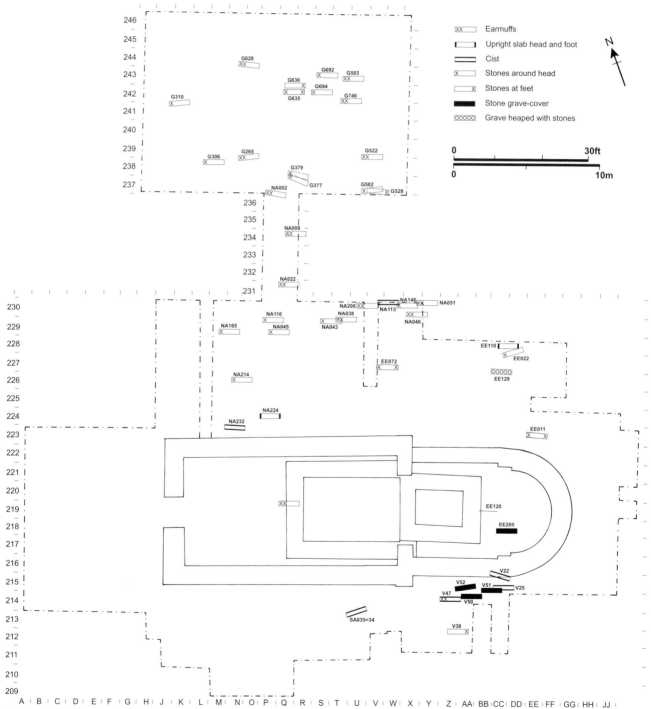

Fig. 130. Stone settings. All numbers shown are burial numbers. (E. Marlow-Mann)

238

5   Footstones are placed beyond the feet, apparently to mark the end of the grave. Sometimes there were pairs of stones either side the feet, probably to hold the feet upright (Plate 101).

6   A few burials were covered with grave-covers, which at Wharram were supported on the sides of the grave.

Many burials show combinations of some of the above, and thus classifying the different arrangements is difficult and probably unprofitable.

Most cemetery sites covering the 11th to 13th centuries include examples of stone settings of some sort (Stroud and Kemp 1993, 153). Although at Raunds, head pillows were usually used for men (Boddington 1996, 41), usually stone arrangements are not attached to a particular type of burial, and this was certainly the case at Wharram: see Table 124.

Table 124. Stone settings plotted by sex of individual.

	All stone setttings	'Earmuffs' only
Male	15	5
Female	12	4
Juvenile	9	2
Not known	10	2
Total	46	13
% of all burials	5%	1%

Plate 98. Burial V47 in sandstone cist with 'earmuffs'.

'Earmuffs' are a familiar and easily distinguished medieval burial arrangement (Rodwell 1989, 171; Plates 98 and 99). The three radiocarbon dated 'earmuff' burials at Wharram give this rite a date-range of 900-1300 (Ch. 14), and their date-range elsewhere is 10th to13th-century (Heighway and Bryant 1999, 205; Boddington 1996; White 1988b, 18, 20; Daniells 1997, 160-61). 'Earmuffs' represent a very small percentage of the burials (1.4% at Raunds, 4-10% of 10th to 13th-century burials at St Oswald's Gloucester), and it is better to view all stone settings as one group.

Plate 99. Site 26 Burial G522 with 'earmuffs'.

Plate 100. Child's grave, Burial NA232, Grid N/223-24, showing stone cist.

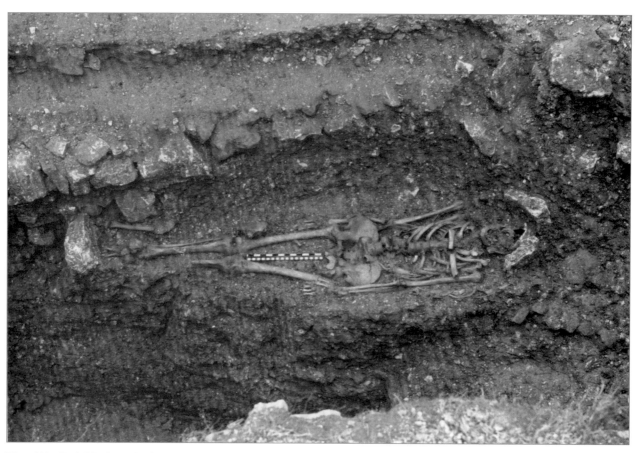

Plate 101. Burial EE011 with footstones and stones around the head.

Table 125. Distribution of stone settings through time: Site 26.

Phase	Date range	'Earmuffs'	%	All stone settings including 'earmuffs'	%	Total burials
1.1		-	-	-	-	1
3.1	960-1100	2	7	4	14	29
3.3	to 1150	1	4	4	16	25
3.4		-	-	-	-	1
3.5	to 1210	-	-	1	13	8
4.1	to 1210	1	3	2	7	30
4.3	to 1305	1	6	1	6	18
4.5	to 1330	-	-	1	8	12
4.6		-	-	-	-	2
U/P		-	-	-	-	2
Total		5	4%	13	10%	128

Stone cists (unmortared) are common in 11th to 12th-century cemeteries (White 1988b, 22-4). The complete cists at Raunds were all provided for children (Boddington 1996, 40). At Wharram out of seven cists, four were juveniles, two male adult and one female adult. (Pl. 100)

Burials could also have the body weighted with stones, as at Raunds. Four were observed in Site 26, and there was one (Burial NA006) north of the church: other examples almost certainly went unrecorded, as the stones can appear to be fortuitous backfill. One grave, Burial EE129, had been covered by a heap of stones.

Only Site 26 provides phasing detailed enough to indicate the popularity through time of these various rites. Although the numbers are small, they indicate for a well-recorded part of the churchyard the frequency of stone settings in the 10th to 13th centuries which is a useful check on the overall distribution for the site.

In no phase was the proportion of stone settings higher than 16%: this is in complete contrast to Raunds where half of all burials of much the same date range contained stone arrangements of some type (Boddington 1996, 13). The reason for this contrast is uncertain. It is possible that some stone settings went unrecognised at Wharram, but even in the well-recorded Site 26, only 10% of burials had stone settings of some sort (Table 125). The site distribution of stone settings suggests that even in the less-well-recorded areas the presence of stone settings was still noted (Fig. 130). There were no stone settings at all from the area west of the church, which was carefully excavated; perhaps this is an indicator of the exceptionally low status of that area, a conclusion which is confirmed by the absence of coffins. The south boundary burials, many of which span the Conquest, also showed no stone settings. The south aisle area was also devoid of stone settings, probably because it was not excavated to a low enough level.

The really high-status rite may well be indicated by the use of cists, and burials with grave-covers; these were relatively rare and only found near the church.

One might conclude that the community at Wharram was poorer even than Raunds - certainly the incidence of coffins seems to be very low - or perhaps that these practices were intensely regional.

Coffins (Table 126)
Several burials with coffins predating Phase II were noted (*Wharram III*, 56). The plot of coffins includes different methods of identification; some are represented only by coffin nails, and these were not usually plotted *in situ*, so it was not possible to be certain that the nails are not strays. Sometimes wood stains survived. The coffins at the eastern area of the site, though only glimpsed in deep excavations, seem to have been better preserved, perhaps by charring (*Wharram III*, 56). Very few coffins were nailed: a plot of wooden coffins (Fig. 129) shows them generally confined to the area near the church. This is to be expected since these are no doubt the most high-status burials.

Table 126. Coffins (omitting post-medieval).

Area	No. of coffins	If nailed	Date
EE	5	?	2 of Phase I
NA	6	3 with nails	10th-13th century
Site 26	-	-	-
SA	-	-	-
V	1	with charred lid	
WCO	1	-	Late medieval
Total	13		

It has been suggested that parallel-sided burials indicate the presence of coffins (Boddington 1996, 35) and so these have been shown as coffins on Fig. 129 (see also Table 127). An alternative explanation, however, is that this type of burial indicates the use of a shroud. This interpretation makes much better sense of the evidence; for instance it means that there are no coffins in the western area (Fig. 129) except for Burial WCO170 which is not certain. This is consistent with the otherwise apparent poverty of the western burials (above, p. 218). Parallel-sided burials are apparently confined to the outer churchyard area (Fig. 129), however, these are the very areas that were dug with most attention to detail, and therefore carry this information; such parallel-sided burials may well have been ubiquitous. If they indicate shroud use, the distribution shown in Fig. 129 makes better sense: it indicates that nearly all coffins were fairly close to the church and were not found in the outlying areas.

Parallel-sided burials can be tracked through time only in Site 26.

Table 127. Parallel-sided burials by phase, Site 26.

Phase	Date range	total	all burials	%
3.1	960-1100	2	27	7
3.3	to 1150	2	26	8
3.5	to 1210	1	9	11
4.1	to 1210	3	29	10
4.3	to 1305	4	18	22
4.5	to 1330	1	12	8
4.6		1	2	50
Total		14	123	11%

Coffin lids

Two burials (Burials V56 and EE112) had above the burial a band of charcoal which may represent a charred coffin lid. Many of the burials which are thought to have had coffins may have had simply a wooden cover placed over an earth grave (cf. Daniell 1997, 163); a reflection in wood of the stone grave-covers described next. No association of age or sex was found related to coffins (p. 86).

Stone grave-covers

The stone grave-covers, probably contemporary with the Phase II church, are discussed elsewhere in this volume (Ch. 14). Though accompanied by head and foot stones (upright slabs at each end of the grave), these stones did not support the slab which was laid directly over the earth-cut grave at a steeply sloping angle to follow the lie of the land. Close by was Burial V47: a grave lined with slabs to form a cist. The grave-cover burials (Burials V50, V51 and V52) were not the earliest burials on the site; some overlay other burials (Burial V51 overlay Burial V56, a so-called charcoal burial). Radiocarbon dates show that burial in this area of the churchyard started *cal AD 960-1040 (95% probability; first_sa)*. The style of the slabs (Ch. 14), and the radiocarbon dates of the burials within them (Burial V50: *cal AD 1000-1260* [95% probability; HAR-2672], Burial V51: *cal AD 1020-1230* [95% probability; HAR-2460], and Burial V52: *cal AD 980-1220* [95% probability; HAR-2462]), date these burials (and by implication those next to and aligned with them and evidently part of the same series) to the 11th century.

Charcoal and ash burials

An often-observed characteristic of late Saxon graves was the laying of the body on a bed of oak charcoal (Biddle forthcoming; cf. also York, St Helen's). Such burials tend to be found in monastic cemeteries of the late Saxon and early medieval periods (Rodwell 1989, 163; Gilchrist and Sloane, 2005, 120-21), so perhaps it is not surprising that although the burials at Wharram range from the 10th to the 13th centuries there are no examples of this rite. Seven of the Vestry burials had traces of charcoal on the bones, but these may have been elements already in the soil. Burial V56 is not a charcoal burial but seems likely to derive from a charred coffin lid (see above).

Gilchrist and Sloane (2005) have identified a later burial practice where a layer of ash is placed under the body in coffined burials. There is no conclusive evidence of this practice at Wharram.

Shroud pins

Elsewhere, the presence of shroud pins indicates earth burial, with shroud but no coffin. No such pins have been identified at Wharram Percy, although it is possible that some of the pins found on the Churchyard sites were used for this purpose (pp 306-7; Fig. 144). The absence of shroud pins is unlikely to be significant, given that the body might often have been sewn into the shroud.

Part Five

The Pottery

by P. Didsbury and A.M. Slowikowski

16 Introduction and Methodology

The pre-Roman and Roman pottery assemblage from Sites 26, 41, 52 and 80 was recorded and analysed according to the methods established for the North Manor sites (Didsbury 2004, 139-83), and the post-Roman to those for the South Manor sites (Slowikowski 2000, 60). The pottery record was input onto a series of Access databases and incorporated into the master database for Wharram (Slowikowski 2004, 139). In the following chapters the pottery from each site is discussed separately. Post-medieval pottery has been recorded but is not discussed further.

The pottery from the excavations in and around the church buildings was recorded for *Wharram III*. The Roman assemblage was mainly published in fiche; problems relating to this and other previously recorded groups have already been discussed in *Wharram IX* (Didsbury 2004, 140-43). The report on the medieval pottery concentrated mainly on its function and purpose within the graveyard.

The disturbed nature of the ground within the churchyard has, unfortunately, limited the usefulness of the pottery in establishing a chronological sequence for activity in this part of the village.

17 The Prehistoric, Iron Age and Roman Pottery

by P. Didsbury

Methodology

Material was quantified by the three measures of sherd count, sherd weight and rim EVEs, according to fabric type within archaeological context. The resulting data, with detailed supplementary observations, were entered onto an Access database, which now forms part of the Site Archive.

The Iron Age and Roman Pottery from Site 26

Introduction

A total of 629 sherds of Iron Age and Roman pottery, weighing 6277 grams, and having an average sherd weight (hereafter ASW) of 9.98 grams, was recovered from Site 26. The assemblage had a rim EVEs value of 2.67. Distribution of the material by period is presented in Table 128.

The material is interpreted as being broadly contemporary with the features from which it derives in

Table 128. Distribution of Iron Age and Roman material by period.

Period	% sherds (n = 679)	% weight (n = 6277 g)	ASW (9.2 g)
1	48.2	64.7	12.4
2	1.6	0.9	4.9
3	28.6	14.0	4.5
4	17.8	17.9	9.3
5	0.4	0.3	6.0
6	0.3	0.1	3.5
7	0.6	0.4	5.8
US/uncertain	2.5	1.8	6.6
Totals	100.0	100.1	

Period 1, and as residual thereafter. This appears to be supported by the data in Table 128, which show the largest proportion of the site assemblage, with the highest ASW, occurring in Period 1. It should be noted that even in Period 1 the ASW value is not high, and does not suggest primary deposition. An almost equal proportion of the site assemblage comes from Periods 3 and 4 combined, when ground disturbance attendant upon interments and other works in the burial ground was probably responsible for releasing further pottery into the archaeological record. The small amounts of material from the latest periods are both negligible and to be expected.

The pottery was examined chiefly in the interests of dating and interpreting the Period 1 activity, and of relating it to the similar assemblages from the North Manor (Didsbury 2004). The site assemblage as a whole also has some limited potential for indicating the overall date-range of Iron Age and Roman activity in this part of the village site.

Fabric nomenclature

This report employs the Wharram Iron Age and Roman fabric series, as formulated in *Wharram IX* (Didsbury 2004, 143-6). Since detailed descriptions are provided in that volume, it will be sufficient here briefly to indicate the fabrics which occur in the Site 26 assemblage (Table 129). New additions to the pre-existing fabric series are indicated by emboldened text and described in greater detail. The distribution of fabrics within the site assemblage is presented in Table 130.

Table 129. Site 26: Iron Age and Roman fabrics present in the site assemblage.

Fabric code	Remarks
CG	Hand-made calcareously tempered wares of indeterminate Iron Age or Roman date
CG4	Hand-made calcareously tempered wares of Iron Age or early Roman date (to c. the 2nd century AD)
RC8	Oxford Red Colour-Coated Ware, as described in the literature (Young 1977, 123)
RG1	Crambeck greyware
RG2	Fine sand-tempered wheel-thrown greywares, not attributable to production centres but probably predominantly of East Yorkshire origin.
RG3	Reduced greywares, tempered with coarse sand and wholly or partially wheel-thrown. The fabrics often include small amounts of chalk. The commonest vessel in this class of fabric on the North Manor was the Huntcliff-type jar, though the fabric type probably has a much wider date range.
RO	Ungrouped wheel-thrown oxidised wares.
RO9	A polished, self-slipped, redware. It has a fairly compact red body, with well-finished brownish red surfaces. There are common dark-coloured and red inclusions c. 0.25mm, and some quartz sand and mica. The ware is represented by only two sherds, both from Period 1, Phase 4, context 255. (No. 17)
RS	Samian.
RW	Ungrouped Roman white wares.
ST3	A hard-fired, medium coarse sandy fabric with a slightly gritty surface texture, used for hand-built jars of Late Iron Age to early Roman date.
ST7	A fine, fully reduced fabric used for hand-built jars of Late Iron Age to early Roman date. It contains some fine sand but is essentially a 'clean' (untempered) fabric.
ST8	A stone-tempered fabric used for hand-built jars of Late Iron Age to early Roman date. For a full fabric description, see No. 2 (below).

Table 130. Fabric distribution within the site assemblage

Fabric	% sherds (n = 679)	% weight (n = 6277)	% rim EVEs (n = 2.67)
CG	0.7	0.2	
CG4	89.1	88.5	76.4
RC8	0.1	0.8	
RG1	1.3	1.4	2.2
RG2	5.2	3.8	9.4
RG3	0.7	2.0	3.7
RO	0.3	0.2	
RO9	0.3	0.2	
RS	0.7	0.3	
RW	0.1	0.04	
ST3	0.1	0.3	
ST7	0.1	0.1	
ST8	0.7	2.1	
Unattributed	0.3	0.1	8.2
Totals	99.7	100.0	99.9

Chronology

As Table 130 shows, the majority of the site assemblage (90- 91% according to measure of quantification) consists of sherds from hand-made vessels in coarse fabrics, mainly calcareously tempered. It will be suggested below that this material belongs to the closing stages of the regional Iron Age, with some material perhaps dating to, as late as the 2nd century AD. Before proceeding to a more detailed discussion of this material, it will be convenient to consider the overall chronology of the Roman wheel-thrown material and the samian.

The Roman material amounted to 60 sherds, weighing 546 grams (ASW 9.1 grams), which represents c. 9% of the Iron Age and Roman site assemblage. The majority of this material (c. 72% - 78%, according to measure of quantification) was found in post-Roman Periods 2-4 and 7. The significance of Roman material from Period 1 is discussed further below.

The earliest chronologically diagnostic material consists of sherds from three South Gaulish samian vessels of 1st-century date, one of them belonging to the Neronian/early Flavian period, and the others to the period c. AD 75-100 (Nos 26, 28 and 32). Unfortunately, all these were residual in Periods 4 or 7. A further vessel comes from Period 1 and is Hadrianic or Antonine (No. 8). The evidence from the South and North Manors (Didsbury 2000, 59; Dickinson and Hartley 2004), and from the North-west Enclosure sites (Evans 2004, 320) suggests that very little samian was received at Wharram Percy until the Hadrianic to early Antonine period. A tiny amount of definite 1st-century material, including a sherd from La Graufesenque, did, however, occur on the South Manor (Didsbury 2000). Three of the Site 26 vessels thus provide valuable additional evidence for the early reception of samian at Wharram. It may be that some of this material reflects the proximity of the fort at Malton. The Neronian/early Flavian vessel (No. 32) belongs to the invasion period itself, and may hint at a degree of earlier contact between Wharram and the Roman army.

There is little other closely datable material among the Roman wares before the later 3rd and 4th centuries, though 2nd-century activity is probably represented by a sherd from a greyware carinated jar (No. 20). Fabric and form considerations suggest a 3rd-century Norton origin for some of the R2 greywares (Nos 21 and 30), but the clearest chronological indicator is the Crambeck greyware (No. 10). This was available in the region from *c*. AD 270/280 (Evans 1989, 79), although it may have taken a few years to move out of its home production area. A late red colour-coated ware, here identified as a probable Oxford product (No. 7), is of a type which was produced from *c*. AD 240-400, though it is perhaps most likely to have been acquired during the latest period of Oxford's market expansion in the later 4th century. There is no unequivocal evidence for later 4th-century material in the site assemblage, though a small number of body sherds of fabric RG3, which was commonly employed for Huntcliff-type jars, was present. It may be noted that Huntcliff jars were present in the Site 41 assemblage, so that their absence here is probably not chronologically significant.

The Period 1 assemblages

Period 1 contexts contained 327 sherds of Iron Age and Roman pottery, with an ASW of 12.4 grams. The period assemblage thus constitutes the majority of material from the site (Table 128). The fabric profile for the period assemblage is shown in Table 131. No material was present in Phase 1. Material from Phases 2-4 is discussed below. Intrusive medieval sherds are listed in Chapter 18, Table 135.

Table 131. Period 1 fabric distribution.

Fabric	% sherds (n = 327)	% weight (n = 4060)	% rim EVEs (n = 1.55)
CG4	89.3	88.3	81.9
RC8	0.3	1.2	
RG1	0.9	1.0	3.9
RG2	5.2	3.0	
RG3	1.2	2.9	
RO9	0.6	0.3	
RS	0.6	0.04	
ST7	0.3	0.1	
ST8	1.5	3.2	14.2
Totals	99.9	100.0	100.0

Period 1, Phase 2

Iron Age and Roman material from this phase amounted to 121 sherds. The great majority (117 sherds) was

recovered from the group of Period 1, Phase 2 post-holes (see Fig. 30). The remainder came from associated layer 700, and from post-hole 732.

Linear cuts 618

The largest single assemblage from the Period 1, Phase 2 post-holes (Fig. 30) was that from fill 619 of opposed linear cuts 618A and 618B. This consisted of 101 sherds of CG4, with an ASW of 14.8 grams, and five sherds of ST8, ASW 25.8 grams. A further two fragments of post-Roman pottery, weighing 2 grams, (Ch. 18, Table 135) are small enough to be regarded as intrusive or the result of contamination during excavation. An estimated six vessels are represented by rim sherds (Nos 1-6). Published parallels for these vessels are cited from a number of Late Iron Age and early Roman assemblages in the region, namely: Levisham Moor Enclosure 'B'; Flixton; Bursea House, Holme upon Spalding Moor; Hawling Road, Market Weighton; the ditches of the so-called 'early fortlet' at Langton Villa; and Rudston Villa. The cited parallels suggest that a date in the late 1st or early 2nd century AD might be the most appropriate for a number of these vessels, particularly Nos 2, 3 and 6. It may be noted that the 'fortlet' ditch at Langton, which provides several useful parallels with vessels in the Site 26 assemblage, also contained a mortarium for which a date *c*. AD 80 to 100/110 has been proposed (Hartley, quoted in Rigby 1980, 48). Approximately 17% of the assemblage (by sherd count) shows traces of carbonised exterior deposits and/or internal residues, suggesting that the material has seen 'normal' domestic use.

There is a possible cross-contextual join with Period 1, Phase 3 deposit 617, discussed below. This includes a distinctive rim sherd which almost certainly belongs to vessel No. 1. Unfortunately, and alone among the material from 617, this sherd is not marked with its context number, so the connection cannot be regarded as certain. Sherds which might belong to vessel No. 6 occur in post-Roman contexts of Periods 3 and 4.

There are some problems in addressing the taphonomy of deposition into this feature. Firstly, it is unclear from the archive whether the material derives from both sections of cut, or only from the southernmost, *i.e.* 618B. Secondly, although only a single fill is accorded to these shallow features (0.19m-0.33m), the archive report refers to vertical colour variations which are sufficiently marked to be taken as indicating 'gradual accumulation' of the deposit, resulting from 'gradual and/or regular clearance'. There are, however, fairly cogent reasons for suggesting that the ceramic material may result from a single deliberate act of deposition. Although the overall ASW value for the assemblage is fairly low, at 15.3 grams, it includes several large sherds, with weights up to 200 grams and maximum dimensions up to 130mm. It has already been suggested that the whole assemblage derives from a limited number of vessels. The material is also markedly unweathered. These facts do not suggest primary rubbish disposal into this feature, but they would be consistent with a coherent portion of an originating assemblage having entered the fill as a single event, before too much dispersal and further breakage had taken place. It is possible, of course, that a period of gradual infilling of this shallow feature culminated in deliberate closure of the feature with material containing potsherds, but it is not possible to demonstrate this. It also seems feasible that the colour variations noted above could have developed post-depositionally *in situ*. Whatever the preferred interpretation, it seems likely that other parts of the originating ceramic assemblage survived elsewhere on the site to be disturbed or redeposited in the post-Roman period.

Post-hole group (Fig. 30): other features
Most of the other cut features associated with this group were aceramic, but small amounts of material were recovered from shallow circular cut 620, from oval cut 730, and from post-holes 615 and 754. All these features, with the exception of post-hole 615, contained only sherds of CG4. These comprised four sherds with an ASW of 5.5 grams in the case of 620, and single sherds with ASWs of 4.0 grams and 11.0 grams respectively in the case of 754 and 730. The only formally diagnostic sherd is a flat-topped jar rim fragment from 620, identical to some of those from cut 618.

The small assemblage from post-hole 615 is markedly different, since three of its four constituent sherds are of Roman date. These consist of two joining flakes of Hadrianic or Antonine samian (2 grams; No. 8), a large sherd from a later 3rd or 4th-century Oxford Red Colour-coated hemispherical flanged bowl (47 grams; No. 7), and a single body sherd of CG4 (7 grams).

It is in the nature of post-holes and similar cut features that they can easily come to incorporate small residual sherds, and the material from three of these features is therefore of limited evidential value. It is undoubtedly of similar date to that from cut 618, but essentially does no more than provide a Late Iron Age or early Roman *terminus post quem* for the features. Although there is a general uniformity in the Period 1 ceramic assemblage, the material from post-hole 615 stands out as anomalous, and compounds, rather than resolves, some of the difficulties which are faced when attempting to organise the features of this phase into a coherent structure. In the case of this post-hole, the samian by itself indicates a *terminus post quem* in the 2nd century AD - perhaps, but not necessarily, early in the century. It has already been suggested above that the colour-coated vessel is likely to be of late 4th-century date. Even if incorrectly identified as an Oxford product, it is certainly best regarded as a late variety of redware post-dating the end of samian importation in the mid-3rd century. However this may be, it does not seem possible simply to explain away the largest and latest sherd in the assemblage as intrusive. If the post-hole is truly a late feature, then it is worth noting the possibility that both the CG4 and the samian might be broadly contemporary, as well as residual within it, perhaps dating from a period in the earlier 2nd century when samian had begun to arrive at Wharram but the

majority of vessels were still being produced in the regional Iron Age tradition.

A number of other features in this phase produced small amounts of pottery, though the material is of no value in furthering our understanding of the post-hole group (Fig. 30). Layer 700, which sealed some of the aceramic cut features noted above, and which has been interpreted as an occupation surface associated with the first use of the post-holes, yielded a single small body sherd (4 grams) of CG4. Part of 700 was in turn sealed by layer 548, into which rectangular post-hole 732 was cut. The fill of this post-hole contained a further small body sherd of CG4 (7 grams).

Period 1, Phase 3
Pottery was recovered from five deposits.

Layer 270, interpreted as 'redeposited natural', contained a single sherd from a CG4 jar with flat-topped rim (No. 9).

Loam deposit 751 contained two small body sherds (ASW 3.0 grams) of Roman greyware (RG2).

Deposit 594 contained a larger, and chronologically very mixed, assemblage. Eighteen sherds of post-Roman pottery (ASW 98 grams) were included (Ch. 18, Table 135). The remainder comprised 23 sherds of CG4 (ASW 6.6 grams) and 14 sherds of Roman greyware (RG1-3, ASW 14.1 grams). The handmade material is indistinguishable from that in the rest of the Period 1 assemblage. The only chronologically diagnostic greyware is a sherd from a Type 1 Crambeck straight-sided flanged bowl, which post-dates *c*. AD 270/280 (No. 10). It has been suggested that this deposit partook more of the nature of a deliberate surface than the others in this phase. The ceramic data confirm that the deposit was likely to have been 'open' for a considerable length of time.

Deposit 617 contained a fairly large assemblage, consisting of 54 sherds (ASW 8.0 grams) of CG4 and a single body sherd of Crambeck greyware (4.0 grams). It should be noted that the greyware, although marked '617', was found among material from context 611, so that some doubt attaches to its correct provenance. The CG4 material (Nos 11-13) is very similar to that from cut 618, and the presence of a possible inter-contextual join has already been noted. The deposit lies over fill 619 of cut 618 and is described as being of very similar nature. It is interpreted as the spreading of part of the same deposit, in conjunction with the clearance phase of the associated structures. This further reinforces the interpretation of 619 offered above, *i.e.* that it represents a deliberate infilling act at closure.

Finally, clay deposit 545, interpreted as either make-up or hill-wash, produced two body sherds of CG4 (20 grams).

Period 1, Phase 4
A large assemblage of pottery was recovered from the fill(s) of ditch 255. It should be noted that pottery was recorded under the cut number. After removal of 23

sherds of post-Roman material (Ch. 18, Table 135) the assemblage amounted to 111 sherds, weighing 1420 grams. The majority was of Late Iron Age to early Roman date (Nos 14-16), and comprised 101 sherds of CG4 (ASW 14.1 grams) and a single sherd of ST7 (6 grams). There was also a small Roman component consisting of seven sherds of RG2 greywares (ASW 10.1 grams) and two sherds of RO9 (No. 17; ASW 5.5 grams). The Roman component is not closely datable. The ditch may have been deliberately backfilled, but the ceramic evidence could be interpreted in a wide variety of ways and does not easily suggest a date for this event.

Other assemblages

Residual material from Periods 2-7 was examined in the interests of site chronology (see above) and of establishing a fully representative illustrated corpus of the hand-made vessels (Nos 18-19, 22-25, 27, 29 and 31). Full details are contained in the archive database.

Conclusions

Some difficulties attach to the interpretation of the Period 1 assemblages, as noted above. Despite these, it is probably reasonable to regard most of them as deriving from a closely contemporary phase of activity connected with the Period 1, Phase 2 post-hole group. The principal Phase 1 assemblage, that from cut 618, seems to belong to the dismantling phase of this structure, while the pottery from most of the other cut features was presumably incorporated during construction. The assemblage from post-hole 615 cannot be satisfactorily explained.

The hand-made pottery tends to suggest a Late Iron Age to early Roman date, perhaps most specifically the later 1st century to early 2nd century AD. It thus appears to be broadly contemporary with the large Iron Age assemblages from the North Manor (Didsbury 2004).

Catalogue (Fig. 131)

Samian identifications in the following catalogue are by Brenda Dickinson, whose help is gratefully acknowledged. There are numerous parallels in the North Manor assemblages (Didsbury 2004) for jars with upright or slightly everted, flat-topped or slightly bevelled rims, such as Nos 2, 6, 11, 12 etc., below. These are not cited individually.

1* Jar. CG4. Hard. Dark grey throughout, with light brown patches on the interior. Abundant relatively small calcite in the 1-3mm range. Patchy carbonised deposits on exterior and interior surfaces. The form is essentially a barrel jar with complex thickened rim. It is difficult to cite a close parallel, though Challis and Harding 1975, fig. 50, no. 9 (from Levisham Moor Enclosure B) and Rigby 1980, fig. 40, no. 140 (from Rudston Villa) have elements in common. There is a *possible* cross-contextual join with deposit 617 (see discussion, above). *Fill of linear cuts 618A and B; 26/619; Period 1, Phase 2*

2* Jar. ST8. Hard. Dark grey core with red margins and patchy light red to dark grey surfaces. Abundant, sub-rounded to angular, non-soluble grits comprising quartz, polymineralic fragments including dark crystals, fine-grained sandstones and other material. Grits are

mainly < 2mm. Jars with a wide variety of everted to upright flat-topped rims are common in eastern Yorkshire in the later Iron Age (Challis and Harding 1975, 97). The expansion of the inner edge of the rim is relatively unusual, but seems to occur, in a less marked fashion, on a vessel from Bursea House, probably dating to the 1st century AD (Creighton 1999, illus. 5.39, no. 8.4). *Fill of linear cuts 618A and B; 26/619; Period 1, Phase 2*

3* Jar. CG4. Hard. Very dark grey core, light red margins and brownish grey surfaces. Abundant calcite and chalk, mainly c. 1-2mm. Cf. Challis and Harding 1975, fig. 38, no. 9 (from Flixton), and Evans with Creighton 1999, illus. 7.18, fabric/form type G32-J02 and cited parallels (from Hawling Road, Market Weighton). The latter vessel is from a Flavian context. *Fill of linear cuts 618A and B; 26/619; Period 1, Phase 2*

4* Jar. CG4. Hard. Grey core with light red interior margin and darker grey surfaces. Abundant calcite to c. 5mm, most 1-3mm. Patchy carbonised deposits on the exterior and on top of the rim. Cf. Corder and Kirk 1932, fig. 7, no. 32 (from Langton Villa). *Fill of linear cuts 618A and B; 26/619; Period 1, Phase 2*

5* Jar. CG4. Hard. Fabric, colouration and form similar to No. 4, above, but with patchy light brown interior surface and a more pronounced shoulder. *Fill of linear cuts 618A and B; 26/619; Period 1, Phase 2*

6 Jar. CG4. Hard. Dark grey, with light greyish brown interior surface. Abundant calcite to c. 5mm. Light carbonised deposits on the exterior and on top of the rim. Cf. Rigby 1980, fig. 32, no. 53 (from Rudston Villa). Non-joining sherds from the same vessel possibly occur in contexts 279, 336 and 627. Vessel not available for illustration at time of publication. *Fill of linear cuts 618A and B; 26/619; Period 1, Phase 2*

7* Hemispherical flanged bowl. RC8. Hard. Grey core, orange margins and rich glossy red colour-coat. Sparse small black and red inclusions, occasional chalk, and much mica. Post-depositional mortar (?) accretions. Cf. Oxford type 51 (Young 1977, fig. 59). *Fill of post-hole 615; 26/616; Period 1, Phase 2*

8 RS. Two joining body sherds (weight 2 grams) from a dish or bowl. Heavily scratched. Hadrianic or Antonine. Not South Gaulish. *Fill of post-hole 615; 26/616; Period 1, Phase 2*

9* Jar. CG4. Flat-topped rim fragment, diameter uncertain. Hard. Very dark grey with brown on top of the rim, and reddish brown on the interior below a neat 10mm deep dark grey band which may indicate use of a lid. Moderate fine calcite, up to 3mm but most < 1mm. *Deposit; 26/270; Period 1, Phase 3*

10* Straight-sided flanged bowl (Corder 1937, type 1). RG1. Burned post-fracture. *Deposit; 26/ 594; Period 1, Phase 3*

11* Jar. CG4. Hard. Dark grey with light red inner margin and variable very dark grey, grey and light brown surfaces. Moderate chalk and calcite c. 1-3mm. Cf. no. 6, above. *Deposit; 26/617; Period 1, Phase 3*

12* Jar. CG4. Hard. Dark grey, with light red interior margin and light brown interior. Moderate calcite, most c. 1-4mm. Carbonised deposits on exterior. *Deposit; 26/617; Period 1, Phase 3*

13* Jar. CG4. Hard. Very dark grey with light brown exterior and patchy dark grey and light brown interior. Sparse to moderate fine calcite c. 0.5-2mm. Thin carbonised deposits on interior. Cf. Challis and Harding 1975, fig. 49, no. 3 (from Levisham Moor Enclosure A). *Deposit; 26/617; Period 1, Phase 3*

14* Jar. CG4. Hard. Abundant calcite, mainly c. 2-4mm, but up to c. 6mm. Fully reduced throughout, with light brown patches on rim bevel. Slight carbonised deposits on interior and exterior. Cf. Didsbury 2004, fig. 104, no. 89 (from Wharram Percy North Manor); Corder and Kirk 1932, fig. 7, no. 22 (from Langton Villa);

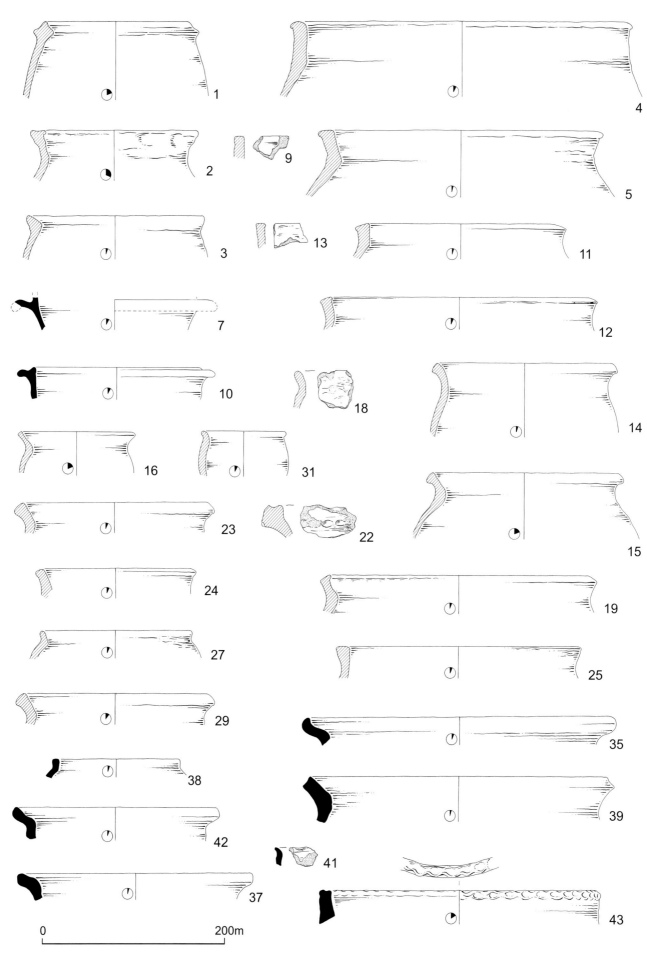

Fig. 131. Iron Age and Roman pottery: Site 26 Nos 1-5, 7, 9-16, 18-19, 22-5, 27, 29 and 31; Site 41 Nos 35, 37-9 and 41-3. Scale 1:4 (C. Marshall)

Challis and Harding 1975, fig. 48, no. 8 (from Normanby); and Evans with Creighton 1999, illus. 7.17, fabric/form type G25-J02, and cited parallels (from Hawling Road, Market Weighton). *Ditch cut/fill; 26/255; Period 1, Phase 4*

15* Jar. CG4. Hard. Grey core with patchy grey and pinkish-brown surfaces. Abundant fine calcite and chalk up to *c.* 3mm. Cf. Rigby 1980, fig. 30, no. 33 and fig. 37, no. 134 (from Rudston Villa), and Challis and Harding 1975, fig. 40, no. 5 (from Faxfleet 'A'). All the vessels cited have less pronounced necks than the example under discussion. *Ditch cut/fill; 26/255; Period 1, Phase 4*

16* Jar. CG4. Hard. Abundant fine calcite with common examples in the *c.* 2-4mm range. Fully reduced throughout, with brownish patches on parts of both surfaces. Extensive thin carbonised deposits, especially on the interior. Cf. Corder and Kirk 1932, fig. 7, no. 23 (a smaller example, from Langton Villa); and numerous other examples from East Yorkshire and north-east England, cf. Challis and Harding 1975, fig. 34, no. 2 (from Garton Slack); fig. 46, nos 1, 4 (from Pale End); and fig. 47, no.13 (from Catcote). *Ditch cut/fill; 26/255; Period 1, Phase 4*

17 RO9. Fragment of turned base, and flake from simple upright rim with two external grooves. *Ditch cut/fill; 26/255; Period 1, Phase 4*

18* Jar. ST3. Hard. Very dark brownish-grey with pale brown to light brown surfaces. Abundant rounded to angular fine quartz sand, most < 1mm but with occasional larger fragments. The fabric is well within the range of Roman sand-tempered wheel-thrown greywares. The vessel bears some resemblance to Challis and Harding 1975, fig. 34, no. 1 (from Garton Slack) and fig. 50, no. 4 (from Levisham Moor Enclosure B), as well as to Didsbury 2004, fig. 103, no. 70 (from Wharram Percy North Manor). *Deposit; 26/598; Period 2, Phase 2*

19* Jar. CG4. Hard. Dark grey throughout. Moderate calcite 1-2mm. Patchy carbonised deposits on exterior. Cf. Rigby 1980, fig. 32, no. 54 (from Rudston Villa), which affords a very close parallel. The lid-seated rim was considered by Rigby to show the influence of Flavian or later wheel-thrown prototypes. A similar rim appears on a larger vessel at Wharram Percy North Manor (Didsbury 2004, fig. 105, no. 113). *Fill of Burial G715; 26/714; Period 3, Phase 1*

20 RG2. Worn rim sherd, probably from a 2nd-century carinated jar. *Fill of Burial G516; 26/515; Period 3, Phase 3*

21 Jar handle. RG2. The fabric appears to be within the Norton range. The loop handle is applied to the wall of the pot, and is deeply grooved on its outer edge, thus bearing direct comparison with a published vessel from the Norton kilns (Hayes and Whitley 1950, fig. 10, type 4b). *Fill of post-hole 572; 26/ 573; Period 3, Phase 3*

22* Jar. CG4. Hard. Very dark grey with pinkish-buff surfaces. Moderate large calcite in the 3-5mm range. The sherd is rather abraded but it is possible that the lower outer edge of the rim had 'thumbnail' decoration. The heavily thickened square-sectioned rim with hollowed upper face is similar to those on two jars from South Cave, cf. Challis and Harding 1975, fig. 36, nos 1 and 3. The second of these cited examples also bears plastic decoration. *Surface; 26/539; Period 3, Phase 4*

23* Jar. CG4. Hard. Fully reduced core with variable light brownish-grey surfaces. Moderate large calcite, 2-5mm. Patchy thin carbonised deposits on both surfaces. Cf. no. 29, below, and cited parallels. *Fill of Burial G597; 26/596; Period 4, Phase 1*

24* Jar. CG4. Fairly hard. Moderate calcite to *c.* 3mm. Mid-grey core with light red surfaces. Perhaps cf. Challis and Harding 1975, fig. 50, no. 1 (from Levisham Moor Enclosure B). *Rubble surface; 26/289; Period 4, Phase 2*

25* Jar. CG4. Hard. Dark grey, with reddish-brown patches on all surfaces. Light carbonised deposits on exterior. Abundant very fine calcite with common larger fragments *c.* 1-5 mm. *Fill of Burial G367; 26/365; Period 4, Phase 3*

26 RS. Body sherd with ovolo (weight 3 grams). Form 30 or 37. First-century, probably *c.* AD 75-100. *Grave cut/fill of Burial G253; 26/320, Period 4, Phase 3*

27* Jar. CG4. Hard. Fully reduced throughout. Moderate ill-sorted calcite, the largest fragments *c.*4mm. Irregular but well-smoothed, almost glossy surfaces. Cf. Rigby 1980, fig. 40, no. 142 (from Rudston Villa); Challis and Harding 1975, fig. 52, no. 3 (from Costa Beck); and perhaps Challis and Harding 1975, fig. 48, no. 10 (from Normanby). *Deposit; 26/69; Period 4, Phase 4*

28 RS. Body sherd with ovolo (weight 9 grams). From a South Gaulish bowl, possibly form 37. There are traces of what may be a repair hole. The ovolo is blurred, possibly from having stuck in the mould, but is apparently intended to be trident-tongued. *c.* AD 75-100. *Deposit; 26/272; Period 4, Phase 4*

29* Jar. CG4. Hard. Dark grey core with patchy light red, brown and dark grey surfaces. Moderate calcite up to *c.* 8mm, much in the 3-5mm range. Similar rims occur at Langton Villa (Corder and Kirk 1932, fig. 7, no. 31), Rudston Villa (Rigby 1980, fig. 30, no. 33), and are particularly well represented at Costa Beck (Challis and Harding 1975, fig. 51, no. 7; fig. 52, nos 5, 7). *Deposit; 26/271; Period 4, Phase 6*

30 Jar. RG2. Fragment of everted rim in hard compact greyware with dark highly burnished surfaces. Perhaps cf. Norton Type 4a (Hayes and Whitley 1950, fig. 10). *Deposit; 26/271; Period 4, Phase 6*

31* Jar. CG4. Hard. Moderate calcite and chalk *c.* 1-3mm. Very dark grey core and interior, with light reddish-brown patches on the exterior surface and the inside of the rim. There is a (?) post-depositional light-coloured fine mortar or plaster deposit on part of the interior. Cf. Didsbury 2004, fig. 101, no. 4, fig. 102, no. 36 and fig. 104, no. 83 (from Wharram Percy North Manor); Challis and Harding 1975, fig. 31, no. 9 (from Eastburn); fig. 46, no. 10 (from Great Ayton Moor). *Deposit; 26/271; Period 4, Phase 6*

32 RS. Body sherd (weight 2 grams). Form 18. South Gaulish. Neronian or early Flavian. *Below turf/humus; 26/36; Period 7, Phase 5*

The prehistoric and Roman pottery from Site 41

Introduction

A total of 392 sherds of prehistoric, Iron Age and Roman pottery, weighing 2262 grams, and having an ASW of 5.77 grams, was recovered from Site 41. The assemblage had a rim EVEs value of 0.50. Distribution of the material by period is presented in Table 132.

Table 132. Distribution of prehistoric and Roman material by period.

Period	% sherds (n = 392)	% weight (n = 2262 g)	ASW (5.8 g)
1	7.4	1.2	1.0
2	84.9	90.8	6.2
3	4.3	3.3	4.4
4	1.3	0.7	3.2
5	1.0	1.9	3.0
US/uncertain	1.0	2.1	10.5
Totals	99.9	100.0	

Fabric nomenclature

Fabric nomenclature is the same as that used for Site 26, with the addition of the fabric code 'BA', used to denote all Bronze Age material.

Fabric distribution is presented in Table 133, below.

Table 133. Fabric distribution within the site assemblage

Fabric	% sherds (n = 392)	% weight (n = 2262)	% rim EVEs (n = 0.50)
BA	7.4	1.2	
CG1	0.3	1.6	30.0
CG4	86.5	94.4	70.0
RG1	0.5	0.2	
RG2	3.6	1.8	
RO	0.3	0.1	
RS	0.5	0.1	
ST7	0.3	0.1	
ST8	0.3	0.3	
Unattributed	0.5	0.2	
Totals	100.2	100.0	100.0

Chronology

The small amount of pottery from Period 1 is all apparently of prehistoric date (see below). The Period 2, Phase 1 to Period 2, Phase 4 assemblages are composed, with the exception of a single sherd, of Late Iron Age and Romano-British material, though this may all be residual (see below). The Iron Age material is closely comparable with that from Site 26.

The Period 1 assemblages

Small quantities of hand-made pottery, amounting to 29 sherds weighing 28 grams, were recovered from Period 1, Phase 4 layers 35 and 36, and Period 1, Phase 1 to Period 1, Phase 5 layer 550. The majority (27 fragments, 5 grams) came from 35 and 36 and comprises miniscule crumbs of oxidised ceramic, several containing fine calcareous inclusions. Two larger sherds (Nos 33 and 34) came from 35 and 550. T. G. Manby kindly examined all this material and concluded that its general characteristics would be consistent with a Middle to Late Bronze Age date.

The Period 2 assemblages

The single most important fact about the Period 2 assemblages is that, in addition to the Iron Age and Roman material tabulated and discussed below, they contain a single sherd of 12th to 14th-century pottery, viz. a rim sherd of medieval fabric B12 (Staxton Ware). It is a jar rim sherd, weighing 41 grams, and comes from Period 2, Phase 1, context 31. Unless the presence of this sherd can be accounted for by intrusion or contamination during excavation, then it would seem that much of the Iron Age and Roman assemblages (certainly those from

Period 2, Phase 2 to Period 2, Phase 4, and possibly much of that from Period 2, Phase 1) must be redeposited. Given the sherd's position, and the marked contrast between its own weight and the average sherd weight of the earlier material (Table 132), intrusion may perhaps seem unlikely.

It will be seen (Table 134) that the great majority of the Period 2 Iron Age/Roman assemblage came from Period 2, Phase 1. It is composed almost entirely of Iron Age sherds in fabric CG4 (Nos 35 and 37-43) and occurred in a number of features: ditches 27 and 535; ditch-fills 529 and 536; gully 534; layers 523 and 528; pit 540; post-holes 30 and 543; and from contexts 31, 551 and 553. Roman material occurred only in three contexts. There was a single small fragment of *possible* wheel-thrown Roman greyware from ditch 27, a definite example from ditch-fill 529, and a tiny chip of samian from layer 523 (No. 36). The samian is of Hadrianic-Antonine date, and the light-grey fabric of the greyware from 529 would be acceptable in a regional Antonine assemblage. None of the Roman material weighs more than 3 grams.

The composition of the Period 2, Phase 2 assemblage was also dominated by CG4, with a small number of possible or definite Roman sherds occurring in two contexts. Iron Age material (No. 44) was present in layer 26, post-hole 520, surface 515 and context 516/527, described as 'cut feature' and 'ditch?' respectively. Roman material came from two of these features, i.e. 26 and 515. The first of these had minute single fragments of possible Roman oxidised ware (RO) and of greyware (RG2). No dating is possible. Surface 515 yielded a further tiny fragment of greyware, possibly Crambeck (RG1) though certainty is impossible.

The small Period 2, Phase 3 assemblage had four pottery-bearing features, viz. layer 508, ditch recuts 510 and 512, and possible pit 514. All of these contained Iron Age material (No. 45), while Roman material occurred in all except 514. The Roman material consisted entirely of tiny fragments of greyware, none of them chronologically diagnostic except for a late 3rd or 4th-century Crambeck greyware from 508.

Finally, Period 2, Phase 4 yielded two body sherds of CG4 from layer 501, and a chronologically undiagnostic sherd of greyware (RG2) from layer 173 (=500).

Table 134. Distribution of Iron Age and Roman material by phase within Period 2.

Period	% of phase by no. (n = 327)	% of phase by wt (n = 2020 grams)
2 Phase 1	81.3	86.8
2 Phase 2	13.1	8.8
2 Phase 3	4.3	3.6
2 Phase 4	0.9	0.5
2 Phase 3/4	0.3	0.2
Totals	99.9	99.9

The Period 3-5 assemblages

Residual Iron Age and Romano-British material, amounting to *c.* 6% of the total site assemblage of this date, comes from these periods. Two vessels (Nos 46 and 47) are catalogued in the interests of publishing a complete samian list for Wharram Percy and of demonstrating the chronological range of the Roman material from Site 41.

Catalogue (Fig. 131)

Samian identifications in the following catalogue are by Brenda Dickinson, and Bronze Age material was examined by T. G. Manby. The help of both is gratefully acknowledged.

33 Form unknown. BA. Lower body/base sherd from a vessel of uncertain basal diameter. 19 grams. Soft to fairly hard red fabric with brownish-grey core/interior margin in the thicker parts of the basal angle. Wall thickness *c.* 9mm. Rather laminated, soapy fabric. Sparse to moderate non-soluble inclusions, generally < *c.* 2mm. The sherd is extremely abraded. *41/35; SF3; Period 1, Phase 4*

34 Form unknown. BA. Body sherd. 4 grams. Wall thickness 8-10mm. Fairly soft, corky fabric. Light brown with dark grey/brown laminae in parts. Sparse to moderate angular calcareous inclusions, probably chalk, <2mm. The outer surface may display traces of a ledge or carination. *41/550; SF 14; Period 1, Phases 1-5*

35* Jar. CG4. Hard mid-grey fabric with darker exterior and reddish-brown interior surfaces. Moderate ill-sorted calcite to *c.* 3mm. Everted rim, dished on the interior. Cf. Challis and Harding 1975, fig. 47, no. 15 (from Catcote), and No. 42, below. *41/523; Period 2, Phase 1*

36 Dish? RS. Body sherd, < 1 gram. Central Gaulish. Hadrianic or Antonine. *41/523; Period 2, Phase 1*

37* Jar. CG4. Hard, very dark grey fabric, with lighter, browner exterior. Moderate ill-sorted calcite to *c.* 5mm. There are neat bands of carbonised residue at both top and bottom of the interior, *c.*15mm and 10mm thick, respectively. The unsooted central band may indicate use of a lid or other closure. Thick, everted rim, with bevelled outer edge. Cf. Didsbury 2004, fig. 102, no. 35 (Wharram North Manor). *41/528; Period 2, Phase 1*

38* Jar. CG4. Fabric as that of No. 37. Short, upright, flat-topped rim. *41/528; Period 2, Phase 1*

39* Jar. CG4. Hard, mid-grey fabric, with light red interior and patchy brown exterior surfaces. Abundant ill-sorted calcite, mainly *c.* 1-3mm, but up to *c.* 6mm. Slightly curved and everted rim, with bevelled edge. Cf. Challis and Harding 1975, fig. 50, no. 1 (Levisham Moor Enclosure B). *Ditch fill; 41/ 529; Period 2, Phase 1*

40 Jar? CG4. Hard, very dark grey fabric with abundant calcite to *c.* 3mm. Fragment of externally thickened rim with flat top. Remains of oblique fingernail slash decoration on the outer edge. *Ditch fill; 41/529; Period 2, Phase 1*

41* Small jar. CG4. Hard, very dark grey fabric with patchy, light brown surfaces. Common fine calcite. Pinched rim on a possibly fairly globular body. Cf. Didsbury 2004, fig. 102, no. 36 and fig. 104, no. 98 (Wharram North Manor) and cited parallels. *Gully; 41/534; Period 2, Phase 1*

42* Jar. CG4. Hard, very dark grey fabric, with light brown interior surface. Moderate calcite to *c.*2mm. Everted rim with dished interior. Cf. No. 35, above. *Ditch fill; 41/536; Period 2, Phase 1*

43* Jar. CG4. Hard, very dark grey fabric, with patchy dark grey, light yellowish-brown and light red surfaces. Abundant ill-sorted calcite to *c.* 4mm. Continuous fingertip decoration along the outer edge of the rim. *Pit, 41/540; Period 2, Phase 1*

44 Form unknown. CG4? Small body sherd (4 grams). Hard grey fabric with very dark grey exterior and light reddish-brown interior. Abundant ill-sorted angular and sub-rounded calcareous temper, perhaps principally limestone, to *c.* 1mm. Remains of at least four thumbnail (?) impressions, in no discernible pattern. *41/26; Period 2, Phase 2*

45 Jar? CG4. Curved everted rim fragment, very worn and of uncertain orientation. Hard, mid grey fabric with greyish-brown surfaces. Common ill-sorted calcite to *c.* 3mm. Perhaps cf. Challis and Harding 1975, fig. 52, no. 6 (from Costa Beck). *41/508; Period 2, Phase 3*

46 Form unknown. RS. Flake, < 1 gram. South Gaulish. First or early 2nd-century. *Topsoil; 41/2; Period 5, Phase 2*

47 Jar. CG1. Rim of Huntcliff jar. *Layer/?ditchfill; 41/102 A and B; Period 5, Phase 2*

18 The Anglo-Saxon and Medieval Pottery
by A.M. Slowikowski

Methodology

The pottery from the Churchyard was recorded and analysed according to the methods used for the pottery from the South Manor (Slowikowski 2000, 57, 60). The pottery from the sites making up this report, Sites 26, 41 and 52, have been discussed separately by site, but the pottery types occurring at all three sites are described together below. Pottery from topsoil was not recorded although the assemblage was examined to extract new or better examples for the type series. The total medieval assemblage for the whole Churchyard was made up of 2313 vessels (12.51 EVEs) comprising 2912 sherds, weighing 22.357kg. The bulk of it was found on Site 26. The sherd count is the unit of quantification used in the discussion and tables, unless otherwise specified. All percentages have been rounded up to two decimal places.

Vessels with more than one sherd from the same context or sherds from different contexts were defined as described in the South Manor pottery methodology (Slowikowski 2000, 60). Sherds and weight were recorded in the relevant context, but as a single vessel can only be recorded once, this was recorded in the context with the largest number of sherds or where it could be shown that the vessel was most likely to have been deposited originally. The other contexts with sherds from the same vessel have a '0' recorded in the vessel field. Tables 135-145, therefore, record some instances where sherds, but not vessels, are noted.

Type descriptions

The pottery was divided into fabric types using the common names published by Le Patourel (1979) and coded following the system used for the South Manor pottery and revised for the assemblage in *Wharram X* (Slowikowski 2005). No new fabric types were identified. Previously published fabric descriptions are not repeated here; they may be found in Slowikowski (2000, 60-98; 2004, 183-191).

The pottery from these sites was recorded and analysed in 1995, before the assemblages from the sites in *Wharram X* and *XII*. Therefore, some types which occurred in quantity on those sites may not have been fully identified in the Churchyard assemblage.

The pottery from the Churchyard has been grouped into broadly similar chronological groupings, in summary:

Ceramic Group 1 - Prehistoric and Roman (for a discussion of this Ceramic Group see Chapter 17)
Ceramic Group 2 - Anglo-Saxon (the presence of eight sherds of Anglo-Saxon pottery was recorded (*Wharram Interim Report* 1979) but the sherds have not been located)
Ceramic Group 3 - 'Anglo-Scandinavian'/Saxo-Norman (2.26% of total assemblage by sherd)
Ceramic Group 4 - Early medieval (58.85% of total assemblage by sherd)
Ceramic Group 5 - High medieval (10.31% of total assemblage by sherd)
Ceramic Group 6 - Late medieval (26.83% of total assemblage by sherd)
Ceramic Group 7 - Late medieval/post-medieval transitional (1.57% of total assemblage by sherd)

Percentages of each fabric type are given in brackets, as a percent of the total site assemblage.

Ceramic Group 3
THET Thetford-type ware (0.03%)
No illustrations
A single sherd was found.

B01 York type A (0.49%)
Fig. 132 (No. 1)
Three jars were recognised, two with external sooting.

1*   Jar. *26/?675; Period 3, Phase 1*

B03 York type D (0.07%)
No illustrations
Undiagnostic body sherds only.

B04 Torksey-type ware (0.56%)
No illustrations
Identifiable forms are jars and bowls.

B05 Stamford-type ware (1.05%)
Fig. 132 (No. 2)
Although jars are the only rim forms present, a handle and a body sherd from two different vessels, both with sparse light yellow glaze, suggest the presence of at least two spouted pitchers or jugs.

2*   Jar. *26/382; Period 3, Phase 4*

B06 Shelly wares (0.07%)
No illustrations
Two sherds were found.

Ceramic Group 4
B07 Pimply ware (7.58%)
No illustrations
Only jars and undiagnostic body sherds were recognised. Four of the jars have been used as cooking pots, resulting in external sooting.

B08 Pimply ware variant (0.31%)
No illustrations
A jar and a jug were recognised, the jug having a simple pulled lip.

B09 Glazed Pimply (0.21%)
No illustrations
All sherds are glazed and are likely to have come from jugs.

B10 Splashed Pimply (0.28%)
No illustrations
Two jugs were recognised, one of which is represented by a handle sherd.

B11 Scarborough Gritty (2.16%)
No illustrations
All recognisable sherds are from jugs. One jug is made up of 40 small and very badly preserved sherds; the glaze is un-fluxed and the vessel has been poorly fired. It may have been sold as a second.

B12 Staxton ware (39.71%)
Figs 132 (No. 4) and 142
Jars, 'peat pots', bowls and curfews were recognised. One sherd was decorated with incised wavy lines. Three sherds, one of them a base, have post-firing holes bored through them, measuring 5mm in diameter. A single body sherd has been reshaped into a disc measuring 45mm in diameter (see p. 298).

3   Disc. *26/65; SF1016; Period 4, Phase 4*
(See Chapter 23, Clay Object No. 9 for description and illustration)

4*   Base sherd with pre-firing hole. *26/3; Period 6, Phase 5*

B13 Glazed Staxton ware (0.14%)
No illustrations
Four body sherds were found, probably all from jugs and having a thin covering of olive green glaze.

B14 Reduced Chalky (0.94%)
No illustrations
Only one jar was recognised; the rest are undiagnostic body sherds.

B16 Beverley 1 (0.03%)
No illustrations
A single sherd from a jug was found.

B18 York Glazed (5.09%)
Fig. 132 (No. 5)
All sherds have a good cover of varying shades of green glaze, often with the addition of copper. Other than the glaze, decoration only survives on one sherd in the form of a red applied pellet, not enough to determine the scheme of decoration.

5*   Jug. *26/247; Period 5, Phase 1. 26/230; Period 6, Phase 2. 26/239; Period 6, Phase 2*

B18U Unglazed whiteware (1.92%)
Fig. 132 (Nos 6-7)
Three jars were recognised. Number 7 is similar in fabric to Tees Valley ware (B34) which will be described more fully in *Wharram XII*.

6*   Jar. *26/336; Period 4, Phase 1*

7*   Jar. *26/453; Period 4, Phase 1*

B27 Splashed glazed orange (0.21%)
No illustrations
Six sherds were recovered, one of which is from a jug.

B28 Splashed glazed chalky (Beverley 1 type) (0.31%)
No illustrations
Nine sherds were found, all from glazed jugs.

Ceramic Group 5
B17 Scarborough (1.67%)
No illustrations
All vessels represented are jugs, largely consisting of single sherds. They are undecorated except for a glaze, which is either yellow-green or, more commonly, dark green.

B19 Gritty (0.45%)
No illustrations
Jugs are the predominant form, but one sherd with an internal orange glaze and external sooting may be from a bowl.

B20 Brandsby (6.39%)
Fig. 132 (Nos 8-12)
Jugs and jars are the predominant forms. The only bowl (No. 10) is comparable to one published by Jennings (1992, 49 no. 104) and dated to the 14th century. The Wharram bowl has a wavy line incised on top of the rim. There is a single sherd from the rim of a urinal (No. 12), not a common form in this fabric.

8*   Jug. *52/5; unphased*

9*   Jug. *52/6; unphased*

10*   Bowl. *41/104; Period 5, Phase 1*

11*   Jug. *26/288; Period 5, Phase 1*

12*   Urinal. *26/3; Period 6, Phase 5*

B21 Hard Sandy (Hard Brandsby) (0.07%)
No illustrations
Two body sherds were found.

B22 Hard orange (0.03%)
No illustrations
Jugs are the only form in this fabric. They are generally plain although there is an example of an applied vertical thumbed strip.

B23 Yorkshire red ware (0.17%)
No illustrations
Undiagnostic body sherds only.

B24 Pinky-buff (0.10%)
No illustrations
Three sherds, one of which could be identified as a jug.

B26 Lightly Gritted (unknown) (0.03%)
No illustrations
A single jug sherd.

B29 Fine buff (unknown) (0.38%)
No illustrations
Where forms could be recognised they are jugs, with pale yellow or green splashed glaze.

B30 Fine micaceous (0.10%)
No illustrations
Three body sherds.

B Unrecognised medieval (0.73%)
Fig. 132 (No. 13)
Nineteen vessels could not be allocated to an existing fabric group. Each is of a different type and largely comprises single small sherds. The most substantial of these vessels is a jar (No. 13), an unglazed whiteware. All have been grouped together under this code but each has its individual description in the Archive.

13*   Jar. *26/598; Period 2, Phase 2. 26/485; Period 3, Phase 2. 26/227; unstratified*

Ceramic Group 6
C01 Hambleton ware (11.86%)
Fig. 132 (Nos 14-16)
Although jugs are the commonest form, jars, cisterns and lobed cups were also identified. The single cistern has an applied frill at the rim; the two lobed cups are small fragments of rim. There is a body sherd with internal glazing and sooting on the exterior which may be from a chafing dish. Vessels are glazed with a thick, but poor quality, dark green glaze, and scars, where vessels have stuck in the kiln, are common on bases and rims. The jar is glazed both internally and externally.

At least eight vessels recorded within this type are reduced to a dark grey internally and should be recorded as C01B late medieval Transitional Reduced ware. This type was defined during the recording of the pottery from

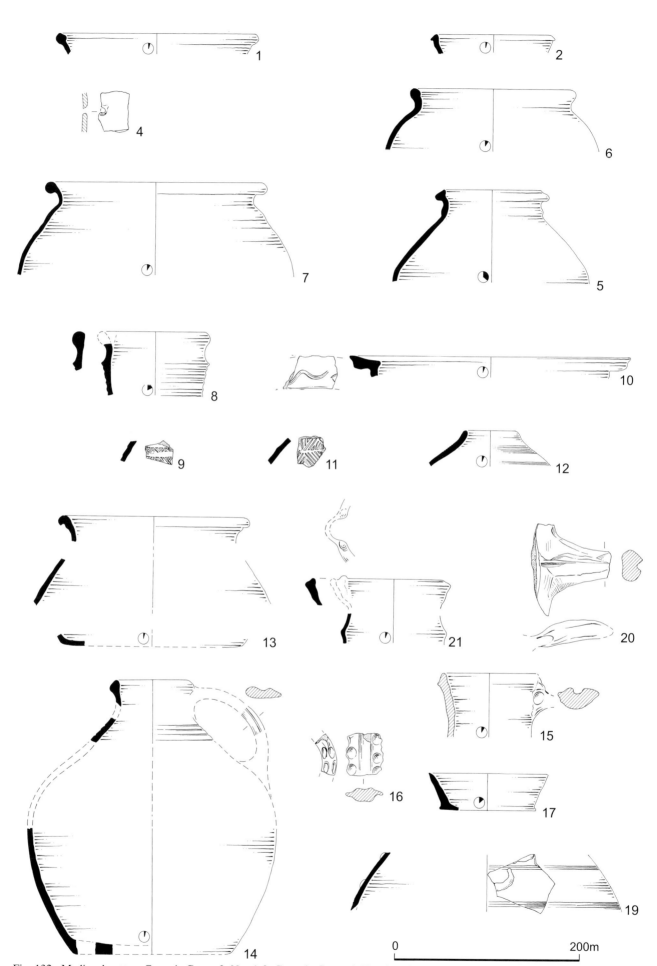

Fig. 132. Medieval pottery Ceramic Group 3, Nos 1-2; Ceramic Group 4, Nos 4-7; Ceramic Group 5, Nos 8-13; Ceramic Group 6, Nos 14-19 and Ceramic Group 7, Nos 20-21. Scale 1:4 (C. Marshall)

Wharram XII and is described fully in that report (Slowikowski forthcoming).

14* Jug. *26/221; Period 7, Phase 4*

15* Jug. *26/221; Period 7, Phase 4*

16* Jug. *26/32; Period 5, Phase 1*

C02 Humber ware (10.92%)
Figs 132 (Nos 17 and 19) and 142
Forms are varied, jugs are the most common, but cisterns, jars and bowls are also found. One of the bowl fragments is possibly from a condiment. Glaze is usually green with brown shades. Apart from two instances each of applied red pellets and applied vertical strips, decoration is absent. One base sherd has been re-shaped into a disc (see p. 298).

17* Bowl. *26/247; Period 5, Phase 1*

18 Disc. *26/36; SF1015; Period 7, Phase 5*
(See Chapter 23, Clay Object No. 10 for description and illustration)

19* Jug. *26/36; Period 7, Phase 5*

C03 Chalky Humber ware (2.65%)
Only jugs occur in this type, mostly as body sherds, although there are two fragments of thumbed base and a single rod handle. The only exception is a sherd with a pre-firing hole drilled through the body (diameter 7mm) which might possibly indicate a chafing dish.
No illustrations

C04 Humber ware spoutless jugs ('Skipton-on-Swale') (0.56%)
No illustrations
This category only includes characteristic small, spoutless, drinking jugs.

C10 Green glazed (0.07%)
No illustrations
Two sherds of unrecognisable form were found. This type was recoded on site by Le Patourel as '15th-century glazed ware'. Although the sherds are small, there are similarities in the glaze to post-medieval Ryedale ware.

Ceramic Group 7
C05 Purple-glazed Humber ware (1.05%)
No illustrations
Mainly jugs, although there is a single jar and two unrecognisable vessels. The jar has spots of purple glaze on the interior. One jug base is concave with a scar and a reduced ring on the base, indicating a heavy load stacked upside down in the kiln.

C07 Raeren (0.03%)
No illustrations
A single jug sherd was found.

C08 Cistercian (0.10%)
No illustrations
Single sherds from four cups were found; one has a rouletted applied white strip.

C09 (Usually unglazed) orange (0.35%)
Fig. 132 (No. 20)
Forms are mainly kitchen vessels, including a foot from a cauldron, a lid-seated jar and a handle from a skillet (No. 20). A possible variant of Ryedale ware.

20* Skillet. *26/45; Period 6, Phase 4*

C Unrecognised late medieval (0.80%)
Fig. 132 (No. 21)
Two single jugs were found which could not be allocated to an existing type. One is brick red in fabric with a purple glaze, similar to a late medieval type occurring in West Yorkshire (Slowikowski 1991, 77; Cumberpatch 2002, 189). The other jug (No. 21) was recorded on site by Le Patourel as '16th-century double-glazed ware'. Only one example of each type was found.

21* Jug. *26/62; Period 4, Phase 6*

C13 Tin-glazed (0.03%)
No illustrations
A single tiny fragment from an unrecognisable vessel was found.

Pottery from Site 26

Period 1: Late Iron Age/Romano-British
A small quantity of medieval pottery was recovered from Period 1 contexts, mainly occurring as single sherds, intrusive from later phases. Grave digging within the churchyard will have resulted in the disturbance of soil both upwards and downwards and assemblages of mixed date should be expected. The mixed assemblage from ditch 255 is likely to have come from near the top. Pottery from Period 1 contexts is listed in Table 135; see Chapter 17 for further discussion.

Period 2: Anglo-Saxon
Although eight hand-made Anglo-Saxon sherds were noted (*Wharram Interim Report* 1979), they have not been located or recorded. Some of the post-Roman pottery found in Period 2 contexts is likely to be intrusive. The deposition of the Saxo-Norman sherds, York type A B01 and Stamford-type wares B05, may have occurred at the very end of this period.

The 35 sherds of No. 13 come from a very mixed assemblage in sealing deposit 598. This vessel also comprises sherds from 227, an unstratified context. The sherds are very small and, although it is not possible to say where 227 was on the site, it does suggest some dispersal of sherds, albeit in relatively discrete amounts.

Table 135. Period 1 pottery (vessel:sherd:weight).

Phase	Ctx	Saxo-Norman			Early medieval						High medieval		Late medieval		
		B04	B05	B06	B07	B08	B12	B14	B18	B18U	B17	B20	C01	C02	C03
1.2	548						2:2:3								
1.2	548													1:1:2	1:1:2
1.2	619						1:1:1			1:1:1					
1.2	731				1:1:2										
1.2	752						1:1:8			1:1:6					
1.3	270						2:2:11				1:1:2	1:2:16			
1.3	545						1:1:4		1:1:4		1:1:4				
1.3	594	1:2:8	1:2:12	1:1:6		1:1:3	10:10:44	1:1:9		1:1:16					
1.3	751						1:1:3			2:2:24					
1.4	255	1:4:20					8:10:53						1:1:22	3:8:74	

Table 136. Period 2 pottery (vessel:sherd:weight).

Phase	Ctx	Saxo-Norman		Early medieval				High medieval		Late medieval
		B01	B05	B07	B12	B14	B18	B29	B	C02
2.1	119		1:1:3							
2.1	640		1:1:5	1:1:2						
2.1	699			2:2:17	3:5:15		1:1:2		1:1:1	
2.1	711			2:2:2	3:3:10					
2.1	729			2:3:38	1:1:1					
2.2	228	1:1:2	1:1:2	12:17:93		1:3:5				
2.2	598		5:5:23	24:81:341	37:37:287 (CC2)	1:6:39	1:1:8	1:1:1		1:1:1

Period 3: Late Anglo-Saxon and Norman (the extended burial ground)

The assemblage from Period 3 contexts is extremely fragmentary, with an average sherd:weight ratio of 1:5.3. The majority of sherds occurred in surfaces and grave fills, and are intrusive. There are, however, a small number of pottery types which date to the Saxo-Norman period, York type A B01, Torksey-type ware B04, Stamford-type ware B05 and Thetford-type ware.

These are the earliest post-Roman types occurring in the churchyard, albeit only 4.8% of the total. These types were mainly found in contexts which produced assemblages of mixed date (Table 137). A possible exception is grave fill 675, which contained a rim sherd of York type A (No. 1) weighing 8g; the smaller Staxton ware sherds from here are likely to be intrusive. Although small in number, these Saxo-Norman sherds do, nevertheless, indicate activity on the site at this time.

Pottery of the early medieval period, mid-12th and 13th centuries, is more frequent but still very fragmentary. Pottery in the grave fills is largely of this date, although there are intrusive late medieval sherds. As may be expected the largest numbers of sherds, 29, are of Staxton ware (B12), ubiquitous on all sites at Wharram.

There were four and five sherds in Reduced Chalky B14 and Pimply ware B07 respectively, while all other types occurred in ones and twos only. Radiocarbon dates for some of the graves range from 960 to 1190 AD, which could conceivably suggest an earlier start date to this pottery. All the pottery, however, came from the fill of the graves; none of it was buried deliberately with the body and, with an overall average sherd weight of only 5.6g, there is no certainty as to where these sherds originated. There is nevertheless an overlap with the latest radiocarbon dates.

In addition to the grave fills, pottery was also recovered from external surfaces 485, 543, 567, 342, 389, 412 and 539, and from pit 484 and dumps 584 and 593 at the eastern edge of the site. The external surfaces produced a very fragmentary assemblage of mixed date ranging from the Saxo-Norman to the late medieval period. The pit and the dumps, on the other hand, only produced pottery of the 12th or 13th centuries. The sherds are sparse and small but there is nothing dated later. The redeposited ditch fill (382) in Period 3, Phase 4 produced an assemblage of largely Saxo-Norman and early medieval pottery, although there was one sherd of Fine buff B29, possibly dating to the 13th to 14th centuries.

Table 137. Period 3 pottery (vessel:sherd:weight).

| Phase | Ctx | Saxo-Norman | | | | Early medieval | | | | | | | | | | High medieval | | | | Late medieval | | | Late med./ Post-med. |
		THET	B01	B04	B05	B07	B08	B10	B11	B12	B13	B14	B18	B18U	B28	B17	B20	B29	B	C01	C02	C03	C05
3.1	303					1:1:3				2:2:6													
3.1	603									2:10:83		1:1:1											
3.1	627									2:2:3												1:1:27	
3.1	675		1:1:8							2:2:9								1:1:2					
3.1	688																						
3.1	691					2:2:11				1:1:3													
3.1	714									1:1:1		1:1:2											
3.1	722											1:1:2											
3.1	745							1:1:1						1:1:2									
3.2	485		1:1:15		1:1:2	4:4:24	1:1:15			18:50:222 (CC2)			1:1:35	1:1:4		1:1:2		1:1:5					
3.2	543					1:1:4				7:7:26			2:2:2	2:2:2		1:1:6			2:2:1		1:1:16	2:2:7	
3.2	567				1:1:3	1:1:2				2:3:48			1:1:3	1:2:2		1:1:2							
3.3	375			1:1:3						2:2:9			2:2:3										
3.3	487									1:1:5													
3.3	494									1:1:3													
3.3	502						1:1:2			1:1:2												1:1:2	
3.3	515									1:1:2													
3.3	584					2:8:33				2:2:8													
3.3	586									2:2:5													
3.3	593									1:1:7													
3.3	669					1:1:3				1:1:4													
3.4	342		2:2:12		2:2:6					3:3:18													
3.4	382				2:3:11					8:8:24		3:3:8	3:3:15										
3.4	389	1:1:3	4:6:28	1:1:2	1:1:3	7:12:21	1:2:23		2:41:133	48:48:239.	1:1:3	2:2:29	5:5:14	12:12:61	1:1:30	3:3:6	7:7:58	1:1:7	2:2:21	1:2:11	9:9:32		1:1:24
3.4	412					1:1:1	1:2:4			9:9:36			4:4:28								3:3:89		
3.4	412.1								1:1:1	5:5:41						2:2:8							
3.4	539					1:1:20				2:2:9											1:1:2	1:1:2	
3.5	310									1:1:4													
3.5	326									1:1:2													
3.5	384					1:1:3						1:1:5											
3.5	397									1:1:1													
3.5	449				1:1:4					1:1:3													

Table 138. Period 4 pottery.

Ph.	Cxt	Saxo-Norman					Early medieval										High medieval								Late medieval				Late med./Post-med.
		B01	B03	B04	B05	B06	B07	B09	B10	B11	B12	B13	B14	B18	B18U	B28	B17	B19	B20	B21	B24	B29	B30	B	C01	C02	C03	C04	C
4.1	292										1:1:5								1:1:7										
4.1	301										2:2:2																		
4.1	325	1:1:3	1:1:4		3:3:3						21:21:106	1:1:3					2:3:54		3:4:166						2:2:9	3:3:38			
4.1	413																	1:1:6									2:3:21		
4.1	415										1:1:8																		
4.1	419										1:1:7																		
4.1	426										1:1:10																		
4.1	435											1:1:3	1:1:3				1:1:3												
4.1	445									1:1:1	6:6:32			2:2:16			3:4:19		1:1:13										
4.1	453										9:15:134					5:9:211													
4.1	455														1:1:13														
4.1	499										1:3:33																		
4.1	509										1:1:2	1:1:8																	
4.2	277						3:3:9				10:11:115			1:1:4		1:1:10	1:1:5	1:1:20	2:2:248			1:1:3			5:9:120	3:3:65	1:1:72		
4.2	289	1:1:35									10:10:7						1:1:3		2:4:26							3:3:26			
4.2	290										1:1:3																		
4.2	336				1:1:1						6:6:43			1:1:2	1:2:124				1:1:2							3:4:27			
4.2	352										9:9:63			2:2:1		1:3:7													
4.2	354						1:1:2				2:2:1																		
4.2	355						3:3:32				27:27:122			1:1:1			3:3:9		1:1:2						2:11:122	7:9:30	1:1:22		
4.2	391	1:1:1	1:1:2	1:1:3	1:1:14		2:2:3				13:13:55															1:1:21	1:1:5		
4.3	265										4:4:9																		
4.3	278										1:1:2														1:1:2				
4.3	306										3:3:4																		
4.3	308														1:1:3														
4.3	316			1:1:4																									
4.3	320										2:2:5																		

Table 138 continued.

Ph.	Cxt	Saxo-Norman					Early medieval										High medieval								Late medieval				Late med./Post-med.
		B01	B03	B04	B05	B06	B07	B09	B10	B11	B12	B13	B14	B18	B18U	B28	B17	B19	B20	B21	B24	B29	B30	B	C01	C02	C03	C04	C
4.3	327																												
4.3	339						1:1:5														1:1:4					2:2:1			
4.3	372																												
4.3	393										1:1:3																		
4.3	403						2:2:4			1:1:3	9:9:50			2:2:5													1:1:50		
4.3	440						1:1:2				1:1:7																		
4.3	570										5:5:22				1:1:3														
4.3	651					1:1:9	2:2:5				2:2:17																		
4.4	65									1:1:1	26:26:164				3:3:3		1:1:3								3:4:61	2:2:6	2:2:14		
4.4	70			1:1:2				1:1:5		2:2:16	23:23:137			2:2:7	2:3:7				5:12:110						1:1:7	13:13:102	4:4:46		
4.4	72																								1:1:2				
4.4	272						1:1:3				3:5:50																		
4.4	294						2:2:10		1:1:2	5:5:9	37:37:215			6:7:76	1:1:7				11:17:123					1:1:14	12:12:134	6:6:64	1:1:3	2:2:34	
4.4	295										15:15:89			2:2:5	1:1:3					1:1:6									
4.4	315				1:1:6			2:2:8			11:12:62				1:1:1		1:1:1		3:4:42	1:1:4			1:1:18			2:2:2	1:1:15		
4.5	254										1:1:1																		
4.5	258										1:1:2																		
4.5	259										4:4:15																		
4.5	261										1:1:1																		
4.5	263																									1:1:2			
4.5	275A										1:1:3			2:2:5															
4.5	281			1:1:1											1:1:14														
4.6	62										26:26:207						5:5:13		6:7:101			1:1:5			10:11:49	3:3:59	6:10:106		1:22:48
4.6	271			1:1:2	1:1:2		1:1:9		1:1:2		34:34:224			2:2:8	2:2:8		2:3:11	1:1:5	2:2:10						7:7:52	2:2:14	5:5:37		
4.6	276										1:1:5																		

259

Period 4: medieval (the reduced burial ground)

Period 4, Phase 1

As in the preceding period, pottery from grave fills is largely early medieval in date, mainly Staxton ware B12, and occurring mainly as single small sherds.

The possible structure to the north of the site (Fig. 36) produced pottery from contexts 292, 301 and 325. The wall footings 292 and 301 produced three sherds of Staxton ware and a sherd of Brandsby ware. Thirty-nine sherds, all from different vessels, came from the collapsed wall 325. They are mainly of early or high medieval date and among the more substantial pieces are two handles from jugs of Scarborough B17 and Brandsby-type B20. The area of bonding material 413 contained a sherd of Gritty ware B19 and three of chalky Humber ware C03, possibly dating to the 14th century.

Two shallow scoops, 444 and 452, north of the structure, both had pottery in their fills. The assemblage in scoop 452 (fill 453) is 12th to 13th-century in date, and is rather more complete than the usual single sherds. It comprises two jars of Staxton ware B12 and Unglazed whiteware B18U (No. 7), with seven and five sherds respectively. The latest pottery types in scoop 444 (fill 445) are Scarborough B17 and Brandsby-type B20 wares, and can be dated to the 13th to 14th centuries. Only one vessel, a Scarborough jug, is made up of more than one sherd, and even then, with a weight of 9g, it could have been a single sherd broken in antiquity.

Period 4, Phase 2

Chalk rubble surfaces 352 and 355 contained a relatively large amount of pottery, mainly Staxton ware B12, but with smaller quantities of high and late medieval ware, including nine sherds from the lower part of a Hambleton jar or possible bowl. The forms are primarily jugs, and at least four have internal white residues, suggesting long term storage of water. Context 354, the fill of oval post-hole 353, contained small sherds of early medieval pottery.

Loam deposits 336 and 391 contained pottery among which were small quantities of late medieval Humber ware. The only substantial vessel is a jar in Unglazed whiteware B18U and even then it consists of only two sherds, weighing 124g. The compacted rubble surface, 277, 289 and 290, in the north-west part of the site contained pottery with a wide date range, indicating a long period of use. The most substantial sherds are two Brandsby-type (B20) jug handles from 277. The presence of soot on the exteriors of at least fourteen sherds suggests a domestic source for the pottery.

Period 4, Phase 3

The pottery in the grave fills of this period is largely early medieval. There are sherds of late medieval pottery in Burials 306 and 339, but these are tiny sherds weighing less than 2g. A single Staxton B12 sherd was found in the fill (393) of post-hole 394 and bonding material 316 contained a residual sherd of Torksey-type ware B04. The rest of the pottery from this period came from disturbed tree root hollows.

Period 4, Phase 4

Deposit 294, in the north-east quadrant of the site, contained a large but fragmentary assemblage of pottery; sooted exteriors and internal white residues suggest a domestic origin. In the assemblage are late medieval Humber wares, including at least two Skipton-on-Swale type C04 drinking jugs, one of which was a larger than average piece weighing 30g.

Deposits 70, 72, 295 and 315, to the south, contained a similar assemblage of pottery of mixed date. The latest sherds are Hambleton C01 and Humber ware C02.

Clay deposits 272 and 65 contained pottery of similar date range, and included a body sherd from a Staxton B12 vessel which had been reshaped into a disc (see p. 298, No. 9).

Period 4, Phase 5

The small fragmentary sherds in the grave fills of this period are Saxo-Norman and early medieval in date. A small sherd of Staxton ware was found in each of post-holes 258 and 263. Post-hole fill 261 contained a sherd of Humber ware C02.

Period 4, Phase 6

The last group of burials was sealed by chalk rubble, contexts 62 and 271. Within these deposits, the latest pottery is Hambleton C01 and Humber ware C02/C03. One of the Chalky Humber ware C03 sherds from 271 has a pre-firing hole, 7mm in diameter, in the body. The vessel probably functioned as a sieve or strainer, but not enough survives to be certain of its form. The jug of unknown type C (No. 21) from deposit 62 could possibly be 16th-century in date (pers. comm. H.E.J. Le Patourel).

Period 5: later medieval to 16th century (1st-2nd quarter)

Layers relating to the robbing and collapse of walls 74 and 20 contained pottery dating from the Early to the late medieval period. The pottery is fragmentary, only one of the Hambleton C01 jugs comprising more than one sherd, and those five sherds weigh only 23g. The pottery in wall 74 included a small modern sherd. Post-holes 286 and 287 in the gap between the two walls contained a sherd of Staxton ware B12 pottery and a sherd of Humber ware C02 respectively. The Staxton ware is residual, but the Humber ware sherd suggests that the robbing of wall 20 and the removal of the posts may have been contemporary. South of the walls, the accumulated deposits 63, 67 and 68 contain Saxo-Norman, early and high medieval pottery with only one sherd of late medieval Humber ware (C04), a Skipton-on-Swale jug.

The path which ran through the walls contained pottery within its make up layers. Foundation layer 283 contained Humber ware (C02) among earlier material, as did layers 32 and 54. A Hambleton jug handle was recovered from deposit 32 (No. 16). Deposits east (244, 245 and 247) and west (288) of the path contained the same mix of pottery, with Hambleton C01 and Humber ware C02 dating to the 14th to 15th centuries, mixed with earlier types, for example a rouletted Brandsby B20 jug

Table 139. Period 5 pottery.

Phase	Cxt	Saxo-Norman		Early medieval						High medieval					Late medieval				Late med./Post-med.		
		B04	B05	B07	B09	B11	B12	B18	B18U	B17	B19	B20	B22	B	C01	C02	C03	C04	C05	C09	C
5.1	20											1:1:1			2:5:55	2:2:7					
5.1	32						4:4:21	1:1:1			1:1:2				3:5:32	4:8:31					
5.1	32.1						2:4:2					2:11:7			2:6:9 (CC6)	5:5:16					
5.1	32.2						5:5:12					4:4:3			0:1:1 (CC6)				1:1:2		
5.1	32.3						1:1:12							1:1:9	1:1:3						
5.1	54			2:2:12			6:6:28								11:12:73	3:16:27					1:1:45
5.1	63	1:1:11	1:1:9				15:15:82					1:1:5						1:1:9			
5.1	67						3:3:15														
5.1	68						5:5:27	1:1:4				2:2:5									
5.1	71			2:2:9		1:1:1	30:30:128	2:2:8		1:1:1		10:10:58			2:7:44	3:3:21	3:3:67				
5.1	74				1:1:2		22:22:118	4:4:2	3:3:19	1:1:4						2:2:2	1:1:1				
5.1	101														1:5:27 (CC4)	1:1:15				1:1:7	
5.1	240.1						5:5:13			1:1:2	2:2:7				1:1:1	3:3:15		1:1:2			
5.1	244						7:7:17			1:1:1							1:1:8				
5.1	245			1:1:7			5:5:45								4:4:68		1:1:3		1:1:20		
5.1	247							1:10:145 (CC1)	2:2:25	1:1:2	1:1:11		1:1:2		8:8:88	2:2:35		2:2:40	1:2:38		
5.1	283	1:1:13					2:2:10					1:1:2				1:1:3					
5.1	286																				
5.1	287			1:1:1												1:1:8					
5.1	288						7:7:54		1:1:1			3:3:9				2:3:6					
5.1	291						2:2:11														
5.1	293											1:1:29									
5.2	64						6:6:37	2:2:4				3:3:49			1:6:26	3:3:21	1:1:6				

Table 140. Period 6 pottery.

Phase	Cxt	S-N B05	B09	B10	Early medieval B12	B13	B16	B18	B17	High medieval B19	B20	B26	B29	Late medieval C01	C02	C03	C04	C10	Late med./Post-med. C05	C08	C09
6.2	49			1:1:16							1:1:14			3:3:34	1:1:12	2:2:11					
6.2	50										1:1:1				1:1:2	1:1:8					
6.2	55														1:1:1						1:1:15
6.2	56													2:2:108					1:1:8		
6.2	59				1:1:17						2:2:11			2:5:32	2:3:158		1:1:5				
6.2	114														1:1:18						
6.2	125														3:3:6					1:1:10	
6.2	159														1:5:134 (CC3)						
6.2	229				1:1:18									4:4:36	1:1:13				1:1:18		
6.2	230				1:1:20			1:2:26 (CC1)			4:11:173	5:5:111		4:11:173	5:5:111		1:1:7			1:1:4	
6.2	232				1:1:14									1:2:23	1:2:102		1:1:18				
6.2	233													13:13:254	1:4:66						
6.2	237				4:4:25									3:3:31	4:7:48						
6.2	238													4:8:47							
6.2	239				3:3:19			2:4:36 (CC1)						2:2:61	3:3:33	1:1:47			1:2:108		
6.3	4	1:1:4			5:5:56			1:1:11	1:1:9		4:4:22				2:2:18						
6.3	14				5:5:76		1:1:12	1:1:3			1:1:2			2:3:79	2:3:34						
6.3	15				5:5:77			2:2:24			5:6:29			1:1:7							
6.3	33				1:1:3									2:5:39 (CC5)	2:2:12						
6.3	34													0:5:28 (CC5)			1:1:3				
6.3	35				5:5:54	1:1:2		1:1:7	3:3:50		1:1:10			1:1:5	3:3:17				1:1:7		
6.3	246										1:1:2										
6.4	45				1:1:3									2:2:58				2:2:28			2:6:162
6.4	46																				
6.4	47														3:6:76					1:1:1	
6.4	148									1:1:4					0:1:21 (CC3)						
6.4	155				1:1:4						2:2:9			1:1:4					1:1:9		
6.5	3		1:1:3		15:15:82			6:6:39	2:2:89		10:10:153	1:1:2	2:2:2	16:18:269	16:18:269	3:5:183					

262

Table 141. Period 7 pottery.

Phase	Cxt	S-N		Early medieval					High medieval		Late medieval				Late medieval/Post-medieval			
		B04	B07	B11	B12	B14	B18	B27	B17	B20	C01	C02	C03	C04	C05	C07	C08	C09
7.1	6									1:3:69		1:1:12						
7.1	7				1:1:4					3:3:55	2:2:36	2:2:8	1:1:2					
7.1	11				1:2:22								1:1:61					
7.2	31				1:1:3							3:4:58	1:1:12					
7.2	218	1:1:2	16:22:92	1:1:3	3:3:22	2:2:5			2:2:37	7:9:36	11:22:124 (CC4)	6:13:96	1:2:1	1:1:10	10:10:83			
7.2	220										2:7:214	4:4:32					1:1:26	2:2:28
7.3	30									1:1:117	1:6:87 (CC6)	1:1:1						
7.3	158				1:1:1													
7.3	222										4:4:64							
7.3	234				1:1:5						8:10:91							
7.4	38													1:1:8				
7.4	217											1:1:1						
7.4	221				1:1:12					2:2:16	8:44:476	2:2:25			2:3:53	1:1:21		
7.5	9				1:1:15					7:8:64		9:15:178			2:2:24			
7.5	36				6:6:48		5:10:72	1:1:1		3:5:113	6:12:111 (CC6)	14:14:274			1:1:1			
7.5	37								1:1:44	2:2:5	3:3:69	3:3:4						
7.5	44						1:1:2				3:3:28							

(No. 11). Two sherds of purple glazed Humber ware C05, dating to the 16th century, were found in 247.

The only context in Period 5, Phase 2 to contain pottery was 64, a deposit south of walls 74 and 20. It was a fragmentary assemblage but did contain six, albeit small, sherds from a Hambleton C01 jug.

Period 6: early/mid-16th century to 18th century
Most of the assemblage found in contexts allocated to Period 6 is residual. In Period 6, Phase 2, the surfaces and deposits contained pottery of mixed dates, although the latest types are generally Hambleton (C01) and Humber wares (C02, C03 and C04). South-east of wall 20, Purple glazed Humber ware C05, dating to the 16th century, was found in surface 56 and Unglazed orange ware C09 in surface 55. The former was also found in a rubble deposit (230), which may relate to a collapsed structure on the east side of the site, north of wall 20. This deposit also contained a fragment from a 16th-century Cistercian cup (C08). Two vessels with cross-matching sherds were noted; although both pottery types are residual here, they indicate soil movement and disturbance. A York Glazed B18 jug (No. 5) is made up of one sherd from deposit 230, two sherds from wall footing 239, both contexts in Period 6, Phase 2, but also of ten sherds from deposit 247, east of the path in Period 5, Phase 1. The latter context is the likely original deposit. The five sherds from a Humber ware C02 vessel from post-hole 159 in Period 6, Phase 2 match with a single sherd from context 148 in Period 6, Phase 4. The original context is most likely to be 159.

In Period 6, Phases 3 and 4, a similar ceramic profile may be seen, mixed assemblages with substantial quantities of late medieval wares but with only one 16th-century Purple Glazed Humber ware jug, in 35, a Phase 3 deposit north of wall 74. Nothing later was recorded in this period. Deposit 35 also produced a Hambleton C01 jug with five sherds and four additional matching sherds from wall footing 34. Phase 4 produced a smaller quantity of sherds but among them were a Purple Glazed Humber ware C05 jug from 155, a Cistercian C08 cup from 148, and an Unglazed orange skillet (No. 20) from 45, all dating to the 16th century.

The latest sherds from deposit 3 in Period 6, Phase 5 are Humber wares C02 and C03. A urinal (No. 12), a vessel type rarely found at Wharram, is in a particularly gritty fabric, possibly a version of Brandsby-type B20, with a thick green glaze which runs into the top of the vessel. These are typically northern vessels and were used to collect urine (Amis 1968, 9), either to gauge the health of an individual from its appearance or for industrial purposes.

No pottery was recovered from Period 6, Phase 6 contexts.

Period 7: late 18th century to 20th century
The latest pottery from Period 7 contexts dates from the 16th century. It is mainly very fragmentary, although there are two substantial Hambleton C01 jugs made up of 30 sherds between them (Nos 14 and 15). These were recovered from spread 221. All the pottery is residual.

Pottery from Site 41

Periods 1 and 2
No medieval pottery was recovered from Period 1 and only a single intrusive sherd of Staxton ware (B12) from Period 2, context 31.

Period 3
No pottery was recovered from gully 168 or hearth 164, but small amounts of early medieval pottery, dating to the 12th or 13th centuries, was found in the layers which sealed them, 163 and 160 respectively. Contemporary with the hearth was a row of post-holes of which 148, 152, 153 and 154 also contained early medieval pottery. Surface 150 contained a sherd of Beverley 1 type B28, as well as a miniscule sherd of Purple Glazed Humber ware C05 which weighs less than 1g and is clearly intrusive.

The possible footing for a boundary wall 131/151 contained early medieval pottery, most of it Staxton ware B12, among which are a number of substantial fragments and vessels with more than five sherds. The recut (19) of gully (22) contained a single sherd of Beverley 1 type B28 of similar date. Surfaces 130D, 133 and 134 also contained early medieval sherds in Staxton B12 and York Glazed B18 types. Cutting these surfaces was a number of scoops and depressions only one of which, 140, contained pottery, two sherds of Beverley 1 type B28 and a single sherd of unknown medieval type but possibly of the same date. Sealing these was a series of chalk surfaces of which 115, 117, 128 and 129 each contained a single sherd of early medieval pottery.

Period 4
Three burials from this period were sent for radiocarbon dating (Chapter 14, Table 117). The first, Burial SA056, was dated to *cal AD 980-1190*. Pottery from the fill of the grave is mostly early medieval in date, although there are intrusive sherds of late medieval pottery mixed in with them. Sealing this are layers 10, 11 and 105, which also contain sherds of possible late medieval date in a largely early medieval assemblage.

The two other dated burials are Burial SA052, dated to *cal AD 980-1220*, and Burial SA053, dated to *cal AD 1020-1220*. Pottery from their fills is early medieval in date, consistent with the second half of the radiocarbon date range. Pottery from pit 108 is of a comparable date to that from the graves, with the exception of the intrusive late medieval sherds.

Period 5: post-medieval and modern
Period 5 contexts produced fragmentary assemblages, containing residual early medieval pottery. There are a number of contexts containing late medieval sherds and these are listed in Table 144. Of the series of dumps and make-up deposits, two contained pottery, contexts 4 and 103. Although primarily an early medieval assemblage, there were sherds of late medieval pottery in 103. Pottery was recovered from the two 'modern' graves, early medieval sherds from Burial SA059 and late medieval sherds from Burial SA060. All other deposits are modern;

Table 142. Site 41 Periods 2 and 3 pottery.

Phase	Ctx	Early medieval					High medieval			Late med. C02	Late med./Post-med. C05
		B07	B10	B12	B18	B28	B19	B29	B		
2.1	31			1:1:41							
3.1	148				1:1:1						
3.1	150					1:1:7					1:1:1
3.1	152			2:2:6							
3.1	153			2:2:5							
3.1	154			1:1:2							
3.1	160			2:2:6							
3.1	163	1:1:5									
3.1	163.2	1:1:1		1:1:1			1:1:3				
3.1	165	1:1:1									
3.2	19					1:1:2					
3.2	130.4			2:5:49							
3.2	131	1:1:1		6:23:181							
3.2	131.2			9:15:97	1:1:4						
3.2	133				0:1:10						
3.2	134			2:2:16	2:3:11						
3.2	140					1:2:26			1:1:19		
3.2	146			2:2:5							
3.2	151		1:1:5	6:8:46				1:1:5			
3.3	115				1:1:3						
3.3	117			1:1:3							
3.3	127			1:1:3						2:2:5	
3.3	128			1:1:2							
3.3	129			1:1:24							

Table 143. Site 41 Period 4 pottery.

Phase	Ctx	Early medieval						High medieval			Late medieval	
		B07	B10	B11	B12	B14	B18	B17	B20	B	C02	C03
4.1	56	1:1:19		1:1:5	1:1:12		1:1:20				1:4:39	
4.1	109		1:2:5			1:1:1						
4.1	113				2:2:8							
4.2	10				1:1:1							
4.2	11	1:1:3		1:1:1	4:4:18							
4.2	50				2:2:3							
4.2	51				1:1:1							
4.2	52			1:1:6	4:4:13				1:1:1			
4.2	53	1:1:1			4:4:16							
4.2	54				1:1:2							
4.2	55								1:1:1			
4.2	57	1:1:8			2:2:4							
4.2	105				3:3:7		2:2:5					1:1:26
4.2	106				3:3:10		1:1:1					
4.2	107							1:1:13				1:1:26
4.2	108				9:9:92		2:2:6			1:1:2		3:3:14

Table 144. Site 41 Period 5 pottery.

Phase	Ctx	Early medieval						High medieval				Late medieval		
		B07	B08	B11	B12	B18	B27	B20	B22	B29	B	C01	C02	C03
5.1	8			1:1:7										
5.1	104			1:1:7	17:17:141	1:2:2	1:2:14	2:2:36			2:2:10	1:3:78	4:4:22	3:4:73
5.2	2	2:2:2	1:2:13		15:15:70			1:1:1			1:1:5	1:1:7	1:1:2	
5.2	4	1:1:1		1:1:4	9:11:54									
5.2	5	1:1:22			2:2:7					1:1:4				
5.2	59			1:1:1	1:1:14	1:1:6								
5.2	60													2:2:21
5.2	101				2:2:27	1:1:1		2:2:21				1:1:5		
5.2	102				7:8:65	7:7:102		2:2:15	1:1:2			1:1:6	2:2:22	
5.2	103				8:8:27	3:3:29				1:1:1		2:2:11	4:4:40	
5.5	119	2:2:30			1:5:75									

Table 145. Site 52 pottery (all periods).

Ctx	Early medieval				High medieval					Late medieval			Late med./ Post-med.
	B07	B12	B18	B27	B17	B19	B20	B23	B	C01	C02	C03	C05
9	1:1:5	1:1:2				1:2:23							
4		17:17:113	3:3:20			1:1:39		3:3:7	1:1:2	2:2:5	3:4:28	3:3:31	1:2:6
5		26:26:142	7:7:46	1:2:14			4:8:82	2:2:5			1:2:10	1:2:16	
6		9:9:47	4:6:112	1:1:11	1:2:8	1:1:4					3:3:13		
11		1:1:5										1:1:33	
15						0:1:21							

Table 146. Comparison of jars and jugs as a percentage of total sherds (all forms).

Form	Early medieval (Ceramic groups 4-5)	Late medieval (Ceramic groups 6-7)	Total
Jar sherds (+ vess)	(1582) 76.09%	(201) 24.42%	(1783) 61.44%
Jar sherds (- vess)	(229) 11.01%	(19) 2.30%	(248) 8.54%
Jug sherds	(477) 22.94%	(605) 73.51%	(1082) 37.28%
Total sherds	2079	823	2902

their assemblages are listed in Table 144 but not discussed further.

Pottery from Site 52

The pottery from Site 52 is very fragmentary and occurs mainly as individual sherds within the various layers/spits. Most of the pottery is early medieval in date, but Burial SA070 (context 11) and Burial SA071 (context 15) contained single sherds of early, high and late medieval date.

Forms

Recognisable forms make up 39.21% of the total vessel assemblage, 46.94% by sherd; a higher percentage than either the South or the North Manors. Most of the assemblage remains as unrecognisable body and base sherds, recorded simply as undiagnostic vessels (VESS). The majority of the glazed body sherds, however, have been counted as jugs.

Jugs make up a large proportion of the total recognisable vessel assemblage, 85.77% by vessel, 79.15% by sherd. The high figure may be an overestimate, due to the presence of glazed body sherds, which would not otherwise have been included. There appears to be an increase in the percentage of jugs used in the late medieval period when compared to the earlier period (Table 146). As a percentage of the total number of jug sherds, 44.08% occurred in the early medieval period, while 55.91% are found in the later period. The rise is not as great as the drop in jar numbers (see below), suggesting that the rate of usage of jugs remained relatively stable throughout the medieval period.

The majority of undiagnostic body and base sherds are most likely to belong to jars, and if the total of all

Table 147. Recognisable forms by fabric, in chronological order, quantified by vessel:sherd. Unrecognisable body and base sherds ('VESS') are quantified by sherd.

FABRIC	JAR	PPOT	BWL	JUG	CIST	CURF	CLDN	SKLT	URNL	LOBC	CUP	VESS
Group 3												
B01	3:3											9
B03												2
B04	2:3		1:1									9
B05	3:4											26
B06	1:1											1
Group 4												
B07	11:54											164
B08	1:2			1:1								6
B09				6:6								
B10				2:2								6
B11				13:52								10
B12	61:143	5:9	2:2			3:5						979
B13				3:3								1
B14	1											19
B16				1:1								
B18				116:139								7
B18U	3:8											45
B27				1:1								5
B28				6:9								
Group 5												
B17				48:52								1
B19			1:1	6:8								4
B20	6:6			134:164					1:1			12
B21				1:1								1
B22				1:1								
B23												5
B24				1:2								1
B26				1:1								
B29				8:8								3
B30												3
B				5								12
Group 6												
C01	2:10			149:239	2:31					2:3		57
C02	2:2		2:2	172:207	4:5							97
C03				46:55								21
C04				16:16								
C10												2
Group 7												
C05	1:1			23:26								3
C07				1:1								
C08											3:3	
C09	2:6						1:1	1:1				2
C				2:23								

Evidence of use	Form and fabric													
	Jar/peat pot						Bowl	Jug						Cauldron
	B01	B05	B07	B12	B18U	B20	B19	B18	B19	B20	C01	C02	C05	C09
lid-type sooting	1													
external sooting (total)			2	3	1	2	1							
external sooting (base)			1	1		1				2				1
internal sooting		1												
sooting above base											1			
internal white residue								1	1	1	1	2	2	

undiagnostic sherds is added to that of all recognisable jars, a figure of 61.23% of the total assemblage is reached. The occurrence of jars decreased however, in the later middle ages due to the more frequent use of metal cooking vessels by people who would not have been able to afford them at an earlier period. The drop in jar (+ vess) totals is very noticeable, with 88.72% occurring in the early medieval period and only 11.27% found in the later period.

The majority of jar and jug fabrics appears to be mutually exclusive (Table 147). The earliest fabrics are used primarily for jars, probably cooking pots. These are primarily in Staxton (B12) and Pimply (B07) wares, but there are three jars (Nos 6 and 7 and one unillustrated) recorded as Unglazed White wares (B18U) which may be datable from their forms to the same period, 12th to 13th centuries. One has a few small splashes of olive green glaze on the exterior, probably accidental, indicating that at least these vessels were fired in the same kiln as glazed wares. Glazed jugs are known to have been made in these fabrics, although not in such large quantities as the jars. Staxton (B12) jugs with poor glazes have been found elsewhere at Wharram, but not in this assemblage; jugs in Pimply (B07) ware, or its variants, are known throughout West Yorkshire and the spots of glaze on the Unglazed White ware (B18U) indicate the presence of glazed jugs, although not at Wharram.

A large number of fabric types are found in jug forms only. Wharram seems to have been getting its jug supplies from a wider source than other forms. This is the same pattern as that seen on other areas of the site (South and North Manors).

Other forms occur on the site in small quantities. In the earlier medieval period, bowls, a curfew and a urinal are found. In the later medieval period, new forms are introduced such as the cistern and cup, but these are sparse in this assemblage.

Although the majority of vessels consisted of no more than one or two sherds, weighing less than 20g, there are vessels, spanning the medieval period, which comprise more than five sherds, or whose constituent sherds are large and weigh over 20g each.

The most significant are Nos 5, 13 and 15 (see illustration catalogue for details) indicating that not all vessels were small, redeposited sherds. Two unillustrated vessels are worthy of mention: a jug in Pink Gritty ware (B11) from (26/389) and a jug in Hambleton ware (C01) from (26/30 and 26/36). The 40 sherds from the Pink Gritty jug weigh 116g, while the fifteen sherds from the Hambleton jug weigh 111g. Average weight, however, is only 2.9g and 7.4g, respectively. Despite the fragmentary nature of these vessels, these sherds had not been widely dispersed.

Function and/or use of the vessels

The relatively large quantity of pottery found in the churchyard is noteworthy, in that the dumping of domestic rubbish in hallowed ground might not be expected. The forms found in this assemblage are varied, both with evidence of use and without. The jars, peat-pots, jugs and bowls are commonly found in most assemblages, but other forms are rarer: cisterns, curfews, cauldrons, skillets, urinals and cups (Table 147).

A number of recognisable forms had evidence of some type of use, among which are sooting and residues (Table 148). Most of the sooted vessels are jars, including a single peat pot, although three jugs, a bowl and a cauldron were also found. All the vessels with internal residues are jugs. These residues are white and flaky and may be water scale, suggesting long term storage of water.

The possibility that some of the finds in the graveyard north of the church have a domestic origin, is discussed in Chapter 20, and the presence of a substantial number of cooking pots, some with sooting, is significant.

The churchyard in the medieval period was an area where communal activities, not necessarily associated with the dead, took place particularly on patron saints' feast days or other holy days, and large numbers of jugs and drinking vessels from Site 26 reinforce Le Patourel's suggestion (1987, 159-160) that the jugs and drinking vessels found in the excavations in and around the church were likely to relate to 'activities of a quasi-religious or even totally secular nature' (see also Rodwell 1989, 148).

19 Post-medieval Pottery

The post-medieval pottery from the Churchyard sites has been catalogued and will be discussed with the pottery from the post-medieval vicarage.

Part Six
The Small Finds
edited by E.A. Clark

20 Introduction

The finds published in this volume are substantially those from Sites 26, 41, 52 and 80. Objects from excavations within the standing walls of the church were published in *Wharram III*. At the time the fashion was for putting most of the data into fiche, and in consequence much of the detailed information on finds is not readily available to those without the appropriate equipment. The present volume gives the opportunity not only to illustrate some objects relevant to the graveyard, for example the stone grave-covers, but also, where scholarship has progressed, to update the reports. A few finds of importance that were totally excluded from *Wharram III* have also been published here.

Although the 1971 Trenches, Sites 20 and 21, are discussed in Chapter 4 (pp 57-8), all the finds from them will be included with those from the post-medieval vicarage buildings (*Wharram XII*, forthcoming).

In 1976 a new recording system was introduced at Wharram; this system, and the need for it, is fully explained in the introduction to *Wharram VII*. The excavation of Sites 26 and 41 was already in progress and finds from these sites recorded under the old system have been retrospectively incorporated into the new one.

In this volume the finds from Sites 26, 41, 52 and 80 are published in the same catalogue sequences and it is important to stress that the periods and phases remain specific to each site. Catalogue numbers for objects from the earlier church excavations, but published here for the first time, continue the sequences in *Wharram III*, and are grouped at the end of the relevant chapter or section. The only exception to this is in Chapter 21, The Funerary Stonework. The very fine series of pre and post-Conquest grave covers, published in fiche in *Wharram III*, have been re-examined and renumbered. The numerical sequence has then been continued for the other stones discussed by Stocker and for the post-Conquest slabs discussed by Ryder. The same sequence is then continued for the other stone objects.

Finds recovery was entirely by eye during excavation. Unless otherwise stated, the objects have been examined by eye during the post-excavation process, with the use of radiography, cleaning, conservation and other techniques as appropriate. The reports include discussions and select catalogues; the full catalogues, including conservation, lithological and scientific reports, form part of the Archive. In each chapter, the published objects are recorded in a single sequence of illustrated and un-illustrated material; the complete archive catalogues continue the same numerical sequence. References to unpublished items appear thus: Archive 208.

Following the pattern of previous Wharram publications, the finds reports are presented by material, and the importance of finds to any particular context is discussed in the text when relevant. Types of object previously unknown or unrecognised in the village are few, but, notably, include a stylus, fragments of unusual red glass, a coin weight and part of a cast-iron memorial.

Coins are an occasional find in most parts of the village, but the relatively large number of medieval ones from the churchyard area presented the opportunity for Barclay to review all such coins from Wharram (Ch. 25). The Roman coins have been similarly reviewed by Sitch in *Wharram IX*, and the post-medieval ones will be discussed in *Wharram XII* (forthcoming).

It is striking that the general impression is of an assemblage very similar to those from other more obviously domestic areas of the village. The medieval pottery, with a considerable number of cooking pots, some sooted, also suggests a domestic origin. The question as to whether the material has been brought from elsewhere or originates from a building in the vicinity will be explored in *Wharram XII*. Apart from an early post-medieval book clasp and other decorative objects that might have been used on books, the only objects recovered from the churchyard that relate to the liturgy of the church are those associated with burials.

The present volume, with its focus on the burials excavated in both the church and its graveyard, provides an opportunity to review the significance of all the burial-related finds, both from within the standing walls and from the external graveyard.

Objects can be associated with burial in a variety of ways: some are directly associated with the body, others are associated with the burial (whether coffined or not), and, finally, others relate to the memorials left in commemoration of the dead. These are discussed below.

Objects associated with skeletons

Due to recording methods in the earlier excavations, few finds can be directly associated with a skeleton, but objects found within the fill of graves, and especially coffins, may have originated from the burial. Very few finds came from the graves within Site 26.

A small number of dress accessories have been found. A copper-alloy hook, (*Wharram III*, 171 and 173, no. 26) was found with one of the group of 11th-century burials under grave slabs (Burial V50) and the ornamental dress pin found under the head of juvenile Burial EE076 (*Wharram III*, 173, no. 41) may be from some form of head covering. Two other dress pins described in *Wharram III* as from graves cannot be ascribed to individual burials. Decorated buttons of copper-alloy were found with post-medieval Burial SA060 (Ch. 26, No. 26), together with a bone-handled gardener's knife (Ch. 28, No. 15) and a possible copper-alloy belt fitting (Ch. 26, No. 14). Burial V42 had ceramic buttons with it (*Wharram III*, 167, fiche fr. 6.D10, no.1). A shoe buckle of 18th-century type (*Wharram III*, fiche, copper-alloy, no. 3) was in the grave of Sophia Robinson who died in 1815 (Burial V05).

Other objects are associated with straps or belts. Part of a narrow strap-end (*Wharram III*, fiche fig. 192, copper-alloy no. 5) was found near the right knee of Burial EE121. Plates from another strap-end (*Wharram III*, 171 and 173, no. 10) were in the fill of Burial WCO010. Three copper-alloy objects (*Wharram III*, fiche fig. 192, nos 21, 15 and 17), all possible fittings from straps, were found with Burials NA167, SA060 and EE122 respectively; No. 17 is described as being above the right hand. A fragment of a leather strap retaining copper-alloy studs (*Wharram III*, fiche fig. 192, no. 11) was with the coffined Burial CN22, and a fragment of a buckle (*Wharram III*, fiche fig. 192, no. 28) was found under the skeleton in Burial EE009 or EE010.

Two items of jewellery were found: a medieval finger ring with Burial CN08 and a glass bead with Burial CN28 (*Wharram III*, 173, fig. 191, no. 34; 170, fiche fr. 6.D13, no. 34,). As both burials are post-medieval they are likely to be chance finds in the fill.

Other burials contained objects that might have been deposited with the body in the form of keepsakes, or they may all be chance finds. A fragment of Roman glass bangle (*Wharram III*, 170, no. 1) was with Burial V46, fragments of triangular loomweights (Ch. 23, Nos 4 and 5) with Burials G597 and G643, and a fossil and decorative piece of calcite were with Burials V20 and CN13 respectively. A folding knife (*Wharram III*, fiche fig. 188, iron no. 42) was in a post-medieval grave, Burial SA017. The fill of the pre-Conquest Burial V56, under what might have been a charred coffin lid, contained a Saxon styca (Ch. 25, No. 8). A medieval bone stylus (Ch. 28, Church 6) in the grave of a juvenile aged 14-15 (Burial V35), adds to those items associated with literacy already known from other sites but showing no evidence of deliberate burial (Gilchrist and Sloane 2005, 179).

Gilchrist and Sloane (2005, 78) cast some doubt on the reported practice of placing pebbles in the mouths of corpses, and the pebbles found in the fills of Burials NA111, G363 and G379 may all be chance finds, as may the nail shown in a photograph in the mouth of Burial NA046 and the cut halfpenny of Henry II (Ch. 25, No. 12) from the fill of Burial G443.

The placing of liturgical goods in the graves of the clergy is well recorded and two burials at Wharram, Burial EE013 and Burial EE080, follow this practice (Ch. 15, Plates 96 and 97; *Wharram III*, 150). A fragment of binding strip (*Wharram III*, 173, fig. 191, no. 56) also came from one of them, Burial EE013.

Graves and coffins

Small fragments of material from shrouds were found in association with six graves. Four of these burials are from the nave (Burials NA092, NA097, NA104 and NA223) and one from the west end of the church (Burial WCO034), four being the graves of children under six years old. The sixth, from the vestry area (Burial V42), is a coffined burial and the fragment may be residual. Three of them are described by Elisabeth Crowfoot (*Wharram III*, 149) as 'simple flax tabby weaves of fairly good quality'.

The pins found in a small number of graves were described in *Wharram III* as possibly being used to fasten shrouds. Recent work by Gilchrist and Sloane (2005, 110) refutes this use, and suggests that, where used, they were a temporary fastening not removed after the shroud was finally sewn. The small pins with simple heads (*Wharram III*, fiche fr. 6.D14, copper-alloy nos 44, 45-47 and 54) found in Burials CN41, CN37 and EE123 would be very suitable for this function, although Burials CN41 and CN37 are both post-medieval graves.

The use of stone in graves is discussed by Heighway (pp 238-241) and the reused fragments of a stone coffin, found around the area of the graveyard, by Stocker (Ch. 21).

Harding discussed the objects in metal, wood and fabric recovered from post-medieval coffined burials within the church (*Wharram III*, 150-53), and a few other examples, found with graves on Site 41, are published in this volume (Ch. 27, Nos 66-69).

Recent work by John Watt has identified the possible nail types being used for making the coffins.

Memorials

Although many of the graves are likely to have been marked originally by earth mounds, none survived.

The medieval grave slabs recovered in excavation or surviving as infill in the aisle arcades were briefly discussed in *Wharram III*, but have been reconsidered in this volume by Stocker and Ryder (Ch. 21), where Stocker also discusses an enigmatic stone cross base.

The up-standing memorial stones in the graveyard, dating from the later 18th to the early 20th centuries, were discussed by Rahtz and Watts in *Wharram II*. Two 19th-century wall monuments, to the Graeme and Wrangthorpe families, were removed from the church after it became redundant and are now in the parish churches of Sewerby and Bainton respectively (*Wharram III*, 149). Together with a few excavated named graves, these late memorials provide the only opportunity to identify those who were buried.

Fragments of polished Purbeck marble and some fragments of worked limestone, all discovered in deposits associated with buildings near the church (*Wharram XII*, forthcoming) suggest that other monuments existed.

No evidence of wooden memorials was recovered, but a fragment from a cast-iron one (Ch. 27, No. 70) is a reminder of other forms of commemoration.

21 Funerary Stonework

Pre-Conquest stonework - the early graveyard in context

by D. Stocker[1]

The excavations in the graveyard of St Martin's church revealed a number of grave-covers and other items of grave furniture which cast some light on the establishment of the graveyard and on its earlier phases. They also offer useful insights into relationships between medieval Wharram and the Roman past. The following report dealing with this material is divided into two main parts:

- A description and discussion of the individual items of grave furniture discovered.[2]
- A general discussion, based on our conclusions regarding the grave furniture, of the character of the earliest phases of the St Martin's graveyard.

The grave furniture

The sixteen stones themselves fall into five groups:
A. Three complete grave-covers discovered *in situ* south of the chancel,
B. Three fragments from at least two grave-covers found reused in the south aisle fabric (left *in situ* and not available for further study),
C. Five fragmentary grave-markers discovered *in situ* alongside the covers of Group A,
D. A single section from a monolithic sarcophagus reused in the south aisle fabric (left *in situ* and not available for further study),
E. Four fragments from a monolithic sarcophagus or sarcophagi discovered during site clearance.

Group A was identified by John Senior (Lang 1991) as Coral Rag. Geoff Gaunt confirms that these stones, and those in the other groups, have a Coral Rag lithology. In lithostratigraphic terms therefore, they are most likely from the Coral Rag Member of the Coralline Oolite Formation. However, localised lenses of appreciably bioclastic limestone occur in places within the underlying Malton Oolite Member of this formation, so it is not inconceivable that some of these fragments could be from these lenses.

Group A – three worked grave-covers found in situ *south of the chancel*
Catalogue
1* (Lang 1991, 222-3 - CASSS Wharram Percy No. 4, *Wharram III*, no. 2) Fig. 133, **Plates 102-105**

This is a complete, small, slightly tapered grave-cover, made of, 'Coarse, shelly, oolitic, very pale brown (10YR 8/4) limestone; Coral Rag, Coralline Oolite Formation, Middle Oxfordian, Upper Jurassic' (Lang 1991, 223).

The sides have been trimmed to near-vertical and the base has been cut flat. The cover's upper surface of 'coped' profile is decorated with a single raised rib of rectangular section (*c.* 30mm broad) which runs the entire length of the stone. It was evidently cut parallel with the left-hand edge of the stone, when viewed with the foot at the base. The rib has been produced by hollowing out the surface of the cover to either side, giving the cover's upper surface panels an irregularly concave profile. The rib has been rounded off in longitudinal profile as it approaches the head-end, but it is unclear whether this was part of the original design or represents

subsequent damage or erosion. Two types of tooling are visible on the base of the stone. The whole surface has been roughly levelled using a mason's 'point' or 'scappling hammer' (a small pick-axe - for the range of potential tools involved see e.g. Bessac 1987) and, in a second operation, probably also carried out during the stone's initial creation, an even surface has been created around the lower edge of the monument by cutting a draft around all four edges, using a broad-bladed tool. This detail suggests that in its original use, the cover was in contact with a stone substructure beneath, either a stone sarcophagus or a mortared cist. In its excavated context, however, the cover was laid over the burial of a child of 3-5years which had no stone setting of any type (Burial V50, which had a radiocarbon date of cal AD 1000-1260).

2* (Lang 1991, 222-3 - CASSS Wharram Percy No. 3, *Wharram III*, no. 5) Fig.133, **Plates 106-111**

When discovered, this was a near-complete, slightly-tapered, grave-cover (now broken into two adjoining stones) made of 'Coarse, shelly, oolitic, very pale brown (10YR 8/4) limestone; Coral Rag, Coralline Oolite Formation, Middle Oxfordian, Upper Jurassic' (Lang 1991, 223).

The right-hand side (as viewed with the foot at the base) has been trimmed to near-vertical whilst the left side is bowed outwards. The upper surface of the cover is of 'coped' profile and is decorated with a single raised rib of rectangular section (*c.* 50mm broad) running the entire length of the stone. It runs centrally down the tapering stone. The rib has been produced by hollowing out the surface of the cover to either side, giving the panels of the cover's upper surface an irregularly concave profile. When discovered the central part of the cover had already been subject to extensive mechanical damage, with the rib itself being broken away. This damage is both too great in depth and too localised in scale to represent mere weathering, and implies either a single episode of deliberate destruction, or a period of prolonged abrasion (e.g. wear caused by constant walking over this part of the stone).

Like No. 1, the base exhibits two styles of tooling. Again the entire surface has been worked roughly flat using a scappling hammer or point, whilst the two long edges have been worked at a slight angle using a broad blade, creating rough chamfers. These chamfers suggest that, again like No. 1, the stone was originally intended to sit above a stone-built grave, either a monolithic sarcophagus or a stone-lined cist. Yet the burial beneath the cover was made within a grave without any surrounding stone setting. It was that of a female probably in her early 20s (Burial V52), which yielded a radiocarbon date of cal AD 980-1220 .

3* (Lang 1991, 222-3 - CASSS Wharram Percy No. 2, *Wharram III*, no. 7) Fig. 133, **Plates 112-117**

This is a complete slightly tapered grave-cover, decorated with a simple cross in low relief, made of 'Coarse, shelly, oolitic, very pale brown (10YR 8/4) limestone; Coral Rag, Coralline Oolite Formation, Middle Oxfordian, Upper Jurassic' (Lang 1991, 222).

The sides have been trimmed to near-vertical. The upper surface of the cover is of 'coped' profile and is decorated with a single raised rib of rectangular section (*c.* 50mm broad) which originally ran centrally down the entire length of the tapered stone. The rib has been produced by hollowing out the surface of the cover to either side, giving the cover's upper surface panels an irregularly concave profile. In addition to the medial rib, the stone clearly shows a second phase of decoration on its upper surface. In the upper half (as viewed from the foot) the ridge-rib has been carefully trimmed away and, in its place, a simple cross has been incised into the surface created. The tooling of the rectangular panel within which the secondary cross was carved in low-relief is clearly visible. It was made with a broad blade and in raking light it can be seen clearly cutting into the rough scappled surface of the original ribbed cover. The cross itself has a slightly splayed head and arms (of *Corpus* type B6) whilst the stem also splays outwards slightly towards the base. There seems little room for doubt that the cross represents a second phase of use. Not only does the tooling pattern demonstrate the point, but the design of the cross is inimical to the original profile of the cover, with its central rib whose original sharply undercut profile still survives on the lower part of the stone.

Like Nos 1 and 2 above, the base of the stone has been cut flat using a scappling hammer or a point whilst a rough draft has been cut along the long edges of the stone using a broad-bladed tool. As with the previous two examples, this feature probably suggests that the stone was originally intended to be placed over a burial within a stone structure beneath; either over a stone sarcophagus or a stone-lined cist. Like the other two examples, this cover was also excavated above a simple burial, presumably made within a shroud or wooden coffin, in a grave that lacked a stone setting. This detail confirms the clear evidence on the cover's upper surface that this monument was reused in the location from which it was excavated. The burial over which the cover was reused (Burial V51) was of a male of between 40 and 50 years which yielded a radiocarbon date of cal AD 1020-1230.

Discussion

The form of decoration on all three covers, with the ridge-rib of squared section created by hollowing-out the panels to either side, is quite distinctive. It is frequently seen on Romano-British sarcophagi lids of the later 3rd and 4th centuries in York and across Britannia. Although grave-covers with a medial ridge-rib are common finds in the 11th and 12th centuries also, unlike the St Martin's examples, typically they have a properly formed ridge roll, often defined between incised lines, and flattened surface panels. The original surface tooling on the three Wharram stones is also distinctive. They seem to have been dressed with a point or a scappling hammer rather than with a bladed tool – again a feature more commonly associated with Roman, rather than Anglo-Saxon masoncraft. Further confirmation that No. 3 was reused in its late Anglo-Scandinavian context is provided by its upper surface being so clearly recut for the insertion of the simple incised cross. It is also possible that the abrasion damage to No. 2 should also be attributed to a previous phase of use, rather than having occurred in St Martin's churchyard. The tooling on the bases of all three covers also shows that they were originally intended to be placed as 'lids' over graves lined with stone, yet all were excavated *in situ* above graves without any such stone structures. This also argues that they were all reused in the context from which they were excavated.

A final confirmation that that these stones were reused in their late Anglo-Scandinavian context may also be provided by their stone type. This particular Corallian ragstone is an unusual stone to find used in local Anglo-Scandinavian grave furniture. There seem to be only three other examples of this stone type in Anglo-Scandinavian Yorkshire (at Amotherby Nos 1 and 2 and Kirby Grindalythe No. 4: Lang 1991, 1245, 151). John Senior suggests that this stone type may have been particularly exploited during the Roman period, and notes its use in Roman Malton (Lang 1991, 15). Whether the pieces at Amotherby and Kirby Grindalythe, which are all approximately contemporary with the Wharram pieces, also reused stones first quarried in the Roman period is no longer ascertainable.

It seems likely, then, that these are three later Romano-British sarcophagi lids which have been brought to the site from elsewhere for reuse as grave-covers in the Anglo-Scandinavian period. The context of discovery establishes that the burials, over which the reused covers were placed, were made in an early phase of the burial

ground at St Martin's (see below). The arrival of the stones at the site can probably be dated by the secondary cross on stone No. 3. Unfortunately this cross is not easy to date precisely through style-critical comparison, but it is very similar in technique and form to examples found from Lincolnshire to Northumberland in the late 10th and 11th centuries. In its simple 'outline' technique it seems similar to several examples from St Mark's church Lincoln (Stocker 1986, e.g. nos III/11, I/5, I/6), which were thought there to date from the early 11th century rather than the late 10th century. A date in the early or mid-11th century may therefore be preferable for the St Martin's examples, and therefore for the introduction of the Romano-British stones to the site for reuse.

The use of such covers over burials made in simple wooden coffins, or even within shrouds without coffins as at St Martin's is not that unusual, and was found at both Raunds (Boddington 1996) and St Mark's, Lincoln (Gilmour and Stocker 1986; see also Gilchrist and Sloane 2005, 181-94). Stone covers of this general type were used to mark the burial and to prevent its early disturbance through grave-digging.

Group B - three fragments from at least two grave-covers reused in the foundations of the south aisle (left in situ *and not available for further study)*
Catalogue
4* (no CASSS number, *Wharram III*, no. 8) Fig. 134
This is a section from a large, apparently undecorated, coped and tapered grave-cover in an unknown stone type. It was laid transversely across a rubble platform to provide a foundation in the central part of the south aisle wall, which was built in the 12th century.

The cover represented was large in size, although it is not known how long this section was. It had dressed vertical sides and a dressed base. The upper surface was of a simple coped profile, without known decoration. The one known end was broken, rather than cut, and as the stone tapers within the known section, it can be said that the visible part represents the central section of the cover. Whilst it is not possible to know whether the head survives, the foot end has certainly been removed. It can also be calculated that, whilst it is geometrically possible for either stone No. 4 or stone No. 6 to have been part of the cover represented by stone No. 5, it is not possible for both Nos 4 and 6 to have come from the same tapered cover, as both represent the same parts of their respective covers.

5* (no CASSS number, *Wharram III*, no. 9) Fig. 134
This is a section from the head end of a large, apparently undecorated, coped and tapered grave-cover in an unknown stone type. It was laid transversely across a rubble platform to provide a foundation in the central part of the south aisle wall, which was built in the 12th century.

The cover represented was large in size, although we don't know how long this section was. It has a dressed end at the maximum of the taper and the known section therefore represents the head end. It had dressed vertical sides and a dressed base. The upper surface was of a simple coped profile, without known decoration. It can be calculated that, whilst it is geometrically possible for either stone No. 4 or stone No. 6 to be part of the cover represented by No. 5, it is not possible for both Nos 4 and 6 to have come from the same tapered cover, as both represent the same parts of their respective covers. It is also the case, however, that, if reconstructed as parts of the cover represented by No. 5, the ridges on both Nos 4 and 6 fall in inappropriate alignments, suggesting, perhaps, that three original covers might be represented by the three stones in Group B, rather than two.

6* (no CASSS number, *Wharram III*, no. 10) Fig. 134

This is a section from a large undecorated coped and tapered grave-cover in an unknown stone type. It was laid transversely across a rubble platform to provide a foundation in the central part of the south aisle wall, which was built in the 12th century.

The cover represented was large in size, although the length of this section is not known. It had dressed vertical sides and a dressed base. The upper surface was of a simple coped profile, without known decoration. The one known end was broken, rather than cut and, as the stone tapers within the known section, it is possible to say that the visible part represents the central section of the cover. It is not known whether the cover's foot survives, but the head end has certainly been removed. It can also be calculated that, whilst it is geometrically possible for either stone No. 4 or No. 6 to have been part of the cover represented by No. 5, it is not possible for both Nos 4 and 6 to have come from the same tapered cover, as both represent the same parts of their respective covers.

Discussion

Large tapered covers of this simple, undecorated, coped type are relatively common finds and eighteen were recovered in the excavations at St Mark's Lincoln. Here they belonged to the second of the two assemblages represented on the site and were though to date between the 11th and 13th centuries. A similar date bracket (perhaps *c.* 1060-1160, rather than much later) is probably appropriate for the St Martin's examples, although the monument form is not precisely datable.

Group C - fragments from five upright grave-markers
Catalogue
7*, 8*, 9* and 10* (no CASSS numbers, *Wharram III*, nos 1, 3, 4 and 6) Fig. 133

These are the lower parts of four small upright grave-markers, of the same Upper Jurassic Coral Rag (G.D. Gaunt) as the covers in Group A, excavated *in situ* south of the chancel (Nos 1, 2 and 3). It seems clear that cover No. 1 was equipped with a grave-marker at either - east and west - end (Nos 7 and 8). Cover No. 2 was also equipped with at least one marker at the head end (marker No. 9), however it remains uncertain whether marker No. 10 was intended to mark the foot (east) end of cover No. 2 or the head (west) end, of cover No. 3.

In form, all four markers are tapered slabs dressed on their broad and narrow faces and with their upper parts broken away. By comparison with other examples of similar markers we can say that approximately two-thirds of each is missing here. It is likely that the uppermost parts of each marker, those projecting above ground surface, were broken away during the life of the cemetery. Numbers 7, 9 and 10 all preserve indications of the very lowest part of the panels showing above ground level, and which may have carried decoration. The transition between the roughly-dressed bases in the ground and the panels above is marked by an instep in the profile of the stones (especially marked on stone No. 10). There are signs also, of the characteristic change from crude tooling used to face the markers' bases (which would have been below ground level) to a finer tooling finish used on the surfaces that were originally visible above ground.

11 (No CASSS number)

This number has been allocated to a fifth upright grave-marker, also broken off at what was contemporary ground level, but incorporated in the footings of the chancel foundation raft of Phase 3. This stratigraphic location allows us to date the stone to the period prior to the 12th century, and its alignment with the markers at the head end of cover No. 3 and the foot end of cover No. 1 may suggest that it marked a burial of similar type and date. No associated grave-cover was noted, however, and the marker was not recovered or drawn in detail, and its stone type is unknown.

Discussion

Such grave-markers are common finds in the 10th and 11th centuries in the Danelaw (Everson and Stocker 1999, 58-62). At St Mark's Lincoln, most examples were tapered, like the St Martin's examples (Stocker 1986, nos I/17, I/19, I/23, II/15, II/16, II/18). Here, too, a single example was discovered *in situ* (I/23), with some decoration surviving above contemporary ground level. Such markers were produced at a number of production centres in Lincolnshire, Yorkshire and the North-east and are usually allocated dates on the basis of their decoration. Having lost any decoration they may once have had, however, the St Martin's markers should be dated to the earlier part of the 11th century on the basis that they are contemporary with the reuse of the covers alongside which they were erected. If No. 10 belonged to cover No. 2 and not to No. 3, No. 3 would be the only burial in this group without an upright marker. Yet this is the only cover in the group decorated with a cross. It may be that similar iconography was provided for the burials under covers Nos 1 and 2 by crosses (now lost) worked on the upper faces of one or both of the markers standing at either end.

Group D - A single fragment from a stone sarcophagus (left in situ *and not available for further study)*
Catalogue
12* (No CASSS number, *Wharram III*, no. 11) Fig. 134

Alongside the three grave-cover sections in Group B (above), a fourth stone, No. 12, was also laid transversely across the rubble footings of the south aisle as building rubble. It probably represents the base of a monolithic sarcophagus. As drawn, however, the stone displays no taper and it is just possible that this represents the remains of some other kind of stone trough or tank. Nevertheless, given its context, it is most likely to represent a sarcophagus. It has been well dressed on the base and side walls, but the upper parts of the side walls have been broken away to make a more suitable shape for reuse in fabric. The original interior of the sarcophagus was dressed with characteristically deep and crude blows with a scappling hammer, point or similar implement.

Discussion

Presuming that this stone does represent a monolithic sarcophagus, and not some other type of basin or trough, it provides two points for discussion. First, the burial chamber is thick-walled and appears not to be tapered, features seen in such sarcophagi only up until the 12th century, but which are particularly associated with Romano-British examples. Secondly, the rough scappling of the interior, though intrinsically undatable, is also often a relatively early feature, and indeed is as characteristic of Romano-British examples as it is of those from the late Anglo-Saxon period. Despite the fact that there are further sarcophagus fragments for which a Roman date might be applicable (Nos 13-16 below), it may be safer, however, to date the sarcophagus represented by stone No. 12 through its proximity to the three covers which were reused in the South Aisle fabric alongside it (Nos 4, 5 and 6), rather than insist that this too is a reused Roman piece. It is likely that all these stones were displaced from the graveyard at a single moment (see below) and therefore that the sarcophagus represented by stone No. 12 may have come from the same high-status burial group represented by

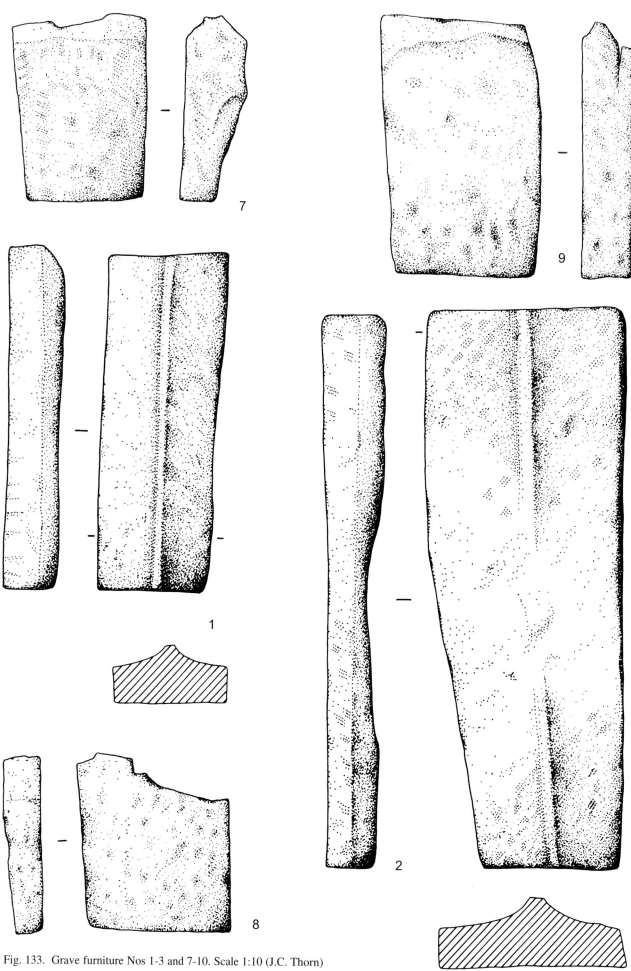

Fig. 133. Grave furniture Nos 1-3 and 7-10. Scale 1:10 (J.C. Thorn)

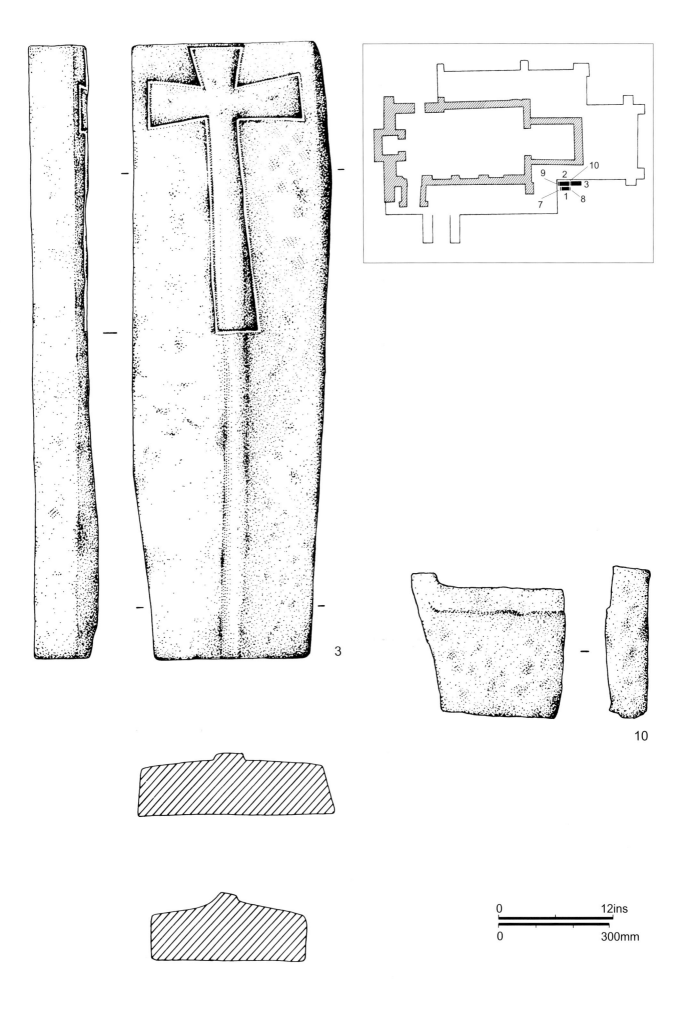

3

10

0   12ins

0   300mm

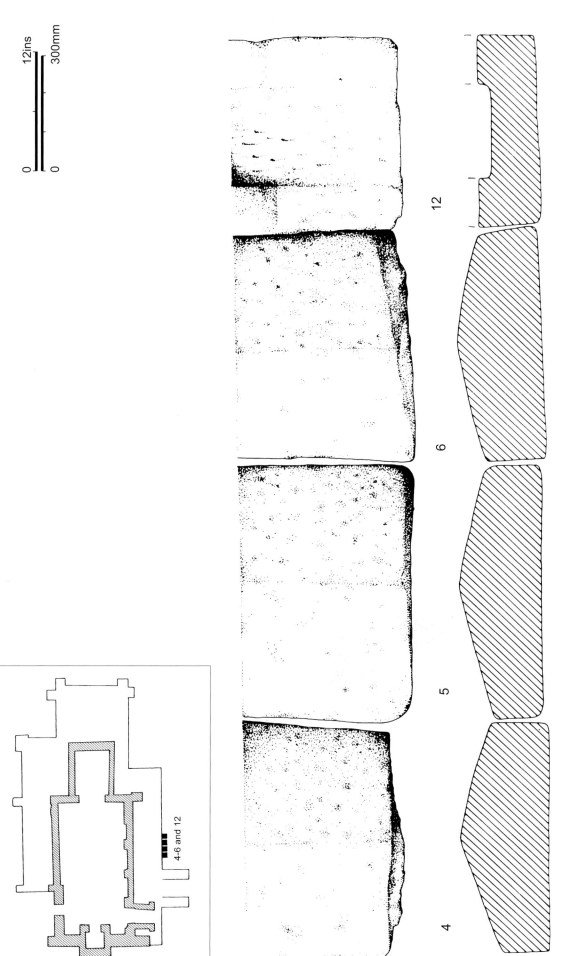

Fig. 134. Grave furniture Nos 4-6 and 12. Scale 1:10 (J.C. Thorn)

12ins

300mm

0

0

12

6

5

4

4-6 and 12

Plate 102. Grave-cover No. 1; view of upper surfaces. Note prominent Roman pick-work or 'scappling'.

Plate 103. Grave-cover No. 1; view of underside. Note the difference in technique between the Roman diagonal tooling along the chamfered edges and the bold pick-work, or 'scappling' in the centre (also Roman).

Plate 105. Grave-cover No. 1; end view showing prominent 'ridge-rib'. Note chamfering on underside angles.

Plate 104. Grave-cover No. 1; view of long edge. Note the prominent Roman vertical tooling, made with the same tool as the chamfered undersides.

Plate 106. Grave-cover No. 2; side view. Note damage to ridge-rib, and prominent vertical Roman tooling, made using a broad-bladed tool similar in size and type to that on the ends and underside chamfers.

Plate 107. Grave-cover No. 2; view of upper surfaces. Note prominent Roman pick-work or 'scappling' and the damage to the central part of the ridge-rib.

Plate 108. Grave-cover No. 2; view of underside. Note the difference in technique between the Roman diagonal tooling along the broad chamfered margins and the bold pick-work, or 'scappling in the centre (also Roman).

Plate 109. Grave-cover No. 2; end view, showing 'ridge-rib'. Note crude, broad, Roman, diagonal tooling, created with a broad blade, similar to that used to cut the chamfers on the underside.

Plate 110. Grave-cover No. 2; view of upper surfaces illustrating the mechanical damage to the ridge rib.

Plate 111. Grave-cover No. 2; view of upper surfaces. Note prominent Roman pick-work or 'scappling' and damage to the central part of the ridge-rib.

Plate 112. Grave-cover No. 3; end view showing the prominent ridge-rib.

Plate 113. Grave-cover No. 3; view of upper surfaces showing the weathered Roman pick-work or 'scappling' and the ridge-rib cut away towards the head end in a reworking of the Anglo-Scandinavian period, to be replaced by the deeply incised cross.

Plate 114. Grave-cover No. 3; view of upper surfaces showing the weathered Roman pick-work or 'scappling' and the prominent original ridge-rib.

Plate 115. Grave-cover No. 3; view of upper surfaces showing the original Roman ridge rib cut away in the Anglo-Scandinavian period to create the deeply incised cross.

Plate 116. Grave-cover No. 3; detail of upper surfaces at head end, showing the panel cut into the Roman cover to receive the Anglo-Scandinavian period cross.

Plate 117. Grave-cover No. 3; side view. Note the original diagonal Roman tooling made with a broad blade.

Plate 118. Sarcophagus Nos 13-16; four fragments perhaps from the same original sarcophagus, of probable Roman date.

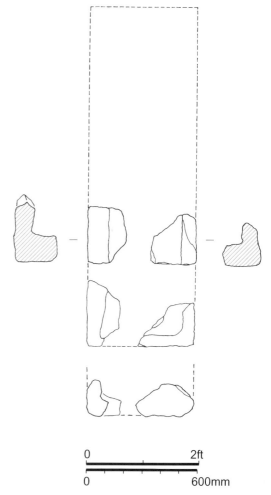

Fig. 135. Schematic reconstruction drawing of sarcophagus, from fragments Nos 13-16: in plan, elevation and section. (P. Pullan)

these grave-covers. These covers apparently represent burials of the period between c. 1060 and c. 1160, and this date would be just as acceptable for what we know of this monolithic sarcophagus as one in the Roman period.

Group E - Four fragments from a stone sarcophagus
Catalogue
13-16* (No CASSS numbers) Fig. 135, **Plate 118**

> The excavations produced four fragments from a stone sarcophagus (or conceivably from more than one such monument) made of the same Jurassic Corallian ragstone as the three excavated reused grave-covers and the markers that accompanied them (see above for petrological description). None of these fragments is decorated and all show signs of having been broken-up for reuse as building rubble. Two of the stones have been recut for placement in walls of something like ashlar construction, and one of them retains a limewashed surface, which must date from the period of its reuse. Further fragments of Coral Rag, but not retaining any surfaces, have been found across the village.

Discussion

It is not possible to say much about the sarcophagus or sarcophagi from which these stones originally derived, as no complete dimension has survived. Neither is it possible to say how these four fragments relate to the sarcophagus fragment incorporated in the footings of the south wall (stone No. 12 above). Two of the stones represent, however, angles of the original monument and they show that this part, at least, was cut square. These angles show no detectable taper on the sarcophagus. Neither is there any sign of a 'cut-out' for the head of the deceased, although this feature could have been at the missing end. Nevertheless, there are several indications that the sarcophagus (or sarcophagi) might be of Roman date, rather than having been newly quarried for the medieval graveyard. First, the stones are made of the same stone type as the three covers which can be shown to be reused Roman funerary monuments (above Group A). All three of these covers show signs of having been intended originally to sit above stone sarcophagi or stone-built cists. Secondly, the sarcophagus, or sarcophagi, represented by Nos 13-16 appears to have been rectangular in plan, than tapered and, although not a conclusive observation, this shape is more frequent in Roman than medieval sarcophagi (see for example the typology of medieval examples developed in Gilchrist and Sloane 2005, 147-51). Unfortunately the archive does not reveal from precisely which part of the church the stones were recovered, but it is thought that some of them, at least, must have come from rubble released in the fall of the tower. If some or all of these fragments had been reused in the tower fabric, it would seem that the sarcophagus (or sarcophagi) represented was already redundant and reduced to building rubble by the central 12th century. This detail, too, might point towards the original monument(s) having been of Roman rather than medieval date.

General discussion – laid to rest at Wharram
Origins of the Roman graveyard furniture
Before considering the significance of the reused Romano-British graveyard furniture in its Anglo-Scandinavian context at St Martin's we have to consider its likely origin

and, initially, we should acknowledge the likelihood that all three reused covers (Nos 1, 2 and 3) came from the same original Romano-British cemetery. It is surely inconceivable that such similar stones should have arrived at Wharram by chance from different sources. It is also likely, given the diversity of types and date range of monuments found in most Romano-British graveyards, that these three monuments were originally provided for related burials, probably lying adjacent to each other in their original cemetery. Broadly speaking, there appear to be three potential origins for such a group of closely related memorials: a small local cemetery attached to, or associated with, a local temple or villa complex; Roman Malton (*Derventio*); or Roman York (*Ebvracvm*). These three possibilities are considered in order below. The sarcophagi fragments of the same Jurassic Corallian ragstone as the grave-covers (Nos 13-16) may have come from this same source, if indeed they also represent a reused Roman artefact or artefacts. It is possible that the stones (also of Jurassic Corallian ragstone) used to make the upright markers (Nos 7, 8, 9 and 10) also originated at the same Roman source, although intrinsic evidence for their being reused at all is absent.

A local temple or villa complex (Fig. 136)
Roman stone sarcophagi with lids originally of the same general type as those reused at Wharram have been recovered from several 'private' cemeteries associated with both villas and temple complexes (EH 1988). Three groups of such villas or temples have now been recognised on the Yorkshire Wolds (Wilson 2003, 52-3): a group of four in the hills around Rudston, of five at the southern end of the Wolds west of Beverley and Hull, and a group of sites around Wharram itself. Here several potential 'villa' or 'temple' sites have been distinguished within Hayfield's study area, from amongst a group of eleven possible settlements of the Romano-British period, through the character of surface finds collected (Hayfield 1988b, 106-14). Although the graveyard furniture reused at St Martin's could, in principle, have come from burial sites associated with any of these locations, cemeteries containing elite burials of the type indicated by our stones, are more usually small and 'private' in character, and we might expect them to be associated with 'villas' rather than with Romanised native settlements (EH 1988). Excluding the Romanised native settlements as likely origins for the elite graveyard furniture from St Martin's, then, we are left with cemeteries associated with four potential 'local' sites: the partly-excavated villa site at Langton, some 7km to the north-west, towards Malton (Corder and Kirk 1932; Ramm 1988); the partly investigated villa at Wharram Grange (*Wharram IV*; Rahtz 1988), less than two kilometres to the north-west; the 'villa' or 'temple' site associated with the source of the Gypsey Race to the east of the modern village of Wharram le Street (*Wharram IV*); and the site of uncertain status at Wharram Percy itself (Rahtz 1988, 127-8). None of these sites has yet produced good evidence for a dedicated cemetery where

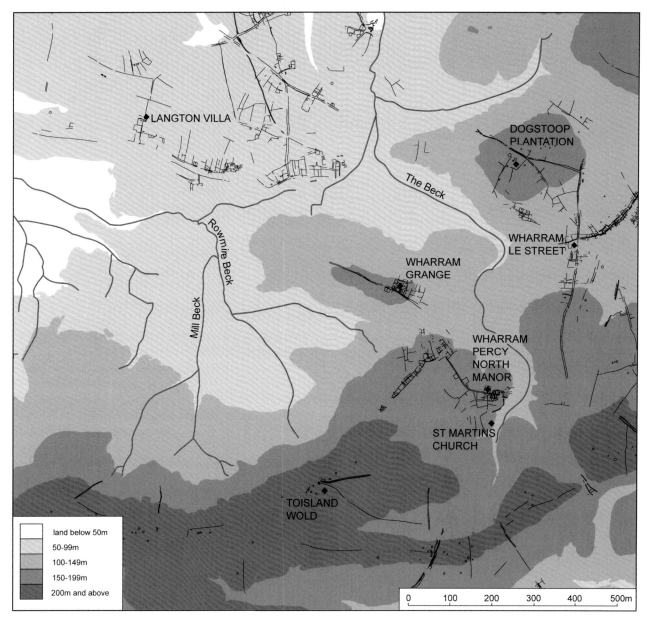

Fig. 136. Map showing relative locations of sites discussed. (A. Deegan after C. Stoertz)

the elite owners of these complexes and their families might have been buried but, as investigations have been within and close to the complexes themselves, such evidence is perhaps not to be expected. Even so, these sites presumably represent the only locations in the general vicinity of St Martin's where members of the Romano-British elite commemorated by this type of stone grave furniture were to be found.

Relationships in the landscape between 'private' cemeteries of the rural elite and the 'villas' or settlement sites with which they were also associated have yet to be systematically explored in England. However, Warwick Rodwell's intelligent analysis of the landscape setting of the Roman villa and estate at Rivenhall (Essex) may be instructive when considering potential sources of the Roman funerary material reused at St Martin's in the late 10th or early 11th century (Rodwell and Rodwell 1986). At Rivenhall, Rodwell showed how the villa site itself took advantage of a dramatic location on the gentle east-

facing slope of a river valley. Yet it was also, Rodwell suggests, aligned on a prominent hill on the opposite side of the river, 600 metres to the east. In a manner reminiscent of Whig landowners of the 18th century (at Castle Howard north-west of Wharram for example), Rodwell suggests that this hill was adopted as the location for the mausoleum of the family of the villa's owners, and there is some evidence for the former existence of mortuary monuments on its brow. This hill would have been selected partly because of its prominence in the landscape viewed from the villa itself but, as well as being visible, it was also of course, 'distanced' from the living. Rodwell was unable to obtain clear proof of his proposals about the relationship between his villa site and the elite cemetery with which he thought it was associated, but his suggestions have yet to be seriously challenged.

Can we use similar thinking about the setting of the 'villas' around Wharram to help us suggest where the 'private cemeteries' of their owners might have been located? The Langton villa is a long way from Wharram Percy; indeed it is nearly at Malton (*Derventio*), and the villa's elite may have buried in the extensive extra-mural cemeteries at Norton there (see below). Furthermore, one might suggest that, if an Anglo-Scandinavian lord of Wharram was searching for prestigious Roman graveyard furniture for reuse by his own family, and was prepared to go as far as Langton, he might have gone a few kilometres further into Norton itself, where such furniture was, presumably, more readily available. On the other hand the Wharram Grange villa was, probably, within the Wharram domain in the 11th century and bringing grave furniture from any associated cemetery would not have posed such logistical problems. There may also have been political capital to be made, with the Anglo-Scandinavian lord – himself perhaps recently established - laying claim to what was still understood to be a domain once owned by the Romans, by acquiring such artefacts and taking them to his new estate centre. Rather than Langton then, perhaps we should ask where the Romano-British owners of the potential villa sites within the Wharram domain itself might have buried. Although Hayfield was initially very cautious about the use of the term (*Wharram IV*, section 20), the description of the site at Wharram Grange as a villa has not been challenged subsequently. It seems to have all the requisite defining characteristics (mosaics, hypocausts, wall plaster etc.), although the period during which it was occupied may still be the subject of some discussion. No Romano-British burial remains were reported from the site but, if it was anything like the Rivenhall villa, we might expect the family of the owners to have buried at a distance. Even so, it may have been important for the family burial site (and perhaps monuments erected there) to be visible from the villa itself. The known barrow field at Toisland Wold, to the south-west of Wharram Grange is not visible from the villa site, but that at Dogstoop Plantation, about 1750m to the north-east across the river valley is not only clearly visible, but it is also a most prominent local landscape feature. Indeed the enclosures within which the Wharram Grange villa sits are orientated in the landscape almost at right-angles to Dogstoop Plantation, in much the same way that the Rivenhall villa is orientated orthogonally on Rodwell's proposed family burial ground. On the knoll at Dogstoop, Catherine Stoertz (1997) plotted a large, irregular rectangular enclosure within and around which are scattered a group of ring-ditches, presumably representing barrows: including two of great size near the brow of the knoll, but located down-slope to the west in such a way that they would have appeared on the skyline from Wharram Grange. The Monument Class Description (EH 1988) notes the frequency with which small rural cemeteries of the Romano-British period contain large barrows.

Turning to face more nearly due west from the Wharram Grange villa, the 'villa' site at Wharram le Street might also have been just visible. Unlike the Wharram Grange site, however, the interpretation of the site at Wharram le Street as a genuine villa, has been challenged, and given its proximity to what must have been a dramatic water source on the high, dry, wolds, the suggestion that the structures here represent some form of temple is certainly persuasive (*Wharram IV*; Rahtz 1988). An interpretation of the site as a temple might also sit more conformably with the suggestion that the Wharram Grange villa was the centre of the estate: at a stroke it removes the possibility of two rival villas in close proximity (although so called 'double' or 'paired' villas are known elsewhere on the Wolds) and would permit the suggestion that the elite family occupying Wharram Grange were in some sense also patrons of the spring and of the religious site associated with it. For our purposes, however, we need to ask whether any such 'temple' site might have also included a 'private' burial ground. Without further investigation at Wharram le Street, it is impossible to answer such a question authoritatively, but an inhumation was found on the site in 1935 and two 'infant' burials were found during excavations of test pits here (*Wharram IV*, section 6). The problem with these burials is that we remain unsure of their date and context and it is far from clear that they represent a formal cemetery of the type that might be represented by the cropmarks at Dogstoop Plantation. They appear to be located close to the centre of the building complex in what would be a very unexpected manner for a formal Roman cemetery. Furthermore, we should notice that rural temple enclosures are not necessarily associated with high-status 'private' cemeteries of the type we are suggesting would have been the origin of the grave furniture reused at Wharram Percy. On the other hand, Early and Middle Saxon burials are ubiquitous on villa sites (Williams 1997) and it may be that these inhumations at Wharram le Street are actually post-Roman in date.

Finally, it has long been clear that a Romano-British settlement site of some importance lay in the vicinity of the North Manor at Wharram Percy village itself. This site has also been proposed as another possible 'villa' (*Wharram IV*, section 27.3; Rahtz 1988, 127-8; *Wharram IX*, 283-4), but Hayfield argues that it is merely another Romanised native settlement, similar to (if perhaps larger than) others within his study area (1988b, 114-16). Hayfield's view was given qualified support in the final consideration of the site by Cool (2004, 343-4). Whether representing a villa or not, the excavated neonatal burials of Romano-British date here do not help us with our search for the burial grounds of the local Romano-British elite, as such infants would not have been accorded burial in such a cemetery (Gowland 2001). Even so, the North Manor site also produced evidence for late Romano-British funeral pyres and cremation burial (Cool 2004, 345-6), so it cannot be entirely ruled out as a potential location for the inhumation of the local rural elite. The more elaborate adult inhumation, grave 17, on the North Manor site, however, is now thought to be early medieval in date (*Wharram IX*, 15; but see also Cool 2004, 346).

Having reviewed the known options, then, we remain unable to demonstrate that the Roman grave furniture was brought to St Martin's in the 11th century from any specific local Roman graveyard. There is little justification for associating it with the Langton villa, but there are some circumstantial reasons why we might suggest that it was brought from the 'private' cemetery, belonging to the elite family who may have occupied the Wharram Grange complex, the least equivocal of the proposed local villa sites. It remains difficult to understand the excavated evidence from the North Manor (for burial as for other activities), so currently there seem to be just two potential locations in the local landscape for such an elite cemetery. It is conceivable that it was associated with the 'villa' or 'temple' site at Wharram le Street, but the landscape setting of the barrow field at Dogstoop Plantation sits more conformably with the Wharram Grange villa site itself, especially if we stress the parallel with the more fully explored example at Rivenhall. The knoll on which the Dogstoop Plantation barrows are located is itself made of chalk, but it stands directly above the quarries in Grimston Hill which are known to have produced a Jurassic Corallian ragstone of precisely the type which was used for the sarcophagi, lids and markers. If the stones were quarried hereabouts, then their original journey to this putative cemetery site in the 3rd or 4th century would have been short: perhaps less than one kilometre. A hypothetical second journey in the late 10th or early 11th century across the river to the new burial ground at St Martin's would have been slightly longer, but still not more than 2km.

Roman Malton (Derventio)
A second possibility is that all three lids and the sarcophagus fragments came from one of the extensive cemeteries around Roman Malton (*Derventio*)(Wenham 1974, 44-6). Jurassic Corallian ragstone was certainly quarried within a few miles of the fort and settlement, and at least one monolithic coffin has been recovered from the Norton cemeteries (Robinson 1978, 36 no. 271; Wilson 2006, 44-5). Unfortunately its stone-type is not known. In 1866, a second 'cist or sarcophagus burial' was found (without any lid) close to the fort at Malton. This item was said to have been moved to the grounds of The Lodge and has subsequently been lost, but the fact that it was moved in this way suggests that it too was a monolithic sarcophagus. It remains the case however, that no sarcophagus lids of the Wharram type have survived from Derventio, although at least six are known from York.

Roman York (Ebvracvm)
All six of the sarcophagus lids found at York that are of the same design as those from Wharram are said to have been cut in 'gritstone' (RCHME 1962, 129-31),[3] although there has been some serious criticism of the petrological analysis which led to that description (Buckland 1984; 1988). The stone supply of Roman York has been much debated, and for a long time it was thought that Roman York did not obtain much (if any) stone from the Jurassic hills to the east. In his two important revisionist papers, however, Paul Buckland demonstrated, not just that Jurassic limestone of the type used for the Wharram covers was widely used in late Roman York, but also that it might have been used,

particularly, for graveyard structures, and that it played a key role in the extensive late Roman pottery trade in the Derwent valley (1984; 1988, 262-5). Peter Wenham excavated a grave at Trentholme Drive, York (1968, 42-4), which was actually covered with slabs of Jurassic Corallian ragstone from the Malton area. Unfortunately this was not a single slab and was unworked, but the discovery demonstrated both that large slabs of this stone were being imported from the Malton area in the late Roman period and that those slabs were being fashioned by masons making burial monuments.

Potential sources for the reused Roman stone: Conclusion
Interesting and informative though this debate over the origins of the reused stones at St Martin's may be, however, we have still not been able to find conclusive evidence locating the original graveyard from which the Romano-British graveyard furniture came. Although it could have come from the *Derventio* graveyards, nothing like it has been recorded from there. On the other hand, similar material has been found in York and, thanks to Buckland's work, the trade in stone for funeral monuments between Roman York and quarries in the Malton area has been identified. Consequently a York origin for the Wharram grave furniture cannot be ruled out. But perhaps it is safest to take a simple functionalist view of the problem and argue that the grave furniture is most likely to have come to St Martin's from the nearest available source. This was probably a 'private' cemetery associated with a local villa. Perhaps the most likely candidate for such a villa is that at Wharram Grange, which (on the Rivenhall parallel) might have been associated with a cemetery at Dogstoop Plantation, although that villa could have been associated, instead or as well, with the 'temple' site at Wharram le Street, where inhumations might also have occurred. At present we can only take this discussion further forward by considering the manner in which the Roman grave furniture was reused at St Martin's, and we should now turn to consider that reuse.

A 'founder's' burial group and its ecclesiastical and political context
Only relatively small areas of the St Martin's graveyard were excavated during the project, and we remain uncertain how representative is the group of covers south of the chancel of the Phase 2 church. Even so, the covers occupy a similar position relative to the chancel to the contemporary group of burials marked with stone at Furnell's Manor, Rounds (Northamptonshire), where the entire graveyard was excavated (Boddington *et al.* 1996, 67 etc.). There, a single burial beneath a carved stone cover (marked with an upright cross) south-east of the chancel of the first church, clearly belonged to a high-status family who, it is presumed, occupied the adjacent manor and founded both the parochial burial ground and the church. This grave has been called a 'founder's grave' and this Rounds evidence has led to the suggestion that many of the worked stone monuments of the period *c.* 950-

1050 or later, relate to the burials of 'founders' of parochial churches; a suggestion which is lent some support from other sources of evidence, at least in Lincolnshire (Everson and Stocker 1999, 76-9; Stocker and Everson 2001). In Lincolnshire, also, we have suggested that the stone marking these 'founder' burials was sometimes provided by the newly re-established Bishop of Dorchester, from quarries opened up around Lincoln, as a way of establishing a physical connection between the newly established parochial graveyard and the newly re-established bishopric. Some of these Lincolnshire monuments reused Roman *spolia* and there is no doubt that burials reusing Roman stone monuments were considered prestigious throughout the Anglo-Saxon period. Bede made a point of describing the search for St Etheldreda's coffin amongst the ruins of Roman Grantchester (Colgrave and Mynors 1969, 394, IV.19) and Charlemagne himself imported a fine late Roman coffin for himself from Italy (e.g. Crook 2000, 77-8, 247). Closer to home, and later in date, it is also significant that St William of York was buried in a Roman sarcophagus in the Minster nave in 1154 (Phillips 1985, 125-7). With such cases in mind, it has been suggested that 10th-century Archbishops of York (as at Lincoln) may also have been keen to establish physical links between the archiepiscopal centre and newly founded parochial graveyards and churches in the archdiocese (Stocker 2000, 197-8). Unlike at Lincoln, however, there was no quarrying industry at York, so any stone dispatched to furnish the new 'founders' graves' in Yorkshire churches would have been prestigious reused Roman *spolia* from the city itself.

As far as we know, the development of St Martin's graveyard was similar to that at Raunds. At approximately the same date, a senior group of three burials, marked with reused carved stones, were located south-east of the chancel of the Phase 2 church. On the basis of the Raunds parallel, in type and location at least, these monuments should relate to the 'founder' of the parochial graveyard and his/her family. If these monuments do represent a 'founder' and his kin group, as at Raunds, then we might speculate that the Roman *spolia* used to mark their graves was intended to make a contemporary political point. Unfortunately that point is no longer made with any clarity today.

On the one hand it might argue that the stones came from a Roman graveyard at York (perhaps in preference to *Derventio*) and were seen as a gesture demonstrating the link between the newly 'founded' parochial churchyard and the archbishopric. This sort of mechanism might help to explain why three such similar sarcophagus lids were brought from elsewhere for reuse together. In such a scenario the 'founder' would be presented with Roman stone grave furniture by the Archbishop as a gift registering his support of his entire family, and they may have been stored as prestige items against the moment when they were needed. But it is equally possible that the political point being made by the reuse of Roman graveyard furniture was more local, and

that it had been brought from a local 'private cemetery' of the Romano-British elite. In such circumstances, it may be that 11th-century lords of the Wharram estate were seeking to confirm themselves and their families as the heirs of the Romano-British owners of the same domain. In their own small way, perhaps, they were emulating Charlemagne himself in appropriating the burial monuments of figures from their own local myth and/or history with whom they wished to associate themselves in the eyes of their contemporaries.

Yet at the same time we should also note that the early lords of Wharram did not seek to make great distinctions between one individual and another. There are certainly no inscriptions on any of the six known covers to identify the individuals commemorated, indeed the deployment of the three reused Romano-British covers serves to submerge the individuality of the deceased, emphasising instead their common kinship as a group, with its single leader marked out by his position to the east and by the use of a simple cross. It is likely that there would have been some decoration on the various markers in Group C, but the evidence of better preserved contemporary examples suggests that these too are unlikely to have stressed the individuality of the deceased. These graveyard memorials, then, seem to emphasise the deceased's membership of the elite kin group, rather than to celebrate their individuality. Consequently, we might suggest that the Wharram monuments' celebration of the kin group, like many other displays of funerary sculpture between the 10th and the 13th centuries, stands between the earlier tradition of more anonymous burial for all but the saintly in a cemetery marked by a single cross, and the later more personal memorial, where an individual is often commemorated by an inscription registering their actual name.

Some early lords of Wharram Percy and their kin
Unfortunately the boundaries of the Phase I graveyard are unknown, but if we presume that the whole earthwork terrace on which the church stands was demarcated for burial, the 'founder' group (above) lies approximately due east of the graveyard's central point. It appears (from Bell *et al.* 1987, fig. 11), however, that they were not the earliest burials within this demarcated space, as they overlie at least three other interments. This conclusion is supported by radiocarbon dates from within the graveyard implying that burial began here between AD 940 and 995; a full generation (and probably more) before the expected style-critical date of the cross on grave-cover No. 3. If these three ornamented burials represent, on the one hand, 'founder' burials, perhaps made with the support of the archbishop and the church hierarchy but, on the other hand, they were made in a graveyard which had already been used for at least one generation of burials, presumably we are detecting a shift in the settlement's sociology. Initially, it seems, burials were made here with less emphasis placed on the expression of social hierarchy, but subsequently, in the 'founder' generation, burial might have been used to express and legitimise a new hierarchical order. Furthermore, it was

argued in the 1987 report that the burial ground was established before the Phase 2 masonry church was constructed (Bell *et al.* 1987, 57). It is possible that this 'founder' phase (more strictly a formal 'refoundation'?) was connected with the construction of that first stone church. In that case, the archiepiscopal connection with the graveyard becomes more overt, as the Archbishop's presence (or more likely that of his representative) may have been necessary for the consecration of the church. Was the occasion marked by the Archbishop's gift of stone grave furniture? Or alternatively, did the 'founder' seek to emphasise, on this occasion, his links with the Roman owners of the domain by reusing their grave furniture for his own family members?

The spatial disposition of the 'founders' group within the graveyard is also interesting. Not only does the great similarity between the monuments strongly suggest that the three burials represent a kin group, but their disposition relative to each other may also be significant, and probably also points to a closely related group of burials. The long section (Fig. 11) shows that the burials and the monuments were cut into a gently sloping bank above the river, facing east. The grave with the cross-marked cover is set further down-slope and east of the other adult. As the burials face east, anticipating the Resurrection, the more easterly position might be considered the more important, or at least in some sense 'leading' the group. It is appropriate, then, that it is this grave-cover which carries the decoration. The grave behind, also an adult, has been dug so close to the marked grave in front that it must have been intended to link the two individuals in death, almost so as to create a single monument. This was the grave of a female, and we can speculate that it represents the wife of a husband in front of her. This reading might be reinforced by the location of the child's burial so close to the right hand. Is this, perhaps, the couple's child, laid alongside the mother?

At Raunds, the 'founder' burial was accompanied by a second grave marked with a small approximately contemporary (or slightly later) carved grave-cover to the north-west (burial no. 5000). This proximity is unlikely to have been coincidental and here too we probably see the burial of a second member of the elite family being associated in death with the 'founder'. In addition to the Raunds 'founder' group, there were at least two other groups of burials marked by graves more elaborate than the norm in this cemetery. In particular, the prominent location south-west of the south door of the first church was occupied by a group of four burials which employed stone both in the construction of the grave (indeed one was in a monolithic coffin) and/or for marking the burials at the surface. Unfortunately, no markers or covers from this second group of burials survived and, although we can say that they were at least one generation later than the 'founder' group, it is not easy to date them absolutely. It is possible, however, that they either represent a second elite family, or (perhaps more likely) that they represent more distant connections of the 'founder' perhaps from two or three generations later. These putatively later

burials clearly relate to the construction of the first stone church at Raunds, whereas the 'founder' could have been buried before the church was constructed.

Presuming that the marked graves at St Martin's are indeed a 'founder' family group, associated in some way with the establishment of the stone church, the burials of subsequent generations of the local elite family, or families, may have been buried nearby, as suggested at Raunds. Consequently, we might suggest that the somewhat later grave-covers (Nos 4, 5 and 6) also came from this part of the burial ground. Such individuals might have wished to locate themselves 'behind' (i.e. to the west) of the 'founding' group to emphasise their legitimacy as descendants and, if they did, their graves would have to be removed when this part of the graveyard was cleared to construct the south aisle in Phase V. We should note, therefore, that another well-constructed grave (lined with stone blocks) was discovered in the vicinity of the south aisle east wall (Burial V47). According to Bell *et al.* (1987, 73), this burial was made in the century between the mid-11th and the mid-12th and was of an individual, perhaps a male, of about twelve years old with a child of about one year placed between the legs. Given its location relative to the 'founders' group, and the possibility that it had a fine stone grave-cover (removed to be incorporated within the aisle fabric), we can speculate that this represents the burial of descendants of the 'founders' kin group, buried a generation or so later than the woman who lay under grave-cover No. 2. The precise stratigraphic relationship between the stone cist of Burial V47 and grave-marker No. 7 to the east was obscured by a trench dug north-south across the churchyard, but it is not impossible that the cist actually employed the grave-marker stone itself to form the end of the burial chamber; literally incorporating the earlier monument into the later. The close physical association between these two burials, one from the 'founders' group and one perhaps only a generation later, is likely to have been an intentional gesture linking the two children in death, and probably more importantly, linking the two families who survived them.

If these speculations are valid, they would indicate that the original kin group was remembered clearly and respectfully for at least a generation after its burial, and that descendants wished to be associated with this group in their own burials. In the late 12th or early 13th century, when the south aisle came to be constructed over the western part of the enlarged 'founder' family plot, Burial V47 was treated with great care, and the interment was not disturbed. The occupant became physically 'incorporated' in the church foundation; a gesture of respect and an acknowledgment of status also found in the contemporary graveyard at St Mark's Lincoln (Gilmour and Stocker 1986, 20, 91, grave 358). The original monument over Burial V47, however, was evidently removed and may be one of those reused in the footings of the new aisle wall. As well as serving a functional purpose, this gesture too would have been one of respect; physically incorporating, as it were, the ancestors in the fabric of the new building. Furthermore, the excavators also noticed that the south aisle east wall (built several generations after the burial of the 'founder' group) was built hard up against the west side of grave-marker No. 9. But the burial marker was retained, and not removed for reuse, and this might suggest that the identity of the 'founder' group itself was still known, and that they were still respected, when the south aisle was built. We should note, also, that there were other burials around Burial V47, although none is recorded as being distinctive, and any of these might have been the original burials marked by the other covers now represented in the south aisle foundations.

Finally we should ask whether we can put a name to this group of elite individuals, whose status and date has been thus defined archaeologically. David Roffe (2000) has explained that *Domesday Book* reports that the two Royal manors of Wharram Percy were tenanted by Lagmann and Karli. Unfortunately the Royal estate and parochial entity (present already in 1086) incorporated a number of other settlements besides Wharram Percy and part of it was probably held alongside Wharram le Street, where there was also a church. The 'founder' monuments are likely to represent individuals senior by no more than a generation to Lagmann and Karli, and monuments, Nos 4, 5 and 6 probably belong to interments close to their own generation. David Roffe suggests that these two individuals were members of a group of more than 300 'King's Thegns' in late Anglo-Scandinavian Yorkshire (Roffe 2000, 9-10), and this fact, as well as their status as tenants on the Royal demesne, distinguishes them in status from the Tenants-in-Chief. Neither need necessarily have been of great power or status, though they would, together, have represented an elite within the Wharram community. It is likely that the 'founder' burial group and the burials marked by monuments Nos 4, 5 and 6 represent their immediate predecessors, their contemporary collaterals and their immediate descendants. Indeed it is even possible that one or two of these monuments might even mark their own graves.

Notes

1 I would like to dedicate this modest offering to the memory of John Hurst who, amongst so many more important tasks, found the time to make me feel welcome in English Heritage in 1986-7.

2 When this report was originally written, most of these stones were not available for inspection, having been reburied following the site's consolidation. Consequently no detailed archive record, to modern standards, was made of, for example, the tooling on the worked stone fragments during the post-excavation process. However, following drafting of the report, at the last moment (October 2006) it became possible to recover many of the stones from the site and transfer them to the English Heritage store at Helmsley. The author and the post-excavation team were able to study them on this occasion and to confirm many of the details suggested in the draft report. Unfortunately, on this occasion there was insufficient time to undertake a detailed metrical study of the tooling evidence, and it has only been recorded photographically.

3 Listing of Romano-British grave-covers of similar type to those from Wharram (RCHME 1962):

    York no. 104 – 'Gabled lid', 'gritstone', from Castle Yard
    York no. 105 – 'Gabled lid', 'gritstone', from railway bridge work north of Railway Station
    York no. 106 – 'Gabled lid', 'gritstone', from railway bridge work north of Railway Station
    York no. 107 – 'Gabled lid', 'millstone grit', from Castle Yard
    York no. 108 – 'Ridged lid', 'gritstone', from north-west of The Mount
    York no. 111 – 'Ridged lid', 'gritstone', from Railway Station

Post-Conquest stonework - medieval cross slab grave-covers
by P.F. Ryder

[Dr L.A.S. Butler catalogued most of these slabs (with comments by J.C. Thorn) for *Wharram III*, but the catalogue and his report were only published in fiche. This volume gave the opportunity to invite the author to place the Wharram stones in their local context and to publish a new report, along with Dr Butler's catalogue and including the author's updated comments on individual slabs (in italics). Dr Butler's original report and catalogue remain in the excavation archive. While the complete catalogue is now numbered within the catalogue sequence for the stone chapters of this volume, the original *Wharram III* catalogue numbers, where relevant, are given as well (Church 1) for ease of comparison.]

Many, if not the majority of the medieval churches in the Wolds retain medieval cross slab grave covers, albeit in fragmentary form; their most usual context today is, as at Wharram, as reused material in later fabric, although, unlike Wharram, this is usually the result of stones being found and then reset in Victorian restorations. Of the eight parishes bordering that of Wharram Percy, seven churches retain cross slabs; none has been recorded at Sledmere (where the church is largely a 19th-century rebuild). A total of 43 slabs were recorded at the churches in Birdsall (1), Fridaythorpe (4), Kirkby Grindalythe (13), Kirkby Underdale (8), North Grimston (3), Wharram le Street (2) and Wetwang (12). In addition, further slabs were photographed and drawn at Garton-on-the Wolds, Kilnwick-on-the-Wolds, Little Driffield and Westow.

The basic cross forms seen at Wharram Percy - straight arm and bracelet - were widely represented. Straight-arm crosses with round leaf occur at Kirkby Grindalythe, Kirkby Underdale and Wetwang, although the later form with the fully developed fleur-de-lys in which the leaf droops and is curled at the tip only occurs at Wharram (Nos 17-20, 28 and 30). Straight arm forms with clustered terminals (Wharram No. 25 and perhaps also No. 15) were well represented among the slabs at Fridaythorpe, Kirkby Grindalythe, Kirkby Underdale, North Grimston and Wharram le Street. Bracelet or four-circle crosses (Wharram Nos 32-34) also occur at Kirkby Underdale and at Wetwang where two are in conjunction

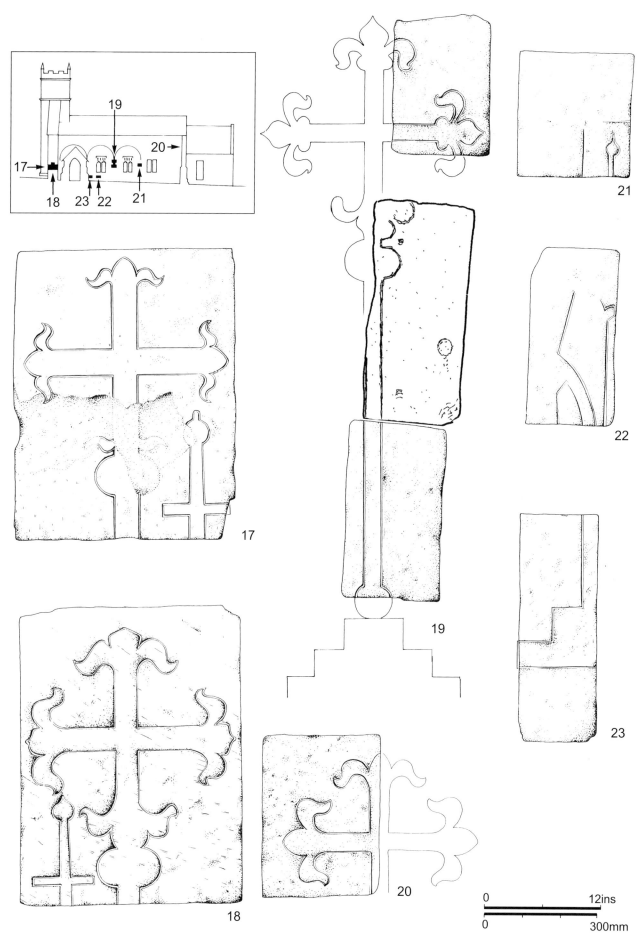

Fig. 137. Medieval cross slab grave-covers, Nos 17-23. Scale 1:10 (J.C. Thorn, middle stone of No. 19, P.F. Ryder)

with straight-arm forms. In general none of the Wharram cross forms is exceptional in any way; the predominance of straight-arm forms is very typical of East and South Yorkshire, whereas further north and west bracelet and four-circle forms become more dominant.

In most parts of the northern England the stepped mount is by far the most common form of cross base of which there are four examples at Wharram Percy (Nos 23, 24, 29 and 37). The neighbouring churches provide a number of examples of another distinctive form, a semi-circular mount with a ball or knop on the shaft just above (Fridaythorpe, Kirkby Underdale and Wetwang); the use of the ball or knop on the cross shaft, either at its top or base, is a common feature in this area.

The way emblems are used in the Wharram area is more unusual. Two slabs at Wharram have swords, one has the priest's emblems of chalice and book, and two others fragmentary or ill-preserved emblems that cannot be identified with any certainty. The 43 additional slabs in the churches of the neighbouring parishes provide only an additional five swords and two more chalice/book combinations.

Butler (1987) has pointed out the strong 'northern' bias in the use of emblems on cross slabs. In many parts of the north of England, the sword (a male emblem, probably relating to the right to bear arms) is the most common, followed by the shears which, after 19th-century controversy, are now generally acknowledged to denote a female burial. A consideration of the numbers of slabs bearing these two emblems in other parts of northern England is instructive:

Northumberland: 221 swords, 108 shears (Ryder 2003)
Durham: 167 swords, 62 shears (Ryder 1985)
Cumbria: 134 swords, 69 shears Cumbria (Ryder 2005)
West Yorkshire: 20 swords, 16 shears (Ryder 1991)
South Yorkshire 46 swords, 26 shears (Ryder, unpubl. research)
Part of Derbyshire 22 swords, 9 shears (Ryder, unpubl. research)
Nottinghamshire: 8 swords, 8 shears (Butler 1987, 251))

North Yorkshire has not as yet been comprehensively surveyed. It is interesting to note, however, that no example of shears was seen at Wharram Percy or at any of the churches around, and Earnshaw's survey of the Bridlington District only revealed one solitary example (Langtoft). It is interesting to speculate why the shears are so rarely used in the Wolds area; it may correlate with the fact that, as Earnshaw pointed out, the vast majority of the slabs are of calcareous grit brought from the north side of the Vale of Pickering. All the other areas in which the shears (and emblems in general) are more commonly used are generally well supplied with locally-available freestone.

In most areas, the emblems of the priest - usually chalice and book - are the third most commonly used. The chalice and book seen on No. 24 at Wharram also occur at Fridaythorpe, although here their relative positions are reversed with the chalice on the right and book on the left.

All the slabs found at Wharram Percy are relatively humble; only No. 34 is carved in relief, and only the priest's slab (No. 24) shows foliage springing from the cross shaft. In nearby parishes, slabs at North Grimston, Wetwang, and a slab lying in the churchyard at Garton-on-the-Wolds, are markedly more elaborate, clearly commemorating persons of some status.

Catalogue (Figs 137-140)

17* (Church 1) Head of rectangular slab. Incised. Fleur-de-lys terminals with pointed bud; ball on cross-shaft. Head of sword to right of shaft. Remainder of slab probably ended in three-step base. Late 13th-century. Surface weathered; 165mm thick.

18* (Church 2) Head of rectangular slab. Incised. Fleur-de-lys terminals with flattened lozenge-shaped bud; ball or knop on cross-shaft. Head of sword to left of shaft may indicate shield or inscription to right. Early 14th-century. 165mm thick.

19* (Church 3) Three fragments forming most of right side of rectangular slab. Incised. Delicate fleur-de-lys terminals with swelling ogee-shaped bud, ball below flower heads; large ball on shaft at head and foot. Early 14th-century. Extremely weathered and may not consist of one slab as reconstructed.

One of the three fragments, that with the cross shaft and lower terminal of the head, also has a small circular object on the right of the shaft, which looks like part of the original design; it is not clear whether this is part of an emblem, or perhaps a letter of an inscription. No foundation for reconstruction of base as in original drawing.

20* (Church 4) Simple fleur-de-lys cross-head. Incised. Slab may have been plain or, more likely, accompanied by symbol of sword. Mid to late 13th century.

21* (Church 5) Worn fragment of rectangular slab. Incised. Symbol may be pommel and hilt of sword (as on Nos 17 and 18); if so, cross-arms are entirely plain or have lost fleur-de-lys terminals when stone reused; alternatively drawing should be reversed, making symbol head of arrow (with point downwards), so that horizontal line is not a cross arm but part of a three or two-step base; if drawing put on its side, could be book with simple binding clasp. Mid to late 13th-century.

The symbol seems too slender to be a sword pommel; perhaps it is some sort of staff, or perhaps a processional cross, with its tip piercing a ball. This means placing it the other way up, with the emblem on the left of the cross shaft. The other transverse line shown on the drawing is now no longer apparent – the stone is quite badly weathered.

22* (Church 6) Central part of rectangular slab. Incised. Slab incomplete so that reconstruction hazardous, but most likely curving lines on left represent suspension belt or loop of hunting horn, while straight line on right is part of sword scabbard, as at Great Salkeld, Cumbria (Cutts 1849, pl.xiii), or part of arrow, as at Papplewick, Notts. (Cutts 1849, pl.xxvii). Late 13th or early 14th-century.

23* (Church 7) Lower left side of rectangular slab. Incised. Two-step base; probably with simple round-leaf (as No. 32) or fleur-de-lys head. 13th-century. South face of south nave arcade near No. 22. Partly weathered but some tooling evident.

24* (Church 8) Four fragments representing the lower part of rectangular slab. Incised. Two or three-step base; pointed leaf trefoil shoots on stem suggesting clustered head of similar foliage (Butler 1964, fig. 6E). Chalice (Oman 1957, group 3) and book flanking shaft. Late 13th or early 14th-century. (see Sidiqui 1987) Found in 1962 clearance of nave. 228mm (9 in) thick. Film of lime mortar around edges suggests it was once part of a flagged floor inside the church.

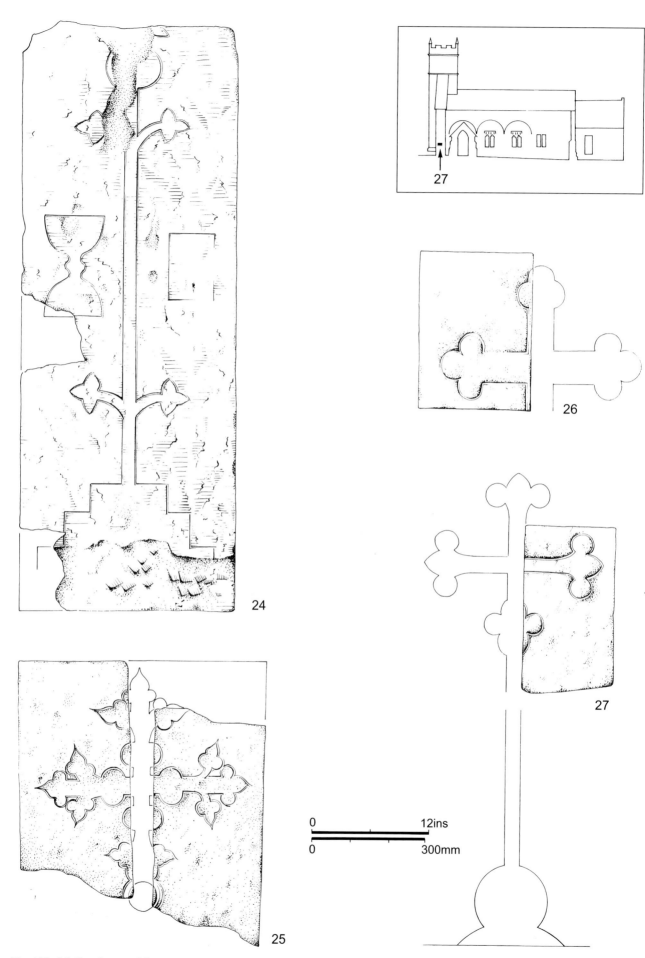

Fig. 138. Medieval cross slab grave-covers, Nos 24-27. Scale 1:10 (J.C. Thorn)

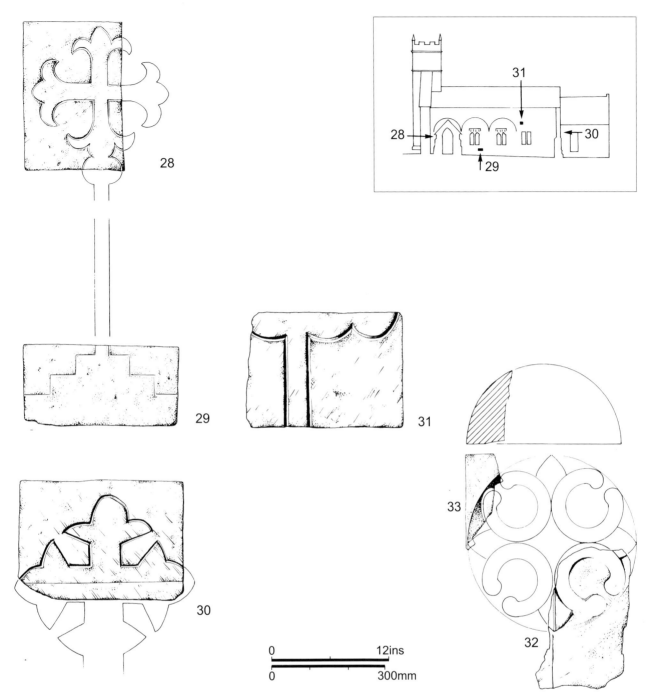

Fig. 139. Medieval cross slab grave-covers, Nos 28-33. Scale 1:10 (J.C. Thorn)

25* (Church 9) Two fragments representing part of head from tapering slab. Incised. Clustered trefoil head with mixed round-leaf and pointed bud. Cross-arms and stem replace by circular knops. Head as restored most probably correct, but stem decoration could be alternately knop and clustered floral head. Mid to late 14th-century. Found in 1962 clearance of nave. Probably cut lengthwise and reused as ashlar. Surface unworn with deeply cut design and diagonal tooling. 304mm (12 in) thick.

26* (Church 10) Part of cross-head. Incised. Simple cross *botonée* terminals on straight cross-arms. Early 13th-century. Found in 1962 clearance of nave. Probably reused as ashlar. Surface slightly weathered, but some tooling evident. 216mm (8? in) thick.

27* (Church 11) Part of cross-head. Incised. Round-leaf terminal with pointed bud. Probably correct as restored with plain shaft. Late 12th or more probably early 13th-century.

No foundation for reconstruction of base as in original drawing.

28* (Church 12) Upper part of rectangular slab. Incised. Simple fleur-de-lys terminal and pointed bud. Knop on shaft. Mid-13th-century.

No foundation for link with No. 29 as on original drawing.

29* (Church 13) Lower portion of rectangular slab. Incised. Simple three-step base.

Inverted; its right half now almost erased by weathering. No foundation for link to No. 28.

30* (Church 14) Head of slab. Poorly carved; deeply incised. Pointed leaves and bud. Coarse design could indicate 13th-century local craftsmanship, although this form has long life (1250-1600). Late examples at Lastingham, N. Yorks, *c*.1560, and Baswich, Staffs., *c*.1600. Surface with diagonal tooling and guide line inside cross.

291

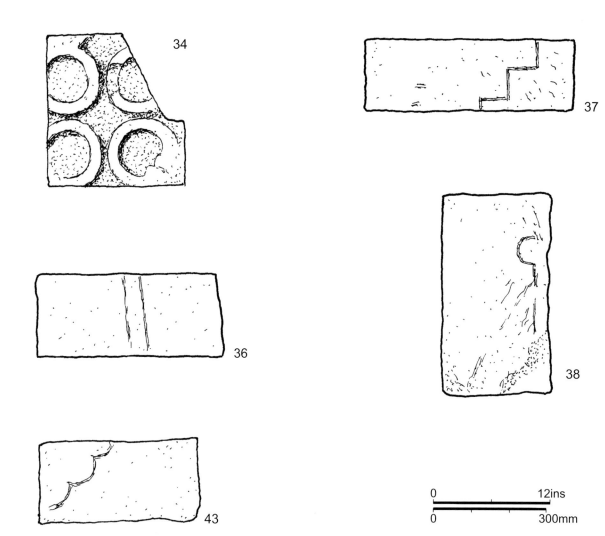

Fig. 140. Medieval cross slab grave-covers, Nos 34, 36-8 and 43. Scale 1:10 (P.F. Ryder)

31 (Church 15) Portion of slab. Deeply incised. Could be part of clustered round-leaf head or part of 'rounded stones' base, although with the latter usually more step form to stones, which represent Mount of Calvary. Probably 12th-century. Appears to have been repointed around edge and may have been reinserted into wall after 1922, when outer facing stones collapsed. Surface with fine diagonal tooling and guide-line along middle of shaft.

This is almost certainly part of a cross head with clustered terminals.

32* (Church 16) Portion of head, either from slab or grave headstone. Design of head in relief in sunk circular roundel. Normal round-leaf head. Shaft incised, apparently as a single line. Late 12th-century. *cf.* Filey and Amotherby, N. Yorks. Found in 1962 clearance of nave. Surface covered by film of lime mortar. Surface with diagonal tooling and guide-line.

Illustration numbered as 17 in Wharram III

33* (Church 17) Slab similar to No. 32 with round-leaf head carved in low relief set within sunken circular panel. Circular profile suggests reuse as half-shaft or respond before being discarded. Found in 1962 clearance of nave. 304mm (12 in) diam.

Illustration numbered as 16 in Wharram III

34* (Church 18) *Four-circle cross head, carved in very high relief, implying that this was a high-status slab.*

35 (Church 19) On south wall of church exterior near south-west buttress and one course above top stone course of porch west wall.

Incised design similar to that in relief on No. 32, but without central leaf terminals.

There is no sign of this now, although there is a badly weathered stone in the area specified that could conceivably have lost its design relatively recently.

36* *Fragment of incised slab, with cross shaft.*

37* (Church unnumbered, discussed with Church 5 in *Wharram III*) *Fragment of incised slab (above No. 21) with stepped base.*

38* (Church unnumbered, discussed with Church 5 in *Wharram III*) *Fragment of incised slab with ?cross shaft, with ball or knop. Below No. 21.*

39 (Church unnumbered, discussed with Church 6 in *Wharram III*) *Fragment of incised slab, with cross shaft. East of No. 22.*

40 (Church unnumbered, discussed with Church 7 in *Wharram III*) Between Nos 22 and 29, stone, 7? in (184mm) long, with two pairs of parallel lines representing book alongside shaft.

A stone with this decoration is no longer apparent, but there is a stone in this position, 690 by 235mm, which has one pair of parallel lines that could represent just about anything.

41 (Church unnumbered, discussed with Church 7 in *Wharram III*) Fragment, 9 in (228mm) thick, with shaft, on reveal of west jamb on inside of south door.

42 (Church unnumbered, discussed with Church 11 in *Wharram III*)
Adjacent to No. 27, base with Calvary mound in three rounded stages. Yellower stone than usual and therefore unlikely to belong with No. 27.

Not found

43* (Church unnumbered, discussed with Church 15 in *Wharram III*)

Fragment of incised slab. Three rounded lobes set diagonally, and therefore likely to be part of a stepped base.

Church 20 and an unnumbered stone discussed with Church 11 in *Wharram III* are both architectural stones and, therefore, excluded from this catalogue.

Stone associated with Burial EE120 (Plates 119-120; see also p. 229 and Fig. 123)

Catalogue
43A Excavations within the chancel uncovered 'an ashlar block, chamfered along its upper edges and with a slot cut in its top' (*Wharram III*, 72). Sandstone, Birdsall Calcareous Grit. It lay on the axis of the church, and appeared to have been set at the east end of a grave (C48), which had been truncated by the east wall of the present chancel (*Wharram III*, fig. 17). It was suggested that the socket had supported a wooden or stone cross which marked the burial, and the burial itself was assigned to the Phase 3 chancel. This dating has since been challenged by David Stocker, who has provided the following discussion.

Discussion
by D. Stocker
This stone shows two clear phases of use.

In its first phase of use the block contained a chamfered angle. This stone was cut using a variety of undecorated tools, skilfully applied, diagonally to the bedding-plane, to produce a 'striated' display surface with very narrow drafts on faces 1, 2, 5 and 6 (see e.g. Stocker 1999, 344-9). These surfaces were subsequently smoothed further, by abrasion, perhaps using a sandstone block, as few tooling impressions remain. The best surviving tooling dating from this initial phase, however, is on what was originally the upper surface (face 10) (which became the base of the stone during its second phase of use). Here an undecorated blade (of about 100mm width) was used to create a neat 'striated' surface finish, with broad draughts, typical of concealed masonry surfaces of the 11th to early 13th centuries (Stocker 1999, 344-9).

In principle a simple chamfered block incorporating a right-angle of this type could have been made for any one of a wide variety of architectural components: a plinth, a string-course, a corbel table etc. In this case, however, the high quality finish on the four surviving display surfaces suggests that it is most likely to have come from an interior location, perhaps from an abacus block, which would have sat above the capital block within the 11th or 12th-century church. Because the stone has been greatly recut, we can't say exactly how big any such abacus block might have been originally, but it must have been large; perhaps large enough to have come from above simple capitals in the original chancel arch, which we know was blocked before Burial EE120 was made.

Plate 119. Socket stone No. 43A; Phase 1 (original) surfaces 1 and 2 (facing), and 5 and 6 (lit, to the right). This is the remaining chamfered return angle of the original architectural detail (perhaps an abacus). Note the fine quality, diagonal 'striated' tooling, subsequently smoothed by abrasion, perhaps with a sandstone block.

Plate 120. Socket stone No. 43A; Phase 2 (secondary) surfaces 3 and 4 (facing), and 7 and 8 (left, unlit). Note the much cruder tooling of the second phase in which the 'socket stone' was created by cutting away large portions of the original stone and excavating the crude rectangular socket.

In a second phase of use, the block was greatly reduced in size and crudely trimmed along two sides to form a rectangular socket stone, with a deep rectangular mortice (approx 120mm deep) cut into what had been the original underside. The tooling on faces 3, 4, 7 and 8 is extremely crude and bears no comparison with that on earlier surviving faces. It was made with an undecorated blade approximately 95mm broad. The mortice has been somewhat more carefully cut, and the interior surfaces also finished with an unornamented blade (about 40mm broad) which had also been used over the primary tooling on faces 3, 4, 7 and 8. The recutting of the original block produced a simple socket-stone for a narrow timber upright (approximately 120mm by 40mm – perhaps 5 x 1^1/$_2$ inches) and, as it was discovered *in situ* at the head of Burial EE120, we must presume that it was intended to support a simple timber grave-marker, probably of cross form. The tooling used for the recutting is not intrinsically datable, but the burial is clearly considerably later in date than the 11th and 12th centuries, later than the destruction of the final phase of the medieval chancel and earlier than the construction of the modern chancel.

Today, grave-markers of this type are extremely rare, if not unknown, as the timber would be prone to both removal for reuse and/or to decay. However, late-medieval references to, and images of, wooden crosses placed over graves have recently been collected by Gilchrist and Sloane (2005, 190-94) where they are shown to have been frequently used in graveyards of this date. It is less clear how common such monuments were following the Reformation, when the site sequence suggests that this example was made. We might guess that such wooden crosses represent a simpler and cheaper form of monument than the more elaborate inscribed stone headstones, which started to become popular following the English Civil War. But if we presume that wooden crosses were also deployed over the more prestigious burials, their rarity after this date might suggest that they became supplanted by inscribed headstones. The site sequence apparently indicates that the Wharram example should be dated to the period between the mid-16th century and the early 19th century. But, if this stone does represent a monument type that preceded the 'headstone' type, a date within the first century of this date bracket may be indicated: i.e. *c*.1550-1650.

22 Stone Objects
by E.A. Clark and G.D. Gaunt, with milling stones by S. Watts

Some 320 fragments of stone were recovered from the Churchyard sites. Much of the stone excavated, including many pieces referred to in this volume, was not retained, and stones of all types may be under-represented compared to other parts of the village. Many of the stones referred to in the excavation text as sandstone were identified as such on site only; they were not seen by Dr Gaunt and not further described lithologically. The spindlewhorls, hone stones and possible rubbing stones are all of stone types and forms already recorded from Wharram.

All the stone described in this chapter has been examined and its lithology identified by G.D. Gaunt using a hand lens and low power microscope in reflected light. No new stone types have been identified in this assemblage and the full lithological and descriptive catalogues form part of the Site Archive.

Measurements, where given, are the maximum possible and usually approximate.

Objects used for decorative and leisure purposes

Pebbles

44 Four joining sections of pebble, chalk. The shape implies an erratic, but possible use is suggested by a small artificial depression, possibly an initial drilling cavity, in the centre of one convex surface, some artificial wear-flattening, and striations around part of the edge. L. *c*. 70mm. *26/220; SF218; Period 7, Phase 2*

Three other pebbles, including two found in the fill of burials (Archive 71-73) have been retained.

Stones used for functional purposes

Spindlewhorls

Spindlewhorls of chalk and mudstone have been found elsewhere in the village; they are classified according to Walton Rogers 1997.

45* Spindlewhorl, chalk. Chalk Group. Sub-circular, with two equal faces, both flat and roughly parallel. The small spindle hole (diameter 5mm) suggests this is a Roman whorl. Max. diameter 30mm; maximum thickness 5mm. *26/315; SF147; Period 4, Phase 4*

46* Spindlewhorl, mudstone. Upper Carboniferous or (more probably) Lower or Middle Jurassic. Form A1. Sloping side decorated with parallel, incised lines. Some damage to face. Diameter of flat face 26mm; diameter of spindle hole 8mm; h.13.5mm. *26/543; SF121; Period 3, Phase 2*

47 Less than half a spindlewhorl, chalk. Ferriby Chalk Formation. Slight heat-reddening. Form A1. Sloping side decorated with two pairs of parallel incised lines. Flat face slightly convex. Height 13mm; diameter of spindle hole *c*. 8-10mm. *26/594; SF134; Period 1, Phase 3*

48* Spindlewhorl, chalk. Chalk Group. Slight heat-reddening. Form A2. Sloping side has traces of incised line around the centre. Larger face (diameter 38mm) slightly convex; smaller face (diameter 19mm) concave; diameter of spindle hole 9-12mm; h. 18.5mm. *26/412A; SF109; Period 3, Phase 4*

49* Spindlewhorl, mudstone. As No. 46. Form A2. Sloping side decorated with two lines of crudely incised ladder-pattern. Diam. of larger face 28mm, the other 15mm; h. 15mm; diam. of spindle hole 6-8mm. *26/412A; SF104; Period 3, Phase 4*

50 Two joining fragments forming complete, but damaged, spindlewhorl, chalk. Ferriby Chalk Formation. Form C. Diam. 28mm; h. 22mm; diam. of damaged spindle hole *c*.10mm. *26/289; SF31; Period 4, Phase 2*

Rubbing stones

51 Fragment of rubbing stone, sandstone. Probably erratic. Upper Carboniferous or Middle Jurassic. One side slightly convex and smooth. Max. remaining l. 47mm. *26/412A; SF151; Period 3, Phase 4*

52 Fragment, sandstone, very fine-grained (i.e. almost siltstone). Probably erratic. Probably Lower Palaeozoic or Carboniferous. One very smooth area could be from artificial use as a rubber or hone. *26/735; SF545; Period 2, Phase 1*

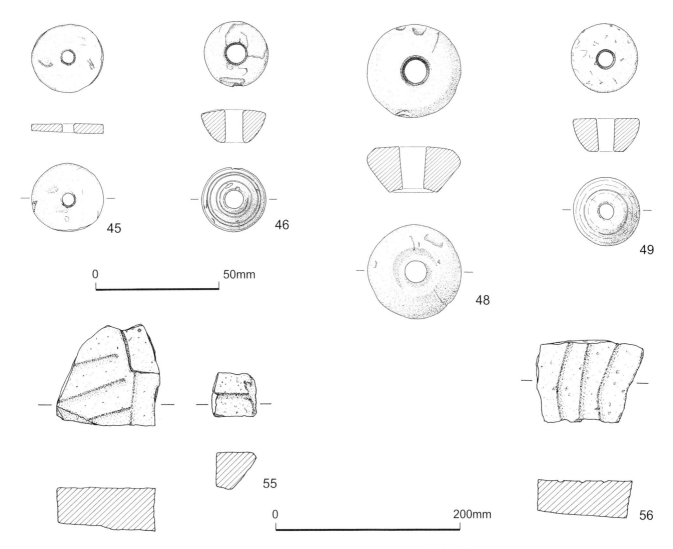

Fig. 141. Stone objects: spindlewhorls, Nos 45-6, 48-9, Scale 2:3, and querns, Nos 55-6, Scale 1:4. (M. Chisnall)

Milling stones

by S. Watts

Excavations within the Churchyard area led to the recovery of some 55 fragments of querns or millstones. Joining fragments, or those that were found together, have, with one exception, been recorded as a single entry and therefore this report is based on a catalogue of 36 entries. Although the assemblage is small compared with other excavated sites within the village it is nevertheless important as, together with that from the church, it demonstrates how extensively material has been redistributed and reused. In addition, it also contains a number of particularly interesting fragments.

The highest proportion of fragments (56%) come from later Anglo-Saxon and medieval contexts and derive from structures and features associated with the burial ground. Seven fragments (19%), however, are probably datable to the Late Iron Age/Roman period and three fragments (8%) to the earlier Anglo-Saxon period (Table 149).

More than half the fragments (55.5%) are of Mayen lava, with Crinoid Grit and sandstones of Millstone-Grit type accounting for 30.5% and 14% of the assemblage respectively (Table 149). Often the percentage of lava is exaggerated due to the friable nature of the stone but in

this instance it appears to be a true representation. Most of the fragments are small and predominantly irregular shaped pieces and, although evidence of a grinding surface survives on more than half the fragments, few retain such diagnostic features as eyes or handle holes, and it is not possible to ascertain, therefore, if they are from upper or lower stones or what the original diameter may have been. Some fragments have no features at all and are only identified as milling stones by the fact that the stone type is not known to have been brought to the village for any other purpose.

Only one fragment, of lava, (No. 53) has the remains of an upright handle hole in its flat upper surface. It was recovered from a Period 1, that is Late Iron Age/Roman, context. The stone, originally c. 460mm diameter, is now only 32mm thick and it is noticeable that its grinding face has worn through to the handle hole. Lava querns were imported in large numbers during the Roman period but this fragment is rather different in form from the lava querns more usually associated with Roman sites, which have a kerb and an L-shaped handle hole. Recent research, however, has shown that lava querns from northern England in particular can vary considerably in design and it has been suggested that they were imported

Table 149. The distribution of quern and millstone fragments by Period and stone type. The plain figures refer to the phasing from Site 26, those in brackets and italics to the equivalent phasing from Sites 41 and 52 respectively. MG = Millstone-Grit type sandstone, CG = Crinoid Grit

Period	(1)	1(2)	2	3	(3-4) 2-3	4	5	6	U/S U/S	(Topsoil) 4	Total	%
Lava		4	1	4	4	3		2	1	1	20	55.5
MG		1		1	2				1		5	14
CG		2	2	1	5				1		11	30.5
Total	0	7	3	6	4	10	0	2	3	1	36	
%	-	19	8	17	11	28	-	6	8	3		100

as blanks to be finished at workshops in Britain. It is noticeable that the grinding surface is pecked rather than furrow dressed which is more usual with Roman lava querns. The fact that the stone has worn through to the handle hole suggests that it may have been re-dressed in local style. A similarly pecked fragment dating to the Roman period was also found on the North Manor site (Gwilt and Heslop 1995, 43; Watts 2004, 221).

Twenty fragments retain evidence of a grinding surface, most of which are randomly pecked. Two fragments of lava, however, are dressed with a pattern of furrows, each of the furrows being formed by a series of indentations made by a sharp pick. The lava fragments in particular show evidence of wear with glazed high spots. The glazing is particularly prominent on a fragment from the edge of a dense, heavy stone (No. 54), originally *c.* 570mm diameter, and the degree of polish is perhaps more consistent with a stone turned by mechanical or animal power rather than by hand. Unfortunately it is from an unphased context.

The two fragments with furrow dressing derive from a Period 6 context and were reused as building stone in the footings of a 16th to 18th-century wall. Furrow dressing, which is found on many Roman querns and millstones, does not seem to have been a feature of the Anglo-Saxon period but came back into use later in the Middle Ages (Watts 2002, 99). No. 55, from the centre of a stone, has straight cut furrows. It also has the remains of the eye or central hole, *c.* 100mm diameter, and a curved rynd chase. These features indicate that the fragment was part of an upper stone and that a forged iron rynd with four curved arms was used to locate and balance the stone on the spindle. Curved rynds appear to be a typical feature of medieval millstones rather than querns and it is likely, therefore, that this fragment originally came from one of the mills that stood in the valley (Watts 2002, 100-102). Although two mills are recorded as being out of use in 1323, one mill appears to have been rebuilt by 1368 and remained in use until the mid-15th century (*Wharram X*, 21-2).

The second fragment (No. 56), from the edge of a different stone, originally *c.* 544mm diameter, appears to have slightly curving furrows at 25mm centres. Stones with curved or sickle dressing have been found on other medieval and post-medieval sites. For example, a piece of lower stone, *c.* 544mm diameter, was reused as a hearth in a 16th-century building in Colchester (Buckley and Major 1988, 36). The pieces of a similarly dressed upper stone, *c.* 570mm diameter, were found during excavations of a medieval brewhouse in Alms Lane, Norwich (Atkin *et al.* 1985, 212) where it is thought to have been used for grinding malt; this raises the possibility that the stone from Wharram may also have had a particular function, although whether it was operated by hand or by animal or water-power is not possible to say.

Finally, at least two fragments show evidence for reuse prior to their deposition. Two pieces of Crinoid Grit stone (Archive 91 and 92), for example, appear to have been reused as sharpening stones. Another fragment (Archive 94) has been trimmed to a roughly circular, slightly domed shape of about 54mm diameter and a maximum of 20mm thick. Its appearance is suggestive of reuse, perhaps as a pot lid or gaming disc.

53   Fragment, lava. From edge of upper stone with remains of upright handle hole, to which grinding surface has worn through. Handle hole is 45mm from edge of stone, maximum diameter *c.* 26mm, narrowing towards grinding surface. Grinding surface appears to slope slightly. Pecked with worn and smoothed high spots towards the periphery. Evidence of tooling across the top surface. Original diameter *c.* 460mm. L. 200mm; w. 147mm; th. 32mm. *26/632; SF136; Period 1, Phase 2*

54   Fragment, lava. From edge of stone. Pecked grinding face. Very worn with glazed high spots. Heavy, close-textured stone with little evidence of vesicles. Original diameter *c.* 570mm. L.179mm; w. 114mm; th. 50mm. *26/227; SF138; unphased part of Site 54*

55*   Two fragments, lava. Not joining but possibly from the same stone. One has remains of grinding face with one deeply pecked furrow across it. L. 49mm; w. 49mm; th. 40mm. The other is from centre of upper stone with evidence of eye, perhaps originally *c.* 100mm in diameter, and the remains of a curving rynd chase *c.* 49mm long, 24mm wide (although stone is broken at this point) and 16mm deep. Retains grinding surface with deeply pecked furrows at *c.* 30mm centres. Top surface damaged. L. 111mm; w. 116mm; th. 50mm. *26/239; SF201; Period 6, Phase 2*

56*   Fragment, lava. From edge of stone with slightly curving furrows on the grinding face at *c.* 25mm centres. Worn with glazed high spots and evidence of concentric wear. Small hole in the upper surface *c.* 12mm diameter and 10mm deep, set 55mm from edge. Original diameter *c.* 544mm. L. 116mm; w. 90mm; th. 41mm. *26/239; SF999; Period 6, Phase 2*

Hones

Other hones of these stone types are discussed and their lithology described in *Wharram VII* and *Wharram VIII*.

57 Two joining fragments of hone, schist. Eidsborg Schist (also known as Norwegian Ragstone). Four smoothed faces, no intact ends. Max. remaining l. 75mm; w. 40-35mm; h. 35-30mm. *26/62; SF148; Period 4, Phase 6*

58 Two joining fragments, schist. Eidsborg Schist (a.k.a. Norwegian Ragstone). One tiny, smooth area. Max. remaining l. 20mm. *52/9; SF38; Period 1, Phase 2*

59 Fragment of hone, sandstone. Lower Palaeozoic. Part of one face and two sides remain, some smoothing on face and one side. Max. remaining l. 50mm; w. 43mm. *26/255; SF153; Period 1, Phase 4*

60 Fragment of hone, sandstone. Upper Carboniferous or Middle Jurassic. One slightly concave end intact. Some smoothing on all faces and end. Max. remaining l. 42mm; w. 40mm; th. 14mm. *26/73; SF155; Period 6, Phase 5*

61 Fragment of hone, sandstone. Upper Carboniferous or Middle Jurassic. End and parts of four surfaces remain, all with some smoothing. Max. remaining l. 90mm; w. 72mm; th. 30mm. *26/412A; SF152; Period 3, Phase 4*

62 Fragment of hone, sandstone. Middle or Upper Jurassic. Broken both ends; parts of four smooth sides remain. Max. remaining l. 28mm. *41/2; SF66; Period 5, Phase 2*

Sarcophagus

Part of a limestone sarcophagus (Archive 106) is discussed in Chapter 21, p. 281.

Objects modified but with no known function

63 Two joining fragments, mudstone. Lower Jurassic. Flat 'slice' with both surfaces naturally rough. Broken at both narrow ends; long edges are very smooth, probably artificially formed, and both curve towards narrower end. The stone is too soft for use as a hone. Remaining l. 38mm; th. 4mm. *26/391; SF165; Period 4, Phase 2*

64 Fragment of limestone. Middle or (less probably) Upper Jurassic. Very fine-grained, semi-porcellanous. With tiny, artificial hole on flat surface. Max. l. 22mm. *26/735; SF542; Period 2, Phase 1*

Stone used in the construction of buildings

Sandstone

Some 120 fragments of sandstone were examined; approximately 25% are of Birdsall Calcareous Grit (BCG), a local stone used throughout the village. Although they occur in contexts from all periods, most are likely to originate from the church. A fragment of calcareous sandstone (No. 69) was found in the fill of a Period 1 feature in Site 26. While some stones are described here, the full catalogue forms part of the Site Archive.

65 Fragment, sandstone. BCG. Worked; curved, possibly part of narrow column. *26/32; SF164; Period 5, Phase 1*

66 Fragment, sandstone. BCG. Worked; part of attached column. 98mm. *26/50; SF205; Period 6, Phase 2*

67 Block, sandstone. BCG. Two sides and part of curved edge and both ends worked. L. 140mm. *26/210; SF213; Period 5, Phase 2*

68 Roughly circular stone, sandstone. BCG. Diam. *c.* 600mm; straight edge, l. 434mm, is probably a secondary cut. A centrally-placed circular recess has a diameter of 410mm and is *c.* 100mm deep. *26/243; SF137; Period 5, Phase 1*

69 Fragment, sandstone, calcareous with abundant finely fragmented calcareous fossil fragments. Middle or (less likely) Upper Jurassic. *26/619; SF546; Period 1, Phase 2*

70 Shaped stone, sandstone (not examined by Gaunt). Reused in gate opening but identified by J.C. Thorn as 'the right hand part of the outer surround to a window'. This stone has not been located. *26/195; SF1026; Period 5, Phase 2*

Limestone

A small number of fragments of limestone (Archive 133-54) were recovered, including North Grimston Cementstone and examples of calcareous concretions from the Upper Jurassic mudstones that form the floor and lower slopes of the Wharram valley.

Roofing stone

More than 70% of all the retained stone from the churchyard excavations is Brandsby Roadstone, the stone normally used at Wharram when a stone roof is needed (Archive 155-245). Over 50% of the 88 fragments, including five complete flags, were in Period 4 and 5 contexts, and another 37% in Periods 6 and 7. The complete stones range from 290mm to 410mm long and from 170mm to 210mm wide. Two fragments show signs of having been used for sharpening or smoothing, and one may have been reused as a weight. Like the building stone, some roof stones are likely to originate from the church, although large numbers were found on Site 77 to the north of this area (*Wharram XII* forthcoming). A single example of a roofing stone of a Middle or Upper Jurassic limestone (Archive 246), was found.

In the post-medieval period, after the railways allowed safe and cheap transport from the quarries, slate was frequently used for roof covering. Slate from two sources in Cumbria has now been recognised at Wharram: one from the Ordovician Borrowdale Volcanic succession and the other from the Silurian Wray Castle Formation, known commercially as 'Burlington Slate'. Examples of both, some virtually complete, were found in the churchyard (Archive 247-73).

Flooring stone

A fragment of possible stone flooring flag (Archive 274) was found in a Period 5 context.

Stone from the church

To enable comparison with the rest of the stone from the village, the stone from the church excavations, both published (*Wharram III*) and unpublished, has been examined by G.D. Gaunt and catalogued. This catalogue forms part of the Site Archive and only selected stones are discussed here.

Thirteen fragments of quern were recovered from the church excavations in addition to the six fragments of lava quern published in *Wharram III* (Church 8). Joining fragments have been recorded together and this discussion is based on a catalogue of eleven entries. Five fragments are of lava, two are of Millstone-Grit type sandstone and four of Crinoid Grit. Apart from one Millstone Grit-type fragment from the edge of a stone, the fragments are mainly small and irregularly shaped, and, although one fragment of Crinoid Grit may also be from the edge of a stone, it is not possible to say if they are from upper or lower stones or what the original diameters may have been.

The remains of a worn grinding surface, however, survive on eight of the fragments. On five the grinding face has been roughly pecked, but two parallel grooves across a fragment of lava are the remains of furrow dressing.

Although the assemblage is small it is nevertheless important as, together with that from the churchyard, it highlights the fact that pieces of broken quern and millstone were reused as building material. For example, two joining fragments of Crinoid Grit were found below the chancel steps and a fragment of Millstone-Grit type sandstone came from the foot of a buttress.

Among the other stones now recorded are a small fragment of a Purple Phyllite hone, recovered from the nave, and a piece of poor quality and possibly worked jet. A large sandstone cobble, smooth on one surface, came from the north churchyard. A small fragment of Purbeck Marble adds to others found in this area of the village. Three fragments of limestone (Coral Rag) sarcophagus, found during excavation but now unprovenanced, are discussed in Chapter 21, p. 281.

23 Clay objects
by S. Elsdon (Nos 1-5), J. Bayley (Nos 6 and 7), P. Didsbury (No. 8) and E.A. Clark and A.M. Slowikowski (Nos 9-12)

The fired clay objects recovered from the churchyard area range in date from Iron Age loomweights to drainpipe from the modern period.

Loomweights (Fig. 142)

1* Base/corner fragment of triangular loomweight with possible attachment groove. Grey to dark brown. *26/272; SF613; Period 4, Phase 4*

2* Four fragments, two joining, plus small fragments some with exterior surfaces, of probable triangular loomweight. Three have corners and two have finger-width grooves near the corners. Clay coarsely wedged with sparse flint ?inclusions. External surfaces blackened in places and smoothed. *26/547; SF117; Period 1, Phase 2*

3 Fragment of loomweight. Unusually thin corner. Brown to dark grey exterior and dark brown core. Local clay with ?chalk. *26/547; SF117; Period 1, Phase 2*

4* Corner fragment of large ?triangular loomweight, probably 70mm thick. No trace of groove for suspension. Brown to black exterior; grey interior. Small quartzite fragments and ironstone inclusions. Probably natural clay. *26/596; SF612; Period 4, Phase 1*

5* Corner fragment of loomweight with clear attachment grooves. Light brown clay with iron staining. *26/642; SF614; Period 3, Phase 1*

These fragments are parts of triangular loomweights typical of the Late Iron Age period in northern Europe.

Typically they have perforations across three corners of the triangle (see Loewe 1977 for illustration of use). They can be quite substantial, up to 3kg, in weight, although most are smaller. They are distributed liberally throughout North Europe in the Late Iron Age, but in southern Yorkshire may overlap with the Roman period.

The weights were attached to the warp threads (several) and probably stood on the floor or in a specially constructed groove below floor level. This enabled the weaver to stand at floor level and to work with warps extended. The later 'belgic' looms were beam weighted, i.e. the fabric was rolled on to a weighted beam rather than individual weights. For comparison see May 1996, 331.

Other fragments were found in Roman contexts on the North Manor (*Wharram IX*, 230).

Miscellaneous objects

6 Small lump of fairly-fine fired clay. It is mainly mid-grey in colour and has the suggestion of a modelled surface on the flat side, now much eroded. It may have been part of a clay mould for casting small metal objects. Max. dimension 19mm. *26/382; SF536; Period 3, Phase 4*

7 Fragment of clay 'wrap', material that covered an iron object that was being coated in brazing metal. Typical brazed objects included barrel padlocks but this fragment is too small for the form of iron object to be identified. *26/255; SF1025; Period 1, Phase 4*

8 Small, 'bun-shaped' object of fired clay, with a flat base. Peter Didsbury comments: 'The fabric is quite fine, soft and slightly sandy, oxidised to light reddish brown, but with greyish surface patches possibly due to weathering. A single stone fragment (*c.* 2mm) is visible on the underside. Probably a deliberately formed item, of unknown function, fired in an open fire'. Diam. *c.* 24mm. *26/216; SF286; Period 7, Phase 5*

9* Clay disc, tear-drop shaped. A. Slowiskowski comments: 'Carefully formed from a concave body sherd of Staxton ware (see p. 252, No. 3). The protrusion on one side may have been formed purposefully – it is formed centrally above a sooting line on the outer surface of the sherd. Pre-firing linear mark on the inner surface'. Diam. 45mm. *26/65; SF1016; Period 4, Phase 4*

10* Clay disc, sub-circular. A. Slowikowski comments: 'Roughly formed from a sherd of Humber ware (see p. 255, No. 18). Pre-firing linear mark across centre of one side'. Max. diam. 65mm; th. 6-10mm. *26/36; SF1015; Period 7, Phase 5*

11 Fragment of heavily fired clay. Surfaces mottled black with some red. Two flat surfaces at right-angles to each other, with mortar in the angle formed by the inner surfaces. W. of arms at inner angle 25mm and 18mm. Total l. 45mm. *26/30; SF207; Period 7, Phase 3*

12 Sphere of clay. Diam. 12mm. *26/36; SF285; Period 7, Phase 5*

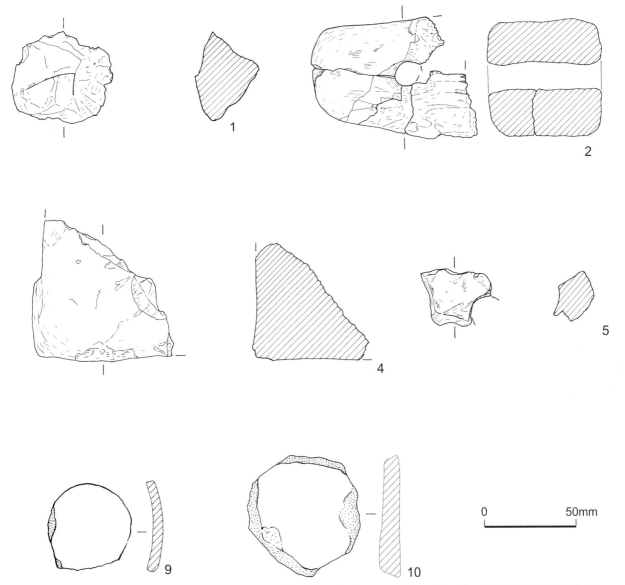

Fig. 142. Clay objects: loomweights Nos 1-2 and 4-5 (M. Chisnall); miscellaneous objects (clay discs) Nos 9-10 (C. Marshall).

Apart from No. 7, all these objects, where identifiable, are further examples of types found elsewhere in the village.

Fragments of chimney pots (Archive 13-15) and clay pipe stems (Archive 16-20) will be discussed with the post-medieval assemblages from the vicarage and farm sites.

Clay tile

Nearly 400 fragments of clay tile were recovered from the Churchyard sites. The vast majority (96%) are from Site 26, where just over 40% were in Phases 4 and 5. The few tiles found in Period 3 contexts may be intrusive, and some 30% were found in post-medieval contexts. The tile fragments were catalogued by Siobhan Watts (see Watts 2000 for a more detailed description of tile from Wharram). The whole tile assemblage will be discussed in the forthcoming volume (*Wharram XII*) on the post-medieval vicarages and farmsteads.

Four thicker and flat fragments (Archive 21-4) may be from floor tiles.

Brick

Some 90 fragments of hard fired clay, probably all brick fragments, were recovered, mainly from Site 26 where some 46% are from Phase 4 contexts. These will be discussed further in *Wharram XII*.

24 Glass Objects
by J. Price, H. Willmott and E.A. Clark

Roman glass (Fig. 143)
by J. Price

1* Romano-British glass bangle. Fragment, plano-convex, D-sectioned bangle (*c*. 40° of circumference). Bluish-green ground, five narrow bands of bl ue and opaque white loosely twisted cords laid horizontally on the convex outside surface and marvered flush. Some damage to the broken edges; iridescent weathering on all surfaces. H. 15mm; th. 7.5mm; inside diam. *c*. 46mm; l. of fragment 23mm. *26/351; SF1012; unstratified*

299

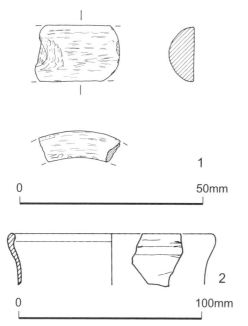

Fig. 143. Glass objects: bangle, No. 1, (Scale 1:1); vessel, No. 2 (Scale 1:2). (M. Chisnall)

This small fragment may be related to a small group of bangles with similar decoration and small internal diameters. Fragments of at least five bangles with bands of fine, loosely twisted, horizontal cords marvered flush with the convex outside surface have been noted from find spots on the North York Moors and in east Yorkshire (Price 1988, 362, nos 45-48, fig. 19.3), but they do not appear to be at all common elsewhere in Britain.

These bangles are, however, strikingly similar in their plano-convex sections and colours, and in the use of twisted cords, to the bangles with one or more prominent horizontal twisted cords which have been found in large numbers in Yorkshire and elsewhere in Britain (see Price 1988, 342-7, 359-62, nos 1-44, fig. 19.2-3 for further information), and it seems likely that they may represent a local variant of the form.

Little evidence has survived for the dating of this small and apparently local group, but their production and circulation may have been broadly contemporary with the large group, which can be assigned to the Flavian-early Trajanic period (c. AD 70 to c. AD 100) in northern Britain.

Another bangle of late 1st or early 2nd-century date was found in the filling of Burial V46 south of the chancel (*Wharram III*, 170).

Post-Roman vessel glass (Fig. 143)
by H. Willmott

A minimum of 41 post-Roman vessels is represented among 110 fragments of glass from the excavations within the Churchyard area. The vast majority of the fragments are from post-medieval bottles but a few are from goblets. The glass has been fully catalogued and will be discussed with the large assemblage of glass from

the post-medieval vicarages and farmsteads (*Wharram XII* forthcoming).

Two fragments of unusual glass were recovered from earlier excavations, one in a trench across the north boundary of the South Manor Area (Site 36) and the other in the fill between natural and first grave level in ditch NA96 in the 1970 north churchyard excavation (the P/Q trench), now ditch 255 on Site 26 (Fig. 31). Neither has been published previously and given both their rarity and similarity they are included together in this report. The most diagnostic fragment, No. 2, is an everted rim with a slight in-turned edge. It is made from a characteristic opaque red glass, sometimes referred to as 'sealing-wax red'. However, the opaque red is marbled with a dark black glass, which shows clearly in the broken section as well as on the surface. The second fragment, No. 3, is made in an identical glass, and is a curving body fragment.

Catalogue
2* Fragment of everted rim with slight in-turned edge from a possible jug. Marbled opaque red and black glass with no weathering. Late 13th to 14th-century. Rim diam. 110mm. *36/16; SF238; Phase 2*

3 Fragment of curving body from a flask or jug. Marbled opaque red and black glass with no weathering. Late 13th to 14th-century? *14/-, C1550; SF330 (Period 1, Phase 4 on Site 26)*

Opaque red glasses generally are rare in Northern Europe, although a number of similarly coloured fragments have been found on some English medieval sites. Red marbled flasks occurred in 14th-century contexts at Drury Hill, Nottingham (Charleston 1980, 69) and at Maison Dieu, Arundel (Harden 1969, 73). The rim of No. 2, however, suggests that it came from a wider-mouthed vessel, such as a jug, although no evidence for a handle or pouring lip survives. Several opaque red jugs, often decorated with trailing, are known from the late 13th and 14th centuries, and it is most likely that the Wharram rim parallels those from Watling House, London (Noel Hume 1957, 104) and Eynsham Abbey, Oxfordshire (Tyson 2000, 119).

XRF analysis undertaken by the Ancient Monuments Laboratory on both fragments showed that they had a near identical composition, and that copper was probably used as the colorant (Bayley nd). Whether this suggests that the two fragments originally came from the same vessel is uncertain, but at the very least they can be argued to be from the same manufacturing tradition. As yet, there is no evidence that opaque red vessel glass was made in England, although fragments have been found on some French and German production sites (Foy and Sennequier 1989, 81; Baumgartener and Krueger 1988, 37).

A note on the window glass
by E.A. Clark

One hundred and fifty-four fragments of window glass were recovered from Site 26 and another four from Site 41. Of these, all on Site 41 and 20 fragments from Site 26 are plain green glass and probably modern. The rest are the same thick dark glass found in the excavations in and around the church (Kerr 1987, 169-70 and fiche). Some fragments are decorated and reflect and/or extend the designs already recorded. Because of its fragmentary nature Kerr assumed that the glass from the church excavations had been smashed prior to lead stripping.

25 The Coins

Roman coins
by B. Sitch

Two Roman coins from the churchyard, one from topsoil and the other from a modern post-hole, are catalogued and discussed, along with all other Roman coins from the village, in *Wharram IX* (234-40) where they are numbered as follows:

41 Valentinian; *Securitas Reipublicae*; AD 367-75. Rev.: Victory with wreath; *LRBCII* (Arles) 477. *26/36; SF475; Period 7, Phase 5*

44 Valens; *Gloria Romanorum*; AD 367-75. Rev.: Victory with wreath; *LRBCII* (Trier) 121A. *26/201; SF479; Period 7, Phase 5*

A review of the medieval coins and jetons from Wharram Percy
by C. Barclay

Introduction
As one would expect on a rural site, the number of medieval coins recovered from the site at Wharram Percy is not large. The chronological coverage (based on date of issue) of the 36 coins and related items recovered, is summarised in Table 150.

Table 150. Numbers of coins from Wharram by date.

8th-9th centuries	8 coins (Church and Churchyard, 5; South Manor Area, 1; North Manor Area Site 39, 1; Area 6, 1)
12th century	4 coins (Churchyard, 1; Post-medieval farmstead and vicarage area, 2; Plateau, 1)
13th-14th centuries	11 coins (Church and Churchyard, 5; North Manor Area, 2; Plateau, 3; Area 6, 1) 1 jeton (Churchyard)
15th-16th centuries	3 coins (Church, 1; North Manor Area, 1; Area 10, 1) 7 jetons (Post-medieval farmstead and vicarage area, 4; South Manor Area, 1; Area 6, 2) 1 coin weight (Churchyard)
Uncertain	1 coin (Pond and Dam Area)

Discussion
A total of eight Anglo-Saxon coins (Nos 1-8) have been recovered during the course of excavations at Wharram Percy. Four of these are silver *sceats* of 8th-century date, whilst the remainder are 9th-century Northumbrian copper-alloy *stycas*. Six have been published and discussed in detail elsewhere (*Wharram I*, 132; *Wharram III*, 174-75; *Wharram VII*, 52-54; *Wharram VIII*, 125-26). The site has produced neither broad Saxon pennies nor any Saxon coins post-dating the Danish conquest of Northumbria.

Excluding Anglo-Saxon material, a total of four English coins of pre-1600 date have previously been published (*Wharram I*, 132; *Wharram III*, 175), whilst a further fifteen have been considered in the course of preparing this report (Nos 9-27). There are four coins of 12th-century date: pennies of Henry I and Stephen from the Post-medieval farmstead and vicarage area (Sites 51 and 54); a cut halfpenny of Stephen from the Plateau (Site 63); and a well-worn cut halfpenny of Henry II (issued 1158-80) from the Churchyard (Site 26). All are scarce coins and would be worthy of note even if found in an urban context. The remaining English medieval material provides a broad general coverage of the period before 1600 and is of a generally more mundane nature, although later medieval and Tudor coins are likewise somewhat under-represented when compared to a range of metal-detected assemblages from elsewhere in Yorkshire.

The presence of a copper-alloy coin weight (No. 36) intended to check-weigh gold nobles may perhaps hint at the possibility that some high value transactions were undertaken on the site, although it is worth observing that numerous other coin weights have been recovered by metal detectorists working on rural sites in North and East Yorkshire during recent years.

In common with many other sites in Yorkshire, the village has produced a quantity of medieval jetons (Nos 30-35). These were used as counters for carrying out arithmetical calculations, and may have served a secondary role as unofficial 'small change'. The earliest jeton recovered is a late 13th-century English piece, but the remaining seven, including three previously-published pieces (*Wharram I*, 132; *Wharram VIII*, 125), are imports struck between *c.* 1500 and the early 17th century.

Area summaries
The Church and Churchyard (Fourteen coins, 39% of total medieval coins)
Medieval coins found during excavation in this area concentrate within the church building and on the east side of Site 26, and range in date from the 8th to 14th centuries. They include two mid-8th-century *sceats* (Nos 3 and 4) from the Churchyard and three copper-alloy *stycas* (Nos 6-8) of 9th-century date. Of the latter, No. 6 was recovered in a possibly redeposited Period 3, Phase 4 ditch fill in the Churchyard, the other two within the church, from a grave (Burial V56) and from the make-up

Table 151. Date ranges of coins from Wharram and other sites in Yorkshire.

Date	Wharram Percy (N= 36)	Brayton (N=39)	Plompton (N=53)	Ryther (N= 92)	Snainton (N=47)
8th-9th centuries	8 (22.2%)	-	-	16 (17.4%)	1 (2.1%)
10th-11th centuries	-	-	-	1 (1.1%)	-
12th century	4 (11.1%)	1 (2.6%)	3 (5.7%)	1 (1.1%)	2 (4.3%)
13th-14th centuries	12 (33.3%)	17 (43.6%)	22 (41.5%)	17 (18.5%)	26 (55.3%)
15th-16th centuries	11 (30.6%)	21 (53.9%)	28 (52.9%)	57 (62.0%)	18 (38.3%)
Uncertain	1 (2.8%)	-	-	-	-

Table 152. Relative numbers of coins, jetons and weights from Wharram and other sites in Yorkshire.

	Wharram Percy (N= 36)	Brayton (N=39)	Plompton (N=53)	Ryther (N=92)	Snainton (N=47)
Coins	27 (75.0%)	31 (79.5%)	32 (60.4)	73 (79.3%)	40 (85.1%)
Jetons	8 (22.2%)	6 (15.4%)	19 (35.8%)	16 (17.4%)	7 (14.9%)
Weights	1 (2.8%)	2 (5.1%)	2 (3.8%)	3 (3.3%)	-

of the Victorian chancel floor. The remaining coins (Nos 12-14, 16, 20, 21 and 25) range from a late 12th-century cut halfpenny to a penny of 1469-70. A late 13th-century jeton and a medieval coin weight (Nos 28 and 36) were also recovered, suggesting the possibility of commercial activity in the area.

North Manor Area (Four coins, 11% of total medieval coins)
A single Northumbrian silver *sceat* of c. 750 (No. 2) was recovered from the fill of the *Grubenhaus* on Site 39. Two medieval coins (Nos 18 and 19) and an Elizabethan halfgroat issued in 1587-89 (No. 26), all of common types, were recovered from other sites within this area.

South Manor Area (Two coins, 5% of total medieval coins)
This area has produced, from Site 90, the earliest medieval coin (No. 1) recorded from Wharram, being an imported Frisian silver *sceat* of early 8th-century date. A late 14th early 15th-century jeton (No. 31) was also recovered.

Post-medieval Farmstead and Vicarage Area (Six coins, 17% of total medieval coins)
Both the Vicarage (Site 54) and the Farmstead (Site 51) have produced very scarce coins of 12th-century date (Nos 9 and 10), but, significantly, no later medieval coins. Nuremberg jetons are, on the other hand, well represented from both buildings (Nos 32-5).

Pond and Dam Area (One coin, 3% of total medieval coins)
A small disc (No. 27), described as 'possible medieval coin silver', was recovered from Site 30, but subsequently lost.

Plateau (Four coins, 11% of total medieval coins)
The sites on the Pleateau produced four medieval coins (Nos 11, 15, 17 and 22), the earliest, from Site 63, being an Awbridge type cut halfpenny in the name of Stephen (issued 1154-58), and the latest being a relatively unworn example of a halfpenny struck between 1351 and 1399 from Site 70.

Area 6 (Four coins, 11% of total medieval coins)
The earliest coin recovered from Area 6 (No. 5) was a *styca* of Eanred (810-40). Other numismatic material included a well-worn post-1377 penny and two 15th-century jetons (Nos 23, 29 and 30).

Area 10 (One coin, 3% of total medieval coins)
The only coin found during the excavation of Area 10 was a well-preserved halfpenny of Henry VI, struck in Calais between 1422 and 1427 (No. 24).

Catalogue
Coins

1 Silver Sceat; Frisia
Rigold (1977) Series E; *c*. 700-710
obv.) Plumed bird right
rev.) Stylised standard
1.15g, little wear
(*Wharram VIII*, 125, no. 7). *Plateau, South Manor Area: 90/21; SF350; Phase 5B-D*

2 Eadberht; sceat
Rigold (1977) Series Y; Booth (1984) Class E; *c*. 750
obv) EOTBERHTV·S [S, as inverted L]; retrograde and letters reversed; cross
rev) Animal moving right; cross under tail and triquetra under body
1.10g; light wear
(*Wharram VII*, 52). *Plateau, North Manor Area: 39/11; SF412; Phase 2*

3 Eadberht; sceat
737-58
rev) fantastic animal
Coin missing. No further details available.
(*Wharram III*, microfiche 272, no. 1). *Church and Churchyard*: *north of north-east chapel, 1964: 14/-; unphased*

4 Eadberht; sceat
737-58
obv) EADBERhTVSi; cross
rev) Animal moving right
1.00g; light wear
Church and Churchyard; surface: 26/539; SF116; Period 3, Phase 4

5 Eanred; styca
810-41
obv) +EANRED REX; cross
rev) +FORDRED; cross with pellets in angles
12mm; weight not recorded
(*Wharram I*, 132, no. 4). *Area 6: SF13771; Period VII*

6 Eanred, styca
810-41
Phase II, Group Ci
obv) +EANRED REX [N reversed]; cross
rev) +FORDRED; cross
1.06g; light wear
Church and Churchyard; redeposited ditch fill: 26/382; SF86; Period 3, Phase 4

7 Archbishop Uigmund; styca
c. 837-54
obv) +VICMVNDIPER; cross with pellets in angles
rev) +COENREDRED; small cross
0.96g
(*Wharram III*, microfiche 272, no. 2). *Church and Churchyard; make up of Victorian floor in present chancel: C250; Phase XII*

8 temp. Aethelred II; styca
Irregular reflective issue; *c.* 841-49/50
obv) EDILRE+ED; retrograde around cross with pellets in angles
rev) X +EDVV+ ; retrograde around cross with pellets in angles
0.96g
(*Wharram III*, microfiche 272, No. 3). *Church and Churchyard; Burial V56: C2051; Phase II*

9 Henry I; penny
Quadrilateral on cross fleury type; 1125-35
BMC xv
rev) [ ] ON [ ]
1.19g, as struck, contemporary loss
(*Wharram XII*, forthcoming). *Post-medieval farmstead area: 51/1034; SF422; Period 2*

10 Stephen; penny
Watford type; 1136-45
BMC i
1.08g, as struck, contemporary loss
(*Wharram XII*, forthcoming). *Post-medieval vicarage area: 54/209; SF753; Period 5, Phase 2*

11 Stephen; cut halfpenny
Awbridge type; 1154-58
BMC vii
rev) [ ]ER [ ] ON [ ]
0.56g, moderate wear, but contemporary loss
(Archive). *Plateau: 63/41; SF1; unphased*

12 Henry II; cut halfpenny
Tealby type; 1158-80
Illegible mint/moneyer
0.67g, light wear, clipped, contemporary loss
Church and Churchyard; Burial G443: 26/442; SF93; Period 4, Phase 1

13 John; cut halfpenny
Short-cross type; class 5b or c; 1205-10
London; William B
0.79g, light wear, probably deposited *c.*1220-40
(*Wharram III*, microfiche 273, no. 1). *Church and Churchyard; south of chancel: C659A; Phases VI-X*

14 John; penny
Short-cross type, class 5c-6c1
London; Walter; 1204-18
1.32g, light wear, contemporary loss
Church and Churchyard; surface: 26/64; SF114; Period 5, Phase 2

15 Henry III; cut halfpenny
Long-cross type, class 5c-g; 1251-72
Canterbury; Willem
0.58g, unworn, deposited by 1272
(Archive). *Plateau: 70/1; SF1; Period 6*

16 Edward I; penny
Class 4d
Canterbury; 1282-89
1.35g, as struck, contemporary loss
Church and Churchyard; surface: 26/51; SF476; Period 6, Phase 2

17 Edward I; penny
Class 10ab6-10cf3; 1301-10
London
1.37g; light wear, unclipped, early 14th-century loss
(Archive). *Plateau: 78/3; SF398; Period 6*

18 Edward I (?); penny
Coin missing, no further details available
(*Wharram IX*, 240). *Plateau, North Manor Area: 602/-; SF21; unstratified*

19 Edward I-II; penny
Sterling type; post-1279
Canterbury
1.14g, moderate wear, probably pre-1350 loss
(*Wharram IX*, 240). *Plateau, North Manor Area: 603/604/181; SF81; Master Period 6*

20 Edward I or later; penny
Sterling type; post-1279
0.54g, moderate wear, clipped, probably 14th-century loss
Church and Churchyard; chalk rubble deposit: 26/62; SF62; Period 4, Phase 6

21 Edward III; penny
Treaty Period, Transitional series; 1361-63
Durham; North (1991) 1229/2
1.13g, as struck, contemporary loss
Church and Churchyard;?hill wash: 26/61; SF477; Period 5, Phase 2

22 Edward III-Richard II; halfpenny
London; 1351-99
rev.) C[IVI/ TAS/] LOn/ DOn
0.46g, moderate wear, early to mid-15th-century loss
(Archive). *Plateau: 70/2; SF18 ; Period 6*

23 Richard II (?) or later; penny
Sterling type; post-1377
Weight not recorded; heavily worn
(*Wharram I*, 132, no. 5). *Area 6: SF12504; Period VII*

24 Henry VI; halfpenny
Annulet issue; 1422-27
Calais; North (1991) 1435
Weight not recorded
(*Wharram I*, 132, no. 8). *Area 10: SF88; Period VII*

25 Edward IV (first reign); penny
Light coinage; Class X; 1469-70
York, Archbishop Neville
0.54g (clipped, broken and mended), fairly heavy wear, probably deposited *c*. 1500
(*Wharram III*, microfiche 273, No. 2). **Church and Churchyard**; *post-hole in nave: C1196; Phases VII-IX*

26 Elizabeth I; halfgroat
im crescent; 1587-89
0.78g, moderate wear, unclipped, late 16th- early 17th-century loss
(*Wharram IX*, 240). *Plateau, North Manor Area: 603/129; SF75; Master Period 6*

27 Possible medieval silver coin
Coin missing, no further details available
(*Wharram X*). *Pond and Dam area: 30/1164; SF84; Phase 4*

Jetons
28 Jeton; English
Pictorial obverse type; 1280s
obv.) shield of England, border of strokes and rosettes
rev.) elaborate cross fleury with interstitial arms, border of strokes and rosettes
cf. Mitchiner (1988) 173b
3.50g, as struck, contemporary loss
Church and Churchyard; *occupation deposit: 26/355; SF61; Period 4, Phase 2*

29 Jeton
15th-century
Inscription Lombardic garbled
obv.) round-bottomed crowned shield with three lys
obv.) 'somewhat similar' to Barnard (1917) pl. xxix, n. 21
rev.) cross fleury, rosettes in angles
26mm; weight not recorded
(*Wharram I*, 132, no. 6). *Area 6: unnumbered; Period VII*

30 Jeton; Nuremberg
Four lys in lozenge/French shield type; *c*. 1480s-1490s
Inscriptions Lombardic garbled
obv.) round-bottomed crowned shield with three lys and something in base
rev.) lozenge of four lys
rev. cf Barnard (1917) xxix, n. 8
cf Mitchiner (1988) 1056
25mm; weight not recorded
(*Wharram I*, 132, no. 7). *Area 6: unnumbered; Period VII*

31 Jeton; Nuremberg
Ship-penny type; 1490-1550
cf. Mitchiner (1988) 1125-86
1.40g, pierced and well worn, perhaps later 16th-century loss
(*Wharram VIII*, 125, No. 8). *Plateau, South Manor Area: 44/5; SF28; Phase 6*

32 Jeton; Nuremberg
Rose and orb type; Hans Krauwinckel II; 1586-1635
rev.) *** GLVCK BECHERT IST IN GWERTT
cf. Mitchiner (1988) 1508-11
1.82g, light wear, contemporary loss
(*Wharram XII*, forthcoming). *Post-medieval farmstead area: 74/300; SF1123; Period 2*

33 Jeton; Nuremberg
Rose and orb type; 16th-early 17th-century
1.22g, light wear, contemporary loss
(*Wharram XII*, forthcoming). *Post-medieval vicarage area: 54/369; SF680; Period 6, Phase 3*

34 Jeton; Nuremberg
Rose and orb type; 16th-early 17th-century
1.40g, moderate wear, contemporary loss
(*Wharram XII*, forthcoming). *Post-medieval vicarage area: 54/516; SF1385; Period 6, Phase 3*

35 Jeton; Nuremberg
Rose and orb type; 16th-early 17th-century
1.22; pierced, moderate wear, contemporary loss
(*Wharram XII*, forthcoming). *Post-medieval vicarage area: 54/990; SF1603; Period 5, Phase 4*

Coin weight
36 Coin weight; English
Noble; circular type; post-1471
cf. Withers and Withers (1993) 170
6.88g (106.16 gr), light wear, late 15th-16th-century loss
Church and Churchyard; *surface: 26/45; SF478; Period 6, Phase 4*

26 Non-ferrous metal objects
by A.R. Goodall

Non-ferrous metal finds from a very wide date range were found in the Churchyard area. The earliest is probably the disc brooch (No. 1), which was found in a context dated to the Iron Age or early Romano-British period. A well-made Romano-British brooch from the 1st to 2nd centuries AD (Church 73) was found in a Period 1 ditch (26/255). Also from Period 1 contexts are part of a buckle frame (No. 5), a pin fragment (A47), a rivet (No. 30), and a curved strip (No. 32) which might be part of a vessel rim.

The late Saxon period is represented by a strap-end with zoomorphic terminal (No. 8), but the majority of the objects date from the medieval and post-medieval periods.

Copper-alloy objects

Brooches and other jewellery
The description of brooch Church 23 appears at the end of the catalogue on p. 307

1* Disc brooch made in parts. This brooch has been described and discussed in detail by Bayley *et al*. (1981). The front disc is decorated with repoussé which is filled with solder. There is a central boss made from non-metallic material, which is secured probably by a rivet. The back plate is flat and the edges are rolled up over the edge of the front plate in order to secure the two parts. On the back is a hinge and catch-plate fashioned from a single strip of metal. The pin is now detached. The brooch comes from the fill of ditch 539/27 dating to the Iron Age or early Romano-British period. Diam. 43mm. *41/544; SF13; Period 2, Phase 1*

2 Wire ring with butted ends, possibly a finger or ear-ring. Diam. 18-20mm. *41/510; SF5; Period 2, Phase 3*

3 Very thin ring with irregular section, probably a finger-ring. Diam. 21mm. *26/543; SF125; Period 3, Phase 2*

4 Very thin ring, possibly a finger-ring. Diam. 20.5mm. *26/343 (in context 294); SF174; Period 4, Phase 4*

Buckles, buckle plates and strap-ends
5* Buckle frame. The front is moulded and has two large knobbed projections. The buckle seems to have been cast in an open mould with the flat rear face finished by filing. A similar knobbed buckle frame was found in excavations at Lurk Lane, Beverley in a late 13th to 14th-century context (A. Goodall 1991, 149, fig.11.590); this is also the dating given for examples illustrated by Fingerlin (1971, 75 and e.g. cat. nos 531, 532 and 534). 21mm x 23mm. *26/255; SF113; Period 1, Phase 4*

6 Ring, possibly an annular buckle frame or a suspension ring. Diam. 31mm. *26/36; SF179; Period 7, Phase 5*

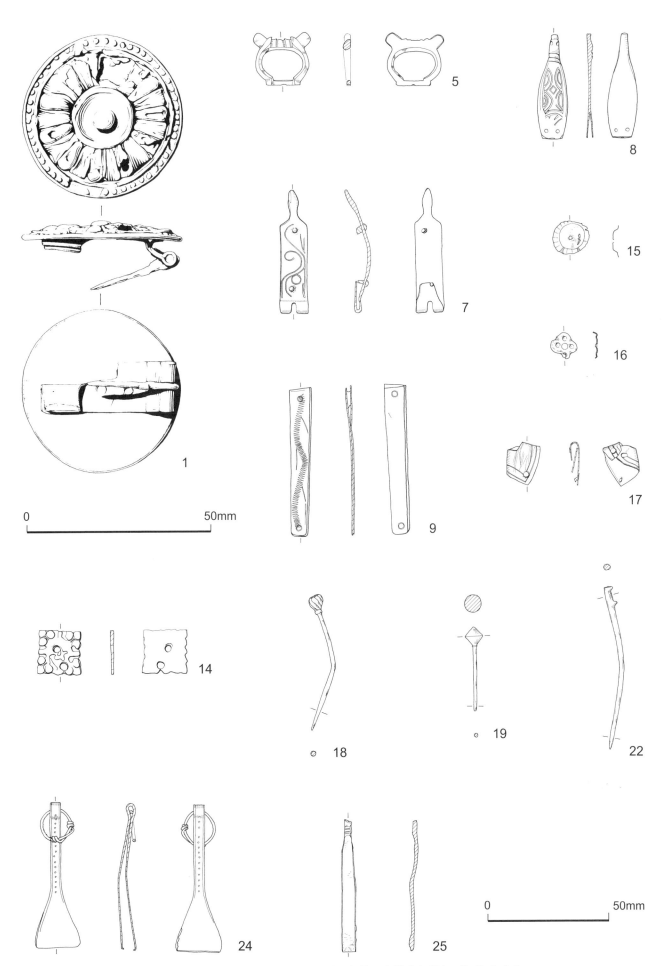

0   50mm

0   50mm

Fig. 144. Copper-alloy: No. 1 (D. Honour), Scale 1:1, Nos 5, 7-9, 14-19 and 22 (M. Chisnall). Scale 2:3

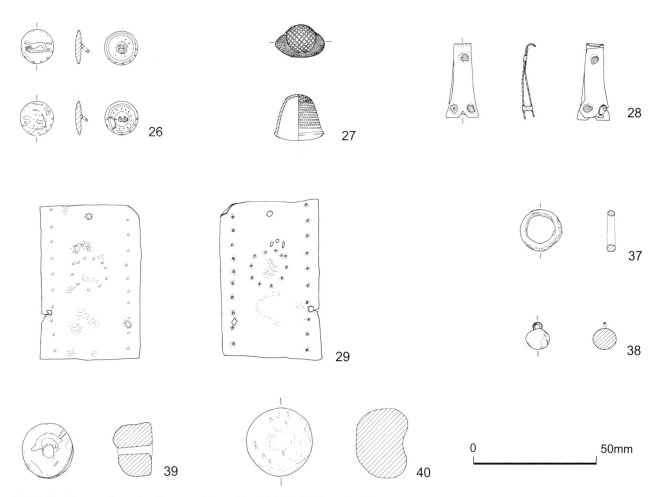

Fig. 145. Copper-alloy miscellaneous objects; Nos 26-9; lead objects buckle No. 37, button No. 38 and weights Nos 39-40. Scale 2:3 (M. Chisnall)

7* Buckle plate made from a strip which has been folded over the pin bar of a buckle. There is incised foliate decoration on one face and the end of the plate has been cut to form an elongated finial. Two domed rivets would have attached it to the strap. L. 49mm. *26/220; SF182; Period 7, Phase 2*

8* Strap-end. There is a split at the top to take the end of the strap, which would have been secured by two rivets and a zoomorphic terminal at the bottom. The front of the leaf-shaped plate has incised geometric decoration, possibly with traces of inlay. It is similar to a strap-end found in a later context in the Area 6 excavations (A. Goodall 1979, 111, fig. 55.12). Late Saxon, 9th-century. L. 41mm. *26/539; SF115; Period 3, Phase 4*

9* Strap-end made from two plates joined by rivets. The front plate is decorated with a wavy line of traced zigzag running from top to bottom of the plate, with short lengths of zigzag line in between. Possible remains of the leather strap between the plates at the upper end. L. 59mm. *26/62; SF226; Period 4, Phase 6*

10 Strap-end, shield shaped with three rivets. The front plate has down-turned edges at the bottom and sides, while the slightly smaller back plate is flat. Possible remains of the leather strap survive between the plates. L. 32mm. *26/180; SF196; Period 6, Phase 1*

11 Possibly an incomplete strap-end, or a patch, with two rectangular pin or rivet-holes and a smaller hole in between. L. 23mm. *26/218; SF186; Period 7, Phase 2*

12 Simple strap-end made from folded sheet with fine incised cross-hatching. A single rivet to attach it to the end of the strap. L. 16.5mm. *26/45; SF190; Period 6, Phase 4*

Strap fittings, studs and mounts

13 Trapeze-shaped strap loop with internal lugs. L.22mm. *26/-; SF228; unstratified*

14* Square mount with cast foliate decoration on the front and a flat back. There are two perforations, one near one edge, the other off-centre. 18mm square. *41/-, Burial SA060; SF 17; Period 5, Phase 2*

15* Repoussé-decorated stud head with central perforation. Diam. 14mm. *26/355; SF78; Period 4, Phase 2*

16* Small repoussé quatrefoil stud head or mount with central perforation. A similar decorative stud head was found in the Area 10 excavations (A. Goodall 1979, 112-3, fig. 57.75). 9mm x 9mm. *26/283; SF172; Period 5, Phase 1*

17* Decorative fragment or mount, V-shaped but now folded, with an incised border and three rivets (one missing). L. 16mm. *26/65; SF188; Period 4, Phase 4*

Pins

18* Dress pin with pear-shaped head above a small collar. The head is decorated with diagonal grooves on the sides and an incised cross on the top. The shank has a slight swelling and is bent. L. 57mm. *26/352; SF60; Period 4, Phase 2*

19* Dress pin with biconical head above a small collar. The shank is broken. L. 33mm. *26/336; SF30; Period 4, Phase 2*

20 Dress pin with large bun-shaped head and incomplete shank. L. 58mm. *26/74; SF183; Period 5, Phase 1*

21 Large pin with flattened head; undecorated. L. 50mm. *26/148; SF223; Period 6, Phase 4*

22* Pin-like object without a distinct head but having two projections near the top end. L. 67mm. *26/218; SF176; Period 7, Phase 2*

23 Possibly part of a pin with a composite head. One hemisphere which would have made the pin head survives. The shank is made from very fine wire and is bent. *41/3; SF21; Period 5, Phase 2*

Ten pins (Archive 47-56) with coiled wire heads and/or fragments of pins were found; Archive 47 was in a Period 1 context and may be intrusive; Archive 53 has white metal plating on the surface.

Toilet implements

24* Tweezers with broad splayed ends, in-turned at the tips. The arms are outlines with incised lines in between which is a row of punched dots. There is a loop made from twisted wire for suspension. A similar but less finely made pair of tweezers was found at Beverley, where they came from a context of late 12th to mid 13th-century date (A. Goodall 1991, 151, fig. 115.617). L. 59mm. *41/-; SF9; unstratified*

25* Arm from tweezers. Unlike the tweezers above, they were made in two parts with the tops of the arms soldered or riveted together. The upper end is damaged but part of the simple transverse moulding remains. L. 53mm. *26/352; SF53; Period 4, Phase 2*

Miscellaneous objects

26* Two buttons with repoussé decorated caps bent over separate back plates with inserted loops. The caps appear to be decorated with hunting scenes, one showing a running animal (a dog or a hare?), the other, possibly a man shooting from the shoulder. Both diam. 13mm. The buttons still have thread attached to them. *41/-, Burial SA060; SF25; Period 5, Phase 2*

A flat button with white metal plating on the surface (Archive 57) was found in the topsoil on Site 52.

27* Thimble with small regular indentations on the sides and a lattice arrangement on the top. The bottom edge is rolled. Probably post-medieval. *26/50; SF227; Period 6, Phase 2*

28* Book-clasp with splayed end and three rivets; no decoration. This is a crudely made example of a common type of book-clasp dating from about the late 16th and 17th centuries. L. 31mm. *26/218; SF187; Period 7, Phase 2*

29* Rectangular plate roughly decorated with repoussé dots. There are two, possibly three, pin holes for attaching the plate to a book binding or chest or other object. 62mm x 40mm. *26/215/216; SF185; Period 7, Phase 5*

30 Rivet with large head. *26/255; SF132; Period 1, Phase 4*

31 Plate from the back or inside of a pocket watch. There is a recess probably to accommodate the spring. Diam. 45mm. *26/215/216; SF189; Period 7, Phase 5*

Three lace ends, or possible lace ends (Archive 58-60), made from rolled sheet, are similar to others found in the village, as are two lengths of wire, Archive 61.

Vessels

32 Curved strip with triangular to D-shaped section. The inner edge is rough, suggesting that the fragment may be the broken rim from, for example, a small vessel, rather than a section of a bangle. L. 56mm. *26/255; SF200; Period 1, Phase 4*

33 Large piece of sheet with a rivet hole near the intact edge and a slight repoussé ridge about 15mm inside the edge. Possibly part of a vessel or a patch from a damaged vessel. L. 57mm. *26/237; SF180; Period 6, Phase 2*

34 Fragment of thick sheet possibly from the body of a vessel. Th. *c.* 2mm. *26/220; SF178; Period 7, Phase 2*

Sheet, strip and fragments

35 Fragment of D-sectioned strip. *41/171; SF18; Period 3, Phase 1*

36 Strip, possibly an offcut or a staple with clenched tapering ends. L. 37mm. *26/62; SF175; Period 4, Phase 6*

Archive 62-68 are pieces of sheet and fragments.

Objects of lead and lead/tin alloy

Buckle

37* Annular shoe buckle frame of lead/tin. Diam. 16mm. *26/218; SF184; Period 7, Phase 2*

Button

38* Small globular button of grey alloy with an inserted loop. L. 11mm. *41/104; SF26; Period 5, Phase 1*

Weights

39* Perforated lead weight. Diam. 19mm. Weight 41gr. *26/62; SF282; Period 4, Phase 6*

40* Probably a lead weight with indentation in flat bottom surface but no perforation. Diam. 24mm. Weight 102gr. *26/36; SF274; Period 7, Phase 5*

Archive 69-87 are fragments of *window lead* from medieval and post-medieval contexts.

Sheet

41 Lead sheet with identical round perforations punched into it. Probably the waste material from the manufacture of buttons or studs. Each disc would have had a diameter of 17mm. *26/9; SF269; Period 7, Phase 5*

42 Lead sheet offcut, folded. *26/232; SF181; Period 6, Phase 2*

43 Piece of lead sheet, possibly associated with roofing, such as a clip to support a tile. *26/45; SF251; Period 6, Phase 4*

44 Large pieces of lead sheet with nail holes, possibly roofing or roof clips. *26/7; SF271; Period 7, Phase 1*

45 Piece of lead with herringbone patterning on one face, possibly a textile impression. L. 22mm. *26/412A; SF275; Period 3, Phase 4*

46 Piece of thin sheet, possibly tin or tin alloy. *26/351; SF245; unstratified*

Archive 88-112 are fragments of *caulking, offcuts, sheet and waste*.

Church catalogue

Church 73* Trumpet-headed brooch. The bow is decorated with a knop between opposing acanthus leaves and there is another knop at the foot. The spring and pin are intact. The brooch is Romano-British and of a type dating from the later 1st to the mid-2nd centuries. This brooch is listed in Bayley and Butcher (2004, 160-61 and 253) with a number of others including some from sites in North and East Yorkshire. The authors suggest a northern source of manufacture. L. 65mm. *14/-, C1550; SF556 (ditch NA96 in the P/Q trench of the north churchyard excavations, now 26/255; Period 1, Phase 4)*

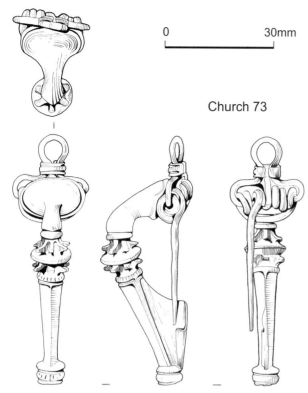

0   30mm

Church 73

Fig. 146. Copper-alloy brooch Church 73. Scale 1:1 (D. Honour)

27 The Iron Objects
by I.R. Goodall and E.A. Clark, spurs by B. Ellis, nails by J.G. Watt

Introduction

More than 1020 iron objects and fragments were recovered from the Churchyard; all were X-rayed before examination. Of these some 800 are identifiable as nails or nail fragments and another 144 objects of other types have been recognised. The remainder are unidentifiable.

Only very few objects relate to the use of the churchyard – a few coffin fittings from burials in Site 41 can be paralleled amongst others from the church and churchyard (Harding 1987), but a fragment of a cast-iron memorial adds another type of grave-marker to those already published (*Wharram II*).

As in preceding Wharram volumes, only selected objects are catalogued here; a complete catalogue forms part of the Site Archive. The symbol + after a dimension indicates that it is incomplete.

Tools

Blacksmithing is indicated by an incomplete forging, while other tools relate to leatherworking, animal husbandry and work with the soil. A file (Archive 75) found in a Period 7 context suggests working with metal. Three wedges (Archive 76-78), ranging from 44-60mm long, and single arms from three pairs of scissors (Archive 80-82) were also found in Period 7 contexts.

1   Incompletely forged knife. Whittle tang drawn out, but blade stub still rectangular in section. L. 56+mm. *26/229; SF609; Period 6, Phase 2*

2*   Awl, complete. L. 111mm. *41/131C; SF53; Period 3, Phase 2*

3   Awl?, tip lost. L. 66+mm. *26/242; SF683; Period 6, Phase 2*

4*   Socketed tool, perhaps agricultural. L. 91+mm. *26/751; SF135; Period 1, Phase 3*

5   Hoe, the small blade set at right angles to the broken whittle tang. L. 64+mm; blade l. 50mm; w. 33mm. *26/242; SF313; Period 6, Phase 2*

6*   Garden fork, broken and distorted. Three tines, one complete, one bent back, one broken. Incomplete tang, curved in side view, wrapped round wooden handle set at right angles to fork. L. 109+mm; w. 60mm. *26/352; SF43; Period 4, Phase 2*

7   Shears blade tip with angled end. L. 54+mm. *26/229; SF603; Period 6, Phase 2*

8   Shears blade tip with angled end. L. 32+mm. *26/155; SF611; Period 6, Phase 4*

9   Ferrule. Circular in section, tapering to pointed tip. L. 95mm; max. diam. 25mm. *26/3; SF617; Period 6, Phase 5*

Knives and table fork

Those knives which are sufficiently complete to be identified, are of three types, without bolsters (10-14), with bolsters (16-19), and clasp knives (20, 21 and Archive 83). The first group all have whittle tangs which were inserted into handles, 10 and 11, the earliest, being the most notable examples. Bolsters, solid forgings between blade and tang, were a post-medieval innovation, and on 16-18 they are of different shapes; 19, with a solid iron handle, is a related type. The clasp knives are also typologically post-medieval in date, as is a table fork found in a late context (Archive 84).

10* Whittle-tang knife, tang broken. Blade back and cutting edge parallel before back angles down to tip. L. 89+mm. *41/508; SF3; Period 2, Phase 3*

11* Whittle-tang knife, tang broken. Blade back and cutting edge parallel before back angles down to tip. L. 113+mm. *26/412A; SF110; Period 3, Phase 4*

12* Whittle-tang knife, blade and tang broken. Blade back and cutting edge taper to tip. L. 57+mm. *26/7; SF620; Period 7, Phase 1*

13   Knife blade fragment, back and edge taper to lost tip. L. 71+mm. *26/218; SF316; Period 7, Phase 2*

14   Whittle-tang knife. Clenched tip to tang, blade back and cutting edge parallel. L. 61+mm. *26/215-216; SF421; Period 7, Phase 5*

15   Scale tang fragment with shaped end and three copper-alloy rivets. L. 64+mm. *26/36; SF643; Period 7, Phase 5*

16   Whittle-tang knife with disc-shaped bolster. Blade and tang broken. Blade back and cutting edge parallel. L. 81+mm. *41/101; SF 42; Period 5, Phase 2*

17   Whittle-tang knife with long tapering bolster. Tang complete, stub of blade. L. 79+mm. *26/215-216; SF415; Period 7, Phase 5*

18   Whittle-tang knife with short bolster. Tang and blade broken. Back of deep blade rises in gentle curve. L. 150+mm. *26/36; SF629; Period 7, Phase 5*

19   Knife with solid handle with knopped terminal. Blade, incomplete, has cutting edge with angled back. L. 134+mm. *26/45; SF648; Period 6, Phase 4*

20   Clasp knife, complete. Bone scales. L. 107mm. *41/-, Burial SA060; SF60; Period 5, Phase 2* (see also Ch. 28, No. 15)

21   Clasp knife, fragmentary. L. 127+mm. *41/512; SF6; Period 2, Phase 3 (intrusive)*

22   Blade fragment from cleaver, the back burred by hammering. L. 107+mm; blade depth 56mm. *26/242; SF312; Period 6, Phase 2*

Building ironwork, fittings, locks and keys

The limited range of building ironwork is similar to that from other areas of Wharram and includes staples, collars, hinge pivots and wire, as well as straps and locks both of which may have been part of furnishings or of doors and gates.

23*   U-shaped staple, complete. One arm distorted. L. 55mm; w. 26mm. *26/228; SF317; Period 2, Phase 2*

24   U-shaped staple, complete but distorted. L. 65mm; w. 32mm. *26/148; SF670; Period 6, Phase 4*

25   U-shaped staple, made from circular-sectioned rod. L. 37mm; w. 18mm. *26/45; SF635; Period 6, Phase 4*

26   U-shaped staple, made from circular-sectioned rod. L. 40mm; w. 18mm. *26/45; SF636; Period 6, Phase 4*

27   U-shaped staple, made from circular-sectioned rod. L. 35mm; w. 22mm. *52/1; SF31; Period 4, Phase 1*

28   U-shaped staple, made from circular-sectioned rod. L. 32mm; w. 13mm. *52/1; SF32; Period 4, Phase 1*

29   U-shaped staple, made from circular-sectioned rod. L. 35mm; w. 12mm. *52/9; SF20; Period 1, Phase 2*

30*   Rectangular staple, one arm broken. L. 70mm; w. 78mm. *26/72; SF398; Period 4, Phase 4*

Another two U-shaped and three rectangular staples (Archive 85, 86 and 87-89) were found in Period 7 contexts on Site 26.

31   Collar, circular. Diam. 35mm; depth 20mm. *26/291; SF6; Period 5, Phase 1*

32*   Collar, circular. Diam. 49mm; depth 16mm. *41/104; SF47; Period 5, Phase 1*

Another collar, a ring and a swivel ring with broken hook (Archive 90-92) were found in Period 7 contexts on Site 26.

33*   Hinge pivot, shank broken. Wear at base of guide arm. Ht 66mm; l. 56+mm. *41/102; SF43; Period 5, Phase 2*

34   Hinge pivot, typologically of 19th or 20th-century date. Guide arm rises from centre of circular expansion at end of broken shank. Ht 83mm; l. 213+mm. *52/3; SF34; Period 4, Phase 1*

35*   Hinge with open loop and broken strap. L. 63+mm; w. 21mm. *26/283; SF407; Period 5, Phase 1*

36   Strap fragment. L. 50+mm; w. 21-26mm. *26/543; SF126; Period 3, Phase 2*

37   Strap fragment. L. 35+mm; w. 17mm. *26/272; SF404; Period 4, Phase 4*

Another hinge with end loop and broken strap and eight more strap fragments, ranging in width from 11 to 38mm, were found in Period 7 contexts on Site 26, as was a rectangular rove and a modern gate hook (Archive 94-104).

38   Wire. L. 77+mm; diam. 2mm. *26/45; SF606, Period 6, Phase 4*

Other fragments of wire (Archive 105-107) were found in Period 7 contexts on Site 26.

39*   Barrel padlock with inverted U-shaped housings at each end to house the padlock bolt. Plain case, bolt damaged and partly withdrawn. L. 38mm; h. 38mm. *26/389.2; SF447; Period 3, Phase 4*

40*   Barrel padlock bolt with shaped end plate which supported free arm and spring arm. Free arm lost, but one of two spines survives on spring arm, though without any leaf springs. L. 45+mm; ht 46mm. *41/140; SF55; Period 3, Phase 2*

41*   U-shaped shackle used in conjunction with barrel padlock to secure limbs. One end hooked, the other with a double-looped fitting. L. 120mm. *41/103; SF44; Period 5, Phase 2*

A tumbler from a lock and a key with an oval bow (Archive 108 and 109) were found in Period 7 contexts on Site 26.

Strips and other domestic ironwork

42   Strip, broken. L. 38+mm; w. 8mm. *26/682; SF399; Period 3, Phase 1*

43   D-sectioned strip fragment with rounded terminal retaining circular stud. L. 53+mm; w. 8mm. *26/289; SF47; Period 4, Phase 2*

These narrow strips are likely to have been used on caskets, two slightly wider ones (Archive 110 and 111) were found in Period 7 contexts on Site 26.

44*   Candleholder, incomplete. Tang, which would have been set in a wooden block or in a ring, supports head which originally had central pricket set between scrolled upright arms with outer cranked arms carrying sockets. Candles would have been impaled on the pricket or placed in the sockets, and rushlights wedged between the pricket and the scrolled arms. L. 104mm; w. 60+mm. *26/45; SF637; Period 6, Phase 4*

45   Arm from candle snuffer, incomplete. Spiked tip, used for uncurling the wick before cutting, has a knobbed foot on its underside, which was originally one of three, the other two being on the finger loops. Open rectangular box on top of arm worked in conjunction with a flat press on the lost arm which carried the cut wick into the box and extinguished it. L. 82+mm. *26/36; SF653; Period 7, Phase 5*

Fragments of cast-iron and other objects of recent date are listed in the catalogue (Archive 112-120).

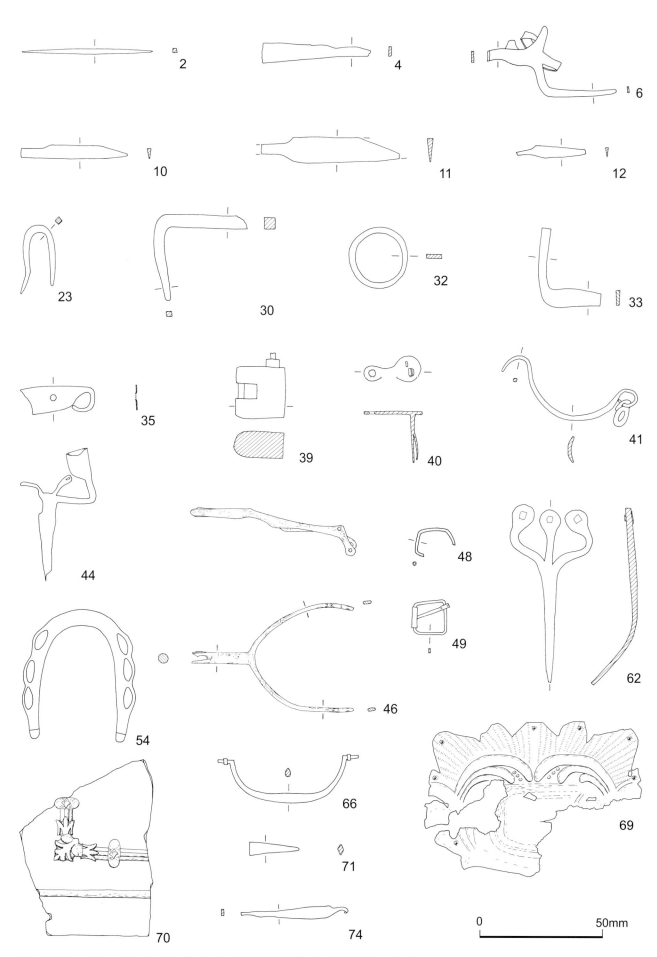

Fig. 147. Iron objects Nos 2, 4, 6, 10-12, 23, 30, 32-3, 35, 39-41, 44, 46, 48-9, 54, 62, 66, 69, 70, 71 and 74. Scale 1:3 (M. Chisnall)

Personal fittings

Spurs
by B. Ellis

46* Rowel spur. Fragile with its surfaces rusted into a coating of soil; a few bright specks may have been non-ferrous plating, probably tin. The neck is long and straight, of round section, with a fragment of the rowel pin remaining in the rowel box although the rowel is lost. The slender spur sides are of flattened-D section. From behind the wearer's heel the sides project very slightly downward, thickening temporarily as they become almost horizontal and tapering forward to extended figure-8 terminals which turn diagonally downward. Overall l. 138mm; l. of neck 51mm (including rowel box 20mm); span about 80mm (one terminal is slightly compressed). *26/220; SF328; Period 7, Phase 2*

The neck length combined with the fairly horizontal plane and extended terminals suggest a date in the first half of the 16th century. Probably 1500-1550.

47 Spur fragment. The fragment consists of one short spur side of D-section, deepest behind the wearer's heel and tapering strongly towards the missing terminal. The fragmentary stump of a small neck projects from the centre of the deepest part and has almost rusted away. Bright traces are probably the remains of non-ferrous plating. Remaining overall l. (positioned as worn) 77mm. *26/218; SF315; Period 7, Phase 2*

This fragment is typical of the small rowel spurs popular in the late 17th century.

Other personal fittings include buckles, pins and parts of pattens.

48* Buckle frame. Trapezoidal shape but distorted and incomplete. W. 34mm; l. 24mm. *41/21; SF35; Period 3, Phase 1*

49* Buckle. Trapezoidal frame with pin resting on sheet-iron cylinder. Frame w. 29mm; l. 30mm. *41/103; SF45; Period 5, Phase 2*

50 Buckle frame, broken. Two sides of rectangular frame, longer side distorted but retains rounded perforated terminal which held one end of lost baluster bar. W. 43+mm; l. 50mm. *26/45; SF605; Period 6, Phase 4*

51 Buckle pin, gently curved in side view. L. 54mm. *26/45; SF639; Period 6, Phase 4*

52 Dress pin. Iron shank, globular non-ferrous head. L. 65mm; head diam. 4mm. *26/351; SF39; unstratified*

53 Single-riveted terminal from patten, long bar distorted and broken. L. 71mm. *41/4; SF40; Period 5, Phase 2*

Two buckle frames, one rectangular (Archive 121), the other D-shaped (Archive 122), were found in Period 7 contexts on Site 26, as was the D-shaped ring from another patten (Archive 123) and two fragments of iron plates from shoes (Archive 124 and 125).

Horsefittings

Horseshoes
The horseshoes are of four types, the earliest, Nos 54-56, having countersunk nail holes, Nos 57 and 58 (and Archive 126-132), with rectangular nail holes, being the succeeding late medieval and early post-medieval type. Numbers 59 and 60 (and Archive 133-138) are typologically post-medieval having their nail holes set in

fullered grooves. Number 61 having a wider web and a distinctive shaped tip, is also typologically post-medieval; Archive 139 has a wide web but lacks the shaped tip.

54* Complete. Wavy edge, 3 x 3 countersunk nail holes, calkins. L. 105mm; w. 94mm; web 15mm. *41/163B; SF56; Period 3, Phase 1*

55 Arm tip. One countersunk nail hole, calkin. L. 53+mm. *41/169B; SF57; Period 3, Phase 1*

56 Arm tip. Calkin. L. 45+mm. *41/132; SF54; Period 3, Phase 2*

57 Arm tip. One rectangular nail hole, calkin. L. 57+mm; web 22mm. *41/127; SF52; Period 3, Phase 3*

58 Arm tip. L. 43+mm; web 20mm. *26/355; SF68; Period 4, Phase 2*

59 Toe fragment, one central nail hole and one in each arm. W. 73+mm; web 28mm. *26/229; SF320; Period 6, Phase 2*

60 Arm. Four rectangular nailholes in fullered groove. Calkin. L. 141mm; web 29mm. *52/1; SF33; Period 4, Phase 1*

61 Complete. Shaped arm tips. 4 x 4 rectangular nail holes. L. 122mm; w. 110mm; web 24mm. *41/103; SF46; Period 5, Phase 2*

Currycomb
62* Currycomb handle with distorted tang and three arms, all with rounded, perforated terminals for attachment to lost iron comb. L. 155mm; w. 66mm. *26/230; SF1014; Period 6, Phase 2*

Bridle bit
63 Bridle bit. Fragment of cheekpiece with incomplete, D-shaped ring for attachment of mouthpiece links and bridle straps. L. 74mm. *26/229; SF321; Period 6, Phase 2*

Stirrup
64 Stirrup. Complete but distorted. Oval body with D-shaped slot for stirrup leather. Open centre to oval tread. W. 133mm; l. 140mm. *26/215-216; SF425; Period 7, Phase 5*

Oxshoes

65 Arm fragment with two nails with broad flat heads. L. 41+mm; web 22mm. *26/45; SF640; Period 6, Phase 4*

Three other fragments (Archive 140-142) were found in late contexts.

Burial fittings

66* Coffin grip, U-shaped with swollen handgrips. Remains of attaching staple on one arm. W. 120mm; h. 37mm. *41/-, Burial SA059; SF61; Period 5, Phase 2*

67 Coffin grip, U-shaped with swollen handgrips. W. 124mm; h. 42mm. *41/-, Burial SA060; SF58; Period 5, Phase 2*

68 Decorated thin tinned sheet. Several fragments of generally indeterminate shape. *41/-, Burial SA059; SF62, Period 5, Phase 2*

69* Decorated thin tinned sheet. Shaped plate with a central plain oval escutcheon and an outer edge resembling a sunburst. L. 179mm; h. 122mm. *41/-, Burial SA060, SF59, Period 5, Phase 2*

70* Cast-iron memorial. Broken fragment with decorative bead close to edge and, further in, one corner of rectangular panel defined by a raised floral band. L. 105+mm; w. 144+mm; th. 8mm. *26/215-216, SF427, Period 7, Phase 5*

Arrowhead

71* Socketed and barbed arrowhead, tip lost. L. 44+mm; socket diam. 12mm. *26/54, SF610, Period 5, Phase 1*

Sheet

72 Sheet fragment. L. 85+mm; w. 38+mm; th. 1.5mm. *26/?62, SF676, Period 4, Phase 6*

73 Sheet fragment. L. 26+mm; w. 25+mm; th. 1mm. *26/51; SF651, Period 6, Phase 2*

Archive 143-146 are cast iron fragments.

Unclassifiable iron fragments

74* Looped object with tapering arm. L. 85+mm; w. 7-10mm. *26/62, SF645, Period 4, Phase 6*

Another 79 fragments (Archive 147-226) are unclassifiable.

Iron objects from the Church

In the 1970s the policy was that only very few iron objects were selected for publication. This, together with the decision to publish most of the objects from the church excavations in fiche only, resulted in many of the iron objects not appearing in either *Wharram III* or its fiche. A complete list of these now forms part of the Archive.

They include many more examples of iron used in buildings and of fragments of knives and horseshoes. Only three handles that may have come from coffins can be directly related to the use of the church and churchyard. A few personal items and a jew's harp add to those from other parts of the village.

Nails
by J.G. Watts

Just over 800 nails and fragments of nails from the Churchyard sites were X-rayed, examined by eye and catalogued. Of these, 34 were totally unidentifiable and are not included in the report. Table 153 shows the identifiable ones by type. Of the 777 identifiable nails and fragments, some 7% are from horse and oxshoes. This is a small proportion compared to those found on the South Manor (16%), or in the North Manor Area (24%) where the relatively large numbers of horseshoe nails were thought to be related to the roadway passing through the site.

Table 153. Total of all identifiable nails by type and as a percentage of the total.

Type of nail	Site 41	Site 26	Site 52	Site 80	Total per Type	% of total
Brodde:Type 4	4	20	1	-	25	3.2
Headed – Deckhead	-	1	-	-	1	0.1
Headed – Rectangular	2	77	1	1	81	10.4
Headed – Circular	10	122	1	-	133	17.1
Headed – Lath	-	18	-	-	18	2.3
Headed – Offset	1	12	-	-	13	1.7
Headed – Oval	2	46	-	-	48	6.2
Headed – Rosehead	2	2	1	-	5	0.6
Headed – Dome	-	2	-	-	2	0.3
Headed – Unidentifiable	4	61	2	-	67	8.6
Point frags	4	196	2	-	202	26.0
Shank frags	5	71	3	-	79	10.2
Roundwire	-	10	-	-	10	1.3
Spike: Type 5	-	18	-	-	18	2.3
Stud: Type 7	-	5	-	1	6	0.8
T-head: Type 3	-	12	-	-	12	1.5
Horseshoe – Fiddle-key	3	8	-	-	11	1.4
Horseshoe – Cruciform	3	2	-	-	5	0.6
Horseshoe – Trapezoidal	-	21	-	-	21	2.7
Horseshoe – Spike	-	2	-	-	2	0.3
Horseshoe – Unidentifiable	5	6	1	-	12	1.5
Oxshoe	-	6	-	-	6	0.8
TOTAL	45	718	12	2	777	99.9

Ninety-three percent of the nails from the Churchyard are joinery nails, the majority probably from building activities – the relatively large numbers of points indicate demolition. The joinery nails include most of the types previously found at Wharram; no new types were identified.

Some of the joinery nails may originate from burials. When the church excavations were published (*Wharram III*) nails were recorded but not examined, so the opportunity has been taken to X-ray those that could be identified as coming from burials. Although the extent of corrosion made identification difficult, the majority of nails from burials in all areas have rectangular, oval or circular heads and are of similar size to those used in post-medieval coffins within the church. It is likely that the coffins were constructed using thin-shanked oval or rectangular-headed nails, and that the lids were secured with large (10-21mm diameter) flat, circular-headed nails. It was possible, from a small number of nails to establish that the average thickness of planks was 16mm (⁵/₈").

28 Objects of Antler and Bone
by I. Riddler

A small group of twenty-one objects of bone and antler consists largely of items from Sites 26 and 41, alongside a group provenanced to the church. They range in date from the later prehistoric to the late post-medieval period, although the majority are of Anglo-Saxon or medieval date. They include a number of items that have not previously been recorded from Wharram Percy and others that are rare finds, both in local and national terms. Thus, although it is a small assemblage of objects, it has a number of points of interest. The objects are described here within broad period bands.

Later prehistoric

A single object can be assigned to this period; it is the earliest object of bone or antler yet to have been recovered from Wharram Percy.

A T-shaped object (No. 1) made from a section of scapula and retrieved from a Period 1 context, probably functioned as a pendant, although it lacks any perforation. It is an unusual object, unparalleled in English later prehistoric bone assemblages but reminiscent of a miniature version of French anciform pendants of Neolithic date which, however, are much larger objects, usually made from antler (Roussot-Larroque 1985).

1* A crudely manufactured T-shaped section of bone, produced probably from the scapula of a small domesticate. The central shaft is circular in section and tapers markedly towards the splayed ends. It is pierced by a long, rectangular perforation, adapted from the natural shape of the bone. The two ends are formed of relatively solid bone and are curved to either side of the shaft. L. 33mm; w. 29mm; th. 2-8mm. Object dating: ?Iron Age. *26/616; SF127; Period 1, Phase 2*

Anglo-Saxon

The Anglo-Saxon assemblage is dominated by fragments of composite combs, as is usually the case, reflecting the situation seen, for example, at the South Manor (MacGregor 2000, 148). There are a few items of textile manufacturing equipment, typical of the Anglo-Saxon period, as well as a bone implement identified as a spearhead, an object type that has only recently been recognised as post-Roman in date.

Composite combs

Five comb fragments and two tooth segments come from single-sided Anglo-Saxon combs of two different types. They include two handled combs and three single-sided composite combs. A bone handle (No. 2) has been cut from a cattle metatarsus and was originally part of a handled comb. In all likelihood, its decoration was confined to the end of the handle and to one of the connecting plates. It can be compared with a series of handles of a similar bone type, decorated in the same way, from Bedford, Birka, Canterbury, *Hamwic*, Ipswich, London, North Elmham, Pakenham, Westbury and York, amongst other sites (Riddler 1990, 11-12; 1995, 390 and fig. 182.1-2; Riddler, Trzaska-Nartowski and Hatton forthcoming; Wade-Martins 1980, fig. 259.1 and 4; West 1998, fig. 119.1; MacGregor 1978, fig. 29.9; Rogers 1993, fig. 679.5697; MacGregor, Mainman and Rogers 1999, fig. 895.7683 and 7686). Few of these combs are closely dated but the sequences from *Hamwic* and Ipswich both suggest that this is essentially a Middle Saxon type of comb, popular above all during the 8th and 9th centuries.

A small fragment of a handle (Church No. 4) stems from an antler-handled comb of a similar type. The decoration is similar to the comb above but includes just three lateral saw-cut lines. Handled combs generally include broader decorative bands consisting of four or more lines, but groups of three lateral lines can be seen on handled combs from Chichester, London and York (Down 1978, fig. 10.44.207; Riddler 1990, fig. 1a; Waterman 1959, fig. 17.2; Rogers 1993, fig. 679.5570; MacGregor, Mainman and Rogers 1999, fig. 896.6788, 6789 and 6793). The overall shape and decorative scheme of the Middle Saxon handled comb is well defined on a near complete comb from York that lacks its front end segment, which was probably curved along its back (MacGregor, Mainman and Rogers 1999, fig. 895.7683). Comparatively few handled combs have come from Wharram Percy, in comparison with combs of other types. A front end segment came from the South Manor and a tooth segment, possibly from a handled comb, was retrieved from one of the Plateau sites (MacGregor 2000, fig. 70.28).

A distinctive single-sided comb fragment made entirely from bone (No. 3) includes ring-and-dot and lattice decoration on both sides. The design of the comb is unusual. The connecting plates widen towards the end segment, suggesting that this might be a fragment of a handled comb. The connecting plates, however, are made from animal ribs, a material that was not used in handled comb production at all. It is more likely therefore, that this is a single-sided composite comb. The end segment is complete, if lacking its teeth, but the connecting plates actually extend beyond it, which is unusual. There are subtle but important differences between the two connecting plates. On one side the decoration is applied with some skill and it incorporates saw marks from the cutting of the teeth. On the other side there are no saw marks and the decoration is more haphazard. On this side each end of the connecting plate is bounded by vertical lines. These do not occur on the better-produced connecting plate, however. These differences, taken in conjunction with the end segment placed seemingly in the wrong position, indicate that this is a comb that has been truncated and repaired. The repair involved shortening the comb, refitting one of the connecting plates and adding an end segment in a new position. The resultant comb, though much shorter than the original, was still suitable for use.

Repaired composite combs are not common. Tempel noted a single-sided comb from Birka which had been shortened, and for which a new end segment had also been added (Tempel 1969, 43 and taf 14.6), and an unpublished double-sided composite comb from *Hamwic* has been treated in a similar manner. A Middle Saxon double-sided composite comb from Red Castle, Thetford has also been shortened and reworked (Knocker and Wells 1967, fig. 15.8). Tempel has noted that at sites like Haithabu comb making was undertaken on such a scale that it was not necessary to retain broken examples (Tempel 1969, 42). Equally, however, Ambrosiani argued that the very fact that some combs were repaired showed that they were not lightly discarded; indeed, they may have lasted for most of the lifetime of the owner (Ambrosiani 1981, 13-14).

The fourth comb fragment (No. 4) consists merely of the end of a connecting plate, once again made of bone, and decorated with bands of vertical lines. The decoration is very common on combs of 7th and 8th-century date. A fragment of an undecorated antler connecting plate (Church No. 5) probably stems from a single-sided composite comb, but too little remains to determine the type. The use of bone - a characteristic of three combs here - is unusual and the majority of Anglo-Saxon combs, of whatever type, were made from antler. Further fragments of bone single-sided composite combs have come from the Plateau (Site 78) and the South Manor (MacGregor 2000, 150, n° 52 and 153, n° 119); they all appear to be of Middle Saxon date. Single-sided composite combs with connecting plates made from animal rib occur during the earlier part of the Middle Saxon period, from the late 7th century to the middle of the 8th century (Riddler 2001a, 66). Handled combs of bone were also made at this time, and their production extended into the 9th century. Thereafter, combs are made entirely of antler until the 12th century.

2* Part of the bone handle for a handled comb, cut from a cattle metatarsus. The end part is decorated around the foramen of the proximal end of the bone by a band of closely-spaced lateral lines, cut with the aid of a saw. Object dating: Middle Saxon. *26/382; SF235; Period 3, Phase 4*

3* A single-sided comb fragment, consisting of an end segment and two tooth segments, secured to two connecting plates by three iron rivets, with traces of a fourth rivet also visible. Both of the connecting plates, which are made of bone, are decorated by a central band of single ring-and-dot designs, enclosed within single bounding lines, with a dense lattice of single crossing diagonal lines above. On the longer fragment this pattern is bounded at either end by a band of four vertical lines. There are five teeth per centimetre. The teeth show noticeable signs of wear, which are more pronounced on one side of the comb. The end segment appears to be made from bone. Object dating: Middle or Late Saxon. *26/272; SF237; Period 4, Phase 4*

4* A fragment of a bone connecting plate for a single-sided composite comb. It is decorated by a band of vertical lines at its end and there are traces of a similar band across its point of breakage. Saw marks from the cutting of the teeth indicate that there were originally five teeth per centimetre. There are also traces of two closely-spaced rivets. Object dating: Middle Saxon. *Site 26/412/A; SF102; Period 3, Phase 4*

5* A tooth segment for a single-sided composite comb, produced from bone or antler. The back of the segment is angled and it is riveted along one edge. It is relatively thick, and quite short. There are six teeth per centimetre and the surviving teeth show traces of considerable wear, which is more pronounced on one side of the segment than the other. L. 8mm; th. 3.5mm. Object dating: Anglo-Saxon. *26/351; SF 45: unstratified*

6 A fragment of an antler tooth segment for a composite comb. Three teeth survive, spaced at six per centimetre; they do not show any traces of wear. Object dating: Anglo-Saxon. *26/ (at the possible interface of) 295 and 336; SF233; Period 4, Phase 4 or 2*

Pin or needle

A roughly facetted point for a bone pin or needle appears to be unfinished. It comes from a Period 2 context and could be of Middle Saxon date, but too little survives to determine the object type.

7 Roughly facetted fragment of the point of a pin or needle, apparently unfinished. Object dating: ?Middle Saxon. *Site 41/528; SF12; Period 2, Phase 1*

Spinning and weaving equipment

The antler pin-beater (No. 8) is of single-pointed form, an implement type that was not current in northern England before the later part of the 9th century (Walton Rogers 1997, 1755; 2001, 163-4). It can be associated with the vertical two-beam loom. It is highly polished and at some point it has been perforated towards the broader end. Few pin-beaters are perforated, although there are several from Ipswich and York (Riddler, Trzaska-Nartowski and Hatton forthcoming; MacGregor, Mainman and Rogers 1999, fig. 923.6687 and 6688). The perforation is well down the shaft in this case, and may be an indication of secondary use.

The antler spindlewhorl (No. 9) conforms with Walton Rogers' type A2, for which one flat face is larger than the other (Walton Rogers 1997, 1736). Type A spindlewhorls belong essentially to the early and Middle Saxon periods and declined in use by the 10th to 11th centuries, at a time

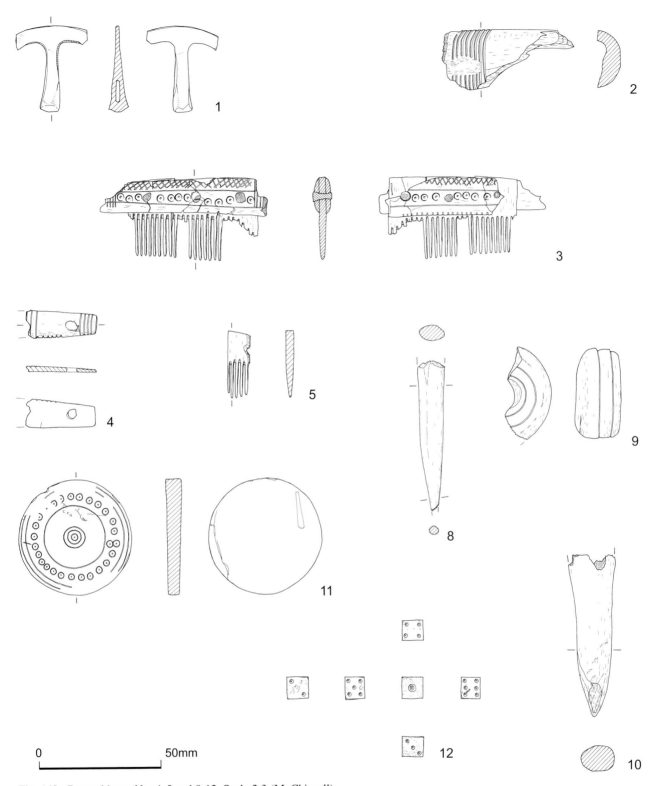

Fig. 148. Bone objects: Nos 1-5 and 8-12. Scale 2:3 (M. Chisnall)

when the bone spindlewhorl became more popular than examples made of antler (Walton Rogers 1997, 1736). Similar antler spindlewhorls have come from the Anglo-Saxon buildings and the South Manor (MacGregor 1992, 58 and fig. 30.22; 2000, 152 and fig. 71.100).

8*   A section of an antler pin-beater of single-pointed form. It has a flattened oval section and has been perforated along the broad face of the shaft. It is polished. Object dating: Late Saxon. *26/?74; SF236; Period 5, Phase 1*

9*   A section of a spindlewhorl made from an antler burr. It is decorated on one broad face by two concentric circles, and this decoration is repeated around the circumference. Original diam. *c.* 40mm; ht 17mm. Object dating: Anglo-Saxon. *26/412A; SF101; Period 3, Phase 4*

Spearhead

The pointed bone implement (No. 10), produced from an ovicaprid radius, can be compared with an object from the South Manor, quite possibly made from a roe deer metatarsus, as well as a similar object from *Sandtun*, made from a juvenile cattle metacarpus and a further example from Brandon, produced from an ovicaprid metacarpus (MacGregor 2000, 153 and fig. 72.113; Riddler 2001b, 251 and fig. 50.116; Riddler forthcoming a). In each case the upper end of the bone has been hollowed axially and two of the objects also have lateral perforations close to the proximal end. Their midshafts have been shaped to short and sharp points. The presence of the lateral hole, which is not obvious with this example (where most of the proximal end is missing), suggests that these objects were fastened to wooden shafts. The South Manor and *Sandtun* objects are of Middle Saxon date and that may also be the case with this example, although it comes from a Period 4 deposit. Comparable pointed bone implements, contemporary with these examples, are particularly common on Slavic sites where most, however, are cut from the distal end of the bone (Schuldt 1985, 110-12 and abbn. 102-5; Becker 2001, 132-4 and figs 4 and 9). A series from Elisenhof are closer in form to these examples, if generally longer (Westphalen 1999, 7-8 and taf. 2). Most have been made from ovicaprid bones, particularly the tibia. Westphalen has suggested that they were used as spear points, either in hunting, or as fish spears, used to catch flat fish from a boat (Westphalen 1999, 8), allowing them to be added to the growing list of implements of bone and antler used in fishing practices (Riddler 2006a).

10* A pointed bone implement, produced from the distal end of an ovicaprid radius. The proximal end has been removed and the midshaft has been trimmed to a point. The object is polished, conceivably from use. Object dating: Middle or Late Saxon. *41/108; SF15; Period 4, Phase 2*

Medieval

The medieval objects are produced entirely in bone and serve as a reminder of the increasingly limited access to antler from the 12th century onwards (MacGregor 1985, 51). The range of objects produced in bone during the medieval period was smaller than in preceding centuries and some of them – and composite combs in particular – are far more common on the Continent than in England. Gaming pieces and styli are both typical and popular object forms of the medieval period.

Gaming pieces

The discoidal bone counter (No. 11) has been cut from the lower mandible of a cow with a circular saw, in the manner of those from Schleswig (Ulbricht 1984, 38 and taf 38). This example belongs to the most common type, for which one face is decorated with designs based on ring-and-dot motifs within concentric circles and the central area is not perforated (Ulbricht 1984, 58; MacGregor 1985, 135-7; Riddler 1994, 186). The English series occur in contexts dated between the 11th and the 13th centuries, at which point a smaller form of discoidal counter, produced in wood as well as bone, replaced these large pieces (Riddler 1994; 1999). They were used for the game of *Tabula*, an ancestor of Backgammon, which was

reintroduced into England during the 11th century (MacGregor 1985, 137; Riddler 1994, 188).

On the cubic die (No. 12) the numbers are arranged so that 1 is opposite 2, 3 is opposite 4, and 5 is opposite to 6. This numbering arrangement is characteristic more of medieval dice, than of those of the Roman period (MacGregor 1985, 131-12; Ulbricht 1984, 59; Brown 1990, 692-3; Riddler in Egan 1998, 290). MacGregor has suggested that this arrangement of numbers is characteristic of dice of 13th-century or later date (MacGregor 1985, 132; MacGregor, Mainman and Rogers 1999, 1983-5).

11* A complete discoidal bone counter for the game of *Tabula*. It has been sawn from the lower mandible of a cow and it is decorated on the upper face by a band of single ring-and-dot motifs enclosed within bounding lines, and by a large, triple ring-and-dot motif at the centre. The upper surface is lightly polished. Diam. 46mm; ht 7mm. Object dating: early medieval. *26/566; SF120; Period 2, Phase 1*

12* A bone or antler die of cubical form, with numbers arranged so that 1 is opposite 2, 3 is opposite 4 and 5 is opposite 6. Dimensions 8.3 x 8.9 x 9.1mm. Object dating: medieval. *26/3; SF234; Period 6, Phase 5*

Stylus

A fragmentary stylus (Church No. 6) lacks its metal point and has a simple, spherical knop with two roll mouldings at the top of the shaft. Its simple design calls several of the styli from York (MacGregor, Mainman and Rogers 1999, fig. 930.8042 and 8054). Styli are common objects of the late medieval and early post-medieval periods, although this is the first example to have been recorded from Wharram Percy. A second bone stylus has come from the North Glebe Terrace (Riddler and Leaf, forthcoming). Most belong to the period from the 13th to the 16th centuries (MacGregor 1985, 124; Riddler 2001c, 278; 2006b, 278). There has been considerable debate concerning their function, but the evidence points strongly towards an identification as styli (MacGregor, Mainman and Rogers 1999, 1975-6; Riddler 2001c, 278). As such, they form a useful indicator of literacy and are not confined to ecclesiastical establishments, occurring also in secular contexts (MacGregor, Mainman and Rogers 1999, 1975; Hurley 1997, 269). In this particular case, the stylus may have come from a burial in the Vestry.

Post-medieval

The small post-medieval assemblage includes two scale tang handles, one probably of 16th-century date and the other belonging to the 18th century and comparable with a large group of similar handles from the North Glebe Terrace. Late post-medieval items include lathe-turned bone rings, a button and a penknife.

A near-complete iron fork (No. 13) includes two scale tang bone plates, fastened by three rivets. The plates have rounded ends and are D-shaped in section. A collection of fifteen implements with similar scale tang plates has come from the North Glebe Terrace (Riddler and Leaf forthcoming). Comparable handles are largely of 18th-century date and include examples from London, Winchester and Galway (Thompson *et al.* 1984, 105 and fig. 52.51; Goodall 1990, fig. 257.2836; Hurley 2004, 470 and fig. 6.9.8a-d). A second handle of bone (Church No. 7) retains its scale tang but has lost most of its knife blade. Two copper-alloy rivets alternate with three of iron and the rounded end has an intimation of a pistol-grip form. A similar alternation of iron and copper-alloy rivets can be seen on a bone knife handle of late medieval date from Site 30 at Wharram (MacGregor and Riddler 2005, 143 and fig. 61.2). In this case, however, the simplicity of the design and the shape of the end, with a rounded terminal and the slight asymmetry of the lower edge, both suggest that it is a little later in date. A handle from Great Lynford has a more overt pistol-grip, as well as an alternation of iron and copper-alloy rivets (Tyrell and Zeepvat 1991, 190 and fig. 96.317). The handle form occurs in 16th-century deposits in London (Egan 2005, 93 and fig. 78.403) and pistol-grip handles of that date are known from Norwich and Winchester (Riddler forthcoming b).

Two bone rings were also recovered, one of which (Church No. 8) was found in the nave. It is lathe-turned with bands of incised decoration, and abundant iron staining is present on its inner surface. It stems from an implement of late post-medieval date, possibly a knife with an iron bolster. A fragment of a ring of D-shaped section (Church No. 9) is also likely to be of late post-medieval date. It has fine machine-made striations on both sides and it can be compared with bone rings and accompanying waste material, produced from cattle tibiae and deposited in a mid-19th-century context at Launceston Castle (Riddler forthcoming c). An incomplete bone button (No. 14) belongs to Biddle's type D, which is mostly of 19th-century date (Biddle 1990, 573). A number were found at the Farmhouse and Vicarage on the North Glebe Terrace (Riddler and Leaf forthcoming). A gardener's knife with antler scale tang plates and a single iron blade (No. 15) is also of late 19th or 20th-century date. Similar knives appear in the Fiskars catalogue of 1897 (Fiskars Aktiebolags 1997, 22 no. 258).

13 An iron fork with two scale tang plates of bone, both undecorated and fastened by three evenly-spaced iron rivets. Object dating: 18th-century. *41/103; SF79; Period 5, Phase 2*

14 An incomplete bone button, perforated by three circular holes arranged in a line. Diam. 11mm. Object dating: late post-medieval. *26/36; SF231; Period 7, Phase 5*

15 A complete gardener's knife with antler scale tang plates and a single iron blade, folded back into the knife. Object dating: late 19th to 20th-century. *41/- Burial SA60; SF 60; Period 5, Phase 2* (see also Chapter 27, No. 20)

Church catalogue

Church 4* Fragment of a handle from an antler handled comb, consisting of part of the outer surface with a band of three lateral lines incised by a saw with a blade 0.5 mm in thickness. The inner part of the handle has been removed to leave a hollow centre. Object dating: Middle Saxon. *14/-, C1574; SF301; north of church*

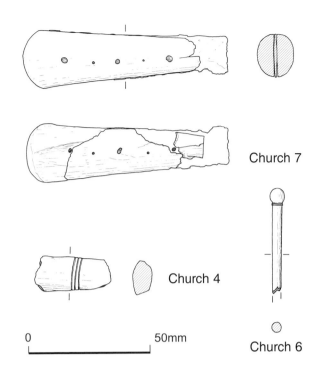

Fig. 149. Church bone: Nos 4, 6 and 7. Scale 2:3. (M. Chisnall)

Church 5 Small fragment of an antler connecting plate for a composite comb, of plano-convex section with a rivet hole at the centre. Probably from a single-sided comb, given the lack of any marks from the cutting of the comb teeth. Object dating: Middle or Late Saxon. *14/-; C1911; SF305; vestry*

Church 6* Fragmentary bone stylus with an oval knop, flattened at its apex, separated from the cylindrical shaft by two thin lateral mouldings. The shaft is circular in section and tapers gradually towards the point, which is missing. *14/-, Burial V35; SF306; vestry*

Church 7* Bone scale tang knife handle, surviving in poor condition but with one tang substantially complete. D-shaped section, flat narrow end, sides widening to rounded butt terminal. Three iron rivets and two of copper-alloy set in an alternating pattern. *14/-, C710; SF300; north aisle*

Church 8 Fragmentary lathe-turned bone ring, decorated with two bands of three incised lines. Abundant iron staining on inner surface. *14/-, C2237; SF303; nave*

Church 9 Fragmentary bone ring of D-shaped section, thin longitudinal machine-made striations on inner and outer surfaces. Internal diameter 23mm. *14/-, C1531; SF304; nave*

29 A note on the wood

Some 26 pieces of wood, some very fragmentary, were recovered from the Churchyard, mostly from Site 26. Small fragments (Archive 12 and 13) were associated with graves but do not represent coffins; larger fragments came from post-holes in Periods 4, 6 and 7. The remains of wood and nails from coffins, as well as post-medieval coffin fittings (see p. 311), were found with Burials SA059 and SA060 (Archive 14-16).

Part Seven
The Environmental Evidence
by J. Richardson

30 The Animal Remains

Introduction

The faunal assemblage from the Churchyard Area of Wharram Percy dates from the prehistoric to the post-medieval period. The animal bones associated with medieval and post-medieval deposits, however, have been excluded from this analysis, as they had been extensively reworked/disturbed during the use of the area as a cemetery. In addition, the prehistoric/Iron Age assemblage was very small and in total, only 1059 fragments were identified to species or a lower-order group (Table 154). Given the small sample size, further analyses have been restricted to the Iron Age/Roman and Anglo-Saxon assemblages. Comparative Roman material has been used from the North Manor Area, North-west Enclosure (Richardson 2004a; 2004b) and Rudston villa (Chaplin and Barnetson 1980), while Saxon data from the South Manor Area have also been employed (Pinter-Bellows 2000).

Methodology

The methodologies used to record bone condition and treatment, the minimum number of bone zones, species presence, age-at-death, pathological and metrical data are the same as those used to analyse the faunal assemblages from the North Manor Area (Richardson 2004a) and the pond and dam (Richardson 2005b). All digital data are held with the Site Archive.

Taphonomic bias

Bone condition and treatment were examined in order to assess the value of the bone assemblage for further analysis. The effectiveness of the recovery of bone fragments (influenced most greatly by the methods of excavation) is also relevant, but unfortunately screening was not systematic here. As a result, the assemblage is likely to be biased in favour of the larger bones and the larger species.

Formation processes

To determine how deposits were formed, bone preservation, weathering and gnawing were assessed and articulated bones were noted. Primary deposits were indicated by articulated parts; a first, second and third phalanx of a pig (Site 26, context 616) and articulated parts (limb and ankle bones) of at least two sheep (Site 26, context 752). Both contexts relate to post-holes in

Table 154. Fragment count by period.

	Prehistoric/ Iron Age	Iron Age/ Roman	Anglo-Saxon
Cattle	3	94	50
Sheep	5	90	23
Sheep/goat	39	230	106
Pig		109	39
Horse	4	14	15
Dog	1	9	5
Hare		1	
Mole		1	
House mouse			
Microfauna			
Amphibian spp.	1	1	5
Domestic fowl		7	1
Domestic fowl/pheasant		9	1
Fowl spp.			3
Domestic goose		9	2
Domestic/wild goose		8	2
Duck sp.		1	
cf. Blackbird		2	
Bird sp.			1
Fish spp.		2	4
Large-size mammal		9	6
Medium-size mammal		9	2
Small-size mammal	3	110	21
Total	56	715	286

Period 1, Phase 2 (see Chapter 4, Fig. 30). The fact that these bones were still articulated when they were deposited indicates that they were rapidly buried. In contrast, the low size index for both periods highlights the fragmented nature of the assemblage, with the majority of bones less than 25% complete (Table 155). Fragmentation of the assemblage is also indicated by the high proportion of loose teeth. These broken bones were probably discarded following carcass reduction, food preparation and/or craft/industrial activities, but it is unlikely that they were middened as relatively few bones were gnawed and high condition and erosion indices indicate that the bones were quickly protected from the effects of trampling and weathering (Table 155).

Table 155. Bone preservation and treatment by period.

	Iron Age/Roman	Anglo-Saxon
Size index	0.28	0.25
Condition index	0.97	0.97
Erosion index	0.92	0.93
% butchered	4.0	3.8
% gnawed	6.1	12.9
% burnt	2.7	5.2
% fresh break	20.8	10.8
% loose teeth	24.8	36.0

For the size, condition and erosion index, values closer to 1.0 indicate more complete or better-preserved bones

Pre-burial processes

The processes that occur prior to bone discard, particularly butchery and burning, can also influence bone survival, although burning apparently had only a negligible effect on the assemblage as a whole (Table 155). Butchery marks were also relatively uncommon and were restricted to the bones of cattle, sheep, pig and goose (Table 156). No butchered horse bones were noted.

Table 156. The proportion of butchered bones by period for all species and knife and chop marks for cattle, sheep, pig and horse.

	Iron Age/Roman	Anglo-Saxon
Knife marks %		
Cattle	2.1	
Sheep	2.8	
Pig	1.8	
Domestic goose	11.1	
Chop marks %		
Cattle	6.4	6.0
Sheep	0.3	
Pig	2.8	5.1

Conclusions

The majority of the fragmentation probably reflects pre-discard processes such as carcass dismemberment and food preparation, as post-discard fragmentation due to trampling and weathering would have been associated with poorer condition and erosion indices and higher proportions of gnawed bones. Instead, it is likely that the bones associated with the Churchyard Area were buried quite rapidly and hence protected from the worst effects of surface disposal and/or middening. Nevertheless, using household waste to manure the fields will have biased the

recovered assemblage (*Wharram V*, 192), and in the absence of systematic sieving, an assemblage skewed in favour of the larger bones and larger species is also proposed.

Animal husbandry

To investigate animal husbandry practices, species proportions, age, sex, metrical and pathological data were assessed. Unfortunately, the fragmented nature of the assemblage meant that very few bones provided metrical data. The few measurements that were taken are not given here, but are held with the Site Archive. On the completion of all faunal analyses for the Wharram Percy excavations, however, a site-wide assessment of the metrical data will be made as part of the final synthesis volume.

Species proportions

Comparing the relative proportions of the main domestic animals over the Iron Age/Roman and Anglo-Saxon periods indicated that while sheep bones were always dominant, they declined at the expense of cattle and horse bones during the Anglo-Saxon period (Fig. 150, Table 154). The proportion of pig bones also declined slightly over time. Such sheep-dominated assemblages are typical of rural sites during the Roman period and have been used as indicators of 'non-Romanised settlements' (King 1991, 17, but cf. Grant 1989, 139). It is likely that the inhabitants of Wharram Percy continued to concentrate on sheep rearing, as the animal was best suited to the free-draining soils of the Yorkshire Wolds, rather than being influenced by the dietary trends introduced by the military and adopted by the towns. Sheep were also important to the Saxon inhabitants, particularly in the later Saxon period as the wool economy developed (King 1991, 18), and the slight decline seen here is probably not significant.

The proportion of the main domestic animals from Iron Age/Roman deposits have been compared to Roman assemblages from the North-west Enclosure and North Manor Area at Wharram Percy, and from Rudston Roman villa located approximately fifteen miles to the east (Fig. 151). Interestingly, the Churchyard data compare most closely with those from Rudston, while the other Wharram sites revealed higher proportions of cattle bones and fewer pigs. This intra-site variability may reflect different activity areas. It is possible, for example, that the larger species tended to be slaughtered and butchered on the outskirts of the village, away from the main living areas. Similar interpretations have been made for Roman Maxey (Halstead 1985, 220 and see Wilson 1994, 64) and it is possible that the North-west Enclosure was used thus. Comparing the Anglo-Saxon deposits from the Churchyard Area to those from the South Manor reveals a similar discrepancy: again cattle bones are more prevalent at the expense of sheep from the South Manor Area (Fig. 152). Given the South Manor's central location, a similar explanation to that given for the

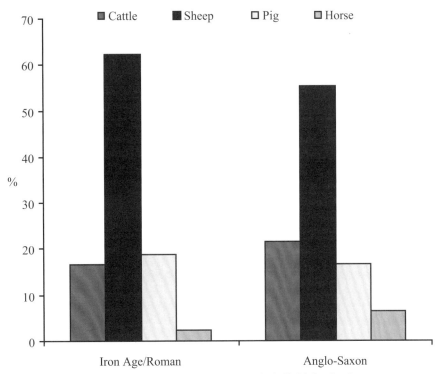

Fig. 150. The relative proportions of the main domestic 'species' by period. (J. Richardson)

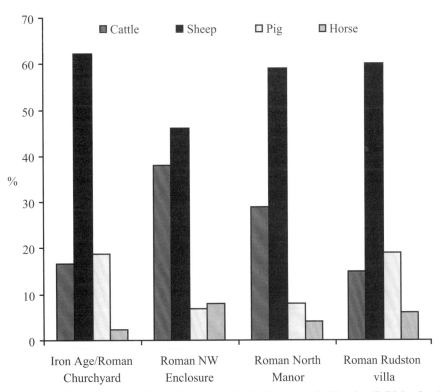

Fig. 151. The relative proportions of the main domestic 'species' in the Roman period by site. (J. Richardson)

peripheral North-west Enclosure is less likely. Instead, perhaps the high cattle percentages reflect variations in the diets of different households.

As has been identified from the other Wharram assemblages analysed to date, the inhabitants of the village, regardless of period, were not hunters. From the Churchyard, only a single duck and hare bone were recovered from Iron Age/Roman deposits, while just a few fish bones were retrieved from both Iron Age/Roman and Anglo-Saxon levels (Table 154).

Age and sex data for cattle, sheep, horse and pig
To investigate the slaughter patterns of cattle and sheep, fusion, dental eruption and wear and sex data have been used. By assessing kill-off patterns and the relative numbers of males and females, specific husbandry

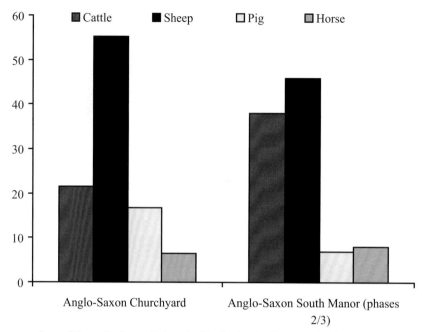

Fig. 152. The relative proportions of the main domestic 'species' in the Anglo-Saxon period by site. (J. Richardson)

regimes, e.g. milk herds or wool flocks, can be proposed. Fusion data are also presented for pig, although these were scarce. Fusion data are given for cattle, sheep and pig in Tables 157 to 159, and dental data for cattle and sheep are given in Tables 160 and 161.

Table 157. Fusion data for cattle by period (zone > 0, F = fused, NF = not fused, neonatal bones excluded).

	Iron Age/Roman			Anglo-Saxon		
	F	NF	% F	F	NF	% F
7-18 months	16	1	94	6	0	100
24-36 months	5	2	71	1	1	50
36-48 months	1	1	50	6	0	100

7-18 months calculated from distal scapula, distal humerus, proximal radius, first phalanx and second phalanx. 24-36 months calculated from distal metacarpal, distal tibia and distal metatarsal. 26-48 months calculated from proximal humerus, ulna, distal radius, proximal femur, distal femur, proximal tibia and calcaneus.

The fusion data for cattle from Iron Age/Roman deposits indicate that only a small proportion of the population had died by 7 to 18 months, but nearly 30% of the animals were slaughtered by 24 to 36 months and 50% by 36 months plus (Table 157). These suggest that milk production was not targeted specifically, as a surplus of juveniles would have been expected, but some sub-adults were slaughtered to provide the inhabitants with high quality beef. The cattle that reached (osteological) maturity would have maintained the viability of a breeding herd, although a minority of milch cows and traction cattle may have been present. Unfortunately, only one sexable pelvis was identified; that of a female, but

possible traction-related stresses (lipping and eburnation) were observed on a first and second phalanx. Insufficient fusion data were available from Anglo-Saxon levels to allow for meaningful interpretation, although what little dental data were available from both periods indicted that some animals were raised specifically for their meat, while others were maintained as breeding stock (Table 160).

Given the relative scarcity of age data for cattle, only the fusion data from Iron Age/Roman deposits have been compared to the slaughter patterns from the North-west Enclosure and Rudston Roman Villa (Fig. 153). These suggest that the slaughter of sub-adults animals (between 24 and 48 months) was most commonly recorded from the Churchyard, although overall, relatively little variation is seen between the three sites. Regardless of site, therefore, cattle appeared to have been used for multi-purpose strategies, including meat, traction, probably some low-intensity milk production, while also maintaining a breeding population.

Table 158. Fusion data for sheep by period (zone > 0, F = fused, NF = not fused, neonatal bones excluded).

	Iron Age/Roman			Anglo-Saxon		
	F	NF	% F	F	NF	% F
6-16 months	53	7	88	13	1	93
18-28 months	21	3	88	2	1	67
30-42 months	17	23	43	3	3	50

6-16 months calculated from distal scapula, distal humerus, proximal radius, first phalanx and second phalanx. 18-28 months calculated from distal metacarpal, distal tibia and distal metatarsal. 30-42 months calculated from proximal humerus, ulna, distal radius, proximal femur, distal femur, proximal tibia and calcaneus.

322

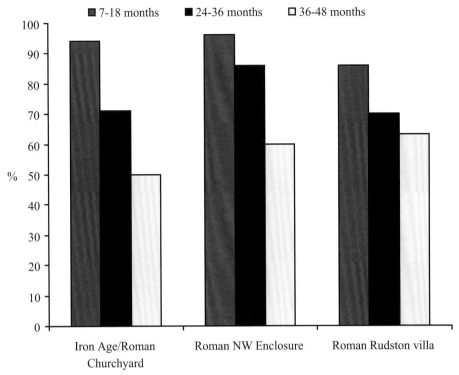

Fig. 153. Fusion data for cattle from Iron Age-Roman Wharram Percy and Rudston Roman villa. (J. Richardson)

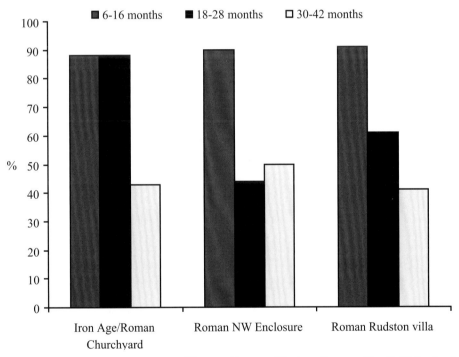

Fig. 154. Fusion data for sheep from Iron Age-Roman Wharram Percy and Rudston Roman villa (J. Richardson)

The fusion data for sheep from the Iron Age/Roman deposits from the Churchyard indicate that few animals were slaughtered up to the age of 18 to 28 months, but by 30 to 42 months the population halved (Table 158). Those slaughtered by 30 to 42 months would have provided only two fleeces at best and would not have become part of the established breeding population. Instead they represent the slaughter of animals that had two or three summers in which to be fattened. It was left to the remaining 43% of the flock to provide breeding stock, fleeces and perhaps small-scale milk production. Two neonatal bones and a newborn's jaw (Table 161) confirm the presence of breeding ewes, although a ratio of two male pelves to one female pelvis is far from compelling. Fusion data were less commonly retrieved from Anglo-Saxon deposits, although there is some evidence that slaughter was more rapid around the age range of 18 to 28 months (Table 158).

Table 159. Fusion data for pig by period (zone > 0, F = fused, NF = not fused).

	Iron Age/Roman			Anglo-Saxon		
	F	NF	% F	F	NF	% F
12 months	6	0	100	4	0	100
24-30 months	6	7	46	0	1	0
36-42 months	0	2	0	0	2	0

12 months calculated from distal scapula, distal humerus, proximal radius and second phalanx. 24-30 months calculated from distal metacarpal, distal tibia, calcaneus, distal metatarsal and first phalanx. 36-42 months calculated from proximal humerus, ulna, distal radius, proximal femur, distal femur and proximal tibia.

Table 160. Number of cattle jaws at various wear stages by period (after Halstead 1985).

	Iron Age/Roman	Anglo-Saxon
A: 0-1 mth		
B: 1-8 mths		
C: 8-18 mths		
D: 18-30 mths	1	1
E: 30-36 mths		1
F: young adult		1
G: adult		1
H: old adult	2	
I: senile		2
Total	3	6

Table 161. Number of sheep jaws at various wear stages by period (after Payne 1973).

	Iron Age/Roman	Anglo-Saxon
A: 0-2 mths	1	
B: 2-6 mths	4	
C: 6-12 mths	7	3
D: 1-2 yrs	1	
E: 2-3 yrs	9	2
F: 3-4 yrs	3	3
G: 4-6 yrs	4	2
H: 6-8 yrs	4	1
I: 8-10 yrs	1	
Total	34	11

In contrast, the dental eruption and wear data indicate the presence of numerous sheep from Iron Age/Roman deposits that were slaughtered before their first year (Table 161). These young animals were not identified in

the same proportions from the fusion data and indicate a disproportionate loss of juvenile bones from the archaeological record when compared to juvenile jaws. Nevertheless, despite this evidence for significant sub-adult slaughter, the multi-purpose strategy of raising sheep for their meat, fleeces and as breeding stock is not discounted. A similar strategy is proposed for the sheep from Anglo-Saxon levels, although dental data were not abundant from this period (Table 161).

In comparing the fusion data from the Iron Age/Roman Churchyard site with the data from the North-west Enclosure and Rudston Roman villa (Fig. 154), it is clear that the proportions of the youngest (up to 6-16 months) and the oldest sheep (up to 30-42 months) to be slaughtered were very similar regardless of site. In contrast, the proportion of animals killed between these age ranges varied more sharply. From the Churchyard slaughter apparently ceased, while at Rudston Roman villa approximately 30% of the flock was killed for its meat and the population from the North-west Enclosure was halved. Although the flocks associated with all three sites were probably still raised to fulfil multi-purpose functions, the differences in slaughter patterns do suggest that husbandry strategies were manipulated to meet local requirements.

Finally, the dental data for sheep from Anglo-Saxon deposits have been compared to data from the South Manor Area (Fig. 155). These indicate that some juvenile animals (up to 6 months) from the South Manor Area were slaughtered, but no comparable evidence was available from the Churchyard Area. Nevertheless, evidence for the availability of prime lamb was identified from both areas. Variations were also apparent in the slaughter of adult animals with a higher proportion of aged animals present in the South Manor assemblage. As with the comparisons of the Iron Age/Roman material given above, however, these differences are not so great as to discount multi-purpose husbandry practices.

The fusion data for pig were scarce from both periods. During the Iron Age/Roman period, some animals did survive beyond 24 to 30 months, but all were slaughtered by 36 to 42 months (Table 159). The pigs were kept for their meat (in the absence of any significant secondary products), but apparently there was only the potential for relatively few litters before slaughter. The potential of the Anglo-Saxon pig herds to be viable breeders appears to be even more compromised as no animals survived beyond their second year. The relevance of this observation, however, is limited by the very small sample size, although the presence of breeding stock from either period is further weakened by the absence of any neonatal bones.

So few horse bones were recovered that age data are extremely limited. Interestingly, however, Iron Age/Roman deposits included a juvenile horse of less than eighteen months, as well as adult animals between six and eight years (based on the dental wear of incisors). The Anglo-Saxon assemblage contained a foetal horse bone, evidence of an animal in its first year and adult

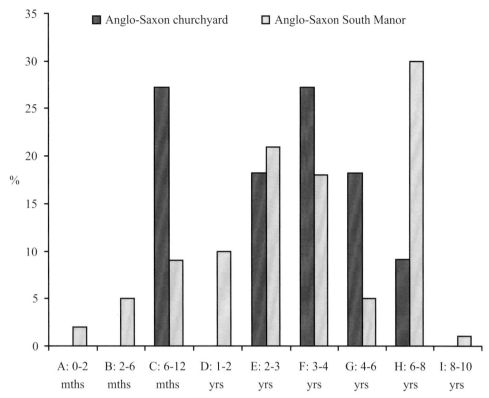

Fig. 155. Dental data for Anglo-Saxon sheep by site. (J. Richardson)

horses of fourteen years or more. Given the presence of sub-adult animals from other parts of Wharram Percy (Richardson 2004a, 271; 2004b, 338), it seems likely that the inhabitants of the village were horse breeders over many hundreds of years. The identification of adult and aged animals indicates that these horses, unsurprisingly, were raised as traction and pack animals rather than for their meat, and certainly the use of horses as work animals is supported by the work-related stress injuries of ring bone to two first phalanges and a second phalanx.

Carcass processing
Some of the cattle and sheep were raised specifically for meat, and pigs exclusively so. Unless these animals were visibly diseased, however, even the aged traction cattle and wool producers would have been utilised for their meat on death. Very few bones were butchered though and this probably reflects the skill of those who dismembered the carcasses (Table 156). Although too few bones were recorded to analyse the presence of particular body parts in any detail, the identification of skull, rib, vertebrae fragments and long bone fragments for the main meat animals suggests that they were slaughtered and processed locally.

Minor domestic species
In addition to meat resources from cattle, sheep and pigs, domestic chickens and geese would have been utilised for their meat as well as their eggs. The number of their bones, however, suggests that they were rarely utilised (Table 154). Dogs, also represented by relatively few bones, were probably kept as guard dogs or to reduce

vermin. No cat bones were identified, although they have been seen from other parts of the village (e.g. Richardson 2004a, 271).

Conclusions

In line with the other faunal assemblages already identified from Wharram Percy, the animal bones from the Churchyard Area were predominantly of sheep. The importance of this animal to the local economy persisted from the Iron Age/Roman to the Anglo-Saxon period and was not influenced by either the Roman or Saxon invasions or subsequent acculturation. The presence of a few neonatal sheep bones indicated that this animal was raised locally and slaughter patterns indicate that it was kept for its meat and its fleeces. In the absence of significant juvenile slaughter, intensive milk production was unlikely, although low-intensity production for home consumption was still a possibility. Cattle were also bred for multi-purpose strategies including traction, while pigs provided a valuable source of prime meat. Finally, the diet was occasionally supplemented by chicken, geese and fish. In addition to the domestic 'meat' animals, horses were represented, although by proportionally fewer bones than from other parts of the village e.g. Sites 30 and 82K (Richardson 2005b, 155-7; 2004a, 268). Nevertheless, the presence of neonatal and sub-adult bones from the Churchyard Area confirms the presence of horse breeders at Wharram from at least the Roman to the later medieval period.

Some variations were observed in the proportion of animals between the different areas of Wharram village and these may reflect activity areas e.g. the use of the peripheral North-west Enclosure for the slaughter of cattle. Dietary preferences may also have affected the range of bones deposited in discrete areas, but taphonomic biases and a site-wide lack of sieving will undoubtedly have influenced the assemblages still further. Additional differences were noted when comparing the slaughter patterns for sheep and cattle from the Churchyard Area with other Wharram sites and with Rudston Roman villa. These variations, however, were not significant enough to suggest that different communities or even different families within the village were undertaking specialised husbandry regimes. Regardless of site or period, therefore, multi-purpose strategies were valued as the means of providing the inhabitants of the Yorkshire Wolds with a variety of meats, as well as eggs, milk, fleeces, skins, traction and pack animals.

31 The mollusca

In total, 308 mollusca shells were examined from the phased deposits of Site 26. Oyster (Ostrea edulis) was the most commonly recovered species and given the roughly equal proportions of lower and upper values, they were most likely introduced to the site unopened and fit for human consumption. The river Humber is the most likely source for this food.

Table 162. Mollusca from Site 26 by period.

Period	Oyster	Cockle	Mussel	Limpet	Periwinkle	Undiagnostic
1	37					
2	4					
3	36	10				
4	34					
5	40				1	
6	57	11	1			1
7	63	12		1		
Total	271	33	1	1	1	1

Part Eight
Conclusions

32 Discussion
by C. Harding and S. Wrathmell

The creation of the cemetery and the foundation of the church

When post-excavation work began on the churchyard it seemed that, beyond providing detailed analysis of the burials for their pathology and aspects of mortuary culture, the existing model of churchyard development would stand, much as proposed in *Wharram III* (213-15, fig. 205). The evidence suggested the earliest burials were around the church, expansion in the medieval period to the north and south, and a possible short phase of medieval burial west of the tower. This was followed by gradual retraction on the north side from the late medieval period to the 19th century, with the full extent of the southern churchyard being used only in the post-medieval period (Harding 1996). Since the earliest burials then known were clustered around the church, it seemed unlikely that there could be much advance in our understanding of the pre-Conquest cemetery.

Since 1987 further work on the plateau has shown the extent of Anglo-Saxon and Anglo-Scandinavian occupation, particularly in the areas of the North and South Manors. This has raised many questions about the nature and status not only of the settlement itself, but also of any church or religious focal point and its relationship to the settlement (Morris 1989, 164; 1991, 23-4; *Wharram III*, 197-9; *Wharram VII*, 89-94; *Wharram VIII*, 198). These should be seen in the context of wider debate (as in Hadley 2000; Lucy and Reynolds 2002; Morris 1989) about the nature of cemeteries, the foundation of churches and their relationship to aristocratic, religious and secular communities before the development of the parochial system.

When Wharram was selected for a large-scale radiocarbon dating programme this was seen as an opportunity to refine the dating of the cemetery development outlined above. The results were totally unexpected, necessitating a re-examination of the proposed model of churchyard development. It now appears possible that the cemetery was established in the second half of the 10th century as a deliberate act of planned burial provision not only for the inhabitants of Wharram Percy but also for surrounding communities. Otherwise, it is difficult to account for the wide scattering of early burials across an area of consecrated ground which seems to have been at its maximum extent well before the Conquest, perhaps even at its inception.

It is, furthermore, tempting to link this act of provision to the formation of Wharram Percy parish. David Roffe has suggested that the parish was an *ad hoc* formation for the payment of tithe to a traditional ecclesiastical centre: 'It was probably only defined as a discrete area at the time, probably in the late 11th or early 12th century, when the render of tithes ceased to be personal and, territorialised, was attached to the church of Wharram Percy' (*Wharram VIII*, 14-15). If the two events were, indeed, linked, the dating evidence for the burial ground presented in this volume indicates a rather earlier date for parochial formation, in the second half of the 10th century. Wharram would not be alone in achieving a defined cemetery area for the first time in the 10th century. Hadley has suggested that it may have been 'only in the tenth century that the majority of people were for the first time told where they must bury their dead' (Hadley 2000, 215).

Whether there was ever a Phase I timber church, as tentatively suggested in *Wharram III* (55-7, 60, fig.1) is a matter of debate. What is clear from the evidence presented here and in *Wharram III* (59-60) is that the cemetery was established before the erection of the first stone church in Phase II: its west wall foundation cut through two burials (though these skeletons have not, unfortunately, survived to be radiocarbon dated), and the stone raft foundation for its chancel cut through others. Other examples of this progression from cemetery to churchyard in the north of England include Kellington and Barton-upon-Humber (Hadley 2002, 221).

The burials beneath the grave-covers south of the Phase II chancel were also not primary, given their radiocarbon dates and that one of them, Burial V51, overlay an earlier burial (Burial V41). Their association with the Phase II church was envisaged in *Wharram III* (58). That line of argument has here been developed by David Stocker (Ch. 21), who suggests that they are the graves of the family that actually founded the Phase II church. He also suggests that the reused Roman sarcophagi may have been provided by the archbishop of York to establish a physical link between the archiepiscopal centre and the new parish church. The motivation for placing the church in this particular location has been considered in an earlier chapter (Ch. 3). Its siting might well have been influenced by a spring, perhaps a 'holy well', forming the focus of the burial ground, which disappeared during the substantial foundation works that preceded the erection of the Phase III chancel. Morris (1989, 86-8) has discussed the construction of parish churches on or near the sites of springs or wells (as at Barton-upon-Humber).

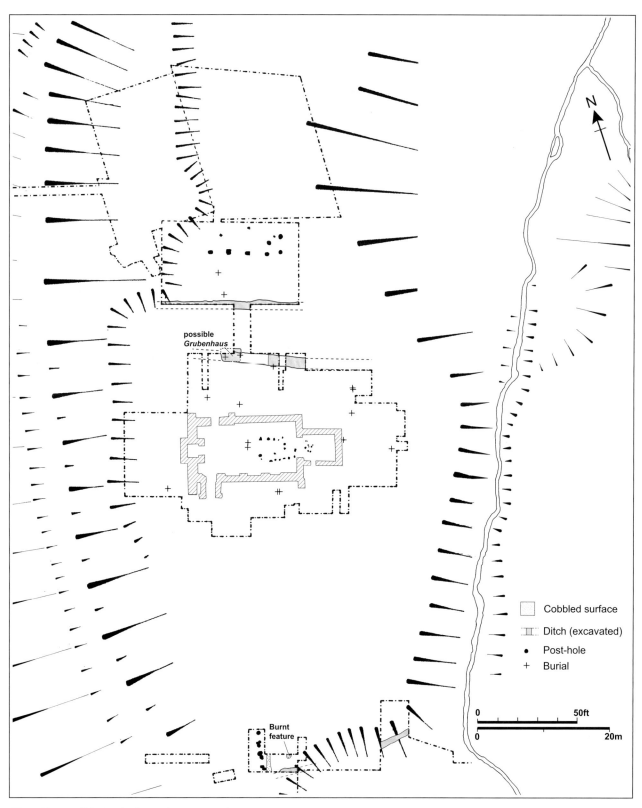

Cobbled surface

Ditch (excavated)

• Post-hole

+ Burial

possible
Grubenhaus

Burnt
feature

N

0   50ft

0   20m

Fig. 156. Possible Anglo-Saxon features pre-dating AD 1000. (C. Philo and E. Marlow-Mann)

Before the cemetery (Fig. 156)

The nature of the pre-cemetery phases of occupation has come primarily from Sites 41 and 26. Nowhere else in the immediate village area, other than Site 41, has revealed evidence of Bronze Age activity, but the phases of Romano-British occupation identified on the terrace may be related to other sites on the plateau. The finds from both Sites 26 and 41 appear to suggest broadly contemporary Late Iron Age to early Roman phases followed by renewed activity in the later 3rd century on Site 26 (Period 1, Phases 2-3, and possibly the Period 1, Phase 4 ditch) and into the early 4th century on Site 41. It is difficult to relate these fragmentary structures and features to the immediate or wider Roman landscape in terms of function and it is very likely that other contemporary post-holes or features in or around the church, in addition to those noted in *Wharram III* (53, fig.10), were destroyed by grave digging or were for other reasons not recorded during the excavations.

It is also difficult to establish an immediate context for the Site 26 Iron Age crouched burial. Whether this burial contributed to any enduring sense of 'special place' or was related to a nearby 'holy spring' can only remain a matter for speculation (Morris 1989, 46-92; 1991, 23-4). Terracing or erosion had clearly altered the ground surface in the post-Roman period and the proximity to this burial of both the Period 1, Phase 4 ditch and, perhaps more significantly, the later burials, suggests that by that time it was not itself a focal feature in the terrace landscape. The early occupation of the terrace will be further discussed in *Wharram XIII*.

Occupation and activity here in the post-Roman, pre-cemetery period is reflected in the prolonged existence of at least the southerly of the two east-west ditches north of the church, in the possible *Grubenhaus* cut into the edge of this ditch, and in the major Period 2 post-hole structure a little further north, on Site 26 (Fig. 156). This post-hole structure may relate to other features on Site 54 to the north, a matter that will be considered further once the analysis relating to that site has been completed (*Wharram XII*). Broadly contemporary, the Period 3 features of a hearth, surfaces and possible wall footings on Site 41 possibly relate to the use of the adjacent Dam and Pond (*Wharram X,* 227-8). Perhaps also pre-dating the cemetery are the 'post-holes' beneath the flooring of the Phase II church. A number of artefacts of pre-cemetery date have been found on this part of the terrace, coins and bone combs among them. It is not known whether these remains represent secular or religious use; but without our knowledge of the later history of this part of the settlement area, they would have been assumed to be secular.

The burials

The 84 samples submitted for radiocarbon dating were selected using criteria determined by the needs of the skeletal analysis (p. 198), but they also addressed other issues. They were used, for example, to establish absolute dating sequences in different zones of the churchyard (where stratigraphic 'strings' could be established) and sequences relative to the phased church structure. It was only possible, however, to submit for dating those burials which were still available with enough collagen remaining in the long bones (Ch. 14, Table 117).

The earliest dated burials were shown to be from the north-east and north-west of the church, with dates in the 9th to 10th centuries (Fig. 156). It is suspected that some of the burials at the east end of the church which could not be submitted might well have been as early or earlier. More surprising, however, were the dates from the extremities of the churchyard. The maximum extents of the cemetery to the south and the north were already in use in the 10th to 11th centuries, while the western cemetery appears to be a post-Conquest expansion, occasionally in use into the post-medieval period, rather than in a relatively short single phase as previously supposed.

The implication that the churchyard was already 'full' at such an early date is unlikely. As suggested above, a more probable explanation is that the cemetery was from this period being used by neighbouring settlements, and that the earliest southern group represents a community that chose to be buried in a separate burial zone from, for example, those of similar date in the north churchyard, without the intervening area already being full. It may be that a future study involving DNA testing could determine whether there is evidence of zoned family groups within the assemblage as a whole (see Zadora-Rio 2003, 2, 13-15).

While to the north of the church something approaching the likely total of burials can be computed, to the south we can only speculate on the density between the south aisle and the sites on the boundary. Nonetheless, Bell (*Wharram III*, 220) and Mays (p. 88) have made informed guesses as to the total number of burials. It is clear that post-medieval burial took place almost exclusively in the southern churchyard. The number of interments, 881, in the period 1570-1899, is, however, represented by only a small number of gravestones (*Wharram II*, fig. 1).

Evidence for preference for burial in specific parts of a churchyard, and particularly in relation to the location of the church, is ambiguous. There are numerous references to a reluctance to be buried on the north side of a church (Porter and Harding 2000), but these appear to reflect superstition and burial choice in the post-medieval and modern periods, rather than in earlier times. Excavation has demonstrated that before the post-medieval period there was a considerable density of burial in the north churchyard, and an analysis of the standing church fabric can be deployed to take the argument a stage further.

The density of burial outside the north nave doorway of the present church has left the modern visitor with a steep incline to negotiate when leaving the church at this point. Both internally and externally, the walling bears evidence of the doorway arch having been raised to

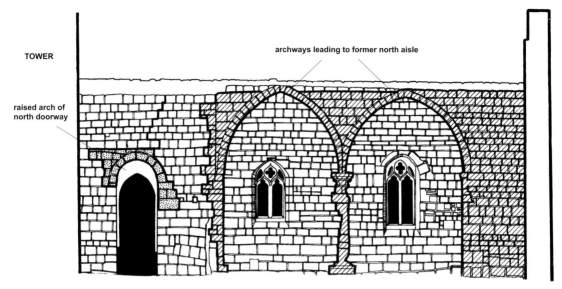

Fig. 157. North wall of standing church showing evidence of raised north doorway arch. (C. Philo)

accommodate access to this heightened ground level. Internally, the opening remained round-headed, though the evidence of rebuilding is clear (Fig. 157). Externally, the doorway was furnished with a pointed arch. This work is thought to have taken place in the late 13th century, indicating that there had already been high-density burial outside the north wall of the nave in the preceding 150 years.

Further burials were located outside the known medieval burial ground, some of which may be medieval in date; these will be discussed further in *Wharram XIII*.

In the period following the final desertion of the village in the early 16th century, when all but a very few burials took place within the church or in the south churchyard, the apparent preference for these areas may be accounted for by other factors. First, the encroachment by the vicarage from the north, starting in the later medieval period, reduced the space available for burial in an area where the extent of the churchyard was poorly defined for much of the time. Secondly, almost all of those to be buried in post-medieval times would have come from the farmsteads to the south of Wharram (Beresford 1987, 13): the south churchyard would have been the logical location for them, especially if the southern townships had traditionally buried there. In terms of the position of the church in relation to the parish as a whole, the effects of depopulation were asymmetric: there would have been far fewer inhabitants north of the church to be buried than from the south.

The characteristics of the burials appear to be typical of similar communities elsewhere in England, on the evidence of other published cemeteries of a similar size and date range (e.g. Boddington 1996; Rodwell and Rodwell 1986). Comparison with more local data is really only possible for urban sites - particularly in York (St Helens, Jewbury). Proportionately, a few more charcoal burials or medieval graves with coffins and shrouds or some dress ornaments might have been expected, but comparative analysis is hampered by the absence of data

from the south churchyard. The range of recorded burial settings may also suggest some regional variation from similarly dated cemeteries elsewhere (Ch. 15).

One interesting parallel for the pattern of cemetery shrinkage and/or encroachment at Wharram is to be found at Rivenhall, Essex (Rodwell and Rodwell 1986; Clarke 2006) where on the north side of the church the graveyard was encroached on in the 13th century by a succession of priests' houses and other ancillary structures. Re-calibrated radiocarbon dates from the 1970s burials and new data from the 1999 excavations have suggested that, there too, the early cemetery (now dated to the late 9th to 10th century) extended to its maximum limits from its inception.

The human remains

The burials studied dated from AD 950 to 1850 but were mostly medieval. While there was no direct evidence of family plots or use of particular areas of the graveyard for different settlements, age-related spatial groupings were evident. The area immediately to the north of the church tended to contain the burials of individuals under eighteen months of age. This area is traditionally used for the unbaptised but it may also be that the transition to adulthood was being recognised.

Of the burial assemblage, about 15% were infants. Analysis of these indicated that low birth-weight and prematurity were not regular problems. Breast-feeding continued until about eighteen months of age, with the infants' diet being supplemented by cereal foods or animal milk some time before its cessation. The fairly modest rate of infant mortality may have been partly assisted by this practice of extended breast-feeding. Once breast-feeding ceased and the benefits of breast milk stopped, growth in bone length, and therefore stature, slowed in comparison to modern children.

During childhood, chronic poor nutrition and disease greatly retarded growth. Wharram Percy children were of similar stature to factory children in the Industrial Revolution, suggesting their health and nutrition were no better than those of the 19th-century urban poor. Despite this, adults were only slightly shorter than modern adults, probably due to the prolongation of the growth period.

Of the adult burials, approximately 40% were aged over 50 years, suggesting reasonable longevity once adulthood was reached, and a chance for age-related diseases to become apparent. Occurrence of osteoporosis was at a similar level to that seen today; among females this may have been due to repeated pregnancy and prolonged lactation, combined with poor nutrition. Compared with a medieval middle class urban population, the frequency of osteoarthritis was greater at Wharram Percy and this may have been due to their physically more demanding lifestyle.

The only suggestion of a secular trend with regard to disease was seen in dental caries. These seemed to increase in the post-medieval period and included a greater proportion of cavities. It appeared to parallel, to a lesser extent, patterns seen in medieval urban material where they were thought to be related to a softer and more cariogenic diet; however, heavy dental wear continued to be a feature in the post-medieval burials.

There was little evidence of differences in health between the sexes or according to social status. Analysis also indicated little evidence of a division of tasks according to gender, with females participating in more physically demanding work. However, heavy work using the upper limbs was more prevalent in males, suggesting they undertook more of this type of work, while female tasks appeared to involve more squatting and working close to the ground.

Among the adult burials, males outnumbered females, and may support the theory of a female-led migration into York from surrounding rural settlements. Skeletal analysis indicated trading links existed between Wharram Percy and other settlements: their diets contained small amounts of seafood, either bought direct from coastal settlements or via trade with inland towns. This evidence is confirmed by the recovery of marine fish bones from excavations in the village (*Wharram X*, 169-75). The human contact brought about by trade enabled diseases such as tuberculosis to be present, despite the village's lower population density.

Comparison with medieval material from York indicated that while there were fewer pathogens and infectious diseases present, infections at Wharram Percy were more likely to lead to death. In contrast, the people of York were more likely to recover, indicating that their long-term exposure to a pathogen-rich urban environment gave individuals a greater resistance to disease.

The cemetery boundaries (Fig. 158)

From the 12th century canon law required that Christian burial grounds had formal bounds, and the failure to maintain such boundaries features frequently in the documentary record (Dymond 1999, 469-71). The apparent absence of any boundary to the north at Wharram is thus clearly not unique. Where earlier boundaries are known the delineation presumably results from the formalisation of landholding around a churchyard or practical matters such as the need to exclude wandering animals, rather than liturgical considerations. The formal enclosure of cemeteries does not seem to have been common in the pre-Conquest period (Gittos 2002, 203-4) and this is born out at Wharram where there was no obvious boundary on the north side until the 15th or 16th century, and even then the boundary was formed incidentally, by a wall enclosing the vicarage, not the churchyard.

The boundaries of the churchyard - walls, ditches and fences, where they could be identified - expanded, shifted and contracted, but not necessarily directly reflecting the changing fortunes of the church and the parish population. The maximum likely area of the churchyard is approximately an acre (1.02 acre: 0.41 ha) of which less than a third has been excavated.

The situation of the church on the edge of a narrow terrace is such that formal bounds to the east or west would have been unnecessary and practically difficult to maintain, other than as fences. The slope upwards along the west side is now very steep and may have been even more so in earlier times: excavation west of the church showed that burials continue westwards straight into the present hillside. Loose chalk and clay (hillwash) have continued to slump down the slope in the post-medieval period masking the original angle of the hillside. The small section of revetment wall on Site 21 may reflect attempts to stem the flow of hillwash and debris. There are indications that such slippages have been occurring here (perhaps intermittently) since the Bronze Age (see Site 41, pp 65-70). The slope down to the beck in the valley east of the church is anthropogenic, the result of the deliberate eastward extension of the terrace.

To the south of the church the influences on the extent of the churchyard were the dam and the pond, and the possible site of a domestic building between the church and the pond. Here we have a full sequence of boundaries extending into the modern period. The earliest boundary at the south-eastern edge of the churchyard, in Site 71, is a pre-Conquest ditch (Site 71, ditch 263) although this may have been a drainage feature associated with the pond to the south. Another ditch followed on a similar alignment but *c*. 1m to the north, with a bank on its south side which was capped in the 13th century by at least two phases of a chalk boundary wall. Rubble and debris carefully dumped against the boundary wall in the early 14th century is seen as an attempt to level up the churchyard terrace and has been tentatively associated with the removal of a possible house to the west (see p. 335).

A new chalk wall maintained the division until the late 15th or 16th century, when it was demolished and replaced by a fence with a gate across a wide path or trackway formed of chalk and ash. This fence alignment continued with minor variations until the present day, the

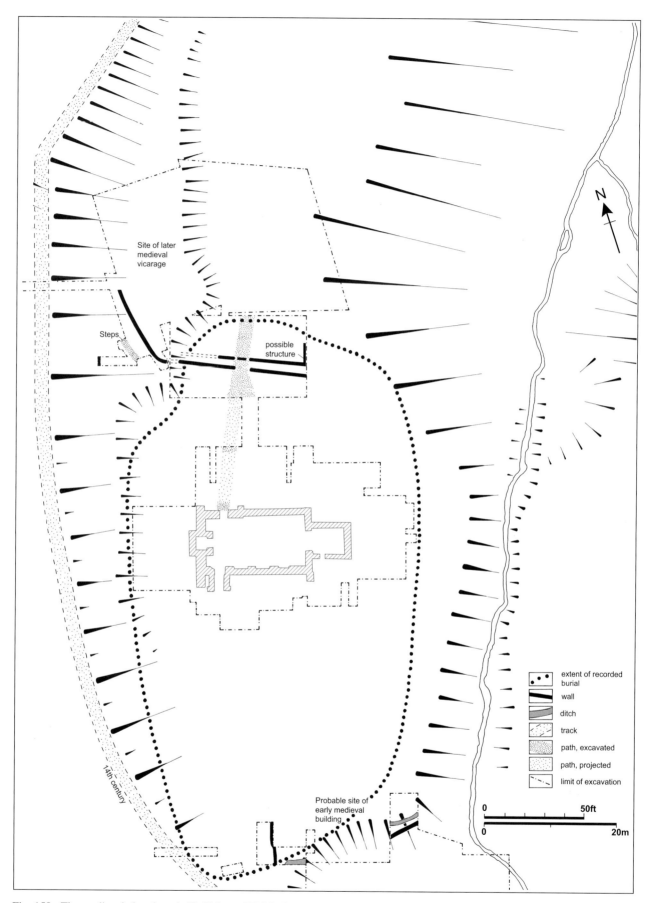

Site of later
medieval
vicarage

Steps

possible
structure

14th century

Probable site of
early medieval
building

	extent of recorded burial
	wall
	ditch
	track
	path, excavated
	path, projected
	limit of excavation

0   50ft

0   20m

Fig. 158. The medieval churchyard. (C. Philo and E. Marlow-Mann)

overall alignment of the boundary having changed only by 1-2m over a period of perhaps 800 years. There were no human remains from this site and no indications of any burials close by. The reason for this is unclear beyond the possibility that this area lay within the curtilage of a house located north of Site 71, or between Sites 71 and 41 (see p. 75).

Site 41 itself produced no definite evidence of any boundaries until a post-medieval fence line, as all deposits sealing the 10th to 11th-century burials had been removed, probably by terracing. It is however possible that a 10th to 11th-century (pre-burial) north-south bedding trench represents a wall foundation rather than just a substantial path make-up. A short section of a ditch (also probably Period 3, Fig. 156), running north-east to south-west and crossing part of the southern boundary of this site, may well relate to one of those on Site 71 (e.g. 265).

A rather different sequence was established in the northern churchyard. The two V-shaped ditches appear to have been cut and disused in the pre-cemetery era, and only the southern one might have still been a usable (though partly filled) boundary as late as the Middle Saxon period. Whether the structure cutting into it was a *Grubenhaus* or lime-kiln, this activity indicated both the visibility and the disuse of the ditch. Burial extended north of these ditches before the Conquest. We can be fairly confident in having found the true northern extent of the cemetery, even though there was apparently no contemporary formal boundary. Subsequent excavation of the areas beyond Site 26 to the north (Sites 54 and 77) found no wall or ditch, nor any more burials.

The earliest burials on Site 26 started a period of intermittent use spanning the late pre- and early post-Conquest periods (from *cal AD 960-1030 (95% probability; GU-5545)* to *cal AD 1040-1130 (95% probability; GU-5537, GU-5539, GU-5540, GU-5541).* Thereafter, the graveyard contracted southwards with the construction of two chalk-founded walls. The earliest wall was very fragmentary and approximately parallel to the church but may have been part of a structure to the north, only incidentally at the same time forming a northern limit to the cemetery. The later wall standing up to six courses high, was on a slightly different alignment and about a metre to the south. A gap in this wall with evidence of a gateway gave access to a gravel path, much patched and re-surfaced, leading from the vicarage to the north door of the church. A new gateway was inserted in the wall using a window jamb probably from the demolished north aisle (*Wharram III*, 215). The alignment of the western end of this wall is interesting, curving up the hillside as a boundary wall to the vicarage. Beside the wall and also climbing the hillside was a flight of stone steps which continued in use into the post-medieval period (Fig. 158).

The area previously available for burial was reduced by the construction of these walls by some 8m (linear). In the 18th and 19th centuries further contraction took place, to a fence line which continued in use until recent times.

The total (linear) retraction was 9.5m (Fig. 159). The surfaces outside the churchyard were clearly in agricultural and/or domestic use and some fragmentary foundations (Periods 4 and 6) on Site 26 suggest that structures used the vicarage boundary wall for support. The vicars were presumably responsible for this shifting alignment, as it increased the area available to the vicarage.

Trackways

As well as burials and boundaries, routeways through the churchyard have also been identified. A medieval track from the settlement on the plateau to the pond, and thence southwards to Thixendale and the other villages, passes along the lowest possible line of the hillside slope beside what is now a steep drop to the churchyard (see Fig. 159). These steep slopes could however have been used for grazing animals and the trees cut for firewood, all rights of the incumbents. The church itself sits on what may also have been a routeway in earlier times along the terrace to the crossing point of the stream, a possible influence on its location.

Other tracks and roads developed in the post-medieval period (Fig. 159). As the site of the vicarage moved eastwards in the 17th to 18th centuries (Site 54, *Wharram XII*) its front door opened onto a rammed chalk road (Site 26 Period 7, phase 2) passing from the east end of the church and continuing north to the farm beyond. The fences associated with this were also located by excavation on Sites 26 and 54. As the churchyard contracted another trackway (also fenced) was established to the west of the church, running initially over the graveyard and in front of the vicarage. Following the demolition of the vicarage in 1834 it took a more westerly route towards the former farm buildings which became cottages for construction workers on the railway in the mid-19th century, and later homes of employees of the Middleton estate.

Other activities in the churchyard

In the medieval period a churchyard relatively uncluttered by monuments was a very useful meeting place for the living. Extensive documentary evidence attests that, in addition to social gatherings and sporting activities, fairs and markets were a common feature and some of the wide range of ceramic vessels may reflect this (for recent discussion of the possibilities see Dymond 1999, 470-71; Daniell 1997, 111-14). Sporting activity or the tethering of livestock may be the explanation of the numerous post-holes amongst the graves, particularly in the north churchyard on Site 26, where mostly they did not seem to have served as grave markers. Sheep were frequently used to keep the grass under control, the responsibility of the incumbent, and some post or stake-holes may relate to grazing control.

Some non-burial activity inferred from the evidence of excavated features and artefacts may, as in the north

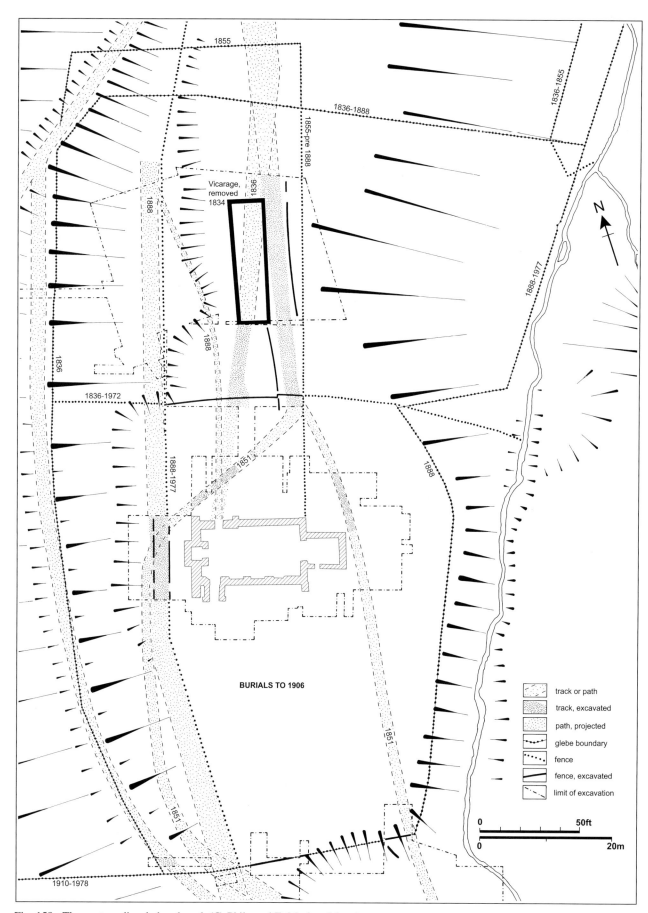

Fig. 159. The post-medieval churchyard. (C. Philo and E. Marlow-Mann)

churchyard (see above), actually define the extent of the graveyard itself at different points in time. Of immediate interest is a quantity of demolition rubble, including building stone, along with significant quantities of ceramics and other artefacts from Site 41 (Period 5) and Site 71 (Phases 4-5), at the south-east corner of the churchyard (p. 75). The pottery is mainly Staxton ware of the 12th to 13th centuries, but includes some vessels of the 13th to 14th centuries. There was, presumably, a domestic building in this area, perhaps a residence connected with the church as suggested in *Wharram III* (214-15). Exactly what this putative structure may have represented will be considered in *Wharram XII*, along with the whole documentary and archaeological evidence for the location of vicarage houses and the dwellings of other ecclesiastical personnel.

No recognisable structures were identified in the excavated area at the west end of the church apart from one of several quarry pits, a recurrent feature of excavations at Wharram, dug for the extraction of chalk rubble and clay for puddling used instead of lime mortar for the bonding of most walls. If the burnt feature north of the church was indeed a lime-kiln rather than a burnt *Grubenhaus*, then it must be related to the first stone church of Phase II, as it was cut by a burial (Burial NA094) with a date range of *cal AD 950-1050 (95% probability; GU-5646).*

Finally, a post-medieval structure (Site 26 Period 6 phase 4) on the north side of the church close to the gateway in the vicarage boundary wall may have served as a sexton's hut or hearse shed. It consisted of a stone and clay foundation using the surviving vicarage boundary wall as its north side.

The relationship of graveyard, church and settlement

The dating of burials and excavated sequences provides a new model of churchyard development which contrasts with that in *Wharram III*. The previous model for the relationship of the church and cemetery to the village settlement therefore also needs to be re-examined. It had previously been assumed that there was a fairly direct relationship in terms of expansion and contraction, but the establishment of some absolute dates for periods of use of the early cemetery contradicts this.

Following the statistical analysis of the radiocarbon dating programme, the cemetery seems not to have served the inhabitants of Wharram Percy before the later 10th century (p. 201). Should we therefore be looking for an earlier church or religious focal point on the plateau, on the terrace, or elsewhere in the parish? Should we be looking for an earlier cemetery in the area of the village or beyond? And what influenced the choice of the terrace for a cemetery in the later 10th century? Christian burial was not 'required' to be in a churchyard or enclosed cemetery at this period and could earlier have been taking place some distance away (Gittos 2002, 202).

Julian Richards has discussed the implications of Middle Saxon occupation on the plateau and its high status material - metalworking, combs, ceramics, sculpture - for the nature and development of the settlement at Wharram (*Wharram VII*, 93-4; *Wharram VIII*, 196-7). In the context of the excavations on the South Manor, Richards also discussed the difficulties of identifying later Saxon/Anglo-Scandinavian material among the finds (with the exception of metalwork), and the general absence of ceramics at this period (*Wharram VIII*, 197), prompting the suggestion that the scarcity of occupation datable to this period may be more apparent than real.

Although the archaeological evidence is somewhat equivocal, one clear option for the planning and laying out of the village framework is the period following the Scandinavian invasions (see also Beresford and Hurst 1990, 84). Thus it may not be without significance that this is also the period of the earliest burials in the cemetery on the terrace. As Richards has also noted, however, the founding of the church, the nucleation of the settlement and the establishment of the parish (in whatever order) are not necessarily related (*Wharram VIII*, 199).

Pre-cemetery activity on the terrace includes a Late Iron Age crouched burial, Romano-British features beneath and to the north of the church, and some Middle Saxon activity. The church and cemetery site is sheltered in a narrow steep-sided section of valley, with springs on the west side and a beck on the east, a far more inviting location than the windswept plateau to the north and west. The question is, therefore, why the main elements of the farming settlement were not, apparently, located in this area: was it a pre-existing 'sacred' or 'religious' site? Was this already a 'special' place at the time of the crouched burial?

Richard Morris has made the interesting suggestion that the valley made have had a ritual use in association with the seasonal trading and penning of livestock - providing a possible function for one or both of the east-west ditches - something likely to have occurred within a social context, perhaps a market accompanying a 'religious' festival or gathering (Morris 1991, 23-4). It is a matter that will be reviewed in *Wharram XIII*, when there will be an opportunity to take into account the results of new earthwork, geophysical and aerial surveys, and analyses.

Appendices

Appendix 1: Catalogue of Burials
by S. Mays

Skeleton	Sex	Age	Stature	Cranial index	Cribra orbitalia	Preservation	Completeness	Phase
CN01	M	40+	165.5	76.96	0	G	40-60	4
CN02	M?	22-25	162.3	78.57	CA	G	40-60	4
CN03	F	ADULT				M	20-40	3-4
CN04	J	7			PA	M	60-80	4
CN05	M	50+	171.4	75.52	0	G	80+	4
CN06	M	22-30	173.0	75.68	0	G	80+	4
CN07	F	50+	164.0	81.67	PA	M	80+	4
CN09	J	5-8				P	<20	4
CN11	M	21-24	173.2			G	80+	4
CN12	M	35-45	166.7	79.21	0	G	60-80	4
CN13	F	30-40	165.2		PA	P	40-60	4
CN14	M	ADULT	168.6			M	80+	4
CN15	-M	14-15			0	G	80+	4
CN16	F	40+	159.1			M	80+	4
CN17	M	30-40	173.2	77.60	0	M	60-80	4
CN18	M	40+	175.2	88.70	0	G	80+	4
CN19	F	40+	162.2	82.78	PPR	G	80+	4
CN20	M	25-35	162.4	79.77	0	G	80+	4
CN22	F	50+	153.9	78.92	0	P	20-40	4
CN24	M	50+	170.3	80.23	0	G	60-80	4
CN27	M	40+	165.0	73.66	0	M	80+	4
CN28	M	22-24	164.6	76.22	0	M	80+	4
CN29	F	ADULT	152.9	79.65	0	G	20-40	4
CN30	F	21-23	160.5		0	M	80+	4
CN31	M	40+	166.3	70.98	0	G	40-60	4
CN32	M	ADULT	169.4		0	G	60-80	4
CN33	M	50+	172.6	77.60	0	G	80+	4
CN36	F	ADULT	159.2		0	P	40-60	4
CN37	M	50+	172.3	67.82	0	P	60-80	4
CN38	M	ADULT	171.3			M	60-80	4
CN39	M	ADULT	170.3			M	40-60	4
CN40	F	50+	162.1	72.77	0	G	40-60	4
CN41	F	40-50	163.8	76.84	0	P	80+	4
CN42	F	ADULT	151.5			G	60-80	4
CN43	M	20-30	160.8			G	60-80	4
CN44	M	40+	168.6			M	40-60	4
CN45	M	50+	172.0			M	40-60	4
CN46	F?	ADULT				P	<20	4
CN47	J	10MONTHS			0	M	60-80	4
EE001	?M	15-18			CPR	G	<20	
EE002	J	10				G	40-60	
EE003	M	25-35	176.5	83.33	0	G	60-80	1-2
EE004	M	40+	172.5			G	60-80	1-2
EE005	?M	11			PPR	G	40-60	
EE006	??F	7-8			PR?	G	40-60	
EE007	F	21-23	166.2	89.09	PR	G	40-60	2
EE009	M?	50+		80.00	0	G	<20	1-2
EE010	M	ADULT				G	20-40	1-2
EE013	M	ADULT	177.7			M	80+	2
EE014	??M	11			0	G	<20	

Skeleton	Sex	Age	Stature	Cranial index	Cribra orbitalia	Preservation	Completeness	Phase
EE015	F	60+	154.4		0	P	60-80	1-2
EE016	F	21-25			0	M	40-60	1-2
EE017	J	4			PA	M	40-60	
EE018	F	21	155.1	81.08	0	G	80+	1-2
EE019	M	30-50	164.6	75.68	0	G	80+	1-2
EE020	M	25-35	172.0	82.98	0	G	80+	1
EE022	F	50+	148.8	80.23		G	80+	1-2
EE024	M?	35-45	161.8	82.42	PR	G	20-40	1-2
EE025	M	50+	163.0		0	M	20-40	1-2
EE026	M	50+	168.9		0	G	40-60	1-2
EE027	M	25-35		75.37	0	G	<20	1-2
EE028	M	25-35			0	G	<20	1-2
EE029	-M	16-18			0	G	80+	
EE030	F	25-35	160.2	87.08	0	G	40-60	1-2
EE031	M	50+		83.05	0	G	20-40	1-2
EE032	M	50+			0	G	<20	1-2
EE033	??F	5-6			PA	G	20-40	
EE034	J	37WIU				G	60-80	
EE035	F	18-25		82.68	CPR	G	<20	1-2
EE036	M	18		78.80	CPR	G	60-80	1-2
EE037	M	40-50	172.1	83.06	0	G	60-80	1-2
EE038	F?	25	168.3	79.79	0	G	40-60	2-3
EE039	-M	16-18			CA	G	60-80	
EE040	M?	20-24	172.3	83.52	0	G	40-60	1-2
EE041	M	21-24	167.5	81.52	CA	M	80+	1-2
EE042	J	6			0	G	60-80	
EE043	F	25-35	155.2		0	G	80+	1-2
EE044	F	17-23		79.55	PA	G	<20	1-2
EE045	M	50+	162.8	76.63	0	G	40-60	1-2
EE046	M	40-50	174.3	82.70	0	G	20-40	1-2
EE047	M	50+		86.86	PR	G	<20	1-2
EE048	J	10-12MON			0	M	20-40	
EE049	J	1			0	G	40-60	
EE050	J	5			0	G	<20	
EE051	J	3.5			0	G	20-40	
EE052	J	9 MONTHS			PA	G	60-80	
EE053	J	48WIU			0	G	40-60	
EE054	J	1-3MONTH			0	M	60-80	
EE055	??F	6			0	G	60-80	
EE056	M?	50+	163.9			M	40-60	1-2
EE057	J	2			0	G	60-80	
EE058	J	2			PR	M	<20	
EE059	J	37-38WIU				G	20-40	
EE060	M	40+		77.78	0	G	20-40	1-2
EE061	F	50+		81.92	0	G	<20	1-2
EE062	M	30-40	176.2	81.91	0	G	80+	1-2
EE063	??F	5-6			PA	G	80+	
EE064	M	50+		81.46	0	G	<20	1-2
EE065	??F	7-8			CA	G	80+	
EE066	??M	8-9			PA	G	80+	
EE067	F	30-50	155.1	75.27		M	20-40	1-2
EE068	J	9 MONTHS			0	G	60-80	
EE069	J	4-5			0	G	60-80	
EE070	F	40-50	158.1	86.71	0	G	80+	1-2
EE071	J	5			PA	G	60-80	
EE072	??F	10			0	G	80+	
EE073	J	4			0	G	80+	
EE074	??F	6			PA	G	40-60	
EE075	??M	8			0	G	60-80	

Skeleton	Sex	Age	Stature	Cranial index	Cribra orbitalia	Preservation	Completeness	Phase
EE076	J	8			CA	G	60-80	
EE077	M?	40-50		78.07	0	G	<20	1-2
EE078	J	42-45WIU			0	G	80+	
EE079	M	ADULT	170.3			M	60-80	2
EE080	M	35-45	162.7	83.24	0	G	80+	2
EE081	??M	10			CA	G	<20	
EE082	M	20-21	173.0	75.00	CPR	G	60-80	1-2
EE083	-F	15-20			0	G	<20	
EE084	??M	8			PA	G	<20	
EE085	M	25-35	170.7	77.25	0	G	80+	1-2
EE086	J	5-6			PA	G	20-40	
EE087	F	40+	160.7			M	20-40	1-2
EE088	J	37WIU			0	G	80+	
EE089	M	ADULT				G	<20	1-2
EE090	J	5-6			0	G	60-80	
EE091	J	1.5			PA	G	<20	
EE092	M	35-45		80.51	0	G	20-40	1-2
EE093	M	35-45		78.72	0	M	<20	1-2
EE094	J	1.5-2			0	G	<20	
EE095	J	5			0	G	<20	
EE096	J	1.5-2			0	G	20-40	
EE097	M?	50+			CA	G	40-60	1-2
EE098	M	ADULT	170.2			G	<20	1-2
EE099	F	30-50	161.1	84.86	0	G	60-80	1-2
EE100	J	4-5				G	80+	
EE101	F	25			PA	G	20-40	1-2
EE102	??F	8				G	80+	
EE103	M	22-25	181.3	81.58		G	20-40	1-2
G251	F?	40+	160.3			M	40-60	2
G253	F	18-19	151.6			M	60-80	2
G254	F	21-23	154.4	84.18	0	M	80+	2
G260	J	2			0	M	40-60	2
G265	M	35-45	170.7	75.27	0	G	80+	2
G273	J	4				G	<20	2
G275A	F	25-35	157.5	78.38	0	G	80+	2
G278	M	ADULT	170.7			M	80+	2
G279	M	50+	166.5	82.01	0	M	60-80	1
G280	??M	8			0	G	60-80	2
G281	J	4			TA	M	60-80	2
G296	M	35-45	171.9	79.35	0	M	80+	2
G297	M	50+	170.6	84.44	0	G	80+	2
G298	J	2			PA	G	20-40	2
G303	M	30-40	178.3	80.22	0	M	60-80	1-2
G304	??M	5-6			CA	G	80+	1
G306	J	3-4				M	20-40	2
G308	J	1-1.5				P	20-40	2
G310	M	30-40	169.2			G	80+	2
G313	J	NEONATE			0	M	20-40	2
G314	J	5-6			PA	G	80+	1-2
G320	J	38-40WIU				G	60-80	2
G327	J	1.5			0	M	40-60	2
G338	J	1-4MONTH			0	M	60-80	2
G339	J	2.5			0	M	20-40	2
G361	F?	35-45	161.6		0	G	80+	2
G363	J	2.5			0	G	80+	2
G364	J	2.5			PA	G	60-80	2
G367	J	3				G	80+	2
G370	M	18-20	161.7		PA	G	80+	2
G377	F	50+	161.2	87.06	0	G	80+	1-2

Skeleton	Sex	Age	Stature	Cranial index	Cribra orbitalia	Preservation	Completeness	Phase
G379	M	45-60	175.1	80.43	0	G	80+	1-2
G381	M	40-50	169.0	78.19	0	G	60-80	1-2
G385	F	35-45	155.7	78.49	0	G	80+	2
G387	J	4				G	<20	1-2
G398	M	21-24	162.8		0	G	80+	2
G406	M	40-50	167.8	77.49	0	G	80+	1-2
G411	M	50+		81.97	CPR	G	40-60	2
G416	F	25-35	159.0		0	G	60-80	2
G419	F	50+	156.6	72.92	0	M	80+	2
G422	J	5			PA	G	80+	2
G424	??F	6-7			PA	G	80+	2
G427	F	25-35	161.0	83.89	0	G	80+	2
G430	J	1.5-2			PR	G	80+	2
G433	??M	5-6			PPR	G	80+	2
G436	M	25-35	168.0	81.62	0	G	80+	2
G438	F	25-35	155.3	76.02	0	G	80+	2
G443	F	21-24	169.2		0	G	60-80	2
G446	J	7				G	<20	2
G451	F?	50+	164.8		0	G	60-80	2
G456	??F	11			PA	G	80+	2
G457	J	30WIU			0	G	60-80	2
G462	M	20-21	178.5	81.32	0	G	80+	2
G467	J	4-5			0	G	80+	2
G470	J	44-46WIU			0	M	80+	2
G474	F	50+	151.3	76.57	PPR	G	80+	1-2
G476	J	32WIU			0	G	80+	2
G478	F	21-23	156.0	79.23	0	G	80+	2
G482	M	50+	178.6		0	G	80+	2
G488	J	3			0	G	60-80	1-2
G492	J	41WIU			0	G	60-80	2
G497	??M	15-16			0	G	80+	2
G500	J	9-10			0	G	80+	2
G503	??F	10			CA	G	80+	1-2
G506	??F	9			0	M	80+	1-2
G510	J	6			PA	G	80+	2
G513	U	ADULT				G	40-60	2
G516	M	40+	169.6			M	80+	1-2
G522	J	15 MONTH			0	G	80+	2
G525	U	ADULT				G	<20	2
G528	M	19-21	166.3	90.48	0	G	80+	2
G531	J	1			0	G	60-80	2
G534	J	3-5MONTH				M	60-80	2
G542	??F	5-6			0	G	80+	1-2
G555	U	ADULT				M	<20	1-2
G558	J	5-7				G	80+	2
G561	M	50+	167.8			M	80+	1-2
G565	M?	ADULT	160.7			G	20-40	2
G571	F	40+	154.5	79.67	0	G	80+	2
G576	J	3-3.5			PA	G	80+	1-2
G579	J	46-48WIU				M	60-80	1-2
G582	F	25-35	154.7	79.33	0	G	80+	1-2
G587	M	35-45	161.0	82.29	0	G	80+	1-2
G592	J	34-35WIU			0	M	40-60	1-2
G597	F	21-25	161.1	86.21	0	G	60-80	2
G601	M	35-45	172.9		0	G	60-80	1-2
G604	M	25-30	174.3	77.08	0	G	60-80	1-2
G607	M	35-45	173.4			G	80+	1-2
G614	J	5-6			0	G	60-80	1-2
G628	F	40+	160.5	82.49	0	M	80+	1-2

Skeleton	Sex	Age	Stature	Cranial index	Cribra orbitalia	Preservation	Completeness	Phase
G635	F	21	152.5	77.01	PA	G	80+	1-2
G636	F	50+	157.8	79.14	0	M	80+	1-2
G643	F	25-35	156.9	77.53	0	G	80+	1-2
G652	F	40-50	154.5	81.92	0	G	80+	2
G655	J	1.5-2			0	G	20-40	1-2
G658	??M	11			CA	G	80+	1-2
G667	??M	7-8			0	G	20-40	1-2
G670	F	40-50	157.3		0	G	60-80	1-2
G673	F	50+	168.5		PR	G	40-60	1-2
G676	M	50+		75.38	0	M	40-60	1-2
G677	U	35-45			0	M	40-60	2
G678	M?	ADULT	171.5			G	20-40	2
G683	J	5			0	G	80+	1-2
G686	J	1-3MONTH			0	M	60-80	1-2
G689	??M	15-18			0	M	80+	1-2
G692	F	50+	159.5	74.87	0	G	80+	1-2
G694	M	25-35	180.3	88.30	0	G	80+	1-2
G697	J	2-3			0	G	80+	1-2
G708	??M	10			0	G	80+	1-2
G710	M	21-30				M	60-80	1-2
G715	M	35-45	168.6	86.19	0	G	20-40	1-2
G720	J	5				G	20-40	1-2
G723	??F	10			0	G	80+	1-2
G746	M	30-50	174.9		0	G	80+	1-2
G747	F	21-30	161.0		0	G	60-80	1-2
G750	F	ADULT	159.7			G	60-80	1-2
G760	F	25	152.3		0	G	80+	1-2
NA002	??F	11			CA	G	60-80	1-2
NA004	-M	17-18			CA	G	60-80	
NA004A	J	38WIU			0	G	40-60	
NA006	F	40-50	162.2	75.98	0	G	80+	1-2
NA006A	J	32-33WIU			0	G	60-80	
NA013	F?	35-45	162.5			M	60-80	1-2
NA014	M	30-40	172.8		0	G	60-80	1-2
NA014A	J	44-47WIU			0	G	60-80	
NA019	??M	8-9			0	G	60-80	
NA022	J	3				G	60-80	
NA023	??M	7			0	G	80+	
NA024	J	5				G	40-60	
NA025	??F	5-6			0	G	80+	
NA026	F	35-45	155.7	90.48	CR	G	60-80	1-2
NA027	J	15MONTHS			0	M	20-40	
NA028	J	1.5			0	G	60-80	
NA029	J	1			0	G	80+	
NA030	J	6			0	G	60-80	
NA031	F	40+				G	40-60	1-2
NA031A	J	2.5			0	M	60-80	
NA032	J	35-36WIU				G	20-40	
NA033	F	50+	151.9	83.04	0	G	80+	1-2
NA034	J	39WIU			0	G	20-40	
NA035	??F	6-7			PA	G	80+	
NA036	J	1.5			0	M	60-80	
NA037	J	1-1.5			PA	G	80+	
NA037A	J	38WIU				G	60-80	
NA038	M	20-25		76.32	0	G	<20	1-2
NA040	J	42-44WIU				M	40-60	
NA042	J	37WIU				M	20-40	
NA043	J	46-47WIU				M	60-80	
NA043A	J	6 MONTHS				M	40-60	

Skeleton	Sex	Age	Stature	Cranial index	Cribra orbitalia	Preservation	Completeness	Phase
NA044	F	18	147.1	84.85	PR	G	80+	1-2
NA045	??F	6			TPR	G	60-80	
NA046	M	50+	176.1	78.42	PR	G	60-80	1-2
NA047	F	35-45	152.9	82.49	0	G	80+	1-2
NA048	J	5-6			0	G	20-40	
NA049	J	4			0	G	60-80	
NA050	J	8-9MONTH			0	G	60-80	
NA051	M	25-35		79.35	0	G	<20	1-2
NA052	J	45WIU				M	60-80	
NA053	J	6			PPR	G	80+	
NA054	J	8-9				M	<20	
NA055	J	NEONATE				G	20-40	
NA056	J	1.5-2			0	M	40-60	
NA056A	J	30WIU			0	G	60-80	
NA057	J	7 MONTHS				M	<20	
NA058	??M	6			CPR	G	80+	
NA059	F	35-45	154.1	77.35	0	G	60-80	1-2
NA060	J	45WIU			0	M	20-40	
NA060A	J	35-36WIU				G	40-60	
NA061	J	33-34WIU				G	60-80	
NA062	J	35WIU			0	G	60-80	
NA063	??M	9-10			0	G	80+	
NA064	J	41-43WIU			0	G	60-80	
NA065	??F	6-7			0	G	80+	
NA066	F	22-30	169.5	83.24	0	G	80+	1-2
NA067	J	35WIU			0	G	60-80	
NA068	F	50+		81.22	0	M	20-40	1-2
NA069	J	41WIU			0	G	80+	
NA070	J	1.5			0	M	20-40	
NA071	J	2			0	G	20-40	
NA073	J	2			0	G	<20	
NA074	??M	5-6			0	G	40-60	
NA075	M	ADULT	164.1			G	40-60	1-2
NA076	J	39WIU			0	G	40-60	
NA077	J	5-6			0	G	20-40	
NA078	M	ADULT	174.8			G	40-60	1-2
NA079	J	3			0	G	80+	
NA080	M	35-45	177.1			G	60-80	1-2
NA081	M	35-45		84.53	0	G	<20	1-2
NA082	J	35WIU			0	G	60-80	
NA083	J	4			0	G	<20	
NA084	F	ADULT	165.4			G	60-80	1-2
NA085	J	45-46WIU			0	M	20-40	
NA086	J	6-7				G	40-60	
NA087	J	3			0	G	80+	
NA088	F	40-50	155.4	86.29	TA	G	80+	1-2
NA089	??M	10-11			0	G	80+	
NA091	M?	40+	166.8		0	M	80+	1-2
NA092	J	4-5MONTH			0	M	60-80	
NA093	J	6 MONTHS			0	P	40-60	
NA094	F	25-35	157.3		0	M	80+	1
NA095	??F	9			0	G	80+	
NA096	J	40-41WIU			0	G	20-40	
NA097	J	2.5			0	G	60-80	
NA098	??F	6			0	G	80+	
NA099	J	35WIU				G	80+	
NA100	M?	40-50	168.5	71.89	0	G	80+	1-2
NA101	F	25-35	158.7		0	G	40-60	1-2
NA101A	J	4				G	80+	

Skeleton	Sex	Age	Stature	Cranial index	Cribra orbitalia	Preservation	Completeness	Phase
NA102	M	50+	170.9	79.78	0	G	60-80	1-2
NA103	??F	7			PR	G	60-80	
NA104	M	25-40	175.6			G	80+	1
NA105	??M	13			0	G	80+	
NA106	J	46WIU			0	G	60-80	
NA107	J	9 MONTHS			PA	M	40-60	
NA108	J	8 MONTHS				M	60-80	
NA109	J	7-9MIU			0	G	20-40	
NA110	J	4			0	G	80+	
NA111	J	6-7			0	G	80+	
NA112	M	50+	170.6	75.92	0	M	60-80	1-2
NA113	M?	ADULT	166.9			G	20-40	1-2
NA114	J	2.5			0	G	60-80	
NA115	M	30-45	159.7	91.19	0	G	80+	1-2
NA116	J	2.5			0	G	80+	
NA117	J	11-12				G	80+	
NA118	J	1.5-2			0	M	40-60	
NA119	J	6 MONTHS			0	M	40-60	
NA120	J	6			0	G	80+	
NA121	M	50-60	168.3	76.11	0	G	80+	1-2
NA121A	J	28WIU				G	<20	
NA122	J	6			TPR	G	60-80	
NA122A	F	25-35	168.9	79.07	0	M	40-60	1-2
NA123	F	21-40	158.8			G	40-60	1-2
NA124	J	33WIU			0	M	20-40	
NA125	J	6			PA	G	60-80	
NA126	J	1-1.5				M	40-60	
NA127	F	25-35		79.26	CA	M	20-40	1-2
NA128	M	ADULT				G	60-80	1-2
NA129	J	35WIU			0	G	60-80	
NA130	J	6-9MONTH			0	M	<20	
NA131	J	6-12MNTH				P	20-40	
NA132	J	2			0	M	20-40	
NA134	M	ADULT	176.1			G	40-60	1-2
NA135	??M	8			CA	G	60-80	
NA136	J	1.5			PA	G	20-40	
NA138	J	11				G	80+	
NA139	J	45-46WIU			0	M	20-40	
NA140	M	ADULT	169.8			G	80+	1-2
NA140A	J	6-7				G	40-60	
NA142	J	37-39WIU			0	G	60-80	
NA142A	J	28-29WIU			0	G	20-40	
NA143	F	ADULT	148.7		CA	G	60-80	1-2
NA144	F	35-45		71.67	0	M	20-40	1-2
NA145	F?	25-35	159.5		0	G	80+	1-2
NA146	M	40-50	162.9	75.27	PR	G	80+	1-2
NA149	F	25-40	165.0			G	60-80	1-2
NA149A	J	8-9MONTH			0	G	40-60	
NA149B	J	40WIU			0	G	40-60	
NA150	J	4-5MONTH			0	G	20-40	
NA151	J	4-5			0	M	20-40	
NA153	J	1.5			0	G	40-60	
NA154	M?	18		83.24	TA	G	60-80	1-2
NA155	J	6 MONTHS				G	20-40	
NA156	?F	14-15			PA	M	20-40	
NA157	F	ADULT	150.1			M	60-80	1-2
NA159	J	45-46WIU			0	G	20-40	
NA160	J	0-3MONTH			0	M	40-60	
NA161	J	32-33WIU			0	G	60-80	

Skeleton	Sex	Age	Stature	Cranial index	Cribra orbitalia	Preservation	Completeness	Phase
NA162	J	47WIU				G	20-40	
NA163	J	9 MONTHS			0	G	<20	
NA164	J	1			0	G	80+	
NA165	J	1.5-2			0	G	80+	
NA166	M	ADULT	166.8			G	60-80	1-2
NA167	F	25-35	158.8	85.71	CPR	G	80+	2
NA168	M?	50+	160.3	78.26	0	G	80+	1-2
NA169	J	3-4MONTH			0	G	<20	
NA170	F?	21-25	152.4	78.89	0	G	60-80	1
NA170A	J	42-45WIU			0	M	60-80	
NA171	M	40-50	174.3	79.68	0	G	40-60	1-2
NA172	M	ADULT	173.1			G	20-40	1-2
NA173	F	21-25	155.6	81.71	0	G	60-80	1-2
NA174	??F	11-12			CA	G	80+	
NA175	??M	8			PR	G	60-80	
NA176	M	25	162.3	93.37	0	G	80+	2
NA177	M	ADULT	174.8			G	20-40	1-2
NA178	-M	17			0	G	60-80	
NA179	J	11-12				G	20-40	
NA180	-M	15-18				G	40-60	
NA181	M	50+	165.1	85.47	0	G	80+	1-2
NA182	J	8-9			0	G	60-80	
NA183	M	ADULT	168.8			M	20-40	1-2
NA184	J	2.5-3			PPR	G	20-40	
NA185	-M	15-18			0	G	40-60	
NA186	J	6-7				G	<20	
NA187	J	12				G	20-40	
NA188	J	7-8				G	20-40	
NA189	J	1-1.5			PA	G	60-80	
NA190	M	35-45	172.2	76.63	0	G	40-60	1-2
NA191	J	3 MONTHS				M	60-80	
NA192	J	10-11				G	20-40	
NA193	J	41-43WIU			0	G	80+	
NA194	J	4-6MONTH			0	M	40-60	
NA195	M	21-24	167.0	81.35	PPR	G	80+	1-2
NA196	J	4			PR	G	60-80	
NA197	M	50+	168.2	82.97	0	G	80+	1-2
NA198	??M	11-12			CA	G	80+	
NA199	M	50+	151.2	87.12	0	G	80+	2-3
NA200	J	11				G	<20	
NA201	J	4-5			PR	G	80+	
NA202	F	60+	155.8	81.36	0	M	80+	1-2
NA203	F	40+	159.3			M	80+	1-2
NA203A	J	6 MONTHS			0	G	80+	
NA204	M	40-50		78.01	0	G	<20	1-2
NA205	J	15-18			0	G	40-60	
NA209	J	42WIU			0	M	20-40	
NA215	F	18-20	155.3		0	G	80+	1
NA216	J	7-9MONTH			0	G	20-40	
NA217	M	50+	165.9	89.39	PR	M	80+	2
NA218	M	50+	168.6		0	G	80+	1-2
NA219	J	4			PPR	G	80+	
NA220	J	42WIU				G	20-40	
NA221	J	46-48WIU			0	G	60-80	
NA222	J	3-4			0	G	60-80	
NA223	J	5-6				G	80+	1-2
NA224	M	ADULT	167.6			G	40-60	1
NA225	J	1.5			0	M	60-80	1
NA227	M	22-25	169.4	83.33	0	M	60-80	1-2

Skeleton	Sex	Age	Stature	Cranial index	Cribra orbitalia	Preservation	Completeness	Phase
NA231	J	6 MONTHS			0	M	20-40	
NA232	J	44WIU			0	G	40-60	
NA233	M	40+	163.1			G	40-60	1-2
NA233A	J	33WIU				M	<20	
NA234	M	40+	174.0			G	40-60	2-3
NA235	M?	17-24		83.68	0	G	20-40	1-2
NA236	J	6-8MONTH				M	<20	
NA237	M	50+		82.39	0	M	<20	1-2
SA002	M	22-24	168.5	74.61	0	G	80+	3-4
SA003	M	50+	175.8	72.77	0	G	80+	3-4
SA005	J	15			CPR	G	60-80	
SA007	?M	12				G	40-60	
SA008	M	25-35	172.9	82.07	0	G	<20	
SA012	M	35-45	174.3		0	G	60-80	1-2
SA0013	F	35-45	166.8	82.49	PPR	G	40-60	2-3
SA014	F	25-35	155.1	82.49	0	G	40-60	2
SA015	M	50+	167.6		0	M	80+	
SA017	F	21-25	160.2	74.73	0	M	80+	4
SA017A	M	25-35	168.6		PR	M	40-60	
SA021	M	50+	167.8	79.57	0	M	60-80	
SA023	F	60+	150.3	78.84	0	M	80+	4
SA029	F	21-24	152.8	71.28	0	M	80+	
SA030	M	30-40		74.60	0	G	<20	
SA033	M?	ADULT	162.0			M	40-60	3-4
SA034	M	50+	162.9		0	G	60-80	1
SA036	F	21-25	156.4	71.58	PR	G	80+	
SA045	J	15-18			CA	G	80+	4
SA047	F	35-45	161.7		PR	G	60-80	
SA048	F	ADULT	160.8		PR	M	40-60	4
SA049	F	50+	159.0		0	M	80+	4
SA050	F	40+	163.3			M	40-60	
SA051	F	50+	158.3	76.54	0	G	20-40	
SA052	M	50+	165.0	77.49	0	G	80+	1-2
SA053	F	50+	149.1	80.79	0	G	80+	1-2
SA054	F	ADULT	156.4			G	20-40	
SA055	J	2-2.5			0	G	60-80	
SA056	M	50+		86.78	0	M	60-80	1-2
SA080	F	17-19				G	60-80	
SA052/16	F	21-23	158.5		0	G	60-80	
SA052/18	M	20-22			CA	G	<20	
V01	J	34-35WIU				G	40-60	4
V03	J	36WIU			0	G	60-80	4
V04	J	43WIU			0	G	<20	
V06	J	45WIU			0	M	20-40	4
V07	??M	13-14			0	G	20-40	4
V10	J	6 MONTHS				G	40-60	
V11	M	40+	169.6		0	G	60-80	
V12	??M	13			0	G	<20	
V14	M	ADULT	173.2			M	<20	
V15	M	50+	168.6	79.26	0	G	40-60	
V16	F	30-40	156.4	83.93	0	G	40-60	4
V17	J	48WIU			0	G	40-60	
V18	M	35-45	173.9	85.64	0	G	40-60	
V19	M?	ADULT	177.2			M	40-60	
V20	J	1.5-2			0	P	<20	4
V21	U	ADULT				M	20-40	4
V22	J	4			PA	G	60-80	
V23	??M	6-7			PA	G	20-40	
V24	-M	14-15			PA	G	80+	

Skeleton	Sex	Age	Stature	Cranial index	Cribra orbitalia	Preservation	Completeness	Phase
V25	J	3-4			PA	M	60-80	
V26	F	50+	165.0		0	G	80+	
V27	M	50+	174.6	74.87	0	G	60-80	
V28	J	1			0	M	20-40	
V29	F	40+	150.0			G	40-60	
V30	M	18-19		75.82	PR	G	80+	
V31	J	10MONTHS				M	20-40	
V32	M?	ADULT	173.4			G	<20	
V33	F	35-45	156.8			G	40-60	
V34	J	10				G	<20	
V35	J	14-15				G	20-40	
V36	M	40+	176.4			M	40-60	
V37	M	40-50	168.6		PR	G	20-40	
V38	M	40-50	167.2		0	G	80+	2-3
V39	M?	ADULT	166.3			G	<20	
V40	M	ADULT	172.8			G	<20	
V41	U	ADULT				M	<20	1-2
V42	M	40-60	175.3	75.96	0	G	80+	4
V43	J	40-41WIU			0	M	40-60	
V44	F?	35-45		90.48	0	G	40-60	
V45	M	40+	165.9	83.43	0	G	60-80	2
V46	F	50+	165.0	86.36	PR	G	80+	
V47	??M	12				G	60-80	
V49	J	7			0	M	40-60	
V51	M	40-50	168.0		0	G	60-80	1-2
V53	J	0-1			0	G	<20	
V55	J	6				G	<20	
V57	J	0.5-1				M	<20	
V59	J	7-8			TA	G	20-40	
V60	J	40WIU			0	G	20-40	
V61	F	35-45	156.8	70.43	0	M	80+	
V62	F	35-45		80.79	0	G	40-60	
V63	J	36WIU				G	20-40	
WCO002	J	3			TA	M	40-60	
WCO003	J	5-6			0	M	60-80	
WCO005	J	10				G	80+	
WCO006	J	12-13			PA	G	40-60	
WCO007	J	4				M	60-80	
WCO009	M	25-40	168.3			G	40-60	2-3
WCO010	M	20		71.51	0	G	60-80	3-4
WCO011	J	11-12				G	40-60	
WCO012	M	ADULT	163.5			G	40-60	
WCO013	M	50+	168.9	85.56	0	G	40-60	
WCO014	M	ADULT	175.7			G	20-40	
WCO015	M	40-50	167.1	81.67	0	G	60-80	
WCO016	F	18-19				G	60-80	
WCO017	F	50+	153.4	87.50	CR	G	80+	
WCO018	M	ADULT	165.4			G	40-60	
WCO019	J	11-12			0	G	80+	
WCO020	J	2.5				G	20-40	
WCO021	-F	16			0	G	20-40	
WCO021A	M	30-40			0	M	<20	
WCO022	F	ADULT	161.9			G	60-80	
WCO023	J	12-13				G	40-60	
WCO026	F	50+	158.2	76.54	PA	G	80+	
WCO027	J	6			PA	G	60-80	
WCO028	F	35-45	165.7	83.33	0	G	60-80	2-3
WCO029	F	50+	158.3		0	G	60-80	
WCO030	M	50+		91.71	0	G	40-60	

346

Skeleton	Sex	Age	Stature	Cranial index	Cribra orbitalia	Preservation	Completeness	Phase
WCO032	M	25-35			0	G	<20	
WCO033	J	6-7			0	G	<20	
WCO034	J	4				M	60-80	
WCO035	J	7				G	20-40	
WCO035A	J	10-11				G	20-40	
WCO036	F	40+	150.5			G	60-80	
WCO037	M	50+	162.8	77.42	0	G	80+	
WCO038	U	ADULT				G	20-40	
WCO039	U	16-20				M	<20	
WCO040	M	20-21	152.8			G	40-60	
WCO041	M	25-40	169.7			G	20-40	
WCO042	J	6 MONTHS				G	20-40	
WCO044	J	11-12			0	G	40-60	3-4
WCO045	F	60+	161.5	78.53	0	G	80+	3-4
WCO052	??M	8			TA	G	60-80	
WCO056	F	35-45	161.1	79.21	CPR	G	80+	
WCO057	M	50+	166.8	79.89	0	G	20-40	
WCO058	?M	13-15				M	80+	
WCO059	M	50+	157.0	77.72	0	G	80+	
WCO062	M	21	155.7			G	20-40	
WCO063	J	4				G	40-60	
WCO067	M	ADULT	171.2			G	<20	
WCO068	M	25-35	171.9		CA	G	60-80	
WCO069	J	13-14				G	60-80	
WCO070	F	25-35		80.57		G	20-40	1-2
WCO071	F	25-35	150.5	84.66	0	G	80+	
WCO072	J	2			0	G	60-80	
WCO077	M	22-25			0	G	20-40	
WCO078	M	22-30	168.2	82.51	0	G	80+	
WCO079	-M	15-18			PR	G	80+	
WCO080	F	30-50		82.29	0	G	<20	
WCO081	M	40+			PR	G	<20	
WCO082	??F	10			CA	G	80+	
WCO085	J	1				M	40-60	
WCO087	F	ADULT	148.6			G	40-60	
WCO088	M	40+		82.68	0	G	<20	
WCO089	F	25-35	158.2			G	40-60	
WCO091	M	25-35	162.3		0	G	80+	
WCO092	-M	17-18			0	G	80+	
WCO093	F	21-25	160.1	77.11	0	G	80+	
WCO097	J	5			0	G	60-80	
WCO098	F?	25-35	163.9	82.53	0	G	80+	
WCO099	??F	8			PA	G	60-80	
WCO100	J	2.5			0	G	60-80	
WCO103	J	13-14			PR	M	80+	
WCO104	J	3 MONTHS			0	M	60-80	
WCO107	J	12-14			PPR	G	40-60	
WCO108	J	2-3			0	G	60-80	
WCO109	F	40+			0	G	80+	
WCO110	M	20-22	162.3		0	G	20-40	
WCO115	M	ADULT				M	20-40	
WCO115A	J	1.5			0	G	40-60	
WCO117	M	50+	161.7			G	80+	
WCO118	M	45+	176.3	79.66	0	G	40-60	2
WCO119	M	30-40	158.4	71.43	PPR	G	20-40	1-2
WCO122	F	19-21	154.0		0	G	80+	
WCO124	F	50+	163.1		CA	M	80+	
WCO125	M	25-35	158.0	82.02	0	G	80+	
WCO125A	J	39-41WIU			0	G	20-40	

Skeleton	Sex	Age	Stature	Cranial index	Cribra orbitalia	Preservation	Completeness	Phase
WCO130	F	50+	161.1	81.40	0	G	60-80	2-3
WCO131	M	50+	175.1	91.81	0	G	80+	
WCO134	-M	16-18			PA	G	20-40	
WCO137	M	50+	165.4		0	G	60-80	
WCO138	M	25-35	165.8	77.78	0	G	60-80	2-3
WCO139	M	45-55	178.3	81.05	0	G	20-40	2
WCO140	J	9			0	G	80+	
WCO142	M	ADULT	167.1			G	40-60	
WCO144	M	50+				G	40-60	
WCO146	M	45-55	160.6	82.87	0	G	80+	
WCO147	??M	9-10			0	G	40-60	
WCO149	F	ADULT		85.80	0	G	<20	
WCO153	M?	40+	151.6			G	20-40	3-4
WCO154	M	17-25		82.04	0	G	<20	
WCO155	J	10-11				G	60-80	
WCO156	M?	21-24	163.0			G	60-80	2-3
WCO162	M	50+	162.0	80.34	CPR	G	60-80	1-2
WCO163	J	4			0	G	60-80	
WCO164	??M	10-11			TA	G	40-60	
WCO164A	M	40+	160.4			G	60-80	
WCO165	F?	35-45	156.4	82.86	0	M	40-60	
WCO165A	M	ADULT	167.7			G	40-60	
WCO166	M	21-25	170.3			G	20-40	
WCO167	F	40+	157.0			M	40-60	
WCO168	M	30-40	172.3			G	40-60	
WCO169	M	ADULT	171.1			G	20-40	
WCO170	F?	50+	152.2	83.61	PR	G	60-80	2-4
WCO173	F	40-50	152.8	87.95	0	G	80+	
WCO174	M	22-24	177.8			G	80+	
WCO175	J	1-1.5			TA	M	20-40	
WCO176	J	10			PA	G	80+	
WCO179	F	40+	147.1	81.50	0	G	60-80	1-2
WCO181	M	25-35	173.4			M	20-40	2-3
WCO183	M	25-35	175.0		0	M	40-60	
WCO184	F	35-45	148.9	78.07	0	M	80+	2
WCO186	J	12				G	20-40	
WCO187	F	40+	160.1			G	40-60	
WCO191	M	50+		82.07	0	G	<20	
WCO192	F	25-35		78.09	0	G	<20	
WCO193	M?	ADULT		71.75	PR	G	<20	
WCO195	J	15-16			CA	G	<20	
WCO199	F	40-50	154.9	80.23	0	G	60-80	
WCO200	M	50+	172.9		0	G	80+	
WCO201	U	20-40		90.36	0	G	40-60	
WCO202	??M	7			0	G	80+	
WCO203	M	ADULT	159.4			M	40-60	
WCO204	F	ADULT				M	40-60	

Notes: Sex, M=male, F=female, U=unsexed adult (aged 18+ years), J=unsexed juvenile (under 18 years), ? used as a suffix or prefix indicates probable sex in adults and juveniles respectively, ?? used as a prefix indicates tentative sex based on the craniofacial morphology technique of Molleson et al. (1998) in juveniles. Age, in years unless stated, wiu=weeks in utero for foetal/perinatal ages. Stature, in cm. Cribra orbitalia, 0=absent, blank denotes orbits missing so condition could not be scored, letter entries indicate condition present, first letter indicates type of lesion (P=porotic, C=cribriform, T=trabecular), other letters indicate status of lesions (A=active, R=remodelled, PR=partially remodelled). Preservation=gross bone preservation, scored on a subjective basis according to the degree of post-depositional erosion shown by the bones G=good, M=moderate, P=poor. Phase, 1=Late Anglo-Saxon (AD 950-1066), 2=Earlier Medieval (AD 1066-1348), 3=Later Medieval (AD 1348-1540), 4=Post-medieval (AD 1540-1850), all dates approximate.

Appendix 2: Notes on Individual Burials
by S. Mays

CN01 R masto-occipital suture obliterated.

CN02 Both maxillary canines bear large lingual tubercles.

There is slight crowding of the anterior mandibular dentition.

CN03 Only a pelvic bone and some foot and leg bones survive. The femoral heads show partial destruction of their joint surfaces; the changes are more marked on the left bone. Where normal joint surface has been destroyed, sclerotic trabecular bone is exposed. In addition to this surface destruction, there are also some discrete cavities extending up to 8mm into the subchondral bone. Those parts of the joint surfaces which do survive are eburnated. Similar changes are present in the left acetabulum and the left sacro-iliac joint (the right pelvic bone is missing).

There is a cavity 3mm deep lined with trabecular bone in the centre of the talar face of the L talo-navicular joint; a similar cavity is present in the talar face or the R talo-navicular articulation. The joint surface around these cavities is porotic, as are both the navicular faces of these joints. The distal joint surface of the right fibula shows marginal erosion.

All elements are very light and friable, and the cortices of the foot bones are paper thin although the trabecular bone within appears normal. The cortical bone of the femoral diaphyses is very porous, and radiography shows loss of cortico-medullary distinction. There is sub-periosteal resorption in the proximal phalanx of the right great toe.

The pathological changes in this specimen are strongly suggestive of hyperparathyroidism (see Mays *et al*. 2001b for full discussion).

Midshaft part of right femur, left and right tibiae and midshaft fibula fragments sacrificed for radiocarbon dating 10-3-95.

CN04 The L maxillary M1 bears a large Carabelli cusp.

There is black staining in the frontal and occipital bones. The bone in the stained areas is rather friable.

CN05 The interdental septa are porotic and have irregular profiles. There is a marked infra-bony pocket around the R maxillary M3. Periodontal disease.

The atlas vertebra shows spina bifida, and its L foramen transversarium is incomplete.

The L third metacarpal lacks its styloid process, there is instead an extension of the trapezoid - a trapezoid process (O'Rahilly 1953, fig. 5c).

There is bony spurring around some interphalangeal joints of the hands, the heads and tuberosities of some of the ribs, the olecranon processes of the ulnae, the radial tuberosities, around the margins of the proximal and distal joint surfaces of the radii and ulnae, around the glenoid cavities of the scapulae, at the insertions of the Achilles tendons on the calcanei, on the tuberosity of the L 5th metatarsal and just anterior to the distal joint surfaces of the fibulae.

C5 and 6 are fused by large, flowing paravertebral osteophytes on the L and R sides of their centra; similar osteophytes on C6 and 7 interlock but are not ankylosed. There are similar, smaller osteophytes on C7 and T1. The bodies of T5-11 are fused by a thick, flowing, R-sided osteophyte and there are smaller articulating osteophytes on the L and R sides of the bodies of T11 and 12 and on the R sides of the bodies of L2 and 3. There are thick osteophytes on the centra of L5 and S1. A large osteophyte on the head of the R 7th rib articulates with one on the body of T7.The R sacro-iliac joint is fused at its superior margin by a thick, smooth osteophyte; its joint surface is normal. DISH.

There is an articulation between the R transverse process of L5 and the R sacral ala. This is probably not partial sacralisation of L5, but rather a novel articulation perhaps formed as a result of excessive movement of the lumbo-sacral articulation due to the extensive spinal fusion.

There is an area of remodelled periostitis on the distal half of the shaft of the R fibula. The tibia is normal. Probably due to local inflammation as a result of infection/injury.
Red-brown staining on the bones.

CN06 The R maxillary canine is unerupted, and X-ray shows that it lies tilted about 30-40 degrees medially; the deciduous canine was retained (although it has fallen from its socket post-mortem).

T12 has lumbar-type facet joints.

There is a concave, porotic area on the anterior margin of the anterior facet of the R calcaneus -probably the site of fibrous attachment for a calcaneum secundarium. The L calcaneus is of normal form.

Red-brown staining on the bones.

Manubrio-sternal synostosis.

CN07 There is a thin bridge of bone between the L transverse process and the posterior arch of the atlas.

The L 3rd metacarpal lacks its styloid process (the R is of normal form).

CN09 The bones show red-brown staining and there are purple/black patches on the internal surface of the frontal bone - here the bone is very friable.

CN11 There is slight rotation of the mandibular central incisors - the mesial parts are turned lingually, the distal parts labially. 'Wing-teeth' (Escobar *et al*. 1977).

There is a pit, 4mm in diameter, 3mm deep, in the anterior facet of the left calcaneus. Possibly osteochondritis dissecans.

Bones stained red-brown.

CN12 The maxillary I2s are somewhat reduced in size.

The interdental septa are porotic and have irregular profiles. Periodontal disease.

There are united fractures of the right trapezoid and the adjoining joint surface of the right second metacarpal.

CN13 There is a crescentic porotic area on the anterior border of the anterior facet of the L calcaneus and a similar one on the R calcaneus. Probably sites for fibrous attachment of calcaneum secundaria.

There is a depression 9 x 4 x 2mm deep on the posterior/inferior facet of the L talus. Osteochondritis dissecans.

There is red-brown staining on the bones. There is green staining on the L mandibular angle.

CN14 T12 has lumbar-type facet joints.

There is superficial destruction of the joint surface of the R acetabulum; the surface in the eroded area is of fine grained amorphous bone. There is slight new bone formation on the ilium around the acetabulum. The proximal part of the R femoral shaft shows fine pitting of the cortex.

There is superficial bony resorption on both ischial tuberosities. X-ray of the skeleton failed to reveal further changes. The cause of these lesions is uncertain, although tuberculosis is one possibility.

The L patella is emarginate, the lateral part is present as a separate ossicle. The adjoining edges of the ossicle and the main part of the bone are porotic, giving the impression that fibrous union existed between them in-vivo.

Some bones have patches of purple staining on them, the bone in affected areas is very friable. The staining is mainly confined to the vertebral bodies.

CN15 The L deciduous maxillary canine has been retained; the permanent one is erupting lingually to it.

The L maxillary M3 is orientated horizontally, and is impacted against the M2, this pressure from the M3 seems to have impacted the M2 against the neighbouring M1, preventing it (the M2) from erupting fully.

A small area on the labial/lateral side of the inferior part of the crown of the R maxillary I1 is denuded of enamel. Probably a developmental anomaly.

Radiography revealed a low, raised area of bone on the endosteal surface of the right radius in the region of the midshaft. This area of new bone is of similar density to the normal cortex which underlies it except for a sclerotic margin at its interface with the medullary cavity. The lesion is about 1cm long. It seems likely that this represents a fibrous cortical defect which has become filled in with bone. Radiography revealed no further lesions in the other long-bones.

CN16 Although the two bones have broken apart post-mortem, the R humerus and ulna were ankylosed in-vivo, in an almost fully extended position. The radius is not ankylosed to either of the other 2 arm bones but its head shows severe osteoarthritis, with broadening, porosis and eburnation of the joint surface. The joint surface on the anterior part of the trochlear surface of the humerus has been resorbed, leaving fragile, porotic bone. This area is no longer involved in the joint as the ankylosis of the ulna and humerus prevented flexion of the elbow. The distal diaphysis and metaphysis of the humerus are somewhat thickened with a pitted cortex. X-ray reveals that its endosteal surface is normal. There is no evidence for fracture of any of the arm bones (although the olecranon process of the ulna is missing post-mortem). Possible diagnoses include septic arthritis and trauma. Radiographic examination indicates that the thickening of the distal humerus is solely due to deposition of new bone beneath the periosteum - this may have occurred as a result of physical injury to the periosteum or it may be due to infection in the elbow area. The former is, perhaps, the more likely explanation given the lack of any other indications of infection (e.g. sequestra or sinus formation).This lack of any unambiguous signs of infection argues against the diagnosis of septic arthritis. It may be that there was a comminuted fracture of the (missing) olecranon process of the ulna and that the humero-ulnar synostosis was a consequence of this injury.

There is some purple staining on the pelvic bones, and on the vertebrae, particularly the neural arches and neural spines of the lumbar vertebrae.

Manubrio-sternal synostosis.

There is a compression fracture of the anterior part of the body of T6, it is firmly healed with slight anterior wedging. T6 and T5 are fused at the anterior/left parts of their centra.

CN17 The photo of this burial *in-situ* shows the letters DT (or DJ) picked out in nails on the coffin lid.

The interdental septa are porotic and have concave profiles. Periodontal disease.

C5-7 have thick osteophytes on the anterior/right sides of their centra. 'Bone former' type changes.

The distal joint surface of the R 1st metatarsal is deflected laterally
.

There is a pit 10 x 7 x 2mm deep, lined with porotic bone, on the medial part of the proximal joint surface of the L tibia. The proximal part of the R tibia is damaged post-mortem, but enough remains to show that it too bore a similar cavity on the medial part of its joint surface. Bilateral osteochondritis dissecans.

Both masto-occipital sutures are obliterated.

There are the beginnings of a sutura mendosa at both asterions.

CN18 The R mandibular canine is unerupted and is rotated through 90 degrees, so that its lingual side faces distally. It is tilted distally so that it would have been impacted against the PM1. The L maxillary canine is similarly rotated and it is tilted mesially so that it is impacted against the I2, and the alveolar bone over its crown is incompletely resorbed. The maxillary third molars are also impacted. The alveolar bone over their crypts is incompletely resorbed.

The bodies of T12 and L1-3 bear short, thick osteophytes – 'bone former' type changes.

There is a concave, porotic area on the anterior margin of the L calcaneus - probably the site for fibrous attachment of a calcaneum secundarium. The R calcaneus is of normal morphology.

The distal joint surfaces of both 1st metatarsals are deflected laterally so that the proximal hallucial phalanges deviate about 30 degrees laterally. The left shows osteoarthritis to Brothwell's (1981) grade 1, the right to Brothwell's grade 2. Hallux valgus.

There are the beginnings of a sutura mendosa at both asterions.

There is green staining near the distal end of the R radius.

Manubrio-sternal synostosis.

CN19 Red-brown staining on sacrum, pelvic bones, spine and vertebral rib ends. There is also patchy purple staining on some bones; where this is present the bone is fragile.

The left acetabulum is rather shallow and there is eburnation on its superior surface near the rim. There is infill of the acetabular floor with new bone. There was probably subluxation of the left hip consequent on the shallow acetabulum.

CN20 The L mandibular M3 is impacted - it is erupting horizontally and its crown is impacted against the distal root of the neighbouring M2.

There is partial sacralisation of L6 - it is completely fused to the L sacral ala but is otherwise a normal lumbar vertebra.

There is a small, flat ossicle bearing an articular facet on one side - a small lumbar rib.

There is an ovoid area with a roughened surface on the medial/posterior surface of the R femur about 3 x 15mm and raised 5mm proud of the surface of the normal cortex. Probably myositis ossificans.

The R 3rd metacarpal lacks its styloid process.

There is much purple-black staining on the pelves, ribs, scapulae and some vertebrae (mainly on their neural arches). There is a white crystalline deposit adhering to the sciatic notch of the L pelvic bone.

CN22 The bones are light with thin cortices - at a post-mortem defect 7-8cm from the distal end of the femur, on its anterior side, the cortex is only 2mm thick.

The bones are stained dark red-brown. There is slight greenish staining on the calvarium and on the bones of the L forearm. There is some white material adhering to the skull. Bone preservation is generally very poor.

CN24 The interdental septa are porotic with flattened profiles. Periodontal disease.

The dorsal part of the distal joint surface of a proximal hand phalanx has been destroyed leaving very sclerotic irregular bone here. No other bones show erosive lesions. Uncertain cause.

Manubrio-sternal synostosis.

CN27 The R maxillary M3 is reduced in size, the relevant part of the L maxilla and the third molar are missing post-mortem.

The R maxillary M3 bears an enamel pearl 1.5mm in diameter on the mesial-lingual aspect of its single root, 3-4mm below the cemento-enamel junction. The R maxillary M2 has a similar sized one at the bifurcation of its distal and lingual roots.

The articulation for the 1st metatarsal on the L medial cuneiform is bi-faceted; that on the R medial cuneiform has a cleft at its centre.

Three R ribs show united fractures, 2 in their sternal thirds, one in its vertebral third.

Slight red-brown staining on the bones.

CN28 Pitting and flattening of interdental septa. Periodontal disease.

Two mid/lower thoracic vertebrae show crescentic depressions in their inferior surfaces. The surfaces of these depressions are of rough, sclerotic bone. Probably avulsion injuries of the vertebral end-plates.

The right calcaneus shows partial separation on a fragment of bone on the anterior/medial side of the anterior articular surface for the talus. Probably an incompletely separated calcaneum secundarium. In the corresponding area on the right calcaneus there is a pitted, crescent-shaped depression, which probably represents the site of fibrous attachment of a calcaneum secundarium.

Purple staining on some bones. Affected parts are poorly preserved.

Both tibiae show well-remodelled deposits of new bone on their posterior surfaces in the midshaft area. There is also a pitted area and some new bone formation at the midshaft of the left fibula.

The joint surface and the whole proximal end of the left ulna is reduced in size compared with the right ulna. To a lesser extent the shaft dimensions are also reduced (although it was not possible to determine maximum length). There is periostitis on the lateral surface of the left ulna, towards the proximal end. Some of this new bone deposit is of woven bone, some is somewhat remodelled. There are also patchy deposits of woven bone further down the shaft.

There are deposits of somewhat remodelled new bone on the left humerus, just above the condyles. The distal joint surface of the left humerus is reduced in size compared with the right, for example its width is about 47mm compared with 55mm on the right bone. The reduction of size of the joint surfaces of the left elbow joint, which are otherwise normal in morphology, suggests that a problem originating before growth was complete; the deposits of unremodelled bone show that the lesion was still active at time of death. The full extent of involvement at the left elbow joint cannot be determined as the left radius is missing.

There is a fusiform swelling in the midshaft area of the right femur. Radiographic examination suggests that this is due to periostitis. The bone at this site is well remodelled, showing that the lesion was quiescent at time of death.

There are two small perforations on the frontal bone. They lie close to the midline, in the area of the bregma. The holes are about 8mm diameter, approximately circular and about 1cm apart. Ectocranially a pitted area surrounds the holes. The cavities are bevelled endocranially. There are deposits of unremodelled new bone on the endocranial surface of the skull in the area of these perforations, showing the cranial disease was active at time of death. There is a small area of pitting on the lateral surface of the right mandibular ramus.

The lesions suggest a systemic infection, which started in the growth period and was active until time of death. A number of specific infectious diseases suggest themselves as the causes of the lesions in this case, but none seems to provide a convincing diagnosis:

1) Smallpox. For: elbow lesions are characteristic of the disease in the skeleton, as are long-bone shaft swellings.

Against: bone lesions in smallpox are generally bilateral in the post-cranial skeleton, the great majority of cases of skeletal smallpox are found in young children, it is questionable whether the prolonged survival with an active infection shown by this individual is likely. In addition, even when it does affect the skeletal system the skull is rarely involved.

2) Tuberculosis. For: the character of the cranial vault lesions is typical - i.e. small size, greater destruction of internal than external table, pitting of ectocranial surface surrounding lesions and spread of infection intra-cranially via the internal periosteum. The elbow region is sometimes a focus for tuberculous infection.

Against: the lack of bone destruction in the elbow lesion is unusual for tuberculosis, as is the sparing of the large joints.

3) Treponemal disease. The long-bone shaft swelling is suggestive but the the cranial and elbow lesions are not typical nor is the general distribution of post-cranial lesions.

CN29 There is an infra-bony pocket around the R maxillary I1. Localised periodontal disease.

There is a lot of stray bone boxed mixed with this burial. The bones treated as the *in-situ* burial are those for which the pattern of bone survival most closely matches that depicted for the burial on the plan. Bones which could not be ascribed to this individual with confidence were not recorded, hence CN29 is rather short of the smaller bones.

CN30 There is articulation between the R navicular and cuboid via extra facets on the lateral/inferior side of the navicular and the posterior/medial side of the cuboid. There is no such articulation on the L foot.

There is severe hypoplasia of the canines and of the occlusal surfaces of the crowns of the only remaining M1. It appears that this defective enamel has predisposed the affected teeth to carious attack. The crown of the L maxillary M1 has been partially destroyed by a large caries cavity which has penetrated the pulp cavity and caused a periapical abscess in the jaw. The R maxillary M1 is missing post-mortem but there is an abscess cavity at its socket, and the mandibular M1s were lost ante-mortem; perhaps this abscessing and ante-mortem loss of the M1s was also precipitated by caries of these teeth.

The bones are stained red-brown. There is purple staining on some parts of the endocranial surface, affected parts are rather fragile.

CN31 The L maxillary PM1 is congenitally absent.

There is a large amount of stray bone boxed mixed with this individual. The bones recorded as CN31 are firmly identifiable as coming from a single individual but the pattern of bone survival is not really consistent with that depicted in the plan for this burial.

Only bones which could be ascribed with confidence to this individual are recorded, hence there is a shortage of the smaller bones for this burial.

There is bony spurring at the sites for insertion of the quadriceps femores on the patellae.

The distal half of the R radius is irregularly swollen and its cortex has a pitted surface. X-ray reveals considerable irregularity of the endosteal surface and much bony sclerosis. Osteomyelitis. The L ulna is missing so it is not possible to determine whether infection extended to this bone.

There are two large cystic defects in the sub-chondral bone superior to the right acetabulum. They communicate with the joint space. Supra-acetabular cysts (Wells 1976).

There is a ragged loss of rim height in the superior part of the right acetabulum. This type of lesion appears to form as a result of trauma causing fatigue failure of the rim edge. Splits in the acetabular cartilage caused by joint injury permit synovial fluid to penetrate subchondral bone causing cystic resorption. If this occurs near the rim edge it may weaken it sufficiently to cause fatigue failure.

CN32 Both CN32 and CN33 (burials FF and GG respectively under the old numbering system) were given finds numbers c1601. It seems that the bones from these 2 individuals from intercutting graves were mixed during or after excavation but it proved possible to separate most of the bones, the exception was the ribs, most of which could not be ascribed to one or other burial with any confidence and so were not recorded. Thus both burials are rather short on ribs.

According to the plan CN32 lacks lower legs but it is not clear whether CN33 is complete or not. One of the individuals represented by the bones lacks lower legs; they are present on the other. That lacking lower legs was treated as CN32, the other as CN33. They were recorded the other way around in an apparent error in the published interim report (Henderson 1987).

The interdental septa are porotic and have very irregular, rather spicular profiles. Periodontal disease.

Much super-eruption of teeth.

The cranium is very thick but not apparently diseased.

L3 and 4 have very large, smooth, paravertebral osteophytes on the R sides of their bodies which articulate but are not fused; the upper R side of the body of L3 bears a similar, smaller osteophyte. 'Bone former' type changes.

Slight purple staining on pelvic bones, affected parts are poorly preserved.

CN33 Excavation problems, see notes for CN32.

Five cervical vertebrae (C2-6) show severe osteoarthritis but only have changes on their right facet joints.

There is slight anterior wedging of the bodies of T6 and 7 giving approximately 30 degree kyphosis. Minor collapse of centra.

The tuberosities of both naviculae bear porotic, sclerotic areas - probably sites for fibrous attachments for os tibiale externa.

The plantar parts of both faces of the articulation between the R intermediate cuneiform and the 3rd metatarsal are porotic, as is the plantar part of the metatarsal face of the same articulation in the L foot. Non-osseous coalition (Regan et al. 1999).

There are small deposits of woven bone on the volar surfaces of both first metacarpals, on the distal parts of the radial shafts, on the left femur adjacent to the lesser trochanter and on the lateral surface of the right tibia one third of the way from the proximal end. There are somewhat heavier deposits, mainly of woven bone, on the distal parts of the tibial shafts. The right fibula bears a mixed deposit of woven and remodelled bone, and there are slight deposits of well-remodelled bone on the left fibula. The widespread and bilaterally fairly symmetrical nature of these deposits is suggestive of hypertrophic osteoarthropathy. The presence of lesions active at death, together with the age of this individual, suggests secondary rather than primary disease.

T6 and 7 are fused at the L and R sides of their centra by large, smooth paravertebral osteophytes. The bodies of T8-10 are fused by similar R-sided osteophytes. There are smaller osteophytes on the L and R sides of the bodies of T11 and 12 and articulating osteophytes on the R sides of the centra of T12 and L1. L1 and 2 are fused by a massive, R-sided osteophyte and there are smaller osteophytes on the L and R sides of the bodies of L3-5. There is bony spurring at the insertions of the quadriceps femores on the patellae, the lesser trochanters of the femora and just anterior to the distal joint surfaces of the fibulae. DISH.

There are small purple patches on some vertebral centra, the bone in these areas is very fragile.

CN36 Dark red-brown staining on the bones.

CN37 Many teeth have infra-bony pockets at their sockets, there is much alveolar resorption and the interdental septa are porotic and have irregular profiles. Severe periodontal disease.

Much super-eruption of teeth.

There are smooth, thick osteophytes on the L and R sides of the body of T12 and the R sides of the bodies of T10 and 11. There is also smooth lipping at the joint margins of the femoral condyles and the proximal joint surfaces of the tibiae. 'Bone former' type changes.

Bones stained red-brown.

CN38 There is bony spurring at the insertions of the quadriceps femorae on the patellae, the soleal lines and tubercles on the tibiae, the linea asperae of the femora, the olecranon processes of the ulnae, the iliac crests and anterior to the distal joint surfaces of the fibulae. 'Bone former' type changes.

Fairly robust bones with thick cortices.

There is some new bone deposition in the acetabular fossae.

Bones stained red-brown.

CN39 There are fractures of 3R ribs, one is united with moderate callus formation, 2 are un-united with sclerotic, porotic broken ends suggesting the formation of pseudarthroses. All the fractures are located in the sternal thirds.

The bones are rather fragmentary with many fresh breaks.

CN40 There is a porotic area on the R sacral ala - it probably represents the site of a fibrous articulation with the transverse process of L5. The L sacral ala is damaged post-mortem. Partial sacralisation of L5.

Localised alveolar resorption, concave and porotic interdental septa. Periodontal disease.

CN41 The interdental septa are porotic and have concave profiles. Periodontal disease.

T12 has lumbar-type facet joints.

There is a porotic facet on the L sacral ala and on the L transverse process of L5, implying a fibrous articulation existed between the

2 in-vivo. Partial sacralisation of L5. The articulation seems to have permitted some movement at the lumbo-sacral joint - there is eburnation of the left L5/S1 facet joint.

CN42 There is an osteophyte on the anterior/superior margin of the sacral face of the L sacro-iliac joint which articulates with a porotic area on the ilium.

The 3rd metacarpals lack their styloid processes.

CN43 T12 has lumbar-type facet joints.

CN44 Forearm bones and left tibia sacrificed for radiocarbon determination 10/3/95 and 26/7/95.

CN45 The interdental septa are porotic with flattened profiles. Periodontal disease.

The bodies of T11, either T9 or 10, and one middle/upper thoracic vertebra show healed compression fractures; there is anterior wedging of T11 and T9/10 and more marked wedging of the fractured middle/upper thoracic vertebra. L2 and 3 also show healed compression fractures of their bodies but as the fractured areas are confined to the middle portions of the centra there is no kyphosis here.

The L 11th rib shows a united fracture 2cm from its head and, a L middle rib shows a united fracture 4cm from its head. The fractures are bridged by woven bone callus indicating that they occurred shortly prior to death.

There is a probable united fracture near the lateral end of the L clavicle; the injury clearly occurred long before death as the callus is smooth and thoroughly remodelled. The orientation of the fracture line is difficult to discern either grossly or radiographically, but it seems likely that it runs through the lateral joint surface approximately parallel to the long axis of the bone. The L acromion is missing so it is not possible to ascertain whether this too was injured.

The bones show dark red-brown staining.

CN47 The course of the fused metopic suture is clearly visible as a line of pitted bone.

This burial has finds number c2207, which corresponds to both burials CN47 and CN48 (numbers UU and VV on the old numbering scheme (Bell 1987)). On the plan CN47 is shown as small child/infant sized, whereas CN48 is adult/adolescent sized. Only one individual is represented by the bones labelled c2207 - an infant aged about 10 months, so it must be CN47 rather than CN48. The remains of CN48 seem to have got lost. According to the burial list CN47 and CN48 may be Ann Vescy (d. 1687) and her brother Ralph Vescy (d. 1695) respectively: this is impossible as CN47 cuts CN48 and hence must the the later of the 2 burials. (Incidentally, the interim report (Henderson 1987) refers to VV (=CN48) as a very incomplete infant skeleton; this must be an error in view of the drawing of the burial on the plan as clearly adult/adolescent sized.)

EE002 Both femora bear a third trochanter.

EE003 There is crowding of the maxillary and mandibular dentition.

The maxillary M2s have rather reduced mesio-distal widths, producing rather narrow teeth.

L6 shows unilateral left-sided spondylolysis; as might be anticipated there are no signs of spondylolisthesis.

Both femora bear a third trochanter.

There is an unhealed linear cut on the L parietal bone, running parallel with the sagittal suture, about 6cm from it; its lower end terminates in the area of the L lambdoid suture. The edges of the cut are straight, clean and well-defined, and the cut surfaces are flat and fairly smooth. There is some post-mortem distortion of the posterior part of the skull so that the edges of the cut no longer line up together. There is some breaking away of the internal table on the lateral side of the cut so that the edge of the lesion is bevelled here. There is a probable perimortal fracture running for about 3cm medially from the upper terminus of the cut.

The cut edges do not show polished surfaces and careful examination under a low-power binocular microscope failed to reveal evidence for parallel scratch marks. Both a polished appearence and the presence of parallel scratch marks are frequent findings in instances of unhealed injuries from edged weapons but despite their absence, the linearity of the cut and the flat, clearly defined cut surfaces are clearly indicative of an unhealed blade injury. The breaking away of small fragment(s) of bone leaving a bevelled edge internally is also a frequent finding in blade injuries (Wenham 1989). Since there is no evidence for healing, the cut must have occurred at or around time of death, and it seems that the cerebral injury which must have resulted was cause of death.

Left humerus and both radii sacrificed for radiocarbon dating 30-1-94 and 26/7/95.

EE004 L5 articulates with the L sacral ala via a joint surface on its transverse process - partial sacralisation of L5.

The L foramen transversarium of the atlas is incomplete.

There is severe (grade III) osteoarthritis of the 1st joint of the R ring finger: the joint surfaces have been totally destroyed leaving rough, irregular surfaces, and there are large marginal osteophytes. No other R hand bones show osteoarthritis; the isolated nature and the severity of the changes suggest local trauma as a cause.

The R 11th rib has an oblique fracture 2cm from its vertebral end. Firmly healed with minimal deformity but much callus. A fragment of another R rib also shows a united fracture.

The weight-bearing parts of the L acetabulum are porotic and show what appear to be minor fissure fractures. A large supra-acetabular cyst (Wells 1976) is also present, measuring about 4 x 3cm on an a-p radiograph; a post-mortem defect reveals that its internal surface is of fairly smooth cancellous bone. There are several smaller supra-acetabular cysts in the right acetabulum. All communicate with the joint space.

EE005 The R foramen transversarium of C7 is incomplete and is larger than its (complete) L-side counterpart.

EE006 The atlas vertebra shows spina bifida.

EE007 The mandibular canines are impacted. The maxillary canines have erupted normally.

There is a depression in the lingual side on the mandible near the border of the socket of the R M2. The hole has smooth borders and exposes the distal root of the M2. No sign of infection.

Left femur sacrificed for radiocarbon determination 30/1/95.

EE010 The box containing these bones is labelled 'DB15 or 17'. DB15, which corresponds to EE014, is a child; the present bones are adult so cannot be part of EE14. Thus they must be old number 17 (which corresponds to EE010) not DB15.

There is slight wedging of the body of T11, its anterior height is 9mm less than its posterior height.

Large, robust bones.

EE013 This skeleton was found with a chalice and paten and is said on the plan to be 'Roger Firby 11th November 1464'. Robert Firby (not Roger), canon of Haltemprice and vicar of Wharram Percy, died in 1464 and requested burial in the 'quire' of the church. Radiocarbon dating indicates that the identification of Burial EE013 as Robert Firby is incorrect.

On the plan a skull is shown as present but now seems lost.

Both third metacarpals lack their styloid processes.

Bones stained red/brown.

Right femur and tibia sacrificed for radiocarbon determination 30/1/95 and 26/7/95.

EE014 The pattern of dental eruption in this individual is slightly unusual: in the permanent dentition the M2s are fully erupted but the canines are not; the maxillary deciduous molars have been shed, the mandibular ones have not. In addition, the pre-molars are at an earlier stage of development than might have been anticipated given the state of development of the anterior dentition.

The skull is very hyperbrachycranic, having a cranial index of 115.8. There is certainly some post-mortem distortion, resulting in a reduced cranial length, but this is fairly minor. The mandibular condyles fit the glenoid fossae in the skull, hence it is unlikely that cranial breadth is significantly affected by post-mortem distortion. The in-vivo cranial index must have been well over 100. Viewed from above, the cranium appears globular in shape, with very prominent parietal eminences. The occipital bone is rather flattened. The endocranial impressions of the cerebral convolutions and the grooves for the meningial arteries are not particularly marked, and there is no separation of the sutures, observations which suggest that there was no increase in intra-cranial pressure as might be expected in, for example, hydrocephalus. There is no evidence for premature closure of coronal or lambdoid sutures which may cause hyperbrachycrany. In summary, the reason why this skull is so hyperbrachycranic is unclear but there is no evidence for any abnormality of suture closure or increased intra-cranial pressure.

EE015 Very thin, atrophied, almost edentulous mandible: the teeth must have been lost a considerable time prior to death. Probably a very elderly individual, well over 60 years at death.

Very light and rarified bones - osteoporosis.

There is a healed fracture one third of the way from the distal end of the shaft of the L 3rd metatarsal. It is united by woven bone callus. The following also show fractures: 9L ribs (2 of which show 2 fractures each), all but one in their mid-shaft areas (the exception is the L 1st rib which is fractured just distal to the articular facet for the vertebral transverse process), 2R ribs (a floating rib which is fractured about 1cm from its head and a middle rib fractured through the articular facet for the vertebral transverse process) and 5 unsided rib fragments. All fracture lines are clearly visible and are united with woven bone callus.

It seems likely that all the above fractures occurred in a single incident, shortly before death. Rates of fracture healing vary greatly between individuals but reference to the discussion of Revell (1986, 207f) suggests that the fractures in EE015 occurred within about 2 months of death.

T2 and 3 are fused at their facet joints. No trace of disease or injury.

There a smooth, slightly raised area of bone on the ectocranial surface of the frontal bone; its surface is indistinguishable from the normal bone. Uncertain cause, probably not pathological.

Green staining on R temple area.

EE016 The L transverse process of L1 is missing; in its place is a joint surface - presumably this articulated with a transverse process present as a separate ossicle - i.e. a small lumbar rib. The R transverse process is reduced in size.

There is a shallow erosion approx 1 x 0.7cm on the visceral surface of the proximal third of a right middle rib. There is a little woven bone formation here too. Two right mid/lower ribs, the right 11th and the left 12th ribs show patches of woven bone toward their proximal ends. The right 11th rib also shows a shallow erosion in this area. A fragment from the sternal third of a rib of indeterminate side shows a deposit of new bone on the visceral surface. The deposit is somewhat remodelled and a post-depositional break reveals that it consists of two thin layers of bone. This individual proved negative for tubercle baccillus DNA (Mays *et al.* 2002b).

EE017 There are small areas of 'labyrinth' type lesions (i.e. superficial, sinuous resorptive lesions) on the internal surface of the occipital bone in the L and R cerebral fossae.

EE018 L3 and 4 both show spondylolysis. No signs of spondylolisthesis.

A L foot sesamoid is bipartite; only one part of the bone has been recovered, and the surface which adjoined the other part of the ossicle is porotic, giving the impression that fibrous union existed between the two parts.

There is periostitis on the medial/posterior angle of the L and R tibiae, in the midshaft areas. The deposits are of somewhat remodelled bone.

There is a probable fissure fracture running in an approximately anterior/posterior orientation across the lateral part of the distal joint surface of the L tibia. There is slight upward displacement of the lateral fragment.

The R hamate lacks its unciform process. There is a porotic area at the site it normally occupies, suggesting that it was present as a separate ossicle (which was not recovered) joined to the main part of the bone by soft tissue. Alternatively it may be an un-united fracture of the unciform process.

The intermediate and terminal phalanges of the L little toe are fused together; those of the R little toe are not.

EE019 The R mandibular canine bears a rudimentary 2nd root on its buccal side.

Left femur sacrificed for radiocarbon determination 30/1/95.

EE020 The interdental septa are porotic and those in the molar areas are also concave. Periodontal disease, more marked in molar areas.

There are the beginnings of a sutura mendosa at the R asterion.

Left tibia sacrificed for radiocarbon dating 20/1/95. Right femur sacrificed for replicate 2-12-96.

EE022 There is an extra facet on the anterior/lateral margin of the L intermediate cuneiform; presumably it articulated with a similar facet on the lateral cuneiform, but the relevant area of this bone is missing.

There is a crescentic, porotic area on the anterior margin of the anterior facet on the L calcaneus. Probably the site of fibrous attachment of a calcaneum secundarium. R calcaneus normal.

A L rib shows an oblique united fracture 5cm from its vertebral end, moderate callus, strongly healed.

EE024 Porotic interdental septa, they are also concave in profile in the molar regions.

Periodontal disease, most marked in the molar areas.

EE025 The R maxillary canine has failed to erupt and lies slanted under the premolars so that the root tip rests under the R maxillary PM2 and its crown under the sockets for the R incisors. The L canine has erupted normally.

EE026 There is marked super-eruption of the R maxillary M1.

The interdental septa are porotic and have irregular profiles. Periodontal disease.

Fragmentary skeleton, many bones show fresh breaks.

Humeri and right tibia sacrificed for radiocarbon determination 30/1/95.

EE027 The interdental septa are porotic and have concave profiles. Periodontal disease.

The maxillary I2s are reduced in size.

EE028 The L molars and premolars show heavy deposits of calculus, partially covering their occlusal surfaces. The deposits on the R side teeth are not as heavy and the occlusal surfaces are not affected. Dental wear is also greater on the R side. It thus seems that the L side of the mouth was not used for chewing for some time before death. Reasons for this are unclear.

The interdental septa in the molar areas are pitted and concave. Periodontal disease.

EE029 There is a deposit of unremodelled bone upon the anterior surface of the body of S2 and smaller deposits on the bodies of S3 and 4. Periostitis.

There is a porotic area on the tuberosity of the R navicular. Probably the site of attachment of an os tibiale externum. The L navicular is missing post-mortem.

EE030 Porotic, flattened interdental septa. Periodontal disease.

There is slight crowding of the mandibular anterior dentition.

There is an oval depressed area of sclerotic, porotic bone at the centre of the proximal joint surface of the R radius. The lesion measures approximately 7 x 5mm, is 1-2mm deep and its edges are sharply delimited. Possibly osteochondritis dissecans.

L frontal foramen.

EE031 Much super-eruption of teeth.

There is severe osteoarthritis of the R proximal humerus - the joint surface is porotic and eburnated, there are large cystic cavities in the subchondral bone which open onto the joint surface and there is heavy marginal lipping inferiorly. The glenoid cavity shows heavy lipping posteriorly - a flange of bone forms a posterior extension to the joint surface and is sufficiently large to touch the acromion. The inferior part of the glenoid cavity is normal but the remainder is porotic and eburnated. The anterior surface of the acromion shows bony lipping, porosis and eburnation -it must have articulated with the humeral head. Rearticulation of the joint shows that there was severe upward/posterior displacement of the humeral head with coracoid as well as acromial impingement. As the humeral head still articulates with part of the glenoid cavity this must be considered as humeral subluxation rather than dislocation. There is a depression in the medial aspect of the surgical neck area of the humerus. This was probably a result of pressure from the inferior edge of the glenoid cavity due to the abnormal conformation of the gleno-humeral articulation.

The acromial face of the R acromio-clavicular joint is obliterated by the heavy spurring on the acromion, and the clavicular face is porotic in its posterior part and eburnated in its anterior part. Re-articulation of the bones suggests that there was dislocation of the acromio-clavicular joint with upward/anterior displacement of the lateral part of the clavical so that the anterior part of its joint surface articulated with the displaced humeral head.

The subluxation of the R gleno-humeral joint and the dislocation of the R acromio-clavicular joint was doubtless due to trauma to the shoulder area.

There are severe degenerative changes in the cervical spine: there is eburnation of facet joints and highly porotic, sclerotic centra with eburnation of some Luschka joints. Perhaps these degenerative changes were precipitated by the same traumatic incident which caused the shoulder injury.

There is a smooth-walled erosion in the right side of the body of C4, 5mm deep, at the transverse foramen. The transverse foramen here is enlarged. There is also a smooth-walled erosion of the left transverse foramen on the axis vertebra. The subchondral bone here is paper thin and at its thinnest point a small pore communicates with the superior articular surface. Differential diagnosis rests between tortuosities of the vertbral arteries and aneurisms. The distinction between these two conditions is difficult but given the severe trauma suffered by this individual, and that multilevel tortuosities are rare (Kricun *et al.* 1992), aneurisms are the favoured option.

EE032 There is porosis of interdental septa and slight alveolar resorption. Slight periodontal disease.

There are fractures of both parietal bones, the frontal bone and L temporal bone. The longest fracture line extends from the squamous part of the L temporal bone across the L parietal, onto the frontal bone, crossing the coronal suture 27mm from the bregma, terminating at the R orbital roof. The next longest fracture zig-zags across the R parietal and R side of the frontal bone from a point below the R parietal eminence to the R frontal eminence. The lines of several other fractures are visible in the bregma area. In some areas (e.g. most of the two longest fractures described above) there seems to be slight separation of fractured edges, but in others this is not the case. All fractures show healing, with some callus, particularly on the endocranial aspects. The callus is of well remodelled bone. There is some pitted bone in the bregma area, indicating infection. This pitting is confined to the ectocranial surface - there is no sign of infection on the internal surface of the cranium. The pitted bone is fairly well remodelled, suggesting the infection subsided some time prior to death. There is a tranverse depression on the vertex of the skull running parallel to and just behind the coronal suture. This suggests that the cranial injuries were caused by a heavy beam or such-like which fell across the skull just behind the bregma. The state of healing suggests that the individual survived the incident for at least several months and perhaps years, and there is no reason to suggests that cause of death was in any way related to the cranial injury.

EE036 Thick cranium, not pathological.

EE037. There is retention of the R maxillary deciduous canine (although it has fallen from its socket post-mortem). The permanent canine has erupted distal to the deciduous tooth and the R PM2 is absent congenitally. The L mandibular canine is impacted against the I2.

There is an infra-bony pocket around the retained deciduous canine. Periodontal infection.

There is a united fracture about 2cm from the end of the neural spine of T1, with slight downward displacement of the fragment. Clay-shoveller's fracture.

L1 has T12-type facet joints.

L6 is an extra segment rather than lumbarisation of the 1st sacral vertebra.

EE038 The interdental septa are porotic and have flattened or slightly concave profiles. Periodontal disease.

Both humeri and both scapulae sacrificed for radiocarbon determination 20/12/94 and 26/7/95.

EE039 The L femur bears a third trochanter.

There is a bifid rib, the bifurcation being near the sternal end.

L frontal foramen.

EE040 There is a bony protruberance on the R side of the occipital bone, 1-1.5cm from the midline between the superior and inferior curved lines. It resembles a small mastoid process and is about 1.5cm long.

EE041 Porotic, concave interdental septa in molar areas. Localised periodontal disease.

T12 has lumbar type facet joints.

Black/grey staining on leg bones.

EE042 The permanent maxillary M1s show large Carabelli cusps, there are small ones on the deciduous maxillary M2s.

EE043 The maxillary and mandibular M1s are smaller than the M2s.

The R maxillary canine is unerupted. It is impacted against the root of the I2, which shows some resorption due to the pressure exerted by its impacted neighbour.

EE044 Both foramen transversaria on the atlas are incomplete.

EE045 The R maxillary molars were lost in-vivo and the alveolar bone here is very resorbed suggesting that they were lost long prior to death. Consistent with this the R mandibular molars have heavy calculus deposits which partially cover their occlusal surfaces.

The R mandibular dentition shows marked super-eruption.

The interdental septa are porotic - periodontal disease.

T11 has a smooth, thick osteophyte on the R side of its body – 'bone former' type change.

EE046 There are infra-bony pockets around the maxillary M3s. The interdental septa in the molar areas are concave and porotic. Periodontal disease confined to posterior dental arcade.

There is ankylosis of C2 and 3 (at the facet joints and the R sides of the centra) and of T3-5 (at the facet joints and anterior parts of centra). Probably congenital block vertebrae.

There are thick, smooth osteophytes on the R sides of the bodies of T5-7; they articulate with one another but are not fused. The head of the 7th rib bears a large osteophyte which articulates with an osteophyte on the body of T6. 'Bone former' type changes.

EE050 The maxillary permanent M1s bear small Carabelli cusps.

EE054 There is slight, unremodelled periostitis on the internal surface of the L scapula, near the glenoid cavity, and on the lateral surfaces of the ilia.

EE056 There is a large cavity on the right side of the superior surface of the body of L1, drained by a sinus piercing an osteophyte which unites the bodies of L1 and T12. There is also a small lytic lesion on the superior surface of the left pedicle of L1. The superior part of the body of T12 is destroyed, as are the centra of T9-11 almost in their entirety. The lower parts of the body of T8 are also destroyed. There are lytic lesions on the superior surface of the body of T8, the superior surface of T7 and the inferior surface of T6. There is ankylosis of the vertebral bodies in this part of the spine (T7-L1) with approximately 90 degree kyphosis. The left 6th-11th ribs show lytic lesions at their heads and/or thickening of their proximal parts between the heads and the tuberosities. The proximal part of only one right rib is present; it shows a lytic lesion at its head and thickening of the adjacent shaft. The surfaces of all lytic lesions are of slightly sclerotic trabecular bone, and new bone formation is negligible. Tuberculosis. DNA analyses (Mays *et al.* 2001a) confirm the diagnosis and indicate the presence of *mycobacterium tuberculosis* rather than *mycobacterium bovis*.

EE060 2 unsided rib fragments show fractures; they are well healed with moderate amounts of thoroughly remodelled callus.

EE061 There is asymmetric closure of the coronal and lambdoid sutures, in each case closure is more advanced on the L than the R side. For the coronal suture the R side is open (Perizonius (1984) stage 0) whereas the L side is obliterated endocranially (Perizonius (1984) stage 4) and is closed but still visible (Perizonius stage 1) ectocranially. For the lambdoid suture the L side is at stage 1 ectocranially and at stage 4 endocranially, the R side is stage 0-1 ectocranially and stage 0 endocranially. There is slight cranial asymmetry, the L side being shorter than the R, suggesting restricted growth on the L side due to earlier cranial synostosis here.

EE062 The atlas vertebra shows spina bifida.

The transverse processes of L1 are present as separate ossicles which articulate with the neural arch via joint surfaces - rudimentary lumbar ribs.

There is periostitis over the general surface of the femora, tibiae, fibulae, lateral surfaces of the ilia, calcanei, metatarsals (particularly the 5th metatarsals), the humeri (mainly towards the distal ends), the radii and ulnae (particularly near the inter-osseous borders), the posterior and anterior surfaces of the scapulae, 9L ribs (mainly near the sternal ends), metacarpals, the middle phalanx of the left little finger and the proximal phalanges of both thumbs. Post-mortem breaks show that the deposits of new bone may be up to several millimetres thick; they are thickest on the bones of the legs and forearms and on the sternal ends of the ribs. On the femora and tibiae deposits are particularly marked at lines of musculo-tendinous insertions - the linea asperae and soleal lines. Most basal hand phalanges show bony deposition at the flexor insertions; these are the only signs of disease in most of these elements. The vertebrae, skull and mandible are not affected. X-ray confirms that the changes consist of the deposition of new bone upon normal cortices. The medullary cavities are normal. Radiographically, deposits range from those which are separated from the underlying cortex by a linear radiolucency to those where the depositions of new bone are firmly merged with the normal cortical bone.

The symmetry of the lesions is striking. The only possible exception to the symmetrical pattern of bone deposits is in the ribs, where only left ribs seem to be affected. The right rib-cage is, however, much less complete than the left so this asymmetry in the lesion distribution here may be at least in part an artifact of the reduced survival of right costal elements. The most likely diagnosis for this individual is hypertrophic osteoarthropathy. DNA analyses proved positive for M. tuberculosis complex DNA, and in addition showed the presence of M. tuberculosis rather than M. bovis. It thus seems likely that pulmonary tuberculosis was responsible for the hypertrophic osteoarthropathy in this case.

EE064 Much super eruption of teeth.

The interdental septa are porotic and have irregular profiles. Periodontal disease.

EE065 There are extra epiphyses at the distal ends of the 1st metatarsals.

EE066 There is hypoplasia of the occlusal surfaces of the crowns of the M1s - they have many more than the usual numbers of pits and fissures and are mottled in appearance. Perhaps this defective enamel precipitated the large caries cavity present in the occlusal surface of the L mandibular M1.

EE067 The interdental septa are concave and porotic and there is localised alveolar resorption. Severe periodontal disease.

Much crowding of mandibular anterior dentition.

EE070 There is a sixth sacral segment which represents an extra segment, not sacralisation of the last lumbar vertebra. It is completely sacralised at the transverse processes, partially at the body, but it has facet joints which articulate with some on S2.

There is a remodelled deposit of new bone on the lateral surface of the R fibula about 1/4-1/3 of the way down the bone and there is a smaller deposit on the R tibia at a similar level. Periostitis.

There is a depression on each side of the internal surface of the mandible, in the sub-lingual fossae, below the sockets for the canines and premolars. The depression is more pronounced on the left side. Anterior lingual depressions of the type described by Shafer *et al.* (1983, 36).

Congenitally absent L maxillary PM1, R maxillary M3 also missing.

EE071 Two R middle ribs are fused by a smooth bridge of bone located between their heads and their tuberosities. The rest of the ribs are normal, as are the vertebrae. Congenital fusion.

EE072 The M1s are reduced in size, in the mandible they are smaller than the M2s, in the maxillae they are of a similar size to the M2s. The maxillary I2s are also reduced in size.

There is a sub-periosteal deposit of bone on the medial surface of the L femur about 1/3 of the way down the shaft. It is of woven bone, although some shows early signs of remodelling. Periostitis.

The R maxillary I1 has a grooved cingulum.

EE073 There is a raised knob of bone on the L side of the posterior arch of the atlas. Its surface is smooth and it rises about 0.5cm proud of the vertebral arch. It seems to articulate with a depression of smooth, slightly sclerotic bone just behind the L occipital condyle. The R sides of the atlas and occiput are normal.

The L spheno-parietal suture is obliterated.

EE076 The L molars have large calculus deposits partially covering their occlusal surfaces. The other teeth are little affected. It thus seems that no chewing occurred on the L side of the mouth for some time before death. The reasons for this are unclear.

EE077 The interdental septa are porotic and some have concave profiles. There is an infra-bony pocket at the socket of the L mandibular canine and there is some alveolar resorption. Periodontal disease.

The R mandibular canine is rotated 90 degrees from its normal orientation so that its lingual surface faces mesially.

EE079 Very robust bones.

C2 and 3 are fused at their facet joints. Probably a congenital anomaly.

Most thoracic and lumbar vertebrae have short, thick osteophytes on their centra, on the R sides in the case of the thoracic vertebrae, near the anterior margins in the case of the lumbar vertebrae. There is bony spurring on the linea asperae and lesser trochanters of the femora, the soleal line and tuberosity of the tibia, just anterior to the distal joint surfaces of the fibulae, at the insertions of the Achilles tendons on the calcanei, on the tuberosities of the ribs and on the tuberosities of the 5th metatarsals. There is also some smooth bony lipping around the glenoid cavities. 'Bone former' type changes.

There is a low ovoid area of raised bone on the lateral side of the L femur in the midshaft area. The lesion measures about 70x22mm with its long axis parallel to that of the bone. It rises 3-4mm proud of the normal cortex, but its surface is heavily eroded post-mortem - the trabecular bone within is exposed and it is not possible to determine the original appearence of the surface of the lesion. X-ray shows that the lesion lies on the surface of the normal cortex. The post-mortem damage means that it is not possible to determine the cause of the lesion.

Deep red-brown staining on the bones.

EE080 The interdental septa in the molar areas are porotic and have concave profiles. Localised periodontal disease.

There is marked super-eruption of the R maxillary M1.

C6 and 7 are fused at their centra and the R sides of their neural arches. Probably congenital block vertebrae.

The L sides of the bodies of L4 and 5 bear large, smooth osteophytes which articulate with one another but are not fused. 'Bone former' type changes.

L5 shows spondylolysis, no sign of spondylolisthesis.

There are pitted, depressed areas of sclerotic trabecular bone on the plantar parts of both faces of the L and R lateral cuneiform-third metatarsal joints. Bilateral non-osseous tarsal coalition (Regan *et al.* 1999).

There is some dark red/brown staining on the bones.

EE082 Flattened, porotic interdental septa. Periodontal disease.

Both foramen transversaria on the atlas are incomplete.

EE083 Slight bathrocrany. There are many wormian bones in the lambdoid suture.

EE085 Porotic interdental septa with flattened or concave profiles. Periodontal disease.

The R transverse process of L1 exists as a separate ossicle which articulates with the neural arch via a joint surface. Unilateral lumbar rib.

C6 is cleft at the R pedicle and the neural arch is asymmetrical, with increased distance between the facet joints and the centrum on the cleft side. Its superior R facet joint lies on the inner side of the neural arch and the R inferior facet joint of C5 is located on the outer aspect of the neural arch. As a result the C5/6 articulation was rather less stable than normal with a probable tendency for C5 to twist to the left. That this placed an increased strain on the C5/6 articulation is demonstrated by eburnation and porosis of the R Luschka joint here. The R pedicle on C7 is longer than the left, an asymmetry which is similar in direction, if not in degree, to than of C6. Conversely the R pedicle of C5 is shorter than the L.

EE086 The R maxillary M1 has a Carabelli cusp.

L pterygoid plate foramen.

EE090 The mandibular deciduous canines bear lingual tubercles.

EE091 There is a tubercle on the buccal/mesial cusp on the R maxillary deciduous M1.

Black/grey staining on parts of the skull.

EE092 There is an abscess at the apex of the right maxillary M1 which penetrates the maxillary sinus. There is no evidence of new bone formation within the sinus but the floor of the sinus is deeper than that on the left side. There is perforation of the inferior part of the medial wall of the sinus adjacent to the opening from the abscess at the medial root of the first molar. The borders of this perforation are of sclerotic trabecular bone. It is not possible to determine the upper limit of the lytic area due to post-mortem damage. Perhaps this represents bone resorption as a result of pressure from a large radicular cyst situated at the medial root of the M1.

EE093 There is a large infra-bony pocket around the L maxillary PM2. The interdental septa are porotic with concave profiles. Periodontal disease.

L frontal foramen.

EE096 There is a foramen on the palate just distal to each deciduous I2. They are 3mm diameter with smooth walls. The roots of the deciduous I2s are visible through them. Probably not pathological.

EE098 Large, robust bones.

There is a deposit of well remodelled bone on the proximal half of the R fibula and on the lateral side of the R tibia, near the proximal end. Periostitis.

There is a smooth bony exostosis on the posterior surface on the L femur on the linea aspera where it divides into the 2 ridges which delimit the popliteal space. The exostosis is a flat flange on bone with its long axis parallel to that of the bone. It is about 2cm wide and rises 1.5cm proud of the normal cortex. Myositis ossificans. 'Rider's bone'.

EE099 The R acetabulum is rather shallow. There are several supra-acetabular cysts (Wells 1976) on its superior margin which communicate with the joint space.

The R maxillary PM1 has three roots.

EE101 The R maxillary M3 is impacted against the neighbouring M2. There is localised alveolar resorption and the interdental septa are porotic and have concave profiles. Periodontal disease.

L pterygoid plate foramen.

The petro-squamous suture of the R temporal bone is still visible although it is fused.

G251 The skull found in this grave near the knees of the skeleton appears to represent redeposited material and does not belong to this individual.

G253 Two unsided rib fragments show un-united fractures. There is woven bone callus at the broken ends indicating that the injuries occurred shortly prior to death.

Three unsided rib fragments show deposits of woven bone on their visceral surfaces. This may be indicative of a chest infection perhaps introduced by the same incident which caused the rib fractures.

G254 The R mandibular M3 is impacted against the M2.

G265 The R maxillary I2 is congenitally absent and the neighbouring canine is unerupted and is orientated medially about 30 degrees to horizontal, with the crown lying impacted against the root of the R I2.

The roots of the maxillary I1s are very short.

The mandibular central incisors are both rotated so that the medial parts of the crowns are turned lingually and the lateral parts turned labially. 'Wing teeth'.
There are large infra-bony pockets at the sockets of the mandibular L M3 and R M2. Periodontal disease.

The R foramen transversarium of the axis is incomplete.

There is bony spurring on the patellae at the insertions of the quadriceps femores, near the anterior margins of the distal joint surfaces of the fibulae, on the calcanei at the insertions of the Achilles tendons, on the ridge on the plantar surface of the L cuboid and at the margins of the glenoid cavity of the R scapula. 'Bone former' type changes.

There is florid bony lipping at the L talo-calcaneal and talo-navicular joints. Both joints show grade II osteoarthritis. These changes were probably induced by trauma to the L ankle.

There is a small cystic defect on the medial side of the head of the R 1st metatarsal and the proximal hallucial phalanx is deflected laterally. Unilateral hallux valgus.

There are the beginnings of a sutura mendosa at the R asterion.

Left tibia sacrificed for carbon-14 determination 23-2-95.

G275 The interdental septa are porotic and there is some localised alveolar resorption. Periodontal disease.

L5 shows spondylolysis, no sign of spondylolisthesis.

There is downward displacement of the L femoral head so that the L femoral length is 10mm shorter than the R. The pit for the ligamentum teres lies rather closer to the inferior margin of the joint surface than is normal. There is shortening of the inferior part of the femoral neck - the distance between the lesser trochanter and the margin of the joint surface is 29mm as opposed to 48mm on the R femur. Slipped capital epiphysis.

L frontal foramen.

Left tibia sacrificed for radiocarbon determination 23-2-95.

The medullary cavities in the clavicles and forearm bones are very narrow and these bones are dense on X-ray. The vertebral bodies show band-like radiodensities near their superior and inferior surfaces with normal bone in between. There is also sclerosis of trabecular bone in the os coxae. These changes are suggestive of renal osteodystrophy. Slipped capital epiphysis, which this individual also displays, is a recognised complication of renal osteodystrophy.

G278 Both transverse processes of L1 and the R transverse process of T12 exist as separate ossicles, articulating with the main parts of the vertebrae via smooth joint surfaces. The ossicles from L1 constitute lumbar ribs.

T7 and 8 are fused at their facet joints and bodies. There is anterior wedging of the body of T8 to produce 25 degree kyphosis here. Compression fracture of the body of T8.

The bodies of L4 and 5 are completely ankylosed and there is a large, thick osteophyte on the R sides of their bodies. The facet joints are normal. There is a large, smooth osteophyte on the R side of the body of S1 and spurring on the calcanei at the insertions of the Achilles tendons. 'Bone former' type changes.

There is a flat, sclerotic, calcified plaque of irregular shape whose maximum dimensions are 3 x 1.5cm. Possibly a pleural calcification.

There is well remodelled sub-periosteal new bone on the L tibia, mainly confined to the subcutaneous surface. Periostitis.

The distal joint surfaces of both 1st metatarsals are both deflected laterally and there are cystic cavities at the medial margins of their heads. Bilateral hallux valgus.

There is a large unilocular cyst in the R ilium adjacent to the superior surface of the R acetabulum. It communicates with the joint surface via a tiny pore. There are small cystic cavities adjacent to the superior margin of the L acetabulum. Supra-acetabular cysts (Wells 1976).

Right femur sacrificed for radiocarbon determination 23-2-95 and 26/7/95.

G279 Porotic interdental septa. Periodontal disease.

Super-eruption of molars.

A R middle-lower rib shows a united fracture one quarter of the way from the vertebral end. There is a moderate quantity of well remodelled callus. The fracture probably occurred long before death.

The mandible has a double aperture for the infra-dental canal on the R side.

There is a pit on the medial facet of the proximal joint surface of each tibia. The pits are lined with sclerotic bone and measure 8 x 5 x 4mm deep. Osteochondritis dissecans.

Distal two-thirds of right femur sacrificed for radiocarbon dating 23-2-95.

G296 The interdental septa are porotic and some have flattened or concave profiles. There is localised alveolar resorption. Periodontal disease.

There is a lytic lesion whose margins are sharply demarcated on the superior surface of the L sacral ala. Its maximum diameter is 4cm, and the superficial part of the sacral ala is destroyed. This lesion communicates with a large cavity within the transverse process of S1. The bone surfaces in the lytic areas show very sparse, sclerotic trabeculae. The cavity within the sacral ala communicates with the bone surface posteriorly via several holes. There is a deposit of pitted sub-periosteal new bone on the anterior part of the L transverse process of S1 adjacent to the superficial lytic lesion. The sacro-iliac joint is normal. The axial skeleton and major long-bones were radiographed but no additional lytic lesions were noted, save for a radiolucency, approximately 5mm diameter, in the body of C7. No changes were visible grossly on this bone.

Diagnosis is problematic. Lytic lesions in the spine are characteristic of tuberculosis, but separate foci in a cervical and sacral vertebra would be rather atypical.

The following sites show slight deposits of woven bone: the shaft of the R tibia (predominantly on the lateral surface), the left fibula (very slight), the lateral surface of the L tibia one third of the way from the distal end, the left and right proximal femora, the radii (mainly on the distal metaphyses, but also toward their proximal ends, the ulnae (mainly on their inter-osseous borders but also a little near their proximal ends), the shafts of the L 1st-4th metacarpals and the R third metacarpal (mainly on their volar surfaces), and the volar surfaces of both proximal pollucial phalanges. The deposits take the form of small, thin patches of bone which show no remodelling.

The symmetrical distribution of thin, new bone deposits suggests hypertrophic osteoarthropathy. Given the age of the individual and the fact that lesions are active and apparently in an early stage suggests secondary rather than primary disease.

The question arises as to whether the lytic spinal lesions are related to the primary condition which caused hypertrophic osteoarthropathy. It is unclear whether the lytic lesions are infectious or neoplastic in origin. Principal causes of hypertrophic osteoarthropathy are lung cancer or chronic lung infections. Perhaps the lytic lesions are metastases from pulmonary carcinoma or infection.

There are pitted, depressed sclerotic areas on both faces of the L and R 3rd metatarsal-lateral cuneiform joints - non-osseous tarsal coalitions (Regan *et al.* 1999).

There is an ossicle in the L masto-occipital suture.

There is a large, bipartite ossicle at the lambda.

G297 The iliac face of the R sacro-iliac joint is double faceted. The sacral face of the joint is missing post-mortem.

Right tibia sacrificed for radiocarbon determination 23-2-95.

Porotic, concave interdental septa - periodontal disease.

G298 There is pitting on the ectocranial surface of the R parietal bone, adjacent to the sagittal suture, 1-2cm from the lambda, with slight thickening of the bone here. Porotic hyperostosis. There is also cribra orbitalia of the porotic type.

G303 L6 shows spina bifida, as do all the sacral vertebrae. L6 has a porotic area on the inferior surface of its L transverse process which articulates with a similar area on the L sacral ala.
Probably a fibrous connection existed between L6 and S1 at this point.

There is well remodelled periostitis over the medial and lateral surfaces of the L tibia and over the general surface of the L fibula.

There is a united fracture one third of the way from the vertebral end of a middle R rib. It is firmly healed with little callus; it has the appearance of a fracture which occurred long before death.

Right femur and midshaft parts of left femur sacrificed for radiocarbon determination 23-2-95 and 26/7/95.

G304 The crown of the R maxillary M2 has a very reduced mesio-distal width. The L maxillary M2 is missing post-mortem.

There is an oval depression on the R parietal bone, 28mm from the coronal suture and 22mm from the lambdoid suture. There is no hole here but the bone fragments are pushed in so that their ends project about 5mm below the endocranial surface and the deepest point of the lesion. On the inner surface of the lesion the inner table of the skull has splintered away leaving the diploe visible.

The splintered parts are still attached to the sides of the lesion and point inwards - they must have injured the brain and overlying soft tissues. The fact that the splintered fragments are depressed inwards still attached to the skull indicates that the injury occurred in-vivo (or at least while the bone was still fresh) and this, together with the lack of healing, suggests that it is a perimortal injury, likely cause of death. The posterior side of the lesion slopes more steeply than the anterior side and the deepest point lies slightly to the posterior/left side of the lesion.

If the injury was a result of inter-personal violence then the blow was probably delivered using a blunt weapon with a fairly small contact area with the assailant standing behind and a little to the left of the victim. Alternatively it could be a result of accidental injury by an object falling on the head.

The L hypoglossal canal is divided by two bony bridges.

Femora, tibiae and humeri sacrificed for carbon-14 23-2-95.

G308 There is marked thickening of the cranial vault, with the diploe visible externally. Thickening is localised but it is difficult to determine the location on the cranial vault as the skull is very fragmentary, poorly preserved and incomplete.

G310 Porotic, flattened interdental septa in molar areas. Localised periodontal disease.

Crowding of mandibular anterior dentition.

There is a fissure fracture of the L fibula, running aproximately parallel to the long axis of the bone. It is located in the distal 4cm of the bone and is visible on both the lateral and medial surfaces (including the distal joint surface). The tibia is normal.

Two R middle ribs show fractures in their sternal thirds. The fractures are at very similar positions on both ribs - they are probably adjacent ribs. The fractures are united by smooth, well remodelled callus. A rib fragment of indeterminate side shows a united fracture of similar appearance, probably also towards the sternal end.

G314 L5 shows spina bifida.

Humeri, tibiae and femora sacrificed for radiocarbon determination 23-2-95.

G327 There is posterior angulation of the proximal third of the right humerus. The posterior surface of the bone here is smooth. A radiograph shows a horizontal line of calcification here. Possibly a united greenstick fracture.

There is a perforation on the occipital bone in the L cerebellar fossa. It is approximately circular, about 4-5mm with sharp edges. The bone is very thin in this area. There is no reactive bone. The lesion is clearly ante-mortem in origin but its precise cause is unclear. Some fragments of occipital bone and of the posterior parts of the parietal bones show a few localised deposits of woven bone. In some instances the woven bone deposit has partially flaked away post-mortem to reveal a depression in the underlying endocranial surface. There is no new bone deposition at the perforation in the occipital bone, but perhaps this has arisen as part of the same process as caused the other endocranial depressions. These changes may be indicative of intra-cranial infection or haemorrhage. Given the evidence of possible trauma to the humerus, it is tempting to speculate whether the cranial lesions were likewise due to trauma (?shaking), but given that the putative humerus fracture is well-healed whereas the endocranial lesions were active at time of death, it may well be that there was no connection between them.

G339 The lower parts of the skeleton are more poorly preserved than the upper parts.

G361 There is a smooth osteophyte on the R side of the superior margin of the body of a lower thoracic vertebra. 'Bone former' type osteophyte.

A sutura mendosa stretches from each asterion about halfway to the midline.

Left femur sacrificed for radiocarbon determination 23-2-95.

G363 The deciduous maxillary and mandibular I2s are absent congenitally, as are all 4 permanent I2s.

The mesial parts of the crowns of the deciduous mandibular canines are under-developed and the R also has a small accessory ridge on its distal side.

G370 There is a concave, crescentic, porotic area on the medial/anterior margin of the R calcaneus. The navicular is normal. Probably the site for fibrous attachment of a calcaneum secundarium. The L calcaneus is normal.

G377 There is a transverse depression across the vertex of the skull, just behind the bregma. Probably due to premature synostosis of the anterior part of the sagittal suture (Lin *et al.* 1998).

G379 The interdental septa are porotic and there is a large infra-bony pocket at the L mandibular canine. Periodontal disease.

There is an oval depression 14 x 9mm diameter on the L side of the frontal bone, 22mm from the midline and 32mm from the coronal suture. The depression lies in a pitted area which covers the central area of the ectocranial surface of the frontal bone. There is a bulge in the endocranial surface corresponding to the location of the depression on the outer surface. It seems probable that the oval lesion represents a well healed depressed fracture and that the pitting represents osteitis as a result of infection of the scalp in the region of the injury.

There is an area of remodelled periostitis on the lateral side of the R tibia, and slight periostitis on the L tibia.

The R foramen transversarium on the atlas is incomplete.

There is a large supra-acetabular cyst (Wells 1976) in the subchondral bone above the left acetabulum, and two above the right acetabulum. All communicate with the joint surface.

G381 The R maxillary I2 has a groove on the cingulum which extends onto the buccal surface of the root.

The interdental septa are porotic and concave in profile. Periodontal disease.

The lateral joint surface of the R clavicle is irregular. Its posterior part has been destroyed - here there is an irregular area of sclerotic bone. There is a fissure across the remaining (anterior) part of the joint surface. Possibly trauma to the acromio-clavicular joint. The acromial face of this joint is missing.

R frontal foramen.

G385 The interdental septa are porotic and, in the molar and premolar regions, they have concave profiles. Periodontal disease.

There is a raised, approximately oval, smooth bony projection on the ectocranial surface of the L parietal bone, 1cm from the parietal notch. It measures 7-10mm in diameter and rises about 5mm proud of the normal outer table. A button osteoma.

There is a smooth-walled cavity in the R side of the body of C4 adjacent to the foramen for the vertebral artery. It is a maximum of 7mm deep. On X-ray the lesion is revealed to possess thin, sclerotic borders. The lesion likely results from tortuosity of the vertebral artery.

L frontal foramen.

Both tibiae, right humerus and fibula shaft fragments sacrificed for radiocarbon determination 23-2-95 and 26/7/95.

G398 There is pitting on the proximal joint surfaces of both proximal hallucial phalanges. Probably not pathological.

There is superficial destruction of the lateral parts of the L zygomatic - in this area the bony trabeculae are very coarse and sclerotic. There is negligible bony regeneration. There is slight superficial destruction of the medial surface of the zygomatic and the bone here as a pitted surface. There is also pitting on the floor of the L orbit. These lesions seem indicative of infection, probably as a result of some overlying soft tissue lesion.

There is an approximately circular 3mm diameter cavity in the dorsal surface of the R third metacarpal, near the proximal end. Unknown cause.

There is a small deposit of woven bone on the lateral surface of the right tibia. Periostitis.

G406 There is irregular alveolar resorption, the interdental septa are porotic and some have concave or flattened profiles. Periodontal disease.

There is ante-mortem chipping on the lingual side of the crown of the L maxillary M3.

There are two shallow depressions lined with sclerotic trabecular bone on the joint surface of the L patella. There is also a pit filled with sclerotic bone which rises proud of the joint surface. Possibly partly healed osteochondritis dissecans.

Bathrocrany.

G411 There is a smooth swelling with a somewhat pitted surface on the posterior side of the R femur, just above the condyles. Both tibiae show build-ups of pitted bone on their medial and lateral surfaces; there are similar deposits on the fibulae. Radiographic examination reveals that the endosteal surfaces of these bones are normal. Well remodelled periostitis.

G416 Impacted maxillary canines. The L maxillary deciduous canine has been retained but has fallen from its socket post-mortem.

G419 The interdental septa are porotic and some have concave or flattened profiles. Periodontal disease.

There is an irregularly shaped deposit of sclerotic bone, maximum diameter 22mm, on the R parietal adjacent to the coronal suture and the temporal line. It rises about 2mm proud of the normal ectocranial surface. Button osteoma.

Bilateral frontal foramina.

The bones are rather light and rarified. Ante-mortem breaks in the vertebral bodies reveal sparse trabeculae with thickened vertical struts. Osteoporosis.

A R middle rib shows a porotic cortex about one quarter of the way from the vertebral end. A radiograph of this area shows marked coarsening of the bony trabeculae with patchy sclerosis and radiolucencies. The demarcation between radiographically normal and abnormal bone is sharp, although this boundary is not apparent on the gross specimen. The radiographic appearance suggests a diagnosis of haemangioma or lymphangioma, with a localised myeloma as a less likely cause (P.B. Guyer, pers. comm. 1992). A fragment of the body of a lumbar vertebra shows very marked coarsening and thickening of the bony trabeculae. This too is a feature of haemangioma (Ortner and Putschar 1985, 376-7).

G424 Both maxillary first molars bear Carabelli cusps.

The first metatarsals have epiphyses at both ends.

G427 L1 has T12 type facet joints.

There is a flat plaque of rather rough bone. It is of irregular shape measuring a maximum of 25mm across.

G430 Bilateral frontal foramina.

G436 Thin skull.

The R transverse foramen on the axis is incomplete.

Both proximal hallucial phalanges deviate laterally.

There are large, bilateral anterior lingual depressions on the mandible, in the subligual fossae below the sockets for I2-PM1.

The intermediate and distal phalanges of both little toes are fused together.

G438 An abscess at the right maxillary M1 penetrates the maxillary sinus, within which there is remodelled new bone.

The right maxillary I2 is reduced, with a conical crown. The crown is only 7mm high. The right I2 is missing post-mortem, but the socket gives the impression that this tooth was also reduced.

There is a raised projection on the upper surface of the right transverse process of the atlas. The surface of this projection is roughened, and articulates with a similar area just posterior to the left occipital condyle. The left atlas facet and occipital condyle are smaller than their right side counterparts. It seems likely that there was a fibrous connection in-vivo between these roughened areas, which must have limited movement at the atlanto-occipital joint.

T3 and 4 are fused at their centra and neural arches. No trace of disease or injury.

It is likely that the block vertebrae and the atlanto-occipital fusion are congenital anomalies.

The left femur has a distal femoral cortical excavation. There is a slightly pitted area at the corresponding point on the right femur.

There is a smooth, multilocular, scalloped erosion on the right side of the centrum of T9, destroying the vertebral body to about one-third of its depth. The lesion under-cuts the vertebral end plates. T10 shows destruction of the inferior part of its body, and the body of T11 has been completely destroyed. There is destruction of the upper parts of the body of T12, leaving a surface of slightly sclerotic trabecular bone. There is destruction of the anterior parts of the bodies of L1 and L2, and these two vertebrae are ankylosed with 45 degree kyphosis. There is a smooth-walled lytic lesion at the head of the right 11th rib. There is thickening of the left ulna at the junction of its middle and proximal thirds; the lesion has a slightly pitted surface and radiography indicates periostitis. There is ankylosis of the left sacro-iliac joint and bone destruction, mainly on the sacral side of the joint, has produced significant transverse narrowing of the pelvic girdle on this side. There is pitting on the lateral surface of the left iliac blade.

Tuberculosis. DNA analyses (Mays *et al*. 2001a) confirm the diagnosis and indicate the presence of *Mycobacterium tuberculosis* rather than *Mycobacterium bovis*.

A 30 week foetus (G457) was found between the femora of this burial. Although it is impossible to be certain, the placement of this infant between the thighs of the woman is strongly suggestive of a mother-child relationship. DNA analyses were performed in an attempt to determine whether a genetic relationship existed between these two skeletons, and to investigate whether there is any evidence that the foetus had contracted tuberculosis trans-placentally. The DNA preservation in the foetal material proved to be too poor to permit resolution of these issues.

G443 Reduced maxillary I2s.

There is heavy wear on the molar teeth, suggesting an age of about 25-35 years. There is only light wear on the anterior dentition. Epiphyseal union suggests an age at death in the early 20s (the epiphyses on the iliac crests and scapular margins are partly unfused and those at the distal ends of the forearm bones are only just fused). The cranial sutures suggest a young adult and the state of the pubic symphyses suggests an age of about 20-50. On balance it seems that this is the skeleton of an adult in her early 20s. Perhaps the heavy molar wear was caused by the habit of tooth grinding (bruxism).

There is a depressed area of exposed trabeculae on the medial side of the surgical neck of each humerus. They resemble the Allen's fossae often found on the necks of the femora (and which are present in this individual) and measure about 13 x 9mm.

G451 There is a probable fissure fracture runing approximately anterio-posteriorly across the distal joint surface of the L tibia, near the base of the medial malleolus.

There is pitting on the proximal joint surfaces of both proximal hallucial phalanges. Probably not pathological.

The distal joint surface of the proximal phalanx of the L ring finger is irregular and flattened in its volar parts. Probably a minor fracture of the joint surface. There is severe osteoarthritis of this joint surface and the adjoining articulation on the intermediate phalanx, presumably caused by the trauma to the joint.

There is a probable fissure fracture near the medial margin of the proximal joint surface of the 1st phalanx of the R index finger.

An abscess cavity at the base of the R maxillary M1 communicates with the maxillary sinus. Where it pierces the sinus it shows a projecting collar of bone around it, suggestive of a radicular cyst.

Left femur sacrificed for radiocarbon determination 23-2-95.

G456 Asymmetrical wear on the deciduous molars - little wear on the R side, much on the L.

L frontal foramen.

G457 See notes for G438.

G462 The L mandibular M3 shows super-eruption.

The R transverse foramen of the atlas is incomplete and the transverse process on this side is enlarged. The L side of the bone is missing post-mortem.

Both calcanei have porotic, crescentic areas on their anterior/medial margins. Probably sites for fibrous attachments for calcanei secundaria.

There is a deposit of woven bone on the shaft of the proximal phalanx of the L index finger. Periostitis.

A foot sesamoid seems to be bipartite. Only one part is present and it terminates in a porotic area suggesting fibrous union with the other part of the bone.

Left tibia sacrificed for radiocarbon determination 23-2-95.

There is a small, smooth exostosis of the lateral surface of the proximal metaphysis of the right tibia, projecting inferiorly. Probably an osteochondroma.

G467 There is ante-mortem chipping of the R deciduous maxillary I1 - most of the crown is broken off and the pulp is exposed. There is a periapical abscess at this tooth position and at the L I1 and the R I2. There is pitting over the anterior surfaces of both maxillae - osteitis as a result of infection from the neighbouring periapical abscesses. It seems probable that the abscesses at the L I1 and R I2 are, like that at the R I1, caused by infection of the pulp of these teeth due to ante-mortem chipping. These teeth have been lost post-mortem so this cannot be confirmed.

There is a deposit of woven bone on the lateral surface of the L fibula, one third of the way from the proximal end. Periostitis.

G474 There are infra-bony pockets at the L maxillary incisors. Periodontal disease.

The mandibular canines are twin-rooted.

Left femur, right tibia and right humerus sacrificed for radiocarbon determination 23-2-95 and 26-7-95.

G478 The following teeth show enamel pearls: R maxillary M3 (on the distal side of its single root 3-4mm below the CEJ) and the R maxillary M2 (one on the mesial and one on the distal side of its single root 3-4mm from the CEJ). The pearls are about 1mm diameter.

There is slight shovelling of the crown of the maxillary L I2. The R maxillary I2 has an accessory tubercle on its lingual side.

Left femur sacrificed for carbon-14 determination 23-2-95.

G482 Bilateral cubo-navicular articulation.

The right acetabulum shows a minor united fracture of the roof near the rim edge. There is a small cyst in the R ilium adjacent to the superior margin of the acetabulum - supra-acetabular cyst (Wells 1976). The cyst communicates with the joint space via holes along the fracture line. Presumably the cystic defect formed as a result of synovial fluid being forced into the subchondral bone along the fracture line.

There is a fissure fracture running in a volar-dorsal direction across the proximal joint surface of the 1st phalanx of the L ring finger. It is healed leaving a step in the joint surface. The adjoining surface of the 4th metacarpal is normal.

The styloid process of the R 3rd metacarpal is missing and there is an area of sclerotic, porotic bone at the site it would normally occupy suggesting that it may have been present as a separate ossicle which was attached via fibrous tissue. The L 3rd metacarpal is of normal morphology.

There is a united fracture about one quarter of the way from the vertebral end of a L middle rib. It is firmly healed with abundant callus.

There is a smooth deposit of bone on the medial side of the shaft of the R humerus about one third of the way from the distal end. Its surface is smooth, it is oval in shape, 3.5 x 1cm in diameter with its long axis parallel to that of the bone. Myositis ossificans.

The anterior part of the tympanic plate is incompletely fused to the squamous part of the temporal bone in L and R temporal bones.

There is destruction of the inferior/posterior part of the body of L3. There is destruction of the superior part of the R pedicle of L4 leaving only a thin bridge of bone connecting the body with the neural arch. There is also a small cavity on the superior surface of the body of L4 measuring about 7mm diameter and 7mm deep. There is a similar lesion on the inferior surface of the body of this vertebra. The surfaces of the lytic lesions in the vertebral bodies are of trabecular bone. None of the lesions shows significant bone regeneration. L5 and thesacral vertebrae appear normal but are very fragmentary. Tuberculosis. DNA analyses (Mays *et al.* 2001a) confirm the diagnosis and indicate the presence of *Mycobacterium tuberculosis* rather than *Mycobacterium bovis*.

G488 There is a small Carabelli cusp on the right maxillary permanent M1. There are also traces of Carabelli cusps on the maxillary deciduous M2s.

G497 There is iron staining on the right side of the mandible. Iron fragments adhere in the molar area.

G500 The L permanent I2 is reduced in size.

G503 The R maxillary M1 bears a small Carabelli cusp.

The L femur bears a third trochanter, the R is normal.

There is a small area of pitting on the L parietal bone adjacent to the lambdoid suture, midway between the asterion and the lambda. Probably porotic hyperostosis. This individual also shows cribra orbitalia of the cribriotic type.

G510 The R maxillary I1 is shovel shaped.

G516 There is spurring at the insertions of the Achilles tendons on the calcanei and on the patellae at the insertions of the quadriceps femores.

G528 The maxillary I2s show grooved cingula.

Both transverse foramina on the atlas are incomplete.

C7 bears a pair of cervical ribs. The R resembles a reduced 1st rib and articulates both with the body and the transverse process of C7. The ends of the rib are damaged but the chord appears to measure about 45-47mm. The L rib is somewhat damaged post-mortem but is much smaller and articulates with the transverse process of C7 only.

There are only 11 thoracic vertebrae but 6 lumbar vertebrae (i.e. there is lumbarisation of the last thoracic vertebra). The presence of the cervical ribs means that there are the usual 12 pairs of ribs.

There is unilateral, left-sided spondylolysis of L1.

There is a slight depression in the L side of the frontal bone adjacent to the frontal eminence; there is a corresponding, larger, bulge on the inner table at this position. The cause of this lesion is unclear.

There is asymmetry in the arm and hand and, to a lesser extent, the leg bones. The bones on the L side are more gracile and shorter.

L R
Humeri:length (with epiphyses)   300 314
Max. diameter at midshaft 18.4 20.7
Min. diameter at midshaft 15.4 16.3

Radii: max. diameter at tuberosity   16.8 19.0
Ulnae: olecranon breadth   23.8 26.7
Metacarpal I : max. length   41 43

(all dimensions in mm; forearm bones were incomplete, precluding maximum length measurements)

The L femur is shorter by 9mm than the right but there is little difference in robusticity.

The cause of these asymmetries is uncertain but a mild episode of poliomyelitis is one possibility. The dentition shows severe enamel hypoplasias corresponding to stress episodes occurring between about 1 and 5 years of age, so perhaps the disease which led to the skeletal asymmetry occurred during this part of childhood.

Left femur, right tibia and right fibula sacrificed for carbon-14 determination 23-2-95 and 26/7/95.

In same grave as G531.

G531 There is pitting on both parietal bones between the parietal eminences and the parietal notches. Porotic hyperostosis.

A fibula fragment of indeterminate side shows partially remodelled periostitis.

There is patchy new bone formation on the internal surface of the occipital bone and posterior parts of the parietal bones. Most deposits are of somewhat remodelled bone although there is some woven bone.

In same grave as G528.

G542 Both femora bear third trochanters.

Bilateral frontal foramina.

G555 There is a cystic cavity 10 x 7mm near the posterior margin of the distal joint surface of the L tibia. It is lined with fairly smooth pitted bone. The cause of this lesion is unclear, although it may represent an intra-osseous ganglion.

G558 There are the beginnings of a sutura mendosa at both asterions.

G561 The interdental septa are porotic and some have concave profiles. Periodontal disease.

There is slight anterior wedging of the bodies of T11, T12 and L1, probably due to minor compression fractures.

The left inferior side of T11 bears a smooth, thick osteophyte, as does the head of a lower rib. 'Bone former' type changes.

Three left ribs show united fractures - 2 lower ribs have fractures about one third of the way from their vertebral ends and a middle rib shows one about one quarter of the way from its sternal end. All are firmly united with moderate, well remodelled callus and probably occurred long before death.

G565 T12 has lumbar-type facet joints.

L6 shows spondylolysis, no sign of spondylolisthesis.

There is minor breakdown of the superior/anterior margins of L3 and 4 and minor compression of the anterior part of the body of L2. These lesions are suggestive of flexion trauma to the lumbar spine with compression fracture of the body of L2 and injury to the discs between L2 and 3, and 3 and 4.

There is a fracture of the L ulna one third of the way from the proximal end. It has united with a very large amount of well remodelled callus. A radiograph reveals that there is a 6-7mm gap between the broken ends bridged by callus. There is slight medial angulation of the part of the bone distal to the injury.

A right middle/lower rib shows a fracture one third of the way from the vertebral end, united with moderate callus.

G571 The L transverse foramen on the atlas is incomplete.

A bony spur from the osteoarthritic L superior facet joint of T1 projects into the canal for the L vertebral artery on C7.

A left rib is fractured near its sternal end. The fracture is united with moderate callus.

There are calcified fragments of a hollow spheroid. The curvature of the fragments suggests that it had a diameter of 4-5cm. The fragments are perforated by small holes, and are smooth on the outer surfaces and rough on their inner surfaces. They are up to several millimetres thick. Probably the remains of a hydatid cyst. Radiographs of the major long-bones, pelves and vertebrae reveal no evidence for cystic cavities within.

There is a small, circular deposit of smooth, sclerotic bone on the ectocranial surface of the frontal bone, 37mm from the bregma just to the L of the midline. Its maximum diameter is 6-7mm. A button osteoma.

Super-eruption of molar teeth.

The interdental septa are porotic and some have concave profiles. Periodontal disease.

Right femur sacrificed for carbon-14 determination 23-2-95.

G576 Two left middle ribs are united by a smooth bridge of bone situated between their heads and their tuberosities. Probably a congenital anomaly.

G582 The maxillary I2s have grooved cingula.

Left femur sacrificed for radiocabon determination 23-2-95.

G587 Porotic, concave interdental septa, irregular alveolar resorption, particularly around the molar teeth. Severe periodontal disease.

The transverse process of L6 and the L sacral ala articulate via smooth joint surfaces.

There are depressions 5-6mm diameter in the posterior facets of both calcanei. Uncertain cause.

Bathrocrany.

G597 There is a large infra-bony pocket at the R maxillary M2. The interdental septa are porotic and have irregular profiles. Severe periodontal disease.

The L 5th metacarpal shows a united Y-shaped fissure fracture on its distal joint surface. It is firmly healed with depression of the medial part producing a 2mm step in the joint surface.

There is a 2mm deep, 4mm diameter circular cavity on the inferior surface of the basi-occipital. The cavity is lined with normal cortical bone. Probably not pathological.

The R maxillary canine is unerupted. It lies within the maxilla in an almost horizontal orientation, with its crown tip near the R margin of the incisive fossa and the tip of its root lying above the socket for the 1st premolar.

G601 C6 and 7 are fused at their facet joints and centra, where osteophytes, which do not project far from the vertebral bodies, are present. The superior part of the body of C6 and the inferior body of C7 have flowing, paravertebral osteophytes, as do the right sides of the bodies of T7-10. There is bony spurring at many entheses, such as the linea aspera of the femurs, and capsular ossifications at various joints which are otherwise normal. 'Bone-former' type changes.

The right elbow joint is very disorganised. The lateral condyle of the right humerus is largely destroyed, and the remaining distal joint surface is eburnated. There are heavy osteophytes at the joint margins. There is eburnation on the proximal joint surface of the right ulna, and it also shows large osteophytes, as does the proximal joint surface of the right radius. There is no sign of infectious disease at this joint. These changes probably reflect an injury with luxation of the elbow joint.

There is partial destruction of both femoral heads. In each, the destruction is focused on the upper parts of the joint surface and penetrates deep within the subchondral bone. The lesions tend to undermine the joint surface. This is particularly true in the case of the left femur where the head is almost completely 'hollowed out' and there is beginning collapse of the joint surface with impacted, fissure fracturing. Both femoral heads show sclerosis on X-ray. The left femur neck shows a little, well remodelled reactive bone and there are small, well-remodelled new bone deposits on the floors of both acetabulae. Probably necrosis of the femoral heads.

Right tibia and distal half of right femur sacrificed for carbon-14 determination 23-2-95.

G604 The interdental septa in the molar regions are porotic and have concave profiles. Localised periodontal disease.

The R transverse foramen on C7 is incomplete.

Right femur sacrificed for carbon-14 determination 23-2-95.

G607 There is a short, thick osteophyte on the L side of the body of L5. 'Bone-former' type change.

The right acetabulum shows a small, cystic cavity near its superior margin which communicates with the joint space. A supra-acetabular cyst (Wells 1976).

There is ragged loss of rim height in the superior part of the right acetabulum. This type of lesion appears to form as a result of trauma causing fatigue failure of the rim edge. Splits in the acetabular cartilage caused by joint injury permit synovial fluid to penetrate subchondral bone causing cystic resorption. If this occurs near the rim margin it may weaken it sufficiently to lead to fatigue failure.

Both naviculae have large tuberosities and there is a cleft between the tuberosity and the posterior joint surface in each case, giving the appearence of incompletely separated os tibiale externa.

There are united fractures of 2 R ribs, one about two-thirds of the way from the vertebral end and the other adjacent to the tuberosity. Both are firmly healed with well remodelled callus.

G614 The maxillary deciduous M2s and permanent M1s show Carabelli cusps.

G628 There is green staining on some ribs and on the palatine bones.

There is a wedge-shaped piece of calcified material, 18 x 14 x 15mm, with irregular surfaces.

Bilateral frontal foramina.

G635 The L mandibular M3 is impacted against the M2.

The R maxillary M3 is a reduced, rather peg-like tooth.

R frontal foramen.

G636 The maxillary I2s have grooved cingula.

The distal joint surfaces of both 1st metatarsals are deflected laterally. The L shows grade II osteoarthritis. Hallux valgus.

There are porotic areas on the ends of the rather short styloid processes of the 3rd metacarpals. Probably the ends of these bones were present as separate ossicles attached by fibrous tissue in life.

The volar part of the R trapezoid is missing, the bone here ending in a roughened area. The joint surface on the scaphoid which articulated with the volar part of the trapezoid is eburnated. The proximal joint surface of the 2nd metacarpal is normal. Perhaps this is an un-united fracture of the R trapezoid. There is severe osteoarthritis at the left and right carpo-1st metacarpal articulations; this too might be viewed as suggestive of trauma to the hands.

G643 The maxillary I2s are somewhat reduced in size.

There are short, thick osteophytes on the superior, L side of the body of L2 and on the L and R sides of the body of S1. 'Bone former' type changes.

The intermediate and distal phalanges of both little toes are fused.

G652 There is a large, curved plaque of calcified soft tissue. It is irregularly shaped and its maximum dimensions are 3x5.5cm and it is 2-4mm thick. It has rough surfaces. Possibly a pleural calcification.

Right femur sacrificed for radiocarbon determination 23-2-95. Proximal right tibia, left tibia and both fibulae sacrificed for replicate 2-12-96.

G658 The R maxillary I2 has a grooved cingulum.

There are 'labyrinth' (sinuous resorptive) lesions on the internal surface of the occipital bone in the fossae for the cerebra and on the arm of the crucial ridge which divides them. The lesions are mainly to the right of the mid-line. They represent superficial and irregular destruction of the endocranial surface. There is no evidence for new bone formation.

There is somewhat remodelled periostitis on the lateral surface of the L tibia. The left fibula shows thickening at the same level. There is also a deposit of well-remodelled periosteal bone in the diaphysis of the left femur. There is a small, superficial destructive lesion on the proximal end of the metaphysis of the left tibia underlying the epiphysial plate, toward the medial margin. There is a similar lesion on the distal surface of the metaphysis of the left femur. There is periostitis on the internal surfaces of the R ribs (except the 1st and the 12th), most pronounced in the vertebral and sternal thirds rather than in the mid-shaft areas. Some remodelling is evident, although many lesions are of woven bone, indicating a disease process active at time of death. Four L ribs show erosive lesions: the 11th rib shows a shallow, irregular erosion on its inferior border. The lesion, which is located in the midshaft area has a slightly pitted surface. The 10th rib has a large erosion on its inferior edge. The lesion has a pitted surface and lies in the anterior third of the rib. Two lower-middle ribs (possibly the 8th and 9th) also show lesions. One shows a shallow erosion with a pitted surface on its inferior aspect just anterior to the tubercle, the other shows a shallow, pitted erosion on its inferior border at the midshaft. There is no sign of bony regeneration at any of these lesions and no left ribs show any signs of periostitis. Six left ribs show thickening near their heads.

DNA analysis was positive for IS6110, indicating the presence of *mycobacterium tuberculosis* complex micro-organism DNA and implying that the infectious lesions described above are due to tuberculosis (Mays *et al.* 2002b).

Both femora bear third trochanters.

The left transverse foramen on the axis vertebra is incomplete.

G670 Porotic, flattened interdental septa. Periodontal disease.

There is a groove on the cingulum and the lingual side of the root of the maxillary L I2.

G673 There are infra-bony pockets at the R maxillary M3 and the R mandibular M3. Periodontal disease.

Thin skull.

There are only 6 cervical vertebrae. There seems to be the normal complement of thoracic and lumbar vertebrae. L1 has T12-type facet joints and transverse processes.

Manubrio-sternal synostosis.

There is an irregular exostosis of smooth, very sclerotic bone on the inferior surface of the R 1st rib, near the medial border. X-ray reveals that it is sitting on the normal cortex and a thin line of radiolucency is visible where it attaches to the rib. Probably an osteoma.

There is an anterior lingual depression in the left sub-mandibular fossa.

G676 Porotic interdental septa with flat or concave profiles. Periodontal disease.

The maxillary incisors and canines show grooved cingula.

There is marked super-eruption of the R mandibular M1.

G677 There is fusion of the R sacro-iliac joint. The ankylosis is smooth, with no osteophyte formation. The bones have broken apart post-mortem revealing that the joint surfaces have been completely destroyed with superficial cavitation of the iliac face. The L sacro-iliac joint is missing. The remainder of the (rather incomplete) skeleton shows no erosive changes. The lesions have the appearance of being due to an infective process at the sacro-iliac joint.

G678 A fragment of the anterior border of a tibia of indeterminate side shows well remodelled periostitis.

G692 There are well remodelled deposits of bone over the general surface of the L tibia and fibula, on the R tibia (mainly on the subcutaneous surface at the junction of the proximal and middle thirds) and over the general surface of the R fibula. A radiograph reveals no changes to the endosteal surfaces of any of these bones. Periostitis.

G694 The R maxillary I2 has a grooved cingulum.

The R superior facet joint of T12 is of lumbar type.

There is a fracture of the distal end of the R 1st metacarpal. The volar part of the distal joint surface is displaced proximally by about 1cm and there is grade II osteoarthritis of both faces of the 1st metacarpo-phalangeal joint. Probably due to a blow on the end of the thumb.

There is a swelling near the distal end of the shaft of the L ulna. The distal end of the bone is broken post-mortem but comparison with the R bone suggests that the lesion lies about 3.5cm from the distal end. It seems likely that this represents a healed fracture.

There are healed fractures of the R parietal and R side of the frontal bone. The focus of the fractures seems to be a point on the coronal suture 4cm to the R of the bregma. The longest continuous fracture line runs from this focus forward to the region of the R frontal eminence and backwards to a point on the lambdoid suture about 4cm from the R asterion. Shorter fractures radiate from this fracture line and from the focus on the coronal suture. The focus on the coronal suture is slightly raised: this represents bulging of

the cranium rather than thickening - there is a corresponding hollow on the endocranial surface. Perhaps this was caused by pressure from haemorrhage in the underlying soft tissues. The fractures are firmly healed and in some places their lines are almost obliterated. There seems to have been slight separation of the broken edges in the long fracture in the area of the R parietal eminence by up to about 1.5mm, with the gap now filled by callus. In the other fractures there seems to have been little or no separation of the broken edges. There is sclerotic bone in the area between the R frontal eminence and the coronal suture, here there may have been many minor fissure fractures which have been obliterated by callus and bony remodelling. There is pitting in the ectocranial surface in the area of the fractures - probably osteitis as a result of superficial infection. The nature of the fractures suggests that a blow from a blunt object was the cause of the injury and that the raised area on the R coronal suture was the point of impact. The state of healing of the fractures suggests prolonged survival of the individual following the injury and there is no reason to suppose that the cause of death was in any way related to the cranial injury.

R frontal foramen.

G697 There is a small foramen in the middle of the occipital squama.

There are deposits of woven bone on the endocranial surfaces of the occipital and left temporal and left sphenoid bones.

G708 The maxillary M1s bear large Carabelli cusps.

There are deposits of woven bone upon the superior surface of the hard palate, mainly on the posterior parts and around the midline. The margins of the pyriform aperture lack their normal sharpness, being thick and rounded. There is reduction of the anterior nasal spine; a short, stubby spine remains. There is pitting on the anterior aspects of the maxillae around the pyriform aperture. There appears to be no resorption of the maxillary alveolar process and the foot bones which are present (the L 3rd and 4th metatarsals) are normal, as are the hand phalanges (although only 3 are present, none being a terminal one). Leprosy. This diagnosis was confirmed by DNA analysis, which was positive for M. leprae.

The L femur bears a third trochanter.

G710 The R mandibular canine is unerupted. It is orientated about 20 degrees from horizontal with its crown against the tip of the root of the L I2. X-ray reveals that it is a morphologically normal canine. The R deciduous canine was retained but has fallen from its socket post-mortem.

The crown of the R mandibular M3 is larger than that of either the M1 or M2.

G715 The maxillary I2s have grooved cingula. The maxillary canines have lingual tubercles. All the maxillary incisors have shovel-shaped crowns. The R maxillary M2 is very flattened mesio-distally and is generally rather reduced in size so that it is smaller than the M3.

The interdental septa are porotic and ragged, particularly in the posterior parts of the dental arcade. There is an infra-bony pocket at the socket of the L maxillary I2. Periodontal disease.

There is a large hole 51x40mm diameter in the L parietal bone/L side of the frontal bone, just to the L of the bregma. It is of rather irregular shape but is very approximately circular. Most of the margins are bevelled ectocranially so that the bone at the edges is generally fairly thin. There are several fractures radiating from this hole, the longest of which crosses the sagittal suture just behind the bregma, runs across the R parietal bone and terminates in the R temporal squama about 2cm from the squamous suture. The lines of the other fractures are difficult to trace in detail; this is particularly true in the area around the hole due to the large amount of knobbly reactive bone. There is a sharply demarcated area of pitting on the frontal and parietal bones around the hole: probably osteitis due to infection of an open wound. On three sides the margins of the pitted area are fairly straight, resembling three sides of a rectangle. There is no sign of infection endocranially. The fractures appear to have occurred long before death and are well healed and the reactive bone around the perforation in the skull is well remodelled. The presence of radiating fractures suggests a blunt injury in the region occupied by the hole. The reason for the hole may be that the blunt impact caused such comminution here that the fragments were resorbed rather than united on healing. Alternatively, the hole may represent a trepanation carried out to treat the injury. The gently bevelled ectocranial surface around the hole would seem to support this interpretation, as would the straight sides of the pitted area which are suggestive of skin flaps being deliberately folded back from the wound. The well remodelled appearance, both of the edges of the hole and of the fractures, suggests prolonged survival after the operation.

G720 The R maxillary permanent M1 shows a Carabelli cusp. The L maxillary M1 is missing post-mortem.

The internal surface of the occipital bone shows 'labyrinth' type lesions (i.e. sinuous resorptive lesions) on the upper arm of the crucial ridge.

G723 Seven left and seven right middle/lower ribs show periostitis on their visceral surfaces. Deposits are generally of woven bone, although some do show a little remodelling. One of the right ribs shows a shallow, scalloped erosion on the visceral surface, towards its proximal end. An upper left rib has a large, scalloped erosion on its inferior surface. The vertebrae appear normal but there is much post-mortem damage. X-ray revealed no further skeletal lesions. This individual proved negative for tubercle bacillus DNA (Mays *et al.* 2002b).

G746 The bodies of the thoracic and lumbar vertebrae show small, smooth osteophytes originating away from the joint surfaces. There is bony spurring on the patellae at the sites for insertion of the quadriceps femores, on the calcanei at the insertions of the Achilles tendons and on the olecranon processes of the ulnae. 'Bone former' type changes.

L1 has thoracic-type facet joints.

L4 shows spondylolysis, L3 shows L-sided unilateral spondylolysis. No sign of spondylolisthesis.

The R third metacarpal is missing its styloid process; there is a porotic area here suggesting that the styloid process was present as a separate ossicle.

There is a hole lined with trabecular bone in the distal joint surface of the L cuboid. Uncertain cause.

The joint surfaces of both faces of the 1st interphalangeal joint of the R index finger and both faces of the 1st interphalangeal joint of the R little finger are very porotic and irregular and have large marginal osteophytes. The remaining finger bones (of which all but three are present) are normal. Probably traumatically induced osteoarthritis.

Bilateral frontal foramina.

There are healed fissure fractures in the right acetabular roof.

There are two cystic cavities in the subchondral bone above the right acetabulum. They communicate with the joint space. Supra-acetabular cysts (Well 1976). Perhaps the cysts formed as a result of synovial fluid being forced into the subchondral bone due to the injury which led to the fracture of the acetabulum.

G747 L4 shows spondylolysis, no sign of spondylolisthesis.

There is a L os tibiale externum. A porotic area on it and on the tuberosity of the L navicular suggests fibrous union in-vivo. There

is no os tibiale externum in the R foot but there is a cleft in the posterior part of the tuberosity of the R navicular suggestive of an incompletely separated ossicle.

There is an ovoid, raised area 5.5 x 2.5cm on the medial surface of the L tibia one quarter of the way from the distal end. It measures 5.5 x 2.5 x 0.8cm high, with its long axis parallel to that of the bone. Its surface is of slightly bumpy cortical bone and there is a small cavity in the surface of the lower part of the lesion. X-ray reveals that the cavity does not penetrate to the marrow cavity, the line of the cortex underlying the lesion is readily apparent and the endosteal surfaces of the bone are normal. This is probably periostitis due to local injury - the cavity suggests that the cause of the lesion might be a penetrating injury from a sharp object.

G750 There is fusion of the proximal and intermediate phalanges of the L index finger at 45 degree flexion. Probably due to a minor fracture near the joint surfaces.

Both hamates lack their unciform processes. The L has a porotic area suggesting that the unciform process existed as a separate ossicle attached to the main part of the bone by soft tissue. An accessory ossicle at this point is termed a hamuli proprium (O'Rahilly 1953). The R hamate bears no such porotic area - the unciform process may have simply been absent.

Left rib, left and right ulnae and right radius sacrificed for carbon-14 determination 23-2-95.

G760 Porotic, irregular interdental septa in the molar areas. Periodontal disease.

Bilateral frontal foramina.

Left femur and right tibia sacrificed for carbon-14 determination 23-2-95.

NA002 There are 6 lumbar vertebrae, the 6th is incompletely sacralised, its right transverse process being of the normal lumbar type the left being fully sacralised. As well as partial sacralisation the 6th lumbar vertebra shows spina bifida - there is a very narrow cleft just to the left of the spinous process.

Right femur and tibiae sacrificed for radiocarbon determination 25/10/95.

NA004 There is a depression 2cm diameter lined with smooth, sclerotic bone in the right upper surface of the vertebral body of S1. It does not have the appearence of a Schmorl's node or an infectious lesion. Cause unknown.

NA004A Slight deposits of woven bone on the shaft of the left humerus. The posterior surfaces of both scapulae and the lingual aspects of the mandible may also show slight deposits of woven bone but it is difficult to be certain as their general surfaces are rather porous, as is expected in an individual of this age.

NA006 There is porosis of the interdental septa, together with some alveolar resorption. Periodontal disease.

Super-eruption of molar teeth.

The left mandibular canine has 2 roots.

There is pitting on the buccal aspect of the left maxilla in the molar area, suggestive of infection. This area is very fragmented post-mortem and the cause of the pitting is unclear but it may be that the abscess cavities at the left maxillary M1 and M2 sockets discharged buccally leading to local infection.

The R calcaneus shows a crescentic area of pitted bone on the anterior border of the anterior facet for the talus. Possibly the site for fibrous attachment of a calcaneum secundarium. Left calcaneus normal.

The L5 shows clefts at the left pedicle and the right pars interarticularis. There are osteophytes on the inferior border of the body of L5 and the superior border of the body of S1, mainly confined to the right side; the anterior wall of L5 shows a little sub-periosteal new bone formation. These changes imply anterior slippage of the body of L5 - spondylolisthesis. The direction of slippage seems to have been slightly to the right, suggesting that the cause was mainly rupture at the left pedicle rather than at the right pars interarticularis.

Left humerus and left tibia sacrificed for radiocarbon determination 26/10/95.

NA013 Porotic interdental septa - periodontal disease.

S6 is an extra segment not sacralisation of the last lumbar vertebra. Sacralisation is incomplete, the left transverse process being full sacral type whereas the right is full lumbar type. This leads to asymmetry in the sacro-iliac joints, the left being extended.

There are the beginnings of a sutura mendosa at both asterions.

Right femur and right humerus sacrificed for radiocarbon determination 26/10/95.

NA014 Robust bones.

There is a crescentic indentation on the anterior border of the anterior calcaneal facet of the left calcaneus; it has a pitted surface with a small area of eburnation. Probably the location of a fibrous attachment for a calcaneum secundarium. The right calcaneus is not present for study.

Left tibia sacrificed for radiocarbon determination 26/10/95.

NA014A Slight deposits of woven bone on tibiae and on ectocranial surfaces of skull vault.

NA019 The right deciduous M1 has been lost ante-mortem although the other 3 deciduous M1s are present in the jaws. The alveolus here is pitted and slightly irregular. A radiograph reveals that the crown of the premolar here is in the process of formation within the mandible. The morphology of the alveolus in this area and the fact that the other deciduous mandibular M1 has not been shed (its roots have not yet begun to be resorbed) suggest that the right mandibular deciduous M1 may have been lost through disease.

The R maxillary I2 is rather broad (mesio-distal width is about 8mm) and there is a groove running up the lingual aspect of the root and partially separating the lower parts of the crown. There is also a notch in the incisive edge. This may be a geminated lateral incisor or fusion between the I2 and a supernumerary tooth.

NA024 The arches of S1-4 articulate via small facet joints.

There are slight woven bone deposits on the internal surface of the occipital bone.

NA025 L4 and 5 show spina bifida, as do all 5 sacral segments.

NA026 There is superficial destruction of the inferior parts of the body of T6 and the superior parts of the body of T7. The surfaces of the lesions are of sclerotic, trabecular bone. The rest of the vertebral column (all cervical vertebrae, T1-8 and 1 lumbar vertebra are present) is normal. The R 6th and 7th ribs show periostitis on their internal surfaces extending from their heads to near the articular facets of their tuberosities, presumably due to extension of infection from the vertebral foci. A fragment of the wing of a scapula of indeterminate side shows deposits of woven bone on both its internal and external surfaces. Tuberculosis. DNA analyses (Mays *et al.* 2001a) confirm the diagnosis and indicate the presence of *Mycobacterium tuberculosis* rather than *Mycobacterium bovis*.

NA031 There is a cleft in the inferior surface of the styloid process of each 3rd metacarpal.

The plantar parts of the distal articular surfaces of the L and R lateral cuneiforms are porotic and slightly raised above the normal joint surface. The proximal joint surface of the R 3rd metatarsal shows similar changes, the L 3rd metatarsal is missing. Non-osseous tarsal coalitions (Regan *et al.* 1999).

The slope of the upper part of the joint surface of the right acetabulum is rather shallow - slight acetabular dysplasia.

There is a small supra-acetabular cyst (Wells 1976) in the subchondral bone above the right acetabulum. It communicates with the joint space.

There is ragged loss of rim height in the superior part of the right acetabulum. This type of lesion appears to form as a result of trauma causing fatigue failure of the rim edge. Splits in the acetabular cartilage allow synovial fluid to penetrate the subchondral bone leading to cystic resorption. If this occurs near the rim edge it may weaken it sufficiently to lead to fatigue failure. Dysplastic hips are particularly prone to this type of problem as their morphology results in greater concentration of mechanical forces near the rim edge than is the case with acetabulae of normal morphology.

NA031A Under the old numbering system this skeleton was 116A; NA031 was old number 116.

An area on the lateral surface of each deciduous mandibular M1 is denuded of enamel, as is part of the lingual cusp of the L maxillary deciduous M1. Probably ante-mortem dental chipping.

NA033 L5 shows unilateral spondylolysis on the L side, and spina bifida. The fragment of neural arch thus created articulates with the L pars interarticularis via a smooth joint surface. There are no signs of spondylolisthesis. The L apophysial joints between L5 and S1 are rudimentary, the L posterior facet joint of L4 has a double articular surface, as does the L superior facet joint of L5.

There are 13 thoracic vertebrae. T13 bears no facets for ribs (there are thus only the usual 12 pairs of ribs) but has normal thoracic-type facet joints. Its L transverse process is of normal lower thoracic type but the R is rudimentary and of lumbar form. T12 has the appearance of a normal T11 and T11 the appearence of a normal T10. There are 7 cervical and 5 lumbar vertebrae, thus T13 represents an extra segment.

There is a crescentic depression with a porotic surface on the anterior margin of the anterior facet joint of the R calcaneus. Probably the site of a fibrous attachment for a calcaneum secundarium. The relevant area of the L calcaneus is missing so it cannot be determined whether the variant is unilateral or bilateral.

The curve of the shaft of the R 5th metatarsal is accentuated. Perhaps this is due to the wearing of constricting footwear. The L 5th metatarsal is normal.

There is a fracture passing through the distal joint surface of the R 2nd metacarpal. Firmly healed.

The skeleton is very fragmentary, with many bones showing fresh breaks.

NA035 Fragments of the pubic bones were bagged with the hands - presumably this individual was buried with the hands placed across the pelvic area.

Both femora bear a 3rd trochanter.

NA036 There is slight porosis of the orbital roofs, although the other cranial bones are normal. The radii and ulnae show abnormal curvature, and the left ilium shows increased lateral curvature. There is also slight bowing of the right fibula. Most of the right tibia is missing, and what remains of the left (about two-thirds of its shaft) appears normal. Post-depositional breaks in the ilia reveal that their trabecular structure is coarse and enlarged. There is enlargement of the costo-chondral ends of the first ribs; the remaining rib ends are missing post-mortem. The ilia are thickened and there is enlargement of the long-bone metaphyses. Rickets. This case is among those discussed by Ortner and Mays (1998).

NA038 Skull and mandible only present although the site photograph shows a complete skeleton - presumably the post-cranials have been lost. The individual is a young adult: using dental attrition he falls into Brothwell's (1981) 17-25 category; the photograph shows that epiphysial fusion is complete. This last was taken into account, giving an age estimate of about 22-25 years. No obvious skeletal pathology is visible on the photograph.

Flattened and porotic interdental septa - periodontal disease.

NA043 There are deposits of woven bone on the tibiae (most marked on the posterior surfaces) and the femora (mainly on the anterior surfaces). Periostitis.

Bones boxed mixed with NA043A (*qv*).

NA043A The bones of this individual were boxed mixed with those of NA043. Many indeterminate fragments and small bones could not be assigned with confidence to one or other individual; these were not recorded.

Slight, unremodelled periostitis on ectocranial and endocranial skull surfaces.

NA044 Porotic and flattened interdental septa. Periodontal disease.

There is the beginning of a sutura mendosa at the L asterion.

There are grooves on the R frontal bone leading to the supra-orbital foramen, they probably conveyed the nerves and/or blood vessels which passed through the foramen.

Both foramen transversaria on the atlas are incomplete.

The L 12th rib shows a firmly healed fracture about 1/3 of the way from its distal end.

NA046 T7-9 are fused at the R sides of their centra by a broad, smooth, flowing osteophyte. Their facet joints and neural arches are normal. The bodies of T10 and 11 bear large R-sided osteophytes which articulate but are not fused. The L sides of T11 and 12 have similar, smaller articulating osteophytes. There is a long, smooth osteophyte on the L side of the body of L4 which overlaps the body of L3, projecting to about half way up it. L2, 3 and 5 and S1 bear short, thick osteophytes on their centra. There is bony spurring on the L radial tuberosity and there is a bony flange on the L linea aspera. There is some ossification of costal and thyroid cartilages. DISH.

There are 6 sacral vertebrae, the 1st of which is incompletely fused to the 2nd: there is complete union at the body and L ala but the R side of S1 bears a free lumbar type transverse process. S6 is an extra segment, there being the normal complement of pre-sacral vertebrae.

L4 has a shallow, irregular cavity on the R side of the superior surface of its centrum. There are also two small lytic lesions on its inferior surface, and a small lesion on the body of L5. The surfaces of the lesions are of sclerotic trabecular bone. These resemble early paradiscal lesions of tuberculosis. The diagnosis of tuberculosis was confirmed by DNA analyses (Mays *et al.* 2001a), which also indicated the presence of *Mycobacterium tuberculosis* rather than *Mycobacterium bovis*.

There is a united fracture in the midshaft area of the L clavicle, with shortening of the bone by about 3cm compared to its

counterpart on the R side due to under-riding of the lateral part of the bone. The fracture line is oblique with respect to the long axis of the bone and there is firm healing with moderate callus.

Femora sacrificed for radiocarbon determination 25/10/95.

NA047 Both masto-occipital sutures are obliterated.

NA048 There is pitting on the superior surface of the hard palate, possibly indicative of intra-nasal infection. The piriform aperture is normal. The anterior nasal spine is missing post-mortem.

NA051 The interdental septa around the molar teeth are porotic and have flattened or concave profiles; those in the anterior part of the mouth are porotic but show no profile changes. Periodontal disease, more severe in molar areas.

NA056A This burial is described on the boxes as 'undisturbed foetal skull fragments and post Cranials'. The remains were given old number 141 which corresponds to NA56, so perhaps the present burial is an infant interred in the same grave with NA56 (or perhaps it is just a numbering error...).

NA059 The interdental septa in the molar area are flattened or concave in profile and there are infra-bony pockets around the mandibular and maxillary L M3s. Severe periodontal disease in molar area.

There are 6 sacral segments, the 6th is an extra vertebra, there being the normal complement of pre-sacral vertebrae. The body of the 1st sacral segment is incompletely united with the 2nd.

NA060 There are deposits of woven bone on the R ulna, the posterior aspects of both humeri and on the internal surface of the occipital bone. Periostitis.

Probably a double burial with NA060A (*qv*).

NA060A The box containing this individual is labelled '145 twin' (old number 145 corresponds to NA60) so this individual was presumably interred in the same grave as NA60.

NA063 The L mandibular canine is twin rooted; the R canine is missing post-mortem.

NA066 Beginning infra-bony pocket formation around the R maxillary M1. The interdental septa are porotic, and those in the molar area have concave profiles. Periodontal disease, most marked in the molar area.

There is scoliosis of the thoracic spine. The heights of the R sides of the centra of T2 and 3 are reduced, as are the heights of the L sides of the bodies of T5-9. This produces an S-shaped curvature of the spine, the scoliosis of the upper thoracic spine being about 25 degrees to the R and that in the mid-lower thoracic area being about 30 degrees to the L. The 2 curves thus approximately cancel one another so that the head would have been maintained roughly in the mid-sagittal plane in life. There is also some asymmetry of the neural arches, the distance from the pars interarticularis to the midline often being reduced on the concave sides of the curves, and the facet joints are in some instances smaller on the concave sides. Ostephytosis of the vertebral bodies, and osteoarthritis of the apophysial joints also occur on the concave sides of the curves, testifying to the increased strains imposed as a result of the spinal deformity.

The tuberosity area on each navicular is roughened and porotic. These were probably sites for fibrous attachments for os tibiale externa.

Bilateral frontal foramina.

There is a depressed, porotic area on the plantar part of the distal joint surface of the R lateral cuneiform. Non-osseous tarsal coalition (Regan *et al.* 1999). The adjoining facet of the 3rd metatarsal and both relevant parts of the L foot are missing post-mortem.

The proximal epiphysis of the R humerus is displaced downwards so that it lies below the level of the greater tuberosity. There is a narrow cleft running around the superior margin of the joint surface and there are small cystic defects at its anterior margin. The humerus is shorter than its counterpart on the L side - by 11mm overall and 12mm if both are measured to the tip of the greater tuberosity. The reduction in length of the R humerus is thus not due solely to the downward displacement of the epiphysis but indicates a deficiency of growth. There is no sign of any bony infection. The above observations are suggestive of an injury to the epiphysial plate. The R scapula shows an apparent os acromiale (whereas the L acromion is of normal form), but in view of the probable injury to the R shoulder perhaps this should be interpreted as traumatic separation of the epiphysial plate here or as a fracture which failed to unite.

NA068 There is a large infra-bony pocket around the mandibular R I1 and there is alveolar resorption in this area. The interdental septa are porotic and show rather ragged profiles. Severe periodontal disease.

The R maxillary canine is not fully erupted and thus is not in occlusion. Its orientation is normal, the tooth is morphologically normal and there is sufficient space in the dental arch for it to erupt. It would thus seem that this should be classified as an embedded rather than an impacted tooth (Shafer *et al.* 1983, 66) - it seems that it was unerupted due to lack of eruptive force rather than prevented from erupting by any physical barrier.

The R mandibular canine is twin-rooted, the L has the usual single root.

There is a large osteoma in the frontal sinus slightly to the L of the midline. It is V-shaped with a maximum length of 2-2.5cm and the width across the arms of the V is about 2cm. The apex of the V is anchored to the L orbital roof with the arms projecting upwards into the frontal sinus. Part of it is visible grossly at a post-mortem break but its full extent is only visible on X-ray. The radiograph reveals an irregular cavity within the cranium around the osteoma; this appears to be localised expansion of the frontal sinus due to pressure from the osteoma.

There is a concave area on the L side of the anterior arch of the atlas to accommodate a large L-sided precondylar tubercle on the basilar area of the occipital bone.

NA070 Described as a 'Disturbed child burial' on the box, and sure enough it is a mixture - fragments of 1 adult and 3 juveniles are present. The plan shows the orientation of the burial - presumably it was sufficiently undisturbed for this to be readily apparent. The most complete child is treated as the burial, the rest of the bone as stray.

NA080 Porotic interdental septa in molar area. Localised periodontal disease. There is crowding of the L anterior mandibular dentition.

NA081 Congenital absence of the L maxillary PM2; there is no space in the dental arch for it.

NA081 (=old number 166) is listed as in boxes 860447 and 860452. The former contains a mixture of bones from several adults and juveniles, the latter contains an adult skull. The plan suggests that NA081 is an adult; the skull was assumed to be part of the *in-situ* burial, but is was impossible to determine which, if any, of the post-cranials belong with it, hence the skull alone is recorded.

Beginning infra-bony pocket formation around the maxillary M2s and the interdental septa in the molar area are porotic with flattened or concave profiles. Periodontal disease.

NA084 Large foramen in the inferior part of the sternal body.

NA088 Reduced, peg-like R maxillary M3.

NA088=old number 173. The boxes are labelled 173A and 173B but all the bones come from 1 individual.

Atlas vertebra shows spina bifida.

Porotic and concave interdental septa in molar area. Localised periodontal disease.

There is a supra-acetabular cyst above the right acetabulum. It communicates with the joint space.

The right acetabulum shows mild acetabular dysplasia.

Fragmentary skeleton. The photograph taken of the burial *in-situ* shows most of the bones intact, thus breakage must have occurred during excavation, cleaning or storage.

NA089 Both foramen transversaria on the atlas are incomplete.

NA091 Light, rarified bones. Osteoporosis.

An unsided rib shows a fracture in its sternal third, firmly healed, little callus.

NA092 There is porosis on the ectocranial surfaces of the temporal bones and skull vault (particularly on the parietal bones) and of the lateral surface of the R ilium. Some sternal rib ends appear swollen. Possibly rickets.

NA094 Tibiae sacrificed for radiocarbon determination 25/10/95.

NA095 The atlas shows spina bifida.

NA098 The L femur shows a 3rd trochanter (the R femur is missing).

NA0100 Reduced maxillary I2s.

The R maxillary M1 is 'dislocated', with the roots tilted buccally and the crown tilted lingually. As a result there is wear on the buccal surface of the lateral root. Only the lingual roots are still embedded in the alveolus.

There are infra-bony pockets around the maxillary M2s, the L mandibular M2 and the R mandibular canine. The interdental septa are porotic. Periodontal disease.

The L mandibular M3 has 3 roots, the extra root being on the buccal side.

Most teeth show super-eruption.

Severe wear on the anterior dentition, most of the crowns are worn away.

NA101 See notes on NA101A.

NA101A This skeleton, partially mixed with NA101, is fairly complete and no stray bone is boxed with it. It it thus probable that this is an *in-situ* burial, probably interred adjacent to NA101.

There are 6 lumbar vertebrae and only 4 sacral segments - complete lumbarisation of the 1st sacral segment.

L foramen transversarium of atlas is incomplete.

NA102 Smooth-walled cystic defects adjacent to margins of joint surfaces of L and R capitates and L hamate. Probably not pathological.

NA103 Buried in same grave as NA107 (*qv*).

Both the L2 and L3 show thickening of the neural arch in the portion between the L pedicle and the pars interarticularis. There is also a little new bone deposition on the left side of the bodies of these two vertebrae. There is also slight erosion of the affected part of the body in the case of L2. 6L and 3R ribs show periostitis as do three unsided rib fragments. Lesions are restricted to the visceral surfaces. Some deposits are of woven bone, some show remodelling, although unremodelled lesions predominate. Sternal, middle and vertebral thirds of ribs are involved. There is also a remodelled patch of bone on the medial side of the shaft of the left femur. Periostitis. The vertebral involvement may be suggestive of tuberculosis, but lesions are insufficient to support a firm diagnosis.

NA104 There is a large erosion near the anterior edge of the inferior surface of the body of T6, and a smaller one near the anterior margin of the superior surface of the body of L1. The surfaces of the lesions are roughened and appear sclerotic on X-ray. Probably avulsion injuries of the vertebral end-plates.

The transverse processes of L1 are rudimentary.

There is a slightly pitted area of unremodelled sub-periosteal bone on the posterior surface of the R radius, towards its distal end. This part of the bone is damaged post-mortem, but enough remains to show that the distal joint surface is normal. Periostitis, probably sequential to local infection.

There are 6 sacral segments, the 6th is an extra segment, rather than sacralisation of a lumbar vertebra.

Left tibia sacrificed for radiocarbon determination 25/10/95. Right tibia sacrificed for replicate 2-12-96.

NA105 The maxillary I2s are rather reduced.

Flattened interdental septa in the molar areas. Periodontal disease.

T12 has lumbar-type facet joints.

L5 shows spina bifida - the tips of the 2 halves of the neural arch meet at the midline but arenot fused together. There is also complete spina bifida of the sacrum which has only 4 segments.

NA107 Field notes say that this is a burial placed on the chest of NA103.

NA108 There are patchy deposits of porous bone on the outer table of the skull vault. The orbital roofs are porous and irregular. The costo-chondral ends of the ribs are flared. The cortex near the costo-chondral rib ends has strands of bone, with long, irregular slits between the stands. There are patchy deposits of woven bone on some rib fragments. The metaphyseal cortices of the major long-bones have irregular, alternating struts and slits. The bone underlying the growth plates has an irregular surface. The scapulae exhibit irregular, porous cortical bone near their margins. The pelvic bones and some long-bones show coarsened trabecular structures. Rickets. This case is among those described by Ortner and Mays (1998).

NA110 There are grooves on both sides of the frontal bone leading to the supra-orbital notches.

NA111 Congenital absence of the L maxillary PM1.

The deciduous L M1 appears to have been lost in life through disease: there is an abscess cavity at this tooth position. There is slight periostitis on the buccal side of the maxilla adjacent to the L deciduous M2, possibly connected with an infection at the deciduous M1 socket.

The interdental septa in the molar areas have flattened or concave profiles. Periodontal disease.

There are 13 R ribs, the supernumary having the appearance of a lumbar rib and having an articular facet on its head only. There is no trace of a corresponding articular facet on the L1.

NA112 The maxillary anterior dentition is very worn, little of the crowns remain; wear is less severe on the mandibular anterior teeth.

Super-eruption of molars.

The R mandibular I1 shows ante-mortem chipping. The lateral side of the crown and top part of the root have been chipped off leaving a polished edge. This smoothing of the edge implies chipping occurred in-vivo, a suggestion which is supported by the presence of an abscess at the base of the tooth which presumably reflects periapical infection as a consequence of the injury. The pulp cavity is filled with secondary dentine, otherwise it would have undoubtedly been breached by the injury to the tooth. The neighbouring I2 is not damaged. The L I1 is missing post-mortem but there is a periapical abscess at its socket - perhaps this tooth, too, was damaged. There is a small abscess cavity on the alveolus near the R mandibular I2 which does not communicate with the tooth socket. Perhaps the infection here was also caused by the same traumatic incident which caused the dental chipping.

There is extensive destruction of the R acetabular floor resulting in a large perforation at its centre. There are small pits lined with sclerotic bone beneath the acetabular joint surface. Radiographic examination reveals further small cavities within the ilium, near the acetabulum. The right femoral head is rather damaged post-mortem, but shows some ante-mortem destruction focused on the site for attachment of the ligamentum teres. The acetabular and femoral head lesions show negligible new bone formation. Tuberculosis. DNA analyses (Mays *et al.* 2001a) confirm the diagnosis and indicate the presence of *Mycobacterium tuberculosis* rather than *Mycobacterium bovis*.

Left femur sacrificed for radiocarbon determination 25/10/95.

NA115 There are deposits of woven bone on the endocranial and ectocranial surfaces of the R side of the frontal bone and the R sphenoid. There is slight woven bone deposition just posterior to the L occipital condyle. The mandibular rami exhibit deposits of woven bone adjacent to the condyles. There is porosis of the cortical bone adjacent to all these lesions. Most ribs and vertebrae show pitting of their surfaces and scattered deposits of sub-periosteal woven bone. They also show deposition of fibre bone endosteally. A few thoracic vertebrae show shallow superficial erosions on their bodies and there is a large lytic area beneath the L upper facet joint of the atlas vertebra, X-ray shows that its margins lack sclerosis. There are smaller areas of destruction on the right neural arch and transverse process of L5, the L sacral ala and the anterior surface of the centrum of S2. The margins of these cavities are of fine-grained woven bone.

Surface pitting and periosteal and endosteal deposits of woven bone are present on both innominates, the right clavicle, the medial third of the left clavicle, the R scapula, the sternum, both humeri, the left femur and the sub-trochanteric area of the right femur.

On radiographic examination, endosteal new bone formation shows as patchy sclerosis, and one additional lytic lesion was found, a radiolucency about 8x10mm in the distal part of the right femoral diaphysis.

The gross and radiographic appearence of the lesions suggests a diagnosis of metastatic carcinoma, probably from a primary focus in the prostate gland (Mays *et al.* 1996). Histological analysis supports this diagnosis (Mays *et al.* 1996).

Most teeth show super-eruption.

Porotic interdental septa and alveolar resorption. Some interdental septa have concave profiles. All changes are most marked in the molar regions. Periodontal disease.

Very brachycranic skull. The occipital bone is flattened posteriorly so that the maximum glabello-occipital length is measured to a point near the lambda.

T12 has lumbar-type facet joints.

There are bilateral anterior lingual depressions (Shafer *et al.* 1983, 36-7) in the sub-mandibular fossae in the canine/premolar areas of the mandible.

The L transverse process of C7 is elongated and has a double foramen. The transverse process has the appearance of a rudimentary cervical rib.

NA116 There is fusion of the axis and C3 at the R facet joints and at the R sides of their neural arches. Probably congenital.

NA117 Both 1st metarsals have super-numary epiphyses at their distal ends; that on the R is unfused, that on the L is fusing.

There are deposits of woven bone on the medial surface of the right femur, about one third of the way from the proximal end, and on the lateral sides of the tibiae, about two thirds of the way up the shafts, the deposit on the L tibia being heavier than that on the R. There is some swelling and pitting of the distal half of the L fibula and of the shafts of the L 4th and 5th metatarsals, suggestive of remodelled lesions. Periostitis.

NA118 The L maxillary M1 bears a large Carabelli cusp. The R M1 is not present.

The bones of NA118 and NA209 were mixed together in the same box. The 2 individuals have been separated as completely as possible but it proved impossible to assign many small fragments to one or other individual with any certainty; these were not recorded.

There are deposits of woven bone on the internal surfaces of the sphenoids, frontal bone and indeterminate skull vault fragments; somewhat remodelled deposits are present on the endocranial surface of the occipital bone. Periostitis.

NA119 The acetabulae are very shallow, showing negligible concavity. There is no evidence for hip dislocation but the proximal epiphyses of the femora are missing post-mortem. Probably a congenital variant.

NA120 Fusion of C3 and 4 at their L facet joints and the L sides of their neural arches. Probably congenital. C4 also shows spina bifida, as do L4 and 5 and all the sacral vertebrae.

NA121 The interdental septa are porotic and those in the molar areas have concave profiles. There is an infra-bony pocket around the R mandibular I1. Periodontal disease.

There is a vertically orientated cleft 1cm long in the superior part of the distal joint surface of the R femur, probably non-pathological. The components of the L knee joint are morphologically normal.

The L scapula and clavicle are more reddish-brown and more eroded than the rest of the skeleton.

See also notes on NA121A.

NA121A This burial is foetal bones boxed mixed with NA121 (=old number 206). NA121A is considered an *in-situ* burial rather than redeposited bone because even though there is some human and animal stray bone mixed with it the foetal bones are all from the same individual.

NA122 See notes on NA122A.

NA122A On the burial list NA122 (=old number 207) is listed as a child and, indeed, NA122 is a child. Two of the 4 boxes which are listed as containing this burial contain adult bones. These bones are considered as burial NA122A - there is no stray bone with them and the burial consists of the top parts of the body only, as though it was an *in-situ* burial truncated by a later feature (?the grave for NA122).

The interdental septa in the molar area are flattened and porotic. Localised periodontal disease.

NA123 Thick skull vault.

The tip of the tuberosity of the R navicular is missing and the bone in this area is porotic. Probably the site for fibrous attachment of an os tibiale externum. The L navicular has a cleft near the tip of its tuberosity - apparently an incompletely separated os tibiale externum.

The L side of the body of T12 lacks a facet for the 12th rib.

This burial is described as a 'disturbed skeleton' on the box, however its orientation is shown on the plan so sufficient must have remained *in-situ* for orientation to be apparent in the field.

NA125 The maxillary deciduous canines each show a tubercle on the distal parts of the lingual aspects of their crowns.

NA127 Clavicles, scapulae, humeri, thoracic vertebrae and ribs sacrificed for radiocarbon determination 25/10/95.

NA131 The flat-bones of the skull are thickened and have irregular and porous outer surfaces. Fragments of the zygomatic and temporal bones show similar features. The right distal radius exhibits abnormal curvature and the surface underlying the growth plate is porous and irregular. The right ilium has a porous and irregular cortex. The femora show areas of sub-periosteal fibre bone deposition. The sternal rib ends are missing post-mortem, but the remaining rib fragments show porous, irregular cortical bone surfaces. There is enlargement of the metaphyses of some of the long-bones. Rickets. This individual is among those described by Ortner and Mays (1998).

NA132 There is remodelled periostitis over the general surface of the tibiae.

NA135 There is pitting of the parietal bones adjacent to the lambdoid suture - cribra cranii. There is also cribra orbitalia of the cribriotic type.

There is irregular destruction of the left side of the mandible from the left I2 area posteriorly. The borders of the lesion lack sclerosis and are fairly smooth, and the area of destruction is an irregular, somewhat scalloped shape. There is minimal bone regeneration, except for a little woven bone at the anterior/medial margin of the lesion. There is slight pitting at the edges of the destroyed area and on the lingual surface of the right side of the mandible. On the temporal bone there is destruction of the left mandibular fossa. Small perforations pierce the temporal bone in this area, and there is slight pitting on the internal surface of the bone. There is marked pitting over the external surfaces of the left temporal bone and the sphenoid bone on its left greater wing, and the bone is also slightly thickened in this area. The impression is of the deposition of a thin layer of well remodelled bone over these surfaces. There is also a small area of pitting on the internal surface of the sphenoid in the region of the left foramen rotundum. Externally, the left pterygoid processes are destroyed with minimal bone regeneration, the margins of the lytic area being of sclerotic trabecular bone. The lateral surface of the left zygomatic bone shows porosis and superficial cavitation.

In summary, there are pathological changes to the left side of the cranium and mandible, and the lesions are mainly lytic in nature. Some of the lesions present a well-remodelled appearence, but some are unremodelled, so it would appear that the process responsible for the pathology was active at time of death (and hence may be implicated in cause of death), but the individual clearly lived with the condition for some time. The distribution of pathological changes is suggestive of a single disease focus in the region of the left mandibular angle or mandibular ramus. The rest of the skeleton (which is fairly complete although it lacks the lower legs and feet) was X-rayed but no further lesions were identified.

The changes here are consistent with a diagnosis of Langerhans' cell histiocytosis, and histological analysis also supports this. This case is described, together with full details of differential diagnoses, in Mays and Nerlich (1997).

NA138 There are deposits of woven bone on the anterior surfaces of S2-5. Periostitis.

NA140 According to the list of burials boxes 860425, 860436 and 860579 contain NA139 (old number 224) and NA140 (old number 225), and 860430 contains only NA139. NA139 is an infant and the bones in the other 3 boxes are those of an adult and a child. The adult was called NA140 and the child NA140A.

There is bony spurring at the insertions of the quadriceps femoris on the patellae, adjacent to the anterior margin of the distal joint surface of the L fibula and on the olecranon process of the R ulna.

The L transverse process of T1 is reduced and terminates in an area of irregular, sclerotic bone. Perhaps the rest of the transverse process was present as a separate ossicle. The articular facet adjacent to the tuberosity of the L 1st rib is present and normal, suggesting that the missing parts of the vertebral transverse process bore a normal joint surface.

NA140A See notes on NA140.

NA142 These bones were boxed mixed with those of a younger foetus, which is numbered NA142A. Some fragments could not be assigned with certainty to one or other individual; these were not recorded.

NA142A See notes on NA142.

NA143 The maxillary PM2s have bifid roots, as does the L mandibular PM1 (the roots of the R mandibular PM1 are not visible).

The transverse processes of the L1 are rudimentary.

NA144 R frontal foramen.

NA145 Porotic, flattened interdental septa; alveolar resorption around the maxillary I1s. Periodontal disease.

The maxillary canines bear lingual tubercles.

There is crowding of the R anterior maxillary dentition and, as a result, the R I2 is deflected lingually.

The L maxillary I2 is congenitally absent.

NA146 There are infra-bony pockets around several maxillary and mandibular teeth. Periodontal disease.

Several metal coffin fittings are boxed with the bones; one of them is adhering to the 4th cervical vertebra. It would seem that this individual was buried in a coffin.

L5 shows spondylolysis, no sign of spondylolisthesis.

The R acetabular floor is filled with new bone; this new bone clearly articulated with the femoral head: both show eburnation. The pit for the ligamentum teres on the R femoral head is obliterated. There are patchy radiolucencies beneath the eburnated area on the femoral head and there is a small amount of new bone in the L acetabular fossa.

The sacrum is fused to the L ilium just posterior to the sacro-iliac joint, the joint itself is normal except for marginal lipping in its superior portion. The R sacro-iliac joint shows slight degenerative changes but is otherwise normal.

The causes of the changes at the hip joints and the sacro-iliac fusion are uncertain.

L frontal foramen.

There are blood-vessel impressions on the lateral surfaces of both tibiae.

Tibiae sacrificed for radiocarbon determination 25-10-95. Left femur sacrificed for replicate 2-12-96.

NA149 The interdental septa are flattened and porotic and there are infra-bony pockets around the mandibular L PM2, R canine and R PM1. Periodontal disease.

Boxed mixed with NA149A (*qv*).

NA149A NA149A is an infant whose bones were boxed mixed with NA149. It is a fairly complete individual and is regarded as an *in-situ* burial adjacent to NA149 and which was inadvertently collected with it.

The distal parts of the tibiae are bowed medially. There is only 1 foot bone present (a fragment of the L 1st metatarsal) and it is normal. The cause of the bowed tibiae is uncertain.

NA149B The bone from this individual is labelled with old number 234 (which corresponds to NA149) although it is boxed separately from NA149 and NA149A. NA149B is fairly complete and there is little stray boxed with it; it thus seems likely that it represents an *in-situ* burial rather than redeposited material, and was presumably double numbered with NA149.

NA150 The superior R side of the posterior arch of the atlas has an area having an appearence identical to bone bearing an epiphyseal cartilage in a growing bone. A similar area is present on the adjoining part of the rim of the foramen magnum. The above suggests that cartilaginous union existed between the atlas and the occipital bone in life; perhaps bony fusion would have occurred as the skeleton matured. There is also asymmetry of these bones: the R side of the posterior arch is thickened compared with the L. The distance between the posterior margin of the occipital condyle and the midline is 18mm on the L side of the occipital compared with 13mm on the R. Presumably a similar asymmetry existed in the lengths of the sides of the posterior arch of the atlas but because the two halves have not yet grown together at the midline it is not possible to verify this.

Two mid-thoracic vertebrae are fused together at the L sides of their neural arches and at their L facet joints.

Both the above probably represent congenital anomalies.

NA151 The L maxillary deciduous I2 has an additional cusp, which projects lingually from the cingulum. X-ray shows that a horn of the pulp cavity projects into this additional cusp. Talon cusp.

The incisive edge of the L maxillary I2 also shows a double labial convexity and both the crown and the root are broader mesio-distally than on the normal right lateral incisor. The tooth count in the upper dentition is normal. This likely represents an example of double tooth, either gemination, or fusion between the I2 and a supernumerary tooth.

Each mandibular deciduous canine shows a circular depression about 1mm diameter in the buccal surface of the enamel of the crown about midway between the cemento-enamel junction and the crown tip. That in the left tooth is sufficiently deep that it exposes the underlying dentine. These defects probably represent localised enamel hypoplasias of the deciduous canines (Skinner *et al.* 1994).

NA154 Congenital absence of maxillary PM2s; the canines and the mandibular premolars are reduced in size and the third molars are absent.

The L foramen transversarium on the atlas is incomplete.

T12 has lumbar-type facet joints.

NA157 Spondylolysis of L5, no sign of spondylolisthesis.

There are channels, having the appearance of rather broad root erosions, on the L femur, L tibia and L pelvic bone and, to a lesser extent, on the R pelvis and the distal end of the R femur. The affected bones are rather poorly preserved, unlike the rest of the skeleton.

NA160 There is an area of somewhat remodelled periostitis on the lateral side of the L tibia, near the proximal end.

NA166 The R superior facet joint on T12 is of lumbar type, the L is of normal thoracic type.

L4 shows spondylolysis, no sign of spondylolisthesis.

NA167 The R maxillary M3 is peg-like, the L is congenitally absent and both mandibular M3s are reduced in size.

There is an infra-bony pocket around the maxillary R I2 and around each mandibular M2. Periodontal disease.

The bones of NA167 and NA172 are boxed commingled. On the list NA167 is referred to as a child and NA172 as 'feet only'. In fact both burials are adults, one consisting of lower legs and feet only (and hence thought to be NA172), the other being fairly complete (thought to be NA167). (The listing of NA167 as a child must simply be an error.)

The L vertebral foramen on the axis is incomplete.

T10 lacks articular facets for ribs on its transverse processes - the 10th ribs have articular facets only at their heads.

There is a healed fissure fracture running along the groove for the insertion of the posterior faciculus of the external lateral ligament in the distal end of the right fibula. There seems to be slight upward displacement of the tip of the malleolus on healing.

There are cystic cavities several millimetres in diameter, lined with trabecular bone in the tuberosities of both naviculae. Probably not pathological.

Tibiae sacrificed for radiocarbon determination 25/10/95.

NA168 The interdental septa are porotic, and those in the molar areas have concave or flattened profiles. Periodontal disease.

L3 shows spondylolysis. There is severe degeneration of the L3/4 disc and considerable new bone on the anterior surface of the body of L4, probably due to activation of the periosteum by anterior slippage of the body of L3 - spondylolisthesis. When the large osteophytes on the bodies of L3 and 4 are rearticulated the body of L3 lies 5-6mm anterior to that of its neighbour, suggesting this degree of slippage in life. There is severe unilateral osteoarthritis of the R hip joint, perhaps initiated by poor gait induced by the spondylolisthesis.

There is a concave crescentic area of porotic bone on the anterior margin of the anterior facet of each calcaneus. These probably represent sites for attachment of calcaneum secundaria.

R frontal foramen.

NA170 There is a diastema between the canine and the PM1 on both sides of the maxillary dental arch, the gap is wider on the R side.

C7 has a thickened, rather elongated right transverse process. This probably represents a rudimentary cervical rib.

L1 has T12-type facet joints.

The ridges for attachment of the deltoid muscles on the humeri are rather large for a female, that on the L is particularly pronounced.

There is a sub-rectangular cavity 9x4mm on the inferior margin of the L femoral head and one measuring 10x5mm in a similar position on the R femur. Probably not pathological.

S1 is not fused to S2 at the facet joints or at the L side of the body: incomplete lumbarisation of S1.

Right femur, both ulnae and right radius sacrificed for radiocarbon determination 25/10/95.

See notes for 170A.

NA170A Said on box to be 'foetus *in situ*' with NA170.

The preservation of the bone is generally good but the anterior parts of the ribs are poorly preserved - very eroded by soil action - as are the L lower leg bones.

NA171 There is a small socket at the position of the R maxillary canine which probably held a retained deciduous tooth which was lost post-mortem. The permanent canine has erupted lingually to this. There is a diastema between the R maxillary canine and the PM1 in which there is embedded a root of a deciduous tooth, it is probably from the deciduous M1.

Small perforation in body of hyoid.

L pterion is of stellate form.

The right humerus shows a small, spindle-shaped swelling on its medial surface at the junction of its middle and distal thirds. The lesion is of smooth, dense-looking bone, but with slight pitting at its margins. It measures approx. 2 x 0.5cm, with its long axis parallel with that of the bone. It stands approximately 2mm proud of the normal cortex. Radiography reveals a diffuse radiolucency within the lesion. Possibly an ossified haematoma. An alternative diagnosis is osteoid osteoma, but the internal radiolucency is rather less well-defined than is customarily seen in that condition.

NA172 Boxed mixed with NA167 (*qv*).

There is heavy bony spurring at the insertions of the Achilles tendons on the calcanei and, to a lesser extent, on the fibulae (near the anterior borders of the distal joint surfaces) and on the patellae at the insertions of the quadriceps femores.

NA173 The R maxillary I2 is much reduced in size; the R is missing.

There is congenital absence of the R mandibular PM2; the deciduous molar is retained here.

Bilateral frontal foramina.

Tibiae sacrificed for radiocarbon determination 25/10/95.

NA174 The central and lateral maxillary incisors have shovel-shaped crowns.

Both femora have 3rd trochanters.

R frontal foramen.

There is a small patch of woven bone on the medial surface of the left femur.

NA175 The L transverse foramen on the atlas is incomplete; the R side is of normal morphology.

NA176 Reduced maxillary I2s.

Flattened occipital bone: measuring from the glabella the maximum cranial length is to a point on the upper part of the occipital squama, near the lambda.

L4 and 5 both show spondylolysis, neither shows any sign of spondylolisthesis.

Both claviculae have deep rhomboid fossae.

There is a pit 1.5mm deep, 7mm diameter, lined with sclerotic trabeculae, on the superior part of the lateral condyle of the L femur. Osteochondritis dissecans. The other components of the knee joint are normal.

There is an exostosis on the dorsal margin of the distal joint surface of the L navicular. Probably traumatic in origin.

The R fibula shows well remodelled periostitis in its lower third. The tibia is normal.

The terminal and intermediate phalanges of a little toe are fused together.

Left tibia sacrificed for radiocarbon determination 25-10-95.

NA177 There is well remodelled periostitis, together with a little woven bone, on the shafts of the tibiae (most marked on the lateral sides) and fibulae (particularly the R). The posterior aspects of the femora, just above the condyles also show slight lesions. There is swelling of the shaft of the R 2nd metatarsal, probably also periostitis.

On the left talus the anterior articular surface for the calcaneus is irregular and rather bumpy, and the trochlear surface shows slight eburnation. Perhaps these changes are due to trauma of the L ankle.

The distal and intermediate phalanges of a little toe are fused together.

NA178 There is an approximately circular depression, 28mm diameter, on the coronal suture about 3cm from the bregma; most of the lesion is located on the frontal rather than the parietal bone. The edges are bevelled ectocranially down to a flat area of thin bone which forms the central part of the lesion. The bevel on the anterior side of the hole is steeper and shorter than on the posterior side. The thin, flat area at the centre of the lesion is about 16mm diameter and the thin bone is perforated along the line of the coronal suture; this perforation is 13mm long by a maximum of 2mm wide. There is no pitting or any other sign of infection - the ectocranial and endocranial surfaces of the skull around the lesion are of normal appearance. The most likely diagnosis is a dermoid cyst, a developmental defect which arises from entrapment of ectodermal cells by underlying mesenchymal tissue during embryogenesis (Barnes 1994, 56-7). Other possibilities include a fibroma or sebaceous cyst.

NA179 The terminal and intermediate phalanges of a little toe are fused together.

NA180 Intermediate and terminal phalanges of some toes fused.

NA181 There is a small acetabular cyst (Wells 1976) above each acetabulum. They communicate with the joint spaces.

There is a fracture running through the proximal joint surface of the proximal phalanx of the R 5th finger; the fracture runs obliquely separating a fragment on the base of the phalanx on the lateral side. Firmly healed.

There is a cleft in the proximal joint surface of the R medial cuneiform. Probably a very incompletely divided cuneiform.

There is a flat plaque of sclerotic bone, 3.5cm long and about 1.5-2cm anterior-posteriorly, on the lateral surface of the R femur, just below the level of the lesser trochanter, rising about 3mm proud of the normal cortex. Myositis ossificans.

The R tibia and fibula show united fractures in their midshaft areas. The fractures are oblique, both running in a superior/lateral

to inferior/medial direction. They are firmly united but the bones are 20mm (tibia) and 16mm (fibula) shorter than their L side counterparts.

C5 and 6 are fused by osteophytes at the anterior parts of their centra, and at their facet joints. C5 has slipped forwards by about 7mm. There is a compression fracture of the anterior-superior part of the body of C6 and this, together with the forward slippage of C5, has caused kyphosis at this point of about 20 degrees. The post-cranial skeleton of this individual is robust and heavily mineralised indicating no lasting neurological deficits as a result of the spinal injury - the degree of anterior luxation of C5 must have been insufficient to damage the spinal cord.

T12 shows a compression fracture of its body and a fracture horizontally across the neural arch at the superior parts of the posterior facet joints. Its body is fused to that of L1 by large osteophytes. The compression of the body of T12 has led to about 20 degree kyphosis at this point in the spine.

L5 shows spondylolysis, no sign of spondylolisthesis. There is a porotic area on the posterior aspect of the neural spine of L4 and on the anterior aspect of the neural arch of L5 at the base of the neural spine. Presumably there was contact between these areas in life, facilitated by the tilting of the detached arch of L5.

NA182 Foramen transversaria on atlas incomplete.

NA183 There is a united fracture about 1/3 of the way from the sternal end of an unsided middle rib. A little well remodelled callus is present; the fracture probably occurred long before death.

NA184 There is pitting on the superior parts of the ectocranial surface of the occipital bone and on the ectocranial surfaces of the parietal bones near the lambdoid suture. Porotic hyperostosis. This individual also shows cribra orbitalia of the porotic type.

Bilateral frontal foramina.

NA185 The inferior facet joints of T12 face anteriorly rather than in the usual lateral orientation. The R transverse process of T12 is missing, as are both those of L1; instead small epiphyseal surfaces are present. Perhaps the transverse processes were present as separate ossicles attached by cartilage. In the L1 these ossicles may be considered as rudimentary lumbar ribs.

NA188 The L 1st metatarsal has an extra epiphysis, at its distal end; it is not fused with the shaft. The R 1st metatarsal is missing post-mortem.

NA189 There is fusion of the mandibular deciduous L I1 and 2. They are fused at their roots and the lower parts of their crowns, but the upper crowns are separate and X-ray shows that the crowns have separate pulp chambers even though the teeth share a single root canal.

The sternal rib ends are somewhat porous and a little thicker than normal. There is slight lateral bending of the distal parts of the tibiae. The long-bones are generally rather thick. These changes are similar to those which may occur in rickets but are insufficient to permit a firm diagnosis.

NA190 Porotic and concave interdental septa, alveolar resorption. Periodontal disease.

T12 has lumbar-type facet joints.

T11 and 12 are fused at the R-anterior parts of their bodies by a thick, flowing osteophyte. There are osteophytes on the L sides of the centra which articulate with one another but are not fused. 'Bone former' type changes.

The body of T12 shows anterior wedging - the anterior height of the centrum is 22mm, 8mm less than the posterior height. There is also more slight wedging of the body of T11. These changes are probably due to minor compression fractures of T11 and 12 and result in about 20 degree kyphosis of this part of the spinal column.

NA191 Parts of the cranial vault show abnormally porous ectocranial surfaces. The forearm bones are thickened and abnormally curved. There is swelling of most sternal rib ends and they show slit-like defects in their cortices. Many bones of the post-cranial skeleton show porosis at their metaphyses and the R scapula exhibits porosis adjacent to the growing margins. Bone surfaces underlying growth plates are porotic, as are the iliac faces of the sacro-iliac joints. The long-bones appear thickened. Rickets. This case is among those presented by Ortner and Mays (1998).

NA192 Both femora show a 3rd trochanter.

NA194 There is widespread formation of fibre bone on the inner surface of the skull vault, and thin sheets of fibre bone also occur on the outer table. The orbital roofs are porous. There is flaring of the sternal rib ends and of the distal end of the right radius. The cortical bone of the ribs is very porous with slits towards the sternal ends. The metaphyses of the long-bones are also porous. The posterior surface of the right scapula has a deposit of woven bone. The bone underlying the growth plates of the long-bones is porous and irregular. There is thinning (craniotabes) of the occipital squama at the R cerebellar fossa. There is some post-mortem flaking but there was probably perforation of the bone in life (the perforation would have been covered by non-mineralised osteoid), but at the very least the bone in this area must have been paper-thin. Rickets. This case is among those described by Ortner and Mays (1998).

NA195 T12 has lumbar-type facet joints.

The humeri have fossae at the insertions of the teres major muscles. The fossa on the L is larger and deeper than that on the R. Benign cortical defects.

Tibiae sacrificed for radiocarbon determination 25-10-95.

NA197 There is an infra-bony pocket around the R mandibular M3. Periodontal disease.

L5 shows spondylolysis, no sign of spondylolisthesis.

T12 lacks facets for ribs - so presumably there were only 11 pairs of ribs.

There are small cystic defects adjacent to the joint margins on the R capitate. Probably non-pathological.

There is a united fracture running medio-laterally across the joint surface of the terminal phalanx of the R middle finger. The intermediate phalanx is un-injured.

There is a depressed, sclerotic area on both faces of the L and R 3rd metatarsal-lateral cuneiform articulations. Bilateral non-osseous tarsal coalition (Regan *et al*. 1999).

There are two fissure fractures in the L navicular; the lateral one seems to penetrate the full anterio-posterior width of the bone, the other affects the proximal joint surface only.

There is a fracture of the shaft of the L 5th metatarsal. Union has occurred with dorsal displacement of the distal part. The callus is well remodelled suggesting healing some time before death.

A L middle rib shows a united fracture in the midshaft area. The L 10th rib shows a united fracture about 1/3 of the way from its head. In both cases there is a little well remodelled callus, suggesting union long before death. Two R ribs show fractures, one about 1/3 of the way from the sternal end and one about 1/3 of the way from the head. The former shows a little well remodelled callus suggestive of an old fracture, but in the latter case the callus shows only a little remodelling, indicating that it occurred in a separate incident nearer to the time of death.

There is a smooth, rounded bony projection rising about 0.5cm proud of the normal cortex on the medial side of the proximal metaphysis of the L tibia. The exostosis points towards the proximal epiphysis and X-ray reveals that the outer surface of the lesion is continuous with the normal cortex. Very probably an osteochondroma. There is a similar bony projection just anterior to the lateral epicondyle of the R humerus. This too has the appearance of an osteochondroma, although they are generally solitary lesions except in cases of hereditary multiple exostoses (diaphysial aclasia), a diagnosis which can be excluded as all other metaphyses are normal.

There is extensive destruction of the R acetabulum, leaving a very shallow socket. The lytic area is of fairly smooth trabecular bone. A large, irregular cavity extends within the ilium from the anterior part of the acetabulum. There is post-depositional damage to the head of the right femur, but some ante-mortem destruction is also evident. There is some irregular new bone deposition on the femoral neck and in the area of the lesser trochanter. All new bone deposits are well-remodelled and the trabeculae in the lytic areas show no sclerosis.

Tuberculosis. DNA analyses (Mays *et al*. 2001a) confirm the diagnosis and indicate the presence of *Mycobacterium tuberculosis* rather than *Mycobacterium bovis*.

NA198 Congenital absence of the R maxillary I2. Both maxillary and the L mandibular M3 are absent.

There is a slightly unusual pattern of dental eruption: the maxillary PM1s have erupted, the mandibular ones have not; the L maxillary and both mandibular canines have erupted but the R maxillary one has not.

There is a pit 10 x 5 x 2mm deep in the L superior articular facet of the axis vertebra. Probably osteochondritis dissecans.

The R vertebral foramen of the axis is incomplete as is the R foramen transversarium of the atlas.

NA199 Marked underbite.

Both femora show 3rd trochanters.

There is incomplete lumbarisation of S1: its R transverse process is free and of lumbar type and its neural arch bears facet joints (the L being much reduced); the L transverse process is united, albeit incompletely, with S2.

There is a probable healed fissure fracture across the cuboid facet of the R calcaneus. This creates a step 2mm high in the joint surface. Small areas of eburnation on both faces of the joint testify to the disruption caused to the articulation.

There is pitting on the proximal surfaces of both proximal hallucial phalanges. Non-pathological.

There is an united fracture of the L clavicle about 1/3 of the way from the lateral end. Negligible callus, the fracture probably healed long before death.

R frontal foramen.

The distal and intermediate phalanges of both little toes are fused together.

Tibiae and fibulae sacrificed for radiocarbon determination 25-10-95.

NA201 Both 1st metatarsals have epiphyses at their distal ends.

NA202 Very thin, highly resorbed mandible.

Slight bathrocrany.

Light bones with thin cortices - osteoporosis.

The joint surface of the head of the R 3rd metacarpal is flattened and broadened. The shaft is thickened, particularly towards its distal end, and the bone is shortened by about 2mm compared with its counterpart in the L hand. It seems probable that this represents Dieterich's disease, a vascular disturbance of the distal epiphysis of the metacarpal, probably as a result of mechanical trauma - i.e. a condition analogous to Freiberg's disease of the metatarsal head. There are no finger bones so the state of the adjacent phalanx cannot be assessed.

Brown staining on lower leg and foot bones.

NA203 There is a probable healed fissure fracture obliquely through the distal joint surface of the L fibula.

The bones are light with thin cortices. A fragment of a lower thoracic vertebral body shows coarsened trabeculae and most of the trabeculae are vertically orientated with few connecting transverse struts. Some other vertebral body fragments also show similar changes. Osteoporosis.

Skeleton rather fragmentary.

NA203A The box containing these bones is labelled with old number 286 (which corresponds to NA201) whereas a label inside the box bears old number 288 (=NA203), as do the bones themselves. The bones constitute an individual distinct from either NA201 or NA203 so there seems to have been a numbering error here. The burial is given number NA203A.

Bilateral frontal foramina.

NA204 Porotic and flattened interdental septa; their profiles are concave in the molar areas. Periodontal disease.

Bilateral frontal foramina; both have grooves on the frontal bone leading to them.

NA205 L5 shows spondylolysis, no sign of spondylolisthesis.

Right masto-occipital suture obliterated.

NA209 Boxed mixed with NA118.

NA215 The occlusal surfaces of the crowns of the M1s are rather irregular and the enamel is thinned so that the colour of the dentine is visible through it. Probably hypoplastic defects associated with a stress episode around time of birth.

The L maxillary canine is impacted - it is tilted forwards so that its crown lies against the neighbouring I2.

Porotic interdental septa - periodontal disease.

L1 has T12-type facet joints.

Right tibia, right ulna and left fibula sacrificed for radiocarbon determination 25-10-95. Left femur sacrificed for replicate 2-12-96.

NA217 There is a small, crescentic depressed area of sclerotic bone on the anterior margin of the anterior facet of the L calcaneus. Probably the site of fibrous attachment for a calcaneum secundarium. The R calcaneus is normal.

The anterior/upper parts of the R sacro-iliac joint are fused by a thick osteophyte. The 2 bones have broken apart post-mortem revealing that the joint surfaces are normal. The bodies of 2 lumbar vertebrae are united by a massive, smooth, paravertebral osteophyte. The other lumbar vertebrae have large, thick osteophytes on their bodies but in all cases the facet joints seem normal.

T1 and 2 have osteophytes on the L sides of their bodies which articulate but are not ankylosed. T4 and 5 are fused at their bodies

by smooth, paravertebral osteophytes. T5 and 6 and T6 and 7 have similar osteophytes which interlock but are not fused. T7-11 are fused at their bodies by a massive, smooth, R-sided osteophyte. In all cases the facet joints are normal. The inferior margins of the body of C3 show large osteophytes. C5 and 6 are fused by large osteophytes on the L and R sides of their centra. The upper margins of the body of C7 bear large osteophytes. There is bony spurring at the grooves for the peroneus longus and the insertions of the Achilles tendons on the calcanei, and the linea aspera and the greater trochanters of the femora. There are osteophytes near the margins of the glenoid cavities of the scapulae, the proximal humeri, proximal L ulna and the proximal R radius. DISH.

The axis vertebrae is fused to C3 at its body, facet joints and neural arch. Fusion at the facet joints and complete fusion of the vertebral bodies without osteophyte formation is not characteristic of DISH. It seems more likely that this fusion of C2 and 3 is a congenital anomaly.

A R rib shows a united fracture one third of the way from its sternal end, a L rib shows a united fracture one third of the way from its vertebral end. In both cases the callus is well remodelled.

The interdental septa are porotic and many have concave or irregular profiles. There is an infra-bony pocket at the maxillary L I1. Periodontal disease.

Left tibia sacrificed for radiocarbon determination 25-10-95.

NA218 Congenital absence of the L mandibular I2. There would have been little space for it in the jaw.

Marked super-eruption of the R mandibular M3 and the L mandibular M2.

Marked underbite, thus, for example, the maxillary M3s occlude with the mandibular M2s, and the mandibular M3s do not occlude at all.

L1 has T12-type facet joints.

There is a united transverse fracture of a R proximal foot phalanx (?from the 3rd toe), near its distal end. The fracture is well healed with some shortening.

There is well remodelled periostitis on the tibiae about 1/4 of the way from their proximal ends; the deposits on the L are mainly confined to the medial surface, those on the R are thicker and lie mainly on the posterior surface. Both fibulae have similar deposits on the proximal parts of their shafts, as does the R femur in the midshaft area and on the posterior surface, just above the condyles. Inflammation of the lower legs which was not active at death.

There is a smooth, approximately circular area of raised bone, about 2cm in diameter on the R parietal bone, 3cm from the midline and 4.5cm from the coronal suture. Probably a button osteoma.

L5 shows spondylolysis. No sign of spondylolisthesis.

The calvarium is very distorted post-mortem.

There is a supra-acetabular cyst (Wells 1976) above each acetabulum. They communicate with the joint spaces.

Right tibia sacrificed for radiocarbon determination 25-10-95.

NA223 Skeleton somewhat fragmentary.

Long-bones sacrificed for radiocarbon determination 25-10-95.

NA224 There are small, crescentic, depressed areas of sclerotic bone on the anterior margin of the anterior facets of the calcanei. Probably sites for fibrous attachments for calaceum secundaria.

There is a 2 x 4mm cystic cavity on the L capitate near the border of the articular surface for the 4th metacarpal. Probably not pathological.

Left tibia sacrificed for radiocarbon determination 25/10/95. Right femur sacrificed for replicate 2-12-96.

NA225 There are deposits of woven bone on the endocranial surfaces of the occipital, temporal, sphenoid, frontal and parietal bones.

NA227 The L maxillary M3 has an enamel pearl 2mm in diameter on its distal aspect, near the bifurcation of its buccal and lingual roots (this tooth only has 2 roots). This tooth also shows a Carabelli cusp.

L5 shows spondylolysis. No sign of spondylolisthesis.

On C7 the anterior root of the L transverse process exists as a separate ossicle (which has been lost post-mortem) - a cervical rib. The R is free at its lateral end and the vertebral foramen is elongated and incomplete as a result. The morphology of the R side could be viewed as the incomplete development of a cervical rib.

Porotic interdental septa, with concave or flattened profiles in molar area. Periodontal disease.

Bilateral frontal foramina.

Left humerus, both radii and right femur sacrificed for radiocarbon determination 25-10-95.

NA233 There is partially remodelled periostitis on the medial surface of the R fibula, 1/4 of the way from the distal end. There is also swelling of the distal end of the R ulna (only the distal 1/4 is present) which probably represents well remodelled periostitis.

There are cystic defects with internal surfaces of trabecular bone on the tali, on margins of the articular surfaces for the naviculae and one lined with smooth bone on the R calcaneus, between the posterior articular surface and the point of insertion of the Achilles tendon. Probably not pathological.

Left femur sacrificed for radiocarbon determination 25-10-95.

See notes on NA233A.

NA233A Foetal bones in the same box as NA233 but bagged separately and given a separate finds number.

NA234 There are two cystic defects in the medial side of the head of the L 1st metatarsal. Probably bunion erosions, although there is no sign of valgus deviation of the great toe. There is also grade II osteoarthritis of the joint surface of the head. The R 1st metatarsal is normal.

The shafts of the L tibia and fibula are thickened by deposits of well remodelled sub-periosteal new bone over their general surfaces. X-ray reveals that their endosteal surfaces are normal. Periostitis.

NA235 The axis vertebra shows spina bifida.

NA236 The deciduous maxillary M2s and the R permanent maxillary M1 show Carabelli cusps (the maxillary L permanent M1 is missing).

There are deposits of porous bone on the ectocranial surface of the skull, particularly in the region of the frontal and parietal eminences. The orbits are very porotic. The trabeculae of the bones of the facial skeleton are sparse and enlarged. The few long-bone cortical fragments that are present are porotic. Rickets. This individual is among those described by Ortner and Mays (1998).

NA237 Porotic and ragged interdental septa. Periodontal disease.

The posterior arch of the atlas has a cleft in the R side at the groove for the R 1st cervical nerve and vertebral artery.

SA002 The R mandibular canine is twin rooted.

There seems to be a numbering error on the list of burials: c1461 is listed as Burial SA003 and c1462 is listed as Burial SA002. It is clear from the plan and photographs, however, that c1461 is Burial SA002 (this one) and c1462 is SA003.

There is porosis of the interdental septa in the molar area - periodontal disease.

There is a pit in the proximal joint surface of the R proximal hallucial phalanx. Not pathological.

There are deposits of woven bone on the lateral surfaces of both tibiae - periostitis.

Double L mental foramen.

There are benign cortical defects on both humeri at the insertions for the pectoralis major and teres major.

Forearm bones and right humerus sacrificed for radiocarbon 20-12-94 and 26-7-95.

SA003 Numbering error in list of burials - see notes for SA002.

There is a slightly depressed area of trabecular bone, about 7x5mm, on the proximal joint surfaces of both ulnae. Probably not pathological.

A fragment of a R rib shows a united fracture, probably situated about 1/3 of the way from the vertebral end.

The bodies of T7-11 have thick, R-sided, paravertebral osteophytes which articulate with one another but are not ankylosed. The superior/right margin of the body of T12 bears a smaller osteophyte of similar type, as does the superior-left margin of L5. There is also slight capsular ossification around the acetabulae. 'Bone former' type changes.

There is a fissure in the R zygomatic bone, running approximately parallel to the zygomaxillary suture, about 0.5cm lateral to it. The lesion is approximately linear and fully penetrates the bone. It is probably a healed blade injury.

There is a supra-acetabular cyst (Wells 1976) in the subchondral bone above the right acetabulum. It communicates with the joint space.

Left femur and right tibia sacrificed for radiocarbon 19-12-94 and 26-7-95.

SA005 The bones from Burials SA005 and SA007 are mixed together in the same boxes; both are juveniles, and the individuals were fairly readily separated. Burial SA005 may also include foot and lower leg bones labelled SA006 on the plan. This suggestion is consistent with the present skeleton, which is fairly complete but lacks tibiae: on the plan a large stone block is shown covering much of the lower leg area, with the foot and ankle bones protruding from it labelled SA006.

SA007 Boxed mixed together with SA005.

There are roughened areas on the lateral parts of S1 and S2 suggesting that a fibrous articulation existed between them.

SA008 The posterior parts of the R squamous suture are obliterated. This has the appearance of a sutural anomaly rather than simply premature closure of this part of the suture. L side normal. The bones received from this individual look rather an odd selection of elements (skull, 1 vertebra, L arm bones, a R rib, a pelvic fragment and a few hand bones) - it seems unlikely that the relative lack of remains from this individual is a result of preservation factors or of damage to the burial by later features. There is no photograph of the burial and the bones were not planned in. The plan implies that SA008 was a double burial with SA009. Perhaps the rest of SA008 got lost - all the bones from SA009 seem to have done.

SA012 Super-eruption of the mandibular M1s.

Skull distorted by soil pressure.

Left femur sacrificed for radiocarbon 19-12-94.

SA013 A thin spit of bone connects the right transverse process with the posterior arch of the atlas.

T5 and 6 bear supernumerary articular facets on adjoining faces of their neural spines.

Of the thoracic vertebrae T1-11 are present. T3-6 show erosions on the L sides of their bodies. The lesions are smallest on T3 and increase in size down the spine so that the largest is on T6 where most of the body has been destroyed by a scalloped lesion which under-cuts the vertebral end-plates. The anterior parts of the bodies of T5-7 show slight sub-periosteal new bone formation. There is partial destruction of the head of the L 6th rib. This rib, and the R 5th rib, show well-remodelled deposits of bone on their outer surfaces between their heads and their tuberosities.

Tuberculosis. DNA analyses (Mays *et al.* 2001a) confirmed the diagnosis, and indicated the presence of *Mycobacterium tuberculosis* rather than *Mycobacterium bovis*.

Left arm bones sacrificed for radiocarbon dating 27-1-95.

SA014 Crescentic, porotic area on the posterior border of the R talus. Probably the site for a fibrous attachment for an os trigonium.

There is a short, smooth projection on the medial part of the posterior surface of the proximal metaphysis of the R tibia. It is about 1cm long and points away from the epiphysial line. X-ray shows that its surface is continuous with that of the normal cortex. Probably an osteochondroma.

Left tibia sacrificed for radiocarbon 19-12-94.

SA015 This burial was boxed with a large amount of stray bone which is probably the disturbed material labelled SA016 on the plan.

C5 and 6 are fragmentary but enough remains to show that they are fused at their bodies and at the L sides of their neural arches. The facet joints are missing post-mortem. Probable congenital block vertebrae.

There is a pitted area on the posterior margin of the L talus. Probably the location for fibrous attachment for an os trigonium.

A fragment of a R rib shows a united fracture.

There is a supra-acetabular cyst (Wells 1976) in the subchondral bone above the left acetabulum. It communicates with the joint surface.

SA017 The L maxillary I2 shows a cingular nodule and both central maxillary incisors show slight shovel-shape.

Probable congenital absence of the R maxillary PM2. There is a flat area of slightly pitted bone here.

Four long-bone and 2 skull boxes are listed as containing the bone from Burial 17. The photograph shows Burial 17 as a complete, adult-sized skeleton in a discrete grave cut. This seems to be the bones labelled with finds number c1455. There are bones from another individual labelled c1456 which may be an *in-situ* burial rather than stray bone on the amount of material present. This latter is recorded as Burial SA017A. Could SA17A be a burial below SA017? The remaining bone (2 long-bone boxes) is treated as stray.

The interdental septa in the molar area are pitted and concave in profile. Periodontal disease.

The intermediate and distal phalanges of a little toe are fused together.

Green staining on temporal bones.

SA017A See notes on SA017.

The L glenoid shows cystic defects on its anterior border. Possibly related to trauma or perhaps not pathological.

R frontal foramen.

Large Carabelli cusps on both maxillary M1s.

SA021 Flattened, porotic interdental septa and beginning infra-bony pocket formation on the distal side of the R mandibular canine. Periodontal disease.

Slight bathrocrany.

There is marked asymmetry in the arm bones - those from the L side are shorter than those from the R. The ends of the L forearm bones are somewhat eroded but their estimated lengths are 237mm for the radius and 245mm for the ulna, compared with 247 and 263mm for their R side counterparts. The L forearm bones are also slightly less robust than the R. The L humerus is 14mm shorter than the R but they are of similar robusticity.

There is an oval hole about 3mm across near the volar margin of the L scaphoid. Probably not pathological.

A L true rib shows a super-numary facet on its superior surface which must have articulated with the transverse process of the neighbouring vertebra (which is missing post-mortem).

Bilateral frontal foramina. There are grooves in the R frontal bone which probably conveyed blood vessels or other structures to the R frontal foramen.

The L side of the skull shows much more post-depositional erosion than the R.

SA023 Very thin, atrophied mandible.

Bathrocrany, lambdoid suture filled with many ossicles.

There is a small amount of preserved hair adhering to the R parietal about 1.5cm from the coronal and 4cm from the squamous suture. The hair is grey-green in colour. The L parietal bone is stained green, as to a slight extent is the R in the region of the adhering hair. The green staining appears to be due to copper corrosion products - perhaps the biocidic effects of copper ions were resposible for preserving the hair.

T4 and 5 are fused at the anterior parts of their bodies, posterior parts of their neural arches and at their facet joints. There is severe osteoarthritis at the apophysial articulations between T2 and 3 and T3 and 4, presumably reflecting the increased strain on these joints as a result of the immobility of their neighbours.

The L transverse process of L5 is elongated - its total length is about 4cm. This has the appearence of a soft tissue ossification (i.e. ossification of the L ilio-lumbar ligament).

Slight capsular ossification around the glenoid cavities.

There is a small oval area of exposed trabecular bone on the proximal joint surface of the L ulna. Probably not pathological.

There is erosion of both external auditory meatuses. Erosion is particularly marked in the inferior and posterior aspects. In both instances the inferior wall of the meatus is completely destroyed, but the changes are more severe in the left temporal bone where the erosion extends deep into the mastoid process. The margins of eroded areas are of cortical bone which in most places is rather rough. The middle ear is normal and the tympanic ring is intact. Only one auditory ossicle is present, the left stapes. It is normal. Radiography shows that the lesion margins are slightly sclerotic. The mastoid processes contain a mixture of small air cells and diploic bone. They are not abnormally sclerotic. These lesions are suggestive of external ear canal cholesteatomas. This case has been described in detail elsewhere (Mays and Holst forthcoming).

SA029 The R zygomatic bone is stained green and there is dark staining near the distal ends of the tibiae.

There is a mass consisting of a small dentinous part and a larger enamel part, measuring about 0.5cm diameter, situated in the maxillary bone immediately posterior to the R I1. A radiograph shows that it has a curved inner canal resembling the root canal in an anterior tooth. It does not impinge upon the socket of the R I1 but it is visible through an aperture in the hard palate. Probably an odontoma; its anatomical resemblance to a normal tooth indicates that it should be classified as a compound composite odontoma.

Porotic and concave interdental septa, particularly around the mandibular molars. Periodontal disease.

There is a porotic area on the anterior borders of the anterior calcaneal facets of both calcanei; the inferior margins of the navicular bones show similar porotic areas. Probably bilateral fibrous calcaneo-navicular bars.

SA030 L lateral pterygoid plate foramen.

Reduced maxillary I2s - the buccolingual and mesiodistal widths of the L are 6.3 and 5.5mm respectively, those of the R are 6.1 and 5.8mm respectively.

Beginning infra-bony pocket formation around the maxillary R PM1. Porotic interdental septa. Periodontal disease.

SA033 There are two supra-acetabular cysts (Wells 1976) above the left acetabulum. They communicate with the joint space.

There is an interruption to the normal sharp edge of the acetabular rim in its superior part, with loss of rim height of several millimetres. This likely represents an acetabular flange lesion (Wells 1976) - traumatic separation of a fragment of the acetabular rim.

Right femur sacrificed for radiocarbon 20-12-94.

SA034 L4 shows spondylolysis. L5 is missing so it is difficult to ascertain whether spondylolisthesis was present.

There is a small crescentic, roughened depression in the anterior edge of the anterior calcaneal facet of the R calcaneus. Probably the site for fibrous attachment for a calcaneum secundarium.

Bony spurring on the R patella and on a thoracic vertebral body.

There are at least three probable blade injuries and one blunt injury on the L side of the frontal bone and the L parietal and temporal bones. One cut, approximately 10cm long, runs from the left frontal eminence and ends on the left parietal. A second describes a curve from the left temporal squama to a point near the vertex of the skull (post-depositional damage makes the precise extent of this cut unclear). A third, approximately 7cm long, runs from the inferior margin of the left temporal bone to a point just above the squamo-parietal suture. A break extends a further 7cm from the superior end of this cut and may represent an associated perimortal fracture. Toward the superior end of this putative perimortal fracture is an ovoid hole (approx. 2 x 3cm) with internally bevelled margins and signs of crushing and flaking on the ectocranial edges. This suggests a perimortal blunt injury. A further fracture, probably perimortal, extends from this hole and terminates in the region of the bregma. No lesions show any signs of healing. In summary, this individual suffered multiple perimortal trauma, consisting of at least three blade injuries and one blunt injury, to the left side of the cranium.

Left tibia sacrificed for radiocarbon 20-12-94.

SA045 The maxillary I1s have a pronounced shovel shape, and the L has 1 and the R 2 secondary tubercles. The R PM2 has an extra cusp; the L mandibular PM2 is missing but its socket is larger than normal - perhaps it too had a 3rd cusp.

SA047 The interdental septa are porotic and some have irregular profiles. Periodontal disease.

L1 lacks its R transverse process.

SA048 L1 lacks transverse processes and has facets on its neural arch where these would normally be. It seems probable that these facets would have articulated with transverse processes present as separate ossicles - i.e. small lumbar ribs - which were not recovered. L1 also has a thoracic-type R superior facet joint, the other 3 are of normal lumbar-type.

Skull distorted by soil pressure.

SA049 There is a roughened area on the posterior parts of the tuberosities of both naviculae. Probably sites for fibrous attachments for os tibiale externae. The accessoria themselves were not recovered.

There is a small deposit of slightly remodelled bone on the medial/posterior angle of the right tibia, one third of the way from the distal end. There is destruction of the joint surface of the left acetabulum, exposing trabecular bone. The destruction of bone is sufficiently advanced to leave the acetabular walls only a few millimetres thick in places. The joint surface of the femoral head is also destroyed leaving a trabecular bone surface. There is no bone regeneration in the affected areas, although there is some new bone in the acetabular fossa. The lesions are likely due to infection. The lack of new bone regeneration at the hip may suggest tuberculosis.

The bones are generally light with thin cortices. At a post-mortem break on the medial side of the L femur, about 7cm from the distal end, the cortex is only about 1.3mm thick. Osteoporosis.

Skull distorted by soil pressure.

SA050 Exostosis on lateral margin of the R patella. Uncertain cause.

There is downward displacement of both femoral heads so that their superior margins lie below the level of the greater trochanters. The depressions for the ligamentum teres are well defined but they are nearer the inferior margins of the joint surfaces than normal. The femoral necks appear rather thick. Probably slipped capital epiphyses.

SA052 There is an infra-bony pocket at the L mandibular canine. Periodontal disease.

A L rib shows a united fracture about halfway along its shaft. There is a little well remodelled callus. It has the appearence of a fracture which occurred long before death.

The terminal phalanx of the R big toe is markedly shorter than the L; its length is 17.6mm compared with 22.2 for the left.

Bathrocrany.

R mental foramen double.

There is a large supra-acetabular cyst (Wells 1976) above the right acetabulum. It communicates with the joint space.

Right tibia sacrificed for radiocarbon 19/12/94.

SA053 The R mandibular condyle is enlarged and has a flattened articular surface. There is porosis in the R mandibular fossa.

The L transverse foramen of the atlas is incomplete.

The top sacral vertebra is only partially fused to S2 at the R ala and centrum, although fusion is complete at the L ala.

There is a small exostosis on the lateral margin of the R patella. Uncertain cause.

The superior part of the distal joint surface of the L 2nd metatarsal is flattened and porotic and the adjacent joint surface of the proximal phalanx is flattened and broadened. Probably trauma to the joint.

Right tibia, fibula and humerus sacrificed for radiocarbon 20-12-94.

SA055 The L mandibular deciduous M1 has three roots and the occlusal surface of the crown is triangular in shape with a large distal/lingual cusp.

There is a deposit of somewhat remodelled bone on the posterior side of the left humerus shaft. Unremodelled new bone deposits are present on the anterior and posterior surfaces of the wing of the left scapula, particularly near the inferior angle. There are slight deposits, also of woven bone, near the inferior angle of the right scapula (posterior surface) and on the inferior surface of the right clavicle, towards its lateral end. Periostitis.

SA056 There is a short, thick osteophyte near the R lower margin of the body of T11. 'Bone former' type change.

The R side of the mandible is very thin where the molars have been lost ante-mortem.

Very fragmentary bones.

Left femur sacrificed for radiocarbon 20-12-94.

SA52/16 Pitting and flattening of maxillary interdental septa. Periodontal disease.

T12 has lumbar-type facet joints.

T8-L1 show erosions on the superior and inferior surfaces of their centra, near the anterior margins. The bone at the erosions is irregular and sclerotic. They reduce the anterior body heights giving rise to slight kyphosis. Many of the affected vertebrae bear Schmorl's nodes. It is possible that these changes are due to Scheuermann's disease. Measurement of the vertebral bodies, using the methodology of Scoles *et al.* (1991), indicates that in only two cases was the wedging of the vertebral bodies greater than 5 degrees. Clinical criteria demand at least three adjacent vertebral bodies show wedging of 5 degrees or more for Scheuermann's disease to be diagnosed.

There are six lumbar vertebrae, the extra vertebrae being a supernumerary segment, there are still the full complement of thoracic and sacral segments. L6 bears an enlarged L transverse process which bears a roughened surface on its inferior side which articulates with a similar roughened area on the L sacral ala. The L facet joint between L6 and S1 is reduced compared to the R.

The L mandibular M3 is impacted against the neighbouring M2.

SA52/18 Small osteoma in R frontal sinus.

Some pitting of interdental septa in molar area of maxilla and mandible. Periodontal disease.

The L maxillary M3 bears a Carabelli cusp.

SA080 L1 has T12-type facet joints.

There is pitting on the posterior parts of the ectocranial surfaces of the parietal bones. Cribra cranii.

There is a benign cortical defect on the right humerus, at the insertion of the teres majoris.

Very fragmentary skeleton.

Vertebral fragments, humeri and left ulna sacrificed for radiocarbon dating 27-1-95 and 27-7-95. Date failed.

V01 Dark red/brown/grey staining on bones.

V07 The interdental septum between the L maxillary PM1 and PM2 is concave and porotic: localised periodontal disease. There is a small fragment of dentine embedded in the buccal side of this septum; this is probably a fragment of the buccal/mesial root of the deciduous M2 which was not shed with the rest of the tooth. This embedded fragment seems to have formed the focus for the periodontal infection.

There is an enamel pearl about 1.2mm diameter at the junction of the distal/buccal root and the lingual root of the R maxillary M2. A smaller pearl (0.8mm diameter) is present on the distal surface of the single, flattened root of the L maxillary M2. The L mandibular M2 bears a tiny pearl about 0.5mm diameter deeply embedded in the dentine on the lateral side of its single root.

V10 There is expansion of the diploe and virtual elimination of the outer table on some cranial vault fragments. The ectocranial aspect of affected fragments is very pitted, with a striated appearence in the areas where changes are most pronounced. Porotic hyperostosis of the cranial vault - cribra cranii. The orbital roofs are missing so it is uncertain whether cribra orbitalia was also present.

V11 Shovel-shaped maxillary I1.

Porotic interdental septa, and infra-bony pocket formation between the buccal roots of the L mandibular M1. Periodontal disease.

T12 has lumbar-type facet joints.

There is a single supra-acetabular cyst (Wells 1976) above the left acetabulum and two above the right acetabulum. They communicate with the joint spaces.

V15 Porotic, concave interdental septa. Periodontal disease.

There are 6 lumbar vertebrae and L6 shows spondylolysis and spina bifida. No evidence for spondylolisthesis.

The humeri each bear a small bridge of bone creating a foramen about 2cm above the medial epicondyle.

The L 11th rib shows a united fracture about one third of the way from the vertebral end. Slight callus, minimal deformity.

The L masto-occipital suture is completely fused.

There is a large supra-acetabular cyst (Wells 1976) in the subchondral bone above the left acetabulum. It communicates with the joint space.

V16 Porotic and concave interdental septa. Periodontal disease.

There are 6 lumbar vertebrae. The L transverse process of L6 articulates via a joint surface with the L sacral ala. The R sacral ala and transverse process of L6 are missing so this side cannot be assessed. A lumbo-sacral transitional variant.

There is a double L epipteric bone.

V18 T12 has lumbar-type facet joints.

There is a 1cm diameter area of exposed trabecular bone on the distal joint surface of the R humerus in the area which articulates with the radial head. This area is slightly depressed below the normal joint surface. Unknown cause.

T7-10 bear large, thick, smooth, R-sided paravertebral osteophytes on their centra, which interlock with one another but are not fused. Probably they would have fused had the individual lived a little longer. There are large capsular ossifications at the heads of the L 10th, R 5th and R 11th ribs, and there is slight spurring at the anterior margin of the iliac face of the R sacro-iliac joint. 'Bone former' type changes.

V19 There is a compression fracture of the body of T12 with anterior wedging (anterior height is reduced by 10mm compared with the posterior side). The fracture is firmly healed with little callus.

T12 has lumbar-type facet joints.

Fragmentary skeleton.

V20 Bones stained dark reddish-brown. Some bones have white powdery material adhering to them.

V21 There is lateral deviation of the distal joint surfaces of both metatarsals; the joint surfaces both show severe osteoarthritis in the form of eburnation and heavy marginal lipping. Bilateral hallux valgus.

Bones stained dark red-brown.

There is a smooth ovoid swelling on the medial side/anterior edge of the L tibia, just below the midshaft. It measures 5.5 by 2.5cm, its long axis parallel to that of the bone. Probably an ossified sub-periosteal haematoma. There is slight swelling near the midshaft on the fibula, probably also due to trauma.

V22 The sockets for the deciduous maxillary central incisors are partially filled with porotic bone so that only shallow depressions remain. A radiograph reveals that the permanent central incisors are within the maxillae and are of normal development for a child of 4 years. It seems probable that the deciduous maxillary I1s were lost ante-mortem through trauma or disease.

V24 The abscess cavity at the socket of the L mandibular M1 is rather large and there is slight periostitis adjacent to the lateral side of this cavity: inflammation of the bone via extension of infection from the abscess.

The L maxillary I2s are markedly shovel-shaped.

There is thickening of the shaft of the R clavicle one third of the way from its lateral end. The thickening is mainly in the anterio-posterior plane. This bone is 6mm shorter than its L side counterpart. Probably a united fracture.

V25 Both mandibular deciduous canines have a small (1mm diameter), roughly circular area on the buccal surface of their crowns denuded of enamel. Localised enamel hypoplasia of the primary canines (Skinner 1986).

V26 The L maxillary I2 shows a horizontal groove on its lingual and distal aspects at the cemento-enamel junction. It is about 1mm wide and a maximum of 1-2mm deep. The groove does not affect the entire lingual or the entire distal side of the tooth but rather is situated around the 'corner' between these 2 sides. It has a slightly polished surface and has the appearence of having been caused by passing a thread against the tooth, perhaps in order to smooth the thread. This is the only maxillary anterior tooth present so it remains uncertain whether this was the only one affected. There is very heavy wear on the mandibular anterior dentition, with the cental incisors being worn to their roots, but none show grooving.

The endocranial surface of the frontal bone shows very deep Pacchionian depressions; they almost penetrate the full thickness of the bone in places, and there is a slight bulge on the outer table over one particularly deep depression on the inner surface.

There is slight pitting of the proximal joint surfaces of both proximal hallucial phalanges - probably not pathological.

The proximal phalanx of the R 4th toe shows an oblique fracture commencing on the lateral side about halfway along the shaft and terminating on the distal joint surface, causing a slight step in the latter. Firmly healed with minimal deformity.

V27 The 1st sacral segment is incompletely united with S2 at its body and articulates with its neural arch via facet joints. Insufficient remains of the sacrum to determine the number of sacral vertebrae. A lumbo-sacral transitional variant.

There are mandibular tori, taking the form of irregular bony outgrowths on the lingual surface of the mandible just below the alveolar border, extending from the PM1 to the M3 on the L side and from the canine to the M3 on the R side.

V28 There are porotic bone deposits on the ectocranial surfaces, primarily in the vault area. The L orbital roof is porous. The right mandibular condyle exhibits abnormal medial/posterior bending. There is flaring of the sternal ends of the ribs. The left ischium shows irregular, porous bone near the growing edges. The cortices of the ribs are porous towards their sternal ends, as are the metaphyses of the long-bones. There is thickening of the long-bones. Rickets. This case is among those described by Ortner and Mays (1998).

V29 The pit for the ligamentum teres on the L femoral head is obliterated. The surface of the femoral head is grooved. X-ray shows that the length of the femoral neck is normal. There seems to be a minor displacement of the femoral head anteriorly/inferiorly. There is no sign of osteoarthritis on either the femoral head or the acetabulum. Probably slippage of the femoral capital epiphysis. The R hip joint is missing.

The plantar surface of the head of the L 3rd metatarsal and the dorsal surface of the head of the L 5th metatarsal are bumpy and irregular. Cause uncertain, possibly related to trauma.

The tuberosities of both navicular bones are present as separate ossicles - bilateral os tibiale externa. The ossicle from the L foot is present, that from the R has not been recovered. The articular surfaces between the naviculae and the ossicles are smooth at their peripheries and porotic and roughened in their central portions, suggestive of fibrous connections for the ossicles.

V30 The crowns of the R maxillary I2 and both maxillary I1s are shovel-shaped.

V32 Large, robust bones.

There is bony spurring at the insertion of the Achilles tendon on the L calcaneus, on the soleal lines of the tibiae and on the anterior borders of the fibulae, adjacent to the distal joint surface.

The proximal articular surfaces of the naviculae have lateral extensions which articulate with the calcanei and cuboids at the superior borders of the cubo-calcaneal joints.

V33 The R maxillary I2 is reduced in size.

L5 shows new bone formation on the anterior surface of its body and marked osteophytosis. These bony changes are probably sequential to anterior herniation of the disc between L5 and S1, the new bone on the body of L5 being a consequence of irritation of the periosteum due to anterior proutrusion of the disc.

T7 and 8 have oblique fissures on the inferior surfaces of their centra. No evidence for fracture or other trauma, probably not pathological.

There is a bony bridge between the posterior arch and the L transverse process of the atlas. R side normal.

There is an oblique fracture of the L clavicle at its lateral curve. The bone is 0.5cm shorter than its counterpart on the R side. Firmly healed, little callus.

V35 There is a deposit of sclerotic bone on the anterior aspect of the body of S1. Uncertain cause.

V36 There is shallow, irregular cavitation on the superior surface of C7. No new bone formation. Unknown cause.

T7 bears an articular facet on the dorsal aspect of its neural spine. It must have articulated with a similar facet on the ventral aspect of the spine of T6 (which is missing post-mortem).

Fragmentary skeleton.

V37 The distal joint surface of the L fibula shows a probable healed fissure fracture running obliquely from the inferior part of the anterior margin to the superior part of the posterior margin. The L tibia is normal.

V38 Porotic and flattened interdental septa. Periodontal disease.

The body of T11 shows slight anterior wedging. No evidence for fracture.

There is a united transverse fracture in the midshaft area of the proximal phalanx of the R 4th toe. There is some well remodelled callus and the shaft of the phalanx is flattened, lacking its normal dorsal curvature.

There is a united oblique fracture about 3cm from the head of the R 11th rib. There is moderate, well remodelled callus.

R frontal foramen.

Right tibia sacrificed for radiocarbon 20-12-94.

There is a large supra-acetabular cyst (Wells 1976) above the right acetabulum. It communicates with the joint space.

V40 Large bones.

V41 Most bones destroyed for C-14 dating 5-6-96.

V42 Congenital absence of the R maxillary I2; the L is missing post-mortem but the small size of the socket indicates that it was of reduced size.

Dental crowding of the anterior mandibular teeth.

The L foramen transversarium on the atlas is incomplete, and a thin bridge of bone connects the L transverse process with the posterior arch. The R side is normal.

The L side of T12 has a small joint surface where the transverse process should be. It seems probable that the transverse process was present as a separate ossicle which articulated with this facet. The ossicle itself was not recovered.

The foramen for the vertebral artery on the R side of C7 is incomplete and rather elongated.

There are short, thick paravertebral osteophytes on the R sides of the bodies of T9-11. The following joint surfaces show smooth marginal ossifications: both femoral heads, the acetabula and the proximal joint surfaces of both proximal hallucial phalanges. There is spurring on the olecranon process of the R ulna. 'Bone former' type changes.

Dark red-brown staining on bones.

Vertebrae rather fragmentary.

V44 The interdental septa are porotic and some show flattened profiles. Periodontal disease.

Five R ribs (the 2nd and probably the 3rd-6th) show united fractures. Those in the 2nd-5th ribs are about one third of the way from their sternal ends; that in the 6th is about half way along its shaft. All are firmly healed with minimal deformity.

V45 The maxillary incisors show grooved cingula. The maxillary canines each have a small tubercle.

Marked super-eruption of the R mandibular M1.

There is a deposit of smooth, sclerotic bone near the inferior border of the L lingual surface of the mandible. It is only slightly proud of the normal bone surface and measures 2cm long by 0.5cm wide. It does not have the appearance of an osteoma or a mandibular torus. Uncertain cause.

The L transverse foramen of the atlas is incomplete, the R side is normal.

The R hamate lacks its unciform process.

T11 and 12 bear large R-sided paravertebral osteophytes on their bodies; they articulate with one another but are not fused. Smaller osteophytes of similar form exist on the borders of T9 and 10. There are slight ossifications around the acetabula. 'Bone former' type changes.

There is a linear indentation 11mm long, 2mm wide and a maximum of 2-3mm deep on the L frontal bone. It is orientated obliquely and lies 1.5cm from the midline and 3cm above the glabella. This probably represents a superficial blade injury. The rounded edges of the lesion indicate healing. The lesion fails to penetrate the full thickness of the frontal bone and there is no corresponding bulge on the endocranial surface.

Right femur sacrificed for radiocarbon 20-12-94.

V46 Remaining molars show marked super-eruption.

Osteophytosis is sufficiently marked on L4 and 5 that the large osteophytes seem to have irritated the periosteum resulting in new bone formation on the anterior surfaces of the centra.

Some bones show iron staining.

A post-mortem break reveals a button osteoma 0.5cm diameter in the L frontal sinus.

The bones are rather light and rarified - osteoporosis.

Bilateral frontal foramina; there are grooves on both sides of the frontal bone which seem to have conveyed the nerves and blood vessels which passed through the frontal foramina.

The intermediate and distal phalanges of both little toes are fused together.

V47 In same grave as V53 (*qv*).

V51 In same grave as V55.

V53 Burial placed over or between knees of V47.

V55 V55 is a child burial in the same grave as V51 (an adult). According to the list of burials V55 is finds number c2062 which is burial LXXVI. The bones labelled c2062 do not appear to be the child burial shown in the photograph as V55; thus they were not treated as V55 despite what the list says. The present bones are labelled c2027 and are the skull and left shoulder area of a child aged about 6. These appear to correspond to the bones identified in the site photograph as burial V55. On the list giving details of individual burials, V51 is said to correspond to JH number 52 (the adult) and 58, which is c2027, the present child. Thus the table of burials appears to be in error - c2027 is burial V55.

V57 The L radius exhibits abnormal curvature and has a porous, irregular cortex. The bone underlying the growth plates is also porous, as is the sub-chondral bone of the iliac face of the sacro-iliac joint. The cortices of the ribs show porosis, as does the ilium near its growing margins. The proximal fragment of the L femur is porous, with sparse, thickened trabeculae visible at post-depositional breaks. Rickets. This case is among those described by Ortner and Mays (1998).

V59 These bones are labelled c2022 (listed as V33) and c2030 (listed as 'misc' bone in grid square AA15, which is the same square in which V33 is located). The box contains no stray bone, all the bones belong to one individual and mainly derive from the upper body. It seems likely that this is an *in-situ* burial, which was not recognised as such on excavation, whose lower parts were destroyed by a later feature (possibly the grave of V33?).

There is periostitis of the L zygomatic, mainly confined to those parts inferior to the zygomatic-facial foramen, and most marked on the medial surface. The neighbouring areas of the skull are normal. These lesions, which are partially remodelled, are probably sequential to local soft tissue infection.

V61 Porotic and concave interdental septa: periodontal disease.

Super-eruption of molar teeth.

Slight hyperostosis frontalis interna.

Probable healed fissure fracture of the proximal joint surface of the R 5th metatarsal. The fracture creates a step in the joint surface. The adjoining surface of the cuboid is normal.

V62 The canines are impacted in the maxillae. X-ray shows that they are of normal form and orientated anteriorly/medially.

The R maxillary I2 is absent congenitally.

The mandibular canines are twin-rooted.

The bones are light, with thin cortices - at a post-mortem defect at the neck of the R humerus the cortical thickness is only 1.4mm. The ribs and vertebrae are particularly light and rarified. Osteoporosis.

WCO007 The R foramen transversarium on the atlas is incomplete; the left side is normal.

WCO009 There is an area of pitted, porotic new bone on the lateral surface of the malleolus of the L fibula. The deposit is somewhat remodelled. Periostitis.

The distal joint surface of the L fibula is elongated superiorly.

There is an elongated exostosis on the medial margin of the proximal metaphysis of the L tibia. It is 6cm long and rises 2-3mm

proud of the normal bone surface. It is smooth, rounded and somewhat irregular, and it points away from the epiphysis. X-ray reveals that the outer surface of the lesion is continuous with the normal cortex. Probably an osteochondroma.

The femora and tibiae are rather asymmetric, the L side being less robust.

Right femur sacrificed for radiocarbon determination 2-2-95.

WCO010 The left maxillary I1 has a narrow groove in its incisal edge; it has the appearance of having been caused by gripping a narrow object (e.g. twine) between the teeth. This tooth's occlusal partner is missing post-mortem so it is impossible to ascertain whether its biting surface bore a similar groove.

Bathrocrany.

T12 has lumbar-type facet joints.

Both humeri, radii and left ulna sacrificed for radiocarbon determination 30-1-95 and 26-7-95.

WCO011 L5 shows spina bifida and spondylolysis. No evidence for spondylolisthesis.

WCO012 There is a probable healed fracture of the R 2nd metatarsal about 1/3 of the way from its distal end. The bone is slightly shortened compared with the L 2nd metatarsal and there is slight callus.

WCO013 There is severe osteoarthritis, with formation of large marginal osteophytes, on all 3 components of the R elbow joint with eburnation of the radio-humeral articulation. Probably traumatic in origin. The L elbow shows only very slight degenerative changes.

Two L ribs (probably neighbours) are fractured in their proximal thirds.

The bodies of T10-12 are fused by a thick, flowing, R-sided osteophyte. T9 has a large R-sided osteophyte which articulates with, but is not fused to, that on T10. The upper surfaces of the bodies of T2 and 4 also show large osteophytes. DISH.

There are the beginnings of a sutura mendosa at the R asterion.

Double mastoid foramen on the L; the R is normal.

WCO014 Large bones.

Lower legs only.

There is heavy bony spurring at the insertions of the Achilles tendons on the calcanei, the soleal line and tuberosity of the R tibia and, to a lesser extent, on the soleal line and tuberosity of the L tibia, and near the anterior/superior margins of the distal joint surface of both fibulae.

The R 1st metatarsal shows a cystic defect on the medial margin of its head. The distal joint surface is deflected laterally and shows osteoarthritic changes in those parts which articulate with the hallucial sesamoids. Hallux valgus. The proximal joint surface of the R proximal hallucial phalanx also shows cystic defects near its margins, presumably associated with the hallux valgus. Similar defects are apparent on the lateral aspects of both 5th metatarsals.

WCO015 T12 has lumbar-type facet joints.

The femoral heads are displaced inferiorly so that their superior articular surfaces lie below the level of the greater trochanters. The femoral necks appear thickened. The pits for the ligamentum teres are normal but lie nearer to the inferior margin of the joint surface than normal. Probably slipped capital epiphyses.

WCO016 There is a groove 1-2mm wide on the incisal edge of the R maxillary I1, probably made by gripping a thin object (e.g. twine) between the teeth. The occlusal partner for this tooth has been lost-post mortem so it cannot be ascertained whether or not it bore a similar groove.

The R foramen transversarium on the atlas in incomplete.

L1 has T12-type facet joints and lacks the lumbar-type transverse process on its R side, although that on the left is normal.

S1 and 2 articulate via apophysial joints.

WCO017 Porosis and some concavity of interdental septa. Periodontal disease.

Double R mental foramen.

New bone formation in the R antrum of Highmore, probably as a result of infection from a dental abscess which healed prior to death.

A lumbar vertebral body shows a healed compression fracture.

There is a 6th sacral segment, it is an extra vertebra.

WCO018 There is a bony bridge between the L transverse process and the superior facet joint of L5; right side normal.

Both acetabulae show porotic defects on their superior joint surfaces which communicate with cavities within the ilia superior to the acetabulae - supra-acetabular cysts (Wells 1976, fig. 11). X-ray shows that the defect in the R ilium is quite large - 2.5 x 1.5cm.

The proximal and intermediate phalanges of the middle finger of the R hand show deposits of sub-periosteal new bone on their palmar surfaces. There is sub-periosteal new bone on the tibiae and fibulae, most marked on the interosseous borders and slight deposits on the femoral shafts (toward their distal ends) and toward the distal ends of the radii. The deposits are mainly somewhat remodelled, but there are also areas of woven bone, indicating a disease process which was active at time of death. There is resorption of the distal end of the left terminal hallucial phalanx. This is the only pedal terminal phalanx present; three manual terminal phalanges are present and are normal. The pattern of symmetrical periosteal deposits of new bone in tubular bones, together with osteolysis of the terminal phalanx, are suggestive of hypertrophic osteoarthropathy.

There is a cystic defect at the medial side of the L 1st metatarsal and the joint surface is deflected laterally. The right 1st metatarsal is normal. Unilateral hallux valgus.

WCO019 Both foramen transversaria on the atlas are incomplete. The anterior arch of the atlas is unfused in the midline, suggesting that, instead of the more usual situation in which the anterior arch is formed from a single ossification centre, it may have been formed from 2 centres or perhaps there was no separate ossification centre for it and the anterior arch formed by growth of the transverse processes towards the midline.

WCO021A R frontal foramen.

This appears to be a burial which was mainly destroyed by WCO021.

WCO022 The skull from this burial seems to have got lost. The skull boxed with these bones can be identified from the photograph of this burial as a stray element in this context.

Large but gracile bones.

There is a thin bony bridge connecting the L transverse process with the posterior arch of the atlas. R side normal.

S6 is present; it is an extra segment rather than sacralisation of the last lumbar vertebra.

WCO023 There are facet joints between S1, 2 and 3.

Both femora show a 3rd trochanter.

WCO026 There is much new bone formation within the R maxillary sinus, and a little in the L. It seems likely that this is due to infection from a dental abscess which healed before death.

There is infra-bony pocket formation at the mandibular M3s and many interdental septa are porotic and flattened or concave in profile. Severe periodontal disease.

The molar teeth show super-eruption.

There is severe osteoarthritis at the left elbow, with destruction of the radio-humeral articulation - porotic, sclerotic bone in place of the normal joint surfaces. The L ulna shows large osteophytes at the margins of its proximal joint surface. The R elbow is free from osteoarthritis. Probably traumatic.

The following bones show large pores in their cortices: pelves, proximal parts of humeri and many ribs, particularly near their sternal ends. Osteoporosis.

L1 bears 2 lumbar ribs which articulate with the vertebral body only.

Double R mental foramen.

WCO027 S1 and 2 articulate via small apophysial joints.

WCO028 There is porosis of interdental septa, and an infra-bony pocket around the L mandibular M2.

Periodontal disease.

L5 shows sub-periosteal new bone on the anterior aspect of its body. Probably anterior herniation of the L4/5 disc.

Forearm bones and right humerus sacrificed for radiocarbon determination 30-1-95.

WCO030 Robust bones. Thick, very brachycranic skull.

WCO032 The L maxillary PM2 has twin roots.

There is a cavity 2-3mm diameter, 3mm deep in the L orbital roof, lined with sclerotic trabeculae. Cause unknown.

WCO035 This burial was boxed as a mixture of 2 individuals. The present individual is the one labelled on the plan as Burial WCO035 but next to this there is another, clearly articulated burial; this was given number WCO035A. Due to the mixing of the 2 individuals there are some foot bones which could not be assigned to a particular individual; these were not recorded.

WCO035A Articulated skeleton to south of WCO035 (see notes on WCO035).

WCO036 There is a small pit in the proximal joint surface of the L 1st metatarsal. Not pathological.

There is a large cystic defect just above the rim of the left acetabulum. It communicates with the joint surface via a small pore, but its main opening is external. There are two smaller defects above the right acetabulum which communicate with the joint space. Supra-acetabular cysts (Wells 1976).

The bodies of T8-10 have large, interlocking, paravertebral, R-sided osteophytes (although they are not fused together). A fragment of the body of another thoracic vertebra (?T7) shows similar osteophytes above and below. There are some capsular ossifications around the acetabular margins and the proximal joint surface of the R ulna, and bony spurring on the linea asperae and the sites for insertion of the Achilles tendons on the calcanei. 'Bone former' type changes.

There is a smooth-walled cystic defect on the L hamate, near the facet for the scaphoid. Probably non-pathological.

WCO037 There is a small cystic defect on the dorsal margin of the head of the R 5th metatarsal.

There is a united fracture of a left false rib, 3cm from the vertebral end, strongly healed with moderate callus.

T11 and 12 are fused by large, thick, paravertebral osteophytes on the L and R sides of their bodies. 'Bone former' type changes.

There is a pit 5mm diameter, 4mm deep, lined with sclerotic trabecular bone, in the distal joint surface of the R tibia. Unknown cause. The trochlear surface of the R talus is normal.

There is a complete L frontal foramen on the L side and an incomplete one on the R side.

There is black/purple staining in the knee area.

WCO038 There is a small R lumbar rib which articulates only with the vertebral body.

T12 has a rudimentary L transverse process in the form of a separate ossicle which articulates with the L side of the neural arch via a joint surface. There is no rib facet on the L side of the body of T12. There is also a further small ossicle but it is unclear what it is.

Of the pubic bones only the left is present. The symphysis has a very narrow contact area with the R pubic bone.

WCO039 The R calcaneus shows a small, concave area of sclerotic trabeculae on the anterior margin of the anterior facet for the talus. Probably the site for fibrous attachment for a calcaneum secundarium. L calcaneus normal.

The L tibia shows a 2 x 3cm area of periosteal new bone on its lateral surface in the midshaft area and another on the interosseous border in the groove for the fibula. There is also a deposit of woven bone 1/3 of the way down the R fibula. Periostitis.

There is a 6 x 9mm cavity lined with sclerotic, irregular bone on the medial side of the proximal metaphysis of the R tibia. There is negligible bony reaction around the cavity. X-ray reveals that the cavity has thin, highly sclerotic borders. Possibly a fibrous cortical defect or an intra-osseous ganglion.

The knee area (excluding patellae) and some foot and ankle bones are stained black. Affected parts are more poorly preserved than neighbouring unstained parts.

WCO040 There is sacralisation of the 1st coccygeal segment.

There is pitting on the proximal joint surface of the R hallucial proximal phalanx. Unknown cause.

WCO041 S6 is an extra segment.

The lower half of the L femur is very swollen, with a pitted, roughened surface. A very large (9 x 12mm) cloaca pierces the posterior wall about 8cm from the distal end, and a smaller one pierces the anterior wall 13cm from the distal end. X-ray shows that there is much bony sclerosis and that the original cortex at the distal end has been completely remodelled away. Osteomyelitis.

The distal joint surface is missing but that of the L tibia is normal, however its shaft shows much remodelled periosteal new bone, mainly on its medial surface. X-ray shows that the endosteal cortical surface of the tibia is normal - i.e. the lesions on this bone represent periostitis, probably extension of the infection from the femur. The R tibia is normal.

The outer surface of the L ilium bears a projection 2cm thick about 1-2cm from the iliac crest. The end of this projection is broken, revealing trabecular bone within. X-ray reveals that there is continuity between the trabecular bone of the exostosis with that of the underlying ilium. Probably an osteochondroma.

WCO044 Right leg bones sacrificed for radiocarbon determination 30-1-95.

WCO045 Very thin edentulous mandible - the teeth must have been lost long before death. This looks like the skeleton of a very elderly individual, probably aged well over 60 years at death.

There is a bridge of bone connecting the L transverse process with the posterior arch of the atlas. The R side is normal.

There is a healed compression fracture of the body of T11 with some anterior wedging (the anterior body height is reduced to 15mm compared with a height of 23mm for the posterior side). There is also a small healed compression fracture in the superior surface of the body of T12 and a large one in the superior surface of L1 giving some lateral wedging here. The superior surface of T10 shows a large Schmorl's node, presumably a result of the same traumatic incident which caused the fractures to the neighbouring vertebrae.

2L and 2R ribs show fractures about 1/3 of the way from their sternal ends. Those on the R ribs are strongly united, but those on the L ribs are un-united.

The proximal phalanx of the R little finger shows a united fracture just behind its head.

There are 2 epipteric bones at the R pterion.

Right femur sacrificed for radiocarbon determination 30/1/95.

WCO056 Porosis and concavity of the interdental septa. There is an infra-body pocket around the mandibular I2. Periodontal disease.

Reduced 12th ribs, the L is 23mm, the R 28mm long.

Partial sacralisation of L5 - the L transverse process and L sacral ala articulate via a joint surface.

There is an 8 x5 mm exostosis rising 4mm proud of the normal bone on the superior surface of a right true rib. It is somewhat irregular, smooth and composed of very sclerotic bone. X-ray reveals that it is sitting upon the normal cortex and a thin line of radiolucency is visible where it attaches to the rib. Probably an osteoma.

The R mastoid foramen is double.

WCO057 The skull was given burial number WCO57, the middle of the body is cut away by Burial WCO82, and the lower legs were given burial number WCO083. Here the whole body is referred to as Burial WCO057.

There are the beginnings of a sutura mendosa at each asterion.

WCO058 According to the list old number W81 is equivalent both to burial number WCO058 and burial number WCO061. This is presumably a numbering error as these 2 burials are not near one another in the cemetery. The site photograph suggests that the bones received are WCO058 rather than WCO061.

The following sites show deposits of sub-periosteal new bone: the right radius, the humeri, the necks of the femurs, the lateral and medial surfaces of the ilia, the posterior and anterior surfaces of the scapulae (slight), the visceral surfaces of 11L ribs and both surfaces of the left first rib, the visceral surfaces of 6R ribs, and the visceral surfaces of many rib fragments. Most deposits are of woven bone although some show a little remodelling. Deposits tend to be laminated. There is new bone within the medullary cavity of the left humerus, right radius, and within the trabecular structure of most rib and some scapula fragments, a fragment of the body of L3 and the neural arch of L4. In the flat-bones and in the metaphyses of long-bones, endosteal bone deposits take the form of cancellous bone within spaces in the existing trabecular structure. Cortices of some long-bones (e.g. femora and humeri) are rather porous. The interpretation of these changes is problematic but perhaps the most likely of the diagnostic options (which include metastatic cancer) is renal osteodystrophy.

WCO059 Porotic interdental septa and alveolar resorption. Periodontal disease.

There is a small cystic defect on the lateral side of the head of the R 5th metatarsal.

Part of the superior margin of the R acetabulum is missing. The area from whence the bone fragment is missing is somewhat porotic and eburnated and is 23mm long and the height of the acetabulum here is reduced by about 3mm. Probably an acetabular flange lesion (Wells 1976) - traumatic separation of a fragment of the acetabular rim.

There are four cystic defects in the subchondral bone above the right acetabulum. All communicate with the joint space. Supra-acetabular cysts (Wells 1976).

T12 shows unilateral spondylolysis - there is a narrow cleft at the R pars interarticularis. The surfaces of the cleft are smooth. No sign of spondylolisthesis.

The bodies of T6-11 have large, smooth, paravertebral, interlocking osteophytes. None is ankylosed but they must have been on the point of fusing had not death intervened. There is slight ossification of costal cartilages and ossification of the thyroid. 'Bone former' type changes.

Black staining on proximal humeri.

WCO067 Large bones.

S1 has a joint surface on its L ala which must have articulated with a facet on the L transverse process of the (missing) L5. The R ala is missing post-mortem. The apophysial joints on S1 are reduced in size.

There is a concave area of porotic bone on the anterior/medial margin of the anterior facet of the R calcaneus. Probably the site of fibrous attachment of a calcaneum secundarium.

WCO068 Porosis and slight concavity of interdental septa. Periodontal disease.

The manubrio-sternal joint is obliquely angled.

There is a roughened, porotic area on the lateral side of the R navicular and on the medial side of the R cuboid. A fibrous connection probably existed between these bones.

There is a depressed, slightly pitted area, 1.5-2cm diameter on the ectocranial surface of the L frontal bone, 1.5cm from the midline and 5cm above the glabella. There is no corresponding bulge on the inner table. Probably due to pressure from an overlying sebaceous cyst or to minor local trauma.

WCO069 In the left femur, the bone beneath the proximal epiphysial plate is convex and the femoral neck and proximal metaphysial area of the bone is thickened. The epiphysis is missing. The right bone is normal. Possibly a slipped capital epiphysis.

WCO070 Slight bathrocrany.

Porosis and flattening of interdental septa around molar teeth and beginning infra-bony pocket formation at M1s. Periodontal disease.

There is a large bony exostosis on the L mandibular condyle.

Bilateral frontal foramina.

Left 1st rib, left scapula, T1, humeri and clavicles sacrificed for radiocarbon dating 30-1-95.

WCO071 Anterior dentition very worn.

T12 has lumbar-type facet joints.

Beginnings of a sutura mendosa at both asterions.

WCO077 Dental crowding in the canine area on mandible and maxilla.

Interdental septa flattened and show slight porosis - periodontal disease.

Bridge of bone between the L transverse process and the posterior arch of atlas.

R frontal foramen.

WCO078 The R maxillary I2 has a deep groove on the lingual surface of its root, giving the appearance of an incompletely divided root.

Porosis and flattening or slight concavity of interdental septa in the region of the premolars and molars. Periodontal disease.

WCO079 The L mandibular canine has 2 roots.

A bridge of bone connects the L transverse process with the posterior arch of the atlas.

WCO080 There is a smooth projection of sclerotic bone 11 x 9mm and 2mm high on the ectocranial surface of the R parietal 5cm from the lambdoid and 5cm from the sagittal suture. A button osteoma.

WCO087 There are 5 boxes of mixed bone supposedly from Burials WCO087 and WCO088. The bones represent at least 8 individuals. The skull of WCO088, however, can be identified from the site photo. It is impossible to determine which post-cranial bones are associated with this skull, so the skull alone is recorded. There is a group of bones which are identifiable as a distinct individual on the basis of their colour and lightness of build; this material is treated as Burial WCO087, although it is impossible to determine whether this is the individual identified as WCO087 on the plan. Only bones which could be confidently determined to belong to this individual are recorded as Burial WCO087, hence it is rather short of the smaller bones. The remaining material was not recorded.

There is a 4mm diameter area of raised bone on the lateral part of the distal joint surface of the R humerus (i.e. the part which articulates with the radial head). Unknown cause.

L5 has facets on its transverse processes which articulate with the sacral alae. L5 lacks a L inferior apophysial joint - in its place there is merely a small bony projection lacking a joint surface. The corresponding apophysial joint on S1 is also lacking. The R apophysial articular surfaces between L5 and S1 are reduced in size. Partial sacralisation of L5.

WCO088 Excavation problems (see notes on Burial WCO087).

WCO089 Porotic interdental septa with rather flattened profiles. Periodontal disease.

Bilateral bony bridging between transverse processes and superior facet joints on L5.

The L humerus has a very large septal aperture - 11mm diameter.

There is a small pore in the proximal joint surface of the proximal phalanx of the L big toe; the corresponding joint surface on the R bone is slightly roughened. Probably not pathological.

WCO091 There are 6 lumbar vertebrae. L6 is a lumbo-sacral transitional vertebra. There seems to have been a fibrous connection between its L transverse process and the L sacral ala - both bear an area of porotic, sclerotic bone - and the R transverse process and sacral ala articulate via articular surfaces. The bodies of L6 and S1 are fully separate.

The medial epicondyle of the right humerus is absent. There is a large irregular exostosis in the area of the lateral epicondyle. The olecranon fossa is rounded in shape rather than having its usual ovoid appearance. The distal joint surface here is enlarged compared with the (normal) contra-lateral side. The lesion has the appearance of a healed, childhood avulsion injury of the growth-plate of the condyle and medial epicondyle (Glencross and Stuart-Macadam 2001). The reason for the enlargement of the distal joint surface is not clear, although it may be a response to altered mechanical forces consequent on the injury, perhaps particularly the non-union of the medial epicondyle.

WCO092 The L mandibular M3 is impacted into the neighbouring M2.

Concave and porotic interdental septa, particularly in the molar area; periodontal disease.

There is depression of the anterior part of the superior surface of the body of L2; the trabeculae in the eroded area are somewhat sclerotic. An avulsion injury of the vertebral end-plate.

The R superior articular surface of the atlas is markedly larger than the L.

WCO093 The R mandibular PM2 is congenitally absent and the deciduous M2 is retained, although it lies below the level of the neighbouring permanent teeth and hence is not in occlusion.

T12 has lumbar-type facet joints.

L5 shows spondylolysis, no sign of spondylolisthesis.

The skull appears very small with a very sloping frontal bone. This is not a reflection of a generally small skeleton - the post-cranial bones are fairly large for a female - the skull is small in relation to body size. There is no sign of increased intra-cranial pressure - the impressions of the cerebral convolutions are no more marked than normal, and there is no sign of premature cranial suture closure.

WCO097 Both 1st metatarsals have a supernumerary epiphysis at their distal ends; that on the R is just fusing, that on the L is unfused.

The squamous sutures are completely obliterated from the parietal notches to the asterions.

WCO098 Many interdental septa show porosis and those around the molars are concave in profile. Periodontal disease.

The femoral heads are rather oddly shaped with slight protrusions beneath the pits for the ligamentum teres, which themselves are rather shallow. No sign of any pathology; probably an anatomical variant.

WCO099 There is a deposit of woven bone 2.5cm diameter in the glabella area, and two further small deposits on the lateral parts of the left and right supraciliary arches. Periostitis.

R frontal foramen.

WCO103 The R maxillary deciduous canine is retained and lies distal to the erupting permanent canine. The deciduous tooth shows resorption of its root on the mesial side due to pressure from the erupting permanent canine.

There is a large buccal tubercle on the crown on the R maxillary M2.

There is a groove on the lingual surface of the root and the lower part of the crown of the maxillary L I2.

The R foramen transversarium on the atlas is incomplete; L side missing.

There is a small pit in the distal joint surface of the L tibia. Probably not pathological.

There is purple staining on the proximal tibiae and distal femora.

WCO107 The L mandibular M1 shows more than the usual numbers of pits and fissures - probably a variant rather than dental enamel hypoplasia.

Both foramen transversaria on the atlas are incomplete.

There are small deposits of woven bone on the distal humeral diaphyses, the left ischium (medial surface) and on the visceral surfaces of two right middle ribs.

WCO108 L foramen transversarium on atlas incomplete. R side missing.

WCO109 Bilateral frontal foramina.

Black staining on proximal tibiae.

WCO110 Fairly robust bones.

WCO115 The L femoral head shows very marked flattening, and both it and the L acetabulum show severe osteoarthritis with eburnation, porosis and formation of massive osteophytes. These osteophytes have irritated the periosteum around the acetabulum and femoral head causing new bone deposition in these areas. The acetabular fossa is filled with new bone. The pit for the ligamentum teres on the femoral head has been obliterated. X-ray and gross inspection indicate that the length of the femoral neck is normal and there is no displacement of the head with respect to the axis of the neck. Perthes' disease.

WCO115a The L foramen transversarium on the atlas is incomplete; no observation possible on R.

There is partially remodelled periostitis on the medial and posterior aspects of the tibiae.

L frontal foramen.

WCO117 There is pitted bone within the maxillary sinus above the L molars. Probably extension of infection from one of the dental abscess cavities which were present in the maxilla.

Super-eruption of the L mandibular M2.

The R transverse processes of L3 and 4 bear joint surfaces which articulate with one another.

T12 has lumbar-type facet joints.

There is bony spurring on the linea asperae, soleal lines of the tibiae, insertions of Achilles tendons on the calcanei, ischial tuberosities, the deltoid ridge of the L humerus, the olecranon process of the L ulna and the R radial tuberosity. There are also capsular ossifications around the glenoid cavities. 'Bone former' type changes. No paravertebral ossifications on vertebrae.

There are united oblique fractures of both claviculae. The callus is well remodelled although the fracture lines are readily visible.

6L ribs (the 4th-9th) show united fractures, those on the 4th-6th about 1/3 of the way from the vertebral ends, the 7th through the facet for the vertebral transverse process, and the 8th and 9th in the area of their tuberosities. The fractures are oblique with respect to the axis of the ribs. 2R ribs also show united fractures, one (the 2nd or 3rd rib) in the midshaft area, the other near the sternal end. The L transverse process of T7 shows a united fracture through the facet for articulation with the rib.

The similar state of healing of all these fractures (the fracture lines are all fairly readily apparent) suggests that they occurred in a single incident, probably a crushing injury to the chest.

There are 2 unidentified soft tissue calcifications, one is long and narrow (38 x 5mm), the other is irregular in shape (11 x 16mm).

There is a large cystic defect in the subchondral bone above the left acetabulum. It communicates with the joint space. A supra acetabular cyst (Wells 1976).

WCO118 The bones from WCO118 and WCO119 were boxed co-mingled. Only those bones which can confidently be ascribed to either individual are recorded, hence both burials are somewhat lacking the smaller bones.

Right femur and right humerus sacrificed for radiocarbon determination 30-1-95. Right tibia sacrificed for replicate 2-12-96.

WCO119 The bones were boxed co-mingled with those of 119 (*qv*)

Porotic interdental septa, alveolar resorption around the molar teeth. Periodontal disease.

Tibiae sacrificed for radiocarbon dating 30-1-95.

WCO122 The inferior L facet joint of T2 and the inferior R facet joint of T7 each show pits lined with sclerotic trabecular bone. Unknown cause.

There is a thin bridge of bone connecting the R transverse process with the posterior arch of the atlas. L side normal.

WCO124 The L mandibular M1 and the R maxillary M3 are the only molars present and show super-eruption. The M1 bears a large amount of calculus; it completely covers the occlusal surface. Its partner was lost ante-mortem, facilitating this large accumulation of calculus.

The bones are rather light with thin cortices - osteoporosis.

WCO125 There is a roughened area on the L talus, just lateral to the groove for the L flexor hallucis longus. Probably the site of a fibrous connection with an os trigonium. R talus normal.

There is a pit on the proximal joint surface of the R proximal hallucial phalanx. Not pathological.

The L 5th and 7th ribs have extra facets on their superior aspects, near their proximal ends, which articulate with the transverse processes on the 4th and 6th thoracic vertebrae respectively.

WCO125A The endocranial surface of the frontal bones are rather porous, especially in the region of the frontal eminences.

WCO130 L4 and 5 both show spondylolysis, no sign of spondylolisthesis.

There are three supra-acetabular cysts (Wells 1976) in the subchondral bone above the right acetabulum. They communicate with the joint space.

There is an osteophyte on the R patella at the insertion of the quadriceps femoris.

There is very slight periostitis on the lateral surface of the L tibia about one third of the way from the proximal end. The deposit is a mixture of woven and slightly remodelled bone.

Left humerus and left femur sacrificed for radiocarbon dating 30-1-95.

WCO131 Robust bones.

C7 has very thick transverse processes; each is pierced by 3 foramina. C5 and 6 have double transverse foramina, C5 on the L transverse process, C6 bilaterally.

The body of L1 shows some new bone deposition on its left anterior surface. There is quite marked osteophytosis on the upper surface of the body of L2. Probably anterior herniation of the L1/2 disc.

There is a pit on the L radial tuberosity which communicates with the medullary cavity. Uncertain cause, perhaps not pathological.

There is perforation of the occipital bone, just to the R of the midline, 28mm above the opisthion. The diameter of the lesion is greatest in the diploe and it may not have completely perforated the inner and outer tables - these may have flaked away post-mortem. The lesion is rounded with a greatest diameter of 12-13mm. There is no bony reaction around it and its internal surfaces are of fairly smooth bone. The complete cranium shows no other perforations. Possibly a dermoid cyst.

WCO134 C7 has facets on its body and transverse processes for a pair of cervical ribs. The ribs themselves were not recovered.

There is a short, smooth projection on the medial margin of the metaphysis of the R tibia, pointing away from the epiphysis. X-ray reveals that the outer surface of the lesion is continuous with the normal cortex of the tibia. Probably an osteochondroma.

WCO137 One left rib and two unsided rib fragments show united fractures. All are firmly healed with well-remodelled callus.

One right rib shows woven bone in its middle third, on its visceral surface. One right rib shows a similar deposit near its head. The sternal 1/3 of a R rib has a deposit of woven bone upon its visceral surface, as does a fragment of another R rib, and five rib fragments of indeterminate side. Periostitis. This individual proved negative for tubercle bacillus DNA (Mays *et al.* 2002b).

WCO138 T12 has lumbar-type facet joints.

A thin bridge of bone connects the L transverse process with the posterior arch of the atlas.

R frontal foramen.

Both humeri, both ulnae and the left radius sacrificed for radiocarbon determination 30-1-95 and 26-7-95.

WCO139 The R mandibular canine is twin rooted.

A thin bridge of bone connects the R transverse process and the posterior arch of the atlas.

Abscess cavities at the R maxillary M2 and L maxillary PM2 and M1 penetrate the maxillary sinus. Those at the left premolar and molar show raised cones of bone around the fistulae in the maxillary sinus, suggestive of radicular cysts. There is also a raised swelling on the R maxillary sinus above the abscess cavity at the M2 (although this abscess does not penetrate the sinus).

There seems to be a failure of formation of most of the maxillary part of the floor of the L orbit. Only the lateral-most part seems to be present (although there is some post-mortem damage in this region). The margins of the defect are of smooth cortical bone, the impression being of failure of formation of part of the bone rather than its resorption due to disease.

There is a united fracture of one right rib.

Right arm bones sacrificed for radiocarbon dating 30-1-95.

WCO142 The bodies of L5 and S1 are united by large osteophytes. A large abscess cavity has partially destroyed the lower part of the body of L5 and sinuses pierce its anterior and posterior walls. There is much pitted new bone on the anterior part of the sacrum beneath the opening of the sinus, suggesting bony reaction to the exudate from the abscess. On the pelvic bones there is slight new bone formation posterior to the acetabulae, and the right ilium shows irregular thickening on its inner aspect in the area between the sacro-iliac articulation and the iliac crest.

Within this irregularly raised area is an approximately circular depression, suggestive of an area where pressure from some soft tissue swelling prevented build up of sub-periosteal bone. On the lower parts of the femoral heads the normal joint surface has been replaced by fine-grained bone, and similar changes are apparent on parts of the acetabular articular surfaces. The left femur also shows new bone on the greater trochanter, the gluteal tuberosity and in a few places on its shaft. The shaft deposits are of woven bone. Both tibiae show deposits of woven bone, particularly towards their distal ends. The right tibia also shows a large deposit of thoroughly remodelled new bone on its lateral side, towards the proximal end. The left tibia shows a raised nodule on its medial surface, within which there is a radiolucent area. The left fibula is thickened by deposits of remodelled and woven bone. The calcanei each show slight deposits of woven bone and slight erosive changes at the margins of the posterior facets for the tali. There is destruction of the head of the left 5th metatarsal and and thickening of its shaft. A proximal foot phalanx shows swelling of its shaft. The entire skeleton above L5 is missing, having been truncated by a later feature.

Tuberculosis. The state of remodelling of the bone deposits shows that the disease process was long-lasting and was active at time of death of the individual. DNA analyses (Mays *et al.* 2001a) confirm the diagnosis and indicate the presence of *Mycobacterium tuberculosis* rather than *Mycobacterium bovis*.

WCO144 Marked overbite.

A R rib is bifurcated at its sternal end.

WCO146 Bathrocrany. The lambdoid suture is filled with many wormian bones.

Reduced R 12th rib - only 31mm long. The L 12th rib was not recovered but there is a facet for it on T12 so it was present.

T12 has lumbar type facet joints.

There is an exostosis on the medial side of the proximal joint surface of the R hallucial proximal phalanx.

There is black staining in the knee area and slightly on the distal tibiae.

WCO149 R frontal foramen.

WCO153 Right femur and tibia sacrificed for radiocarbon determination 30-1-95.

WCO154 Porotic and concave interdental septa. Periodontal disease.

WCO156 An area on the anterior edge of the anterior facet of the R calcaneus is slightly roughened and there is a slightly roughened depression on the inferior/medial border of the R navicular. Suggestive of a soft tissue calcaneo-navicular bar. The L foot bones are normal.

Left femur destroyed for radiocarbon determination 30-1-95.

WCO162 Super-eruption of the molars.

Porotic and concave interdental septa. On the distal side of the L mandibular canine there are the beginnings of infra-bony pocket formation. Periodontal disease.

Slight dishing of the body of L3 – 'codfish'-type deformity.

There is a partial metopic suture - it extends only 4cm from the bregma. It may be that it has been partially obliterated as a result of the normal process of suture closure.

There is slight black staining in the knee area.

Right lower leg bones sacrificed for radiocarbon dating 30-1-95. Left lower leg bones sacrificed for replicate 2-12-96.

WCO164 L foramen transversarium of atlas incomplete, R side normal.

There are deposits of woven bone about 1/3 of the way from the distal ends of the R radius and ulna.

WCO164a There is an extra articular facet between the cuboid and the navicular on both feet.

Adjoining surfaces of the spinous processes of L2 and 3 are pitted and eburnated as, to a lesser extent, are those of L3 and 4. This together with the Schmorl's nodes and severe osteoarthritis of the facet joints here is perhaps suggestive of trauma to the lumbar spine.

There is a healed fissure fracture across the cuboid facet of the L calcaneus. There is a united oblique midshaft fracture of the L 1st metatarsal; although union is strong the bone is shortened by 7mm compared to its R side counterpart. There is severe osteoarthritis of the L talo-calcaneal articulation. The above lesions are suggestive of severe trauma to the L foot.

There is a large cystic cavity in the subchondral bone above the right acetabulum. It communicates with the joint space. A supra-acetabular cyst (Wells 1976).

WCO165 Small, gracile bones.

Infra-bony pocket around the L maxillary M1. Resorption and pitting of interdental septa. Periodontal disease.

There is a linear depression 25mm long, 7mm wide on the R frontal bone approximately parallel to the coronal suture, 32mm from it, starting 29mm from the midline. It is about 3mm deep and there is no corresponding bulge on the inner table. The surface of the lesion is slightly pitted. Probably a healed, superficial injury.

On the cranium, the L posterior condylar canal is double.

WCO165a Both foramen transversaria on the atlas are incomplete.

There is an exostosis about 5mm long on the dorso-lateral side of the proximal end of the L 2nd metacarpal. Probably traumatic.

Black staining on proximal tibiae.

WCO166 The L mandibular M2 has 3 roots.

Large bones.

The R foramen transversarium is incomplete, L side normal.

Bones from Burials 166 and 167 have been boxed in a co-mingled state, together with a lot of stray bone. It is unclear which skeleton is 167 and which is 166 but on the plan 166 looks like a large adult so the larger skeleton was regarded as 166.

WCO167 Boxed mixed with 166 (*qv*)

WCO168 Large, robust bones.

Super-eruption of mandibular M2s.

Left 5th metatarsal has a rather laterally flattened, porotic head.

WCO170 Gracile bones.

T12 has lumbar-type facet joints.

There is a cystic space above the right acetabulum and three above the left which communicate, via a hole, with the joint surfaces. Supra-acetabular cysts (Wells 1976).

The axis vertebra is fractured: the fracture line runs obliquely from the L pedicle, beneath the odontoid process and terminates beneath the R superior articular facet. A further fracture line runs across the R superior articular facet. There is some compression of the bone beneath the R superior articular facet, and the R transverse process and inferior articular facet are ankylosed with C3, whose R transverse process and inferior facet joint are, in turn, ankylosed with those of C4. The odontoid process of the axis vertebra is displaced anteriorly and rightwards a few millimetres and leans to the R by about 20 degrees from the vertical. The fissure fracture of the R articular process and the compression of the bone beneath it appears to have been caused by the R inferior articular facet of the atlas being forced down upon it. When rearticulated, the atlas appears to be slightly rotated to the L, and there is a smooth, concave area just to the left of the midline on the internal surface of its posterior arch - perhaps resorption of bone due to slight pressure of the posterior arch upon the spinal cord and associated structures - the spinal canal has been somewhat narrowed as a result of slight anterior/rightward slippage of the atlas relative to the axis. The fractures are quite firmly healed (showing the individual survived the injury) although the fracture lines are easily traced. It seems likely that the injury occurred through the neck being bent forcibly to the right, perhaps as a result of a fall on the head.

The bones are rather light with thin cortices. The vertebrae are particularly rarefied. Osteoporosis.

Right femur sacrificed for radiocarbon determination 2-2-95.

WCO173 Congenital absence of both maxillary PM1s.

Alveolar resorption, and pitting and irregularity of interdental septa, mainly confined to the molar sockets. Periodontal disease. There is heavy calculus on the molar teeth - perhaps this irritated the periodontal tissues helping to precipitate the periodontal disease in this individual.

There is an area missing from the superior edge of the acetabular rim about 35mm long. This area is irregular and sclerotic. Probably an acetabular flange lesion (Wells 1976) - traumatic separation of a fragment of the acetabular rim.

R frontal foramen.

There is a 6th sacral segment; it is an extra vertebra not sacralisation of the last lumbar segment.

There are two cystic defects above the right acetabulum. Each communicates with the joint space. Supra-acetabular cysts (Wells 1976).

WCO174 Spondylolysis of L5. No sign of spondylolisthesis.

The 1st coccygeal segment is fused to S5 at its R transverse process

WCO175 There are marked 'labyrinth' lesions (i.e. sinuous resorptive lesions) on the endocranial surface of the occipital bone. There appears to be no new bone formation, although it is just possible that these lesions represent well-remodelled deposits as the cranium here is rather thick.

WCO176 There is a circular depression about 7mm diameter, lined with sclerotic bone in the posterior part of the distal joint surface of the L tibia. Osteochondritis dissecans.

WCO179 Gracile bones.

C6 has a smooth-walled cavity on the L side of its body at the foramen for the vertebral artery. It is about 1cm deep running under the inferior and superior surfaces of the body. It also erodes the anterior part of the pedicle and the transverse foramen is enlarged. The anterior surface of the lamina is normal. On X-ray the lesion is revealed to have thin, sclerotic borders. The lesion may have been caused by tortuosity of the vertebral artery.

Left humerus and tibia, right ulna and right tibia sacrificed for radiocarbon determination 2-2-95 and 26-7-95.

WCO181 Large, robust bones.

There are deposits of woven bone on the femora, mainly on the posterior aspects; the L bone is the more affected. Periostitis.

Right femur sacrificed for radiocarbon dating 2-2-95.

WCO183 The left and right sub-lingual fossae of the mandible each show a depression in the I2-PM1 regions. Anterior lingual depressions of the type described by Shafer *et al.* (1983, 36-7).

Left femur sacrificed for radiocarbon determination 30-1-95.

WCO184 Porotic interdental septa, particularly in the molar area. Periodontal disease.

The L scaphoid has a smooth hole 8mm deep on the volar margin of the articular surface for the radius. Probably not pathological.

There are 2 button osteomata on the ectocranial surface. The larger is 2cm diameter and lies on the sagittal suture 6mm from the bregma, the smaller is 6mm diameter on the R parietal 0.5cm from the bregma adjacent to the sagittal suture.

There are root impressions on many of the bones.

Right tibia sacrificed for radiocarbon determination 2-2-95.

WCO187 Gracile, fairly small bones.

The R facet joint between T11 and 12 is lumbar type, the L is normal thoracic type.

WCO191 Burials 191, 192 and 193 have became mixed and have been boxed together, together with a large amount of stray bone. There are 3 complete skulls with mandibles. These are recorded as Burials 191, 192 and 193, although in the absence of a photograph of the skeletons *in-situ* it is impossible to determine which is which, so they have been assigned numbers arbitrarily. Since it is impossible to ascertain which post-cranial bones belong to which skull the skulls alone are recorded.

There are vascular channels on the frontal bone.

Interdental septa are pitted and many have concave profiles. Periodontal disease.

WCO192 Bones mixed with those of Burials WCO191 and 193 (see notes for 191).

Bilateral frontal foramina.

WCO193 Bones mixed with those of WCO191 and 192 (see notes for 191).

Crowding of anterior mandibular dentition.

Porotic interdental septa; those around the L mandibular M2 and 3 are concave. Periodontal disease.

WCO195 R frontal foramen.

WCO199 Concave and pitted interdental septa. Periodontal disease.

There are small deposits of woven bone on internal aspects of both scapulae.

Bilateral frontal foramina.

WCO200 S6 is an extra segment rather than sacralisation of the last lumbar vertebra.

The following sites show thin, patchy deposits of new bone: the tibiae, fibulae, femora, external aspects of both ilia, and both radii and ulnae, mainly toward their distal ends. Some deposits are of woven bone, some of remodelled bone. Deposits of bone are particularly marked on muscular insertions, such as the soleal lines on the tibiae and the linea asperae of the femora. There is also new bone formation at the flexor insertions on some first row hand phalanges. The strikingly symmetrical distribution and the thinness of bone deposits is suggestive of hypertrophic osteoarthropathy. Given the likely age at death of this individual, and the presence of active lesions, it is likely to be secondary rather than primary disease.

In addition, two left and one right ribs bear deposits of woven and partially remodelled bone upon their visceral surfaces. These would seem to be indicative of an intra-thoracic infection. This individual proved negative for M. tuberculosis complex DNA (Mays and Taylor 2002), so it would seem probable that these costal lesions are indicative of non-tuberculous pulmonary infection. Presumably this is the disease condition which caused the hypertrophic osteoarthropathy.

Three middle/lower R ribs show united fractures, two at the facet for the vertebral transverse process and one about 3cm from its proximal end. The fractures show quite abundant, well remodelled callus. In addition 2 other R ribs show exostoses, one at its head, the other in the region of the articular facet for the vertebral transverse process. These were probably caused in the same incident which fractured the ribs.

The intermediate and distal phalanges of the R middle finger are ankylosed; there appears to be a minor fracture at or near the medial part of the distal joint surface of the intermediate phalanx.

The acetabula are rather shallow.

There is a supra-acetabular cyst (Wells 1976) above the right acetabulum and two above the left. All communicate with the joint surfaces.

Appendix 3: Key Words for Individual Burials
by S. Mays

CN01	Misc.
CN02	Dental
CN03	Hyperparathyroidism, Radiocarbon
CN04	NMT, Pres.
CN05	Pres., Periostitis, DISH, Periodontal Disease, Spina Bifida, Misc.
CN06	Unerupted Canine, Misc., Accessory Tarsal Bone, Pres.
CN07	Misc.

There is ragged loss of rim height in the superior part of the right acetabulum. This type of lesion appears to form as a result of trauma causing fatigue failure of the rim edge. Splits in the acetabular cartilage caused by joint injury permit synovial fluid to penetrate the subchondral bone causing cystic resorption. If this occurs near the rim edge it may weaken the bone sufficiently to cause fatigue failure.

WCO201 At the distal end of the R humerus the medial epicondyle is lacking. The olecranon fossa is elongated superio-inferiorly. The distal joint surface appears somewhat enlarged, although this cannot be confirmed as the left bone is missing. The general appearence is similar to the R humerus of WCO091 (*qv*). Probably a childhood avulsion injury involving epiphysial separation of the condyle and medial epicondyle (Glencross and Stuart-Macadam 2001).

Many bones show fresh breaks with one broken part missing - some parts must have been lost on excavation or at the post-excavation stage.

WCO202 There are several severe enamel hypoplasias. There is one line on the incisors, 3.9mm from the CEJ measured on the mandibular I1s. The crowns of the M1s are malformed; they have rather more than the usual numbers of pits and fissures and these are rather irregular in form. There are also pitted bands of depressed enamel on the M1 crowns, on the maxillary M1s the defects are so severe that areas of the crown on the medial side are completely denuded of enamel. The location of the band is 3.4mm from the CEJ measured on the mandibular M1s. The M1s also bear a linear hypoplasia; this is located 1.0mm from the CEJ, measured on the mandibular M1s.

WCO203 Quite large but gracile bones.

Roughened area on the anterior border of the L calcaneus. Probably the site for fibrous attachment of a calcaneo-navicular bar or a calcaneum secundarium, it is impossible to determine which as the navicular bone is missing.

3 middle thoracic vertebrae are fused at their bodies and, for the lower 2 also at their facet joints. There is trabecular continuity across the centra of the upper two but the lower 2 are only fused at the periphery of their centra. The bodies of all 3 vertebrae are very damaged; their R sides show a thick, sclerotic deposit of bone but the post-mortem damage makes it impossible to determine whether the L sides were similarly affected. Probably congenital block vertebrae.

There is a large cystic defect within the subchondral bone superior to the right acetabulum. It communicates with the joint space. A supra-acetabular cyst (Wells 1976).

WCO204 Fairly robust bones.

There are three cystic cavities within the subchondral bone above the right acetabulum. They communicate with the joint surface. Supra-acetabular cysts (Wells 1976).

CN09	Pres.
CN11	Pres., Dental, ?Osteochondritis Dissecans
CN12	Periodontal Disease, Localised Microdontia, Fractures
CN13	Pres., Accessory Tarsal Bone, Osteochondritis Dissecans
CN14	Misc., NMT, Pres.
CN15	Dental, Unerupted Third Molar, Neoplasm
CN16	Misc., Pres., ?Trauma, Fracture
CN17	Misc., Osteochondritis Dissecans, Exc., Periodontal Disease, Bone Former
CN18	Pres., Hallux Valgus, Misc., Accessory Tarsal Bone, Unerupted Canines and Third Molars, Bone Former

CN19	Pres., Slight Acetabular Dysplasia
CN20	Lumbar Rib, Unerupted Third Molar, NMT, Misc., Myositis Ossificans, Pres.
CN22	Misc., Pres.
CN24	Misc., Periodontal Disease
CN27	Localised Microdontia, Dental Enamel Pearls, Misc., Fractures, Pres.
CN28	Infection, Pres., Misc., Periodontal Disease, Trauma, Accessory Tarsal Bone
CN29	Exc., Periodontal Disease
CN30	Pres., Misc., Dental
CN31	Trauma, Supra-Acetabular Cysts, Exc., Hypodontia, Misc., Osteomyelitis
CN32	Pres., Dental, Misc., Bone Former, Exc., Periodontal Disease
CN33	Exc., Misc., Fractures, Accessory Tarsal Bones, Tarsal Coalition, Hypertrophic Osteoarthropathy, DISH, Pres.
CN36	Pres.
CN37	Periodontal Disease, Dental, Bone Former, Pres.
CN38	Misc., Pres.,Bone Former
CN39	Fractures, Pres.
CN40	NMT, Periodontal Disease
CN41	NMT, Periodontal Disease, Misc.
CN42	Misc.
CN43	Misc.
CN44	Radiocarbon
CN45	Fractures, Pres., Periodontal Disease
CN47	Exc., Misc.
EE002	NMT
EE003	Radiocarbon, Fracture, Dental, Spondylolysis, NMT, Localised Microdontia
EE004	Supra-acetabular Cyst, Trauma, Fractures, Misc., NMT
EE005	Misc.
EE006	Spina Bifida
EE007	Radiocarbon, Misc., Unerupted Canines
EE010	Misc., Exc.
EE013	Radiocarbon, Exc., Misc., Pres.
EE104	Hyperbrachycranic Skull, Dental
EE015	Pres., Block Vertebrae, Misc., Fractures
EE016	Lumbar Rib, Periostitis
EE017	Misc.
EE018	Spondylolysis, Misc., Periostitis, Fracture
EE019	Radiocarbon, Dental
EE020	Radiocarbon, Periodontal Disease, Misc.
EE022	Fracture, Misc., Accessory Tarsal Bone
EE024	Periodontal Disease
EE025	Unerupted Canine
EE026	Radiocarbon, Pres., Periodontal Disease, Dental
EE027	Periodontal Disease, Localised Microdontia
EE028	Periodontal Disease, Dental
EE029	Periostitis, Accessory Tarsal Bone
EE030	NMT, Periodontal Disease, Dental, ?Osteochondritis Dissecans
EE031	Dental, Subluxation, Dislocation, ?Aneurisms
EE032	Fracture, Periodontal Disease
EE036	Misc.
EE037	Dental, Hypodontia, Unerupted Canine, Periodontal Disease, Fracture, Misc., NMT
EE038	Periodontal Disease, Radiocarbon
EE039	NMT, bifid rib
EE040	NMT
EE041	Periodontal Disease, Misc., Pres.
EE042	NMT
EE043	Unerupted Canine, Localised Microdontia
EE044	Misc.
EE045	Dental, Bone Former, Periodontal Disease
EE046	Bone Former, Block Vertebrae, Periodontal Disease
EE050	NMT
EE054	Periostitis
EE056	Tuberculosis
EE060	Fractures
EE061	Craniostenosis
EE062	Hypertrophic Osteoarthropathy, Spina Bifida, Lumbar Ribs
EE064	Periodontal Disease, Dental
EE065	Misc.
EE066	Dental
EE067	Periodontal Disease, Dental
EE070	Anterior Lingual Depressions, Hypodontia, NMT, Periostitis
EE071	Fused Ribs
EE072	Localised Microdontia, Periostitis, Dental
EE073	Supernumerary Atlanto-occipital Articulation, Misc.
EE076	Dental
EE077	Periodontal Disease, Dental
EE079	Block Vertebrae, Bone Former, Misc., Pres.
EE080	Periodontal Disease, Block Vertebrae, Bone Former, Spondylolysis, Tarsal Coalition, Pres., Dental
EE082	Periodontal Disease, Misc.
EE083	Bathrocrany
EE085	Periodontal Disease, Lumbar Rib, Cleft Pedicle
EE086	NMT
EE090	Dental
EE091	Dental, Pres.
EE092	Dental
EE093	Periodontal Disease, NMT
EE096	Misc.
EE098	Periostitis, Misc., Myositis Ossificans
EE099	Slight Acetabular Dysplasia, Dental, Supra-acetabular Cysts
EE101	Unerupted Third Molar, Periodontal Disease, NMT, Misc.
G251	Exc.
G253	Periostitis, Fractures
G254	Unerupted Third Molar
G265	Radiocarbon, Unerupted Canine, NMT, Hypodontia, Dental, Periodontal Disease, Misc., Trauma, Hallux Valgus, Bone Former
G275A	Radiocarbon, Misc., Slipped Capital Epiphysis, Periodontal Disease, Spondylolysis, NMT

G278	Radiocarbon, Lumbar Ribs, Misc., Fracture, Bone Former, Periostitis, Hallux Valgus, Supra-acetabular Cysts	G528	Radiocarbon, Exc., Skeletal Asymmetry, Dental, Misc., Cervical Ribs, Spondylolysis
G279	Radiocarbon, Periodontal Disease, Dental, Fracture, Misc., Osteochondritis Dissecans	G531	Exc., Periostitis, Porotic Hyperostosis
		G542	NMT
G296	Hypertrophic Osteoarthropathy, Periodontal Disease, ?Infection, Misc., NMT, Tarsal Coalition	G555	?Neoplasm
		G558	NMT
		G561	Bone Former, Periodontal Disease, Fractures
G297	Periodontal Disease, Radiocarbon, Misc.	G565	Fractures, Spondylolysis, Misc.
G298	Porotic Hyperostosis	G571	Radiocarbon, Dental, Periodontal Disease, Misc., Fracture, Hydatid Cyst, Neoplasm
G303	Spina Bifida, Radiocarbon, NMT, Periostitis, Fracture		
		G576	Fused Ribs
G304	Radiocarbon, Localised Microdontia, Fracture, NMT	G582	Radiocarbon, Dental
		G587	Periodontal Disease, Misc., Bathrocrany, NMT
G308	Misc.		
G310	Periodontal Disease, Dental, Fractures	G597	Unerupted Canine, Periodontal Disease, Misc., Fracture
G314	Radiocarbon, Spina Bifida		
G327	Misc., Fracture, Periostitis	G601	Radiocarbon, Trauma, Bone Former, Misc., Femoral Head Necrosis
G339	Pres.		
G361	Radiocarbon, Bone Former, NMT	G604	Radiocarbon, Periodontal Disease, Misc.
G363	Hypodontia, Dental, Localised Microdontia	G607	Trauma, Supra-acetabular Cysts, Misc., Fractures, Bone Former
G370	Accessory Tarsal Bone		
G377	Misc.	G614	NMT
G379	Supra-acetabular Cysts, Periodontal Disease, Fracture, Periostitis, Misc.	G628	Pres., Misc., NMT
		G635	Unerupted Third Molar, Localised Microdontia, NMT
G381	Dental, Periodontal Disease, ?Trauma, NMT		
G385	Radiocarbon, Misc., NMT, Periodontal Disease, Neoplasm	G636	Dental, Trauma, Hallux Valgus, Misc., Fracture
		G643	Misc., Bone Former, Localised Microdontia
G398	Misc., Infection, Periostitis	G652	Radiocarbon, Misc.
G406	Bathrocrany, Periodontal Disease, Dental, ?Osteochondritis Dissecans	G658	NMT, Dental, Periostitis, Misc.
		G670	Periodontal Disease, Dental
G411	Periostitis	G673	Neoplasm, Periodontal Disease, Misc., NMT, Anterior Lingual Depression
G416	Unerupted Canines		
G419	Misc., Periodontal Disease, Neoplasm, NMT	G676	Dental, Periodontal Disease
G424	NMT, Misc.	G677	Infection?
G427	Misc.	G678	Periostitis
G430	NMT	G692	Periostitis
G436	Misc., Anterior Lingual Depressions	G694	Fractures, NMT, Dental, Misc.
G438	Tuberculosis, Dental, Misc., Atlanto-Occipital Fusion, Exc., Localised Microdontia, Block Vertebrae	G697	Misc., Periostitis
		G708	NMT, Leprosy
		G710	Unerupted Canine, Dental
G443	Localised Microdontia, Misc.	G715	Dental, Localised Microdontia, Periodontal Disease, Fracture, Trepanation
G451	Radiocarbon, Fractures, Misc., Dental		
G456	Dental, NMT	G720	Dental, Misc.
G457	Exc.	G723	Periostitis
G462	Neoplasm, Radiocarbon, Periostitis, Dental, Misc., Accessory Tarsal Bones	G746	Supra-acetabular Cysts, Fracture, Bone Former, NMT, Misc., Spondylolysis, Trauma
		G747	Accessory Tarsal Bone, Periostitis, Spondylolysis
G467	Dental, Periostitis		
G474	Radiocarbon, Dental, Periodontal Disease	G750	Trauma, Radiocarbon, Misc.
G478	Radiocarbon, Dental Enamel Pearls, Dental	G760	Radiocarbon, Periodontal Disease, NMT
G482	Misc., Supra-acetabular Cyst, Fractures, Myositis Ossificans, Tuberculosis	NA002	Radiocarbon, NMT, Spina Bifida
		NA004	Misc.
G488	NMT	NA004A	Periostitis
G497	Pres.	NA006	Radiocarbon, Spondylolisthesis, Periodontal Disease, Dental, Accessory Tarsal Bone, Cleft Pedicle
G500	Localised Microdontia		
G503	Porotic Hyperostosis, NMT		
G510	Dental		
G516	Misc.	NA013	Radiocarbon, NMT, Periodontal Disease, Misc.

NA014	Radiocarbon, Accessory Tarsal Bone, Misc.	NA112	Tuberculosis, Radiocarbon, Dental
NA014A	Periostitis	NA115	Cervical Rib, Neoplasm, Anterior Lingual Depressions, Dental, Periodontal Disease, Misc.
NA019	Dental, Double Tooth		
NA024	Periostitis, Misc.		
NA025	Spina Bifida	NA116	Block Vertebrae
NA026	Tuberculosis	NA117	Periostitis, Misc.
NA031	Slight Acetabular Dysplasia, Misc., Tarsal Coalition, Supra-acetabular Cysts	NA118	Periostitis, Exc., NMT
		NA119	Slight Acetabular Dysplasia
NA031A	Exc., Dental	NA120	Block Vertebrae, Spina Bifida
NA033	Fracture, Pres., Misc., Accessory Tarsal Bone, NMT, Spondylolysis, Spina Bifida	NA121	Periodontal Disease, Misc., Pres., Exc.
		NA121A	Exc.
NA035	Exc., NMT	NA122	Exc.
NA036	Rickets	NA122A	Periodontal Disease, Exc.
NA038	Exc., Periodontal Disease	NA123	Exc., Misc., Accessory Tarsal Bone
NA043	Exc., Periostitis	NA125	NMT
NA043A	Periostitis, Exc.	NA127	Radiocarbon
NA044	Misc., NMT, Periodontal Disease, Fracture	NA131	Rickets
NA046	Radiocarbon, Fracture, NMT, DISH, Tuberculosis	NA132	Periostitis
		NA135	Langerhans' Cell Histiocytosis, Porotic Hyperostosis
NA047	Misc.		
NA048	Misc.	NA138	Periostitis
NA051	Periodontal Disease	NA140	Exc., Misc.
NA056A	Exc.	NA140A	Exc.
NA059	NMT, Periodontal Disease	NA142	Exc.
NA060	Periostitis, Exc.	NA142A	Exc.
NA060A	Exc.	NA143	Dental, Misc.
NA063	Dental	NA144	NMT
NA066	Periodontal Disease, Scoliosis, Accessory Tarsal Bones, NMT, Tarsal Coalition, Epiphysial Plate Injury	NA145	Periodontal Disease, Hypodontia, Dental
		NA146	Radiocarbon, NMT, Misc., Periodontal Disease, Exc., Spondylolysis
NA068	Neoplasm, NMT, Dental, Unerupted Canine, Periodontal Disease	NA149	Periodontal Disease, Exc.
		NA149A	Exc., Misc.
NA070	Exc.	NA149B	Exc.
NA080	Periodontal Disease, Dental	NA150	Atlanto-Occipital Fusion, Block Vertebrae
NA081	Exc., Periodontal Disease, Hypodontia	NA151	Dental, Talon Cusp, Double Tooth
NA084	NMT	NA154	Hypodontia, Localised Microdontia, Misc.
NA088	Pres., Slight Acetabular Dysplasia, Supra-acetabular Cyst, Exc., Localised Microdontia, Spina Bifida, Periodontal Disease	NA157	Pres., Spondylolysis
		NA160	Periostitis
		NA166	Spondylolysis, Misc.
NA089	Misc.	NA167	Radiocarbon, Localised Microdontia, Periodontal Disease, Exc., Misc., Fracture
NA091	Fracture, Misc.		
NA092	?Rickets	NA168	NMT, Spondylolisthesis, Periodontal Disease, Accessory Tarsal Bones
NA094	Radiocarbon		
NA095	Spina Bifida	NA170	Cervical Rib, Exc., Radiocarbon, Dental, Misc., NMT
NA098	NMT		
NA100	Localised Microdontia, Dental, Periodontal Disease	NA170A	Exc., Pres.
		NA171	?Trauma, Dental, Misc., NMT
NA101	Exc.	NA172	Misc., Exc.
NA101A	Exc., NMT, Misc.	NA173	Radiocarbon, Localised Microdontia, Hypodontia, NMT
NA102	Misc.		
NA103	Periostitis,Exc.	NA174	Periostitis, NMT, Dental
NA104	Radiocarbon, Trauma, Misc., Periostitis, NMT	NA175	Misc.
NA105	Localised Microdontia, Misc., Periodontal Disease, Spina Bifida	NA176	Radiocarbon, Periostitis, Trauma, Misc., Osteochondritis Dissecans, Spondylolysis, Localised Microdontia
		NA177	Misc., Periostitis, ?Trauma
NA107	Exc.	NA178	Dermoid Cyst
NA108	Rickets	NA179	Misc.
NA110	Misc.	NA180	Misc.
NA111	Lumbar Rib, Hypodontia, Periodontal Disease, Dental		

NA181	Fractures, Spondylolysis, Misc., Myositis Ossificans, Supra-acetabular Cysts
NA182	Misc.
NA183	Fracture
NA184	NMT, Porotic Hyperostosis
NA185	Misc., Lumbar Ribs
NA188	Misc.
NA189	Double Tooth, ?Rickets
NA190	Fractures, Misc., Periodontal Disease, Bone Former
NA191	Rickets
NA192	NMT
NA194	Rickets
NA195	Radiocarbon, Misc.
NA197	Tuberculosis, Neoplasm, Fractures, Tarsal Coalition, Spondylolysis, Misc., Periodontal Disease
NA198	Misc., Osteochondritis Dissecans, Dental, Hypodontia
NA199	Radiocarbon, Misc., NMT, Fractures, Dental
NA201	Misc.
NA202	Pres., Aseptic Necrosis, Misc., Bathrocrany
NA203	Fracture, Misc., Pres.
NA203A	Exc., NMT
NA204	Periodontal Disease, NMT
NA205	Spondylolysis, Misc.
NA209	Exc.
NA215	Radiocarbon, Unerupted Canine, Misc., Periodontal Disease, Dental
NA217	Radiocarbon, Block Vertebrae, Accessory Tarsal Bone, Fractures, DISH, Periodontal Disease
NA218	Radiocarbon, Misc., Pres., Neoplasm, Periostitis, Fracture, Dental, Hypodontia, Spondylolysis, Supra-acetabular Cysts
NA223	Radiocarbon, Pres.
NA224	Radiocarbon, Accessory Tarsal Bones, Misc.
NA225	Periostitis
NA227	Radiocarbon, Spondylolysis, NMT, Dental Enamel Pearl, Periodontal Disease, Cervical Rib
NA233	Exc., Radiocarbon, Misc., Periostitis
NA233A	Exc.
NA234	Periostitis, Misc.
NA235	Spina Bifida
NA236	Rickets, NMT
NA237	Periodontal Disease, NMT
SA002	Dental, Misc., Radiocarbon, Exc., Periodontal Disease, Periostitis, NMT
SA003	Misc., Supra-acetabular Cyst, Radiocarbon, Exc., Fractures, Bone Former
SA005	Exc.
SA007	Misc., Exc.
SA008	Misc., Exc.
SA012	Radiocarbon, Pres., Dental
SA013	Tuberculosis, Misc., Radiocarbon
SA014	Radiocarbon, Accessory Tarsal Bone, Neoplasm
SA015	Exc., Block Vertebrae, Accessory Tarsal Bone, Fracture, Supra-acetabular Cyst
SA017	Misc., Hypodontia, Dental, Exc., Periodontal Disease, Pres.
SA017A	NMT, Exc., Misc.
SA021	Periodontal Disease, Bathrocrany, Misc., NMT, Pres.
SA023	Pres., Cholesteatoma, Misc., Bathrocrany, Preserved Hair, Block Vertebrae
SA029	Pres., Neoplasm, Periodontal Disease, Tarsal Coalition
SA030	NMT, Localised Microdontia, Periodontal Disease
SA033	Acetabular Flange Lesion, Supra-acetabular Cysts, Radiocarbon
SA034	Radiocarbon, Fractures, Accessory Tarsal Bone, Spondylolysis, Misc.
SA045	Dental
SA047	Misc., Periodontal Disease
SA048	Pres., Lumbar Ribs
SA049	Infection, Pres., Misc., Accessory Tarsal Bone
SA050	Slipped Capital Epiphyses, Misc.
SA052	Radiocarbon, Supra-acetabular Cyst, Periodontal Disease, Fracture, Misc., Bathrocrany, NMT
SA053	Radiocarbon, Misc., Trauma
SA055	Dental, Periostitis
SA056	Radiocarbon, Misc., Pres., Bone Former
SA052/16	Unerupted Third Molar, Periodontal Disease, ?Scheuermann's Disease, Misc., NMT
SA52/18	Periodontal Disease, NMT, Neoplasm
SA080	Misc., Porotic Hyperostosis, Radiocarbon, Pres.
V01	Pres.
V07	Periodontal Disease, Dental Enamel Pearls
V10	Porotic Hyperostosis
V11	Periodontal Disease, Dental, Supra-acetabular Cysts, Misc.
V15	Supra-acetabular Cyst, Periodontal Disease, Spondylolysis, Spina Bifida, Misc., Fracture
V16	NMT, Periodontal Disease
V18	Bone Former, Misc.
V19	Pres., Misc., Fracture
V20	Pres.
V21	Trauma, Pres., Hallux Valgus
V22	Dental
V24	Dental, Fracture
V25	Dental
V26	Dental Grooving, Fracture, Misc.
V27	NMT
V28	Rickets
V29	Accessory Tarsal Bones, Slipped Capital Epiphysis, Misc.
V30	Dental
V32	Misc.
V33	Fracture, Misc., Localised Microdontia
V35	Misc.
V36	Pres., Misc.
V37	Fracture
V38	Supra-acetabular Cyst, Radiocarbon, Periodontal Disease, Fractures, Misc., NMT

V40	Misc.	
V41	Radiocarbon	
V42	Pres., Misc., Hypodontia, Localised Microdontia, Dental, Bone Former	
V44	Periodontal Disease, Fractures	
V45	Radiocarbon, Fracture, Bone Former, Dental, Misc.	
V46	Dental, Misc., Pres., Neoplasm, NMT	
V47	Exc.	
V51	Exc.	
V53	Exc.	
V55	Exc.	
V57	Rickets	
V59	Periostitis, Exc.	
V61	Fracture, Periodontal Disease, Hyperostosis Frontalis Interna, Dental	
V62	Misc., Hypodontia, Dental, Unerupted Canines	

WCO007 Misc.
WCO009 Radiocarbon, Periostitis, Misc., Neoplasm
WCO010 Radiocarbon, Bathrocrany, Misc., Dental Grooving
WCO011 Spina Bifida, Spondylolysis
WCO012 Fracture
WCO013 Trauma, Fractures, DISH, Misc.
WCO014 Misc., Hallux Valgus
WCO015 Misc., Slipped Capital Epiphysis
WCO016 Dental Grooving, Misc.
WCO017 NMT, Periodontal Disease, Misc., Dental, Fracture
WCO018 Supra-acetabular Cysts, Misc., Hypertrophic Osteoarthropathy, Hallux Valgus
WCO019 Misc.
WCO021A Exc., NMT
WCO022 NMT, Exc., Misc.
WCO023 NMT, Misc.
WCO026 Misc., Dental, Periodontal Disease, Trauma, NMT, Lumbar Ribs
WCO027 Misc.
WCO028 Radiocarbon, Periodontal Disease, Misc.
WCO030 Misc.
WCO032 Misc., Dental
WCO035 Exc.
WCO035A Exc.
WCO036 Supra-acetabular Cysts, Misc., Bone Former
WCO037 Misc., Fracture, Bone Former, NMT, Pres.
WCO038 Lumbar Rib, Misc.
WCO039 Accessory Tarsal Bone, Periostitis, ?Neoplasm, Pres.
WCO040 Misc.
WCO041 NMT, Osteomyelitis, Neoplasm
WCO044 Radiocarbon
WCO045 Radiocarbon, Misc., Fractures, NMT
WCO056 Neoplasm, Periodontal Disease, NMT, Misc.
WCO057 Misc., Exc.
WCO058 Misc., Exc.
WCO059 Acetabular Flange Lesion, Bone Former, Periodontal Disease, Misc., Spondylolysis, Supra-acetabular Cysts, Pres.

WCO067 Misc., NMT, Accessory Tarsal Bone
WCO068 Periodontal Disease, Misc., Tarsal Coalition
WCO069 ?Slipped Capital Epiphysis
WCO070 Radiocarbon, NMT, Bathrocrany, Periodontal Disease, Misc.
WCO071 NMT, Dental, Misc.
WCO077 NMT, Periodontal Disease, Dental, Misc.
WCO078 Dental, Periodontal Disease
WCO079 Misc., Dental
WCO080 Neoplasm
WCO087 Exc., Misc., NMT
WCO088 Exc.
WCO089 Periodontal Disease, Misc., NMT
WCO091 Trauma, NMT
WCO092 Unerupted Third Molar, Periodontal Disease, Trauma, Misc.
WCO093 Hypodontia, Misc., Spondylolysis
WCO097 Misc.
WCO098 Periodontal Disease, Misc.
WCO099 Periostitis, NMT
WCO103 Pres., Dental, Misc.
WCO107 Periostitis, Misc., Dental
WCO108 Misc.
WCO109 Pres., NMT
WCO110 Misc.
WCO115 Perthes' Disease
WCO115A Periostitis, Misc., NMT
WCO117 Supra-acetabular Cyst, Misc., Fractures, Dental
WCO118 Radiocarbon, Exc.
WCO119 Radiocarbon, Exc., Periodontal Disease
WCO122 Misc.
WCO124 Dental, Misc.
WCO125 Accessory Tarsal Bone, Misc.
WCO125A Misc.
WCO130 Supra-acetabular Cysts, Radiocarbon, Periostitis, Misc., Spondylolysis
WCO131 ?Dermoid Cyst, Misc.
WCO134 Cervical Ribs, Neoplasm
WCO137 Periostitis, Fractures
WCO138 Radiocarbon, NMT, Misc.
WCO139 Fracture, Radiocarbon, Misc., Dental
WCO142 Tuberculosis
WCO144 Dental, bifid rib
WCO146 Bathrocrany, Misc., Pres.
WCO149 NMT
WCO153 Radiocarbon
WCO154 Periodontal Disease
WCO156 Radiocarbon, Tarsal Coalition
WCO162 Radiocarbon, NMT, Pres., Periodontal Disease, Misc., Dental
WCO164 Periostitis, Misc.
WCO164A Supra-acetabular Cyst, Misc., Trauma, Fractures
WCO165 Fracture, NMT, Misc., Periodontal Disease
WCO165A Trauma, Misc., Pres.
WCO166 Misc., Exc., Dental
WCO167 Exc.
WCO168 Dental, Misc.

WCO170 Radiocarbon, Supra-acetabular Cysts, Fractures, Misc.

WCO173 NMT, Acetabular Flange Lesion, Supra-acetabular Cysts, Hypodontia, Periodontal Disease

WCO174 Spondylolysis, Misc.

WCO175 Misc.

WCO176 Osteochondritis Dissecans

WCO179 Radiocarbon, Misc.

WCO181 Radiocarbon, Misc., Periostitis

WCO183 Radiocarbon, Anterior Lingual Depressions

WCO184 Radiocarbon, Neoplasms, Pres., Periodontal Disease, Misc.

WCO187 Misc.

WCO191 Exc., Misc., Periodontal Disease

WCO192 Exc., NMT

WCO193 Periodontal Disease, Exc., Dental

WCO195 NMT

WCO199 Periostitis, NMT, Periodontal Disease

WCO200 Supra-acetabular Cysts, Slight Acetabular Dysplasia, Hypertrophic Osteoarthropathy, Fractures, Trauma, Periostitis, NMT

WCO201 Trauma, Pres.

WCO202 Dental

WCO203 Supra-acetabular Cyst, Misc., Block Vertebrae

WCO204 Supra-acetabular Cysts, Misc.

Notes: Misc. = miscellaneous; NMT = non-metric trait; Pres.= bone preservation; Spina Bifida = spina bifida occulta in pre-sacral vertebrae; Porotic Hyperostosis = porotic hyperostosis of cranial vault; Exc. = notes on excavation or post-excavation processing of burial

Appendix 4: A Note on the Burnt Clay

The 134 fragments recovered from Sites 26 and 41 are mainly of two types, a sandy clay matrix with chalk and flint inclusions, some quite large, and a more homogeneous type with a soapy feel. Both have been found across most areas of the village. The sandy variety occurred only on Site 26 with the majority appearing in Periods 5, 6 and 7. Both sites produced the soapy type which predominates in the medieval and earlier phases.

Appendix 5: A Note on the Coal

Just over 1000g of coal were recovered from Site 26. Seventy-eight percent of it was from contexts in Periods 6 and 7 and is likely to relate to the post-medieval buildings in the vicinity of the churchyard.

Appendix 6: A Note on the Charcoal

Charcoal was recovered from Sites 26 and 41. On Site 41 large samples were taken from the earliest levels (Period 1) and these will be fully examined as part of the charcoal survey to be undertaken at the end of the project.

On Site 26 charcoal was retrieved from a wide variety of contexts, only a few of which produced suitable samples for the survey. Of the 245g recovered, some 60% was in Periods 3 and 4, with some small amounts in the post-hole groups of Period 1, Phase 1 and 2. Charcoal associated with some of the graves was merely in the fill and of no significance.

Appendix 7: The Metalworking Residues
by G. McDonnell

Introduction and methodology

Just over 7kgs of metalworking debris recovered from the Churchyard area has been examined and catalogued. As in other parts of the village, diagnostic smithing slags predominate with other types present in small quantities, including Iron Age Grey which also occurred on the North Manor sites (McDonnell 2004, 255). More detailed discussion of the slags from Wharram is in the report on the smithing site in the South Manor area (McDonnell 2000, 155-8).

Discussion

A hearth bottom weighing 385g, a tiny fragment of SSL and some corroded iron were in Roman contexts on Site 41. On the same site, 11g of Iron Age Grey, a fuel ash slag diagnostic of Iron Age sites, occurred in a medieval layer, along with some 680g of smelting slag of a type which is neither Roman nor medieval and may be contemporary.

As in the North and South Manor areas, the vast majority of the metalworking debris (4316g) occurred in the late Saxon and early medieval periods. Table 163 shows the distribution for Site 26 where some 3774g (79%) were in these periods.

Table 163. Metalworking debris from Site 26 by period and weight.

Period	SSL	HB	HL	FE	TOTAL	CIN
1	228	-	-	+	228	-
2	161	-	2	+	163	<1
3	1502	142	5	-	1649	42>
4	1113	976	36	-	2125	30>
5	181	-	18	-	199	21
6	19	-	-	-	19	36>
7	38	-	-	-	38	10>
-	26	313	-	-	339	2
Total	3268	1431	61	+	4760	

SSL=Smithing Slag Lumps, HB=Hearth Bottoms, HL=Hearth Lining, CIN=Cinder

Appendix 8: Concordance of the Contexts containing Pottery, Small Finds, Metallurgical and Environmental Remains, and of all Contexts mentioned in this volume, by Site, Phase and Context

The concordance lists pre-medieval and medieval pottery by sherd count and weight; catalogue numbers of illustrated sherds are given in brackets. The presence of prehistoric and post-medieval pottery is indicated. The published or Archive catalogue numbers are given for small finds of stone, clay, metal, wood, bone or ivory, leather and for published glass objects and window glass. The remaining vessel glass is listed by number of fragments (bracketed), as are brick, nails, clay tile, burnt clay and published animal bone; animal bone in other contexts is not recorded here. Metallurgical waste, cinder, coal and charcoal are listed by weight and, finally, mortar and molluscs by presence.

   The concordance lists those contexts from the Church discussed in the text or appearing in a figure but no finds are included.

Abbreviations

Pottery:
Pre.: Prehistoric pottery
Rom.: Iron Age and Roman pottery
Med.: Saxon and medieval pottery
PM: post-medieval pottery

Small Finds:
Bone: bone or ivory artefact
Brick: brick fragments
Clay: clay artefact
Coin: coin
Copper: copper-alloy artefact
Glass: glass object
Iron: iron artefact
Lead: lead artefact
Lst.: limestone
Nail: nail including fragments (the second number is nails from animal shoes)
Quern: quernstone
Roof.: roofing stone (including slate)
Sst.: sandstone
St.: other stone
Stone: stone artefact other than quern, including stone possibly used for flooring
Tile: clay tile
Vess.: vessel glass
Window: window glass
Wood: wooden artefact

Environmental and Technological Remains:
An.: animal remains
Burnt: burnt clay fragments
Char.: charcoal
Cin.: cinder
Coal: coal
Moll.: molluscs
Mortar: mortar and plaster samples
Slag: metallurgical waste

Description
Str.: Structure

Phase	Context	Description	Fig. Nos	Artefacts and environmental remains

Site 26

Phase	Context	Description	Fig. Nos	Artefacts and environmental remains
7.5	1	topsoil		Iron A123
7.1	2	?topsoil formation	45	
6.6	3	chalk rubble deposit	44	Med. 60:822 (4, 12); PM; Bone 12; Brick (4); Iron 9; Lead A76; Lst. A147; Nail 6:-; Roof. A155-A160; Tile (8); Window A1, A2; Coal 6g
6.4	3A	surface	44	Finds are included in context 3
6.3	4	bonding-type material/floor make-up	43	Med. 14:120; Moll.
6.3/5.1	4 or 74	-		Iron A205
6.6	5	chalky deposit	45	
7.1	6	fill of conduit 84 Str. M		Med. 4:81; Roof. A161
7.1	7	pit cut/fill		Med. 9:105; PM; Brick (1); Clay A16; Iron 12; Lead 44; Nail 1:-; St. A350; Tile (2)
6.5	8	demolition rubble		
7.5	9	topsoil		Rom. 2:15; Med. 26:281; PM; Clay A17; Iron A78, A130, A147; Lead 41, A87; Nail 6:1; Roof. A162; St. A351; Vess. (3); Window A3; Coal 2g
5.2	10	hill wash/silt	41	
7.1	11	construction trench of conduit 84, Str. M	45	Med. 3:83
6.6	13	chalk cobble surface Str. L	44	
6.3	14	loam deposit	43	Med. 14:206
6.3	15	chalk rubble surface	43	Med. 14:137
4.1	16	chalk surface		
6.3	17	demolition rubble	43	
5.1	20	Wall 20	39, 41 42, 44	Med. 9:64; Tile (1); Coal 2g (or CXT76)
5.2	21	path	41	
7.2	22	large rubble deposit	45	
7.3	27	post-hole cut/fill	45	
7.3	28	post-hole cut/fill	45	
7.2	29	rubble deposit	45	
7.3	30	scoop cut/fill	45	Med. 8:205; PM; Clay 11; Vess. (1); Window A4
7.2	31	rubble deposit	45	Med. 6:73; PM; Nail 1:-; St. A390; Tile (1)
5.1	32	path and make-ups	39, 41; 42, 43	Med. 19:87 (16); Iron A148; Nail 39:1; Sst. 65; St. A364, A391; Tile (17); Char. ≤ g; Coal 2g; Moll.
5.1	32A	path and make-ups		Med. 26:34; Window A5
5.1	32B	path and make-ups		Med. 11:18; Window A6
5.1	32C	path and make-ups		Med. 3:24
5.1	32D=283	path and make-ups	39	
6.3	33	path repair	43	Med. 1:40; PM; Nail 1:-
6.3	34	wall footing Str. K	43	Med. 9:57; PM; Nail 5:-
6.3	35	demolition rubble		Med. 20:175; PM; Nail 1:-; Tile (1)
7.5	35/36	-		Clay A12; Nail 2:-; Tile (7)
7.5	36	turf and humus		Rom. 1:2 (below 36), 32; Med. 49:620 (19); PM; Bone 14; Brick (3); Clay 10, 12, A13, A13a, A14, A18, A21; Coin 41 (*Wharram IX*); Copper 6, A53; Iron 15, 18, 45, A76, A77, A79, A83, A84, A86, A88, A89, A97, A98, A101, A104, A107-A109, A111-A114, A122, A134, A136-A139, A145, A149, A150; Lead 40, A92, A111; Nail 87:1; Roof. A163-A168, A247, A248; St. A352, A392; Tile (80); Vess. (17); Window A7-A12; Burnt (1); Char. 25g; Cin. ≤ g; Coal 77g; Moll.
7.5	?36	-		Tile (1)

Phase	Context	Description	Fig. Nos	Artefacts and environmental remains
7.5	37	topsoil		Med. 10:124; PM; Clay A14; Copper A54; Lead A86, A110; Nail 4:-; Roof. A169; St. A353, A365, A393, A394; Vess. (2); Window A13; Char. ≤1g; Cin. 2g; Coal 23g
	?37	-		PM
7.4	38	?fill/?levelling deposit		Med. 1:8
7.4	39	?surface repair/ ?wall footing	40	
7.2	40	road surface	45, 40	
7.2	42	rubble deposit	45	
7.2	43	?rut in road	45	
7.5	44	?post-packing		Med. 3:28; PM; Clay A15; Iron A87, A105, A106, A121, A124; Nail 10:-; Roof. A249; Tile (4); Vess. (13); Window A14; Char. 14g; Coal 25g finds from 44A and 44B may be included
6.5	?44A	demolition rubble		Rom. 1:4; Nail 6:-
6.4	44B	area of burning	44	
7.5/6.2	44/49	-		PM; Iron A142; Nail 3:1; Roof. A170; Tile (1); Window A15; Wood A1; Char. 1g; Coal 19g; Slag 38g
6.4	45	surface	44	Med. 10:248 (20); PM; Brick (1); Coin 36; Copper 12, A60, A61; Iron 19, 25, 26, 38, 44, 50, 51, 65, A151; Lead 43; Nail 7:-; St. A284, A354; Tile (3); Vess. (2); Cin. 9g; Coal 82g
6.4	46	surface	44	Rom. 1:3; Med. 1:3; PM; Nail 6:-; Vess. (1); Cin. 1g; Coal 7g; Moll.
6.4	47	surface	44	Med. 7:80; Lead A103; Nail 6:1; St. A347, A348; Tile (8); Window A16;Burnt (1); Char. 15g; Cin. ≤1g; Coal 19g; Moll.
6.2	48	chalk cobbles	42	Brick (3); Nail 1:-; Cin. 2g; Coal ≤1g; Moll.
6.2	49	clay and chalk rubble	42	Med. 8:87; PM; Nail 6:-; Roof. A171, A172; Sst. A107; Vess. (1); Burnt Coal 1g
6.2	50	rubble deposit	42, 40	Med. 2:10; PM; Brick (1); Copper 27; Nail 6:-; Sst. 66; St. A285; Burnt (2); (3); Char. 6g; Coal 3g; Moll.
6.2	50/55	-		PM; Nail 3:-; Tile (3); Coal 13g; Moll.
6.2	51	surface	42, 40	PM; Coin 16; Iron 73; Nail 10:-; Roof. A173; Tile (3); Window A17; Wood A2
6.2/5.1	51/74	-		Rom. 1:2
6.2	52	wall footing Str. F	40	
6.2	53	bonding material/ ?wall foundation	42	
5.1	54	path	39; 41	Med. 34:173; Iron 71, A152, A153; Nail 12:-; Tile (6); Window A18; Char. 2g; Coal 3g; Moll.
6.2	55	silt deposit	42	Med. 3:17; Nail 1:-; Char. 1g
6.2	56	surface	42, 40	Med. 3:116; Moll.
5.2	57	surface		Nail 4:-; Roof. A250; Window A19; Char. 1g; Slag 41g
5.2	58	area of burning	41	PM; Char.; Coal 8g
6.2	59	clay and chalk rubble	42	Med. 12:223; Iron A154, A155; Nail 17:2; Roof. A174; Sst. A108; Tile (5); Wood A3; Burnt (1); Char. ≤1g; Coal 22g; Slag 19g
-	60	surface	42	Med. 1:1; Nail 3:-; Window A20; Coal 2g; Moll.
5.2	61	?hill wash	41	Coin 21
5.2	61A	hill wash/silt	41	
4.6	62	chalk rubble deposit		Rom. 3:34; Med. 85:588 (21); Coin 20; Copper 9, 36, A67; Iron 74, A156, A157, A158; Lead 39, A70; Nail 5:-; Quern A74 (joins 382); Roof. A175, A176; Stone 57; Sst. A109- A112; Tile (14); Window A21-A23; Wood A4; Burnt (1); Char. 5 ≥ Coal 27g; Moll.; Slag 53g
-	?62	-		Iron 72; Roof. A177
5.1	63	hill wash	39, 42	Med. 21:128; PM; Iron A159; Lst. A138; Nail 6:1; Roof. A178, A179; Stone A274; Tile (2); Burnt (5); Moll.; Slag 118g
5.1	?63	-		Lead A72; Nail 1:-; Tile (3); Window A24
5.2	64	surface	41, 40	Med. 21:143; PM; Coin 14; Nail 2:-; Roof. A180-A182; Tile (7)
5.2/6.5	64/?73	-		Roof. A183

Phase	Context	Description	Fig. Nos	Artefacts and environmental remains
4.4	65	loam deposit	38	Rom. 1:6; Med. 39:252; PM; Clay 9, A22; Copper 17, A58; Iron A160; Nail 12:-; Roof. A184-A186; Wood A5, A6; Char. ⊴g; Cin. 8g; Coal 5g; Moll.
5.1	67	hill wash	39	Med. 3:15; Iron A161; St. A367; Coal 4g; Moll.
5.1	68	hill wash	39, 40	Rom. 1:5; Med. 8:36; PM; Vess. (1)
4.4	69	loam deposit	38	Rom. 4:38, 27; Tile (1)
4.4	70	loam deposit	38, 40	Rom. 8:53; Med. 62:439; PM; Brick (4); Lst. A133; Roof. A187; Sst. A113, A114; Tile (4); Window A25, A26; Burnt (1); Char. ⊴g; Cin. 7g; Coal 8g; Moll.
?5.1	71	bonding material/ collapsed Wall 20	40	Rom. 2:7; Med. 53:293; Brick (23); Roof. A188-A191; Nail 5:1; Sst. A115; Tile (1); Window A27; Char. 1g; Cin. 1g
?5.1/4.4	71/?72	-		Brick (8)
4.4	72	loam deposit	38	Med. 1:2; Iron 30
4.4/4.6	72/?271	-		Rom. 1:4
6.6	73	wall, Str. L	44	Stone 60
6.6	?73	-		Roof A192
5.1	74	Wall 20	39, 41; 42, 44; 40	Rom. 1:3; Med. 41:192; PM; Clay 18a; Copper 20, A51; Lead A98, A99; Nail 2:-; Roof. A193; St. A355, A395; Tile (2); Window A28-A30; Burnt (2); Char. 4g; Cin. 15g; Coal 13g; Mortar A1, A2; Slag 2g
5.1	?74	-		Bone 8; Tile (1)
6.4	76	wall, Str. J	44	Window A31, A32; Nail 4:-; Moll.
6.4	?76	-		Nail 1:-
6.6	77	post-hole cut/fill	44	
6.6	78	post-hole cut/fill	44	
6.6	79	post-hole cut/fill	44	
6.6	80	post-hole cut/fill	44	
6.6	81	post-hole cut/fill	44	
6.6	82	post-hole cut/fill	44	
4.1	83	wall		
7.1	84	conduit, Str. M	45	
5.1	88	wall, Structure E	39, 42	
6.6	89	post-hole cut/fill	44	
6.6	90	post-hole cut/fill	44	
7.3	91	post-hole cut/fill	45	
7.3	92	post-hole cut/fill	45	
7.3	93	post-hole cut/fill	45	
7.3	94	post-hole cut/fill	45	Lead A83, A89
7.3	95	post-hole cut/fill	45	
7.3	96	post-hole cut/fill	45	
6.3	97	post-hole cut/fill Str. K?	43	
6.3	98	post-hole cut/fill Str. K?	43	
5.2	99	post-hole cut/fill	41	
6.6	100	post-hole cut/fill	44	
5.1	101	?make up/?external surface	39; 40	Med. 7:49
7.3	102	post-hole cut/fill	45	
5.1	103	?make-up/?external surface	39	
5.1	104	?make-up/?external surface	39	Nail 1:-; Vess (1)
5.1	105	?make-up/?external surface	39	
7.3	106	post-hole cut/fill	45	
7.3	107	post-hole cut/fill	45	
7.3	108	post-hole cut/fill	45	
7.3	109	post-hole cut/fill	45	
7.3	110	post-hole cut/fill	45	

Phase	Context	Description	Fig. Nos	Artefacts and environmental remains
7.3	111	post-hole cut/fill	45	
6.2	113	post-hole cut/fill		PM; Vess. (1); Wood A7
6.2	114	post-hole cut/fill	42	Med. 1:18
6.2	115	post-hole cut/fill	42	
1.2	116	post-hole cut/fill Str. A	30	
1.2	117	stake-hole Str. A	30	
1.2	118	stake-hole Str. A	30	
2.1	119=639	cut feature Str. B?	32	Med. 1:3; An. (5)
1.2	120	post-hole cut/fill Str. A	30	An. (1); Char. 1g
1.2	121	post-hole cut/fill Str. A	30	
1.2	122	post-hole cut/fill Str. A	30	
1.2	123	stake-hole Str. A	30	
7.3	124	post-hole cut/fill	45	
6.2	125	post-hole cut/fill	42	Med. 4:16; Nail 1:-; Tile (1); Vess. (1); Coal 12g
1.2	126	post-hole cut/fill Str. A	30	
1.2	127	post-hole cut/fill Str. A	30	
1.2	128	post-hole cut/fill Str. A	30	
7.5	130	post-hole cut/fill fence		Nail 1:-
7.5	134	post-hole cut/fill fence		Iron A99
7.5	138	post-hole cut/fill fence, gatepost		PM; Iron A85, A144, A162; Nail 5:-; Burnt (2)
7.5	140	post-hole cut/fill fence		Copper A55
7.5	141	post-hole cut/fill fence		Stone A71
7.3	142	post-hole cut/fill	45	
7.3	143	post-hole cut/fill fence	45	Nail -:1
6.5	144	robber trench		
6.4	145	demolition debris Str. H	44	
6.4	146	demolition debris Str. H	44	
6.4	148	wall footing Str. G	44	Med. 2:22; Copper 21, A52; Iron 24; Nail 4:1; Vess. (1); Window A33; Cin. ≤1g; Coal 6g
7.3	149	post-hole cut/fill	45	PM
7.3	150	post-hole cut/fill fence	45	Nail 1:-; Tile (1)
7.3	151	post-hole cut/fill fence	45	
7.3	152	post-hole cut/fill fence	45	
7.3	153	post-hole cut/fill fence	45	
7.3	154	post-hole cut/fill fence	45	Vess. (1); Char. 1g
6.4	155	wall foundation Str. H	44	Med. 5:26; Iron 8; Nail 5:1; Tile (1); Window A34
7.3	156	post-hole cut/fill fence	45	
7.3	158	post-hole cut/fill fence	45	Med. 1:1
6.2	159	post-hole cut/fill	42	Med. 5:134
7.3	160	post-hole cut/fill fence	45	Nail 3:-; Burnt (1); Coal ≤1g
7.3	162	stake-hole cut fence	45	
7.3	163	post-hole cut/fill fence	45	
7.3	165	post-hole cut/fill fence	45	Lead A109; Roof. A251
7.3	166	post-hole cut/fill fence	45	
7.3	167=185	post-hole cut/fill fence	45	
7.4	168	post-hole cut/fill	40	
7.3	169	post-hole cut/fill fence	45	
6.2	170=177	post-hole cut/fill	42	
6.2	171	stake-hole cut/fill	42	
7.3	172	post-hole cut/fill fence	45	
7.3	173	post-hole cut/fill fence	45	
7.3	174	post-hole cut/fill fence	45	
6.2	175	post-hole cut/fill	42	
6.2	177=170	post-hole cut/fill	42	Wood A8

Phase	Context	Description	Fig. Nos	Artefacts and environmental remains
6.2	178	post-hole cut/fill	42	PM; Nail 1:-; Tile (1); Vess. (1); Coal ⊴ g
6.2	179	post-hole cut/fill		
6.1	180	loamy soil with ?animal disturbance		Copper 10; Lead A73
6.2	182	post-hole cut/fill		
6.2	183	post-hole cut/fill		
7.3	185=167	post-hole cut/fill fence	45	
6.2	186	post-hole cut/fill	42	Nail 3:-
6.2	190	post-hole cut/fill	42	
6.2	191	gully cut/fill	42	
6.2	192	post-hole cut/fill	42	
6.2	193	post-hole cut/fill	42	
7.3	194	?post pit 160	45	
5.2	195	reused stone, gate setting	41	Sst. 70
5.1	199	stake-hole cut/fill	39	
7.5	201	post-hole cut/fill fence		Coin 44 (*Wharram IX*); Nail 2:-; Window A35; Coal 2g
6.5	202	post-hole cut/fill animal disturbance		PM; Char. 2g; Cin. 6g
4.6	203=250	grave cut/fill Burial G250		PM; Tile (4)
4.6	204	post-hole cut/fill		
4.6	205	post-hole cut/fill		
7.3	206=249	post-hole cut/fill fence		Tile (1)
5.2	207	stone block, gate setting Wall 20	41	
5.2	208	stone block, gate setting Wall 20	41	
5.2	209	repair to surface of 32		
5.2	210	stone block gate setting Wall 20	41	Sst. 67
5.2	211	post-hole cut/fill Wall 20		
5.2	212	post-hole cut/fill Wall 20	41	Nail 5:1
6.1	213	burnt clay		
7.5	214	turf and humus		PM
7.5	215	topsoil		
7.5	214/215	topsoil		Lst. A148; Nail 4:-
7.5	215/216	rubble and topsoil		PM; Clay A19; Copper 29, 31; Iron 14, 17, 64, 70, A75, A80, A81, A82, A91, A94, A100, A110, A115, A116, A117, A119, A120, A125, A127, A128, A129, A133, A135, A163; Lead A85; Nail 17:2; Roof. A194, A195; Tile (2); Vess. (43); Window A36-A38; Wood A9; Cin. ⊴ g
7.5	?214/215/ 216		40	Brick (1)
7.5	216	rubble and topsoil		Clay 8
7.5	?216			PM; Tile (6); Coal 9g
7.4	217	rubble dump		Med. 1:1; PM; Iron A90, A103; Nail 4:-; Vess. (1)
7.4	?217			Brick (3); Tile (6); Window A39
7.2	218	road	45	Med. 88:511; PM; Brick (4); Copper 11, 22, 28; Lead 37, A77, A79, A80, A82, A104, A106-A108; Iron 13, 47, A95, A96, A118, A126, A140, A143, A146, A164; Nail 78:8; Roof. A196-A200; St. A356; Tile (5); Vess. (3); Window A40-A52; Wood A10; Burnt (3); Cin. 6g; Coal 84g; Moll.
7.2	219	rut in road surface	45	
7.2	220	large rubble deposit	45, 40	Med. 14:300; PM; Copper 7, 34; Iron 46; Lead A78; Nail 10:1; Roof. A201; St. A368; Stone 44; Tile (2); Window A53-A57; Char.; Coal 61g

Phase	Context	Description	Fig. Nos	Artefacts and environmental remains
7.4	221	rubble spread east? surface		Med. 53:603 (14, 15); PM; Iron A141; Lead A84; Nail 14:1; St. A357; Tile (1); Window A58, A59; Cin. 1g; Coal 6g; Moll.
7.3	222	scoop	45	Med. 4:64; PM; Lead A81, A105; Nail 5:-; Roof. A202; Tile (3); Window A60-A62; Char. ≤g;
7.2	223	rubble deposit	45	
7.2	224	large rubble deposit	45	
7.2	225	rubble deposit	45	Rom. 1:6
-	227	-		Rom. 8:39; Med. 126:933; PM; Iron A93, A102, A165, A166; Nail 9:1; Quern 54; Roof. A203; Tile (18); Vess. (1); Window A63; Char. 1g; Cin. 2g; Coal 13g; Slag 18g
2.2	228=598	hill wash?/silt		Rom. 1:6; Med. 22:102; Iron 23; An. (3);
6.2	229	surface	42	Med. 6:67; PM; Clay A23; Copper A68; Iron 1, 7, 59, 63; Lead A74, A88; Nail 15:1; St. A358; Tile (4); Window A64, A65; Cin.6g; Coal 33g; Moll.
6.2	230	rubble deposit	42, 40	Med. 22:359; Iron 62; Lead A75, A102; Nail 4:-; St. A359; Tile (1); Window A66; Coal 224g; Moll.
6.2	231	surface	42	
6.2	232	chalk rubble deposit	42	Med. 3:37; Brick (1); Lead 42; Nail 1:-; Tile (7); Window A67; Char. 1g
6.2	233	chalk rubble deposit	42	Med. 16:374; Nail 4:-; Tile (1); Window A68, A69; Burnt (2); Cin. 1g; Coal 8g; Moll.
7.3	234	mixed rubble	45	Med. 11:94; Iron A92; Nail 6:1; Moll.
7.3	235	linear cut/fill	45	PM; Nail 1:1; Cin. 1g; Coal 1g
6.2	236	rubble deposit	42	
6.2	237	wall footing Str. F	42	Med. 11:122; PM; Copper 33; Iron A167; Window A70; Moll.
6.2	238	surface Str. F	42	Med. 15:95; Nail 8:-; Tile (2)+; Window A71; Coal 1g
6.2	239	wall footing Str. F	42	Med. 15:304; Lead A101; Nail 2:1; Quern 55, 56; Roof. A204, A205; St. A360; Tile (2); Char. 1g; Cin. 9g; Coal 33g; Moll.
6.1	240	loamy soil	40	
5.1	240A	core of Wall 20		Med. 12:38
6.2	241	chalk rubble deposit	42	
6.2	242	pit cut/fill	42	Iron 3, 5, 22; St. A361
5.1	243	surface	39	Sst. 68
5.1	244	chalk rubble deposit	39, 40	Med. 9:26; Coal ≤g
5.1	245	chalk rubble deposit	39	Med. 16:208; Lead A71; Nail 5:-; Tile (1); Window A72
6.3	246	demolition rubble	43	Med. 2:7; Nail 1:2
5.1	247	chalk rubble deposit	39, 40	Med. 25:321 (5, 17); Nail 13:1; Roof. A206, A207; St. A362; Tile (7); Char. ≤g; Cin. 5g; Coal 36g; Moll.
6.2	248	pit cut/fill	42	
5.2	252	sandstone block, gate setting Wall 20		
4.5	253	grave cut/fill Burial G253		Rom. 2:27; St. A396; Slag 121g
4.5	254	grave cut/fill Burial G254		Med. 1:1
1.4	255	ditch cut/fill	31, 40	Rom. 111:1508, 14-17; Med. 23:169; Clay 7; Copper 5, 30, 32; Lst. A137; Nail 2:-; Quern A88; Sst. A116; St. A286, A287; Stone 59; Tile (1); Window A73; An. (72); Burnt (2); Char. 1g; Coal 2g
4.5	257	post-hole cut/fill	38	
4.5	258	post-hole cut/fill	38	Med. 1:2
4.5	259=279	grave cut/fill Burial G279		Rom. 5:93; Med. 4:15; Quern A84; Slag 8g
4.5	261	post-hole fill		Med. 1:1; Iron A168; St. A288, A369; Burnt (10); Cin. 2g; Coal ≤g
4.5	?262	post-hole cut/fill	38	Char. 1g; Slag 31g;
4.5	263	post-hole cut/fill		Rom. 1:14; Med. 1:2; Nail 2:-; Wood A11; Burnt (8);
4.5	263/267	post-hole cut/fill	38	
4.5	264	post-hole cut/fill	38	

404

Phase	Context	Description	Fig. Nos	Artefacts and environmental remains
4.3	265	grave cut/fill Burial G265		Med. 4:9; Lead A96; Char. 1g; Moll.; Slag 46g
4.5	266	post-hole cut/fill	38	
4.5	268	post-hole cut/fill ?marker for Burial G275A	38	
4.5	269	post-hole cut/fill	38	
1.3	270	clay and rubble deposit	31	Rom. 1:10, 9; Med. 5:29; Tile (1); An. (10); Burnt (3); Moll.; Slag 2g
4.6	271	chalk rubble deposit		Rom. 5:54, 29-31; Med. 62:384; PM; Copper A49; Iron A169; Lead A97; Lst. A139; Nail 6:-; Roof. A208, A209; St. A289Tile (9); Window A74; Moll.; Slag 413g
4.6	?271	-		Rom. 2:10
4.4	272	loam deposit	38	Rom. 4:76, 28; Med. 6:53; Bone 3; Clay 1; Copper A66; Iron 37, A134, A170; Lst. A149; Nail -:1; Roof. A210, A211; Tile (2); Char. 1g; Moll.; Slag 405g
4.5	273	grave cut/fill Burial G273		Rom. 8:56; Char. 1g; Slag 13g
4.5	274	post-hole cut/fill	38	Rom. 2:18
4.5	275A	grave cut/fill Burial G275A		Slag 117g
4.6	276	?animal burrow		Med. 1:5; Char. ⊴g; Slag 15g;
4.2	277	rubble surface	37, 38, 39	Rom. 2:25; Med. 31:662; Tile (1); Char. ⊴g
4.3	278	grave cut/fill Burial G278		Rom. 1:6; Med. 1:2; Roof. A212
3.1	279=259	grave cut/fill Burial G279		Rom. 3:52; Nail 1:-
4.5	280	grave cut/fill Burial G280		Coal 2g
4.5	281	grave cut/fill Burial G281		Med. 2:15; Slag 41g
3.3	282	post-hole cut/fill	34	St. A290
5.1	283	path make up for 32D	39	Med. 3:18; Copper 16; Iron 35; Nail 3:-; Slag 20g
4.5	284	post-hole cut fill ?marker for Burial G254	38	Slag 14g
4.3	285	post-hole cut/fill	37	Moll.
5.1	286	post-hole cut/fill Wall 74/20		Med. 2:10
5.1	287	post-hole cut/fill Wall 74/20	39	Med. 1:8
5.1	288	rubble deposit ?Str. E	39, 42	Med. 15:71 (11); Iron A171, A172; Roof. A213-A226; Slag 18g
4.2	289	rubble surface	37	Rom. 1:13; 24; Med. 22:177; Iron 43, A173; Lead A95; Nail 5:1; St. A291-A293; Stone 50; Slag 8g
4.2	290	rubble surface	37	Med. 1:3; Nail 1:-
5.1	291	?hearth/?scoop/fill	39	Rom. 1:10; Med. 2:11; Iron 31; Nail 1:-; Moll.
4.1	292	linear rubble spread	36	Med. 2:12; Roof. A227
5.1	293	scoop	39	Med. 1:29
4.4	294	external yard surface	38, 40	Rom. 4:17; Med. 92:691; Copper 4 (see context 343); Iron A174, A175 Lead A70; Nail 26:2; Roof. A228-A230; Sst. A117; St. A294, A397; Tile (31); Window A75; Char. 17g;Cin. 7g; Coal 40g; Moll.
4.4	295	loam deposit	38, 40	Rom. 6:31; Med. 19:103; Bone 6 (and context 336); Iron A176; Nail 2:-; Roof. A252; Sst. A118; St. A349; Tile (2); Slag 46g
4.4	?295	-		Rom. 1:6; PM; Brick (3); Burnt (2)
4.5	299	post-hole cut/fill	38	Rom. 1:7

Phase	Context	Description	Fig. Nos	Artefacts and environmental remains
4.5	300	post-hole cut/fill	38	Slag 4g
4.1	301	linear rubble spread	36, 37 40	Med. 2:2
3.3	302	post-hole cut/fill	34	
3.1	303	grave cut/fill Burial G303		Med. 2:6; Burnt (1)
3.1	304	grave cut/fill Burial G304		Slag 1g
1.1	305	grave cut/fill Burial G305		Slag 8g
4.3	306	grave cut/fill Burial G306		Rom. 1:2; Med. 4:6; St. A295; Moll.; Slag 11g
4.3	308	grave cut/fill Burial G308		Med. 1:3; Slag 7g
3.5	310	grave cut/fill Burial G310		Rom. 1:17; Med. 1:4; Nail 1:-
3.3	311	post-hole cut/fill	34	
4.3	312	post-hole cut/fill	37	
4.5	313	grave cut/fill Burial G313	38	
4.4	315	loam deposit	38, 40	Rom. 5:43; Med. 26:159; Brick (9); Nail 10:-; Quern A89-A91; Roof. A253; Sst. A119; St. A277, A278; Stone 45; Tile A108, A109; Vess. (3);Window A76, A77; Burnt (3); Char. 2g; Cin. 8g
4.3	316	?demolition debris		Rom. 1:8; Med. 1:4
5.1	318	post-hole cut/fill	39	
4.5	319	post-hole cut/fill	38	
4.3	320	grave cut/fill Burial G320		Rom. 1:3, 26; Med. 2:5; Nail 3:-
4.1	321	wall Wall C	36	Lead A90; Roof. A231; Moll.; Mortar A3
4.3	322	post-hole cut/fill	37	
u/s	324	?animal disturbance		Med. 1:23
4.1	325	rubble	36, 37	Rom. 12:99; Med. 39:386; Lst. A150; Nail 3:-; Quern A75; St. A296, A398, A399Tile (3); Moll.
3.5	326	Cut, ?grave/?quarry		Med. 1:2
4.3	327	grave cut/fill Burial G327		Rom. 3:22; Med. 1:4
4.3	329	post-hole cut/fill	37	
4.3	330	post-hole cut/fill	37	
4.3	331	post-hole cut/fill	37	
4.3	333	post-hole cut/fill	37	
4.3	334/336	-		PM
4.1	335	rubble	36, 37	
4.2	336	loam deposit	40	Rom. 4:69; Med. 15:199 (6); Brick (2); Copper 19; Iron A177, A178; Lst. A106; Nail 3:-; Sst. A120; St. A279; Tile (2); Char. ⊴g; Cin. ⊴g; Moll.; Slag 17g
4.2	337	loam deposit		Rom. 1:12
4.3	339	grave cut/fill Burial G339		Rom. 2:11; Med. 3:6
4.3	341	post-hole cut/fill	37	Rom. 1:3
3.4	342	Chalk and chalk rubble deposit (see context 536)	35	Med. 5:24; Roof. A232; Cin. 9g
4.4	343	object in context 294		Copper 4
4.1	344	post-hole cut/fill ?Str. C	36	Rom. 1:9
4.1	345	post-hole cut/fill ?Str. C	36	Rom. 2:9

Phase	Context	Description	Fig. Nos	Artefacts and environmental remains
4.1	346	bonding material/ wall foundation Str. C	36	
3.4	347	clay deposit	35	
4.1	348	bonding material	36, 37	
u/s	351	unstratified finds		Rom. 3:11; Med. 53:599; PM; Bone 5; Brick (1); Glass 1; Iron 52, A132, A179, A180, A181; Lead 46, A112; Roof. A233-A236; St. A297, A400-A402; Tile (13); Nail 17:-; Vess. (2); Window A78; Burnt (1); Coal 16g; Moll.; Slag 313g
4.2	352	chalk cobble surface	37	Rom. 1:6; Med. 14:71; Copper 18, 25; Iron 6, A182; Nail 2:1; Roof. A237; St. A298, A299; Tile (3); Burnt (2); Moll.; Slag 37g
4.2	353	post-hole cut	37	
4.2	354	fill of post-hole 353		Med. 3:19; Iron A183; Tile (3); Burnt (1); Char. 1g
4.2	355	occupation deposit	37	Med. 56:340; Coin 28; Copper 15; Iron 58; Nail 30:1; Roof. A238; Tile (17); Burnt (1); Char. 10g; Coal ≤1g; Moll.; Slag 407g
3.5	357	grave fill, Burial G361		Nail 1:-
4.3	358	post-hole cut	37	
4.3	359	fill of post-hole 358		Tile (1)
4.3	366	grave fill, Burial G367		Rom. 5:49, 25; Tile (1)
4.3	369	grave fill, Burial G370		Rom. 1:20
4.3	372	grave fill, Burial G430		Rom. 1:33; Med. 1:1; Slag 43g
3.3	375	grave fill, Burials G363, G379		Rom. 1:20; Med. 5:15; Stone A72
3.4	382	?redeposited ditch fill	35, 40	Rom. 7:66; Med. 20:77 (2); Bone 2; Clay 6; Coin 6; Iron A184; Lst. A151; Quern A74 (joins 62); Sst. A121; St. A275; Char. 1g; Cin. ≤1; Slag 24g
3.4/4.2	382/391	-		Burnt (1); Coal ≤1g
3.5	384	grave fill, Burial G385		Med. 2:8; Nail 1:-
4.1	388	collapsed wall, ?footing, Str. C	37	Nail 6:-; Tile (1)
3.4	389	surface	35, 40	Rom. 3:11; Med. 141:741; PM; Nail 16:2; St. A300, A370-A372; Tile (1); Char. 3g; Coal 40g; Moll.; Slag 221g
3.4	389/1	surface		Roof. A239; St. A363; Tile (6); Window A79; Char. 50g; Cin. 2g; Coal 10g;
3.4	389/2	surface		Brick (1); Iron 39, A185; Tile (2); Window A80; Char. 6g; Coal 15g; Moll.
3.4/3.2	389/485	-		Moll.
3.4	390	surface	35, 40	Rom. 3:10; Moll.
4.2	391	loam deposit	37, 40	Med. 21:104; Stone 63; Tile (3); Char. 36g; Coal ≤1g; Moll.; Slag 158g
4.3	392	post-hole cut	37	
4.3	393	fill of post-hole 392		Rom. 2:7; Med. 1:3; St. A301; Moll.
4.1	395	fill of post-hole 394		Brick (22)
3.5	397	grave fill, Burial G398		Rom. 1:7; Med. 1:1; Iron A186; St. A302; Char. ≤1g;
1.3	401	clay and rubble deposit	31	
4.3	402=439	?scoop/root hole	37	
4.3	403=440	scoop fill/root hole		Med. 15:112; Quern A85, A92; Sst. A122, A123; Tile (1); Moll.
3.3	405	grave fill, Burial G406		Quern A76
4.1	407	shallow scoop	36	
4.1	408	fill of scoop 407		Nail 1:-
3.5	410	grave fill, Burial G411		Nail 2:-; Quern A77
3.4	412	surface	35, 36	Rom. 6:33; Med. 19:158; Iron A187, A188; Nail 9:-; Quern A86; St. A280; Char. 1g; Moll.; Slag 390g

407

Phase	Context	Description	Fig. Nos	Artefacts and environmental remains
3.4	412A	surface		Rom. 9:48; Med. 8:50; Bone 4, 9; Copper A48; Iron 11, A189, A190; Lead 46; Lst. A135, A140; Sst. A124; St. A342, A343, A373; Stone 48, 49, 51, 61; Vess. (2); Burnt (2); Char. ⩽g; Moll.; Mortar A4; Slag 73g
	413	bonding material	36	Med. 4:27
4.1	415	grave fill, Burial G416		Med. 1:8
4.1	415/418	grave fills, Burials G416, G419		Iron A191; St. A281, A374; Stone A73
4.1	419	skeleton Burial G419		Med. 1:7
4.1	426	grave fill, Burial G427		Med. 1:10; Vess. (1)
4.1	435	grave fill, Burial G436, G438		Med. 2:6; Lst. A141; Quern A78; St. A382 Moll.
4.3	439=402	scoop/root hole	37	
4.3	440=403	fill of 439		Med. 2:9; Quern A93
4.1	442	grave fill, Burial G443		Coin 12
4.1	444	shallow scoop	36	
4.1	445	fill of scoop 444		Med. 14:81; Char. ⩽g
3.5	449	grave fill upper, Burial G451		Med. 2:7; Iron A192; Char. ⩽g
3.5	450	grave fill lower, Burial G451		Iron A193; St. A303; Char. ⩽g; Slag 8g
4.1	452	shallow scoop	36	
4.1	453	fill of scoop 452		Med. 24:345 (7); Nail 1:-
3.4	454	burnt clay, ?hearth	35	
4.1	455	grave fill, Burial G456		Med. 1:13
4.1	458	post-hole cut	36	
3.3	463	post-hole cut	34	
3.3	473	grave fill, Burial G474		Roof. A240; Slag 1g
3.3	477	post-hole cut	34	
4.1	479	grave fill, Burial G478		Lst. A152; St. A375
3.3	483	post-hole cut	34	
3.2	485=567	chalk surface	34, 40	Rom. 4:31; Med. 61:324; Iron A194; Nail 2:1; Char. ⩽g; Coal 2g; Moll.
3.3	487	grave fill, Burial G488		Rom. 1:3; Med. 1:2; Iron A195
3.3	489	post-hole cut (fill 490)	34	Rom. 1:5
3.2	491	chalk surface	34, 40	
3.3	493	pit cut	34	
3.3	494	fill of pit 493		Med. 1:5
4.1	496	grave fill, Burial G497		Iron A196
4.1	499	grave fill, Burial G500		Med. 3:33
3.3	502	grave fill, Burial G503		Med. 2:5; St. A304
3.4	507	burnt clay, ?hearth	35	
4.1	509	grave fill, Burial G510		Rom. 2:5; Med. 2:10
3.3	515	grave fill, Burial G516		Rom. 2:14; 20; Med. 1:2; Wood A12; Burnt (1);
3.3	517	post-hole cut	34	

Phase	Context	Description	Fig. Nos	Artefacts and environmental remains
1.2	523	post-hole cut	30	
4.6	525	skeleton Burial G525		Slag 1g
3.5	536	Burial G536 finds within context 342		Slag 9g
3.3	537	?scoop/dump		Rom. 1:1; Window A81
3.4	539	surface		Rom. 87:132, 22; Med. 5:33; Coin 4; Copper 8; Iron A197; Lst. A142, A143; Nail 1:1; Quern A79, A94; St. A403; Cin. 31g; Coal ≤1g; Moll.
3.3	540	grave cut Burial G542		Coal 1g (or context 148)
3.2	543	firm silty clay	34	Rom. 20:97; Med. 16:62; Copper 3; Iron 36, A198, A199; Lst. A144; Nail 3:- ; Quern A80; St. A344, A376; Stone 46; Burnt (2); Char. 5g; Moll.; Slag 329g
1.2	544	hearth, Str. A	30	
-1.3	545	make up?/hill-washed silt?		Rom. 2:20; Med. 3:12; Quern A87; St. A404, A405; An. (8)
1.2	547	fill of post-hole 546		Clay 2, 3
1.2	548	make up?/surface repair	30	Med. 4:7
3.3	551	post-hole cut	34	
3.3	552	fill of post-hole 551		Lst. A153
4.1	557	grave fill, Burial G558		Moll.
3.3	560	grave fill, Burial G561		Rom. 2:12
2.1	562	post-hole cut Structure B	32	
2.1	563	fill of post-hole 562		Rom. 1:3; Brick (1); Lst. A145; Quern A95; Roof. A241, A242; Sst. A125; St. A276, A377; An. (30); Burnt (3); Char. 2g; Moll.; Slag 38g
2.1	566=660	fill of post-hole 659		Bone 11
3.2	567=485	east surface		Med. 9:60; St. A305, A406; Moll.
4.3	570	grave fill, Burial G571		Med. 6:25; Brick (1)
3.3	572	post-hole cut	34	
3.3	573	fill of post-hole 572		Rom. 1:30; 21; St. S306
3.3	575	grave fill, Burial G576		St. A378
3.3	583	scoop	34	
3.3	584	fill of scoop 583		Med. 10:41; Nail 1:1; Burnt (1); Char. 4g
3.3	586	grave fill, Burial G587		Rom. 33:168; Med. 2:5; Char. ≤1g; Moll.; Slag 130g
3.3	593	dump	34	Rom. 1:3; Med. 1:7; St. A307; Moll.; Slag 30g
1.3	594	loam deposit	31, 40	Rom. 37:348, 10; Med. 18:98; Iron A200; Nail 1:1; Sst. A126; St. A308, A309; Stone 47; An. (72); Burnt (1); Char. ≤1g; Coal 1g; Moll.; Slag 10g
4.1	595	grave cut, Burial G597	40	
4.1	596	grave fill, Burial G597		Rom. 12:109, 23; Clay 4; Window A82; Slag 109g
4.1	597	skeleton, Burial G597	40	
2.2	598=228	hill wash/rain-washed silt	40	Rom. 3:24, 18; Med. 166:700 (13); Lead A93; Quern A81, A96; St. A310, A379, A407; An. (105); Burnt (1); Char. 6g; Cin. ≤1g; Slag 87g
3.1	600	grave fill, Burial G601		Rom. 1:27
3.1	602	grave cut, Burial G604	40	Slag 121g
3.1	603	grave fill, Burial G604		Rom. 1:5; Med. 2:4

Phase	Context	Description	Fig. Nos	Artefacts and environmental remains
3.3	606	grave fill, Burial G607		St. A311
3.3	608	post-hole cut	34	
2.1	610	post-hole cut Str. B	32	
2.1	611	fill of post hole 610		Rom. 1:1; An. (8); Moll.; Slag 24g
3.3	613	grave fill, Burial G614		Nail 1:-
1.2	615	post-hole cut Str. A	30	
1.2	616	fill of post-hole 615		Rom. 4:56, 7, 8; Bone 1; St. A312, A380; An. (62); Char. 1g; Slag 208g;
1.3	617	occupation deposit		Rom. 55:435, 11-13; An. (21)
1.2	618A	linear cut Str. A	30	
1.2	618B	linear cut Str. A	30	
1.2	619	fill of linear cuts 618A+B		Rom. 106:1621, 1-6; Med. 2:2; Lst. A154; Sst. 69; An. (28)
1.2	620	post-hole cut Str. A	30	Rom. 3:15; Quern A82; St. A313; An. (23)
1.2	621	fill of post-hole 620 Str. A		Rom. 1:7
1.2	622	post-hole cut Str. A	30	
1.2	624	post-hole cut Str. A	30	
3.1	627	grave fill, Burial G628		Rom. 2:34; Med. 11:110; Iron A201; Nail 2:-; Moll.; Slag 308g
1.2	629	post-hole cut Str. A	30	
1.2	631	post-hole cut ?Str. A	30	
1.2	632	fill of post-hole 631		Quern 53; An. (1)
1.2	637	post-hole cut Str. A	30	
2.1	640	fill of ?pit/?post-hole 639		Med. 2:7; Lead A91; An. (17)
3.1	642	grave fill, Burial G643		Clay 5; St. A314
1.2	644	post-hole cut Str. A	30	
2.1	646	post-hole cut Str. B	32	
2.1	647	fill of post-hole 646		Nail 1:-; An. (2); Slag 2g
2.1	648	post-hole cut Str. B	32	
2.1	649	fill of post-hole 648 Str. B		An. (7); Slag 12g
4.3	651	grave fill, Burial G652		Rom. 2:21; Med. 5:31; St. A283, A315
3.3	653	grave cut, Burial G655	40	
3.3	655	skeleton, Burial G655	40	
3.3	657	grave fill, Burial G658		Wood A13; Char. 1g
2.1	659	post-hole cut Str. B	32	
2.1	660=566	fill of post-hole 659	32	An. (5)
1.2	661	post-hole cut Str. A	30	
1.2	662	fill of post-hole 661		Char. 7g
1.2	663	post-hole cut	30	
1.2	664	fill of post-hole 663		An. (23); Burnt (40)
3.3	667	skeleton, Burial G667	40	
3.3	668	grave cut, Burial G670	40	
3.3	669	grave fill, Burial G670		Med. 2:7
3.3	670	skeleton, Burial G670	40	
3.1	672	grave fill, Burial G673		St. A316; Char. 1g
3.1	674	grave cut, Burial G676	40	
3.1	675	grave fill, Burial G676		Med. 3:11 (1)
3.1	682	grave fill, Burial G683		Rom. 2:6; Iron 42; Sst. A127; St. A317, A408; Moll.; Slag 4g

Phase	Context	Description	Fig. Nos	Artefacts and environmental remains
3.1	688	grave fill, Burial G689		Med. 3:11
3.1	691	grave fill, Burial G692		Med. 1:3; Iron A202; St. A318 Moll.
3.1	696	grave fill, Burial G697		Tile (3)
2.1	698	depression	32	
2.1	699	fill of depression 698		Med. 9:35; St. A319, A345; An. (17)
1.2	700	internal? surface Str. A	30	Rom. 1:4; Lst. A146; Quern A83; St A346; An. (8)
1.2	703	post-hole cut Str. A?	30	
1.2	705	post-hole cut	30	
3.1	709	grave cut in 680, Burial G710		Copper A63
2.1	711	post-hole cut Str. B	32	Rom. 3:15; Med. 5:12; An. (2)
3.1	714	grave fill, Burial G715		Rom. 1:46, 19; Med. 4:14
3.1	713	grave cut, Burials G715, G716, G717	40	
3.1	722	grave fill, Burial G723		Med. 1:2
1.2	724	post-hole cut Str. A	30	
1.2	725	fill of post-hole 724		An. (6)
1.2	726	post-hole cut	30	
1.2	727	fill of post-hole 726		St. A320; An. (1)
2.1	728	post-hole cut Str. B	32	
2.1	729	fill of post-hole 728		Rom. 2:5; Med. 4:39; Iron A203; St. A321; An. (8); Moll.
1.2	730	post-hole cut Str. A	30	
1.2	731	fill of post-hole 730		Rom. 1:11; Med. 1:2; Copper A47; St A322; An. (1); Moll.
1.2	732	post-hole cut	30	
1.2	732A	stake-hole cut	30	
1.2	733	fill of post-hole 732		Rom. 1:7
2.1	734	post-hole cut Str. B	32	
2.1	735	fill of post-hole 734		Iron A204; Stone 52, 64; An. (48); Char. 4g; Moll.
2.1	736	post-hole cut Str. B	32	
2.1	737	fill of post-hole 736		Copper A62; An. (6); Char. 1g
2.1	738	linear cut	32	
1.2	740	post-hole cut Str. A	30	
1.2	741	fill of post-hole 740		
2.1	742	oval cut Str. B	32	
2.1	743	fill of oval cut 742		St. A381; An. (2)
3.1	745	grave fill, Burials G746, G747		Med. 2:3; St. A323; Moll.
3.1	748	grave cut, Burial G750	40	
1.3	751	loam deposit	31, 40	Rom. 2:6; Med. 3:27; Iron 4; An. (31); Moll.
1.2	752	organic dump Str. A	30	Med. 2:14; St. A409; An. (213)
1.2	753	clay pad?	30	
1.2	754	post-hole cut Str. A	30	
1.2	755	fill of post-hole 754		Rom. 1:4; Moll.
1.2	756	post-hole cut Str. A	30	
1.2	761	post-hole cut Str. A	30	
1.2	763	post-hole cut Str. A?	30	
1.2	766	post-hole cut Str. A	30	
1.2	768	post-hole cut Str. A	30	
1.2	769	fill of post-hole 768		An. (1)
1.2	770	post-hole cut Str. A	30	
1.2	771	post-hole cut Str. A	30	
1.2	773	post-hole cut	30	
2.1	775	stake-hole cuts	32	
1.2	777	post-hole cut	30	
1.2	778	stake-hole, fence?	30	

Phase	Context	Description	Fig. Nos	Artefacts and environmental remains
1.2	779	stake-hole, fence?	30	
1.2	780	stake-hole, fence?	30	
1.2	781	stake-hole, fence?	30	
1.2	782	stake-hole, fence?	30	
1.2	783	stake-hole, fence?	30	
1.2	784	stake-hole, fence	30	
3.3	785	post-hole cut	34	
1.2	787	stake-hole Str. A	30	
1.2	789	post-hole cut Str. A	30	
1.2	791	3 stake-holes ?Str. A	30	
1.2	792	stake-hole Str. A	30	
1.2	796	post-hole cut	30	
1.2	797	?post-hole cut Str. A	30	
1.2	799	stake-hole	30	
-	802	unstratified		Rom. 1:8; St. A324
1.2	805	stake-hole ?Str. A	30	
1.2	806	stake-hole ?Str. A	30	
1.2	807	stake-hole ?Str. A	30	
7.1	810	destruction debris, Building H		
6.6	811	wall, Building L	44	
6.6	812	destruction debris Building K	44	
6.3	813	burnt deposit, ?floor Str. K	43	
6.3	814	wall, Str. K	43	
7.3	818	mixed rubble	45	
6.3	822	chalk and clay deposit Str. K	43	
1.3	823	loam deposit	40	
2.2	824	cut of possible pit	40	
5.1	825	post-hole cut/fill	39, 42	
7.3	828	post-hole cut	45	
4.1	829	shallow scoop	36	
7.3	830	post-hole cut/fill	45	
7.3	831	post-hole cut/fill	45	
1.2	832	post-hole cut/fill	30	
4.2	833	chalk rubble deposit	40	
5.1	834	surface	39, 40	
1.2	835	stake-hole, Str. A	30	
1.2	836	stake-hole, Str. A?	30	
4.1	837	bonding material (in section)	36, 40	
4.1	838	wall footing?, Wall C?	36, 37	
6.6	839	inner? surface	44	
1.2	846	post-hole/stake-hole		
-	-	unstratified		Rom. 2:50; PM; Copper 13; Iron A131, A206; Nail 14:-; Roof. A243, A244, A246, A254-A70, A272, A273; Tile (2); Vess. (3); Window A83-A86; Cin. 1g; Coal 4g; Mortar A5-A7

Site 41

Phase	Context	Description	Fig. Nos	Artefacts and environmental remains
5.2	2	topsoil		Rom. 1:1; 46; Med. 23:100; Nail 5:-; Stone 62; Burnt (1); Coal <1g; Slag 80g
5.2	3	post-hole	61	
5.2	4	layer/fill	61, 54	Med. 11:57; Iron 53, A207; Nail 2:-
5.2	5	surface	54	

Phase	Context	Description	Fig. Nos	Artefacts and environmental remains
5.2	5/7	-		Med. 4:33
5.1	6B	post-hole	54	
5.2	7	layer		Rom. 2:5
5.1	8	layer	54	Med. 1:7; Char.; Moll.; Slag 362g
4.2	9	layer	59	
4.2	10	chalk surface	59, 54	Rom. 1:2; Med. 1:1; Quern
4.2	11	chalk surface	59, 54	Med. 6:22; Iron A208; Nail 1:-
5.2	13	post-hole	61	
5.2	14	post-hole	61	
5.2	15=124	post-hole	61	Copper A56
4.2	16	disturbance	59	St. A325; Cin. 2g
-	17	-	54	
4.1	17A	layer		
3.3	17B	layer		Quern A97
3.3	18	layer	54	St. A327; An. (7)
3.2	19	ditch	58, 54	Med. 1:2; An. (4)
3.2	20	layer	58, 54	Rom. 1:3; An. (6)
3.1	21	layer	57, 54, 56	Iron 48
3.1	22	gully	57, 54	An. (2)
3.1	23	post-hole	57	An. (2)
3.1	24	post-hole	57, 54	An. (1)
2.4	25	layer	54	Rom. 7:38; An. (3)
2.2	26	layer	54	Rom. 30:114, 44; Iron A209; Quern A102; St. A328; An. (3); Moll.
2.1	27=539	ditch	54	Rom. 16:208; Iron A210; An. (17); Char. ⊴g
2.1	28	post-hole		
2.1	29	post-hole		
2.1	30	post-hole		Rom. 2:11
2.1	31	-	54	Rom. 2:5; St. A329
3.3	32	layer	54	St. A382; Burnt (1)
-	33/34	layer	54	Burnt (1)
1.4	35	surface	54	Pre.; Rom. 1:19, 33; St. A383; Char. 182g+; St.
1.4	35/36	surface		Pre.; Rom. 28:24
1.4	36	surface		Burnt (1); Char. 260+
1.3	38	layer	54	
1.3	39	layer	54	Char. 115g+
1.2	40	layer	54	
1.2	41	layer	54	
1.1	42	?natural	54	
1.1	43	?natural	54	
1.1	44	?natural	54	
5.2	101	layer		Med. 6:54; Iron 16, A211; Nail 11:2; Sst. A128; Vess. (1)
5.2	102=102A and B			Rom. 1:36, 47; Med. 5:17; Iron 33; Lead A100; Nail 3:-; Sst. A129; Tile (2); Window A87
5.2	102A	rubble	61	
5.2	102B	make-up deposit	61, 60	
5.2	103	layer	61, 60	Med. 18:108; Bone 13; Copper 23; Iron 41, 49, 61; Nail 3:-; Quern A98; Burnt (1)
5.1	104	layer	60	Med. 37:383 (10); Copper A50, A59; Lead 38; Iron 32, , A212; Nail 4:5; Tile (1); Window A88; Slag 94g
5.1	104B	layer	60	
4.2	105	chalk surface	59	Med. 6:38
4.2	105A	chalk surface	59	
4.2	105B	chalk surface	59	
4.2	105C	chalk surface	59, 60	
4.2	105D	chalk surface	59	
4.2	106	recut of 108	59, 60	Med. 4:11; Iron A213; Nail -:1; St. A330; Tile (2)

Phase	Context	Description	Fig. Nos	Artefacts and environmental remains
4.2	107	?fill	60	Med. 2:39
4.2	108	pit	59, 60	Rom. 1:4; Med. 15:114; Bone 10; Iron A214; Tile (1); Slag 99g
4.1	109	disturbance		Med. 3:6
4.2	112	surface	59	
4.1	113	surface		Med. 2:8
4.1	114	surface		
3.3	115	surface		Med. 1:3; Nail -:1
4.2	116	post-hole	59	
3.3	117	surface		Med. 1:3
3.3	119	layer		Med. 7:105
5.2	120	post-hole	61	
5.2	121	post-hole	61	
4.2	122	post-hole	59	
5.2	123A	post-hole	61	
5.2	123B	post-hole	61	
5.2	123C	post-hole	61	
5.2	124=15	post-hole	61	
5.2	124A	post void	61	
3.3	127	layer		Med. 4:13; Iron 57, A215
3.3	128	surface		Rom. 1:7; Med. 1:2
3.3	129	surface		Med. 2:25; Mortar A8
3.2	130	layer	58	
3.2	130A	layer	58	
3.2	130B	layer	58	
3.2	130C	layer	58	
3.2	130D	ditch/gully	58	Med. 5:49
3.2	131=131B and C		58	
3.2	131B	slot		Med. 16:101; Lst. A136
3.2	131C	?wall base		Rom. 1:4; Med. 20:163; Copper A65; Iron 2; Nail 2:-; Char. 15g
3.2	132	layer	58	Rom. 1:3; Med. 1:3; Iron 56; Quern A99
3.2	133	layer	58	Rom. 1:4; Med. 1:3
3.2	134	layer	58	Rom. 2:19; Med. 5:27; Nail 1:-
3.2	135	post-hole	58	
3.2	136	surface	58	
3.2	137	depression/scoop	58	
3.2	138	layer	58	
3.2	139	depression/scoop	58	Rom. 1:8
3.2	140	depression/scoop	58	Med. 3:45; Iron 40; St. A384
3.1	144	post-hole	57	
3.1	145	post-hole	57	
3.2	146	post-hole		Med. 2:5
3.1	146B	post-hole	57	
3.1	147B	depression	57	
3.1	148	post-hole	57	Med. 1:1
3.1	149	post-hole	57	
3.1	150	layer	57	Rom. 1:2; Med. 2:8; Sst. A130; Quern A100; Slag 697g
3.2	151	fill/layer	58	
3.2	?151	fill/layer	58	Med. 10:56; Nail -:1
3.1	152	post-hole	57	Med. 2:6
3.1	153	post-hole	57	Med. 2:5; Burnt (1)
3.1	154	post-hole	57	Med. 1:2; Cin. ⊴g
3.1	155	post-hole	57	Rom. 1:2
3.1	156	post-hole	57	
3.1	158	gully	57	Rom. 1:10; Slag 9g
3.1	160	layer	57	Med. 2:6

414

Phase	Context	Description	Fig. Nos	Artefacts and environmental remains
3.1	163=163A and B		57	Iron 54; Nail -:1; St.
3.1	163A	layer		Rom. 1:3; Med. 1:5; St. A331
3.1	163B	layer		Rom. 2:3; Med. 3:5; Iron 54
3.1	164A+B	hearth	57	Rom. 2:4
3.1	165A	rubble		Med. 1:1; Slag 1g
3.1	165B	rubble		Rom. 1:3
3.1	167	layer		Med. 2:2
3.1	168	gully	57	
3.1	169B	layer		Iron 55; St. A332
3.1	171	surface		Copper 35; Slag 334g
2.4	173=500	layer		Rom. 1:5; Sst. A131; Burnt (1)
2.4	500	layer	60	An. (7)
2.4	501	layer	60	Rom. 2:6; Lead A94; St. A385; An. (9); Slag 385
2.3	505	layer	56	
3.1	506	ditch	57	
2.3	507	ditch	56	St. A333; An. (2); Moll.
2.3	508	layer	56, 60	Rom. 5:55, 45; Iron 10; An. (25); Moll.
2.3	509	post-hole	56	
2.3	510	ditch recut	56	Rom. 6:7; Clay A24; Copper 2; St. A334; An. (55); Moll.
2.3	511	ditch	56	An. (3)
2.3	512	ditch recut	56, 60	Rom. 2:6; Iron 21; An. (2); Slag ⊴
2.3	513	ditch	56	Nail 1:-
2.3	514	?pit	56	Rom. 1:5; Quern A101; An. (13)
2.2	515=521	surface	60	Rom. 11:38
2.2	516	cut feature		An. (9)
2.2	516/527	cut feature/?ditch		Rom. 1:2; Moll.
2.2	520	post-hole		Rom. 1:2
2.3	521=515	layer	60	St. A335; An. (2)
2.1/2.2	522	post-hole	60	
2.1	523	layer		Rom. 23:139, 35, 36; Iron A216; Nail 1:-; St. A336; An. (2)
2.1	528	layer	60	Rom. 54:291, 37, 38; Bone 7; Iron A217; Stone A386; An. (6)
2.1	529	fill of ditch		Rom. 19:199, 39, 40; An. (6); Moll.
2.1	531	gully		An. (1)
2.1	532	post-hole	55	
2.1	533	post-hole	55	Rom. 31:70
2.1	534	gully		Rom. 12:41, 41; An. (7)
2.1	535	ditch		Rom. 67:406; St. A337; An. (11); Burnt (2)
2.1	536	fill of ditch 535		Rom. 9:62, 42
2.1	539=?27	ditch	55	
2.1	540	pit		Rom. 17:262, 43; Iron A218; Slag 518g
2.1	543	post-hole	55	Rom. 1:4; St. A338; An. (1)
2.1	544	fill of ditch 539/27		Copper 1
2.1	545	post-hole	55	
2.1	547	post-hole	55	
1.5	548	layer		An. (1); Burnt (7)
1.1-1.5	550	surface		Pre.; Rom. 1:4, 34; An. (1)
2.1	551	fill		Rom. 4:51; An. (3)
2.1	553	general number for ditches		Rom. 10:5; An. (2); Moll.
4.2	-	Burial SA050		Med. 2:3; Copper A65
4.2	-	Burial SA052		Rom. 2:3; Med. 6:20
4.2	-	Burial SA053		Med. 5:17
4.2	-	Burial SA054		Med. 1:1
4.2	-	Burial SA055		Med. 1:2

Phase	Context	Description	Fig. Nos	Artefacts and environmental remains
4.2	-	Burial SA056		Rom. 1:7; Med. 8:95
4.2	-	Burial SA057		Med. 3:12
5.2	-	Burial SA059		Med. 3:21; Iron 66, 68; Tile (4); Wood A15, A16
5.2	-	Burial SA060		Med. 2:21; Bone 15 (same as Iron 20); Copper 14, 26; Iron 20, 67, 69; Wood A14
4.2	-	Burial SA061		Med. 1:1
-	-	unstratified		Roman 4:47; Med. 4:22; Copper 24

Site 52

-	1	topsoil		Med. 5:50; Brick (1); Copper A57; Iron 27, 28, 60, A219, A220, A221; Nail 5:-; St. A339; Tile (1)
-	3	topsoil		Iron 34; Nail -:1
-	4	layer/spit		Med. 36:251; Iron A222, A223; An. (6); Nail 6:-; Roof. A245; St. A340, A341, A410; Slag 33g
-	5	layer/spit		Med. 49:315 (8); Clay A20; Iron A224; Tile (1); An. (10); Slag 76g
-	6	layer/spit		Med. 22:195 (9); Quern A103; An. (5); Slag 115g
-	8	unstratified		Med. 2:35
-	9	layer/spit		Med. 4:30; Iron 29; Quern A104; Stone 58
-	11	fill of Burial SA070		Med. 2:28
-	15	fill of Burial SA071		Med. 1:21; St. A411; Slag 47
-	21	layer		
-	101	-		Med. 20:79; Iron A227; St. A387; Tile A139
-	103	-		Med. 2:11; Quern A105; Sst. A132; St. A388
-	105	-		Med. 10:23

Site 71

This concordance only lists contexts mentioned in this volume, the phasing is that given in *Wharram X;* see that volume also for finds.

8	2	topsoil	65
8	7	chalk rubble	65
8	8	turf line	65
6	15	occupation surface	68, 69
			65
7	18	post-hole	69
7	57	post-hole	69; 65
7	59	post-hole	69
7	61	wooden stake	69
7	62	post-hole	69
8	67	chalk rubble	68
7	68	post-hole	69
6	70	post-hole	68
4	71	silt organic deposit	65
6	74	post-hole	68
6	77	post-hole	68
8	78	wooden stake	68
5	80	chalk rubble surface	67, 68
			65
4	81	silt/chalk deposit	65
5	82	ash/rubble deposit	67
6	83	post-hole	68
5	95	silt surface	65
5	96	post-hole	67
5	98	post-hole	67
4	102	channel recut	66, 65
1.1	110	natural clay	63

Phase	Context	Description	Fig. Nos	Artefacts and environmental remains
5	123	pit	65	
5	124	post setting	67, 68	
5	125	post setting	67, 68	
5	127	fence slot	67, 68	
4	130	wall	66, 67 65	
4	132	channel recut	66, 67 65	
5	145	clay/silt deposit	65	
4	155	chalk surface	66, 65	
8	165	clay/silt deposit	65	
8	166	clay/silt deposit	65	
8	167	chalk rubble	65	
8	169	clay/silt deposit	65	
8	170	topsoil/chalk mix	65	
8	171	post-hole	65	
8	180	post-hole	65	
8	183	layer	65	
8	184	layer	65	
8	185	modern debris	65	
5	189	ash/chalk pebbles	67	
4	191	ash/organic deposit	65	
4	193	silt/chalk deposit	65	
4	195	ash deposit	65	
4	196	carbonised grain deposit	65	
4	197	rubble deposit	65	
4	200	slumpage layer	66	
3	202	wall	64	
4/5	203	silt/chalk surface	65	
4/5	204	construction surface	65	
4	208	ash deposit	65	
3	209	chalk yard surface	65	
3	214	wall	64	
3	217	chalk rubble	64	
3	218	wall	64	
3	219	chalk layer	65	
3	220	gravel lens	65	
4/5	222	silt/chalk deposit	65	
4/5	223	silt/chalk deposit	65	
4	224	carbonised grain deposit	65	
4	226	silt/clay deposit	65	
4	227	ash/organic deposit	65	
4	228	chalk rubble	65	
4	229	ash deposit	65	
4	230	clay/chalk deposit	65	
4	231	ash deposit	65	
3	233	clay/silt deposit	64	
3	234	channel recut	65	
3	235	clay bank	64, 65	
3	236	earth and clay bank	64	
1.1	238	clay bank	65	
3	239	chalk layer	65	
1.1	245	chalk platform	64, 65	
1.1	258	clay deposit	63, 65	
2.1/1.2	259	clay bank	63, 65	

Phase	Context	Description	Fig. Nos	Artefacts and environmental remains
1.1	260	clay bank	63, 65	
3	261	channel	65	
2.1/1.2	262	channel recut	63, 65	
1.1	263	channel	65	
7	264	trackway	68, 69 65	
2.1/1.2	265	channel	63, 64 65	
2.1/1.2	268	channel recut	63	
2.1/1.2	269	channel recut	63	
1.1	270	post setting	63	
1.1	271	post setting	63	
1.1	272	post setting	63	
1.1	273	depression	63	

Site 80

-	2	-		Tile (1); Vess. (1)
-	3	skeleton, Burial SA080		Pottery
-	5	-		Iron A226; Nail 2:-; Roof. A271; St. A389; Tile (3); Vess. (2)

Site 99/77

3	182	wall	48	

Site 100/77

4	79=175 =177	flight of steps	47, 48	

Church Contexts

	C26	stone block		
	EE42	chalk raft	9, 118	
	EE92	layer	9	
	EE93	layer	9	
	EE95	layer	9	
	EE97/99	layer	9	
	EE101/ 206/207	mortar dump		
	EE104	surface	9	
	EE105	surface	9	
	EE106	chalk platform	9	
	EE108	layer	9	
	EE109	layer	9	
	EE110	clay dump	9	
	EE119	sandstone surface	9	
	EE121	surface	9	
	EE202	layer	9	
	EE204	layer	9	
	EE205	layer	9	
	EE207	layer	9	
	EE215	surface	9	
	(EE104 & EE105)			

Phase	Context	Description	Fig. Nos	Artefacts and environmental remains
	EE219	layer	9	
	NA4	building debris	24, 26, 27	
	NA9	surface	26	
	NA10	building debris	26	
	NA21	group no.	26	
	NA28	post-hole	26	
	NA29	post-hole	26	
	NA30	post-hole	26	
	NA31	post-hole	26	
	NA32	path	24, 26	
	NA35	ditch	20, 23	
	NA36	ditch fill		
	NA37	ditch fill	22	
	NA38	ditch fill		
	NA51	burnt chalk		
	NA96	ditch	20	
	NA97	?Grubenhaus/ 'lime kiln'	20, 23	
	NA98	stake-hole group	26	
	NA99	post-hole	26	
	NA123	layer	27	
	NA173	deposit	27	
	NA196	deposit	27	
	NA198	deposit	27	
	NA217	deposit	27	
	NA218	deposit	27	
	NA233/ 215	deposit	27	
	NA234	deposit	27	
	V1	layer	9	
	V2	layer	9	
	V20	ceramic drain		
	39*	layer	11	
	59*	gravecover	11	
	67*	headstone	11	
	75*	gravecover	11	
	78*	headstone	11	
	79*	headstone	11	
	V89	sandstone surface	9, 11, 118	
	V90	layer	9, 11	
	V91	chalk raft	9, 11	
	V96	layer	11	
	V99	layer	11	
	V103	layer	9, 11	
	WCO18	surface	14	
	WCO19	surface	14	
	WCO22	ceramic drain	17	
	WCO23	hillwash		
	WCO24a	chalk packing	16	
	WCO25	conduit trench	16	
	WCO26	water conduit	16	
	WCO28	shallow pit	15	
	WCO29	pit	15	
	WCO31	pebble surface	17	
	WCO35	chalk pebbles	17	
	WCO36	post-hole	17	
	WCO37	post-hole	17	

Phase	Context	Description	Fig. Nos	Artefacts and environmental remains
	WCO38	post-hole	17	
	WCO39	post-hole	17	
	WCO40	post-hole	17	
	WCO41	post-hole	17	
	WCO42	sandstone surface	17	
	WCO43	chalk packing	17	
	WCO44	cemetery soil		
	WCO45	post-hole	17	
	WCO46	post-hole	17	
	WCO48	post-hole	16	
	WCO49	post-hole	16	
	WCO50	post-hole	16	
	WCO51	post-hole	16	
	WCO52	post-hole	16	
	WCO53	post-hole	16	
	WCO54	post-hole	16	
	WCO55	post-pipe	16	
	WCO56	post-hole	14	
	WCO57	post-hole	14	
	WCO58	post-hole	15	
	WCO239	quarry	14	
	WCO244	?quarry	14	
	WCO248	post-hole	17	
	WCO250	burnt deposit	16	
	WCO251	sandstone rubble	16	

Appendix 9: Burial Concordance

The following concordance has been compiled using data from numerous sites with varying recording techniques. An *
after the Burial Number indicates a number assigned from photographic evidence during post-excavation work; it is
possible that some of these may duplicate burials already with a Burial Number. All the burials have been reviewed:
where possible the overall church phasing from Wharram III has been retained (Roman numerals), but many have
subsequently been rephased as detailed below:

The East End, South Aisle, Vestry, Site 52 and Site 80 burials are phased partly by the church phases (as Roman
numerals). Those that could not be closely phased are instead recorded as: EM = Early Medieval, M = Medieval, PM =
Post-medieval

Sites 26 and 41 are phased numerically (i.e. 2.1 = Period 2, Phase 1). NB: phasing is individual to each site.

North Churchyard burials were originally recorded on a series of five plans, A – E, with plan E recording the first
plan drawn and so probably the most recent burials. In some areas the superimposition of burials was more precisely
recorded but during a different season of excavation and in a different area. Here the sequence of burials is numbered
AA, AB, AC etc, where AA represents the earliest burials. In Grids JKL 223-230 the same process uses the numbering
KA, KB etc and in the PQ trench (linking the North Churchyard to Site 26) the phase numbering is prefixed P, with PA
being the earliest burials. Where possible the PQ trench burials have been linked to Site 26.

West End burials were not individually phased (see Ch. 14 for range of dates)

Site codes have been abbreviated as follows:
CN: Church Nave
Ch: Chancel
EE: East End
NA: North Churchyard
SA: South Aisle
V: Vestry
WCO: West End

Burial No.	Previous Ref.	Site	Grid	Phase	Equiv. Site 26 Phase	Mays' Phase	RC date	Studied by Mays	Fig. No.	Table No.	Pl. No.
CN01	A	CN	N/21	XI		4		Y	124		
CN02	B	CN	N/21	XI		4		Y	124		
CN03	C	CN	P/20	VIII-IX		3-4	GU5575	Y	124	117	71, 72
CN04	D	CN	O/20	XI		4		Y	124		
CN05	E	CN	N-O/20-21	XI		4		Y	124	64, 98, 103	
CN06	F	CN	K-N/20	XI		4		Y	90, 124		
CN07	G	CN	N-O/21	XI		4		Y	124		
CN08	H	CN	O/20	XI					124		
CN09	I	CN	N-O/19	XI		4		Y	124		
CN10	J	CN	N/19	XI					124		
CN11	K	CN	L-M/19	XI		4		Y	124		
CN12	L	CN	M/18	VIII-X		4		Y	90, 124	61, 84	
CN13	M	CN	M/18	XI		4		Y	124	101	
CN14	N	CN	L-M/16	XI		4		Y	124	53	
CN15	O	CN	L-M/16	IX-XI		4		Y	124		23
CN16	P	CN	O/17	IX-XI		4		Y	124	84	
CN17	Q	CN	M-N/17	XI		4		Y	124	101	
CN18	R	CN	M-N/17	XI		4		Y	124		
CN19	S	CN	O-P/17	XI		4		Y	124		
CN20	T	CN	O-P/17-18	XI		4		Y	124		
CN21	U	CN	N-O/19	XI					124		
CN22	V	CN	N-O/18	XI		4		Y	124		
CN23	W	CN	N-O/19	?					124		
CN24	X	CN	T-U/13	XI		4		Y			
CN25	Y	CN	U/20-21	IX-XI					124		
CN26	Z	CN	U/20-21	IX-XI					124		
CN27	AA	CN	T-U/17	XI		4		Y	124	61, 84	
CN28	BB	CN	T-U/17-18	XI		4		Y	90, 124		63
CN29	CC	CN	T-U/19	XI		4		Y	90		
CN30	DD	CN	T-U/19	?		4		Y	90		
CN31	EE	CN	S-T/19-20	XI		4		Y	90	61	
CN32	FF	CN	T-V/18	IX-XI		4		Y	90		
CN33	GG	CN	T-V/18	IX-XI		4		Y	90, 124	84, 98	
CN34	HH	CN	AA/2	X-XI					123		
CN35	II	CN	Y-Z/20	VII-X					123		
CN36	JJ	CN	S-T/19	?		4		Y	124		
CN37	KK	CN	U-V/21	XI		4		Y	124		
CN38	LL	CN	S/19	XI		4		Y	124		
CN39	MM	CN	S/18	XI		4		Y	124	84	
CN40	NN	CN	U-V/20	XI		4		Y	124		
CN41	OO	CN	T-U/19	?		4		Y	124	54	
CN42	PP	CN	U-V/21	XI		4		Y	124		
CN43	QQ	CN	V-W/19	VII-X		4		Y	124		
CN44	RR	CN	V-W/19	VIII-X		4	GU5576	Y	124	117	
CN45	SS	CN	T/19	IX-XI		4		Y	124	84	
CN46	TT	CN	U-W/18	VIII-XI		4		Y	124		
CN47	UU	CN	V-W/19	XI		4		Y	124		
CN48	VV	CN	V-W/19	?							
CN49	WW	CN	T-U/21-22	?					124		
CN50	XX	CN	T-U/21-22	?					124		
CN51	YY	CN	Q/20	I?					119		
CN52	ZZ	CN	Q/19	I?					119		
CN53	-	Ch	Y/19	VII-IX					123		
CN54	-	Ch	Z/19	VII-IX					123		
CN55	-	Ch	Y-Z/19	VII-IX					123		

Burial No.	Previous Ref.	Site	Grid	Phase	Equiv. Site 26 Phase	Mays' Phase	RC date	Studied by Mays	Fig. No.	Table No.	Pl. No.
CN56	Context 47	Ch	AA-BB/19	VII-IX					123		
EE001	1(1963)	EE	JJ/24	EM		?		Y			
EE002	2(1963)	EE	JJ/24	EM		?		Y			
EE003	3(1963)	EE	HH-JJ/24	EM		1-2	GU5507	Y	90	61, 62, 84, 117	32
EE004	4 (1963)	EE	HH/23	EM		1-2		Y		84	53
EE005	5	EE	HH/23	EM		?		Y			
EE006	6	EE	JJ/23	EM		?		Y		64	
EE007	7	EE	JJ-KK/22	EM		2	GU5508	Y		117	
EE008	15	EE	DD-EE/24	EM							
EE009	16	EE	DD/24	EM		1-2		Y			
EE010	17	EE	DD/24	EM		1-2		Y			
EE011	18	EE	DD-EE/23	EM					130		101
EE012	20	EE	FF/22	EM							
EE013	-	EE	DD-FF/21	M		2	GU5506	Y	123, 129, 118	53, 117	96
EE014	DB5	EE	?EE-FF/28	?		?		Y			
EE015	DB19	EE	FF/27-28	EM		1-2		Y		65, 84	
EE016	DB21	EE	EE-FF/27	EM		1-2		Y		103	
EE017	DB22	EE	DD-FF/27-2	EM		?		Y			
EE018	DB18	EE	DD-FF/27	EM		1-2		Y	90	54, 62, 84, 103	43
EE019	DB20	EE	DD-EE/26	EM		1-2	GU5510	Y	118	117	
EE020	DB20	EE	DD-EE/26	EM		1	GU5511/ GU5683	Y	90, 118	117	
EE021	DB20	EE	DD-EE/26	EM							
EE022	DB25	EE	CC-DD/28	EM		1-2		Y	129, 130	84	
EE023	DB23	EE	DD-EE/28	EM							
EE024	DB24	EE	DD/28	EM		1-2		Y			
EE025	DB32 Or 32A	EE	CC/28	EM		1-2		Y			
EE026	DB31	EE	CC/28?	EM		1-2	GU5509	Y		117	
EE027	DB2 (1963)	EE	JJ/18-19	EM		1-2		Y		61	
EE028	RK2 (1963)	EE		?		1-2		Y			
EE029	DB3	EE	DD/15	?		?		Y		103	
EE030	DB4	EE		?		1-2		Y			
EE031	DB6	EE		?		1-2		Y			44, 45
EE032	DB7	EE	JJ/18-19	EM		1-2		Y		84	
EE033	DB8	EE		?		?		Y			
EE034	DB9	EE		?		?		Y			
EE035	9	EE		?		1-2		Y			
EE036	11 (1963)	EE	JJ/17	?		1-2		Y			
EE037	12	EE	JJ/17	?		1-2		Y	90	61, 84	38
EE038	DB12	EE	JJ/17-18	?		2-3	GU5452	Y		117	
EE039	13 (1963-4)	EE		?		?		Y			
EE040	DB13 (1964)	EE		?		1-2		Y			
EE041	14 (1963)	EE		?		1-2		Y			
EE042	DB14 (1964)	EE		?		?		Y			
EE043	23 (1964)	EE		?		1-2		Y		54, 61	
EE044	26 DB27	EE		?		1-2		Y			
EE045	-	EE		?		1-2		Y			
EE046	DB28	EE		?		1-2		Y		65	
EE047	DB16	EE	JJ/18	?		1-2		Y			

Burial No.	Previous Ref.	Site	Grid	Phase	Equiv. Site 26 Phase	Mays' Phase	RC date	Studied by Mays	Fig. No.	Table No.	Pl. No.
EE048	33	EE		?		?		Y			
EE049	DB32	EE	BB-CC/28?	?		?		Y			
EE050	DB36	EE		?		?		Y			
EE051	DB37	EE		?		?		Y			
EE052	DB59	EE		?		?		Y			
EE053	DB69	EE		?		?		Y			
EE054	DB38	EE		?		?		Y		103	
EE055	DB39	EE		?		?		Y			
EE056	DB39A	EE		?		1-2		Y		102	
EE057	DB40	EE		?		?		Y			
EE058	DB41	EE		?		?		Y			
EE059	DB144	EE		?		?		Y			
EE060	DB45	EE		?		1-2		Y		84	
EE061	DB46	EE		?		1-2		Y			
EE062	47	EE		?		1-2		Y		64	
EE063	48 = DB48	EE		?		?		Y			
EE064	DB49	EE		?		1-2		Y			
EE065	50	EE		?		?		Y			
EE066	DB51	EE		?		?		Y			
EE067	52	EE		?		1-2		Y			
EE068	DB53	EE		?		?		Y			
EE069	54	EE		?		?		Y			
EE070	55	EE		?		1-2		Y		61, 103	
EE071	DB56	EE		?		?		Y			
EE072	57 = DB57	EE	V-W/27	?		?		Y	130	61, 103	94
EE073	DB58	EE		?		?		Y			
EE074	60	EE	X-Y/27	?		?		Y			95
EE075	DB61	EE	X-Y/27	?		?		Y			95
EE076	DB62	EE	X-Y/28	?		?		Y			95
EE077	63	EE		?		1-2		Y			
EE078	DB66	EE		?		?		Y			
EE079	DB67	EE	Z/24	M		2		Y	123	65	97
EE080	DB68	EE	X-Z/24	M		2		Y	90, 123	62, 65	97
EE081	DB70	EE		?		?		Y			
EE082	72	EE		?		1-2		Y			
EE083	74	EE		?		?		Y			
EE084	75	EE		?		?		Y			
EE085	DB76, DB76B	EE		?		1-2		Y	90		
EE086	DB77	EE		?		?		Y			
EE087	DB78	EE		?		1-2		Y			
EE088	DB79	EE		?		?		Y			
EE089	80	EE		?		1-2		Y			
EE090	DB82	EE		?		?		Y			
EE091	DB83	EE		?		?		Y			
EE092	DB86	EE		?		1-2		Y			
EE093	87	EE		?		1-2		Y			
EE094	DB89	EE		?		?		Y			
EE095	DB91	EE		?		?		Y			
EE096	92	EE		?		?		Y			
EE097	DB93	EE		?		1-2		Y			
EE098	DB94	EE		?		1-2		Y		103	
EE099	DB96	EE		?		1-2		Y			
EE100	97	EE		?		?		Y			
EE101`	98	EE		?		1-2		Y			

Burial No.	Previous Ref.	Site	Grid	Phase	Equiv. Site 26 Phase	Mays' Phase	RC date	Studied by Mays	Fig. No.	Table No.	Pl. No.
EE102	102	EE		?		?		Y			
EE103	105	EE		?		1-2		Y			
EE104	Context EE152	CC/24	?								
EE105*	Context EE180	EE	Y/28-9	?							
EE107*	-	EE	Z/24	?							
EE108*	-	EE	Z/24	PM					123, 124		
EE109*	DB5	EE	EE-FF/28	EM							
EE110*	EE026	EE	CC/28	EM					130		
EE111	-	EE	DD/23	EM					129		
EE112	-	EE	CC-DD/20	EM					9B, 129		
EE113*	Context EE154	EE	JJ/22	M							
EE114*	Context EE155	EE	JJ/21	M							
EE115*	Context EE161	EE	EE-FF/28	EM							
EE116*	Context EE179	EE	FF-GG/17	M					129		
EE117*	Context EE181	EE	V/28-9	EM							
EE118*	Find 658	EE	V/27	?							
EE120	Context C48	EE	BB/19	M					123, 130		
EE121*	Find 658b	EE	FF/15	?							
EE122*	Find 658A	EE	BB/18	?							
EE123*	Find 657a	EE	DD/19	?							
EE124*	Find 621	EE	FF-GG/16	?					129		
EE126*		EE	Z/25	M					123		97
EE127*		EE	Y-Z/24	M					123		
EE128*		EE	BB-CC/26-8	PM					124		
EE129*		EE	BB-CC/27	?					130		
EE130*		EE	BB-CC/27	?							
EE131*		EE	DD/27	?							
EE133*		EE	Y/28 app	?							
EE137*		EE	Y/28?	?							95
EE139*		EE	Y-Z/28	?							
EE140	-	EE	FF/23	EM							
EE183*	Context EE183	EE	Z-AA/23	?							
EE184*	Context EE184	EE	JJ/16	EM							
EE205	Context EE205	EE	CC-EE/19	EM					9A, 130		
EE214	Context EE214	EE	CC-DD/20	EM			HAR3575		9A, 118	117	
-	8	EE	?	?							
-	10	EE	?	?							
-	19	EE	?	III-VIII							
-	DB10	EE	JJ/17-18	III-IX							
-	DB11	EE	JJ-KK/17-18	III-IX							
-	DB15	EE	EE-FF/28	III-VII							
-	DB26	EE	?	?							
-	DB29	EE	?	?							

Burial No.	Previous Ref.	Site	Grid	Phase	Equiv. Site 26 Phase	Mays' Phase	RC date	Studied by Mays	Fig. No.	Table No.	Pl. No.
-	DB30	EE	?	?							
-	DB17	EE	JJ/19-19	EM							
G250	Skeleton 317	Site 26	K-L/237	4.6					129		
G251	Skeleton 318	Site 26	J-K/240	4.5		2		Y	38, 121, 129		
G253	Skeleton 320	Site 26	L-M/238	4.5		2		Y	38, 121	84, 103	
G254	Skeleton 319	Site 26	L-M/239	4.5		2		Y	38, 90,	138, 121	
G260	Skeleton 321	Site 26	L/239	4.5		2		Y	38, 121		
G265	Skeleton 322	Site 26	N-O/238-9	4.3		2	GU5544	Y	37, 90, 121, 129 130	53, 61, 117, 138	
G273	Skeleton 324	Site 26	M/241	4.5		2		Y	38, 121		
G275A	Skeleton 325	Site 26	L-M/237-8	4.5		2	GU5543	Y	38, 90, 121	12, 62, 117, 138	46
G278	Skeleton 326	Site 26	J-K/240	4.3		2	GU5547	Y	37, 121	84, 103, 117, 138	54
G279	Skeleton 327	Site 26	N/240	3.1		1	GU5542	Y	33, 121	84, 101, 117	
G280	Skeleton 328	Site 26	N-0/240	4.5		2		Y	38, 121		
G281	Skeleton 329	Site 26	M/230	4.5		2		Y	38, 121	12, 138	
G296	Skeleton 323	Site 26	N-0/240	4.5		2		Y	38, 90, 121		
G297	Skeleton 330	Site 26	N-O/237	4.3		2	GU5546	Y	37, 90, 121	53, 117	
G298	Skeleton 331	Site 26	N-O/239	4.3		2		Y	37, 121		
G303	Skeleton 332	Site 26	N-O/237	3.3		1-2	GU5541	Y	34, 121	64, 84, 103, 117, 137	
G304	Skeleton 332	Site 26	N-O/238	3.1		1	GU5545	Y	33, 121, 129	61, 84, 117	34, 35
G305	Skeleton 334	Site 26	H/238	1.1			HAR-2208		29, 117		
G306	Skeleton 335	Site 26	L-M/238	4.3		2		Y	37, 121, 129, 130	138	
G308	Skeleton 336	Site 26	M-N/237	4.3		2		Y	37, 121	138	
G310	Skeleton 337	Site 26	J-K/241-2	3.5		2		Y	35, 121, 130	84, 137	
G313	Skeleton 338	Site 26	L/240	4.5		2		Y	38, 121		
G314	Skeleton 339	Site 26	O-P/237-8	3.3		1-2	GU5540	Y	34, 121	64, 117	
G320	Skeleton 340	Site 26	P/328	4.3		2		Y	37, 121	138	
G327	Skeleton 342	Site 26	N/237	4.3		2		Y	37, 121	84, 103, 138	
G338	Skeleton 341	Site 26	P-Q/239	4.3		2		Y	37, 121		

Burial No.	Previous Ref.	Site	Grid	Phase	Equiv. Site 26 Phase	Mays' Phase	RC date	Studied by Mays	Fig. No.	Table No.	Pl. No.
G339	Skeleton 343	Site 26	O/237	4.3		2		Y	37, 121	138	
G361	Skeleton 344	Site 26	J-K/243	4.3		2	GU5553	Y	37, 121	117	
G363	Skeleton 348	Site 26	Q-R/237	4.3		2		Y	37, 121	61, 137	
G364	-	Site 26	T-U/239-40	4.3		2		Y	37, 121		
G367	Skeleton 346	Site 26	T-U/238	4.3		2		Y	37, 121, 129		
G370	Skeleton 347	Site 26	R-T/237-8	4.3		2		Y	37, 90, 121, 129		
G377	Skeleton 349	Site 26	Q-R/237-8	3.3		1-2		Y	34, 90, 121, 130		
G379	Skeleton 350	Site 26	Q-R/237-8	3.3		1-2		Y	34, 121, 130	84, 103, 137	
G381	Skeleton 351	Site 26	P-Q/237-8	3.3		1-2		Y	34, 90, 121		
G385	Skeleton 352	Site 26	P-R/241	3.5		2	GU5552	Y	35, 90, 121	115, 117, 137	
G387	Skeleton 353	Sitc 26	Q-R/237-8	3.3		1-2		Y	34, 121		
G398	Skeleton 354	Site 26	Q-R/240-1	3.5		2		Y	35, 90, 121, 129	103, 137	
G399	Skeleton 355	Site 26	Q-R/241	3.5					35, 121		
G406	Skeleton 356	Site 26	P-R/239	3.3		1-2		Y	34, 90, 121	83	
G411	Skeleton 357	Site 26	Q-R/241	3.5		2		Y	35, 121	103	
G416	Skeleton 358	Site 26	R-S/238-9	4.1		2		Y	36, 121	138	
G419	Skeleton 359	Site 26	R-S/239	4.1		2		Y	36, 121	115, 138	77
G422	Skeleton 360	Site 26	R-S/238	4.1		2		Y	36, 121		
G424	Skeleton 361	Site 26	T-U/237	4.1		2		Y	36, 121		
G427	Skeleton 362	Site 26	R-S/239	4.1		2		Y	36, 121	138	
G430	Skeleton 363	Site 26	R-S/240	4.1		2		Y	36, 121	138	
G433	Skeleton 364	Site 26	T-U/238-9	4.1		2		Y	36, 121		
G436	Skeleton 365	Site 26	S-T/238	4.1		2		Y	36, 90, 121	53, 138	
G438	Skeleton 366	Site 26	S-T/238	4.1		2		Y	36, 121	12, 61 65, 102	
G443	-	Site 26	S-T/239	4.1		2		Y	36, 121	61	
G446	-	Site 26	S-T/239	4.1		2		Y	36, 121		
G451	-	Site 26	O-P/245-6	3.5		2	GU5551	Y	35, 121	84, 117, 137	
G456	-	Site 26	S-T/239-40	4.1		2		Y	36, 121, 129	138	
G457	-	Site 26	S/238	4.1		2		Y	36, 121	12	
G462	-	Site 26	T-U/239	4.1		2	GU5550	Y	36, 90, 121	103, 117	

Burial No.	Previous Ref.	Site	Grid	Phase	Equiv. Site 26 Phase	Mays' Phase	RC date	Studied by Mays	Fig. No.	Table No.	Pl. No.
G467	-	Site 26	U/238	4.1		2		Y	36, 121	83, 103	25, 26
G470	-	Site 26	U/240	4.1		2		Y	36,121		
G474	-	Site 26	P-Q/238-9	3.3		1-2	GU5539	Y	34, 121	117	
G476	-	Site 26	U-V/238	4.1		2		Y	36, 121		
G478	-	Site 26	Q-R/238-9	4.1		2	GU5549	Y	36, 121	117	
G482	-	Site 26	R-S/238	4.1		2		Y	36, 121	84, 102	
G488	-	Site 26	L-M/244	3.3		1-2		Y	34, 121, 129	137	
G492	-	Site 26	U/238	4.1		2		Y	36, 121		
G497	-	Site 26	U/239	4.1		2		Y	36, 121		
G500	-	Site 26	U-V/239	4.1		2		Y	36, 121, 129	61, 138	
G503	-	Site 26	T-U/243	3.3		1-2		Y	34, 121, 130	137	
G506	-	Site 26	S-R/240	3.3		1-2		Y	34, 121		
G510	-	Site 26	T/237	4.1		2		Y	36, 121, 129	138	
G513	-	Site 26	M/236-7	4.3		2		Y	37, 121		
G516	-	Site 26	O-P/242	3.3		1-2		Y	34, 121	137	
G522	-	Site 26	U-V/238-9	4.1		2		Y	36, 121, 130		99
G525	-	Site 26	O/236-7	4.6		2		Y			
G528	-	Site 26	U-V/237	4.1		2	GU5548	Y	36, 90, 121, 130	12, 62, 117	
G531	-	Site 26	V/237	4.1		2		Y	36, 121	12, 103	
G534	-	Site 26	V/237	4.1		2		Y	36, 121		
G535	-	Site 26	P/238	3.5					35, 121		
G536	-	Site 26	M/241-2	3.5					35, 121		
G542	-	Site 26	P-Q/244	3.3		1-2		Y	34, 121		
G555	-	Site 26	O-P/240	3.3		1-2		Y	34, 121		78
G558	-	Site 26	U-V/238-9	4.1		2		Y	36, 121		
G561	-	Site 26	N-O/242-3	3.3		1-2		Y	34, 121	84	
G565	-	Site 26	Q-R/241	3.5		2		Y	35, 121	62, 84	
G571	-	Site 26	S-T/245	4.3		2	GU5538	Y	37, 90, 121	84, 115, 117, 138	64
G576	-	Site 26	U-V/240	3.3		1-2		Y	34, 121		
G579	-	Site 26	U-V/237	3.3		1-2		Y	34, 121		
G582	-	Site 26	U-V/237	3.3		1-2	GU5537	Y	34, 90, 121, 129, 130	117	
G587	-	Site 26	M-N/241	3.3		1-2		Y	34, 90, 121	137	
G592	-	Site 26	M/239	3.3		1-2		Y	34, 121		
G597	-	Site 26	R-S/237	4.1		2		Y	36, 90	84	
G601	-	Site 26	U-V/237	3.1		1-2	GU5554	Y	33, 90, 121	117	50
G604	-	Site 26	W/237	3.1		1-2	GU5558	Y	33, 90, 121	117, 137	
G607	-	Site 26	L-M/243	3.3		1-2		Y	34, 121	84	
G614	-	Site 26	N/245	3.3		1-2		Y	34, 121		
G628	-	Site 26	N-O/243-4	3.1		1-2		Y	33, 90, 121, 130	137	
G635	-	Site 26	Q-R/242	3.1		1-2		Y	33, 90, 121, 130	61	
G636	-	Site 26	Q-R/242	3.1		1-2		Y	33, 90, 121, 130	84	

Burial No.	Previous Ref.	Site	Grid	Phase	Equiv. Site 26 Phase	Mays' Phase	RC date	Studied by Mays	Fig. No.	Table No.	Pl. No.
G643	-	Site 26	P-Q/243	3.1		1-2		Y	33, 90, 121	61	
G652	-	Site 26	U-W/243	4.3		2	GU5557/ GU5680	Y	37, 121	117, 138	
G655	-	Site 26	W/239	3.3		1-2		Y	34, 121		
G658	-	Site 26	N-O/237	3.3		1-2		Y	34, 121	103	61
G667	-	Site 26	W/240	3.3		1-2		Y	34, 121		
G670	-	Site 26	W/241	3.3		1-2		Y	34, 121	137	
G673	-	Site 26	T/241	3.1		1-2		Y	33,121		
G676	-	Site 26	W/239	3.1		1-2		Y	33, 121	137	
G677	-	Site 26	L-M/236-7	4.5		2		Y	38, 121		
G678	-	Site 26	N-O/236-7	4.5		2		Y	38, 121	103	
G679	-	Site 26	L/236-7	3.1					33		
G683	-	Site 26	R-S/242	3.1		1-2		Y	33, 121		
G686	-	Site 26	R/244	3.1		1-2		Y	33, 121		
G689	-	Site 26	S-T/244	3.1		1-2		Y	33, 121	137	
G692	-	Site 26	R-S/243	3.1		1-2		Y	33, 90, 121, 130	54, 103, 137	
G694	-	Site 26	R-S/242	3.1		1-2		Y	33, 121, 130	53, 84	
G697	-	Site 26	U-V/238	3.1		1-2		Y	33, 121	103	
G708	-	Site 26	R-S/241	3.1		1-2		Y	33, 121		98
G710	-	Site 26	R-T/242	3.1		1-2		Y	33, 121		24
G715	-	Site 26	W/238	3.1		1-2		Y	33, 121	61, 84, 137	36, 37
G716	-	Site 26	W/238	3.1					33, 121		
G717	-	Site 26	W/238	3.1					33, 121		
G720	-	Site 26	R-S/243	3.1		1-2		Y	33		
G723	-	Site 26	T-U/244	3.1		1-2		Y	33, 121, 33	103, 137	60
G746	-	Site 26	T-U/242	3.1		1-2		Y	33, 121, 130	53, 62, 84	
G747	-	Site 26	T-U/241	3.1		1-2		Y	33, 121	62, 103	
G750	-	Site 26	W/237	3.1		1-2	GU5556	Y	33, 121	117	
G760	-	Site 26	L-M/242	3.1		1-2	GU5555	Y	33, 121	117	
NA001	=G381	NA	P-Q/37	PB	3.5						
NA001A	-	NA	P-Q/37	PC	4.1, 4.3, 4.5						
NA002	291	NA	O-P/36	PB		?	GU5641	Y	105, 129, 130	64, 117	
NA003	-	NA	O-P/35	PA	3.3				21, 129		
NA004	292	NA	O-P/34-35	PB		?		Y	129		
NA004A	292 (1965)	NA		?		?		Y		103	
NA005		NA	P-Q/34-35	PC	4.1, 4.3, 4.5						
NA006	293	NA	O-P/34	PB		1-2	GU5642	Y	129	62, 117	
NA006A	293 (1965)	NA		?		?		Y			
NA007	-	NA	O-P/34	PC	4.1, 4.3, 4.5						
NA008	-	NA	O-P/33-34	PC	4.1, 4.3, 4.5				129		
NA009	-	NA	P-Q/34	PA	3.3				130		
NA010	-	NA	Q/34	PB	3.5						
NA011	-	NA	Q/33-34	PC	4.1, 4.3, 4.5						
NA012	-	NA	P/33	PA	3.3						

428

Burial No.	Previous Ref.	Site	Grid	Phase	Equiv. Site 26 Phase	Mays' Phase	RC date	Studied by Mays	Fig. No.	Table No.	Pl. No.
NA013	294	NA	O-P/33	PB		1-2	GU5643	Y	22, 105, 129	117	
NA014	295	NA	P-Q/33	PA		1-2	GU5644	Y	105	117	
NA014A	295 (1965)	NA		?		?		Y		103	
NA015	-	NA	O-P/32-33	PA	3.3						
NA016	-	NA	O-P/32	PC	4.1, 4.3, 4.5						
NA017	-	NA	O/32	PA	3.3						
NA018	-	NA	O-P/32	PB	3.5						
NA019	296	NA	P-Q/32	PC		?		Y	129		
NA020	-	NA	O-P/31-32	PA	3.3				25		
NA021	-	NA	O-P/31	PA	3.3				25		
NA022	297	NA	P-Q/31	PA		?		Y	25, 129, 130		
NA023	298	NA	P-Q/31	PA		?		Y	25		
NA024	299	NA	P-Q/30	PB		?		Y	25	103	
NA025	110	NA	T/30	E		?		Y		64	
NA026	111	NA	T/29	E		1-2		Y		102	56
NA027	112	NA	Q/30	E		?		Y			
NA028	113	NA	R-S/29	E		?		Y			
NA029	114	NA	R/30	E		?		Y			
NA030	115	NA	W/30	E		?		Y			
NA031	116	NA	W/29	E		1-2		Y			
NA031A	116A	NA	W/29	E		?		Y		83	
NA032	117	NA	S/27	E		?		Y			
NA033	118	NA	Q/30	E		1-2		Y		62, 64, 84	
NA034	119	NA	R/30	E		?		Y			
NA035	120	NA		?		?		Y			
NA036	121	NA	O/30	E		?		Y			68
NA037	122A	NA	O/30	E		?		Y			
NA037A	122B	NA	O/30	E		?		Y			
NA038	123	NA	T/29	D		1-2		Y	129, 130		
NA039	124	NA		?							
NA040	125	NA	O/30	E		?		Y			
NA041	126	NA	P/29	E							
NA042	127	NA	T/28	D		?		Y			
NA043	128	NA	S/29	D		?		Y	130	103	
NA043A	-	NA	S/29	D		?		Y		103	
NA044	129	NA	R/28	D		1-2		Y	90	84	
NA045	130	NA	P/29	E		?		Y	130		
NA046	131	NA	X/30	D		1-2	GU5645	Y	130	84, 98, 102, 117	
NA047	132	NA	W/30	D		1-2		Y	90		
NA048	133	NA	P/30	D		?		Y			
NA049	134	NA	P/29	D		?		Y			
NA050	135	NA	S/30	D		?		Y			
NA051	136	NA	X/30	D		1-2		Y	130		
NA052	137	NA	V/30	D		?		Y	22		
NA053	138	NA	P/28	C		?		Y			
NA054	139	NA	V/29	C		?		Y			
NA055	140	NA	X/30	D		?		Y			
NA056	141	NA	R/29	D		?		Y			
NA056A	141	NA	R/29	D		?		Y			
NA057	142	NA	W/30	C		?		Y			
NA058	143	NA	X/30	C		?		Y	129		

Burial No.	Previous Ref.	Site	Grid	Phase	Equiv. Site 26 Phase	Mays' Phase	RC date	Studied by Mays	Fig. No.	Table No.	Pl. No.
NA059	144	NA		?		1-2		Y	90		
NA060	145	NA	K/28	D		?		Y		12, 103	
NA060A	145 twin	NA	K/28	D		?		Y		12	
NA061	146	NA	K/28	E		?		Y			
NA062	147	NA	S/30	D		?		Y			
NA063	148	NA	T/30	C		?		Y	129		
NA064	149	NA	P/28	D		?		Y	129		
NA065	150	NA	T/30	C		?		Y	129		
NA066	151	NA	T/29	B		1-2		Y	90		47
NA067	152	NA	S/30	E		?		Y			
NA068	153	NA	M/29	D		1-2		Y			75
NA069	154	NA	P/28	D		?		Y			
NA070	155	NA	P/28	E		?		Y			
NA071	156	NA		?		?		Y			
NA072	157	NA		?							
NA073	158	NA	S/29	E		?		Y			
NA074	159	NA		?		?		Y			
NA075	160	NA		?		1-2		Y			
NA076	162	NA	Q/29	D		?		Y			
NA077	162	NA	N/30	E		?		Y			
NA078	163	NA		?		1-2		Y			
NA079	164	NA	N/29	E		?		Y			
NA080	165	NA	N/29	E		1-2		Y			
NA081	166	NA	M/30	E		1-2		Y		61	
NA082	167	NA	T/30	C		?		Y			
NA083	168	NA		?		?		Y			
NA084	169	NA		?		1-2		Y			
NA085	170	NA		?		?		Y			
NA086	171	NA	P/30	D		?		Y			
NA087	172	NA	P/30	D		?		Y	129		
NA088	173	NA		?		1-2		Y	90	61, 64	
NA089	174	NA		?		?		Y			
NA090	175	NA		?							
NA091	176	NA	N/30	D		1-2		Y		84	
NA092	177	NA	O/30	D		?		Y			
NA093	178	NA	O/30	D		?		Y			
NA094	179	NA	O/30	C		1	GU5646	Y	23, 105	117	
NA095	180	NA	S/30	C		?		Y		64	
NA096	181	NA	R/30	C		?		Y			
NA097	182	NA	R/30	C		?		Y			
NA098	183	NA	R/29	C		?		Y			
NA099	184	NA	P/28	C		?		Y			
NA100	185	NA	W/29	B		1-2		Y		61	
NA101	186	NA	W/30	B		1-2		Y			
NA101A	-	NA	W/30	B		?		Y			
NA102	187	NA	W/30	B		1-2		Y			
NA103	188	NA	S/30	B		?		Y		12, 103	
NA104	189	NA	O-P/30	C		1	GU5647/ GU5681	Y	23, 105	103, 117	
NA105	190	NA	R/29	B		?		Y		61, 64	
NA106	191	NA	S/30	B		?		Y			
NA107	192	NA	S/30	C		?		Y		12	
NA108	193	NA	Q/30	B		?		Y			
NA109	194	NA	R/27	D		?		Y			
NA110	195	NA	T/30	B		?		Y			

Burial No.	Previous Ref.	Site	Grid	Phase	Equiv. Site 26 Phase	Mays' Phase	RC date	Studied by Mays	Fig. No.	Table No.	Pl. No.
NA111	196	NA		?		?		Y		61	
NA112	197	NA	X/30	B		1-2	GU5648	Y	105	83, 102, 117	92
NA113	198	NA	V/30	B		1-2		Y	130		
NA114	199	NA		?		?		Y			
NA115	200	NA	N/29	D		1-2		Y			79, 80
NA116	201	NA	O/29	C		?		Y	130	65	
NA117	202	NA	T/27	C		?		Y		103	
NA118	203	NA	U/28	C		?		Y		103	
NA119	204	NA	S/30	B		?		Y			84
NA120	205	NA	Q/30	C		?		Y		64, 65	
NA121	206	NA	U/30	B		1-2		Y	90		
NA121A	-	NA	U/30	B		?		Y			
NA122	207	NA	U/28	C		?		Y			
NA122A	207	NA		?		1-2		Y			
NA123	208	NA	M/28	C		1-2		Y			
NA124	209	NA		?		?		Y			
NA125	210	NA	R/30	B		?		Y			
NA126	211	NA	M/29	C		?		Y			
NA127	212	NA	K/30	KC		1-2	GU5649	Y		117	
NA128	213	NA	T/27	B		1-2		Y			
NA129	214	NA		?		?		Y			
NA130	215	NA	T/30	B		?		Y			
NA131	216	NA		?		?		Y			
NA132	217	NA	T/30	B		?		Y		103	
NA133	218	NA		?							
NA134	219	NA		?		1-2		Y			
NA135	220	NA	U/28	B		?		Y			81, 82
NA136	221	NA	X/30	B		?		Y			
NA137	222	NA	V/29	C							
NA138	223	NA	W/29	C		?		Y		103	
NA139	224	NA	T/29	B		?		Y			
NA140	225	NA		?		1-2		Y		53	
NA140A	225	NA		?		?		Y			
NA141	226	NA	S/30	A							
NA142	227	NA	Q/30	B		?		Y	129		
NA142A	-	NA	Q/30	B		?		Y			
NA143	228	NA	T/29	B		1-2		Y			
NA144	229	NA	U/30	B		1-2		Y			
NA145	230	NA	S/29	B		1-2		Y	90	61	
NA146	231	NA	X/30	A		1-2	GU5650/ GU5679	Y	90, 105, 129, 130	62, 117	92, 93
NA147	232	NA		?							
NA148	233	NA	U/27	B							
NA149	234	NA	U/29	B		1-2		Y			
NA149A	234	NA	U/29	B		?		Y			
NA149B	234	NA		?		?		Y			
NA150	235	NA		?		?		Y		65	
NA151	236	NA	T/26	B		?		Y			
NA152	237	NA	T/26	E							
NA153	238	NA	O/28	B		?		Y			
NA154	239	NA	T/30	B		1-2		Y		61	
NA155	240	NA	N/29	D		?		Y			
NA156	241	NA		?		?		Y			
NA157	242	NA	N/29	B		1-2		Y		62	

Burial No.	Previous Ref.	Site	Grid	Phase	Equiv. Site 26 Phase	Mays' Phase	RC date	Studied by Mays	Fig. No.	Table No.	Pl. No.
NA158	243	NA	Q/29	B							
NA159	244	NA	Q/29	B		?		Y			
NA160	245	NA	Q/28	B		?		Y		103	
NA161	246	NA	P/28	B		?		Y			
NA162	247	NA	R/29	B		?		Y			
NA163	248	NA		?		?		Y			
NA164	249	NA	R/29	B		?		Y	23, 24		
NA165	250	NA	M/29	B		?		Y	23, 24,		
	Context 49								129, 130		
NA166	251	NA	T/29-30	B		1-2		Y		62	
NA167	252	NA	N/29	B		2	GU5651	Y	90, 105	61, 84, 117	
NA168	253	NA	P/28	B		1-2		Y	90	62	
NA169	254	NA	T/29	B		?		Y			
NA170	255	NA	T/29	A		1	GU5652	Y	90	12, 117	
NA170A	-	NA	T/29	A		?		Y		12	
NA171	256	NA	Q/29	B		1-2		Y			
NA172	257	NA	M/29	B		1-2		Y			
NA173	258	NA	M/29	A		1-2	GU5653	Y	105	61, 117	
NA174	259	NA	K/30	D		?		Y		103	
NA175	260	NA	K/30	B		?		Y			
NA176	261	NA	J/30	?		2	GU5654	Y	90	53, 61, 62, 101, 103, 117	
NA177	262	NA	J/30	?		1-2		Y		103	
NA178	263	NA	K/28	?		?		Y			21
NA179	264	NA	J/29	?		?		Y			
NA180	265	NA	J/29	?		?		Y			
NA181	266	NA	J/28	D		1-2		Y	90	53, 62, 84	41, 42
NA182	267	NA	J/28	B		?		Y			
NA183	268	NA	J/28	E		1-2		Y		84	
NA184	269	NA		?		?		Y			
NA185	270	NA	K/28	D		?		Y			
NA186	271	NA	J/27	?		?		Y			
NA187	272	NA	J/27	?		?		Y			
NA188	273	NA	J/27	?		?		Y			
NA189	274	NA	K/27	E		?		Y			
NA190	275	NA	K/27	?		1-2		Y	90	84	
NA191	276	NA	J/27	?		?		Y			
NA192	277	NA	J/26	?		?		Y			
NA193	278	NA	O/28	B		?		Y			
NA194	279	NA		?		?		Y			
NA195	280	NA	J/26	?		1-2	GU5655	Y	90	117	
NA196	281	NA	K/26	?		?		Y			
NA197	282	NA	J/26	B		1-2		Y	90	62, 84, 102	56
NA198	283	NA	K/25	D		?		Y		61, 101	
NA199	284	NA	J/25	D		2-3	GU5656	Y	90, 105	84, 117	
NA200	285	NA	J/25	D		?		Y			
NA201	286	NA		?		?		Y	23, 24		
NA202	287	NA	T/26	B		1-2		Y			52
NA203	288	NA	J/29	C		1-2		Y		84	
NA203A	-	NA		?		?		Y			
NA204	289	NA	U/30	?		1-2		Y			

Burial No.	Previous Ref.	Site	Grid	Phase	Equiv. Site 26 Phase	Mays' Phase	RC date	Studied by Mays	Fig. No.	Table No.	Pl. No.
NA205	290	NA	U/29	A		?		Y		62	
NA206	130	NA	X/29	D							
NA207	-	NA	X/30	C							
NA208	153	NA	U/30	D					130		
NA209	203	NA	U/28	C		?		Y			
NA210	253	NA	P/29	A							
NA211	264	NA	K/28	B							
NA212	-	NA	K/27	C							
NA213	284	NA	K/25	D							
NA214	250	NA	N/26	E					129, 130		6
NA215	300	NA	L-M/25-26	KA		1	GU5659	Y	105	117	
NA216	301	NA	K/26	KA		?		Y			
NA217	302	NA	K-L/24	KB		2	GU5640	Y	105	65, 84, 98, 117	
NA218	303	NA	K-L/24	KA		1-2	GU5639	Y	105	61, 62, 84, 103, 115, 117	
NA219	304	NA	K-L/23-24	AC		?		Y			
NA220	305	NA	P-Q/25	AC		?		Y			
NA221	306	NA	P/25	AC		?		Y			
NA222	307	NA	P-Q/25	AC		?		Y			
NA223	308	NA	P/24	AC		1-2	GU5638	Y	105	117	
NA224	309	NA	P/24	AB		1	GU5657/ GU5677	Y	105, 130, 118	53, 117	
NA225	310	NA	P-Q/24	AA		1		Y		103	
NA226	311	NA		?							
NA227	312&1 (1962)	NA	R/24	AC		1-2	GU5658	Y	105, 118	62, 117	
NA228	312A	NA		?							
NA229	312B	NA		?							
NA230	312c	NA		?							
NA231	313	NA	R/25	AC		?		Y			
NA232	314	NA	N/23-24	E		?		Y	130		100
NA233	315	NA	K-L/25	KB		1-2	GU5637	Y	105	103, 117	
NA233A	315	NA	K-L/25	KC		?		Y			
NA234	316	NA	K-L/25	D		2-3		Y		103	
NA235	291 (1965)	NA		?		1-2		Y		64	
NA236	294 (1965)	NA		?		?		Y			
NA237	296 (1965)	NA		B		1-2		Y			
NA238	2 (1962)	NA	R/27	?							
NA239	9 (1962)	NA	R/27	?							
NA240	4 (1962)	NA	R/27	?							
NA241	3 (1962)	NA	R-S/25	B							
NA242	-(1962)	NA	K/24	?							
NA243	-	NA	R/25	?							
NA244	-	NA	R/24	?							
NA245	-	NA	M/27	?					27		
NA246	-	NA	M/28	?					27		
NA247	-	NA	M/29	?					27		
NA248	-	NA	M/29-30	?					27		
SA001	-	SA	L-M/15	M							
SA002	XXVI	SA	L-M/15	M		3-4	GU5453	Y	90, 118	53, 103, 117	
SA003	XXV	SA	L-M/14	M		3-4	GU5454	Y	118	84, 117	33
SA004	-	SA	K-L/12-13	PM					124		

Burial No.	Previous Ref.	Site	Grid	Phase	Equiv. Site 26 Phase	Mays' Phase	RC date	Studied by Mays	Fig. No.	Table No.	Pl. No.
SA005	XXXI	SA	M/11	EM		?		Y			
SA006	-	SA	N-L/12	EM							
SA007	-	SA	M/11-12	M		?		Y			
SA008	VI	SA	N/11-12	EM		?		Y			
SA009	VII	SA	N/11-12	EM							
SA010	VIII	SA	N-O/11	EM							
SA011	-	SA	N/14	EM							
SA012	XXX	SA	N-O/12	EM		1-2	GU5455	Y	118	117	
SA013	XXVII	SA	N-P/12	M		2-3	GU5491	Y	118	102, 117	57
SA014	XXVIII	SA	N-O/12	M		2	GU5456	Y	118	117	
SA015	XXIX	SA	O-P/11-12	M		?		Y		65, 84	
SA016	-	SA	O-P/11-12	M							
SA017	XXI	SA	O-P/11	PM		4		Y	90, 124	61	
SA017A	-	SA	O-P/11	PM		?		Y	124		
SA018	XXIII	SA	P-Q/10	PM					124		
SA019	XXII	SA	P-Q/10-11	PM					124		
-	I	SA	U/13	X-XII							
SA020	-	SA	P-Q/12	PM					124		
SA021	IV	SA	Q-R/12	PM		?		Y	124		
SA022	III	SA	Q-R/12	PM					124		
SA023	V	SA	R-S/12	PM		4		Y	124	65	83
SA024	-	SA	P-Q/13	EM							
SA025	-	SA	Q/14	EM							
SA026	-	SA	P-Q/14	M							
SA027	-	SA	Q/14	M							
SA028	XVII	SA	S/11	M							
SA029	IX	SA	T/11	M		?		Y	90		30
SA030	XVI	SA	S/11	PM		?		Y	124	61	
SA031	XV	SA	T/11	M							
SA032	X	SA	T-U/14-15	M							
-	XI	SA	T/11	?							
SA033	II*	SA	T-U/14	M		3-4	GU5457	Y	118	117	
SA034	XX	SA	T-U/14	EM		1	GU5458	Y	130, 118	62, 84, 117	31
SA035	-	SA	T-U/14	EM					130, 118		
SA036	XIV	SA	U-V/14-15	M		?		Y			
SA037	-	SA	W/15	EM							
SA038	-	SA	W/14-15	EM							
SA039	-	SA	W/14	EM							
SA040	-	SA	V/14	EM							
SA041	-	SA	W/13-14	EM							
SA042	-	SA	I-J/13	M							
SA043	-	SA	J-K/13	M							
SA044	-	SA	K-L/12	PM					124		
SA045	XXIV	SA	O-P/10	PM		4		Y	124		
SA046	XIX	SA	T/13-14	EM							
SA047	-	SA		?		?		Y	90		
SA048	XII	SA	S/11	PM		4		Y	124		
SA049	XIII	SA	V/12-13	PM		4		Y	124		
SA050	XXXIV	Site 41	R/185	4.2		?		Y	59, 60	143	
SA051	XXXVI	Site 41	S/185	4.2		?		Y	59	143	
SA052	XXXVII	Site 41	R-S/184	4.2		1-2	GU5461	Y	59, 90	84, 117, 143	
SA053	XXXX	Site 41	R-S/185	4.2		1-2	GU5462	Y	59, 90	117, 143	
SA054	XXXXIb	Site 41	R-S/183	4.2		?		Y	59	143	

Burial No.	Previous Ref.	Site	Grid	Phase	Equiv. Site 26 Phase	Mays' Phase	RC date	Studied by Mays	Fig. No.	Table No.	Pl. No.
SA055	XXXXIa	Site 41	R-S/183	4.2		?		Y	59	103, 143	
SA056	XXXXII	Site 41	U-V/182	4.2		1-2	GU5463	Y	59	117, 143	
SA057	XXXVIII	Site 41	R-S/184	4.2					59	143	
SA058	XXXIX	Site 41	S/185	4.2					59		
SA059	XXXIII	Site 41	R/184	5.2					60, 61	144	
SA060	XXXII	Site 41	R/183	5.2					60, 61	144	
SA061	XXXV	Site 41	S/184-5	4.2					59		
SA062	XXXI	Site 41	X/184	5.1					61		
SA063	in section	Site 41	R/183	4.2					60		
SA064	in section	Site 41	R/185	4.2					59, 60		
SA070	Context 12	Site 52	J/182	M					51		
SA071	Context 16	Site 52	L/182	M		?		Y	51		
SA072	Context 18	Site 52	L/182	M		?		Y	51		
SA080	Context 3	Site 80	N-P/179-180	M		?		Y			
SA101	1 (1967)	SA	S-T/13	EM							
SA102	2 (1967)	SA	S-T/13	EM							
SA103	3 (1967)	SA	S-T/14	EM							
SA104	4 (1967)	SA	S-T/14	EM							
SA105	XVIII	SA	R/11	M							
SA106	V	SA	T/12	M							
SA107	-	SA	T-V/15	EM							
V01	XXXII	V	BB-CC/14	PM		?		Y	9, 124		
V02	XXXIII	V	BB/13	PM							
V03	XXXIV	V	CC/14	PM		?		Y	9A, 124		
V04	XXXV	V	AA/12	PM		4		Y	124		
V05	XXXVI	V	X-Y/12-13	PM					124		
V06	XXXVII	V	BB-CC/15	PM		4		Y	9A, 124		
V07	XXXVIII	V	AA-BB/12	PM		4		Y	124		
V08	XXXIX	V	X/12	M?							
V09	XL	V	X/12	PM					124		
V10	XLI	V	Z-AA/12	PM		?		Y	124		
V11	XLII	V	CC/14-15	PM		?		Y	9A, 124		
V12	XLIII	V	AA-BB/12	PM		?		Y	124		
V13	XLIV	V	X-Y/12-13	PM					124		
V14	XLV	V	CC/13	PM		?		Y	9A, 124		
V15	XLVI	V	CC/12	PM		?		Y	9A, 124	62, 64, 84	
V16	XLVII	V	CC/14	PM		4		Y	9A, 124		
V17	XLVIII	V	CC/15	PM		?		Y	9A, 124		
V18	XLIX	V	CC/14	PM		?		Y	9A, 90-, 124		
V19	L	V	CC/13	PM		?		Y	9A, 124	84	
V20	LI	V	AA/13	PM		4		Y			
V21	LII	V	CC/13	PM		4		Y	9A, 124		
V22	LIII Context 51	V	CC/15-16	EM		?		Y	9A, 130		
V23	LIV	V	Y-Z/12	PM		?		Y	124		
V24	LV	V	Y-Z/12	PM		?		Y	124	84	
V25	LVI Context 54	V	CC/15	M		?		Y	9A, 130		22
V26	LVII	V	Y-Z/15	PM		?		Y	124	84	29
V27	LVIII	V	CC/14-15	PM		?		Y	9A, 124		
V28	LIX	V	CC/14	EM		?		Y	9A		67
V29	LX	V	Z-AA/12	PM		?		Y	124		
V30	LXI	V	Y-Z/13	PM		?		Y	90, 124		
V31	LXII	V	CC/13	EM		?		Y	9A		

Burial No.	Previous Ref.	Site	Grid	Phase	Equiv. Site 26 Phase	Mays' Phase	RC date	Studied by Mays	Fig. No.	Table No.	Pl. No.
V32	LXIII	V	CC/14-15	EM		?		Y	9A		
V33	LXIV	V	AA/15	PM		?		Y	124	61, 84	
V34	LXV	V	CC/14-15	EM		?		Y	9A		
V35	LXVI	V	CC/14	EM		?		Y	9A		
V36	LXVII	V	CC/12-13	EM		?		Y	9A		
V37	LXVIII	V	Z-AA/15	PM		?		Y	124	84	
V38	LXIX	V	Z-AA/13	M		2-3	GU5460	Y	129, 130	53, 84, 117	
V39	LXX	V	BB-CC/14	EM		?		Y	9A		
V40	LXXI	V	CC/13	EM		?		Y	9A		
V41	LXXII	V	CC/15	EM		1-2	GU5669	Y	9A, 118	117	
V42	LXXIII	V	Z-BB/13-14	PM		4		Y	124	61	
V43	LXXIV	V	CC/14	EM		?		Y	9A		
V44	LXXV	V	CC/15	EM		?		Y	118	84	
V45	LXXVI	V	Y-Z/13	M		2	GU5459	Y	90	53, 84, 117	
V46	LXXVII	V	Y-Z/14	PM		?		Y	90, 124		
V47	LXXVIII	V	Y-AA/14-15	EM		?		Y	120, 130	12	98
V48	LXXIX	V	CC/14	EM					9A, 118		
V49	LXXX	V	AA/14	EM		?		Y			
V50	LXXXI	V	AA-BB/14-1	EM			HAR 2672		120, 129, 130	117	
V51	LXXXII	V	BB-CC/15	EM		?	HAR 2460	Y	9A, 11, 120, 129, 130, 118	12, 117	
V52	LXXXIII	V	AA/15	EM			HAR 2462		11, 120, 129, 130	117	
V53	LXXXIV	V	Z/14	EM		?		Y		12	
V54	LXXXV	V	AA/15	EM							
V55	LXXXVI	V	BB-CC/15	EM		?		Y		12	
V56	LXXXVII	V	CC-DD/15	EM			HAR 2631		9A, 129, 118	117	
V57	LXXXVIII	V	CC/15	EM		?		Y	9A		66
V58	LXXXIX	V	CC/14	PM					124		
V59	-	V	AA/15	?		?		Y		103	
V60	-	V	CC/15-16	M		?		Y			
V61	-	V	BB-CC/15	?		?		Y		84	73
V62	-	V	AA/14	?		?		Y		61	
V63	-	V	Z/14	EM		?		Y			
V64	Context 45	V	BB/13	?							
WCO001	-	WCO	H-J/23								
WCO002	W1	WCO	H-J/22			?		Y			
WCO003	W2	WCO	H/22			?		Y	129		
WCO004	W3	WCO	H/21								
WCO005	W4	WCO	A-B/22			?		Y			
WCO006	W5	WCO	B/18			?		Y			
WCO007	W6	WCO	C-D/20-21			?		Y			
WCO008	W7	WCO	F-G/15								
WCO009	W8	WCO	D-E/14			2-3	GU5515	Y	102	103, 117	
WCO010	W9	WCO	A-B/14			3-4	GU5513	Y	90, 102	117	27
WCO011	W10	WCO	A-B/14-15			?		Y		62, 64	
WCO012	W11	WCO	A-B/14			?		Y		84	
WCO013	W12	WCO	B-C/14			?		Y		84, 98	
WCO014	W13	WCO	A-B/15			?		Y			
WCO015	W15	WCO	B-C/16			?		Y	90, 129		

Burial No.	Previous Ref.	Site	Grid	Phase	Equiv. Site 26 Phase	Mays' Phase	RC date	Studied by Mays	Fig. No.	Table No.	Pl. No.
WCO016	W16	WCO	A-B/15-16			?		Y	129		28
WCO017	W17	WCO	A-B/17			?		Y	90, 129	84	
WCO018	W18	WCO	A-B/17			?		Y			65
WCO019	W19	WCO	A-B/18			?		Y	129		
WCO020	W20	WCO	A/19			?		Y			
WCO021	W21	WCO	B/19			?		Y			
WCO021A	-	WCO				?		Y			
WCO022	W22	WCO	A-B/19-20			?		Y			
WCO023	W23	WCO	A-B/20			?		Y			
WCO024	W24	WCO	A/21								
WCO025	W25	WCO	A-B/21								
WCO026	W26	WCO	A-B/21-22			?		Y	90, 129		
WCO027	W27	WCO	A-B/23			?		Y			
WCO028	W28	WCO	B/23			2-3	GU5512	Y	90, 102	117	
WCO029	W29	WCO	B/22			?		Y			
WCO030	W30	WCO	B/22			?		Y			
WCO031	W31	WCO	B/22								
WCO032	W32	WCO	B/23			?		Y			
WCO033	W60	WCO	B/21			?		Y			
WCO034	W34	WCO	C-D/23			?		Y			
WCO035	W35	WCO	C/23			?		Y			
WCO035A	W35A	WCO	C/22			?		Y			
WCO036	W36	WCO	C-D/22			?		Y		54	
WCO037	W37	WCO	C-D/22			?		Y	90, 129	84	
WCO038	W38	WCO	C/21			?		Y			
WCO039	W39	WCO	C-D/20			?		Y		103	
WCO040	W40	WCO	C-D/20			?		Y			
WCO041	W41	WCO	C/19			?		Y			62
WCO042	W42	WCO	C-D/19			?		Y			
WCO043	W43	WCO	C-D/18								
WCO044	W44	WCO	C-D/17			3-4	GU5495	Y	102	117	
WCO045	W46	WCO	C-D/16			3-4	GU5516	Y	102, 124	84, 117	69,70
WCO046	W49	WCO	A/23								
WCO047	-	WCO	B/22								
WCO048	W61	WCO	A-B/21								
WCO049	-	WCO	A-B/19								
WCO050	-	WCO	B/17								
WCO051	W59	WCO	B-C/16								
WCO052	W51	WCO	B-C/15			?		Y			
WCO053	W14	WCO	B-C/15								
WCO054	-	WCO	C/22								
WCO055	W56	WCO	C/21								
WCO056	W90	WCO	C-D/20			?		Y	90		76
WCO057	W62	WCO	C-E/19			?		Y			
WCO058	W81	WCO	C-D/18			?		Y			85, 86, 87, 88
WCO059	W45	WCO	C-D/17			?		Y		53, 62	
WCO060	W71	WCO	C/16-17								
WCO061	W81	WCO	C/16								
WCO062	W85	WCO	C/16			?		Y			
WCO063	W84	WCO	C/16			?		Y			
WCO064	-	WCO	C-D/16								
WCO065	W95	WCO	C-D/15								
WCO066	W75	WCO	C-D/14								
WCO067	W47	WCO	C-D/15			?		Y			

Burial No.	Previous Ref.	Site	Grid	Phase	Equiv. Site 26 Phase	Mays' Phase	RC date	Studied by Mays	Fig. No.	Table No.	Pl. No.
WCO068	W122	WCO	C-D/14-15			?		Y			
WCO069	W92	WCO	D-E/14			?		Y			
WCO070	W93	WCO	D-E/14			1-2	GU5494	Y	102	117	
WCO071	W83	WCO	C-D/15-16			?		Y	90		
WCO072	W82	WCO	D/16			?		Y			
WCO073	-	WCO	D/17								
WCO074	-	WCO	D/17								
WCO075	-	WCO	D/17								
WCO076	-	WCO	D/17								
WCO077	W86	WCO	D/17-18			?		Y			
WCO078	W87	WCO	D-E/17-18			?		Y	90	53	
WCO079	W88	WCO	D-E/17			?		Y			
WCO080	W64	WCO	D/18			?		Y		115	
WCO081	W63	WCO	D/19			?		Y			
WCO082	W78	WCO	D/19			?		Y			
WCO083	W62	WCO	D-E/19								
WCO084	-	WCO	D/19								
WCO085	W48	WCO	D-E/20			?		Y			
WCO086	W66	WCO	D/21								
WCO087	W58	WCO	D/20-21			?		Y			
WCO088	W57	WCO	D-E/20-21			?		Y			
WCO089	W55	WCO	C-E/21			?		Y			
WCO090	-	WCO	D/22								
WCO091	W53	WCO	D-E/22-23			?		Y			
WCO092	W65	WCO	D-E/23			?		Y			
WCO093	W52	WCO	D-E/23			?		Y	90	61, 62	
WCO094	W120	WCO	E-F/23								
WCO095	-	WCO									
WCO096	-	WCO	E-F/22-23								
WCO097	W74	WCO	E-F/22			?		Y	129		
WCO098	W73	WCO	F/22			?		Y			
WCO099	W68	WCO	E-F/22			?		Y	129	103	
WCO100	W67	WCO	E-F/21-22			?		Y			
WCO101	W75	WCO	E-F/21								
WCO102	W76	WCO	F/21								
WCO103	W96	WCO	D-E/20			?		Y			
WCO104	W80	WCO	E-F/20			?		Y			
WCO105	W79	WCO	E/19-20						129		
WCO106	W106	WCO	E/19								
WCO107	W117	WCO	E/19			?		Y		103	
WCO108	W104	WCO	D-E/18-19			?		Y			
WCO109	W89	WCO	E-F/17			?		Y			
WCO110	W100	WCO	E-F/17			?		Y			
WCO111	-	WCO	D-E/16-17								
WCO112	-	WCO	D/16								
WCO113	-	WCO	E/16								
WCO114	-	WCO	E/16								
WCO115	W91	WCO	E-F/15			?		Y			51
WCO115A	-	WCO	E-F/15			?		Y		103	
WCO116	-	WCO	E-F/15								
WCO117	W138	WCO	F-G/14-15			?		Y		84	
WCO118	W98	WCO	E-F/14			2	GU5503/ GU5682	Y	102	117	
WCO119	W99	WCO	E-F/14			1-2	GU5502	Y	102	117	
WCO120	-	WCO	GH/14								

Burial No.	Previous Ref.	Site	Grid	Phase	Equiv. Site 26 Phase	Mays' Phase	RC date	Studied by Mays	Fig. No.	Table No.	Pl. No.
WCO121	-	WCO	G/14								
WCO122	W133	WCO	G-H/14			?		Y	90		
WCO123	W134	WCO	G/14								
WCO124	W132	WCO	G-H/14-15			?		Y	90		
WCO125	W168	WCO	G-H/15			?		Y	90		
WCO125A	-	WCO	G-H/15			?		Y			
WCO126	-	WCO	G/21								
WCO127	-	WCO	G-H/21								
WCO128	W97	WCO	G-H/21								
WCO129	-	WCO	H/22								
WCO130	W70	WCO	F-G/22-23			2-3	GU5493	Y	102	62, 103, 117	
WCO131	W54	WCO	G-H/23			?		Y			
WCO132	-	WCO	F/23								
WCO133	W77	WCO	F-G/23								
WCO134	W72	WCO	C-D/15			?		Y			
WCO135	W69	WCO	F/22								
WCO136	W131	WCO	H/14								
WCO137	W101	WCO	B/18			?		Y	90, 129	84, 103	59
WCO138	W102	WCO	B-C/17			2-3	GU5499	Y	90, 102, 129	117	
WCO139	W103	WCO	B/17			2	GU5498	Y	102	84, 117	
WCO140	W105	WCO	B-C/16			?		Y	129		
WCO141	W124	WCO	C-D/15								
WCO142	W123	WCO	C-D/16			?		Y		102	
WCO143	W119	WCO	C-E/19						129		
WCO144	W121	WCO	D/18			?		Y			
WCO145	-	WCO	D/18								
WCO146	W156	WCO	E-F/18			?		Y	90		
WCO147	W149	WCO	D-E/18			?		Y			
WCO148	-	WCO	E/18								
WCO149	W150	WCO	D-E/18			?		Y			
WCO150	-	WCO	D-E/17-18								
WCO151	-	WCO	D-E/17								
WCO152	-	WCO	D/17								
WCO153	W140	WCO	D-E/17			3-4	GU5497	Y	102	117	
WCO154	W139	WCO	D-E/16			?		Y			
WCO155	W158	WCO	D-E/16			?		Y	129		
WCO156	W141= W100	WCO	E-F/16			2-3	GU5496	Y	102	117	
WCO157	W151	WCO	E/16								
WCO158	-	WCO	D-E/15-16								
WCO159	-	WCO	D-E/15-16								
WCO160	-	WCO	D-E/15-16								
WCO161	-	WCO	D-E/15-16								
WCO162	W143	WCO	E-G/14			1-2	GU5517/ GU5678	Y	90, 102	53, 117	
WCO163	W146	WCO	E-F/15-16			?		Y			
WCO164	W147	WCO	E/16			?		Y		103	
WCO164A	-	WCO	E/16			?		Y		53, 84	
WCO165	W145	WCO	E-G/16			?		Y	129	84	
WCO165A	-	WCO	E-G/16			?		Y			
WCO166	W157	WCO	F-G/16			?		Y			
WCO167	W157	WCO	F-G/16			?		Y			
WCO168	W159	WCO	F-G/16			?		Y			
WCO169	W160	WCO	F-G/17-18			?		Y			

Burial No.	Previous Ref.	Site	Grid	Phase	Equiv. Site 26 Phase	Mays' Phase	RC date	Studied by Mays	Fig. No.	Table No.	Pl. No.
WCO170	W162	WCO	F-G/18			2-4	GU5492	Y	102, 129	84, 117	39, 40
WCO171	-	WCO	F/18								
WCO172	-	WCO	G/18								
WCO173	W110	WCO	F-G/18-19			?		Y	90	61	
WCO174	W119	WCO	F-G/19			?		Y		62	
WCO175	W111	WCO	G/20			?		Y			
WCO176	W107	WCO	F-G/20			?		Y		101	49
WCO177	W126	WCO	G/21								
WCO178	-	WCO	G/21								
WCO179	W117	WCO	G-H/21			1-2	GU5501	Y	102	117	20
WCO180	W106	WCO	G/21								
WCO181	W118	WCO	G/21			2-3	GU5500	Y	102	103, 117	
WCO182	-	WCO	F-G/22								
WCO183	W142	WCO	G-H/22-23			?		Y	102		
WCO184	W155	WCO	G-J/17			2	GU5514	Y		54, 115, 117	74
WCO185	W163 = 196	WCO	G/16								
WCO186	W161	WCO	G/16			?		Y			
WCO187	W153	WCO	G-H/16			?		Y			
WCO188	W154	WCO	F-G/16								
WCO189	-	WCO	G/16								
WCO190	W152	WCO	G/16								
WCO191	W136	WCO	G-H/15			?		Y			
WCO192	W137	WCO	G-H/15	IV		?		Y			
WCO193	W135	WCO	G/15			?		Y			
WCO194	-	WCO	C/16								
WCO195	W148	WCO	E-F/15-16			?		Y			
WCO196	-	WCO									
WCO197	-	WCO	G/22								
WCO198	-	WCO	F-G/20								
WCO199	W94	WCO	C/20			?		Y	90	103	
WCO200	W108	WCO	?			?		Y		84, 103	
WCO201	W129	WCO	?			?		Y			48
WCO202	W130	WCO	?			?		Y			
WCO203	W144	WCO	E-G/14			?		Y		65	
WCO204	W167	WCO	G/20			?		Y			
WCO21A	W50	WCO	B/19								
-	W33	WCO	B/21								
-	W109	WCO	?	VI-IX							
-	W112	WCO	?	VI-IX							
-	W113	WCO	?	VI-IX							
-	W114	WCO	?	VI-IX							
-	W115	WCO	?	VI-IX							
-	W116	WCO	?	VI-IX							
-	W125	WCO	E/21	VI-IX							
-	W127	WCO	?	VI-IX							
-	W128	WCO	?	VI-IX							
-	W164	WCO	?	VI-IX							
-	W165	WCO	?	VI-IX							
-	W166	WCO	?	VI-IX							

Bibliography

Abbreviations

Borthwick, Borthwick Institute for Archives, University of York

BMC, Broke, G.C., 1916, *English Coins in the British Museum: The Norman Kings*

EH 1988, *English Heritage Monument Class Descriptions: Cemeteries (Romano-British)*. English-heritage.org.uk

Interim Reports, Interim Reports of the Wharram Research Project from 1953-1990 (various titles and editors)

LRBC II, Carson, R.A.G., Hill, P.V. and Kent, J.P., 1960, *Late Roman Bronze Coinage AD 324-498 II*

PR WP, Parish Registers Wharram Percy

RCHME 1962, *Inventory of the Historical Monuments in the City of York, Volume I, Ebvracvm, Roman York*

References

Abrahams, P., 1977, *Soil Report From Wharram Percy, North Yorkshire,* Ancient Monuments Lab. Rep. 2360

Abramson, S.J, 1997, 'Adrenal Neoplasms in Children', *Radiol. Clin. North Am.,* 35, 1415-53

Adams, J.E., 1997, 'Vitamin D' in Feldman, D., Glorieux, F. and Pike, J. (eds), *Radiology of Rickets and Osteomalacia,* 619-42 (New York)

Ali, A., Tetalman, M.R., Fordham, E.W., Turner, D.A., Chiles, J.T., Patel, S.L., and Schmidt, K.D., 1980, 'Distribution of Hypertrophic Pulmonary Osteoarthropathy', *Am. J. Roentgenology* 134, 771-80

Aloia, J.F., Vaswani, A.N., Yeh, J.K., Ross, P., Ellis, K. and Cohn, S.H., 1983, 'Determinants of Bone Mass in Postmenopausal Women', *Arch. Intern. Med.* 143, 1700-1704

Ambrosiani, K., 1981, *Viking Age Combs, Comb Making and Comb Makers in the Light of Finds from Birka and Ribe,* Stockholm Studies in Archaeology 2 (Stockholm)

Amis, P., 1968, 'Some Domestic Vessels of Southern Britain: a Social and Technical Analysis', *J. Ceram. Hist.* 2

Anderson, D.L., Thompson, G.W. and Popovich, F., 1976, 'Age of Attainment of Mineralisation Stages of the Permanent Dentition', *J. Forensic Sci.* 21, 191-200

Andersen, J.G. and Manchester, K., 1992, 'The Rhinomaxillary Syndrome in Leprosy: A Clinical, Radiological and Palaeopathological Study', *Int. J. Osteoarchaeol.* 2, 121-9

Anderson, T., 1986, 'The Churchyard on the Folkebibliotekstomt (Library Site), Trondheim. An Interim Osteological Report', in Anderson, T. and Göthberg, H., *Olavskirchens Kirkegård. Humanosteologisk Analyse og Faseinndeling,* Fortiden I Trondheim Bygrunn: Folkebibliotekstomten, Meddelelser Nr 1, 1-15 (Trondheim)

Anderson, T., 1994, 'Medieval Example of Cleft Lip and Palate from St Gregory's Priory, Canterbury', *The Cleft Palate – Craniofacial J.* 31, 466-72

Anderson, T., 1997, 'A Medieval Case of Bilateral Humerus Varus', *J. Paleopathology* 9, 143-6

Anderson, T. and Andrews, J., 1993, 'A Recently Excavated Odontome From Medieval Canterbury, Kent', *Int. J. Osteoarchaeol.* 3, 99-104

Annett, M. and Kilshaw, D., 1983, 'Right and Left Hand Skill II: Estimating the Parameters of the Distribution of L-R Differences in Males and Females', *Br. J. Psychology* 74, 269-83

Arcini, C., 1999, *Health and Disease in Early Lund,* Investigationes de Antiqvitatibus Urbis Lundae VIII (Lund)

Atkin, M., Carter, A. and Evans, D.H., 1985, *Excavations in Norwich 1971-8, pt 2,* East Anglian Archaeol. Rep. 26

Aufderheide, A.C. and Rodriguez-Martin, C.,1998, *The Cambridge Encyclopaedia of Human Palaeopathology*

Bagchi, K. and Bose, A.K., 1962, 'Effect of Low Nutrient Intake During Pregnancy on Obstetrical Performance and Offspring', *Am. J. Clin. Nutr.* 11, 586-92

Baker, B., 1999, 'Early Manifestations of Tuberculosis in the Skeleton' in Pálfi, G., Dutour, O., Deák, J. and Hutás, I. (eds), *Tuberculosis Past and Present,* 301-7 (Budapest)

Barber, G., Watt, I. and Rogers, J., 1997, 'A Comparison of Radiological and Palaeopathological Diagnostic Criteria for Hyperostosis Frontalis Interna', *Int. J. Osteoarchaeol.* 7, 157-64

Barnard, F.P., 1917, *The Casting-Counter and the Counting Board*

Barnes, E., 1994, *Developmental Defects of the Axial Skeleton in Palaeopathology* (Niwot, Colorado)

Bass, W.M., 1987, *Human Osteology. A Laboratory and Field Manual* (3rd ed.) (Columbia)

Bateman, N.C.W, 1997, 'The Early 11th to Mid 12th Century Graveyard at Guildhall, City of London' in de Boe, G. and Verhaege, F. (eds), *Death and Burial in Medieval Europe,* Papers of the Medieval Europe Brugge 1997 Conference, Volume 2, Instituut voor het Archeologisch Patrimonium, 115-20 (Zellik)

Baumgartener, E. and Krueger, I., 1988, *Phonix aus and und asche, glas des mittelalters* (Munich)

Bayley, J.,1976, Ancient Monuments Lab. Rep. 2293

Bayley, J., nd, 'The analysis of some glass from Wharram Percy, Yorks', Ancient Monuments Lab. Rep. 3701

Bayley, J., and Butcher, S., 2004, *Roman Brooches in Britain. A Technological and Typological Study based on the Richborough Collection*. Reps Res. Comm. Soc. Antiq. London No. 68

Bayley, J., Foard, G. and Simpson, G., 1981,'An Iron Age disc brooch from Wharram Percy, Yorkshire', *Antiquaries J.* 61, 346-9

Beals, K.L., Smith, C.L. and Dodd, S.M., 1983, 'Climate and the Evolution of Brachycephalisation', *Am. J. Phys. Anthropol.* 62, 425-37

Becker, C., 2001, Bone Points – no longer a mystery? Evidence from the Slavic Urban Fortification of Berlin-Spandau, in Choyke, A.M. and Bartosiewicz, L., *Crafting Bone: Skeletal Technologies through Time and Space,* Br. Archaeol. Rep. Int. Series 937, 129-48

Bell, R., 1987, 'Conclusions' in *Wharram III,* 189-220

Bella Estate, 1806, *Survey and Valuation of the Estate of Sir Henry Englefield Barot, and George Isted Esqr. Situate in the Parishes of Wharram le Street and Wharram Peircey in the East Riding of the County of York*. Ms book, Birdsall Estate Office

Bennett, J.M., 1987, *Women in the Medieval English Countryside*

Beresford, M.W., 1979, 'Documentary Evidence for the History of Wharram Percy' in *Wharram I*, 5-25

Beresford, M.W., 1987, 'The Documentary Evidence', in *Wharram III*, 5-46

Beresford, M.W. and Hurst, J.G., 1990, *Wharram Percy: Deserted Medieval Village*

Berry, A.C. and Berry, R.J., 1967, 'Epigenetic Variation in the Human Cranium', *J. Anat.* 101, 361-79

Berryman, H.E. and Haun, S.J., 1996, 'Applying Forensic Techniques to Interpret Cranial Fracture Patterns in an Archaeological Specimen', *Int. J. Osteoarchaeol.* 6, 2-9

Bessac, J.-C., 1987, *L'outillage traditionnel du tailleur de pierre de l'Antiquité à nos jours*, Revue Archéologique de Narbonnaise, Supplément 14 (Paris)

Bevan, B., 1999, 'Land, life, death, regeneration: interpreting a middle Iron Age landscape in eastern Yorkshire' in Bevan, B. (ed.), *Northern Exposure: interpretative devolution in the Iron Ages of Britain*, Leicester Archaeol. Monogr. 4

Biddle, M., 1990, *Object and Economy in Medieval Winchester,* Winchester Studies 7ii

Biller, P.P.A., 1982, 'Birth-Control in the West in the Thirteenth and Early Fourteenth Centuries', *Past and Present* 94, 3-26

Black F.L., 1975, 'Infectious Disease in Primitive Societies', *Science* 187, 515-18

Black, S. and Scheuer, L., 1997, 'The Ontogenic Development of the Cervical Rib', *Int. J. Osteoarchaeol.* 7, 2-10

Boddington, A., 1987, 'Raunds Northamptonshire: analysis of a country churchyard', *World Archaeol.* 18.3, 411-25

Boddington, A., (ed.), 1996, *Raunds Furnells, The Anglo-Saxon Church and Churchyard*, Engl. Heritage Archaeol. Rep. 7

Bogin, B., 1988, *Patterns of Human Growth*

Booth, J., 1984, *Sylloge of Coins of the British Isles 48: Northern Museums*

Boucher, B.J., 1957, 'Sex Differences in the Foetal Pelvis', *Am. J. Phys. Anthropol.* 15, 581-600

Boyle, A. and Keevill, G., 1998, 'To the Praise of the Dead and Anatomie: The Analysis of Post-Mediaeval Burials at St Nicholas, Sevenoaks, Kent, in Cox, M. (ed.), *Grave Concerns*, Counc. Br. Archaeol. Res. Rep. 113, 85-95

Brahee, D.D. and Guebert, G.M., 2000, 'Tortuosity of the Vertebral Artery Resulting in Vertebral Erosion', *J. Manipulative Physiol. Ther.* 23, 48-51

Brickley, M. and Miles, A., 1999, *The Cross Bones Burial Ground, Redcross way Southwark, London*, Mus. London Archaeol. Serv. Monogr. 3

Bridges, P.S., 1991, 'Degenerative Joint Disease in Hunter-Gatherers and Agriculturalists From the Southeastern United States', *Am. J. Phys. Anthropol.* 85, 379-91

Bridges, P.S., 1994, 'Vertebral Arthritis and Physical Activities in the Prehistoric Southeastern United States' *Am. J. Phys. Anthropol.* 93, 83-93

Bridges, P.S., 1996, 'Skeletal Biology and Behavior in Ancient Humans', *Evol. Anthropol.* 4, 112-20

Brodie, N., 1994, '*The Neolithic - Bronze Age Transition in Britain*. Br. Archaeol. Rep., Br. Ser. 238

Bronk Ramsey, C., 1995, 'Radiocarbon calibration and analysis of stratigraphy', *Radiocarbon* 37, 425-30

Bronk Ramsey, C., 1998, 'Probability and dating', *Radiocarbon* 40, 461-74

Bronk Ramsey, C., 2000, 'Comment on "The use of Bayesian statistics for 14C dates of chronological ordered samples: a critical analysis"', *Radiocarbon* 42, 199-202

Brook, A.H., 1984, 'A Unifying Aetiological Explanation for Anomalies of Human Tooth Number and Size', *Arch. Oral Biol.* 29, 373-8

Brothwell, D.R., 1963, *Digging up bones* (1st ed.)

Brothwell, D.R., 1972, *Digging Up Bones* (2nd ed.)

Brothwell, D.R., 1972, 'Palaeodemography and earlier British populations', *World Archaeol.*, 4, 75-87

Brothwell, D.R., 1981, *Digging Up Bones* (3rd ed.)

Brothwell D.R. and Browne, S., 1994, 'Pathology' in Lilley, J.M., Stroud, G., Brothwell, D.R. and Williamson, M.H. (eds), *The Jewish Burial Ground at Jewbury,* Archaeol. York 12/3, 457-94

Brothwell, D.R., Powers, R., Hirst, S.M., Wright, S.M. and Gauthier, S., 2000, 'The Human Bones' in Rahtz, P., Hirst, S.M. and Wright, S.M., (eds) *Cannington Cemetery*, Britannia Monogr. Ser. 17, 131-256

Brown, D., 1990, 'Dice, a Games-Board, and Playing Pieces' in Biddle, 692-706

Bryant, A., 1829, *Map of the East Riding of Yorkshire from an Actual Survey by A. Bryant, In the years 1827 and 1828*, scale one inch to a statute mile [1:63360]

Buck, C.E., Cavanagh, W.G. and Litton, C.D., 1996, *Bayesian Approach to Interpreting Archaeological Data*

Buck, C.E., Christen, J.A, Kenworthy, J.B, and Litton, C.D., 1994, 'Estimating the duration of archaeological activity using 14C determinations', *Oxford J. Archaeol.*, 13, 229-40

Buck, C.E., Kenworthy, J.B., Litton, C.D. and Smith, A.F.M., 1991, 'Combining archaeological and radiocarbon information: a Bayesian approach to calibration', *Antiquity* 65, 808-21

Buck, C.E., Litton, C.D., and Scott, E.M., 1994, 'Making the most of radiocarbon dating: some statistical considerations', *Antiquity* 68, 252-63

Buck, C.E., Litton, C.D. and Smith, A.F.M., 1992, 'Calibration of radiocarbon results pertaining to related archaeological events', *J. Archaeol. Sci.*, 19, 497-512

Buck, C.E., Christen, J.A. and James, G.N., 1999, 'BCal: An on-line Bayesian radiocarbon calibration tool', *Internet Archaeol.* 7, http:intarch.ac.uk/journal/issue7/buck_index.html

Buckland, P.C., 1984, 'The Anglian Tower and the use of Jurassic limestone in York' in Addyman, P.V. and Black, V.E. (eds), *Archaeological Papers from York presented to M.W. Barley*, 51-7

Buckland, P.C., 1988, 'The Stones of York. Building Materials in Roman Yorkshire' in Price and Wilson (eds), 237-87

Buckland-Wright, J.C., Spring, M.W., Mak, R.H.K., Turner, C., Compston, J., Vedi, S., Haycock, G.B. and Chantler, C., 1990, 'Quantitative Microfocal Radiography of Children with Renal Osteodystrophy; Comparison with Laboratory and Histological Findings', *Br. J. Radiol.* 63, 609-14

Buckley, D.G. and Major, H., 1998, 'Quernstones' in Crummy, N., *The post Roman small finds from excavations in Colchester 1971-85*, Colchester Archaeol. Rep. 5, 36-9

Buhr, A.J. and Cooke, A.M., 1959, 'Fracture Patterns', *Lancet* 1, 531-6

Buikstra, J.E. and Cook, D.C., 1981, 'Pre-Columbian Tuberculosis in West-Central Illinois: Prehistoric Disease in Biocultural Perspective' in Buikstra, J.E. (ed.), *Prehistoric Tuberculosis in the Americas*, Northwestern University Archaeological Program, Scientific Papers No. 5, 115-39 (Evanston)

Bullough, V. and Campbell, C., 1980, 'Female Longevity and Diet in the Middle Ages', *Speculum* 55, 317-25

Butler, L.A.S., 1964, 'Minor medieval monumental sculpture in the East Midlands', *Archaeol. J.* 121, 111-53

Butler, L.A.S., 1987, 'Symbols on Medieval Memorials', *Archaeol. J.* 144, 246-55

Buxton, L.H.D., 1937, 'The Anthropology of Medieval Oxford', *Oxoniensia* 2, 118-28

Buxton, L.H.D., 1938, 'Platymeria and Platycnemia', *J. Anat.* 73, 31-6

Capasso, L., 1997, 'Osteoma: Palaeopathology and Phylogeny', *Int. J. Osteoarchaeol.* 7, 615-20

Challis, A.J. and Harding, D.W. 1975, *Later Prehistory from the Trent to the Tyne*, Br. Archaeol. Rep. 20

Chambers, C.H., 1950, 'Congenital Anomalies of the Tarsal Navicular With Particular Reference to Calcaneo-Navicular Coalition', *Br. J. Radiol.* 23, 580-86

Chaplin, R.E. and Barnetson, L.P., 1980, 'Animal bones', in Stead, I.M., *Rudston Roman Villa* 149-161

Charleston, R.J., 1980, 'Glass of the high medieval period', *Bulletin de l'Association International pour l'Histoire du Verre* 8, 65-76

Clarke, R., 2006, 'Rivenhall revisited: further excavations in the churchyard of St Mary and All Saints 1999', Essex Archaeol. Hist. 35 (2004) 26-77

Clay, R.M., 1909, *The Mediaeval Hospitals of England*

Colgrave, B. and Mynors, R.A.B. (eds), 1969, *Bede's Ecclesiastical History of the English People*

Connell, B., 1997, 'Scurvy Among The Juvenile Skeletal Remains From Wharram Percy', unpubl.

Connell, B. and White, W., forthcoming, 'The Human Bone' in Steele, A. (ed.), *Excavations at the Monastery of St Saviour, Bermondsey – Southwark*

Cooke, C. and Rowbotham, T.C., 1968, 'Dental Report', in Wenham, L.P. (ed.), *The Romano-British Cemetery at Trentholme Drive, York*, 177-216

Cookson, P.J., 1974, 'Delayed Osteoblastic Metastasis From a Childhood Bronchial Carcinoid Tumour', *Hum. Pathol.* 5, 493-6

Cool, H.E.M., 2004, 'An Overview of the Sites' in *Wharram IX*, 341-6

Corder, P., 1937, 'A pair of fourth-century Romano-British pottery kilns near Crambeck', *Antiq. J.* 17, 392-413

Corder, P. and Kirk, J.L., 1932, *A Roman Villa at Langton, near Malton, East Yorkshire*, Roman Malton Dist. Rep. 4

Cox, M., 1999, 'The Human Bones' in Haughton, C. and Powesland, D. (eds), *West Heslerton, The Anglian Cemetery. Volume I: The Excavation and Discussion of the Evidence*, 172-88

Cox, T., Cox, S. and Thirlaway, M., 1983, 'The Psychological and Physiological Response to Stress' in Gale, A. and Edwards, J.A. (eds), *Physiological Correlates of Human Behaviour* 1, 255-76

Creighton, J., 1999, 'The Pottery' in Halkon and Millett, 141-64

Croft, P., Coggon, D., Cruddas, M. and Cooper, C., 1992, 'Osteoarthritis of the Hip: An Occupational Disease in Farmers', *Br. Med. J.* 304, 1269-72

Crook, J., 2000, *The Architectural Setting of the Cult of Saints in the Early Christian West c. 300-1200*

Cumberpatch, C.G., 2002, 'The Pottery' in Roberts, 169-226

Cutts, E.L., 1849, *A Manual for the Study of the Sepulchral Slabs and Crosses of the Middle Ages*

Daniell, C., 1997, *Death and Burial in Medieval England 1066-1550* (London and New York)

Davies, P.D., Humphries, M.J., Byfield, S.P., Nunn, A.J., Darbyshire, J.H., Citron K.M. and Fox, W., 1984, 'Bone and Joint Tuberculosis. A Survey of Notifications in England and Wales', *J. Bone Joint Surg.* 66B, 326-30

Davis, P.J. and Brook, A.H., 1986, 'The Presentation of Talon Cusp: Diagnosis, Clinical Features, Associations and Possible Aetiology', *Br. Dental J.* 160, 84-8

Dawes, J., 1980, 'The Human Bones' in Dawes and Magilton, 19-120

Dawes, J.D and Magilton, J.R, 1980, *The Cemetery of St Helen-on-the-Walls, Aldwark*, Archaeol. York 12/1

Day, S.P., 1996, 'Dogs, Deer and Diet at Star Carr: A Reconsideration of C-isotope Evidence From Early Mesolithic Dog Remains From the Vale of Pickering, Yorkshire, England', *J. Archaeol. Sci.* 23, 783-7

Dehling, H., and van der Plicht, J., 1993, 'Statistical problems in calibrating radiocarbon dates', *Radiocarbon* 35, 239-44

de Smet, L., 1998, 'Avascular Necrosis of the Metacarpal Head', *J. Hand Surg.* 23B, 552-4

Dias, G. and Tayles, N., 1997, "Abscess Cavity' – A Misnomer', *Int. J. Osteoarchaeol.* 7, 548-54

Dickinson, B. and Hartley, B., 2004, 'The samian' in Didsbury, 169-70

Didsbury, P., 2000, 'The Iron Age and Roman Pottery' in *Wharram VIII*, 57-9

Didsbury, P., 2004, 'The Iron Age and Roman pottery' in *Wharram IX*, 139-83

Dobney, K. and Brothwell, D., 1987, 'A Method for Evaluating the Amount of Dental Calculus on Teeth From Archaeological Sites', *J. Archaeol. Sci.* 14, 343-51

Down, A., 1978, *Chichester Excavations III*

Dykes, W., 1836a, 'Plan of an Estate comprising Wharram Percy, Bella and Wharram Grange in the East Riding of the County of York, the Property of Henry Willoughby Esq[re]', Birdsall Estate Office, Bi M 21

Dykes, W., 1836b, 'Plan of an Estate comprising Wharram le Street (*sic*), Bella and Wharram Grange in the East Riding of the County of York, the Property of Henry Willoughby Esq[re]', surveyed 1836, Borthwick PR WP9/5

Earnshaw, J.R., 1971, Medieval Grave Slabs from the Bridlington District. *Yorkshire Archaeol. J.* 42, 333-44

Eastell, R., 1993, 'The Role of Calcium and Exercise in the Prevention of Postmenopausal Osteoporosis', *J. Obstet. Gynaecol.* 13, Suppl. 1, 5-7

Eaton, S.B., Konner, M. and Shostak, M., 1988, 'Stone Agers in the Fast Lane: Chronic Degenerative Diseases in Evolutionary Perspective', *Am. J. Med.* 84, 739-49

Edynak, G.J., 1976, 'Life Styles From Skeletal Material: A Mediaeval Yogoslav Example' in Giles, E. and Friedlaender, J.S. (eds), *The Measures of Man: Methodologies in Biological Anthropology*, 408-32 (New York)

Egan, G., 1998, *The Medieval Household. Daily Living c. 1150-c. 1450*, Medieval Finds from Excavations in London 6

Egan, G., 2005, *Material Culture in London in an Age of Transition. Tudor and Stuart period Finds c. 1450-c. 1700 from Excavations at Riverside Sites in Southwark*, Mus. London Archaeol. Serv. Monogr. 19

Eisenstein, S., 1978, 'Spondylolysis. A Skeletal Investigation of Two Population Groups', *J. Bone Joint Surg.* 60B, 488-94

Eley, J. and Bayley, J., 1975, *Stonar Human Bones*, Ancient Monuments Lab. Rep. 1903

Ellis, H.A. and Peart, K.M., 1973, 'Azotaemic Renal Osteodystrophy: A Quantitative Study on Iliac Bone', *J. Clin. Pathol.* 26, 83-101

El-Najjar, M.Y., Ryan, D.J., Turner, C.G. and Lozoff, B., 1976, 'The Etiology of Porotic Hyperostosis Among the Prehistoric and Historic Anasazi Indians of the Southwestern United States', *Am. J. Phys. Anthropol.* 44, 477-88

Escobar, V., Melnick, M. and Conneally, P.M., 1977, 'The Inheritance of Bilateral Rotation of Maxillary Central Incisors', *Am. J. Phys. Anthropol.* 45, 109-116

Eshed, V., Latimer, B., Greenwald, C.M., Jellema, L.M., Rothschild, B.M., Wish-Baratz, S. and Hershkovitz, I., 2002 'Button Osteoma: Its Etiology and Pathophysiology', *Am. J. Phys. Anthropol.* 118, 217-30

Ettinger, B., Black, D.M., Nevitt, M.C., Rundle, A.C., Cauley, J.A., Cummings, S.R. *et al.*, 1992, 'Contribution of Vertebral Deformities to Chronic Back Pain and Disability', *J. Bone Miner. Res.* 7, 449-55

Evans, J., 1989, 'Crambeck; the development of a major northern pottery industry', in Wilson, P.R. (ed.), *The Crambeck Roman Pottery Industry*, Yorkshire Archaeol. Soc., 43-90

Evans, J., 2004, 'The Iron Age and Roman Pottery' in *Wharram VIII*, 312-24

Evans, J. with Creighton, J., 1999, 'The Hawling Road ceramic series' in Halkon and Millett, 200-229

Eveleth, P.B. and Tanner, J.M., 1990, *Worldwide Variation in Human Growth*, (2nd ed.)

Everson, P. and Stocker, D., 1999, *The Corpus of Anglo-Saxon Stone Sculpture Volume V. Lincolnshire*

Fazekas, I.G. and Kósa, F., 1978, *Forensic Foetal Osteology* (Budapest)

Feldesman, M.R., 1992, 'Femur/Stature Ratio and Estimates of Stature in Children', *Am. J. Phys. Anthropol.* 87, 447-59

Feldman, F. and Johnston, A., 1973, 'Intraosseous Ganglion', *Am. J. Roentgenology* 118, 328-43

Field, R.K., 1965, 'Worcestershire Peasant Buildings, household Goods and Farming Equipment in the Later Middle Ages', *Medieval Archaeol.* 9, 105-45

Fildes, V.A., 1986, *Breasts, Bottles and Babies. A History of Infant Feeding*

Fingerlin, I., 1971, *Gürtel des hohen und späten Mittelalters*

Finnegan, M., 1978, 'Non-Metric Variation of the Infracranial Skeleton', *J. Anat.* 125, 23-37

Fiskars Aktiebolags, 1997, *Illustrerad Katalog å Fiskars Aktiebolags tillverkning af Finsmiden*, Facsimile reproduction (Helsinki)

Foy, D. and Sennequier, G., 1989, *A travers le verre du moyen age a la rennaissance*, Musee Departemental des Antiquites (Rouen)

Fredrickson, B.E., Baker, D., McHolick, W.J., Yuan, H.A. and Lubicky, J.P., 1984, 'The Natural History of Spondylolysis and Spondylolisthesis', *J. Bone Joint Surg.* 66A, 699-707

Freeman, J.V., Cole, T.J., Chinn, S., Jones, P.R.M., White, E.M. and Preece, M.A., 1995, 'Cross-Sectional Stature and Weight Reference Curves for the UK, 1990', *Arch. Dis. in Child,* 73 17-24

Gall, E.A., Bennett, G.A. and Bauer, W., 1951, 'Generalised Hypertrophic Osteoarthropathy', *Am. J. Pathol.* 27, 349-85

Garn, S.M., 1970, *The Earlier Gain and Later Loss of Cortical Bone* (Springfield)

Garn, S.M., Lewis, A.B. and Bonne, B., 1962, 'Third Molar Formation and Its Developmental Course', *The Angle Orthodontist* 32, 270-79

Gejvall, N-G., 1960, *Westerhus. Medieval Population and Church in the Light of the Skeletal Remains* (Lund)

Gelfand, A.E., and Smith, A.F.M., 1990, 'Sampling approaches to calculating marginal densities', *J. Am. Stat. Assoc.*, 85, 398-409

Gies, F. and Gies, J., 1990, *Life in a Medieval Village*

Gilchrist, R. and Sloane, B., 2005, *Requiem. The Medieval Monastic Cemetery in Britain*

Gilks, W.R., Richardson, S., and Spiegelhalter, D.J., 1996, *Markov Chain Monte Carlo in Practice*

Gilmour, B.J.J. and Stocker, D. (eds), 1986, *St Mark's Church and Cemetery*, Archaeol. Lincoln 13/1

Gittos, H., 2002, 'Creating the sacred: Anglo-Saxon rites for consecrating cemeteries' in Lucy and Reynolds (eds)

Glencross, B. and Stuart-Macadam, P., 2001, 'Radiographic Clues to Fractures of the Distal Humerus in Archaeological Remains', *Int. J. Osteoarchaeol.* 11, 298-310

Goldberg, P.J.P., 1986, 'Female Labour, Service and Marriage in the Late Medieval Urban North', *Northern Hist.* 22, 18-38

Goodall, A., 1979, 'Copper alloy objects' in *Wharram I,* 108-15

Goodall, A., 1991, 'The copper alloy and gold' in Armstrong, P., Tomlinson, D. and Evans, D.H., *Excavations at Lurk Lane Beverley 1979-82*, Sheffield Excavation Rep. 1, 148-54

Goodall, I., 1990, 'Knives' in Biddle, 835-60

Goodman, A.H. and Armelagos, G.J., 1985, 'Factors Affecting the Distribution of Enamel Hypoplasias Within the Human Permanent Dentition', *Am. J. Phys. Anthropol.* 68, 479-93

Goose, D.H. , 1962, 'Reduction of Palate Size in Modern Populations', *Arch. Oral Biol.* 7, 343-50

Gowland, R., 2001, 'Playing dead: implications of mortuary evidence for the social construction of childhood in Roman Britain' in Davies, G., Gardiner, A. and Lockyear, K. (eds), *TRAC 2000, Proceedings of the tenth annual Theoretical Roman Archaeology Conference*, 152-68

Graber, L.W., 1978, 'Congenital Absence of Teeth: A Review With Emphasis on Inheritance Patterns', *J. Am. Dent. Assoc.* 96, 266-75

Grahnén, H., 1956, 'Hypodontia in the Permanent Dentition; A Clinical and Genetical Investigation' *Odontologisk Revy* 7, Supplement 3

Grant, A., 1989, 'Animals in Roman Britain' in Todd, M., (ed.), *Research on Roman Britain 1960-89,* 135-46

Grauer, A.L., 1991, 'Patterns of Life and Death: The Palaeodemography of Mediaeval York', in Bush, H. and Zvelebil, M. (eds), *Health in Past Societies*, Br. Archaeol. Rep. Int. Ser. 567, 67-80

Grauer, A.L., 1993, 'Patterns of Anaemia and Infection From Mediaeval York, England' *American J. Phys. Anthropol.* 91, 203-13

Grauer, A.L. and Roberts, C.A., 1996, 'Palaeoepidemiology, Healing and Possible Treatment of Trauma in the Mediaeval Cemetery Population of St Helen-on-the-Walls, York, England', *Am. J. Phys. Anthropol.* 100, 531-44

Greenfield, G.B., 1972, 'Roentgen Appearance of Bone and Soft Tissue Changes in Chronic Renal Disease', *Am. J. Roentgenology* 116, 749-57

Greenfield, G.B., Schorsch, H.A. and Shkolnik, A., 1967, 'The Various Roentgen Appearances of Pulmonary Hypertrophic Osteoarthropathy', *Am. J. Roentgenology* 101, 927-31

Greenwood, C., 1818, *Map of the County of York*, surveyed in 1815, 1816 and 1817. [1:87120]

Grupe, G. and Bach, H., 1993, 'Life Style, Subsistence and Mortality in the Slavonic Village at Espenfeld (Kr. Arnstadt, FRG). A Trace Element Study', *Anthropologisher Anzeiger* 51, 317-32

Guatelli-Steinberg, D. and Lukacs, J.R., 1999, 'Interpreting Sex Differences in Enamel Hypoplasia in Human and Non-Human Primates: Developmental, Environmental and Cultural Considerations', *Yearb. Phys. Anthropol.* 42, 73-126

Gustafson G. and Koch, G., 1974, 'Age Estimation up to 16 Years of Age Based on Dental Development', *Odontologisk Revy* 25, 297-306

Gwilt, A. and Heslop, D., 1995, 'Iron Age and Roman querns from the Tees Valley' in Vyner, B. (ed.), *Moorland Monuments: studies in the archaeology of north-east Yorkshire in honour of Raymond Hayes and Don Spratt*, Counc. Br. Archaeol. Res. Rep 101, 38-45

Hackett, C.J., 1981, 'Microscopic Focal Destruction (Tunnels) in Exhumed Bone', *Med., Sci. Law* 21, 243-65

Hadler, N.M., Gillings, D.B., Imbus, H.R., Levitin, P.M., Makuc, D., Utsinger, P.D., Yount, W.J., Slusser, D. and Moskovitz, L., 1978, 'Hand Structure and Function in an Industrial Setting', *Arthritis Rheum.* 21, 210-20

Hadley, D., 2000, 'Burial Practices in the Northern Danelaw, *c.* 650-1100', *Northern Hist.* 36, 199-216

Hadley, D., 2002, 'Burial practices in northern England in the later Anglo-Saxon period', in Lucy and Reynolds (eds), 209-28

Halkon, P. and Millett, M., *Rural Settlement and Industry: Studies in the Iron Age and Roman Archaeology of Lowland East Yorkshire*, Yorkshire Archaeol. Rep. 4

Halstead, P., 1985, 'A study of mandibular teeth from Romano-British contexts at Maxey' in Pryor, F., French, I.M., Crowther, D., Gurney, D. Simpson G. and Taylor, M., *Archaeology and Environment in the Lower Welland Valley Volume 1*, 219-24

Hanawalt, B.A., 1986, *The Ties That Bound: Peasant Families in Mediaeval England*

Hanson, D.B. and Buikstra, J.E., 1987, 'Histomorphological Variation in Buried Human Bone From the Lower Illinois Valley: Implications for Palaeodietary Research', *J. Archaeol. Sci.* 14, 549-63

Harden, D.B., 1969, 'Glass', in Evans, K.J., 'The Maison Dieu, Arundel', *Sussex Archaeol. Collect.* 107, 73-4

Harding, C., 1987, 'Post-medieval coffin furniture' in *Wharram III*, 150-153

Harding, C., 1996, 'Wharram Percy (North Yorkshire): Topography and Development of the Churchyard', in Galinie, H. and Zadora-Rio, E., (eds), *Archéologie du Cimetière Chrétien*, Actes du 2e colloque ARCHEA, 183-191 (Tours)

Hardwick, J.L., 1960, 'The Incidence and Distribution of Caries Throughout the Ages in Relation to the Englishman's Diet', *Br. Dent. J.* 108, 9-17

Hatcher, J., 1994, 'England in the Aftermath of the Black Death', *Past and Present* 144, 3-35

Hauser, G. and de Stefano, G.F., 1989, *Epigenetic Variants of the Human Skull*, E. Schweizerbart'sche Verlagsbuchhandlung (Stuttgart)

Hayes, R.H. and Whitley, E., 1950, *The Roman Pottery at Norton, East Yorkshire*, Roman Malton Dist. Rep. 7

Hayfield, C., 1988a, 'Cowlam Deserted Village: A Case Study of Post-medieval Village Desertion. *Post-medieval Archaeol.* 22, 21-109

Hayfield, C., 1988b, 'The Origins of the Roman Landscape around Wharram Percy, East Yorkshire' in Price and Wilson (eds), 99-122

Heaney, R.P., 1993, 'Bone Mass, Nutrition and Other Lifestyle Factors' *Am. J. Med.* 95, Supplement 5A, 29-33

Hedges, R.E.M. and Law, I.A., 1989, 'The Radiocarbon Dating of Bone', *Appl. Geochem.* 4, 249-53

Hedges, R.E.M., Millard, A.R. and Pike, A.W.G., 1995, 'Measurements and Relationships of Diagenetic Alteration of Bone from Three Archaeological Sites', *J. Archaeol. Sci.* 22, 201-9

Heighway, C. and Bryant, R., 1999, *The Anglo-Saxon Minster and Later Medieval Priory of St Oswald at Gloucester*

Henderson, J.D., 1987, 'Human Skeletal Remains From the Nave' in *Wharram III*, 181-8, mf 7.F4

Hengen, O.P., 1971, 'Cribra Orbitalia: Pathogenesis and Possible Aetiology', *Homo* 22, 57-76

Hershkovitz, I., Greenwald, C.M., Rothschild, B.M., Latimer, B., Dutour, O., Jellema, L.M. and Wish-Baratz, S., 1999, 'Hyperostosis Frontalis Interna: An Anthropological Perspective', *Am. J. Phys. Anthropol.* 109, 303-25

Hershkovitz, I., Greenwald, C.M., Latimer, B., Jellema, L.M., Wish-Baratz, S., Eshed, V., Dutour, O. and Rothschild, B.M., 2002, 'Serpens Endocrania Symmetrica (SES): A New Term and a Possible Clue for Identifying Intrathoracic Disease in Skeletal Populations', *Am. J. Phys. Anthropol.* 118, 201-16

Hewlett, B.S., 1991, 'Demography and Childcare in Preindustrial Societies', *J. Anthropol. Res.* 47, 1-37

Himes, J.H., Matorell, R., Habicht, J-P., Yarbrough, C., Malina, R.M. and Klein, R.E., 1975, 'Patterns of Cortical Bone Growth in Moderately Malnourished Preschool Children', *Hum. Biol.* 47, 337-50

Hooke, B.G.E., 1926, 'A Third Study of the English Skull With Special Reference to the Farringdon Street Crania', *Biometrika* 18, 1-55

Horowitz, M. and Nordin, B.E.C., 1993, 'Primary Hyperparathyroidism' in Nordin, B.E.C., Need, A.G. and Morris, H.A. (eds), *Metabolic Bone and Stone Disease* (3rd ed.), 119-31

Howell, D.C., 1992, *Statistical Methods for Psychology* (3rd ed.) (Belmont)

Howells, W.W., 1973, *Cranial Variation in Man. A Study by Multivariate Analysis of Patterns of Difference Among Recent Human Populations*, Pap. Peabody Mus. No. 67 (Cambridge, Massachusetts)

Hurley, M.F., 1997, 'Artefacts of Skeletal Material' in Cleary, R.M., Hurley, M.F. and Shee Twohig, E., *Skiddy's Castle and Christ Church Cork. Excavations 1974-77 by D. C. Twohig*, 239-73 (Cork)

Hurley, M.F., 2004, 'Bone Artefacts' in FitzPatrick, E., O'Brien, M. and Walsh, P., *Archaeological Investigations in Galway City, 1987-1998*, 463-76 (Bray)

Hurst, J.G., 1984, 'The Wharram Project: Results to 1983', *Medieval Archaeol.* 28, 77-111

Inglemark, B.E., 1946, 'Über die Längenasymmetrien der Extremetäten und ihren Zusammenhang mit der Rechts-Linkshändigkeit', *Upsala Läkareförenings Förhandlingar N.F.*, 52, 17-82

Jacobs, S.C., 1983, 'Spread of Prostatic Cancer to Bone', *Urology* 21, 337-44

Janssen, H.A.M. and Maat, G.J.R., 1999, *Canons Buried in the "Stifskapel" of the Saint Servaas Basilica at Maastricht, AD 1070-1521*, Barge's Anthropologica No. 5 (Leiden)

Jefferys, T., 1775, *The County of York*, survey'd in MDCCLXVII, VIII, [X and MDCCLXX]. Engraved by Thomas Jefferys, Geographer to His Majesty. MDCCLXXI, Corrected and Published according to Act of Parliament 25 March 1775. [1:63360] Sheet IX covers Wharram Percy

Jennings, S., 1992, *Medieval Pottery in the Yorkshire Museum*

Johnson, P. and Nicholas, S., 1995, 'Male and Female Living Standards in England and Wales, 1812-1857: Evidence From Criminal Height Records', *Econ. Hist. Rev.* 48, 470-81

Jordan, D., Haddon-Reece, D., and Bayliss, A., 1994, *Radiocarbon dates from samples funded by English Heritage and dated before 1981*

Judd, M.A. and Roberts, C.A., 1999, 'Fracture Trauma in a Mediaeval British Farming Village', *Am. J. Phys. Anthropol.* 109, 229-43

Julkunen, H., Heinonen, O.P. and Pyorala, K., 1971, 'Hyperostosis of the Spine in an Adult Population' *Ann. Rheum. Dis.* 30, 605-12

Jurmain, R.D., 1977, 'Stress and the Etiology of Osteoarthritis' *Am. J. Phys. Anthropol.* 46, 353-66

Jurmain, R., 1999, *Stories From the Skeleton: Behavioral Reconstruction in Human Osteology*

Kalkwarf, H.J., Specker, B.L., 1995, 'Bone Mineral Loss During Lactation and Recovery After Weaning', *Obstet. Gynaecol.* 86, 26-32

Kamboulis, C., Bullough, P.G. and Jaffe, H.L., 1973, 'Ganglionic Cystic Defects of Bone', *J. Bone Joint Surg.* 55A, 496-505

Katzenberg, M.A., Herring, D.A. and Saunders, S.R., 1996, 'Weaning and Infant Mortality: Evaluating the Skeletal Evidence', *Yearb. Phys. Anthropol.* 39, 177-99

Kaye, M., Pritchard, J.E., Halpenny, G.W. and Light, W., 1960, 'Bone Disease in Chronic Renal Failure With Particular Reference to Osteosclerosis', *Med.* 39, 157-90

Keeley, H. (n.d.). 'Wharram Percy, Yorkshire, Soil Report', unpubl. manuscript on file at the Ancient Monuments Laboratory, English Heritage

Keiley, F., 1989, 'On-Site Recovery of Human Bones', Paper presented at the one-day meeting of the Palaeopathology Association (British Section), May 1989

Kelley, M.A. and Micozzi, M.S., 1984, 'Rib Lesions in Chronic Pulmonary Tuberculosis', *Am. J. Phys. Anthropol.* 65, 381-6

Kendall, G., 1982, 'A Study of Grave Orientation in several Roman and post-Roman Cemeteries from Southern Britain', *Archaeol. J.* 139, 101-23

Kent, S. and Dunn, D., 1996, 'Anaemia and the Transition of Nomadic Hunter-Gatherers to a Sedentary Lifestyle: Follow-Up Study of a Kalahari Community', *Am. J. Phys. Anthropol.* 99, 455-72

Kent, S., Weinberg, E.D. and Stuart-Macadam, P., 1994, 'The Etiology of Anaemia of Chronic Disease and Infection', *J. Clin. Epidemiol.* 47, 23-33

Kerr, J., 1987, 'Excavated Window Glass', in *Wharram III*

King, A., 1991, 'Food production and consumption – meat', in Jones, R.F.J. (ed.), *Roman Britain: Recent Trends*, 15-20

King, S.E. and Ulijaszek, S.J., 1999, 'Invisible Insults During Growth and Development' in Hoppa, R.D. and Fitzgerald, C.M. (eds), *Human Growth in the Past: Studies Using Bones and Teeth*, 161-82

Kjølbye-Biddle, B., 1975, 'A cathedral cemetery: problems in excavation and interpretation', *World Archaeol.* 7.1, 87-108

Knocker, G.M. and Wells, C., 1967, 'Excavations at Red Castle, Thetford', *Norfolk Archaeol.* 34, 119-86

Knodel, J. and Kintner, H., 1977, 'The Impact of Breastfeeding Patterns on the Biometric Analysis of Infant Mortality', *Demogr.* 14, 391-409

Knüsel, C.J., Roberts, C.A. and Boyleston, A.,1996, 'When Adam Delved … An Activity-Related Lesion in Three Human Skeletal Populations', *Am. J. Phys. Anthropol.* 100, 427-34

Knüsel, C.J., Goggel, S. and Lucy, D., 1997, 'Comparative Degenerative Joint Disease of the Vertebral Column in the Mediaeval Monastic Cemetery of the Gilbertine Priory of St Andrew, Fishergate, York, England', *Am. J. Phys. Anthropol.* 103, 481-95

Kohlmeier, L. and Marcus, R., 1995, 'Calcium Disorders of Pregnancy', *Endocrinol. Metab. Clin. North America* 24, 15-39

Kósa, F., 1989, 'Age Estimation From the Foetal Skeleton', in Iscan, M.Y. (ed.), *Age Markers in the Human Skeleton*, 21-54 (Springfield)

Kricun, R., Levitt, L.P. and Winn, H.R., 1992, 'Tortuous Vertebral Artery Shown by MR and CT', *Am. J. Roentgenol.* 159, 613-15

Lamb, H.H., 1984, 'Climate and History in Northern Europe and Elsewhere' in Mörner, N.A. and Karlén, W. (eds), *Climatic Changes on a Yearly to Millennial Basis*, 225-240 (Groeningen)

Lang, J., 1991, *The Corpus of Anglo-Saxon Stone Sculpture Volume III. York and Eastern Yorkshire*

Larsen, C.S., 1997, *Bioarchaeology*

Laskey, M.A. and Prentice, A., 1999, 'Bone Mineral Changes During and After Lactation', *Obstet. Gynaecol.* 94, 608-15

Leonard, M.A., 1974, 'The Inheritance of Tarsal Coalition and Its Relationship to Spastic Flatfoot', *J. Bone Joint Surg.* 56B, 520-26

Le Patourel, H.E.J., 1979, 'Medieval Pottery' in *Wharram I*, 74-107

Le Patourel, H.E.J., 1987, 'Medieval Pottery' in *Wharram III*, 154-165

Lethbridge, T. C. and Tebbutt, C. F., 1933-4, 'Ancient Lime-Kilns at Great Paxton, Hunts', *Proc. Cambridge Antiq. Soc.* 35, 97-105

Lewis, A.B. and Garn, S.M., 1960, 'The Relationship Between Tooth Formation and Other Maturation Factors', *Angle Orthodont.* 30, 70-77

Lignereux, Y. and Peters, J., 1999, 'Elements for the Retrospective Diagnosis of Tuberculosis on Animal Bones From Archaeological Sites' in Pálfi, G., Dutour, O., Deák, J. and Hutás, I. (eds), *Tuberculosis Past and Present*, 339-48, (Budapest)

Lilley, J. H., Stroud, G., Brothwell, D. R. and Williamson, M.H., 1994, *The Jewish Burial Ground at Jewbury,* Archaeol. York, 12/3

Lin, K.Y., Gamppner, T.J. and Jane, J.A., 1998, 'Correction of Posterior Sagittal Synostosis', *J. Craniofacial Surg.* 9, 88-91

Lingström, P. and Borrman, H., 1999, 'Distribution of Dental Caries in an Early 17th Century Swedish Population With Special Reference to Diet', *Int. J. Osteoarchaeol.* 9, 395-403

Liversage, H.M., 1994, 'Accuracy of Age Estimation From Developing Teeth of a Population of Known Age (0 to 5.4 Years)', *Int. J. Osteoarchaeol.* 4, 37-45

Locke, E.A., 1915, 'Secondary Hypertrophic Osteo-Arthropathy and its Relation to Simple Club-Fingers', *Arch. Intern. Med.* 15, 659-713

Loewe, G., 1977, in Wilhelmi, K., 'Zur Funktion und Verbreitung dreieckiger Tongewichte der Eisenzeit', *Germania* 55, 178-85

Loudon, I.S.L., 1981, 'Leg Ulcers in the 18th and Early 19th Centuries', *J. Royal College Gen. Pract.* 31, 263-73

Lovell, N.C., 1994, 'Spinal Arthritis and Physical Stress at Bronze Age Harappa', *Am. J. Phys. Anthropol.* 93, 149-64

Lucy, S. and Reynolds, A.J. (eds), 2002, *Burial in Early Medieval England and Wales*, Soc. Med. Archaeol. Monogr. 17

Lukacs, J.R., 1999, 'Enamel Hypoplasia in Deciduous Teeth of Great Apes: Do Differences in Defect Prevalence Imply Differential Levels of Physiological Stress?, *Am. J. Phys. Anthropol.* 110, 351-63

Lunar Corporation, 1993, *Lunar DPX Technical and Operator's Manuals*, Version 3.6 (Madison)

Lynch, B.M. and Jeffries, R.W., 1982, 'A Comparative Analysis of the Nitrogen Content of Bone as a Means of Establishing a Relative Temporal Ordination of Prehistoric Burials', *J. Archaeol. Sci.* 9, 381-90

Maat, G.J.R. and Mastwijk, R.W., 2000, 'Avulsion Injuries of Vertebral Endplates', *Int. J. Osteoarchaeol.* 10, 142-52

MacDonell, W.R., 1904, 'A Study of the Variation and Correlation of the Human Skull, With Special Reference to English Crania', *Biometrika* 3, 191-244

MacDonell, W.R., 1906, 'A Second Study of the English Skull, With Special Reference to the Moorfields crania', *Biometrika* 5, 86-104

MacGregor, A., 1978, 'Industry and Commerce in Anglo-Scandinavian York' in Hall, R.A. (ed.) *Viking Age York and the North,* Counc. Br. Archaeol. Res. Rep. 27, 37-57

MacGregor, A., 1985, *Bone, Antler, Ivory and Horn. The Technology of Skeletal Materials since the Roman Period*

MacGregor, A., 1992, 'Bone and Antler Objects' in *Wharram VII,* 54-8

MacGregor, A., 2000, 'Bone and Antler Objects' in *Wharram VIII,* 148-54

MacGregor, A. and Riddler, I.D., 2005, 'Bone and Ivory Objects' in *Wharram X,* 143-5

MacGregor, A., Mainman, A. and Rogers, N.S.H., 1999, *Bone, Antler, Ivory and Horn from Anglo-Scandinavian and Medieval York*, Archaeol. York 17/12

Manchester, K., 1984, 'Tuberculosis and Leprosy in Antiquity: An Interpretation', *Med. Hist.* 28, 162-73

Manchester, K., 1991, 'Tuberculosis and Leprosy: Evidence for Interaction of Disease' in Ortner, D.J. and Aufderheide, A.C., (eds), *Human Palaeopathology*, Current Syntheses and Future Options, 23-35 (Washington)

Maresh, M., 1955, 'Linear Growth of the Long-Bones of the Extremeties From Infancy Through Adolescence' *Am. J. Dis. in Children* 89, 725-42

Marlow, M., 1992, 'The Population', in Sherlock, S.J. and Welch, M.G. (eds), *An Anglo-Saxon Cemetery at Norton, Cleveland*, Counc. Br. Archaeol. Res. Rep. 82, 107-118

Martin, L. and McCluskey, B., 2004, 'Land at High Street, Gargrave, North Yorkshire', Archaeol. Serv. WYAS, Rep. 1234 (unpubl.)

Martin, R., 1928, *Lehrbuch der Anthropologie in Systematischer Darstellung* (Jena)

May, J., 1996, *Dragonby: Report on Excavations at an Iron Age and Romano-British Settlement in North Lincolnshire*

Mays, S., 1985, 'The Relationship Between Harris Line Formation and Bone Growth and Development', *J. Archaeol. Sci.* 12, 207-20

Mays, S.A., 1987, 'Social Organisation and Social Change in the Early and Middle Bronze Age of Central Europe: A Study Using Human Skeletal Remains' PhD Thesis, Univ. Southampton

Mays, S.A., 1989, *The Anglo-Saxon Human Bone From School Street, Ipswich, Suffolk*, Ancient Monuments Lab. Rep. 115/89

Mays, S.A., 1991, *The Medieval Burials From the Blackfriars Friary, School Street, Ipswich, Suffolk (Excavated 1983-1985),* Ancient Monuments Lab. Rep. 16/91

Mays, S., 1993, 'Infanticide in Roman Britain', *Antiquity* 67, 883-8

Mays, S., 1995, 'The Relationship Between Harris Lines and Other Aspects of Skeletal Development in Adults and Juveniles', *J. Archaeol. Sci.* 22, 511-20

Mays, S.A., 1996a, 'Age-Dependent Cortical Bone Loss in a Medieval Population', *Int. J. Osteoarchaeol,* 6, 144-54

Mays, S. 1996b, Data recorded on skeletal remains from Zwolle, Netherlands, unpubl.

Mays, S.A., 1997, 'Carbon Stable Isotope Ratios in Mediaeval and Later Human Skeletons From North-East England', *J. Archaeol. Sci.* 24, 561-7

Mays, S., 1998a, *The Archaeology of Human Bones*

Mays, S., 1998b, Data recorded on skeletal remains from Trondheim, Norway, unpubl.

Mays, S., 1999a, 'Linear and Appositional Long Bone Growth in Earlier Human Populations: A Case Study From Mediaeval England', in Hoppa, R.D. and Fitzgerald, C.M. (eds), *Human Growth in the Past: Studies Using Bones and Teeth,* 290-312

Mays, S., 1999b, 'A Biomechanical Study of Activity Patterns in a Medieval Human Skeletal Assemblage', *Int. J. Osteoarchaeol.* 9, 68-73

Mays, S., 2000a, 'New Directions in the Analysis of Stable Isotopes in Excavated Bones and Teeth' in (Cox, M. and Mays, S. (eds), *Human Osteology in Archaeology and Forensic Science,* 425-38

Mays, S., 2000b, 'Diffuse Idiopathic Skeletal Hyperostosis (DISH) in Skeletons From Two Mediaeval English Cemeteries', *J. Paleopathol.* 12, 25-36

Mays, S., 2002, 'The Relationship Between Molar Wear and Age in an Early 19th Century AD Archaeological Human Skeletal Series of Known Age at Death', *J. Archaeol. Sci.* 29, 861-71

Mays, S.A., 2003a, 'Bone Strontium: Calcium Ratios and Duration of Breastfeeding in a Mediaeval Skeletal Population', *J. Archaeol. Sci.* 30, 731-41

Mays, S.A., 2003b, 'An Unusual Deciduous Incisor in a Mediaeval Child', *J. Paleopathol.* 15, 159-66

Mays, S.A., 2003c, 'The Rise and Fall of Rickets in England', in Murphy, P. and Wiltshire, P. (eds), *The Environmental Archaeology of Industry,* 144-53

Mays, S., forthcoming a, 'Talon Cusp in a Primary Lateral Incisor From a Medieval Child', *Int. J. Paediatr. Dent.* 14

Mays, S. forthcoming b, 'Supra-acetabular Cysts in a Mediaeval Skeletal Population', *Int. J. Osteoarchaeol.*

Mays, S. and Cox, M., 2000, 'Sex Determination in Skeletal Remains' in Cox, M. and Mays, S. (eds), *Human Osteology in Archaeology and Forensic Science,* 117-30

Mays, S. and Holst, M., forthcoming, 'Palaeo-otology of Cholesteatoma', *Int. J. Osteoarchaeol.*

Mays, S. and Nerlich, A., 1997, 'A Possible Case of Langerhans' Cell Histiocytosis in a Medieval Child From an English Cemetery', *J. Paleopathol.* 9 73-81

Mays, S. and Taylor, G.M., 2002, 'Osteological and Biomolecular Study of Two Possible Cases of Hypertrophic Osteoarthropathy From Mediaeval England', *J. Archaeol. Sci.* 29, 1267-76

Mays, S., de la Rua, C. and Molleson, T., 1995, 'Molar Crown Height as a Means of Evaluating Existing Wear Scales of Estimating Age at Death in Human Skeletal Remains', *J. Archaeol. Sci.* 22, 659-70

Mays, S., Strouhal, E., Vyhnánek L. and Nemecková, A., 1996, 'A Case of Metastatic Carcinoma of Medieval Date From Wharram Percy England', *J. Paleopathol.* 8, 33-42

Mays, S., Lees, B. and Stevenson, J.C., 1998, 'Age-Dependent Bone Loss in the Femur in a Medieval Population', *Int. J. Osteoarchaeol.* 8, 97-106

Mays, S., Taylor, G.M., Legge, A.J., Young, D.B. and Turner-Walker, G., 2001a, 'Palaeopathological and Biomolecular Study of Tuberculosis in a Medieval Skeletal Collection From England', *Am. J. Phys. Anthropol.* 114, 298-311

Mays, S., Rogers, J. and Watt, I., 2001b, 'A Possible Case of Hyperparathyroidism in a Burial of 15th-17th Century AD Date From Wharram Percy, England', *Int. J. Osteoarchaeol.* 11, 329-35

Mays, S.A., Richards, M.P. and Fuller, B.T., 2002a, 'Bone Stable Isotope Evidence for Infant Feeding in Mediaeval England', *Antiquity* 76, 654-6

Mays, S., Fysh, E. and Taylor, G.M., 2002b, 'Investigation of the Link Between Visceral Surface Rib Lesions and Tuberculosis in a Medieval Skeletal Series From England Using Ancient DNA' *Am. J. Phys. Anthropol.* 119, 27-36

McKenzie, D., 1936, 'Surgical Perforation of a Mediaeval Skull With Reference to Neolithic Holing', *Proc. R. Soc. Med.* 24, 895-8

McManus, I.C., 1991, 'The Inheritance of Left-Handedness' in Bock, G.R. and Marsh, J. (eds), *Biological Asymmetry and Handedness,* CIBA Foundation Symposium 162, 251-67

Meema, H.E., Oreopoulos, D.G., Rabinovich, S., Husdan, H. and Rapoport, A., 1974, 'Periosteal New Bone Formation (Periosteal Neostosis) in Renal Osteodystrophy', *Radiol.* 110, 513-22

Mensforth, R.P., Lovejoy, C.O., Lallo, J.W. and Armelagos, G.J., 1978, 'The Role of Constitutional Factors, Diet and Infectious Disease in the Etiology of Porotic Hyperostosis and Periosteal Reactions in Prehistoric Infants and Children', *Med. Anthropol.* 2(1), 1-59

Merbs, C.F., 1996, 'Spondylolysis and Spondylolisthesis: A Cost of Being an Erect Biped or a Clever Adaptation?', *Yearb. Phys. Anthropol.* 39, 201-28

Miles, A.E.W., 1963, 'The Dentition in the Assessment of Individual Age in Skeletal Material' in Brothwell, D.R. (ed.), *Dental Anthropology,* 191-209

Miles, A.E.W., 1989, *An Early Christian Chapel and Burial Ground on the Isle of Ensay, Outer Hebrides, Scotland With a Study of the Skeletal Remains,* Br. Archaeol. Rep. Br. Ser. 212

Miles, A.E.W. and Bulman, J.S., 1994, 'Growth Curves of Immature Bones From a Scottish Island Population of 16th to mid 19th Century: Limb Bone Diaphyses and Some Bones of the Hand and Foot', *Int. J. Osteoarchaeol.* 4, 121-36

Milne, G., 1979, 'The Peasant Houses' in *Wharram I*, 67-73

Mitchiner, M., 1988, *Jetons, Medalets and Tokens: The Medieval Period and Nuremberg*, vol. 1

Mittler, D.M. and van Gerven, D.P., 1994, 'Developmental, Diachronic, and Demographic Analysis of Cribra Orbitalia in the Medieval Christian Populations of Kulubnarti', *Am. J. Phys. Anthropol.* 93, 287-97

Møller-Christensen, V., 1961, '*Bone Changes in Leprosy*' (Copenhagen)

Møller-Christensen, V., 1982, *Aebelholt Closter* (Copenhagen)

Molleson, T.I., 1992, 'The Anthropological Evidence of Change Through Romanisation of the Poundbury Population', *Anthropologischer Anzeiger* 50, 179-89

Molleson, T., Cruse, K. and Mays, S., 1998, 'Some Sexually Dimorphic Features of the Human Juvenile Skull and Their Value in Sex Determination in Immature Skeletal Remains', *J. Archaeol. Sci.* 25, 719-28

Mook, W.G., 1986, 'Business meeting: Recommendations/ Resolutions adopted by the Twelfth International Radiocarbon Conference', *Radiocarbon* 28, 799

Moore, W.J. and Corbett, M.E., 1978, 'Dental Caries Experience in Man' in Rowe, N.H. (ed.), *Diet, Nutrition and Dental Caries*, 3-19 (Chicago)

Moore, W.J. and Corbett, M.E., 1983, 'Dental and Alveolar Infection', in Hart, G.D. (ed.), *Disease in Ancient Man*, 139-55 (Toronto)

Moore, W.J., Lavelle, C.L.B. and Spence, T.F., 1968, 'Changes in the Size and Shape of the Human Mandible in Britain', *Br. Dent. J.* 125, 163-9

Morant, G.M., 1950, 'Secular Changes in the Heights of British People', *Proc. R. Soc. London* 137B, 443-52

Morant, G.M. and Hoadley, M.F., 1931, 'A Study of the Recently Excavated Spitalfields Crania', *Biometrika* 23, 191-248

Morris, R., 1989, *Churches in the Landscape*

Morris, R., 1991, 'Baptismal Places: 600-800' in Wood, I., and Lund, N. (eds) *Peoples and Places in Northern Europe, 500-1600, Essays in Honour of Peter Hayes Sawyer*, 15-24

Nguyen, T.V. and Eisman, J.A., 1999, 'Risk Factors for Low Bone Mass in Men' in Orwoll, E.S. (ed.), *Osteoporosis in Men*, 335-61

Nielsen-Marsh, C.M. and Hedges, R.E.M., 2000, 'Patterns of Diagenesis in Bone I: The Effects of Site Environments', *J. Archaeol. Sci.* 27, 1139-50

Noel Hume, I., 1957, 'Medieval bottles from London', *The Connoisseur* 139, 104-8

North, J.J., 1991, *English Hammered Coinage. vol. 2: Edward I to Charles II, 1272-1662*

O'Connor, T.P., 1993, 'The Human Skeletal Material' in Rodwell, W. and Rodwell, K., *Rivenhall: Investigations of a Roman Villa, Church, and Village 1950-1977, Volume 2: Specialist Studies*, Counc. Br. Archaeol. Res. Rep. 80, 96-102

Oman, C., 1957, *English Church Plate 597-1830*

O'Rahilly, R., 1953, 'A Survey of Carpal and Tarsal Anomalies' *J. Bone Joint Surg.* 35A, 626-42

Ordnance Survey 1854, *Yorkshire, sheet 143*, surveyed in 1850-51, scale six inches to one statute mile, [1:10560]

Ordnance Survey 1890, *Yorkshire (East Riding), Sheet CXLIII.9*, surveyed in 1888, Scale 1:2500

Ordnance Survey 1910, *Yorkshire (East Riding), Sheet CXLIII.9*, re-surveyed in 1888, revised in 1909, edition of 1910, Scale 1:2500

Ortner, D.J. and Eriksen, M.F, 1997, 'Bone Changes in the Human Skull Probably Resulting From Scurvy in Infancy and Childhood', *Int. J. Osteoarchaeol.* 7, 212-20

Ortner, D.J. and Mays, S., 1998, 'Dry-Bone Manifestations of Rickets in Infancy and Early Childhood', *Int. J. Osteoarchaeol.* 8, 45-55

Ortner, D.J. and Putschar, W.G.J., 1985, *Identification of Pathological Conditions in Human Skeletal Remains* (Washington)

Ossenberg, N., 1976, 'Within and Between Race Distances in Population Studies Based on Discrete Traits of the Human Skull', *Am. J. Phys. Anthropol.* 45, 701-16

Otlet, R.L., 1977, 'Harwell radiocarbon measurements II', *Radiocarbon* 19, 400-423

Otlet, R.L., 1979, 'An assessment of laboratory errors in liquid scintillation methods of 14C dating' in Berger, R. and Suess, H.E. (eds), *Proceedings of the ninth International Radiocarbon Conference*, 256-67

Otlet, R.L., and Warchal, R.M., 1978, 'Liquid scintillation counting of low-level 14C dating', *Liquid Scintillation Counting* 5, 210-18

Otlet, R.L., Walker, A.J., Hewson, A.D. and Burleigh, R., 1980, '14C interlaboratory comparison in the UK: experiment design, preparation, and preliminary results', *Radiocarbon* 22, 936-46

Papp, T. and Porter, R.W., 1994, 'Changes of the Lumbar Spinal Canal Proximal to Spina Bifida Occulta', *Spine* 19, 1508-11

Parker, B.R., 1997, 'Leukemia and Lymphoma in Childhood', *Radiol. Clin. North Am.* 35, 1495-516

Parker, M.J. and Pryor, G.A., 1993, 'Mortality and Morbidity After Hip Fractures', *Br. Med. J.* 307, 1248-50

Parsons, F.G., 1908, 'Report on the Hythe Crania', *J. R. Anthropol. Ins.* 38, 419-50

Parsons, F.G., 1910, 'Report on the Rothwell Crania', *J. R. Anthropol. Inst.* 40, 483-504

Pavelka, M.S.M. and Fedigan, L.M., 1991, 'Menopause: A Comparative Life History Perspective', *Yearb. Phys. Anthropol.* 34, 13-38

Payne, S., 1973, 'Kill-off patterns in sheep and goats: the mandibles from Asvan Kale' *Anatolian Stud.* 23, 281-83

Peavy, P.W., Rogers, J.V., Clements, J.L. and Burns, J.B., 1973, 'Unusual Osteoblastic Metastases From Carcinoid Tumours', *Radiol.* 107, 327-30

Perizonius, W.R.K., 1984, 'Closing and Non-Closing Sutures in 256 Crania of Known Age and Sex From Amsterdam (AD 1883-1909)', *J. Hum. Evol.* 13, 201-6

Philips, J.T., 1960, 'An Iron Age site at Driffield, East Riding, Yorks', *Yorkshire Archaeol. J.* 40, 183-91

Phillips, D., 1985, *The Cathedral of Archbishop Thomas of Bayeux. Excavations at York Minster Volume II*

Pineda, C.J., Guerra, J., Weisman, M.H., Resnick, D. and Martinez-Lavin, M., 1985, 'The Skeletal Manifestations of Clubbing: A Study in Patients With Cyanotic Congenital Heart Disease and Hypertrophic Osteoarthropathy', *Semin. Arthritis Rheum.* 14, 263-73

Pinter-Bellows, S., 1992, 'The Vertebrate Remains From Sites 94 and 95', in *Wharram VII*, 69-79

Pinter-Bellows, S, 1996, 'The Human Remains' in Stone and Appleton-Fox, 58-61

Pinter-Bellows, S., 2000, 'The animal remains' in *Wharram VIII*, 167-84

Plato, C.C., Wood, J.L. and Norris, A.H., 1980, 'Bilateral Asymmetry in Bone Measurements of the Hand and Lateral Hand Dominance', *Am. J. Phys. Anthropol.* 52, 27-31

Platt, C., 1996, *King Death: the Black Death and its aftermath in late medieval England*

Porter, R.T. and Harding, C., 2000, unpubl. report, Wharram Percy Project archive

Powell, F., 1996, 'The Human Remains' in Boddington (ed.), 113-24

Powers, N., 2004, 'Cranial Trauma and Treatment: a Case Study from the Medieval Cemetery of St Mary Spital', *Int. J. Osteoarchaeol.* 14

Prader, A., Tanner, J.M. and von Harnack, G.A., 1963, 'Catch-Up Growth Following Illness or Starvation', *J. Paediatr.* 62, 646-59

Price, J., 1988, 'Romano-British glass bangles from East Yorkshire' in Price and Wilson eds, 339-66

Price, J. and Wilson P.R. (eds), 1988, *Recent Research in Roman Yorkshire. Studies in honour of Mary Kitson Clark (Mrs Derwas Chitty)* Br. Archaeol. Rep. (Br. Ser.) 193

Radin, E.L., Paul, I.L. and Rose, R.M., 1980, 'Osteoarthritis as a Final Common Pathway' in Nuki, G., ed., *The Aetiopathogenesis of Osteoarthritis*, 84-9

Rahtz, P.A., 1978, 'Grave Orientation', *Archaeol. J.* 135, 1-14

Rahtz, P.A., 1979, *The Saxon and Medieval Palaces at Cheddar*, Br. Archaeol. Rep. Br. Ser. 65

Rahtz, P.A., 1981, *Wharram Percy Data Sheets*, Univ. York (2nd ed.)

Rahtz, P. 1988, 'From Roman to Saxon at Wharram Percy' in Price and Wilson (eds) 123-37

Ramm, H., 1988, 'Aspects of the Roman Countryside in East Yorkshire' in Price and Wilson (eds), 81-8

Regan, M.H., Case, D.T. and Brundige, J.C., 1999, 'Articular Surface Defects in the Third Metatarsal and Third Cuneiform: Nonosseous Tarsal Coalition', *Am. J. Phys. Anthropol.* 109, 53-65

Reid, D.J. and Dean, M.C., 2000, 'The Timing of Linear Hypoplasias on Human Anterior Teeth', *Am. J. Phys. Anthropol.* 113, 135-9

Resnick, D. and Niwayama, G., 1981, *Diagnosis of Bone and Joint Disorders* (1st ed.)

Resnick, D. and Niwayama, G., 1988, *Diagnosis of Bone and Joint Disorders* (2nd ed.)

Revell, P., 1986, *Pathology of Bone* (Berlin)

Reynolds, N., 1976, 'The structure of Anglo-Saxon graves' *Antiquity* 50, 140-43

Richards, M.P. and Hedges, R.E.M., 1999, 'Stable Isotope Evidence for Similarities in the Types of Marine Foods Used by Late Mesolithic Humans at Sites Along the Atlantic Coast of Europe', *J. Archaeol. Sci.* 26, 717-22

Richards, M.P., Mays, S.A. and Fuller, B.T., 2002, 'Stable Carbon and Nitrogen Isotope Values of Bones and Teeth Reflect Weaning Age at the Medieval Wharram Percy Site, Yorkshire, UK', *Am. J. Phys. Anthropol.* 118

Richardson, J., 2004a. 'The animal remains' in *Wharram IX*, 257-72

Richardson, J., 2004b, 'The animal remains' in *Wharram IX*, 332-339

Richardson, J., 2005a, 'The Pit Alignment' in Roberts, I. (ed.), *Ferrybridge Henge: The Ritual Landscape*

Richardson, J., 2005b, 'The animal remains' in *Wharram X*, 153-69

Riddler, I.D., 1990, 'Saxon Handled Combs from London', *Trans. London Middlesex Archaeol. Soc.* 41, 9-20

Riddler, I.D., 1994, 'Bone Objects' in Mynard, D.C., *Excavations on Medieval Sites in Milton Keynes*, Bucks. Archaeol. Soc. Monogr. Ser. 6, 30-33, 36 and 185-8

Riddler, I.D., 1995, 'Bone, Antler and Ivory' in Ivens, R., Busby, P. and Shepherd, N., *Tattenhoe and Westbury. Two Deserted Medieval Settlements in Milton Keynes*, Bucks. Archaeol. Soc. Monogr. Ser. 8, 318-19 and 390-93

Riddler, I.D., 1999, 'The Wooden Gaming Piece' in Killock, D., 'Late Medieval and Post-Medieval Developments at 100-104 Bermondsey Street Southwark' *Surrey Archaeol. Collect.* 86, 133

Riddler, I.D., 2001a, 'The Spatial Organisation of Bone and Antler Working in Trading Centres' in Hill, D. and Cowie, R. (eds), *Wics. The Early Medieval Trading Centres of Northern Europe*, Sheffield Archaeol. Monogr. 14, 61-6

Riddler, I.D., 2001b, 'The Small Finds' in Gardiner, M., Cross, R., Macpherson-Grant, N. and Riddler, I., 'Continental Trade and non-Urban Ports in Middle Anglo-Saxon England: Excavations at *Sandtun*, West Hythe, Kent', *Archaeol. J.* 158, 228-52

Riddler, I.D., 2001c, 'The Small Finds' in Hicks, M. and Hicks, A., *St Gregory's Priory, Northgate, Canterbury. Excavations 1988-1991*, Archaeol. Canterbury New Ser. II, 267-87

Riddler, I.D., 2006a, 'Early Medieval Fishing Implements of Bone and Antler' in Pieters, M., Verhaege, F. and Gevaert, G., *Fishing, Trade and Piracy. Fishermen and Fishermen's Settlements in and around the North Sea Area in the Middle Ages and Later*, Archeologie in Vlaanderen 6, 171-80 (Brussels)

Riddler, I.D., 2006b, 'Objects and Waste of Bone and Antler' in Cramp, R.J., *Wearmouth and Jarrow Monastic Sites. Volume 2*, 267-81

Riddler, I.D., forthcoming a, 'Objects of Bone and Antler' in Carr, B. and Tester, A., *A High Status Middle Saxon Settlement on the Fen Edge*, East Anglian Archaeol.

Riddler, I.D., forthcoming b, 'Ivory Knife Handle' in Shepherd Popescu, E., *Norwich Castle: Excavations and Historical Survey, 1987-98. Part II: c. 1345 to Modern*, East Anglian Archaeol.

Riddler, I.D., forthcoming c, 'Stone, Bone, Antler and Ivory Finds' in Saunders, A., *Excavations at Launceston Castle, Cornwall*, Soc. Medieval Archaeol. Monogr. Ser.

Riddler, I.D. and Leaf, H., forthcoming, 'Bone, Antler and Ivory Objects' in *Wharram XII*

Riddler, I.D., Trzaska-Nartowski, N.I.A. and Hatton, S., forthcoming, *An Early Medieval Craft. Objects and Waste of Bone, Antler and Ivory from Ipswich Excavations, 1974-1994*

Rigby, V., 1980, 'The coarse pottery', in Stead, I.M., *Rudston Roman Villa*, Yorkshire Archaeol. Soc.

Rigold, S.E., 1977, 'The Principal Series of English Sceattas', *Br. Numis. J.* 47, 21-30

Roberts, C. and Manchester, K., 1995, *The Archaeology of Disease* (2nd ed.)

Roberts, C. and McKinley, J., 2003, 'Review of Trepanations in British Antiquity Focusing on Funerary Context to Explain Their Occurrence' in Arnott, R., Finger, S. and Smith, C.U.M. (eds), *Trepanation: History, Discovery, Theory*, 55-78

Roberts, C.A., Lucy, D. and Manchester, K., 1994, 'Inflammatory Lesions of Ribs: An Analysis of the Terry Collection', *Am. J. Phys. Anthropol.* 95, 169-82

Roberts, C.A., Boylston, A., Buckley, L., Chamberlain, A.C. and Murphy, E.M., 1998, 'Rib Lesions and Tuberculosis: The Palaeopathological Evidence', *Tubercle Lung Dis.* 79, 55-60

Roberts, I., 2002, *Pontefract Castle Archaeological Excavations 1982-86*, Yorkshire Archaeol. 8

Robinson, J.F., 1978, *The Archaeology of Malton and Norton*

Roche, M.B. and Rowe, G.G., 1951, 'The Incidence of Separate Neural Arch and Coincident Bone Variations', *Anat. Rec.* 109, 233-52

Rodwell, W., 1989, *Church Archaeology* (2nd ed.)

Rodwell, W.J., 1981, *The Archaeology of the English Church*

Rodwell, W., 2001, *Wells Cathedral Excavations and Structural Studies 1978-93*

Rodwell, W.J. and Rodwell, K.A., 1986, *Rivenhall: investigations of a villa, church, and village, 1950-1977*, Counc. Br. Archaeol. Res. Rep. 55

Roffe, D., 2000, 'The Early History of Wharram Percy', in *Wharram VIII*, 1-16

Rogers, J. and Waldron, T., 1995, *A Field Guide to Joint Disease in Archaeology*

Rogers, J. and Waldron, T., 2001, 'DISH and the Monastic way of Life', *Int. J. Osteoarchaeol.* 11, 357-65

Rogers, J., Watt, I. and Dieppe, P., 1985, 'Palaeopathology of Spinal Osteophytosis, Vertebral Ankylosis, Ankylosing Spondylitis, and Vertebral Hyperostosis', *Ann. Rheum. Dis.* 44, 113-20

Rogers, J., Waldron, T., Dieppe, P. and Watt, I., 1987, 'Arthropathies in Palaeopathology: The Basis of Classification According to Most Probable Cause', *J. Archaeol. Sci.* 14, 179-93

Rogers, N.S.H., 1993, *Anglian and other Finds from Fishergate*, Archaeol. York 17/9

Rösing, F.W. and Schwidetsky, I., 1984, 'Comparative Statistical Studies on the Physical Anthropology of the Late Mediaeval Period (AD 1000-1500)', *J. Hum. Evol.* 13, 325-9

Rothschild, B.M. and Rothschild, C., 1998, Recognition of Hypertrophic Osteoarthropathy in Skeletal Remains, *J. Rheum.* 25, 2221-7

Rozanski, K., Stichler, W., Gonfiantini, R., Scott, E.M., Beukens, R.P., Kromer, B. and van der Plicht, J., 1992, 'The IAEA 14C intercomparison exercise 1990', *Radiocarbon* 34, 506-19

Ruff, C.B., 2000a, 'Body Mass Prediction From Skeletal Frame Size in Elite Athletes', *Am. J. Phys. Anthropol.* 113, 507-17

Ruff, C.B., 2000b, 'Biomechanical Analyses of Archaeological Human Skeletons' in Katzenberg, M.A. and Saunders, S.R., (eds), *Biological Anthropology of the Human Skeleton*, 71-102 (New York)

Ruff, C.B. and Walker, A., 1994, 'Body Size and Body Shape' in Walker, A. and Leakey, R. (eds), *The Nariokotome* Homo Erectus *Skeleton*, 235-65 (Cambridge)

Ruff, C.B., Scott, W.W. and Liu, A.Y-C., 1991, 'Articular and Diaphysial Remodelling of the Proximal Femur With Changes in Body Mass in Adults', *Am. J. Phys. Anthropol.* 86, 397-413

Russell, J.C., 1937, 'Length of Life in England 1250-1348', *Hum. Biol.* 9, 528-41

Russell, J.C., 1948, *British Medieval Population* (Albuquerque, New Mexico)

Ryder, M.L., 1974, 'Animal Remains From Wharram Percy', *Yorkshire Archaeol. J.* 46, 42-52

Ryder, P.F., 1985, *The Medieval Cross Slab Grave Cover in County Durham*, Archit. Archaeol Soc. Durham Northumberland Res. Rep. 1

Ryder, P.F., 1991, *Medieval Cross Slab Grave Covers in West Yorkshire*

Ryder, P.F., 2003, 'Medieval Cross Slab Grave Covers in Northumberland, 3 North Northumberland', *Archaeol. Aeliana* 5th ser. 2391-136

Ryder, P.F., 2005, *The Medieval Cross Slab Grave Covers in Cumbria*, Cumberland Westmorland Antiq. Archaeol Soc. Extra Series 32

Salmi, A., Vuotilainen, A., Holsti, L.R. and Unnerus, C.E., 1962, 'Hyperostosis Cranii in a Normal Population', *Am. J. Roentgenology* 87, 1032-40

Santos, A.L. and Roberts, C.A., 2001, 'A Picture of Tuberculosis in Young Portuguese People in the Early 20th Century: A Multidisciplinary Study of the Skeletal and Historical Evidence', *Am. J. Phys. Anthropol.* 115, 38-49

Saunders, S.R. and Barrans, L., 1999, 'What Can be Done About the Infant Category in Skeletal Samples?' in Hoppa, R.D. and Fitzgerald, C.M. (eds), *Human Growth in the Past: Studies From Bones and Teeth*, 183-209

Saunders, S.R. and Hoppa, R.D., 1993, 'Growth Deficit in Survivors and Non-Survivors: Biological Mortality Bias in Subadult Skeletal Samples', *Yearb. Phys. Anthropol.* 36, 127-51

Saunders, S.R., Hoppa, R.D. and Southern, R., 1993, 'Diaphysial Growth in a Nineteenth Century Skeletal Sample of Subadults From St Thomas' Church, Belleville, Ontario', *Int. J. Osteoarchaeol.* 3, 265-81

Saunders, S.R., Herring, D.A. and Boyce, G., 1995, 'Can Skeletal Samples Accurately Represent the Living Populations They Come From? The St Thomas' Cemetery Site, Belleville, Ontario' in Grauer, A.L. (ed.), *Bodies of Evidence: Reconstructing History Through Skeletal Analysis*, 69-89 (New York)

Scheuer, J.L., Musgrave, J.H. and Evans, S.P., 1980, 'Estimation of Late Foetal and Perinatal Age From Limb Bone Lengths by Linear and Logarithmic Regression', *Ann. Hum. Biol.* 7, 257-65

Schmorl, G. and Junghanns, H., 1971, *The Human Spine in Health and Disease* (2nd American ed., translated by E.F. Beseman) (New York)

Schour, I. and Massler, M., 1941, 'The Development of the Human Dentition', *J. Am. Dent. Assoc.* 28, 1153-60

Schuldt, E., 1985, *Groß Raden. Ein slawischer Tempelort des 9./10. Jahrhunderts in Mecklenburg,* (Berlin)

Schulter-Ellis, F.P., 1980, 'Evidence for Handedness on Documented Skeletons', *J. Forensic Sci.* 25, 624-30

Schultz, A. H., 1967, 'Notes on Diseases and Healed Fractures of Wild Apes' in Brothwell, D.R. and Sandison, A.T. (eds), *Diseases in Antiquity,* 47-55 (Springfield)

Schultz, M., 2001, 'Palaeohistopathology of Bone: A New Approach to the Study of Ancient Diseases', *Yearb. Phys. Anthropol.* 44, 106-47

Schuurs, A.H.B. and van Loveren, C., 2000, 'Double Teeth: Review of the Literature', *J. Dent. Child.* 67, 313-25

Schwarcz, H.P. and Schoeninger, M.J.,1991, 'Stable Isotope Analyses in Human Nutritional Ecology', *Yearb. Phys. Anthropol.* 34, 283-321

Scoles, P.V., Latimer, B.M., DiGiovanni, B.F., Vargo, E., Bauza, S. and Jellema, L.M., 1991, 'Vertebral Alterations in Scheuermann's Kyphosis', *Spine* 16, 509-15

Scott, E.M., Harkness, D.D. and Cook, G.T., 1998, 'Inter-laboratory comparisons: lessons learned', *Radiocarbon* 40, 331-40

Sellevold, B.J., 1997, 'Children's Skeletons and Graves in Scandinavian Archaeology' in de Boe, G. and Verhaege, F. (eds), *Death and Burial in Medieval Europe*, Papers of the Medieval Europe Brugge 1997 Conference, Volume 2, 15-25 (Zellik)

Shafer, W.G., Hine, M.K. and Levy, B.M., 1983, *A Textbook of Oral Pathology* (4th ed.)

Shahar, S.,1990, *Childhood in the Middle Ages*

Shneerson, J.M., 1981, 'Digital Clubbing and Hypertrophic Osteoarthropathy: The Underlying Mechanisms', *Br. J. Dis. Chest* 75, 113-31

Siddiqui, K.S., 1987, 'Geology of Building and Monumental Stones', fiche, KS 2289 in *Wharram III*

Signorelli, L. and Wheelhouse, P., 2004 , 'A165 Reighton Bypass, Reighton, North Yorkshire', Archaeol. Serv. WYAS Rep. 1276 (unpubl.)

Sillen, A., 1989, 'Diagenesis of the Inorganic Phase of Cortical Bone', in Price, T.D. (ed.), *The Chemistry of Prehistoric Human Bone*, 211-29

Sillen, A. and Parkington, J., 1996, 'Diagenesis of Bones From Eland's Bay Cave', *J. Archaeol. Sci.* 23, 535-42

Silveira, L.H., Martinez-Lavin, M., Pineda, C., Fonseca, M-C., Navarro, C. and Nava, A., 2000, 'Vascular Endothelial Growth Factor in Hypertrophic Osteoarthropathy', *Clin. Exp. Rheumatol.* 18, 57-62

Silverberg, S.J., Shane, E., De la Cruz, L., Dempster, D.W., Feldman, F., Seldin, D., Jacobs, T.P., Cafferty, M., Parisien, M.V., Lindsay, R., Clemens, T.L. and Belizikian, J.P., 1989, 'Skeletal Disease in Primary Hyperparathyroidism', *J. Bone Min. Res.* 4, 283-91

Silveri, F., DeAngelis, R., Argentati, F., Brecciaroli, D., Muti, S. and Cervini, C., 1996, 'Hypertrophic Osteoarthropathy: Endothelium and Platelet Function', *Clin. Rheumatol.* 15, 435-39

Silverman, F.N. and Kuhr, J.P., 1993, *Caffey's Paediatric X-Ray Diagnosis* (9th ed.)

Simon, S.R., Radin, E.L., Paul, I.L. and Rose, R.M., 1972, 'The Response of Joints to Impact Loading – II In Vivo Behavior of Subchondral Bone', *J. Biomechanics* 5, 267-72

Sjøvold, T., 1990, 'Estimation of Stature From Long Bones Utilising the Line Organic Correlation', *Hum. Evol.* 5, 431-47

Skinner, M.F., 1986, 'An Enigmatic Hypoplastic Defect of the Deciduous Canine', *Am. J. Phy. Anthropol.* 69, 59-69

Skinner, M.F. and Newell, E.A., 2003, 'Localised Hypoplasia in the Primary Canine in Bonobos, Orangutans, and Gibbons', *Am. J. Phys. Anthropol.* 120, 61-72

Skinner, M.F., Hadaway, W. and Dickie, J. 1994, 'Effects of ethnicity and birth month on localised enamel hypoplasia of the primary canine', *J. Dentistry Children* 61, 109-113

Slowikowski, A.M., 1991, 'The Archaeological Evidence for the Character and Uses of Medieval Pottery in the Lowlands of West Yorkshire', unpubl. MPhil thesis, Univ. Leeds

Slowikowski, A.M., 2000, 'The Anglo-Saxon and Medieval Pottery' in *Wharram VIII*, 60-98

Slowikowski, A.M., 2004, 'The Anglo-Saxon and Medieval Pottery', in *Wharram IX,* 183-212

Slowikowski, A.M., 2005, 'The Anglo-Saxon and Medieval Pottery' in *Wharram X,* 73-121

Slowikowski, A.M., forthcoming, 'The Anglo-Saxon and Medieval Pottery' in *Wharram XII*

Smith, B.H., 1991, 'Standards of Human Tooth Formation and Dental Age Assessment' in Kelley, M.A. and Larsen, C.S. (eds), *Advances in Dental Anthropology*, 143-68

Smith, R., 1988, 'Human Resources', in Astill, G. and Grant, A. (eds), *The Countryside of Mediaeval England*, 188-212

Stead, S., 1991, 'The Human Bones', in Stead, I.M. (ed.), *Iron Age Cemeteries in East Yorkshire*, Engl. Heritage Archaeol. Rep. 22, 126-39

Steele, J., 2000 'Skeletal Indicators of Handedness', in Cox, M. and Mays, S. (eds), *Human Osteology in Archaeology and Forensic Science*, 307-23

Steele, J. and Mays, S., 1995, 'Handedness and Directional Asymmetry in the Long Bones of the Human Upper Limb', *Int. J. Osteoarchaeol.* 5, 39-49

Steier, P. and Rom, W., 2000, 'The use of Bayesian statistics for 14C dates of chronologically ordered samples: a critical analysis', *Radiocarbon* 42, 183-98

Steinbock, R.T., 1976, *Palaeopathological Diagnosis and Interpretation* (Springfield)

Stenhouse, M.J. and Baxter, M.S. 1983 '14C dating reproducibility: evidence from routine dating of archaeological samples', *PACT* 8, 147-61

Stevens, P., 1992, 'The Vertebrate Remains From Site 39' in *Wharram VII*, 67-9

Stewart, T.D., 1968, 'Identification By the Skeletal Structures' in Camps, F.E., (ed.) *Gradwohl's Legal Medicine* (2nd ed.), 123-54

Stinson, S., 1985, 'Sex Differences in Environmental Sensitivity During growth and Development', *Yearb. Phys. Anthropol.* 28, 123-47

Stloukal, M. and Hanáková, H., 1978, 'Die Länge der Längsknochen Altslawischer Bevölkerungen – Unter besonder Berücksichtigung von Wachstumfragen', *Homo* 29, 53-69

Stocker, D., 1986, 'The excavated stonework' in Gilmour and Stocker (eds), 44-82

Stocker, D.A., 1999, *The College of the Vicars Choral of York Minster at Bedern: Architectural Fragments*, Archaeol. York 10/4

Stocker, D., 2000, 'Monuments and Merchants: Irregularities in the Distribution of Stone Sculpture in Lincolnshire and Yorkshire in the Tenth century' in Hadley, D. and Richards, J. (eds), *Cultures in Contact: Scandinavian Settlement in England in the Ninth and Tenth Centuries,* 179-212 (Turnhout)

Stocker, D. and Everson, P., 2001, 'Five Towns Funerals: decoding diversity in Danelaw stone sculpture' in Graham-Campbell, J., Hall, R., Jesch, J. and Parsons, D.N. (eds), *Vikings and the Danelaw Select Papers from the Proceedings of the Thirteenth Viking Congress, Nottingham and York, 21-30 August 1997,* 223-43

Stoertz, C., 1997, *Ancient Landscapes of the Yorkshire Wolds. Aerial photographic transcription and analysis*, R. Comm. Hist. Monuments Engl.

Stoessiger, B.N. and Morant, G.M., 1932, 'A Study of the Crania in the Vaulted Ambulatory of Saint Leonard's Church, Hythe', *Biometrika* 24, 135-203

Stone, N. and Appleton-Fox, N., 1996, *A View From Hereford's Past* (Almeley)

Stone, R. and Appleton-Fox, N., 1996, *A View from Hereford's Past: a report on the archaeological excavation of Hereford Cathedral Close in 1993*

Stroud, G., 1993, 'The Human Bones' in Stroud, G. and Kemp, R.L., *Cemeteries of the Church and Priory of St Andrew, Fishergate*, Archaeol. York 12/2, 160-241

Stroud, G. and Kemp, R.L., 1993, *Cemeteries of St Andrew, Fishergate*

Stroud, G., Brothwell, D.R., Browne, S., Watson, P. and Dobney, K., 1994, 'The Population' in Lilley, J.M., Stroud, G., Brothwell, D.R. and Williamson, M.H., *The Jewish Burial Ground at Jewbury*, Archaeol. York 12/3, 424-51

Stuart-Macadam, P., 1985, 'Porotic Hyperostosis: Representative of a Childhood Condition', *Am. J. Phys. Anthropol.* 66, 391-8

Stuart-Macadam, P., 1987, 'Porotic Hyperostosis: New Evidence to Support the Anaemia Theory', *Am. J. Phys. Anthropol.* 74, 521-6

Stuart-Macadam, P., 1989, 'Nutritional Deficiency Disease: A Survey of Scurvy, Rickets and Iron Deficiency Anaemia' in Iscan, M.Y. and Kennedy, K.A.R. (eds), *Reconstruction of Life From the Skeleton,* 201-22 (New York)

Stuart-Macadam, P., 1992, 'Porotic Hyperostosis: A New Perspective', *Am. J. Physical Anthropol.* 87, 39-47

Stuiver, M. and Kra, R.S., 1986, 'Editorial comment', *Radiocarbon*, 28(2B), ii

Stuiver, M., and Polach, H.A., 1977, 'Reporting of 14C data', *Radiocarbon* 19, 355-63

Stuiver, M., and Reimer, P.J., 1986, 'A computer program for radiocarbon age calculation', *Radiocarbon* 28, 1022-30

Stuiver, M., and Reimer, P.J., 1993, 'Extended 14C data base and revised CALIB 3.0 14C age calibration program', *Radiocarbon* 35, 215-30

Stuiver, M., Reimer, P.J., Bard, E., Beck, J.W., Burr, G.S., Hughen, K.A., Kromer, B., McCormac, F.G., van der Plicht, J. and Spurk, M., 1998, 'INTCAL98 radiocarbon age calibration, 24,000–0 cal BP', *Radiocarbon* 40, 1041-84

Suchey, J.M., Wisely, D.V. and Katz, D., 1987, 'Evaluation of the Todd and Stuart-McKern Methods of Ageing the Male Os Pubis' in Reichs, K.J. (ed.), *Forensic Osteology: Advances in the Identification of Human Remains,* 33-67 (Springfield)

Suchey, J.M., Brooks, S.T. and Katz, D., 1988, *Instructions for the Use of the Suchey-Brooks System for Age Determination of the Female Os Pubis*, Instructional materials accompanying the female pubic symphyseal models of the Suchey-Brooks System distributed by France Casting (Fort Collins, Colorado)

Tamers, M.A., 1965, 'Routine carbon-14 dating using liquid scintillation techniques' in Chatters, R.M. and Olson, E.A. (eds), *Radiocarbon and tritium dating: proceedings of the sixth international conference on radiocarbon and tritium dating*, 53–67 (Washington D.C.)

Tanner, J.M., 1981, 'Growth as a Target-Seeking Function', in Falkner, F. and Tanner, J.M. (eds), *Human Growth: A Comprehensive Treatise*. Vol. 1, *Developmental Biology and Prenatal Growth*, 167-79

Tanner, J.M., 1989, *Foetus Into Man* (2nd ed.)

Tanner, J.M., Whitehouse, R.H. and Takaishi, M., 1966, 'Standards From Birth to Maturity for Height, Weight, Height Velocity and Weight Velocity; British Children', *Arch. Dis. Child.* 41, 454-71, 613-35

Tattersall, I., 1968a, 'Multivariate Analysis of Some Mediaeval British Cranial Series', *Man* 3, 284-92

Tattersall, I., 1968b, 'Dental Palaeopathology of Mediaeval Britain', *J. Hist. Med.* 23, 380-85

Teesdale, H., 1828, *To the Nobility, Gentry, and Clergy of Yorkshire this map of the County…* corrected in the years 1827 and 1828 is respectfully dedicated by the Proprietors Henry Teesdale, and Co and C. Stocking [1:84480]. This has no 'corrections' to Greenwood in Wharram Percy township

Tempel, W.-D., 1969, *Die Dreilagenkamme aus Haithabu. Studien zu den Kämmen der Wikingerzeit im Nordseekustengebiet und Skandinavien*, Unpubl. Doctoral Dissertation (Gottingen)

Termine, J.D. and Posner, A.S., 1966, 'Infra-Red Determination of the Percentage of Crystallinity in Apatitic Calcium Phosphates', *Nature* 211, 268-70

Thompson, A., Grew, F. and Schofield, J., 1984, 'Exavations at Aldgate, 1974', *Post-medieval Archaeol.* 18, 1-148

Thomson, D.L., 1999, 'Intraindividual Variance in Trait Size and the Analysis of Developmental Instability', *Anim. Behav.* 57, 731-34

Trinkaus, E., 1975, 'Squatting Amongst the Neanderthals: A Problem in the Behavioural Interpretation of Skeletal Morphology', *J. Archaeol. Sci.* 2, 327-51

Trinkaus, E., 1981, 'Neanderthal Limb Proportions and Cold Adaptation', in Stringer, C.B. (ed.), *Aspects of Human Evolution*, 187-224

Trinkaus, E., Churchill, S.E. and Ruff, C.B., 1994, 'Post-Cranial Robusticity in Homo II: Humeral Bilateral Asymmetry and Bone Plasticity', *Am. J. Phys. Anthropol.* 93, 1-34

Turner-Walker, G., Mays, S. and Syversen, U., 2000, 'Do High Parity and Prolonged Lactation Have Long-Term Consequences for Bone Mineral density?', *J. Bone Min. Res.* 18(6), S530 (abstract)

Turner-Walker, G., Syversen, U. and Mays, S., 2001, 'The Archaeology of Osteoporosis', *J. European Archaeol.* 4, 263-8

Tyrell, R. and Zeepvat, R. J., 1991, 'The Finds' in Mynard, D.C. and Zeepvat, R.J., *Excavations at Great Linford, 1974-80. The Village*, Bucks. Archaeol. Soc. Monogr. Ser. 3, 137-240

Tyson, R., 2000, *Medieval Glass Vessels found in England AD 1200-1500*, Counc. Br. Archaeol. Res. Rep. 121

Ulbricht, I., 1984, *Die Verarbeitung von Knochen, Geweih und Horn im mittelalterlichen Schleswig*, Ausgrabungen in Schleswig. Berichte und Studien 3 (Neumünster)

Vallois, H.V., 1965, 'Anthropometric Techniques', *Curr. Anthropol.* 6, 127-43

van der Plicht, J., 1993, 'The Gröningen radiocarbon calibration program', *Radiocarbon* 35, 231-7

Virtama, P. and Helelä, T., 1969, 'Radiographic Measurements of Cortical Bone. Variations in a Normal Population Between 1 and 90 Years of Age', *Acta Radiologica*, Supplementum 293

Vitzthum, V.J., 1994, 'Comparative Study of Breastfeeding Structure and Its Relation to Human Reproductive Ecology', *Yearb. Phys. Anthropol.* 37, 307-49

Wade-Martins, P., 1980, *Excavations in North Elmham Park 1967-1972*, East Anglian Archaeol. 9

Waldron, T., 1985, 'DISH at Merton Priory: Evidence for a "New" Occupational Disease?', *Br. Med. J.* 291, 1762-3

Waldron, T., 1993, 'The Health of the Adults', in Molleson, T. and Cox, M., *The Spitalfields Project: Volume 2 - The Anthropology*, Counc. Br. Archaeol. Res. Rep. 86, 67-89

Waldron, T., 1994, *Counting the Dead*

Waldron, T. and Antoine, D., 2002, 'Tortuosity or Aneurism? The Palaeopathology of Some Abnormalities of the Vertebral Artery', *Int. J. Osteoarchaeol.* 12, 79-88

Walker, J.B., 1981, 'The Children in the Cemetery: Child Mortality and Public Health in Lyme Regis 1856 to 1979', *Proc. Dorset Nat. Hist. Archaeol. Soc.* 103, 5-12

Walton Rogers, P., 1997, *Textile Production at 16-22 Coppergate*, Archaeol. York. The Small Finds 17/11

Walton Rogers, P., 2001, 'The re-appearance of an old Roman Loom in Medieval England' in Walton Rogers, P., Bender Jørgensen, L. and Rast-Eicher, A. (eds), *The Roman Textile Industry and its influence*, 158-71

Ward, G.K., and Wilson, S.R., 1978, 'Procedures for comparing and combining radiocarbon age determinations: a critique', *Archaeometry* 20, 19-31

Warwick, R., 1968, 'The Skeletal Remains', in Wenham, L.P., (ed.), *The Romano-British cemetery at Trentholme Drive, York*, Minist. Public Build. Works Archaeol. Rep. No. 5, 113-209

Waterman, D.M., 1959, 'Late Saxon, Viking and Early Medieval Finds from York' *Archaeologia* 97, 59-105

Watson, C.L., Mays, S., Lockwood, D.N.J. and Taylor, G.M., 2004, *Ancient DNA Analysis of a Case of Lepromatous Leprosy From the Deserted Mediaeval Village of Wharram Percy*. Paper Presented at the Annual Meeting of the British Association for Biological Anthropology and Osteoarchaeology, Bristol, September 2004

Watts, M., 2002, *The Archaeology of Mills and Milling*

Watts, N.B., 1996, 'Introduction: Osteoporosis 1996', *Am. J. Med. Sci.* 312, 249-50

Watts, S., 2000, 'Clay tile' in *Wharram VIII*, 119-21

Watts, S., 2004, 'Querns' in *Wharram IX*, 219-24

Wells, C., 1976, 'Ancient Lesions of the Hip Joint', *Med. Biol. Illus.* 26, 171-7

Wells, C., 1980, 'The Human Bones' in Wade-Martins (ed.), 247-374

Wells, C., 1988, 'An Early Mediaeval Case of Death in Childbirth' in White, W. *The Cemetery of St Nicholas Shambles*, 71-3

Wenger, D.R. and Frick, S.L., 1999, 'Scheuermann Kyphosis', *Spine* 24, 2630-39

Wenham, L.P., 1968, *Excavations at Trentholme Drive, York*

Wenham, L.P., 1974, *Derventio (Malton). Roman Fort and Civilian Settlement*

Wenham, S.J., 1989, 'Anatomical Interpretation of Anglo-Saxon Weapon Injuries' in Hawkes, S.C., (ed.), *Weapons and Warfare in Anglo-Saxon England*, Oxford Univ. Comm. Archaeol. Monogr. 21, 123-39

West, S., 1998, *A Corpus of Anglo-Saxon Material from Suffolk*, East Anglian Archaeol. 84

Westphalen, P., 1999, 'Die Kleinfunde aus der frühgeschichtlichen Wurt Elisenhof', *Offa-Bücher* 80, 1-232

Wharram I (Andrews, D.D. and Milne, G., 1979) *Wharram. A Study of Settlement on the Yorkshire Wolds, I. Domestic Settlement 1: Areas 10 and 6*, Soc. Medieval Archaeol. Monogr. 8

Wharram II (Rahtz, P. and Watts, L., 1983) *Wharram Percy: The Memorial Stones of the Churchyard*, York Univ. Archaeol. Publ. 1

Wharram III (Bell, R.D., Beresford, M.W. and others, 1987) *Wharram. A Study of Settlement on the Yorkshire Wolds, III. Wharram Percy: The Church of St Martin*, Soc. Medieval Archaeaol. Monogr. 11

Wharram IV (Rahtz, P., Hayfield, C. and Bateman, J., 1986), *Wharram. A Study of Settlement on the Yorkshire Wolds, IV. Two Roman Villas at Wharram le Street*, York Univ. Archaeol. Publ. 2

Wharram V (Hayfield, C., 1987) *An Archaeological Survey of the Parish of Wharram Percy, East Yorkshire. 1, The Evolution of the Roman Landscape*, Br. Archaeol. Rep. Br. Ser. 172

Wharram VI (Wrathmell, S., 1989) *Wharram. A Study of Settlement on the Yorkshire Wolds, VI. Domestic Settlement 2: Medieval Peasant Farmsteads*, York Univ. Archaeol. Publ. 8

Wharram VII (Milne, G. and Richards, J.D., 1992) *Wharram. A Study of Settlement on the Yorkshire Wolds, VII. Two Anglo-Saxon Buildings and Associated Finds*, York Univ. Archaeol. Publ. 9

Wharram VIII (Stamper, P.A. and Croft, R.A., 2000) *Wharram. A Study of Settlement on the Yorkshire Wolds, VIII. The South Manor Area*, York Univ. Archaeol. Publ. 10

Wharram IX (Rahtz, P.A. and Watts, L., 2004) *Wharram. A Study of Settlement on the Yorkshire Wolds, IX. The North Manor Area and North-West Enclosure*, York Univ. Archaeol. Publ. 11

Wharram X (Treen, C. and Atkin, M., 2005) *Wharram. A Study of Settlement on the Yorkshire Wolds, X. Water Resources and their Management*, York Univ. Archaeol. Publ. 12

Wharram XII forthcoming (late and post-medieval vicarage and post-medieval farmstead)

Wharram XIII forthcoming (synthesis)

White, W., 1988a, 'The Human Bones: Skeletal Analysis' in White, 28-69

White, W., 1988b, *The Cemetery of St Nicholas Shambles*

White, W., 2002, 'The Human Skeletal Remains From the Burial Ground of St Benet Sherehog' in Miles, A. and White, W. (eds), *Excavations at No. 1 Poultry. Volume 3: The St Benet Sherehog Burial Ground*

Whittaker, D.K., 1993, 'Oral Health' in Molleson, T. and Cox, M. (eds), *The Spitalfields Project. Volume 2: The Anthropology*, Counc. Br. Archaeol. Res. Rep. 86, 49-66

Whittaker, D.K. and Molleson, T., 1996, 'Caries Prevalence in the Dentition of a Late Eighteenth Century Population', *Arch. Oral Biol.* 41, 55-61

Williams, H., 1997, 'Ancient Landscapes of the Dead: the Reuse of prehistoric and Roman monuments as Early Anglo-Saxon Burial Sites', *Medieval Archaeol.* 41, 1-32

Wilson, B., 1994, 'Projects modelling the spatial patterning of bones: limited success in publication' in Luff, R. and Rowley-Conwy, P. (eds), *Whither Environmental Archaeology*, Oxbow Monogr. 35, 57-66

Wilson, P., 2003, 'The Third, Fourth and Fifth Centuries' in Butlin, R.A. (ed.) *Historical Atlas of North Yorkshire*, 52-5

Wilson, P., 2006, 'A Yorkshire Fort and Small Town: Roman Malton and Norton Reviewed', *Yorkshire Archaeol. J.*

Wiltse, L.L., Widell, E.H. and Jackson, D.W., 1975, 'Fatigue Fracture: The Basic Lesion in Isthmic Spondylolisthesis', *J. Bone Joint Surg.* 57A, 17-22

Withers P. and Withers B.R., 1993, *British Coin Weights*

Workshop of European Anthropologists, 1980, 'Recommendations for Age and Sex Diagnosis of Skeletons, *J. Hum. Evol.* 9, 517-49

Wrathmell, S., 2005, 'The Documentary Evidence' in *Wharram X*, 1-8

Wright, T.C. and Dell, P.C., 1991, 'Avascular Necrosis and Vascular Anatomy of the Metacarpals', *J. Hand Surg.* 16A, 540-44

Wrigley, E.A., 1968, 'Mortality in Pre-Industrial England: The Example of Colyton, Devon, Over Three Centuries', *Daedalus* 97, 546-80

Wynne-Davis, R. and Gormley, J., 1978, 'The Aetiology of Perthes' Disease', *J. Bone Joint Surg.* 60B, 6-14

Young, C. J., 1977, *Oxfordshire Roman Pottery*, Br. Archaeol. Rep. 43

Zadora-Rio, E., 2003, ' The Making of Churchyards and Parish Territories in the Early-Medieval Landscape of France and England in the 7th-12th Centuries: A Reconsideration', *Medieval Archaeol.* 47, 1-19

Index

by S. Atkin

Page numbers in *italics* refer to illustrations. Page numbers in Roman refer to both text and tables

Henry I 301, 303
Henry II 270, 301, 303
Henry III 303
Henry VI 302, 303
John 303
medieval 11, 301-4
Richard II 303
Roman 9, 269, 301
Stephen 301, 302, 303
combs, antler/bone 39, 313-14, *315*, 317, 329
conduit 19, 30, 42, 54, 55, *55*, 59, 64, 65
context recording system 2, 4
Corallian ragstone (Coral rag) 271, 272, 273, 281, 284, 298
counters *see* gaming pieces
craft activities 123
cranial measurements 103-13, 191, 198
    PCA 106, 108-9, *108*
criminals 119, 120
cropmarks 60, *282*
cross base, stone 270, 289, 293-4
currycomb, iron 51, *310*, 311

dam 4, 7, 65; *see also* pond and dam
daub, burnt 34
demography 84-95
dental and oral disease 99, *99*, 110, 133-43, 190-1, 198, 331
    abscesses 133, 136, 137
    ante-mortem tooth loss 133, 135-6, 137
    calculus 137-8
    caries 133, 134-5, 137, 190, 198, 331
    dental development 84-5, 92
    dental trauma 140-41
    enamel hypoplasias (DEH) 138-40
    hypodontia 127, 128
    impacted and embedded teeth 140
    localised hypoplasia of the primary canines (LHPC) 140
    microdontia 127, 128
    odontoma 142-3
die, bone/antler *315*, 316
diet (and nutrition) 85, 93, 94-5, 99, 100-1, 102, 103, 110, 133, 137, 159, 165, 166, 179, 190, 191, 330-31
discs, pottery 260, 298, *299*
diseases 99, 101-2, 133, 138, 140, 190, 191-2; *see also* bone disease; dental and oral disease; infectious disease
ditches *see* boundary ditches
DNA analyses 86, 164-5, 167, 169, 175, 191, 329
Dogstoop Plantation *282*, 283, 284
Domesday Book 204, 287
domestic refuse (Site 71) 74, 75
drains, ceramic 12, 15, 20
Dykes, William, plans (1836) 5, *6*, 7

earmuffs, stone 39, 224, 238, *238*, 239, *239*, 241
ear-ring(?), copper-alloy 304
east of church *see* church east end (EE)

emigration *see* migration
Ensay (Scotland) 97, *98*, 132
Espenfeld (Germany) 90

fairs 333, 335
families (kinship), and burials 45, 61, 75, 85-6, 123-5, 189, 233, 329, 330
    early lords and their kin 285-7
farmhouse (Site 74)
    conduit 55, 64
    jeton 304
farmsteads 1, 30, 330
    Iron Age/Romano-British (Site 41) 66-7, 75
    Site 51, coins 301, 302, 303
fees for burial 87
fences and fencelines 5, *6*, 7, 19, 20, 42, 51, 55, 57, 64, 74, 75, 331, 333, *334*
ferrule, iron 308
file, iron 308
finger-rings, copper-alloy 270, 304
Firby, Robert 205
fish 95
fish bone 319, 321, 325, 331
fittings, iron 309, *310*
flint
    Bronze Age 66
    in Burial G305 31, *31*
floor tiles 12, 299
flooring stone 297
foetuses *see under* burials
folding knife 270
footstones *see under* stone settings
fork, iron 308, 316, 317
fork handle, bone 316-17
fossil, in burial 270
'founder's' burial group 284-7, 327
fractures 143-50, 192
    cranial (blunt injuries, edged weapons) 143-8, 192
    post-cranial 148-50, 181
funerary stonework 271-94; *see also* grave-covers; grave-markers; grave slabs; sarcophagi

gaming pieces (counters), bone 36, *315*, 316
garden fork 308, *310*
gardener's knife 270, 317
gates/gateways 5, *6*, 7, 48, 49, 62, 74, 331, 333
geology 1, 84, 179
glass, vessels 300, *300*; *see also* bangles; bead
glebe lands 4-5
Gloucester (Glos.), St Oswald's 232, 233, 235, 236, 239
Gothenburg (Sweden) 135
Graeme family 270
grave-covers, stone 237, 238, *238*, 239, 241, 242, 269
    11th-century *in situ* 14, 221, 224, *224*, 226, *237*, 242, 271-2, *274-5*, 284, 285, 286, 327
    reused in south aisle wall 224, 271, 272-3, *276*, 286-7
    medieval *see under* grave slabs
    grave-markers 16, 25, 45, 61, 125, 229, 271, 273, *274-5*, 281, 284, 287, 294

466

soils 101-2, 148
south boundary (SA) 68, *78*, 79, 86, 87, 233, 241
    arm positions 233, 234
    fence 70
    orientation 236, *236*
    pre-Conquest burials 216, *216*, 217, 221
    radiocarbon dating *204*, 206, *206*, 213, 215
    see also boundary ditches; farmhouse (Site 74);
        Site 41; Site 52; Site 71; Site 80
South Manor *xx*, 327, 335
    animal bone 319, 320-21, *322*, 324
    coins and jetons 301, 302, 304
    finds 300, 312, 313, 314, 315, 316
    pottery 244, 251, 266, 268
spearhead, bone, Anglo-Saxon 313, 315-16, *315*
spindlewhorls
    antler/bone 314-15, *315*
    stone 294, *295*
Spitalfields *see* London
springs 1, *6*, 29, 55, 60, 65, 283, 327, 335
spurs *310*, 311
squatting facets 125-7, 191, 331
stable *6*, 51
stable isotope analyses 102, 103, 166
    carbon 85, 93, 94-5, 191, 197
    nitrogen 85, 93, 189, 190, 191, 197
stains (red-brown) 80
staples, iron 309, *310*
stature 95, 97-100, 118-20, 148, 190, 330-1
steps/stepped track 58, 59, *59*, *60*, *332*, 333
stillbirths 87, 89, 90
stirrup, iron 311
Stonar 90
stone and stonework
    from the church 297-8
    medieval cross slab grave-covers 287-93
    pre-Conquest grave furniture 271-87
    reused in gateway (from north aisle?) 49, 62, 297,
        333
    stone objects 294-8
    used in building construction 297
    see also cross-base; grave-covers; grave-markers;
        grave slabs; hones; querns (millstones); rubbing
        stones; sarcophagi; spindlewhorls
stone settings 39, 42, 45, 198, 216, 238-41, *238*
    bed of chalk blocks 226, *227*
    footstones 14, 239, *240*
    head and footstones *22*, 39, 45, 226, *227*, 238, 242
    head marker 16
    heap of stones covering *238*, 241
    'pillow stones' 238, 239
    stones around head 226, 238, *240*
    weights on leg/body 39, 241
    see also cists/stone cists; earmuffs; grave covers;
        headstones
strap-ends, copper alloy 22, 29, 270, 304, *305*, 306
strap fittings, copper alloy 270, *305*, 306
stream 30, 75, 333

studs, copper alloy 270, *305*, 306
stylus, bone 269, 270, 316, 317, *317*
sugar 133, 137, 190

Tabula bone counter *315*, 316
tapeworm 74
Teesdale (1828) 5
temple (local?), Roman 281, 281-4
terriers 4-5
tethering posts 61, 333
textiles, from shrouds 270
thimble, copper alloy *306*, 307
Thixendale *xix*, 1, *2*, 5, 15, 204, 333
tiles, clay 299; *see also* floor tiles; roof tiles
timber structure 42
tin/tin alloy sheet 307
Tirup (Denmark) 119
toilet implements, copper alloy *305*, 307
Toisland Wold *282*, 283
tombstones 233
tool storage, structure for? 54
tools, iron 308, *310*
Towthorpe *xix*, 1, 2
tracks (trackways) 5, *6*, 7, 14, 15, 19-20, 29, 55, 57, 58,
    59, *59*, 60, 331, *332*, 333, *334*; *see also* paths; roads
trading links 191, 331
trepanation 147, 192
Trondheim (Norway) 119, 135
    St Olav's churchyard 87, 90
tuberculosis 86, 163-6, *164*, 167, 169, 175, 191, 331
tweezers, copper alloy *305*, 307

urine and urinals 264, 268
USA, skeletal material 97, 98, *98*, 118

vessel glass 300, *300*
vessels, copper alloy 307
vicarage boundary wall (182) 59-60, *60*, 62, 211, 331,
    333, 335
vicarages 1, 4, 5, 7, 29, 30, 42, 48, 49, 55, 57, 62, 64,
    330, 333
    coins and jetons (Site 54) 301, 302, 303, 304
    Site 54: 55, 64
    yard surfaces (Site 71) 74
villa complex 281, 282-4

wall monuments 270
walls 42, *42*, 45, *45*, 51, 52, *52*, 54, 62, 64
    construction 62, 64
    walls 73/811 54, *54*, 55, 64
    walls 74/20 30, 45, *45*, *46*, 48, *48*, 51, 54, 55, 59-
        60, *60*, 62, 64
water source 283
weaning 102-3, 173, 177, 181, 189-90
wedges, iron 308
weights, lead *306*, 307; *see also* coin weights
West Heslerton, burials 117, 119, 135
Westerhus (Sweden) 90, 119